1 MONTH OF
FREE
READING

at

www.ForgottenBooks.com

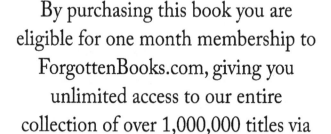

By purchasing this book you are eligible for one month membership to ForgottenBooks.com, giving you unlimited access to our entire collection of over 1,000,000 titles via our web site and mobile apps.

To claim your free month visit: www.forgottenbooks.com/free892551

ISBN 978-0-265-80791-0
PIBN 10892551

[*Supplement to The Journal of the Department of Agriculture, Victoria,*
10th January, 1913.]

ᘓ.　　　ᘘ.

THE JOURNAL

OF THE

DEPARTMENT OF AGRICULTURE

OF

VICTORIA,

AUSTRALIA.

PUBLISHED FOR AND ON BEHALF OF THE GOVERNMENT BY DIRECTION

OF THE

HON. GEORGE GRAHAM, M.L.A.,

Minister for Agriculture.

VOLUME X.

1912.

𝔅𝔶 𝔄𝔲𝔱𝔥𝔬𝔯𝔦𝔱𝔶:

ALBERT J. MULLETT, ACTING GOVERNMENT PRINTER, MELBOURNE.

1912.

17265.

THE JOURNAL OF THE DEPARTMENT OF AGRICULTURE, VICTORIA.

VOLUME X. Parts 1—12.

INDEX.

The Journal of THE DEPARTMENT OF AGRICULTURE OF VICTORIA, AUSTRALIA.

January, 1912.

BEE-KEEPING IN VICTORIA.

PRICE THREEPENCE.   (Annual Subscription—Victoria, Inter-State, and N.Z., 3/-; British and Foreign, 5/-.)

THE JOURNAL

OF

THE DEPARTMENT OF AGRICULTURE,

VICTORIA, AUSTRALIA.

A. T. SHARP, Editor.

CONTENTS.—JANUARY, 1912.

COPYRIGHT PROVISIONS AND SUBSCRIPTION RATES.

The Journal is issued monthly. The subscription, which is payable in advance and includes postage, is 3s. per annum for the Commonwealth and New Zealand, and 5s. for the United Kingdom and Foreign Countries. Single copy Threepence.

Subscriptions should be forwarded to the Director of Agriculture, Melbourne. A complete list of the various publications issued by the Department of Agriculture will be supplied by the latter.

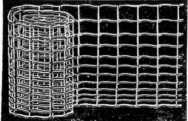

DEPARTMENT OF AGRICULTURE, VICTORIA.

GOVERNMENT STUD BULLS.

AVAILABLE FOR SERVICE OF COWS BELONGING TO BONA FIDE SETTLERS UNDER THE CLOSER SETTLEMENT ACTS.

Fee, 5s per cow.

Jersey Bull "DERRIMUT," (Calved 22nd October, 1908).
Sire—Sir Jack (888). *Dam*—Lady Kitchener by Lord Melbourne.
(*In charge of Mr. H. Crumpler, Block 148, Bamawm.*)

Jersey Bull "ROSE FOX," (Calved 19th August, 1909).
Sire—Starbright Fox (90). *Dam*—Taboose by Magnet Progress (545 A. H. B.).
(*In charge of Mr. E. W. Porter, Block 65, Bamawm.*)

Jersey Bull "VERBENA'S BOY," (Calved 10th January, 1908).
Sire—Acrobat. *Dam*—Verbena 2nd by Sword by Progress 2nd.
(*In charge of Messrs. Cunningham, Block 707, Bamawm.*)

Jersey Bull "NOBODY," (Calved 22nd April, 1910).
Sire—Lucky Noble of Oaklands. *Dam*—Winnie of Melrose 3rd by Royal Blue.
(*In charge of Mr. E. T. Partington, Block 636, Bamawm.*)

Jersey Bull "MILKY WAY," (Calved 20th June, 1909).
Sire—Starbright Fox (90). *Dam*—Milkmaid 3484 (5090) by Ellimoon (imp. 262 H. B.).
(*In charge of Mr. S. H. Harland, Block 91, Nanneella.*)

Jersey Bull "GOOD MEDAL," (Calved 3rd April, 1910).
Sire—Gold Medal Fox (424 A. H. B.). *Dam*—Melba by Greystones 2nd.
(*In charge of Messrs. Johnston and Kennedy, Block 842 and 444, Nanneella.*)

Jersey Bull "MAGNET'S FOX," (Calved 6th November, 1909).
Sire—Foxie Laddie. *Dam*—Magnet 2825 by Defender (imp. 228 H. C. H. B.).
(*In charge of Mr. C. W. Wade, Block 292, Koyuga.*)

Jersey Bull "CRAMP ROSE," (Calved 22nd March, 1910).
Sire—Lord Cramer (555 A. H. B.). *Dam*—Daisy of Prospect (347 A. H. B.), by Cardigan.
(*In charge of Mr. L. H. Holloway, Block 2, Koyuga.*)

Jersey Bull "ZODIAC," (Calved 10th November, 1908).
Sire—Starbright Fox (90). *Dam*—Zoe 4040 (5095) by Hohenzollern.
(*In charge of Mr. R. W. Chipple, Block 212, Sunday Hill.*)

Jersey Bull "GAY FOX," (Calved 2nd May, 1909).
Sire—Starbright Fox (90). *Dam*—Flossy by Ellimoon (imp. 262).
(*In charge of Mr. F. Cox, Block 106, Sunday Hill.*)

DEPARTMENT OF AGRICULTURE,
VICTORIA.

GOVERNMENT STUD BULLS.

AVAILABLE FOR SERVICE OF COWS BELONGING TO BONA-FIDE SETTLERS UNDER THE CLOSER SETTLEMENT ACTS—*continued.*

Fee, 5s. per cow.

Jersey Bull "WILLIAM OF AYRE"; CALVED, February, 1910.
Sire :—Favourite's Fox 2nd.   *Dam* :—Bessie McCarthy, by Snowflake's Progress.
(*In charge of Mr. J. S. Dickinson, Block* 13, *Nyah.*)

Jersey Bull "FOX'S LAD"; CALVED, 5th October, 1908.
Sire :—Fox, by Snowdrop's Progress 2nd.   *Dam* :—Pansy 2nd, by Duke.
(*In charge of Mr. Ernest E. Borley, Block* 6, *Nyah.*)

Ayrshire Bull "PETER OF WILLOWVALE"; CALVED, 30th Sept., 1909.
Sire :—Annetta's Pride (243).   *Dam* :—Madge 2nd (Appendix A.H.B.), by Red
Chief (359).
(*In charge of Mr. F. McIvor, Block* 12F, *Swan Hill.*)

Particulars of extended pedigrees, milking records, &c., can be obtained from each bull holder, from the resident Dairy Supervisors **(Mr. O'KEEFE, Rochester, or Mr. S. J. KEYS, Swan Hill),** or from **The Department of Agriculture, Melbourne.**

AVAILABLE FOR SERVICE OF COWS THE PROPERTY OF BEET GROWERS AT BOISDALE.

Red Danish Bull "CLAUDIUS"; CALVED, 10th November, 1909.
Sire :—Ernst Bellinge (imp.).   *Dam* :—Kirsten IX. (imp.).
Fee, 5s. (available to 30 cows).

Red Danish Bull "HAMLET"; CALVED, 1st August, 1910.
Sire :—Ernst Bellinge (imp.).   *Dam* :—Marianne IV.   *G. Dam* :—Marianne III. (imp.).
Fee, 5s. (available to 10 heifers).

Red Polled Bull "TABACUM"; CALVED, 12th November, 1908.
Sire :—Acton Ajax (imp.).   *Dam* :—Janet, by Primate by Laureate (imp.).
Fee, 7s. 6d. (available to 20 cows).

Jersey Bull "GAY LAD II."; CALVED, 8th August, 1906.
Sire :—Acrobat, by Cherry's Pride (imp.).   *Dam* :—Gaiety, by Snowdrop's Progress II.,
by Lady Superior's Progress (imp.).
Fee, 5s. (available to 40 cows).   (Winner of 7 first prizes.)

Particulars of extended pedigrees, milking records and prizes may be obtained from, and arrangement for service made with, **Mr. E. STEER,** at the Homestead Block 21, where the bulls are kept.

THE JOURNAL

OF

The Department of Agriculture

OF

VICTORIA.

| Vol. X. | Part 1. | 10th January, 1912. |

BEE-KEEPING IN VICTORIA.

F. R. Beuhne, Bee Expert.

I.—LOCATION.

Bee-keeping in Victoria is carried on under different conditions to those existing in other countries. In the Northern Hemisphere, and also in New Zealand, the principal supply of nectar comes from ground flora on meadows, roadsides, fields and woods. In Victoria, we depend almost exclusively on our eucalypts and a few other native trees and shrubs. Owing to our hot summers, which prevent the secretion of nectar in soft herbaceous plants, except on irrigated land and in exceptionally cool districts, the amount of honey obtained from other than native flora is small in comparison with the quantity harvested from eucalypts.

. Even where climatic conditions are favourable to the secretion of nectar, the system of closely feeding down pastures. which is largely practised in Australia, does not permit of the proper development of the nectar-producing plants and the maximum production of nectar. As probably over 90 per cent. of the honey produced in Victoria is obtained from eucalypts, this fact should be borne in mind when selecting a district in which to commence bee-keeping.

With the opening up of country to settlement, the natural honey resources are to a large extent destroyed. It is a natural and inevitable result and no claim can be made on behalf of bee culture to have the whole of the country kept in its natural state.

Every country, however, must have forests and timber reserves to maintain the supply of timber, to protect the sources of water supply, and to exercise a beneficial influence on the climate. As the forests of Victoria are now permanently reserved and are being improved by thinning, protection against fires. and new plantations, they afford ample scope for apicultural enterprise and a great expansion of the bee-keeping industry. Moreover, the advent of irrigation settlement on a large scale, together

17862. A

with the practice of cutting fodder crops instead of feeding them off, will make bee-keeping profitable in many places where, under the old system of continuous eating off, it could not be engaged in.

SELECTION OF LOCALITY.

For the purpose of becoming conversant with the habits of bees, to get some practice in handling them, and to gain the knowledge and experience not obtainable from literature, bee-keeping may be commenced almost anywhere. When, however, it is taken up as a business, a suitable district is essential to success. In selecting a site, due consideration should be given to the two main factors ; namely, the amount and variety of bee flora within a radius of two or three miles of the site chosen. The permanency of the bee flora is, however, the most important consideration, and the intending bee-keeper should locate on, or close to, some permanent forest or other reserve, so as to avoid the risk of having his honey resources destroyed by the ring-barking of the trees.

A BEE FARM IN EAST GIPPSLAND—AN IDEAL SITUATION FOR AN APIARY.

In some of the best honey country in Victoria, consisting almost entirely of yellow box and red gum for many miles in extent, there is a deficiency of pollen-producing plants before and after the honey-flow. With a scarcity of pollen, colonies cannot attain their maximum development, and therefore the best results can only be obtained where the bees, prior to the honey-flow, are kept elsewhere. Thus, a practice has sprung up amongst bee-keepers of having two sites for an apiary—one for breeding up in spring and wintering ; the other for securing the honey crop. The moving of the bees from the winter site to the honey country, and back again when the honey-flow is over, entails a considerable amount of work, which can be avoided if a site is secured on the border line of the two classes of country.

LICENCES.

When locating on forest or other Crown lands, it is necessary to obtain two licences—a bee-farm licence for one acre upon which to place the apiary, and a bee-range licence which secures to the holder the exclusive use of the bee flora for a radius of one mile. No other bee-farm licence is allowed at a lesser distance than two miles. The payments to be made are 1s. a year per acre for a bee-farm site, and ½d. per acre for the radius of the bee range, or about £4 4s. a year.

Site of Apiary.

Having decided upon the locality, the spot upon which the hives are to be set out should be selected, with due regard to its suitability for the bees and convenience of working the apiary.

An even, gently sloping surface, of gravelly or sandy soil, will be found most suitable. It should, if possible, be sheltered by a natural or artificial breakwind on the south and west. A slope to the north or east is preferable to one to the south or west.

The honey-house should be placed at the lower end, and the hives arranged in such a way that a good general view can be obtained from the door and windows of the building, so that during the swarming season the apiary may be under observation while necessary indoor work is being done. Having the building at the lower end of the ground has the double advantage of getting a better view of the whole apiary and of moving the supers of heavy honeycombs down hill at extracting time.

It is not advisable to stand hives under evergreen trees, such as pines or eucalypts. Colonies in permanently shaded positions never thrive so well as others out in the open. If placed under deciduous trees, as for instance in an orchard, the hives will have shade during the hottest part of the day in summer, and sunshine during the cold months of the year when the trees are not in leaf.

Arrangement of Hives.

In laying out the apiary, it is better to place the hives in groups of twos, threes, or fours, with a longer distance between the groups, than to stand the hives singly in rows. The group system lends itself better to the various necessary operations of uniting or dividing colonies and in moving about amongst the hives; it gives more space between the groups than would be the case between the same number of hives placed singly.

When grouping hives, the entrances should point in different directions. None, however, should face the south, as the strongest and coldest winds come from that quarter. It is also advisable to vary the grouping so that no two adjoining groups will be exactly alike. This will to a great extent prevent the straying of returning field bees and the loss of virgin queens returning from their mating flight. The latter frequently occurs when hives stand in symmetrical rows and without any variation in the arrangement and without distinguishing landmarks.

(To be continued.)

BEES AND SPRAYING.

*E. E. Pescott, Principal, Horticultural School, Burnley, and
F. R. Beuhne, Bee Expert.*

The establishment of an apiary at the Burnley Horticultural Gardens has furnished an opportunity for observing and recording data regarding the working of bees among fruit trees, and the effect of the various orchard operations upon the bees. The apiary was established during the spring of last year; and, although it is too early to establish any definite conclusions, certain observations have already been made which may somewhat upset various theories regarding the action of sprays upon the bees.

It is an accepted fact that the bee is the most useful of all insects for the purposes of conveying pollen from flower to flower for fertilization purposes. It was pointed out last year, in the January and April numbers

A PORTION OF THE BURNLEY APIARY.

of the *Journal*, that bees were of great service to the orchardist in assisting to increase the yield of fruit. It is also known that to exclude bees and other insects from the trees at the time when they are in blossom is sure to result in a considerably reduced fruit crop.

It is often considered that bees are able to collect a good store of honey from fruit tree blossom, and that the yield of fruit tree honey comes at a time when the bees urgently need it for brood rearing. That may be so in other countries, but it does not appear to be so in Australia. Here, the nectar flow seems to be somewhat weak, and insufficient in quantity for the necessities of the bees. A Victorian apiarist during the past season removed his bee colonies from his home to a district where the bees had an available range over 15,000 fruit trees. He ultimately found that the bees were starving, and he had to remove them to a more suitable locality. It may thus be found that the chief use of bees in the orchard will be for cross-fertilization purposes.

It has been frequently stated, especially in publications dealing exclu·
sively with the honey bee, that spraying the fruit trees, at the time when
the trees are in blossom, will cause great mortality amongst the bee
colonies, particularly if the spray be a poisonous one.

Whenever losses of bees occur in apiaries located in or near orchards
in which spraying is practised, the owners assume that the mortality is due
to the poisons used in the spraying mixtures. So far, there appears to be
no proof that bees gather poison along with nectar and pollen, nor is there
any instance on record of the poisons having been proved, by analysis,
to be present in dead bees, bee larvæ, pollen, or honey.

Dead bees may often be found not only on the blossoms of fruit trees
which were not sprayed, but also on acacia and other flowers blossoming
at the same time. Heavy losses of bees from unknown causes occasionally
occur at the time of fruit bloom in localities where there are no fruit
trees at all; while, on the other hand, apiaries located close to orchards
in which the trees were sprayed repeatedly, suffered no perceptible loss
and were in a thriving condition. Again, bees might not be affected by
the amount of poison gathered with the nectar, but it might be sufficient
to kill the brood. In an independent experiment made last season, iron
sulphate, 1 part in 400 of sugar syrup, was quite harmless to bees, but
killed all the brood.

In the *A B C and X Y Z of Bee Culture* it is stated definitely that
spraying trees during bloom is destructive to bees and brood. We quote—

Now that spraying with various poisonous liquids has come to be almost universal
among fruit-growers, the question arises, "Shall such spraying be done during the
time the trees are in bloom, or before and after?" If it is administered when
the petals are out, bees are almost sure to be poisoned, much brood will be killed,
and many times valuable queens are lost. About the first thing one notices during
fruit-blooming time, if trees are sprayed while in bloom, is that a good deal of
the brood dies, until the bee-keeper begins to wonder whether the bees have foul
brood, black brood, or pickled brood—unless the truth dawns upon him that they
have been carrying in poisonous liquids from the trees that have just been sprayed.

It is not advocated in this article that fruit trees should be sprayed
when in full blossom; the spraying operations can usually be conducted
either before or after the flowering stage.

It was pointed out in the January, 1911, article previously referred to,
that rain at the blossom time seriously interferes with pollen action, and
naturally liquid sprays would have the same effect. But there may be times
when necessity compels the grower to spray at this season.

At the Burnley orchards, there are altogether over 1,800 varieties of
fruit trees, which bloom at various times—from the end of August to the
beginning of November. Hence, the trees, particularly the apple and pear
trees, must be sprayed at a time when some of them are in bloom, with
both Bordeaux mixture and arsenate of lead. And this occurs every
season.

During last year, the pear trees were sprayed with Bordeaux mixture
when some were in blossom; while, later on, a number of apple trees were
sprayed with lead arsenate when in bloom. Under these circumstances
it was decided to make observations in order to establish reliable data on
this question.

At the Burnley apiary, the bee hives are right under the fruit trees,
and at the time of spraying with Bordeaux mixture the ground had not
yet been ploughed, so that the spray fell not only on any fruit blossoms
which were open, but also on the Cape weed then abundantly in bloom.

Neither the spraying with Bordeaux mixture nor the subsequent one with arsenate of lead had any effect whatever upon the bees, the colonies developing normally and without any check; there was not at any time dead brood in the hives.   There is no doubt that under the atmospheric conditions prevailing at the time the spraying of the trees proved quite harmless to bees.   Observations will, however, be continued in future, to demonstrate whether spraying is injurious to bees at all; or, if so, under what conditions.

DAIRY PRODUCTS FROM THE LONDON MARKET.

R. Crowe, Exports Superintendent.

Since it was impracticable to afford visitors to the Royal Agricultural Society's Show a trip to London to see how our products compare there with those from other countries, the next best thing was adopted.   Certain products from countries with which we have to compete against in London were procured there in the open market and displayed side by side with our own at the last Show in Melbourne   The whole of the exhibits excited the keenest interest, and the movement proved an unqualified success. The educational effect upon all concerned was most marked, and was greatly appreciated.

BUTTER.

Butter from Denmark, Siberia and Ireland was shown alongside some from Victoria that had been purchased on the London market at the same time as the others and returned to Melbourne.   The cask of Danish butter contained one cwt.   The butter itself was of excellent quality, and as pleasing to the eye as on the palate.   In appearance, it was of a nice straw colour, with a seemingly transparent surface characteristic of fresh well-made butter which has not been overworked, or plastered in finishing. A small label about 4 in. x 2 in., bearing the national trade mark (the "Lur" brand—the old vikings' trumpet) rested on top of the butter. On endeavouring to remove the label it was found to break away, the reason being obvious—to prevent its transference from one package to another.   A disc of fine quality butter paper, corresponding in diameter to the top of the cask, covered the butter before the lining paper was folded in.   The folding was so regularly and daintily accomplished as to resemble a circular fan.   The cask was made of white beech, with white willow hoops.   One of the staves bore the impression of the national trade mark, while the factory's brand occupied a place on the head of the cask.   The flavour of the butter was all that could be desired.   Upon analysis, it was found to contain 94.19 per cent. butter fat, 13.97 per cent. moisture, 1.2 per cent. salt, 0.64 per cent. casein, and no boric acid.   Reichert value, 30.

The cask of Siberian butter was of the same size as the Danish, but the package and contents were inferior to it in every respect.   The package consisted of material more roughly dressed and put together. The butter was lifeless in appearance; in flavour, it was not comparable to the Danish, and about a quarter of an inch of dairy salt was spread over the top surface.   There was no national brand, and the contrast generally was quite pronounced.   Upon analysis, the butter was found to contain 86.7 per cent. butter fat, 10.88 per cent. moisture, 1.72 per cent. salt, 0.7 per cent. casein, and no boric acid.   Reichert value, 28.

DANISH BUTTER.   SIBERIAN BUTTER.

IRISH BUTTER.   AMERICAN LARD.

The Irish butter was packed in a deal box containing 56 lbs., which was slightly wider each way at the top than at the bottom, no doubt to enable the contents to be more readily placed on the grocer's counter. As regards quality and appearance, there was not much to choose between the Siberian and Irish butters. The latter contained 84.53 per cent. butter fat, 12.8 per cent. moisture, 2.07 per cent. salt, 0.6 per cent. casein, and no boric acid. Reichert value, 30.7.

The box of Victorian butter bore the Commonwealth stamp and certificate number, and upon looking up its record it was discovered that originally it comprised portion of a parcel dealt with for export over five months previously. Notwithstanding its age, the butter opened up in good condition. In the first place, it was not a superfine butter, and, of course, was not up to the Danish standard. In any case, that could not be expected, as the Danish was probably not more than 9 or 10 weeks old. The Victorian butter was decidedly better than the Siberian or Irish, and it opened up in accordance with the grade originally awarded to it. Slight depreciation had taken place, but not sufficient to warrant it being placed in a lower grade.

ENGLISH CHEDDAR CHEESE.   CANADIAN CHEDDAR CHEESE.

The lessons to be deduced were, first of all, the thoroughness apparent in every detail connected with the Danish product, the make and cleanliness of the package, the dainty finish, and the impression of the national mark; the butter itself left nothing more to be desired.

Since the Show it is pleasing to note that some Victorian butter factories have materially improved the appearance of their butter, by paying more attention to the finish and the folding in of the paper, and completing it with an attractive paper seal.

Cheese.

English Cheddar, Canadian Cheddar, English Cheshire, Dutch Edam and Gouda cheeses were shown, the two latter being typical of the kind for which there is a great demand in the East. The Cheshire and Cheddar cheeses were 90 lbs. each, and symmetrical in shape. The quality of all varieties was very fine indeed. Comparisons could not be drawn, so regular and characteristic was each make. Upon cutting, the texture was close, meaty, and everything that could be wished for.

When advising makers of cheese during the previous season as to the sizes required for the English market, the greatest difficulty was experienced in persuading some manufacturers to depart from the 40 lbs. size and to make cheese of 60 lbs. each.   Not the slightest trouble was encountered in convincing all who saw the exhibits of the advantages possessed by the larger cheese.   Locally, small cheeses are probably preferred because, on account of the plentifulness of meat, cheese does not enter largely into the diet of the people, and the average grocer takes a long time to cut the last of a cheese.   In England, however, where the population is dense, and cheese forms no inconsiderable pioportion of the working man's diet, a number of large cheeses may be cut out in a single day.

From the manufacturer's point of view, everything is to be gained by making the large sizes for export, since less surface is exposed for evaporation and loss in weight per lb. than is the case with small sizes. In a climate such as ours, with a comparatively dry atmosphere, this is most important.   In addition, two large 90 lb. cheeses go in one case, whilst a slightly smaller case will hold only three of 40 lbs. each, or two of 60 lbs. each.   It will therefore be recognized that a ton of the larger size cheese would cost much less for casing than a ton comprising the smaller sizes.   Again, the grocer in London is prepared to pay more for the large sized cheese, because there is less rind or waste per lb. than is the case with small ones.

Briefly, then, the cheese-maker by making large sized cheese has more to sell, it costs less to pack for market, and a higher price can be realized. The analyses were as follow :—

—	Moisture.	Ash.	Proteids.	Fat.	Milk Sugar.
	%	%	%	%	%
English Cheddar ...	36·25	3·75	{ 26·33 Nitrogen 6·37 }	29·95	3·74
Cheshire	39·11	2·00	24·50	31·28	3·11
Gouda	40·12	5·95	25·01	24·60	4·32
Canadian Cheddar ...	33·53	3·55	25·33	35·58	2·01

PIG PRODUCTS.

Bacon from Ireland, Canada, Denmark and Holland; hams from Yorkshire, Ireland and United States; and lard from Ireland, Denmark and United States were displayed.   All of the sides of bacon were much larger than is favoured locally, and were dusted over with ground pea meal. Upon cutting, the quality did not impress experts, and their verdict was confirmed by frying rashers in the pan.   They were mild cured, and the flesh was coarse and flabby, proving that feeding had not been considered in order to "top off" and harden the flesh.   In curing, also, the minimum loss in weight was evidently aimed at.

The one great lesson was that baconers from 130 to 170 lbs. represent the typical weights required in England, 150 lbs. being the ideal weight, whilst here the weights range from 120 to 150 lbs.   Nearly all breeders know that it costs less per lb. to produce a pig of 180 lbs. weight than one of 130 lbs. weight, the cost per lb. for the last 50 lbs. being much less than for the first 130.

The hams were not in any way exceptional, and did not call for special mention.   The Yorkshire ham was unsmoked and on that account appeared less attractive than the others.

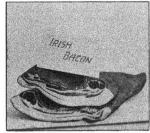

IRISH BACON.

CANADIAN BACON.

DANISH BACON.

DUTCH BACON.

YORKSHIRE HAM.   IRISH HAM.   AMERICAN HAM.

The lard from Ireland and Denmark was put up in bladders, whilst the American was packed in a pail, very attractively got up. It is improbable, however, that either of these forms will be adopted here when an export trade is developed. At various times lard has been exported from Victoria packed in butter boxes; the stowing on board ship for long voyages is the determining consideration.

POULTRY.

Sussex, Surrey, Irish, Canadian and French chickens were shown, and a glance was sufficient to enable one to recognize the difference in breeding, quality and packing. The case of French chickens stood out from all the rest as regards regularity of size, colour and plumpness.

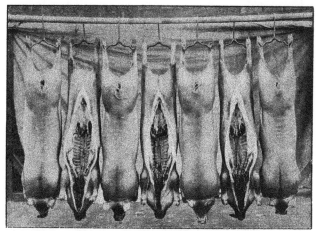

VICTORIAN PORK.

There was little to choose between the Sussex and Surrey chickens; they were uniform in colour, size, weight and condition, with white legs, and cleanly got up.

In the case of 12 Irish chickens, at least eight different colours and shades of colour could be distinguished. The birds were not uniform in size and condition, and of course were discounted in consequence.

The get up of the Canadian birds was even worse. The variety of colours was not so great, but the want of regularity in size and condition was more apparent; in addition, the feet had not been washed before killing.

A glance at the exhibits as a whole was sufficient to impress one with the advantages resulting from grading into uniform classes and exercising care in regard to every detail in trussing and packing.

BUILDING HINTS FOR SETTLERS.

XVI.—TWO-BAIL MILKING SHED.

J. Wilson, Silo Builder.

The accompanying plan of a milking shed is the first of a series which it is proposed to publish from time to time in the *Journal*. This is a simple and sanitary shed meeting all the requirements of the Milk

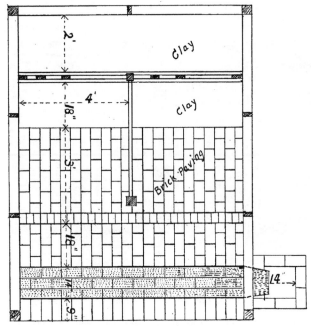

PLAN OF TWO-BAIL MILKING SHED.

and Dairy Supervision Act. It can be erected at a small cost, without the assistance of outside labour. The woodwork is all sawn timber, as follows :—

Angle studs, 4 in. x 4 in. hardwood.
Plates, rafters, runners for bails, tongues, and two short braces for front and all other studs, 4 in. x 1½ in. hardwood.
Purlins and runners for iron, 3 in. x 1½ in. hardwood.
Braces, 3 in. x 1 in. hardwood.

The shed is lined on the inside with galvanized corrugated iron, the small corrugations making a neat finish. Lining the walls on the inside.

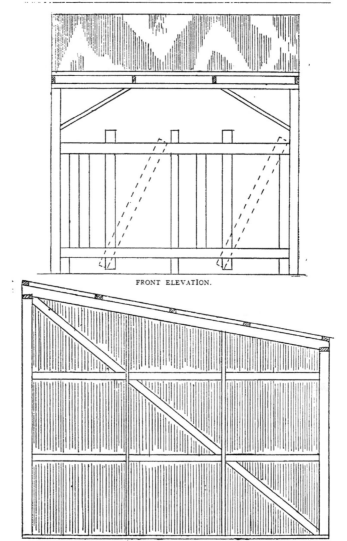

FRONT ELEVATION.

SIDE ELEVATION.

does away with the angles and corners which are formed where the usual
practice is followed. This prevents cobwebs, dirt, &c., from accumulating, and the walls can also be more readily washed with a mop or swab.

As shown, the floor provides a raised kerbing, dung space, and gutter
at the rear of the cow. A brick cess pit is also provided on the outside
of building; this is connected with the brick gutter by an open iron
gutter, the end of which projects 1½ in., and allows the fluid to flow into
a kerosene tin placed in the pit.

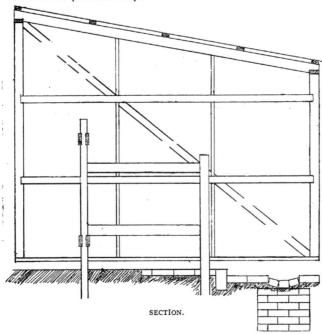

SECTION.

Timbers should be tarred or painted, preferably before erection. The
approximate cost of material landed on truck at Melbourne is £6 17s.

Material for Two-bail Milking Shed.

Hardwood—
    4 in. x 4 in.—two 9 ft.; three 7 ft. lengths.
    3 in. x 3 in.—one 7 ft. length.
    4 in. x 1½ in.—four 12 ft.; two 11 ft.; eleven 9 ft.; two 8 ft.; four 5 ft.;
        two 4 ft.; two 3 ft. lengths.
    3 in. x 1½ in.—four 12 ft.; seven 9 ft. lengths.
    3 in. x 1 in.—two 14 ft.; one 12 ft. length.
    Corrugated galvanized iron, 26 gauge—ten 6 ft. lengths (roof).
    Small corrugated galvanized iron, 26 gauge—eleven 9 ft.; four 8 ft. lengths
(walls).
    Springhead nails, 2½ in.—2 lbs.

Galvanized clout tacks, 1½ in.—3 lbs.
Bolts and nuts—two 5 in. x ½ in.; two 7 in. x ½ in.
Cement—two bags.
Sand—two loads.
Bricks—268.

SILOS AND SILAGE.

G. H. F. Baker, Silo Supervisor.

A silo is a practically air-tight receptacle in which green fodder is stored in a succulent state.   In this condition it will remain for as long a period as required without deteriorating in value.   The material thus preserved is known as ensilage or silage.   Correctly, the word "silo" means a pit; but it may be a square, round, or oblong receptacle of any size below or above ground.

METHODS OF SILAGE-MAKING.

There are various methods of silage-making, and it is immaterial which is followed, as long as care is exercised and a good sample is obtained.   The farmer should never neglect an opportunity to have some such fodder stored on the farm.

PIT SILO.—The underground or pit silo was the first style adopted in Victoria and it met with varying success.   It may be of any shape, provided the wall surface is comparatively smooth and as plumb as possible, the bottom being the full width of the upper portion.   The reason for this is that, as the silage settles down, any unevenness of the wall surface is liable to allow of air entering the mass and decomposition occurring at that place.

In hillside situations or porous soil, the wall or floor surfaces may be left in their natural conditions, but where drainage is necessary it should be walled with slab, brick or cement; also provide a pipe or other means to carry off any sub-surface moisture to prevent the silage being damaged thereby.

The difficulty of properly draining the underground silo and of hoisting the silage, together with the cost of excavating, bricking, &c., has militated against the adoption of this system to any great extent.

STACK SILAGE.—Stack silage has also been more or less popular in many districts for a few years, and it is a very good makeshift method of preserving green fodder in years of superabundant growth.

TUB SILO.—Some fourteen years ago the overground, or tub silo as it is now called, was introduced to Victoria from America; and, owing to the ease with which it is both filled and emptied, it has almost superseded all other forms of silo.   It was first introduced to the Victorian farmers by the late David Syme.   Professor Cherry, then lecturer on Scientific Dairying to the Department of Agriculture, was so favourably impressed with its utility that he advocated its adoption far and wide.   It has been considerably improved and cheapened since its introduction; and now, with the assistance given by the Government by the extended payment system, it is within the reach of all Victorian farmers.

The tub or overground silo may be built of brick, concrete, all steel, all wood, or wood and iron combination, all of which have proved satisfactory and have stood the test of time.

The brick and concrete silos are the most costly, but their period of use-fulness is greater.

PIT SILO.

The all-steel portable silo, known as the Russell, is recommended where white ants are prevalent, where there is danger from bush fires,

WOOD AND IRON SILO.

or where the farmer is on a leased property. Being all steel, the white ants cannot destroy it, there is no fear of it being burnt, and it can be easily dismantled and rebuilt.

The all-wood silo can be cheaply constructed where sawn timber is readily procurable.

CONCRETE SILO.

STEEL AND ALL WOOD SILOS.

The wood and iron type of silo is very popular in all parts of the State; when properly constructed and limewashed before filling and after emptying, it will last many years.

When to Cut a Crop for Silage.

The time at which to cut a crop for silage varies with the different varieties usually ensiled. Thus, maize, one of the principal crops grown for silage, is ready when the bottom leaves are drying off and the grain is doughy and glazing. The same applies to sorghum, amber cane, planter's friend, millet, or teosinte. Oats, wheat, barley, rye, &c., should be ensiled when on the turn from the green to ripening stage; the grain will then be fairly full but milky. With weeds, thistles, wild oats, &c., it is necessary to ensile them as soon as the pollen appears, so as to prevent the seed from fouling the ground during the following season. When ensiling any immature growth it is necessary to mix some drier fodder with it to counteract the excessive moisture and thus prevent a soft mushy sour silage resulting.

As legumes, such as beans, clovers, lucerne, peas, and vetches, have been found to give as good value when dry cured as hay, it is not advisable to ensile them, except as portion of a mixture. When ensiled by themselves the loss of food properties is greater than the gain in palatability and digestibility, the loss in the most valuable nutrients being the heaviest.

Filling the Silo.

Briefly, it may be stated that the preservation of green fodder as silage depends on the fermentation going on in the mass, which is controlled by the amount of air present. Should an excess of air be allowed entry, then decomposition sets in and the material is ruined.

There are two recognized varieties of silage—sweet and sour. By sour, it must not be understood that the material is in any way offensive; it is pale greenish yellow in colour with a vinous odour. Sweet silage, on the other hand, is of a brown colour and has a sweet luscious odour. The sour variety is found more suitable for milking cows, while the sweet has been recommended for fattening stock.

Slow filling and well trampling, by keeping a minimum of air in the silo, arrests the fermentation; the temperature does not rise above 90 deg. Fahr., and sour silage is produced, whilst by quick filling the air is not so well drawn out, the temperature rises to 120 deg., or even to 150 deg. Fahr., and sweet silage is obtained.

Filling too quickly is not considered an advantage on account of the liability of the mass to generate too great a heat with the result that the silage is liable to decompose. On the other hand, filling too slowly is liable to result in a cooling off of the material before sealing the mass down, with the result that loss ensues.

Before commencing to fill the silo, the interior wall should be lime washed with a thick wash made of lime and skim milk. This may be done each evening after filling, using the silage as a stage. The wash is put on to protect the lining of the silo against the acid juices of the silage, and must never be neglected nor applied thinly.

Unless unavoidable, the crop or material intended for silage should not be cut until it has reached the proper stage of maturity.

Every effort should be made to ensile the material the same day as it is cut in the field.

In order to exclude as much air as possible and economize space, it is necessary to reduce the fodder to a fine mass before filling into the silo. It is therefore necessary to pass it through a chaff or silage cutter and cut it into half to three-quarters of an inch in length. From the

cutter it is carried by means of an elevator or blower, which should
deliver the material as near the centre of the silo as possible. This may
be done by the aid of bag chute attached to the mouth of the elevator
or the blower, whichever method is in use.

The labour of distributing the fodder is thus minimized, and an even
sample of the material will be distributed all over the silo. If the
fodder be allowed to fall direct from the mouth of the conveyor, the
heaviest parts will fall on one side, and the lighter parts on the other—
the silage will not settle evenly and loss will eventuate. To assist in
the close packing of the silage it is absolutely essential to well trample
it all over the silo. Trampling the sides or around the edges is not
sufficient, for with the shrinking of the centre the outer edges creep
towards it and away from the walls, thus allowing access of air and
consequent loss. The centre should always be kept a little higher than
the outer edges.

The rate of filling should not be under 5 ft. nor over 12 ft. per
day. Avoid, as much as possible, delays in filling; a day or less is not
serious but a longer period will have adverse results. The amount of
settlement that takes place after the silo has been filled, sealed, and
weighted is a fair index as to how it has been filled and packed. In
a well filled silo it will amount to close on 3 ft., and more in those
that have not received proper attention. The writer has seen a shrinkage
of 10 ft. in a 21-ft. silo that had been filled to the top but was not
trampled. The owner of this silo believed that trampling was injurious,
but after one season's trial he is now a greater advocate for trampling
and packing than he was for the other method. *Too much stress cannot
be laid on the importance of well packing the silage in the silo.*

Sealing and Weighting.

The satisfactory sealing and weighting of the silo are also very important features that make for success. Many devices have been tried
with more or less success, but all that is necessary is to cover the green
fodder with a sheet made of tarred bags and upon this place a foot of
chaffed straw or other waste material, and well wet same. This
is to encourage mould growths which act as an air-tight seal and thus
preclude air from gaining access to the silage. Upon the top of this
material place a foot deep of some weighty substances, such as sand,
earth, logs, brick or stone, to press down the top 4 or 5 ft. of silage;
all under that depth is pressed down by the weight above. If the precautions mentioned are taken, the farmer will be pleased with both silo
and silage.

The same precautions are necessary when filling a pit silo, whether
the fodder be chaffed or not. When ensiling whole sheaves in a pit silo,
start building from the centre by first making a heap there and laying
the sheaves in such a manner that they are placed lengthwise along the
walls, not butt ends as in a stack. In this case the order is reversed to
assist in excluding the air. Always build with centre higher than the
sides; if time permits, cut the bands and remove them.

If the pit is a large one, the ends of the pit should be sloped to
admit of the waggons or drays being driven right through the silo and
over the silage; this will aid very much indeed in consolidating the
silage. If a small silo is in use, take a draught horse into it and walk
him around, after every load is added, to pack the fodder.

Seal in the same way as a tub silo, and weight with the earth taken
out of the excavation. As shrinkage will be considerable, build the silage

several feet higher than the surface.   If it has been well filled and?
packed, it will only shrink to surface level.   Cut drains around the pit
to prevent water flowing in.

STACK SILAGE.

A stack of silage is built in the same way as a stack of hay.   The
necessary precautions to take are to guard against building the stack large
in area and low in height, as a large amount of green material can be
placed in a small area.   Hay stack dimensions are of no value for silage
stacks.   In general practice, it is found that one-fourth the area of a
ton of hay will hold a ton of silage.

During building, the stack should be weighted every night after
ceasing work.   This can be done by suspending weights on wires across
the stack, or placing some weighty material on it.   Finish off the stack
in a suitable shape to resist the weather, and weight it to assist settling
and exclusion of air.

Several devices for weighting stack silage have been tried, but none
are so satisfactory as the dead weight on top.   It is ever doing its
duty and does not require any attention after being placed there.   Logs,
stones, sand, bricks or earth may be used for weighting.   One good
plan is to make a framework of heavy saplings.   Lay these around the
edges, cutting notches in them so that they will fit into each other where
joined; then fill between them and all over the stack with earth.   This
device will do good work and give satisfaction.

OPENING THE SILO.

When opening a silo carefully remove the weight and seal.   The
latter, together with any mouldy silage that may be on top, should be
placed on the manure heap for future use as humus for the soil.

The silage required should be daily scraped off in layers from the top
and bagged or passed down a chute to the feed truck.   Avoid, as far
as practicable, sinking holes in the silage; in fact, keep as little of the
silage exposed to the air as possible.   Remember, air is the chief
factor in destroying silage.   Some careful farmers cover their silage with
a tarred bag sheet immediately they have removed all they want for the
day.

DAILY RATION.

The daily ration of silage for a dairy cow is from 30 to 40 lbs., when
fed with other fodders; when there is some grass available, 30 lbs. per
day is ample.   Sheep will eat as much as 3 lbs. a day, but 2 lbs. will
keep big wethers or ewes in good condition. . It is advisable to give
horses small quantities only of silage, otherwise there may be trouble from
stomach derangements; limit the amount fed to a few lbs. per day.
Pigs and poultry will only eat small quantities.

ADVANTAGES OF SILAGE.

Silage may be made of all plants that animals are allowed to eat in
the green state and such fodder preserved by this means loses but little
of its feeding properties in the process.   In one way there is a slight
improvement, that is, the tougher fibre of siloed fodder is softened and
made thereby more digestible and acceptable to animals.

At no time of the year do animals do better than in the height of
spring; they then rapidly make flesh and yield their maximum flow of

milk. It is for these reasons that the silo is recommended to the farmer so that the surplus growth of spring may be carried on in the same succulent condition to a leaner time. Dry fodder never equals the rich spring growths. No other method of fodder conservation can hope to approach the rational one of ensiling, for by that all the succulent juices are retained, the fibre is softened, and little of the food properties are lost; while, by dry curing the fodder, all the natural juices are lost.

No fodder is relished so much by stock. as silage. Its influence is very beneficial to the animal system, is invigorating, and prevents cripples and impaction. Succulent silage makes for good health and heavy milk flow.

With the help of a silo a farmer can take two crops off the same area in a year, for when a crop reaches the right stage of maturity it can be chaffed direct from the field into the silo, leaving the land free to be manured, prepared, and sown with a succeeding crop for silage.

The silo enables a farmer to make good use of all undesirable growths on the farm and to eradicate objectionable weeds; seed of any kind that has passed through the mild fermentation which goes on in a silo will not germinate. Silage made from any fodder can therefore be fed to animals without fear of spreading weeds.

It is safe from the ravages of birds and vermin. There is no danger from fire, and when properly made it will remain in a tempting easily-digested condition for years.

In times of drought, as many animals die of impaction as of starvation for the system is unable to deal continuously with toughened hard-to-digest fodder with the consequent result that death takes place, whereas had the crop been converted into silage a soft succulent easily digested fodder would have been available to tide the animals over the period of scarcity.

Crops can be ensiled at their best and placed ready for feeding at any time. On farms where green fodder crops are grown, and where ensiling is not practised, it is necessary to start carting the fodder for succulent feed before it is at its best. In many cases where the crop is an autumn one, reaping is continued into winter long after the crop has reached maturity and been damaged by frosts. The loads must of a necessity be light to enable the horse to pull it out of the paddock. The land is cut into ruts, making ploughing the following spring very difficult, whereas if this crop had been ensiled it could have been left till it reached the right stage of maturity and then ensiled in the long days when it is pleasant to work and when the ground is firm. The silage is ready for feeding in the short days of winter and unpleasant tasks are escaped.

Every year, in all parts of the State, there is a shortage of succulent fodder, from late summer to early spring, but by the aid of the silo cattle can, with profit, be tided over this time of stress. The dairy returns can be kept up—prices for dairy produce are highest in the lean times.

Silage therefore keeps up the dairy returns, keeps the stock healthy and thriving, enables the farmer to carry more stock, spurs him on to better efforts in all his farming pursuits by increasing the profits of the farm and aids in keeping up the fertility of the soil. No one who has fed silage to his stock would hesitate a moment before stating that a farm is not complete without a silo.

Throughout the whole of the State every spring there is an abundance of growth which goes to waste.   A few weeks later it would be of great benefit and assistance to the animals on the farm in enabling them to digest the hard dry innutritious fodder at their disposal, which is only eaten when necessity compels.   It is therefore the duty of every farmer to equip his farm with a silo.

THE ARTIFICIAL MANURES ACTS.

UNIT VALUES FOR 1912.

P. Rankin Scott, Chemist for Agriculture.

The Amending Artificial Manures Act of 1910 requires that manufacturers or importers shall, on or before 1st November in each year, register the brands of their several fertilizers, and at the same time supply to the Secretary for Agriculture, under declaration, the name and address of manufacturer or importer, the place of manufacture, the raw material from which the manure is manufactured or prepared, a statement of the percentages of nitrogen, phosphoric acid, and potash contained in the manures, and the retail price per ton.   From these percentages of plant foods and prices, the unit values of the constituents which have a commercial value are calculated, and these unit values constitute the basis of calculating the values of all manures for the period during which the registered brands continue in force, *i.e.*, until the publication in the *Government Gazette* of the list of registered brands for the following season.

A fixed limit of deficiency is allowed in all fertilizers (see schedule hereunder).   When a manure is shown to contain less nitrogen, phosphoric acid, or potash than the proportions stated on the label or in the invoice certificate, to the extent set forth in the schedule, the vendor is liable to a fine of £10 for a first offence, and £50 for any subsequent offence.

SCHEDULE.

Description of Manur	Percentages of Deficiency allowed in regard to Ingredients of Fertilizing Value.				
	Nitrogen.	Potash readily Soluble.	Phosphoric Acid.		
			Water Soluble.	Citrate Soluble.	Citrate Insoluble.
All manures containing nitrogen ..	0·50				
All manures containing potash .	..	1 ·00			
All manures containing water soluble phosphoric acid	..	..	1 .00*		
All manures containing citrate soluble phosphoric acid	..	..	..	1 ·00*	
All manure containing citrate insoluble phosphoric acid	..	..	..	..	1 ·00*

* NOTE.—Provided that the total phosphoric acid deficiency shall not exceed 1·50 per cent.

The label and invoice certificate referred to above are those mentioned in sections 5 and 7 of the principal Artificial Manures Act of 1904. These clauses require the vendor to attach to each bag a label or tag, declaring the composition of the manure sold in quantities exceeding 56 lbs., and to deliver to all purchasers of manures, at the time of sale, an invoice certificate conveying similar information to that required to be stated on the label.

Practical Utility of Unit Value System.

From the unit values and the guarantee contained on the tags or invoice certificates, it can be readily ascertained whether the price asked for a fertilizer is its reasonable commercial value (see method of calculation).

It will be noted that the price asked for mixed manures is generally higher than the commercial value which would be arrived at by means of a calculation from the unit value, but it must be remembered that in fixing the unit values no allowance is made for the cost of mixing and other incidental expenses, but only the actual value of the constituents which have a commercial value is taken into account.

The unit values and methods of calculation are shown hereunder :—

Unit Values of Manures for 1912.

(Calculated from declared prices of Fertilizers registered at the Office of the Secretary for Agriculture.)

	s.	d.
1 per cent. of nitrogen in the form of nitrate ...	17	5
1 per cent. of nitrogen in the form of ammonia ...	14	9
1 per cent. of nitrogen in the form of blood ...	12	9
1 per cent. of nitrogen in the form of fine bone ...	12	9
1 per cent. of nitrogen in the form of coarse bone and unspecified	12	0
1 per cent. of phosphoric acid as water soluble ...	4	9
1 per cent. of phosphoric acid as citrate soluble ...	4	0
1 per cent. of phosphoric acid as fine bone ...	4	6
1 per cent. of phosphoric acid as coarse bone ...	4	0
1 per cent. of phosphoric acid as insoluble, in bone superphosphates, and Thomas phosphates ...	3	0
1 per cent. of phosphoric acid as insoluble, in all other manures ...	2	0
1 per cent. of potash in the form of sulphate ...	5	5
1 per cent. of potash in the form of chloride ...	4	8

Method of Calculating the Commercial Value of a Manure.

The commercial value per ton of a manure sold in Victoria is obtained by multiplying the percentages stated of the fertilizing substances by the corresponding unit values fixed therefor, and adding the separate values together. Examples :—

1. **Nitrate of Soda—**

Invoice certificate or tag, 15·50 per cent. nitrogen.

Calculation—	£	s.	d.
15·50 × 17s. 5d. =	13	10	0
Calculated value per ton =	13	10	0

2. SUPERPHOSPHATE—

Invoice certificate or tag—

Water soluble phosphoric acid	17 per cent.
Citrate soluble phosphoric acid	1 ,,
Insoluble phosphoric acid ...	2 ,,
Total phosphoric acid	20 ,,

Calculation—

	£	s.	d.
Phosphoric acid (water soluble)—17 × 4s. 9d. = ...	4	0	9
,, ,, (citrate soluble)—1 × 4s. = ...	0	4	0
,, ,, (insoluble) —2 × 2s. = ...	0	4	0
Calculated value per ton	4	8	9

3. BONEDUST—

Invoice certificate or tag—

Nitrogen	3.50 per cent.
Phosphoric acid	19.50 ,,
Mechanical condition—	
Fine	40 per cent.
Coarse	60 ,,

Calculation—

			£	s.	d.
Nitrogen, fine	$\dfrac{3\cdot50 \times 40}{100}$	= 1·40 × 12s. 9d. =	0	17	10
Nitrogen, coarse	$\dfrac{3\cdot50 \times 60}{100}$	= 2·10 × 12s. =	1	5	2
Phosphoric acid, fine	$\dfrac{19\cdot50 \times 40}{100}$	= 7·80 × 4s. 6d. =	1	15	2
Phosphoric acid, coarse	$\dfrac{19\,50 \times 60}{100}$	= 11·70 × 4s. =	2	6	9
Total value per ton			6	4	11

4. MIXED MANURE—

Invoice certificate or tag—

Nitrogen as sulphate of ammonia	1·60 per cent.
Phosphoric acid—	
Water soluble	11·50 per cent.
Citrate soluble	·65 ,,
Citrate insoluble	1·25 ,,
Potash as muriate (chloride)	1·50 ,,

Calculation—

	£	s.	d.
1·60 × 14s. 9d. = ...	1	3	7
11·50 × 4s. 9d. = ...	2	14	7
·65 × 4s. = ...	0	2	7
1·25 × 2s. = ...	0	2	6
1·50 × 4s. 6d. = ...	0	6	9
Calculated value per ton	4	10	0

GENERAL REMARKS.

All substances containing nitrogen, phosphoric acid, or potash, manufactured or prepared for the purpose of fertilizing the soil, come under the operation of the Artificial Manures Acts.

Nitrogen is the most expensive of the three essential fertilizing elements. It exists in three forms—organic, ammonia, and nitrate. Organic nitrogen is widely distributed through the animal and vegetable kingdom, and its chief source for manurial purposes is from blood, bones, and other organic substances.

Nitrogen as ammonia is obtained chiefly from the destructive distillation of coal in gas manufacture. It combines with an acid radicle forming sulphate of ammonia, and in this form it is more readily soluble than organic nitrogen.

Nitrogen as nitrate is found in natural deposits in South America. It exists as nitrates of soda and potash. Like ammonium sulphate, it is completely soluble in water and diffuses readily through the soil. It is available as food to the plant without further change.

Phosphoric acid is derived from phosphates, the chief source of which is phosphate of lime. It occurs in fertilizers in three forms, which are distinguishable by their solubility (water-soluble, citrate-soluble, and insoluble), and these terms express the forms in which phosphoric acid is readily available, moderately so, or difficultly so, respectively.

The first mentioned form is, of course, soluble in water, the second is the portion soluble in citrate of ammonia after the extraction of the water soluble content. Citrate soluble form is generally considered to be available as plant food, and is of importance in arriving at the value of a fertilizer. The insoluble phosphoric acid is not of any immediate value to the plant, its action on soils is slow, and its value doubtful. Experience has shown the necessity of fertilizers which are immediately available to the plant, and for this reason insoluble phosphate is treated with sulphuric acid, and so converted into soluble superphosphate.

Bonedusts contain phosphoric acid and nitrogen, the phosphoric acid content being insoluble in water ; but, in a finely divided state, the particles have more surface exposure, and, consequently, decay quicker and become available to the plant. The fineness of a bonedust has, therefore, an important bearing on its availability.

Bone fertilizers are distinct from bonedusts, in that some are composed of bonedust, animal refuse, ground phosphate rock, and generally superphosphate, while others are bonedusts diluted with gypsum.

Ground phosphates and guanos differ from the organic phosphates such as bonedusts and animal fertilizers. They contain practically no organic matter, are denser in structure, and, except in extreme cases, they are not used to any extent without treatment with acid. They are used as raw material for the manufacture of superphosphates.

Thomas phosphate is the by-product obtained in the manufacture of steel, through the use of phosphatic iron ore. The phosphoric acid content is more readily soluble than in bones or rock phosphates.

Potash is obtained from natural deposits, and is supplied in the form of sulphate and chloride (muriate). Both forms are readily soluble.

The following is a list of fertilizers registered in the office of the Secretary of Agriculture for the year 1912, showing the particulars of each manure, as required by the Artificial Manures Acts, to be published in the *Government Gazette*.

LIST OF FERTILIZERS REGISTERED AT THE OFFICE OF SECRETARY FOR AGRICULTURE UNDER THE ARTIFICIAL MANURES ACTS.

Description of Manure.	Brand.	Nitrogen.	Phosphoric Acid.				Potash.	Price asked for the Manure per ton.	Where Obtainable.
			Water Soluble.	Citrate Soluble.	Insoluble.	Total.		£ s. d.	
		%	%	%	%	%	%		
Mainly Phosphoric, Phosphoric Acid readily Soluble.									
Concentrated Superphosphate	Sickle	…	40·00	4·00	…	44·00	…	12 10 0	Cuming, Smith, and Co., Melbourne
"	M.L.	…	40·00	4·00	…	44·00	…	12 10 0	Mt. Lyell M. and R. Co., Melbourne
Superphosphate	Alberts	…	40·00	4·00	2·00	44·00	…	12 10 0	Wischer and Co., Melbourne; Aust. Explosives and … Co.
"	Federal, O.S.	…	17·00	1·00	2·00	20·00	…	4 7 6	J. Cockbill, Post Office place, Melbourne
"	Florida, Sickle	…	17·00	1·00	2·00	20·00	…	4 10 0	Cuming, Smith, and Co., Melbourne
"	Hasell's	…	17·50	0·50	2·00	20·00	…	4 7 6	A. H. Hasell, Melbourne
" No. 1	M.L.	…	17·00	1·00	2·00	20·00	…	4 6 0	Mt. Lyell M. and R. Co., Melbourne
" No. 1	Rohs	…	17·00	1·00	1·00	19·00	…	4 6 0	P. Rohs, Bendigo
"	Wischer's	…	17·00	1·00	2·00	20·00	…	4 12 6	Wischer and Co., Melbourne
Containing Nitrogen also.									
Nitro Superphosphate	Sie	1·39	14·28	0·84	2·22	17·34	…	4 7 6	Cuming, Smith, and Co., Melbourne
"	Gardiner's	1·14	1·03	5·41	9·56	16·00	…	5 0 0	Exrs. G. Gardiner, Geelong
"	Hasell's	1·50	13·00	1·00	2·00	16·00	…	4 12 6	A. H. Hasell, Melbourne
"	M.L.	1·60	13·00	1·00	2·00	16·00	…	5 0 0	Mt. Lyell M. and R. Co., Melbourne
Blood, Bone, and Superphosphate	Wischer's	1·50	13·18	1·52	2·30	17·00	…	5 0 0	Wischer and Co., Melbourne
"	Federal	1·10	13·00	1·00	5·00	19·00	…	5 0 0	Aust. Explosives and Chem. Co., Melbourne
Bone and Superphosphate	Federal, B.B.S.	2·63	8·50	0·50	5·50	14·50	…	5 7 6	" " "
"	Federal, B.S., No. 1	1·50	8·50	0·50	10·00	19·00	…	5 7 6	" " "
"	Federal, 1 and 3	0·75	12·75	0·75	6·00	19·50	…	5 0 0	" " "
"	S. and F. Bugg	1·45	8·05	7·20	5·05	20·30	…	5 15 0	S. and F. Bugg, Kyneton
"	Cockbill's	1·50	12·75	1·50	4·75	19·00	…	5 5 0	J. Cockbill, Post Office-place, Melbourne
Dissolved Bone and Superphosphate	Sie	1·00	10·01	3·88	5·48	19·37	…	5 2 6	Cuming, Smith, and Co., Melbourne
Bone and Superphosphate (A)	"	1·50	8·50	0·50	10·00	19·00	…	5 7 6	" " "

		2·62	·50	0·50	5·50	14·50				Manufacturer
Blood, Bone, and Superphosphate (B)	Sickle						:	5 7	6 0	Cuming, Smith, and Co., Melbourne
Bone and Superphosphate (7)										
" " (⅓ and ⅔)	Gardiner's	0·75	12·75	0·75	6·00	19·50	:	5 0	0 0	Exrs. G. Gardiner, Geelong
" " (⅓ and ⅔)	Hasell's	1·25	2·82	8·00	9·82	17·00	:	4 15	0 0	A. H. Hall, Melbourne
" " No. 1		1·50	9·00	1·00	9·50	17·00	:	4 0	5 0	
" " No. 2	M.L."	1·50	12·75	1·25	9·50	19·50	:	5 5	7 6	M. Lyell M. and R. Co., Melbourne
Dissolved Bones and Superphosphate		1·50	8·50	1·30	9·00	19·00	:			
" Dissolved Bones and Superphosphate		0·90	12·75	1·00	5·75	19·50	:	5 5	6 0	" " "
Blood, Bone, and Superphosphate	A.N.A., Surprise	1·00	10·00	3·75	5·25	19·00	:	5 5	7 6	" " "
Animal Fertilizer and Superphosphate	Rohs	2·50	7·59	1·30	5·60	16·05	:	5 10	2 0	G. W. Hall, Braybrook
Bone and Superphosphate No. 1	Wischer and Co.	1·50	8·00	2·95	5·31	17·50	:	5 5	10 0	P. Rohs, Geo Bribo
" " No. 2		1·00	8·50	4·00	5·50	19·50	:	5 5	6 0	Wer and Co., Mel urne
Dissolved Bones and Superphosphate	" "	0·75	12·75	0·50	6·00	19·50	:	5 5	7 6	" " "
Blood, Bone, and Superphosphate	" "	2·63	10·01	0·75	0·48	19·37	:	5 5	2 6	" " "
			8·50	3·50	5·50	14·50	:	5 7	7 6	
Phosphoric Acid moderately Soluble.										
Thomas Phosphate	Federal	:	:	14·00	3·00	17·00	:	4 5	0 0	ukt. Exes and R Co.,
" "	Sickle	:	:	14·00	3·00	17·00	:	4 5	5 0	Cuming, Sth, and Co., Mel- bourne
" "	Hasell's	:	:	14·00	3·00	17·00	:	4 2	2 6	A. H. Hall, Melbourne
" "	M.L.	:	:	14·00	3·00	17·00	:	4 5	5 0	Mt. Lyell M. and R. Co., Mel- bourne
" " "Star"	Wer and Co.	:	5·00	14·00	3·00	17·50	:	4 5	6 0	Wer and Co., Melbourne
Thomas Phosphate and Superphosphate	Federal, T.S.	:		11·00	1·50	17·50	:	4 15	15 0	Aust. Explosives and R Co.
" "	Slo	:	5·00	11·00	1·50	17·50	:	4 15	0 0	Cuming, Sth, and Co., Mel
" "	M.L.	:	5·00	11·00	1·50	17·50	:	4 15	0 0	Mt. Lyll M. and R. Co., Mel- bourne
" "	Wischer and Co.	:	5·00	11·00	1·50	17·50	:	4 15	0 0	Wischer and Co., Melbourne
Phosphoric Acid difficultly Soluble.										
Bone Fertilizer	B.F., Sejal	5·00	:	3·00	13·00	16·00	:	6 15	0 0	Aust. Explosives and Chem. Co., Melbourne
" "	B.F.	3·00	:	3·50	14·50	18·00	:	6 17	6 0	S. and F. Bugg, Kyneton
" "	S. and F. Bugg	3·68	:	5·67	15·78	21·45	:	6 0	0 0	J. Cockbill, Post Office-place, Melbourne
" "	Cokbill's	3·50	:	3·50	14·75	18·25	:	5 10	10 0	
Bone Manure	Sickle, Special	6·00	:	5·00	10·00	15·00	:	7 0	0 0	Cuming, Smith, and Co., Mel- bourne
Bone Fertilizer		5·00	:	3·00	10·00	16·00	:	6 15	15 0	
" "	Sickle	3·00	:	3·50	14·50	18·00	:	5 17	10 0	P. Fitzgerald, Bentleigh
" "	Horseshoe	3·50	:	4·70	10·70	15·40	:	5 10	0 0	Exrs. G. Gardiner, Geelong
" "	No. 1, Magic	3·00	:	6·68	15·00	18·00	:	5 5	5 0	" " "
" "	No. 2, Magic	3·00	:	3·10	9·42	16·00	:	4 15	0 0	" " "
" "	Magic	2·47	:	4·61	12·90	16·08	:	6 0	0 0	A. H. Hasell, Melbourne
" "	Hasell's (A)	4·28	:	3·77	16·03	20·64	:	6 0	0 0	" " "
" "	" (B)	3·48	:		15·43	19·20	:	6 2		" " "

LIST OF FERTILIZERS REGISTERED AT THE OFFICE OF SECRETARY FOR AGRICULTURE UNDER THE ARTIFICIAL MANURES ACTS—continued.

Description of Manure.	Brand.	Nitrogen.	Phosphoric Acid.				Potash.	Price asked for the Manure per ton.	Where Obtainable.
			Water Soluble.	Citrate Soluble.	Insoluble.	Total.			
		%	%	%	%	%	%	£ s. d.	
Phosphoric Acid difficultly Soluble—continued.									
Bone Fertilizer	Hasell's (C)	2·52		2·73	15·51	18·24	...	5 5 0	A. H. Hasell, M·bourne
"	M.L. (A)	5·00		3·00	13·00	16·00	...	6 15 0	Mt. Lyell M. and R. Co., Melbourne
"	(B)	3·50		3·50	15·50	19·00		6 7 6	" " "
"	C)	3·00		3·50	14·50	18·00		6 17 6	" " "
"	(D)	5·00		2·60	11·40	14·00		6 7 6	A. Murphy, nat
"	Ark	3·72		3·98	12·90	16·88		6 10 0	G. W. nill, Braybrook
"	A.N.A., Surprise	3·00		6·00	9·00	15·00		6 10 0	Wischer and Co., Melbourne
"	Wischer and Co.,	5·00		9·00	7·00	16·00		6 15 0	
Ground Phosphate	Wischer and Co.	3·00		3·50	14·50	18·00	...	5 17 6	Aust. Explosives and Chem. Co.,
"	Federal, G.P.				36·50	36·50		5 5 0	
Pacific Island Guano	Flag, A.G.C.	0·50		3·50	12·50	16·00	...	3 7 6	H. R. Black, Collins-street. Melbourne
Ground Phosphate	Sickle				36·65	36·65		5 0 0	Ong, nith, and Co., Melbourne
Maldon Island Guano	Hasell's				22·90	22·90		3 10 0	A. "Hasell,"
Guano (Ground Rock Phosphate)	"				27·50	27·50		4 0 0	Mt. Lyell M. and L Co., Melbourne
Ground Phosphate	M.L.				36·65	36·65		5 0 0	bourne
Guano	Wischer and Co.				23·00	23·00		3 10 0	Wischer and Co., Melbourne
"	"				23·00	23·00		3 10 0	" " "
Ground Phosphate	"				36·50	36·50		5 0 0	
Containing Nitrogen, Phosphoric Acid, and Potash.									
Sugar Beet Manure	Federal, Beet.	4·50	11·00	0·75	1·25	13·00	5·50	8 0 0	Aust. Explosives and Chem. Co., Melbourne
Citrus Manure, Special	S.C.P.	1·00	6·40	0·38	5·56	12·34	15·00	8 10 0	" " "
Maize Manure	M.Z.	2·36	10·20	0·60	6·20	17·00	2·00	6 0 0	" " "
Top Dressing for Grass	T.D.	1·60	11·00	0·60	1·30	12·94	1·50	5 0 0	" " "
Grass Laying Manure	G.L.	1·50	8·50	0·50	5·50	14·50	2·00	5 0 0	" " "
Horticultural Manure	H.M.	2·50	11·02	0·68	1·38	14·68	10·00	5 0 0	" " "
Pea, Bean, and Clover Manure	P.B.	0·50	10·00	0·60	4·20	14·80	3·00	6 0 0	" " "
Onion Manure	M.G.	2·00	11·00	0·64	1·30	12·94	5·00	6 0 0	" " "
Apricot and Peach Manure	A.P.P.	2·46	9·00	0·53	1·06	10·59	12·00	9 0 0	" " "
Orchard Manure	F.M.	1·80	13·22	0·78	1·55	15·55	8·00	7 0 0	" " "

Manure	Brand	Company						
			6 0	**5·00**	**16·44**	**1·64**	**0·80**	**14·00** / **1·00**
Potato Manure	Federal, Potato	Aust. Explosives and Chem. Co., Melbourne	6 0	5·00	16·44	1·64	0·80	14·00 / 1·00
Rape Manure	Rape	,,	5 0	2·00	15·30	4·18	0·62	10·50 / 0·98
Vine Manure	V.S.P.	,,	12 0	12·00	8·41	0·84	0·42	7·15 / 7·00
Grass Manure	V.N.P.	,,	10 0	12·00	8·91	0·89	0·45	7·57 / 5·53
	Sickle	,,	5 0	2·70	20·75	9·05	0·65	11·05 / 0·30
... Manure	,,	Cuming, Smith, and Co., Melbourne	8 0	8·38	13·20	1·32	0·96	11·22 / 4·00
... Manure	,,	,,	12 0	13·94	14·00	0·72	0·38	6·18 / 3·94
... Manure	,,	,,	6 0	1·80	16·40	1·64	0·82	13·94 / 2·38
Onion Manure	,,	,,	6 0	3·59	16·00	1·60	0·80	13·60 / 2·40
Orchard Manure	,,	,,	7 0	7·18	15·20	1·52	0·76	12·92 / 1·20
... Manure	,,	,,	6 0	5·18	17·28	6·18	3·10	8·00 / 1·30
... Manure	,,	,,	6 0	4·15	15·20	1·72	0·86	14·62 / 4·00
... Manure	Hasell's	A. H. Hasell, Melbourne	5 0	7·18	13·00	1·62	0·76	12·92 / 1·20
Sugar Beet Manure / Crop Manure	,,	,,	9 0	8·20	13·10	1·25	0·75	11·00 / 4·00
... and	,,		6 0	1·00	14·25	1·50	0·75	11·00 / 4·00
Grass Manure	,,		8 0	1·50	21·66	7·40	1·10	12·50 / 3·00
Onion Manure	,,	,,	7 0	3·06	11·95	1·30	0·50	9·55 / 3·40
Horticultural and Tomato Manure	,,		10 0	8·32	13·50	2·00	0·75	11·00 / 2·00
Orchard and ... Manure	,,		6 0	7·14	15·00	0·25	0·50	14·00 / 3·00
Potato Manure	,,	Mt. Lyell M. and R. Co., Melbourne	6 0	4·10	10·20	2·90	0·75	9·75 / 3·20
... Crop Mixture	M.L.	,,	10 0	1·00	10·20	1·75	1·25	6·80 / 3·00
Fodder Crop Manure	,,	,,	6 0	4·75	10·25	2·00	1·00	7·25 / 3·25
... Crop Manure	,,	,,	6 0	2·70	20·75	9·05	0·65	11·00 / 0·30
Grass, Laying Down	,,	,,	5 0	1·00	14·00	1·75	1·25	11·00 / 3·00
... Manure	,,	,,	8 0	14·00	7·50	1·45	0·75	11·00 / 4·00
Horticultural Manure	,,	,,	7 0	8·25	15·20	1·50	1·00	11·00 / 3·35
... Manure	,,	,,	10 0	3·00	12·10	1·50	0·50	13·50 / 3·00
Onion Manure	,,	,,	6 0	8·80	16·30	7·30	1·00	8·50 / 1·05
Potato Manure (with Bone)	,,	,,	6 0	4·15	17·20	2·00	1·00	13·00 / 1·20
Rape Manure	,,	,,	5 0	1·00	16·00	1·45	0·75	13·00 / 4·00
Tomato Manure	,,	,,	8 0	8·25	13·20	1·51	0·75	13·00 / 2·35
... Manure	,,	,,	7 0	7·20	17·25	1·75	0·85	14·65 / 0·75
Maize Manure	,,	,,	5 0	2·55	18·00	1·95	0·90	9·80 / 0·50
Grass Manure	Wischer and Co.	Wischer and Co., Melbourne	5 0	2·60	18·00	1·80	0·75	15·30 / 3·38
... Manure (Key Fertilizer)	,,	,,	7 0	2·55	16·50	0·95	0·55	9·80 / 3·00
M.G. Manure (Special)	,,	,,	10 0	9·70	11·00	1·10	0·55	9·35 / 5·00
Horticultural Manure	,,	,,	6 0	13·00	10·00	1·39	0·50	8·50 / 3·38
Nurseryman's ... Food	,,	,,	6 0	5·00	11·00	1·00	0·50	9·15 / 2·50
Orchard Manure	,,	,,	12 0	4·50	16·00	1·10	0·96	15·00 / 2·50
... Manure	,,	,,	6 0	6·50	11·68	1·58	0·75	8·50 / 0·94
Onion Manure	,,	,,	10 0	4·50	16·30	7·30	0·50	4·45 / 1·05
... Manure (with Bone)	,,	,,	12 0	6·50	5·25	0·55	0·25	8·50 / 7·75
... Manure	,,	,,	6 0	7·78	16·30	7·31	0·50	8·50 / 1·65
Vine Manure	,,	,,	7 0	7·65	10·90	1·45	0·95	8·50 / 3·00

LIST OF FERTILIZERS REGISTERED AT THE OFFICE OF SECRETARY FOR AGRICULTURE UNDER THE ARTIFICIAL MANURES ACTS—*continued.*

Description of Manure.	Brand.	Nitrogen. %	Phosphoric Acid. Water Soluble. %	Phosphoric Acid. Citrate Soluble. %	Phosphoric Acid. Insoluble. %	Phosphoric Acid. Total. %	Potash. %	Price asked for the Manure per ton. £ s. d.	Where Obtainable.
Containing Nitrogen and Phosphoric Acid.									
Special Citrus Manure	Federal, S.C.	2·36	5·21	0·30	7·71	13·22	...	5 10 0	Aust. Explosives and Chem Co., Melbourne
Apricot and Peach Manure	A.P.	3·70	12·00	0·70	1·41	14·11	...	7 0 0	,, ,, ,,
Vine Manure	V.S.	6·70	11·30	0·66	1·33	13·29	...	9 5 0	,, ,, ,,
Grass Manure (Top Dressing)	V.N.	5·74	10·70	0·63	1·26	12·59	...	8 5 0	,, ,, ,,
	Sickle	0·70	10·40	0·97	1·93	19·30	...	5 0 0	Cuming, Smith and Co., Melbourne
Rape Manure	Hasell's	1·39	14·28	0·84	2·22	17·34	...	5 0 0	A. H. Hasell, Melbourne
,, ,,	,,	1·20	14·25	1·00	2·25	17·50	...	5 0 0	,,
Containing Phosphoric Acid and Potash.									
Grain Manure (Special)	Federal, S.G.	...	16·50	1·00	2·00	19·50	0·75	4 15 0	Aust. Explosives and Chem. Co., Melbourne
Orchard Manure	Sickle	...	12·00	0·71	1·41	14·12	14·00	7 10 0	,, ,, ,,
Leguminous Manure	N.N.	...	15·30	0·95	2·59	18·84	2·99	5 0 0	Cuming, Smith, and Co., Melbourne
Lawn Manure	Hasell's	...	12·00	1·00	3·00	16·00	4·59	5 0 0	A. H. Hasell, Melbourne
Lawn Manure ,,	M.L.	...	7·00	11·00	1·00	19·00	2·00	5 0 0	Mt. Lyell M. and R. Co., Melbourne
Grass Manure (Top Dressing)	,,	...	7·00	11·00	1·00	19·00	2·00	5 0 0	Wischer and Co., Melbourne
Leguminous Manure	,,	...	11·50	2·00	1·50	17·00	4·75	5 0 0	,, ,,
Pea Manure	Wischer's	...	14·45	0·85	1·70	17·00	7·78	6 2 0	,, ,,
Leguminous Manure	,,	...	15·30	1·00	1·90	18·20	2·60	5 0 0	,, ,,

LIST OF FERTILIZERS REGISTERED AT THE OFFICE OF SECRETARY FOR AGRICULTURE UNDER THE ARTIFICIAL MANURES ACTS—*continued.*

Description of Manure.	Brand.	Nitrogen.	Phosphoric Acid.	Potash.	Price asked for Manure per ton.	Where Obtainable.
		%	%	%	£ s. d.	
Mainly Nitrogenous.						
Sulphate of Ammonia	Federal, A.S.	20·00			15 0 0	Aust. Explosives and Chem. Co., Melbourne
,, ,,	Sickle	20·00			15 0 0	Cuming, Smith, and Co., Melbourne
,, ,,	Hasell's	20·00			15 0 0	A. H. Hasell, Melbourne
,, ,,	M.G.Co.	20·00			15 0 0	Metropolitan Gas Co., Melbourne
,, ,,	M.L.	20·00			15 0 0	Mt. Lyell M. and R. Co., Melbourne
,, ,,	Wischer and Co.	20·00			15 0 0	Wischer and Co., Melbourne
Nitrate of Soda	Federal, S.W.	15·50			13 10 0	Aust. Explosives and Chem. Co., Melbourne
,, ,,	Sickle	15·50			13 10 0	Cuming, Smith, and Co., Melbourne
,, ,,	Hasell's	15·50			13 10 0	A. H. Hasell, Melbourne
,, ,,	M.L.	15·50			13 10 0	Mt. Lyell M. and R. Co., Melbourne
,, ,,	Wischer and Co.				13 10 0	Wischer and Co., Melbourne
Blood	Federal Pure Bld Fertiliser	11·50	1·00	0·18	8 10 0	W. Angliss and Co., Melbourne
,,	Ciampion	11·00	2·00		7 15 0	John Cooke and Co., Melbourne
,,	Sickle	7·50	1·00		6 0 0	Cuming, Smith, and Co., Melbourne
,,	M.C.C.	7·50			4 3 0	Melbourne City Council, Melbourne
,, (A.)	M.L.	11·00	1·00		8 16 0	Mt. Lyell M. and R. Co., Melbourn
,, (B.)	M.L.	7·50	f·00		6 0 0	,, ,,
,,	Wischer and Co.	7·50			6 0 0	Wischer and Co., Melbourne
Mainly Potassic.						
Kainit	Sickle			12·40	5 0 0	Cuming, Smith, and Co.,
,,	M.L.			12·40	5 0 0	Mt. Lyell M. and R. Co.,
,,	Wischer and Co.			12·40		Wischer and Co.,
Nitrate of Potash	Federal, P.N.	15·00		46·00	28 0 0	Aust. Explosives and ... Co., Melbourne
,,	Sickle	13·00		46·00	28 0 0	Cuming, Smith, and Co.,
,,	M.L.	13·00		46·00	28 0 0	Mt. Lyell M. and R. Co.,
,,	Wischer and Co.	15·00		46·00		Wischer and Co.,
Potash Chloride (Muriate)	Federal, P.M.			60·50	14 5 0	Aust. Explosives and ...
,, ,,	Sickle			60·00	14 10 0	Cuming, 1 ifth, and Co.,
,, ,,	Hasell's			60·00	14 5 0	A. H. Hasell,
,, ,,	M.L.			60·00	14 5 0	Mt. Lyell M. and R. Co.,
,, ,,	Wischer and Co.			64·00	14 5 0	Wischer and Co.,
Potash Sulphate	Federal, P.S.			52·00	14 7 6	Aust. Explosives and ...
,,	Hasell's			52·00	14 12 6	A. H. Hasell,
,,	M.L.			52·00	14 7 6	Mt. Lyell M. and R. Co.,
,,	Wischer and Co.			52·00	14 7 6	Wischer and Co.,

List of Fertilizers Registered at the Office of Secretary for Agriculture under the Artificial Manures Acts—*continued.*

Description of Manure.	Brand.	Nitrogen.	Phosphoric Acid.	Mechanical Condition.		Price asked for the Manure per ton.	Where Obtainable.
				Fine.	Coarse.		
		%	%	%	%	£ s. d.	
Containing Phosphoric Acid and Nitrogen—Phosphoric Acid moderately Soluble.							
Bonedust ...	Lara ...	2·10	18·60	28·00	72·00	5 5 0	J. W. Branch, Geelong West
Bonemeal ...	Sickle ...	3·00	21·00	30·00	70·00	6 10 0	Cuming, Smith, and Co., Melbourne
Bonedust ...	Horseshoe ...	3·90	15·45	52·20	47·80	7 0 0	P. Fitzgerald, Bentleigh
Bone and Blood ...	Hasell's ...	5·50	17·60	40·00	60·00	7 0 0	A. H. Hasell, Melbourne
Bonedust ...	Jopling's ...	3·52	19·17	18·50	81·50	6 5 0	J. R. Jopling, Ballarat
„ ...	Vauxhall ...	3·86	23·25	33·70	66·30	6 0 0	W. Moore, Panmure
Bonemeal ...	M.L. ...	3·00	21·00	30·00	70·00	6 10 0	Mt. Lyell M. and R. Coy. Ltd., Melbourne
Bonedust ...	Rohs ...	4·00	18·00	66·00	34·00	5 15 0	P. Rohs, Bendigo
Bonemeal ...	Wischer's ...	3·00	21·00	30·00	70·00	6 10 0	Wischer and Co., Melbourne
*Animal Fertilizer ...	Champion ...	6·00	9·00	50·00	50·00	5 15 0	John Cooke and Co., Melbourne

* Not sold retail.

1st December, 1911.

P. RANKIN SCOTT,
Chemist for Agriculture.

NHILL FARM COMPETITIONS, 1911.

A. E. V. Richardson, M.A., B.Sc. (Agric.), Agricultural Superintendent.

In connexion with the Nhill Farm Competitions for 1911, entries were received in the following sections:—Large Farms, Small Farms, Crops, Fallow.

SECTION I.—LARGE FARMS.

The following scale of points was used in judging these farms:—

A. Best system of cropping, rotation, cultivation	35
B. Character, condition, and value of farm crops	20
C. Condition of the fallow, taking area into consideration ...	20
D. Live Stock—	
(a) Horses	25
(b) Sheep	20
(c) Cattle	10
(d) Pigs	5
(e) Poultry	5
E. General farm equipment	20
F. Boundary and subdivisional fences and gates	20
G. The most complete and efficient system of water storage ..	45
H. Arrangement, character, and condition of farm buildings ...	20
I. Best kept and most suitable orchard and vegetable garden ...	10
J. Best provision of reserve fodder	20
K. Best efforts in direction of tree planting	5
L. Farm and live stock insurance	5

DETAILS OF JUDGING.

System of Cropping, Cultivation, Rotation, and Manuring.

The general scheme of rotation and cropping varied within very small limits among the competitors in all sections. In most instances, the general plan followed was a four-course rotation in which wheat, preceded by a bare fallow, headed the series. The wheat stubbles are usually burnt off; and, after a preliminary discing, oats, either with or without manure, are sown as the second crop in the series. These oats are invariably stripped; and, during the third year, the self-sown oats are grazed with sheep. Finally, the rotation is brought to a close with a season of bare fallowing, which serves as a preliminary to the next wheat crop. Under such a scheme of rotation, it is apparent that only one-fourth of the holding is under wheat and one-fourth in bare fallow, whilst the remainder is either grazed or partially devoted to oats. On the larger holdings, the rotation is still further extended by interposing two years of grazing between each successive round of wheat crops. The rotation is thus a five years' course, comprising 1, wheat; 2, oats; 3, grazing; 4, grazing; 5, fallow; 6, wheat; *i.e.*, one wheat crop in five years.

In other cases, two wheat crops were taken off in succession, thus necessitating one wheat crop being placed on stubble land—a very risky practice in a dry season—and the rotation then worked out as follows:—1, wheat; 2, wheat; 3, oats; 4, grazing; 5, grazing; 6, fallow.

Whatever may be the merits of these various practices, it must be clearly apparent that they may only be profitably practised when land values are comparatively low, and when each individual holder has a relatively large area of land. With a considerable rise in the price of land, and the inevitable increase of population that must be ahead of Victoria, these practices must undergo considerable modification in favour

TURKEY RED AND KUBANKA WHEAT AT MR. GEORGE BATSON'S, NHILL.

of rotations which will yield higher net returns per acre. Indeed, the time will soon come —if prices for land increase at a rate even approximating that of the last decade—before those who are now practising such rotations will find it more profitable to sell their land and invest the money at fixed deposit rather than continue a system of rotation by which only one crop of importance is obtained in four or five years. In this connexion, systematic and continued experimental work, having for its object the testing of every possible rotation likely to be suitable to the Wimmera district, would be of invaluable service to the primary producers of the district. Some of the farmers of the district have been experimenting in this direction, but it must be recognized that the scope of any experimental work that may be carried out on a private farm under ordinary conditions is very strictly limited.

The Man on the Land, though he may have the inclination and the patience, may not always have the necessary time and facilities for carrying on experimental work of a far-reaching character. In this connexion it is pleasing to find that there are some in the district who do find time to tackle experimental work, and not solely on their own account, but for the general advancement of the agricultural practice of the district.

Mr. Batson, for example, has a most interesting collection of plots, which include, *inter alia*, Swedish oats, Polish wheats (*Triticum Polonicum*), Emmer (*T. dicoccum*), and many American wheats of the Durum class, like Kubanka, Chul, Galgalos, Fretes, Turkey Red, as well as Egyptian wheat, rye and rye grasses, rape, barley, and lucerne.

The American wheats referred to above are supposed to be very drought resistant in the United States, but they have yet to prove that claim in competition with the best of our Australian wheats.

It is interesting to note that these

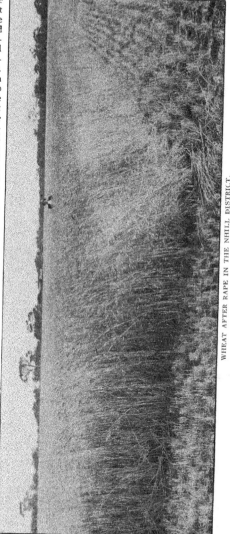

WHEAT AFTER RAPE IN THE NHILL DISTRICT.

American wheats did rather badly when first introduced, but Mr. Batson persevered with them; and now, having become acclimatized, they are showing up well in comparison with varieties like Federation, Dart's Imperial and Jumbuck.

Besides these variety tests, Mr. Batson has conducted manurial tests, and has experimented with forage crops such as rape and barley. This year, he has a fine crop of wheat grown after a rape crop which was fed down with sheep. Though, with Mr. Batson and Mr. H. E. Dahlenburg, the rape crop has not been too successful, the principle involved in this departure from the traditional practice of the district is of the very greatest importance. What is needed in the Wimmera is a hardy quick-growing winter forage, which, sown in autumn, will come up with the first rains; and, maturing quickly, will be available in July and August before the natural herbage has made much growth. Could such a fodder be obtained, it is safe to say that it would lead to great developments in the Wimmera district, and the necessity for relying on the natural pasture and wild oats would be obviated. Further, if such a fodder were of a leguminous character, the additional advantage of increasing the organic nitrogen content of the soil would be gained.

Barley is not appreciated to any large extent in the district, and this may be due to the fact that most attempts to grow good samples of malting barley have failed. The six-rowed barleys for feed are very drought resistant, especially if suitable varieties are chosen; and, with proper treatment, they will be found a most profitable adjunct in any system of mixed farming in the drier districts of the State.

Experimental work, however, is absolutely necessary for the continuous and progressive advance of agricultural practice, and Mr. Batson stands out prominently by his enterprise in testing new varieties of wheat, oats, barley, rye, rape, grasses and lucerne, also in growing those that are most successful on a large scale, as well as in conducting manurial and other trials.

The system of cultivation, manuring and rotation, adopted by Messrs. Crouch and Dahlenburg, differs very little in detail. Mr. Sanders, besides lengthening the chain of rotation, grows two wheat crops in succession, one of which is on stubble land. It is not a practice, however, which could be generally followed with success; and, if this season has not fully demonstrated the futility of growing wheat on stubble land in the Wimmera, it has, at least, done so in the other wheat-growing portions of the State.

Cleanest and Best Crops.

Many of the crops examined were not nearly so clean as was expected, owing to the prevalence of wild oats. There can be no doubt that the presence of such oats in the wheat crops will reduce the yield in the Nhill district by bushels per acre this season. As these oats shed their grain long before harvest, it is safe to assume that the 1911 crop will leave a legacy of rubbish for future crops; and, providing that the usual rotation is practised, considerable difficulty will be experienced in ridding the land of this pest.

In spite of the acknowledged damage done to the crop by wild oats, many wheat-growers solace themselves with the fact that some of the damage done by this pest will be counterbalanced by the grazing value of the wild oats, which spring up spontaneously from the stubbles with the fall of the first rains. In spite of the prevalence of wild oats, some tolerably good crops were seen.

Mr. Batson's crop was, on the whole, the best and most regular of the large farm crops.   Mr. Crouch's crops were very good, but, in one paddock of Federation pickled with ½ lb. of bluestone to the bag, the crop was very badly smutted.   This empirical method of pickling, as I subsequently discovered, was largely practised in the district, and should be displaced by a system in which solutions of known strength and concentration are used.

Condition of the Fallow.

In awarding points for fallow, the area, depth and character of the soil, mulch, freedom from weeds, regularity and evenness, and amount of moisture conserved below the mulch, were taken into consideration.

Mr. Sanders lost heavily in this section on account of the comparative absence of moisture in the fallows, the rough and crusty nature of a fair area of fallow and the prevalence of weeds.

READY FOR WORK—HORSES AND STABLE ACCOMMODATION AT
MR. C. E. DAHLENBURG'S.

Mr. Crouch's fallow was in good condition, and the conservation of soil moisture was assisted by a liberal and effective soil mulch.

Live Stock.

Horses.—In all instances the display of horses was very creditable, and more especially was this the case with draught stock. Messrs. Sanders, Dahlenburg, and Crouch each possess a number of roomy, strong-boned, good-quality mares. With the exception of Mr. Sanders, however, little use has been made of them; for there were only a few young stock coming on.   Mr. Batson's horses are more uneven in quality than the other competitors, and he has allowed them to get in rather low condition.   Mr. Dahlenburg's horses, I think, are the best and most even in quality, though Mr. Sanders has more young stock of good quality.

Sheep.—In all cases, the sheep are used for wool only, and breeding lambs for freezers does not, therefore, come into consideration.   The selection of pure merino ewes and rams of hardy constitution, with big frames, good length of staple, and dense in the fleece, is therefore a most important consideration.

The sheep of both Messrs. Sanders and Batson possess the characteristics mentioned above, and they have taken care to see that the ewes are mated with rams of good quality.

Other Stock.—On none of the farms were cows, pigs and poultry relied upon to swell the farm income. While the holdings of the district remain comparatively large, it is perhaps inevitable that wheat and sheep will monopolize the attention of the large wheat-farmer, and cattle, pigs, and poultry be considered as mere appendages to the farm.

Certainly, the difficulty of obtaining an adequate supply of labour in country districts will prevent many from undertaking any other activities than those which can be immediately performed by the members of the family. At the same time. it is certain that the returns from every farm could be greatly augmented by the systematic exploitation of these avenues of profit. The cows. poultry, and pigs have been regarded merely as ministering to the domestic comforts of the home. and a policy of *laissez faire* has, therefore, been adopted in regard to these.

Very little attention was given anywhere to the housing of the pigs and poultry. The most popular structure for pigs was the familiar pole and thatch, which has, at least, the merit of coolness on a summer day ; and, for feeding receptacles, the hollowed-out log had many faithful devotees. With respect to the policy adopted in regard to poultry, it is with some satisfaction I noted that, even if, in some cases, houses were not provided, the hens were at least prevented from roosting on the reels of the binders by the erection of wire screens on the implement sheds, and by inducing the fowls to make a home in a clump of shady trees adjoining the farm buildings.

Farm Implements and Machinery.

The efficiency of the farm operations is largely dependent on the type of implements and machinery used. Except in one instance, all farms. large and small were provided with portable engines, either oil or steam. and these performed such diverse duties as sawing wood, chaffcutting, winnowing. and running a machine shearing plant.

There was little to choose between the various farms in the completeness of the equipment. A comparison of the present day implements with those in use a decade ago affords very striking proof of the advancement made in recent years in the direction of improved machinery. The only weak point in an otherwise excellent equipment was the general absence of suitable seed graders. These should be looked upon as indispensable implements on every wheat farm, and their systematic use for the preparation of seed wheat will lead to a considerable improvement in the average yields.

Among many ingenious time and labour-saving novelties was a useful seed-covering appliance invented by Mr. Batson. It consists of a shaft, attached to the footboard of the drill. and fitted with a number of long narrow tines, which, by means of a lever, may be inclined at any obtuse angle with the soil. These tines act as a set of harrows ; and, inasmuch as they are attached immediately behind the hoes. and in a position constantly fixed with respect to the hoes. they bring about a more regular covering effect than that of an ordinary harrow.

For mallee land where stumps have not yet been eliminated, the tines are provided with a clock spring attachment which permits them to safely negotiate the stumps.

Fences.

The boundary and subdivisional fences were, for the most part, fairly substantial, in good order and sheep proof.   Some lines of fence, how-

A SEED COVERING APPLIANCE.
Invented by Mr. George Batten, Nhill.

ever, are old and need immediate renewing.   Good fitting, well swung gates are of some importance in economic working, and much delay is

PATENT SEED COVERER FOR MALLEE LAND.
Made by Mr. Davis, Nhill.

caused, as well as mental irritation, when the familiar "barb wire" gate is continually encountered in passing from paddock to paddock.

Mr. Crouch, with his 30 wooden and 8 "cyclone" gates, has now banished these nerve-racking, unsightly structures from his property, and the equanimity with which he may now contemplate his gates will more than compensate him for the trifling cost of installation.   Mr. Crouch has also replaced several miles of old fence by a neat substantial post and dropper structure.

Water Storage.

This is one of the most important features to be considered in the drier portions of the State.   Though Nature has not provided the Wimmera farmer with running creeks and rivers, she has provided an unlimited supply of underground water of very good quality which may be obtained from wells or bores.   Over the greater portion of the district the sub-soil is eminently suited for holding water, and very little is lost by

RESIDENCE OF MR. C. E. DAHLENBURG; KIATA.

seepage and drainage from properly constructed dams.   However large and numerous dams may be on any given property, it is always a commendable practice to tap the unlimited underground stores of moisture, by a bore or a well.

Mr. Sanders has a well 278 feet deep, fitted with a windmill and pump.   A 7,000-gallon storage tank is located on the highest portion of his holding, and from this the water gravitates through pipes and ball taps to water several 320-acre blocks.   There are thirty-nine dams, conveniently placed in various parts of the holding, and varying in capacity from 700 to 5,000 cubic yards.   In addition, there is a large swamp occupying over 1,000 acres on a portion of the property; and this, in latter years, has been covered with a fine body of perfectly fresh water.

Windmills placed conveniently near the homestead furnish a supply of water from neighbouring dams for the houses and gardens of Messrs.

Batson and Dahlenburg, whilst Mr. Crouch has a windmill attached to a well 160 feet deep, from which water is lifted into two tanks of 2,000

THE ÆSTHETIC SIDE OF FARM LIFE.

gallons each. The whole of the rainwater from the homestead and farm buildings is conserved, either in underground cement tanks or in numerous

ANOTHER VIEW OF MR. C. E. DAHLENBURG'S GARDEN.

overground galvanized-iron tanks, at the properties of Messrs. Dahlenburg, Crouch, and Sanders.

Farm Buildings, Etc.

Pride of place must be given in this regard to Mr. Dahlenburg. Besides the modern commodious 11-roomed brick residence with all conveniences, there is a fine array of substantial farm buildings. Foremost among these is the stable, 90 ft. x 40 ft., well ventilated, solidly built, and blocked throughout with well-set sleepers. Attached to this is a large galvanized-iron chaff shed, 40 ft. x 22 ft., and engine shed. Near by is a barn 50 ft. x 24 ft., built on piles, with a fine wooden floor, and capable of accommodating 3,000 bags of wheat, and a circular iron silo 15 ft. x 10 ft., in which oats for feed are stored. Other features of interest are the implement shed, dairy, smithy, fowlhouse, and drafting yards for sheep.

RESIDENCE OF MR. GEORGE BATSON, NHILL.

Mr. Crouch's homestead and buildings have not been laid out on the same generous plan, but they are very well suited for the purpose for which they were intended. Mr. Crouch has a fine stable, well appointed implement shed, smithy, buggy shed, chaffhouse and engine house; and, in addition, he has a commodious hayshed, and an up-to-date, well-built woolshed, 55 ft. x 27 ft., with drafting yards attached.

In all the farms examined in this section, provision was made for lighting the house with gas, either acetylene or ærogen.

Orchard and Garden.

One of the most pleasing features in the competition is the recognition of what might be called the æsthetic side of farm life.

On Mr. C. E. Dahlenburg's property, there was a beautiful display of flowers in the gardens and greenhouse. Neatly clipped privet hedges. 80 varieties of roses, a bewildering array of poppies, godetias, dahlias, and carnations, pleasantly set in lawns of well-kept buffalo and couch grass, with ornamental trees and shrubs in the background, combine to make a most artistic effect.

One cannot help feeling that here, at least, an effort has been made to make farm life attractive, and to make the farm what it should be— a home.   Primarily, of course, a farm must be profitable, but it does not succeed, in the highest sense, unless it appeals both to youth and old age, by reason of its intrinsic attractiveness.   The practical value of the gardens is not overlooked; for, in addition to a well regulated series of vegetable beds, there are over 2 acres of assorted fruit trees, the majority of which are in full bearing.

The orchards of Messrs. Batson, Dahlenburg, and Sanders were well kept and nicely laid out, and provide an excellent variety of fruit for

PORTION OF MR. BATSON'S ORCHARD AND VEGETABLE GARDEN.

domestic purposes.   The vegetable garden of Mr. Batson, as well as his well-kept vineyard, is worthy of special mention.

Tree Planting.

Very little systematic work has been done in this direction.   In all cases, belts of natural timber have been reserved in various paddocks for shelter purposes, and these, it may be considered, to a large extent, render tree planting unnecessary.   The native bulloak and box. however, cast very little shade, and small clumps of thickly planted sugar gums and pines would serve the dual purpose of adequate shelter and subsequent profit.

Summary.

Mr. Dahlenburg has secured first place in the competition with a fine all-round display.   System and method are to be observed in every department of farm work.   The stock are very creditable, and the farm stands out prominently with respect to the equipment, orchard and garden, farm buildings, reserves of fodder. and for system in tree planting.

Mr. Batson is a creditable second, and has scored consistently in nearly all the sections, and established a comfortable lead in his system of cropping and condition of his crops.

Mr. Crouch is deserving of the greatest encouragement, especially in view of the trouble he has evidently taken in erecting an entirely new set of farm buildings. By attending to a few small details pointed out in the above discussion, he should be a hard competitor to beat next season.

Points Awarded.

Competitor.	A.—Cropping.	B.—Crops.	C.—Fallow.	D.—Stock. (65).				E.—Equipment.	F.—Fences.	G.—Water Storage.	H.—Buildings.	I.—Orchard.	J.—Reserve Fodder.	K.—Tree-planting.	L.—Insurance.	Total.
				Horses.	Sheep.	Cattle.	Pigs. Poultry.									
	35	20	20	25	20	10	5	5	20	20	45	20	10	20	5	5	285
1. C. E. Dahlenburg ..	27	15	14	20	16	8	2	4	19	13	37	17	10	18	4	1	225
2. G. Batson ..	31	18	16	17	17	4	3	3	17	13	35	14	10	15	3	2	219
3. W. Crouch ..	27	17	17	18	16	7	2	2	18	16	38	16	5	12	2	2	215
4. W. Sanders ..	25	15	10	20	18	6	3	2	18	14	42	10	7	14	2	4	210

SECTION II.—SMALL FARMS.

There were only three entries for these sections and the points allotted were as follow :—

Points Awarded.

Competitor.	A.—Cropping, System of Cultivation.	B.—Crops.	C.—Fallow.	D.—Stock.	E.—Implements and Equipment.	F.—Fences.	G.—Orchard and Garden.	H.—Water Storage, &c.	I.—Dwelling and Farm Buildings.	J.—Reserve Fodder.	K.—Tree-planting.	L.—Insurance.	Total.
	30	20	20	40	20	15	10	10	20	10	5	5	205
1. J. Diprose ..	20	14	17	31	17	12	9	8	15	8	2	..	153
2. W. Dahlenburg ..	20	12	19	32	16	10	6	5	18	4	4	3	149
3. J. & A. Anderson	18	12	16	16	14	14	6	10	19	3	5	..	133

The Messrs. Anderson have the makings of a first-class farm; and, with careful management, it should be difficult to beat next season. They stand out from other competitors in the very fine provision made for water storage and the condition and arrangement of the farm fences and gates. There is an excellent orchard, but it is sadly in need of cultivation, and fine systematic work has been done in the direction of tree planting. The Messrs. Anderson, however, have only recently purchased the farm, and it is not yet in full working order. Neither pigs nor cows are kept on the farm; and, though there are excellent poultry yards, they are practically empty.

Mr. Diprose has a fine well-kept orchard in full bearing, and a vegetable garden showing evidence of care and system in working. His draught stock were good, particularly the yearlings and 2-year olds. He had the most complete collection of implements and the best all-round crops.

Mr. Dahlenburg had a fine set of buildings, and has made rapid strides during the few years he has had possession of his farm. The outbuildings are well laid out, commodious and substantial. More attention, however, needs to be paid to the fences and gates, and a windmill and tanks with water laid on to the farm and homestead are urgently required for economic working.

SECTION III.—CROPS.

There were 10 entries for this section; and, of these, 3 were for crops grown on mallee land. Farmers who enter for such crop competitions naturally wish to know the reasons which actuate a judge in awarding the prizes. Before discussing the details, I should like to indicate what I conceive to be the objects of such a competition and the manner in which such objects may be realized by a scheme of judging.

These competitions, I take it, have for their general object, the stimulation and improvement of the farm practice of the district, and they are successful in proportion to the extent to which they realize such an object. In crop judging, it seems natural to infer that the best crop and the one most deserving of the prize is that which pans out financially the best. But, if this is to be the sole criterion, I am inclined to the belief that the general object of the competition, namely, the stimulation and improvement of farm practice, would be defeated. To award the prize to the heaviest yielding crop, irrespective of other considerations, would mean a severe handicap for those necessarily placed on holdings of comparatively poor soil. It may be a much harder proposition to raise a 20-bushel average on some types of soil than to secure 30 bushels off a rich black flat. The yield of a crop in any given district, assuming other things to be equal, is dependent on the fertility of the soil on which the crop is grown; and, in the Nhill district, at least, there are areas on each farm that regularly produce bushels better results than others.

Though heaviness of yield, therefore, is an important consideration. and, in a measure, an indication of a farmer's calibre, it is clearly not the only consideration. Under normal conditions, the efficiency of a farmer's work is judged by the condition of his crop, the relative freedom from weeds and undergrowth, its regularity and evenness, the judgment displayed in sowing the right quantity of seed per acre. the extent to which he has tried to suppress diseases such as smut and bunt, and, lastly, the care with which the seed has been chosen, and with which he has attempted to keep it true to type and of a high standard of productivity. In nearly all crops, wild oats were very prevalent, and in some instances, overshadowed the wheat. Wild poppy, charlock, and various members of the thistle family were common intruders, though the amount of damage done by these was far less than by the wild oats.

Disease was noticeable in all the crops examined, the commonest being ball smut (*Tilletia tritici*) loose smut (*Ustilago tritici*) and flag smut (*Urocystis occulta*).

The dryness of the season evidently had a very salutary effect on the development of rust, as well as on takeall, though many patches of the latter were noticeable. An interesting occurrence of takeall disease was observed on virgin land on Mr. Greenwood's property. Here the disease was observed on stray patches of barley grass in takeall affected patches of crop.

The prevalence of ball smut this season in the Nhill crops raises the question of the efficacy of the pickling solutions adopted. On inquiry it was noticeable that many of the crops were pickled at the rate of ½ lb. bluestone to the bag. How much water was used in preparing the solution does not seem to have troubled the farmers concerned. Bluestone is an efficient fungicide *only* if proper precautions are taken, and only when solutions of definite strength and concentration are employed. It is not sufficient to merely guess the strength of the pickle by the depth of colour or tint. Solutions of definite strengths should be employed, say, 2 lbs. to 10 gallons of water, and the inevitable losses of solution due to continued pickling should be made up by adding a definite weight of water and bluestone, and not in an arbitrary way by pitching a handful of bluestone at occasional intervals into the pickling tub.

So far as the regularity and evenness of the crop is concerned, this is, in many ways, an indication of careful farming, though it is not always an infallible sign. In spite of the variable and patchy nature of most of the land on which the crops were grown, it is pleasing to note that many of the crops were almost perfectly even and uniform in character, displaying care in handling the soil during the previous fallowing season, and in drilling both seed and manure.

With regard to trueness to type, it is a matter for regret to find that most of the crops are very badly mixed, and contain an inordinate number of strange heads of wheat.

One would experience but little difficulty in gathering a large sheaf of "strangers" from a square chain of crop. Not only is it evident that the crops are becoming badly mixed, but there are unmistakeable signs of degeneration in the Federation crops of the district. Evidences of this may be gathered from the large number of barren spikelets at the basal portions of the ears, amounting, in many cases, to one-quarter and one-third of the total number of spikelets. Also, the marked tapering nature of so many of the heads is another indication of this phenomenon. These are no mere physiological derangements due to the effect of an abnormally dry season, but are undoubted signs of a falling away in character and type from the original square headed compact variety introduced some years ago.

This degeneracy of type is not, however, confined to the Nhill district, but is noticeable in other portions of the State, and it is what might logically be expected from any wheat, or indeed any crop in which special pains are not taken to prevent the natural tendency to degeneration observable in all cultivated plants. We have heard a great deal lately about selection of stock—draught horses, dairy cattle, stud sheep. We know that it was by continuous, patient selection that the famous Booth and Bates types of Shorthorn cattle were evolved. Is it logical to assume that selection, which has had so potent an influence in raising the standard of our domestic animals, shall prove unavailing when applied to the vegetable kingdom? In systematic, careful, long continued selection, we have an instrument in which we may truly mould plants at will. The sugar content of beets has been trebled, the percentage of starch in potatoes and protein content of maize greatly augmented by systematic selection.

Does it then require much faith to believe that wheat—our staple crop —can be vastly improved, both in quality and in prolificacy by the application of those scientific principles which have proved so useful with other crops and with live stock? Will it be admitted for one moment that this degeneracy of type, which has been observed in the crops, cannot be counteracted? It is a common saying among farmers that such and such types of wheat are "running out." This will be the fate of Federation unless some enterprising individual takes it in hand, and prevents it, by a rigorous systematic course of selection, from falling with ever-increasing momentum to the low level of mediocrity.

With these preliminary observations we may proceed to examine the results of the competition.

Points Awarded.

Competitor.	Freedom from Weeds.	Evenness and Regularity.	Freedom from Disease.	Trueness to Type.	Apparent Yield.	Total.
	15	15	15	20	35	100
1. G. Parkin	14	15	11	9	35	84
2. W. G. Greenwood	11	14	12	13	25	75
3. G. Crouch	12	13	11	12	24	72
4. { J. and A. Anderson	14	11	13	10	23	71
{ P. Bone	12	13	12	12	22	71
6. W. Dahlenburg	10	12	12	12	21	67
7. Reichelt Bros.	10	11	12	8	22	63

Mr. G. Parkin secures the highest marks in this section. His was a magnificent crop of Federation standing 5 feet high, almost perfectly level and remarkably free from weeds. He also secured the maximum for yield.

Mr. Greenwood was second with a good sample of Federation, which, in comparison with other crops, was very true to type.

The figures for the apparent yield are proportional, but not equivalent to, the estimated yield per acre.

CROPS GROWN ON MALLEE LAND.

Points Awarded.

Competitor.	Freedom from Weeds.	Freedom from Disease.	Regularity and Evenness.	Trueness to Type.	Apparent Yield.	Total.
	15	15	15	20	35	100
1. E. F. Schultz	11	10	13	11	27	72
2. R. L. Simon	9	13	11	14	22	69
3. Marshall Bros.	13	13	10	12	19	67

SECTION IV.—FALLOW LAND.

The competition in this section was very keen; and, with one or two exceptions, the fallowing was very thoroughly done. The principal object in bare fallowing is, of course, the conservation of soil moisture, and fallowing is successful just in proportion to the amount of moisture conserved. The amount that may be thus conserved is governed by the moisture present in the soil at the commencement of fallowing operations, and by the amount of moisture that subsequently falls as rain. The ideal is to conserve all the moisture that falls. That ideal, however, can never be wholly achieved, simply because losses through evaporation and percolation are inevitable. The farmer's object, however, should be to reduce the amount of loss by evaporation to a minimum, and this can be done by providing that, at all times, the moisture reservoir of the subsoil shall be covered with an adequate and loose soil mulch.

It is not necessary that the surface should be harrowed down to the consistency of an onion bed, for this may defeat the object in view, by assisting rather than retarding capillary activity. The ideal should be to have a fairly liberal surface mulch with the fine particles below and clods of moderate size on the surface. This is achieved by stirring the surface as often as is necessary. This means that the soil should be stirred only when it becomes apparent that the loose surface mulch is in danger of becoming consolidated after showers of rain. Many over-zealous farmers often work the land too much, though this is far less frequent an occurrence than those who do not put sufficient work into their fallow. Hence, in judging the fallow, the following points have been taken into consideration :—

(*a*) The amount of moisture conserved in the soil and subsoil below the mulch.
(*b*) The depth, character, and efficiency of the mulch and its suitability for the prevention of further losses of moisture by evaporation.
(*c*) Freedom from weeds.
(*d*) Regularity and evenness of the surface, for this is an indication of the judgment displayed in working.
(*e*) The size and condition of the surface particles and clods.

The following table summarizes the result :—

Points Awarded.

Competitor.	Moisture conserved.	Depth and Character of Soil Mulch.	Freedom from Weeds.	Regularity and Evenness.	Condition of Surface Clods.	Total.
	10	10	10	10	10	50
1. W. Greenwood ..	10	10	9	9	9	47
2. {J. Reichelt ..	9	10	8	8	9	44
{W. Crouch.. ..	9	10	8	8	9	44
4. P. Bone	9	9	8	9	8	43
5. {Borgelt Bros. ..	8	8	9	8	8	42
{W. Dahlenburg ..	9	9	8	8	8	42
7. R. D. McKenzie ..	6	8	7	7	9	37

Mr. Greenwood's fallow was in excellent condition, and he displayed great judgment in handling the patchy nature of the soil on his holding. He gave his land a liberal soil mulch, and its effectiveness was demonstrated by the amount of moisture conserved below. It was also very free from weeds of any kind, regular and even in character, and the tracks left by the implements displayed system and method in working the different blocks

Messrs. Crouch and Reichelt also exhibited very creditable areas of fallow.

    *   *   *   *   *   *   *

In conclusion, I would like to add that these competitions have been productive of a vast amount of good. Not only have they attracted general attention to the different aspects of rural life on some of our best farms, but they have evidently had a most stimulating influence on the competitors in preceding years, inasmuch as very considerable improvements have been effected on many of the farms quite recently, with a view of bringing them up to a standard suitable for competition. It is, of course, inevitable that, in any given district, there will always be a few farmers who stand out conspicuously from their fellows, in the efficiency with which they conduct the various farm operations, and in regard to the general standard of cultivation. From the point of view of the State, it is of the highest degree of importance that the great bulk of the farming population should follow the lead set by the more progressive farmers of a given district.

In a word, it is of the highest importance to encourage the *many* to do what the *few* are doing at the present time. From the standpoint of the State, true progress will come, not by increasing the size of the individual holding, but by encouraging higher class farming, and I feel sure that the yearly focussing of the farmers' attention on the merits of the best farms of a district must lead to great general improvement in the farm practice of that district. In this direction, the Nhill Agricultural Society has done most valuable work during the past eleven years, and it is sincerely to be hoped that this good work will continue.

I cannot allow this opportunity to pass without pointing out the great amount of good work Mr. C. H Towns, the popular secretary of the Nhill society, has done. The success of a society is very largely dependent on the energy and enthusiasm of its chief officers; and, for the able direction of the work of the farm competitions for the past eleven years, Mr. Towns is almost wholly responsible.

FARM BLACKSMITHING.

(*Continued from page* 799, *Vol. IX.*)

George Baxter, Instructor in Blacksmithing, Working Men's College, Melbourne.

V.—WELDING (*Continued*).

SWINGLE-TREE MOUNTINGS.

Figs. 42 and 43 show two methods of mounting a *swingle-tree*. The first is much simpler than that depicted in Fig. 43, but is not as strong. Holes must be bored through the timber to receive the ironwork. whereas in the second instance the iron is made to surround the wood, thereby preventing it from splitting, which would easily happen if the first method be adopted. Notwithstanding this disadvantage, it is commonly used; and, to overcome the loss of strength due to boring the holes referred to, wood of a larger section is employed.

It would undoubtedly be advisable to first make one of the simplest nature. The following information concerning both methods will, it is hoped, be sufficiently clear to enable one to make either. Fig. 42 will be considered first.

Take a piece of $\frac{1}{2}$ in. or $\frac{5}{8}$ in. round iron of any convenient length and start by making a wedge-shaped point in the same manner as that described for the hinge (Fig. 40); then bend it over the beak of the anvil, using a drift to make the hole the correct size and shape. (See *a*, Fig. 42).

In taking the welding heat care must be exercised to prevent the eye being burnt. Cooling the eye occasionally will have the desired effect. When properly heated, weld with the hand hammer. To obtain the best results, start by striking light and quick blows on the thin edge of the scarf and gradually increase the weight of blows as the thicker part is hammered. It is desirable that the welded portion should be left thicker than the original bar for several reasons, one of which is that it fits the hole tightly, and therefore prevents it from turning round; another reason is that it strengthens what would otherwise be the weakest part.

One welding heat should be quite sufficient to insure satisfactory results; in fact, much stronger than if two or more heats are needed to join the parts together. It must be remembered that each welding heat wastes

42. SWINGLE-TREE MOUNTING.

a. Ready for welding; *b.* Welded, ready for screwing; *c.* Completed swingle-tree.

away so much metal, and the inevitable result is that the work is in many cases rendered useless.

Cutting to length is the next operation; then screwing to fit a nut. It is always best to purchase nuts already screwed. It saves a lot of time

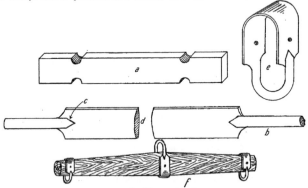

43. SWINGLE-TREE MOUNTINGS.

a. Fullering preparatory to drawing down; *b.* End drawn and swaged; *c.* Mitre; *d.* Shows cross section; *e.* Finished forging; *f.* Completed swingle-tree.

and they are so cheap that it would not pay to make them. They may be purchased from any ironmonger.

The eye-bolt (Fig. 42*b*) may be used for purposes other than in the case illustrated; for instance, if there are children in the home they will want a swing, and no safer and better way of fixing the rope to the cross beam can be found than by making two eye-bolts out of $\frac{5}{8}$ in. diameter iron for the purpose. Again, it is sometimes necessary to attach a block and tackle to the roof for lifting heavy weights—the eye-bolt is just the article required for the purpose. Where an underground tank is on the farm the cover requires to be lifted; if an eye-bolt made from $\frac{3}{8}$ in. diameter iron, with a round ring attached to the eye, be connected in the same manner as previously described it will be found to be very convenient.

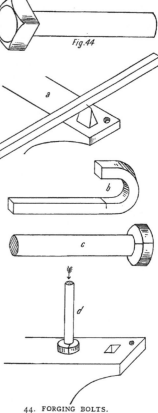

Fig.44

To accomplish the forging connected with Fig. 43 is a much more difficult matter. The sketches show the various stages of construction; *a* is a piece of flat iron, say $1\frac{1}{2}$ in. x $\frac{1}{2}$ in., with grooves formed in it with the *fuller* and the beak of the anvil in such position that the central portion will, on being flattened out, be of the necessary length for the swingle-tree. As the size will vary, it will be impossible to state the length.

After the fullering is done, each end is raised to a welding heat and drawn down to a circular shape like *b* (Fig. 43). In drawing out work of this nature the iron is roughly rounded with the hammer and afterwards swaged smooth and to exact size. Illustrations of swage and swage block appeared in the September, 1911, issue.

The next operation is to flatten out the central part to about $\frac{1}{4}$ in. thick at the middle section and gradually taper it away to $\frac{1}{8}$ in. at the edges as illustrated at *d*. The breadth is allowed to increase to about 2 in., whilst flattening. The mitre (*c*) is made with the fuller and sett-hammer.

When this is satisfactorily done it is bent at the centre of the flattened portion, to fit the swingle-tree, which is usually made semi-circular; then scarf the round ends like a link and weld up.

44. FORGING BOLTS.

a. Cutting the iron for collar; *b.* Partly bent; *c.* Collar correctly shaped; *d.* Preparing for the welding heat.

To attach to the wood, drill a small hole through the flat part; and, after fitting tightly, either put a screw in each side, or bore a hole through the wood and drive a piece of iron right through and slightly rivet the ends to prevent it dropping out. Another method of fastening is to forge the mount slightly smaller than the wood; and, by making the iron red hot and quickly driving on and cooling out before the iron burns too deep, the contraction of the iron will hold it tight, just as a tyre is held on to a wheel.

Forging a Bolt.

The majority of bolts are made by machinery; but, at the same time, blacksmiths are continually being called upon to make them for special purposes and where it is not convenient to buy them. Machine made bolts are short, rarely exceeding 10 in. long; so that when a longer bolt is required it is either made outright by the smith or else a shorter one is lengthened. Screwed ends, *i.e.*, plain circular pieces of iron cut off in 9 in. or 10 in. lengths, are screwed at one end, and a nut fitted to them at the bolt factories and sold cheaply by most ironmongers. They are very convenient and save a great deal of hard work in screwing, particularly in large bolts.

If a long bolt, say 2 ft., be required, a head would be made on a piece of iron and a screwed end welded on to the other end.

A bolt head is made by wrapping a piece of square or flat iron around the end of the required sized round iron; and, after raising to a welding heat, forging the head to shape.

In order to do this in an intelligent and systematic manner, several things require to be taken into consideration. In the first place, it will be understood that in the United Kingdom bolt-heads and nuts are made to fixed measurements, known as Whitworth's standard, so that a bolt made in one shop will fit a nut made in another; also, that a spanner may be made to suit the nuts of all bolts of a given size. The size of a bolt is known by the diameter of iron in its circular part.

The farmer who has an American as well as an Australian made machine has no doubt found out that a nut from one will not fit a bolt from the other. This is on account of the United States engineers having adopted a standard known as the Sellars, which is slightly different to the English. But, even in American machines made by different makers, the nuts are in many instances not interchangeable.

The importers of agricultural machinery, besides selling the completed machine, also sell duplicate parts, and they are particularly careful that the duplicates of their machines will not be exactly suitable for others. Consequently, the user of the machine is practically compelled to buy his renewals from the agent from whom he bought his machine. Whilst one cannot blame the manufacturer for protecting his own interests, the practice is at times aggravating to the farmer. When a nut drops off a screwed end, he finds that, although he has some of the same sized nuts on hand, the threads are differently cut, and so cannot be made use of, necessitating a journey of often many miles for the proper article.

The Whitworth standard of sizes for bolt heads, nuts, and the width of spanner jaws, is found by taking the diameter of the iron in the body of the bolt as the unit, and multiplying that diameter by $\frac{3}{2}$ and adding $\frac{1}{8}$ in. to the product. The depth of nut equals the diameter of the bolt, whilst the depth of head is $\frac{7}{8}$ that of the nut, but in ordinary practice, is made the same. When making a bolt, it would be well to bear this in mind, for it is far more satisfying and no more difficult to make the head right than wrong.

The ordinary method of making a bolt in a blacksmith's fire is, as previously stated, to wrap a piece of square or flat iron around a circular bar. Now, as the heads are to be made to fixed sizes, the size of the bar used for forming the head requires to be carefully selected so as to make the bolt with a minimum of labour. The following table is compiled to enable the maker to at once select the most suitable size for bolts ranging from $\frac{1}{2}$ in. to 1 in:—

TABLE OF SIZE OF IRON FOR BOLT HEADS, WITH FINISHED DIMENSIONS OF HEAD.

	in.	in.	in.	in.	in.
Diameter of bolt	$\frac{1}{2}$	$\frac{5}{8}$	$\frac{3}{4}$	$\frac{7}{8}$	1
Size of square iron for head ..	$\frac{3}{8}$	$\frac{7}{16}$	$\frac{1}{2}$	$\frac{9}{16}$	$\frac{5}{8}$
Width of head across the flats ..	$\frac{7}{8}$	$1\frac{1}{16}$	$1\frac{1}{4}$	$1\frac{7}{16}$	$1\frac{5}{8}$
Depth of head	$\frac{1}{2}$	$\frac{5}{8}$	$\frac{3}{4}$	$\frac{7}{8}$	1

The correct method of making the collar to form the head is to first of all find out the length which will exactly encircle the round bar. Thus, to the diameter of bolt, add the thickness of square bar and multiply the sum by $3\frac{1}{7}$. The end of the square bar is now heated to bright red and placed on the hardee at a distance from the heated end equal to the required length when it is cut about half-way through, as shown at *a* in Fig. 44, and then bent to *b* when it is broken off, and the circular bar inserted and the ends knocked down as shown at *c*.

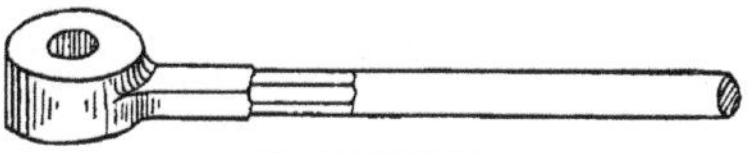

45. BOLT-TOOL.

The collar is now driven off and the round bar heated to redness and placed in the collar similar to *d*, and driven down on the top. The object is to swell the round bar slightly where it will be wasted by obtaining the welding heat. By altering the position of the bolt from vertical to horizontal and resting the collar on the anvil, a blow struck on it tightens it so that it will not slip off in the fire.

In welding, the head is struck sufficiently hard to crush the metal and so form a flat surface on opposite sides. It is quickly turned at right angles and struck. By this means the square head is roughly formed; and, at the same time, the weld is partly made. To complete the welding and to obtain correct shape a *bolt-tool* (Fig. 45) or *fork-tool* (Fig. 46) is required.

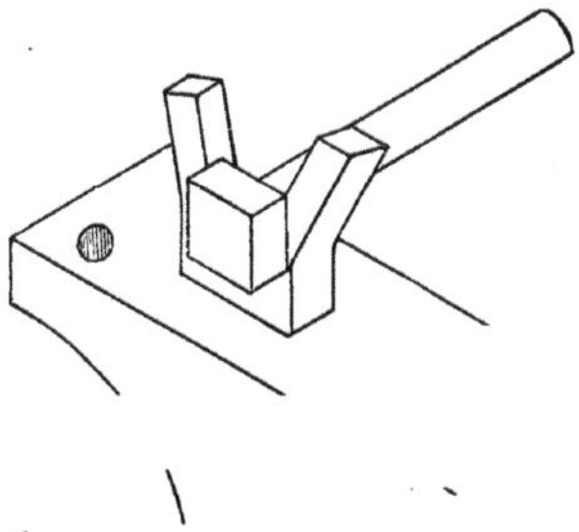

46. METHOD OF USING A FORK-TOOL.

When a bolt-tool is used, the bolt is immediately placed through the hole and the square hole of the anvil, and hammered down to the required depth, then removed, and again hammered on the sides. A pair of calipers should be previously set to the width of the head for testing the size.

The fork-tool may be used for heading various sized bolts, and in that respect is a better tool than the bolt-tool, which can only be used for one size, so that a set of such tools would be necessary.

The swage block has a number of round holes in it which may be used in the place of a bolt-tool.

The sketch clearly shows the manner in which the fork-tool is utilized. A great many bolts are made with hexagonal heads ; but, as they are more difficult to forge and the square head is likely to fulfil all the requirements of the farm, they will not be described.

(To be continued.)

VINE DISEASES IN FRANCE.

(Continued from page 676, Vol. IX.)

F. de Castella, Government Viticulturist.

FUNGICIDE SPRAYS.

Though there is no reason to fear that copper sprays will ever be required in Victoria to combat the various vine fungi which wreak such havoc in French vineyards, since we are protected from them by climatic conditions, other branches of our agriculture are vitally interested in the question. Orchardists are only too familiar with the need for copper sprays, and, more recently still, potato-growers are being forced to resort to the same specific in order to overcome the Irish Blight.

The fungus diseases, with which these two industries have to deal, present many features in common with those against which French vine-growers use such sprays. The mycelium of all these fungi grows in the interior of the tissues of the host plant, the spores alone appearing on the outside. They are, therefore, not amenable to direct treatment and can only be fought by the indirect or preventive method. The latter consists, briefly, in spreading over the whole of the growing surface liable to invasion, a very thin coating of a slightly soluble copper salt so that every drop of rain or dew must dissolve sufficient of it to render it an unsuitable medium for the germination of the spores of the fungus.

In view of this similarity it will no doubt prove of interest and use, to both orchardists and potato-growers, to know something of the different sprays employed in France since there is no country where they are more extensively applied nor where a greater variety of formulæ are in general use. In Victoria, so far, we only know copper lime and copper soda. In France, numerous other copper-containing substances are in every-day use, some of which present advantages in certain directions.

Some idea of the extent to which spraying is practised in France will be gathered from the total quantity of sulphate of copper used for the purpose in that country ; this was estimated by Professor Chuard, in 1909, to amount to no less than 50,000 tons of sulphate of copper annually—a quantity equivalent to 12,500 tons of metallic copper. This was prior to 1910. In view of the extraordinary prevalence of fungus diseases during that disastrous season, even the above huge consumption must have been considerably exceeded.

Brief reference must here be made to some general considerations which have a bearing on all the different copper sprays. They are all based on the original Bordeaux mixture, the efficacy of which, as a specific against Downy Mildew, was accidentally discovered through the practice, common among several small growers whose vines abutted on main roads, to protect themselves from the depredations of passers, by sprinkling their grapes with a mixture of lime and bluestone. Grapes so treated, being looked upon as poisonous, were left severely alone. When Downy Mildew, recently introduced from America, commenced to ravage the vineyards, it was noticed how free from mildew were these poisoned outer rows. The general adoption of the copper lime spray immediately followed, and even now it is the most widely used of all sprays, though several other compounds tend to supersede it in certain quarters.

The hydrated oxide of copper which is formed when lime is added to a copper sulphate solution* is the active agent in Bordeaux mixture; though only slightly soluble in water, it is sufficiently so to render each drop of rain or dew coming in ·contact with it unfit for spore germination. Its very slight solubility, in fact, causes its influence to be more lasting, since it is only entirely washed off by very heavy rain. This brings us to one of the most important points in connexion with copper compounds, *viz.*, their power of adherence. It is mainly because some of the more recent sprays possess it in a high degree that they tend to displace the original Bordeaux. Even with this, however, adherence varies considerably according to the procedure followed in its preparation, as will be seen later.

Whatever be the spraying compound used, the following are the most important points to be considered in order that the best results may be obtained :—

1. Even distribution of spraying material.
2. Sufficient, but not excessive. solubility.
3. Adherence, so that frequent repetition of spraying may be obviated.
4. Convenience of preparation.

The first of these is; no doubt, largely dependent on the spray pump employed. It cannot be too emphatically stated that satisfactory results are not to be expected from a faulty pump. Protection cannot be complete unless distribution is so thorough that no dew drop, however small, can escape contact with some of the spray material. The futility of throwing a few large drops every here and there, leaving large spaces of leaf surface untouched, and consequently, so many open doors for the entry of the fungus parasite, is obvious. Such a course is absolutely incompatible with the essentially preventive nature of the treatment. The subject of the present article, however, is spraying mixtures, not spray pumps, and the composition of the former exercises a greater influence on the facility for even distribution than might, at first sight, be imagined.

WETTING POWER OF SPRAYING MIXTURES.

This is a question which has quite recently received a good deal of attention in France. The lower the surface tension of a liquid, the smaller the drops which it can form, and consequently the greater its wetting power. It is for this reason that the wetting power of alcohol is much greater than that of water.

By the addition of certain substances it is possible to reduce the surface tension of the spraying liquid and consequently its wetting power, with the result that the facility for even and thorough distribution is considerably increased. Soap is one of the substances used for this purpose, but it presents the drawback of combining with the copper hydrate and modifying the composition of the mixture, thus necessitating alteration in the

---

* According to Pickering (*Eleventh Report of the Woburn Experimental Fruit Farm*) the active agent would be a basic sulphate, and not hydroxide. Whether this view be correct or not is of little consequence, so far as its mode of action is concerned.

proportions of its constituents. Several copper soap formulæ are recommended in standard French works. Only certain kinds of soap are suitable; with others, the gain in wetting power is either insufficient, or counterbalanced by loss in adherence.

A kind of mucilage known as *Saponine* appears to possess, in a high degree, the power of reducing surface tension without the drawbacks of the majority of soaps. The usual source from which it is obtained is the powdered bark of certain plants such as *Quillaia, Saponaria,* &c., and these have been successfully tried for the purpose. Quite recently, the powdered fruit of *Sapindus utilis,* the Soap Tree, has been recommended for the same purpose.* Used in the proportion of 2 per 1,000 of the spraying liquid, it very considerably increases its wetting power, without exerting any chemical action on the copper compounds contained in it.

OTHER CONDITIONS.

Solubility conditions seem to be fulfilled by all the sprays in common use.

Adherence is, perhaps, the most important property of all, especially when dealing with severe visitations. It stands to reason that, the better the deposit adheres to the foliage, the longer will its protective action be felt and the less often will it need to be repeated. If adherence be satisfactory, it will require heavy rain to wash it off, whilst if it be faulty it will be removed by a few light showers. The more recently a mixture has been prepared, and the cooler it has been kept, the better it will adhere. This applies particularly to copper-soda which deteriorates very rapidly, especially if the weather be warm†. Copper-soda deteriorates much more rapidly in this way than copper-lime (Bordeaux) or copper-potash; the latter, strange to say, is not at all generally used. In order to increase adherence, several substances are added to mixtures. We may mention the following :—Soap, rosin, sugar or molasses, linseed oil, and gelatine. Some of these will be referred to later.

As regards percentage of copper, though various strengths have been recommended at different times, practical men now seem to be agreed, after long years of experience, that 1½ to 2 per cent. is most satisfactory; 2 per cent. is the most usual strength—anything over this is unnecessary.‡ These percentages are estimated as sulphate of copper, or its equivalent, if other copper compounds of copper be employed.

Convenience of preparation is of great practical importance. It is mainly on this account that several of the newer preparations are gradually displacing Bordeaux mixture in spite of their higher price. Most of these innovations require to be merely mixed with the proper quantity of water immediately before use. Their freedom from grit or lumps of any kind obviates trouble through the clogging of nozzles, so frequent with badly prepared Bordeaux.

It is, of course, impossible to deal here with more than a few of the many spray formulæ now in use in France. It will suffice to refer briefly to the way in which Bordeaux is prepared and to those of the newer substitutes which appear to have most to recommend them.

(To be continued.)

---

* G. Gastine. *Revue de Viticulture,* 4th May, 1911, p. 525. This tree, which is somewhat extensively grown in Algeria, would do well in Northern Victoria. Its value for increasing the efficiency of spraying mixtures alone would justify its introduction to Victoria.
† J. M. Guillon and G. Gouirand, *Revue de Viticulture,* Vol. XI., p. 29.
‡ This applies to France. In the moist climate of Switzerland, where downy mildew is very virulent, anything less than 2 per cent. is considered insufficient, whilst sprays containing up to 3 per cent. copper sulphate are often used.

PROPAGATION OF FRUIT TREES.

(Continued from page 831, Vol. IX.)

C. F. Cole, Orchard Supervisor.

PRUNING.

The writer wishes it to be clearly understood that the methods advocated in this article are for general use in a nursery, and not when planting out trees permanently in an orchard. When planting out certain of the types illustrated, it would, however, be as well to practice the same or a very similar method of cutting, if the grower wishes to secure suitable growths so as to enable him from the start to frame his trees upon sound lines.

The object of the propagator, when pruning young trees in the nursery rows, should be to start the future head growths from, or as near as possible to, the main stem of the young tree. This can only be accomplished by cutting the branches hard back to the basal buds, or by removing all branch growths, thus framing a straight-stemmed tree and pruning it as such.

By practising either of the above methods, the future trees will be framed with uniform vertical or somewhat similar head growths. It is not only an advantage to the propagator when packing for transit, but also to the grower, who will have a tree framed upon sound principles. Whichever method is put into execution will be controlled by the position and condition of the buds. No hard-and-fast rule can be laid down of how and where to cut, owing to the many different types to be found growing in the nursery row.

52. CARELESS PRUNING.

Before cutting, the propagator will need to have a clear conception of the future position of the growths and type of tree he wishes to attain.

The sole object is to get good, sound, healthy growth, and at the same time frame a tree with an evenly-balanced and shapely head carrying no more than three or four healthy vertical growths. The position of the buds upon the branches, also the many types of trees, varies considerably. Hardly two branched trees of a variety are alike; some carry buds evenly spaced to the base of the branches, whilst others have them irregularly, and in many instances the buds near the base are blind. At times, the most expert hand is at a loss how to prune some types to advantage.

The ten different types selected by the writer for illustrative purposes cover a fairly wide field outside of the simplest types.

Before commencing the operation examine the collars upon a branched tree, *i.e.*, the basal portion of the branches where they join the main stem, to see if there are any sound collar buds. Should any be present, reduce the centre of the tree, if necessary, and leave the required number of branches—three or four. Then cut these branches back to the main stem and buds, care being taken not to cut or injure the buds. The result will

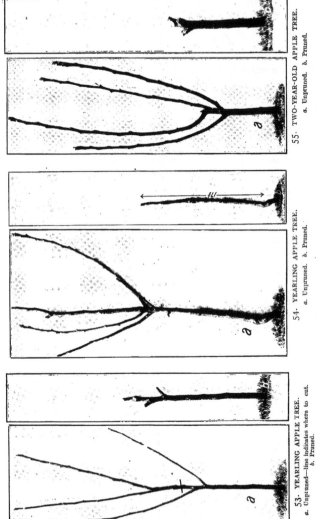

55. TWO-YEAR-OLD APPLE TREE.
a. Unpruned.   *b.* Pruned.

54. YEARLING APPLE TREE.
a. Unpruned.   *b.* Pruned.

53. YEARLING APPLE TREE.
a. Unpruned—line indicates where to cut.
b. Pruned.

NOTE.—For the sake of clearness, the pruned tree, in each case, is reproduced on a somewhat larger scale.

be that the full flow of ascending sap will elaborate the collar buds and cause them to make strong, clean growths, and so form a tree equal to one from a pruned " straight " *i.e.*, an unbranched yearling tree.

Many propagators prefer pruning upon similar lines to those practised upon trees when first planted out in the orchard, *i.e.*, leaving three to four branches and cutting them back to within 3 or 4 in. from the main stem. This method is sound when pruning two-year-old trees in the nursery rows, or where there are no buds at the basal part of the branches, or no collar buds to operate upon. But, where possible, especially with yearling trees, cut back to the basal or collar buds, particularly in the case of almonds, apricots, nectarines, peaches, plums (all kinds), and quinces.

Another method that may be practised at times, more so upon stone than seed fruits, especially nectarines and peaches, is to reduce the tree back to an inside bud, if any, upon the stem close to where the bud and stock are united, see Fig. 59*a*, where the position of the bud is shown by ——→ . A line through the stem indicates where to cut. This operation is performed the same as when heading back a budded stock to the united bud. The result from such treatment is that a tree, equal to a strong one-year-old from an inserted bud, is produced.

A very common type in the nursery row is a tree on which the branches on one side are stronger than those upon the other. If the head formation is similar to Fig. 60*b*, *i.e.*, with regard to the number of branches, treat it when pruning, the same as Fig. 60*a*, by cutting the stronger branches back the same length as the weaker ones. Then, during the early part of the vegetative period, and when the stronger shoots have made about 12 in. of growth, check them by nipping the terminal ends. This will give the weaker ones a chance to pull up.

When such a type is being planted out in the orchard, the root conditions should receive attention, if necessary (see Fig. 25). The top should receive somewhat similar treatment during the first season as if standing in the nursery row.

A difficult tree at times to prune is a two-year-old cherry, especially varieties that are free bloomers, and of which the bloom and wood buds are similar. The method of cutting back to the basal buds upon the branches should not be practised, owing to the buds, in all probability, being bloom ones. Cherries rarely break growth from a bloom bud, differing in this respect from most fruits. Therefore, the pruner will need to exercise care. Cut close to the buds, selecting those upon the outside of the branches. It is only upon rare occasions that it is necessary to cut at an inside or upper bud upon a branch to obtain a vertical growth.

When pruning, it is just as easy to cut correctly as incorrectly. It is purely a matter of making one cut. Fig. 52 shows a pruned tree where the cuts have been carelessly done. Compare this with Fig. 55*b* ; the cuts in this case are neatly made, and the tree correctly pruned.

Fig. 53*a* is a common type of a yearling apple tree carrying a head growth of four branches. The central branch has a somewhat crooked growth, and is the one that would, if left, receive the direct flow of ascending sap. To remedy this, and bring about the equalization of the sap, which means uniform growths, it will be necessary to remove the central branch where indicated by line. Having done this, and there being no collar buds, select outside buds upon the three remaining branches so that when cut each branch will be of equal length and form an evenly-balanced pruned head. This, with proper treatment and care, will not only be a perfect specimen of a two-year-old tree by the following winter, but will be framed upon sound lines.

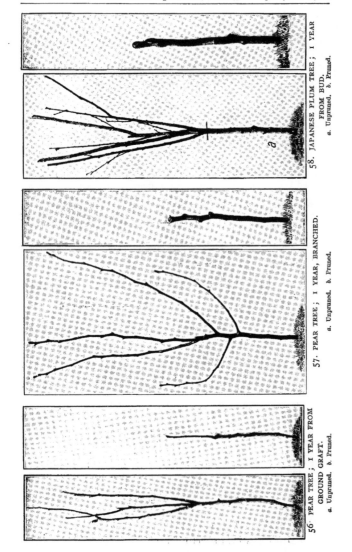

58. JAPANESE PLUM TREE ; 1 YEAR FROM BUD.
a. Unpruned. b. Pruned.

57. PEAR TREE ; 1 YEAR, BRANCHED.
a. Unpruned. b. Pruned.

56. PEAR TREE ; 1 YEAR FROM GROUND GRAFT.
a. Unpruned. b. Pruned.

Fig. 54*a* is another type of a strong well grown one-year-old apple tree with low branch growths. With trees of this type the main stem or central vertical growth should never be reduced back to the branches —the future head of the tree should not be formed by utilizing these branches. All of the latter should be cut away, close to the main stem. Then reduce back to where there are three or four good sound buds, see Fig. 54*b*. The result will be, by the following autumn, a tree with sound head conditions that may be packed without fear of breakage during transit.

Fig. 55*a* is a sound type of an apple tree, produced from

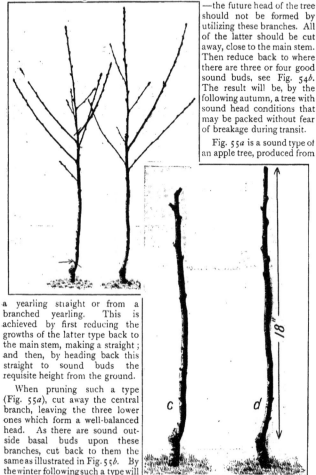

a yearling straight or from a branched yearling. This is achieved by first reducing the growths of the latter type back to the main stem, making a straight; and then, by heading back this straight to sound buds the requisite height from the ground.

When pruning such a type (Fig. 55*a*), cut away the central branch, leaving the three lower ones which form a well-balanced head. As there are sound out-side basal buds upon these branches, cut back to them the same as illustrated in Fig. 55*b*. By the winter following such a type will be what is termed a three-year-old, and hard to separate from a well-grown one-year-old branched pruned.

59. YEARLING PEACH TREES.
a and *b*. Unpruned. *c* and *d*. Pruned.

When planting out permanently and pruning a type like Fig. 55*a* there is no necessity to cut so hard back.

Fig. 56*a* is a yearling pear tree produced from ground grafting a mis-budded stock. Such a type, if the stem is long enough, should be treated by reducing it back below the branches. But as the type illustrated has branched too low it will be necessary to cut away the two outside branches so as to form a tree having a stem of suitable length. The central growth should then be cut back as shown in Fig. 56*b*.

Fig. 57*a* shows a typical branched one-year-old pear tree from bud, well grown and having sound head conditions. As there are sound collar buds at the basal end of the branches, reduce back to these buds; first, by cutting away the terminal branch upon the main stem. Owing to the terminal portion being some-

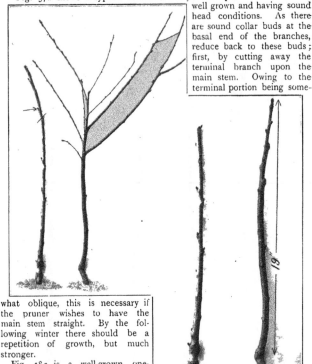

what oblique, this is necessary if the pruner wishes to have the main stem straight. By the following winter there should be a repetition of growth, but much stronger.

Fig. 58*a* is a well-grown one-year-old Japanese plum. It is rarely that this variety of fruit is not plentifully supplied with collar buds upon the main stem at the base of the branches, and

60. YEARLING CHERRY AND PEACH TREES.

a. Unpruned Cherry.   *c.* Pruned Cherry.
b. Unpruned Peach.   *d.* Pruned Peach.

also upon the stem below the head growths. If the stem is long enough to form the future head of the tree, cut upon the stem below the branches where indicated by line, *i.e.*, if there are suitable buds. If the stem is too short, or there are no suitable buds, reduce back the branches to the collar buds, the same as Fig. 58*b*. Failing collar buds, branch prune at the basal buds.

Fig. 59*a* and *b* are common types of yearling peach or nectarine trees. Fig. 59*a* requires to be differently pruned to Fig. 59*b*. By examining the branches upon the former, it will be seen that they have sound basal buds to work upon. All branches not required to form the future head upon this type (Fig. 59*a*) should be cut away close to the main stem. Then harden back the vertical growth to where marked thus —, and prune back the three branches left to the basal buds. (See Fig. 59*c*.)

Fig. 59*b* is a very simple type to prune, having sound buds upon the main stem, and above the strong oblique growth, to operate upon. To get clean growth and form an evenly-balanced head condition, it will be necessary to utilize these buds. When pruning such a type, the correct method is to remove all branches close to the main stem. Then prune back to where there are three or four sound buds evenly spaced to form the future head growths. (See Fig. 59*d*.)

Fig. 60*b* is a distinct type of a one-year-old tree from Figs. 59*a* and *b*. Allowing the two stronger branches to grow unchecked, and thereby utilizing the greater quantity of the sap flow and plant food, has been the means of starving the opposite branches and the top of the tree. If such a type had a sound bud upon the stem near the union of the stock, like Fig. 59*a*, the better plan would be to reduce back to such a bud. To correctly prune such a type, so as to get an evenly-branched head, the two stronger branches as well as the three lower ones should be cut back close to the main stem. This will leave the three higher ones, and these should be cut back to the sound basal buds. (See Fig. 60*d*.)

Fig. 60*a* is a straight type very easily pruned correctly, but is so often pruned otherwise. If the growth made is long, vigorous and straight, it simply means reducing back to a bud the desired height from the ground so as to form a tree with a stem the requisite length. But with a type like the one illustrated, having made a short sturdy growth, and the terminal end being bent, it is necessary to cut so as to form a well-balanced head upon a straight stem. To obtain this end, it will be necessary to cut at bud marked thus —, and not at bud indicated by ⟫→. This type of yearling tree is more prevalent amongst cherries than other kinds in the nursery row.

(*To be continued.*)

ORCHARD AND GARDEN NOTES.

E. E. Pescott, Principal, Horticultural School, Burnley.

The Orchard.

The necessity for constant surface cultivation is apparent every summer, but more so in dry seasons. Not only in non-irrigable districts is this a necessity, but also in those districts where the trees can be watered, and more so in the latter case. In irrigated orchards, the tendency of the soil, as a result of artificial waterings, is to set and harden. Consequently, stirring the surface must be resorted to, in order to keep up a good mechanical condition of the soil, and also to prevent loss of irrigation water by evaporation.

In non-irrigated orchards, the cultivation work is necessary to conserve what water has entered the subsoil as a result of the winter and spring rains. Soil crusts should not be allowed to form. Summer showers are not alone the cause of these formations; dry weather conditions cause the soil to consolidate, and any trampling, or vehicular traffic tends to harden the surface, and thus to allow of the escape of moisture that the trees must need.

Pests and Spraying.

If woolly aphis is at all existent, a spraying with a strong nicotine solution will reduce it considerably. A paint, the basis of which is any of the petroleum oils, or one of the miscible oil preparations now on the market, will be useful where this pest is not very frequent. The method is to mix the oil with lime, or sulphur, potash, or some other crude chemical of an insecticidal value, and to paint the parts attacked with a good strong brush.

The sulphur-potash remedy has been previously mentioned in these notes, and it is especially effective in not only killing out the pest where-ever applied, but also in rendering that particular spot obnoxious to any other aphides that may come along later. It is made by dissolving 2lbs. sulphate of potash in ½ gallon of water and then mixing with 2lbs. of sulphur. The whole is worked up to the consistency of house paint with linseed oil. It is applied to the affected parts with a brush.

Codlin moth spraying will still require to be carried on. All affected apples should be gathered and destroyed. None should be allowed to remain on the trees or on the ground. As soon as the workings or marks of the insect are observed, the fruit should be gathered and destroyed. If the fruits are left, there is always the danger of the larvæ escaping to a crevice or hiding place and so continuing the loss.

Cherry and pear trees may be sprayed with arsenate of lead wherever the slug is present; vines may be sprayed similarly wherever the vine moth caterpillars are found.

Budding.

January and February are the suitable months for budding. · In budding, it is necessary that the bark shall run or open freely; and, to do this, the tree must have a good sap flow at the time of performing the operation. If such does not occur, the trees to be worked, or the stocks, should be given a good watering, and the budding deferred for a day or two. Full instructions for budding were given in Mr. Cole's articles on the Propagation of Fruit Trees in the September and October, 1911, *Journals*.

Summer Pruning.

In January and February, trees that require it may be summer-pruned. In performing this work, care should be observed that as much of the leafage as possible is retained on the trees.

Unduly long laterals of fruiting trees may be shortened back, always cutting to a leaf. Unnecessary terminal leader growths, of which there are sometimes three or four, all strong growing, may be reduced to one; retaining this one as a leader. In no case should this growth be cut or interfered with in any way.

The result of these cuts will be to divert the sap which was flowing into growths that would subsequently be pruned, into more profitable channels, so that weak buds and growths may be strengthened, and induced into fruit bearing.

Vegetable Garden.

The vegetable section should be kept in good condition by alternate cultivation and watering. A good surface scarifying with the Planet Jr., or with a hoe, should be given when the soil has well settled after each watering. This will keep the soil in good condition, and the crops in good growth. Where crops are growing, an occasional overhead watering will be beneficial; it will clean and invigorate the leaves.

. As soon as a crop has been removed from a plot, the ground should be well manured and dug over. If any pest, such as aphis or caterpillars, has been prevalent, it would be advisable to burn all crop refuse, to destroy any insects that may remain.

Seedlings of such crops as cabbage, celery, lettuce, cauliflower, &c., may be transplanted; and seeds of peas, French beans, turnip, cauliflower, &c., may be planted.

Keep the tomatoes well watered and fed, pinching out surplus and strong growing laterals. In early districts the onion crop will be ripening. In late districts, or with late crops, the ripening may be hastened by breaking down the top. An autumn crop of potatoes may be planted.

Flower Garden.

The lawns, flower beds, and shrubberies will need frequent waterings. Such plants as cannas, delphiniums, perennial phloxes, and penstemons, will require a good water supply. These and similar plants will benefit by a good mulching.

Much hand work will be of great benefit in the flower garden and borders at this season of the year. Regular hoeings do much to improve the texture of the soil, and to conserve the soil moisture. In shallow and undrained soils, constant waterings will be a necessity, if the plants are to be kept alive; at the same time, there is always the danger of excessive water in undrained soils.

Mulching will also be an important work this month. This work will greatly assist the retention of soil moisture; at the same time, it will greatly reduce the temperature of the soil. Any material that will ultimately be incorporated with the soil in the form of humus is useful for mulching purposes.

Dahlias and chrysanthemums should be kept growing and in good heart, by watering, light feeding, and mulching. They should also be tied to the stakes as the growths extend.

Pests, such as caterpillars of several species, and red spider, will now shortly appear. For the former, weak sprayings with arsenate of lead, or Paris green, may be given. Wherever the red spider is observed, the attacked parts should be cut off and burned. Not only should this be done to the chrysanthemums and dahlias, but also to all plants in the beds similarly affected. Constant waterings will often relieve the plants of this trouble, but the most efficacious method is to burn all parts affected as the insect makes its appearance.

Carnations may now be layered and seeds of pansies and perennial and biennial plants may be sown. A few late gladioli and a few spring flowering bulbs for early flowering, may also be planted.

A NEW LUCERNE TROUBLE.

Downy Mildew (*Peronospora trifoliorum*, De Bary).

C. C. Brittlebank, Assistant to the Vegetable Pathologist.

Some crowns of lucerne were recently forwarded to the office of the Vegetable Pathologist for examination, and were found to be affected with Downy Mildew. As this disease is evidently a recent introduction, the following notes will be of interest.

17862.

Peronospora trifoliorum is a common parasite on various legumes in America and Europe, and in the former country there is record of damage to lucerne by this pest. Until the specimens under notice came to hand there was no record of it for Victoria.

As this fungus belongs to a genus, many of which are destructive to cultivated plants, it behoves the growers of lucerne, especially in irriga- tion areas, to be on watch, lest their crops be invaded by this pest; if once established, it would be most difficult, if not impossible, to ex- terminate. It is spread not only by conidia, which are blown from plant to plant, but also by oospores or resting spores formed within the tissue of diseased leaves. The latter, falling into the crowns of the plants and on to the soil, serve as fresh sources of infection, from which the disease spreads during the following year. Even if the lucerne be eaten down to the crowns by sheep or other stock, a certain number of fallen leaves would be trodden into the soil and start the disease afresh in the following spring.

Although only a few specimens of this disease have been brought under notice, and probably but few lucerne growers have seen it up to the pre- sent time, it does not follow that the disease is of no economic importance. Until a few years ago, the Lucerne Rust had not been observed in Vic- toria ; the first specimens obtained were found by the writer on the rail- way embankment at Garden Vale, near Melbourne. At the present time, many parts of the State are infested by this disease, and tons of valuable fodder are destroyed every year. Lucerne rust was, without doubt, imported with consignments of seed from other countries, as in nearly every shipment of lucerne seed spores could be obtained in abundance. Most probably, the resting spores of the downy mildew of lucerne have reached Victoria in fragments of diseased leaves, mixed through shipments of seed.

GENERAL APPEARANCE OF DISEASED PLANTS

The specimens under notice had a stunted and unthrifty look, the upper portions of the stem and leaves being covered by a thick greyish, or violet-grey downy layer Many of the diseased leaves were coated on both surfaces and had their edges curled downwards and inwards towards the mid-rib. Others again, were of a yellowish grey, more especially those exhibiting the downy coating on the under side only. Several of the stalks were almost bare of leaves on their lower portions and clearly showed the disastrous effects of the disease.

If a small portion of the grey felted coating be mounted for examina- tion by the microscope, it will be found to consist of minute tree-like structures, bearing, at the tips of the many forked branches, oval egg- shaped bodies known as conidia. These minute bodies are capable of infecting any lucerne or clover plants on which they may fall, weather conditions being favourable.

If small patches only of the field be attacked, they should be at once covered with straw and burnt over to destroy all diseased plants and fallen leaves. By taking this precaution, it is possible that the disease may be arrested in its destructive course.

As irrigation colonies become more numerous, so will the conditions be more favourable to the spread of various diseases—warmth and mois- ture constitute suitable conditions for the development of fungoid pests. Settlers should therefore be continually on the lookout for the appearance of any disease such as the one under review.

VICTORIAN EGG-LAYING COMPETITION, 1911-12,

CONDUCTED AT BURNLEY HORTICULTURAL SCHOOL.

(Continued from page 820, Vol. IX.)

H. V. Hawkins, Poultry Expert.

No. of Pen.	Breed.	Name of Owner.	April to Oct.	Nov.	Total to Date (8 months).	Position in Competition.
12	White Leghorn	W. G. Swift	938	153	1,091	1
31	,,	R. W. Pope	901	161	1,062	2
40	,,	A. J. Cosh (S.A.)	905	140	1,045	3
20	,,	H. McKenzie	819	141	960	4
33	,,	Range Poultry Farm (Qld.)	826	130	956	5
37	,,	E. Waldon	790	143	933	6
18	,,	S. Brundrett	775	121	896	7
13	Black Orpington	D. Fisher	736	117	853	8
46	Minorca	G. W. Chalmers	736	114	850	9
21	White Leghorn	R. L. Appleford	718	126	844	10
39	,,	A.W. Hall	693	146	839	11
25	,,	B. Mitchell	702	127	829	12
55	,,	W. G. McLister	698	124	822	13
44	Black Orpington	T. S. Goodisson	700	114	814	14
38	White Leghorn	Mrs. C. R. Smee	662	138	800	15
32	Silver Wyandotte	M. A. Jones	696	101	797	16
10	Black Orpington	H. A. Langdon	659	137	796	17
9	White Leghorn	J. O'Loughlin	661	130	791	18
36	,,	F. A. Sillitoe	652	128	780	19
1	,,	A. Brebner	647	129	776	20
67	,,	C. L. Sharman	657	118	775	} 21
49	,,	W. J. Thornton	627	148	775	
24	,,	F. Hannaford	621	148	769	23
3	,,	K. Gleghorn	634	134	768	24
28	,,	J. Campbell	628	135	763	25
2	,,	E. P. Nash	611	150	761	26
66	White Wyandotte	J. E. Bradley	662	97	759	27
50	White Leghorn	C. H. Busst	619	136	755	28
19	,,	A. Jaques	632	120	752	29
4	Golden Wyandotte	H. Bell	636	112	748	30
22	Black Orpington	P. S. Wood	630	116	746	31
5	White Leghorn	L. C. Payne	609	134	743	32
65	,,	H. Hammill (N.S.W.)	605	128	733	33
45	,,	T. Kempster	601	131	732	34
47	,,	C. W. Spencer (N.S.W.)	588	141	729	35
27	,,	Hill and Luckman	593	135	728	36
51	,,	J. W. McArthur	623	104	727	} 37
63	Black Orpington	A. J. Treacy	635	92	727	
8	White Leghorn	T. W. Coto	590	128	718	39
62	,,	P. Hodson	563	149	712	40
59	,,	W. H. Dunlop	582	126	708	41
57	,,	G. E. Edwards	559	144	703	} 42
60	,,	J. J. Harrington	575	128	703	
58	Faverolles	K. Courtenay	585	117	702	44
43	White Leghorn	W. B. Crellin	572	128	700	45
11	Brown Leghorn	F. Soncum	556	141	697	46
41	White Leghorn	Morgan and Watson	579	109	688	47
53	,,	A. Stringer	551	135	686	48
42	White Orpington	P. Mitchell	585	93	678	49
52	White Leghorn	W. J. McKeddie	540	136	676	50
30	Black Orpington	Rodgers Bros.	554	112	666	51
6	Silver Wyandotte	Mrs. H. J. Richards	552	110	662	52
35	White Leghorn	J. H. Brain	488	143	631	53
34	,,	E. Dettman	508	122	630	54
54	,,	F. N. Hodges	524	97	621	55
7	,,	H. Stevenson	486	134	620	56
16	Silver Wyandotte	Miss A. Cottam	515	104	619	57
26	White Leghorn	F. Seymour	488	125	613	58
23	Golden Wyandotte	G. E. Brown	511	88	599	59
64	White Leghorn	J. D. Read	446	146	592	60]
56	,,	Mrs. C. Thompson	438	130	568	61
61	Silver Wyandotte	J. Reade	456	87	543	62
17	White Leghorn	W. J. Eckershall	432	104	536	63
14	Black Orpington	W. J. Macauley	425	96	521	64
15	Minorca	H. McChesney	351	105	456	65
48	,,	G. James	242	104	346	66
			40,378	8,240	48,618	

INSECTIVOROUS BIRDS OF VICTORIA.

FRONTAL SHRIKE TIT.

(*Falcunculus frontatus*, Gould.)

C. French, Junr., Acting Government Entomologist.

The Frontal Shrike Tit, a very handsome bird, is fairly plentiful in most localities a few miles from Melbourne. They are usually seen in pairs, generally amongst the topmost branches of eucalypts and other trees.

FRONTAL SHRIKE TIT.
(*Falcunculus frontatus*, Gould.)

The male has a beautiful dark coloured crest, and a black throat; but the throat of the female is green. The bill of this bird. being short and very strong, is admirably adapted for destroying the hard wing-cases, &c., of the destructive insects which hibernate under the bark and in the crevices of the trees. They also break open hard galls and scales and eat the insects contained therein. They are very active and seem to devote most of their time hunting for insects, and they do a considerable amount of good in keeping the strawberry cockchafer, cherry green beetle, codlin moth, longicorns, wire worms, and other pests in check. Remains of these insects have been found in stomachs of the Frontal Shrike Tit. .

The nests are very beautiful structures. In form, they are cup-shaped, being slightly contracted at the rim. The outside is generally composed of the inner bark of the eucalypt, mosses, lichens, cobwebs, and grasses, whilst the inner lining consists of grasses and fine shreds of bark. They are usually placed on the topmost branches of eucalypts, and though often found are most difficult to obtain, being fortunately out of the reach of boys.

As this bird is one of the best destroyers of noxious insects, it should, needless to say, receive every protection.

THE OLIVE.

L. Macdonald, Horticulturist, Dookie Agricultural College.

(Continued from page 839. Vol. IX.)

PROPAGATION.

The olive is one of the easiest trees to raise. It is propagated either from seeds, cuttings (as truncheons, hard wood, or terminal cuttings), sprouts, stools, or the excrescences found on the base of the tree.

SEEDS.—Like the peach, apricot, and other deciduous trees, the olive fails to come true from seed ; and, in the majority of cases, there is a reversion to more or less wild and worthless types. Hence, all seedlings, except those that are retained where it is desired to raise new varieties, should be worked over with selected varieties, either by budding or grafting.

The seed may be planted out in the open nursery or started in small beds where conditions can be controlled better, and planted out in their second season's growth. The latter is, perhaps, the more suitable method. In either case, the soil should be well prepared. The seed should be obtained, if possible, from selected trees. The pulp should be thoroughly removed before planting. A good method of doing this is by soaking the seed in an alkaline solution made up of $\frac{1}{4}$ to $\frac{1}{2}$ lb. of caustic soda to 1 gallon of water. Cracking the outer shell can also be adopted, but should be carried out with care so that no injury may be done to the kernel. This is a slow process and is not recommended for general purposes.

The seed should be sown 1 to 2 in. in depth and covered with some friable material. Where surface watering is adopted, a light mulch of short horse manure, or some such material, is advantageous, as it prevents the ground "caking" on top or cracking.

Germination is often tardy and irregular where no injury has been done to the outer shell, the seed sometimes remaining in the ground many months without making growth. Quicker results are obtained with those seeds whose outer shell has been injured in some way, thus permitting the moisture to gain more ready access to the kernel. Seeds may be sown as soon as the fruit is fully ripe or at any time through the winter months, say from May to September.

CUTTINGS.—The various sorts of cuttings are used chiefly for reproducing selected varieties. They may, however, be worked over with other kinds by either budding or grafting. This is sometimes done to diminish or increase the vigour of certain varieties.

TRUNCHEONS.—These may be obtained from heavy limbs split in quarters, or from round branches 1 to 3 in. in diameter. Those of a diameter from 2 to 3 in. are the most suitable for planting out. They should be about 15 to 20 in. in length and should be taken from the trees in June, July, or August. All side shoots should be removed and care taken not to bruise the bark. When planting in the nursery, it is a good plan to place the truncheons at an angle in the furrow, tread firmly, and cover over completely with soil, taking care to leave the top of the cutting close to the surface in such a manner that it will remain moist and gain a sufficiency of air. Several trees may be obtained from each truncheon in this manner, as they often develop sprouts and roots along the greater part of their length. If only one shoot is desired, the most suitable should be selected and the others removed.

TERMINAL CUTTINGS.—These are made from the tips of the shoots after they have passed the herbaceous stage ; they should be cut about 6 in. in height. All of the lower leaves should be removed immediately after cutting, to prevent evaporation of moisture and consequent wilting. The

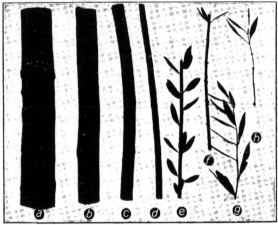

7. OLIVE TRUNCHEONS AND CUTTINGS.

a, b, and *c.* Truncheons, 3in., 2in. and 1in. diameter respectively ; *d* and *e.* Cuttings ; *f.* Cutting prepared for planting ; *g.* Terminal cutting ; *h.* Terminal cutting prepared for planting.

end for planting should be cut off close to a node, as they callus and root better when cut in such manner. Those cuttings with the buds close together are the best. They should be planted in a compost containing a good proportion of sharp sand and be kept continually moist. This kind of cutting is best started in lath or shelter houses or in frames, and planted out when well rooted. Cuttings of old wood below an inch in thickness should be of lesser length than the truncheons, and should be started in the nursery.

Cuttings are considered the quicker method of raising selected varieties. They come into bearing earlier, but are supposed to be shorter lived. It is possible that, in poor soils or trying situations, the seedling may be the more thrifty and long lived tree, but experience in this country has not gone to prove that this is the case. Many of the oldest trees in Australia were raised from truncheons and are still doing well. However, their age is comparative youth in the life of the olive tree, and perhaps it is as well to accept the opinion of continental writers on the greater longevity of seedling trees until there is greater evidence at hand to the contrary.

SPROUTS.—These may be obtained from the base of old trees, a good shield-shaped piece being cut off with each. They should then be shortened and treated in the same manner as terminal or small cuttings. They may also be obtained from truncheons where good growth is made and a rapid multiplication of numbers is necessary.

STOOLS.—This is a rapid and effective method of obtaining rootlings for transplanting and working over or for increasing a selected variety. Well established young trees are cut down close to the ground. A number of shoots develop from the adventitious buds that break out on the stub. The earth is then moulded up over the base of these and if kept moist rooting soon takes place. When the shoots are well-rooted, the soil is broken away and the shoots removed with a sharp knife or secateur. A fresh batch may then break out and can be treated in the same manner.

EYES.—This is a term used for the excrescences that occur around the lower part of aged trees. They may be used for propagation and succeed best where bottom heat is available. After removal with a sharp knife, they should be planted about an inch in depth in the same manner as seeds, covered with some friable material, and kept continually moist. When sprouting occurs, they should be removed to the nursery. They require skill in handling, and are not recommended except under circumstances where conditions may be controlled.

(To be continued.)

ANSWERS TO CORRESPONDENTS.

The Staff of the Department has been organized to a large extent for the purpose of giving information to farmers. Questions in every branch of agriculture are gladly answered. Write a short letter, giving as full particulars as possible, of your local conditions, and state precisely what it is that you want to know. *All inquiries forwarded to the Editor must be accompanied by the name and address of the writer.* This is very necessary, as sometimes insufficient information is furnished by the inquirer.

TOPPING UP COCKERELS FOR MARKET.—E.D. inquires as to method of feeding.

Answer.—Give equal parts pollard, barley meal, and bran, with the addition of steamed lucerne chaff (about a third), and sufficient skim milk to mix the whole to a crumbly consistency. For the last few days, add a little mutton fat or glycerine to mash. Feed a little at first, and gradually increase quantity as the appetite improves. Avoid grains. Skim milk to drink will improve and whiten the flesh. Birds should be kept off green grass when fattening. Grit must always be available.

NON-PREGNANCY.—H.E.M. states that he has a cow that will not get in calf, but has returned to the bull regularly for the past year.

Answer.—Syringe out with 2 per cent. solution of lysol. The day previous to service flush with a solution of baking soda. If this treatment be not successful, an impregnator should be tried.

REMOVAL OF AFTERBIRTH.—H.E.M. asks how to remove afterbirth that does not come away naturally.

Answer.—Insert the hand and detach from the button-like protuberances to which it is attached in a manner somewhat resembling the end of a finger in a glove. Pay special attention to cleanliness, and irrigate the womb with an antiseptic solution, such as lysol or Condy's fluid.

WORMS.—E.C.P. inquires as to treatment for worms. His yearling colt is not in as good condition as he should be, evidently owing to the prevalence of worms.

Answer.—Give one teaspoonsful of liquor arsenicalis in feed twice daily. Most yearling colts suffer from worms.

ITCH.—E.J.D. states that his mare is suffering from itch, near the mane being affected the worst.

Answer.—Wash with a solution of phenyle, and smear well with carron oil.

REMINDERS FOR FEBRUARY.

LIVE STOCK.

HORSES.—*At Grass.*—Supplement dry grass, if possible, with some greenstuff. Provide plenty of pure water and shade shelter. *In Stable.*—Supplement hard feed with some greenstuff, carrots, or the like, and give a bran mash once a week at least.

Avoid over-stimulating foods, such as maize and barley. Give hard feed in quantities only consistent with work to be performed. Stable should be well ventilated and kept clean. Remove manure promptly to a sufficient distance. Exclude flies. When at work, give water at short intervals. Always water before feeding.

CATTLE.—For milking cows the food should be of a succulent nature. Water should be pure, plentiful, and easily accessible. Provide shade shelter and salt licks. Keep milking sheds and feed boxes scrupulously clean. Remove attractions for flies. Care should be taken that the remainder of the cows required to calve next spring should be served this month.

If succulent feed not available, calves should be given milk until green grass appears. Their condition will thus be maintained and enable them to winter well.

PIGS.—If hard fed, some green vegetable food should be added. Give an ounce of Epsom salts in the feed occasionally; also a handful of charcoal. Water baths are appreciated in hot weather. Keep free from lice by brushing occasionally with an oil brush.

SHEEP.—Drench any weaners scouring; Cooper's tablets are handy for this work. Lime dams and pools; thick water and dry feed are responsible for many troubles with ewes later on. Keep salt available.

Do not wait until in-lamb ewes, or good wool-growing sheep are poor, before commencing to feed a little oats or oaten hay; it means better mothers and more shafty fleeces.

Coarse crossbred ewes are not in season till now. Downs' rams should be mated with this class for lambs; merino rams for graziers' sheep.

POULTRY.—Chickens should now be trained to perch; they will be more healthy and less liable to develop wry tails.

Provide plenty of green feed and give less grain and meat. Avoid condiments. Keep water in cool shady spot and renew three times each day. Keep dust bath damp.

Birds showing symptoms of leg weakness should be given 1 grain of quinine per day (three months old chickens, ½ grain) and plenty of skim milk.

CULTIVATION.

FARM.—See that haystacks are weatherproof. Cultivate stubble and fallow, and prepare land for winter fodder crops. Get tobacco sheds ready for crop. In districts where February rains are good, sow rye, barley, vetches, and oats for early winter feed.

ORCHARD.—Spray for codlin moth. Search out and destroy all larvæ. Cultivate the surface where necessary and irrigate where necessary, paying particular attention to young trees. Fumigate evergreen trees for scale. Continue budding.

FLOWER GARDEN.—Cultivate the surface and water thoroughly during hot weather. Summer-prune roses by thinning out the weak wood and cutting back lightly the strong shoots. Thin out and disbud dahlias and chrysanthemums. Layer carnations. Plant a few bulbs for early blooms. Sow seeds of perennial and hardy annual plants.

VEGETABLE GARDEN.—Continue to plant out seedlings from the seed-beds. Sow seeds of cabbage, lettuce, cauliflower, peas, turnip, and French beans. Keep all vacant plots well dug.

VINEYARD.—February is the month for the "Yema" or Summer bud graft. Select scion-bearing vines; mark with oil paint those conspicuous for quality and quantity of fruit, regular setting and even maturity.

Sulphur again, if necessary, but avoid applying sulphur to wine grapes too short a time before gathering.

Cellars.—Prepare all plant and casks for the coming vintage. An ounce of bisulphite of potash to each bucket of water used to swell press platforms, tubs, &c., will help to keep it sweet. Keep cellars as cool as possible. Complete all manipulations so as to avoid handling older wines during virtage.

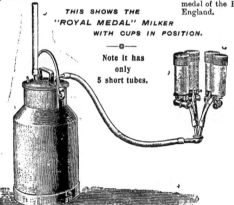

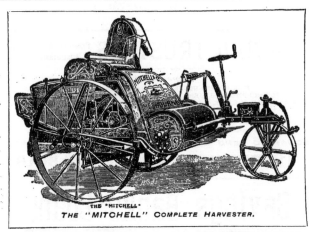

[Registered at the General Post Office, Melbourne, for transmission by Post as a Newspaper.]

The Journal of

THE DEPARTMENT OF AGRICULTURE OF VICTORIA, AUSTRALIA.

February, 1912.

The Pig Industry.

PRICE THREEPENCE.   (Annual Subscription—Victoria, Inter-State, and N.Z., 3/-; British and Foreign, 5/-.)

THE JOURNAL

OF

THE DEPARTMENT OF AGRICULTURE,

VICTORIA, AUSTRALIA.

T. HOPKINS, Acting Editor.

CONTENTS.—FEBRUARY, 1912.

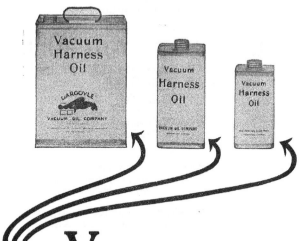

Vacuum Leather Oil

replaces the original and natural oils in leather which quickly disappear when harness is exposed to the weather.

Vacuum Leather Oil

preserves the leather; keeps it soft and pliable as a kid glove; gives a black finish; makes it water-proof; and prevents it from breaking and cracking.

Write for booklet: "How to Take Care of Leather."

Vacuum Oil Co. Pty. Ltd.

90 William Street, Melbourne.

DEPARTMENT OF AGRICULTURE,
VICTORIA.

GOVERNMENT STUD BULLS.

AVAILABLE FOR SERVICE OF COWS BELONGING TO BONA-FIDE SETTLERS UNDER THE CLOSER SETTLEMENT ACTS.

Fee, 5s. per cow.

Jersey Bull "DREADNOUGHT"; CALVED, 22nd October, 1908.
Sire :—Sir Jack (188). *Dam* :—Lady Kitchener, by Lord Melbourne.
(In charge of Mr. H. Crumpler, Block 148, Bamawm.)

Jersey Bull "ROSE FOX"; CALVED, 19th August, 1909.
Sire :—Starbright Fox (190). *Dam* :—Tuberose, by Magnet's Progress (54 A.J.H.B.).
(In charge of Mr. E. W. Prater, Block 106, Bamawm.)

Jersey Bull "VERBENA'S BOY"; CALVED, 10th January, 1908.
Sire :—Acrobat. *Dam* :—Verbena 2nd, by Snowdrop's Progress 2nd.
(In charge of Messrs. Laing and Mundie, Block 70, Bamawm.)

Jersey Bull "NOBILITY"; CALVED, 2nd April, 1910.
Sire :—Lucy's Noble of Oaklands. *Dam* :—Winnie of Melrose 3rd, by Royal Blue.
(In charge of Mr. E. T. Partington, Block 136, Bamawm.)

Jersey Bull "MILKY WAY"; CALVED, 20th June, 1909.
Sire :—Starbright Fox (190). *Dam* :—Milkmaid 34th (590), by Plinlimmon (imp. 62 A.H.B.).
(In charge of Mr. L. S. Hulands, Block 91, Nanneella.)

Jersey Bull "GOLD MEDAL"; CALVED, 3rd April, 1910.
Sire :—Golden Fox (142 A.J.H.B.). *Dam* :—Melba, by Greystanes 2nd.
(In charge of Messrs. Jacobs and Kennedy, Blocks 43 and 44, Nanneella.)

Jersey Bull "MAGNET'S FOX"; CALVED, 6th November, 1909.
Sire :—Fox's Laddie. *Dam* :—Magnet 28th, by Defender (imp.) (2288 H.C.J.H.B.).
(In charge of Mr. C. C. Woods, Block 29, Koyuga.)

Jersey Bull "CREAM PROSPECT"; CALVED, 22nd March, 1910.
Sire :—Lord Creamer (155 A.J.H.B.). *Dam* :—Daisy of Prospect (347 A.J.H.B.),
by Cardigan.
(In charge of Mr. L. H. Radclyffe, Block 2, Koyuga.)

Jersey Bull "ZODIAC"; CALVED, 10th November, 1908.
Sire :—Starbright Fox (190). *Dam* :—Zoe 4th (805), by Handsome Hero.
(In charge of Mr. R. J. Chappell, Block 12F, Swan Hill.)

Jersey Bull "GAY FOX"; CALVED, 12th May, 1909.
Sire :—Starbright Fox (190). *Dam* :—Floss, by Plinlimmon (imp. 62).
(In charge of Mr. F. Cox, Block 6D, Swan Hill.)

DEPARTMENT OF AGRICULTURE,
VICTORIA.

GOVERNMENT STUD BULLS.

AVAILABLE FOR SERVICE OF COWS BELONGING TO BONA-FIDE SETTLERS UNDER THE CLOSER SETTLEMENT ACTS—*continued.*

Fee, 5s. per cow.

Jersey Bull "WILLIAM OF AYRE"; Calved, February, 1910.
Sire:—Favourite's Fox 2nd.   *Dam:*—Bessie McCarthy, by Snowflake's Progress.
(In charge of Mr. J. S. Dickinson, Block 13, Nyah.)

Jersey Bull "FOX'S LAD"; Calved, 5th October, 1908.
Sire:—Fox, by Snowdrop's Progress 2nd.   *Dam:*—Pansy 2nd, by Duke.
(In charge of Mr. Ernest E. Borley, Block 6, Nyah.)

Ayrshire Bull "PETER OF WILLOWVALE"; Calved, 30th Sept., 1909.
Sire:—Annetta's Pride (243).   *Dam:*—Madge 2nd (Appendix A.H.B.), by Red Chief (359).
(In charge of Mr. F. McIvor, Block 12F, Swan Hill.)

Particulars of extended pedigrees, milking records, &c., can be obtained from each bull holder, from the resident Dairy Supervisors (**Mr. O'KEEFE, Rochester,** or **Mr. S. J. KEYS, Swan Hill**), or from **The Department of Agriculture, Melbourne.**

AVAILABLE FOR SERVICE OF COWS THE PROPERTY OF BEET GROWERS AT BOISDALE.

Red Danish Bull "CLAUDIUS"; Calved, 10th November, 1909.
Sire:—Ernst Bellinge (imp.).   *Dam:*—Kirsten IX. (imp.).
Fee, 5s. (available to 30 cows).

Red Danish Bull "HAMLET"; Calved, 1st August, 1910.
Sire:—Ernst Bellinge (imp.).   *Dam:*—Marianne IV.   *G. Dam:*—Marianne III. (imp.).
Fee, 5s. (available to 10 heifers).

Red Polled Bull "TABACUM"; Calved, 12th November, 1908.
Sire:—Acton Ajax (imp.).   *Dam:*—Janet, by Primate by Laureate (imp.).
Fee, 7s. 6d. (available to 20 cows).

Jersey Bull "GAY LAD II."; Calved, 8th August, 1906.
Sire:—Acrobat, by Cherry's Pride (imp.).   *Dam:*—Gaiety, by Snowdrop's Progress II., by Lady Superior's Progress (imp.).
Fee, 5s. (available to 40 cows).   (Winner of 7 first prizes.)

Particulars of extended pedigrees, milking records and prizes may be obtained from, and arrangement for service made with, **Mr. E. STEER,** at the Homestead Block 21, where the bulls are kept.

THE JOURNAL

OF

The Department of Agriculture

OF

VICTORIA.

L
N.
BOTAN
Q....

| Vol. X.   Part 2. | 10th February, 1912. |

THE PIG INDUSTRY.

I.—PRODUCTION AND CONSUMPTION.

R. T. Archer, Senior Dairy Inspector.

In all the leading dairying countries the revenue from the pig represents a very considerable portion of the farmer's income and is the means of utilizing to the best advantage the by-products of the dairy, viz., skim-milk, butter-milk, and whey. While this applies to the countries against which we have to compete on the markets of the world, it must be admitted that the condition of the industry in the State of Victoria is at present very unsatisfactory, and is likely to continue so, until it is placed on a better basis. The problem is how to accomplish it. Fortunately, we have sufficient information to indicate the lines upon which it is advisable to move.

Twenty-two years ago the financial conditions of Victoria were very depressed and the various products of the soil were correspondingly low in value. Fortunately, other countries had had similar experiences and had overcome them. Our statesmen found a solution of our difficulties in the experiences of Denmark. About 40 years ago, when the principal industry in that country was the production of grain, the farmers had a great struggle to keep their heads above water. Then came the establishment of the dairying industry, which has been the means of bringing prosperity to them.

It was the experience of the Danes that influenced our legislators to do so much to develop the export trade of dairy produce from Victoria. This had the desired effect on the finances, and paved the way to the present prosperity. It has become our third staple industry, and enabled us to export in the season 1910-11 butter to the value of two and a half million pounds sterling.

52.   D

Later on, the Danes discovered that they were not getting all that was possible out of their industry, and that they could do better with their skim-milk and butter-milk by converting them into bacon for export to Britain, which already provided the outlet for the bulk of their butter.

To enable them to start on sound lines, qualified men were sent by the Government to discover the class of meat that brought the best returns and how to produce it, with the result that they forthwith started breeding stations. These were placed under the control of experienced breeders who were subsidized to breed pure pigs, so that pure boars should be available at a reasonable rate to dairy farmers for crossing with the native breed of pigs. The breed decided on was the Large Yorkshire, and regular importations are still being made to keep up the standard.

Breeders' associations were started in different districts to provide boars for use by the members. This system of breeding, combined with proper methods of feeding, has enabled them to produce a type of bacon which commands the highest price on the British markets. The importance of this will be evident from a study of the figures given below, taken from *The Grocer:*—

IMPORTS INTO GREAT BRITAIN, 1910.

Source of Supply.	Product.	Quantity.	Value.	
		cwt.	£	£
Denmark ..	Butter	1,726,091		10,208,192
	Bacon	1,794,416		6,341,726
Canada ..	Butter	117,000		117,498
	Cheese	1,607,074		4,424,806
	Bacon	411,935	1,449,637	
	Hams	37,621	138,232	
	Lard	..	25,052	
	Pork	1,768	4,205	
	Total Pig Products	..	..	1,617,126
United States ..	Cheese	38,247		105,400
	Bacon	1,306,921	£4,453,293	
	Hams	665,771	2,329,516	
	Lard	1,342,257	4,201,013	
	Pork (Salt) ..	38,866	101,645	
	Total Pig Products	..	..	11,085,467
Holland ..	Cheese	231,318	..	567,360
	Fresh Pork	366,180	..	1,025,301
	Total Fresh Pork Exported	465,229	..	1,302,641
Victoria . ..	Butter	..	..	2,483,565
	Cheese	..	..	13,601
			1909–10. 1910–11.	
	Ham and Bacon ..	232,200	£489 £6,772	
	Pork (carcases) ..	4,439	592 9,988	
			£1,081 £16,760	16,760

EXPORTS OF PIG PRODUCTS FROM UNITED STATES, 1910.

(Kindly supplied by the Consul for the United States of America.)

Product.	Country.	Quantity.	Value.
		cwt.	£
Bacon	Belgium	19,699	48,317
	France..	210	547
	Germany	2,482	6,118
	Netherlands	9,511	21,749
	Other European Countries	23,331	54,815
	British North America	16,852	65,737
	Other Countries..	..	261,456
	Total Exports	..	458,739
Lard	Belgium	80,361	208,008
	France..	4,206	10,029
	Germany	833,416	2,261,703
	Netherlands	212,121	555,337
	Other European Countries	90,512	219,555
	British North America	85,949	253,272
	Other Countries..	..	370,480
	Total Exports	..	3,878,384
Hams	Belgium	47,368	117,549
	France..	..	..
	Germany	455	1,234
	Netherlands	972	2,445
	Other European Countries	2,863	7,844
	British North America	24,328	83,355
	Other Countries..	..	232,966
	Total Exports	..	445,393
Pork	Belgium	1,242	2,573
	Germany	3,561	7,995
	Netherlands	415	860
	Other European Countries	15,010	29,923
	British North America	111,881	274,629
	Other Countries..	..	368,433
	Total Exports	..	684,413

These tables will serve to illustrate the importance of the trade to the United States and what a large proportion of the whole exports is sent to Britain. It also shows that, in addition to the United Kingdom, there are many other ever-expanding markets the trade of which we may hope to share should we choose to develop the industry. The English figures are the Board of Trade returns, and are reproduced from *The Grocer:*—

IMPORTS OF PIG PRODUCTS TO BRITAIN.

Product.	Source of Supply.	Quantity.			Value.		
		1908.	1909.	1910.	1908.	1909.	1910.
		cwt.	cwt.	cwt.	£	£	£
Bacon ..	Denmark ..	2,049,513	1,809,745	1,794,416	5,680,923	5,801,382	6,341,726
	United States..	2,858,312	2,189,053	1,306,921	6,726,084	6,057,473	4,453,293
	Canada ..	687,759	443,386	411,935	1,827,636	1,364,357	1,449,637
	Other Countries	90,158	183,279	350,117	245,936	578,453	1,146,618
	Total ..	5,685,742	4,625,463	3.863,389	14,480,579	13,801,665	13,391,274
Hams	United States..	1,169,601	1,073,569	665,775	2,936,960	2,952,084	2,329,516
	Canada ..	52,657	53,593	37,621	138,472	154,222	138,232
	Other Countries	2,969	1,867	15,730	9,237	6,590	58,837
	Total ..	1,225,227	1,129,029	719,126	3,084,669	3,112,896	2,526,585
Pork (Salted) ..	United States..	81,119	55,639	38,866	139.178	113,555	101,645
	Other Countries	189,489	202,900	188,325	189,673	199,307	202,523
	Total ..	270,608	258,539	227,191	328,851	312,862	304,168
Lard	United States..	1,924,881	1,703,578	1,343,257	4,258,051	4,694,353	4,201,013
	Other Countries	62,610	57,022	109,236	149,359	163,673	319,061
	Total ..	1,987,491	1,760,600	1,452,493	4,407,410	4,858,026	4,520,074
Lard (Imitation)	.. ..	174,064	231,847	275,402	306,700	438,909	603,444
Pork (Fresh) ..	.. ..	..	..	..	..	1,023,322	1,196,797
		7,343,132	8,005,478	6,537,601	22,609,209	23,547,680	22,442,342

CANADIAN BACON TRADE.

In a report on trade between Canada and Britain, published in *The Grocer*, Lord Strathcona, High Commissioner for Canada, states—

In respect of bacon, it will be noted that a decrease of £463,279 (or 25.35 per cent.) took place in 1909 in the imports of this important product. The shortage in the supply of bacon for the market of the United Kingdom during the year under revision has created an interesting situation. Bacon is unquestionably the staple breakfast dish in England, and the demand has been a steady and increasing one for some years past. Up to 1905, the rapid growth and expansion of the Canadian bacon exports to the United Kingdom was so gratifying that it was hoped that the Dominion would eventually find it one of the largest and most profitable of her industries. This hope has not, however, been borne out, though a leading agricultural journal recently pointed out, in speaking of the excellent reputation established on the British market for Canadian bacon, that had the supply been equal to the demand, it is difficult to estimate the magnitude that might have been reached

A glance at the following import statistics will show the falling off in the supply of Canadian bacon which has taken place.

Country.	1907.	1908.	1909.	1910.
	cwt.	cwt.	cwt.	cwt.
Canada	873,340	687,759	443,386	411,935
Denmark	1,799,787	2,049,513	1,809,745	1,794,416
United States	2,599,817	2,858,312	2,189,053	1,306,921
Other Countries.. ..	92,661	90,158	183,279	350,117
	5,365,605	5,685,742	4,625,463	3,863,389

UNPRECEDENTED RISE IN PRICES.

Whatever may be the cause of this decrease, the effect of smaller supplies from Canada and elsewhere has been to cause a serious and unprecedented rise in price of bacon in this country.   A comparison of prices is given below :—

Bacon.	1908.	1909.	1910.	1911.
Irish	54s. to 63s.	70s. to 77s.	75s. to 83s.	64s. to 73s.
Danish	42s. ,, 55s.	66s. ,, 75s.	68s. ,, 78s.	60s. ,, 69s.
Canadian	47s. ,, 50s.	69s. ,, 71s.	72s. ,, 76s.	57s. ,, 67s.
Swedish	51s. ,, 53s.	70s. ,, 72s.	74s. ,, 77s.	62s. ,, 66s.
American	42s. ,, 47s. 6d.	58s. ,, 64s.	..	..
Russian	..	..	64s. to 70s.	50s. to 58s.
Dutch	..	..	72s. ,, 76s.	59s. ,, 64s.

Such abnormal prices at once reduce consumption.   It has been stated that 70 per cent. of the households in the United Kingdom are maintained on 45s. per week or less, and higher prices therefore operate at once to diminish purchases.   The prospect of Canadian and United States supplies of bacon continuing to be restricted causes concern in the provision trade in Great Britain, and it is being pointed out that attention in that country could profitably be directed towards increasing home supplies. It is urged there would be, in consequence, less dependence on outside sources, while the prohibitive prices ruling at the present time may perhaps be avoided in the future.

NEW SOURCES OF SUPPLY.

New sources of supply are being found.   Russia, Siberia, and Holland are being drawn upon, while consignments of pigs have been received from China.   Canadian farmers must maintain an abundant supply of hogs if the Dominion is to successfully compete with a country like Denmark, where painstaking attention is devoted not only to the successful production of bacon, but also to the maintenance of regular supplies to this great market.   It is to be noted that a large British co-operative society has decided to establish three factories in Denmark, where the conditions are so favorable for production, and at least one of the largest private bacon curers in the United Kingdom, whose products have a high reputation has also decided to follow this example.

As an evidence of the direct interest taken by the Danish Government in the development of this important trade, it may be pointed out that advertisements are officially inserted in the British provision trade journals stating that the business is under Government control, and that bacon from perfectly sound pigs is guaranteed to buyers.   It must be realized that, while an enormous market exists in Great Britain for bacon, there will always be competition of a formidable character to meet in it, and great efforts will be required if Canada is to retrieve the position which was obtained prior to 1905.

The following are the total exports of bacon from Canada :—

						£.
1903	...	...	...	...	...	3,000,000
1904	...	...	...	...	...	4,000,000
1905	...	...	...	...	...	5,000,000
1910	...	...	...	...	...	1,617,126

CONSUMPTION IN GREAT BRITAIN PER HEAD OF POPULATION.

Product.		1905.	1906.	1907.	1908.	1909.
Bacon and Hams ..	lbs.	17·28	17·14	16·12	17·07	14·06
Beef (Salt and Fresh)	,,	13·34	14·49	14·82	14·31	15·49
Mutton (Fresh) ..	,,	9·87	10·47	11·61	11·01	11·83
Butter	,,	10·57	10·92	10·48	10·45	9·93
Cheese	,,	6·19	6·63	5·89	5·65	5·80
Eggs	..	51·75	51·48	50·11	48·65	46·95
Spirits	gals.	·91	·90	·91	·85	·65
Beer	,,	27·70	27·97	27·58	26·62	25·83

It will be seen from this that, except for beef and mutton which show an increased consumption, the other products show a decrease.   But, as we have seen above, the price has increased, and this goes further. to illustrate that there is an opening for us to develop an export trade in pig products.   Especially so, as it can be shown that this country possesses facilities over those we have to meet in competition, so as to admit of production at a cost that will leave a fair margin for profit.

FRESH OR FROZEN PORK.

Supply in Smithfield Market, London.

Source of Supply.	Quantity.
	tons.
United Kingdom	8,520
Australasia	191
Canada and United States of America	136
South America ..· ..	5
Holland and Other Countries ..	22,555
	31,407 at £56 per ton = £1,758,792.

In a paper by Mr. London M. Douglas, the well-known English authority, is the following comment on the meat industry :—

The year 1910 will be memorable in connexion with the meat industry of England, because of its having witnessed such a crisis in the history of the meat supply as is likely to have far-reaching results.   During last year it began to be realized in some of the larger European States that the home supplies of meat of all kinds were not keeping pace with the increase in the population, and as meats from other countries and from British colonies were refused entry into these States the home prices became consequently higher and higher.   Agitation has now gone so far that it is most likely that Germany, Austria, Hungary, Switzerland, France, and Italy will be compelled to open their frontiers to supplies of foreign meat. In Portugal, the prohibitions have already been removed, with the result that in that country the prices of meat have fallen to their normal level.

This is of extreme importance to all interested in agricultural matters· in Australia, as it means in the near future the opening up of enormous markets.   Instead of having a share of the British trade only to depend upon, as an outlet for our surplus products, we shall have millions of Europeans as customers.   In the *Age* of 20th December, 1911, mention was made that the Minister of Customs had been notified that the new Swiss duty on frozen meat, smoked meat, and bacon would be 4s. 0$\frac{3}{4}$d. per cwt from 1st January, 1912.   The old duty varied from 10s. 2d. on frozen meat to 4s. 0$\frac{3}{4}$d. on fresh bacon.

In *The Grocer* of 16th September, 1911, it was stated that the French Government, owing to dearness of food in that country, is allowing live pigs to be imported from Denmark subject to duty, the late prohibition being removed.   The import duty on bacon and ham to France is 15s. to 25s. per cwt., and nearly as much on fresh pork.   It will be noticed that the greatest quantity of the fresh pork is sent from Holland to Britain.

Considerable shipments of frozen pork have been sent to Great Britain from China.   Two shipments, comprising about 10,000 carcases, were taken to Liverpool, but as they did not comply with the regulations of the Local Government Board in certain technicalities the health authorities refused to allow them to go into consumption.   They were to be landed and placed in bond under cold storage until reshipped, probably to the Isle of Man for curing into bacon and ham for re-exporting.   It was stated at a meeting of produce merchants that the Chinese frozen pork was being cured and sold as English bacon.   Whether that is so or not it is certain that if there is a glut of frozen pork it can be cured and sold as bacon.

In a report in an English paper on the pork trade last season appears the following statement :—

A fair quantity of Victorian pork is on Smithfield, 90 to 100 lbs. weight. It is said to be rather too fat for the pork butcher, but it is of first-rate quality. About 5$\frac{1}{2}$d. per lb. is the price.   The pork trade is a disappointment to those people who were last year anticipating heavy prices.   Old sows this time last year were making 6$\frac{1}{2}$d.; now they would be worth only half of that figure.   There is a slump in pigs, caused partly no doubt by the fact that the Chinese pigs are now arriving regularly, and of good quality, and are accepted by the trade.

In support of this we have copies of complete account sales giving the results of operations of Victorian farmers on the London market, but which still yielded a satisfactory return.   The charge for slaughtering has since been increased to 4s. 6d. per pig over 100 lbs. weight.

COST OF MARKETING PORK IN LONDON.

Particulars of 11 Carcases Pork (1,621 lbs.) per s.s. " Aeneas."

	£	s.	d.
By 11 carcases, 1,593 lbs., at 5½d.	36	10	2

Melbourne Charges :—

	£	s.	d.
To Slaughtering 11 pigs, and delivery to freezing works, at 3s. 6d.	1	18	6
„ Freezing (including handling, wrap, bagging, and storage), at 1s. 6d.	0	16	6
„ Ocean freight, 1,621 lbs., at ⅝d.	4	4	5
„ Marine insurance	1	11	3
„ Railage to ship..	0	4	0
„ Labour (loading into ship) and stamps B/s Lading	0	1	9
„ Agency, correspondence, postage, &c. ..	0	10	6
Total Melbourne Charges	9	6	11 = 1·408d. per lb.

London Charges :—

	£	s.	d.
To Discount, 2 months, at 5 per cent.	0	6	2
„ Landing charges, &c.	0	18	0
„ Port rates	0	1	0
„ Commission and full guarantee, at 3 per cent.	1	1	11
Total London Charges	2	7	1 = 0·355d. per lb.

Charges—Grand Total	11 14 0 = 1·763d. per lb.	..	11	14	0
Net Proceeds	3·737d. per lb.	..	24	16	2

(Loss in weight, 28 lbs., or 1·73 per cent.)

	£	s.	d.
Net Return per Pig—(Average, 147 lbs. dressed weight) ..	2	5	1
Less freight	0	3	3
Net Return	2	1	10

CHINESE PORK.

A correspondent of the *Globe* writing on the subject of Chinese pork says :—

I have recently returned from China, and am able to state that the frozen pigs that are being exported to England are of breeds quite equal to many raised in England and far superior to those coming from several countries in Europe. I had an opportunity of speaking to our Ambassador at Pekin, and also to the Consul-General in the town from which the pigs are imported, upon the question. They both assured me that the English company which inaugurated this business deserves every credit for its enterprise in tapping a valuable source of food supply, that the pigs were of a special breed from a district that had been noted for generations for their excellence in quality, and that they were fed on rice which is exceedingly cheap in the district. There is no doubt that the food of these pigs is far and away superior to that of those raised in the neighbourhood of all large towns in England.

In the *Argus* of 11th November last is published the following cable :—

Inspector Farrar, who was sent to China by the Local Government Board when charges were made that pork bred in that country and shipped to Great Britain was not sound, has made his report. He says that all pigs in China which are intended for home consumption and for export are grain fed and bred on farms, the conditions of which compare favorably with those in England.

Dear Bacon in Great Britain.

While Victorian farmers are obtaining low prices for their pigs we frequently see comments on the dearness of bacon in Great Britain and in this country too.   In Great Britain various reasons are given for the decrease in the number of pigs kept, the principal of which are:—

1. That yearly an increased amount of milk is being consumed in its natural condition as a beverage, making less skim milk and whey available for pig feed.
2. Owing to more stringent sanitary regulations, fewer pigs are kept by cottagers.   These formerly aggregated a considerable total.

In the trade there have been deductions on pigs over 180 lbs., and also on overfat bacon.

Disease has played its part in checking production, as swine fever, tuberculosis, and measles cause considerable loss and trouble.   This last-named disease is not known in Victoria, but in America nearly every pig has to be examined microscopically for the purpose of detecting its presence or otherwise.   All these are handicaps in favour of Victorian farmers.   The principal cause, however, of the high price of bacon in Great Britain is the restricted supply from foreign countries.   On the other hand, the reason that pigs in Victoria are bringing such low prices is that there are far more fat pigs produced than can be handled by those in the trade.   They pick what they require from those offering.

British Bacon-curing Factories.

The following table gives the products of British bacon-curing factories principally for the wholesale trade.   The products by farmers, pork butchers, provision merchants, &c., for private trade are as far as possible eliminated:—

Product.					Quantity.	Value.
					cwt.	£
Bacon	..	..	..	..	1,716,000	5,365,000
Hams	..	..	..	..	457,000	1,658,000
Pork (Salt)	..	..	..	..	18,000	31,000
Lard	..	..	..	..	587,000	1,414,000
Sausages	..	..	..	..	..	751,000
Heads	..	..	..	..	..	182,000
Sausage Casings	..	..	..	..	..	290,000
Preserved Meats (Brawn, Tinned Meats, &c.)				..	..	383,000
Offals	..	..	..	..	..	278,000
Other Products	..	..	..	..	..	157,000
					..	10,509,000

A very interesting feature of these figures is that the recognised output of the bacon factories, viz., bacon, hams, pork, and lard, totals £8,468,000, while the by-products give £2,041,000—nearly one-fourth additional.   So it appears that they could sell bacon, &c., at cost price and have 25 per cent. over for working expenses.   At most bacon factories in this country, a private individual can get a pig killed and cured for 1d. per lb.   It, therefore, stands to reason that it will not cost 1d. per lb. to turn out the bacon, as the work will not be done for nothing. As about one-fifth the weight of the carcase is lost in curing, it should be possible to buy at 4d. per lb. carcase weight, and sell at 5d. for bacon.

The Byron Bay Co-operative Bacon Factory Company (New South Wales) claims that it can place bacon on any market at 5d. to 5¾d. per lb.

At the present time we see the market quotations as follows :—

Best Porkers, suitable for first-class counter trade, realized from 4d. to 4½d , a few medium to good realized from 3¼d. to 3½d. ; prime bacon sizes, 3d. to 3¾d. : medium, from 2½d. to 2¾d. ; and heavy lots less.

Bacon.—There was an improved demand yesterday. Prime light-weight sides are selling at from 6¼d. to 6¾d., special lines commanding higher rates; medium to good realize from 5d. to 5¾d., and occasionally to 6d.; shoulders offering at down to 4½d. per lb.; middles, 8½d. to 9d.

Hams.—In anticipation of Christmas, trade was brisk. Prime light weights are quoted at from 10d. to 10½d., up to 1s. being mentioned for special cures, whilst for medium weights and quality, down to 9d. is being accepted.

These quotations show a considerable margin between the buying and selling prices.

The Future Prospects of the Industry.

The future prospects of the industry, so far as this country is concerned, may be considered decidedly hopeful. While it is temporarily under a cloud, experience goes to show that all that is required is proper organization to place it on a sound footing. With this it should develop into a very important branch of the export trade.

Statistics show that two great sources of supply to the British market (United States and Canada) are gradually but surely declining, and ere long must cease altogether on account of the rapid increase in population and the consequent increased food requirements in those countries. In Denmark, we cannot expect to see any great increase in production as the limit has been almost reached. Holland and Sweden are the only other European countries from which we may anticipate competition. The rapid growth of the population in central Europe increases the food requirements of those countries where there is already a short supply of animal foods generally. As we have seen, China is likely to become a rival.

CHAMPION PEN OF PORKERS (LARGE YORKSHIRES).

(To be Continued.)

DISEASES OF FARM ANIMALS.

Anthrax and Blackleg.

In response to many enquiries for information concerning the above-named diseases, the following article by Dr. S. S. Cameron, M.R.C.V.S., is reprinted from the *Journal of Agriculture* for July, 1906.—EDITOR.

ANTHRAX.

SYNONYMS :—*Cumberland Disease—splenic fever—splenic apoplexy—
black rot.*

Anthrax is the most ancient contagious disease of animals that is known. The sixth plague of Egypt, referred to by Moses, was anthrax, and elsewhere he indicates the transmission of the disease from cattle to man by means of soiled clothing. Homer, Ovid, Plutarch, Dionysius, Livius and other ancient writers frequently refer to this disease ; and in some cases their descriptions are most exact and plainly manifest the disease as we know it now-a-days.

Anthrax exists in most countries of the world and has been prevalent throughout Australia for a long period, affecting cattle and sheep principally but horses and pigs in lesser degree. In New South Wales it was known prior to the seventies as Cumberland Disease (from its particular prevalence in the County of Cumberland) and the credit of definitely identifying and announcing this disease as anthrax belongs to the late Graham Mitchell, F.R.C.V.S., of Melbourne. Early in 1876 there was great mortality of sheep in the Western District of Victoria which was recognized as being analogous with Cumberland disease and identified by Mitchell as anthrax. His announcement was, however, officially discredited, much bitter feeling being engendered, and it was not till after Mr. Mitchell's death in 1888 that the correctness of the diagnosis was publicly admitted. A detailed history of the controversy on the subject, which was a lengthy one, is given in a brochure on " Cumberland Disease in Australian Sheep " published by Graham Mitchell in 1877.

DEFINITION.—An acute contagious febrile blood disease, affecting herbivorous and omnivorous animals (including man) principally, caused by the *bacillus anthracis*, and characterized by a general hæmolysis with engorgement of the spleen and other organs and by sudden onset, rapid course and almost uniformly fatal termination.

CAUSATION.—The *bacillus anthracis* was discovered in the blood of animals dead of the disease in 1850 by Davaine, and was demonstrated by him to be the specific cause of the disease thirteen years later (1863). It was the first disease-producing organism to be recognized, and the science of bacteriology may be said to date from its discovery. Usually, but not without exception, it is found in the blood of all parts of the body and in the spleen and other organs. Compared with others since discovered it is a large bacillus (5 to 20 microns long by 1 to 1.15 microns thick) and is distinctly rod-shaped with square ends. It is non-motile, ærboic, stains by Gram's method or any aniline dye and grows freely on a variety of culture media. Grown outside the body it assumes a filamentous form and bears spores which are particularly resistant to extremes of temperature.

---

* A micron equals $\frac{1}{25,400}$ part of an inch.

The anthrax bacillus is quickly destroyed in the presence of putrefaction and septic ferments, and as decomposition of an unopened anthrax
carcase is very rapid the search for the bacilli may be fruitless if the
examination is delayed till putrefaction is advanced.   Not only may the
bacilli not be found by microscopic examination, but the blood and tissues
will not be infective to other animals after a few days except in those
cases where, through admission of air, the bacilli have sporulated.   In
such cases the bacilli would have become disintegrated but the spores
would produce anthrax in any susceptible animal inoculated.   This fact
has an important bearing on the diagnosis of the disease and also upon
the suppression of its spread.   It will be obvious that microscopical and
bacteriological methods of diagnosis cannot be relied on except when the
examination is conducted on comparatively fresh specimens, taken in a
manner to minimize risk of contamination with putrefactive organisms.
Even as regards inoculation, Friedberger and Frohner set out that " inoculation gives negative results when the matter containing the bacilli is
soiled by other microbes or is in a state of putrefaction.''

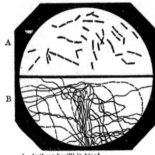

A. Anthrax bacilli in blood.
B. Filamentous development of anthrax
    bacilli on artificial culture.

On the second point, as to preventing the spread of the disease,
seeing that spore formation in the
bacilli does not occur in the living
animal nor in the carcase to any
extent if air and oxygen are excluded and that the bacilli themselves are quickly destroyed after
the death of the animal, it follows
that the risk of spread of the disease is greatly lessened if the carcase is not cut or opened up to contact with air.   The germs are im-
prisoned, so to speak, and die
from oxygen starvation.   Any risk
there is lies in the possibility of
the discharges from the carcase
containing bacilli which, on contact
with the air, form spores by which the contagion may be propagated.   If,
however, such discharges are collected and burnt along with the carcase,
or buried deeply with it, the risk of spread of anthrax may be reduced to a
minimum.   It is this quick destruction of the bacillus by decomposition
and the absence of sporulation that accounts for that sudden cessation of an
anthrax outbreak which is so frequently observed and which appears so
inconsistent with the expected behaviour of a contagious disease.

When the bacillus has become liberated from the carcase it may be
preserved in the soil and propagate for an almost indefinite length of
time.   This is more likely to occur if the soil is rich in organic matter,
and hence moist alluvial lands are notoriously more retentive of anthrax
infection than dry uplands.   A paddock with anthrax-infected soil may
not produce anthrax for years, until the occurrence of conditions which
favour the transmission of the germs from the soil to the herbage.   In
very damp seasons the germs may be brought to the surface by the elevation of the water level on swampy ground; or they may be washed out by
floods and deposited on the surface; or the excessive moisture may bring
up earth worms whose earth casts may contain bacilli from an anthrax

grave or infected soil; also grass or plants springing from deeply-buried seed and pushing up through rain-loosened soil may carry bacilli to the surface on their growing leaves. Again, anthrax may occur in very dry seasons when infected water-holes, swamps and morass land dry up and leave the germ-mixed mud accessible to stock. A growth of vegetation springs up on the mud coating, and stock often pull up such vegetation by the roots and so run further risk. Flies and insects of various kinds are also much more numerous during the dry summer season, and they are undoubted carriers of contagion.

METHOD OF INFECTION.—It will have been gleaned from what has been said about infection from pasturage that one of the principal ways in which the germ gains entrance to the system is in the food by *ingestion.* In addition to pasture, hay or other fodder grown on infected land is a frequent cause of anthrax breaking out on previously uninfected properties. In New Zealand, anthrax in sheep has been traced to the feeding of growing root crops, in which case the likelihood of ingesting soil along with the food is very great. Root crops that have been manured with bone-dust supposed to have been contaminated with anthrax germs have been particuarly blamed. Since the investigation of this phase of the subject by Professor Gilruth, when Government Veterinarian in New Zealand, imported Indian bonedust has been held responsible for a number of outbreaks in Victoria and elsewhere throughout Australia.

INOCULATION is another form of infection, flies and insects conveying the germs from anthrax carcases to wounds and abrasions on other animals. Inoculation may also occur through accidental wounds made with knives and instruments previously used on an anthrax carcase; in fact, this is the most common way in which man becomes infected with the form of anthrax known as "malignant pustule."

It is questionable whether the disease in animals is ever caused by INHALATION, but in man the pulmonary anthrax called "woolsorters' disease" is most likely caused through inhalation of the particles contaminated with anthrax germs which rise when dried skins, hides and wool are being handled.

FORMS OF ANTHRAX AND SYMPTOMS.—As a general infection anthrax occurs in hyper-acute, acute and sub-acute forms. The first of these is more usually described as *Apoplectic or Fulminant* anthrax. The animals, cattle or sheep mainly, are affected suddenly without premonitory symptoms; they have convulsions and die in the course of from a few minutes to an hour. The earlier cases in the anthrax outbreak at Keilor, Victoria, in the beginning of 1903 were of this form, some of the cows being found dead within an hour of their having been observed feeding, and apparently perfectly well. Others were seen to suddenly stop feeding, look round wildly, stagger and fall as if in a fit and die after struggling for a few minutes. The fulminant form of anthrax appears to afford an illustration of the phenomenon observed by various investigators that the bacilli are less numerous in the blood in proportion to the more rapid course of the infection. Quite often in these cases the bacteriological examination of the blood gives negative results because the bacilli are located or colonized in one particular organ or spot; they have not had time to multiply to an extent sufficient to pervade the whole body before death results from the lethal effects on the central nervous system of the anthrax toxin formed locally.

ACUTE GENERAL ANTHRAX is a little less rapid.   Death occurs in
from two to twenty-four hours.   During this time there is high fever
with increase of temperature, tremors, excitement, grinding of the teeth,
groaning, stupefaction, or frenzy, staggering gait, spasms, laborious
breathing, prostration and finally the convulsions which precede death.
There may be great straining to pass fæces and urine, with frothy and
blood-tinged discharges from the natural orifices.   Emphysema or a
gaseous distension under the skin may also be observed.

SUB-ACUTE GENERAL ANTHRAX.—In this the features are somewhat
similar to those of the acute form, only that the course is less rapid and
the steps from one set of symptoms to another are more prolonged and
defined.   There may be intermission of symptoms for a time and the
fatal culmination does not usually occur until the lapse of 36 or 48
hours, and it may be postponed for five or even seven days.

GLOSS-ANTHRAX.—In horses and pigs anthrax often assumes a local
form affecting the tongue and region of the neck and throat.   These
become swollen and there may be also swellings on the shoulder flank
and thigh, which are at first hard, hot and painful and later on become
doughy, fluctuating and cold.   The tongue is greatly enlarged and
blackened and may protrude from the mouth.   There is inability to
swallow and great difficulty in breathing.

POST-MORTEM APPEARANCES.—The carcase has a tendency to swell
quickly, decomposition of the abdominal contents being very rapid.   There
is also a gaseous distension (emphysema) under the skin which on pressure gives out a crackling sound.   Blood-tinged fluid effusions are noticed
under the skin.   In what may be described as typical cases, but to
which there are many exceptions, the blood is profoundly changed, being
black in colour and remaining black on exposure to air.   It does not clot
freely and has a tarry appearance.   The lining membrane of the chest
and abdominal cavities is dotted with patches of blood extravasation
(ecchymosis) as also are the heart sac, the kidneys and the liver.   The
heart and large veins leading from it are filled with black liquid blood
and the heart muscle is soft and relaxed.   The lymphatic glands are
always congested, and may be spotted with hœmorrhages.   The liver is
usually enlarged, soft, friable and easily broken down.   The lungs are
engorged with blood and dropsical.   The trachea and bronchial tubes
contain bloody mucus.   The mucous lining of the stomach and bowels is
reddened and spotted with blood extravasations.   In the spleen the
most decided changes are observed.   It is enlarged to two or three times
its natural size, and its structure or spleen pulp is softened, broken down,
and heavily charged with blood and fluid of a deep colour.

The appearances described are not likely to be all met with in every
case, in point of fact "in the rapidly fatal cases the changes in the
blood and tissues are often little marked" (Law); but even in fulminant
anthrax there may usually be found localizations of the described appearances in some organ or group of lymphatic glands where colonization of
the bacilli has occurred, and blood or tissues from such part will be found
loaded with bacilli.

PREVENTION.—The carcases of animals dead of anthrax and all matter
likely to have become contaminated should be destroyed by fire as
described under the headings "Disposal of Carcases" and "Disinfection"

in the chapter on Prevention of Disease.   Lands upon which anthrax has become " enzootic," *i.e.*, where the soil is impregnated with the bacilli and the disease breaks out periodically, should if possible be turned from grazing use for a time and cultivated.   The underdraining of low-lying, damp land is also to be recommended, not only because of the removal of stagnating moisture but also because of the soil aeration which draining effects.   Under the slow influence of oxygen, anthrax bacilli are gradually robbed of their virulence.   Seeing that anthrax is not usually conveyed from animal to animal by direct contact but is most often contracted from the pasture or food, a practical measure towards the prevention of its spread is the removal of all apparently healthy animals from the paddock in which the disease has been occurring to dry upland country.   The mortality will almost at once cease, and even if an odd animal does succumb after removal the risk of contaminating the new paddock will be small if the precautions previously mentioned, as to disinfection and the non-opening of the carcase before burning or deep burial, are strictly observed.   Besides, the anthrax germs are not likely to become permanently fixed on dry sandy soils.

PREVENTIVE INOCULATION.—Immunization of flocks and herds by inoculation with an " anthrax vaccine " has been practised for many years with varying degrees of success.   Some of the " vaccines " used consist of an attenuated or weakened culture of the bacillus and others of sterilized anthrax toxins.   They are prepared in various ways—(a) by the action of heat (Toussaint), sunlight (Arloing), compressed oxygen (Chauveau) or antiseptics (Chamberlain and Roux); (b) by the cultivation of the bacillus in an oxygen atmosphere (Pasteur); and (c) by sterilizing anthrax blood and dissolving out the soluble toxins (Law).

Pasteur's method is the one that has given the best results and by it protective virus of two grades of virulence are usually used.   The first is a very weak virus (" 1st vaccin ") resulting from cultivation in oxygen at a high temperature (42 degrees C.), to prevent the formation of spores for twenty-four days.   The second or stronger virus (" 2nd vaccin ") is got when cultivation under the same conditions is carried on for twelve days.   To inoculate, the prescribed dose of 1st vaccin is injected under the skin on the inner aspect of the thigh (sheep) or behind the shoulder (cattle) and fourteen days later the 2nd vaccin is similarly injected.   The dose must be regulated according to size and age, but the average is ⅛th of a cubic centimeter for sheep and double that amount (¼th c.c.) for cattle.   The protection lasts for about a year or more, after which re-inoculation is necessary.

It cannot be confidently recommended to practise inoculation for anthrax indiscriminately   It should never be practised except on anthrax lands, that is, where the disease occurs periodically as an enzootic, as " elsewhere it may lead to the stocking of a new area with a malignant germ (the anthrax bacillus) which in young and susceptible animals re-acquires its original virulence."   Another drawback as regards sheep is that different breeds and families appear to possess a very irregular sensitiveness to the same virus; hence in large part doubtless, the many fatalities that result from inoculation of sheep on the one hand and the many failures to protect on the other.   In Australia the best results are obtained between May and September.

Law's method of anthrax protection by injection of sterile solution of anthrax toxins has been practised with success in America.   The blood of an anthrax animal is heated for half-an-hour at 212 degrees F. to destroy the germs; it is then washed with boiled water to dissolve out the toxins, and the resulting solution is injected in doses of 2 to 4 c.c., as the protecting virus. The advantages claimed are:—(*a*) That the material can be prepared on the spot when dealing with an outbreak; and (*b*) that, as the germs are destroyed, the risk of inoculating virulent anthrax or introducing it to a new area is avoided.

BLACKLEG.

Synonyms :—*Black-quarter—Quarter-Ill—Symptomatic Anthrax— Emphysematous Anthrax.*

Definition.—An acute infectious febrile disease, affecting almost solely young cattle, caused by the *bacillus Chauveauii* and characterized by fever, lameness and hot, painful swellings on the quarter, thigh, neck, shoulder or elsewhere which tend to become emphysematous and gangrenous.

This disease has only become prominently prevalent throughout Australia during recent years. It is a disease so common in England that it would be well known to imported veterinarians, and its occurrence would scarcely have escaped their notice, yet it was not till the late nineties that its existence was chronicled. Since then it has been the cause of considerable mortality amongst calves and young stock in many dairying districts. The incidence of the disease is practically confined to young cattle between the age of three months and two years. It seldom, if ever, attacks calves while still on a milk diet solely; this because of the fact that the germ is usually introduced from the soil when grazing.

Nature and Causation.—For a long time blackleg was looked upon as a modification of anthrax but it is now known to be caused by a difference bacillus, and while it has many features of an anthracoid character its clinical history, local symptoms and age period of incidence serve to easily differentiate it from true anthrax.

The actual cause is a bacillus, called the *bacillus Chauveauii* or *bacillus anthracis emphysematosus,* having the following features :—Rod-shaped with rounded ends one end being often larger than the other on account of the presence of a spore, so making the bacillus club-shaped. It is anærobic, living in the tissues without utilizing the oxygen of the blood and being but rarely found in the blood in which oxygen is abundant; motile, the movements being both undulatory and rotary; and sporulates within the body. It withstands putrefaction, and is found abundantly in the tissues a long time after death, even up to six months. A reference to the description of the anthrax bacillus will show that in regard to all the features just mentioned the bacillus of blackleg is the direct antithesis of the anthrax bacillus. Like the latter, however, this bacillus persists in the soil for an almost indefinite period, and blackleg can be readily produced by inoculating the washings of marshy soils that have been contaminated a long time previously. The disease occurs under the same conditions and on the same class of country as anthrax. An obvious preventive measure, therefore, is to avoid depasturing young cattle on wet clayey or marshy soils during the age period of this disease. It would seem to be necessary for there to be wounds or scratches of the mucous lining of the mouth or alimentary tract before the disease can be contracted, for it is probably only conveyed by inoculation. In this connexion it is significant that the age period of the disease is synchronous with dentition changes, and it is likely that in the great majority of cases the inoculation occurs through the raw edges of the gums when the milk teeth are being cast. Pasturing on scrub or on spear grass or other rough herbage is also likely for obvious reasons to predispose to the contracting of the disease.

Lack of vigour through high condition on the one hand or through poverty on the other is a noticeable auxiliary cause, as also are chills and sudden changes of weather during the spring when young stock are shedding their winter hair.

Symptoms.—The period of incubation or time elapsing from inoculation to the manifestation of symptoms varies from one to five days, the average being two days. The animal then becomes dull, feverish and depressed ; there is loss of appetite and rumination, and a marked increase of temperature. A stiffness or lameness in walking is then observed. This is usually confined to one limb and there quickly succeeds a swelling or tumefaction of the affected limb or of some other part of the body. The swelling is small at first but extends very rapidly and may acquire a considerable size in a few hours. It is hot and painful, and when rubbed or pressed with the hand a crackling noise is heard due to the distension of the tissues beneath the skin with gas. Later, the swelling becomes cold and insensitive, and on being lanced a dark-red frothy and offensive fluid exudes along with bubbles of gas. As the disease advances the animal rapidly weakens, the breathing becomes very distressful and, pre-

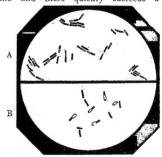

A. Bacillus of blackleg.
B. Bacillus of blackleg showing drumstick development.

ceded by a rapid fall of temperature, death results in from one to three days.

Post-mortem Examination.—The carcase—the internal organs as well as the tissues underlying the skin—will be found greatly bloated or distended with gas. The tissues in the region of the swelling are engorged with dark, frothy blood ; they are friable, breaking down readily under finger pressure and have a bruised pulpy appearance. The bacillus is present in this pulpy mass in large numbers. The lymphatic glands in the neighbourhood are enlarged and congested. The lungs, liver and kidneys are also usually congested but the spleen is rarely enlarged.

Prevention.—Recovery practically never occurs and curative treatment is useless so that quick destruction of all cases definitely diagnosed as blackleg is a wise procedure. The carcases should be burnt and the disinfection methods and other preventive measures recommended in anthrax cases and for infected areas should be carried out in every detail. Cultivation of infected land is more successful in eradicating blackleg than anthrax, the aeration of the soil effected by the cultivation operations being inimical to the development of the anaerobic germ.

PREVENTIVE INOCULATION.—Immunity against blackleg can be produced artificially by subjecting the system of an animal to the action of the weakened toxins of the bacillus.   This may be done by different methods, but that which has been most successful is the use of a weakened virus or "vaccine" prepared from the diseased flesh according to the method of Arloing.   "Forty grammes of the diseases muscle are dried rapidly at 32 degrees C. (90 degrees F.) and triturated in 80 grammes of water.   This is divided in 12 equal parts and put on plates in two thermostats, six at 100 degrees C. (212 degrees F.) and six at 85 degrees C. (185 degrees F.) where they are kept for six hours, when it forms a dry, brownish powder.   One-tenth of a gramme (1½ gr.) of this powder is dissolved in five grammes of distilled or boiled water and will furnish ten doses.   The animal to be protected is first injected in the tip of the tail or elsewhere with the virus prepared at 100 degrees C., and ten days later with that prepared at 85 degrees C."   (Law.)   A peculiar fact about the weakened virus so prepared is that its full virulence is regained by the addition to it of a small quantity of lactic acid.

The Pasteur Institute prepares the vaccine, and issues it in the form of short threads that have been soaked in a virus of required strength and afterwards dried.   The threads are introduced under the skin by a special needle after the manner commonly practised in inoculation for pleuro-pneumonia.   An American firm also distributes virus prepared by the Arloing method but in the form of solid pilules which are injected under the skin by means of a syringe fitted with a canula, needle and spring piston.

For the successful prevention of the disease on infected farms or in infected districts all the young cattle between three months and two years old should be inoculated in the spring and autumn.   The two inoculations are necessary because the protection which it conveys only lasts about six months.

It should be mentioned that this method of immunizing stock against blackleg should be restricted to cattle in infected areas otherwise there is grave risk of introducing the disease into new country.   Such risk is much greater if the inoculation is carried out during the hot summer season.

In New South Wales, blackleg is a notifiable disease, the penalty for failure to report being £50, and for selling or purchasing stock affected with it the fine is £100.   Under the *Noxious Microbes Act* 1900 preventive inoculation by private owners without a licence from the Chief Inspector of Stock constitutes an offence.

WHEAT AND ITS CULTIVATION.

I.—INTRODUCTION.

A. E. V. Richardson, M.A., B.Sc. (Agric.), Agricultural Superintendent.

Ever since the dawn of history civilized man has used wheat as a staple article of diet; and, in competition with foods of other races, it is displacing rice, millet, and other grains to such an extent that its production has become one of the most fundamental problems of the time. No problems in the realm of agriculture should be of greater moment than those relating to the production and distribution of our daily bread. Particularly is this true with respect to Australia, for the prosperity of her people and the stability of her finances are in a very large measure dependent on the success of her wheat harvests.

It is estimated that the world's average annual production of wheat for the past five years has been 3,150 million bushels. Of this vast quantity, Australia has only contributed about 2 per cent. Although the wheat industry of the Commonwealth has made enormous progress during the past decade, it will be many years before Australian production will exert any appreciable influence on the price of wheat in the great markets of the world.

Importance of the Wheat Industry.

Some idea of the importance of the wheat industry to Australia may be gained from a perusal of the latest figures of the Commonwealth Statistician. Of the total area under cultivation for all crops in 1909-10, namely, 10,972,299 acres, no less than 6,586,236 acres were reaped for wheat, or 60 per cent. of the total, whilst 2,228,029 acres or 20 per cent. of the total were cut for hay, the greater portion being wheaten hay, that is, probably 75 per cent. of the total area under cultivation to all crops was placed under wheat in 1909-10.

The man in the street naturally seeks some explanation for the extraordinary popularity of this cereal, and under the existing economic conditions convincing reasons are readily forthcoming. Wheat is an excellent pioneer crop, and it lends itself admirably to the *extensive* system of farming common to all comparatively new countries, where, compared with densely-populated countries, land is cheap, and individual holdings considerable, high class farming is rarely practised, and the object of the cultivator is rather to secure a small average return from an extensive acreage than a large average return from a small area. With our multiple-furrow ploughs, 20-tine cultivators, and 4-horse drills, large areas can be cultivated with the minimum of hand labour, and the complete harvesters enable the grain to be taken off with the greatest facility. With the increase of population, and the inevitable increase in land values ahead of us, this system of farming, particularly in Victoria, will gradually be modified, and a new era will be ushered in, characterized by smaller areas under individual cultivation and higher averages per acre.

Under existing conditions of cultivation, it does not require the exercise of much skill, or of a great deal of labour, to secure a *payable* crop of wheat, though it does require the very highest skill, ability, and intelligence to secure the maximum crop the soil and season will allow.

As long as the wave of expansion continues in Russia, Canada, Argentine and Australia, enormous supplies will be raised for many years to come under pioneer conditions—under conditions of extensive farming—and it is owing to the capacity of these countries during the last generation for raising cheap wheat that wheat is being displaced from its position in the rotation systems of highly farmed and densely populated countries.

An additional reason for its popularity lies in the fact that for wheat there is always a ready market, and that, unlike many agricultural products, it does not suffer by storage or transportation over long distances. Moreover, it is a most reliable crop, especially when treated in a rational manner, and, being more resistant to drought than any of the other cereals, it is more likely to succeed under arid Australian conditions than other crops.

Finally, during the last decade, prices have been most satisfactory, and the standard of efficiency in wheat cultivation has been considerably raised by the recognition of the value of fallowing, judicious crop rotation, rational soil cultivation, and systematic manuring. The wheat farmer has, therefore, greater confidence in the future, for he feels that he knows more of the essentials for successful cropping than he did a decade ago.

In subsequent articles, some of the more important phases of the wheat industry will be discussed, including problems relating to the cultivation and manurial requirements of the crop, seeding and harvesting operations, crop rotation, wheat improvement, and experimental and research work.

To pave the way for future discussion, it would be well to indicate in a general and elementary manner the position of our staple crop in the vegetable kingdom, and the nature and structure of the grain under consideration.

CLASSIFICATION.

Wheat belongs to the great family of grasses (*Gramineæ*), which are characterized by the possession of hollow stems, closed joints, alternate leaves, with sheaths split on the side opposite the blade.

Wheat, rye, barley and rye-grass all belong to the tribe *Hordeæ* of this order. In all these, the flowers are arranged in what botanists call spikes, and each spikelet is one or many flowered. Other important farm crops are included under the *Gramineæ*, and the following rough classification shows in simple manner the more important members of the order.

		Maydeæ ..	..	Maize.
	Spikelets	Andro pogoneæ	..	Sorghum.
	(One Flowered)	Paniceæ ..	..	Millet.
Gramineæ ..		Oryzeu ..	..	Rice.
		Phalarideæ ..	..	Canary Grass.
	Spikelets	Aveneæ ..	..	Oats.
	(Many Flowered)	Festuceæ ..	..	Fescue, Brome Grass.
		Hordeæ ..	..	Wheat, Barley, Rye.

Although the number of varieties of wheat in the different wheat-growing countries of the world runs into thousands, all these varieties are included in the one genus—*Triticum*. It is generally admitted that there are eight general types in cultivation, with differences sufficiently great to enable them to rank as separate species or sub-species. Hackel,* however, recognises but three true species, and classifies the remainder as sub-species.

---

* *Die Naturlichen Pflanzen familien.*

Now, though many of these species are likely to be of very little value to the Australian farmer, they are of the highest interest to the breeder of wheats suitable for our local conditions. By the crossbreeding of some of these species with those wheats in general cultivation in Australia, some very desirable characteristics, *e.g.*, drought resistance, non-shattering of grain, rust resistance, and early maturity, may deliberately be imparted to our local varieties.

The eight types of wheat referred to above may be classified thus :—

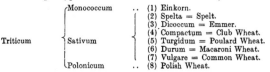

Triticum	Monococcum	..	(1) Einkorn.
			(2) Spelta = Spelt.
			(3) Dicoccum = Emmer.
			(4) Compactum = Club Wheat.
	Sativum		(5) Turgidum = Poulard Wheat.
			(6) Durum = Macaroni Wheat.
			(7) Vulgare = Common Wheat.
	Polonicum	..	(8) Polish Wheat.

(1) *Einkorn*, (2) *Spelt*, and (3) *Emmer.*—Of these different types, the first three (Einkorn, Spelt, and Emmer) are to be found on most wheat-breeding stations, and are frequently of service in imparting such properties as hardiness, drought resistance, ability to hold the grain, and capacity for thriving on poor soil. They have all been cultivated from the very earliest times, but their cultivation is now chiefly confined to portions of Germany, Spain, Italy, and Russia. Both for forage and for food purposes, however, they are gradually being displaced, even in those countries by varieties of *Triticum sativum vulgare*—common bread wheat.

(4) *Club or square-head* wheat differs from common wheat, principally in its short stiff straw and short but compact head. Its yield is unsatisfactory, however, and it is very susceptible to rust.

(5) *Poulard* wheat is grown principally in the hot dry areas bordering the Mediterranean. It very closely resembles the durum or macaroni wheats in the appearance and characteristics of the grain. Egyptian, and the so-called mummy wheat with branched and compound heads, belong to this sub-species.

(6) *Polish wheat* (*T. Polonicum*) has not done well in experimental plots under Australian conditions, though it is successfully cultivated in the drier portions of southern Europe. The grains of this wheat are very long and somewhat resemble rye.

(7) *Sativum vulgare*—common bread wheat—is the most widely cultivated of all the species, and it enjoys this popularity on account of its high yielding power, and because it makes such excellent bread. The greater majority of the varieties of wheat grown in Australia belong to this important sub-species.

The future of the Australian wheat industry is largely dependent on the profitable utilization of those vast areas at present considered outside the margin of " safe " farming.

From the remarkable developments that have resulted during the last decade in the profitable opening up of lands that hitherto were considered practically useless, it is quite apparent that it is not safe for any one to predict the possible confines of profitable wheat farming in the future. To further extend the zone of profitable cultivation, it is evident that attention must be concentrated on those factors which will enable the grower of the future to raise wheat successfully on the more arid portions of the Commonwealth.

In the past, efforts have been mainly directed to the question of cultivation and the devising of methods to secure the maximum conservation of soil moisture.   While great improvements have been effected in the system of cultivation and manuring during the last decade, are we to assume that further advance with respect to these practices is impossible?

There is, however, another important factor to be considered, but this is frequently ignored in discussions relating to the ultimate utilization of our arid areas, viz., the influence of the plant.   Very little attention has been devoted to the question of raising varieties of wheat which will thrive

FIG. 1. LE HUGUENOT, 4¾ TONS OF HAY PER ACRE.

under extremely arid conditions, though, manifestly this is a problem worthy of the best efforts of our wheat-breeders.   Though the wheats, which are at present popular with growers, seem to be well adapted to the conditions under which they are grown, there is not a single variety which can be safely described as free from defect.

While a great deal may be accomplished by scientific effort in the production of new varieties suitable for our driest areas, it is not reasonable to expect that more would be accomplished in a decade in this way than by centuries of care by past generations of wheat-growers under arid climes. That is to say, the production of drought-resistant varieties is likely to be successful if we use as foundation stocks those varieties which have been grown for generations under the very driest conditions.

There is always a difficulty attendant on the introduction of varieties from foreign shores. Very rarely does an introduced wheat do well during the initial stages of its introduction to an unfamiliar climate, and very often its merits are overlooked by those who are inclined to hasty judgments. This difficulty may be appreciated from the experience at the Parafield Wheat Station (South Australia) where over 200 varieties of wheat from different portions of Russia, India, United States, Canada, and Argentine have been grown for some years. Many of these varieties were total failures during the first season or two, but they gradually became "acclimatized," and some of them promise to equal and excel the very best of the local varieties.

The most probable method, then, of securing suitable varieties for our arid areas would appear to be—

(a) The systematic testing for a period of years of the best of our local wheats and foreign wheats, when grown under conditions similar to those that obtain in the very driest areas, and

(b) The gradual improvement of such varieties either by systematic selection or by crossbreeding combined with selection.

(8) *Triticum sativum durum*—durum or macaroni wheat. Among the many thousands of varieties grown in different parts of the world the durum wheats promise to be of some value in the production of drought-resistant varieties. They are tall and erect, with smooth, bright green leaves, and long, narrow translucent grain of exceptional hardness, which is invariably rich in gluten, but poor in starch. The heads are usually heavily bearded and vary in colour from light yellow to a bluish black. During recent years these durum wheats have become very popular with the wheat-growers of the arid portions of the United States, and this is simply because, under their conditions of climate, these wheats are more productive than those hitherto cultivated.

Durum wheat, on account of its relatively high gluten content and its density, is well suited for the manufacture of macaroni, but it is not generally regarded as suitable for milling purposes, on account of the dark colour of the flour and of the resultant bread.

This question of colour in flour is very important, both to the miller and the baker. The consuming public, whether rightly or wrongly, we need not consider here, demands bread of snow white colour, and looks upon dark-coloured bread as inferior in quality. So long as this demand for snow-white colour in bread continues, so long must both miller and baker consider the question of colour in flour of supreme importance.

Incidentally, it might be mentioned that Victoria and South Australia have always been able to produce wheats which on milling give a flour of excellent colour; and it is principally on this account that these wheats have met with a ready sale on the English market. We cannot, however, overlook the fact that, generally speaking, they are low in gluten content and in strength. It may be that these deficiencies are a characteristic of the climate, and if so we might be inclined to infer that improvement in these respects is beyond the limit of possibility. While admitting, however, that these important qualities are, in a large measure, dependent on the climate, there is reason to believe that these properties may be greatly improved by crossbreeding and selection.

If proof of this were necessary, the case of Comeback, Bobs, and John Brown—varieties raised by the late Mr. Farrer—might be mentioned. Whether their properties can be retained in ordinary cultivation, or whether they will gradually fall to the level of our ordinary wheats, can only be determined by testing the milling properties of these varieties through a succession of years. Bobs and Comeback, however, are not grown in quantities sufficient to influence appreciably the *f.a.q.* sample of wheat. Nor are they likely to come into general cultivation until it is proved that they will yield as heavily as the best of our wheats, or until millers encourage farmers to grow them by offering an increased price sufficient to compensate the grower for any monetary loss by reason

FIG. 2. A HEAVY CROP OF DURUM WHEAT.

of a possible shortage of yield. If Comeback and Bobs could be further improved by making them as prolific as, say, Federation, the farmer would grow them as readily as he now grows Federation.

The Australian wheats, then, at present have the reputation of producing flour of unrivalled colour, and for this reason, they are always welcome on the English wheat market. Voller,* who is regarded as an authority on milling problems, gives the following useful information for British millers in making blends :—

For *largest* loaf, use good Minnesota or Manitoba.
For *whitest* flour, use good white English, Oregon, or *Australian*.
For *sweetest* flour, use good English and Manitoba in equal parts.

* Modern Flour Milling.

The production of flour of good white colour is therefore a matter of considerable importance.   Of course, it does not follow that snow-white bread is more digestible or more nutritious than dark bread.   As a matter of fact, the nutritive qualities of whole meal bread are well known. The public, however, have a decided preference for snow-white flour as against dark flour.   The durum wheats, therefore, when first introduced into cultivation in America were looked upon by millers with dismay. They promptly docked the growers of durum wheat, but in spite of the docking, it soon became evident that these wheats, on account of their prolificacy and adaptability, had come to stay.

To meet the taste of the consuming public, therefore, they had no alternative but to bleach the flour with various oxidizing agents to rid it of its objectionable colour.   Nitrogen peroxide is most commonly used for this purpose, and ordinary flours as well as the durum flours are treated in this way.

As much controversy has been waged in connexion with this question of bleaching, a short summary may be of interest to possible growers and millers of durum wheat.

Ladd utterly denounces the practice of bleaching durum and other flours as " undesirable, dangerous, and fraudulent."[†]   He contends that injurious nitrites are left in the flour, that the quality of the gluten is lowered, and that the bleaching permits of low-grade flours being used.

On the other hand, Wesener and Teller[‡] examined a number of flours and foodstuffs, and, *inter alia*, found that rain-water contained eight times as much nitrogen trioxide as ordinary bleached durum flour, and that ham contains five hundred times more of this compound than the highest amount found in a series of bleached flours.   They also affirm that bleaching has no injurious effects on the gluten, and entirely disagree with Ladd's views.

Snyder,[§] in an exhaustive review of the subject of bleaching of flour, concludes that in bread-making tests of commercially bleached flours, no difference could be observed between the bread made from bleached and ordinary flour of the same variety of wheat, except that the bleached flours produced a whiter bread and also showed a tendency to produce larger loaves.   No difference was observed in the digestibility with pepsin solution, and the bleaching did not impart any odour or taste to the bread or leave in it any residue.

It is interesting to note that the question of flour bleaching, both of durum and ordinary bread-wheats, was discussed at length before Lord Warrington in the High Court of England in a dispute over a patent for bleaching flour (*vide* Reports of Patent Cases, XXVI., 1909); and, after hearing evidence from such specialists as Ladd, Halliburton, Hehner, Dewar, Ballantyne, and Wilcox, His Honour, during the course of a lengthy judgment, found—

(1) That there is no substantial difference in point of digestibility between bread made from unbleached flour and bread made from bleached flour.

(2) No deleterious action on the flour is caused by bleaching with nitrogen peroxide.

It might be mentioned that several varieties of this sub-species are grown in different parts of the Commonwealth, but those most in favour at the present time are grown entirely for forage purposes, and not for

[†] Bulletin No. 72, North Dakota Experiment Station.
[‡] American Food Journal, September, 1907.
[§] Bulletin No. 111, University of Minnesota.

grain.   Among many that might be mentioned are Kubauka, Medeah, Atalanta, and Huguenot.

The first three are heavily bearded, and are therefore somewhat objectionable for hay, though they give exceptionally heavy cuts.   Huguenot is quite free from beard, but in all other respects closely resembles Medeah.

These wheats make very sweet hay, which is much relished by stock. Owing to the fact that they tiller rather badly it is necessary to sow them rather thickly, otherwise the hay is very coarse.   It is often advantageous to mix these varieties with wheats like Majestic and Baroota Wonder, when sowing them for hay.   The illustrations represent two crops of hay grown at the Parafield Wheat Station on stiff, red clay soil during 1910. No. 1 weighed 4¾ tons per acre, whilst No. 2 gave over 5 tons per acre of dried hay.

Though these two varieties give heavy yields of hay, they give poor yields of grain, and on this account will never rank as dual purpose wheats.

Having considered in outline the various sub-species of the genus *Triticum*, let us now consider the internal structure of a typical kernel. For this purpose, we will take the variety most commonly grown, viz., Federation.

Microscopic Structure of the Wheat Kernel.

If a thin section be taken longitudinally through a wheat grain and examined under a microscope with a lower power objective, three distinct structures will be observed (Fig. 3) viz. :—

1. Embryo or germ.
2. Endosperm.
3. Protective coats.

Embryo.—At the end opposite the *brush* will be found the embryo or germ, which is destined to form the future wheat plant.   Careful examination of the embryo will reveal— .

(a) The *plumule*, that portion of the germ which develops into the stem and leaves of the young plant, consisting of minute rudimentary leaves enveloped within the plumule sheath.

(b) The *radicle* or rudimentary root, with its root sheath and root cap.

(c) *Absorptive epithelium*, a series of elongated cells lying between the embroyo proper and the endosperm, lying with their long diameters being directed towards the endosperm.

According to Brown and Morris,* this epithelium secretes diastase during the process of germination, and this enables the starchy contents of the endosperm to be transformed and assimilated by the developing germ. It is thus the means whereby the germ derives its sustenance from the stored up food in the endosperm until it has developed sufficiently to maintain itself by its own root activities.

Compared with other portions of the grain the embryo is rich in protein. fat, and ash constitutents, and, though it contains a considerable amount of sugar, it has but little starch.   Nearly one-sixth of the embryo consists of fat and oil and about one-third protein, so that these two constituents make up practically one-half the germ.

Endosperm.—By far the greatest portion of the kernel is made up of the endosperm, which acts as a storehouse of food for the young plant

---

* Germination of the Gramineæ.

during the time it is seeking to establish itself in the soil. The endosperm occupies, on an average, about 80 per cent. of the kernel.   It is principally composed of what are known as *starch cells*—large elongated cells with their long diameters arranged radially to the surface of the kernel. These starch cells, however, are found, on examination, to consist of an

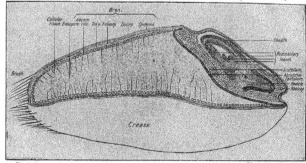

Photo.]   [C. C Brittlebank

FIG. 3. LONGITUDINAL SECTION OF A GRAIN OF WHEAT SHOWING THE
INTERNAL STRUCTURE.

outer covering of cellulose containing within a large number of starch grains.   Besides these starch grains, the starch cells contain a considerable amount of gluten, and Fleurent has shown that the amount of such gluten varies with the position of the starch cell in the endosperm.   From a detailed examination of a number of Indian, Russian, and French

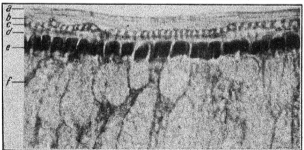

Photo.]   [C. C. Brittlebank.

FIG. 4. LONGITUDINAL SECTION OF FEDERATION WHEAT.

wheats, he was able to show that the amount of gluten in the endosperm increased from the centre to the periphery.   In an Indian variety, *e.g.*, the amount of gluten varied from 8 per cent. at the centre to $10\frac{1}{4}$ per cent. at the peripheral portion of the endosperm.

It is the endosperm which forms the flour in the process of milling the grain.

Protective coats.—The starchy endosperm and the embryo are both protected by a firm tough coat, which, on superficial examination appears to be homogeneous in structure. When examined under a microscope,

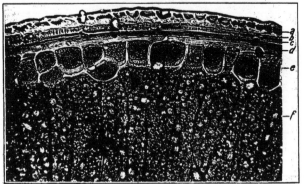

Photo.]   [C. C. Brittlebank.

FIG. 5. TRANSVERSE SECTION OF FEDERATION GRAIN.

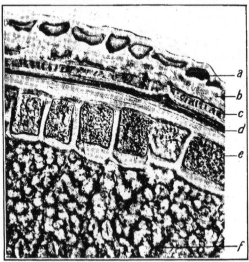

Photo.[[C. C. Brittlebank.

FIG. 6. TRANSVERSE SECTION OF FEDERATION WHEAT. *x* 400, SHOWING
STRUCTURE OF PROTECTIVE COATS AND ENDOSPERM.

however, this covering membrane is found to consist of several layers of sharply differentiated cells.   These various structures serve as a protection for germ and endosperm, and, in the process of milling, become detached from the remainder of the kernel and collectively form the *bran*.

At least five different layers may be distinguished under the microscope besides several irregular, vaguely defined intermediate layers.   Examination of a number of varieties of wheat commonly grown in Victoria reveals wide differences in their microscopic appearance, especially in regard to the structure and characteristics of the layers immediately covering the endosperm, and it may be that these microscopical characters are correlated with important external characteristics of the varieties concerned.

An examination of Fig. 6 will reveal the following structures :—

(a) The *epidermis*, which consists of a layer of longitudinal cells with their long axes in the direction of the length of the kernel.

(b) A second layer, the *epicarp*, very similar to the former in general appearance resting on an irregular layer apparently devoid of cellular structure.

(c) The *endocarp*, placed at right angles to the cells above described.   In cross section the cells of the endocarp appear to be very regular in character, with thick cell walls which in longitudinal section display minute pits.

(d) The *testa*, consisting in the unripe kernel of two distinct layers of cells closely applied to the aleurone layer.   The testa is very tough in character, not readily permeable to water and homogenous in structure.

(e) The *aleurone* layer, consisting of large more or less rectangular cells, with thick cell walls containing oil and granular nitrogenous matter.   It is frequently called the gluten layer, though this is a misnomer, as the gluten found in the flour is derived from the starch cells of the endosperm and not from the aleurone layer.

What is known as the bran consists of the five layers described above. The micro-photographs of the sections illustrated above were prepared by Mr. C. C. Brittlebank, Acting Vegetable Pathologist of this Department.

To be Continued.

PROPAGATION OF FRUIT TREES.

(Continued from page 63.)

C. F. Cole, Orchard Supervisor.

DISBUDDING.

Cutting off, *i.e.*, reducing the stocks back to the inserted bud will be the cause of numerous shoots pushing out around and below the bud.   The growth of these shoots is generally earlier and more rapid with stone than with seed fruits.   As such shoots are robbers they will, if neglected too long, seriously affect the growth of the buds.   The probable result will be either death to the moving bud or a weakened condition of growth. To prevent this, it is necessary to remove all superfluous shoots before a certain period elapses.   This period is controlled by the species, variety of fruit, and the quickness of the growths.·

Deciduous stone fruits, such as the apricot, nectarine, peach, and plum will first require attention.   All shoots should be removed before they become hardened at the base of the growth and before they are more than 6 or 8 in. in length.   With healthy and well grown stocks there is no danger of leaving the shoots to attain this length.   Such shoots are a protection to the growing bud until this time.   With the apple, cherry, pear, &c., the shoots should be removed earlier.

When disbudding, as this operation ·is termed, the operator should carry an old knife to remove any shoots from the stock just below the surface of the soil.   Shoots may be removed from the stock by rubbing them off with the thumb and finger, *i.e.*, if soft enough, or cut off close to the stock with a sharp knife.

61. DISBUDDING STOCKS.
a. Stock showing robber shoots.   *b.* Same stock disbudded, showing growing bud.

Before starting to remove the shoots, first locate the inserted and growing bud.   The bud is the terminal point.   When the stock is reduced shoots cannot sprout around or about the bud.   If there is any likelihood of injuring it while disbudding, hold the growing bud carefully with the one hand to insure ·its safety, and remove the useless shoots with the other. Growing buds are very easily broken away from the stocks.   When disbudding stone fruits, remove all shoots, if the inserted bud has not started to grow and is alive.

If the bud is dead, and one wishes to save the stocks for future use, cut off to a shoot close to the ground; failing a shoot, reduce to the ground.   During the following winter, such stocks should be carefully removed, trimmed, and planted out again for budding upon.   Almond.

apricot, and peach stocks carrying dead buds are not worth while bother-
ing about when disbudding; either remove or rub off all shoots.

With the apple, select a strong vertical shoot and remove all others.
Trim and train into a tree the same as a growing inserted bud.   Such
a tree should either be Northern Spy, Winter Majetin, or some other
blight-proof variety used for stock purposes.   If not wanted for sale
during the winter, it may be head-grafted the following spring with some
other desired variety.   When removing trees for sale from the nursery
row the propagator should be careful not to mix them with the worked
varieties.   To guard against mistake the rows should be carefully ex-

62. DISBUDDING STOCKS.

a. Yearling tree, pruned, showing robber shoots. *b.* Same disbudded.

amined in the autumn, and all trees marked by tying a short piece of
raffia or some other suitable material around the stems.

When disbudding the pear and quince it will repay the operator to cut
off the shoots with a sharp knife close to the butt of the stock.   Whilst
doing so he should be careful to remove the fleshy basal portion of the
shoots.   If rubbed off, the shoots will probably sprout again.   By
cutting, the risk of doing so is greatly lessened.

All propagated trees unsold and left standing in the nursery rows
should be pruned.   Such trees require to be disbudded in the spring.
Remove all superfluous shoots that push out upon the stem, &c., only

leaving those required to form, or reform, the future head of the young tree.

Fig. 62A shows a yearling branched tree that has been pruned back to a straight stem. The operation of disbudding should have been performed earlier, *i.e.*, when the shoots were soft and easily removed with the thumb and finger. Consequent upon this delay, it has thus become necessary to remove the shoots with a sharp knife. By the early removal of shoots that are not required the ones left to form the future head benefit greatly by receiving the whole of the nourishment. When removing

63. DISBUDDING STOCKS.
a. Two-year-old tree, pruned, carrying too many shoots. *b.* Same disbudded.

hardened shoots from the stems of young trees, cut close so that the cambium will heal quickly and neatly across the scars.

Fig. 63A shows a two-year-old tree that has been branched pruned, *i.e.*, the three branches operated upon to form the future head have been reduced back to their basal buds. Consequent upon this, more shoots than what are necessary have shot from the basal buds. Where this occurs, all shoots not required should be removed either by rubbing or cutting ; the former action takes precedence whilst the shoots are soft. With two-year-old trees very few shoots push out upon the stems. This is owing to the previous season's disbudding.

With several varieties of plums, such as Hill End, Grand Duke, and Diamond, that start and make strong rapid growth at the beginning, it is not unusual for the stems of many of the growing buds to split upwards, starting a little above the basal portion of the growth. This splitting occurs if the stocks are strong and the season favorable for vigorous growths.   The writer's experience is that the splitting is more prevalent when worked upon the myrobolan stock, and attributes this largely to the stock forcing too rapid and also too strong a growth at the beginning upon varieties that are naturally strong growing.   To mini. mize this, disbudding should be delayed a little longer with varieties subject to splitting, so as to allow the superfluous shoots to utilize some of the rapidly ascending sap and nourishment.   Where the stems have split. cut back to a basal bud to start a fresh vertical growth.

Staking.

Staking, *i.e.*, placing a wooden stake in a vertical position close to a bud requiring support so that its growth may be tied to it and thereby insure its safety until the stem is sufficiently hard to be self-supporting. The stake will also be utilized to train any bud that is growing otherwise than vertical.

This operation is an important one and should not be overlooked. The time is controlled by a knowledge of the growth of species and the varieties that are being propagated.

Very good stakes can be made by cutting 5 feet palings in halves and then splitting them into stakes 1 in. wide.   Stakes should be pointed with a tomahawk.   If the pointed ends are dipped into tar and left to dry before using the stakes will last for years.   Whatever class of stake is used they should be rigid.

Immediately after disbudding all varieties of plums the growing bud should be supported by tying to a stake.   If not, there is a great risk of the bud being blown out by the first strong wind.   The writer has found if the growing buds are any length, that the best plan is to disbud a few, stake and tie at once, and so on until finished.   If a strong wind should spring up the superfluous shoots will protect the growing bud somewhat until operated upon.   The writer has seen hundreds of plum buds with a growth of from 6 to 8 inches broken off by a sudden gust of wind immediately after being disbudded.   The stakes should not be removed until the wood of the bud is hardened.   About December is a suitable time.   Fig. 64B shows a growing bud properly staked and tied.

Citrus, loquat, medlar, mulberry, and walnut buds should be staked early and no risks with them taken.   With the almond, apple, cherry, nectarine, peach, and quince only buds of crooked growth require staking. But the propagator should always bear in mind that there is a risk of losing unstaked buds up to a certain stage of growth.

The apricot is a fruit that at times makes strong growth in late summer and early autumn if the weather is favorable.   It should therefore be staked after being topped and trimmed.

Stakes should be strong and of a fair length.   If the stakes are short, there is a big risk of the young tree, when carrying a good head growth, breaking off at the terminal end of the stake during wet windy weather. Again, if the apricot is growing freely, it differs from other trees in the nursery row, owing to that part of the stem above where it is callused

52.   E

to the stock not hardening simultaneously with the part below.   Owing
to this feature there is always the risk of breakage at this particular place
if the stakes are removed previous to late autumn, especially if the head
growth is heavy.   Some varieties are worse than others in this respect.

Although staking is a simple operation, it takes practice to place the
stakes in a vertical position.   The butt of the stock, if vertical or nearly
so, will be a guide.   By holding the stake in a vertical position, and
keeping the pointed end away from the butt, and at the same time gauging
the same distance apart between the stake and the terminal end of the
stock, will facilitate this operation.   In Fig. 64A the dotted line indicates
the correct position of the stake, the butt having been used as a guide.

64. STAKING.

a. Growing bud requiring staking; dotted lines indicate correct position of stake.   *b.* Same bud, properly staked and tied.

In sandy or loose soils the stakes can either be pressed into the soil
with the hands, or tapped into position with a hammer, or mallet;   the
latter being necessary if the soil is firm.   Fig. 64A also indicates the
position of the stake when placed in position alongside a bud growing
obliquely.   With vertical ones the stake should be placed directly behind.

The operator will require to exercise great care when bending the growth
upward, so as to place it in the correct position against the flat of the
stake, so as to be ready for tying.   Growing buds are tender and brittle,
some more so than others.   There is also a risk of causing injury if the

stake is placed too close to the stock or growing bud. When tying to the stake, select that part just below the nodes, *i.e.*, the swelling or knot below the buds. Do not tie too close to the terminal end of the buds. If so, there is every likelihood of the stems buckling owing to its upward growth being checked by the string.

It will be necessary to keep going over the rows and tying the buds as they grow until they attain a certain height. When tying bind twice around and not too tightly. By doing so there is not the same risk of the string cutting into the expanding growth of stem as when using a single strand. Owing to the rapid growth and quick expansion a close watch should be kept upon the buds to see that the strings are not cutting. If so, release by cutting the string at the back of the stake; renew the string, if necessary. When tying to the stake growing buds

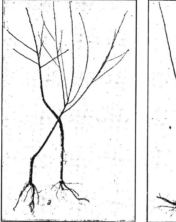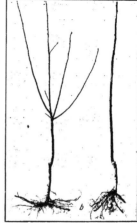

65. STAKING.

a. Results of not staking. *b.* Results of staking

that are branching see that the growths are not cramped or tied so as to cause them to become deformed or crooked. Almonds, apricots, nectarines, and peaches should be staked, if necessary, as soon as trimmed.

The best material to use for tying with is threads drawn from sujee bagging (Fig. 3).

Much unnecessary staking can be prevented by budding the stocks upon the side facing the prevailing winds that blow during the first five months of the bud's growth and previous to the hardening of the stems. Such winds generally blow from a northerly direction. Failing a knowledge of the winds of a locality, the native or other timber is a guide at times : it has a tendency to lean in the opposite direction. With some species of trees, the growth is greater and denser upon the sheltered side. Young and quick growing trees that branch early and catch the wind. like nectarines and peaches, are greatly influenced.

(To be continued.)

THE SHIPMENT OF GRAPES AND OTHER SOFT FRUITS.

F. de Castella, Government Viticulturist, and E. Meeking, Senior Fruit Inspector.

The shipments of soft fruits from this State by the *Somerset* and other vessels during the past two seasons, and also the shipments forwarded from South and Western Australia during the same period, have demonstrated beyond doubt that, provided certain conditions are complied with, all classes of soft fruits may be successfully exported. It is therefore considered that the following points in connexion with the handling, transportation, and other details of preparing these fruits for export will be of value to growers and exporters.

CONDITION AND MATURITY OF FRUIT.

It is essential to ship only varieties of proved carrying power. If from irrigated vines or trees, the final watering should have been given some weeks before time of shipment. In the case of grapes this watering should not be later than 1st January. Grapes or fruits from recently-irrigated vines or trees will not carry well.

In the absence of up-to-date pre-cooling and transport arrangements in this State, picking peaches, pears, or plums on the unripe side is recommended, since slightly unripe peaches and plums carry better than those picked quite ripe. Grapes, in particular, ripen but little after picking—far less than most other fruits. They should, therefore, although not quite ripe, be nearly so, before picking; otherwise, on arrival at their destination, though sound, they will be of poor quality.

PACKAGES (SIZES, MARKING, ETC.).

Any shape of package may legally be used, provided the nett weight or number of fruits be legibly stamped thereon. In addition to the weight or number, the name or registered brand of the grower or exporter, the name of the State, the word "Australia," and the name and variety of the fruit should be also stamped or stencilled on cases. The variety of fruit need not be shown in full, but may, with advantage, be abbreviated; for example, "Dora" for "Doradillo" grapes; "B. Bosc" for "Beurré Bosc" pears; "Dia" for "Diamond" plums; "Yorks" for "Early York" peaches. The following are the different sizes recommended for the various kinds of fruit:—

Grapes:—The cases used by West Australian shippers are recommended. These are made in two sizes. Larger size:—22½ in. x 13½ in. x 7 in.; nett capacity 28 lbs. grapes. Smaller size:—26½ in. x 13½ in. x 5 in.; nett capacity 25 lbs. grapes. Cases should be lined with white or coloured lining paper, cut to size, not only on account of appearance, but also to prevent loss of cork through cracks, joints, etc.

Peaches, Pears and Plums:—These should be packed in trays measuring 18 in. x 14 in. x 2⅞ in. Three of these trays cleated or hoop-ironed together make a standard bushel.

GATHERING.

None but first grade fruits should be exported. They should be carefully picked the day before they are packed and left overnight in a shed or other convenient place, protected from dew. For this purpose, a shed with open sides, allowing free ventilation of air, may be recommended. The very slight wilting which occurs to the fruit during this period, toughens the skin, reduces internal pressure, and, in the case of grapes, minimizes danger of berries bursting through compression when lid is nailed down. During this time, the bunch of grapes or the other fruits must, on no account, be stacked one on top of another but should be placed in layers, side by side.

No fruit should be handled too much. It should be carefully severed from the tree with specially made clippers having blunt points, and handled by the projecting stalk, thus avoiding, as far as possible, the hands coming into actual contact with the fruit itself. Grapes should be carefully laid in the picking receptacle, and, during the whole operation of handling and packing, should be manipulated from the stalk. The same rule holds good regarding the handling of peaches, pears and plums.

PACKING.

Grapes :—Export grape cases are packed on the flat. Line with white or coloured lining paper, cut to size, not only on account of appearance, but to prevent loss of cork through crack joints, etc. Clips should be used to avoid tearing by the wind. Cover bottom (side) of cases with about ½ inch of finely granulated cork free from dust and also from chips or larger fragments, which prevent the cork penetrating between the berries. On this, place a layer of bunches; if these are very large and especially if berries are very close, the bunch should be cut into several smaller ones. Any damaged or doubtful berries must be removed with scissors or special pointed secateurs—on no account pulled off.

Do not press grapes against sides; leave a little room for the cork. When the first layer of grapes is in, cover with cork; shake well and add more cork, if necessary; then more grapes, and so on until the case is full, shaking frequently. The whole top surface is then covered with cork until the grapes are completely hidden. The cork should be slightly above the level of sides of case so that some pressure must be applied before the lid can be nailed down. Before doing this, draw the paper carefully and evenly into place. It is essential that the fruit be tightly packed and that plenty of cork be used. When the case is opened, only cork should be seen, all grapes being buried in it. Beginners are apt to use too little cork. The larger case described above which holds 28 lbs. of grapes, requires nearly 5 lbs. of cork to pack it properly. Beginners would do well, at least for the first few cases, to weigh both grapes and cork. A measure capable of holding 5 lbs. of cork will be found convenient.

Peaches, Pears and Plums:—The trays to contain these should be lined with a layer of wood-wool about ½ inch thick. The fruits should then be carefully placed in layers or rows with a very thin portion of wood-wool between each. Japanese or other large plums, peaches, nectarines, and pears should be wrapped in paper cut to size according to dimensions of fruits. The usual sizes to which wrapping-paper is cut are:—10 in. x 7½ in. for smaller sizes, and 10 in. x 10 in. for the larger varieties. To carry out this operation, the wrapper should be placed in the left hand, the fruit carefully lifted by the stalk, and the calyx or " eye " end placed in the centre of the paper. The hand holding the fruit and wrapping-paper is then closed, bringing the edges of the paper around stalk end of the fruit, and the operation is completed by twisting the ends of the paper in the right hand around the stalk. When the tray is filled a thin lining of wood-wool, sufficient to pack the fruit tightly without undue compression, should be placed on top of the rows.

Three trays so packed should be placed together, the lid carefully nailed on the topmost tray and the three firmly cleated or hoop-ironed together to form a rigid package. For this purpose, hoop-iron is recommended as forming a neater and firmer package than those fastened together with wooden cleats. The method for fastening the trays together, is as follows :—One end of the hoop-iron is affixed to the top left-hand corner of the uppermost tray. The hoop-iron is then brought around the edge and pulled taut. For this purpose a special tool is used, consisting of a piece of iron having a handle about one foot in length with a cross handle, which is about 3 inches on either side. From the lower end of this tool, two rounded pieces of iron, each about 2 inches in length, project horizontally. These projections are separated by about ¼ inch from each other. The hoop-iron, after being fastened to the top end of the tray, is carried between these two projections. The packer then, by using the package as a fulcrum, draws the iron taut, and, holding it in this position with his body, leaves his hand free to nail the hoop-iron around the edges of the trays.

FORWARDING.

Where no district cool storage accommodation is available, fruit should be consigned to cool stores at Melbourne, and not to the ship's side direct. There is no disadvantage in forwarding a week before the ship sails. In fact, such a course is recommended. Consignments must, at latest, be forwarded in time to get into cool stores in Melbourne at least three or four days before the exporting vessel is to sail. This will enable consignments to go into the ship's refrigerator in cool condition and give them a better chance to be successfully carried than if shipped uncooled, and, moreover, minimizes risk of missing the boat. They must, at latest, be forwarded in time to get into cool stores in Melbourne on the Friday before sailing owing to the impossibility of handling during the intervening Saturday and Sunday. Where facilities are available, fruit should be cooled to 30 degrees Fah. as soon as possible after picking and transported direct to ship in refrigerator cars.

The exporter, or prospective exporter, of soft fruits must remember that to place soft fruits on distant markets, attention to the above details must be rigidly adhered to. Unfortunately, many other details of equal importance connected with the transportation of his fruits do not come under his control. But the effect of any remissness on the part of those concerned in the transportation side of the business may be greatly minimized if avoidable errors on his part are not committed.

THE LIGHT BROWN APPLE MOTH.

(Tortrix (Cacæcia) responsana.)

C. French, Junr., Acting Government Entomologist.

During last October several growers at Mildura forwarded, for examination, several bunches of young Zante currant grapes that were almost destroyed by caterpillars.   On examining them, I was of opinion that the cause of the trouble was the larva of the Light Brown Apple Moth, a very destructive insect which attacks almost any kind of garden plant, as well as apples, and other fruits.

This moth is found in most parts of Victoria.   The larva is of a greenish colour, and measures about ½ in. in length.   The moth itself is about the size of the well known Codlin Moth, and is of a pale yellowish brown colour.   The accompanying illustration shows the life history of the moth :—

EXPLANATION OF PLATE.

Fig. 1. Apple branch and fruit, showing damage done to pips, with larvæ escaping. Natural size.
  „ 2. Moths on wing. Natural size.
  „ 3. Upper portion of apple when newly formed, showing where eggs of moth are deposited.
  „ 3. Larvæ. Magnified.

Some additional specimens of the caterpillars were sent at my request. These I placed in the breeding cages on 19th November. and on the 24th they pupated or turned into the chrysalis ; on the 12th December they emerged as perfect moths.   When about to pupate, the caterpillar spins a loose silken web in which it turns into the chrysalis.   In this stage of its existence it is often attacked by parasitic wasps and other useful insects, which to a certain extent keep it in check.

Fortunately, in arsenate of lead, we have an excellent remedy, The spray must be forced well into the bunches of young grapes as it is in the middle of the bunch that the caterpillars are generally found.

Trapping the moths by lights has also proved effective.   An ordinary hurricane lamp placed on a brick in a basin of kerosene will answer admirably.   The moths are attracted to the light, fly against the glass and fall into the kerosene, and are destroyed.

If this pest is not kept in check it will cause heavy losses to growers of grapes.   It is therefore advisable that immediate action be taken to stamp it out.

*   *   *   *   *   *   *

Mr. F. de Castella, Government Viticulturist, submits the following note :—

" I have read with interest the proof of your note on the Light Brown Apple Moth, now appearing as a vine pest.   I have long known vines, in different parts of the State, to be attacked, at flowering time and after. by small green caterpillars, which spin a web and make a nest in the young bunches, thereby interfering with their development and causing more or less serious damage.   I distinctly remember these at St. Hubert's, on the Yarra, as long ago as the early seventies ; in general appearance, at least, they were the same as the caterpillars which I recently saw at Mildura.

It is reassuring to know that this is an Australian native, and not one of the French bunch caterpillars, for we have but little idea here, of the fearful havoc which is sometimes wrought in Europe by allied species.

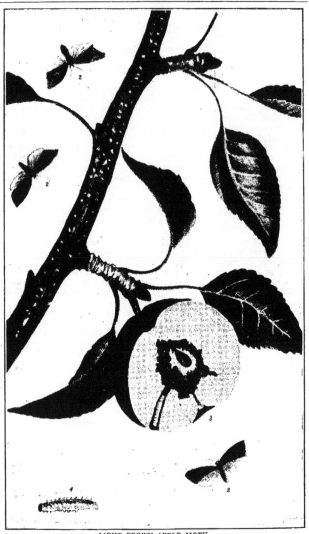

LIGHT BROWN APPLE MOTH.
(Tortrix (Cacæcia) responsana.)

The 1910 vintage, in parts of Burgundy and Champagne, was reduced by fully one-half, owing to the ravages of two web-forming, bunch caterpillars, known locally as *Cochylis* and *Eudemis.* Another species, the common name of which is *Pyrale,** is often very destructive, especially near Bordeaux.

Though satisfactory to know that we have not to deal with either of these, we must not underestimate the enemy, for we have no guarantee that the Australian *Cacœcia*, if left to itself, might not develop into an equally redoubtable pest, especially under such conditions as prevail at Mildura, where the vine-planted areas are so continuous as to practically constitute one vast vineyard, as is also often the case in France. I do not wish to be thought an alarmist, but I consider that we have here a pest which requires careful watching, and I am glad that you are advising growers to take immediate steps to stamp it out.

At the time of my last visit to Mildura (15th November) though little damage had been done, bunches with webs in them were quite numerous, so much so that I requested several growers to send you specimens for identification. At that time, most of the insects had already left their webs. It was, in fact, rather difficult to find one. A second generation will no doubt make its appearance shortly, when I hope fresh specimens will be forwarded to you; it is not impossible that we have to deal with more than one species, and we cannot have too much information on the subject. Growers would not only be studying their own interests, but also those of the industry at large, if they would immediately forward to you specimens of any strange insects that may appear from time to time in their vineyards or orchards."

BEE-KEEPING IN VICTORIA.

F. R. Beuhne, Bee Expert.

(Continued from page 3.)

II.—THE BEES.

There are many terms used in connexion with bees which are liable to cause misunderstanding when wrongly applied by the uninitiated. Some of these words have a general as well as a specific meaning. Any community of bees may be called a colony, but in practice the term is only applied to bees established in a dwelling provided by man. Colonies in trees, rocks, or other natural abodes are known as bees' nests. While a hive of bees denotes a colony in an artificial dwelling the dwelling itself without bees or combs is known as a bee hive. Communities of bees on the wing, clustered outside away from the hive, or inside the hive without combs, are called swarms.

Every normal colony of bees in the active season consists of three classes of individuals, viz., the queen, a large number of workers, and a variable number of drones. The queen is the mother of all the other

* According to French authorities the scientific names of these are—for the first, *Cochylis roserana* (or *Tortrix ambiguella*): for the second, *Eudemis botrana*: whilst that of *Pyrale* is *Tortrix (Œnophtira) Pilleriana*.

bees and the only fully-developed female. The workers are sexually undeveloped females, and constitute the largest part of the colony, numbering
from 40,000 to 70,000 in a strong colony in the height of the season.
On the average, it takes 4,500 worker bees to equal one pound in weight.
The drones, which are of larger size than the workers, are the males, and
their only use in the economy of the hive is to mate with the virgin queen.
Towards autumn, when they are no longer required, or at any time during
a scarcity of nectar, they are driven out of the hive by the workers and
left to die of starvation, except in the case of a colony with an old or
failing queen, or a queenless stock.   Both of these will retain their
drones and also admit those expelled from other hives—a provision of
Nature to enable the mating of the future young queen to take place.

Life History.

A knowledge of the life history of bees will assist any one to better
understand what conditions are necessary to the highest welfare of the
colony and the maximum profit to the bee-keeper.   While such knowledge

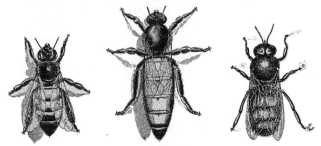

WORKER BEE, QUEEN AND DRONE OF THE ITALIAN BEE.

will not take the place of practical experience in the management of bees,
it will form a good basis for an understanding of the various manipulations.

The bee, like other insects, goes through four stages of development,
viz., (1) egg, (2) larva, (3) chrysalis, and (4) imago or perfect insect.

The ovaries of the queen contain up to 500,000 eggs, which she
deposits in the cells of the comb during the breeding season—after the
cells have been prepared for her by the worker bees.   The life of a
queen bee is about three years.   Under the most favorable conditions, she
will deposit up to 3,000 eggs in twenty-four hours.   The eggs in the
ovaries of the queen are all alike as to sex.   The act of fertilization
takes place in the oviduct when the egg is on its way out, *i.e.*, it is to
produce a female—a queen or a worker bee; the egg producing a drone
is not fertilized.   Thus, even a queen which has never met a drone will,
after a delay of two or three weeks, deposit eggs.   None of these, however, can produce anything but drones.   This reproduction without fertilization was first discovered by Dr. Dzierszon in 1853.   It is known
as parthenogenesis or virgin-development, and has a very important bearing
on practical bee culture.

The drones of a pure bred queen of any race are always pure of the same race, even though the queen herself was mated to a drone of a different variety. Thus, by having one single pure bred and purely mated queen, and raising from her eggs a new queen for each colony, the race or strain of bees of an entire apiary of hundreds of colonies may be changed in one season. As each young queen is pure bred, her drone progeny are also pure, irrespective of how she mated. The following season there will therefore be none but pure drones in the apiary. All young queens will then be mated to pure drones; and, if from a pure bred mother, will produce queens, workers, and drones of pure race. The mating takes place in the air, often a considerable distance away from the apiary, and some of the queens will most likely be mis-mated when other bees exist within two miles of the place.

Fertilized eggs are deposited by the queen in the smaller or worker cells of the comb; the cells are 1·5 in. in diameter—twenty-five to a square inch of comb surface. Unfertile eggs are laid into drone cells, which are ¼ in. wide—sixteen to the square inch. By the use of full sheets of comb foundation in the frames of the modern hive, the raising of drones is reduced to a minimum, because the wax sheets are embossed with the pattern of worker comb only. Any egg which is fertilized, and would in the ordinary course produce a worker bee, can at the will of the nurse bees be made to produce a queen, when necessary. This fact is made use of in what is known as artificial queen-rearing, by depriving a suitable colony of its queen and brood and substituting a comb containing eggs or young larvæ from a queen of the race or strain desired.

After the egg which produces a worker is laid, it remains unaltered for three days. It is then supplied with a minute quantity of larval food by the nurse bees, and a scarcely visible grub or larvæ, which lies coiled at the bottom of the cell in the shape of the small c of ordinary type emerges. It grows rapidly; and, on the sixth day after emerging from the egg, it assumes an upright position in the cell. The worker bees cap the cell with a paper-like substance, the grub meanwhile spinning a cocoon round itself in the cell. The young bee has now entered the third or chrysalis stage, from which it emerges as the perfect insect, eighteen days from the time the larva first appeared, or twenty-one days since the egg was laid. In the case of the queen, the time of development is five days less, *i.e.*, three days in the egg stage, six days in the larval state, and seven days as chrysalis, or sixteen days in all from the time the egg was laid to the young queen emerging from the sealed cell.

The drone is in the egg for three days, larva seven days, and chrysalis fourteen days, or a total of twenty-four to twenty-five days from the egg to the perfect insect. The following table may be useful in showing the variations in the time of development:—

NUMBER OF DAYS OF DEVELOPMENT.

	In the Egg.	Larva.	Sealed Cell.	Total.
Worker Bee ...	3 days	6 days	12 days	21 days
Queen ...	3 "	6 "	7 "	16 "
Drone ...	3 "	7 "	14 "	24 "

(To be continued.)

VINE DISEASES IN FRANCE.

(Continued from page 56.)

F. de Castella, Government Viticulturist.

FUNGICIDE SPRAYS—*continued.*

FRENCH BORDEAUX MIXTURE OR COPPER-LIME.

The usual formula is:—Sulphate of copper, 6 lbs. ; quicklime, 3 lbs. ᵻ
water, 30 to 40 gallons; according as one wants a 2 per cent. or a 1½ per
cent mixture. The copper sulphate is dissolved in the greater part of
the water and a milk of lime made with the balance; the latter is poured
into the former in a thin stream, with constant stirring. Authorities are
emphatic as to the necessity of pouring the lime into the copper sulphate ;
if the reverse were done, a coarser grained and less adherent form of copper
hydroxide would be obtained.

The chief difficulty in properly preparing the mixture is due to the
variable composition of the lime; it is, on this account, impossible to
exactly gauge the proper quantity by weight. The correctness of the lime
dose is of vital importance. If too little is used the mixture will be acid
and burn the foliage; if too much, it will be alkaline, less adherent, and
will not run through the spray nozzles so easily. Exact neutrality is
most desirable ; in order to obtain it, a slight excess of milk of lime should
be prepared, which is added carefully until neutralization is shown by an
indicator. Litmus paper may be used for the purpose, but phenolphthalein
paper† is more convenient, the pink colour to which it changes being more
readily noticed than the blue of the litmus. The following instructions
are concise and easily followed. They are taken from a sheet, distributed
by the Viticultural Station at Lausanne (Switzerland) :—

Weigh 2 lbs. of bluestone, and dissolve in 5 gallons of water in an open cask, in
which the 10 gallon level is marked by a peg. Solution is facilitated by suspend-
ng the bluestone in a basket just below the surface of the water, a day beforehand.
Thoroughly mix the blue liquid so as to have an even solution.

Take about 2 lbs. of quicklime and place it in another tub; slake it gradually
with small quantities of water at a time; when thoroughly slaked, make up to about
5 gallons with water and stir carefully so as to make a thin milk of lime.

Prepare the mixture, dipping out the milk of lime with a dipper and pouring
it through a fine sieve into the bluestone solution, carefully stirring with a stick,
meanwhile; do not dip too deeply into the lime, so as to avoid lumps. As soon
as a couple of gallons have been thus added, an assistant (a child will do) with
clean hands and who has particularly avoided touching either bluestone or lime,
takes a strip of the white indicator paper, cuts off a small piece, and drops it into
the mixture. Usually, if the milk is thin enough, the first piece remains white.
The operator then adds more milk, stirring well. The assistant drops in a second
fragment of the paper, and so on until the piece of paper becomes pink; the other
pieces previously dropped, change colour also. There is now enough lime; make
up to 10 gallons with pure water and stir well. The rest of the milk of lime may
be thrown away.

Thanks to the indicator paper, weighing the lime may be dispensed with; all
that is necessary is good, fresh lime, from a builder, slaked to a very thin milk.

If one is prevented from using the mixture at once, add, to every 10 gallons,
2 ozs. of sugar dissolved in a little water. This will cause it to keep its power for
several weeks. It is, nevertheless, better to use freshly prepared mixture.

Many substances in addition to sugar are often added to increase adherence. Gelatine seems to be one of those which has most to recommend it.

---

† Strips of white blotting paper dipped in a 2 per cent. solution of Phenolphthalein and allowed to
dry, make a very good indicator.

BURGUNDY MIXTURE (COPPER-SODA).

The chief objection to this mixture is its rapid deterioration, especially in hot weather. It must therefore be prepared in small quantities, as required. The usual formula is :—Copper sulphate, 2 lbs. ; crystallized carbonate of soda (common washing soda), 2½ lbs. ; and water, 10 gallons. Owing to the variable composition of washing soda, it is better to proceed according to the last directions given for Bordeaux mixture, checking neutrality with phenolphthalein paper. The sheet quoted above recommends the use of water free soda (Solvay soda) instead of washing soda. Two solutions are made, one of 2 lbs. copper sulphate in 5 gallons water, and one of 1 lb. of Salvoy soda in 5 gallons of water. The second is poured into the first with constant stirring.

Any dry spraying substance, from previous lots, causes rapid deterioration ; all vessels must, therefore, be kept thoroughly clean. The addition of sugar will have no effect in keeping it in good order, as with Bordeaux, but cream of tartar or Rochelle salt may be used for the purpose ; 2 ozs. of whichever salt is preferred should be dissolved in the water for the second solution before the Solvay soda is added. In other respects, the preparation is the same. The addition of either of the above salts will enable the copper soda mixture to keep for a few days. Any copper soda mixture which shows a heavy greenish sediment is useless, since it will no longer adhere.

According to R. Brunett (*Revue de Viticulture,* 19th January, 1911), Burgundy growers were dissatisfied, last season, with copper soda, which they have hitherto mainly used, and are preparing to adopt Bordeaux mixture in future.

COPPER-SOAP MIXTURES.

Owing to its alkalinity, soap can take the place of lime or soda in the preparation of copper mixtures. Its action in lowering surface tension augments the wetting power considerably, and this is perhaps the main advantage to be derived from its use. Adherence is good whilst fresh, but diminishes rapidly with keeping. Like copper-soda, copper-soap must be prepared immediately before it is used. Equal quantities of copper sulphate and soap powder are used. For a 1½ per cent. mixture this would mean, for every 10 gallons of water, 1½ lbs. copper sulphate, and 1½ lbs. powdered soap. Dissolve each substance in 5 gallons of water and mix thoroughly, pouring soap into copper, not the reverse.[*]

Copper-soap mixtures are not new ; they have been in favour in some quarters since first recommended by M. G. Lavergne at the close of the last century, but they have not come into very general use. Several of the proprietary spray powders, which merely require mixing with water to be ready for use, are mixtures of soap and copper sulphate.

Quite recently, MM. Vermorel and Dantony have recommended a new copper-soap[†] which seems to have much to recommend it. It is of colloidal nature ; when diluted, it wets well and does not deteriorate on keeping. It is prepared as follows : —

Dissolve 1 lb. of copper sulphate in 10 gallons of water ; dissolve 4 lbs. soap (free from alkali in excess) in 10 gallons of water. Pour the copper into the soap (contrary to the usual practice). Opertaing thus, instead of the usual voluminous, greasy precipitate of copper soap, one obtains an opaque, greeny-blue liquid, with a surface tension as low as plain soap solution, which wets the bunches just as alcohol would. . . . .

---

[*] L. Degrully. *Progres Agricole,* 24th April, 1910.
[†] *Revue de Viticulture,* 1st June, 1911.

The kind of soap used is important ; it should be as rich as possible in oleate of soda and free from alkali in excess. Australian soaps, mostly made from animal fat, would probably prove unsuitable for the purpose, since they contain much soda stearate.

Stearate of soda . . . renders the preparation of colloidal copper soap difficult. In a general way, stearate should be proscribed from all insecticide or fungicide formulæ containing soap. Our experiments show that its presence brings about an important increase in surface tension and a decrease in the solubility co-efficient.

ACETATE OF COPPER, OR "VERDET."

Two sorts of acetate of copper have come into prominence of late years for spraying purposes. These are the neutral acetate, known in French as *verdet neutre*, and what is known as *verdet gris*, which is a mixture of several basic acetates. This substance, of which the English common name is verdigris, has long been used by colour manufacturers, calico dyers, &c. Its manufacture constituted an important industry in Southern France many years ago, where it was a by-product of wine-making, being obtained by treating copper plates with grape-marc which had undergone acetic fermentation. It is therefore rather curious that it should now turn out to be a valuable specific for the treatment of vine diseases. This use, in fact, appears likely to bring about the revival of the almost extinct verdigris industry.

Neutral acetate is readily soluble in water ; *verdet gris*, though not soluble, mixes readily with water to form a sort of semi-solution.

In water, the basic verdets do not give a true solution, such as neutral acetate does. Hydration phenomena occur ; the viscous paste at first formed, if diluted slightly, becomes colloidal. If maceration is sufficiently prolonged and the quantity of water is sufficient, dissociation brings about the separation of a soluble part which colours the solution blue (neutral acetate) and light flakes which float in it, gradually falling to the bottom, but which the slightest agitation again places in suspension. . . .*

. Both substances constitute excellent fungicides. On the whole, neutral verdet is most highly recommended by authorities. Though quite soluble, its adherence is satisfactory, owing to a partial decomposition which takes place after spraying.

The copper salt must undergo a chemical change and pass from a soluble to an insoluble colloid state, in order that it may both adhere to the surface and set free a sufficient quantity of copper to contaminate the water drops in which conidia and zoospores might (otherwise) germinate. . . . . With neutral verdet it is an insoluble and colloid basic acetate which is spontaneously produced after spraying ; whereas with dilute liquid mixtures of basic verdets, it is a mixture, difficult to define, so far as proportions are concerned, of copper hydroxide, gelatinous basic acetate and soluble neutral acetate, the latter itself giving rise to the insoluble basic salt (Bencker).*

Sufficient has been said to show that the verdets should constitute an excellent spray, insoluble enough to insure adherence, and yet soluble enough to constitute a powerful germicide. These theoretical considerations have been amply borne out in practice, and the verdets are coming into general use in France. In Switzerland, where downy mildew is particularly virulent, they are held in high esteem. Either the soluble (neutral), the insoluble (verdet gris), or a mixture of the two are used.

---

* A. Dejeanne—Les Verdets. *Revue de Viticulture,* 30th June, 1910.
* Ibid.

The solutions or semi-solutions are very fluid, and never clog spray nozzles.

Being richer in metallic copper* than sulphate, considerably less is required. In other words, verdet may be looked upon as being twice as strong as sulphate, so that 1 lb. to 10 gals. of water (1 per cent.) would be equivalent to a Bordeaux mixture containing 2 lbs. to 10 gals. Preparation is almost instantaneous and very simple; it is only necessary to thoroughly mix with a small quantity of water for a few moments, and then to dilute to the required bulk.

As verdet does not leave such visible marks on the sprayed plants as copper-lime or copper-soda, supervision of the work done is more difficult. This slight defect is easily corrected by the addition of plaster of Paris at the rate of ½ lb. to 10 gals. of spray mixture.

POTATO DIGGING MACHINES.

G. Seymour, Potato Expert.

The harvesting of the potato crop by hand has always proved a tedious and expensive operation. Especially so has this been the case in late years, owing to the scarcity of labour, and the indifferent manner in which the work is carried out by those available. Rates for this work have increased during the last 20 years by 50 per cent. to 75 per cent. This increase, coupled with the fact that the delay has frequently caused the harvesting to be prolonged into the wet season, and thereby injuring the condition of the soil for the succeeding cereal crop, especially barley, has created a want for a satisfactory potato-raising machine The following points, some of which have hitherto proved insurmountable, are required in a satisfactory digger :—

1. That it shall lift the crop clean from the soil and not cover those lifted.
2. That it shall leave them in convenient rows for picking up.
3. That it shall not bruise or damage the tubers.
4. That it shall leave the land in a level and workable condition.

Inventors have followed two well-defined lines in their efforts to solve these problems. One is the separation of the tubers from the soil, generally by scattering them to one side of the machine; the other, by raising the soil and tubers as with a scoop or shovel and passing the whole on to an endless band or elevator provided with spaces for the soil to pass through, the tubers being deposited in a neat row at the rear of the machine. The soil is returned to its place again, leaving the field quite level.

The history of potato-raising machinery is one of many failures and some partial successes. Probably the most primitive attempt was the potato plough made by Howard and others more than 40 years ago. This was as simple as it was possible to make it, being neither more nor less

---

* Neutral acetate contains 31·7 per cent. of copper. Verdet gris, which is a mixture of bi-, sesqui-, and tri-basic acetate varies somewhat according to the preponderance of one or other of these salts; if pure, its copper strength varies between 34 and 35 per cent. The commercial form contains about 33 per cent. (Dejeanne).

than the sole and sock of an ordinary drill plough with a series of grids instead of breasts.   The action of the grids was to raise the tubers to the surface as the plough passed along the drill under the crop.   Given a friable soil and dry weather, this implement gave satisfactory results as far as recovering the tubers was concerned.   One serious drawback was that it left the land in a succession of ridges, and made it impossible to restore the field to its former condition.

This drawback was recognised and an effort was made nearly 40 years ago to overcome it by Mr. Cockerell, of Morang, who invented an attachment for the ordinary single plough.   It may be described as a wheel through which the upturned sod containing the tubers had to pass ; this wheel was fitted with short spokes or prongs.   The machine was put on the market with the very comprehensive title of " Cockerell's Prize Patent Potato Raiser and Setter, Moulder-up and Land Cleaner," and was awarded First Prize at Smeaton Agricultural Show in November, 1873. As a potato raiser. it proved a failure.

JACK'S IMPERIAL POTATO DIGGER.

The urgent necessity of some mechanical means of harvesting the potato crop was brought under the notice of the Government in 1891 by the West Bourke and other Agricultural Societies, with the result that the sum of £250 was offered in prizes for a machine capable of lifting the tubers without damage or loss.   A trial was arranged, and took place at Romsey on 12th July, 1892.   Forty-eight machines entered for the competition, but only 10 put in an appearance.   The judges' report stated that only 3 of the machines entered did work that came near the conditions laid down.   These were :—

   1. F. W. Lee, of Woodend, who was awarded £25.
   2. Garde & Chrystal, " The Boss," £20.
   3. John Hatch, " The Hoover," £20.

The machine entered by Mr. Lee was a purely Victorian invention, and was probably the first attempt to raise the potato crop mechanically by forks.   This machine gives satisfaction in dry friable soils.   The other two machines were of American make, the " Boss " being what is known as the spinner pattern, and very similar to machines made by Alex. Jack and Sons, of Maybole, Scotland.   The object of this and the fork type is to remove the tubers from the ground without handling the soil.   The

Hoover, on the other hand, elevates the tubers and soil together, trusting to the former passing through spaces between the bars on the elevators.

As stated, the "Boss" was of the spinner pattern. It was fitted with a strong share that passes under the drill, the upraised crop coming in contact with a set of arms forked at the end. These are attached to a wheel that revolves rapidly, scattering the tubers on the surface up to 6 ft. in breadth. This great width makes the work of gathering the crop very tedious, but a more serious objection is the large quantity of tubers bruised by the rapidly revolving arms. The Hoover or elevator principle has many points to commend it. This machine is fitted with a shovel-like share, which passes under the drill and raises the soil and tubers on to an elevator, through which the earth falls as it is carried along by an endless belt fitted with slats. The tubers are delivered at the rear of the machine in an even row, no wider than the space in which they grew, and very convenient for gathering. This, together with the fact that, when working at the proper depth, the tubers are not damaged, seemed to stamp it as the most perfect machine for the purpose. But when the land is wet the bars of the elevator soon become clogged, with the result that the whole of the tubers and the earth are carried up the elevator

LEE'S POTATO DIGGER.

which soon becomes blocked up; the draught is increased so enormously that requires four horses to work the machine.

On reference to the illustrations, it will be noticed that the Lee machine digs with two forks. In this respect it imitates hand digging very closely. The forks throw the tubers on to a grid where they are separated from the soil and left in a row clear of the track where the horses walk, so that digging may proceed whether the tubers are picked up or not. The inventor of this machine has made some improvements recently which he claims will render it perfect.

Until about two years ago no important improvement was to be found in potato-raising machinery since the Royal Agricultural Society of England's trial in 1896, held at Leicester. However, several new designs have come on the market. This society carried out trials at Littleworth on 27th September, 1911. One of the machines at this competition, made by Alex. Jack and Sons, was on the Harder principle. As this machine was noticed by the Hon. the Premier when in the past season in Scotland to be doing very satisfactory work, he purchased one and forwarded it to Melbourne.

A very satisfactory trial of this machine was held at Messrs. Clement Bros.' Market Garden, South Oakleigh, on 29th November. The soil, a very hard sandy loam, put the machine to a good test as regards draught, which was satisfactory as it was worked by two medium draught horses without strain. The crop was a light one, with a fair amount of weeds and haulm.   The work done was very satisfactory—a trial with the fork proved that the crop lifted clean without bruising or damage.

A second trial was held at Mr. Crowe's farm at Crossley, in a light friable soil very suitable for machine digging.   The crop here was very light, and the field free from weeds.   The trial was witnessed by a large number of local growers who expressed themselves well pleased with the work.

RANSOME'S ROTARY POTATO DIGGER.

A further trial was held at Messrs. Callaghan Bros. farm at Wollaston, near Warrnambool. This trial was under more difficult conditions.   The soil was rather lumpy, and there was also a fairly heavy growth of tall weeds and green potato tops. The crop was an average one containing a high percentage of large tubers.   These conditions gave the machine a severe test on the most vital points; viz., cleanness of digging, small amount of damage to crop, ability to handle weeds and green plants, and level condition of land after the machine.

A careful examination of the bottom of the drill after the machine showed that fewer potatoes were left in the ground than by ordinary fork digging.   Three drills, each about seven chains long, were carefully examined, and only 21 tubers cut by the share could be found.   Two

HOOVER POTATO DIGGER.

bags were turned out and examined carefully for potatoes damaged by the forks, but none were found.   The result of these trials must be considered very satisfactory, and proves that this machine is a great improvement on any yet tried in this State.   The leading growers at these trials expressed themselves highly pleased with the way the crops were handled under different conditions of soil and crop.

FARM BLACKSMITHING.

(Continued from page 54.)

George Baxter, Instructor in Blacksmithing, Working Men's College, Melbourne.

V.—WELDING *(continued).*

LENGTHENING BOLTS.

In the article in the January issue mention was made of lengthening or shortening a bolt by welding. The success of doing this is dependent to a great extent upon the manner in which the scarf is formed. Whilst a bolt is taken here as an illustration, the form of procedure would be similar if pieces of square, flat, or, in fact, almost any shaped bars required to be joined together. This form of scarf is known by the name of the *lapped scarf.*

So that the finished bolt may be of the required length, allowance must be made for the waste of material which, as previously mentioned, occurs during welding. In nearly all cases this can be taken as the thickness of the bar. Certainly there are exceptions to the rule, but as some of the more intricate are not likely to occur in the simpler and comparatively rough work of a farm, no mention need be made of them. To do so, might have a tendency to bewilder the amateur smith, and consequently the information would be more harmful than beneficial.

Still using the bolt as an illustration, let it be supposed that one 2 ft. in length is required and that another 8 in. long is at hand. It would then be far easier to lengthen it than to make a new one outright. A start would be made by cutting the existing bolt in two at the middle section. Then obtain a piece of iron of the same diameter as the bolt. It need not be of any particular length, excepting that it should be longer than is required to make up the deficiency.

Take hold of the bolt head in a pair of tongs and the plain bar by the hand, or, if too short for that, in another pair of tongs. Then place both in the fire in such a position that the length of the heated part will be about 2 in. When a white heat has been reached take either to the anvil for the purpose of scarfing; but, previous to shaping the scarf, *upsetting* or "jumping up" is necessary. This means thickening the part at and adjacent to the weld. This is necessary to ensure having the welded part equally as strong as the remaining portion of the bolt.

In the several cases of welding already dealt with, it would be observed that a reduction of sectional area had taken place, particularly at the part where the point of the scarf joins the other bar. Therefore, it is weaker there than anywhere else. In the case of a bolt where there is great longitudinal strain placed upon it by tightening up the nut, it becomes necessary to have the weld securely made without any reduction in size.

If the head be the first piece taken from the fire, the upsetting is best accomplished by standing the head on the anvil in an upright position and striking the heated end with the hammer until it becomes increased to about one and a quarter times its original diameter; *e.g.,* if the bolt be $\frac{1}{2}$ in., then the end would be *upset* to $\frac{5}{8}$ in. diameter at the point. At the same time, it would gradually become smaller as the distance from the end increased, until the original diameter of the bolt is reached, which would be where the heat does not rise sufficiently high to assume the red colour.

If the plain bar be long enough to conveniently hold in the hand without burning it, the best means of upsetting it is to catch hold of the cold end and hold it in a vertical position. By repeatedly raising it to a good height and bringing the heated end down with as much force as possible, it will become enlarged. In most cases, the bar will bend before being sufficiently upset, but it can be straightened and the upsetting proceeded with.

To form the scarf, the best plan is to follow each successive step shown in Fig. 47, where *a* shows the bar upset, *b* with the end bent so as to be conveniently struck with the hand-hammer in the direction and position of the arrow, whilst *c* shows the shape made with the hammer, as well as the fuller in its place to receive the first blow. As each blow

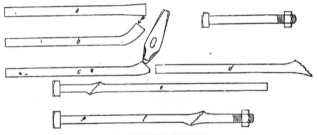

47. LENGTHENING BOLT.

a. Bar upset. *b.* End bent for strikung with hammer. *c.* Shape made with hammer. Fuller in position to receive the first blow. *d.* Effect of using fuller. *e* and *f.* Correct position for hammering.

is delivered, the fuller is moved slightly forward, leaving in its trail a succession of little steps as shown at *d*. It should always be the object of the operator to obtain the shape shown, for a bad weld is sure to follow a badly formed scarf.

Particular attention should be paid also to the manner in which the pieces are laid together; *e* and *f* show the correct position previous to hammering. For welding small iron, the hand-hammer is heavy enough, but the blows should be delivered as quickly as possible so that the union is made complete before the temperature has fallen below the welding point. If it is noticed that the weld is only partially made, then the work should be returned immediately to the fire and again raised to the welding heat and hammered.

When a weld is properly made, there should be no part of the scarf visible. If that is the case and the size has been maintained, then there will be no reduction of strength.

.Before welding on the screwed end, the proper length should be measured off, making sufficient allowance for the waste. To upset the screwed end, proceed as directed for the head, with the exception that a block of hardwood should be substituted for the anvil as the latter would damage the thread.

Maul Rings.

Maul rings may be made by bending and welding either iron or mild steel, or from a solid bar of mild steel by splitting and forging. The first named is the more common method adopted.

The ring made from the solid bar of mild steel is the strongest, but entails considerably more labour than one made by bending and welding, either from the same material or from iron. One made from iron on the splitting and forging principle would be weaker than a bent and welded one. This is entirely due to the nature of the materials; iron is fibrous, whilst mild steel is granular in structure. Mild steel is equally strong in all directions, but iron is weakest when the strain is opposed to the direction of the fibre. To obtain the greatest amount of strength when iron is used, the ring should be bent and welded. By this means the fibre is placed in the best position to resist the internal pressure.

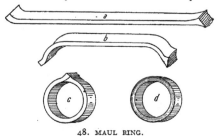

48. MAUL RING.
a. Ends upset.   *b* and *c.* Bending.   *d.* Finished ring.

Mild steel possesses greater strength than iron, as well as the property of being drawn out, punched, split and forged without the liability of bursting apart, as iron would if similarly treated. It is therefore especially adapted for intricate forgings, or where strength combined with lightness is desirable, as in the case of bridges, girders, agricultural machinery, &c.

To make an iron ring, the first consideration is the length of the bar. A suitable size of bar is 1 in. x $\frac{1}{2}$ in. The ends are upset in the same manner as described above, one end being scarfed and the other slightly bent, as shown in Fig. 48 *a*. It is then further bent like *b*, and afterwards heated along the straight part, and bent as at *c*. When thus formed, it is ready for the welding heat, which is rather more difficult to obtain than any form of welding previously dealt with. It requires close attention whilst in the fire. It will be found by practice that flat bars are always harder to weld than square or round ones.

After heating, it is first placed on the beak of the anvil and vigorous blows are directed on to the scarfed part, when it is removed to the face of the anvil, and knocked down edgeways, and also on the inside at the point of the scarf, with the hand-hammer. When the weld is completed, the ring should be rounded on the beak.

To make a solid mild steel ring of the same dimensions, a piece of $1\frac{1}{8}$ in. square steel would be necessary. In order to make it the right size, it is requisite that the quantity of metal be calculated. This may be done as follows:—Ascertain the cubical contents of the ring and divide the product by the cross sectional area of the bar it is to be made from. If the required internal diameter be 5 in., then the solidity of the ring will be equal to the product of the sum and difference of the internal and external diameters multiplied by the depth of the ring and 11-14 or .7854. This product, divided by $1\frac{1}{8}$ squared, will be the theoretical length required. But, in forging work, this quantity is not sufficient, because there is always a loss of material by heat and compression in hammering, for which allowance must be made. This allowance is variable, according to number of heatings necessary; but, in most cases, an addition of 5 per cent. will suffice for mild steel, whilst 10 per cent. is requisite for iron forgings. On working out the equation, the length will be found to be $7\frac{1}{4}$ in. nearly. When the piece is cut off the bar, two marks should be made on it, each one being $\frac{3}{8}$ in. from the ends.

Heat to bright red for the entire length, and then split with the hot chisel, care being taken to make the cut through the centre of the bar lengthwise, and between the two marks before mentioned, so as to prevent having a thick and thin side. In cutting anything of this description, the chisel should never be driven right through the piece from one side. The cut should be made about half-way through and then treated the same from the opposite side. After splitting, it is opened out to a rough shaped ring by up-ending it on the anvil whilst the middle is hot, and by striking the top. By heating and beating out on the beak of

49. OBLONG FRAME.

a. End scarfed. *b.* First corner bent. *c.* Second corner bent. *d.* Third corner bent, and ready for welding. *e.* Finished frame.

the anvil, a correct circle will be formed.

The bands on the nave of a wheel or the tyre are made by bending and welding. They are afterwards "shrunk on." The iron for nave bands is now rolled thinner on one edge than the other, so that when the band is made the inside diameter will be larger on one side than the other, which will enable it to be driven on tightly. At the same time, there are many still made from the ordinary flat bars and the taper is given to the band in forging.

When a band is to be shrunk on, it should be forged slightly smaller than the external diameter of the wheel or whatever it is intended for. If a band has to be shrunk on to wood, it would be made smaller than if it had to be shrunk on to iron, on account of wood being more compressible than iron, and also for the reason that wood becomes charred with the heat from the iron, and is thereby reduced in size.

In agricultural machinery, there are a number of parts made of cast iron, such as the cog and pulley, which are connected with its mechanism. Sometimes, as the result of accident, they are broken, and there are occasions when the break can be repaired, by making a band of wrought iron and shrinking it on to the projecting boss of the wheel, together with patches of steel plate which can be cut out, fitted, drilled and riveted over some of the fractures.   For making the ring for the boss of a wheel, square iron is usually the most suitable.   In making a ring of round or square iron, the ends should be upset and bent and scarfed like a link.

A square or oblong frame or band is sometimes required.   One use that may be pointed out is that of a post which has split at the end; another, the anvil block, which may split by the hammering on the anvil. A band made and shrunk on will prevent any further damage being done.

The illustration, Fig. 49, should not be hard to follow, especially as instruction in bending a pole clip has been previously given.

(To be continued.)

THE OLIVE.

L. Macdonald, Horticulturist, Dookie Agricultural College.

(Continued from page 71.)

BUDDING AND GRAFTING.

It was pointed out in connexion with propagation that the olive does not come true from seed.   Hence, it is necessary to bud or graft seedling stock with selected varieties.   Undesirable varieties may be worked over in the same manner.   Either method of propagation, if carried out in the proper manner and at the right season, should be attended with good results.   For general purposes, however, budding is considered the most suitable method of working.

It is not intended here to give a detailed account of the operation of either budding or grafting, as in almost any work dealing with the propagation of fruit trees such details will be found.   However, as there are some few points of difference between the nature of the olive wood and its treatment, and that of many other fruit trees, it is thought advisable to mention some of the more important points to observe in the work. Therefore, in carrying out the work of budding or grafting, it is important—

1. To see that the sap layers of both scion and stock have as great a contact as possible.

2. To use only scions and stocks that "run" well and on which the barks lifts easily.

3. To exclude the air from the wound as soon after the operation as possible by using some bandage.

4. To remove the leaves from all scions shortly after cutting and keep moist until used.

5. To see that the necessary tools are in good order, so that the work may be carried out as quickly and cleanly as possible.

6. To carry out the work at the right time.

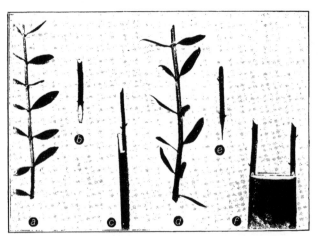

8. TONGUE AND CLEFT GRAFTS.

a. Scion ; *b* Prepared Scion ; *c.* Tongue graft; *d.* Scion; *e.* Prepared for cleft graft; *f.* Cleft graft on old tree.

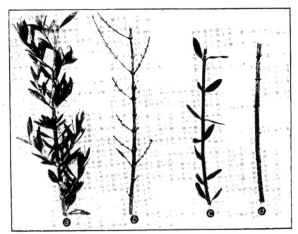

9. SCIONS FOR TWIG AND AXILLARY BUDS.

a. Scion for twig buds unprepared ; *b.* Same, prepared ; *c.* Scion for axillary buds, unprepared *d.* Same, prepared.

Spring is the most suitable time to carry out either budding or grafting on the olive. Budding may also take place again in late summer; but, unless forced, such buds remain dormant over winter, and break into growth in the spring. Spring buds, on the other hand, break into growth straight away; and, as they gain a good hold, the tops of the stock or branches are shortened back to concentrate the growth of the tree in the bud.

Scions.—The same care should be exercised in selecting olive scions, either for budding or grafting, as is taken with other trees. They should be obtained from the strongest and most prolific trees, and should be of well-matured, but not over-matured, wood and of a suitable size. A good method of obtaining suitable ones where little growth is made is to cut back some of the branches on a selected tree. This will cause the growth of vigorous wood. All leaves should be removed from the scions immediately after cutting to prevent evaporation of moisture, and they ought to be placed with their ends in water or kept moist in some other way until used. Upright wood of good growth and sufficiently matured should be selected.

BUDDING.—Quite a number of different forms of buddings are adopted in various places and some difference of opinion exists among propagators as to which is the better method, also with regard to the removal of the wood from the buds. In budding the olive, the writer favours the removal of the wood, unless the stock is very sappy or unless the buds are cut in such manner that only a thin film of wood fibre is left adhering to the bud. The two chief forms of budding that are adopted and generally give excellent results are—(1) twig buds; (2) axillary buds.

Twig Buds.—These are made from small shoots that are cut from the scions in the same manner as ordinary leaf or axillary buds. They succeed best in spring. Some of the disadvantages in twig budding are that the right kind of twig is not always easily obtained. It often happens that these short twigs have only well developed fruit buds, not only at the axils of the leaves but also at the terminal point, and do not make the best stock. Hence, it is necessary to

10. TWIG BUD.

use some judgment in selecting only the right class of scion. More time is also needed in this form of budding, but if it is carried out in spring excellent results should be obtained.

Axillary buds.—These are the common forms of buds used in the propagation of fruit trees generally. They are easily made and quickly inserted, and can be used with success, either in spring or late summer.

GRAFTING.—This work is carried out in early spring just when the trees begin to make new growth. Many different forms of grafting may be adopted. For general purposes, however, the tongue or whip graft and the cleft graft will be found suitable.

The tongue or whip graft is used chiefly on young stock, or where the diameter of the stock is not great. It is found to be the most satisfactory graft in such cases.

The cleft graft is used chiefly for working over old trees or larger stock.   When working with either of these grafts on stock of greater diameter than the scion, care should be taken to get as great a contact between the sap layer of one side of the scion and stock as possible. Also, materials should be at hand for bandaging up the wound to exclude the air and hold the scion firmly in position. Raffia, strips of waxed paper, or cloth will be found suitable for this purpose.

Two scions are usually put in each cleft in working over old trees; if too many shoots spring from them, they should be removed in the next season.   A great many adventitious buds spring out on limbs that have been cut back for grafting—these should be thinned out so as not to interfere with the growth of the scions.

Old trees may be successfully worked over, by heading down the top. When the strong young shoots develop they may be budded; the buds usually take better in the new growths.

(To be Continued.)

ORCHARD AND GARDEN NOTES.

E. E. Pescott, Principal, Horticultural School, Burnley.

The Orchard.

GREEN MANURE.

The benefits accruing from growing a cover crop for green manure are everywhere recognised.   The crop should be planted as soon as possible after the early autumn rains have prepared the ground for the plough. As the crop makes no growth in winter, and very little in the spring time— it being advisable to plough it in as early as possible in spring—it is advantageous to get a good and abundant growth in the autumn.   Consequently, the earlier the crop is planted, the greater the amount of herbage there will be for manurial purposes.

The crop may be sown towards the end of February.   A leguminous crop should be preferred before any other, owing to the amount of nitrogen which this class of plants contains.   The sowing will need to be a plentiful one, as it is well to have a good dense growth.   Field peas and tares or vetches are generally grown for the purpose.   The partridge variety of the field pea is coming into favour for this work.   In some instances, the tick bean has also been used with good success.

In ordinary orchard soils, it is often advisable to sow 1 cwt. each of bonedust and superphosphate per acre, to stimulate the crop into a quick and good growth.

SPRAYING.

Another spraying for codlin moth will probably be required for the later varieties of apples and pears. The coolness of the present summer has not been favorable to the rapid development of this pest, and it has not been so prevalent during this season.

A spray with nicotine solution or with a resin wash may now be given for either woolly aphis or bryobia mite, but only after the crop has been gathered. If these pests are not very prevalent, the spraying may be left until winter, when a good red oil emulsion, or a lime-sulphur spray may be given.

FUMIGATION.

Citrus and other evergreen trees that are attacked by scale insects should be freed from the scale at this time. Although spraying with such mixtures as resin compound, crude petroleum emulsion, and lime-sulphur emulsion, will do good work in keeping scale insects in check, the only effective means of complete eradication is by fumigation. The trees are enclosed in a tent that will prevent the escape of any gas through its texture. The gas is generated inside the tent, and the tent is kept over the tree for a period of from half to three-quarters of an hour. The best remedy is hydrocyanic acid gas, which is generated by placing cyanide of potassium in a mixture of sulphuric acid and water. As both the cyanide and the gas are deadly poisons, every care should be exercised in using them. The operator must take care that not the slightest portion of the fumes is breathed. Fumigation should be carried out at nighttime, or on a cloudy day, and the foliage of the trees must be thoroughly dry.

YOUNG TREES.

Young trees of the citrus family should now be making a good thrifty growth. The foliage should be glossy, and the general appearance should be a healthy one. Occasional light waterings, as well as a mulching of grass or of well rotted manure will be helpful to the trees.

Young deciduous fruit trees will also benefit by having a manure mulch; and, if it has not been previously done, unnecessary growths in the centre of the tree should be removed.

BUDDING.

It is now a suitable time to carry out any required budding work. In budding, it is necessary that the bark shall run or open freely; and, to do this, the tree must have a good sap flow at the time of performing the operation. If such does not occur, the trees to be worked, or the stocks, should be given a good watering, and the budding deferred for a day or two. Full instructions for budding were given in Mr. Cole's articles on the Propagation of Fruit Trees in the September and October, 1911, Journals.

CULTIVATION AND GENERAL WORK.

Guava trees have just finished flowering, and a good watering will be of benefit to them. Persimmon and loquat trees may also be watered to their advantage.

The soil should be kept loose and well worked between the trees, especially if the weather be at all hot. The surface must also be well worked after every irrigation.

Journal of Agriculture, Victoria. [10 FEB., 1912.

Vegetable Garden.

Celery crops will now be a prominent feature in the vegetable section. The seed may be sown from January to March, and succession plantings should be carried out occasionally during those months. The growth of celery should be quick; a fair supply of water, and a good rich loose soil are helpful to its growth. The plants should be earthed up as they make growth.

Ample water will now be required in the vegetable garden. The surface should be kept well hoed and mulchings of manure should be given wherever possible.

Cabbage, carrot, turnip, radish, lettuce, peas, cauliflower, &c. seeds may now all be sown; and young plants from any seed beds may be planted out.

Flower Garden.

Ample waterings and sprayings, with subsequent cultivation, will be helpful in hot, dry or windy weather.

Weak plants, herbaceous plants, and surface rooting plants will be greatly benefited by a cool and nutritious mulch. Old stable manure will be helpful.

Dahlias may be mulched and disbudded, thinning out the weak and useless shoots. Where sufficiently advanced, chrysanthemums may be disbudded. Stake all tall growing plants to prevent any damage from winds or from their own weight.

All old flower heads, and weak wood may now be removed from the rose bushes. They should then be well watered, so as to induce good growth for the autumn blooms. They may be fed towards the end of the month.

Flowering trees and shrubs that have passed their blossom time should be pruned and thinned out freely.

A few bulbs may be planted for early blooming; also prepare beds for the main planting next month.

REMINDERS FOR MARCH.

LIVE STOCK.

HORSES.—Feed as advised last month. Those in poor condition should be "fed up" in anticipation of winter.

CATTLE.—Feed as last month. Where grass is plentiful, cattle can be profitably bought this month. Secure heifers to calve in autumn to replenish the herd. Old cows in good condition should be sold. Cows not in calf should also be sold; otherwise they will come in next season too late to be profitable. Only exceptional cows, and those required for town milk supply, should be served between now and July.

PIGS.—Feed as last month. Breeding sows should be served; the young pigs will sell well in early spring when milk is plentiful. Fatten stores for winter curing. Weaners should not be allowed to go back; if markets are favourable, may be sold as porkers when ready.

SHEEP.—Merino and fine comeback breeding ewes should be kept strong for lambing. Crutch those most woolly and clear their eyes. Rams should not be running with merino or fine comeback ewes at this time. Pure British ewes and very coarse crossbreds are only properly in season now. If possible, spell a paddock from now, to draft ewes with lambs into during April.

POULTRY.—Cull out the drones and get rid of surplus cockerels. Keep forward pullets well fed—eggs are rising in value. Repairs to houses should be done this month. Thoroughly cleanse all houses and pens. Spray ground and houses with a 5 per cent. solution of crude carbolic acid, to which should be added a little lime—this will act as a safeguard against chicken pox; burn all refuse and old feathers. Provide a liberal supply of green food. Add a small quantity of sulphur to mash; also, for each moulting hen, add a teaspoonful of linseed to the morning mash. Use tonic in water, which should be kept in cool shady spot.

CULTIVATION.

FARM.—Work fallow where possible for autumn sowing of cereals. Sow winter fodder crops, such as rye, barley, and vetches. Prepare land for lucerne plots for autumn seeding. Make silage of maize and other crops for winter use.

ORCHARD.—Prepare new land for planting; plough deeply and sub-soil; leave surface rough. Plant out strawberries after first rain. Plant crops for green manure. Continue to fight the Codlin Moth.

VEGETABLE GARDEN.—Prepare ground for winter crops. Plant out seedlings in moist soil. Sow cabbage, cauliflower, lettuce, early peas, swede turnip, beet, carrot, radish, and early onions.

FLOWER GARDEN.—Cultivate and water. Feed dahlias, chrysanthemums, and roses. Plant out shrubs, trees, and all kinds of bulbs. Sow hardy annuals. Plant geranium and pelargonium cuttings. Spray for Aphis, Red Spider, and Mildew.

VINEYARD.—Select scions, if not done last month. Where ripening is difficult, assist by removing basal leaves only, as soon as berries change colour. This is the month for drying currants, sultanas, and gordos (Lexias and Clusters). Do not pick before grapes are properly ripe. For instructions for packing grapes for export, apply to Department. Shipments should be made in March and early April.

Cellars.—Vintage month. For light dry wines, pick as soon as grapes are ripe; do not wait for over-maturity, as is so often done. Pay attention to acidity; correct same if necessary with tartaric acid or late grapes. Acidimeter supplied by Department; price, 3s. 6d. Sulphiting and the use of pure yeasts are strongly recommended, as they insure production of sound wine; further information supplied on application.

STATISTICS.

Rainfall in Victoria.—Fourth Quarter, 1911.

TABLE showing average amount of rainfall in each of the 26 Basins or Regions con stituting the State of Victoria for each month and the year, with the corre sponding monthly and quarterly averages for each Basin, deduced from all available records to date.

Basin or District.	October.		November.		December.		Year.	
	Amount	Average.	Amount.	Average.	Amount.	Average.	Amount.	Average.
	points.	points.	points.	points.	points.	points.	points.	points.
Glenelg and Wannon Rivers	170	287	26	188	314	145	510	620
Fitzroy, Eumeralla, and Merri Rivers	242	290	29	193	333	156	604	639
Hopkins River and Mount Emu Creek	148	251	25	193	355	159	528	603
Mount Elephant and Lake Corangamite	167	243	30	191	371	157	568	591
Cape Otway Forest ...	233	345	97	238	429	222	759	805
Moorabool and Barwon Rivers	156	247	46	196	413	185	615	628
Werribee and Saltwater Rivers	153	242	95	193	386	215	634	650
Yarra River and Dandenong Creek	270	338	157	269	497	320	924	927
Koo-wee-rup Swamp ...	196	346	79	253	536	267	811	866
South Gippsland ...	211	386	120	264	469	321	800	971
Latrobe and Thomson Rivers	278	365	104	265	591	305	973	935
Macallister and Avon Rivers	134	233	121	187	264	270	519	690
Mitchell River ...	82	284	159	200	296	247	537	731
Tambo and Nicholson Rivers	120	300	141	180	340	279	601	759
Snowy River	197	354	114	209	353	279	664	842
Murray River	34	183	77	137	185	141	296	461
Mitta Mitta and Kiewa Rivers	103	336	170	256	419	239	692	831
Ovens River	112	337	92	235	317	230	521	802
Goulburn River	91	242	35	181	213	175	339	598
Campaspe River ...	77	207	13	169	210	175	300	551
Loddon River	52	170	15	142	222	120	289	432
Avon and Richardson Rivers	54	145	7	123	188	87	249	355
Avoca River	58	152	10	129	179	108	247	389
Eastern Wimmera	61	201	16	161	311	113	388	475
Western Wimmera	71	199	4	142	257	82	332	423
Mallee District	32	121	21	96	144	80	197	297
The whole State	109	234	55	172	283	166	447	572

100 points = 1 inch.

H. A. HUNT,

Commonwealth Meteorologist.

10th January, 1912.

Fruit, Bulbs, Plants, Grain, &c.

Goods.	Imports. Inter-State.	Imports. Oversea.	Exports. Oversea.	Goods.	Imports. Inter-State.	Imports. Oversea.	Exports. Oversea.
Apples	7,150	111	100	Linseed ...	—	146	—
Apples, Custard ...	2	—	—	Loquats ...	3	--	—
Apricots... ...	—	—	181	Logs	1,967	18,655	—
Bananas, bunches ..	24,639	81,903	—	Mace	—	99	—
Bananas, cases ...	3,992	25,175	—	Maize	449	728	—
Barley	19,282	22,702	—	Melons	136	—	--.
Beans	37	317	—	Nutmegs ...	—	285	—.
Bulbs	1	261	—	Nuts	103	2,102	—
Cherries... ...	1,019	—	3,064	Oats	3,856	4	—
Chillies	.1	64	—	Oranges	112,315	2,134	3,127
Cocoa beans ...	.	1,272	—	Passion	275	—	—
Cocoanuts ...	—	315	—	Paw Paws ...	14	13	—
Coffee beans ...	—	506	—	Peaches	28	—	118
Copra	—	76	—	Pepper	—	197	—
Cucumbers ...	10,973	—	20	Peas, dried ...	1,577	3	—
Currants, black ...	1	—	—	Pineapples ..	17,242	217	381
Dates	—	13,734	—	Plants	101	274	26
Figs	—	780	—	Plums	—	—	312
Fruit—				Potatoes ...	5	—	..
Canned ...	—	—	4,303	Rice	6,670	9,337	—
Dried ...	—	3,013	652	Seeds	477	4,378	—
Mixed ...	69	18	—	Spice	—	177	--.
Grapes	1	—	—	Strawberries ...	1	—	—
Green ginger ...	—	87	—	Tomatoes ...	4,649	18	35
Hops	—	224	—	Vegetables ...	7,681	482	—
Jams, Sauces, &c....	—	—	1,377	Wheat. Grain, &c.	1,336	14	—
Lemons ...	2,817	1,697	1,948	Yams	36	—	—
Totals ...	69,984	152,255	11,645	Grand Totals ...	228,905	191,520	15,044

Total number of packages inspected for quarter ending 31st December, 1911 = 436,069.

E. MEEKING, *Senior Fruit Inspector.*

Perishable and Frozen Produce.

Description of Produce.			Exports from State (Oversea). Quarter ended 31.12.1911.	Exports from State (Oversea). Quarter ended 31.12.1910.	Deliveries from Government Cool Stores Quarter ended 31.12.1911.	Deliveries from Government Cool Stores Quarter ended 31.12.1910.
Butter ...	...	lbs.	24,450,852	25,253,752	24,917,984	19,941,600
Milk and Cream ...		cases	2,930	801	51	80
Cheese ...	...	lbs.	15,480	264,840	500	255,172
Ham and Bacon	...	"	62,500	46,560	...	...
Poultry ...	...	head	5,310	9,879	4,759	5,489
Eggs... ...	...	dozen	...	30	500	3,811
Mutton and Lamb		carcases	1,118,555	998,883	66,454	113,287
Beef		quarters	5,457	2,759	...	...
Veal... ...		carcases	935	1,468	79	343
Pork... ...	...	"	1,491	1,078	858½	851
Rabbits and Hares	...	pairs	159,450	5,490	11,763	3,804
Sundries ...	...	lbs.	...	...	52,365	80,296

R. CROWE, *Superintendent of Exports.*

VICTORIAN EGG-LAYING COMPETITION, 1911-12,

CONDUCTED AT BURNLEY HORTICULTURAL SCHOOL

(*Continued from page 67.*)

H. V. Hawkins, Poultry Expert.

No. of Pen.	Breed.	Name of Owner.	Eggs Laid during Competition.			Position in Competition.
			April to Nov.	Dec.	Total to Date (9 months).	
12	White Leghorn	W. G. Swift	1,091	152	1,243	1
31	„	R. W. Pope	1,062	143	1,205	2
40	„	A. J. Cosh (S.A.)	1,045	181	1,176	3
20	„	H. McKenzie	960	148	1,108	4
33	„	Range Poultry Farm (Qld.)	956	134	1,090	5
37	„	E. Waldon	933	141	1,074	6
18	„	S. Brundrett	896	114	1,010	7
39	„	A.W. Hall	839	150	989	8
13	Black Orpington	D. Fisher	853	121	974	9
21	White Leghorn	R. L. Appleford	844	128	972	10
46	Minorca	G. W. Chalmers	850	95	945	11
55	White Leghorn	W. G. McLister	822	115	937	12
25	„	B. Mitchell	829	102	931	13
38	„	Mrs. C. R. Smee	800	130	930	14
10	Black Orpington	H. A. Langdon	796	118	914	15
9	White Leghorn	J. O'Loughlin	791	121	912	16
49	„	W. J. Thornton	775	135	910	17
32	Silver Wyandotte	Mrs. M. A. Jones	797	111	908	18
44	Black Orpington	T. S. Goodisson	814	93	907	19
24	White Leghorn	F. Hannaford	769	137	906	20
1	„	A. Brebner	776	1.5	901	21
2	„	E. P. Nash	761	138	899	} 22
28	„	J. Campbell	763	136	899	
3	„	K. Gleghorn	768	129	897	} 24
36	„	F. A. Sillitoe	780	117	897	
50	„	C. H. Busst	755	136	891	26
19	„	A. Jaques	752	132	884	27
5	„	L. C. Payne	743	127	870	28
45	„	T. Kempster	732	136	868	} 29
67	„	C. L. Sharman	775	93	868	
47	„	C. W. Spencer (N.S.W.)	729	135	864	31
22	Black Orpington	P. S. Wood	746	118	864	}
62	White Leghorn	P. Hodson	712	143	855	33
4	Golden Wyandotte	H. Bell	748	102	850	34
57	White Leghorn	G. E. Edwards	703	145	848	35
8	„	T. W. Coto	718	127	845	36
66	White Wyandotte	J. E. Bradley	759	85	844	37
65	White Leghorn	H. Hammill (N.S.W.)	733	107	840	38
11	Brown Leghorn	F. Soncum	697	139	836	39
59	White Leghorn	W. H. Dunlop	708	122	830	40
27	„	Hill and Luckman	728	101	829	41
51	„	J. W. McArthur	727	100	827	42
60	„	J. J. Harrington	703	113	816	43
43	„	W. B. Crellin	700	115	815	44
63	Black Orpington	A. J. Treacy	727	80	807	45
53	White Leghorn	A. Stringer	686	113	799	46
41	„	Morgan and Watson	688	108	796	47
58	Faverolles	K. Courtenay	702	93	795	48
52	White Leghorn	W. J. McKeddie	676	106	782	49
42	White Orpington	P. Mitchell	678	97	775	50
30	Black Orpington	Rodgers Bros.	666	96	762	51
6	Silver Wyandotte	Mrs. H. J. Richards	662	97	759	52
35	White Leghorn	J. H. Brain	631	121	752	53
34	„	E. Dettman	630	121	751	54
7	„	H. Stevenson	620	123	743	55
64	„	J. D. Read	592	146	738	56
26	„	F. H. Seymour	613	115	728	57
54	„	F. Hodges	621	89	710	58
16	Silver Wyandotte	Miss A. Cottam	619	87	706	59
56	White Leghorn	Mrs. C. Thompson	568	124	692	60
23	Golden Wyandotte	G. E. Brown	599	84	683	61
61	Silver Wyandotte	J. Reade	543	108	651	62
17	White Leghorn	W. J. Eckershall	536	88	624	63
14	Black Orpington	W. J. Macauley	521	74	595	64
15	Minorca	H. R. McChesney	456	83	539	65
48	„	G. James	346	87	433	66
			48,618	7,680	56,298	

DOOKIE AGRICULTURAL COLLEGE.
(SHEPPARTON DISTRICT.)
H. PYE, Principal.

The College offers every facility to students to become competent agriculturists and dairymen. The work is carried out on a large commercial scale, the ploughing, drilling, manuring, harvesting, threshing, and shearing being done by students under competent instructors. Over 2,000 sheep and lambs, 150 cattle, and 50 horses, including stallion, are on the farm, which comprises over 6,000 acres.

FEES (per Annum)—*First Year*, £32 5s.; *Second Year*, £27 5s.; *Third Year*, £22 5s.; Payable half-yearly.

LONGERENONG AGRICULTURAL COLLEGE.
(HORSHAM DISTRICT.)
W. D. WILSON, B.Sc., Principal.

One aim of this institution is to fill in the gap between the State School and Dookie, *i.e.*, to take students between the ages of fourteen and sixteen years.

The farm contains an area of 2,386 acres, and is admirably adapted for demonstrating what can be done in farming with irrigation. There is a large area of the farm under cultivation, and the orchard and vineyard cover an area of 30 acres.

FEES—*Resident*, £20 per annum; *Non-resident*, £5 per annum; Payable half-yearly.

Applications relative to the above Colleges should be sent to the Secretary, Council of Agricultural Education, Department of Agriculture, Melbourne. On receipt of Post Card a copy of the Prospectus of either College will be posted.

NEXT SESSION COMMENCES MARCH, 1912.
INTENDING STUDENTS MAY NOW BE ENROLLED.

DEPARTMENT OF AGRICULTURE,
VICTORIA.

Burnley Horticultural School.

E. E. PESCOTT, Principal.

ANNOUNCEMENT.

The curriculum and management of the Burnley Horticultural School have now been arranged so that greater advantages and facilities will be given to students of both sexes in Horticulture and allied subjects.

The present course of Horticulture for male students includes a two years' course, students being charged a fee of £5 per annum.

Classes have been formed at Burnley, whereby students of both sexes may receive instruction on two afternoons of each week—Tuesdays and Fridays.

Instruction includes theoretical and practical work, and will commence at 2 p.m. This will be a two years' course, and the fee charged will be £2 per annum.

It has also been arranged that several short lecture courses shall be given on subjects which are suitable adjuncts to Horticulture, such as Poultry Farming, Bee-keeping, and Fruit Preserving, and these courses will be open and free to the general public. The subjects and dates of the Short Course Lectures will be announced monthly in this Journal.

1912 Session commences 12th February.

Application for admission should be made at once to **The DIRECTOR OF AGRICULTURE,**

PUBLIC OFFICES, MELBOURNE,

OR TO THE PRINCIPAL.

DEPARTMENT OF AGRICULTURE,
VICTORIA.

AGRICULTURAL CLASSES, 1912.

At least thirty students, exclusive of school children, must be enrolled at each centre, the rent of the hall and all local charges to be paid by the Agricultural Society under whose auspices the Class is held.

As only a limited number of classes can be held during the year, it is essential that Agricultural or other Societies should make early application prior to 1st March.

LECTURES ON AGRICULTURAL SUBJECTS, 1912.

Agricultural or other Societies wishing to have public lectures delivered are requested to make application prior to 1st March. The hall, advertising, &c., must be provided locally, free of cost, but all other charges are borne by the Department.

Staff—The Director (Dr. S. S Cameron), and Messrs. Archer, Carmody, Carroll, de Castella, Cother, Crowe, French Jr., Griffin, Ham, Hart, Hawkins, Johnstone, Kendall, Knight, McFadzean, Pescott, Richardson, Robertson, Sawers, Seymour, Smith, Strong, Turner, and Expert of the State Rivers and Water Supply Commission.

Applications relative to the above Institutions and Lectures should be sent to the Director of Agriculture, Melbourne.

"WATERLOO BOY", 4 h.p. PORTABLE OIL ENGINE.

ABSOLUTELY THE SIMPLEST AND CHEAPEST EFFICIENT ENGINE IN THE WORLD.
USES BENZINE OR KEROSENE.

IGNITION.—Is make and break style, charge fired by electric spark. Igniter, which in other Engines is difficult to get at, in the "Waterloo" can be completely removed by loosening two cap screws
Both **Magneto** and **Battery Ignition**,—a very useful arrangement, as work can never be stopped.

SPEED LEVER.—Acts same as throttle of a steam engine. You can speed up or down, or stop altogether with it. Makes the Engine easy to start, prevents "kicking back," and saves fuel.

MIXER.—Is a great idea, patented because it is worth patenting. Has an adjustable mixing cup that can, by a winged nut, be slipped up or down to give more or less air. No valve springs or pump to get out of order; makes Engine easy to start; aids the governor and speed lever in getting more power out of the fuel.

GOVERNOR.—Centrifugal type, sure and sensitive. Allows a charge in the cylinder only when the work requires it.

FUEL.—Works on either benzine or kerosene, but benzine is better, as it is not so dirty. The speed-saving devices, Speed Lever, Patent Mixer, and Governor make the "Waterloo" consume the least fuel. Compare it for **simplicity, fuel cost,** and **power** with other engines, and you will send your order to us.

HOPPER COOLED.—That is, there are **no** Tank, Pipes, and Pump to cool the cylinder. Makes the Engine easy to move about; less space, less weight, and no water pump troubles, as there is no Pump. Also lessens the fuel bill.

TRANSPORT.—Is a very strong one. Through axles in both front and rear wheels. Turntable on front axle is simple and strong.

☞ SEND FOR CATALOGUES OF OUR OTHER FARM REQUISITES.

MITCHELL & COMPANY PTY. LTD.

FACTORY & OFFICE:SHOW ROOM:
WEST FOOTSCRAY, MELBOURNE.   596 BOURKE ST., MELBOURNE.

[Registered at the General Post Office, Melbourne, for transmission by Post as a Newspaper.]

The Journal of THE DEPARTMENT OF AGRICULTURE OF VICTORIA, AUSTRALIA.

March, 1912.

MAFFRA BEET SUGAR FACTORY.

THE JOURNAL

OF

THE DEPARTMENT OF AGRICULTURE,

VICTORIA, AUSTRALIA.

T. HOPKINS, Acting Editor.

CONTENTS.—MARCH, 1912.

COPYRIGHT PROVISIONS AND SUBSCRIPTION RATES.

THE JOURNAL

OF

The Department of Agriculture

OF

VICTORIA.

| Vol. X.   Part 3. | 10th March, 1912. |

THE BEET SUGAR INDUSTRY AND CLOSER SETTLEMENT.

Harry T. Easterby, General Manager Maffra Sugar Factory.

HISTORICAL.

The fine building which is depicted on the front cover of the *Journal* in which this article appears was erected by the Maffra Beet Sugar Company in 1897-8, and cost for machinery and plant some £70,000. This company was subsidized by the Victorian Government to the extent of £2 for every £1 subscribed by shareholders. They carried on operations for two seasons.

Due to a number of adverse conditions, which are within the memory of most people, the factory was closed after the second campaign, and the Government entered into possession as mortgagee. The adverse conditions referred to exist no longer, and beet growing, which was then totally new to farmers, has become quite a familiar operation owing to the efforts of the Government during the interval 1900 to 1909 in inducing farmers to carry out experiments. For the best crops of beet a series of prizes has been offered each year.

In 1909 it was, upon the advice of Dr. Maxwell, the eminent sugar expert, decided to re-open the Maffra Factory in a purely experimental way in order that it might be demonstrated:—

Firstly—That beets could be grown commercially and profitably by farmers, and,

Secondly—That a standard marketable sugar could be produced, which would compare favorably with the best manufactured in the Commonwealth.

The details of securing the necessary acreage, to make a trial run worth while, were put into the hands of Mr. F. E. Lee, who, originally

2098.   F

an officer of the old Beet Company, had for many years been associated
with the industry and with the carrying out of the field experiments.   To
his enthusiasm and belief in the ultimate success of the industry must be
credited the fact that sufficient growers were found to justify the re-open-
ing.   Upon Mr. Lee's relinquishing this work, to take up a position on
the Closer Settlement Board, the writer relieved him of the out-door management in connexion with the scheme.   The next step was the selection

MAFFRA SUGAR BEET FACTORY—BEET BINS.

of a capable factory manager, and here the Government were fortunate in
securing the services of one of America's most prominent Beet-sugar men,
Mr. G. S. Dyer, whose family has been most honorably connected with
the Beet Industry in America ever since its inception.
     The first campaign under the auspices of the Government was started
in April, 1911, and despite many initial difficulties, it has successfully
proved that which it was intended to do.   Many of the crops realized

a very handsome profit after paying all expenses, and it was clearly shown that beet-growing could be made a most successful industry. The sugar produced was of the finest quality, notwithstanding the fact that the machinery had been lying idle for twelve years and that a totally inexperienced and raw crew were operating in the factory. When placed on the market it commanded the highest market rates for first-class sugar. The success of this experimental campaign was considered so satisfactory that the Government decided to continue operations and build up the Beet-sugar industry in Victoria upon a sound foundation.

PRESENT DEVELOPMENT.

Those farmers who had made a financial success of beet growing with few exceptions replanted on a larger scale for this year, notable increases being from 5 to 17 acres, 2 to 10 acres, 5 to 9 acres, 18 to 28 acres. and so on. But beyond this, relatively few of the farmers surrounding the Maffra Factory have undertaken to grow beets. The majority of them are successful dairymen and graziers rather than cultivators of the soil, and, as they can make money at these pursuits, they have hitherto not given the question of growing beet a great deal of attention.

However, it was clear that a larger acreage must be secured in order to provide more beet for the factory than in the previous year, and that this securing of area and larger supply of beets must be progressive until the full capacity of the Maffra Factory (40,000 tons of beets) was reached.

This will necessarily occupy some two or three years, for farmers generally will only come in by degrees, and when they see that other people can make good money from beet-growing. This year large numbers of persons are beginning to recognise the advantage they derive as beet-growers from being able to obtain supplies of pulp as fodder for their cows and pigs. This aspect of the question will be dealt with at a later stage.

In addition to the Maffra District, other parts of Victoria have this year been given an opportunity of demonstrating whether beet-root growing is suitable to their localities. In Gippsland itself beet is being grown from Bairnsdale to Nar-nar-goon.

Experimental half acres have also been planted at Rochester. Bamawm. Shepparton, Colac, Bacchus Marsh, Portland, &c., &c. Upon the irrigation areas in the North beet-root can undoubtedly be made a profitable crop, and one which the settlers would be keen to cultivate, because they know it has an assured market value.

Seeing that beet growing will not be taken up by the farmers of the Maffra and surrounding districts upon a large scale immediately, the Victorian Government, recognising clearly the value of the Sugar-beet industry as an important asset to the country, determined to make this question in some respects a closer settlement one. A tide of immigration is now setting in to our shores, and it is necessary that new settlers should have a staple payable crop to engage upon. What better crop could there be than sugar-beet, with its sure and certain market, its big money returns, and its by-products of pulp, tops, and molasses, to assist the dairying business? Therefore in suitable localities the growth of beet is to be bound up with closer settlement.

F 2

CLOSER SETTLEMENT—BOISDALE ESTATE.

The first move in the above direction was the purchase of some 2,500 acres, portion of the well-known Boisdale Estate, one of the finest areas in Victoria. The land was bought in two sections, the first subdivision consisting of 785 acres, being divided into 18 blocks. These were thrown open to settlers in August, 1911, and were immediately applied for. The second subdivision was bought a little later, and was not ready for settlement till September, 1911. This consisted of 1,728 acres, and was divided into 39 allotments. Of these, 26 blocks have been taken up, 6 of the remaining blocks are still open to applicants, while 7 blocks are held by the Department of Agriculture for the present, for the purpose of growing beet-root and assisting to make up the supply to the factory. The land thus made available was intended for combined beet and dairy

CORA LYNN BEET CROP, BUNYIP DISTRICT.

farming. The soil is a rich alluvial deposit and is several feet in depth. Blocks vary from 40 to 60 acres.

The Boisdale purchase promising so well, another purchase of 8,000 acres of the far-famed Kilmany Park was made in the spring. This estate has now been subdivided and made available for settlement in blocks of from 60 acres upwards. Particulars concerning the settlement of this estate are given at the end of this article.

The first fact that strikes an intending settler applying for land at Boisdale is that there is no pioneering work to be done. Here is no necessity to wrest with the axe a hard-won home from the giant forest or the tangled scrub; he can set himself, his family and household goods,

down in the midst of a well-ordered community with most of the adjuncts
of civilization.   A well-equipped Butter and Cheese Factory is upon the
Estate, to which settlers can sell their milk.

State School, Public Hall, Post Office, and Railway Station are all
within easy distance of settlers, while the roads are good, and a plentiful

BOISDALE CHEESE AND BUTTER FACTORY.

STATE SCHOOL.   PUBLIC HALL.

BOISDALE.

supply of water is easily obtained by sinking from 15 to 25 feet.   Many
of the blocks are also well watered by billabongs.   The River Avon
bounds the property on the East, while the lofty Australian Alps lend

beauty to the landscape on the North.   Altogether, the settler can congratulate himself upon his surroundings and the value of his land.

The type of house provided varies according to the requirements of the settler.   For a young man just commencing, the style of house shown below is all that is at present needed.

SETTLER'S HOUSE—TWO ROOMS.

The man with a family, however, requires something better than this, and the Closer Settlement Board accordingly erect a house of the following type :—

SETTLER'S HOUSE—FOUR ROOMS.

for which easy terms are given in the shape of annual repayments spread over a series of years.   The settler generally builds his own outbuildings, such as stables and cowsheds.

The houses originally upon portion of the Estate are also utilized, some of the best of these being built of brick, forming most substantial homesteads with necessary silos, milking sheds, stables, &c.

Beet Growing and Dairying at Boisdale.

In order to provide that beet-root growing should be made part and parcel of the scheme of Closer Settlement at Boisdale the following clause was inserted in the terms and conditions of purchase :—

> For a period of at least ten years, unless remission is given by the Agricultural Department, a minimum area of 10 acres shall be utilized for beet culture each year, the cultivation of the crop to be carried out to the satisfaction of the Agricultural Department. A system of three-course rotation to be followed (*i.e.*, the 10 acres under beet in any year shall not be put under beet again until the third year following) unless remission of this condition be approved by the Agricultural Department, and the whole resulting crop of manufacturable beet shall be supplied to the Maffra Factory, which will pay for same at a rate per ton of topped clean roots delivered at the factory, such rate to be determined by the Factory Manager from year to year during the ten years or until this condition is remitted, which may be done at any time by the Board. At the present time £1 per ton is being paid for beet roots.

A BOISDALE BEET AND DAIRY HOMESTEAD.

As the blocks were only taken up between August and October, it was necessary for the Department to at once prepare the 10 acres of ground upon each settler's block so that beet-growing could be immediately put in hand for the present campaign. Accordingly the land was ploughed, rolled, harrowed, and seeded, in most cases in advance of settlement, each successful applicant taking over his beet plot upon arrival. Owing to the fact that the Government did not obtain possession of the land until late in the year, no autumn fallowing, which is very advisable, could be carried out, but omitting this, the land generally was put into as good a condition for seeding as the circumstances would permit. For next season, however, the whole of the preliminary cultivation for beet-root should be properly carried out. While the beet crops throughout the District are upon the lighter side this year, partly on account that sowing was a little late and partly owing to the season, it is evident that given right treatment the Boisdale soils can be made to

MR. RAEBURN'S BEET CROP, BOISDALE (1912).

produce heavy yields of beet. The following two photographs are of Messrs. Raeburn and Bedggood's crops, which are equal to any in the Maffra District and are superior to the majority.

MR. BEDGGOOD'S BEET CROP, BOISDALE (1912).

The first subdivision of the Estate was prepared and seeded first, and had, on the whole, better preparation in the shape of ploughing and sub-soiling. Good crops, however, are also to be found upon the second sub-division, as the following photograph will show :—

MR. HUETON'S BEET CROP, BOISDALE (1912).

MR. HARVEY'S DAIRY HERD, BOISDALE.

Dairying is being carried on simultaneously with the growing of beet, and excellent returns are being secured by settlers from the sale of their milk and cream to the Boisdale Butter Factory.   Mr. Trevor Harvey, one of the Boisdale settlers, has a herd of dairy cows which are mostly of the Jersey type.

RED DANISH BULL, CLAUDIUS.
Placed by the Government for the use of settlers at Boisdale.

Mr. Harvey weighs all his milk and cream, and keeps a tabulated record of the yield of each cow.   He has also a miniature chemical laboratory, and makes his own tests.   He is thus enabled to know exactly what he is doing and what progress he is making.   His milking sheds and general surroundings are the most advanced of the new beet farms on Bois_dale.

The following figures, supplied by some of the settlers, show that a good living can be made by dairying on the small area that each man holds :—

Settler.		No. o: Cows.	Monthly Returns.		
			£	s.	d.
A.	.. ..	11	21	0	0
B.	.. ..	14	20	0	0
C.	.. ..	11	19	8	0
D.	.. ..	12	18	0	0
E.*	.. ..	10	14	0	0
F.	.. ..	12	18	0	0
G.†	.. ..	28	32	0	0
H.	.. ..	14	21	0	0
I.	.. ..	17	18	0	0
J.	.. ..	12	16	0	0
K.	.. ..	13	18	0	0
L.	.. ..	16	21	0	0
M.	.. ..	21	18	0	0
N.	.. ..	12	16	0	0
O.	.. ..	9	12	0	0

* Six of these are two-year-old heifers.
† Two blocks.

The Department has a number of Red Polled and Danish cattle at Boisdale, which are being retained to form the nucleus of a dairy herd on one of the State experimental farms.

Lucerne grows exceptionally well, and many settlers have had three fine cuttings recently.

BEET GROWING FOR NEXT SEASON.

Farmers who intend growing beet for next season (1913) are strongly advised to get their land fallowed as early as possible—not later than in the Autumn, so that the final ploughing and subsciling and the working up of the seed-bed can be carried out just prior to sowing.

Sowing should invariably be done in August, and early thinning is an immense advantage, fully 25 per cent. greater yield being secured by carrying out this important act in the cultivation of the crop at the right time, viz. :—upon the appearance of the fourth leaf.   Farmers generally this year were too late, both with sowing and thinning, and the yields would have been much more satisfactory had both these operations been carried out at the proper time.   Cultivation is now particularly easy with the special beet cultivators imported from America by the Department, and which are lent free to farmers under conditions which are ascertainable at the Sugar Factory.

GOVERNMENT HERD—RED POLLED DAIRY CATTLE, BOISDALE.

Full details· as to preparation of ground for beet, and subsequent cultivation, were given in the last August number of this *Journal*, copies of which can be obtained. upon application to. the Department of Agriculture or to the Sugar Factory, Maffra.

These may be briefly epitomized as under :—

Always select the best lands for Sugar Beets. Tilled land is always preferable. Avoid poor land—land where sheep have just pastured, sandy land that will blow or drift, cold, wet or late land.

See that the land is cleared of all cornstalks and roots, and rubbish of any kind before being ploughed, so that nothing will interfere with the perfect working of the Cultivator.

Use only well rotted manure or artificial fertilizers approved for beet on land intended for beets. Do not put a coat of heavy, coarse manure on your land just previous to planting beets. It is very apt to interfere with. the proper seeding and cultivating, to cause a poor stand, and to hurt the quality of the beets.

The land should be ploughed in the Autumn, and allowed to mellow by lying.

fallow through the early winter. · Then in July a second ploughing 8 or 10 inches deep and subsoiling another 6 inches should be carried out.   The

SYNDICATE BEET CROP.   MAFFRA.

subsequent cultivation before seeding involves harrowing and rolling to an extent sufficient to provide a smooth, level, and well-tilled seed-bed.

STACKING LUCERNE HAY, BOISDALE.

Get your soil in the very best possible condition; put beets in early, not later than August, and work them early, thinning out carefully to only one in a place; then cultivate the soil often.   This always pays well.

Never plant more than three-quarters of an inch deep in the early part of the season, and from three-quarters to one inch in the latter part of the season.

BREAKING UP LAND FOR BEET AT BOISDALE.

Plant the beets in rows never more than 18 inches apart and thin out to 8 inches between the plants in a row, unless the land is

CULTIVATOR FOR BEET.

very rich, when the beets can be left 6 inches apart, so as to control the size of the plant.

In thinning, always select and leave the strongest, healthiest, and most uniform sized plants. Great care should be taken to leave the young plant in as good a condition as possible by placing a little earth around the root, so that it cannot fall down nor get sunburned.

Start your cultivator as soon as the beets are well through the ground, so as to keep the weeds from starting. Cultivate often, particularly after every rain, always leaving the surface level and never hilling or ridging up the beets.

The beet is one of the best crops to give profitable returns in proportion to the care and attention bestowed on it. Various important points are:—Secure a good stand by using plenty of seed and properly preparing the soil; thin properly when the young beet has reached the proper size; avoid thinning out too far apart in the rows; maintain a good state of cultivation.

The proper time to thin is upon the marked appearance of the third or fourth leaf. The secret of raising beets cheaply and of good yield and quality is—keep a clean field.

On the Value of Beet Pulp as Cattle Fodder.

An important feature of the beet-sugar industry is the supply of pulp which it returns to the farmer. This beet-pulp forms a valuable stock food, and the testimony of farmers and others entitled to speak upon the subject will be read with interest.

The United States Secretary for Agriculture states :—

"In order to get the benefit of beets as a rotator and to get the pulp to feed to his cows the farmer could actually afford to furnish to the factory the sugar from his beets free, and then would be only selling the air—for the sugar in beets comes wholly from the air."

I take the following from a recent article in the *American Sugar Industry* relative to the value of beet pulp as a stock feed :—

"Sugar beets will yield from fifteen to twenty tons per acre. About two-thirds of this will be returned as pulp The tops make additional feed. The dry matter contained in a pound of beet pulp is about equal to the dry matter in an equal amount of ordinary roots, such as mangels. It has been found that one pound of corn is equal to eight pounds of wet beet pulp when fattening lambs. Beet-pulp, either wet or dry, constitutes an important addition to the list of feeds that the dairyman may feed to his cows."

"Experiments in feeding both wet and dried pulp have been carried on at some of the stations. The Utah Station found that horses will eat as high as twenty pounds of wet pulp daily Combined with oats and lucerne, 9.5 pounds of the wet pulp were found equal to 1.5 pounds of oats. At this rate, with oats at two shillings a bushel, wet beet pulp is worth about sixteen shillings a ton. Nine pounds of wet pulp were equal in feeding value to 2.8 pounds of lucerne. If lucerne is worth £2 10s. a ton, then pulp is worth nearly sixteen shillings."

Some Experiences with Wet Pulp.

Interesting as may be the experimental work, the experience of some of the farmers who have been using the feed carries much weight. The following statements are from men who have been feeding wet pulp :—

No. 1.—"I cannot speak too highly of the feeding value of sugar-beet pulp for cattle. I have had nothing but excellent results from feeding it to my live stock.   My cows have increased their flow of milk one-third through feeding the wet pulp.   Young live stock will get· fat on it."

No. 2.—" I am very·much satisfied with wet beet pulp as a cattle food. My cows gave an increase in the flow of milk when fed with the pulp.   To the best of my knowledge I think it is worth about £1 per ton."

No. 3.—" Sugar-beet pulp is another good feed for milch cows.   I am sorry that I cannot get another carload at the present time.   With the present prices of feed, I think sugar-beet pulp is worth about sixteen shillings per ton.   It made a difference of from fifty to sixty pounds of milk in one day when I quit feeding it.   I earnestly recommend the feeding of beet pulp to dairy cows."

SOME EXPERIENCES WITH BEET PULP IN THE MAFFRA DISTRICT.

".I am feeding my cows solely on beet pulp.   I cart it out in the paddock, and distribute it in small heaps on the grass, allowing about a heap of 80 lbs. per day to each cow, and find they waste very little.   I am milking 65 cows, and since I have been using pulp the milk supply has increased from 113 gallons to 140 gallons a day, or slightly under half a gallon per cow.   I consider beet pulp is equal to green oats for winter feeding—in fact I proved it so when the factory was working last May, and I have also proved it to be as good as millet for this time of the year (Summer), and consider these two crops to be the best milking fodder in their respective seasons.   I have never used lucerne or bran to any extent and therefore cannot compare them, but I consider it far ahead of green maize.   I think that pulp would give even better results by the use of oaten hay or chaff with it."   *W. J. Dwyer, Maffra.*

" *Re* the value of beet pulp as fodder for milch cows, I have been feeding my cows on the pulp alone, and the quantity of milk has increased about half a gallon per day for each cow.   I think beet pulp is equally as good as any other fodder grown."   *A. A. Martin, Maffra.*

" I have been feeding beet pulp to my cows, the pulp being fed alone, being placed in the paddock in small heaps.   It has resulted in an increase in the daily milk yield equal to about half a gallon per cow.   In my opinion there is no better fodder, and at the present price is cheaper than chaff or bran, and cows will yield more milk on the pulp."   *J. Robertson, Maffra.*

"I have been feeding my cows on pulp from the factory, and am desirous of informing you that it is an excellent food for producing milk. Since I have been using the pulp my cows have just given one-third more milk than before I used it.   I am feeding my cows on pulp alone, twice a day, and I consider cows fed on pulp will produce more milk than those fed on lucerne or green oats.   My cows eat the pulp greedily and will lick it off the ground, and I can safely say that any one who can get pulp need never worry about growing anything else.   I have poddy calves fed on beet pulp, and they are all vealers and could be sent to market I would thoroughly recommend it to anybody with cows."   *John A. Mitchelmore, Maffra.*

KILMANY PARK ESTATE.

This property abuts on the main Gippsland Railway line, about 120 miles from Melbourne and 6 miles from Sale, and the Nambrok and Fulham railway stations are practically on the estate.   The whole of the blocks lie between the railway line on the north and the Latrobe River on the south, the latter being one of the finest rivers in Gippsland.

The soil ranges from light grazing and cultivation land on the north-east, thence slopes southwards and westwards to mixed farming and dairying land, and finally to extensive areas of river flats, highly suitable for dairying and beet growing.

There is a good supply of timber on the estate for fencing and firewood purposes. Water is obtainable at easy depths on the lower land by sinking, and good catchments exist on the higher slopes.

The area has been subdivided in such a way as to meet the requirements of practically all kinds of farming. Some of the blocks range up to 270 and 280 acres of a lighter class of land suitable for cereal growing, and grazing, at values from below £10 to £6 10s. per acre. Then there are mixed farming blocks of somewhat small area, and finally the blocks carrying beet-growing conditions similar to those imposed in the case of the Boisdale settlement previously described. There are 56 beet blocks available, varying in size from 20 acres to 195 acres. On the larger areas 10 acres of beet are to be grown annually, and 4 acres on the smaller areas, which are intended as small farm homes for workmen on the estate. On the majority of the blocks, however, it is contemplated that settlers will combine beet-growing with dairying, for which latter there is, in every case, a sufficiency of land, exclusive of the beet area, and they will be able to follow the plan which has been so successfully adopted in connexion with the Boisdale Estate. The fact that some of the lighter land on the estate is relieved of the beet-growing conditions is an indication of the desire of the Government that only land that is fully suitable for beet-growing, and on which profitable crops of beet may be grown, should have the beet-growing conditions attached.

In the acquirement of these blocks, the transaction, so far as the purchase of the land is concerned, will be with the Closer Settlement Board, it being a requirement that the deposit and subsequent instalments be paid by the settler without assistance from the Government. It is probable, however, that, in order to more quickly establish the industry and provide an acreage of beet up to the maximum capacity of the factory, the Department of Agriculture will be authorized, as in the case of Boisdale, to make advances to desirable and suitable settlers of a sufficiency of money to purchase stock and implements adequate to the running of the dairy portion of the farm, to the extent of making a living in the interval between the acquirement of the land and the harvesting of the first beet crop. The repayment of all such loans will be secured by a lien on the stock so purchased and on the resulting crop of beet; but repayment may not, in all cases, be insisted on after the first harvest.

BOISDALE BEET SIDING AND STATION.

WORMS IN SHEEP.

By S. S. Cameron, D.V.Sc., M.R.C.V.S.

Of the domestic animals that are kept in large numbers to minister to the wants of man the sheep is the least subject to attacks of disease. True, the goat, the donkey, the mule, and the cat are much more disease-resistant, but amongst domesticated animals in the economic sense these may be considered a negligible quantity. Sheep are but slightly liable to the ordinary ailments of an inflammatory or sporadic nature, which are of frequent occurrence in horses and cattle, such as colic, pneumonia. pleurisy, enteritis, impaction, or constipation. They are also remarkably immune against germ diseases; and except for anthrax, malignant catarrh, foot and mouth disease, braxy, and one or two other contagious diseases of somewhat mild character the ovine species is free from the attack of disease scourges which decimate the equine, bovine, and porcine species respectively, such as glanders, pleuro-pneumonia, and swine fever. Nevertheless sheep, like mortals, have "troubles of their own" in the shape of a truly worrying number of parasitic diseases. Invasion by macroscopic (naked eye) animal parasites such as worms— as distinguished from microscopic vegetable parasites called bacteria— occurs more frequently in the sheep than in any other domestic animal, and the diseases caused through such invasion, by their untoward effect on growth and fattening and by their frequent fatalities, are a great source of loss to the sheep raiser. These losses are practically perennial in certain districts, but in other localities they are only troublesome inter-mittently, *i.e.*, during certain seasons.

PREVENTIVE MEASURES.—Before proceeding to a detailed treatment of the diseases of sheep caused by parasites, it will be well to discuss generally the factors favorable to parasitism and the measures which can be most advantageously adopted to counteract them. Nearly all the harmful worm parasites, and indeed many insect parasites, require moist ground or stagnant water to live in while they are in the egg or larval stage. Hence if sheep could be kept to country free from stagnant water, marshy ground and boggy spots, the chances of their becoming affected with parasitic diseases would be practically non-existent. This statement is particularly true in regard to such diseases as fluke, lungworm and stomach worm, and, apart from its scientific foundation, is supported by the practical experience that during and after years of drought the pre-valence of fluke and worms in sheep is very much lessened. In England and other closely-settled agricultural countries it has also been found that along with the reclamation of swamps and marshes and the under-draining of wet lands, parasitic diseases of animals have declined enormously. This, because the natural harbours in the shape of stagnant water for snails, molluscs, and the like animalculæ, in which the parasites have to live during some period of their life history, is done away with.

Obviously then, to avoid infestation with parasites, sheep should not be grazed on low-lying, damp or marshy land, and for this reason as well as because it also predisposes to foot rot, it is an axiom of the sheep breeder that such land is not good sheep country. But, equally obviously, in Australia, where the runs are so large, it is next to impossible to confine sheep grazing to dry uplands. On many runs, at all events in some districts, some parts of the extensive paddocks are low-lying and wet. and if sheep are grazed on these parts during the spring and early summer there will always be more or less danger of them becoming infested with worms. On such runs great efforts should be made to fence off the wet parts so that they could be left bare of sheep during the months when the temperature is favorable for the development of the immature stages of the various parasites. September, October, November, and December are the months during which parasitic developmental processes are most active. Before this the eggs of the parasites have either not been passed out on to the ground, or if they have they may be eaten with impunity, because they are only in a "half-hatched" condition and incapable of development. Later than December the likelihood of their development is not great, because as a rule the conditions of the land as regards moisture are not favorable. This statement does not at first sight appear to be in accord with the fact that worm troubles in sheep are most markedly manifested during the late summer, but it must be remembered that a considerable time elapses after invasion of the system before the effects are pronounced. Associated with wet land as a causative agency in the prevalence ot parasitic diseases is the fact that on many extensive grazing areas the only available supply of water for stock is that contained in natural or artificial waterholes or tanks. Such stagnant water supplies frequently become foul and fœtid from pollution by animal discharges and surface drainage from adjacent camping grounds, and they are always likely to be highly charged with the immature forms of animal parasites, for which they constitute an ideal developing medium. Hence the extraordinary prevalence of intestinal and other parasites in Australian domestic animals; and hence also, perhaps in great measure, the fact that, excepting Iceland only, hydatid disease in man is more prevalent in Australia than in any other country in the world. The remedy, and it is one that will have to be carried out if the prevalence of worm diseases is to be minimized, lies in the fencing of all water-holes so that no stock can gain access to them, and the provision of troughs for drinking purposes. The troughs to be situated near by the water holes and automatically supplied with water from them by pumping with wind mill power. Even without the fencing-off of water holes the provision of troughs would greatly lessen the trouble because there is nothing in the objection sometimes raised that it is of no use providing drinking troughs as stock will not make use of them. It will be found *on trial* that stock will always go naturally to clean water and may be frequently observed to refuse, or drink but sparingly of, contaminated water.

Overstocking of sheep pasture should be rigidly avoided, for it is the opinion of those best qualified to judge that it is in great degree responsible for the spread of the worm pest. In addition to the excessive fouling of the land with a greater amount of parasite-impregnated droppings from infested sheep, the depletion of the land of its most nutritious grasses and plants results in a lack of thriving which predisposes to worm infection. One of the best means for improving flukey or worm-infested pastures is to burn them; but it is not usually practicable. For lambing ewes nothing is better than a paddock that has been burnt in the autumn. The feed that springs after the burning produces a good flow of milk and the burnt ground will be comparatively free from the eggs of parasites with which the young lambs are so liable to become infested. The periodical dressing of lambing paddocks with freshly burnt lime is also of great advantage, but such preventive procedure is scarcely practicable on larger areas. From what has been previously said as to the beneficial effects of draining, this preventive measure should not be neglected. Of course, the expense of under-draining will be an effective bar to its adoption on a large scale, but where stud sheep are being reared the expense will show ample recompense. Pipe draining is not necessary; an equally effective and much cheaper plan is to place two straight saplings, 8 or 9 inches thick, 3 or 4 inches apart in the bottom of the cut drain, then put a third sapling on the top to keep the other two apart and form an eye or channel, and fill in a covering of scrub or brushwood over the saplings before replacing the earth. Surface draining by the running of plough furrows and helping here and there with the spade, can be done at moderate expense even on large areas, and it should be done wherever surface water is apt to remain, so that likely breeding places for parasites may be done away with.

Preventive and Tonic Licks.

Except in so far as the licks usually recommended act as tonics and alteratives and so help to keep the sheep in robust health and thriving condition, it may be doubted whether they are really preventive of parasitic invasion. Their use should certainly never be allowed to excuse the carrying out of the previously detailed measures which, being based on scientific knowledge of the nature of the invasion and means of spread of its cause, are truly preventive. Nevertheless custom and experience have spoken to the usefulness of these licks and a word or two may be said about them.

Salt.—Experienced authorities hold that, apart from the question of preventing attacks of parasites, it pays well to give sheep all the salt they will take, the expense and trouble showing a good return in more and better mutton and more and better wool. In some districts where the salt bushes have not been eaten out and where the land and herbage are of a saline nature sheep may not need an artificial supply, but wherever on trial it is found they will take it an ample supply of rock salt should always be made available. Liverpool salt (*i.e.*, coarse, crushed rock salt) is preferred by some, and it certainly constitutes a good vehicle for the admixture of other worm medicines. Whatever salt or lick is used should be protected from waste by rain by being placed in covered troughs.

Salt and Iron.—Sulphate of iron, finely powdered and mixed well with Liverpool salt in the proportion of one part ($\frac{1}{2}$ cwt.) of the former to 40 parts (1 ton) of the latter. This to be constantly available to sheep in country at all subject to fluke and worms, and to be given in even sound country (other than true salt-bush country), when the season is such as is likely to favour parasitic infection. Where sheep are actually infested this lick may be improved as an appetite stimulant by the addition of flowers of sulphur and ground ginger in the proportion of one-half the amount of the sulphate of iron.

Salt and Lime.—A mixture of slaked lime, 1 part, and Liverpool salt, 12 parts, to which may be added one half-part of sulphate of iron or ground ginger or both.

Salt and Turpentine.—Mix thoroughly one pint of turpentine with from 28 lbs. to 56 lbs. Liverpool salt according to condition and age of sheep ; spread thinly in weather-protected troughs. As an active vermifuge for tapeworms half-a-pound of powdered areca nut may be added to this lick.

REMEDIAL MEASURES.—It may be truly said that while it is comparatively easy, by the carrying out of the measures previously indicated, to keep sheep free from worms, it is a heart-breaking and patience-taxing struggle to get a mob in order again that has got low from worms or fluke.

So far as fluke is concerned a flock should never be given the chance of getting emaciated or poor from it. Whenever, by the observance of any of the usual symptoms (which in regard to fluke as also in regard to other parasitic affections of sheep are too well known to need recapitulation in an article of this character), it becomes known that the sheep are infected with fluke, advantage should be taken of the fact, that in the first stages of the trouble they thrive exceptionally well, to draft them off to the butcher before the wasting stage commences. When the flukes first invade the liver their presence stimulates an increased flow of bile whereby for a time the process of digestion is greatly assisted, and consequently a fattening tendency is promoted. This fact is so well known that many years ago it was seriously proposed in·England (and actually put into practice by some breeders) to artificially infest sheep with fluke so as to quickly fatten them. If the sheep are closely watched and preliminary fattening noted, not much loss will result; but once this stage is past, and emaciation with its accompanying dropsy sets in, no remedial treatment is of much avail in arresting the " rot." Where it is possible to treat sheep individually or where stud sheep are concerned, the following prescription may be used :—

> Powdered oak bark.
> ,,   calamus root.
> ,,   gentian root.
> ,,   juniper berries of each 1 lb.
> ,,   sulphate of iron, ½ lb.
> ,,   common salt, 2 lbs. for sheep; 3 lbs for lambs.

Mix dry and give at the rate of a teaspoonful per sheep once a day mixed with a feed of chaffed ensilage or green oats, bran, crushed oats or chaffed hay.

As regards stomach, intestinal and lung worms medicinal treatment is greatly aided by the provision of artificial fodder; in fact, the cure of a mob is less certain, and certainly more troublesome, by the use of drenches, than by changing them on to lightly-stccked artificial feed such as young oats, rape, prairie, rye, or other sown grass, or by giving them a liberal allowance of chaffed hay or ensilage strengthened with crushed-oats or bran. The latter course has to be frequently adopted because it is difficult to get the artificial pastures mentioned in the green state during the months when treatment is most often wanted, viz., January and February, unless its requirement has been anticipated, as it should be on a well-managed sheep farm. Especially is this artificial feeding needed as a help in treatment when it is found that lambs are affected at weaning time.

WORM DRENCHES.—(1) *The Arsenic drench.*—For stomach worms (the " thread " worm or *Hæmonchus contortus*) and intestinal worms (the sheep tape worm or *Moniezia*). The dose of arsenic is about 2 grains for a grown sheep, 1½ grains for a weaner and up to 1 grain for a lamb:

> White arsenic, 2 ozs. avoirdupois.
> Washing soda, 4 ozs.   ,,
> Water, 1 gallon.

Boil slowly, stirring meanwhile for half-an-hour until the arsenic is all dissolved; then add water to make the mixture measure 3 gallons; let sediment settle and decant clear liquid or pour it quietly off. Bury or otherwise destroy sediment.

Dosage.—For grown sheep—1 fluid ounce (two tablespoonfuls) the three gallons sufficing for 480 grown sheep. *For weaners*—Add one gallon of water, making four gallons, which, with a dose of one ounce, will suffice for 640 weaners *For lambs*—Add water to make $5\frac{1}{2}$ gallons, which, with a dose of one ounce, will suffice for 880 lambs.

The greatest care and exactness should be exercised in preparing and measuring the drench. The arsenic should be ordered in packages which do not require breaking or re-weighing and the quantity prepared should correspond to the number of sheep to be drenched. The mixture should be frequently shaken while drenching,   .

(2) *Turpentine drench*—For lung worm (*Filaria bronchialis*) or (*strongylus filaria*).

Rectified oil of turpentine, 1 oz.
Milk or white of egg, 2 ozs.
or Rectified oil of turpentine, Linseed oil and starch gruel of each 1 oz.

Dose.—Grown sheep, 3 ozs.; weaners, 2 ozs.; lambs, $1\frac{1}{2}$ ozs. If the sheep are weak the dose to be proportionately reduced. The turpentine drench has also been found to be very effective for stomach and intestinal worms.

(3) *Thymol drench.*—In view of the great success which has recently attended the treatment of allied forms of intestinal worms in man with thymol, this drug is worthy of a trial for stomach worms in sheep. The dose for a sheep would be from 5 to 20 grains according to age and condition and it should be given dissolved in half an ounce of turpentine and diluted with about two ounces of milk or linseed oil.

Directions for Drenching.—The sheep should be yarded on the evening before the morning on which the drenches are to be given and kept without food. They must be drenched on an empty stomach and kept away from food and water for three hours at least after they are drenched. One drenching will often suffice, but if no improvement occurs repeat in a fortnight. If the sheep continue to show signs of worms drench every two months.

Intra-tracheal Injection for Lung Worm.—This direct method of treating lung worm is certainly very tedious, but equally certainly it is very effective, and may be adopted with advantage over all other methods of treatment when small lots of sheep are concerned or in the case of valuable studs. Its efficiency lies in the fact that the medicaments used have a chance of coming into actual, and therefore destructive, contact with the worms lodged in the air passages. Coughing fits are also promoted by which the worms are dislodged and expelled. The operation is comparatively simple but requires care—otherwise the losses may be considerable.

To operate the sheep is "turned," set on its rump and held between the knees of a standing assistant with its head and neck outstretched. The wool must be carefully "parted" in the middle line of the throat midway down the neck, an incision lengthways of the windpipe and about an inch long is then made with a sharp blade down on to the rings of

the windpipe.   The needle of the syringe is then inserted in a downward
direction in the space between any two rings and the contents of the
syringe injected forcibly towards the lungs.   A dab of sheep dip or
other antiseptic dressing may be applied to the wound after withdrawal
of the syringe.   An ordinary hypodermic syringe of large size may be
used, but if it is fitted (as intra-tracheal syringes are) with short stout
needles the preliminary incision of the skin may be dispensed with, *i.e.*,
in the hands of an expert operator who by practice can hit the windpipe
between the rings every time.

The vermicidal solution to be injected may be compounded as follows :—

(1) Syrup of poppies ·
    Rectified oil of turpentine of each one fluid ounce.
    Pure carbolic acid, ten drops.
    Olive oil, two drams.

Sufficient for eight sheep.   Dose, two drams (1 dessertspoonful).

(2) Rectified oil of turpentine, one ounce.
    Laudanum or chloroform, half an ounce.
    Carbolic acid, pure liquefied, ten drops.
    Olive oil, half an ounce.

Sufficient for eight sheep.   Dose, two drams (1 dessertspoonful).   Half
doses of either prescription for young lambs.   Two-third doses for
weaners.

FUMIGATION OR INHALATION FOR LUNG WORM.—This treatment involves the introduction into the air passages of some gaseous agent which
will have a poisonous effect on the worms lodged there, or by inducing
coughing will cause their expulsion.   It is a rapid method of dealing with
large numbers, as a hundred or two at a time may be subjected to the
treatment.   The process may be illustrated by instancing fumigation with
sulphur, although chlorine gas or volatilized formalin may be used with
equal safety and success.

The sheep are placed in a woolshed or other building, all the openings
into which should be effectively closed.   Bags may be stuffed into air
holes, louvres and other openings, and cracks and crevices in doors, floors,
ceilings, and windows may be pasted over temporarily with paper.   Rock
brimstone or flowers of sulphur is ignited inside the building and kept
burning so giving off sulphurous acid gas (SO_2) .   This is done perhaps
most conveniently by placing the ignited sulphur on an iron plate or
shovel kept at a dull red heat by the flame of a lamp underneath.   It
may be also vaporized by placing it on top of a layer of live wood or
coal ashes on a shovel or plate.   Two or three persons should remain in
the building seated on their haunches at different parts so that they are
practically in the same position as the sheep with regard to the inhalation
of the sulphur flames.   When the fume-laden atmosphere approaches the
unbearable for the men it will be time to throw open the doors and let
the sheep have some fresh air but they may be left in the building (with
open doors) until the fumes have dissipated.   If any of the sheep cough
violently or are otherwise overcome they should be immediately removed
to the outer air and in no event should the inhalation be pushed to the
point of suffocation.   It is better to repeat the process at an interval of
a few days rather than run any undue risk.

THE PIG INDUSTRY.

(Continued from Page 82.)

R. T. Archer, Senior Dairy Inspector.

II.—THE NEED FOR CO-OPERATIVE EFFORT.

DENMARK'S EXAMPLE.

What is the remedy for these unsatisfactory conditions? Co-operation. The results of co-operation in Denmark will surely indicate the lines on which we should act. The trade in that country was entirely controlled by private or proprietary firms until the year 1888, when the first co-operative bacon curing factory was established. The following figures will give a good idea of the results :—

Year.			Number of Co-operative Bacon Factories.	Number of Pigs killed.	Average Price paid for Pigs.		
					£	s.	d.
1888	..	..	..	1	23,400	2	9	0
1889	..	..	..	8	131,500	2	18	0
1893	..	..	..	14	317,780	3	5	0
1894	..	..	..	15	385,700	2	18	0
1895	..	..	..	17	528,800	2	8	0
1896	..	..	..	20	626,850	2	5	0
1897	..	..	..	25	583,400	2	15	0
1900	..	..	..	26	660,000	2	16	0
1901	..	..	..	26	651,000	3	0	0
1902	..	..	..	27	777,200	3	4	6
1903	..	..	..	29	About 800,000	..		

In addition to the co-operative factories, there were 25 private factories. Each factory serves a tract of country about 16 miles in radius, within which the pigs are fattened, and the average number supplied by each farmer per year runs from 10 to 12. They reckon to supply a pig for each cow they milk. In 1902, 777,200 pigs killed by the co-operative factories averaged 129 lbs. in weight. The price realized averaged 64s. 6d., or 6d. per lb. free to the owner.

In the Danish factories no part of the pig is lost, even the bristles are of value. The blood is dried and prepared for feeding horses, cows, and poultry. For the disposal of the cheaper cuts of bacon, liver, sausages, &c., the factories have established shops in their local towns. The tails, feet, and heads nearly all go to Ireland in barrels, while the cured bacon almost wholly goes to Great Britain. The cost per pig of killing and curing averages 2s. 6d., while the charges for freight and selling, in the British markets, &c., come to about 2s. 9d., equal to about ½d. per lb.

Strong evidence of the soundness and prosperity of the pig industry is shown by the increasing numbers of swine in Denmark :—

Year.			Total of Pigs.
1881	..	..	527,000
1888	..	..	771,000
1893	..	..	829,000
1898	..	..	1,168,000
1903	..	..	1,456,699

To complete their wonderful organization, the district factories are each represented on a Central Association of Co-operative Bacon Curers in Copenhagen. Funds of £400 or £500 a year are subscribed by the local factories for running this association, which costs considerably under a farthing per pig.

The duties of the Central Organization are:—

1. To deal with strikes of workmen.
2. To deal with insurance of workmen against accidents.
3. To deal with insurance of bacon to Britain.
This mutual insurance system has resulted in a great saving over the former practice of each factory doing its own insurance.
4. To hold exhibitions of bacon.

The simple method of conducting these exhibitions is worth noting, also the practical steps taken to benefit by the results. The Exhibition Committee of Copenhagen telegraphs at any time, and without notice, to the managers of local factories to forward some sides of bacon, just as they are ready for shipment to the British markets. The judges' decisions are thereafter intimated to the managers of co-operative factories, along with remarks stating whether any defects are due to faults in the manufacture, or to the breeding and quality of pigs.

With this information, managers are enabled to correct and improve their methods, while an expert in pig-breeding is sent by the Central Association to visit the farmers in districts where the quality of pigs is defective, and to instruct them in the breeding and feeding of a better class of animal. Of paramount importance is the fact that no skim milk is allowed by law to leave the creameries or butter factories without being pasteurized. It is believed that this practice has almost eliminated tuberculosis from pigs.

Before a factory is started, it is considered necessary to make sure of a supply of pigs to be regularly delivered, and to obtain security for a sufficient loan to provide buildings, plant, and working capital. Farmers who fail to supply the number of pigs they guarantee are liable, according to the signed conditions of co-operation, to a fine of 11s. 3d. per head on the deficiency, but the fine has seldom been incurred or imposed.

In providing the capital no money is actually raised from the farmers, but is obtained by loan on their personal security from banks and various other sources. "Each for all and all for each" is their motto. At the beginning, some difficulty was experienced in getting farmers to sign such a deed; but, since the benefits of co-operation have become known, farmers are not only willing but anxious to share in all the responsibilities. Only one factory, it is believed, has been unsuccessful, and that was due entirely to the want of a sufficient supply of pigs.

About the beginning of 1903 the Agricultural Department of Ireland sent a representative committee to Denmark to obtain full information with regard to the system adopted by the Danes in the development of their bacon industry. The Canadian Government also sent a delegation, and later a body of Scotchmen visited Denmark for the same purpose.

In the case of the first two countries reference elsewhere proves that, by following the Danish methods, great improvement in their trade was effected, and the relative positions of the produce from these two countries on the British market show that we should be guided by their experience. Although the United States of America produces and exports the greatest quantity of pig products, it will be seen that the prices obtained for the same are very much below what is received by the other countries named, and is sufficient proof that we must aim at the quality produced by Denmark and Ireland.

At a meeting of those interested in the improvement in the condition of trade in pig products in England, as reported in *The Grocer* of 5th March, 1910, Mr. Hannon, who was one of the delegates sent to Denmark, and who has large experience in the trade in Ireland, said:—

There was needed (1) a systematized improvement of breeds; (2) assistance in carrying out experiments to guide the farmer in producing pigs for the curers at a minimum cost; (3) demonstrations to see if food production on the farms for pigs could be extended; and (4) increased facilities for obtaining information on phases of the question.

Mr. W. H. Butt, President of the Bristol Grocers' Association, confirmed what other speakers had said about consumers preferring lean bacon, and stated that there had *been a considerable improvement in Irish bacon in the last five years,* and the breeders there had bred to produce a pig to meet the popular demand.

That improvement in Irish bacon dates from the time the Commission was sent to Denmark to inquire into the methods of breeding, feeding, &c., and may be taken as an additional proof of the lines we should follow.

Roscrea Farmers Co-operative Bacon Factory.

The first farmers' co-operative bacon factory in the United Kingdom was inaugurated at Roscrea, Tipperary, Ireland, in January, 1908, and it was able, under adverse circumstances to show a successful record in its first year.

The Roscrea factory has a nominal capital of £15,000, of which rather less than £12,000 was subscribed, about £7,000 being the outlay for site, buildings, and plant. The initial expenditure left a little over £4,000 for working capital. Experience showed that this was too little, and that the working capital of such a factory, having a capacity of about 750 pigs per week, should be at least £10,000.

At the end of the first year's working, notwithstanding the fact that the capital was limited and that the markets had been unsettled, the balance-sheet showed a gross profit of £4,000. After paying all expenses of working and depreciation there was a credit balance of £308. The experience of the directors of the factory was unique, as they had constantly to decline business which they could have secured if more capital had been available. For the same reason, it is anticipated that, with an additional £5,000 of capital, the gross earnings of the factory would approximate £8,000.

3. ROSCRAE CO-OPERATIVE BACON FACTORY.

Figures like these speak more eloquently than words, and it may now be safely stated that the principle of co-operation in bacon curing has been established in the United Kingdom, and the recognition of this will bear fruit in the immediate future in the general impetus which will thus

4. BLEEDING PASSAGE.

be given to the pig industry, and the general construction of bacon factories in the country as an essential part of agricultural development.

This undertaking is purely co-operative. Each shareholder has to sign a bond under a penalty of 10s. per pig to supply such bacon pigs as he produces and *all* of them to the factory. Every shareholder shares in the profits in the form of a bonus proportionate to the number of pigs he supplies.

Of the 2,800 shareholders the majority were small farmers. As already stated, shareholders sign a guarantee to supply all their pigs of weights required in the bacon trade, to their own factory. This defeats unfair competition, where enhanced prices are offered to induce them to send pigs away.

In constructing the buildings, it was arranged that each department or set of operations should follow in sequence as far as possible. Pigs are landed at the receiving platform where they are weighed alive, and the suppliers can be paid on that basis at once, if they so desire. The dead weight is ascertainable usually the day following delivery, and averages about 25 per cent. less.

After weighing, the pigs are driven into sties, allowed to remain overnight and usually killed next morning.   They are driven one by one into the catching pen, where they are shackled or caught up by means of leg chains, a running noose being formed by means of a chain slipped through a ring; this noose is passed over one hind foot.   The chain is then attached to a hook at the end of a steel rope which is governed by

hand or power hoist. Hoisted to overhead bar in this position, they are slaughtered by sticking in the direction of the heart, letting the blood out quickly. This operation does not take more than one minute.

The carcases are pushed along the overhead bar to the bleeding passage and allowed to hang some little time, and are then pushed off the bar on to the dumping table. This dumping table forms part of what is known as a *slaughtering tack*, which is the main part of the pig abattoir. While on the dumping table, the leg chains are removed, and the carcases are then rolled into a rectangular

5. PIGS HANGING UNDER SINGER.

scalding vat capable of holding some five pigs at once. The vat is partially filled with water at about 180 deg. F., and the carcases are turned round and round until the hair becomes loose.   One by one, they are then tilted on to a scuttling table where they are scraped almost free from hair.   A hook is inserted into the apex of the lower jaw, and the animals suspended to the track bar head upwards.   They are pushed along this bar until they come under the opening of a vertical singeing furnace, which is so constructed that the carcase of the pig may be hoisted through a circular fire, and so the whole carcase is burned or singed. This operation takes only a quarter of a minute, and the carcase is again lowered to the track bar, pre senting a very black and shrivelled appearance. This burning is a great advantage to Wiltshire bacon, giving the bacon a peculiar piquant flavour. The fat under the skin becomes momentarily melted, and subsequently becomes firmer than it would be otherwise.

After leaving the singeing furnace, the carcases are thrown into a cold water bath, cooled, and the sinews of the hind feet exposed, whilst a gambrel is inserted to spread the hind feet apart. By the gambrel the carcases are hoisted to the track bar, where they are scraped quite clean and washed. The intestinal and general offal are removed and taken to a separate apartment to be sorted for various uses. The flake

lard is always left with carcases and is weighed in together with head and feet. This forms the *dead weight*, which is sometimes taken while the carcase is warm, and sometimes when cold. The difference allowed between warm and cool weight is 4 lbs. Cooling in the open air usually occupies about 6 hours. After weighing, the carcase is split up into sides, the head and fore feet severed, and the lard removed. The head and feet are chilled and put into pickle to be cured.

Curing. — The sides are pushed into the hanging house, in case they have not already been allowed to hang, after which they are pushed

6. DISEMBOWELLING DEPARTMENT.

along the track bar into the chill room, where they are kept at a temperature of 38 deg. F. until, on inserting a meat thermometer into the gammon end, it registers 40 deg. F. On the average, it takes 36 hours to reach this degree of coolness. When it has been attained, the sides are taken into the curing cellar, where finally they are trimmed and at once pumped with a recognised pickle in fourteen different places. They are then laid on the cellar floor and stacked in tiers ten sides deep. The cellar is kept at a temperature of about 42 deg. F. Each side is covered over, first of all, with an equal mixture of curing antiseptic and saltpetre, in

7. VIEW IN HANGING HOUSE AFTER BRANDING OF THE SIDES HAS TAKEN PLACE.

a finely granulated state, and on top of this is placed a thick layer of salt.

For mild cured bacon, this is all the curing that is required, and in about 14 days the process is complete, after which the bacon is taken out and washed in cold water, and then should be in a state for selling as green bacon. If wanted as dried bacon, it must be hung in a drying

8. CURING ROOM, SHOWING PICKLING PUMP.

room for 3 days in a temperature of 90 deg. F., and is then available as pale dried bacon.   If it is wanted as *smoked* bacon, it must be hung

9   LARD ROOM.

3 days in a smoke stove where the temperature does not exceed 90 deg. F., and where a thick volume of smoke is produced from hardwood saw-dust, *i.e.*, oak, ash, or beech.

10. REFRIGERATING MACHINE.

These operations refer to what is technically known as Wiltshire bacon, *i.e.*, whole side bacon.   In conjunction with the production of

Wiltshire bacon, are sausage-making, lard-refining, hams, middles, rolls, or other special products. Competent management and a staff acquainted with the various operations are indispensable.

The writer is indebted to Mr. Loudon M. Douglas, the authority previously referred to, for the descriptive matter and illustrations of the Roscrea Factory.

MODEL SIDES OF BACON.

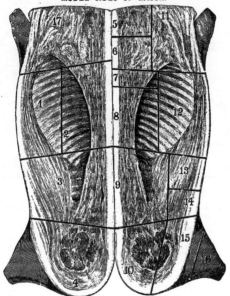

11. A TYPICAL WILTSHIRE FLITCH.

British Dairy Farmers' Association Comparative Prices.

							d.	
1. Streaky Quarter	..	..	..	..	..	..	11	per lb.
2. Rib Quarter ..	..	..	..	..	..	..	11	,,
3. Middle Quarter	..	..	..	..	..	..	8½	,,
4. Ham Quarter ..	..	..	..	..	..	..	8½	,,
5. End of Neck ..	..	..	..	..	..	..	7½	,,
6. Middle of Neck	..	..	..	..	..	..	8½	,,
7. Thick Back and Sides ..	..	..	..	..	..	10	,,
8. Prime Back and Ribs ..	..	..	..	..	..	11	,,
9. Loin ..	..	..	..	..	..	..	10	,,
10. Fillet	..	..	..	..	..	..	10	,,
11. Shoulder ..	..	..	..	..	..	..	8	,,
12. Prime Streaky	..	..	..	..	..	..	11	,,
13. Thin Streaky ..	..	..	..	..	..	..	8½	,,
14. Flank	..	..	..	..	..	..	6½	,,
15. Middle of Gammon	..	..	..	..	..	..	11	,,
16. Knuckle of Gammon	..	..	..	..	..	..	7	,,
17. Fore end ..	..	..	..	..	..	..	6	,,

WEIGHTS OF PARTS OF A PIG OF TOTAL DEAD WEIGHT (WITHOUT OFFAL) OF 194 LBS.

							lbs.	oz.
Bones from back (chine)	..	..	..	..	..	..	5	12
Blade bone	..	..	..	..	..	..	2	4
Steaks	..	..	..	..	..	..	2	4
Cuttings ..	..	..	..	..	..	..	2	0
Kidneys ..	..	..	..	..	..	..	0	6
Flake fat	..	..	..	..	..	..	7	0
Fat (intestinal, &c.)	..	..	..	..	..	..	2	4
Feet	..	..	..	..	..	..	4	0
Blades	..	..	..	..	..	..	0	8
Skull (upper part of head)	..	..	..	..	..	..	14	8
Chap (lower jaw) ..	..	..	..	..	..	..	2	8
Two sides	..	..	..	..	..	..	150	0
Total	..	..	..	..	..	..	193	6

STANDARD OF EXCELLENCE FOR JUDGING A CARCASE OF PORK.

1. Dressing of carcase	5
2. General appearance and firmness of flesh and fat	10
3. Proportion of meat to bone	15
On splitting the carcase into halves, the following points are to be noted :—	
4. Plumpness of legs	20
5. Thickness of loin and smallness of proportion of fat to lean	20
6. Streakiness of belly part	10
7. Fleshiness of forequarter..	15
8. Smallness of head	5
	100

(To be continued.)

PROPAGATION OF FRUIT TREES.

(Continued from page 107.)

C. F. Cole, Orchard Supervisor.

TOPPING.

The practice of topping growing buds at a certain period to encourage branched growth, and then trimming away superfluous growths not required to form a head, is considered by many to be unnecessary. Others maintain that it is a faulty practice, the forced branched growths not being suitable to prune upon, so as form the future base of the tree when planting out permanently in the orchard, owing to the wood being immature.

Topping, when performed at the proper time upon certain kinds and varieties of growing buds, is decidedly an advantage. Under normal conditions a tree is produced, the stability of which is unquestionably sound and equal in all respects to a two-year-old tree produced from a yearling straight.

With many varieties topping is not an advantage, and should not be practised. Amongst these are apples, cherries, pears, and plums (Japanese and cherry plums excepted).

2)9 ş.   G

Before practising this operation a thorough knowledge of the varieties and their habit of growth is necessary, the climatic conditions of the district, and the action of the soil with regard to growth. When performed upon unsuitable varieties short stunted growths are generally encouraged. Such growths are unsuitable to prune upon. With varieties that are suitable and branch freely of their own accord, topping will need to be restricted. Only those buds growing freely and strongly should be operated upon, *e.g.,* take the Jonathan apple under favorable conditions. Growing buds of this variety branch freely and strongly, yet there are many buds of this variety unsuitable for topping to be found in the nursery row. Those with a weak tendency should be left untopped. If operated upon, weakly branch growth is encouraged.

Almonds, apricots, nectarines, peaches, and plums (Japanese and cherry) should be topped when the buds have made about 16 to 18 in.

66. TOPPING AND TRIMMING.
a. Untreated. *b.* Result of correct treatment.

of growth. This check will be the means of causing the rapidly ascending sap to excite the buds upon the stem into strong branch growths. These growths will be dealt with when trimming. Fig. 66B shows the result of topping a growing peach bud in October. The bud was trimmed in early November, and photographed late in the same month. This young tree is of sound type. Fig. 66A shows a growing peach bud untopped carrying thin and weakly branch growths. Compare this with Fig. 66B which is the same age, the same variety (Hale's early), and worked upon the same kind of stock and growing in the same row. Cherries, if not branching of their own accord, should not be topped to force them to do so.

Fig. 67A shows a strong young apple-bud growing and branching freely, the variety is Rome Beauty. By topping such a type, and removing the lower branch growths, the terminal buds will break, making strong growths in a few weeks. Fig. 67B shows the result of such treatment. This young tree, two months' growth from the dormant bud, will by the autumn be a strong and well-developed tree carrying thoroughly matured branch growths and in every respect a most suitable type to plant out in the orchard.

Late topping should be avoided; from the middle of October to the middle of November is the best time to operate upon deciduous fruits.

The reader will gather from the foregoing remarks and illustrations that, if the method of topping is intelligently practised upon certain kinds of fruits and varieties suitable for such treatment, a sound type of branched yearling trees is produced. But, if practised indiscriminately,

67. TRIMMING.

a. Untreated. *b.* Result of correct treatment.

unsuitable trees, inferior to untopped ones of the same variety will be produced.

TRIMMING.

Trimming growing buds carrying branch growths upon the stem is a necessary and important operation. If the superfluous shoots are not removed from the stem, the basal ones, being the stronger, will utilize the greater quantity of the nourishment and sap flow. By so doing, the terminal portion is weakened. The result is that a most unsuitable tree is produced.

Shortly after the young growing buds have been topped in the nursery row, and when the lateral growths are long enough to operate upon, all shoots that are not required to form the head growths should be carefully removed. If using a sharp knife, cut them close to the stem so that they will not break again from the basal part.

Soft shoots upon certain varieties may be removed with the thumb and finger. If the propagator wishes to produce a sound type of yearling .

tree he must now take the opportunity.   This is the last stage in propagating a sound and useful type of tree.

Stone fruits will first require attention; remove all branches, leaving only those to form the head (see Fig. 66B).

With many varieties of seed fruits that have been topped, only three to four of the terminal buds make branched growth.   Where this occurs. no trimming is necessary.   Again, many varieties branch well before the stem growth is of any length.   Such types should be topped at a bud when the necessary height is attained, and all branched growths removed.   The removal of these growths will give the terminal portion a greater supply of nourishment.   Fig. 67A shows such a type, the arrow marking where to top at bud.   Fig. 67B shows the result of this treatment a few weeks later.   Fig. 68A is a type more often found amongst almonds, apricots, nectarines, peaches, and plums.   This type should not

68. TRIMMING.

a. Young tree being ill-formed. *b* Correct treatment.

be neglected.   If so, the strong growing lower branch will utilize the greater quantity of ascending sap and nourishment, and starve that portion of the stem above, also the branch growths necessary to form a well-balanced head.   Such a growth should be removed close to the stem as shown in Fig. 68B.   If neglected an ill-shaped tree will be the result, besides being a most unsuitable type to prune the following winter.

TREATMENT OF STOCKS.

Stocks grown for budding purposes should be attended to early in the vegetative period and before the superfluous shoots are of any length. The stocks should not be allowed to carry heavy head growths.   The heavier the head growth, the greater the draw upon the soil.

Some stocks require different treatment from others at the beginning. Apricot and peach stocks, if grown direct from the stone for working upon, should be stripped with the thumb and finger when the shoots upon the stems have just started growth.   Perform this operation by taking hold of the top of the stock with the one hand and with the other start three parts of the way up the stock, stripping down to the ground.   Remove all shoots and leaves.

With planted-out peach stocks, treated the same as Fig. 28, all shoots excepting one should be removed.   This is left to trim and bud upon. When removing any shoots upon the stocks below ground level, do not break them off.   First remove the soil, and then rub or cut off close to the stock.

Following the stripping treatment it will be necessary to keep all shoots rubbed off upon the stems, and the head growths reduced to a few branches.

Apples, cherries, pears, and plum stocks should be trimmed to carry not more than three branched growths.   When trimming stocks, do not rub off any shoots that are hard or are getting hard, as there is a risk of tearing the bark.   Remove with a knife, cutting close to the stem. Cut all shoots close to, not $\frac{1}{8}$ in. or $\frac{1}{4}$ in. from, the stem.

The stocks should be kept well cultivated in order to conserve the moisture in the soil.   If irrigation is possible, keep the stocks growing. Do not allow them to get a check.   Pear stocks should be kept growing well from the beginning, as they will be the first of the deciduous fruits to be budded.   If they have not made suitable growth by January, there is very little likelihood of them being suitable for budding the same summer.

If the weather is dry it is an advantage to water all stocks, if possible, a few days before budding.   If the budded stocks are allowed to suffer from the want of moisture before the autumn, there is always a risk of the buds dying out, even if unity with the stock is perfect.

(To be continued.)

VINE DISEASES IN FRANCE.

(*Continued from page* 119.)

F. de Castella, Government Viticulturist.

FUNGICIDE SPRAYS.

OXYCHLORIDE OF COPPER.

The introduction of this novel fungicide is due to Professor Chuard, of Lausanne University (Switzerland), who was anxious to find some spraying substance capable of permitting a reduction in the quantity of copper annually absorbed by the soil.*   The use of verdet already permits a

---

* Analysis shows that as the result of twenty years' use of copper sprays, the surface foot of soil in the vineyards of the Lausanne "Station Viticole" contained 3½ milligrammes per kilogramme (3·5 parts per 100,000).   This was rather more than half of the total quantity sprayed.   In some other vineyards higher quantities were found ; in one case as much as 112 milligrammes (11·2 parts per 100,000).—*Comptes rendus de l'academie des Sciences*, Paris, 29th March, 1910.

saving, as pointed out above, but an even greater saving is possible by the use of oxychloride. To quote Professor Chuard—

This product, now on the market, is obtained directly from copper, in the electrolytic manufacture of soda or potash by the Granier process, which is based on the use of metallic copper anodes.

It is a pale green, non-crystalline powder, insoluble in water, but capable of remaining in suspension sufficiently to permit of its regular application. It possesses remarkable adherence, a fairly general property, in fact, of oxychlorides.

This product contains 50 per cent. of copper. At the rate of 500 grammes per hectolitre (1 lb. to 20 gals.) it has regularly given results at least equal to those obtained from a mixture based on 2 per cent. copper sulphate. This means a reduction of 50 per cent. in the quantity of copper used.

He explains the efficacy of reduced doses of this substance as follows :—

Oxychloride of copper exposed to air and moisture, as it is after its application on the leaf, undergoes oxidation which gives rise, progressively, to small quantities of soluble cupric chloride. This formation . . . . of a readily ionizable compound, explains in the clearest and most satisfactory manner the superiority of copper oxychloride over hydrate or carbonate,* those much less dissociable forms under which copper is to be found in copper-containing sprays.

Apart from theoretical considerations, however, oxychloride has been extensively tried on a practical scale and has given excellent results. It appears, in fact, to be the recent introduction which has most to recommend it from all points of view. In addition to its use as a spray, it constitutes an excellent fungicide powder when used in the dry state. As we shall see presently, copper-containing powders are becoming very popular, not as substitutes for, but as a complement to, spray mixtures.

Substitutes for Copper.

Other metallic salts besides those of copper possess fungicide properties, and some of them have been tried for the treatment of fungus vine diseases of the vine. A few years back, mixtures containing mercury were recommended, and, after trial, abandoned as being less satisfactory than the copper sprays they were intended to replace.

More recently still, silver has been suggested as a substitute for copper. Though the employment of a noble metal for spraying purposes might seem extravagant at first sight, it is economically feasible; the deadly effect of silver salts on fungi rendering possible the use of very much weaker sprays. The strength recommended is $\frac{1}{3}$ oz. of nitrate of silver to 10 gals. of water. It is made into a mixture with soap, of which $2\frac{1}{2}$ ozs. are mixed with the above quantities. This silver soap spray possesses excellent wetting power, which renders it suitable for treatment directed against mildew of the bunch (*Rot Gris*); the greasy nature of the new-formed fruit causing it to be difficult to properly wet with Bordeaux mixture. It appears to have more effect on bunch mildew than against the same fungus on the leaves. It has been tried on a practical scale with contradictory results, and does not appear likely to displace copper as the basis of fungicide sprays for general use.

Copper-Containing Powders.

Being much easier and cheaper to apply, powders were long since extensively experimented with as substitutes for liquid sprays. It

---

* In copper-soda mixtures the copper is present in the form of hydrated carbonate.

is now generally recognised that they cannot, when used alone, be relied upon as efficient protection, and for a good many years little has been heard of their use. Since the disastrous mildew visitations of the 1910 summer, they have once more come to the fore, not, however, as substitutes for, but as a complement to the usual copper sprays. An application of suitable powder, applied with the bellows or, preferably, with the knapsack machine, in the same way as sulphur, immediately after spraying, very considerably increases the efficiency of the protection afforded by the latter. It will be readily understood that a powder can easily be blown into the interior of the vine, thus making it possible to reach parts which it would be difficult to get at with the liquid spray.

Numerous forms of copper-containing powders are now for sale in France. Some are mixtures of sulphur and sulphate of copper, so that the same application may serve to combat oidium as well as mildew. In other cases the copper sulphate is simply mixed with an inert substance, serving to dilute it and to enable it to be ground into a finer powder than would otherwise be possible. Such is *Sulphosteatite* a very popular preparation which is a finely powdered mixture of talc and copper sulphate. In some powders, again, the copper is in the form of oxide, or of acetate (verdet), whilst the oxychloride of copper, previously referred to as a spray, constitutes an excellent powder for use in the dry state. These latter substances have the advantage of not burning the foliage. If the copper is present in the form of sulphate it is recommended to add a certain quantity of lime before use to prevent damage to the foliage.

Conclusion.

The above is a brief review of modern French and Swiss opinions on the whole question of fungicide sprays, so far as their composition is concerned. It will be remarked that they do not agree on all points with modern English views as stated in the *Eighth Report of the Woburn Experimental Fruit Farm* (1908) which was reviewed by Mr. McAlpine, late Vegetable Pathologist for Victoria, in the *Journal* for November, 1910. The chief difference consists in the proportion of copper considered necessary in order to secure adequate protection. Even with verdet and oxychloride, which permit a reduction in the quantity of copper used, very much stronger mixtures are recommended than the 10 ozs. to 50 gals. provided for by the Woburn formula.

A point of the most vital importance, of greater importance, perhaps, than the composition of the spraying mixture, is the absolute necessity for early treatment if protection is to be achieved. *The first spraying must be carried out before there are any visible signs of the disease.* This was emphatically impressed upon the Societé des Agriculteurs de France by M. Capus in February last, as follows:

. . . For the defence of leaf, bunch and grape, one moment alone is of importance : that of invisible invasion or contamination, after which the enemy being in occupation, any intervention by the vine-grower is rendered futile. What we must guard against by treatment is thus, not the visible invasion, but the hidden invasion.

The exhaustive inquiry conducted by *La Revue de Viticulture* on the results obtained during the disastrous 1910 summer led to the following conclusions* :—

The efficacy of copper salts in the treatment of mildew does not admit of any doubt, provided such treatment is applied at a suitable time.   The failures which occurred in 1910 were due in the majority of cases to late treatments, to treatments which were not plentiful enough, to incomplete , treatments not followed up by application of powders, or to treatments with liquids which did not contain a sufficient dose of copper.

As the result of its inquiry, *La Revue* issued the following practical instructions as to what should constitute efficient treatment :—

1. Spray with copper mixtures *in a preventive way* before mildew appears in the region, no matter what the length of the vine shoots may be.

2. Repeat such spraying, *in an opportune manner*, every time the vine is in a receptive state; that is, each time that a fall in barometric pressure corresponds with a fall in temperature.

3. Execute sprayings *very rapidly* over the whole vineyard, irrespective of weather; even if it be raining.

4. Spray abundantly and see that the workmen apply the liquid to all organs of the vine; gangers to follow up workmen instead of walking in front of them.

5. Each spraying to be simultaneously carried out on each side of each row.

6. In districts where vines are trellised, they should be tied up as early as possible.

7. As soon as the flowers are formed, spraying to be followed, whilst the vines are still wet, by sulphuring with sulphur containing 10 per cent. of copper sulphate or applications of powders of talc, &c., containing 5 to 10 per cent. of copper sulphate; these powders to be spread in a cloud in such a way as to cover the whole surface of the grapes; such applications to be made between sprayings, as soon as setting is over.   After the fruit commences to colour apply no more sulphur, but only copper-containing powders.

8. Vine-growers should make the necessary arrangements to assure rapid execution of copper treatments.

9. Vines should be kept in a good state of vegetation, so that they may offer greater resistance to the attacks of mildew.

BEE-KEEPING IN ·VICTORIA.

(Continued from page 115.)

F. R. Beuhne, Bee Expert.

III.—RACES OF BEES.

Of some twenty known varieties of the honey bee (Apis mellifica) four only have been introduced and established in Australia, viz., the Black Bee; the Italian; the Cyprian; and the Carniolan.

The Black Bee, it has been stated, was first brought to Tasmania from Great Britain in 1824. From Tasmania some hives were taken to Sydney and from thence the variety has spread pretty well over the whole of Australia.   It is hardy and will fly on cold and wet days when some

---

* Raymond Brunet, Report read at the Tours Viticultural Congress, 14th January, 1911.

of the other races will not leave the hive, and it commences brood rearing very early in spring—almost in midwinter. As in the raising of brood, pollen, the fertilising dust of flowers, is required, the black bee is a most important factor in the fertilisation of the blossoms of the earliest flowering kinds of fruit trees. In cool districts, or when the pollination of fruit blossom is of greater importance than the yield of honey, the black bee or one of its crosses with Italian or Cyprian is probably the best kind of bee to keep. On the other hand, Blacks, although commencing to breed early, do not maintain a high rate of re-production for long and, where the main honey flow occurs in summer, do not give as good a yield of honey per hive as Italians. They are excessive swarmers, more excitable when handled than the other races, offer less resistance to foulbrood, and often allow wax moth grubs to infest their combs.

The Italian Bee was introduced in the seventies. It is of somewhat lighter build than the Black and has three yellow or light orange coloured bands across the abdomen. It is gentle and little inclined to sting when properly handled. Italian queens, even those imported direct from Italy, vary greatly in colour, some are quite yellow, and some almost as dark as black queens; whilst others have dark and yellow bands. The colour of the queen is therefore no indication of purity of race, the best proof of which is the uniform markings of all her worker progeny. Italian bees cling tightly to the combs when the frames of combs are handled, while black bees or hybrids often drop off without shaking. Pure bred Italians, and, to a lesser degree their crosses with others, are more immune from foulbrood, and rarely allow wax moth grubs to get into their combs. They begin breeding later in spring than Blacks, but at the approach of warm weather soon overtake the latter and maintain a greater worker force throughout the season. A variation of the Italian is the Golden Italian which was secured by select breeding for colour, or by crossing with Cyprians. It has five yellow bands instead of three—practically the whole of the abdomen is yellow. Bees of this variety are more susceptible to cold and wet than the three banded Italians and rather predisposed to Bee-Paralysis. Italians, when pure, do not cap their combs so white as black bees do, and are therefore less suitable for the production of comb honey.

The Cyprian in appearance, and many other respects, resembles the Italian. It is somewhat slimmer, the yellow rings are of a deeper shade, and the fuzz rings of the segments whiter. Cyprians are good breeders, sometimes continuing brood rearing when a honey-flow has stopped till all stores are consumed. They raise a large number of fine queen cells at swarming time or when made queenless. Their undesirable characteristic is viciousness during a dearth of nectar, when even the use of smoke, so effective with other races, will not subdue them. As they are not superior to Italians in honey gathering they are not desirable, and not many are now kept in Victoria.

The Carniolan is one of the more recent introductions, in appearance and habits resembles the black bee, from which it is distinguished by the greyish colour of the segment rings. Carniolans are excessive swarmers, as gentle as Italians when pure, but owing to their close resemblance to blacks it is difficult to maintain purity of race. Taking the experience of the largest honey producers of this State for guidance the three banded Italians can be recommended as the best bees to keep for honey production.

HANDLING OF BEES.

The sting of the bee is an important factor in preventing over production of honey. There are many persons who have an almost unreasonable fear of bees, or, rather of getting stung, and yet there are very few people to whom a sting causes more than a sharp pain for a short time and some discomfort through swelling of the affected part. Both pain and swelling become less and less after a number of stings have been received and the seasoned beekeeper, while reducing the number of stings he receives to a minimum by observing certain rules, takes little notice of the stings he does receive beyond removing them promptly. There are, however, some individuals to whom a sting causes serious pain and protracted discomfort, and to whom bees have a lasting dislike—attacking them whenever they come near hives. Such people should have nothing to do with bees.

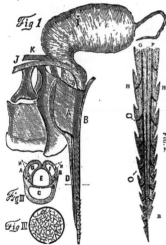

Most, however, after being stung a number of times become more or less immune, even though the first few stings caused considerable pain and swelling. With the right strain of bees; an understanding of their habits; correct methods of handling; and a knowledge of irritating causes the largest apiary can be run without more than an occasional sting being received.

Of late years bee stings have been used by medical men for the cure of certain forms of rheumatism. That the poison of the sting has no lasting injurious effect upon the human system seems evident from the fact that many prominent men who have lived amongst bees all their lives have attained to extreme age, *e.g.*, Dr. Dzierszon, Rev. Langstroth, Dr. C. C. Miller, A. T. Root, and others.

To avoid stings as much as possible one should dress in light coloured clothes, bees have a rooted objection to anything black, and more so when it is rough or fuzzy The odours of such things as camphor, kerosene, turpentine, eucalyptus oil, carbolic acid, lysol, dogs, horses, ants, or meat, on the hands or clothes of the operator, or anywhere near the hive, will cause bees to sting. In their attacks on trespassers (as in their search of nectar) bees are largely guided by the sense of smell. The odour of flowers attracts them to the spot where the flowers grow, while the sense of sight locates the blossom.

When approaching a hive one should walk lightly and avoid standing in the line of flight of the bees leaving the hive or returning to it. Before opening the hive blow a whiff of smoke from the smoker in at the entrance, and another one or two over the top of the frames as soon as the hive cover is raised sufficiently. When these precautions are taken there need be little fear of stinging unless the bees are of a vicious strain, in which case the queen should be removed and one from a gentler stock introduced. There are, however, occasions when even the best tempered bees will sting more or less viciously. For instance, when a honey flow has suddenly ceased and bees have had access to honey other than the nectar in flowers; or when a colony has become hopelessly queenless, which means that they have no queen and no brood to raise one from. The remedy in the first case is never to allow bees access to honey outside the hive, and not to open hives when robber bees are seen hovering round. In the second, give the queenless colony a comb of brood from another hive, or introduce a queen.

To reduce the effect of a sting to a minimum it should be quickly removed, when very little of the poison will have entered the puncture. The sting itself is a sharp-pointed and barbed hollow shaft connected with the poison sac in the body of the bee. When the sting has entered the rubberlike human skin it cannot be withrawn on account of the barbs, and in the effort of the bee to free itself the sting with the poison bag, and the actuating muscles attached, is torn from the abdomen. The muscles may be seen to continue working sometimes for many seconds after the sting has become detached from the bee and it is therefor advisable to immediately remove it from the skin. This is best done by scraping it away with the fingernail or if both hands are engaged rubbing it off on your clothes. On no account should a sting be picked off with the finger tips because that cannot be done without pressing the poison bag and injecting the whole of its contents into the skin.

To neutralise the effects of a sting a number of remedies are recommended. The blue bag is the most commonly advocated cure—I am not at all sure whether green or yellow would not do as well.

Ammonia is certainly more effective, but it has the disadvantage of irritating the bees, and more stings are likely to be the result. Washing the part stung with soap and water allays irritation, whilst if many stings have been received bathing with hot water will diffuse the poison, lessen the pain, and reduce the swelling. For the average individual the best thing to do is to quickly remove the sting and think no more about it.

(To be continued.)

ORCHARD AND GARDEN NOTES.

E. E. Pescott, Principal, Horticultural School, Burnley.

The Orchard.

Green Manure.

As emphasized in last month's notes, the importance of a cover crop for green manure should not be overlooked. Where the physical properties of the soil require improving, or where the soil needs humus, this class of crop is an urgent necessity.

The sowing of the crop should not be delayed, so that a good herbage may be produced before the cold of winter stops the growth. It is generally found that it is far better to secure as good a growth as possible in the autumn.

Cultivation.

Late in the month, or early in April, a start may be made with the autumn ploughing. Advantage should be taken of the first rains to get this work done.

The present season has been entirely opposite to that of last year, when, summer and early autumn rains were abundant, and the first opportunity must be taken to open up the soil to let the moisture in.

Planting.

It is advisable to open up and prepare early the new areas for plant- ing. If at all possible, the soil should be well aerated and sweetened' before planting. It is possible to grow young trees in freshly opened soil, but the general experience is against such work, it being preferable to have· the soil as sweet as possible for the young orchard. In anticipation of planting, the soil at first need only be ploughed roughly, and it should not: be afterwards harrowed.

Strawberries.

Strawberries may be planted during the month. If planted early, they become established this season, and so are enabled to bear a light crop in the springtime. Strawberries require good soil ; new soil, or old grass land' is always preferable.

In planting, ample room should be left for cultivation between the rows, as all weeds should be kept down.

Pests.

No codlin-moth-affected, or diseased fruit of any kind should be left: on the ground after the crop has been gathered. These should all be destroyed by boiling.

Rust infested plum and peach leaves, as well as all foliage of stone- fruits that have been attacked by this and other fungus diseases, such as shot hole, &c., should be burned if possible. This will minimize the possibility of future attacks.

The same treatment should be given to foliage where either red spider or the bryobia mite have been in evidence.

Vegetable Garden.

Autumn weeds must be kept out of the kitchen garden. These rapidly grow, and remain as robbers right through till springtime. It is doubtful whether any chemical means should be taken to keep the weeds in check in this section. Both red oil emulsion and the lime-sulphur wash have been used for this purpose ; but the work is only in an experimental stage, and this treatment cannot be generally recommended. It will be best for the present to resort to hoeing or to hand weeding.

The section should be well dug over for planting the winter crops. Before digging, a light sprinkling of bone dust, and a good top dressing of stable manure should be spread on the surface. These may then be dug in, as they provide humus for the soil.

Large plots should be avoided in winter ; where such occur, a path should be run down the centre. This will provide more efficient drainage. The beds too may be more raised than in the summer time.

Early onions may be planted out in the beds, and if not already done, onion seeds should be planted at once.

All classes of seedlings may be planted out ; and seeds of lettuce, early peas, beet, carrot, radish, cabbage, cauliflower, and swede turnip may be sown.

Asparagus beds should be cleaned out and cut down as soon as the berries begin to colour. Celery rows should be kept earthed up ; rhubarb beds should be given a dressing of manure to encourage the coming winter crop, and new rhubarb plantations may now be established.

Flower Garden.

The hot dry weather has made havoc in some flower gardens, and, as a result of this weather, red spider has been prevalent on some succulent and herbaceous plants. These should be destroyed, particularly where dahlias are growing ; or a good nicotine spraying should be given if the plants are to be retained.

Chrysanthemums, roses, and dahlias will now all be coming into bloom ; and as these show their bloom buds, they should be fed with liquid manure weekly.

All classes of spring flowering bulbs, as well as hardy annual, biennial, and perennial seeds, should be planted and sown.

Roses should be watched for mildew attacks, and the sulphur should be freely used for this. Plantings of shrubs and trees may now be made, and wherever flowering shrubs have ceased to bloom, they may be pruned. Frequent cultivation and watering will be necessary, especially if the weather continues hot and dry.

WHEAT AND ITS CULTIVATION.

(Continued from page 101.)

A. E. V. Richardson, M.A., B.Sc. (Agric.) Agricultural Superintendent.

II.—ITS STRUCTURE AND NUTRITION.

One of the most interesting chapters in the history of agricultural science is that relating to the discovery of the food requirements of plants. More than a century of careful scientific investigation was necessary to establish the fundamental facts of plant nutrition and on this basic know-

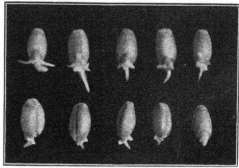

7. GERMINATING WHEAT GRAINS.

ledge the superstructure of modern agricultural science rests. The aim of the present article is to supply a simple account of the more important of the facts of plant nutrition by using our staple farm crop as an illustration.

8. LONGITUDINAL SECTION
THROUGH THE ROOTCAP OF A
YOUNG WHEAT ROOT.

In the preceding article we noted that the wheat kernel consists of three distinct portions (1) Embryo or germ (2) Protective coats (3) Endosperm—the latter consisting mainly of starch and serving as reserve material for nourishing the young plant.

To bring about the germination of this kernel three factors are necessary, namely (1) moisture, (2) air (3) warmth. Under these stimulating agencies the germ soon enlarges and the plumule and radicle bursting through the pericarp form respectively the miniature stem and the root of the young plant.

The first supply of food for the young plant is derived from the reserve materials of the endosperm. As these reserves of food, however, are insoluble in water, they are manifestly incapable of passing out of the cell walls in which they are enclosed. They must be brought into a condition in which they may diffuse readily from cell to cell. This transformation is effected by the chemical activity of a substance called diastase, which is secreted by the epithelial cells of the scutellum (*vide* p. 99, Fig. 3).

Diastase belongs to a class of bodies called unorganized ferments or enzymes and a very small amount of diastase is able to transform practically an unlimited amount of starch into a soluble form. It is diastase which is responsible for the conversion of the starch of the germinating barley grain into maltose— one of the sugars—in the manufacture of malt. This diastase transforms the starch of the grain into maltose which being soluble diffuses from cell to cell until it reaches the growing points of the developing embryo and supplies it with some of the nourishment necessary to its growth.

Similarly, the protein matter of the endosperm, which, like the

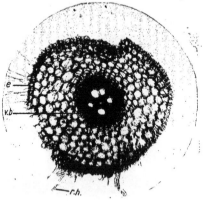

9. TRANSVERSE SECTION OF A YOUNG WHEAT ROOT SHOWING ROOT HAIRS (*r.h.*), VASCULAR BUNDLE (*v.b*), EPIDERMIS (*e*), AND GROUND TISSUE.

starch, is insoluble in water, is acted on by a ferment present in the grain, and is broken down into diffusible proteids called peptones. These soluble peptones, as well as other nitrogenous compounds of lesser importance (amides and amido-acids) diffuse from cell to cell and nourish the growing tissues of the young embryo. It is not long before the reserves of food in the seed are exhausted, and henceforth the young plant must lead an independent existence. At this stage an examination of the root system will reveal several interesting features.

Along the greater portions of the roots, minute delicate fibrils will be observed. These are the tender root hairs which push their way through the minute interstices between the soil particles and apply themselves

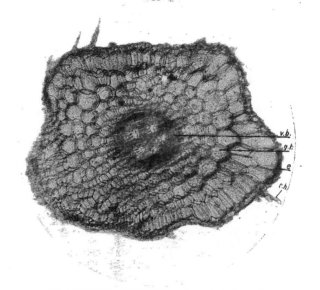

10. TRANSVERSE SECTION OF WHEAT ROOT (X 270).

closely to the uneven edges of the soil grains. Microscopical examination proves them to be long tubular appendages—mere delicate prolongations of the epidermis. The epidermis forms the external layer of the root, and, as may be seen in Fig. 10, it is composed of cells closely packed together with no interstitial spaces or openings of any kind. In this respect, as will be shown later, it differs markedly from the epidermis of the leaf. From this absence of openings it will be clearly apparent that the plant, so far as the root system is concerned, is quite incapable of appropriating food of a solid character from the soil. Whatever nutrients are obtained from the soil, therefore, must be liquid or gaseous in character. Now the particles that compose a normal soil in good condition are very irregular in shape, and are invested with a film of water. This film of moisture surrounding each soil particle is really a very dilute solution containing various substances dissolved from the mineral constituents of the soil. It is this film surrounding each soil particle which is the source of the plant food obtained from the soil. The mode of entry of this dilute solution to the epidermal cells of the root may be illustrated by a very simple experiment.

If a lamp chimney covered over one end with a piece of bladder or of parchment be partially filled with strong brine, and then placed in a vessel of water, the two liquids will diffuse merely by the thin membrane. Under these circumstances, each of the liquids will diffuse through the membrane and mix with the liquid on the other side. The attraction for water inwards will be greater the stronger the brine. The movement will continue until the liquids on both sides of the diaphragm have the same composition.

This process is called osmosis, and each cell in the epidermal layer of the root is a small osmotic apparatus. The cell sap corresponds to the salt solution, the cell wall and protoplasm to the diaphragm or the bladder separating the liquids, and the soil solution on the surface of the soil particles corresponds to water in the vessel. But there is one important difference to be borne in mind. While the protoplasm of the cell readily allows the soil water bearing in solution plant food to diffuse inwards and mix

11. EPIDERMIS OF ROOT OF FEDERATION WHEAT (X 270).

with the cell sap it refuses to allow the bulk of the dissolved substances in the cell sap to diffuse outwards. The osmosis of plant nutrition is therefore a controlled osmosis, the control being exercised by the living protoplasm of the cell.

The density or concentration of the cell sap must on fertile soil be always greater than that of the dilute solution investing the soil particles, so that the solutions outside may be carried inside the cell and tend to make it tight with water or turgid. The solutions which penetrate the epidermal cells by osmosis, pass from cell to cell in the root tissue by the same process. In the lower types of plants, such as the algæ, which are composed entirely of simple cellular tissue, the movement of water within the plant may be accounted for by osmosis alone

In the higher plants the transference of water from cell to cell by osmotic agencies alone would be far too slow to keep pace with the water requirements of the leaves. Specially developed structures are therefore found in these plants, and serve as conducting media whereby the water taken in at the root finds its way rapidly to the leaf. Fig. 10 shows a cross section of a young root of Federation wheat. Several delicate root hairs (*r.h.*) will be observed, each forming simply an elongated cell of the epidermis. In the centre of the root is the axillary vascular bundle (*v.b.*) which runs throughout the length of the root and ultimately merges into similar structures in the stem.

Fig. 15 is a longitudinal section through one of the vascular bundles of the stem.

Each bundle consists, mainly, of a series of elongated cells with ligni-fied thickened cell walls, and a variety of long cylindrical vessels forming continuous open tubes, with and without spiral thickenings. These vessels originally contained protoplasm, but during the course of growth the protoplasm was used for thickening the cell walls, and the matured vessels are merely long tubes specially adapted for con-ducting water.

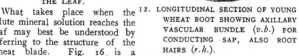

The dilute solution of mineral plant food, which has diffused through the root hair, epidermis, and root tissue, now finds its way to the conducting tissues of the axillary vascular bundle, and is conveyed through similar tissues in the stem to the leaf.

STRUCTURE AND FUNCTION OF
THE LEAF.

What takes place when the dilute mineral solution reaches the leaf may best be understood by referring to the structure of the wheat blade. Fig. 16 is a

12. LONGITUDINAL SECTION OF YOUNG WHEAT ROOT SHOWING AXILLARY VASCULAR BUNDLE (*v.b.*) FOR CONDUCTING SAP, ALSO ROOT HAIRS (*r.h.*).

transverse section of a leaf of Federation wheat. Above and below, the leaf is bounded by a single layer of epidermal cells, and lying between is the mesophyll. The upper portion of the mesophyll is typically closer in structure than the lower portion, which is usually spongy in character and contains a large number of intercellular spaces. These intercellular spaces form labyrinthic chambers in which air freely circulates in the interior of the leaf. Scattered through the body of the mesophyll are the vascular bundles which form in wheat a set of parallel strands serving not only as a skeleton for the support of the remaining leaf tissue, but also as media for the conduction of the sap to every part of the leaf. The cells of the mesophyll contain a large number of green bodies called chloroplasts or chlorophyll corpuscles, which give the leaf its characteristic green colour. The epidermis (Fig. 17) of the leaf in contrast to that of the root is studded with microscopic openings called stomata, more or less regularly placed. Each stoma or pore consists of two sausage-shaped guard cells joined together at the extremities in such a manner as to leave a very narrow slit-like pore between them. The opening and closing of these stomata are brought about by changes in the curvature of the guard cells, and this in its turn is dependent on the turgidity or water content of the cells.

It is interesting to note that in this specimen of wheat the number of stomata on the *upper* surface per square centimetre amounted to 3,681, whilst the number on the *lower* surface was 3,321 per square c.m.

Respiration.—These stomato are the breathing pores of the plant. Respiration is quite as necessary for the life process of plants as it is for animals and the process is essentially the same in animals. The stems, roots and leaves of a plant are constantly in need of oxygen for respiration, and while under ordinary conditions the aerial portions of a plant can secure a sufficiency of oxygen for their requirements, it not infrequently happens that the roots suffer from lack of proper supplies of air in the soil. This may readily be seen in the unhealthy, sickly yellow appearance of wheat growing in low-lying portions of fields after heavy winter rains, or in badly drained water-logged soils. Respiration goes on throughout a plant's existence and its general effect is to destroy the carbonaceous material of the plant and liberate carbonic acid gas.

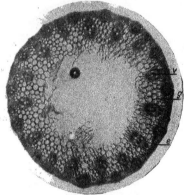

13. TRANSVERSE SECTION OF THE STEM OF FEDERATION WHEAT, SHOWING VASCULAR BUNDLES.

Assimilation or Photosynthesis.—This process of respiration in green plants is overshadowed by the opposite process of assimilation. The leaf is the medium whereby all green plants are enabled to obtain from the air the carbon which forms the greater portion of their bulk. Carbonic acid gas is present in ordinary air to the extent of about four parts in 10,000. Air containing carbonic acid enters the stomata and circulates freely in the intercellular spaces. Under the influence of sunlight which supplies the necessary energy and in the presence of the chlorophyll and moisture in the leaf, the carbon of the carbonic acid is fixed by being converted into carbohydrates and oxygen is set free and exhaled by the plant. This process is called "carbon fixation," "assimilation," or as it is dependent on light "photosynthesis." The energy necessary to effect these changes is of course obtained from the light and the leaf has transformed the energy of sunlight into potential energy possessed by the newly formed carbohydrate. Stephenson for this reason described coal as "bottled sunlight," because the energy it possessed was derived from the sunlight, which, ages ago assisted to grow the vegetation which we now mine as coal.

This process is of enormous practical importance in the economy of nature. All animals directly or indirectly are dependent on the preliminary life of plants to store up food, and green plants have the power of securing the greater portion of the solid matter of which they are composed from the carbonic acid gas of the air. Much discussion has taken place as to exactly what happens in the process of assimilation. In any case starch may be regarded as the first visible product formed. Starch, however does not accumulate in the leaf, but is transferred from the leaf to the stem and roots to be stored till required. The starch is transferred by the agency of an enzyme—diastase—such as is formed in the germinating grain. The starch is thus converted to sugar, which being soluble may diffuse to such parts as require it. Photosynthesis takes place only in the day time, whereas respiration is constantly in progress. Respiration, however, is never so rapid as the opposite process of assimilation so that the net result is an increase in dry weight as a result of assimilation.

Transpiration.— A third function of the leaf is to get rid of the superfluous water taken in by the root-hairs. As the mineral plant food taken in by the root is in the form of a very dilute solution, it follows that a large amount of water must be evaporated in order that the plant may receive sufficient mineral matter to build up its tissues. The

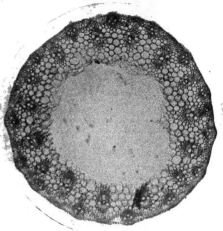

14. TRANSVERSE SECTION OF A STEM OF FEDERATION WHEAT (X 50).

superfluous water is vaporized in the intercellular tissues of the mesophyll and passes out through the stomata, whilst the mineral substances remain behind. This important process is called transpiration and by its means the absorption of fresh supplies of mineral food from the soil is rendered possible.

A large number of experiments have been made to determine the amount of water lost by transpiration from the ordinary farm crops. Though the actual amount is very considerable it is less than would be evaporated from an equal surface of water exposed to the same conditions. Lawes and Gilbert's experiments tend to show that for every ton of dry matter elaborated in ordinary farm crops about 250 tons of water require to be evaporated from the leaves. Hellriegel's observations in Germany show that for wheat 453 tons of water are required for each ton of dry matter produced. It is probable that under Australian conditions the amount required would be even higher than this. Assuming, however, in the absence of definite figures for Australian conditions, the results obtained by Hellriegel, and assuming that the ratio of grain to straw in an average wheat crop is 2 : 3, then a 20-bushel wheat crop would need to transpire an equivalent of 6 inches of rain, and a 30-bushel crop would need approximately 9 inches of water. In other words 6 inches of *absolutely effective* rain during the growing period should be theoretically sufficient for the requirements of a 20-bushel crop of wheat provided the soil was in good condition at the time of germination. Such results are not obtained in practice, however, because under the most perfect methods of soil cultivation, losses of moisture from the soil other than by the transpiration current are inevitable. Obviously there should be a sort of equilibrium existing between the amount of water transpired and the amount absorbed by the roots. Frequently the former is in excess of the latter and wilting results. This often takes place in a wheat field in early spring when hot

15. LONGITUDINAL SECTION OF A FEDERATION WHEAT STEM THROUGH THE VASCULAR BUNDLE SHOWING THE CONSTRUCTION OF THE CONDUCTING VESSELS.

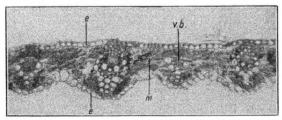

16. CROSS SECTION OF A WHEAT LEAF SHOWING EPIDERMAL CELLS, MESOPHYLL, AND VASCULAR BUNDLES.

winds are prevalent or when wheat has been thickly sown or manuring has been excessive. Under these circumstances transpiration from leaf and stem is not infrequently in excess of the amount of water taken up by the roots and injury results. The water is mainly transpired through the stomata of the leaves and as the number of stomata is usually greater on the under surface, transpiration is more active from that surface. The guard cells of the stomata regulate the amount of diastomatic transpiration and the relative position of these cells is largely dependent on their turgidity. The more turgid the guard cells the more they curve away from one another, the wider the opening and the greater the transpiration. Conversely when they become flaccid they straighten out and completely close the aperture. Transpiration is therefore largely influenced by the turgidity of the guard cells.

The most important external conditions governing the processes are—
    (a) Temperature.
    (b) Humidity.
    (c) Intensity of light.
    (d) Air movements.
    (e) Water content of soil.

Some of these influence transpiration through the agency of the guard cells and some of them act independently.

The absorption of the dilute mineral solution by the root hairs from the soil grains and the mode of its transference to the manufacturing organs of the plant—the leaves—has already been described. It is now necessary to consider the nature of the food thus absorbed.

This may be determined synthetically by means of water cultures, *i.e.*, by growing wheat plants in vessels containing distilled water to which certain mineral substances of known chemical composition have been added. Carbon we have already seen is obtained from the air, hydrogen and oxygen, which are also necessary, are obtained from water. Water cultures show that besides these three there are other seven chemical elements necessary, and that these can only be obtained from the soil.

These seven are nitrogen, phosphorus, sulphur, iron calcium (lime), magnesium and potash. If the soil is wanting in but one of these elements there is no crop. Three other elements drawn from the soil are always found in the ash of plants but they are regarded not as essential, but as accidental elements. These are silicon (silica), sodium (soda), and chlorine. A number of other accidental elements may be found in crops from special soils.

For the farmer practical interest centres in the seven essential constituents of the ash enumerated above. Each of these is usually present in sufficient quantity in Australian wheat soils save phosphoric acid. Even on such soils there is usually from fifty to one hundred times more phosphoric acid than is required for one wheat crop. But the roots have no openings and they must absorb their ash constituents in solution and the great bulk of phosphoric acid in soils is insoluble in water. Given sufficient soil moisture and good physical condition it is the most deficient soil constituent which determines the size of the crop, and for this reason it is usual to supply a little soluble phosphoric acid in superphosphates to improve the soil in its weakest point.

Soils may be classed as sand, clay, lime and peat or humus soils. As regards the grain the ash varies little in composition according to the soil. The straw however varies considerably—*e.g.*, on clay soil the ash may contain about 70 per cent. of silica, on peat hardly any. A 20-bushel crop of wheat may contain 35 lb. nitrogen, 14 lb. phosphoric acid, and 20 lb. of potash, the first two being chiefly in the grain and the last-named in the straw.

While the composition of the ash of the whole crop varies according to the soil it is grown on, it is evident that the crop exercises to some extent a power of selection, absorbing in largest quantity those particular constituents which it requires :—Thus the ash of wheat contains a relatively high percentage of phosphoric acid and a low percentage of lime. The ash of mangolds, on the other hand, is rich in potash, whilst that of clover and lucerne is rich in lime. What probably happens is that the nutrient solution for any given soil is more or less of constant composition. The root hairs allow this soil solution to enter by osmosis until the concentration inside the cell is the same as that

17. EPIDERMIS OF FEDERATION WHEAT (UNDER SURFACE OF LEAF) SHOWING STOMATA (3321 PER SQUARE CENTIMETRE).

without. No more can enter until the living cells of the plant withdraw some of the nutrient solution for constructive purposes and thus lower the concentration of the cell sap in that ingredient. Soda is more abundant in the soil than potash, yet in the ash of wheat potash is far more abundant than is soda.

In the case of wheat the plant cells keep utilizing the potash for the construction of tissue and thus lowering the concentration and permitting more to enter. On the other hand very little soda is used by the plant cells and the cell sap is therefore as concentrated in soda as that of the soil solution.

STORAGE AND MIGRATION OF FOOD.

The leaf is the manufacturing organ of the plant. It has already been shown that it is responsible for the forma-

18. EPIDERMIS OF LEAF (X 300) OF WHEAT SHOWING STRUCTURE OF STOMATA.

tion of carbohydrates such as starch and sugar from simple inorganic materials. It also builds up organic compounds containing nitrogen such as the proteins. The intermediate stages between the absorption of nitrates, sulphates, and phosphates by the roots and the elaboration of proteins by the living cells of the leaf are not known, but it seems probable that intermediate products like asparagine and other amido acids are first formed and that these are subsequently elaborated into protein. Most of the compounds elaborated by the leaf are used for building up new cells, cell walls and in nourishing the living tissue. During active vegetation and under ordinary conditions of growth there is more material constructed than is needed for the immediate requirements of plants. In the case of wheat sown in April or May the early growth is usually vigorous. As winter comes on the temperature of the soil gradually falls and growth appears to be at a standstill.

In reality, however, assimilation is going on actively but the products are utilized in the formation of new roots and the ultimate success of the crop is in a large measure dependent on the nature of the root system built up in this stage of apparent inactivity. With a gradual rise of temperature characteristic of early spring the wheat plant enters on the most vigorous period of its existence. Assimilation now proceeds actively and the products move off as fast as they are produced and are stored in the stems of the plant for future use. At a later stage the lower leaves begin to die off, and the carbohydrates together with the important nitrogen phosphoric acid and potash compounds are gradually moved to the more active portions of the plant.

After the fertilization of the grain takes place the absorption of food supplies from the soil practically ceases and the whole energies of the plant are concentrated on the migration to the grain of the already elaborated material stored in the leaves and stem.

There is a general movement of water from the lower portions of the plant to the upper parts, and with the moisture the sugars, amides and proteins are transferred to the grain. Desiccation now sets in, and in the case of wheat about two-fifths of the whole dry matter of the plant is found in the grain. Of the nitrogen and phosphoric acid found in the whole plant no less than three-fourths of the former and about two-thirds of the latter substance are found in the kernel.

The microphotographs and sections illustrating this article were prepared by the Acting Vegetable Pathologist, Mr. C. C. Brittlebank.

(To be continued.)

FARM BLACKSMITHING.

(Continued from page 127.)

George Baxter, Instructor in Blacksmithing, Working Men's College, Melbourne.

V.—WELDING *(continued).*

FORGING A HOOK.

It is not a very difficult matter to forge a hook provided one has a good idea of the shape and strength required.

An easily remembered approximate rule to determine the size of iron to make the hook is to reckon the diameter of bar equal to the square root of. the load to be lifted, and, for the length of bar, eight times its diameter.

When the piece has been cut off one end is heated and upset to form the eye; it is then flattened as shown at A (Fig 50). A hole is then punched through it (see B), and the eye worked to shape on the beak of the anvil so as to make the iron forming the eye circular, similar to C. The hole should not be too large; it is sufficient if large enough to allow a link of the chain to which it is to be attached to work freely.   In a

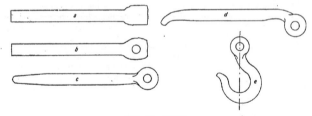

FIG. 50. HOOK.

(*a*) The bar upset and flattened.   (*b*) The hole punched.   (*c*) Eye finished and point prepared.   (*d*) Shows ends bent.   (*e*) The finished hook.

hook made of 1 inch diameter iron a hole $\frac{5}{8}$-in. diameter would be quite large enough.   To make it larger would weaken it.

When the eye is finished the opposite end is heated and drawn tapered, making the diameter at the end about half that of the original bar; and the length of tapered part about three times the diameter of bar, as shown at C.

Bending is the next consideration, and the best way to effect this is to first bend the point and eye as shown at D.   Then heat the straight portion evenly, and on removing it from the fire cool off each end so as to prevent alteration, and bend the remaining part on the beak of anvil, bringing it to the shape shown at E.

When a hook is properly made a line drawn through the centre of it should pass through the centre of its eye.

To join a hook of this kind to a chain either a connecting link is welded in or a shackle is used.   When a link is used it should be made larger than the links comprising the chain, to permit its being easily welded, and because of the fact that, being a larger link, it must be forged of thicker iron to be of equal strength.

To give some idea of the proportions of a chain, hook, and connecting link, let it be supposed that a piece of ⅜-in. chain is to be used. Now the safe load to apply to a ⅜-in. chain of good quality, would be .9 tons ; *e.g.*, the number of eighths of inches contained in the iron from which the chain is made, being squared and divided by 10.

The size of iron for the hook would be the square root of load which, taking the nearest size of bar obtainable, would be ·1 inch diameter and the length to make it 8 inches.

The diameter of iron for the connecting link would require to be ½ inch. Adding one-eighth to the diameter of chain will in most instances be sufficiently correct.

Welding in the connecting link, particularly when the link is small, is a rather awkward proposition, requiring a fair amount of practice. It is therefore always advisable to have the length of connecting link about double that of the links in the chain.

A Pair of Tongs.

This is a very useful thing to be able to make, and as the accomplishment embraces such exercises as punching, forging, riveting, welding,

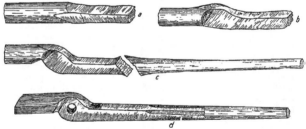

FIG 51. BLACKSMITH'S TONGS.

(*a*) Forming the handle.   (*b*) Forming the eye.   (*c*) Ready for welding.   (*d*) The finished jaw.

making two objects alike and fitting them together, it affords excellent practice. Tongs are not made to fixed measurements and so the symmetry of the work is dependent upon accuracy of eye, combined with the taste and judgment of the operator.

Mild steel is the best material to use for forging the jaws of tongs. It is much stronger than iron, and consequently the tongs can be made lighter than if iron be selected. The size of steel used will vary with the work required of the tongs. The smallest size generally used being ¾-in. diameter.

The illustration, Fig. 51, shows the evolution of each jaw previous to riveting together.

About the best advice that the writer can tender the novice attempting his first tongs is to obtain a well shaped pair to copy from, and then proceed by drawing out similar to shape shown at A. Next, lay on the near edge of the anvil about ¾ of an inch of the round bar, and flatten it out to, roughly, ½ inch thick (see B). The *fuller* should then be requisitioned to form like C. When the two jaws are thus formed the handles are prepared for welding on. For a light pair made from ¾-in. diameter ⁷⁄₁₆-in. round is quite heavy enough.   Two pieces of that size 18 inches long are cut off and one end of each upset to, say, ⅝-in. at the end, gradually tapering back about 3 inches. . The welding together requires no explanation further than that given in the *Journal* for January.

When each jaw has been welded on to its handle, it is reheated and flattened out to the required shape, and a hole punched for the rivet. Fitting the jaws to each other and riveting them together are the next operations.   To make the rivet, select a round bar about ⅛-in. larger than the hole; heat to welding and round down to slightly less than the diameter of hole. Cut nearly through at a short distance (about ½ inch is usually sufficient) back from the shoulder formed by reducing the bar; this enlarged piece forms the head of rivet. Cut the drawn out part off, just long enough to go through both jaws, and project out sufficient for riveting.   Heat the rivet before finally separating from the bar, and place in the hole.   By a backward and forward motion the bar will break off, leaving the rivet in the hole ready for hammering.

After riveting it will be found that the tongs will not

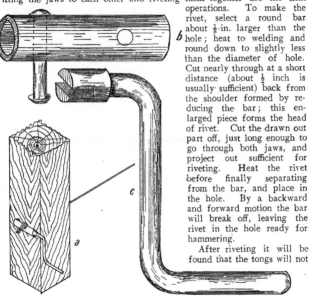

FIG. 52. WIRE STRAINER.
(*a*) Shows the strainer in position. (*b*) The barrel and stop.   (*c*) The key.

work unless put into the fire and made red hot. This has the effect of releasing the tension of the rivet.   Whilst still hot, set the tongs to the iron they are intended to hold, and cool out.

A · WIRE STRAINER.

A simple, and at the same time effective, wire strainer may be cheaply and quickly made by pursuing the following method :—

The materials required are a short piece of gas or water pipe 5 inches long and 1 inch internal diameter ; a piece of ⅜-in. round iron to make the stop ; about 4 inches of 1-in. round iron or mild steel (the latter for preference) and 12 inches of ⅝-in. iron.   A, Fig. 52, is a sketch of the strainer in position, with the wire attached.   B is the barrel, and C the key for operating it.

To make the strainer, cut the pipe to length and bore two $\frac{3}{8}$-in. diameter hole through it at right angles to each other, and about 1 inch from either end.   One hole is to receive the wire, and the other is for the purpose of containing the stop.   The stop is made from a piece of $\frac{3}{8}$-in. round iron by heating one end immediately at the point, gripping it tightly in the vice, leaving half an inch of the heated end projecting above the jaws, and hammering it down to form the head, somewhat similar in shape to the head of a nail.   The opposite end is treated in the same way, but before making the head the iron must be placed through the hole of the pipe, and then held in the vice and beaten.   When finished the stop will resemble the handle of the vice.   It should be free to move up and down when the pipe is revolved.

The key, only one of which is required for any number of strainers, is more difficult to forge.   It is made by reducing several inches of the 1-in. bar to $\frac{5}{8}$-in. diameter, with the hammers and swages, and then welding on to it the piece of $\frac{3}{8}$-in. iron.   Before bending the handle to shape, the slot requires to be made either by making a slot hole with a flat punch, or by drilling a hole at the back, slitting with a chisel, and forging to shape.   The former is the better plan.   The slot must be made sufficiently wide to easily slip over the fencing wire it is intended to tighten.

The fencing wire will be passed through a hole bored in the straining post and reeved through the strainer; then doubled back, and again reeved through the hole in the strainer only, and thus prevented from drawing out when the strain is placed upon it.   To tighten the wire the key is placed in the end of the pipe so that the slot fits over the wire, then by revolving it the wire is wound around the barrel and at each half revolution the stop drops down, and, coming into contact with the post, prevents the wire from unwinding.   When the wire is sufficiently tightened the key is removed.

Although this strainer is simple in construction and application it is thoroughly efficient.

(*To be continued.*)

THE OLIVE.

By L. Macdonald, Horticulturist, Dookie Agricultural College.

(Continued from page 130.)

Soil Preparation.

It pays to give soil preparation thorough consideration when an orchard is being planted, and the same applies also to laying out an olive grove. If the soil be ploughed and subsoiled to a good depth, the young trees have a much better chance of establishing a good root system; and, in future years, are able to withstand, without injury, conditions that would seriously affect trees planted on poorly prepared soil.

11. TPYICAL YOUNG SEEDLING OLIVES.

The soil should be broken up to as great depth as possible and left with a fine tilth on top. This is particularly so in the somewhat dry lands where irrigation cannot be adopted, as it admits of a better conservation of available moisture and gives the young roots more genial conditions in which to develop.

Transplanting.

Little difference exists between the actual operation of planting olive trees and that of any other of our fruit trees. They are planted during the winter months—May, June, or July. However, it will be found that, in some districts, they succeed better if planted at certain times according to the locality. Again, some varieties show a disposition to succeed better if planted early, while the opposite is the case with others.

In transplanting, it is important to see that the roots are not exposed to the sun or wind and not allowed on any account to become dry. In dry districts, where irrigation is not available, it is advisable to plant early; that is, in May or June, so that the winter rains will set the soil well around the roots. With late planting under such conditions there is always the likelihood of the weather taking up and the soil drying out. In any case, however, the soil if moist should be trampled firmly around the roots; and, if dry, watered to force the air out and set the soil well around the roots.

The tops should be pruned hard back in proportion with the root surface. This will give the tree a better chance of adapting itself to its new situation. If the top were not reduced, it would mean that the roots, many of which were lacerated and broken in removal, would not be able to supply a sufficiency of sap to meet the demand made by the respiration of such a large leaf surface. Consequently, drying out of the bark and tissues would result to the detriment of the tree. All broken or damaged roots should be removed.

It often happens that the young trees shed their leaves after transplanting, sometimes remaining through a whole season without making any
growth.   This is particularly so if planted out of season.   No alarm,
however, should be occasioned at this; so long as the bark remains green
and plump, they may be depended on to start into growth again.   In
the first season after transplanting, the young trees should be allowed to
make as much growth as possible, even though a number of shoots come
from below the crown.   This is to encourage as great a root extension as
possible; shaping up can be undertaken before the next season.

The distance to plant the trees apart will depend chiefly on local conditions, variety and methods of culture.   Various distances from 20 to
30 ft. apart are recommended by different authorities.   Some varieties,
such as the Verdale, are not such
strong growers, as, for instance,
Polymorpha; hence, they can be
planted closer together.   The
writer is inclined to favour the
lesser distance, between 20 to 25
ft.; that is, where hand picking is
intended.   This will necessitate
the practice of careful pruning
each year, as with our other fruit
trees, to keep the trees low and in
proper shape.   If the trees are
allowed to grow unrestrained, they
will eventually crowd at this distance.   Such crowding will cause
the exclusion of light from the
lower parts of the trees and result
in bad setting of the fruit, and
dying back of the lower branches.
The tops of the trees will become
so broad and unwieldy that beating down the fruit will have to be
resorted to.   Where this method
of gathering the fruit is intended,
the trees may be planted further
apart and allowed to grow to a great size.

12. CROWN AND TOP OF YOUNG TREES
SUITABLE FOR TRANSPLANTING.

In some localities, it is found that certain varieties show a tendency
to be self-sterile, if planted in isolated blocks.   Hence, it is advisable to
plant other varieties adjacent to insure cross-pollination, which is likely
to result in more regular crops.

CULTIVATION.

It is thought, by many, that good cultivation is unnecessary for the olive.
In fact, it is claimed, by some growers, that the trees do better where cultivation is not adopted.   Quite a number of the plantations in this
country are either not cultivated at all, or at odd times with intervals of
years between.   This system of cultivation at periods of long intervals is
perhaps more detrimental than none at all, owing to the strong tendency of
the small feeding roots of olive trees to rise close to the surface of the soil.
If the soil is undisturbed for several years it becomes a network of fibrous
roots, these will be destroyed if the ploughing takes place again. · Constant cultivation encourages deeper rooting.

In those districts where the rainfall is light, and the conservation of all available moisture is one of the most important contributories to successful culture, there can be no question that good cultivation is essential.   The well broken surface soil absorbs readily any water that falls.   The " run off " is minimized and the maintenance of a fine tilth through the dry season hinders evaporation of moisture from the lower soil layers. Although the surface soil through being frequently disturbed is not of direct value as a feeding ground for the roots during the current season, it serves a valuable purpose in maintaining more congenial conditions for root develop-ment in the underlying soil.   Besides, the plant foods that are liberated by the action of light and air on the frequently disturbed soil will be washed down and made available during subsequent seasons.

Where irrigation is practised, constant and thorough cultivation should be carried out.   It is important that the cultivation following irrigation should take place as soon after watering as possible, otherwise cracking

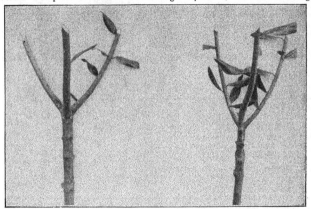

13. TOPS OF YOUNG TREES HEADED BACK READY FOR TRANSPLANTING.

and drying out of the soil will quickly take place.   The furrow system of irrigation is the most satisfactory, and two or three waterings will usually be found sufficient ; this will, of course, be governed by conditions and the nature of the soil.   It is a mistake to use water too frequently or make it take the place of cultivation.

In some soils where constant irrigation with clean cultivation is carried out, the land eventually becomes inert, cold, and irresponsive to the use of artificial fertilizers.   The trees become pale, drawn, and vigourless, owing to the physical deterioration of the soil.   In such cases, provision should be made for the addition of humus or plant fibre on which the soil bacteria may continue their activities.   This is usually best done by growing legumi-nous crops between the trees.   In the drier parts, such crops should be grown only during the winter months and turned in before the land dries out in the spring.   Owing to harvesting operations taking place during the winter, some judgment should be exercised in planting such crops, other-wise the best results will not be obtained.

(To be continued.)

REMINDERS FOR APRIL.

LIVE STOCK.

HORSES.—Those stabled should be fed liberally. Food of a more stimulating nature can now be given to get them well over the "changing coat" season. Those doing fast or heavy work should be clipped; if not wholly, then trace high. The legs should not be clipped. Those not rugged on coming into the stable at night sweating freely should be wiped down and in half-an-hour's time rugged or covered with bags until the coat is dry. Weaned foals should have a little crushed oats daily, if available.

CATTLE.—As the nights become colder the dairy cows should be rugged. The rugs should be removed in day-time when the shade temperature reaches 60 degrees. If new grass is plentiful, give a ration of hay or straw, whole or chaffed, to counteract the purging effects of young grass. Cows may now be spayed.

PIGS.—Sows not already served should be put to the boar. Supply all pigs with plenty of bedding, and see that sties are warm and well ventilated. Supply sows liberally with grain. Castrate young boars.

SHEEP.—Where early lambs are being bred for local markets, transfer ewes and lambs to best pasture as soon as dropped. Castrate ram lambs when a few days old; defer tailing them until the ewe lambs are ready. After first rain (when dust is settled) clear wool from the eyes of young merino sheep; whilst yarded put weak weaners in hospital paddock, and any unprofitable woolled sheep in fattening paddock.

POULTRY.—Do not feed much grain this month—soft food aids moult; add a teaspoonful of linseed to each bird's ration once daily. The more exercise the hens get the better they moult. Remove all male birds from pens. Add Douglas mixture to drinking water. Keep a sharp look-out for chicken pox. Forward pullets should now be in their winter quarters, with plenty of scratching litter, and fed liberally—including ration of animal food.

CULTIVATION.

FARM.—Dig potatoes as they mature. Cart out and spread stable manure. Prepare and plough land for main cereal crops. Sow Chou Moellier seed in beds for transplanting. Sow the following mixture per acre for green feed during the winter months for the dairy herd :—1½ bushels, New Zealand Black Oats; ½ bushel, Cape Barley; ½ bushel, Tick Beans; ½ bushel, Vetches. Sow Giant Drumhead Cabbage for transplanting (1 lb. sufficient for 1 acre, in rows 3 feet apart); provided the soil is in good friable condition, plants from seed sown last month should be planted out. Sow wheat and oats according to locality; also rape for winter feed or green manuring. Prepare clean seed-bed for lucerne; and sow Hunter River, Arabian, Turkestan, or Peruvian seed, free from dodder, in drills 7 inches apart and at the rate of 10 lbs. of seed per acre. Sow permanent pastures with grasses and clovers.

ORCHARD.—Prepare land for planting; plough deeply and sub-soil. Plant legumes for green manure. Plant out strawberries. Clean up Codlin Moth from trees as soon as all fruit is gathered.

FLOWER GARDEN.—Plant out evergreen shrubs, trees, and Australian plants, divisions of herbaceous plants, seedlings, layers, and rooted cuttings. Feed chrysanthemums with liquid manure weekly until flowers begin to open. Prepare land for future plantings of roses and shrubs.

VEGETABLE GARDEN.—Plant out seedlings from the seed beds. Dig all vacant spaces roughly. Sow onions for early crop; also peas and broad beans. Clean out asparagus beds wherever the seeds are ripening.

VINEYARD :—

Vintage operations occupy the greater part of April. See last month's notes.

Cellars.—Cleanliness is emphatically urged. Carefully remove all fermentable refuse—skins, lees, skimmings, &c. Such odds and ends favour multiplication of vinegar flies (*Drosophila funebris*). If present, destroy these with formalin or insecticide powders. A little bisulphite or sulphurous acid in washing water is recommended; also free use of lime on floors, &c.

VICTORIAN EGG-LAYING COMPETITION, 1911-12,

CONDUCTED AT BURNLEY HORTICULTURAL SCHOOL.

(*Continued from page 67.*)

H. V. Hawkins, Poultry Expert.

No. of Pen.	Breed.	Name of Owner.	Eggs Laid during Competition.			Position in Competition.
			April to Dec. 31.	Jan.	Total to Jan. 31 (10 mths)	
12	White Leghorn	W. G. Swift	1,243	132	1,375	1
31	"	R. W. Pope	1,205	145	1,350	2
40	"	A. J. Cosh (S.A.)	1,176	132	1,308	3
20	"	H. McKenzie	1,108	138	1,246	4
37	"	E. Waldon	1,074	136	1,210	5
33	"	Range Poultry Farm (Qld.)	1,090	114	1,204	6
39	"	A.W. Hall	989	145	1,134	7
18	"	S. Brundrett	1,010	97	1,107	8
21	"	R. L. Appleford	972	113	1,085	9
13	Black Orpington	D. Fisher	974	104	1,078	10
46	Minorca (Black)	G. W. Chalmers	945	98	1,043	11
34	White Leghorn	F. Hannaford	906	135	1,041	12
25	"	B. Mitchell	931	107	1,038	13
55	"	W. G. McLister	937	100	1,037	14
10	Black Orpington	H. A. Langdon	914	121	1,085	15
9	White Leghorn	J. O'Loughlin	912	122	1,034	16
38	"	Mrs. C. K. Smee	930	100	1,080	17
2	"	E. P. Nash	899	130	1,0.9	18
19	"	A. Jaques	884	141	1,025	19
50	"	C. H. Busst	891	128	1,019	20
36	"	F. A. Sillitoe	897	117	1,014	21
28	"	J. Campbell	899	114	2,013	22
3	"	K. Gleghorn	897	111	1,008	23
49	"	W. J. Thornton	910	97	1,007	24
1	"	A. Brebner	901	104	1,005	25
44	Black Orpington	T. S. Goodisson	907	95	1,002	26
32	Silver Wyandotte	Mrs. M. A. Jones	908	88	996	27
45	White Leghorn	T. Kempster	868	124	992	28
62	"	P. Hodson	855	131	986	29
5	"	L. C. Payne	870	108	978	30
47	"	C. W. Spencer (N.S.W.)	864	112	976	31
11	Brown Leghorn	F. Soncum	836	136	972	32
57	White Leghorn	G. E. Edwards	848	118	966	33
65	"	H. Hammill (N.S.W.)	840	114	954	34
67	"	C. L. Sharman	868	84	952	35
8	"	T. W. Coto	845	106	951	} 36
22	Black Orpington	P. S. Wood	864	87	951	
4	Golden Wyandotte	H. Bell	850	96	946	38
43	White Leghorn	W. B. Crellin	815	118	933	39
66	White Wyandotte	J. E. Bradley	814	85	929	40
60	White Leghorn	J. J. Harrington	816	109	925	41
59	"	W. H. Dunlop	830	93	923	42
53	"	A. Stringer	799	114	913	43
51	"	J. W. McArthur	827	83	910	} 44
41	"	Morgan and Watson	796	114	910	
27	"	Hill and Luckman	829	81	910	
63	Black Orpington	A. J. Treacy	807	86	893	47
58	Faverolles	K. Courtenay	795	92	887	48
35	White Leghorn	J. H. Brain	752	130	882	49
52	"	W. J. McKeddie	782	93	875	50
34	"	E. Dettman	751	117	868	} 51
64	"	J. D. Read	738	130	868	
30	Black Orpington	Rodgers Bros.	762	105	867	53
42	White Orpington	P. Mitchell	775	90	805	54
6	Silver Wyandotte	Mrs. H. J. Richards	759	101	860	55
7	White Leghorn	H. Stevenson	743	110	853	56
26	"	F. H. Seymour	728	87	815	57
56	"	Mrs. C. Thompson	69?	119	811	58
16	Silver Wyandotte	Miss A. Cottam	706	79	785	} 59
54	White Leghorn	F. Hodges	710	75	785	
23	Golden Wyandotte	G. E. Brown	683	87	770	61
61	Silver Wyandotte	J. Reade	651	103	754	62
17	White Leghorn	W. J. Eckershall	624	74	698	63
14	Black Orpington	W. J. Macauley	595	65	660	64
15	Minorca	H. R. McChesney	539	66	605	65
48	"	3. James	433	76	509	66
			56,298	7,062	63.360	

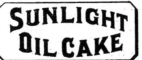

BULLS FOR SALE.

SHORTHORN Bull (Milking Strain) "Hayle Duke of Pentland."

Dropped July 31st, 1905.   Bred by JAS. LIDYETT, Myrniong.

Sire :—Hayle Prince, 836)4 (imp.), three times Champion at Melbourne Royal Show.
Dam :—Jessamine III.   First and Champion Melbourne Royal Show 1905 in Milking Shorthorn Class, and gave 68 lbs. of milk with 3·9 test.

"Hayle Duke of Pentland" has been used at the Wyuna Irrigation Farm for the last five years, and most of the young cows tested to remain in the herd are by him.   Hence the reason for sale.

Price, **10** guineas.   Inspection at Wyuna Irrigation Farm, *viâ* Tongala.

SHORTHORN Stud Bull "John Murray."   5 years.

Sire :—Earl Summerton 4th.   *Dam :*—Oxford Summerton 8th.

Price, **5** guineas.   Inspection at Wyuna Irrigation Farm, *viâ* Tongala.

JERSEY Bull "Cream Prospect."   Dropped March 22nd, 1910.

Sire :—Lord Creamer (155 A.J.H.B.).   *Dam :*—Daisy of Prospect (347 A.J.H.B.).

Price, **12** guineas.   Inspection on application to Dairy Supervisor O'KEEFE, Rochester.

Extended pedigrees and particulars on application to DEPARTMENT OF AGRICULTURE, MELBOURNE.

DEPARTMENT OF AGRICULTURE,
VICTORIA.

Burnley Horticultural School.

E. E. PESCOTT, Principal.

ANNOUNCEMENT.

The curriculum and management of the Burnley Horticultural School have now been arranged so that greater advantages and facilities will be given to students of both sexes in Horticulture and allied subjects.

The present course of Horticulture for male students includes a two years' course, students being charged a fee of £5 per annum.

Classes have been formed at Burnley, whereby students of both sexes may receive instruction on two afternoons of each week—Tuesdays and Fridays.

Instruction includes theoretical and practical work, and will commence at 2 p.m. This will be a two years' course, and the fee charged will be £2 per annum.

It has also been arranged that several short lecture courses shall be given on subjects which are suitable adjuncts to Horticulture, such as Poultry Farming, Bee-keeping, and Fruit Preserving, and these courses will be open and free to the general public. The subjects and dates of the Short Course Lectures will be announced monthly in this Journal.

Demonstrations in Fruit Preserving will be given by Miss MENDOZA, Fruit Preserving Expert, in the Hall, on March 1st, 8th, and 15th, at 2.45 p.m. These Demonstrations are Free to the Public.

STUDENTS SHOULD ENROLL WITHOUT DELAY.

Application for admission should be made to

The Director of Agriculture, Public Offices, Melbourne,

OR TO THE PRINCIPAL.

DEPARTMENT OF AGRICULTURE,
VICTORIA.

~~~~~~~~

AGRICULTURAL CLASSES, 1912.

At least thirty students, exclusive of school children, must be enrolled at each centre, the rent of the hall and all local charges to be paid by the Agricultural Society under whose auspices the Class is held.

As only a limited number of classes can be held during the year, it is essential that Agricultural or other Societies should make early application

——>∘<——

LECTURES ON AGRICULTURAL SUBJECTS, 1912.

Agricultural or other Societies wishing to have public lectures delivered are requested to make early application. The hall, advertising, &c., must be provided locally, free of cost, but all other charges are borne by the Department.

Staff—The Director (Dr. S. S. Cameron), and Messrs. Archer, Carmody, Carroll, de Castella, Cother, Crowe, French Jr., Griffin, Ham, Hart, Hawkins, Johnstone, Kendall, Knight, McFadzean, Pescott, Richardson, Robertson, Sawers, Seymour, Smith, Strong, Turner, and Expert of the State Rivers and Water Supply Commission.

Applications relative to the above Institutions and Lectures should be sent to the Director of Agriculture, Melbourne.

The Journal of

THE DEPARTMENT OF AGRICULTURE OF VICTORIA, AUSTRALIA.

April, 1912.

FARM BLACKSMITHING

PRICE THREEPENCE. (Annual Subscription—Victoria, Inter-State, and N.Z., 3/-; British and Foreign, 5/-.)

THE JOURNAL

OF

THE DEPARTMENT OF AGRICULTURE,

VICTORIA, AUSTRALIA.

CONTENTS.—APRIL, 1912.

COPYRIGHT PROVISIONS AND SUBSCRIPTION RATES.

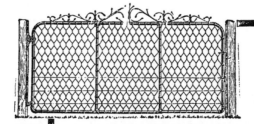

Alston's Patent Windmills

——AT THE ROYAL SHOW.——

At the recent Royal Show a fine collection of **Windmills** was exhibited by **James Alston,** of **Queen's Bridge,. Melbourne.** Mills of all diameters, from 6 ft. to 25 ft. were shown at work, suitable to all requirements of farmers or stock raisers, the small Mills being suitable for lifting moderate supplies from shallow wells, while the larger sizes are capable of dealing with almost any depth's. A splendid Mill, 25 feet diameter on a 50 ft. Steel Tower, working an 18″ pump, and throwing a stream of water of about 15,000 gallons per hour, attracted much attention. This, we believe, is the largest Mill ever shown on the Show Ground. **Alston's Patent Steel Windmills** have all the most up-to-date improvements in their construction. Pumps of many descriptions were shown, including the latest Draw Plunger Pumps for bore use, which admits of the plunger being drawn without disturbing the pipes in the bore.

THE JOURNAL

OF

𝔗ʜe 𝔇epartment of 𝔄gricuⅼture

OF

VICTORIA.

| Vol. X. | Part 4. | 10th April, 1912. |

WHEAT AND ITS CULTIVATION.

(Continued from page 191.)

A. E. V. Richardson, M.A., B.Sc. (Agric.) Agricultural Superintendent.

III.—FOOD REQUIREMENTS AND CHEMICAL COMPOSITION.

The manner in which the young wheat plant builds up its tissues from simple inorganic materials has been described, and it now remains to consider from an analytical point of view the composition of the grain and straw elaborated by the plant's activity. We need not enter at this stage into a discussion of the effect of environment on the chemical composition of the product or on the milling quality of the kernel. It is sufficient to note that the climate, the nature of the soil, the mode of fertilization, and even the cultivation of the soil are all important factors in influencing the quality and character of the grain. It has already been remarked that the food of plants consists of 10 essential elements, namely, carbon, hydrogen, oxygen, nitrogen, sulphur, phosphorus, iron, magnesium, potassium and calcium ; and that three other elements, though invariably present in the ash, are not regarded as essential to plant life.

Now of these essential elements seven are obtained from the soil, whilst three, carbon, hydrogen and oxygen are obtained either from air or from water. One of the most interesting and astonishing facts in agricultural science is that no less than 95 per cent. of the total dry-matter of the plant is obtained not from the soil at all.

The importance of this fact is more evident when we consider that, whilst the air contains practically an inexhaustible supply of carbon, constantly replenished by the vital activity of animals and by the processes of

3831.   H

combustion, the soil contains a limited quantity of several essential mineral ingredients which may only be replenished by the application of fertilizers.

The constituents other than carbon, hydrogen, oxygen and nitrogen are called the inorganic or ash constituents of the plant.

To properly appreciate the food requirements of wheat it is necessary to consider the amount of nitrogen and ash constituents removed from the soil by an average crop. For our purpose, in the absence of sufficient local data, we may consider a summary of the results obtained at Rothamstead where scientific experimental work has been systematically conducted for over seventy years.

Tables I. and II. are digests of the elaborate tables given in the *Rothamstead Memoirs* (Vol. VI.), p. 104. Table I. represents the total produce, dry-matter, ash constituents and nitrogen obtained from plots 2, 3, 5 and 10, treated respectively for 20 years with—

> (a) Farmyard manure.
> (b) No manure.
> (c) Mixed mineral manures.
> (d) Ammonium Salts only.

TABLE I.

QUANTITY PER PRODUCE, DRY-MATTER, NITROGEN AND ASH CONSTITUENTS REMOVED PER ACRE BY WHEAT TREATED WITH VARIOUS MANURES.

(Average of 20 years.)

No. of Plot.	Total Produce.	Dry Matter.	Ash Constituents per acre.	Nitrogen per acre.	Nitrogen and Ash Constituents expressed as per cent. of Dry Matter.	Balance of dry matter obtained from Air.
	lbs.	lbs.	lbs.	lbs.		
Plot 3—No manure ..	2,364	1,988	93·44	20·3	5·72 %	94·28 %
Plot 5—Mixed minerals ..	2,808	2,360	115·71	24·3	5·92 %	94·08 %
Plot 10—Ammon. salts ..	4,421	3,727	145·11	40·0	4·96 %	95·04 %
Plot 2—Farmyard manure	6,064	5,098	246·84	51·7	5·85 %	94·15 %

Of these four plots the unmanured plot (plot 3) approximates more closely to the average wheat yield of Victoria than do any of the other plots, and may therefore be studied in greater detail.

Its yield of grain (15.2 bush.) is commonly reached and exceeded in many parts of the State, though the average yield of the State has never equalled it.

Table II. has been arranged to show the following details :—(1) total yield; (2) dry-matter; (3) essential soil constituents, and (4) non-essential plant constituents removed by the grain and by the straw of a 15.2 bush. crop.

TABLE II.

AMOUNT OF PRODUCE, DRY-MATTER, ESSENTIAL AND NON-ESSENTIAL SOIL CONSTITUENTS REMOVED PER ACRE FROM PLOT 3 (UNMANURED).

AVERAGE OF 20 YEARS' RESULTS.

Plot 3.				Grain.	Straw.	Total Produce.
Yield	..	..	..	15·2 bushels	12·96 cwt.	2,364 lbs.
Dry Matter	..	..	..	766 lbs.	1,222 lbs.	1,988 ,,
Essentials—						
1. **Nitrogen**	..	..	..	14·1 lbs.	6·2 lbs.	20·30 lbs.
2. **Phosphoric Acid**	..	..	7·83 ,,	2·4 ,,	10·23 ,,
3. **Potash**	..	..	..	5·22 ,,	11·92 ,,	17·14 ,,
4. Iron Oxide (ferric)	..	..	·10 ,,	·53 ,,	·63 ,,
5. Lime	..	..	..	·49 ,,	3·92 ,,	4·42 ,,
6. Magnesia	..	..	..	1·64 ,,	1·18 ,,	2·82 ,,
7. Sulphuric Acid	..	..	·22 ,,	2·99 ,,	3·21 ,,
Non-essentials—						
1. Silica	..	..	..	·10 ,,	52·98 ,,	53·08 ,,
2. Soda	..	..	..	·03 ,,	·20 ,,	·23 ,,
3. Chlorine	..	..	..	·01 ,,	1·64 ,,	1·65 ,,

Careful perusal of these tables, representing the averages of 20 years' work, suggests the following remarks :—

(1) In a 15.2 bushel crop the ratio of grain to straw is approximately 60 : 100—that is, for every bushel of grain obtained there are 100 lbs. of straw.

(2) The most important of the essential ash constituents are concentrated in different portions of the wheat plant, *e.g.*, 70 per cent. of the nitrogen and 75 per cent. of the phosphoric acid is found in the grain, whilst 70 per cent. of the total potash is present in the straw.

(3) Between 5 per cent. and 6 per cent. of the total dry-matter of wheat is obtained from the soil, whilst no less than 94-95 per cent. is obtained from the atmosphere.

(4) A 15-bushel crop of wheat removed from the soil 20 lbs. of nitrogen, 10 lbs. of phosphoric acid, and 17 lbs. of potash.

(5) Assuming that the grain is carted off the farm and the straw is used for litter and ultimately returned to the soil. the two main constituents taken from the soil are phosphoric acid and nitrogen, whilst the greater part of the potash, together with more than half the organic matter are returned to the soil.

(6) Assuming, however, that the straw is burnt, as is frequently done in Victoria, and the whole of the grain is sold, then 1,145 lbs. of organic matter of the straw is converted into carbonic acid gas, water, and ammonia, and thus absolutely lost, whilst 77½ lbs. of ash, of which 53 lbs. represent silica, are left behind.

The loss of organic matter is going on fairly rapidly in the wheat areas of the State, owing to the continual oxidation of the organic matter of the soil consequent on fallowing, and partly due to the continual practice of stubble burning.

In later articles it will be necessary to consider the probable ultimate effect of such losses and the possible methods of counteracting them.

(7) Each of the essential ash constituents mentioned above, though aggregating less than 5 per cent. of the dry-matter, are nevertheless absolutely necessary for the life and full development of the plant, and it is the most deficient of these constituents which determines what the harvest shall be.

(8) The four constituents, lime, magnesia, iron, and sulphur are contained in such small quantities in the wheat plant and in such large quantities in the soil that the soil supply is never likely to be depleted in these ingredients.

Thus in most cases the problem of maintaining soil fertility, so far as it is governed by purely chemical consideration, centres round the adequacy of the nitrogen, phosphoric acid, and potash content of the soil.

Lime sometimes becomes of great importance in the maintenance of soil fertility, but the necessity for lime in such cases invariably arises from a faulty biological and physical condition of the soil.

(9) All these mineral substances can enter plants *only* through the roots and root hairs and in the form of a dilute mineral *solution.*

We may now turn from the elementary composition of the wheat plant to a consideration of its proximate constituents, and particularly with the proximate composition of the kernel itself.

The composition of the kernel may, perhaps, be best understood by considering it in relation to the products obtained in the process of milling. To gain some information on this point a sample of Federation wheat, grown at the Parafield Wheat Station (S.A.) in 1910, was milled in the Departmental Flour Mill, and the original wheat, together with the flour, bran, and pollard was analyzed by the Chemist for Agriculture of this Department (Mr. P. R. Scott). The following table gives the amount of the proximate constituents—water, fat, carbo-hydrates, fibre, protein, and ash in the bran, flour, pollard and wheat:—

TABLE III.

Constituents.	Federation Wheat.	Federation Flour.	Federation Bran.	Federation Pollard.
	%	%	%	%
1. Moisture	10·99	10·48	9·47	9·08
2. Fat	2·37	1·58	4·42	4·90
3. Carbo-hydrates, Starch, &c.	73·54	78·56	60·72	63·03
4. Fibre	1·87	·30	7·62	6·13
5. Ash	1·34	·63	4·09	2·94
6. Protein	9·89	8·45	13·68	13·92

1. *Water.*—It will be noted that this particular sample of Federation contains about 11 per cent. of moisture, whilst lesser quantities of this ingredient are found in the flour, bran, and pollard prepared from it.

This discrepancy is accounted for by the evaporation that has taken place in the process of milling, during which process considerable heat is developed.

The percentage of moisture present in wheat varies within very wide limits, and it has even been known to fluctuate considerably from day to day with variations in the humidity of the air.   The amount of moisture in the grain becomes a matter of considerable commercial importance in the drier portions of the Commonwealth, especially in parts of South Australia where at harvest time the temperatures are very high and the atmosphere exceedingly dry.   Under such circumstances, the moisture content of the ripe grain is very low.   When such grain is stored for a considerable time, or shipped to a more humid climate, a considerable gain in weight may result.   For example, judging from the evidence given to the South Australian Royal Commission on the Marketing of Wheat, it would appear that .75 per cent. to 3.5 per cent. of the total weight of wheat was gained by merely storing the wheat at the local railway station for six months.

On the other hand, it is conceivable that transferred from a moister district the grain may even lose in weight by storage, more especially if it were stored in a district relatively drier than that in which it was produced.

2. *Fat.*—It will be noted from the table that the flour contains a much smaller percentage of fat than either bran, pollard or the grain itself.   Small as this percentage is, however, it is probably much higher than the amount found in commercial flour made from the same variety of wheat.   This arises from the fact that, in the experimental mill with which this sample was milled, it is rather difficult to get rid of the whole of the germ and to keep it out of the flour.

Fat, of course, occupies a high position as a food stuff, but the amount present in flour is so small as to make it of secondary importance.   The fat of wheat is not found uniformly distributed throughout the kernel, but is almost wholly concentrated in the germ and in the bran.

It is owing to the high fat-content of the germ that it is so necessary to eliminate it from the flour in the process of milling.   The germ not only discolours the flour, but is also a positive source of danger to the keeping quality of the product, inasmuch as the fat of the germ readily develops rancidity and impairs the value of the flour.

3. *Carbo-hydrates.*—The principal constituents of the carbo-hydrate group are starch, dextrin, and sugar, of which starch is by far the most abundant.   It forms from 65 to 70 per cent. of the wheat grain, and the great bulk of the endosperm from which the flour is ultimately derived.   The amount of dextrin and sugar vary considerably in different varieties of wheat, but generally speaking, the amount is very small. In sound wheat and flour the sugar is usually cane sugar.   The presence of much maltose, however, is an indication of unsoundness.

Cellulose, the substance which makes up the " skeleton " of vegetable organisms, the " fibre " which holds the various parts of the plant together, belongs to this group, and is found in the kernel in three forms—

(a) The woody fibre, or lignified cellulose of the bran.
(b) The parenchymatous cellulose forming the partitions of the endosperm.
(c) The delicate fabric forming the envelope of the starch cells.

4. *Ash.*—The composition of the ash or inorganic portion of the grain, the residue left on igniting the crushed grain, is very interesting.

The following figures give the mean of the results of twelve representative samples of Victorian wheat recently analysed in this Department by the Chemist for Agriculture :—

TABLE IV.

COMPOSITION OF ASH OF TWELVE TYPICAL VARIETIES OF VICTORIAN WHEAT.

			%
Phosphoric anhydride		(P_2O_5)	40·87
Potash ..		(K_2O)	29·93
Magnesia		(MgO)	14·61
Lime ..		(CaO)	3·72
Soda ..		(Na_2O)	3·24
Sulphuric anhydride		(SO_3)	3·02
Brown oxide of manganese		(Mn_3O_4)	1·62
Silica ..		(SiO_2)	1·51
Chlorine		(Cl)	·90
Alumina		(Al_2O_3)	·58
Iron oxide		(Fe_2O_3)	·50
			100·50
Less oxygen = Chlorine			·50
			100·00

With regard to the essential ash constituents, it is interesting to note the relatively large amounts of phosphoric acid and potash present, and it is not difficult to understand why manuring with superphosphate has produced such remarkable results during the last decade on soil naturally deficient in this constituent. When we realize that practically *all* the phosphoric acid absorbed by a wheat crop is transferred to the grain and thus carted off the farm each year, it is not hard to understand the necessity for continuous phosphatic fertilization. A comparatively large amount of magnesia is found in the wheat ash, but soils generally contain an abundance of this constituent.

PROTEIN.

The nitrogenous compounds of the wheat kernel have been the subject of much painstaking research. In a communication to the *American Chemical Journal* of 1893, Osborne and Voorhees pointed out that the nitrogenous compounds of wheat consist principally of proteids, of which they recognised five.

Wigner, however, has since shown that nitrogen, combined in other forms than proteid, is present in the wheat kernel, and in quantities far larger than has been generally supposed. He shows that, while the flour contains very little non-coagulable nitrogenous matter, there is a considerable quantity of non-proteid nitrogen in the bran or husk.

The principal proteid of wheat is *gluten*, which, however, really consists of *gliadin* and *glutenin*. If a small quantity of flour be mixed with water so as to make a dough, and this dough be kneaded out under a gently flowing stream of water, the starch and other non-gluten compounds are gradually washed away, and a sticky elastic mass of gluten is left behind. This gluten is composed of two proteids, viz., *gliadin;* which is soluble in dilute solutions of alcohol, but is insoluble in neutral aqueous solutions, and glutenin, which is insoluble in alcoholic solutions. Gliadin may, therefore, be separated from glutenin by digesting the gluten with

.a 70 per cent. solution of alcohol.   If this solution be filtered and care-fu'ly evaporated, the gliadin may be obtained in transparent laminæ. The gliadin forms with water a sticky medium, and it helps to bind the particles of flour toge:her, making the dough tough and coherent.

The glutenin imparts solidity to the gluten and evidently forms a nucleus to which the gliadin adheres.   It is distinguished from gliadin by being ncn-adhesive and ncn-plastic, and by the fact that it is in-soluble in dilute alcohol.   These two proteids together constitute the gluten of wheaten flour, and it is owing to the presence of this gluten that it becomes poss:ble to make a porous bread from flour.   The carbonic acid gas evolved during the fermentative action of the yeast becomes im-prisoned in the gluten, and the expansion of this gas during leavening and baking causes the bread to " rise " and become light and porous. The gliadin and glutenin together amount to 80-90 per cent. of the total proteids of the wheat kernel.

It is found that the amount of gliadin compared with glutenin varies very considerably in d.fferent wheats, and, cn this account, it was for-merly suggested that what is known as *strength* in wheat was dependent on the gliadin-glutenin ratio.   Subsequent investigations, however, have failed to establish any relation between the strength and the gliadin-glutenin ratio.

It may be mentioned that the gliadin-glutenin ratio of four different samples of Federation wheat from the Parafield Wheat Station in 1909 was found by the writer to be 42 : 58.   The gliadin-glutenin ratio in these samples was not connected by any definite relation to the strength or other physical properties of the flour.   This may be seen from Table V.*   The four samples of wheat referred to were all samples of Federa-tion.   Grade I. consisted of fine plump grain weighing 68¼ lbs. per bushel, obtained by sieving a parcel of wheat with a mesh of .275 c.m. Grade II. weighed 67¾ lbs. per bushel, and was composed of grains passing through a .25 c.m. sieve, but retained by a .225 c.m. mesh. Grade III. weighed 63 lbs. per bushel and was obtained with a .2 c.m. sieve, wh'lst the lowest grade was hand-picked from shrivelled grain which passed through the .2 c.m. sieve.

Table V. summarizes the density, volume, and milling products of each grade of wheat and the gliadin-glutenin ratio and strength of the resultant flours.

TABLE V.

Grade.	Bushel Weight.	Weight of 100 Grains.	Average Weight of each Kernel.	Average Volume of each Kernel.	Percentage of Milling Products.			Gluten Content.		Ratio Wet : Dry.	Gliadin percentage.	Glutenin percentage.	Strength—quarts per 200-lb. sack.
					Flour.	Bran.	Pollard.	Wet Gluten.	Dry Gluten.				
	lbs.	grams.	grams.	c.c.m.	%	%	%	%	%		%	%	
I. ..	68·25	4·899	·489	·0369	77·4	11·7	10·9	25·91	9·24	2·71	42·51	57·49	49·0
II. ..	67·75	4·048	·405	·0290	74·4	12·5	13·1	23·86	8·25	2·89	44·1	55·9	48·3
III. ..	63·1	2·687	·268	·0188	69·1	15·3	15·6	22·77	7·92	2·87	42·93	57·07	48·1
IV. ..	55·2	1·481	·148	·0124	58·2	14·0	27·8	26·7	9·4	2·83	42·44	57·56	46·5

* *Vide* " Milling Qualities of High and Low-grade Wheats" by A. E. V. Richardson.   Bulletin No 61. S.A. Department of Agriculture.

Besides the two proteins already described, namely, gliadin and glutenin, three others have been isolated and described.   These are—

(1) *Leucosin.*—A protein soluble in water, coagulating at 50-60 degrees, and similar to albumin.

(2) *Globulin.*—A protein soluble in a dilute salt solution and coagulated by heat.

(3) *Proteose*, which is soluble in water and not coagulated by heat.

It will be necessary at a later stage, when reviewing the milling qualities of various wheats, the effect of environment on the composition and properties of the kernel, the factors underlying strength in wheat and flour, and in discussing the possibility of improving the quality of our wheats, to consider in greater detail the elementary notions outlined above

(To be continued.)

PROPAGATION OF FRUIT TREES.

(Continued from page 173.)

C. F. Cole, Orchard Supervisor.

LIFTING.

When lifting young trees from the nursery rows for sale or planting out care should be exercised to see that the branches are not broken or injured, also that the roots are not mutilated.   If a branch upon a tree carrying well balanced head growths is broken it will probably give difficulty when pruning to reform such head conditions, particularly if the tree be carrying only two or three branch growths and has no suitable buds upon the stem to head back to.   The method of removing the soil to enable the trees to be lifted will be controlled by the class of soil, the roots, and the kind of tree to be lifted.   Very often, in light or sandy soils, and after a heavy rain, all that is necessary, with kinds that are chiefly surface-rooting, is to force the spade well down upon each side or around the trees to be removed, keeping the spade a suitable distance off so that the roots will not be cut or injured close to the butts.   Then by taking hold of the tree by the butt, below the bud mark, with one hand gently pulling whilst forcing the spade upwards beneath the tree with the other, it will be removed without injury.   In heavy, deep rooting, or soils having a stiff clay sub-soil, it will be necessary to open out well upon each side, keeping well away from the butts.   When doing this the spade should be used side on to the trees, the opening being parallel with the row.   After removing the soil the required depth upon either side the spade may be used flat on, so that the operator may be enabled to get well beneath to cut any small tap roots.   If two persons are working together one should take hold of the tree by the butt whilst the other forces the spade well beneath, using it as a lever by pressing the handle upwards towards the trees at the same time that the other person is pulling. The handle should not be pressed downwards or away from the trees; by so doing there is a risk that the blade, when forced upwards, will scrape the bark upon the roots, or else break them close to their basal parts.

When the tree has been lifted the soil should be shaken from the roots by giving the butt a few sharp clouts with the palm of the hand.   The practice of tapping the butts against something hard is faulty in that it involves great risk of causing injury to the bark or cambium.   Deciduous trees carrying foliage at the beginning of the lifting season should have the foliage removed as soon as they are lifted.   The operation of removing the leaves from most kinds is easily performed by drawing the hand down the growths towards the crown, upwards with others.   It is a matter of choice whether the leaves are removed before or after lifting, but if the leaves are not removed the trees will wilt to some extent.

When evergreen trees, such as the loquat, are destined for a long journey it will be found beneficial to remove the foliage, and any tender or immature growths, by using a sharp knife.   This applies also to the citrus family with regard to tender and immature growths.

Apple trees, if a portion of the roots are required for root-grafting, should be opened out well in order that all the length of root possible be obtained.   The pieces of roots cut off should be healed in and not allowed to get dry before being grafted.   When trees having brittle roots, like the apricot, cherry, &c., are being lifted care must be exercised in pulling because of the risk of breakage.   Yearling loquats worked upon the quince stock should be handled with care when being lifted from the soil, tied together, or packed, as they are very liable to break away at the union with the stock.   As soon as the trees have been lifted all those belonging to the one variety should be tied together and labelled, the name being written distinctly upon a waterproof tag, such tag to be affixed to a portion of the tree where there is least likelihood of its detachment.   Lifted trees should be healed in if not required for early despatch or planting-out.   Deciduous trees will receive no hurt for a day or two if packed in a sheltered position, the roots being kept well watered and covered with sacks or some such suitable material.   Evergreen trees should not be allowed to lie about; they should not be lifted until required, and packing should proceed as soon as possible if for transit.

Packing.

The manner in which trees should be packed for transit will be determined chiefly by the distance, the time occupied in reaching their destination, and the botanical order to which they belong.   Evergreen require rather more care than deciduous trees.   The chief factor in packing is to keep the roots moist and cool, care being exercised in seeing that no material is used that will develop heat when damped and kept away from the air.   When deciduous trees are being packed for a short journey, straw, grass hay, rushes, or some similar suitable material may be used for the outside covering.   No obnoxious grasses or weeds should be used as that would be the means of disseminating the seeds of such plant pests.   Some partly decayed straw or grass hay well damped, should be packed about the roots.   To secure this class of packing for the roots the straw or grass should be placed in a heap, kept covered and well watered some short while before using.   The straw or grass will thus become partly decayed by the time it is required, and if damped well before using it will keep moist about the roots for some weeks with no fear of heating.   When straw or rush is used for packing the operator should place upon the ground, about 1 foot apart, and parallel to one another, 8 to 10 strands of hay lashing (rope), first tying a loop upon one end of each of the strands. Then the straw or rush is laid upon the strands, beginning from the centre of the ropes and kept as nearly as possible all one way; the width is to be judged by the quantity of trees to be packed. If the bundle is to be bottle-shaped, *i.e.*, a bundle in which the roots of the trees are placed all at one end, about 18 inches of the material used should overlap the last strand of rope at the bottom, or root end, of it, and the bedding should be laid wider at the bottom, and tapering off to the top. If a double end bundle is required, that is one having the roots of the trees placed at each end, the packing material should overlap at both ends, and its length will be determined by the growth of the trees. The ropes and packing material having been placed in position, a light covering of the damp root material is to be spread upon the bedding at the end, or ends, where the roots are to lie. Then a strand of rope is laid across the top of the bedding parallel to, and over, the second rope from the bottom; also one near the top of the bundle. If all the trees to be packed in the bundle are of the one variety there is no necessity to tie them up into small lots, and each lot labelled separately, but they may be allowed to lie loosely, and only the one tag affixed. The trees are laid upon the bedding, the roots of the first layer or two placed over and midway between the two last strands of rope at the basal end, and the first layer of trees having been placed in position the damp root material is packed well amongst the roots. This process is continued until all the trees are placed in position. It is not necessary to place all the roots of the trees directly upon one another; a certain quantity of them may be worked forward toward the head growths, care being observed that the roots receive attention in regard to damp material with a little of the dry packing worked in amongst the head growths to prevent them from breaking. The ends of the two strands that were placed upon the top of the bedding should now be passed through the loops, drawn taut, and tied off. A covering is to be placed upon the top of the trees, equal in length to the bottom bedding and overlapping the material at the root end. Each strand is to be taken separately, one end passed through the loop, drawn fairly taut and half-hitched off. All the strands having been fixed each rope in turn is to be undone and drawn tight, slacking to be prevented by tying off with two half-hitch knots. The bottom of the bundle must now receive attention; the roots are to be covered with moist material and a piece of rope tied to the second last strand, hitched to the last, and enough length of rope left to insure that where a loop is tied it will reach to the centre of the bottom of the bundle. Half of the overlapping material is to be folded well in, the loop end of the short rope drawn down, and a short stick placed through the loop; press carefully into the bundle in order to keep the folded-in material in position whilst turning the bundle over. This done, take a strand of rope and begin strapping half-way along, working down to the bottom of the bundle and hitching off at the last strand. Finish folding in the other half of the overlapping material, withdraw the stick, pass the end of the rope through the loop, draw taut, and hitch off: quarter off the bundle by strapping in the same manner; cut away any superfluous ends of rope and the bundle is finished. To guard against breakage care must be exercised when the ropes are being drawn taut over the basal portion of the branched growths. When fruit trees are being packed, those having brittle or projecting roots should always be placed in the centre, and those having fibrous roots upon the outside. When the branch growths of trees are being tied together preparatory to inclusion in a bundle straw should be carefully and liberally used to prevent breakage, particularly two-year-old pruned trees, or one-year-old branched pruned. When a double-ended bundle is being packed it is treated in practically the same manner as the bottom of a single or bottle-shaped one. A piece of hessian or bagging strapped around the root end of the bundle will help to conserve the moisture for a longer period. Deciduous trees so packed, will carry safely over a seven to ten days' journey in the winter months. To water the root end of the bundles when packed is an advantage; the roots must always be well watered before packing takes place. The number of trees and the name of the variety should be written on a tag, and the tag attached to that particular parcel before its inclusion in the bundle. Ever-green trees, such as citrus and loquats, if the roots are packed first in partly-decayed straw or grass hay, then in bagging, and finally, in straw or rush, will carry without hurt upon a short journey, but the better method is to pack them in cases standing the trees upright and covering the top with hessian. This is done by nailing two pieces of wood upright about 3 in x $\frac{1}{2}$ in., the height being controlled by the growth of the trees to be packed; nail these uprights in the centre, one at each end of the case, upon the outside. Then nail a crosspiece to the top of the uprights (if the case is a large one it will be necessary to duplicate the uprights and crosspiece); bore two holes at each end of the case, horizontal to each other, and about 7 in. apart; take a short piece of stout rope, pass the ends through from the outer side, tie a knot at each end and nail it down to the inside of the case. The rope should be long enough that when this operation is finished the case will have two crude handles for lifting purposes. Before the trees are packed in the box all bruised or injured roots should be cut away. Then, using fresh water, puddle clay, until it is the consistency of cream, dab the roots well into it, and having done this, pack the trees closely together in the case in an upright position, filling in amongst the roots with wet sawdust. Shake down the sawdust well to ensure that the roots are sufficiently covered; lightly water to settle the sawdust. Finally, draw the tops of the branches together, if neces-sary, with a piece of twine and provide a covering of hessian, tacked to the uprights, cross piece, sides and ends of the case. If the package is to be forwarded by steam-boat it should be clearly labelled by stencilling:— "Keep from heat of engines." Deciduous trees destined for a long sea voyage should be packed in cases; the roots first puddled in clay and then packed around with some suitable material that will hold the moisture and not generate heat. Sphagnum moss is preferable. The trees should be laid lengthwise in the case; those well matured and not overgrown should be selected for long journeys. Trees properly packed will carry in good condition from any of the Australian States to South Africa and South America. A limited number of trees is being exported annually to those countries from Victoria.

(To be continued.)

THE OLIVE.

(*Continued from page* 198.)

By L. Macdonald, Horticulturist, Dookie Agricultural College.

Pruning.

Compared with the advances that have been made in the treatment of many other of our fruit trees very little has been done, as yet, towards the scientific pruning of the olive. This fact is more remarkable when it is considered that the olive has held such a proud position in the economic field for so many centuries and is destined, no doubt, to bear its great reputation for ages yet to come.

It is due probably to the longevity and hardihood of the trees, which have proved themselves capable of bearing good crops for years without pruning. Hence it is often contended that pruning is unnecessary. However this may be under some circumstances, it is obvious, nevertheless, that careful and scientific pruning must contribute largely towards the ultimate success of olive culture.

True, in some places pruning is performed periodically, but in such a crude manner that it is almost unworthy of the name. The methods referred to consist of thinning out some of the large branches of the trees at long intervals of time or promiscuously cutting out the branches from the centre of the tree. Such methods are not based on the lines on which proper treatment should rest, and must inevitably fail to bring about the desired end. Sunscalding frequently takes place in the exposed portions of the remaining limbs and permanent injury is thereby caused.

It will be found that after reaching a full fruit bearing age, the olive, like many other trees, when left to itself has a strong tendency to alternate between the production of heavy crops and light crops during a series of years. The wanton prolificacy of the good years carries almost as many disadvantages as the barrenness of the lean years, for many reasons that are obvious. Therefore it is to pruning that we must look to modify these wayward tendencies and maintain uniformity and economy in cropping both advantageous to the grower and to the tree. Furthermore, where diseases are prevalent pruning will facilitate their successful treatment.

It is first of all essential that the pruner understands the nature of the fruiting wood, and habit of the tree's growth, before he can make any intelligent progress in carrying out the work. It is often stated that the olive bears its fruit on two-year-old wood. As this is a matter that vitally affects any theory in regard to treatment, it would be well, at the outset, to examine it closely, so that the beginner may understand exactly how far it is true. It will depend greatly on the time of the year at which the wood is examined, to define what is meant when speaking of its age. If the laterals are taken when the fruit is on the tree they will be found to be carrying the bulk of their fruit on the previous season's growth and may at that time be spoken of as two-years-old or in their second season's growth.

However, it is only to be expected that any classification of the wood designed to assist the beginner must be made to suit the wood at pruning time, that is in the winter after the crop is off and before the spring growth sets in; not when the fruit is on the tree; otherwise, a great many complications might occur. Hence, we find that, like other drupaceous fruits, *e.g.*, plum, peach, and apricot, the olive bears its fruit chiefly on the previous season's growth. It differs, however, in this, that, although the bulk of the crop is borne on last season's growth, it also bears on the wood made the previous season and also on the current season's growth. So that fruit

14. DIFFERENT TYPES OF LATERALS, SHOWING FRUITING HABIT.

will sometimes be found growing on three separate seasons' growth. Although this takes place at times, the quantity of fruit borne on other than

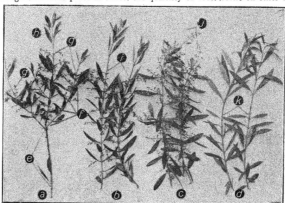

15. DIFFERENT TYPES OF LATERALS IN BLOOM.

the previous season's growth is so unimportant that it should not be reckoned with in the pruning of the tree.

At this point, perhaps, the different types of fruiting laterals in No. 14 might be examined. These will indicate, to some extent, the manner in which those laterals that are classed as one-year-old at pruning bear their fruit and also suggest the most satisfactory method of handling them for fruit production.

Fig. B. in No. 14 shows a good type of fruiting lateral. It will be observed that this lateral is fruiting right to its terminal point. It will be of no value for fruit production during the following season owing to no fresh growth being made. If allowed to remain on the tree it may eventually break into fresh growth and subsequently bear fruit. However, in a well-regulated tree the object is to remove such shoots after they have fruited well, and encourage fresh ones from year to year.

Fig. C. in the same plate shows two vigorous laterals carrying a good supply of fruit. This type, and that shown at B., are best for fruit production on the olive. They, with all the other laterals depicted in this plate except E., are in their second season's growth, or are what would be one-year (or season)-old at pruning. The arrows at *H* indicate the terminal

16. BRANCH SHOWING DETERIORATED LATERALS.

point of the previous season's extension. Further growth is being made, which may fruit in the ensuing season.

Fig. D. is an example of a lateral, bearing fruit both on the previous season's growth, which terminates at *i*, and on the current season's growth, which is indicated at *j*.

The next lateral on the same plate, indicated at E., is from the Polymorpha variety. It is in its third year's growth. The fruits borne on the old wood at *k* have sprung from what might be termed adventitious buds. This frequently takes place; more especially on some varieties, as Uvaria or Polymorpha, that are in a vigorous state of growth. The letter *l* indicates the terminal point of the first season's growth, while *m* is the terminal of the second season's growth. Fruit alone has been produced in its third season, no further extension of wood growth being made. Although this type is of some value for fruiting it is by no means amongst the best of the olive laterals.

Two different types are again illustrated at F and G. The former are from Conditiver and show the solitary, terminal fruiting habit of this variety. The latter are from Nigerrima and show the clustering at the terminal point that often occurs on this and other varieties. The branches of fruit at A are from the Uvaria variety.

Before stopping to review the various types of wood depicted on No. 14, it would, perhaps, be better to consider the nature of the various types shown on No. 15. They represent four of the most characteristic laterals found on well-cared-for trees.

Fig. A is a branching lateral in its third season's growth. A couple of leaves may be noticed still growing on that portion that is indicated at e, which is the extent of the first year's growth. Where those leaves remain on wood of this age, it often happens that fruit is born from buds that break out at their axils, as was shown at Fig. E. on No. 14. The fruit buds may be observed at f springing from the axils of the leaves. This is on the second season's growth, which terminates at g. A further extension is being made at h during the third season.

The three remaining types shown in this plate belong to what are known as one-year (or season)-old laterals at pruning. They were photographed at the beginning of their second season's growth, in which they subsequently develop fruit. A very free development of fruit buds may be noticed practically the whole length of those at B and C. The difference occurs only at the terminal point. On those shown at B a further extension is being made at i, while at j, in the other pair, the terminal point has ceased to make any further wood extension and has developed only flower buds. This terminal fruiting habit is most apparent in those shoots that have a downward or drooping tendency and are not likely to recontinue in active growth. Those shown at D are what are commonly known as barren laterals. The terminal point of the first season's growth is indicated at K, while a further fresh extension is being made. These laterals often serve a useful purpose by sheltering the more permanent parts of the tree, besides sometimes developing fruit in their third or fourth season's growth.

After a careful examination of the types of wood illustrated in Nos. 14 and 15 it is manifest that the olive is essentially a " lateral-bearing " tree. That is, it produces its fruit chiefly on comparatively long slender growths that extend from year to year from the more permanent parts of the tree; also, that the great bulk of the fruiting wood is of last season's growth. The best class of this fruit bearing wood is represented by those types depicted at Figs. B and C in No. 14 and at B and C in No. 15. In the majority of cases, however, once these laterals fruit, their decline sets in. This tendency is more marked in those that have assumed a drooping or downward tendency. Hence, one of the most important objects in the treatment of established trees is the encouragement from year to year of a good supply of these fresh laterals for fruiting in the following season.

If the trees are left to themselves the laterals extend very slowly owing to the crowding that usually results and the deterioration that takes place in the wood. The fruit is then borne on the few inches of growth that is made at the terminal points and chiefly on the outside of the tree. The branch shown on No. 16 gives a fair indication of what happens where the vigour is diminished and continual subdivisions take place. It is plain that any fruit borne on the terminals of these many deteriorated laterals will be inferior in quality and more difficult to gather than that which is produced on the strong-growing ones.

17. BRANCH UNPRUNED.

The crowns of the young trees should be formed about 18 inches from the ground and a good set of main arms encouraged. The standard system of training the trees is adopted in some places. This consists of training the tree to a single stem for about 5 feet from the ground and then allowing the head to assume a globular form. The gooseberry bush method of training several trunks from the ground is also adopted, but neither of these methods is recommended here.

The writer favours the establishment of a low crown and the maintenance of a modified vase form; that is, more branches are retained than is usual with some of our other fruit trees. Care should be taken, however, that ample space is afforded for the free development of laterals on all the main branches, as the wood will not mature when crowding takes place and the best results cannot be maintained. For the first three or four years after planting the main object in pruning should be the establishment of a good frame-work and the maintenance of good growth in the tree.

The trees should be kept well in hand and fruiting wood encouraged right from the base upwards. It will be necessary, as stated before, that provision be made for the renewal of the supply of fruiting wood from year to year. This is best done by maintaining a reserve of strength in the tree, by cutting back and thinning out. Thus more general growth throughout the tree is encouraged each season, and the possibility of it spending its strength in any one season by excessive cropping and being unable to produce sufficient wood for a crop in the following season is minimized.

Owing to the pliable nature of the wood the direction and rigidity of the main limbs should be carefully maintained; otherwise a pronounced ten-

18. BRANCH AS IN NO. 17 PRUNED
SHOWING THINNING OF LATERALS
AND CUTTING BACK OF LEADER.

dency to spread will be observed where heavy crops occur and the limbs will not easily regain their original position. This tendency is more marked, of course, in some varieties than in others, owing to the habits of growth being entirely dissimilar.

The pruning season may start as soon as the crop is off the trees, and may continue until just before the spring growth sets in. That is, the work should be carried out usually about June or July in most of our districts, varying somewhat with the locality and variety.

If the frame-work has been properly established the chief care at each annual pruning will be the selection and encouragement of the right class of laterals for fruiting. As a general practice the spurring back of the laterals is not advised. It is better to practice thinning, leaving the remaining ones long.

(*To be continued.*)

FARM BLACKSMITHING.

(*Continued from page 195.*)

George Baxter, Instructor in Blacksmithing, Working Men's College, Melbourne.

V.—WELDING (*continued*).

FORGING SPANNERS.

Figure 53 shows two methods of forging spanners. A is the usual manner in which they are made from steel out of a solid bar, and B is the best method of making from iron.

To forge the first named a piece of mild steel is required equal in thickness to the depth of the nut and in width about one and three-quarters the breadth of the nut.

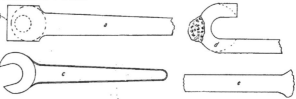

FIG. 53. SPANNER.

(*a*) Roughing out. (*b*) Position to cut off bar. (*c*) The completed spanner. (*d*) and (*e*) Scarfed ready for welding.

Such a piece of metal is first drawn down to form the handle, as shown in A ; the length of handle requiring to be fifteen times the diameter of the bolt. It would then be cut off at B, the enlarged portion roughly rounded, and a hole punched as shown by dotted lines. The hole being then drifted out to the breadth of nut the gap would be cut out with the chisel and the spanner afterwards forged as near as possible to shape shown at C. The handle should be the last part finished by rounding the edges with a top and bottom swage, so that it will be comfortable in the hand.

For an iron spanner (best made as shown at D and E) take a square bar equal in size to the diameter of bolt it is intended for; cut off a piece long enough to make the handle, upset and lap-scarf it, and allow the point of scarf to spread out as shown. To make the jaw, heat and upset the bar at the place where the weld is to be, then bend and scarf with the ball end of the hand hammer. After welding, forge to shape by cutting off the corners to dotted line and finish.

The following proportions of spanners will no doubt be found useful.

Taking the breadth of the nut as 1, then the outer diameter of jaw will be 2; thickness of jaw ⅝ths. for steel, and ¾ths for iron; length of handle 15; greatest breadth of handle 1; least breadth of handle, ½.

WORKING AND TEMPERING STEEL.

It may be considered an accomplishment to know sufficient about the nature of steel, and the manner in which it is manipulated at the forge, to be able to make a useful tool. It certainly should be eminently useful to the farmer, removed as he is, in many cases, by miles from a blacksmith's shop. Proficiency in the art of tool-making can only be acquired by long practice, close observation, and extreme care.

Whilst the farmer does not require to enter into all the intricate details of tool-making, or study all the phenomena connected with steel, yet if he is desirous of making or repairing a tool he wants to understand more about it than could be learned by simply watching some one else do the work. He wants to know something of the causes of failure, and of the effect that heat has upon the metal, etc. By carefully following the directions given in this article he should be able to meet with a fair measure of success at first, and with further practice there is no reason why he should not become quite an expert.

Steel is produced by mechanical means, the process chiefly consisting of adding a small percentage of carbon to wrought iron. The effect of the combination is that the character of the iron is altered to such an extent that it almost appears to be a different metal. The structure has been altered from fibrous to granular; the hardness intensified; the weight increased, and the property of welding so affected that it becomes extremely difficult and in some cases impossible of accomplishment. When steel is heated to redness and suddenly cooled it becomes very hard and brittle, and it is this property which makes it the most useful of all metals. It can be made to cut glass; it can be rendered so soft that it may be cut by another piece of steel such as the blade of a pocket knife; it can be forged and bent into any conceivable shape. It can be made so elastic that thousands of oscillations will not alter its shape. (For example take a watch spring, which will remain visibly perfect for years). It can also be made of any degree of hardness between the two extremes, and the process by which this is done is called *tempering*.

Tempering by which elasticity is produced, is effected by reducing some of the hardness given to steel by heating and quickly cooling it. The degree of hardness of a tool varies: firstly, by the hardness of the material to be cut and, secondly, by the manner in which it is to be cut; for instance if the work is to be performed by means of a blow then the tool needs to be made as elastic as possible and at the same time retain sufficient hardness to maintain a cutting edge; but if the tool be required to work in a lathe where the pressure is fairly constant then it may be made much harder.

A piece of steel that has been heated to redness and cooled out will if polished be of a silvery whiteness, and if slowly reheated changes in the colour of its surface will be noticed. These changes are due to the oxidation of the surface of the metal exposed to the atmosphere and heat. As the temperature rises the colours darken. The first indication of change takes place when the temperature rises to 250 deg. Fahr. It will then be noticed to be of a dirty white colour. As the heat increases it assumes a yellow colour, then dark straw, brown, purple, and varying shades of blue. The changes, which are called the tempering colours, are followed as guides in determining the hardness of the steel.

The first essential to the production of good tools is the selection of suitable steel. Manufacturers of steel make it in many grades, and as each grade is intended for a specific purpose if steel be used for a purpose that it is not intended for then good results cannot be obtained. Notwithstanding this there are many who have an idea that the high priced qualities are the best for all purposes. That is a mistake; there are times when the cheapest is best. In purchasing steel it is always well to state the purpose for which it is to be used and the merchant will know what grade to supply.

The tools about a farm do not as a rule require to be made of high-grade steel, *e.g.*, steel containing a large percentage of carbon. The quality used for miners' drills would suit most purposes and give very good results if properly treated. It costs about 4d. per lb.

In working steel, greater care must be exercised than in forging iron or mild steel. It will not permit of being heated to a temperature above bright red without injury, because when so heated the carbon becomes burnt out and so it is destroyed. Neither must it be hammered after the redness has left it, for such treatment would cause it to crack. Low grade steel may be welded, but the operation requires considerably more skill than the welding of iron. Welding steel should therefore be avoided, excepting in the case of pointing picks, crow-bars, or plough-shares. What is known as *blister steel* is most suitable for welding purposes.

Forging a Cold Chisel.

To make a cold-chisel (Fig. 54) for cutting metal, take a piece of $\frac{3}{4}$-in. octagonal steel, and cut off a piece $6\frac{1}{2}$ in. long. Heat one end to redness and form the head, which is done simply with the hand hammer. In drawing out the chisel end, do so with as few heats as possible, for the reason that each heating reduces the carbon value. For ordinary purposes the shape of the chisel should be as shown in the sketch. The width of blade does not require to be more than $\frac{7}{8}$ in., and the length of tapered part about 3 in. It is now ready for tempering and grinding.

To temper, heat the tool slowly and evenly to a low red for a distance of about 2 in. from the point, place about 1 in. of the heated portion in water which has previously been heated to about 70 deg. Fahr., and after a period of about five seconds, slowly raise the tool about $\frac{1}{2}$ in.; let it remain there for several seconds longer. Remove from the water, and with a piece of sandstone, brick, or emery cloth rub vigorously to remove the scale from the surface, when the part which was cooled will be white, and as the heat is conducted to the point from the back so the colours will appear on the surface. When the point assumes a purple hue, quickly plunge again into the water; cool right out, and grind. In grinding a chisel to cut iron the angle formed at the point should not be less than 70 degrees. If ground too thin it will not stand up to the work, no matter how well it may be tempered.

The punch (Fig. 55) needs no further comment than that it requires the same treatment as the chisel.

A drill (Fig. 56) is made to fit the socket of a machine or ratchet-brace by forging; the cutting end is first formed like a punch, then flattened at the end as shown, and the corners cut off. The temper of a drill needs to be dark straw at the point, which is slightly harder than the chisel.

A cross-cut chisel (Fig. 57) is used for cutting key-ways in wheels that are fixed to a revolving shaft; or when it is necessary to remove a large amount of metal from a large flat surface the cross-cut is used for chipping a number of grooves, and the ridges so left are cut off with a flat chisel. The process of making a cross-cut needs but little description, the shape being suggestive of the mode of procedure. One point about it is that the end of the chisel needs to be made wider than the remaining part of the blade. If it is not widened out as shown in the drawing it will stick in the groove formed by cutting, and so cause trouble. It is tempered in exactly the same manner as the cold chisel.

If a tool when put to use after forging and tempering is found to quickly blunt, it shows that the temper has been reduced too much. In such a case, retemper it to a lighter colour, *e.g.*, if it were tempered, say,

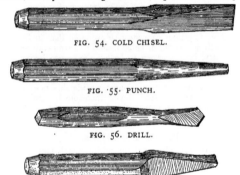

FIG. 54. COLD CHISEL.

FIG. 55. PUNCH.

FIG. 56. DRILL.

FIG. 57. CROSS CUT CHISEL.

to a purple hue, then let it be dark straw. It will further be found that whilst one piece of steel will be sufficiently hard at purple, another will require a higher temper—due to the quality of the steel.

When a tool breaks in working, it may be through being tempered too hard, or through overheating in forging or tempering. If from the first cause the fracture will be quite white, and on examination of the fracture it will be found to be of a very fine grain. When overheating has been the cause then the break will be partly black and partly bright and the fracture will be always curved; if badly burnt the break will show a very coarse and crystalline grain.

POINTING A PICK.

Picks are made of iron, with a small piece of steel welded on to the point. This, of course, wears away, and necessarily requires to be relaid. Sometimes only a very short piece of steel has been welded on, and when such is the case a new piece may be welded on by splitting the end of the pick with a hot chisel (so as to make it look like the letter Y), a piece of steel first made wedge-shaped and inserted into the split; a welding heat

taken, and then hammered to required shape.   In making the wedge, have
the surfaces roughened by driving a chisel into them, and previous to putting
into position make the pick point red hot ; the wedge cold.   The reason
for doing so is that by having the Y heated, and the steel cold, the iron
is embedded in the cuts made in the wedge by striking a good hard blow
on it, and the wedge is thus prevented from falling out in the fire.

When very much worn it becomes necessary to lengthen the pick point
by first welding a wedge-shaped piece of iron on the back of the pick some
distance from the point, as shown at A in Fig. 58, so that the point of the
pick and the piece of iron form the Y shape for the reception of steel—
B, same figure.   It is then treated as mentioned above.   The best steel
for welding to picks, crow-bars, or plough-shares is *blister steel*, which may
be bought in sizes suitable for requirements ; but if not available then a piece
of miners' drill steel may be used.   In taking a welding heat on steel great
care must be exercised to secure good results.   Steel, being much more difficult to weld than iron, has to be done at a much lower temperature.   It is
always advisable, and in most cases necessary, to use a flux for the purpose.
For welding blister steel to iron, sand will do for a flux, or if a small
quantity of borax (about 1 in 4) be added, the work is facilitated.   When

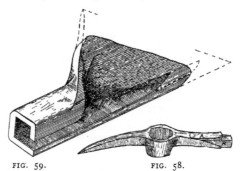

FIG. 59.   FIG. 58.

higher grade steel is to be welded, there are special welding mixtures that
may be purchased, but if borax alone be used it makes a very effective flux.

The heat for welding steel is of a yellowish colour.   If heated the same
as iron the steel would fly to pieces when struck with the hammer.

RELAYING A PLOUGH SHARE.

All plough shares cannot be relaid.   Some are made of cast iron, which
is unweldable.   Those made of wrought steel can be repaired time after
time.   Fig. 59 shows one well worn, and the dotted lines indicate the
original shape.   To make them up to those lines, a piece of iron is welded
on, a start being made at the top corner and working towards the point.
It is impossible to weld the piece all the way along at one heating, about
4 inches being about the maximum length that can be done at once.   When
the iron is welded on a piece of steel is then put on the point.   It is almost
impossible to describe in detail how this may be done, the condition of the
shares being different in each instance.   Ingenuity and common sense are
required to carry out the work successfully.

(Concluded.)

SOIL MOISTURE AND CROPPING.

By John W. Paterson, B.Sc., Ph.D., Experimentalist.

A twenty-bushel crop of wheat (grain, straw and roots) contains at harvest about 450 lb. of water. This water is present as water in the crop. Chemical analysis further shows that it contains about 170 lb. of hydrogen chiefly in its starch and protein compounds. This hydrogen would nearly all come from water which was decomposed as water by the plant while growing. It requires 1,530 lb. of water to yield 170 lb. of hydrogen.

Adding 450 and 1,530 we get 1,980 lb. of water. One inch of rainfall per acre weighs just over 100 tons, so that 1,980 lb. of water equals 0.0088 inches, or 0.88 points. If water only played the part of phosphoric acid or any ordinary food material to plants then 0.88 points of rain would satisfy the requirements of this crop for water.

The insufficiency of such a rainfall is abundantly manifest. About 2,000 times as much rain must fall on the ground annually, and such a rainfall must have a suitable periodic distribution, to give a yield of wheat such as is here contemplated.

What then was the use of all this rain of which the crop has nothing to show at harvest, but which was nevertheless required to produce the desired yield? There are three answers :—

(1) Part of it was used in the vital processes, and afterwards discarded from the stems and leaves during the growth of the plant.

(2) Part of it was necessary for the soil changes whereby food materials are prepared for the plant.

(3) Part of it was inevitably lost from the soil.

First:—As to the water discarded by the plant.—The crop of wheat under consideration would weigh dry about 1½ tons. In producing this dry matter it is essential that very much water must pass through the plant during growth. It has been variously estimated that from 200 to 600 lb. of water must pass through the plant for each 1 lb of dry increase. Taking 400 as a middle figure, it would thus be necessary for 1½ × 400 = 600 tons of water to be absorbed from the soil and evaporated from the leaves to produce the crop of wheat.

This amount of water equals 6 inches of rainfall. Satisfactory figures are wanting. It is certain however that different crops, and probably in an important degree different varieties of the same crop, make widely different demands in regard to water per unit of dry matter formed. The subject is an important one as bearing upon the best crops, and the best variety of crop to cultivate in dry districts.

Economy in the use of water is not however everything in a crop; ability to obtain the water under various conditions is not less important. The power of any crop to obtain water depends upon several factors among which are :—

(1) The percentage of water in the soil.

(2) The readiness with which its water is gradually given up by the particular class of land.

(3) The amount of pure air (oxygen) at the rootlets.

(4) The soil temperature.

(5) The concentration (osmotic value) of the weak salt solution forming the soil moisture.

(6) The variety and vigour of the crop.

(7) Climate—particularly as regards sunshine, humidity and wind.

Secondly:—As to water necessary for the soil processes whereby food materials are rendered available for crops.—On the average a soil will contain 100 times more plant food than the crop then growing on it requires. But the crop cannot use it because the soil constituents must be easily soluble before they can be taken up or absorbed as plant food. The soil constituents which the crop finds most difficulty in obtaining enough of in soluble forms are nitric and phosphoric acids, and sometimes potash.

There is extremely little available phosphoric acid and also sometimes little available potash left in a poor soil at harvest. For the next crop, unless manured, the chief source of supply is the amount which can be rendered available in the interval. A year's fallow gives longer time. But in order that the process whereby the phosphoric acid is made available may go on, the soil must be sufficiently moist. Chemical change scarcely occurs between dry solids. In addition to chemical change, solution of mineral plant foods is to some extent effected by the soil bacteria, but these also require moisture. In fallow, it is desirable to conserve moisture apart from the water requirement of the next crop, because the moisture facilitates the solution of mineral plant food during the period of fallow.

But probably soil moisture is most important from the point of view of nitric acid formation. Deficiency of phosphoric acid can be made good at relatively small cost by a small application of superphosphate and its use is perfectly safe. Nitric acid on the other hand is not only much dearer, but its application artificially as nitrate tends to force on a kind of growth which renders the crop more subject to damage by drought at a later date. The process whereby nitric acid is formed from the insoluble nitrogenous compounds of decaying crops is termed nitrification.

The change is brought about by several different kinds of bacteria. There are three stages. One kind attacks the nitrogen of the decaying crop residues ; a second carries the work through another stage ; the third yields the finished nitric acid. It is known that sufficient moisture must be present to allow these germs to work, and that they may be killed by severe drought. Exactly how much water they require to do their best work, and at what stage of dryness they cease work altogether is a subject however upon which there appears no reliable information.

Nitrification is a necessary antecedent to crop-production on any land growing grain or roots, and to provide suitable conditions for it is of primary importance. It is of particular importance on soils continuously under crop without any return of fresh vegetable matter to them, because on such land nitrification becomes each year more difficult.

Thirdly:—As to water lost inevitably from the soil.—There are three ways in which water is lost from soils :—

    (1) Surface drainage into ditches and watercourses.

    (2) Percolation into underground springs.

    (3) Evaporation from the surface.

(1) Surface drainage causes most loss on baked surfaces, lying on the slope, and when the rainfall is concentrated in a short period of time. More particularly in autumn and winter, when the land is hard, is much water lost in this way. Early ploughing after harvest avoids loss, as not only is the surface left rough to impede surface flow, but at the same time the upper portion of the soil is rendered sufficiently open and porous to take in what falls upon it.

    (2) Percolation into underground springs. This loss is unavoidable, and in many cases it is an advantage preventing the soil becoming waterlogged. In some classes of land, particularly clays, when no natural

escape for surplus water exists it is necessary to underdrain to get the same result.

(3) Evaporation from the surface. All soils are subject to this loss and the amount may represent the total annual rainfall. According to Greaves the yearly amount evaporated from a water surface in the vicinity of London equals 20.6 inches. There is more loss than this from a soil kept fully saturated. While fully saturated all soils lose water at the same rate. As different soils are allowed to dry those with largest particles (sands) lose water fastest. After a time those with finest particles (clays) lose most because they have most to lose. Finally, both kinds of soils come to a balance losing or gaining moisture according to the humidity of the air.

Evaporation may be greatly diminished by protecting the soil from the action of sun and wind. Under ordinary circumstances as the soil loses moisture by evaporation, more water reaches the surface from below. It rises by capillary attraction through the pores of the soil. The smaller these pores are (within limits) the higher the water will rise; if they are very large it will practically not rise at all Leaves or loose litter spread on the surface have very wide pores and water cannot rise through them. At the same time they prevent rapid evaporation because they shield the soil surface from sun and wind.

Litter spread on the surface to limit evaporation is called a mulch. Instead of spreading litter the soil itself may be used as a mulch. For this purpose it is only necessary to stir it to a depth of 2 or 3 inches when it is not too wet. By this means the surface pores become too large to raise the water above the lower layer of the stirred soil. The stirred soil soon appears to dry while an unstirred portion may appear to remain wet, but that is because in the latter case the water is continuing to rise to the surface and dissipate by evaporation, while in the former case no water is rising to the surface and none is lost, because the surface layer is not getting any from underneath to lose. Beneath the apparently dry surface water is being saved from loss in the body of the soil. Working with a 3-inch soil mulch on a clay loam, Professor King of Wisconsin found that 63.13 per cent. of the evaporation on similar unmulched land was saved in 100 days.

When referring to the water requirements of a wheat crop it was observed that about 400 tons probably was required to produce 1 ton dry increase, equal to approximately 100 tons for each ton of the crop in the green sappy state. In greater or less degree the same is true for the requirements of weed plants, and so weeds, whether in the crop or on fallow, rob the land of much moisture. As the making of a soil mulch, whether on fallow land or by way of intertillage in growing crops, kills weeds at the same time as it makes a mulch it has thus a double effect in conserving moisture.

The particular importance of soil moisture conservation in Australian farming arises in large part from the powerful evaporation which occurs during the summer months. In some ways the conditions are special and more exact information is required. With this object, experiments are being conducted during the present season bearing on the relation of soil moisture to the requirements of the plant, to the conditions for nitrification in soils, and to different methods of bare fallowing and intertillage. To the reporting of the results of the experiments designed under those heads the present article will serve us as an introduction.

AN EFFECTIVE SPARROW TRAP.

J. Wilson, Silo Builder.

The prevalence of sparrows throughout the State frequently causes great loss to producers, and to combat this pest the writer has designed a simple, yet effective, trap, by which as many as 200 sparrows have been caught in a single day. The following details of construction and the accompanying illustrations will enable readers to give the method a trial.

Cut a 12-ft. piece of 3-ft. x 2-ft. hardwood into 3-ft. lengths, and check them out 3-in. x 1-in. on two sides at both ends to take the top and bottom rails, so as to make all the outside faces flush. Also cut four 9-ft. lengths of 3-in. x 1-in. Lay two lengths of 3-in. x 2-in. on edge on a level piece of ground, and nail the 3-in. x 1-in. pieces temporarily in the checks. Square the side and spike together firmly. Then deal with the other side in the same manner. Next cut six 3-ft. lengths of 3-in. x 1-in. and nail them in the other checks at the ends. Fix the other two lengths 12 inches from each end at the top of trap to carry the wire netting.

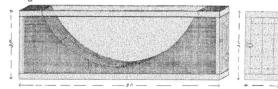

Cover the frame with ½-in. wire netting. Keep the netting 6 inches from the ground in the centre of trap. Cut out five holes of 1½-in. diameter in the centre of the netting. Insert points of snips and give a turn to form round holes. Cover the side with netting and lace top and sides together with wire. Then cut out sides to the sweep of the top wire. Make and fix two ledge doors at each end of the trap.

The following material will be required :—

Timber.—One 12 ft., 3 x 2 hardwood. Four 9 ft.; one 18 ft., 3 x 1; 35 ft, 6 x ⅞, T. and G.
Galvanized wire netting, 3-ft. wide, ½-in. mesh, 11 yards.
T-hinges and screws, 12 inches, two pairs.
Clout tacks, ½ inch, 1 lb.
Wire nails, 3 inches, 1 lb.

As sparrows often congregate near poultry runs, it is suggested that one or two fowls be placed in the trap for the first day to attract the sparrows. It is also advisable, when emptying the trap, to leave one or two birds to act as decoys. Bait the trap with a handful of grain.

BEE-KEEPING IN VICTORIA.

(Continued from page 179.)

F. R. Beuhne, Bee Expert.

IV.—Hives.

The hive most generally in use in Victoria is the "Langstroth" either eight or ten frame. There are however a number of beekeepers who use a modified form of the Heddon hive. Whatever hive is adopted the walls should not be less than $\frac{7}{8}$ inch in thickness, otherwise extremes of temperature will affect the bees, and during very hot weather combs may melt down. All hives sold by manufacturers are made of $\frac{7}{8}$-inch wood, and I strongly advise beginners who intend to make their own hives not to use thinner boards.

The eight-frame Langstroth hive, as shown in Fig. 5, is made of $\frac{7}{8}$-inch shelving, pine, or Californian redwood. It measures 20 in. by $13\frac{5}{8}$ in. outside, and is $9\frac{1}{2}$ inches deep, giving an inside measurement of $18\frac{1}{4}$ x $12\frac{1}{8}$ x $9\frac{1}{2}$. The ten-frame Langstroth is of the same length and depth, but of 16 inches outer and $14\frac{1}{4}$ inches inner width, thus giving room for two more frames. The end boards of the hive are rebated inside to a distance of $\frac{7}{8}$ inch down and $\frac{1}{2}$ inch into the thickness of the board. On to the shoulder of this rebate is nailed a runner of folded tin so as to project $\frac{1}{4}$ inch upwards. On this metal runner rest the top bars of the frames, and its purpose is to prevent the crushing of bees when handling frames and to avoid the gluing down of the latter by the bees.

Two kinds of frames are sold by dealers, the Simplicity and the Hoffmann. The outer dimensions of both are the same, viz., $17\frac{5}{8}$ in. x $9\frac{1}{8}$ in., with the top bar $19\frac{1}{2}$ inch long, but while in the Simplicity, or loose hanging frame, top, side and bottom bar are all of the same width, viz., $\frac{7}{8}$ inch, in the Hoffmann, or self-spacing frame, the upper part of the side bars is $1\frac{3}{8}$ inch wide. When pushed close together in the hive, they give the correct spacing of the combs, viz., $1\frac{3}{8}$ inch, which is the average distance at which bees build combs when in a state of nature. Eight or ten frames in the respective hives leave a small space, this is occupied by a thin board of the dimensions of the frames and called the follower and its object is to more easily remove or handle the frames after it is withdrawn. The thickness of the bars of the Simplicity frame is top bar $\frac{1}{2}$ inch or $\frac{5}{8}$ inch, reduced to $\frac{3}{8}$ inch at the projecting ends; side bars $\frac{3}{8}$ to 7-16 inch; bottom bar $\frac{1}{4}$ to $\frac{3}{8}$ inch. In the Hoffmann frame the thickness and width of the top bar varies with different manufacturers, American frames having a top bar 1 inch wide and $\frac{7}{8}$ inch thick, while some frames of local make have a top bar $\frac{7}{8}$ inch wide, and $\frac{1}{2}$ inch or $\frac{5}{8}$ inch thick. The bottom bar is $\frac{3}{4}$ inch x $\frac{1}{4}$ inch in all the different makes. Whatever the thickness of the bars the outside measurement of the frame is always the same.

The Simplicity frame is the cheapest and easiest to uncap for the extraction of honey, but, being a loose hanging frame, it has some serious disadvantages. Each frame has to be spaced separately every time bees are handled, and as there is a $\frac{1}{4}$-inch space between the frames when correctly spaced the bees will often build comb into these spaces and on to the end wall of the hive. Further, every time a hive is moved the

FIG. 5.--Eight-frame Langstroth Hive, Two Storey.

FIG. 6.—End and General View of Simplicity Frame.

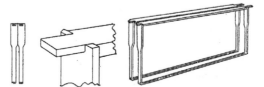

FIG. 7.—End and General View of Hoffmann Frame.

FIG. 8.—End and General View of New Frame.

frames have to be secured in some way to prevent them knocking against one another and crushing bees, and for these reasons self-spacing frames are more advantageous. The difference in the first cost between Simplicity and self-spacing frames is only 2s. to 2s. 6d. per hundred frames. Wide top bar Hoffmann frames as used in America are somewhat difficult to uncap when extracting; as the comb of honey when sealed does not project beyond the wide top bar, it cannot be used as a guide for the uncapping knife, as can be done with the Simplicity or the Hoffmann, with a $\frac{7}{8}$ inch x $\frac{5}{8}$ inch top bar as shown in Figure 7.

One drawback of Hoffmann frames is that the bees often fasten the side bars of the frames together with wax or propolis. The latter is a substance gathered by the bees for the purpose of filling up any interstices or crevices in the hive. It consists of resin, wattle-gum, tar, paint, cart-grease, and similar substances. In some districts, propolis is a great nuisance to the beekeeper. Some strains of bees will daub it everywhere inside the hive. To overcome this difficulty, and also that of uncapping Hoffmann wide top bar frames, and yet have a self-spacing frame, a number of apiarists, including the writer, have adopted the frame shown in Figure 8. It has a top bar $\frac{7}{8}$ inch wide, $\frac{1}{2}$ inch thick, bottom bar $\frac{7}{8}$ inch x $\frac{3}{8}$ inch, and side bars $1\frac{1}{8}$ in. x $\frac{1}{2}$ in. The top and bottom bars are nailed on so that the side bar projects on the reverse side at the opposite end. The spacing is obtained by four stout flat-headed nails driven into the side bars and projecting $\frac{1}{4}$ inch, as shown in the illustration (Fig. 8). These frames are not stocked by manufacturers, but will be made to order if ordered in sufficient quantities. They can however easily be made by any one at all handy with tools, the only difference between them and the Simplicity frames being that the side bars are 1 inch instead of $\frac{7}{8}$ inch, and that the frames are nail spaced instead of loose hanging.

The Heddon hanging frame hive, also known as the Bolton hive, is what is called a sectional hive. The hive consists of shallow bodies $5\frac{3}{4}$ inches deep, with self-spacing frames $5\frac{3}{8}$ inches deep. The advantages claimed for it are that it can be readily expanded or reduced in size according to conditions and season by adding or removing stories; that swarming can be prevented or controlled by means of inverting the sets of frames at intervals, thus causing the destruction of queen cells, and that shallow supers are easier to lift and handle when full of honey, and the shallow combs easier to uncap than deep ones.

As an offset against these advantages, it must be mentioned that the Heddon hive costs more, that double the number of combs have to be handled when extracting, and that the splitting up of the hive into so many sets of frames by the intervening bee spaces has a tendency to retard breeding up in spring.

In connexion with this, I should like to say that the correct bee space between set of frames in the stories of a hive is $\frac{1}{4}$ inch. In the hives purchased from manufacturers too much allowance is made (generally) for shrinkage of timber, leaving up to $\frac{5}{8}$ inch between the stories. This excessive space first acts as a great check on the bees entering the super in spring, while later on it is filled with comb and honey, and is a hindrance and nuisance every time a hive is opened, also causing the death of many bees when frames are replaced in supers without first removing the pieces of comb which connected the upper and lower frames. With a $\frac{1}{4}$ inch bee space between the stories there will be little or no bur comb.

(To be continued.)

GENERAL NOTES.

By J. W. P.

AGRICULTURAL RESEARCH IN UNITED STATES OF AMERICA—

According to the report of the Secretary of Agriculture of the United States for 1910, there are now 62 agricultural experiment stations in active work in that country.   Fifty-five of these stations receive appropriations provided for by Acts of Congress, which amounted to £269,000 in the fiscal year 1909-10; in addition £200,000 was contributed by the State Legislatures, and £150,000 was received by the stations as fees for analyses of fertilisers, sales of farm products and from other local sources. The total annual revenue is over £600,000 as compared with half that sum in 1905.   Generally speaking, the State funds are mainly used for the more practical work, including maintenance of sub-stations, demonstration fields, agricultural surveys and a great variety of local experiments, while the funds provided by Acts of Congress are chiefly devoted to original research in difficult problems of agriculture generally.

COOL STORAGE OF FRUIT—

Annually for some years past the New Zealand Department of Agriculture has placed in the cool chambers of the Auckland Farmers' Co-operative Freezing Company considerable quantities of fruit, comprising a large number of varieties of apples and pears.   The object of the tests was to regulate the markets during periods of glut and thus avoid losses to the growers. In the December issue of the *Journal of the Department* the following important points are noted in connexion with the cool storage of apples and pears :—

(1) "Cool storage retards the normal rapid or fairly rapid ripening of the fruit.   Consequently, most varieties should be well matured and well coloured, but gathered a little on the green side, to achieve the best results."

(2) "Bruised or blemished fruit, or fruit attacked by pest or disease, should not be placed in cool storage."

(3) "Ripe or over-ripe pears will not keep sound."

(4) "Immature fruits shrivel."

(5) "Apples of soft texture when ripe should be gathered for cool storage before becoming fully ripe."

It is believed that the development of cool storage in the Dominion will do much to improve the prospects of fruit-growers there.

GERMINATION OF WEED SEEDS—

Wonder is often expressed at the sudden appearance of weeds upon land under cultivation where no signs of the same plants were visible while the land lay in pasture.   In the *Journal of the Board of Agriculture* (London) an account is given of some interesting investigations.   The weeds experimented with were the ribwort or "rib-grass" (*Plantago lanceolata*) and wild mustard (*Sinapis arvensis*). In 1899, pots containing 100 seeds of each weed were placed at a depth of 12 inches below the surface of the ground.   From 1900 onwards a pot was dug up each year and the seeds allowed to germinate.   With rib-grass two-thirds of the seeds were dead by 1900, but after ten years 8 per cent. still retained their germinating capacity.   With the yellow-flowered mustard the germinating capacity was as high after ten years (87 per cent.) as after one year. For purposes of comparison seeds kept in dry storage since 1899 have been allowed to germinate in each year from 1900 onwards.   The seeds of rib-grass germinated fairly well the first few years, but by 1909 were all dead.   The percentage of seeds of mustard germinating after one year was 82 per cent., and after ten years 24 per cent.   In other experiments lasting for six years it was found that those buried deepest in the ground retained their germinating power best   The seeds of cultivated plants, especially grasses, lost their germinating power in the soil much more quickly than the related weed seeds.   Weed seeds were found to retain their germinating power after passing through the digestive tract of a cow or pig, but when eaten by fowls were, as a rule, destroyed.

MILK RECORDS—

With the object of demonstrating the value of milk records to the dairy farmer the Lancashire (England) County Council has been carrying out tests during the last three years—in 1908 on fourteen farms, in 1909 on twelve farms, and in 1910 on twelve farms.   Each herd was tested as regards the yield and composition of the milk once every three weeks, this having been found to give results sufficiently correct for practical purposes.   The total yield for the three weeks was got by multiplying the yield on the day of testing by 10.5, and the estimated yield half-way between two testings by 10.5, and adding the two results.   A number of points elucidated by the records obtained are discussed in this report. The usual great differences were found in the capacity of individual cows. Taking the two best and the two worst cows at various ages (twelve good and twelve bad cows in all) the average yield of milk of the best cows was found to be nearly double that of the worst.   It is estimated that in the case of the former, after paying for the cost of keep, a gross profit of £10 per annum per cow is left, but with the latter a loss of 3s. 8d. per cow.   This Department has arranged a scheme and prepared cards for keeping milk records, and is ready to supply information to those wishing to improve their milking herds along those lines.

HARVESTING THROUGH THISTLES—

An ingenious invention has been made by Mr. L. N. I'anson, a farmer in the Grenfell district of New South Wales.   Last year he sowed a crop of wheat in an old thistly paddock; the crop was put in late and the thistles beat it.   They were chiefly star thistles and a few black ones, and as it was impossible to make hay owing to the thistles being so thick it was decided to strip it.   This however was also found to be impracticable as they clogged up the combs of the harvesters.   Mr. I'anson did not wish to abandon the crop, however, so he hit upon another plan.   He fixed a bar from which long prongs projected in front of and above the comb of the harvester.   These prongs were wide enough to allow the wheat to pass through to the comb of the harvester, but were sufficiently close to catch the thistles.   The arrangement was worked by a lever and was kept pointing forward above the crop when a clean patch was being stripped, but on coming to a thistly patch the prongs were lowered and pointed backward beneath the comb, so that the thistles were pushed down beneath it.   Instead of having to abandon the crop the inventor stripped 16 bushels to the acre.   A brief description of the above is given in the *Agricultural Gazette of New South Wales* for January, and it is anticipated that the contrivance, which the inventor was advised to patent, will prove of real benefit on thistly crops.

LUCERNE—

Regarding the needs of lucerne we could almost sum the matter up in four words—lime, drainage, humus and inoculation.   Perhaps we have given these in the order of their relative importance.   Lime is necessary on soils not naturally of limestone formation or filled with limestone pebbles.   The importance of this is impressed on us more and more each year ; in fact, we believe to-day that there have been more failures throughout the United States on account of insufficient lime in the soil than from any other cause.   Then as to drainage ; there is no use in planting lucerne on any soil where water may ordinarily be found at a depth of less than 3 feet.   The lucerne may grow all right until its roots strike this water, but then it will d e.   Fertile soils contain enough humus.   Impoverished soils may be so deficient that special preparation must be made before lucerne can possibly succeed.   Where stable manure is not available, on impoverished soils we would recommend preparation for lucerne one or two years in advance growing such crops as crimson clover, mammoth clover, cow peas, Canada field peas or soja beans, and preferably turning them under, or else pasturing them off so as to give the soil the greatest benefit possible from them.   We recommend inoculation, not that it is always necessary, but it is an inexpensive process, and in five cases out of six it will actually pay.—*Irrigation Age, Chicago.*

THE NEW NITROGENOUS MANURES—

There is an increasing demand for nitrogenous manures in the more humid districts of the State, and this is likely to extend as cultivation becomes of older date. In view of this fact and the present excessive price of some of these manures the discovery and rapid development of two chemical processes whereby nitrogenous manures are manufactured from atmospheric gases has more than passing interest. The two new fertilisers are known as nitrate of lime, and cyanamid of lime. They are both products of the electric furnace, the necessary energy being obtained for cheapness at waterfalls.	During the past year it is estimated that from 170,000 to 180,000 horse-power was used in this way to manufacture nitrates and 20,000 horse-power in the manufacture of cyanamid.	The new manures have been tested against the old at a number of experiment stations in Europe and America with most satisfactory results.	At Rothamsted the old manures, nitrate of soda and sulphate of ammonia, were tested alongside the new manures—nitrate of lime and cyanamid of lime; and it is reported that "if there is any difference as regards effectiveness on the Rothamsted soil between these sources of nitrogen it does not exceed 10 per cent."	From experiments elsewhere it would seem that with the cyanamid certain precautions should be observed as to harrowing or otherwise covering the material after it is applied, and also as to not applying too much, but nitrate of lime has an action absolutely similar to nitrate of soda, and is probably superior to it on soils poor in lime. So far no bulk samples have reached Australia, but they are sure to come.

SWAN HILL HOME-MILKING COMPETITION, 1911.

S. J. Keys, Dairy Supervisor.

The above competition was successfully carried out under the auspices of the Swan Hill Agricultural Society, the following conditions being observed by competitors:—

1. The cows to be milked at their homes under the supervision of officers of the Department of Agriculture for a period of 24 hours during the two weeks previous to the show, the day's butter production to be taken as the basis in deciding the cow's yield.

2. In the event of two cows obtaining the same highest yield of butter, the prize to go to the cow that gave the most milk.

3. All cows entered to be shown on the day of show.

4 No test or butter returns to be made available until cows are in pens in show yard on the day of show.

Greatest Butter Production.

In the section for cows giving the greatest butter production 10 cows were entered.	Last year's high returns were easily eclipsed, notwithstanding that, during the trial, a heavy wind prevailed, which no doubt affected the yields.

The first prize fell to a beautiful Ayrshire cow, " Pearl," owned by Mr. Robert Hastings, and purchased from Mrs. Smith at her dispersal sale two years ago.	Pearl is blood-red in colour, showing strong constitution, beautiful conformation, and splendid condition; she had just come into profit from a somewhat lengthy spell, was full of vigor, and in splendid heart for making an ideal milker.	In general appearance and in colour

"PEARL," WINNER OF TEST. 72 LBS. MILK—21.27 LBS. COMMERCIAL
BUTTER PER WEEK.

this cow appears to show as much of the North Devon breeding as of the
Ayrshire, but Mr. Hastings assures me she was got by a pure Ayrshire
bull and is out of an Ayrshire cow—; she gave the fine yield of
72 lbs. milk showing a 3.6 test, equivalent to 2.59 lbs. butter fat per
day, or a butter production of 21.16 lbs. weekly.

"DULCIE," SECOND PRIZE, $63\frac{1}{2}$ LBS. MILK—20.224 LBS. COMMERCIAL
BUTTER PER WEEK.

The second prize was won by "Dulcie," also owned by Mr. Hastings. "Dulcie," 5 years old, easily beat her record of last year by producing 63½ lbs. of milk showing a 3.9 butter fat test, equivalent to 2.47 lbs. butter fat, or 20.224 lbs. of commercial butter weekly. Like her herd mate, "Pearl," she was bred by Mrs. Smith and sold at the high figure of £14, which was a record for Swan Hill, and considered ridiculous, but Mr. Hastings has never regretted his bargain. On her first calf she gave up to 50 lbs. of milk daily. "Dulcie," a medium sized cow, of an even, quiet, and kind temper, with light bone, and carrying no surplus flesh, had had only 6 weeks' spell before calving, and had been in milk 60 days when tested. She was got by the same Ayrshire bull as the winner, and shows a good deal of the Ayrshire type, although black or brown and white in colour.

GREATEST WEIGHT OF MILK.

Section 2 was for the cow giving the greatest weight of milk in 24 hours. The first and second prizes went to the same cows and in the same order as in section 1, with the third prize cow, a Jersey and Shorthorn cross, 18 lbs. behind the winner.

The two winning cows were chiefly run on a growing crop of oats, and after each milking were given a little damp bran, which assisted them materially. The rest of the cows competing were run on natural pastures, as well as lucerne. Had they received a little special attention and hand feed as well, no doubt some of them would have been closer up in the contest. The full returns from the whole of the cows competing are as follow :—

Owner.	Cow.	Milk, lbs. in 24 Hours.	Butter Fat Test.	Butter Fat.	Commercial Butter per Week.
				lbs.	lbs.
R. Hastings	"Pearl"	72	3·6	2·59	21·21
R. Hastings	"Dulcie"	63½	3·9	2·47	20·224
T. Binns	"Dolly"	48½	5·2	2·26	18·50
F. McIver	"Spot"	50½	4·2	2·12	17·36
R. Hastings	"Spot"	43	4·4	1·89	15·47
R. Prince	"Darkey"	53¼	3·4	1·84	15·06
R. Prince	"Jess"	47½	3·6	1·71	14·00
R. Prince	"Beauty"	52	3·0	1·56	12·77
F. McIver	"Plum"	46½	3·0	1·41	11·54
R. Prince	"Nancy"	43¼	3·2	1·41	11·54

In 1910, eleven cows competed, the highest butter return being 16.986 or 4.182 lbs. behind this year's winner. The lowest this year was 11.113 lbs. of butter, while last year's lowest return was 9.775, being 1.338 better for 1911. The average for 1910 was 15.171 lbs., and 15.7 lbs. for 1911.

The greatest weight of milk given by one cow in 1910 was 63.75, while in 1911 it was 72 lbs., being a difference of 8.25 lbs. in favour of this year's winner. The lowest weight in 1910 was 31½ lbs., while in 1911 the lowest was 43¾ lb., being 12.25 lbs. better than in the previous year. The average weight for the whole of the cows competing was, in 1910, 41.25 lbs., and 51.56 lbs. in 1911, or 10.31 lbs. in favour of this year, when the show was held much earlier than usual, and before the lucerne and grasses were as well advanced.

VALUE OF IRRIGATION AND LUCERNE.

The high yields of these cows prove plainly the special value of the Northern country for dairying when put under a thorough system of irrigation, and sown down in lucerne. There is no reason why all of the settlers should not have cows competing next year, and keep up or eclipse the high average attained this year.

The best of the Swan Hill flats has been acquired by the Lands Purchase Board for closer settlement purposes, and has been subdivided into blocks containing about 50 acres each. · This land is equally well suited for citrus fruit growing, and will, in course of time, return a large revenue from that source alone to the occupiers.

The settlers are a very desirable class of men and women, who are · working with a will. Up to 40 and 45 cows are being carried on blocks of 53 acres and under, and throughout the winter the whole of the stock were in splendid condition. A better class of dairy cow is entering the district than has hitherto been seen here. The Department of Agriculture is doing its best to assist the settlers. During the last six months it has purchased four pure Jersey bulls and one Ayrshire bull from leading studs, and located them amongst the settlers at Nyah and Swan Hill, where they are available for service at a nominal fee. It will be a matter of only a few years before their influence will be felt in the cream results from their stock, as well as their higher value in the open market, when any surplus stock have to be sold.

So well have the settlers taken to dairying that most of them keep milk charts, and numerous applications are received to test individual cows. With such regular attention, and the growing and conservation of fodder, success is assured to the settlers in the Swan Hill district.

ANNUAL GRANT TO AGRICULTURAL SOCIETIES.

AMENDED REGULATIONS FOR 1912.

The regulations providing for the conditions hitherto in force to qualify for participation in this grant have been amended. Conditions B, 1 and 2 and C 1 and 2 have been abolished, but condition A remains as under :—

The awards of prizes in all classes for stallions three years old and over at the Society's Show must be subject· to the possession by the exhibit of a Government certificate of soundness.

Stallion Inspection Parades will be held at different centres throughout the State prior to the commencement of the Show season (Time Table of Stallion Parades for 1912 will be available shortly after 1st April, 1912). The parade centres are so arranged that all owners of Show stallions have the opportunity of submitting them for examination for the Government Certificate of Soundness before the closing of entries for the Show. Show Secretaries will require to obtain evidence of the possession of the Government Certificate in respect of exhibits at the time of entry, and should not accept entries of other than certificated horses.

Immediately after the Show, Secretaries of Societies are required to forward the names *of all the horses* that have won the prizes in stallion classes, together with the names of the owners, to the Director of Agriculture.

The new regulations further provide, in lieu of the compulsory conditions concerning the holding of agricultural classes and a series of lectures, that encouragement shall be given to those Agricultural Societies which carry out classes or lectures by providing for them a greater proportional participation in the grant. Thus :—

1.—AGRICULTURAL CLASSES.

A sum of £10 as a special subsidy will be added to the *pro ratâ* grant to such Societies as carry out agricultural classes in strict conformity with the following conditions and to the satisfaction of the Department:—

Applications must be submitted not later than 1st May, 1912.

Thirty students at least must be enrolled before a class can be held.

The rent of hall and all local charges are to be paid by the Agricultural Society; all other expenses by the Department. Arrangements must be made to insure the uninterrupted use of the hall during the time the lectures are going on.

A roll of attendances at lectures and demonstrations shall be kept.

The agricultural classes will extend over two weeks, five days a week, a demonstration being given each morning and afternoon, and four limelight lectures on evenings to be arranged for by the Secretary of each Society.

At the conclusion of each class, a written examination of about 1½ hours duration will be held, a medal to be awarded by the Department to the student in each district obtaining the highest number of marks for examination work and regular attendance combined. Two-thirds of the maximum marks obtainable will be given for examination work, and one-third for regular attendance. The Department reserves the right to withdraw the offer of the medals in the event of there being less than five students remaining for examination. Students in attendance at Agricultural High Schools and Colleges, or at the Continuation Schools, and teachers from such institutions or State Schools shall not be allowed to sit for such examination.

A special examination for the Gold Medal offered by the Australian Natives' Association will be held at the close of the year, and only winners of Departmental medals will be eligible to compete thereat.

Subjects of First Week.

Agriculture.
Live Stock and Veterinary Science.

Subjects of Second Week.

Two or more of the following, to be selected :—(*a*) Sheep Breeding and Management (including Wool Classing and Lambs for Export); (*b*) Dairy Farming (including Management and Breeding of Pigs); (*c*) Poultry Breeding and Management; (*d*) Orchard and Garden Work.

II.—LECTURES.

A sum of £5 as a special subsidy will be added to the *pro ratâ* grant to such Societies as arrange for and carry out a series of four lectures throughout the year in strict conformity with the following conditions and to the satisfaction of the Department :—

Applications must be submitted not later than 1st May, and accompanying the application must be a list of the subjects (see below) which the Society chooses for the series.   The dates of lectures will then be fixed by the Department, and if Societies will state the most suitable seasons for their districts the lectures will, as far as possible, be arranged accordingly.

An attendance of at least fifteen *bonâ fide* farmers, farmers' sons or farm-hands will be required, otherwise the lecture will not count for the special subsidy.

The President or Secretary or a member of the Council or Committee of the Society must take the chair at each lecture and must certify as to the number and *bona fides* of the attendance as above required.

The rent of the hall, advertising and all other local charges are to be paid by the Agricultural Society ; all other expenses by the Department.

The Department will recognise any suitable lecture, paper, or address that a Society may arrange to have delivered by any person other than a Departmental officer, and such lecture will count as one of the four required, provided due notification prior to delivery of lecture is given, and the President of the Society afterwards certifies as to *bona fides* and suitability of the lecture and the number and character of the attendance.

SYNOPSIS OF LECTURES AND DEMONSTRATIONS.

PRINCIPLES OF AGRICULTURE.

1. The plant food of the soil.
2. Cultivation methods and management.
3. Principles of manuring.
4. Valuation of artificial manures.
5. The management of the farm.
6. Special crops and catch crops.
7. Irrigation principles and methods.

VETERINARY SCIENCE AND LIVE STOCK SUBJECTS.

1. The structure and care of the horse's foot (lantern).
2. Brood mares and breeding mishaps (lantern).
3. Colic, constipation, and other bowel complaints.
4. Ailments of dairy cows—milk fever, impaction, udder complaints.
5. Contagious diseases of stock—abortion, blackleg, tuberculosis, anthrax, pleuro pneumonia, &c.
6. Ailments of swine, or ailments of sheep.
7. Unsoundness in horses (lantern).
8. Principles of stock breeding—stud horses.

DAIRY FARMING.

1. Breeding and management.
2. Dairy buildings.
3. Dairy management.
4. Milk and cream testing.
5. Foods and feeding.
6. Pig breeding, feeding, and management.

POULTRY BREEDING AND MANAGEMENT.

1. The poultry industry : its importance. Locality—suitability or otherwise.
2. Housing (construction of, materials, insect proof, aspect, &c.). How to select stock.
3. Breeds : payable or otherwise, eggs and table. Breeds adapted for export—modes of crossing.
4. Turkeys : their care and management. Chicken raising and care.
5. Foods and feeding demonstrated.
6. Common ailments of poultry. Incubation—natural and artificial.

ORCHARD AND GARDEN WORK.

1. Fruit growing—Varieties suitable to the different localities, soils and sites.
2. Preparation of land—Planting and pruning.
3. Cultivation—Manuring and management.
4. Insect pests and fungus diseases and their treatment.

VITICULTURE.

1. Wine making.
2. Phylloxera and resistant stocks—Preparation of land.
3. Propagation and grafting—Best varieties to grow.
4. Pruning and seasonable operations.
5. Wine-making and cellar management.
6. Drying raisins, sultanas and currants—Packing fresh grapes for export.
7. Vine diseases and treatment.

POTATO CULTURE.

1. The soil and its cultivation—Care of the growing crop, manures.
2. Seed and its selection—Keeping of seed potatoes.
3. Diseases and their treatment.

SUBJECTS AND STAFF.

Principles of Agriculture—Mr. A. E. V. Richardson, M.A., B.Sc. ; Dr. J. W. Paterson, Ph.D., B.Sc. ; and Mr. Temple Smith.

Veterinary Science, Stock Management, Dairy Sanitation and Education—Messrs. Robertson, Kendall, Griffin, Cother, and Johnstone.

The Dairying Industry and Export Trade—Messrs. Crowe, Archer, and Carroll.

Orchard and Garden Work—Messrs. Carmody and Pescott.

Sheep Breeding and Management—

Viticulture—Mr. F. de Castella.

Flax Culture and Demonstrations at Shows—Mr. Knight and staff.

Poultry Breeding and Management—Mr. H. V. Hawkins.

Poultry Dressing Demonstrations—Mr. A. Hart.

Potato Culture—Mr. G. Seymour.

Tobacco Culture—Mr. Temple Smith.

Pig Breeding and Management—Mr. R. T. Archer.

Fruit Industries—Mr. J. G. Turner and staff.

Insect Pests—Mr. C. French. Junr.

Plant Diseases—Mr. W. Laidlaw and Mr. C. C. Brittlebank.

Irrigation—Expert of State Rivers and Water Supply Commission.

THE PIG INDUSTRY.

(Continued from page 169.)

R. T. Archer, Senior Dairy Inspector.

III.—BREEDS.

We have now to consider the type of bacon in greatest demand, that
gives the highest return, and how to produce it.   Years ago the popular
demand was for heavy fat bacon but during the last three decades the
popular taste has undergone a complete change, not only in the warmer
climate of Australia but also in Britain, and now the requirement is young
and tender bacon—juicy, lean, sweet, mildcured.   Fortunately for the
producer this is what should return the greatest profit, for the light-weight
pig is cheaper to produce than the heavy-weight—for two reasons :

FIG. 12. BERKSHIRE EOAR, "HIGHCLERE TOPPER."

1st—owing to the greater powers of digestion and assimilation of the
young pig a greater weight of meat is produced from a given weight of
food, consequently the less it costs to produce; 2nd—the lighter-weight
pig brings the highest price per lb.

In this country the most popular breed has been the Berkshire.   This
breed has many good characteristics.   It is a rapid grower, well improved,
which enables it to make good use of the food supplied, and it can be
kept ready for market at any time either as sucker, porker, or baconer.
Two faults of the Berkshire lie in the facts that they average small litters
(about six) and they produce rather too great a proportion of fat to lean.
There are strains of the breed however that average litters of ten or twelve,
and those are the pigs to breed from, provided they possess the good
features of the breed.

FIG. 13. VICTORIAN BRED BERKSHIRE SOW.

FIG. 14. VICTORIAN BRED BERKSHIRE BOAR.

FIG. 15. VICTORIAN BRED BERKSHIRE SOW WITH LITTER.

The " Standard of Excellence " adopted by the Berkshire Society of Victoria, as published in the first volume of their *Herd Book*, 1911, is as follows :—

Colour—Black, with white on face, feet, and tip of tail.
Skin—Fine, and free from wrinkles.
Hair—Long, fine, and plentiful.
Head—Moderately short, face dished, snout broad ; and wide between the eyes and ears.
Ears—Fairly large, carried erect or slightly inclined forward, and fringed with fine hair.
Neck—Medium length, evenly set on shoulders ; jowl full, and not heavy.
Shoulders—Fine and well sloped backwards, free from coarseness.
Back—Long and straight, ribs well sprung, sides deep.
Hams—Wide and deep to hocks.
Tail—Set high, and fairly large.
Flank—Deep and well let down, making straight underline.
Legs and feet—Short, straight, and strong, set wide apart, and hoofs nearly erect.
Objections—A perfectly black face, foot, or tail ; a rose back ; white or sandy spots or white skin on the body ; a white ear ; a very coarse mane, and inbent knees.

FIG. 16. BERKSHIRE SOW, " MANOR EMPRESS QUEEN."

THE LARGE WHITE YORKSHIRE.

It has already been mentioned that the large White Yorkshire is the breed with which the Danes have built up their bacon industry, also that many other European countries are large purchasers of the breed in England. It has done more for the improvement of pigs than any other breed. In 1890, the Canadian Government introduced pigs to its Central Experimental Farm, the breeds first introduced being Berkshire, Large Yorkshire, and Essex. Since that time Chester Whites, Poland Chinas. Tamworths, Duroc Jerseys, and Large Blacks, have all been tested, with the result that the only breeds now kept are Large Yorkshire, Tamworths, and Berkshires ; the others having been found more or less faulty for the production of Wiltshire bacon. In this country the breeds selected by the Canadian Government have proved satisfactory, with the exception of the Large Yorkshire, which, I believe, is only to be found at the Dookie Agricultural College. Instead of the Large Yorkshire, the Middle York-shire is largely bred here ; it makes a very excellent cross with the

Berkshire, although the large Yorkshire has everywhere proved its superiority; and in all those countries, especially European, where the improvement of pigs is seriously entered upon, the Large Yorkshire is the most favoured breed.

FIG. 17. LARGE WHITE YORKSHIRE SOW.

LARGE YORKSHIRE.

Scale of Points. (By Sanders Spencer.)

	Points.
Colour—White, freedom from blue spots on skin desirable	2
Head—Long and light, wide between the ears	4
Ears—Thin, long, slightly inclined forward, and fringed with fine hair ..	3
Jowl—Small and light	2
Neck—Long and muscular	3
Chest—Wide and well let down	5
Shoulders—Oblique and narrow on top	4
Girth—Around the heart	4
Back—Long and straight	5
Sides—Deep	5
Ribs—Well sprung	5
Loin—Broad and not drooping	3
Belly—Full and thick, with at least twelve teats	2
Flanks—Thick and well let down	4
Quarters—Long, wide, and straight from hip to tail	7
Hams—Broad, full, and meaty to the hocks	8
Tail—Set on high, not coarse	3
Legs—Straight, with flinty flat bone	6
Ankles—Strong and compact	4
Pasterns—Short and yet springy	2
Feet—Firm and strong	3
Evenness—Freedom from wrinkles on skin	2
Coat—Long, straight, and silky	4
Action—Free, clean, and not rolling in hindquarters	5
Symmetry—General style and contour, showing evidence of careful breeding..	5
	100

FIG. 18. LARGE YORKSHIRE SOW AND LITTER.
(Dookie Agricultural College.)

FIG. 19. LARGE WHITE YORKSHIRE BOAR, "HOLYWELL ROYALTY II."

FIG. 20. MIDDLE YORKSHIRE BOAR, "JUMBUNNA'S PRIDE."
1st prize Royal Agricultural Show Melbourne, 1911—under 15 months.

Objections.

Head—Narrow forehead or short pug nose.
Ears.—Thick, coarse, or much inclined forward.
Jowl—Fat and full.
Neck—Short and very thick.
Chest.—Narrow, with both forelegs apparently coming from almost the same point.
Shoulders—Coarse, heavy, wide, and open on the top.
Girth—Light round the heart, and foreflank light.
Back—Weak and hollow when the pig is standing at rest.
Sides—Shallow, not well let down between the forelegs.
Ribs—Flat and short curved ; light back rib.
Loin—Narrow and weak.
Belly—Flaccid or wanting in muscle, or gutty or podgy.
Flank—Thin, and not well let down.
Quarters—Short, narrow, or drooping.
Hams—Narrow, wanting in depth or deficiency of muscle in second thigh.
Tail—Coarse, and set on low.
Legs—Crooked, weak, and with round and coarse bone.
Ankles—Extra large, round, and weak.
Feet—Flat, splayed, and extra wide and large.
Evenness—Wrinkles on sides, neck, or shoulders.
Coat—Coarse, curly, bristly, or mangy, with fringe along top of neck or shoulders.
Action—Sluggish and clumsy.
Symmetry—Predominance of certain points, especially heavy shoulders or forequarters generally, with weak loins and light hams.

Disqualifications.

Colour—Black hairs or black spots.
Boars—Rupture, one testicle only down.
Sows—Deficiency in or very irregularly placed or blind teats, injured or diseased udder.

FIG. 21. MIDDLE YORKSHIRE SOW, "LADY-BIRD."
Champion Royal Agricultural Show, Melbourne, 1911.

The "Standard of Excellence" for Middle White Yorkshire.

(Yorkshire Herd Book of Victoria.)

Colour—White, freedom from blue spots.
Hair—Long, plentiful, and silky.
Head—Short and light, wide between ears and eyes, face slightly dished.
Ears—Medium, carried erect, slightly inclined forward, fringed with fine hair.
Shoulders—Well sloped backward and free from coarseness.
Chest—Wide, and well let down.
Neck—Medium length, evenly set on shoulders, jowl full and not heavy.
Back—Long and straight, sides deep, ribs well sprung.
Loin—Broad, and not drooping.
Belly—Full, thick, with at least twelve teats.
Flank—Thick and well let down.

Hams—Broad, full, and meaty to hocks.
Tail—Set on high, and not coarse.
Legs—Short, straight, and strong ; feet firm and strong, hoofs nearly erect.
Action—Free, clean, and not rolling in hindquarters.

FIG. 22. YORKSHIRE SOW "AURUM" AND LITTER.

FIG. 23. MIDDLE YORKSHIRES—VICTORIAN BRED.

FIG. 24. TAMWORTH SOW, "WHITEACRE BEAUTY."

THE TAMWORTH.
(By Sanders Spencer.)

	Points.
Colour—Golden red, without black spots...	5
Head—Long, snout straight, wide between the ears	4
Ears—Thin, pricked and fringed with fine hair	3
Jowl—Small and light ..	2
Neck—Long and muscular	3
Chest—Wide and well let down ..	5
Shoulders—Oblique and narrow on top ..	4
Girth—Around the heart	4
Sides—Deep and long ..	8
Ribs—Well sprung	6
Loin—Wide and strong, not drooping	4
Belly—Full and thick, with straight underline, and at least twelve teats	3
Flank—Thick and well let down	4
Quarters—Long, wide and straight from hip to tail	7
Hams—Broad, full, and meaty to the hocks	8
Tail—Set on high, not coarse	3
Legs—Straight and with flinty flat bone ..	6
Ankles—Strong and compact	4
Pasterns—Short and yet springy	2
Feet—Firm and strong, not splayed	3
Evenness—Freedom from wrinkles in skin	2
Coat—Long, straight, and silky ..	3
Action—Free and clean	3
Symmetry—General style and contour giving evidence of good breeding	4
	100

Objections.

Head—Narrow forehead or upturned nose.
Ears—Thick and coarse, or inclined forward.
Jowl—Thick and coarse, fat and full.
Ribs—Flat or short curved ; light back ribs.
Loin—Narrow or weak.
Belly—Flaccid or wanting in muscle, gutty or podgy.

Disqualifications.

Colour—Black hairs or black patches on the skin.
Boars—Rupture ; one testicle only down.
Sows.—Deficiency in or very irregularly placed or blind teats.

THE LARGE BLACK.
Scale of Points formulated by the Large Black Pig Society.

Head—Medium length, and wide between the ears	5
Ears—Long, thin, and inclined well over the face ..	6
Jowl—Medium size	3
Neck—Fairly long and muscular	3
Chest—Wide and deep ..	3
Shoulders—Oblique, with narrow plate	6
Back—Long and level (rising a little to centre of back not objected to)	12
Sides—Very deep	10
Ribs—Well sprung	5
Loin—Broad ..	5
Quarters—Long, wide, and not drooping ..	8
Hams—Large and well filled to hocks	10
Tail—Set high, and not coarse ..	3
Legs—Short and straight	5
Belly and Flank—Thick and well filled ..	8
Skin—Fine and soft	4
Coat—Moderate quantity of straight silky hair	4
	100

Objections.

Head—Narrow forehead or dished nose.
Ears—Thick, coarse, or pricked.
Coat—Coarse or curly, bristly mane.

Disqualifications.

Any other colour than black.

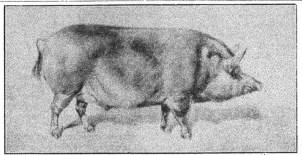

FIG. 25. TAMWORTH BOAR, "MIDDLETON MAINSPRING."

FIG. 26. LARGE BLACK SOW, "HASKETON LONG LADY."

FIG. 27. LARGE BLACK BOAR, "ROYAL BODMIN."

Herd-book entries.—The Regulations for the registration of boars and sows provide that no boar or sow is eligible for registration if known to have a cross of any other breed within four generations, or if showing any white spot or mark. The name and registered number of the sire and dam must be stated, and a distinctive ear-mark must be given to each animal entered for registration. In the case of animals entered by persons other than the breeder, the correctness of the pedigree must (if required) be certified by the signature of the breeder. Applications for registration are received subject to inspection of the animals entered, if deemed necessary. All entries must be made on the Society's printed form, and must be accompanied by the necessary fees as follows :—Members.—Registration fees : Boars, 5s. per head ; sows, 2s. 6d. per head. Non-Members.—Boars : 10s. per head. Boars and sows must be entered for registration at time of service, or at not exceeding twelve months from date of birth. Double fees will be charged for registration of animals exceeding the age of twelve months at time of entry.

SELECTION OF BOAR.

In breeding, the selection of the boar is of the greatest importance, as he directly influences every pig one may have to fatten, and it depends on his breeding, very largely, whether or not the pigs can make profitable use of the food given to them. As in the case of all sires the boar should be pure bred, of approved strain both with regard to capacity to put on flesh rapidly, and to influence the sow in the production of large litters, for certain it is that the boar does exercise that influence, and in proportion to his breeding.

BACON TYPE OF BOAR.

We have to bear in mind that the object in view is the production of pigs that will give the greatest weight of lean meat in those parts which bring the highest price in the market. All meat in front of the girth is of comparatively low value, so the less we have there the better as long as the conformation is consistent with constitutional development. The boar should have a masculine appearance, forelegs set wide apart ; thick through the heart or behind the elbow ; deep from top to bottom behind the shoulder, full behind the shoulder, giving good heart girth ; jowl broad and strong, but not fat and flabby ; forehead broad, and poll broad and full ; neck of medium length, strongly muscled but not showing heavy crown of fat ; eye large, full, and bright (this denotes sexual energy) ; general appearance alert and active. The shoulder should be compact on the top, and blend well with the top line and ribs at this point ; an upright shoulder, from a bacon producer's point of view, is not regarded as a serious objection ; the lengthening from the back of the shoulder to the ham, gives the largest development where the meat is most valuable ; ribs well sprung, arching out boldly from the backbone, then dropping suddenly, almost vertically, giving a flat straight side. This is most important, indicating strong development of muscle along the back, and muscle is lean meat. The top line should rise very slightly above the straight line, giving a very slight arch, the highest point being over the loin ; back medium and uniform width throughout ; loin same width as the back, full, strong, and heavily muscled ; rump same width as the back and loin, slightly rounded from side to side over the top and from hips to tail ; ham should taper towards the hock, and carry flesh well down towards the hock, especially on the inside; underline trim and straight, no tendency towards a sagging belly; hind flanks full, giving a good thickness of meat at this point; legs of medium length, bone clean and flattish in appearance (rough puffy legs are very undesirable); pasterns should be upright, causing the animal to walk on the toes. Pigs with weak pasterns should not be bred from. Hair abundant, but fine, straight, and silky. A row of bristles along the top of the neck and shoulders is extremely objectionable. Carriage easy, walking without apparent exertion and without a swaying movement.

In selecting a boar it should be from a large, and above all, even litter, which is a good indication of prepotency on the influence of blood.

Mr. Sanders Spencer, the noted English breeder, says with regard to this :—" Although some persons make mere size a great point when choosing a boar, our experience leads us to consider this to be a mistake; a very large boar seldom lasts long; he becomes too heavy for the sows; he probably proves to be slow, and his litters few and small in number. A very large and heavy boar is also more likely to suffer from weakness of the spine or hindquarters, and is frequently weak in his joints, and crooked in his legs. These latter failings especially should be avoided, as they are hereditary, and will frequently crop up for several generations. Weakness of ankles and roundness of bone, two qualities which should be avoided in a sire, are often allied with great size. A medium, compact boar, heavy in the hindquarters, and light in the forequarters, will frequently continue fruitful for at least twice as long as will the heavy shouldered and coarse boned boar. Nearly all of the most successful pigs have been on a small rather than a large scale."

The boar should be purchased from a breeder of repute, thus insuring that the pedigree of the animal will be reliable, and of value. The longer the pedigree the surer will be the result, and so even greater care must be taken to see that he is of proper conformation. If he is a bad one he will just as surely leave his imprint on his offspring. If one is not sure of his own judgment, or has not had sufficient experience, the advice and assistance of a good judge should be secured. When we see what the pig is in a state of nature, and know that neglect brings about very rapid degeneration, it should make us extremely careful in the selection of the boar. The sexual organs should be well developed. This denotes constitutional vigour. Never use a ruptured pig nor one with only one testicle showing. These conditions are hereditary. A ruptured pig may be castrated in the ordinary way, provided a few stitches are inserted in the purse, but the animal with only one testicle showing is very difficult to treat. On no account use a savage or bad tempered boar, for besides being a continual menace to his attendants and to live stock, his offspring will be restless, unsettled, and slow feeders. The old proverb "a contented mind is a continual feast " applies undoubtedly to the pig, and the best feeders are those that do not waste their food and energy in uselessly tearing about, but feed and rest most of the time between meals. The teats in the boar are also of great importance, they should be of full number and well developed. Sows with undeveloped udders should not be bred from as the defect is hereditary.

MANAGEMENT OF THE BOAR.

On this point we cannot do better than quote Mr. Sanders Spencer, as he is one of the leading and most successful breeders. " We hold strongly to the belief that it is advisable to select the boar when it is young; if it be possible to see it on its dam, and to see its sire, so much the better. We will, therefore, assume that the delivery of the boar follows the weaning of it. It should be placed with other pigs of about the same age, and fed generously on pollard with a little barley meal added; this two or three times a day; and then between the morning and the midday meal give them a few peas or a little whole wheat or oats. If skim milk can be obtained, the young pigs will pay as much for it as will any other kind of stock, and further, they will make far greater progress with than without it. A run in a small paddock or enclosure for a few minutes each day will help to keep the pigs in health. This system may be followed until the young boar is some five months old, when any unspayed sow pigs in the lot should be weeded out; the food may be increased in richness by the addition of more meal, without any fear of the boar becoming too fat, provided sufficient exercise be allowed; this is most important, as good feet and ankles can only be retained in this way, and further, as soon as the boar has been used, it is seldom possible or advisable to allow him much liberty."

As strength of bone without coarseness is a most desirable feature, the best way to obtain this is by mixing with the feed daily about a tablespoonful of bone meal. Repeated trials have demonstrated that the density or breaking strength of the bones in those pigs fed bone meal is more than double that of those not fed bone meal. If the boar has been well reared he may be used for service at eight months, sometimes they are used before that age. It is a mistake to let him run with the sows, the litters are smaller, and not so strong, and the vigour of the boar is impaired from the too frequent service of the sows. He should be kept in a special enclosure; when the sow has been in use a day or two put her into the boar's sty, and remove her after one complete service. Care must be taken in handling the boar, never trust him, but don't ill-use him. Under this system a boar will serve fifty sows in a season, and they are known to work up to 150. The food requirements of the boar depend largely on his age, and the amount of work he has to perform. He must be kept in a vigorous healthy condition, not allowed to get too fat. If he has plenty of clover or lucerne he will require very little grain. The more work he has to do the more grain feed will he require. If he is used too frequently the litters may be fewer in number and less vigorous, but on the other hand a long rest is not likely to be productive of the best results. The generative organs are in the most healthy condition when in regular use. If carefully managed the boar may give satisfaction for eight years or more. When finished with the cheapest way of disposing of him is to destroy and bury him, for it will not pay to fatten him.

SELECTION OF THE SOW.

The sow need not necessarily be pure bred provided she is of a good type. She should be selected from a prolific mother, as fecundity is hereditary. The teats should number at least twelve, fully developed (any with defective teats should be discarded), set well apart, even in size, and the front teats well forward on the body. The number of teats does not indicate always the number of pigs she is likely to have. Sometimes sows with ten or eleven teats will have big litters.

BACON TYPE OF SOW.

The head, neck, shoulder and bone should be finer than in the boar, and except for these points the description of the boar will apply to the sow. Extremes should be avoided. A long, scrawny neck, narrow chest, and long coarse legs indicate a slow feeder and an undesirable quality of bacon. The carcase of such an animal contains too much bone, is deficient in muscle, or lean meat. The thick short type is also undesirable, the best bacon type being between the two extremes. Weak bones which tend to break down at the pasterns should not be tolerated. The bone should be clean and strong, not coarse, there should be enough of it to insure a good sized animal. An overgown or clumsy sow should not be used, and a savage animal should be got rid of, for often it is necessary to be in the sty with her for various purposes, and if she is bad tempered there is risk of loss of young, and she will not milk so well.

MANAGEMENT OF THE SOW.

Having chosen the young sow, she must be well reared to develop her into the best frame possible. Many people breed the young sow at six months old, but this is not advisable, as it is more than likely that her growth will be checked to such an extent as to materially lessen her value as a brood sow. If she is put to the boar at eight or ten months old the result will be more satisfactory. If the first service is not successful, she will return in three weeks. The period of gestation is sixteen weeks. The variation being comparatively slight. Old or weakly sows frequently pig a few days before, but those in fair condition usually pig on the 112th day. A strong and vigorous sow may go a day or two over. She may run out in a grass, clover or lucerne paddock until within a few days of farrowing, when she may be put in a sty. The sows are more healthy running in a paddock than kept in a sty, getting plenty of exercise and green food, and it is the cheapest way of working them. Care must be taken that the sow has plenty of food to enable her to keep up her own condition, and at the same time to develop her young. In the paddock she must be provided with shade, shelter, and water, especially shade and water in the summer. The approaching parturition is generally preceded by enlargement of the vulva, the distension of the udder, and the giving way of the muscles on either side of the tail. As soon as the udder becomes smooth and heated, and milk can be drawn from the teats by the pressure of the thum and forefinger, the arrival of the pigs may be confidently looked for within the next twelve hours, unless it be a first litter, when the rule will not hold good.

A few days before she is due to farrow she may be put into a roomy sty, 10 feet square, with a yard for exercise, will be sufficiently large, with a guard rail all round 9 inches from the floor and 9 inches from the wall, and provided with a limited quantity of short litter. An hour or two before farrowing she will begin to prepare her nest, and she should then be continually watched to prevent overlaying any of the little ones —which may be taken away as they appear, first being rubbed with a cloth, put to the teat to get a taste of the milk, and then placed in a box in which some dry straw has been laid. If the weather is cold, cover the box with a bag. If any of the pigs get a chill and turn cold, limp and damp, a teaspoonful of spirit will help to revive them, and a suck at the teat will complete the cure. The little pig will often give a peculiar

squeal which indicates that it is approaching a condition of helpless uncon-
sciousness. There is a difference of opinion as to how many pigs a sow
should be allowed to rear. It is generally considered by those of the
greatest experience that seven or eight for a first litter, and ten to twelve
for mature sows are sufficient. Many pick the best up to the required
number, and either destroy the rest or rear them by hand, or it may so
happen that they may be reared on another sow, the litter of which is
short of the desired number. As a rule the placenta will come away
shortly after the last pig, and it should be removed right away at once.
It sometimes happens that a little pig's teeth are so sharp and long that it
pricks and hurts the sow so much that she will refuse to allow them to
suckle. This often causes serious trouble, and the little ones should be
examined, and the offending teeth removed. To remove the teeth take
the pig under the left arm, open the mouth with the left hand, and with
the right hand and a small pair of pinchers break off the offending teeth,
and place the pig back to the teat. A little coaxing and scratching will
make the sow lie down, and the pigs will then soon relieve the distended
and inflamed udder, giving her comfort, and there will be no more trouble
from that source. If the noise of the little pigs squealing excites the
sow, take them out of hearing. When the sow's pen is cleaned out the bed
should not be disturbed as it unsettles her.

As a rule the sow will not have much difficulty in farrowing, and, if
possible, it is better that she should do so unaided If she is an exceptionally long time in starting, or if there is a long interval after the first
portion of the litter arrives, and the sow appears to be in pain, the hand
should be smeared with carbolic oil and gently inserted, and if a pig is
presented crosswise it should be gently pressed back into the womb and
turned, or if the head is presented it may be taken away gently. Should
the little one have difficulty in getting its breath, open the mouth and
blow down the throat. If the pigs are not removed as they arrive they
may be placed to a teat, and will immediately commence to suckle, and
will nestle up to the mother, and the heat of her body will help to keep
them warm.

In two or three days the little ones will be strong enough to take care
of themselves. The health of the sow must be carefully watched, and
any indications of constipation corrected at once, 2 oz. of sulphur and
a pinch of nitre may be mixed in the food as a corrective. As soon as
she will take it a warm slop of bran and milk should be given. Her
feed for four weeks should be in a sloppy condition, consisting of bran
and pollard with skim milk if available. If whey is used it should be
scalded, or it may have the effect of producing diarrhœa in the young pigs.
The condition of the excreta is one of the best indications of the health
of the pig, and this should neither be hard formed nor yet liquid. Either
of these conditions requires immediate attention; to a very large extent
the disability may be regulated by the proportion of bran in the food.
A few hours after farrowing, if her bowels and other organs are not
acting healthily, the sow should be given a little gentle exercise.

A sow may be managed to bear five litters in two years, but this is
not advisable; two litters a year will be more satisfactory. The main object
now is to bring the young along as quickly as possible, and that can only
be done by feeding the sow for production of milk. In three or four
weeks the little pigs may be taught to drink from a small trough, fenced

away from the sow so that the little ones can run under the rails ; skim-milk to commence with, and then a little pollard added. Any males not required for breeding should be operated upon at as early an age as possible, say at two or three weeks old. The longer it is delayed the worse the effect on the pig. Great care must be taken with regard to cleanliness. The parts and instruments should be cleansed with an antiseptic such as $1\frac{1}{2}$ to 2 per cent. solution of lysol. Hundreds of farmers take no sanitary precautions whatever, and probably lose no pigs, but one has only to pay a visit to the public abattoirs to see that the effect of this neglect is often the loss and destruction of much valuable meat. The little extra care does not make many seconds difference in the time required for the operation. In England the female pigs not required for breeding purposes are spayed, which improves them for fattening and curing. The little ones may be weaned at six to eight weeks. The sow, if in good condition, may come in season in about three days after they are removed. If she has suckled herself into a low condition, it may be necessary to miss once or twice before sending to the boar, or a good plan is to leave the young with her a while longer. This often results in benefit to both sow and pigs, and the trouble which sometimes follows from a rest from breeding, of getting the sow in pig when she is mated, is avoided. When there is trouble in getting the sow to breed, particularly if she has put on too much condition, it may often be overcome by feeding rich rather than bulky food, for instance, a few beans or peas will prove far more suitable food for a sow about to be put to the boar than a comparatively large quantity of sloppy and innutritious food. The sow is more likely to hold if put to the boar just before going off heat than when she first comes on. It possible, she should be kept for a day or so by herself after being served. When there is difficulty in getting a sow to breed it may often be overcome by trying different boars, one after another. As soon as she proves in pig she should be fed nutritious, muscle forming food to keep up her own condition, and to develop her young. She should not be fat, but in good hard condition with a good store of lean meat which will help her to retain her condition while providing plenty of milk, whereas the fat would rapidly waste without assisting her in milk production. From the sixth to the fifteenth week of the sow's pregnancy she should be fed liberally on those kinds of food which are best suited for the production of lean meat and muscle rather than fat, as the drain on her system in building up the framework of some fifteen little pigs is very extensive. A week or so before she is due to farrow she may be fed on the same sort of feed she will get after farrowing. Pollard and bran with skim-milk if available should be the food for the sow for a month after farrowing. Then may be added barley meal or other crushed grain. If she shows signs of constipation the proportion of bran should be increased. If oats are fed the husk should be removed, as this is likely to be injurious to the young pigs. She may now be fed three times instead of twice a day. If it is not possible to give the sows a grass run, it will be found beneficial to throw tares, lucerne, or other green stuff to them.

MANAGEMENT OF THE YOUNG PIGS.

The management of the young pig depends upon its ultimate destination, whether it is intended for stud, show, or fattening. The show may be looked upon as an advertisement, and it is not always the animal that takes the prize at the leading shows that will give the best results at the stud. This depends largely on its treatment. It is an old and true saying that the young animal must never be allowed to lose its baby flesh. As above-mentioned, we fed the mother in such a way that the little ones have a good start, commencing life in good condition, and then not only maintain that condition, but continually improve upon it. The sow is fed on milk producing food, pollard and bran, with skim-milk if available, or water, in a sloppy condition. When the little ones are about a month old she may have barley or other meal in addition. Those that are intended for show purposes are sometimes kept from the mother, but put to her at regular intervals of two hours for a feed, and at the same time given as much cow's new milk as they will take. This brings them along evenly and rapidly, and is responsible for the wonderfully even litters that we see in the show pen. For stud purposes this is not the best system to work upon. Better to let the little ones run with the sow, and when about three weeks old provide them with a little trough fenced off from the mother so that they can run under the rail at will. In this provide them with skim-milk at about body temperature, giving them little and often as much as they will take. A few whole peas or wheat may also be given them. A little pollard may gradually be worked into it. In this way they will, by degrees, learn to eat, so that when weaning time arrives they will hardly feel the loss of the sow, and it will also take a great amount of the strain off her. It must be remembered that a pig has a comparatively small storage capacity, that is why it must be fed little and often, and also of concentrated food. If allowed to become too hungry it will feed ravenously, which will probably upset the digestive organs. The food must be continued in a sloppy condition for the young pigs. Injudicious feeding will often bring about feverish conditions. The first indication of stomach derangement is almost invariably by the droppings becoming hard and dry, like peas. This is followed by diarrhœa. Any appearance of constipation must be corrected at once. A supply of a condition powder, the composition of which is given below, should be kept on hand, and a little put into the food regularly. It has been proved that young pigs will keep in health and thrive much better when this is done. Another great trouble in young pigs is a sort of rheumatic affection, especially if they are not provided with suitable houses or shelter. Whatever form this shelter may take, the most important points to provide for are dryness, freedom from draughts, reasonable warmth, light, ventilation, and convenience. Whatever is provided for a bed, it must be dry. In warm weather a hurdle of close lattice providing for good drainage may suffice, but in cold weather dry straw or similar material on the hurdle will be necessary. On no account should they be allowed to lie on damp fermenting bedding. This is a frequent cause of pneumonia, which often results in death in twenty-four hours. With young pigs in cold weather at least, the food should be given to them warm, about 100° Fah. This economizes a certain amount of food, and anything that increases the comfort of the animals will favour more rapid development. After weaning, the food should be continued for some time about the same as before. As they advance in age the proportion of barley or other meal may be increased. If oats are used these should be husked, as the fibrous husk often acts as an irritant to the stomach of a young pig. A few whole peas or a little whole wheat may be given to them at midday instead of the ordinary food. At ten or eleven weeks old they may be fed three or four times daily.

This is the most critical stage of the pig's life, and the treatment that we give those intended for the stud will be the most suitable for those destined for pork or bacon. The old idea of allowing the pigs to become stores is wrong, and unprofitable from every standpoint. Provided there is a demand for it, the younger the pig the more per lb. you will get for it, and the less per pound will it cost to produce. The young pig has greater powers of digestion and assimilation, and can, therefore, produce a greater weight of meat from a given amount of food than an old one. The younger it is the greater the proportion of lean to fat, it is also tender and juicy, and when mild cured is what the consumer will pay the most money for. The older and heavier they are, the greater the proportion of fat, the more it costs to produce, and the less per lb. will the curers pay for it. The aim should be to fatten the pig right from the time it is born, first through the sow, then as above indicated, then if the price for porkers at 70 to 90 lbs. is good, let them go. If not, they should be suitable for the bacon-curer at 120 lbs. carcase weight. This is the weight in greatest demand, and should be produced at five to six months old. To obtain these results we must have the right class of pig, quick growing, and strong constitutioned, of those breeds that naturally produce lean or muscle more than fat.

Sometimes little pigs are affected with fits, they suddenly fall over, remain motionless for a few minutes, and gradually recover. After repeated attacks they die. This is due to over feeding or too rich food, but with the use of the powder above mentioned this is not likely to occur. Another way of working the little pigs is when they are about three or four weeks old, to turn the sow out for an hour or two in the middle of the day, and during her absence give them some milk in a trough. They will soon learn to feed, and by degrees add some pollard, and give a few whole peas or wheat. Any left in the trough will be eaten by the sow on her return. In this way they will learn to become independent of the mother, so that in eight or nine weeks time they can be weaned without feeling her loss, and the sow will gradually dry off without any inconvenience to herself. At weaning time a little barley meal may be given in addition to the pollard, and at ten weeks old they may have about one-fourth meal and three-fourths pollard.

About a tablespoonful of bone meal per pig per day should be given in the food. This will greatly economize the food, and help to keep them healthy.

POWDER FOR PIGS.

U.S.A. Bureau of Animal Industry.

Wood charcoal	..	..	..	..	..	..	1 lb.
Sulphur	..	..	..	..	..	..	1 ,,
Salt ..	..	..	..	..	..	..	2 ,,
Bi-carbonate of soda (baking soda)		..	..	..	..	..	2 ,,
Hyposulphite of soda	..	..	..	..	..	..	2 ,,
Sulphate of soda	..	..	..	..	..	..	1 ,,
Sulphide of antimony (black antimony)	..		..	..	..	..	1 ,,

Thoroughly pulverize and mix and give one tablespoonful daily per 100 lb. live weight of pig.

THE INFLUENCE OF SUPERPHOSPHATES ON THE GERMINATION OF WHEAT.

By Alfred J. Ewart, D.Sc., Ph.D., F.L.S., Government Botanist of Victoria, and Professor of Botany and Plant Physiology, in the Melbourne University.

It has frequently been stated that when wheat lies in a dry soil for a long time in contact with superphosphate of lime, its germination may be very seriously affected. The fact was mentioned as long ago as 1905 in the *Journal of Agriculture* of South Australia, page 135, and recent work has confirmed this fact. It appears however that the injurious action only becomes pronounced when there is a little free moisture to begin with and the soil subsequently dries, and when this is so, any seeds which had begun to germinate would die in any case if the soil remained dry for a sufficient length of time. When the germination takes place fairly rapidly, a stimulating rather than an injurious action appears to be exercised. In order to avoid the possibility of the superphosphate injuriously affecting the germination of the grain when it lay for a long time in contact with the seed in a dry soil, a drill has been invented and placed upon the market which plants the grain and superphosphate at different depths. Some plots planted in the ordinary way and with this drill were inspected last year, but it was not possible to make any definite conclusions from them, except that the planting of the superphosphate beneath the wheat did not seem to retard the growth in any way. Of course it should be remembered that the special value of this mode of planting would only become strongly apparent when the special condition mentioned prevailed, namely, a long period of delayed germination owing to the dryness of the soil.

In any case it seemed worth while to try whether mere contact with dry superphosphate would affect the germination of wheat and also to carry out small plot experiments with the grain and superphosphate planted at exactly measured depths. This is necessary because the very best drill varies a little in the depth at which the seed is planted, particularly where the seed bed contains many stones or unbroken clods.

The experiments were carried out by the Second Year Agricultural Students (1911) under supervision. In the first place experiments were tried by storing dry wheat with an equal quantity of dry superphosphate for three to six weeks, and noting the germination at the end of those times. The following are the results :—

Experiment.	% Germination control 3 weeks.	% Germination superph. 3 weeks.	% Germination superph. 6 weeks.
I. ..	90%	86%	84%
II. ..	91%	94%	92%
III. ..	96%	91%	93%
IV. ..	85%	91%	80%
Average ..	91%	9 %	87%

Evidently when the grain and superphosphate are dry, little or no injurious effect is exercised in a moderate length of time. In the following plot experiments, in the plots " A," the grain and phosphate were planted 1 inch deep. In " B " the grain was planted 1 inch and the phosphate 2 inches, and in " C " the grain was 1 inch deep and the phosphate 4 inches deep. The heads and straw were harvested and weighed separately, the former being cut off just before the grain ripened. All the plots were slightly affected with " rust " and plot " B " in series 5 was badly affected. They were carefully hand weeded, but the weeding in series 6 was not quite so thorough as in the other plots. The superphosphate was applied at the rate of 1 cwt. per acre except in series 2 where the quantity was doubled. The following are the detailed results :—

Series I.	Series II.	Series III.	Series IV.	Series V.	Series VI.
Control.	2 cwt. super. per acre.	1 cwt. super. per acre.	1 cwt. super. per acre.	1 cwt. super. per acre.	1 cwt. super. per acre.
	C. Heads, 31 Straw, 228	C. Heads, 13 Straw, 128	C. Heads, 30 Straw, 180	C. Heads, 33 Straw, 160	C. Heads, 14 Straw, 105
No Manure. Heads, 8 Straw, 72	B. Heads, 21 Straw, 157	B. Heads, 12 Straw, 116	A. Heads, 25 Straw, 160	B. Heads, 16 Straw, 102 Badly infested with Rust	B. Heads, 19 Straw, 132
	A. Heads, 16 Straw, 144	A. Heads, 10 Straw, 123	B. Heads, 34 Straw, 196	A. Heads, 19 Straw, 119	A. Heads, 19 Straw, 140

A. Grain and phosphate, 1 inch.
B. Phosphate, 2 inches ; grain, 1 inch.
C. Phosphate, 4 inches ; grain, 1 inch.

Summarizing these results, the weights were :—

—	Heads.	Straw.
A. Grain and Phosphate 1 inch	89	686
B. Phosphate 2 inches, Grain 1 inch	103	703
C. Phosphate 4 inches, Grain 1 inch	121	801
Control, no manure	27	240

Apparently, therefore, so far as experiments on a small scale can be relied on, planting the superphosphate from 1 to 3 inches below the grain seems to slightly increase the yield both as regards heads and straw, and since with the exception of one series of plots and with the badly rusted plot in series 5, the results in each series are consistent with the averages of the whole plots, it seems probable that field tests would give similar results. In any case this method of planting is worthy of extended trial, since it is impossible to predict how long the grain may have to lie in the ground, and planting the superphosphate under the grain instead of in contact with it, certainly does not seem to injuriously affect the yield. It is possible that where a beneficial influence is exercised it may be because the presence of the manure under the grain encourages the young roots to grow more vertically downwards and so obtain a better supply of water. If this is the case the effect would be most pronounced on a loose friable soil in which moisture descends quickly. It was in a soil of this character that the above tests were made.

Mr. A. E. V. Richardson, Agricultural Superintendent, adds the following interesting note to the above :—

With reference to your article on " Influence of Superphosphates on the Germination of Wheat," there is one point which perhaps may have escaped notice, but which I think would serve to make the figures you use still more striking.

If you take the average of the 1 cwt. A, B and C plots and compare them with the 2 cwt. plots they work out something like this :—

Manure.			Heads.		Straw.	
			2 cwt.	1 cwt.	2 cwt.	1 cwt.
A. Plots—						
Manure sown with seed	..	..	16	18¼	144	135½
B. 1″ under seed	..	..	21	20¼	157	136½
C. 3″ ,,	..	..	31	22½	228	143¼

The manure placed deep as at C, was an advantage all round, but the advantage was much greater with the larger than with the smaller dressing of manure. Taking the whole of the plots (15) the best · yield was obtained from 2 cwt. super., but in order to give this result, the manure had to be drilled deep.

The whole of the results indicate that deeper drilling of the manure may enable the farmer to use larger quantities of manure with profit than has hitherto been possible with the ordinary drill.

INSECTIVOROUS BIRDS OF VICTORIA.

THE WHITE-HEADED STILT.

(Himantopus leucocephalus, Gould.)

By C. French, Junior, Acting Government Entomologist.

During the months of October, November and December these beautiful birds which are noted destroyers of noxious insects, also the fresh-water snails which are the hosts of the dreaded Liver Fluke, have been breeding near Laverton, on the Geelong line. This is probably the first authentic record for Victoria.

The nests, about 10 to 15 feet apart in the middle of a fairly large swamp, placed on clumps of the dwarf Salt-marsh plant Salicornia, and principally composed of dried *Lyngbya destuarii* and other aquatic plants, measured approximately 8 inches across, and were built up about 9 inches above the water. Dead twigs of the Salicornia were placed on the tops of the nests, several of which were placed on burnt clumps of the " Awned Sword Sedge " (*Gahnia trifida*) about 12 inches above the water. The majority of the nests contained 4 eggs (one with five was discovered) and most of the eggs were placed with the small ends pointing towards the middle of the nest, though in some instances several of the eggs had the small ends pointing outward.

Unfortunately, before all the eggs were hatched out the swamp commenced to dry up; the old birds left the locality, and deserted a number of eggs and young birds.

The accompanying photograph is taken from a group of birds, nests, eggs, and young, in the National Museum, Melbourne. The specimens were collected by myself and presented to the Museum.

THE WHITE-HEADED STILT (HIMANTOPUS LEUCOCEPHALUS).

ORCHARD AND GARDEN NOTES.

E. E. Pescott, Principal, Horticultural School, Burnley.

The Orchard.

The exceptionally dry season has been one of the causes in reducing the fruit crop to a large extent. Large quantities of fruit have not fully developed; and many varieties, notably the London Pippin, have been badly affected with the so-far mysterious trouble known as " pig face " or " crinkle."

Another feature was the prevalence of fruit blossoms early in March. Cherry, plum, pear, apple, and other fruit trees were in full blossom, the latter varieties carrying at the same time, crops of fruit.

This was mainly the result of the hot week experienced in February. Where the trees were well forward, and had matured their foliage, or where trees were shallow rooted, the excessively hot weather caused the dropping of the foliage. The subsequent cool change, with light rains, was sufficient to cause the fruit buds to fully develop, and to burst into blossom.

The blossom, and if fruit subsequently formed, the fruit should be removed from the trees, so as to bring them back, as far as possible, to normal conditions.

The continued dry weather has prevented the sowing of green manure crops. But with the showers that have fallen at the end of March, it will now be possible to have these sown without delay. As previously mentioned, one of the main objects in connexion with cover crops should be to obtain as abundant growth as possible in the autumn, so that a greater quantity of organic matter may be added to the soil.

In stiff clay and in sour soils, it will be an advantage to give the autumnal dressing of lime. From 4 to 5 cwt. per acre will be all that is necessary.

For the successful coping with the Codlin Moth pest, it is essential that all fallen and diseased fruit should be gathered and destroyed. Where bandages are used, these should be removed and thoroughly cleaned, or preferably, they should be burned.

Strawberries may now be planted out; if planting is carried out at once, they will take a firm roothold of the soil before winter sets in.

Vegetable Garden.

The vegetable garden should now be well dug over and left in a fairly rough state. Various seedlings from the seed-bed, such as cabbage, cauliflower, onions, and celery may now be planted. The celery beds should be well drained, as blanched stems will rot in the winter, if much soil water accumulates around the plants.

Asparagus beds should be cleaned over, and all plants that have ripened their seeds should be cut back. The weeds too should all be cleaned out, and their seeds should not be allowed to settle in the beds.

Early peas, broad beans, and onions may now be sown.

Flower Garden.

Seeds of all hardy annual and perennial plants should be planted without delay. It is advisable to have these well advanced in growth before the cold weather sets in and retards their growth for the winter.

Towards the end of the month a start should be made with the winter digging. A top dressing of either manure or lime may be given before digging, the latter wherever the soil is at all sour, where sorrel is present, or in stiff clay soils. In addition all garden refuse and litter should be dug in; this will all form plant food, it will assist in lightening the soil, and it will be a means of easy disposal of all garden rubbish.

The winter digging may be as deep as possible, and the soil may be left in a fairly rough condition for the rains and frost to mellow down.

Chrysanthemums will now require weekly supplies of liquid manure, which should be maintained until the blooms begin to open.

All bulbs should now be planted and these should be preserved from attacks of snails and slugs. A plentiful supply of such remedies as tobacco dust, Pestend, lime, carbolized sawdust, &c., will all assist to protect the young growths.

As each season continues, some formerly neglected, and so-called old-fashioned flower is brought into prominence in a considerably improved form. Previous seasons have seen improved forms of Scabious, the old pincushion, Zonale Geraniums, Sweet Peas, and so on. The present form of such plants are vast improvements upon the old strains, and are valuable additions to our garden flowers.

Among the latest additions to this class of flowering plants is the strain of Gloxinia-flowered Pentstemons. For years the cultivation of this useful herbaceous perennial has languished, but with the advent of the improved type, we are enabled to furnish our gardens with clumps of a very fine improved strain.

The late Mr. Kerslake of Sydney was the pioneer in Australia in advancing this plant again to the front, and some very fine varieties are now purchasable. The flowers are unusually large, as compared with the older types, and well merit their name " Gloxinia-flowered." The trusses carry very many large flowers, and for summer flowering hardy plants, these pentstemons are extremely desirable.

Some of the valuable varieties are:—Unique, rose pink, with dark streaked throat; Brilliant, rich pink, white throat; Iris, petunia, streaked throat; Hercules, pink, streaked throat; John Louder, deep purple; A. J. Tymms, bright rose red, with marked throat; and Louis Laplastrier, rose purple, with brightly streaked throat.

ANSWERS TO CORRESPONDENTS.

The Staff of the Department has been organized to a large extent for the purpose of giving information to farmers. Questions in every branch of agriculture are gladly answered. Write a short letter, giving as full particulars as possible, of your local conditions, and state precisely what it is that you want to know. *All inquiries forwarded to the Editor must be accompanied by the name and address of the writer.* This is very necessary, as sometimes insufficient information is furnished by the inquirer.

COUCH GRASS.—E.S. has a couch grass bowling green in some parts of which the grass is not growing as well as usual. He asks whether the constant watering which. it gets in the summer is likely to leach out some of the requisite plant foods in the soil and affect the growth.

Answer.—Couch grass thrives in the poorest as well as in the richest of soils. Consequently, any soil leaching from excessive watering would hardly interfere with its growth. This grass discolours badly in winter, and loses most of its foliage. Excessive rain or water in winter would kill out the weaker growths, of which there would be a considerable quantity, owing to the close cutting in summer necessary for bowling greens. It would be advisable to re-sow the bare patches with a light seeding, 'op dressing with fresh soil, and giving a light sprinkling of blood manure, about 3 ozs. to the square yard.

EROSION.—A.J. writes " What is the best method of stopping the formation of a gully by erosion in a gently sloping paddock with a clay sub-soil? The gully is forming in a paddock within 30 yards of my fence. It is 12 to 14 feet deep, and about 6 feet wide, and seems to be advancing at about the rate of a yard ever year. Prevention would have been better than cure as it will cost a very large sum to repair the damage already done, but I am apprehensive for my own land and would like to present a scheme before the owner for stopping the trouble."

Answer.—Your best plan would be to cut drains above the cutaway, with a slight fall to prevent the water running into the gully, and fill the cutaway with scrub placed across the fall of the water to hold the silt. When the scrub is covered put in fresh layers until the hole is full. Plant trees (willows) in and around the edges, and sow paspalum or other grasses on the top.

WHITE PAINT FOR FARM BUILDINGS.—H.C.B. asks for directions for making white paint suitable for painting farm gates, out-buildings, &c.

Answer.—Dissolve 56 lbs. of white lead in 9 pints of raw and 9 pints of boiled linseed oil, then add 2 lbs. of ultramarine blue (previously dissolved in oil), 1 pint of turps and ½ lb. of patent driers. Mix thoroughly, and strain through a fine sieve. For porous work, add more oil, and use less oil for second coat. This quantity will cover 100 square yards.

COVERING STACK.—W.N. inquires as to cheap method of covering a haystack. He asks whether hessian soaked in coal tar and dried would keep out the rain.

Answer.—Thatching with straw is the cheapest and safest means of covering a stack, unless a proper hay shed is built. Hessian soaked in tar would not be capable of keeping out all rain; a good tarpaulin canvas would be better.

SWINGLE BARS FOR FIVE-HORSE TEAM.—J.W. writes " Can you give particulars of necessary bars and chains to yoke five horses three and two, instead of all abreast, so as to avoid having to work offside horse on the ploughed ground."

Answer.—The swingle bars required for a team of five horses worked two and three abreast are one three-horse bar, one two-horse bar, and three single bars. The leading horses (two) can be yoked with leading chains to the two land and furrow horses, or a furrow and land horse to chains behind the hames, or can be yoked to a double set of bars connected with a chain running up between the back furrow and land horses from the double bar. This system will necessitate a greater length of the three-horse bar to distribute the draught evenly for the outside third horse, and is objectionable in turning as the bars, if slackened, are liable to interfere with the back horses.

CRUSHED OATS FOR DRAUGHT HORSES.—J.W. asks whether there is any advantage in feeding working draught horses on crushed instead of whole oats.

Answer.—Crushed oats are quite 20 per cent. better as feed than whole oats, being easily and more completely digested. All the principal firms dealing in agricultural implements sell grain-crushing machines.

VICTORIAN EGG-LAYING COMPETITION, 1911-12,

CONDUCTED AT BURNLEY HORTICULTURAL SCHOOL.

(Continued from page 200.)

H. V. Hawkins, Poultry Expert.

No. of Pen.	Breed.	Name of Owner.	Eggs Laid during Competition.			Position in Competition.
			April to Jan.	Feb.	Total to date (11 mths)	
31	White Leghorn	R. W. Pope	1,350	123	1,473	1
12	"	W. G. Swift	1,378	81	1,459	2
40	"	A. J. Cosh (S.A.)	1,308	111	1,419	3
20	"	H. McKenzie	1,246	114	1,360	4
37	"	E. Waldon	1,210	114	1,324	5
33	"	Range Poultry Farm (Qld.)	1,204	71	1,275	6
39	"	A. W. Hall	1,134	112	1,246	7
18	"	T. Brundrett	1,107	81	1,188	8
13	Black Orpington	D. Fisher	1,078	84	1,162	} 9
21	White Leghorn	R. L. Appleford	1,085	77	1,162	
24	"	F. Hannaford	1,041	106	1,147	11
19	"	A. Jaques	1,025	120	1,145	12
2	"	E. P. Nash	1,029	110	1,139	13
10	Black Orpington	H. A. Langdon	1,035	103	1,138	14
9	White Leghorn	J. O'Loughlin	1,034	103	1,137	} 15
50	"	C. H. Busst	1,019	118	1,137	
46	Minorca	G. W. Chalmers	1,043	84	1,127	17
25	White Leghorn	B. Mitchell	1,038	83	1,121	18
28	"	John Campbell	1,013	107	1,120	19
3	"	K. Gleghorn	1,008	109	1,117	} 20
55	"	W. G. McLister	1,037	80	1,117	
38	"	Mrs. C. R. Smee	1,030	81	1,111	22
1	"	A. Brebner	1,005	94	1,099	23
45	"	T. Kempster	992	106	1,098	24
36	"	F. A. Sillitoe	1,014	83	1,097	} 25
11	Brown Leghorn	F. Soncum	972	125	1,097	
62	White Leghorn	P. Hodson	986	105	1,091	27
49	"	W. J. Thornton	1,007	82	1,089	28
32	Silver Wyandotte	Mrs. M. A. Jones	996	79	1,075	29
44	Black Orpington	T. S. Goodisson	1,002	68	1,070	30
57	White Leghorn	G. E. Edwards	966	85	1,051	31
5	"	L. C. Payne	978	70	1,048	} 32
65	"	H. Hammill (N.S.W.)	954	94	1,048	
67	"	C. L. Sharman	952	93	1,045	34
22	Black Orpington	P. S. Wood	951	92	1,043	35
47	White Leghorn	C. W. Spencer (N.S.W.)	976	64	1,040	36
4	Golden Wyandotte	H. Bell	946	91	1,037	37
8	White Leghorn	T. W. Coto	931	71	1,022	} 38
60	"	J. J. Harrington	925	97	1,022	
66	White Wyandotte	J. E. Bradley	929	92	1,021	40
43	White Leghorn	W. B. Crellin	933	82	1,015	41
35	"	J. H. Brain	882	130	1,012	42
41	"	Morgan and Watson	910	84	994	43
51	"	J. W. McArthur	910	69	979	44
53	"	A. Stringer	913	64	977	45
64	"	J. D. Read	868	106	974	46
59	"	W. H. Dunlop	923	49	972	47
58	Faverolles	K. Courtenay	887	84	971	48
34	White Leghorn	E. Dettman	868	97	965	49
52	"	W. J. McKeddie	875	80	955	50
27	"	Hill and Luckman	910	42	952	51
6	Silver Wyandotte	Mrs. H. J. Richards	860	89	949	52
63	Black Orpington	A. J. Treacey	893	55	948	53
30	"	Rodgers Bros.	867	65	932	54
42	White Orpington	P. Mitchell	865	64	929	55
7	White Leghorn	H. Stevenson	853	47	900	56
56	"	Mrs. C. Thompson	811	85	896	57
26	"	F. H. Seymour	815	70	835	58
16	Silver Wyandotte	Miss A. Cottam	785	77	862	59
54	White Leghorn	F. Hodges	785	71	856	60
23	Golden Wyandotte	G. E. Brown	770	79	849	61
61	Silver Wyandotte	J. Reade	754	90	844	62
17	White Leghorn	W. J. Eckershall	698	61	759	63
14	Black Orpington	W. J. Macauley	660	63	723	64
15	Minorca	H. R. McChesney	605	33	638	65
48	"	G. James	509	69	578	66
			63,363	5,668	69,031	

REMINDERS FOR MAY.

LIVE STOCK.

HORSES.—Those stabled can be fed liberally. Those doing fast or heavy work should be clipped; if not wholly, then trace high. Those not rugged on coming into the stable at night should be wiped down and in half-an-hour's time rugged or covered with bags until the coat is dry. Old horses and weaned foals should be given crushed oats. Grass-fed working horses should be given hay or straw, if there is no old grass, to counteract the purging effects of the young growth.

CATTLE.—Cows, if not housed, should be rugged. Rugs should be removed in the daytime when the shade temperature reaches 60 degrees. Give a ration of hay or straw, whole or chaffed, to counteract the purging effects of young grass. Cows about to calve, if over fat, should be put into a paddock in which the feed is not too abundant. Calves should be kept in warm dry shed.

PIGS.—As recommended in Reminders for April.

SHEEP.—Attend lambing ewes first thing each morning. Avoid overcrowding in lambing paddocks, and consequent shortage of feed. Scarcity of feed means inattentive mothers. Breeds of ewes having more than half of British blood should be kept in good strong condition, as they will not lamb until July or August. Young ram weaners of all breeds should now be classed, and rejects castrated or blocked. Be suspicious of weak fore-quartered ewes. If castrating, slit, tie with fine cord soaked in antiseptic, cut off, and apply Stockholm tar liberally inside and out. Blocking, whilst most humane in the case of rams two years old and over when the latest appliance is used, is not desirable for two-tooths. Clear wool from eyes of merino rams, and cut horns with pruning shears.

POULTRY.—Feed animal food to forward pullets, about ½ oz. daily, and equal parts short oats and maize at night. Give 2 ozs. lucerne chaff, mixed with mash, to each bird daily. Watch young stock for Roup (watery discharge from nostrils, with unpleasant breath). Late chicks are likely subjects. Isolate all cases, and use disinfectants freely. Keep head and throat clean by washing with either Condy's fluid or boracic acid. In cases of Chicken Pox isolate birds and apply to affected parts ointment made of sulphur, eucalyptus oil (three or four drops), carbolic acid (two drops), and a little vaseline mixed well.

CULTIVATION.

FARM.—Dig main crop of potatoes. Push on with ploughing and sowing of cereal crops, including peas and beans. Green fodder (as for April) may still be sown. Land for maize, potatoes, and other root crops should be prepared and manured. Flax may be sown. Transplant Chou Moellier and Giant Drumhead cabbage plants in rows 3 feet apart. Complete sowing permanent pastures with grasses and clovers.

ORCHARD.—Plough, manure; apply lime to orchard lands at rate of 5 or 10 cwt. per acre where soil is sour. Spray trees infested with scale insects, Woolly Aphis, and Bryobia Mite with red oil or crude petroleum. Clean all rough bark from trees. Commence pruning at end of month.

FLOWER GARDEN.—Digging, manuring, and pruning; trench and drain where necessary. Dress the surface with lime. Continue to sow hardy annuals. Bury all leaves, soft-wooded cuttings, and weeds. Continue to plant spring blooming perennials and other plants. Plant cuttings of carnations and roses.

VEGETABLE GARDEN.—Cut down and clean out asparagus beds. Apply manure and lime dressings. Cultivate deeply. Plant out seedlings and early potatoes; sow peas, broad beans, carrots, and parsnips.

VINEYARD.—Subsoil land for new plantations if not already done. It is very undesirable to perform this work immediately before planting. Vine-growers are warned against the too common practice of feeding off foliage after vintage. Any small advantage in the form of stock feed is only gained at the cost of a reduction in the following season's crop, owing to interference with accumulation of reserves, which continues so long as the leaves remain green. Sheep should not be allowed into the vineyard until all leaves have changed colour. Early and deep ploughing is strongly recommended (*see* March *Journal*, page 198).

Cellars.—Rack or fill up (preferably the former) dry wines as soon as a lighted match, introduced at bung hole, is no longer extinguished. Sweet wines should also be racked and fortified to full strength.

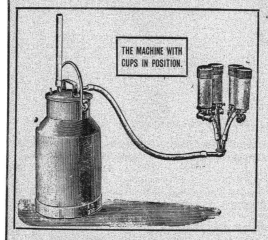

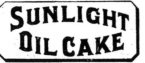

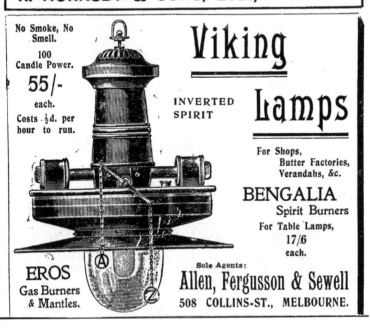

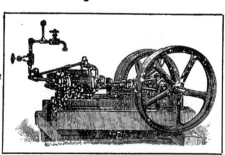

LITERATURE FOR AGRICULTURISTS.

PLAN AND SPECIFICATION OF SHEEP-SHEARING SHED. 2s. 6d. *Postage*, 1d.

MILK CHARTS (Monthly and Weekly), 6d. per dozen, post free. When ordering, dairy farmers should mention " Monthly " or " Weekly."

By *Professor A. J. Ewart, Government Botanist*.

WEEDS, POISON PLANTS, AND NATURALIZED ALIENS OF VICTORIA. 2s. 6d. *Postage :* Commonwealth, 1½d. ; N.Z., 5d. ; British and Foreign, 10d.

PLANTS INDIGENOUS TO VICTORIA. Vol. II., 10s. *Postage :* Com., 2d. ; N.Z., 8d. ; Brit. & For., 1s. 4d.

By *C. French, F.E.S., Government Entomologist*.

DESTRUCTIVE INSECTS OF VICTORIA. Parts I., II., III., IV., V. 2s. 6d. each. *Postage :* Parts I. and III., C., 1d. ; N.Z., 3d.; B. & F., 6d. each. Parts II. and IV., C., 1½d. ; N.Z., 4d. ; B. & F., 8d. each. Part V., C., 1d. ; N.Z., 4d. ; B. & F., 7d.

By *D. McAlpine, Government Vegetable Pathologist*.

RUSTS OF AUSTRALIA. 5s. *Postage :* C., 2d. ; N.Z., 8d. ; B. & F., 1s. 4d.

SMUTS OF AUSTRALIA. 4s. *Postage :* C., 2½d. ; N.Z., 9d. ; B. & F., 1s. 6d.

FUNGUS DISEASES OF CITRUS TREES IN AUSTRALIA. 2s. *Postage :* C., 1d. ; N.Z., 3d. ; B. & F., 6d.

FUNGUS DISEASES OF STONE FRUIT TREES IN AUSTRALIA. 2s. 6d. *Postage :* C., 1½d. ; N.Z., 5d. ; B. & F., 10d.

SYSTEMATIC ARRANGEMENT OF AUSTRALIAN FUNGI. 3s. *Postage :* C., 2d. ; N.Z., 8d. ; B. & F., 1s. 4d.

THE DEPARTMENT OF AGRICULTURE,
MELBOURNE, VICTORIA.

Remittances from places outside the Commonwealth to be by Money Order only.

Pamphlets obtainable from the Director of Agriculture, Melbourne, Free on Application.

NEW SERIES.

1. SILO CONSTRUCTION. *A. S. Kenyon, C.E.*
2. HINTS FOR NEW SETTLERS. *T. A. J. Smith.*
3. APPLE GROWING FOR EXPORT. *P. J. Carmody.*
4. BOOKKEEPING FOR FARMERS. *W. McIver, A.I.A.V., A.S.A.A., Eng.*
5. CIDER MAKING. *J. Knight.*
6. FARM PLUMBING. *C. H. Wright.*
7. CITRUS FRUIT CULTURE. *E. E. Pescott.*
8. BUILDING HINTS FOR SETTLERS. *A. S. Kenyon, C.E., and others.*
9. TOBACCO CULTURE. *T. A. J. Smith.*
10. SILOS AND SILAGE. *G. H. F. Baker.*
11. THE BEET SUGAR INDUSTRY AND CLOSER SETTLEMENT. *H. T. Easterby.*

The Journal of

THE DEPARTMENT OF

AGRICULTURE

OF VICTORIA, AUSTRALIA.

May, 1912.

A PRESENT DAY CLYDESDALE STALLION.

PRICE THREEPENCE. (Annual Subscription—Victoria, Inter-State, and N.Z., 3/-; British and Foreign, 5/-.)

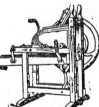

THE JOURNAL

OF

THE DEPARTMENT OF AGRICULTURE,

VICTORIA, AUSTRALIA.

CONTENTS.—MAY, 1912.

COPYRIGHT PROVISIONS AND SUBSCRIPTION RATES.

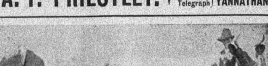
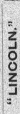

Vacuum

Gargoyle

Prepared

Red Spraying Oil

**Needs no Soft Soap
or other ingredient.**

**Requires only
Clean Soft Water.**

Vacuum Gargoyle Red Spray Oil
now obtainable in prepared form
is the same Oil as that originally
introduced to Australia for fruit-
tree spraying.

Full particulars—

**Horticultural Department,
Vacuum Oil Co. Pty. Ltd.,**
90 William Street, Melbourne.

THE JOURNAL

OF

The Department of Agriculture

OF

VICTORIA.

LIBRARY'
NEW YORK
BOTANICA
GARDEN.

Vol. X. Part 5.	10th May, 1912.

WHEAT AND ITS CULTIVATION.

(*Continued from page* 208.)

No. 4.—SEEDING OPERATIONS.

*By A. E. V. Richardson, M.A., B.Sc. (Agric.), Agricultural
Superintendent.*

No activities in the farm calendar arouse such speculation and anxiety
to the Australian wheat-grower as those pertaining to seeding operations.
The nature and peculiarities of the Australian climate are such as to
render a close study of the factors underlying successful seeding quite
imperative. In some of the more favoured countries of Europe the distribution of the rainfall is so even throughout the year that the wheat-
grower may sow his wheat at leisure in autumn ; or, if weather conditions
be unfavorable for autumn seeding, he may defer operations until the
advent of spring. and still secure a heavy crop.

The uncertainty of the spring and early summer rainfall and the long
hot and relatively dry summers characteristic of the bulk of the wheat-
growing areas of Australia, preclude such spring sowing from being a
success in these districts. Autumn sowing, or early winter sowing, must
therefore he regarded as essential to success over the greater portion of
the State.

Wheat-growers in the drier districts have learned, from long experience, that in the great majority of seasons the ultimate success of the crop
depends very largely on getting the seed sown on soil in good physical
condition at the *right time*—within what may be called the *normal* seeding
period, which, under the most favorable conditions extends over some six
to eight weeks. When, however, heavy showers fall intermittently during
this period the seeding is considerably delayed, and much of the crop must
be sown too late to secure optimum results. Where large areas are to be
sown, and difficulties arise either from a dearth of labour or teams, the
sowing season must be prolonged beyond the period necessary to insure
the best results.

Time to Sow.

Autumn, then, is the season for seeding, and the actual date to commence operations will vary with the district, and the general character of the season. Much, of course, depends on the weather. In some years the rains hang back until late in autumn, and seeding often commences on a dry seed bed. In other years, again, the autumn rains are timely, frequent and copious, and the seed is sown under conditions which bring about rapid, even, and vigorous germination. Speaking generally, it may be said that it is safe to sow seed during the *normal* seeding period when the soil is either sufficiently dry to leave the seed ungerminated, or else when the soil is so thoroughly moist as to induce immediate germination. There is an intermediate stage, however, between these extremes when it is dangerous to sow wheat. This condition arises when the soil is neither dry nor wet, but contains sufficient moisture to induce germination, yet insufficient to keep the young plant fully supplied with moisture. Under these circumstances, unless rain opportunely falls, the soil begins to dry out and the grain malts.

While wheat and other naked seeds are very susceptible to malting in slightly moist and rapidly drying soils, oats and barley, with their tough, fibrous, protective envelopes, are not so susceptible. Hence, while it may be unsafe to sow wheat under such conditions, barley and oats may be sown with much less likelihood of loss. Generally speaking, the latter portion of April, and the month of May are the most favorable months for the drier areas, whilst the seeding may often be prolonged till June in more certain districts. Where large areas are to be sown a start must be made as early as possible to finish the seeding in a reasonable time.

Many farmers in their anxiety to get over large areas frequently commence seeding operations earlier than is indicated above. One of two things may happen. Dry weather may continue after the seed is sown, and induce a considerable amount of malting, in which case some re-sowing will require to be done. On the other hand, timely showers may supervene and bring the young plants on with exceptional vigor, and result in rank, heady growth. Not only are such crops liable to be cut later on with frosts, but they are also prone to lodge with the heavy winter rains.

These contingencies may be obviated either by administering a check to the rapid growth by judicious feeding down with sheep, or by taking the precaution to sow comparatively late maturing varieties in the early part of the seeding, and reserving very early varieties till the end of the season.

Very late sowing, in the drier areas, can only be successful when the winter proves to be exceptionally mild and the spring and summer rains ample, frequent, and timely, a combination of circumstances we may hardly hope for. Hence, in the drier districts the wheat-grower is well advised to reduce the late sown crops to a minimum.

Treatment of the Land.

To adequately discuss the possible preparatory modes of soil treatment for wheat cultivation would take more space than can be given here, and discussion will, therefore, be reserved for special consideration in later articles. For the present it is assumed that the wheat is to be sown on well-prepared bare fallow.

Varieties to Sow.

The choice of varieties is governed by the physical character of the soil, the climate in which the wheat is to be grown, and the purpose for which the wheat is required. The farmer must select those particular wheats which prove the most favorable and profitable under his particular conditions. The difference between the yields of two varieties of wheats grown on the same farm, under absolutely identical conditions, is often sufficient to more than pay the rent or interest on the land on which the crop was grown. This has been frequently demonstrated in departmental experiments, and indicates the prime importance of selected experimental stations in each of the important districts of the State where, among other lines of investigation, continuous and systematic tests of all approved varieties of cereals may be made in the interests of growers of that district.

In the drier districts, in normal seasons, the earlier varieties are generally the most suitable, whilst in districts where the rainfall is heavy and growing season more protracted late maturing wheats may be expected to yield better results than early wheats. Some wheats of outstanding excellence, like Federation, may do well in any district, but it rarely falls to the lot of any variety to have such a wide range of usefulness. It is a good maxim for the wheat-grower not to confine himself to a single variety of wheat.

Fortunately, owing to the work of the late W. Farrer, of New South Wales, and to the enterprise of private farmers like Mr. W. Marshall, of Parkside, South Australia, there is a considerable number of good wheats to choose from. A portion of every farm is usually set apart for hay, and for this purpose it is well to grow some recognised hay varieties. A good hay-wheat should retain its colour well, produce an abundance of straw and flag, and should be sweet and palatable to stock. It should be fairly solid in the straw, and preferably beardless. For purposes of grain production the principal and essential requirement is prolificacy under the conditions in which it is grown. It is, of course, highly desirable that the grain should be of good milling quality, *i.e.*, of good colour, high flour strength, and satisfactory gluten content. It very frequently happens, however, that the high quality wheats are shy yielders. Comeback and Bobs, for example, stand out prominently among Australian wheats on account of their high flour strength, but, unfortunately, they do not produce such heavy yields as varieties like Federation and Yandilla King. Under conditions existing at present in Victoria the farmer has no alternative but to grow prolific wheats irrespective of quality. Indeed, it would appear that the best he can hope for at present is f.a.q. prices for his product. Before high quality wheats can be popular and profitable in this State—(1) The millers must be prepared to purchase high quality wheats like Comeback and Bobs, at prices considerably in advance of those ruling for f.a.q. wheat in order to give adequate encouragement to the grower; (2) the wheat-breeder must produce varieties in which the high quality of Comeback, and the prolificacy of Federation, will be combined.

Among the numerous varieties now at the disposal of the farmer are the following :—

> *Hay-wheats.*—Baroota Wonder, Correll's No. 7, Firbank, Huguenot, Majestic, Marshall's No. 3, Thew, Triumph, White Tuscan and Zealand.
>
> *Grain-wheats.*—Bayah Bunyip, Dart's Imperial, Federation, Gluyas, King's Early, Steinwedel, Marshall's No. 3, Yandilla King.
>
> *Forage and Ensilage.*—Medeah, Huguenot, Kubanka.

RATE OF SEEDING.

The amount of seed to be sown varies within very wide limits, and is governed by several considerations. The amount of seed required varies with—

(1) *Climate.*—The lower the average rainfall of the district, the less seed is required. The minimum is required in dry, mallee districts.

(2) *Time of Sowing.*—Early sown wheat requires less seed than the same variety sown late. As the seeding progresses it is well to gradually increase the amount sown, since late sown wheat has much less opportunity to stool out and establish itself before the winter sets in than the early sown wheat.

(3) *Character of Seed Bed.*—Early sowing on clean land requires the minimum. Land, foul with weeds, must, if it has to be sown, be sown thickly to give the wheat an opportunity to choke the weeds.

(4) *The Character* of the wheat, its stooling capacity, the size of the grain, whether it is an early or late maturing variety, and its germinating capacity. Obviously all these influence the amount of seed required.

(5) *The Use* to which the wheat is put—whether for grain, hay, green forage or ensilage. The minimum will be required in the former case; the maximum in the latter.

(6) *Method* of sowing—whether drilled or broadcasted. About 20-25 per cent. more seed is required with the broadcasted to give the same braird as the drill.

With these reservations, it may be said that the average amount of seed for grain is 45-60 lbs., while for hay and forage 1-2 bushels may be used.

For grain the amount sown may be as low as 30 lbs. in dry, mallee districts to 65-70 lbs. in moister districts. Generally speaking, sow early crops thin, and late crops thick; sow light land thicker than rich, heavy land; and be sparing with good stooling varieties, and correspondingly liberal with varieties of poor tillering capacity.

METHOD OF SOWING.

Since the introduction and general use of superphosphates in the wheat-growing areas of the State the old broadcaster has been superseded by drills which sow seed and manure through the same hoes.

The advantages of broadcasting are—(1) The small cost per acre; (2) the large areas that may be sown in a day.

Bearing in mind what has already been said regarding the necessity for sowing seed quickly when once the " normal seeding period " arrives, we may readily appreciate, even in this age of drills, the merits of broadcasting; for, should unfavorable weather conditions prevail at seed time, the broadcaster may be useful in making the most of whatever intervals of fine weather may occur in an unusual seeding season.

In a normal season, however, when seeding conditions are favorable, the best place for the broadcaster is in the implement shed. The advantages possessed by the drill more than outweigh those of the broadcaster. With the drill seed and manure may be sown in the one operation. This not only economizes labour, but it also enables young plants to rapidly find the superphosphate and make vigorous growth in the earlier stages of its existence. Whatever weeds may lie between the drills are not so fortunately situated as the young wheat plants, and the latter are thus better able to cope with such weeds. Moreover, the drill is more economical with seed than is the broadcaster, as it requires at least 25 per cent. more seed with the broadcaster to get the same braird. Wherever a farmer values his seed-wheat at prices considerably above those ruling for f.a.q. wheat—wherever selected seed of high quality is sown—this saving of seed is a most important item.

Moreover, with the drill the germination is far more regular, because it is sown at a uniform depth.

Finally, the depth of sowing may be regulated with the drill to suit the condition and nature of the seed bed.

TREATMENT OF THE SEED.

(1) Is Change of Seed Necessary?

There is a notion, very prevalent among wheat-growers, to the effect that change of seed at periodical intervals is more or less necessary. It is very difficult to obtain, even from those who hold this view most stoutly, the grounds which render such a change of seed necessary. Perhaps the most obvious reason lies in the farmers' expressive phrase that the "wheat has run out." This is an expression of the belief that the continued cultivation of the same variety of wheat under the same soil conditions for a number of years results in the deterioration of that particular strain of seed to such an extent as to render a change absolutely imperative. In other words, it is the practical farmer's expression of the belief that varieties of wheat, under ordinary conditions of cultivation, tend to degenerate. Such a view is by no means new. It dates back at least to Roman times, for in the Georgics Vergil tell us—

> " Unless the peasant with his annual pain
> Renews his choice, and selects the largest grain,
> Thus all below, by Nature's curse,
> Or Fate's decree, degenerates still to worse."

It is difficult, indeed, to see how, if careless and slipshod methods of cultivation are practised, and no care taken to preserve the very best of the crop for the next season's seed, the prolificacy of any given variety of wheat can be maintained at a high level. It is still more difficult to see how such a grower can improve matters by securing a change of seed from persons equally careless as himself. *Unless the change be for the purpose of obtaining a better variety, or more vigorous seed, or for seed that has been subjected to careful and continued systematic selection, there can be no advantage resulting from change of seed.* Indeed, if it be merely a promiscuous exchange, it is more than probable the change would be a decided disadvantage. This would happen in all cases, for example, in which wheat is transferred from a favorable to an unfavorable environment. Again, in extreme cases, such as would happen, *e.g.*, in introducing new varieties from foreign climes, several years must elapse before the new seed becomes "acclimatized." (*Vide* p. 95.) Moreover, such change of seed is often the cause of introducing new weed pests and diseases from one district of the State or country to another. The balance of evidence goes to prove that farmers should rely on locally-developed seed, and should give more attention to their own seed, and the prevalent idea that *mere change of seed* gives good results would appear to be founded more on opinion than upon well ascertained fact.

(2) Grading the Seed.

Another widespread notion which, fortunately, can be proved experimentally to have no foundation in fact is that shrivelled grain is as good for seed purposes as plump grain. Some years ago it was not an uncommon practice for some farmers to sell their best wheat as f.a.q.

to the miller or merchant, and keep the shrivelled grain for seed. If there is one thing that has been conclusively demonstrated by carefully conducted experimental work it is the fact that plump grains are greatly superior to shrivelled grains from a productive point of view.

As no local experimental results are available to assist us on this subject, we may consider what has been done at the Ontario Agricultural College, Canada. Professor Zavitz reports results extending over six successive years with winter wheat, and eight years with spring wheats. Large, plump grain, of winter-sown wheat, gave 46.9 bushels per acre, as against 39.1 bushels of shrivelled grain of the same variety, *i.e.*, 7.8 bushels per acre extra. Again, with spring wheats the difference amounted to 5 bushels in favour of graded grain, the large, plump grain yeilding 21.7 bushels, whilst the shrivelled grain of the same variety gave 16.7 bushels.

In view of what has been said above, it follows that growers should make every endeavour to secure the very best seed— large, plump, vigorous —and if the seed represents the progeny of strong, *selected*, vigorous plants, good results will be assured. Great emphasis must be laid on the necessity for the *selection* of hardy, vigorous prototypes, because, under favorable conditions, small, but well-developed seeds from highly productive, vigorous plants, may give better results than large grains from unproductive plants.

It can readily be shown, however, that, in general, the more vigorous plants possess the larger kernels, and that, by mere grading, the bulk of the grain obtained would come from the more vigorous plants.

The large grains, obtained as a result of such grading, might be expected to give more vigorous, and, inferentially, more productive plants, because of the greater reserve food supply for the young plant in the early stages of its growth.

(3) Pickling the Seed.

Pickling of the seed for the prevention of "stinking smut," or Bunt (Tilletia Tritici), is now regarded as a regular part of the farm routine. Much effort has been spent on the evolution of bunt-proof wheats, and it would appear that already a considerable amount of success has been obtained. Florence and Genoa, *e.g.*, have been shown in experimental trials to be practically immune from smut, whilst wheats like Medeah and Huguenot have long been known to be smut-resistant. The same cannot be said, however, for the varieties in general cultivation, for some of the most prolific yielding wheats we grow are very susceptible to smut.

The advantages of securing a bunt-resistant prolific wheat must be manifest. The process of pickling would be unnecessary, and the time, labour, and expense, involved in the operation, would be saved to the farmer. Seeing that the quality of smut-resistance has already been observed in a few varieties, it is not difficult to impart the quality to other more prolific, but more susceptible, varieties.

The cost of the actual pickling operations is not great, but as a considerable proportion of seed is destroyed by most of the fungicides in general use, it follows that the total cost, including the damaged seed, is very considerable.

The production of a *bunt-proof prolific* variety is, therefore, a legitimate aim of the wheat-breeder, and it is not too much to expect that such a variety will materalize in the near future.

To understand why any treatment for smut should be effectual it is necessary to realize that bunt is caused by a fungus which reproduces itself by small bodies called spores, which are analogous to the seeds of the higher plants. This smut fungus is parasitic in its growth, and attacks the wheat plant just when germination takes place. The mycelium of the fungus then penetrates the wheat plant, lives on its host, grows with it, and ultimately produces myriads of spores which collectively form the " bunt balls " of the infected heads. The effect of the fungicides, used in pickling. is to kill all the spores in any way adhering to the grain.

Most of the spores adhering to infected grains will be found in the " brush " of the kernel, whilst a lesser number are usually found in the crease of the grain. If a number of grains of wheat be poured into a vessel of water, it will be noted that small bubbles of air invariably become entangled in the tuft of hairs constituting the " brush," and in such cases the grain does not become moistened at these points, even after prolonged immersion. This will explain the need for vigorous agitation of the seed whilst immersed in the pickling solution.

Reinfection may, and often does, take place after the seed has been pickled. This commonly occurs where the pickled seed has been transferred to smutty bags which have not been treated with the pickling solution. Again, in sowing the seed the bunt balls, left among the grain by careless pickling, may be broken in the drill, and the contents of the ball scattered over the seed. It must, of course, be borne in mind that while loose bunt spores are killed by contact with the pickling solution, the spores contained within the unbroken bunt balls, which float on the surface of the pickle. are unaffacted by the fungicide. Steps must, therefore, be taken during pickling to remove or break any bunt balls which may be present in the seed.

An ideal fungicide for pickling purposes would require to be (*a*) *cheap;* (*b*) *effective, i.e.,* capable of destroying all the spores adhering to the grain ; (*c*) capable of preventing *reinfection* of the seed ; (*d*) without effect on the *germination* of the grain. The fact that so much controversy has arisen respecting the various fungicides on the market is proof that the ideal fungicide has not yet been obtained.

Bluestone is a most popular fungicide, and, when properly used, is very effective.

The stronger solutions have a very deleterious effect on the germination of the grain, as they not only reduce the germinable power of the seeds, but also delay the germination considerably. Many instances were observed last season by the writer when judging farm crops and farm competitions, in which crops were badly affected with bunt, although the seed had been pickled with bluestone. In all these cases, however. the cause was undoubtedly the arbitrary method of pickling adopted. Instead of using a solution of fixed and definite concentration, the practice followed was that of dissolving a handful of bluestone in a small but unknown quantity of water and pouring it over a bag of seed. Such a method of procedure is most unsatisfactory. What the grower needs to realize is that the strength or concentration of the solution is all important to successful work, for there is an optimum concentration at which the best results are obtained. Below this strength the fungicide is ineffectual, and with higher concentrations the germination of the seed is greatly interfered with.

In practice the amount of bluestone which gives the best results is $1\frac{1}{2}$ lbs. to 10 gallons of water, *i.e.,* $1\frac{1}{2}$ per cent. Of course, smutty seed may require as much as 2 lbs. to 10 gallons, but the farmer should make it his business not to sow dirty seed. He should make it an habitual practice to reserve each year the very cleanest and best-grown portion of his crop for next season's seed.

Various substances have been used to lessen the corrosive action of the bluestone, and among these the use of lime and salt have been recommended ; but the results of experimental work at present tend to show that the benefit obtained is not commensurate with the extra labour involved.

Formalin has been known for many years to be an effective fungicide and is now widely used for pickling wheat. It is a solution of formaldehyd gas in water, and the usual concentration of the commercial article is 37-38 per cent.

It is a cheap fungicide, efficient in preventing smut, but it apparently has little power to prevent reinfection. Bluestone, however, is highly efficient, both in destroying spores adhering to the seed, and also in preventing further reinfection by fresh spores falling on the seed after it has been pickled.

It follows, therefore, that in pickling with formalin more care must be taken with bunt balls than when pickling with bluestone.

Formalin is generally considered to have a depressing influence on the germination, and the effect depends on the length of time the seed has been pickled before sowing, the nature of the seed bed, and the concentration of the solution used. I may remark, however, that at the Parafield Experimental Farm a packet of Federation seed, which was immersed in a 1/400 solution of formalin for five minutes, on 1st April, 1909, gave a germination of 89 per cent. when planted on 25th May, 1910—nearly 14 months later.

The strength usually recommended is 1 in 400, *i.e.*, 1 lb. of formalin to 40 gallons of water. It is not desirable, nor is it necessary, to use stronger solutions than this. Indeed, unless the seed is smutty, it may even be advisable to use a weaker solution than this, and for general purposes 1 lb. to 45 gallons, or 1 lb. to 50 gallons, *i.e.*, 1 in 450, or 1 in 500, may be recommended.

Fungusine is a proprietary preparation, which has been used as a fungicide for the prevention of smut, but considerable difference of opinion exists as to its merits.

There seems to be little doubt that fungusine does not have that deleterious effect on the germination of the grain which has been noted with formalin and bluestone. Indeed, in nearly all cases in which it has been tried, the germination has for some reason or other been materially stimulated by the pickling. Were it absolutely effective as a fungicide, and proved itself capable of preventing reinfection, there would be no question as to its value as a pickle. Before one can come to a conclusion in this matter, it is necessary to test it over a period of years, in a systematic manner, side by side with standard fungicides.

Until such experiments have been conducted it is not safe to indulge in hasty generalizations. It is interesting to note, however, that investigations have been conducted at the Cowra Experimental Farm, New South Wales, with these various fungicides for the past two years. The results are given in the *Agricultural Gazette* of New South Wales (April, 1911). The following table has been extracted from the results to illustrate the point at issue :—

—	(1) Efficiency of the Fungicide. Bunty plants. (Average 1909–10.)	(2) Effect on Germination. Plants killed. (1909–10.)	(3) Efficacy in preventing reinfection. Clean plants after reinfection. (1910 only.)
	%	%	%
1. Bluestone 2%	1·4	22·4	96·6
2. Formalin 1/400	9·6	14·5	67·2
3. Fungusine ..	3·4	− ·7	96·4

NOTE.—In all these tests the seed was purposely infected until it was literally black with smut. It was thus infinitely dirtier than seed sown under ordinary farming conditions.

The results of these experiments are thus summarized—

> " As a smut-preventive fungusine gave practically as good results
> as any method tried, and had no injurious effect on the
> germination of the seed.   .   .   .   In preventing rein-
> fection it was correspondingly efficient."   (*Agricultural
> Gazette* of New South Wales, April, 1911.)

This result is in accord with the results of experiments conducted at the
Parafield Wheat Station (South Australia) during 1909, where, in comparative tests, fungusine acquitted itself remarkably well. (*Vide Journal
of Agriculture* of South Australia, January, 1910—Bunt Tests—A. E. V.
Richardson).

Hot Water Treatment. — This has been recommended at various
times, but, in practice, though the treatment is efficient, the method is
very cumbersome, slow, and unwieldy. The method consists in immersing
the seed for 10 minutes in hot water at a temperature of 130° to 132° F.
The practical difficulty is to keep the temperature constant. A considerable
lowering of temperature results immediately the seed is introduced, but this
may be avoided by pre-heating the seed in a vessel of water, the temperature
of which is approximately 130° F., before immersing it in the main bath.
It is a method, however, which requires skilful handling and careful
supervision.

Methods of Pickling.—Seed-wheat may be pickled with formalin or
bluestone, either by immersion for a stated time in a solution of given concentration, or by pouring the solution over several bags of wheat on a
cement floor, and shovelling over the mass until every grain has been
thoroughly wetted with the solution.

The advantage of the barn-floor method of pickling is the rapidity
with which it may be done. The disadvantage, however, is that it is not
possible to remove any bunt balls that may be present, and reinfection may
subsequently take place. This, as pointed out above, is of more consequence with the formalin pickle than with the bluestone, for the reason
that formalin appears to be less able to prevent reinfection than bluestone.
With fungusine, the floor method is the only one possible. Pickling by
immersion is less expeditious, but, on the whole, it is more efficacious.
The whole of the grain comes in contact with the pickle, especially when
the vessel containing the grain is agitated. Moreover, any bunt balls which
may be present can be removed by skimming, and danger of reinfection
avoided. Several patent picklers are now on the market for expediting
this work, and with these much of the old-time drudgery associated with
pickling is avoided. With bluestone pickling the apparatus needs to be constructed of copper and wood.

MANURING OF THE WHEAT CROP.

The manurial requirements of the wheat crop under diverse soil and
climatic conditions, the comparative merits of different forms of artificial
manures and the principles upon which the maintenance of soil fertility
depend may be reserved for discussion in subsequent articles.

AFTER-TREATMENT OF WHEAT.

Very frequently the crop requires some kind of attention after sowing,
and the treatment will vary considerably with the type of growth made,
the character of the season, and the nature and preliminary treatment of
the seed bed.

Rolling the crop after it has grown some 6 inches—8 inches is frequently
practised.

With hay or ensilage crops this is often beneficial, as it helps to make a level surface for the binder, thus facilitating the harvesting of the crop. Moreover, on light, open land, the consolidation of the soil effected by rolling is very beneficial to the growing crop. Rolling may also be practised where the operations, preparatory to seeding, have not been of such a character as to provide for that soil consolidation so essential to the success of a wheat crop. On heavy lands which tend to set hard, and which are likely to run together with the winter rains, the roller should be displaced by the harrows.

Harrowing is always beneficial to a young wheat crop, provided it be not already too thin. Certainly, a percentage of the young plants is dragged out in the operation, but it is well in this connexion to remember the healthy proverb, " The man who harrows should never look behind."

This disadvantage is more than compensated for by the increased vigor of the remaining plants, and by the great stimulus given to stooling; nor must it be forgotten that the harrows assist in subjugating the weeds, and in the drier portions of the State it assists in conserving the limited supplies of soil moisture by retarding capillary activity and lessening evaporation.

In harrowing the growing crop the work should be done at right angles to the drills.

Feeding Down the Crop.—It has already been remarked that, in favorable seasons, the early sown crops are likely to come away very rapidly and make heavy, vigorous, rank growth in May and June. Such heady growth is exposed to two dangers :—

    1. Lodging in wet weather.
    2. Blighting either from late spring frosts, or by a premature burst of hot weather in spring.

Such growth may be arrested by feeding down with sheep. This is a decided advantage on light land, or on land which has, for various reasons, not been consolidated sufficiently through adequate tillage operations; but on heavy land it may be a positive disadvantage to feed down a crop with sheep. This would happen if the land were wet, and more or less boggy; under these circumstances the sheep would do more harm than good. In any case, unless the feeding be done fairly rapidly, little benefit will accrue from the process.

In dealing with large paddocks, difficulty arises in putting on a sufficient number of sheep to carry out the work in reasonable time. Complications arise where the crop is not uniform, and where the rank portions occur in patches. Under such circumstances it becomes necessary to " shepherd " the flock, as, if left to themselves, the sheep will invariably graze those portions which do not require feeding off.

One point must not be overlooked in this connexion, and that is the time such operations may, with safety, be performed. Late feeding down is generally decidedly detrimental, and can only be performed with any prospect of success when the spring rains are frequent and copious.

In the drier portions of the State it is a good maxim for the wheatgrower, at all times, to plan his work with the expectation of the present season being a dry one, and, in the event of such expectation being realized, crops requiring to be fed off will give best results when fed early. In addition to checking the rank growth, judicious feeding-off assists the stooling propensities of the plant, and reduces the proportion of flag and straw to grain, thereby avoiding the danger of blighting by hot, spring winds.

(To be continued.)

THE INFLUENCE OF SOIL MOISTURE UPON NITRIFICATION.

By J. W. Paterson, B.Sc., Ph.D., Experimentalist, and P. R. Scott, Chemist for Agriculture.

INTRODUCTION.

Nitric acid or nitrate contains nitrogen in the highest state of oxidation. Ammonia is a compound of nitrogen which has no oxygen. To convert ammonia into nitric acid, its nitrogen must be oxidized. This happens in fertile soil, and the oxidation is brought about by certain bacteria. The process of oxidizing ammonia to nitric acid is termed nitrification.

Besides nitrogen and oxygen plants require eight other elements in their food materials. Each of these must be in the highest state of oxidation commonly occurring in Nature. Phosphites, sulphites, nitrites, and ferrous salts either kill the plant outright, or they give an unsatisfactory return. This is also true of ammonia for ordinary crop plants. Ammonia is not poisonous in practical amounts, but it gives a much smaller yield than the

A.	B.	C.
Without nitrogen.	With nitrogen in form of nitrate.	With nitrogen in form of ammonia.

highly oxidized nitrogen found in nitrates. The accompanying figure* shows very fairly the action of ammonia and nitrate nitrogen under conditions where nitrification is impossible.

The reason why nitrates should be better than ammonium salts as a food of plants is somewhat obscure. The first organic compounds formed by plants from the absorbed nitrogen are amino-acids and their derivatives. As these contain the amidogen radical (NH_2) which is closely related to ammonia (NH_3), one might have expected the ammonium salts to give the better result. As the primary amide formation always occurs in the plant cell where oxidizable carbohydrate is present along with the absorbed nitrogen compound, it may be that nitrate possesses an advantage in that

---

* From *A Manual of Agricultural Botany*, by Prof. Frank, Berlin; translated by John W. Paterson. Edinburgh: Wm. Blackwood and Sons.

it contains easily available oxygen which is useful, while at the same time it yields NH_2 in the nascent state in the process of its reduction. This, however, is merely a suggestion; whatever the physiological reasons the superiority of nitrate to ammonia nitrogen for direct crop production may be taken as an established fact.

It has been indicated that nitrification is the work of certain soil bacteria. There are two kinds of bacteria and two stages in the change, but apparently both have very much the same requirements, save in the nature of their nitrogenous food. One kind changes ammonia into nitrite, the second changes nitrite into nitrate. The conditions for growth of these bacteria are therefore the conditions for nitrification. They require—

1. The ordinary plant food of crops except iron.
2. An available base to neutralize the acids produced—carbonate of lime being the best.
3. An ammonium salt—probably the carbonate.
4. Free aeration of the soil.
5. Sufficient moisture.
6. Darkness.
7. Temperature between 41 deg. and 130 deg. F., 97 deg. being the best.

FILLING THE BOTTLE.

If moisture is necessary for nitrification, it follows that conservation of soil moisture has a double purpose. The moisture is held in reserve for the use of a future crop, but its presence meanwhile tends to the production of nitrates. To find how far exactly, and within what limits the presence of soil moisture has an effect upon the production of nitrates was the object of these experiments.

METHOD OF WORK.

The method of investigation was as follows :—Air-dry soil equal to 300 grams dry soil was placed in a bottle of 3 inches diameter, 6 inches high, neck $1\frac{1}{2}$ inches, and of 500 c.c. capacity. Sufficient tapping was given to make the soil compact. A mark was placed on the bottle at the soil level, the soil was replaced by water to the same mark, and from the weight of water required the apparent S.G. of the soil was determined. From this and the real S.G. as found by the displacement method, the porosity of the soil, and from this the total water-holding capacity was found by calculation. There were two sets of experiments in consecutive periods, using about 100 bottles each. In the first experiments water was added to bring the original soil moisture up to 10, 20, 30, 40, 50, 60, and 70 per cent. of its total water-holding capacity in different bottles. In the second, the steps were 10, 20, 30, 50, 70, and 90. All the bottles were marked to the same volume, and the same weight of dry soil was used in every case.

Before charging the bottles, the weighed soil was thoroughly mixed with its proper quantity of water in a Wedgewood mortar. One-half of the bottles got water only, the other half got 5 c.c. standard ammonium sulphate solution in their water. After filling, the bottles were placed in a dark cupboard in the laboratory, and the temperature of the cupboard was read daily at 9 a.m. and 5 p.m. The bottles in the cupboard were corked. Twice weekly each bottle was taken out, uncorked, aspirated for 5 seconds with the suction pump, corked, and replaced in the locker.

The method of using closed bottles and aspirating seemed better than the method of using open bottles and adding water lost, which has been adopted elsewhere in investigating this subject. In order to judge of the two methods, six bottles were left open, and the results compared with closed aspirated bottles after a period of twenty-eight days. The following figures were obtained :—

TABLE I.

Original moisture per 100 of dry soil	2·67	5·35	8·03	13·38	18·73	24·08
Loss from Closed Bottles	0·31	0·31	0·39	0·56	0·58	0·68
Loss from Open Bottles	1·7	4·0	6·3	9·5	8·3	8·8

With closed bottles the losses were insignificant, while with open bottles usually more than one-half of the original moisture was lost. The lost water in open bottles cannot be replaced in a satisfactory manner, because at the point where the water is added the soil will be much wetter than at other points in the soil mass. To demonstrate this, a glass tube of 1-inch bore was packed with soil to the same degree as in the experiment bottles, and to a depth of 10 inches. Water was then added from the top equal to 10.70 parts per 100 dry soil (40 per cent. of its water-holding capacity). At the end of seventeen days the tube was cut into four sections of $2\frac{1}{2}$ inches and the moisture in each determined. Of the total water in the soil there was found in the top section 35; in the second, 31; the third, 24; and in the fourth, 10 per cent. With a smaller quantity of water, or with a shorter time allowed, the differences would probably have been greater than here noted.

In each experiment the ammonia bottles and the control blanks were done in duplicate, and the average results are taken where the figures are close, when wider, the average is marked doubtful. This happens in two instances with the very wet soils of the second experiments.

THE SOILS.

The first experiment uses one sample of sandy soil from the Horticultural School, Burnley. The second experiments employ a medium clay soil from the same place in addition. In preparation the air-dry soils were put through a 2 mm. sieve. The mechanical analyses of the prepared soils were as follow :—

TABLE II.

—	Diameter in millimetres.	Sandy Soil.	Clay Soil.
		Per cent.	Per cent.
Fine Gravel	1 −2 ..	·10	·48
Coarse Sand	·5 −1 . ..	·97	1·61
Medium Sand ·..	·25 − ·5 ..	·75	2·06
Fine Sand	·1 − ·25 ..	6·76	11·70
Very fine Sand	·05 − ·1 ..	74·10	46·20
Silt	·01 − ·05 ..	3·29	5·15
Fine Silt	·005 − ·01 ..	2·14	7·25
Clay	·005 and under..	8·03	18·64
Moisture	.. .. ..	·86	2·15
Loss on ignition	.. .. ..	3·00	4·76

The clay soil contains a higher percentage of the finer particles, and inferentially a larger superficial area of soil grains. One would expect therefore that an equal quantity of water would be further spread out and form a thinner film in the clay than in the sand, and be less available for the purpose of nitrification. As will be seen later, this result was obtained. The higher percentage of water in the clay analysis is connected with the same cause.

The chemical analyses of the soils were as follow :—

TABLE III.

—	Sandy Soil.	Clay Soil.
	Per cent.	Per cent.
Water	·86	2·15
Loss on ignition (1)	3·00	4·76
Soluble Silica	·31	1·40
Iron and Alumina	2·22	4·11
Manganese	·037	·03
Lime	·19	·48
Magnesia	·15	·27
Potash (2)	·046	·134
Soda .. .. ·.	·123	·139
Chlorine	·014	·008
Phosphoric Acid (3)	·032	·061
Sulphuric Acid	·06	·03
Carbonic Acid (4)	·032	·12
Insoluble Residue	92·96	86·29
(1) Containing—Nitrate Nitrogen	·00094	·000868
Ammonia Nitrogen	·00182	·002460
Organic Nitrogen	·09224	·116672
Total Nitrogen	·095	·120
(2) Containing available K₂O	·0353	·0847
(3) Containing available P₂O₅	·0218	·0179
(4) Equal Carbonate of Lime	·073	·273

In the chemical analysis the larger percentage of lime, and particularly of carbonic acid, in the clay is notable as representing available base. The sandy soil with .032 carbonic acid falls below the minimum requirements,* and is apparently deficient in available lime—a point which will be referred to later on.

ANALYTICAL METHODS.

Before going on to the results, the analytical methods must be briefly described.

Moisture.—At the close of the experiments, the soil in the bottles was mixed, and 25 grams dried at 212 deg. F. for five hours in a tarred dish.

Nitrate Nitrogen.—Fifty grams of the mixed moist soil from the bottles was transferred to a small bag of nainsook, and 250 c.c. of a solution containing 5.36 c.c. sat. potash alum + .64 c.c. formalin was poured over the soil in the bag placed in a mortar. After kneading for 2 min. as much of the solution as possible was transferred to a Mason jar, and 'left over

READING THE RESULTS.

night to settle. Fifty c.c.'s of the clear solution was evaporated to dryness on the water bath, cooled, and 20-30 drops disulphonic acid (Gill) added, stirred, and left ten minutes. There was then added 15 c.c. distilled water, potash till alkaline, the solution was filtered if necessary, and made up to 50 c.c.'s. This solution was read in the colorimeter against standard nitrate of potash. Allowance was made for the water in the moist soil. All solutions and salts used were tested for nitrate, and care was taken in washing the bags, and preparing nitrate-free water. Chlorides were eliminated with a measured quantity of saturated silver sulphate. The analytical work was carried out by Mr. W. C. Robertson, chief deputy chemist.

RESULTS OF THE FIRST EXPERIMENTS.

Table IV. gives the progress of nitrification in sandy soil, with different degrees of moisture. Ammonia nitrogen added = .02121 gram per 300 grams soil = 70.7 parts per million. Length of incubation period—27 days. Mean temperature, 66 deg. F.

* In Minnesota soils. Suvder regards ·1 per cent. combined carbonic acid as the minimum from which good results can be got : Hall at Rothamsted adopts a similar view.

TABLE IV.

Water in Soil as—		Nitrate Nitrogen per 1,000,000 Parts Dry Soil.			Percentage of added Ammonia Nitrified.
Percentage of Saturation.	Percentage of Dry Soil.	Control Blanks.	Ammonia Bottles.	Excess with Ammonia.	
10	2·67	4·76	4·86	·10	·141
20	5·35	7·51	14·24	6·73	9·52
30	8·03	10·08	41·68	31·60	44·69
40	10·70	10·60	52·41	41·81	59·14
50	13·38	11·64	59·97	48·33	68·36
60	16·05	12·89	57·64	44·75	63·29
70	18·73	13·02	59·08	46·06	65·15

Between 40 and 70 per cent. of the water-holding capacity, rate of nitrification did not vary in any important degree. At the various steps below 40, there was a notable falling away; 10 per cent. practically stopped nitrification, and at 20 the rate was only one-seventh of the best case. Another duplicate set of bottles set up at the same time, but analyzed one week earlier, showed results on a lower plane for each degree of moistness, but placed them in the same order of merit.

RESULTS OF THE SECOND EXPERIMENTS.

Here two classes of soil were used—the one a fresh sample from the same spot as in the first experiments, the other a medium clay. The water added to the sandy soil formed as before a percentage of its saturation capacity; the clay soil was brought up to the same content of water without reference to its water-holding capacity. Ammonia added = 0.1 gram per 300 grams soil = 333.33 parts per million. Length of incubation period, 42 days. Mean temperature taken from bi-daily readings, 68.5 deg. F.

TABLE V.

(a) Sandy Soil.

Water in Soil as—		Nitrate Nitrogen per 1,000,000 Parts Dry Soil.			Percentage of added Ammonia Nitrified.
Percentage of Saturation.	Percentage of Dry Soil.	Control Blanks.	Ammonia Bottles.	Excess with Ammonia.	
10	2·67	8·33	10·03	1·70	·51
20	5·35	16·30	60·12	43·82	13·15
30	8·03	19·25	82·79	63·54	19·06
50	13·38	21·71	110·35	88·64	26·59
70	18·73	19·18	117·65	98·47	29·55
90	24·08	9·11(?)	27·68	18·57 (?)	5·57 (?)

The results here agree with those of Table III., and indicate that for this soil there is a long range in the medium degrees of moistness which are about equally favorable for nitrification. This sandy soil contained .86 per cent. moisture (see analyses) in the air-dry condition; when exposed in a thin layer for four days in a saturated atmosphere at the temperature of the laboratory, it held 2.35 per cent. of moisture. As seen from the top line in both tables, neither of these amounts is sufficient to maintain nitrification. In the 90 per cent. of saturation introduced in the second experiments, the result was poor owing probably to the water excluding air from the pores of the soil. If, as would appear, the best degree of saturation for this soil runs from 40 to 70 per cent., the figures indicate that, beyond those limits, increasing wetness acts more sharply than increasing dryness.

Table VI. gives the results on the clay soil.

TABLE VI.

Water as Percentage of Dry Soil.	Nitrate Nitrogen per 1,000,000 Parts Dry Soil.			Percentage of added Ammonia Nitrified.
	Control Blanks.	Ammonia Bottles.	Excess with Ammonia.	
2·67	9·00	10·55	1·55	·46
5·35	13·65	14·52	·87	·26
8·03	24·23	198·80	174·57	52·37
13·38	34·65	277·80	243·15	72·96
18·73	38·50	340·50	302·00	90·61
24·08	1·78 (?)	262·60	260·82 (?)	78·26 (?)

Referring to their mechanical analyses, and the water content of the two varieties of soil, it was apparent that clay holds its water more firmly than the sand. The effect of this is now seen upon the nitrifying action, because while with sand it was the driest series only which remained stationary, with clay the second driest also failed to act. With sand, 5.35 per cent. of water induced nitrification although slowly, with clay it had no effect. With sufficient moisture, nitrification proceeded rapidly in the clay, and the water optimum is apparently higher with clay than sand. This is no doubt owing to its greater absorptive power, and in connexion with this it is further noticeable that the largest supply of water (24.08 per cent.) which gave a very poor result with sand gave a high return with the clay soil.

On comparing the last columns of tables V and VI. it will be observed that nitrification was altogether more active in the clay than the sand. In the best case of the former just over 90 per cent. of the total nitrogen was nitrified. This result closely agrees with Professor Wagner's* investigations into the comparative effects of nitrate of soda and sulphate of ammonia, when applied as manures. Referring to the chemical analyses above, it was noticed that the clay soil probably contained sufficient available base, while the sand was deficient in lime—as are a large number of Victorian soils. It is not clear that this deficiency has affected in kind the action of soil moisture in promoting nitrification, although in the sandy soil it has probably affected it in degree. Lime, however, lies outside the scope of the present experiments—their object was rather to obtain experimental data on the relation of moisture to nitrification in two types of Victorian soils as they came to hand.

The effect upon nitrification of lime and other substances added to the soil will be investigated in a future set of experiments.

---

* Die Stickstoffdüngung der landw. Kulturpflanzen, by Prof. Dr. Paul Wagner. Berlin, Paul Parey.

SUMMARY.

1. Nitrification is inactive in these soils while they still contain about three times more moisture than in their average air-dry condition.

2. At the lower lmits of moisture less water starts nitrification in sand than in the clay.

3. At the higher limits of moisture less water stops nitrification in sand than in the clay.

4. While the optimum amount of water probably varies for each soil, and is higher for clay, still for both soils it lies within the range of fourteen to eighteen parts per 100 of dry soil.

5. A rise above the optimum amount of water is more harmful than an equal fall below it.

6. If the summer working of fallow land helps to retain water in the surface soil, this water may have a powerful influence upon the production of nitrates for the next crop.

7. A growing crop may reduce the nitrate supply for the next crop in two ways—it may use up all the nitrates actually present, and it may so dry the land that nitrification in the interval between crops is reduced to a minimum.

8. The moisture requirements for nitrification suggest that in dry seasons a single flooding of fallow land might be followed by good results.

THE PORT OF HULL AS A DISTRIBUTING CENTRE FOR AUSTRALIAN PRODUCE.

By Austin Wilson, Special Trade Commissioner, Port of Hull, England.

The object of my visit to Australia is to supplement the efforts of our agent, Mr. E. Bechervaise, of Geelong, in endeavouring to arouse interest in the Port of Hull, and to bring before the notice of growers and shippers of Australian produce the special advantages, which this port offers in the way of facilities, for reaching the British consumers in the densely populated northern and midland counties of England. History records that in the year 1296 King Edward I. granted Hull its first charter; and the city was named Kingston (or Kingstown)-upon-Hull. In all legal and official documents it still bears this name, although in general use it has been shortened to Hull. Modern Hull is the largest port on the north-east coast of England, and is situated on the north bank of the Humber estuary. This estuary is formed by the confluence of the Rivers Ouse, Trent, Aire and Calder, and Hull, and has a wide and deep channel leading directly to the sea. Outside the Alexandra Docks there is 40 feet of water at low tide in the channel, and the port is therefore accessible to large steamers at any time.

The docks cover a river frontage of about 6 or 7 miles and are up-to-date and well equipped At present a new dock and deep-water quay, both of which will be available this year, are being built. The new dock when fully completed will be the largest commercial dock in the world, having a water area of 85 acres, and will be equipped with all the best modern appliances for dealing with ships and their cargoes. At the deep-water quay, steamers will be able to come alongside at any state of the tide to discharge or load. Coaling appliances capable of delivering 600 tons per hour are already installed on this quay and are in daily use.

Hull is served by five railway companies, and has in consequence a fast service of trains to all parts of the country.   As an instance perishable traffic leaving Hull 6.30 p.m. arrives in London 2.30 a.m. next morning (200 miles).   In addition to the railway services there is an unrivalled system of navigable rivers and canals radiating north, south, and west of Hull which serve over 1-6th of the total area of England.

All river craft have the privilege (secured to them by Act of Parliament) of using the docks free of dues, and they compete very strongly with the railway companies for the carriage of goods to and from inland towns. In consequence of this competition the railway rates from Hull are on a lower basis than from any other United Kingdom port.   Rates of conveyance, &c., consequently as cheap or cheaper than from any other port, serve a district carrying a population of between ten and twelve million people, or more than quarter of the total British population.

Hull is well placed as regards coal.   It has access by rail to over 380 collieries, and during 1910 nearly 7,000,000 tons coal came into Hull by rail and river chiefly for export abroad.   The South Yorkshire Coalfield is proven nearer to the sea each year, and new pits are being sunk from time to time.   It is estimated that within ten years from now over 20,000 tons of coal will be raised per day in excess of what is being raised now, and over 100,000 more people will be congregated in consequence of these developments.   With the geographical position of the port and inland transit facilities, and the vast and increasing population which it serves, it is contended that Hull is an ideal distributing centre for Australian produce and well worthy of the serious attention of producers and shippers.   Australia has hitherto sent the bulk of its refrigerated produce to London which is generally acknowledged to be the dearest port in Great Britain.   The dues and charges on goods landed there form a serious handicap when in competition with similar produce reaching the British consumers through cheaper channels, and as an instance of that Hull can deliver meat and apples *ex* ship Hull to London markets at practically the same cost as from *ex* ship London docks.   A shipper of produce therefore who uses Hull as a distributing centre can serve London as cheaply as his competitors and at the same time he has the benefit of the northern markets.

In sending apples to London a grower finds usually the London expenses amount to about 1s. 3d. per case.   If a northern wholesaler buys at Covent Garden, he has to pay cost of transit from London and delivery to retail shops, and also to allow for his own profit on the transaction.   If he pays a high price for the apples, his retailers only have a limited sale, while if he buys the apples at a low price, the grower suffers.   Both conditions are unsatisfactory as it is to the interest of the grower to sell as much produce as possible at remunerative prices.   Up to recent times London has been able to absorb all that has been sent, and maintain uniform prices, but this market, like all others, has its limits, and for some time past it has been frequently glutted and an increasing proportion of the produce has had to be sold to buyers away from London.   In these instances the grower not only gets poor prices from the London buyers, but he has to bear the cost of transport from London on the produce which is sent north, as buyers when bidding always bear in mind the expenses they will incur in getting produce to the ultimate destination. The cost of handling, cataloguing, and selling apples by public auction at Hull does not exceed 6d. per case as against 1s 2d. to 1s. 3d. in London.

In the case of butter the freight to London can be reckoned at 4s. per cwt., cost of transit to Tooley-street 1s. per cwt., and London commissions at 3 per cent., say, 3s. per cwt., making altogether 8s. per cwt., without reckoning insurance and other expenses, which will probably bring the cost up to 10s. per cwt.   If a northern wholesaler buys from London,· the rail transit will cost at least 2s. per cwt.   His profit and cost of retail distribution will be about 5s. per cwt., making altogether 17s. per cwt. Danish butter can be delivered from Copenhagen *via* Hull to Leeds for 2s. per cwt. against 17s. for Australian butter, and the producer must bear this difference.   If the butter for northern towns was sent to Hull for distribution, about 6s. per cwt. would be saved which is now needlessly paid away.   There is a large and densely populated area served by the port of Hull which is at present being neglected by Australia, and we consider it is worthy of consideration.

In regard to meat sent to London, it is well known to many that the system of handling there is far from perfect.   The meat is landed to quay and barrowed round to lighters which convey it to cold stores.   These cold stores are 20 miles from the Royal Albert and Victoria Docks, and 27 miles from Tilbury, and when the meat arrives at the cold stores it is frozen up again.   If sold to a northern buyer it is carted through the London streets to a railway station, loaded into insulated cars and forwarded to its destination where it is usually carted to a cold store before being distributed to retail shops.   This means that the meat is handled excessively and usually frozen twice before reaching the northern retailer, besides incurring unnecessary charges.   In Hull steamers can berth alongside the cold stores and sling the meat direct from their holds to the stores. Insulated cars load alongside and convey the meat quickly, cheaply, and what is extremely important, with a minimum of handling to the towns in the area which are served by Hull.   Another most important point is that although Australian produce ranks amongst the finest in the world, it very largely loses its identity before reaching the British consumer.   The time has surely come when Australian produce should make a name for itself. The quality is all right and the price, but the method of marketing at present does not give it a fair show.

Most of the emigrants come from provincial centres in Great Britain. They leave friends and relations behind who receive letters regularly, describing the splendid quality of the produce, and it is only reasonable to presume that there is a good chance of building up a large and growing trade amongst these people if they are catered for.   It is claimed justly that people at home have vague ideas respecting the extent and general features of Australia, but I think the people in the provinces may legitimately claim that Australians have so far looked upon London as England so to speak in the marketing of produce.

There are 30,000,000 people outside the London distributing area who can be reached through the out ports at a lower cost than *via* London, and Hull being the third port in importance in Great Britain serves a larger population than any other out port.   So long as it is endeavoured to serve this area *via* London the cost of this expensive and roundabout method of distribution must come out of the growers' pockets.   Competitors from Canada, North and South America, Russia, Denmark are sending their produce to the British consumers through the cheapest channels.   Australia is already sufficiently handicapped by its distance from Great Britain and European markets, without still further handicapping itself by unnecessary transport and handling charges.   At the rate the country is progressing it will be more and more dependent on the oversea markets each year, and if the progression continues on present lines the London markets will be glutted more and more frequently.   In its own interests it is high time the importance of the British out ports was realized, and I have shown that the Port of Hull is a proper and suitable port for the distributing of Australian produce. Any grower or shipper of produce

Showing method of discharging meat, ex steamer, Alexandra Docks, Hull. The meat is slung direct from hold to the cold store, alongside which the steamer is berthed.

This shows the same meat being landed and transferred to the store. The sorting of the meat is done in the store, and not on the quay, as in London. Refrigerated cars load the meat direct from the store and convey it to inland towns with a minimum of handling.

desiring information at any time regarding Hull can obtain same on application to Mr. E. Bechervaise, 17 Malop-street, Geelong.

GENERAL NOTES.

By J. W. P.

ERADICATION OF BRACKEN—

From time to time various methods have been adopted for the permanent removal of bracken such as the use of spiked rollers or the application of manures to encourage other herbage, but apparently the old-fashioned method of repeated cuttings is the most effective yet tried. In this connexion the recent experience on a large estate in England is described in the *Mark Lane Express* of 19th June. When the bracken was cut down continually its growth became less vigorous each year. Clean cutting with a scythe or hook was the most effective, and care should be taken to cut below the lowest leaves which if left will go on seeding. Cutting should begin early in the year, and the more the growth of the plant is stimulated by the process the quicker will be its ultimate exhaustion. Burning and chain harrowing only encourage the evil by manuring and otherwise improving conditions favorable to the growth of the plant.

STRENGTH IN WHEAT—

Much of the wheat exported from India is lacking in strength, and except for its remarkable dryness has little to recommend it to the miller. For some years the Indian Agricultural Research Institute at Pusa has been collecting stock, both by selection and breeding new varieties, with a view to providing a higher class wheat for export. From Bulletin 22 recently issued the efforts seem to have met with success. Wheats have been produced which in the climate of Western Bengal give not only a much higher yield than the native wheats, but also are characterized by great strength, and are therefore likely to command a higher price in the home markets. Commenting on the successful issue of the experiments the *Journal of the Board of Agriculture* (London) observes :—"The work at Pusa confirms what has been established at Cambridge—that it is possible, by the scientific methods of breeding associated with the name of Mendel, to combine high quality with good yield. The results obtained last year with Burgoyne's Fife—a new Cambridge wheat—shows that it gives a grain equalling the Canadian in milling quality combined with the cropping capacity of the best British wheats." There is a considerable field here for the Australian wheat grower.

AGRICULTURAL IMPORTS OF THE UNITED KINGDOM—

The value of the principal articles of food imported into the United Kingdom in 1911 was £190,712,000. Of this vast total 40 per cent. represented value of grain and flour, 24 per cent. live and dead meat, 19 per cent. dairy produce, and 4 per cent eggs. The leading sources of wheat were India (20,161,518 cwts.), Russia (18,106,100), Argentina (14,748,600), Canada (14,373,000), Australia (13,910,720), and United States (12,939,229). Of beef less than one-fourth came as live cattle, the great bulk being chilled and frozen beef (7,362,434 cwts.), and of this Argentina contributed 83 per cent. Live sheep were unimportant, frozen mutton being the principal source of supply. Of this 93 per cent. came from three countries, New Zealand sending 1,981,467 cwts., Argentina 1,782,066, and Australia 1,291,696. Rabbits were imported as fresh rabbits (57,808 cwts.) chiefly from Belgium, and as frozen rabbits from Australia (394,155) and New Zealand (73,703). The value per cwt. of these frozen rabbits was, however, only about one-third of the value per cwt. of the fresh Continental supply. Of bacon consignments (4,868,738 cwts.), Denmark sent 44 per cent., United States 37, and Canada 13 per cent. The chief imports of butter (4,302,956 cwts.) were from Denmark 40 per cent., Australia 20 per cent., Russia 15 per cent., Sweden 8 per cent., New Zealand 6 per cent., France 4 per cent., Holland 2 per cent. Of cheese (2,348,322 cwts.) supplies were drawn chiefly from Canada, 63 per cent., and New Zealand. Russia was a large exporter of eggs. Turning to wool imports (795,091,310 lbs.), Australia sent 41 per cent., New Zealand 22 per cent., South Africa 13 per cent., and India 7 per cent. From the above it is apparent that Australia as exporter to the United Kingdom stands first in the matter of wool and rabbits, second in butter, and in mutton third, while for wheat it has the fifth place.

HOURS FOR MILKING—

It is the common practice to milk cows twice a day, but in the evening the milk will usually be richer in butter-fat than it is in the morning. Milk has a tendency to lose fat when it remains long in the cow's udder, and as there is usually a longer interval before the morning milking this causes the morning milk to be poorer in fat. Did twelve hours elapse between each milking this result would not be found; indeed, the morning milk might be slightly richer owing to the greater restfulness of the animals over-night. Regarding the influence of times of milking upon the percentage of fat some useful facts are published by Professor S. H. Collins, of Durham University, England. When the intervals between milking were twelve hours, *e.g.*, cows milked at 6 a.m. and 6 p.m., the morning milk contained 0.18 per cent. more fat than the evening milk on the average of 22 tests. When, however, the intervals were thirteen and eleven hours by milking at 6 a.m. and 5 p.m. the results were the other way, and the evening milk was then richer in fat than the morning milk by 0.33 per cent. on the average of 192 tests. With intervals of about fourteen and ten hours (6 a.m. and 4 p.m.) the excess in the evening milk was 0.70 per cent. on the average of 18 tests. With greater irregularity in the intervals the differences became still greater, and when the cows were milked at 6 a.m. and 3.30 p.m. the evening milk contained more fat than the morning by 1.09 per cent. on the average of 391 tests. As milk usually contains about 4 per cent. of fat (Official Standard — 3.5) a difference of 1.09 per cent. represents about one-quarter of the total fat in the milk. The other milk-solids are not affected by irregular milking, just the fat. From two milkings therefore the best results are obtained by milking as nearly as practicable at equal intervals of twelve hours.

PIG-FEEDING—

Pig-feeding experiments with sweet and sour skim milk were conducted at the Dairy Institute, at Proskau, by J. Klein (*Milckw. Zentbl.*, 6 (1910), No. 5, pp. 215-222).—Twelve pigs, three months of age, were divided into two groups and fed for twelve weeks a basal ration of ground barley and potato flakes to which fish meal was also added during the latter half of the period. Group 1 received an average of 5.5 kg. of sweet milk per head as a supplementary ration and made an average daily gain per head of 0.661 kg. and dressed 81 per cent. of the live weight. Group 2, which received 5.5 kg. of sour milk per head per day, made a corresponding gain of 0.655 kg. and dressed 80.65 per cent. This result agreed with that of previous experiments.

There seemed to be no advantage in souring the milk as there was a slight loss of sugar, though it was thought that sour milk had a slight dietetic effect which offsets the loss of sugar. There was no noticeable difference in the chemical composition of the flesh.—*Experiment Station Record.*

CERTIFICATION OF STALLIONS.

FIFTH ANNUAL REPORT—(SEASON 1911-12).

By W. A. N. Robertson, B.V.Sc.

The Stallion Parades arranged for during the season just completed, marking the fifth in which the scheme for the Examination and Certification of Stallions has been in operation, were carried to a successful issue by the veterinary officers engaged in the work.   As in previous years, the major portion of such work was performed by four members of the staff—the object of limiting the examining staff in this manner being an endeavour to attain, to the utmost, uniformity in the examination.   A perusal of the table showing the work of the individual officers would, at first sight, tend to indicate that this uniformity had not been obtained; but a more careful analysis shows that the variation which exists is due to a difference in the number of stallions rejected for type, and this number stands in inverse proportion to the progressiveness of the districts visited; for example, in the more progressive centres the unsound sire has been forced to make way for the sound and the animal of lower type for that of a higher; whilst the more backward portions of the State have a larger percentage of horses which are below a reasonable standard; and so an officer attending the majority of such centres will reject a higher percentage.

The work of the officers during the season under review is shown in the following table:—

OFFICERS' EXAMINATIONS OF STALLIONS, SEASON 1911-12.

Officers.	No. Examined.	No. Certificated.	No. Rejected.	Percentage Rejected.
Mr. E. A. Kendall, B.V.Sc.	305	247	58	19·01
Mr. R. G. Griffin, M.R.C.V.S. ...	252	201	51	20·23
Mr. G. S. Bruce, F.R.C.V.S	243	169	74	30·45
Mr. R. N. Johnstone, L.V.Sc. ...	165	127	38	23·03
Mr. W. J. Cother, G.M.V.C.	10	10	...	...
	975	754	221	...
Appeal Boards	4	4	..	
Grand Total	979	758	221	22·57

Of the 130 parades held, 97 were carried out under the auspices of various agricultural societies; and it is pleasing to note that in the majority of cases secretaries rendered all the assistance in their power, and helped to lighten the duties of the examining officer by adhering to the official time-table, and making suitable arrangements for presenting all stallions submitted for examination.

The total number of stallions examined by members of our own staff is shown in the table of analysis given at a later stage of this report to be 979; to this must be added 91 for which certificates were transferred, making a total of 1,070 certificated in this State.

The season stands out prominently as one of great activity in the draught horse industry as evidenced by the increase in the importations from New Zealand and the United Kingdom, the figures for the last two seasons being as under :—

STALLIONS IMPORTED TO VICTORIA.

Year.	From New Zealand.	From Great Britain.
1910	207	13
1911	254	53

EXAMINATION AND REJECTION.

The 979 stallions examined were dealt with as is shown in the following table :—

ANALYSIS OF DEFECTS OF REJECTS, SEASON 1911-12.

	DRAUGHTS.		LIGHTS.		PONIES.		TOTALS.	
—	No. Examined.	No. Certificated.	No. Examined.	No. Certificated.	No Examined.	No. Certificated.	No. Examined.	No. Certificated.
	692	554	165	121	122	83	979	758

Unsoundness.	No. Rejected.	Per cent. Rejected.	No. Rejected.	Per cent Rejected.	No. Rejected.	Per cent.. Rejected	No. Rejected.	Per cent. Rejected.
	138	19·94	44	26·66	39	31·96	221	22·57
Sidebone ...	58	8·38	...	...	...	...	58	5·92
Ringbone ...	14	2·02	2	1·21	...	.	16	1·63
Spavin (Bone)	3	·43	6	3·66	3	2·45	12	1·22
Bog Spavin...	3	·43	1	·6	...	...	4	·4
Curb ...	4	·57	4	2·42	2	1·63	10	1·02
Roaring ...	...	...	...	...	...	...	...	...
Shivering ...	2	·28	...	...	...	...	2	·2
Nasal Disease	...	...	...	...	...	...	...	...
Total unsound	84	12·13	13	7·87	5	4·09	102	10·42
Disapproved	54	7·8	31	18·78	34	27·86	119	12·15
Total rejected	138	19·94	44	26·66	39	31·96	221	22·57

It will be seen that 221, or 22.57 per cent., were rejected. This is a decrease of 4.12 per cent. as between the number refused certificates last year which in turn was a 3 per cent. decrease over that of the previous season. Comparing last season's work with that of 1910-11 it is seen that the percentage of draught horses rejected has fallen from 28.58 per cent. to 19.94. This great reduction is due entirely to the diminished number of unsound ones met with, the number refused as being below standard being practically the same, viz., 7.01 per cent. in 1910-11 and 7.8 per cent. in 1911-12. Analysing the reasons for rejection still further it is found that sidebone is the diminishing factor, for whereas 19 per cent. of draught horses were rejected in 1910-11 only 8.38 per cent. were rejected on this account in 1911-12—a difference of 10.62 per cent. Light horses show an increase of 2.05 per cent. in the number rejected and this is seen to be due to a decrease of 2.61 per cent. in respect of unsoundness and an increase of 4.70 per cent. in respect of type. Ponies show a similar state of affairs ; in the number rejected there is an increase of 10.87 per cent., being due to a decrease of 1.38 in regard to unsoundness and an increase of 12.34 per cent. in regard to type. It would be premature at present to claim from these figures a general decrease of unsoundness in our stallions. but it may be regarded as an indication of the trend towards the goal which is sought. During the season 287 stallions which had been previously certificated were presented for re-examination They were dealt with as follows :—

SUMMARY OF FIVE YEARS' WORK, 1907-1912.

Season	DRAUGHTS Examined	Certificated	Rejected Unsound	Disapproved		Percentage			LIGHTS Examined	Certificated	Rejected Unsound	Disapproved		Percentage			PONIES Examined	Certificated	Rejected Unsound	Disapproved		Percentage			TOTALS Examined	Certificated	Rejected Unsound	Disapproved		Percentage		
1907-8	403	271	96	36	132	23·82	8·93	32·75	301	246	32	23	55	10·63	7·64	18·27	214	186	10	18	28	4·67	8·41	13·08	918	703	138	77	215	15·04	8·38	23·42
1908-9	501	341	137	23	160	27·33	4·59	31·92	295	242	29	24	53	9·83	8·13	17·96	199	159	5	35	40	2·5	17·58	20·10	995	742	171	82	253	17·17	8·24	25·41
1909-10	410	275	96	39	135	23·52	9·56	33·08	191	147	12	32	44	6·27	16·77	23·04	156	112	5	39	44	3·29	25·65	28·94	757	534	113	110	223	15·04	14·65	29·69
1910-11	542	387	117	38	155	21·57	7·01	28·58	143	108	15	20	35	10·53	14·08	24·61	128	101	7	20	27	5·47	15·62	21·09	813	596	139	78	217	17·09	9·6	26·69
1911-12	692	554	84	54	138	12·13	7·8	19·94	165	120	13	31	44	7·87	18·78	26·66	122	83	5	34	39	4·09	27·86	31·96	979	758	102	119	221	10·42	12·15	22·57
Grand Total																									4,462	3,333	663	466	1,129	14·86	10·44	25·3

HORSES SUBMITTED FOR RENEWAL OF CERTIFICATE, SEASON 1911-12.

Four years old.				Five years old.			
Passed.	Rejected.	Per cent.	Total.	Passed.	Rejected.	Per cent.	Total.
123	17	12·14	140	123	24	16·32	147

The summary, on page 290, of the five years' work will show the total number of animals examined and the action taken. The detailed analysis of the reasons for rejection have been given in previous reports, and may be found in full in Bulletin No. 30.

ENGLISH EXAMINATIONS.

Considerable zest was given to the breeding of draught horses last season by the great increase in importations from Great Britain, a total of 53 stallions composed of 39 Shires and 14 Clydesdales being introduced as against nine Shires and four Clydesdales the previous year. Importers realizing the necessity of introducing only sound animals were careful to obtain certificates in England that would be accepted here. They experienced some trouble however in doing this in respect of Scottish horses; and it was not until late in the year that the Glasgow Agricultural Society, realizing the difficulties which faced both breeders and shippers, took the matter in hand and appointed four veterinary officers to examine on their behalf horses for export to Victoria. So that for the coming season there should be little difficulty encountered.

TRANSFERRED CERTIFICATES.

The number of stallions examined in Great Britain, New Zealand, and other States of the Commonwealth for which certificates were transferred by this Department totalled 91, 44 being from New Zealand, 42 from Great Britain, and 5 from New South Wales.

In respect of the certificates issued in these countries some little confusion has existed in the mind of holders thereof, to the extent that they have presented them at shows, &c., and have been surprised that they were not accepted. These certificates are issued as a guarantee that a Victorian one covering a similar period for which a certificate would be issued if the examination were carried out by a Victorian officer, will be issued without further examination. Until however they are so transferred for a Victorian certificate or endorsed by the Chief Veterinary Officer of this State as "recognised for Victorian Shows," they cannot be regarded officially. Importers or buyers would therefore be wise in effecting a transfer as soon as convenient after entering Victoria. More care is also necessary on the part of buyers in noting the date upon which a certificate expires. This applies more particularly to New Zealand certificates which, if issued prior to April the 1st in any year, are only transferable for a Victorian certificate expiring on the ensuing 30th June, whereas New Zealand certificates issued after that date are exchanged for the Victorian one terminable the 30th June 12 months. In respect of certificates obtained in the United Kingdom, if such are obtained prior to January 1st, they are considered as certificates for the current season, while examinations conducted on or after January 1st are transferred as for a certificate for the subsequent season. These months of grace are allowed to enable stallions to be got ready in Victoria for the season's sales, &c., opening in July.

ALTERATIONS TO REGULATIONS.

As a result of experience gained in the five seasons during which examinations have been conducted it has been found that some alteration of the regulations can be made. Perusal of the regulations issued with this report will reveal the following principal alterations and additions :—

(1) In respect of stallions refused a certificate as being below standard—Part II. of the Regulations, Clause (3) has been added which for the future will allow a three or four year old stallion refused a certificate under this heading to be re-presented the following year for examination, unless the owner in the meantime avails himself of the appeal conditions, when the opinion of the Board shall be considered final. Any five-year-old stallion however rejected by a veterinary officer under this heading will not be eligible for re-examination except as provided for by the appeal conditions.

(2) With regard to the notification of reasons for rejection a new Clause (3) has been added to Part III. providing for an official notification being sent to owners of rejected stallions intimating the fact of such rejection and the reasons for the same. This will further an owner's opportunity of appealing against the decision within the stipulated period of 30 days. Clause (8) has also been added to this section of the regulations which may be regarded as a machinery section and refers to the dates upon which certificates will be issued.

APPEALS.

During the season six appeals were lodged—four being on the question of unsoundness and two in respect of type, breed and conformation. Two of the former were successful and both of the latter.

LIST OF CERTIFIED STALLIONS.

The list of certificated stallions issued with this report is one of horses which were examined in the past season only. Those which have received life certificates must be added to the list published in .Bulletin No. 30, whilst the list of terminable certificates published in that Bulletin is now obsolete and need not be further considered, whilst in its place must be read the list of terminable certificates issued herewith. Secretaries of agricultural societies are specially requested to make themselves familiar with this principle, which it is intended shall be followed for the future. In order to make this list as complete as possible it is specially requested that holders of certificates become familiar with the notice on the back thereof and report to the Department the death of any stallion in order that the name may be removed.

REGULATIONS

Governing the Examination of Stallions for the Government Certificate of Soundness and Approval.

I.—Examination Parades.

(1) Societies within whose district an Inspection Parade is appointed are required to provide a suitable place for the examinations to be conducted, and to suitably and reasonably advertise the holding of the parade on receipt of notice from the Department of the fixture. The secretary or some member of the committee of the society is required to be in attendance at the appointed time to assist the examining officer in the arrangements for the inspection.

(2) The Parades will be conducted and the Veterinary Officer will attend without expense to Societies other than that involved in advertising and making known the occasion to the public and the Stallion owners in the district, and providing the examination ground.

(3) The Examining Officer will attend Inspection Parades held at times and places set out in the official Time Table for the year, and all examinations of Stallions for the Government Certificate will be made at such Parades or on some such publicly advertised occasion, *unless* under special circumstances as provided for in clause 5.

(4) In the event of it being found impossible for local reasons to hold the Parade in any district at the time and date set out in the Time Table, notice to that effect—together with suggestions for alternative date and time compatible with the rest of the Time Table—should be given *not later than 1st June*, after which no alteration in the Time Table can be made.

(5) The special examination of stallions for the Government Certificate of Soundness at other than the advertised stallion parades may be arranged for in cases where, through accidental circumstances, the owner has failed to submit the horse at such parade.

Such examinations will only be arranged when the attendance of the Examining Officer will not interfere with the requirements of the Department for his services in other directions.

An owner requesting such special examinations will be required to prepay a fee of £1 1s. for each horse examined; also the railway fare (first class return), and travelling expenses at the rate of 14s. per day, of the visiting officer.

II.—Grounds for Rejection.

(1) Refusal of Certificate on the ground of unsoundness will be made only when in the opinion of the Examining Officer the horse is affected at the time of examination with one or more of the following hereditary unsoundnesses in any degree, viz. :—

Roaring	Curb	Thoroughpin and Bursal Enlargements
Ringbone	Bog Spavin	Nasal disease (Osteo-porosis)
Sidebone	Bone Spavin	Chorea (" Shivering " or " Nervy ")

or such other hereditary unsoundness as the Minister may at any time declare. (Blemishes or unsoundness, the result—in the opinion of the Examining Officer on appearances then presented—of accident, injury, and over-strain or over-work, will not disqualify.)

(2) The Certificate will also be refused in the case of animals considered by the Examining Officer to be below a reasonable standard for Government approval, as regards type, conformation and breeding.

(3) Stallions three or four years old, which are refused a Certificate as regards type, conformation and breeding may, unless dealt with under the Appeal Board Condition, be re-submitted annually until five years old, after which the refusal shall be subject to review under Part V. of these regulations only.

III.—CERTIFICATES.

(1) Particulars concerning the identity of the horse—name, breeder, pedigree, age, prior ownership, &c.—must be furnished to the Examining Officer at the time of examination. If deemed necessary in any case the owner may be called upon to furnish a statutory declaration as to the correctness of such particulars.

(2) Certificates will be issued within seven days of the holding of the Parades, and will be forwarded to the Secretaries of the Societies under whose auspices the Parades are held, and who will either forward them to the owner direct, or deliver them to him on application.

(3) The owners of stallions for which a Certificate is refused will within seven days of such refusal be officially notified of the fact; the reason for such rejection will also be given.

(4) Until the issue of a certificate, or until the publication of the official list of certificated stallions, the result of the Veterinary examination will not be communicated to any person except as herein provided or under circumstances as follow :—The Examining Officer may, on request on proper occasion, communicate to the owner or his agent—duly authorized in writing to inquire—the result of the examination. In case of refusal of the certificate the reasons for refusal will not under any circumstances, save in legal proceedings under the direction of the Court, be communicated to any person except the owner or his agent duly authorized in writing. Secretaries of Societies, persons in charge of the horse, grooms or relatives of the owner will not be considered authorized agents for that purpose unless they deliver to the officer the owner's signed authority to receive the information.

(5) The Victorian Government Certificate of Soundness can only be issued in respect of horses three years old and over, that have been examined by a Victorian Government Veterinary Officer, or horses in respect of which any of the following certificates are produced : —

The Government Certificate of Soundness of New South Wales, Queensland, South Australia or New Zealand.

The Veterinary Certificate of the Royal Shire Horse Society (England).

The Veterinary Certificate of Royal Agricultural Society (England).

The Veterinary Certificate of Royal Dublin Society (Ireland).

The Veterinary Certificate of Highland and Agricultural Society (Scotland).

The Veterinary Certificate of Glasgow and West of Scotland Agricultural Society.

Any horse which has been rejected by the Veterinary Examiners for any of the above certificates will not be eligible for examination for the Victorian Government Certificate of Soundness.

(6) The form of the Victorian Government Certificate of Soundness is as follows:—" G.R.—Department of Agriculture, Victoria, No.   .
Certificate of Soundness and Approval, issued for the season
(or issued for Life as the case may be), given in respect of the *(breed)* stallion *(name and description of stallion)* submitted for Government inspection by the owner *(name of owner)* at *(place of examination)* such horse having been found suitable for stud service and free from hereditary unsoundness and defects of conformation predisposing thereto on examination by *(signature of Examining Officer)* Veterinary Officer on the day of   19   .

(Signature).

Chief Veterinary Officer.

Issued by direction of the Minister of Agriculture.

(Signature).

Secretary for Agriculture."

(7) Two-year-old colts may be submitted for examination and a temporary certificate will be issued in respect of such as pass the examination Such temporary certificate must not be taken to imply suitability for stud service of approval as regards type, nor is the issue of it intended as an indication of the likelihood of a certificate being issued when submitted for examination at a more mature age.

(8) The season in respect of Government Certificates shall be considered as opening on July 1st, stallions passing the examination any time during the three months previous to this date in New Zealand or Australia will be granted a Certificate for the season next following. In respect of stallions examined in Great Britain examinations on or after 1st January will be considered as examinations for the following season.

IV.—Tenure of Certificate.

(1) Certificates issued during the seasons 1907 and 1908 are life certificates.

(2) Certificates issued during the season 1908 in respect of horses four years old and over are life certificates; those for three-year-olds are season certificates only, and the horse must be submitted for re-examination at four and five years before a life certificate will be issued.

(3) In 1910, and subsequently, only stallions *five* years old and over will be given life certificates. *Three-year-old* and *four-year-old* stallions will be certificated for the *season only*, and will be required to be submitted for *re*-examination each season *until five* years old, when a Life certificate will be issued.

(4) The Season certificate issued in respect of any horse must be handed to the Examining Officer at the time of re-examination or forwarded to the Chief Veterinary Officer before a subsequent Season certificate or a Life certificate will be issued.

(5) The Minister retains the right to at any time have a certificated stallion submitted for re-examination, and to withdraw the certificate, in the event of the animal being declared, to his satisfaction, unsound.

V.—Board of Appeal.

(1) Any owner of a stallion who is dissatisfied with the refusal of a Government certificate in respect of his horse may appeal against the decision to the Minister at any time within *thirty* days of the examination, under the following conditions :—

(*a*) That the appeal be in writing and be accompanied by the lodgment of £5, such amount to be forfeited in the event of the appeal *not* being upheld, unless the Board shall for good cause otherwise direct.

(*b*) That the appeal be accompanied by an undertaking to pay any railway fares and hotel expenses incurred by the Board of Appeal in connexion with the settlement of the appeal.

(*c*) That, in the event of refusal having been on the ground of unsoundness, the appeal be accompanied by a certificate from a registered Veterinary Surgeon setting out that the horse has been found by him on examination since the refusal appealed against, to be free from all the unsoundnesses set out in Part II. of these Regulations.

(*d*) That, in the event of refusal having been on the ground of being below standard for Government approval, the appeal be accompanied by a certificate from the President and two members of the Committee of the Society under whose auspices the parade was held, setting out that in their opinion the horse is of fit and proper type, conformation, and breeding to be approved as a stud horse.

(2) On receipt of Notice of Appeal in proper form, and with the above conditions complied with, the Minister will appoint a Board of Appeal, which shall consist of :—

(*a*) In the case of appeals against refusal of certificate on the ground of unsoundness, the Chief Veterinary Officer and two practising Veterinary Surgeons.

(*b*) In the case of appeals against refusal of certificate as being below standard for Government approval, the Chief Veterinary Officer and two horsemen of repute and standing.

Such Board shall act and decide on the appeal, and its decision shall be final, and *not subject to review.*

(3) In the event of the appeal being allowed, refund shall be made of the deposit, and any expenses paid by the appellant under Clause 1 (*b*). Further, the Board may recommend to the Minister the allowance of such of the expenses of the appellant in supporting his appeal as it may consider reasonable under the circumstances of the case, and the Minister may, in his discretion, confirm the recommendation in whole or in part, whereupon allowance shall be made to the appellant accordingly.

(4) No stallion in respect of which a Government certificate is refused will be allowed to be re-submitted for examination except in the case of an appeal or in such case as when a three or four years old stallion has been refused on account of type as herein provided for. In the event of any rejected stallion being re-submitted for examination under another name or under such circumstances as in the opinion of the Minister are calculated to mislead the Examining Officer into the belief that the horse has not previously been examined, the owner of such rejected stallion, if proved to the satisfaction of the Minister that he is responsible for such re-submission, shall be debarred from submitting any horse for examination for such period as the Minister shall determine.

NOTICE TO SECRETARIES OF AGRICULTURAL SOCIETIES.

Section " A " of the conditions to be complied with by Agricultural Societies before being eligible for participation in the annual Government grant is as follows:—

"*A.—That the awards of prizes in all classes for stallions, three years old and over, at the Society's Show must be subject to the possession by the exhibit of a Government certificate of soundness.*"

In order to comply with the above, the special attention of show secretaries is invited to the receiving of entries in stallion classes. No entry should be received unless at the time of entry the Government certificate is produced, or unless satisfactory evidence is given that a Government certificate is held by the owner in respect of the exhibit. The awarding of a prize card and the withholding of prize money in respect of any exhibit shall not be deemed as compliance with the condition. Care should be taken also to see that the certificate is not out of date, that is to say:—

For three-year-olds a 1912 three-year-old certificate must be held.
For four-year-olds, a 1912 four-year-old certificate must be held (the 1911 three-year-old certificate is out of date).
For horses five years old and over, a life certificate must be held.

Secretaries are strongly urged to become familiar with the regulations, particularly Regulation IV., which deals with the tenure of certificates.

Secretaries are required to forward immediately after the show a return (forms for which will be sent to each society) giving required particulars concerning 1st, 2nd, and 3rd prize winners as under:—

RETURN to be forwarded to the Chief Veterinary Officer concerning Stallions (3 years old and over) awarded Prizes at the.....................
Agricultural Society's Show held............ ....,...................

Name of Stallion.	Certificate Number.	Name of Class and Section (not Number).	Prize Awarded.			Owner's Name.	Owner's Address.
			1st.	2nd.	3rd.		

(Signed)........ ....
Secretary...................... Agricultural Society.
Date.....................

Particular atten...on is directed to the method now in vogue of classifying certificated stallions. The list is now divided into horses carrying a life certificate and those which are terminable, and supplementary lists will be issued annually which should be added to those listed in Bulletin No. 30.

4878. 1.

SUPPLEMENTARY LIST OF LIFE CERTIFICATED STALLIONS.

Cert. No.	Name of Horse.	Age.	Owner.	Parade.	Date of Examination.	Officer.
				DRAUGHTS.		
1999	Admiral Sperry	5 years	A. Duff	Maryborough	16.8.11	R.N.J.
1978	Admiral Sperry	5 years	W. Barnes	Rainbow	8.8.11	E.A.K.
2022	Advance	Aged	H. McGregor	N.Z. Govt. Cert.	29.7.11	..
2149	Albert of Tandridge	5 years	M. J. Caffrey	English Exam.	30.10.11	..
2045	Albyn's Victor	5 years	Jas. Rigney	Ballan	26.8.11	E.A.K.
1979	Bancor's Heir	5 years	C. J. Freeman	Rainbow	8.8.11	E.A.K.
1917	Baron Aldie	5 years	G. and W. Lord	Rosedale (Special)	26.5.11	W.J.C.
2145	Baron Belmont	5 years	Falkiner Bros.	English Exam.	23.3.11	..
1965	Baron Clinton	5 years	R. N. Herkes	Clyde	2.8.11	R.N.J.
2046	Baroone Saxon	5 years	Jas. Booth	Ballan	26.8.11	E.A.K.
2066	Barrow Oak	5 years	J. T. Brown	Seymour	1.9.11	E.A.K.
1941	Bengal 2nd	5 years	Arch. Kirk	City Horse Bazaar	22.7.11	R.N.J.
2125	Black Prince	5 years	Roberts Bros.	Trafalgar	18.9.11	G.S.B.
1956	Blair Athol	Aged	Caffrey and Murphy	N.Z. Govt. Cert.	18.5.11	..
2024	Borderside	5 years	Geo. Nield	Swan Hill	22.8.11	E.A.K.
1910	Bramhope Druid	5 years	James Cowie	Melbourne (Special)	10.4.11	E.A.K.
1909	Bramhope Royal William	6 years	F. W. Griffin	Melbourne (Special)	10.4.11	E.A.K.
1911	Bramhope Sampson	6 years	F. W. Griffin	Melbourne (Special)	10.4.11	E.A.K.
1920	Bruiser 2nd	6 years	F. W. Griffin	English Exam.	20.4.11	..
2013	Carol Redwood	5 years	C. H. Feldtmann	Benalla	18.8.11	G.S.B.
2025	Cashier	Aged	W. Teague and Sons	Swan Hill	22.8.11	E.A.K.
2116	Cedric's Favourite	5 years	J. Wallace	Warrnambool	14.9.11	E.A.K.
2030	Champion of Kelmscott	5 years	W. A. Milvain	Kerang	23.8.11	E.A.K.
2100	Clan Donald	6 years	A. Kay	Ballarat	16.9.11	R.G.
1918	Clydeside	Aged	Mitchell and O'Brien	Melbourne (Special)	15.5.11	G.S.B.
2157	Contraband	5 years	C. W. Tindall	English Exam.	28.12.11	..
1922	Copperplate	5 years	F. W. Griffin	English Exam.	21.4.11	..
2002	Coronation 2nd	5 years	Jno. McGillivray	Geelong	20.8.08	G.S.B.
1928	Dalrymple Jock	6 years	A. Dufty	N.S.W. Exam.	10.4.11	..
1974	Dan	5 years	Christopher Bourke	Donald	8.8.11	R.G.
1967	Dreadnought	5 years	R. Semmler	Murtoa	2.8.11	E.A.K.
2018	Drumoolin	5 years	Quinn Bros.	Elmore	21.8.11	R.G.
2001	Dunmore	5 years	B. J. Hughes	Inglewood	17.8.11	R.N.J.
2014	Ettrick	5 years	E. Louby	Benalla	18.8.11	G.S.B.
2083	Ettrick Lad	6 years	A. Colvin	Agricultural Offices	9.9.11	G.S.B.
1936	Evanyett	5 years	J. R. Kent	Horsham	11.7.11	R.N.J.
2102	Everlasting King	5 years	Geo. Fraser	Ballarat	16.9.11	R.G.
2096	Federal Prince	5 years	J. Pasco	Sale	14.9.11	R.N.J.
2019	Federation King	5 years	D. Trewick	Elmore	21.8.11	R.G.
2126	Forest King	5 years	A. J. Ryan	Trafalgar	18.9.11	G.S.B.
2008	Frogmore	5 years	J. Giddings	Melbourne	18.8.11	E.A.K.
2103	Gay Garland	5 years	W. R. Clarke	Romsey	18.9.11	R.G.
1976	Girvan Chief	Aged	R. C. Hannah	Donald	8.8.11	R.G.
1996	Glenroy	5 years	J. Long	Heathcote	14.8.11	R.N.J.
1956	Glen Stuart	5 years	Geo. Hill	N.Z. Govt. Cert.	26.1.11	..
2016	Glenview	5 years	Smythe Bros.	Daylesford	21.8.11	G.S.B.
1927	Glen William	5 years	L. Hutchesson	Horsham	11.7.11	E.A.K.
1954	Grampian 2nd	5 years	J. McLeod	Korumburra	25.7.11	R.G.
2158	Hacconby Kingmaker	5 years	C. W. Tindall	English Exam.	28.12.11	..
2041	Hamilton Star	5 years	R. Steer	Hamilton	24.8.11	R.N.J.
1945	Heather King	5 years	F. Rae	City Horse Bazaar	24.7.11	R.N.J.
2112	Hero Ben	5 years	E. Bodey	Camperdown	13.9.11	E.A.K.
2057	Highland Laddie	5 years	J. Robble	Wangaratta	28.8.11	R.G.
1991	Honest Oak	Aged	G. R. Burrell	Balmoral	11.8.11	R.N.J.
1988	Ian North	5 years	C. H. Warne	Watchem	10.8.11	R.G.
1935	Kelms Pride	5 years	Jno. Dugdale	Agricultural Offices (Special)	17.7.11	G.S.B.
2020	Kelsman	5 years	M. O'Grady	Elmore	21.8.11	R.G.
1914	Kelvin Lad	6 years	Walter and Agar	Agricultural Offices	13.5.11	G.S.B.
2043	Kingsway 2nd	5 years	Executors of D. Archibald	Kyabram	22.8.11	R.G.
2106	Knight of Kildare	5 years	E. Boland	Terang	11.9.11	E.A.K.
2139	King Alexander	5 years	S. McNabb	Morwell	3.10.11	E.A.K.
1948	King William	5 years	Benson Bros.	City Horse Bazaar	24.7.11	R.N.J.
2082	Laird of Burnbrae	5 years	W. Cameron	Melton	2.9.11	R.N.J.
1943	Leek Baronet	Aged	W. H. Robinson	City Horse Bazaar	22.7.11	R.N.J.
1953	Lieutenant Mac	5 years	R. G. Anderson	City Horse Bazaar	25.7.11	E.A.K.
2065	Lorne Ruby	5 years	K. C. Harper	Bundoora (Special)	31.8.11	R.N.J.
1913	Luxall	5 years	A. Robertson	Melbourne (Special)	15.5.11	G.S.B.

SUPPLEMENTARY LIST OF LIFE CERTIFICATED STALLIONS—*continued.*

Cert. No.	Name of Horse.	Age.	Owner.	Parade.	Date of Examination.	Officer.
			DRAUGHTS—*continued.*			
1908	Lymn Bouncer ..	5 years	H. S. Ruddock ..	Melbourne (Special)	10.4.11	E.A.K.
2086	Lymn Truffle ..	5 years	Jno. Smith ..	Royal Show ..	4.9.11	E.A.K.
2122	Lord Clyde ..	5 years	H. Reynolds ..	Werribee ..	16.9.11	E.A.K.
2077	Lord Glengyle ..	5 years	R. Allen ..	Numurkah ..	29.8.11	E.A.K.
1929	Lord Harperland ..	5 years	E. Harders ..	Horsham ..	12.7.11	R.N.J.
2094	Macauley	5 years	Jno. Findlay ..	Alexandra ..	14.9.11	G.S.B.
1989	McLeish	5 years	W. Crozier ..	Agricultural Offices	12.8.11	W.J.C.
2120	Major Gordon ..	5 years	P. McIntosh ..	Colac	15.9.11	E.A.K.
1951	Major Mac ..	5 years	Stuckey Bros. ..	City Horse Bazaar	24.7.11	R.N.J.
1939	Manoravon Rosason	6 years	H. G. Leslie ..	English Exam. ..	11.4.11	..
2127	Master Wattie ..	5 years	Brock Bros. ..	Traialgar ..	18.9.11	G.S.B.
1919	Mazemoor Topper ..	5 years	M. J. Caffrey ..	Newmarket ..	12.6.11	Appeal Board
2131	Mellington Colonel	5 years	T. O'Donohue ..	Bunyip	19.9.11	G.S.B.
1994	Melville Lad ..	5 years	F. H. Dunn ..	Cobram ..	14.8.11	G.S.B.
2029	Merry Prince ..	5 years	G. Pearse ..	Swan Hill ..	22.8.11	E.A.K.
2032	New Blood ..	5 years	T. Bagnall ..	Pyramid ..	24.8.11	E.A.K.
1982	Newton Stewart ..	5 years	E. Devereaux ..	Warracknabeal ..	11.8.11	E.A.K.
2044	One O'clock ..	5 years	D. Robertson ..	Bacchus Marsh ..	28.8.11	E.A.K.
2006	Orbost Oak ..	5 years	J. and C. Wallace	Kaniva	17.8.11	E.A.K.
2070	Orphan Boy ..	5 years	J. Burns ..	Euroa	1.9.11	R.G.
1983	Patrician	5 years	R. McKenzie ..	Warracknabeal ..	11.8.11	E.A.K.
2107	Peerless	5 years	J. and A. Clarke	Terang	11.9.11	E.A.K.
2071	Pimpernel	5 years	F. Cann ..	Euroa	1.9.11	R.G.
2084	Powisland Pure Blood	5 years	Chas. Mills ..	Pyramid Hill ..	24.8.11	E.A.K.
1959	Premier's Fancy of Willowbank	5 years	R. Jack.. ..	N.Z. Govt. Cert. ..	9.6.11	..
1962	Premier Ward ..	5 years	J. Carrol ..	Sea Lake ..	19.7.11	G.S.B.
1924	Pride of Aldowrie ..	5 years	J. Mackintosh ..	Newmarket (Special)	5.7.11	G.S.B.
2036	Pride of Lochiel ..	5 years	J. T. Ovens ..	Kyabram ..	22.8.11	R.G.
2148	Prince Aerial ..	5 years	O'Leary Bros. ..	Penshurst (Special)	22.2.12	Appeal Board
2000	Prince Albert 2nd ..	5 years	F. Berger ..	Maryborough ..	16.8.11	R.N.J.
1963	Prince Charlie ..	5 years	C. Umbers ..	Sea Lake ..	19.7.11	G.S.B.
1952	Prince of Albyn ..	6 years	J. Rousch ..	City Horse Bazaar	25.7.11	R.N.J.
1925	Prince Percival ..	5 years	W. Langley ..	Horsham ..	11.7.11	E.A.K.
2124	Robin Hood ..	5 years	C. H. Gimblett ..	Tallangatta ..	19.9.11	E.A.K.
2052	Royal Blue ..	5 years	Alf. Buckley ..	Hopetoun ..	23.8.11	G.S.B.
1964	Royal Conqueror ..	5 years	J. Millstead ..	Sea Lake ..	19.7.11	G.S.B.
2004	Royal Dandy ..	5 years	A. W. Warren ..	Geelong ..	17.8.11	G.S.B.
2109	Royal Favourite ..	5 years	M. O'Keefe ..	Port Fairy ..	12.9.11	E.A.K.
1950	Royal Knight ..	5 years	Baldwin and Carruthers	City Horse Bazaar	24.7.11	R.N.J.
2017	Royal Mint ..	5 years	Donald Blair ..	Boort	15.8.11	R.G.
2071	Royal Nugget ..	5 years	Papworth Bros. ..	Charlton ..	17.8.11	R.G.
2108	Royal Ribbon ..	Aged	B. McNulty ..	Terang ..	11.9.11	E.A.K.
2058	Sandy's Heir ..	5 years	R. J. Mason ..	Wangaratta ..	28.8.11	R.G.
2005	Scotland's Fancy ..	5 years	D. Lamb ..	Geelong ..	17.8.11	G.S.B.
2059	Scottish King ..	5 years	Geo. Luckie ..	Wangaratta ..	28.8.11	R.G.
1934	Scottish King ..	6 years	Donald Blair ..	City Horse Bazaar	22.7.11	R.N.J.
2079	Severn Marlow ..	Aged	A. Lummis ..	N.S.W. Exam. ..	3.8.11	..
2054	Shepherd	5 years	J. Liddle ..	Beulah	22.8.11	G.S.B.
1972	Silver King ..	5 years	S. Farrell ..	N.Z. Govt. Cert. ..	4.7.11	..
2142	Solomon IV. ..	5 years	A. Williams ..	N.S.W. Exam. ..		..
2072	Sunflower ..	5 years	S. Dunn ..	Tatura ..	31.8.11	R.G.
1984	Sir Charles ..	5 years	S. Atkin ..	Warracknabeal ..	11.8.11	E.A.K.
2136	Sir Principal ..	Aged	P. Quirk ..	Romsey.. ..	18.9.11	R.G.
2055	Sir Simon Percival ..	5 years	H. Naylor ..	Beulah	22.8.11	G.S.B.
1915	Tamhorn Hugo ..	6 years	T. Maddern ..	English Exam. ..	3.3.11	..
1921	Thorney Vulcan ..	5 years	R. F. Anderson ..	English Exam. ..	20.4.11	..
2049	Tongala	5 years	J. J. Downey ..	Ballan	26.8.11	E.A.K.
2098	True Blue ..	5 years	J. Strawhorn ..	Kyneton ..	12.9.11	R.G.
1968	The Macdonald ..	5 years	A. Wohlers ..	Murtoa ..	2.8.11	E.A.K.
1955	The Standard ..	5 years	W. J. Plant ..	Newmarket ..	24.7.11	G.S.B.
2007	United	5 years	J. McDonald ..	Kaniva	17.8.11	E.A.K.
1912	Willaston Hero ..	5 years	Caffrey and Murphy	English Exam. ..	3.3.11	..
2023	Willaston Matchless 2nd	5 years	J. McMurray ..	English Exam. ..	23.2.11	..
1993	Young Bonaparte ..	5 years	J. Mulraney ..	Goroke	9.8.11	G.S.B.
2078	Young Federation ..	5 years	H. J. Hansen ..	Numurkah ..	29.8.11	E.A.K.
2128	Young Highland Lad	5 years	N. G. Martin ..	Trafalgar ..	18.9.11	G.S.B.

SUPPLEMENTARY LIST OF LIFE CERTIFICATED STALLIONS—*continued.*

Cert. No.	Name of Horse.	Age.	Owner.	Parade.	Date of Examination.	Officer.

DRAUGHTS—*continued.*

Cert. No.	Name of Horse.	Age.	Owner.	Parade.	Date of Examination.	Officer.
2050	Young Prince of Albyn	Aged	C. Lipplatt	Ballan	26.8.11	E.A.K.
1931	Young Royal Blue	Aged	A. C. Hately	Horsham	12.7.11	E.A.K.
2074	Young Topgallant	Aged	J. McKenna	Nathalia	30.8.11	E.A.K.

THOROUGHBREDS.

Cert. No.	Name of Horse.	Age.	Owner.	Parade.	Date of Examination.	Officer.
2009	Amberite	Aged	A. Cairns	Charlton	17.8.11	R.G.
2075	Berriedale	Aged	P. Russell	Beaufort	30.8.11	G.S.B.
2114	Blent	Aged	J. Jenkins	Warrnambool	14.9.11	E.A.K.
2111	Calvanite	5 years	E. Manifold	Camperdown	13.9.11	E.A.K.
1980	Crash	6 years	A. J. Pyers	Minyip	10.8.11	E.A.K.
2052	Curtain Lecture	Aged	J. O'Keefe	Shepparton	25.8.11	R.G.
1990	Emblem	Aged	J. R. McDonald	Balmoral	11.8.11	R.N.J.
2099	Little Gun	5 years	J. C. H. Graves	Mansfield	15.9.11	G.S.B.
2146	Mr. John	Aged	C. Bath	Eltham (Special)	22.2.12	R.G.
2147	Posture	Aged	J. D. Lewis	Agricultural Offices	2.3.12	R.N.J.
2080	Winteriga	6 years	D. Coutts	Condah (Special)	31.8.11	G.S.B.

LIGHT HORSES.

Cert. No.	Name of Horse.	Age.	Owner.	Parade.	Date of Examination.	Officer.
1946	Abydos	Aged	D. Mitchell	City Horse Bazaar	24.8.11	W.J.C.
2035	Ajax	5 years	J. T. Ovens	Kyabram	22.8.11	R.G.
2110	Almont, J.	5 years	G. J. Vagg	Camperdown	13.9.11	E.A.K.
2141	Anist	6 years	D. C. Chllcott	Dookie (Special)	19.10.11	Appeal Board
1966	Billy Mac	Aged	W. Greaves	Bendigo	2.8.11	R.G.
2069	Bleriot	5 years	R. W. Storey	Euroa	2.9.11	R.G.
2039	Brilliant	5 years	C. and E. Cameron	Hamilton	24.8.11	R.N.J.
2051	Canary's Pride	5 years	G. W. Anderson	Hopetoun	23.8.11	G.S.B.
1985	Child Abdallah	Aged	T. Brennan	Agricultural Offices (Special)	14.8.11	E.A.K.
2048	Cosmopolitan 2nd	5 years	A. Wade	Ballan	26.8.11	E.A.K.
2101	Dashaway	6 years	Woolcock and Sons	Ballarat	16.9.11	R.G.
1923	Derando	5 years	W. E. J. Craig	Yuille and Co. (Special)	23.6.11	R.G.
2068	Dictator	5 years	J. McNamara, jun.	Yarrawonga	29.8.11	R.G.
2117	Dixie Brown	6 years	W. Vaughan	Colac	15.9.11	E.A.K.
2003	Emulation	5 years	A. McFarlane	Geelong	17.8.11	G.S.B.
2056	Ercildoon Dick	5 years	C. Gardner	Wangaratta	28.8.11	R.G.
2012	Fashion Direct	5 years	T. F. Hogan	Quambatook	15.8.11	R.G.
1969	Firestone	5 years	R. N. Scott	Agricultural Offices	5.8.11	E.A.K.
2137	Fitz Bell	5 years	G. W. Booth	Frankston	23.9.11	G.S.B.
1932	General Cass	5 years	E. J. Glossop	Agricultural Offices	6.5.11	G.S.B.
2138	Governor Dixie	5 years	J. Heffernan	Kilmore	28.9.11	G.S.B.
2067	Gundaroo	5 years	G. Howe	Seymour	1.9.11	E.A.K.
2139	Harkaway	5 years	M. Harper	Warragul	19.9.11	G.S.B.
2028	Honest	5 years	W. J. Gillard	Swan Hill	22.8.11	E.A.K.
1961	Jardiniere	5 years	Gunsser Bros	Sea Lake	19.7.11	G.S.B.
2053	King Almont	5 years	H. Reid	Beulah	22.8.11	G.S.B.
2035	Kingski	5 years	H. V. McLeod	Casterton	23.8.11	R.N.J.
1977	Lyntourie	5 years	W. A. Morgan	Donald	8.8.11	R.G.
1942	October	5 years	J. Graham	City Horse Bazaar	22.7.11	R.G.
2089	Ohio	5 years	Howard Smith	Royal Show	4.9.11	G.S.B.
2064	Oster Huon	6 years	A. J. Pitman	Yarrawonga	29.8.11	R.G.
2033	Ostermeyer Direct	5 years	McLaren Bros.	Pyramid	24.8.11	E.A.K.
2093	Ostrich	Aged	A. Colvin	Agricultural Offices (Special)	12.9.11	G.S.B.
2095	Pasha's Son	5 years	J. P. Buntine	Bairnsdale	13.9.11	R.N.J.
2010	Prince Almont	5 years	Geo. Davies	Charlton	17.8.11	R.G.
1970	Prince Maurice	5 years	J. Zander	Agricultural Offices	5.8.11	G.S.B.
2113	P.S.	5 years	Wm. Garvie	Camperdown	13.9.11	E.A.K.
2084	Ringer	6 years	W. Marshall	Agricultural Offices	9.9.11	G.S.B.
2097	Robert Alto	6 years	Thomson Bros.	Kyneton	12.9.11	R.G.
2037	Rockefeller	5 years	D. McLeod	Kyabram	22.8.11	R.G.
2073	Splendour	5 years	J. McKenna	Nathalia	30.8.11	E.A.K.
2123	Standish Direct	5 years	W. Walter	Werribee	16.9.11	E.A.K.
2105	Togo	5 years	H. Tomkins	Mansfield	15.9.11	G.S.B.
2135	Tracey Boy	5 years	Turner Bros.	Whittlesea	22.9.11	R.N.J.
2143	The General	6 years	D. Shelley	Ballarat Show	16.11.11	R.G.
1998	Yelretso	Aged	— Grogan	Dunolly	15.8.11	R.N.J.
2144	Young Larrican	6 years	T. Sutherland	Ballarat Show	16.11.11	R.G.

SUPPLEMENTARY LIST OF LIFE CERTIFICATED STALLIONS—*continued.*

PONIES.

Cert. No.	Name of Horse.	Age.	Owner.	Parade.	Date of Examination.	Officer.
2134	Bobby Dazzler	5 years	H. Samson	Dandenong	21.9.11	R.N.J.
2115	Brigham Again	Aged	Geo. Smith	Warrnambool	14.9.11	E.A.K.
2047	Bygauley	5 years	J. J. Downey	Ballan	26.8.11	E.A.K.
2051	Canary's Pride	5 years	G. W. Anderson	Hopetoun	23.8.11	G.S.B.
1947	Chumale	Aged	A. Bennett	City Horse Bazaar	22.7.11	R.G.
2026	Commodore Nut	5 years	W. D. McCormack	Swan Hill	22.8.11	E.A.K.
1973	Cymro Bach	Aged	W. A. Morgan	Donald	8.8.11	R.G.
1940	Cymro Dau	6 years	H. C. Lees	English Exam.	11.4.11	
2027	Dandy Bones	5 years	J. L. Loutit	Swan Hill	22.8.11	E.A.K.
1975	Dandy Brick	5 years	J. W. Baker	Donald	8.8.11	R.G.
1986	Dandy Chief	5 years	E. O'Meara	Birchip	9.8.11	R.G.
2133	Dawalight	6 years	Wm. Lobb	Korumburra	20.9.11	R.G.
2035	Fiction	5 years	W. G. Wilkinson	Royal Show	4.9.11	E.A.K.
2140	Gilbert	Aged	J. Hancock	Mildura	5.10.11	G.S.B.
2040	Gilbert	5 years	W. J. Brown	Hamilton	24.8.11	R.N.J.
1938	Greylight	Aged	E. Jones	English Exam.	11.4.11	
2118	Gwalia Cæsar	5 years	P. Sim	Colac	15.9.11	E.A.K.
2104	Interest	5 years	W. Marshall	Romsey	18.9.11	R.G.
2076	Jock Frisk	5 years	D. Stewart	Beaufort	30.8.11	G.S.B.
2119	King Olie	5 years	J. James	Colac	15.9.11	E.A.K.
2081	Limerick	5 years	M. McKay	Penshurst	1.9.11	G.S.B.
1933	Little Jack	5 years	P. W. Pollock	Horsham	12.7.11	E.A.K.
1949	Look He Comes	5 years	W. E. Rosling	City Horse Bazaar	24.7.11	W.J.C.
1937	Lord Towyvale	6 years	A. E. Bowman	English Exam.	11.4.11	
2087	Lou Lou's Dandy	5 years	C. Jones and Sons	Royal Show	4.9.11	R.N.J.
2088	Magic Blend	5 years	Frank D. Brown	Royal Show	4.9.11	E.A.K.
1944	Master Brigham	6 years	W. R. Smith	Newmarket	22.7.11	E.A.K.
2132	Mountain Bells	5 years	R. Clulow	Leongatha	20.9.11	R.N.J.
2042	Piper	Aged	A. Walter	Hamilton	24.8.11	R.N.J.
2030	Prince Dandy	5 years	F. Irish	Royal Show	4.9.11	E.A.K.
1957	Prince Harold	5 years	S. Pollock	Agricultural Offices	22.7.11	G.S.B.
1992	Radium	5 years	F. H. Lackmann	Goroke	9.8.11	G.S.B.
2015	Rubicon	Aged	M. Evans, jun.	Benalla	18.8.11	G.S.B.
1981	Sarsfield	5 years	T. Long	Minyip	10.8.11	E.A.K.
2129	Sirdan	5 years	R. Reid	Tallangatta	19.9.11	E.A.K.
2121	Spectator	6 years	W. J. Trask	Colac	15.9.11	E.A.K.
2091	Sunrise	Aged	F. Fountain	Royal Show	4.9.11	R.N.J.
2092	Trotting Railway 2nd	Aged	Mrs. D. T. Davies	Royal Show	4.9.11	E.A.K.
2060	The Doctor	Aged	H. Younger	Wangaratta	28.8.11	R.G.
2061	Valve	6 years	W. Younger	Wangaratta	28.8.11	R.G.
1987	Welsh Flyer	5 years	J. F. Beasley	Birchip	9.8.11	R.G.
2021	Welshman	5 years	— Hanson	Rochester	21.8.11	R.G.
1907	What is Wanted	5 years	W. E. Rosling	Agricultural Offices	25.3.11	G.S.B.
1971	Wilkes Jr.	5 years	S. Armstrong	Ararat	8.8.11	G.S.B.
2008	Young Comet	Aged	T. Bourke	Seymour	1.9.11	E.A.K.
1995	Young Dandy Jr.	5 years	G. Anderson	Cobram	14.8.11	G.S.B.

LIST OF TERMINABLE CERTIFICATED STALLIONS.

(Four-year-old Certificates expiring 30th June, 1912).

Cert. No.	Name of Horse.	Owner.	Parade.	Date of Examination.	Officer.
			DRAUGHTS.		
270/4	Abbotsford	A. Cameron	N.Z. Govt. Cert.	23.5.11	
254/4	Abbotsford's Pride	H. J. Kortum	Elmore	22.7.11	E.A.K.
376/4	Admiral Sperry	H. S. Gibson	Traralgon	13.9.11	R.N.J.
220/4	Agate	J. Caffrey	English Exam.	4.3.11	
340/4	Aladdin	Geo. Muir	Bacchus Marsh	28.8.11	E.A.K.
302/4	Albyn	D. Scott	Maryborough	16.8.11	R.N.J.
223/4	Aldfield Ben	O. Wills	English Exam.	20.4.11	
349/4	Attraction's Pride	W. Curtain	Rutherglen	30.8.11	R.G.
244/4	Bardon Napoleon	E. Jones	English Parade	10.4.11	
357/4	Baron	Craven Bros.	Tatura	31.8.11	R.G.
360/4	Baron Bombay	Shields Bros.	Dookie	31.8.11	E.A.K.
416/4	Baron Bute	Geo. Chirnside	Scottish Exam.	5.8.11	
284/4	Baron Irvine	C. H. Perkins	Rainbow	8.8.11	E.A.K.
382/4	Baron McLeod	R. Kerr	Lilydale	15.8.11	R.N.J.
278/4	Baron McNair	A. E. Bowman	N.Z. Govt. Cert.	7.4.11	
368/4	Baron's Best	J. Glenn	Royal Show	4.9.11	G.S.B.
213/4	Bellringer	Caffrey and Murphy	Melbourne (Special)	10.4.11	E.A.K.
422/4	Biddulph Bondsman	M. J. Caffrey	English Exam.	24.11.11	
211/4	Birdsall Harold	F. W. Griffin	Melbourne (Special)	10.4.11	E.A.K.
288/4	Blue Bell	H. Collins	Minyip	10.8.11	E.A.K.
271/4	Bonnie Chief	J. Roberts, jun.	City Horse Bazaar	28.7.11	G.S.B.
359/4	Bonnie Clyde	S. Delvin	Portland	31.8.11	G.S.B.
333/4	Bonnie Scott	Miss Henty	Casterton	23.8.11	R.N.J.
248/4	British Leader	W. Underwood	City Horse Bazaar	22.7.11	R.G.
285/4	Brown King	A. G. Cust	Rainbow	8.8.11	E.A.K.
309/4	Cairnbrogie Stamp	J. Binns	Nhill	16.8.11	E.A.K.
338/4	Carlyon	A. Robinson	Murchison	24.8.11	R.G.
326/4	Cashman	Burke Bros.	Kerang	23.8.11	E.A.K.
411/4	Centrewood	C. E. Gomm	Frankston	23.9.11	G.S.B.
384/4	Channel Flight	P. Fraser	Ballarat	16.9.11	R.G.
286/4	Charmer Jun.	Mackenzie Bros.	Rainbow	8.8.11	E.A.K.
237/4	Chieftain	Jno. McLean, jun.	Horsham	12.7.11	R.N.J.
215/4	Clumber Baronet	M. J. Caffrey	Melbourne (Special)	15.5.11	G.S.B.
279/4	Clyde Boy	J. Walder and Sons	Donald	8.8.11	R.G.
219/4	Coedy's Forest Hero	Hill Bros.	English Exam.	23.2.11	
249/4	Crown Derby	W. S. Graham		22.7.11	E.A.K.
396/4	Crown Prince	A. Simon	Tallangatta	19.9.11	E.A.K.
257/4	Croydon	R. H. Lanyon	City Horse Bazaar	24.7.11	R.N.J.
319/4	Cumloden	J. Crawford	Rochester	21.8.11	R.G.
402/4	Dainty Davie	J. Low	Korumburra	20.9.11	R.G.
228/4	Dalmuir Prince 2nd	A. Ross	Horsham	11.7.11	R.N.J.
269/4	Defiance	J. E. Small	N.Z. Govt. Cert.	26.5.11	
418/4	Dominion Chief	M. Rocks	Preston (Special)	21.11.11	R.G.
247/4	Douglas	Mitchell and O'Brien	City Horse Bazaar	22.7.11	R.N.J.
423/4	Dreadnought	M. J. Caffrey	English Exam.	20.10.11	
364/4	Dreadnought	F. Metherall	Numurkah	29.8.11	E.A.K.
336/4	Drumflower's Bud	Wm. Stokes	Echuca	22.8.11	R.G.
252/4	Drum Laddie	C. R. Roper	Newmarket	22.7.11	E.A.K.
369/4	Drummer	Anderson Bros.	Royal Show	4.9.11	G.S.B.
394/4	Drummer Boy	Jno. Ball	Werribee	16.9.11	E.A.K.
335/4	Enfield	A. S. Brewis	Hamilton	24.8.11	R.N.J.
273/4	Evelyn Lad	J. Carter	Bendigo	2.8.11	R.G.
240/4	Earl of Newton	R. Ward	Horsham	12.7.11	E.A.K.
424/4	Fairfield Dray King	M. J. Caffrey	English Exam.	20.10.11	
283/4	Federal Laddie	J. Kurtzmann	Stawell	7.8.11	E.A.K.
343/4	Federal Star	C. Gardner	Wangaratta	28.8.11	R.G.
274/4	Fine View	H. C. Hately	Murtoa	2.8.11	E.A.K.
245/4	Finstall Forest Victor	J. Archibald	English Exam.	11.4.11	
306/4	Gay Lad	Phillips Bros.	Geelong	17.8.11	G.S.B.
387/4	General Hunter	R. E. MacArthur	Camperdown	13.9.11	E.A.K.
232/4	Gentleman Chief	Jno. Gifford	Horsham	11.7.11	R.N.J.
289/4	Glenalbyn	D. McGilp	Minyip	10.8.11	E.A.K.
225/4	Glen Avon	J. Patrick	Melbourne (Special)	5.7.11	R.G.
421/4	Glen Donald	J. Henderson	Leongatha (Special)	27.2.12	.W.J.C.

LIST OF TERMINABLE CERTIFICATED STALLIONS—*continued.*

Cert. No.	Name of Horse.	Owner.	Parade.	Date of Examination.	Officer.
		DRAUGHTS—*continued.*			
212/4	Glengarry	A. J. Donaldson	Melbourne (Special)	10.4.11	E.A.
370/4	Glenmore Again	A. Aitken	Royal Show	5.9.11	G.S.B.
221/4	Hawton Burly	T. McMillan	English Exam.	23.2.11	
216/4	Highland Boy	P. Mangan	Melbourne (Special)	15.5.11	E.A.K.
209/4	Highland Chief 3rd	H. S. Ruddock	Melbourne (Special)	10.4.11	E.A.K.
323/4	Howlet	Andrew Scott	Rochester	21.8.11	R.G.
280/4	Jack O'Connell	Letcher Bros.	Donald	8.8.11	R.G.
205/4	Jock	A. Colvin	Nathalia (Special)	31.8.11	G.S.B.
239/4	John Hamilton	A. Mibus	Horsham	12.7.11	E.A.K.
350/4	Jolly Native	Wm. Wood	Rutherglen	30.8.11	R.G.
412/4	Knight Dunmore	D. J. Kelleher	Kilmore	28.9.11	G.S.B.
229/4	Knottingley President	A. and J. H. Young	Horsham	11.7.11	R.N.J.
403/4	King Jimmy	C. N. Byriell	Korumburra	20.9.11	R.G.
388/4	King of Clubs	M. Skeyhill	Camperdown	13.9.11	E.A.K.
287/4	King of the Shepherds	W. Gould	Rainbow	8.8.11	E.A.K.
203/4	Lavington King	H. S. Ruddock	Melbourne (Special)	10.4.11	E.A.K.
313/4	Linkwood	Robt. Cairns	Charlton	17.8.11	R.G.
281/4	Lion King	J. Maloney	Donald	8.8.11	R.G.
320/4	Loch Albyn	T. Brown	Elmore	21.8.11	R.G.
372/4	Lolworth Premier	P. Hart	Royal Show	6.9.11	G.S.B.
361/4	Lorryman	W. Grattan	Dookie	31.8.11	E.A.K.
400/4	Lord Galloway	R. G. Kiell	Corryong	20.9.11	E.A.K.
267/4	Lord Garthland	J. F. Nicholls	Newmarket	22.7.11	E.A.K.
419/4	Lord Glencairn	R. Gilby	Melton (Special)	18.12.11	G.S.B.
304/4	Lord Haldon	N. Ramsay	Inglewood	17.8.11	R.N.J.
282/4	Lord Hopetoun	P. Sullivan	Donald	8.8.11	R.G.
420/4	Lord Islington	J. W. Wilson	Tatura (Special)	14.2.12	E.A.K.
404/4	Lord Jock	W. J. Wilson	Korumburra	20.9.11	R.G.
299/4	Lord Leeston	H. Doidge	Agricultural Offices	12.8.11	W.J.C.
250/4	Lord Lindsay	D. Lang	Newmarket	22.7.11	E.A.K.
227/4	Lord Newton	J. Patrick	Melbourne	5.7.11	R.G.
264/4	Lord Roland	J. S. W. Parker	Newmarket	24.7.11	G.S.B.
236/4	Mac's Fancy	G. W. Francis	Horsham	11.7.11	E.A.K.
346/4	Major	E. Walker	Shepparton	25.8.11	R.G.
337/4	Major Style	C. Hall	Echuca	22.8.11	R.G.
218/4	Melbourne Prince	J. Caffrey	English Exam.	23.2.11	
314/4	Mick O'Shanter	P. Glasheen	Charlton	17.8.11	R.G.
251/4	Middlemarch	J. and M. J. Egan	Newmarket	22.7.11	E.A.K.
347/4	Milton's Pride	P. Downes	Yarrawonga	29.8.11	R.G.
324/4	Moira Lad	J. W. Barton	Swan Hill	22.8.11	E.A.K.
231/4	Montgomery	A. Robertson	Horsham	11.7.11	E.A.K.
392/4	Montrave's Pride	Geo. Crabbe	Colac	15.9.11	E.A.K.
217/4	Mountain Chief	D. White	Melbourne (Special)	15.5.11	G.S.B.
266/4	Nambrok	H. J. Nixon	Newmarket	22.7.11	E.A.K.
329/4	Napoleon	C. Marfleet	Pyramid Hill	24.8.11	E.A.K.
365/4	Newton's Sensation	J. Meiklejohn	Numurkah	29.8.11	E.A.K.
303/4	Newton's Style	Gordon and Williamson	Maryborough	16.8.11	R.N.J.
258/4	Oakburn	A. C. Petrass	City Horse Bazaar	24.7.11	R.G.
321/4	Oliver Twist	Ingram Bros.	Rochester	21.8.11	R.G.
253/4	Patrick's Pride	E. L. Edwards	Newmarket	22.7.11	E.A.K.
310/4	Percy's Hero	J. Vennell	Kaniva	17.8.11	E.A.K.
294/4	Peter's Pride	J. Cameron	Warracknabeal	11.8.11	E.A.K.
328/4	Powisland Blue Blood 2nd	D. J. Milne	Kerang	23.8.11	E.A.K.
207/4	Primley Achilles	R. A. Smales	Melbourne (Special)	10.4.11	E.A.K.
393/4	Pride of Kelvern	W. Phalp	Colac	15.9.11	E.A.K.
315/4	Pride of Milton	J. McKenna	Charlton	17.8.11	R.G.
300/4	Prince Charlie	A. McClure and Sons	Goroke	9.8.11	G.S.B.
268/4	Prince Charlie	H. F. Ogilvie	N.Z. Govt. Cert.	29.5.11	
272/4	Prince Harold Boy	Love, Royle, and Thurgood	Agricultural Offices	15.7.11	G.S.B.
259/4	Prince Margam	H. J. Bodey	City Horse Bazaar	25.7.11	R.G.
362/4	Prince Newton	W. G. Down	Dookie	31.8.11	E.A.K.
265/4	Prince of Elderslie	W. J. Baikie	Newmarket	24.7.11	G.S.B.
366/4	Prince Robin	E. W. Fowler	Numurkah	29.8.11	E.A.K.
348/4	Ranfurly	J. Blackwood	Yarrawonga	29.8.11	R.G.
330/4	Red Ensign	Jno. Ervin, sen.	Pyramid	24.8.11	E.A.K.

LIST OF TERMINABLE CERTIFICATED STALLIONS—*continued.*

Cert. No.	Name of Horse.	Owner.	Parade.	Date of Examination.	Officer.
		DRAUGHTS—*continued.*			
417/4	Royal Charlie	W. J. Black	Benalla (Special)	19.10.11	Appeal Board
316/4	Royal Charlie	Donaldson Bros.	Charlton	17.8.11	R.G.
206/4	Royal Gift	W. McKnight	Agricultural Offices	8.4.11	G.S.B.
351/4	Royal Park	T. Oliver	Rutherglen	30.8.11	R.G.
380/4	Salisbury Hero	A. and J. Rankin	Kyneton	12.9.11	R.G.
317/4	Sandy McNab	H. S. McFarlane	Wycheproof	17.8.11	R.G.
409/4	Searchlight	W. J. Craig	Lang Lang	22.9.11	G.S.B.
234/4	Shepherd Chief	P. T. Gildea	Horsham	11.7.11	E.A.K.
410/4	Signaller	H. E. Mapleson	Lang Lang	22.9.11	G.S.B.
399/4	Stirling Castle	R. V. Colliver	Bunyip	19.9.11	G.S.B.
263/4	Sunflower	J. C. Wightman	Newmarket	24.7.11	E.A.K.
390/4	Surprise	J. Jenkins	Warrnambool	14.9.11	E.A.K.
344/4	Sweet William	Geo. Smith	Wangaratta	28.8.11	R.G.
241/4	Sir Isaac	McCann Bros.	Horsham	12.7.11	E.A.K.
275/4	Sir Malcolm	A. Wohlers	Murtoa	2.8.11	E.A.K.
243/4	Sir Patrick	H. Hill	Horsham	12.7.11	R.N.J.
260/4	Sir Percival Jun.	G. Hicks	City Horse Bazaar	25.7.11	R.N.J.
226/4	Sir William	Mitchell and O'Brien	Melbourne (Special)	5.7.11	G.S.B.
353/4	Tam McKenzie	V. C. Reid	Agricultural Offices	2.9.11	E.A.K.
352/4	Tam o'Again	C. Hands	Boort	15.8.11	R.G.
443/4	Tibberton Dray King	C. W. Tindall	English Exam.	28.12.11	
210/4	Tom Walton	F. W. Sallmann	Melbourne (Special)	10.4.11	E.A.K.
386/4	Trafalgar	R. H. Gibson	Traralgon	13.9.11	R.N.J.
325/4	True Scott	W. McKnaight	Swan Hill	22.8.11	E.A.K.
406/4	The Colonel	Jno. Wuchatsch	Korumburra	20.9.11	R.G.
242/4	The Pirate	McCann Bros.	Horsham	12.7.11	E.A.K.
222/4	The Rigg Fashion	M. J. Dooley	Agricultural Offices	24.6.11	G.S.B.
415/4	Udale	H. A. Currie	Scottish Exam.	28.7.11	
261/4	Uxbridge Fyvie	J. McCulloch	City Horse Bazaar	25.7.11	E.A.K.
262/4	Victor's Pride	G. Wright	Newmarket	24.7.11	E.A.K.
230/4	Waikato	G. H. Hill	Horsham	11.7.11	R.N.J.
342/4	Wally	W. E. Poulton	Hopetoun	23.8.11	G.S.B.
233/4	Warkworth	Haustorfer Bros.	Horsham	11.7.11	R.N.J.
246/4	Western Herdsman	H. McCall	N.Z. Govt. Cert.	25.4.11	
341/4	Young Harrington	J. P. Arandt	Bacchus Marsh	28.8.11	E.A.K.
331/4	Young Hopetoun	Fehring and Sons	Pyramid	24.8.11	E.A.K.
236/4	Young Officer	O. Bodey	Horsham	12.7.11	R.N.J.
377/4	Young Royal Stuart	A. J. Jessop	Maffra	14.9.11	R.N.J.
290/4	Young St. Albans	G. R. Goods	Minyip	10.8.11	E.A.K.
		THOROUGHBREDS.			
391/4	Beau Brocade	T. T. Mulder	Colac	15.9.11	E.A.K.
356/4	Harmattan	R. W. Storey	Euroa	1.9.11	R.G.
354/4	Kerrisdale	T. McKimmie	Seymour	1.9.11	E.A.K.
		LIGHTS.			
408/4	Almont's Pride	Jas. Downie	Lang Lang	22.9.11	G.S.B.
291/4	Almont S.	F. W. Shickerling	Warracknabeal	11.8.11	E.A.K.
383/4	Almont 2nd	G. Bryant	Ballarat	16.9.11	R.G.
301/4	Arrel	Jno. Dempster	Heathcote	14.8.11	R.N.J.
345/4	Ashville Boy	Thos. Moore	Shepparton	25.8.11	R.G.
238/4	Black Tracker	Gifford and Sons	Horsham	11.7.11	E.A.K.
298/4	Clarida	O'Donnell Bros.	Birchip	9.8.11	R.G.
305/4	Decorator	T. Jennings	Inglewood	17.8.11	R.N.J.
292/4	Gerald Clive	P. Seclander	Warracknabeal	11.8.11	E.A.K.
395/4	Glynne	Geo. Collis	Yarram	18.9.11	R.N.J.
378/4	Honest Laddie	Grant Bros.	Kyneton	12.9.11	R.G.
323/4	Howlet	A. Scott	Rochester	21.8.11	R.G.
385/4	Jack Huon	P. Donovan	Ballarat	16.9.11	R.G.
327/4	Joy Bells	M. Peacock	Kerang	22.8.11	E.A.K.
358/4	Kent Cleve	Jno. Devlin	Tatura	31.8.11	R.G.
308/4	King Osterley 2nd	Geo. Anderson	Geelong	17.8.11	G.S.B.
371/4	King Osterley	D. Taylor	Royal Show	4.9.11	G.S.B.
379/4	Kingspring	W. McDonald	Kyneton	12.9.11	R.G.
214/4	Lord McKinney	G. H. Dunlevey	Agricultural Offices	29.4.11	G.S.B.
363/4	Middy Huon	C. Baurchier	Numurkah	29.8.11	E.A.K.
293/4	Millionaire	J. Rossiter	Warracknabeal	11.8.11	E.A.K.

LIST OF TERMINABLE CERTIFICATED STALLIONS—*continued.*

Cert. No.	Name of Horse.	Owner.	Parade.	Date of Examination.	Officer.
		LIGHTS—*continued.*			
373/4	Oakwood ..	J. T. Folland	Royal Show	9.4.11	E.A.K.
256/4	Osterwynne	W. R. Smith	Horsham	12.7.11	R.N.J.
311/4	Owyhee Chief	Geo. Showell	Castlemaine	18.8.11	R.N.J.
277/4	Prince Douglas	Mrs. C. White	Agricultural Offices	5.8.11	G.S.B.
272/4	Prince Harold Boy	Love, Royle, and Thurgood	Agricultural Offices	15.7.11	G.S.B.
322/4	Reality Rex	S. O'Brien	Rochester	21.8.11	R.G.
367/4	Sir Hampden	J. H. Fraser	Numurkah	29.8.11	E.A.K.
332/4	Sports Huon	J. T. Ovens	Kyabram	22.8.11	R.G.
276/4	Verm McKinney	M. Mulligan	Bendigo	2.8.11	R.G.
255/4	Victor Direct	J. Schrieber	City Horse Bazaar	24.7.11	W.J.C.
397/4	Weeho ..	Jos. Park	Tallangatta	19.9.11	E.A.K.
296/4	Young Almont B. ..	J. Mitchell	Warracknabeal	11.8.11	E.A.K.
297/4	Young Harold	E. Wyatt	Warracknabeal	11.8.11	E.A.K.
		PONIES.			
312/4	Billie Barlow	Wm. Donaldson	Charlton	17.8.11	R.G.
414/4	Bonnie Argyle	Wm. Connors	Myrtleford	11.10.11	G.S.B.
389/4	Brigham's Last	Wm. Rodgers	Warrnambool	14.9.11	E.A.K.
398/4	Chamberlain	A. L. Hardie	Warragul	19.9.11	G.S.B.
407/4	Dandy O'More	L. Tatterson	Dandenong	21.9.11	R.N.J.
307/4	General Gordon	H. Dunn	Geelong	17.8.11	G.S.B.
355/4	Little Tam	L. Moody	Seymour	1.9.11	E.A.K.
401/4	Masher Boy	T. Canty	Leongatha	20.9.11	R.N.J.
374/4	Prince Taff	Mrs. B. F. Sandford	Royal Show	4.9.11	E.A.K.
322/4	Reality Rex	S. O'Brien	Rochester	21.8.11	R.G.
295/4	Rob Roy 2nd	W. T. Clarke	Warracknabeal	11.8.11	E.A.K.
318/4	Rysharold Hambletonian	W. B. Metherall and Son	Agricultural Offices	19.8.11	G.S.B.
405/4	Starlight ..	J. M. Brown	Korumburra	20.9.11	R.G.
381/4	Tichbourne	A. E. Godden	Kyneton	12.9.11	R.G.
334/4	The Hero ..	D. G. Tomkins	Coleraine	22.8.11	R.N.J.
375/4	Wonderful	W. H. D. McNabb	Royal Show	4.9.11	G.S.B.
339/4	Young Brigham	R. W. Nichol	Clunes ..	25.8.11	G.S.B.

(Three-year-old Certificates expiring 30th June, 1912.)

DRAUGHTS.

Cert. No.	Name of Horse.	Owner.	Parade.	Date of Examination.	Officer.
598/3	Abbot McArthur	J. Lawson	N.Z. Govt. Cert. ..	5.7.11	..
536/4	Abbot's Fancy	A. Robertson	Melbourne (Special)	5.7.11	R.G.
535/3	Abbotsford	Colvin Bros.	Melbourne (Special)	5.7.11	G.S.B.
669/3	Abbot Smith	White Bros.	N.Z Govt. Cert. ..	5.5.11	..
599/3	Abbot's Pride	Jos. Johnson	N.Z. Govt. Cert. ..	31.5.11	..
735/3	Abbot's Pride	W. Haebich	Tungamah	29.8.11	R.G.
587/3	Acorn	W. Bodey	Horsham	12.7.11	E.A.K.
728/3	Admiral's Champion	H. Cronk	Wangaratta	28.8.11	R.G.
790/3	Admiral Sperry	Jno. E. Coulthard	Yarram	18.9.11	R.N.J.
468/3	Albion	Oakes Bros.	Nathalia (Special)	31.3.11	G.S.B.
755/3	Aldebaron..	Abbot Bros.	Royal Show	4.9.11	E.A.K.
725/3	Alexander's Best	A. Robertson	Agricultural Offices	26.8.11	R.N.J.
537/3	Alexander's Own	A. Robertson	Melbourne (Special)	5.7.11	G.S.B.
736/3	Attraction	J. J. Mackay	Tungamah	29.8.11	R.G.
740/3	Attraction's Champion	W. Morley	Rutherglen	30.8.11	R.G.
782/3	Australia's Favourite	M. Mahoney	Terang ..	11.9.11	E.A.K.
646/3	Avonmore..	J. Harper	City Horse Bazaar	25.7.11	E.A.K.
665/3	Ayrshire ..	Jesse Stokes	N.Z. Govt. Cert. ..	5.5.11	..
772/3	Balfour's Pride	Jas. Anderson	Maffra ..	14.9.11	R.N.J.
730/3	Balmoral ..	E. S. Green and Son	Shepparton	25.8.11	R.G.
471/4	Baron Argyle	W. Hegarty	Melbourne (Special)	15.5.11	G.S.B.
780/3	Baron Bold 2nd	N. W. Quick	Ballarat	16.9.11	R.G.
640/3	Baron Erskine	E. Roberts	City Horse Bazaar	24.7.11	R.G.
804/3	Baron Fenwick	Jno. H. Sargood	Raywood (Special)	25.10.11	R.G.
472/3	Baron Glazebrook	Mitchell and O'Brien	Melbourne (Special)	15.5.11	G.S.B.
664/3	Baron Gleniffer	S. J. Lynn	N.Z. Govt. Cert.	28.4.11	..
538/3	Baron Grant	Jas. Patrick	Melbourne (Special)	5.7.11	R.G.
473/3	Baron Humber	Mitchell and O'Brien	Melbourne (Special)	15.5.11	G.S.B.

LIST OF TERMINABLE CERTIFICATED STALLIONS—*continued.*

Cert. No.	Name of Horse.	Owner.	Parade.	Date of Examination.	Officer.
		DRAUGHTS—*continued.*			
568/3	Baron Milton	A. Slocum	Newmarket	30.6.11	R.G.
509/3	Barons Prince	Ingram Bros.	Digger's Rest	22.5.11	R.G.
474/3	Baron Stuart	A. Robertson	Melbourne (Special)	15.5.11	G.S.B.
747/3	Baron Woodlea	Wm. Williams	Numurkah	29.8.11	E.A.K.
783/3	Barrabool	Jas. Axford	Terang	11.9.11	E.A.K.
775/3	Bay Knight	Jas. McRae	Kyneton	12.9.11	R.G.
464/3	Bay Star ..	J. and M. J. Egan	Agricultural Offices	3.4.11	E.A.K.
671/3	Belted Ben	A. Giddings	Sea Lake	19.7.11	G.S.B.
693/3	Ben Hampton	W. F. Schickerling	Warracknabeal	11.8.11	E.A.K.
622/3	Ben Lomond	G. Carey	City Horse Bazaar	24.7.11	R.G.
539/3	Bit of Fashion	W. Kilpatrick	Melbourne (Special)	5.7.11	G.S.B.
567/3	Black Lion	Graham Bros.	Newmarket	30.6.11	R.G.
753/3	Black Mac	J. T. Peterson	Melbourne (Special)	6.9.11	E.A.K.
600/3	Black Points	J. R. Henry	N.Z. Govt. Cert. ..	31.5.11	..
721/3	Blue Royal	Balkin and Gerdts	Hamilton	24.8.11	R.N.J.
675/3	Bold Baron	H. Jackman	Bendigo	2.8.11	R.G.
617/3	Bold McGregor	J. P. Belleville	Newmarket	22.7.11	E.A.K.
732/3	Bonaparte	—. McGregor	Pakenham (Special)	29.8.11	R.N.J.
581/3	Bonnie Boy	Tucker Bros.	Horsham	12.7.11	R.N.J.
475/3	Bonnie Charlie	A. Robertson	Melbourne (Special)	15.5.11	G.S.B.
545/3	Bonny Glen	H. Hill	N.Z. Govt. Cert. ..	8.6.11	..
639/3	Border Lad	W. Foster and Son	City Horse Bazaar	24.7.11	W.J.C.
532/3	Boro' Albert Victor..	R. N. Scott	English Exam. ..	20.4.11	..
533/3	Boro' Candidate	Jno. Widdis	English Exam. ..	20.4.11	..
534/3	Boro' Marmion	Arthur Hart	English Exam. ..	20.4.11	..
528/3	Boro' Sportsman	J. P. Belleville	English Exam. ..	20.4.11	..
642/3	Boy Model	J. Mills	City Horse Bazaar	25.7.11	R.N.J.
578/3	Bramhope Paladin ..	F. Hickman	Horsham	11.7.11	R.N.J.
508/3	Braw Scot	Alex. Sands	Digger's Rest	22.5.11	R.G.
808/3	Bridge Hill King	M. J. Caffrey	English Exam. ..	20.10.11	..
524/3	Brilliant Lad	Mitchell and O'Brien	Agricultural Offices	10.6.11	E.A.K.
540/3	Britain's Flag	Mitchell and O'Brien	Melbourne (Special)	5.7.11	G.S.B.
737/3	British Heather	S. H. Wilson	Tungamah	29.8.11	R.G.
476/3	British Pride	Mitchell and O'Brien	Melbourne (Special)	15.5.11	E.A.K.
738/3	Captain Grigg	J. Blackwood	Yarrawonga	29.8.11	R.G.
733/3	Carmichael	Jno. Gooden	Warrnambool (Special)	29.8.11	R.N.J.
758/3	Carolyn	Jno. Wm. Dean	Royal Show	4.9.11	R.N.J.
601/3	Carson's Fancy	Jas. Lawson	N.Z. Govt. Cert. ..	31.5.11	..
478/3	Champion Again	A. Robertson	Melbourne (Special)	15.5.11	G.S.B.
511/3	Chatsworth Warrior	J. Caffrey	English Exam. ..	3.3.11	..
627/3	Clan McArthur	E. Roberts	City Horse Bazaar	24.7.11	R.G.
479/3	Clydesdale Bill	Hermann Schneider	Melbourne (Special)	15.5.11	G.S.B.
723/3	Clydesdale Prince	E. and A. Breen	Kyabram	22.8.11	R.G.
791/3	Clydesdale Prince	R. C. Buchanan	Tallangatta	19.9.11	E.A.K.
647/3	Colonel Keith	A. J. Williams	City Horse Bazaar	25.7.11	E.A.K.
756/3	Comet ..	Brock Bros.	Royal Show	4.9.11	E.A.K.
580/3	Coronation	G. Oxley	Horsham	12.7.11	R.N.J.
541/3	Cranbourne Stewart	W. Abram	Melbourne (Special)	5.7.11	R.G.
574/3	Creslow Kingmaker	Geelong Harbor Trust	English Exam. ..	11.4.11	..
480/3	Crown Tenant	W. Langley	Melbourne (Special)	15.5.11	G.S.B.
796/3	Darnley's Pride of Rythesdale	Syme Bros.	Dandenong	21.9.11	R.N.J.
624/3	Defender ..	Hooper Bros.	City Horse Bazaar	25.7.11	R.G.
542/3	Derby Royal	Jno. Grant	Melbourne (Special)	5.7.11	R.G.
481/3	Devondale Chief	A. Robertson	Melbourne (Special)	15.5.11	G.S.B.
666/3	Diamond Crest	Walter and Agar	N.Z. Govt. Cert. ..	5.5.11	..
482/3	Diamond King	A. Robertson	Melbourne (Special)	15.5.11	G.S.B.
517/3	Dividend ..	Mitchell and O'Brien	Melbourne (Special)	15.5.11	E.A.K.
748/3	Dreadnought	J. C. Rockliffe	Numurkah	29.8.11	E.A.K.
722/3	Drummer's Style	Neil Anderson	Murchison	24.8.11	R.G.
569/3	Drummond King	R. C. Pearse	Newmarket	30.6.11	R.G.
461/3	Duncraig Colt	Alex. Robertson	Agricultural Offices	1.4.11	E.A.K.
602/3	Dunmore ..	Jas. Lawson	N.Z. Govt. Cert. ..	31.5.11	..
573/3	Dunsby Menestral 3rd	Evan Jones	English Exam. ..	11.4.11	..
809/3	Eaton Charmer	M. J. Caffrey	English Exam. ..	24.11.11	..

LIST OF TERMINABLE CERTIFICATED STALLIONS—*continued.*

Cert. No.	Name of Horse.	Owner.	Parade.	Date of Examination.	Officer.
		DRAUGHTS—*continued.*			
591/3	Earl Erskine	G. F. Meyers	N.Z. Govt. Cert.	10.4.11	..
663/3	Erskine Yet	H. Graham	N.Z. Govt. Cert.	6.5.11	..
514/3	Earl of Darnley	W. R. Smith	Agricultural Offices	27.5.11	G.S.B.
759/3	Fairfield	Glenn Bros.	Royal Show	4.9.11	G.S.B.
712/3	First Choice	R. H. Lanyon	Boort	15.8.11	R.G.
777/3	Fitz Lion	Mrs. Roberts	Kyneton	12.9.11	R.G.
582/3	Flashlight	Graham Bros.	Horsham	12.7.11	R.N.J.
694/3	Flashwood's Model	Chas. Mason	Warracknabeal	11.8.11	E.A.K.
543/3	Forest King	A. Chrystal	Melbourne (Special)	5.7.11	R.G.
687/3	Fyvie Blacon	R. C. Hannah	Donald	8.8.11	R.G.
717/3	Gaer Conqueror	Jno. Archibald	Kyabram	22.8.11	R.G.
577/3	Gamekeeper	Hermann Hill	Horsham	11.7.11	R.N.J.
629/3	Gay Gordon	J. Ferguson	City Horse Bazaar	24.7.11	R.G.
544/3	Gay Newton	Jas. Patrick	Melbourne (Special)	5.7.11	G.S.B.
762/3	General Mac	J. K. Marum	Royal Show	4.9.11	E.A.K.
786/3	Glen Donald	Alex. Gibson, jun.	Port Fairy	12.9.11	E.A.K.
631/3	Glenhope	T. Standing	City Horse Bazaar	24.7.11	R.G.
603/3	Glen Lyon	Jas. Lawson	N.Z. Govt. Cert.	31.5.11	..
483/3	Glen Lyon	A. Robertson	Melbourne (Special)	15.5.11	E.A.K.
739/3	Glenmuick	Jas. Clark	Yarrawonga	29.8.11	R.G.
661/3	Goldfinder	A. E. Freshney	N.Z. Govt. Cert.	6.5.11	..
670/3	Good Enough	Jno. Mills	N.Z. Govt. Cert.	8.4.11	..
606/3	Good Shepherd	D. McClure	City Horse Bazaar	22.7.11	R.N.J.
546/3	Halden Shepherd	D. McClure	Melbourne (Special)	5.7.11	G.S.B.
691/3	Halley's Comet	C. Ruowldt	Minyip	10.8.11	E.A.K.
727/3	Hampden Ben	H. Allen	Beulah	22.8.11	G.S.B.
462/3	Harry Herd	A. Colvin	Nathalia (Special)	31.3.11	G.S.B.
547/3	Harry Lauder	Jas. Patrick	Melbourne (Special)	5.7.11	G.S.B.
469/3	Hatfield's Pride	W. J. McKay	Agricultural Offices	13.5.11	E.A.K.
460/3	Heather Jock	Mitchell and O'Brien	Agricultural Offices	25.3.11	G.S.B.
649/3	Heather Lad	Geo. Stokes	City Horse Bazaar	25.7.11	R.G.
618/3	Hector Grant	L. Bagnell	City Horse Bazaar	22.7.11	R.G.
792/3	Hiawatha	A. L. Hamilton	Corryong	20.9.11	E.A.K.
570/3	Highland Fame	C. McMicking	Newmarket	30.6.11	R.G.
641/3	Highland Prince	F. Mentha	City Horse Bazaar	24.7.11	R.G.
484/3	His Excellency	Mitchell and O'Brien	Melbourne (Special)	15.5.11	E.A.K.
477/3	His Grace	Mitchell and O'Brien	Melbourne (Special)	15.5.11	G.S.B.
519/3	His Lordship	R. Jack and Son	Agricultural Offices	3.6.11	G.S.B.
492/3	His Majesty	H. J. Whittingham	Melbourne (Special)	15.5.11	E.A.K.
761/3	His Majesty	E. J. Rickey	Royal Show	4.9.11	R.N.J.
485/3	Ian Moore	Mitchell and O'Brien	Melbourne (Special)	15.5.11	E.A.K.
635/3	Innismore	P. F. D'Arcy	City Horse Bazaar	24.7.11	R.G.
614/3	Jack's the Lad	H. Hart	Newmarket	22.7.11	E.A.K.
763/3	Kelm's Best	L. W. Andrews	Royal Show	4.9.11	R.N.J.
531/3	Kelvin's Fancy	A. H. Reed	Newmarket (Special)	19.6.11	R.G.
548/3	Kia Ora	Jno. Grant	Melbourne (Special)	5.7.11	R.G.
576/3	Kingfisher	R. P. Young	Horsham	11.7.11	R.N.J.
778/3	Kingston	Henebery and Hawkins	Maffra	14.9.11	R.N.J.
584/3	Kinloch Again	W. T. Bodey	Horsham	12.7.11	E.A.K.
486/3	Knight Commander	A. Robertson	Melbourne (Special)	15.5.11	E.A.K.
487/3	Knight of the Garter	A. and A. Kennedy	Melbourne (Special)	15.5.11	G.S.B.
729/3	King George	G. Docker	Wangaratta	28.8.11	R.G.
588/3	King Pippin 2nd	A. and J. H. Young	Horsham	12.7.11	E.A.K.
549/3	Laird of Glengarry	A. Chrystal	Melbourne (Special)	5.7.11	G.S.B.
575/3	Laird of Glenkenich	Geo. Gill	N.Z. Govt. Cert.	25.5.11	..
781/3	Landlord	D. McCallum	Ballarat	16.9.11	R.G.
489/3	Lautevar	A. Robertson	Melbourne (Special)	15.5.11	E.A.K.
470/3	Llynely's First Lord	J. Caffrey	English Exam.	3.3.11	..
490/3	Lock Allen	T. Smith	Melbourne (Special)	15.5.11	E.A.K.
579/3	Longford's Fashion	Jas. Gildea	Horsham	11.7.11	R.N.J.
512/3	Lymm Champion 2nd	J. Caffrey	English Exam.	3.3.11	..
513/3	Lymm Forest Boy	J. Caffrey	English Exam.	3.3.11	..
510/3	Lymm Raider	J. Caffrey	English Exam.	3.3.11	..
764/3	Lord Ashmore	R. A. Ash	Royal Show	4.9.11	E.A.K.
793/3	Lord Donald	A. Harris	Corryong	20.9.11	E.A.K.
529/3	Lord Garthland	J. R. Henry	Newmarket (Special)	19.6.11	R.G.

LIST OF TERMINABLE CERTIFICATED STALLIONS—*continued.*

Cert. No.	Name of Horse.	Owner.	Parâde.	Date of Examination.	Officer.

DRAUGHTS—*continued.*

Cert. No.	Name of Horse.	Owner.	Parâde.	Date of Examination.	Officer.
491/3	Lord Hampden	Pat. Mangan	Melbourne (Special)	15.5.11	G.S.B.
653/3	Lord Islington	R. Hornbuckle	N.Z. Govt. Cert.	..	..
607/3	Lord Lindsay	Caffrey and Murphy	City Horse Bazaar	22.7.11	R.G.
571/3	Lord Mitchell	H. McLaren	Newmarket	30.6.11	R.G.
525/3	Lord Roseberry	Mitchell and O'Brien	Agricultural Offices	10.6.11	E.A.K.
649/3	McGregor ..	J. Lawson	City Horse Bazaar	25.7.11	E.A.K.
608/3	McKenzie's Pride	A. Lawrie	City Horse Bazaar	22.7.11	R.G.
700/3	Maironga Prince	Wm. Blair	Watchem	10.8.11	R.G.
768/3	Major's Pride	Stuckey Bros.	Traralgon	13.9.11	R.N.J.
493/3	Marksman	D. F. Hourigan	Melbourne (Special)	15.5.11	G.S.B.
494/3	Mark Ward	J. Schinnick	Melbourne (Special)	15.5.11	E.A.K.
707/3	Marshall ..	Jno. Stafford	Geelong..	17.8.11	G.S.B.
672/3	Mataura ..	W. Widdis	N.Z. Govt. Cert.	23.5.11	..
495/3	Merry Maker	Mitchell and O'Brien	Melbourne (Special)	15.5.11	E.A.K.
749/3	Merton's Pride	H. Rolls	Numurkah	29.8.11	E.A.K.
658/3	Model Prince	Jno. Gifford	N.Z. Govt. Cert.	23.5.11	..
526/3	Monarch ..	Mitchell and O'Brien	Agricultural Offices	10.6.11	E.A.K.
636/3	Moravian ..	Hugh Boyd	City Horse Bazaar	24.7.11	R.N.J.
702/3	Murray King	C. Milson	Cobram	14.8.11	G.S.B.
465/3	Neil Marshall	T. Coogan	Agricultural Offices	8.4.11	G.S.B.
551/3	Nelson Lyon 2nd	Jno. Grant	Melbourne (Special)	5.7.11	G.S.B.
696/3	Neotsfield Rufus	Jno. Munro	N.S.W. Exam.	23.6.11	..
552/3	Netherhall	Jas. Patrick	Melbourne (Special)	5.7.11	G.S.B.
637/3	Never Despair	Thos. Kelly	City Horse Bazaar	24.7.11	R.N.J.
554/3	Newton Moore	Jas. Patrick	Melbourne (Special)	5.7.11	R.G.
656/3	Newton's Best	J. J. McCarron	N.Z. Govt. Cert.	23.5.11	..
520/3	Nobleman	Mitchell and O'Brien	Agricultural Offices	3.6.11	G.S.B
555/3	Perfection	Jas. Patrick	Melbourne (Special)	5.7.11	R.G.
609/3	Perfect Motion	Peter Byrne	City Horse Bazaar	22.7.11	R.G.
683/3	Powlett ..	Hocking Bros.	Bendigo	2.8.11	R.G.
515/3	Premier ..	Geo. Smith	Rosedale (Special)	26.5.11	W.J.C.
468/3	Premier Grey	Mitchell and O'Brien	Agricultural Offices	22.4.11	G.S.B.
596/3	Premier Lauder	P. Kelleher	N.Z. Govt. Cert.	9.6.11	..
673/3	Premier McNab	Jno. Burns	N.Z. Govt. Cert.	9.6.11	..
662/3	Premier Millar	C. J. Coles	N.Z. Govt. Cert.	9.6.11	..
674/3	Premier Montgomery of Willowbank	A. Lummins	N.Z. Govt. Cert.	9.6.11	..
690/3	Purves ..	F. L. McIntosh	Jeparit ..	9.8.11	E.A.K.
556/3	Pride of Albury	A. Chrystal	Melbourne (Special)	5.7.11	R.G.
676/3	Pride of Clifton	W. T. Caldwell	N.Z. Govt. Cert.	23.5.11	..
677/3	Pride of Cray	A. E. Cockram	N.Z. Govt. Cert.	23.5.11	..
557/3	Prince Albert	A. Chrystal	Melbourne (Special)	5.7.11	R.G.
750/3	Prince Cedric	Joseph Jeffrey	Numurkah	29.8.11	E.A.K.
724/3	Prince Edwin	Jas. Dwyer	Rushworth	24.8.11	R.G.
648/3	Prince Imperial	Sir S. McCaughey	City Horse Bazaar	25.7.11	E.A.K.
779/3	Prince Imperial	J. Mansfield	Kyneton	12.9.11	R.G.
496/3	Prince Thornley	C. McFarlane	Melbourne (Special)	15.5.11	G.S.B.
521/3	Quality ..	Mitchell and O'Brien	Agricultural Offices	3.6.11	G.S.B.
751/3	Quality Prince	J. McMurray	Numurkah	29.8.11	E.A.K.
704/3	Rantin Robin	Jas. Galloway	Maryborough	16.8.11	R.N.J.
610/3	Referendum	J. F. Farrer	City Horse Bazaar	22.7.11	R.G.
466/3	Right Royal	Caffrey and Murphy	Melbourne (Special)	10.4.11	E.A.K.
731/3	Robbin ..	J. R. W. Powles	Shepparton	25.8.11	R.G.
621/3	Roseneath Clan	W. G. Wilkinson	City Horse Bazaar	24.7.11	R.G.
588/3	Russell Yet 2nd	Graham Bros.	Horsham	12.7.11	E.A.K.
553/3	Royal Barclay	A. Robertson	Melbourne (Special)	5.7.11	G.S.B.
497/3	Royal Ben	Mitchell and O'Brien	Melbourne (Special)	15.5.11	G.S.B.
795/3	Royal Carlyle	R. H. Biggar	Korumburra	20.9.11	R.G.
716/3	Royal Champion	W. Hercus	Pyramid	24.8.11	E.A.K.
572/3	Royal Edward	Graham Bros.	Newmarket	30.6.11	R.G.
498/3	Royal Edward	Mitchell and O'Brien	Melbourne (Special)	15.5.11	G.S.B.
788/3	Royal Gartley	Sydney Knight	Warrnambool	14.9.11	E.A.K.

LIST OF TERMINABLE CERTIFICATED STALLIONS—*continued.*

Cert. No.	Name of Horse.	Owner.	Parade.	Date of Examination.	Officer.
			DRAUGHTS—*continued.*		
597/3	Royal Gordon	Philip Bolte	N.Z. Govt. Cert.	30.5.11	..
558/3	Royal Gordon	E. S. Bailliere	Melbourne (Special)	5.7.11	G.S.B.
499/3	Royal Hurry	A. Robertson	Melbourne (Special)	15.5.11	E.A.K.
611/3	Royal Newton	A. G. Hildyard	City Horse Bazaar	22.7.11	R.G.
550/3	Royal Oak	J. D. Mitchell	Agricultural Offices	8.7.11	G.S.B.
650/3	Royal Palmer	McNabb Bros.	Newmarket	24.7.11	E.A.K.
566/3	Royal Review	J. D. Mitchell	Agricultural Offices	8.7.11	G.S.B.
500/3	Royal Review	A. Robertson	Melbourne (Special)	15.5.11	G.S.B.
744/3	Royal Robin	P. and R. Ferrari	Nathalia	30.8.11	E.A.K.
626/3	Royal Saxon	E. Roberts	City Horse Bazaar	24.7.11	R.G.
657/3	Royal Signal	P. Rogers	N.Z. Govt. Cert.	6.5.11	..
518/3	Royalty	Mitchell and O'Brien	Melbourne (Special)	15.5.11	G.S.B.
501/3	Royal Willie	Allan Boyd	Melbourne (Special)	15.5.11	E.A.K.
645/3	Sandy McKenzie	Mitchell and O'Brien	City Horse Bazaar	25.7.11	R.N.J.
530/3	Saxon Hall	J. J. Murphy	Newmarket (Special)	19.6.11	R G.
810/3	Scarcliffe Memento	M. J. Caffrey	English Exam.	20.10.11	..
742/3	Scottish Chief	W. Ford	Dookie	31.8.11	E.A.K.
585/3	Scottish Lad	A. Hoff	Horsham	12.7.11	R.N.J.
638/3	Scottish Premier	Wm. Walter	City Horse Bazaar	24.7.11	R.N.J.
805/3	Scottish Pride	A. J. Tozer	Blackwood Forest (Special)	3.11.11	R.G.
745/3	Shepherd Boy	J. H. Tuckett	Nathalia	30.8.11	E.A.K.
741/3	Shepherd Charlie	E. P. Bedwell	Tatura	31.8.11	R.G.
619/3	Shepherd Signal	J. O'Brien	N.Z. Govt. Cert.	21.4.11	..
743/3	Shepherd's Pride	W. Church	Dookie	31.8.11	E.A.K.
746/3	Shepherd's Style	Jas. Ross	Nathalia	30.8.11	E.A.K.
811/3	Sherwood Royal Tom	M. J. Caffrey	English Exam.	20.10.11	..
604/3	Silver King	James Lawson	N.Z. Govt. Cert.	31.5.11	..
800/3	Son of Champion	Turner Bros.	Whittlesea	22.9.11	R.N.J.
697/3	Southern Star	H. Green	Birchip	9.8.11	R.G.
713/3	Spanish King	R. Heywood	Kerang	23.8.11	E.A.K.
559/3	St. Ambrose	Jas. Patrick	Melbourne (Special)	5.7.11	R.G.
516/3	Statesman	N. C. Teychenne	Melbourne (Special)	15.5.11	E.A.K.
634/3	Sir Edwin	R. H. Landale	City Horse Bazaar	24.7.11	R.N.J.
502/3	Sir James	P. Mangan	Melbourne (Special)	15.5.11	E.A.K.
560/3	Sir John Small	A. Chrystal	Melbourne (Special)	5.7.11	G.S.B.
678/3	Sir Norman Ivanhoe	H. J. Bodey	N.Z. Govt. Cert.	20.6.11	..
705/3	Sir Regulus	—. Howe	Inglewood	17.8.11	R.N.J.
612/3	Sir Robin	C. H. McCulloch	City Horse Bazaar	22.7.11	R.N.J.
660/3	Sir Thomas	Caffrey and Murphy	N.Z. Govt. Cert.	6.6.11	..
561/3	Sir Walter Royal Bush	Jno. Grant.	Melbourne (Special)	5.7.11	R G.
704/3	Sir Rantin Robin	Jas. Galloway	Maryborough	16.8.11	R.N.J.
586/3	Sir Walter Scott	S. H. Bleakley	Horsham	12.7.11	E.A.K.
659/3	Sir William	Wm. McClelland	Lara (Special)	29.7.11	G.S.B.
714/3	Tasman	W. G. Hastie	Kerang	23.8.11	E.A.K.
632/3	Time o'Day	Anson Bros.	City Horse Bazaar	24.7.11	R.G.
503/3	Top Sail	Olsen and Hammond	Melbourne (Special)	15.5.11	G.S.B.
504/3	The Baron	P. Mangan	Melbourne (Special)	15.5.11	G.S.B.
505/3	The Bruce	Mitchell and O'Brien	Melbourne (Special)	15.5.11	G.S.B.
562/3	The Chief	Jas. Patrick	Melbourne (Special)	5.7.11	G.S.B.
563/3	The Earl	Mitchell and O'Brien	Melbourne (Special)	5.7.11	G.S.B.
652/3	The Gift	T. Maddy	Newmarket	24.7.11	E.A.K.
488/3	The Laird of Craigieburn	P. Mangan	Melbourne (Special)	15.5.11	G.S.B.
703/3	The Liberal	A. Borland	Dunolly	15.8.11	R.N.J.
620/3	The McDonald	Jas. Hamilton	City Horse Bazaar	24.7.11	R.G.
506/3	The Premier	T. Haley, jun.	Melbourne (Special)	15.5.11	E.A.K.
613/3	The Scout	W. J. White	City Horse Bazaar	22.7.11	R G.
630/3	The Squatter	J. H. Cornfoot	City Horse Bazaar	24.7.11	R.G.
522/3	The Star	Jno. McLeod	Agricultural Offices	3.6.11	G.S.B.
523/3	The Stockman	Walter and Agar	Agricultural Offices	3.6.11	G.S.B.
507/3	The Success	Mitchell and O'Brien	Melbourne (Special)	15.5.11	G.S.B.

LIST OF TERMINABLE CERTIFICATED STALLIONS—*continued.*

Cert. No.	Name of Horse.	Owner.	Parade.	Date of Examination.	Officer.
		DRAUGHTS—*continued.*			
527/3	The Thistle ..	Mitchell and O'Brien	Agricultural Offices	10.6.11	E.A.K.
615/3	The Vet.	C. K. Peel ..	Newmarket ..	22.7.11	E.A.K.
679/3	Undaunted Knight ..	Hay and Thonemann	N.Z. Govt. Cert. ..	23.5.11	..
593/3	Union Jack ..	G. W. Pickford ..	Horsham ..	12.7.11	E.A.K.
564/3	Ury Park ..	Jno. Rousch ..	Melbourne (Special)	5.7.11	G.S.B.
651/3	Wallace ..	H. J. Nixon ..	Newmarket ..	24.7.11	E.A.K.
605/3	Wallace 2nd ..	Jas. Lawson ..	N.Z. Govt. Cert. ..	31.5.11	..
668/3	Wee Laddie ..	Andrew M. Johnston	Sale (Special) ..	20.7.11	R.N.J.
643/3	Welcome Boy ..	J. Mills ..	City Horse Bazaar	25.7.11	R.N.J.
565/3	Woodlands ..	Jas. Patrick ..	Melbourne (Special)	5.7.11	R.G.
628/3	Wrangler ..	P. S. Oppenheim..	City Horse Bazaar	24.7.11	R.N.J.
784/3	Young Admiral ..	D. H. James ..	Terang	11.9.11	E.A.K.
698/3	Young Ben ..	King Bros. ..	Birchip	9.8.11	R.G.
635/3	Young Clyde ..	O. G. Richner ..	City Horse Bazaar	26.7.11	E.A.K.
710/3	Young Coronation ..	W. J. Bennett ..	Quambatook ..	15.8.11	R.G.
699/3	Young Kelmscott ..	Thos. Bellett ..	Watchem ..	10.8.11	R.G.
715/3	Young King ..	E. G. Denyer ..	Kerang ..	23.8.11	E.A.K.
692/3	Young Kinloch ..	Jno. Maher ..	Minyip ..	10.8.11	E.A.K.
594/3	Young Laird of Lanark	W. Johns ..	Horsham ..	12.7.11	E.A.K.
633/3	Young Timekeeper ..	Anderson Bros. ..	City Horse Bazaar	24.7.11	R.G.
		THOROUGHBREDS.			
802/3	Brown Peer ..	Geo. Nixon ..	Orbost	3.10.11	R.N.J.
807/3	The Bachelor ..	J. Bird ..	Ballarat Show ..	16.11.11	R.G.
467/3	Warrough ..	T. McKimmis ..	Melbourne (Special)	10.4.11	E.A.K.
		LIGHT HORSES.			
686/3	Abbey ..	Harricks Bros. ..	Ararat	8.8.11	G.S.B.
754/3	Admiral Sperry ..	E. Batson ..	Royal Show ..	4.9.11	R.N.J.
684/3	Bonny McKinney ..	R. Matchett ..	Bendigo ..	2.8.11	R.G.
803/3	Direction ..	R. R. Corbould ..	Mildura ..	5.10.11	G.S.B.
680/3	First Voyage ..	W. Greaves ..	Bendigo ..	2.8.11	R.G.
760/3	Game Boy ..	E. Batson ..	Royal Show ..	4.9.11	R.N.J.
681/3	Harold Direct ..	T. Cawsey ..	Bendigo ..	2.8.11	R.G.
706/3	Highland Cleve ..	T. Larcombe ..	Geelong ..	17.8.11	G.S.B.
688/3	Jack Christian ..	R. C. Hannah ..	Donald ..	8.8.11	R.G.
806/3	King ..	C. Bartlett ..	Agricultural Offices	4.11.11	G.S.B.
789/3	Lord Lincoln ..	Geo. Trigg ..	Colac	15.9.11	E.A.K.
718/3	Lord Lyndsey ..	J. T. Ovens ..	Ayabram ..	22.8.11	R.G.
682/3	Oakwood King ..	R. Matchett ..	Bendigo ..	2.8.11	R.G.
799/3	Odd Patch ..	G. A. Finlay ..	Lang Lang ..	22.9.11	G.S.B.
589/3	Osterly Grange ..	O. Maroske ..	Horsham ..	13.7.11	R.N.J.
778/3	Preston Junior ..	McLure and Sons..	Kyneton ..	12.9.11	R.G.
726/3	Prince Harold ..	C. Darley ..	Hopetoun ..	23.8.11	G.S.B.
701/3	Quickshot ..	J. Jackman ..	Balmoral ..	11.8.11	R.N.J.
769/3	Silver Bells ..	W. Widdis ..	Traralgon ..	13.9.11	R.N.J.
695/3	Sir Carlaw ..	J. Bunge ..	Warracknabeal ..	11.8.11	E.A.K.
685/3	Sir Hambletonian ..	A. J. Mitchell ..	Agricultural Offices	5.8.11	E.A.K.
752/3	Triport ..	Jno. Shinnick ..	Numurkah ..	29.8.11	E.A.K.
767/3	Walter Bell Boy ..	Alf. West ..	Royal Show ..	4.9.11	R.N.J.
734/3	Yarpeet ..	J. Fisher ..	Hopetoun ..	23.8.11	G.S.B.
		PONIES.			
785/3	Advance ..	L. Harper ..	Port Fairy ..	12.9.11	E.A.K.
720/3	Bantam ..	Brown Bros. ..	Hamilton ..	24.8.11	R.N.J.
776/3	Black Osterley ..	H. Morris ..	Kyneton ..	12.9.11	R.G.
787/3	Bobs ..	W. H. Podger ..	Camperdown ..	13.9.11	E.A.K.
757/3	Coronation ..	Jno. Ellis ..	Royal Show ..	4.9.11	R.N.J.
689/3	Cutty Sark ..	J. Oliver ..	Jeparit	9.8.11	E.A.K.
794/3	Dandy Boy ..	Grieves Bros. ..	Leongatha ..	20.9.11	R.N.J.
625/3	Dandy Premier ..	J. Meheron ..	City Horse Bazaar	25.7.11	R.G.
711/3	Little Wonder 2nd ..	H. Burness ..	Benalla ..	18.8.11	G.S.B.
719/3	Lord Lonsdale ..	W. Coe ..	Coleraine ..	22.8.11	R.N.J.
765/3	Nimble Boy ..	R. Ridley ..	Royal Show ..	4.9.11	E.A.K.
766/3	Prince Leo 3rd ..	J. R. Brien ..	Royal Show ..	4.9.11	E.A.K.

LIST OF TERMINABLE CERTIFICATED STALLIONS—*continued.*

Cert. No.	Name of Horse.	Owner.	Parade.	Date of Examination.	Officer.
		PONIES—*continued.*			
798/3	Robin	R. Masters ..	Dandenong ..	21.9.11	N.J.
797/3	Robin	L. Beazley ..	Dandenong ..	21.9.11	N.J.
771/3	Roy	C. F. Jenkins ..	Bairnsdale ..	13.9.11	N.J.
708/3	Satan	Wm. Day ..	Geelong ..	17.8.11	S.B.
774/3	Wee MacGregor ..	W. S. McCole ..	Maffra	14.9.11	R.N.J.
812/3	What's Wanted 3rd	Miss S. L. Robinson	Agricultural Offices (Special)	23.3.12	B.N.J.
709/3	Young Ballygauley	C. Anderson ..	Geelong ..	17.8.11	G.S.B.

(Two-year-old Certificates expiring 30th June, 1912.)
DRAUGHTS.

Cert. No.	Name of Horse.	Owner.	Parade.	Date of Examination.	Officer.
123/2	Admiral Gun ..	McNabb Bros. ..	Newmarket ..	24.7.11	E.A.K.
127/2	Altona	G. H. Lister ..	Kyabram ..	26.7.11	G.S.B.
146/2	Baron Again ..	R. Ralston ..	Euroa	1.9.11	R.G.
136/2	Blenheim ..	C. F. Menzel ..	Hamilton ..	24.8.11	R.N.J.
122/2	Bonnie Carlyle ..	H. McCue ..	City Horse Bazaar	25.7.11	G.S.B.
128/2	Chilo	A. Ross ..	City Horse Bazaar	26.7.11	G.S.B.
147/2	Cock of the North ..	L. McLeod ..	Tatura	31.8.11	R.G.
140/2	Coronation ..	C. Marshman ..	Beulah	22.8.11	G.S.B.
130/2	Defender's Pride ..	Henry Bunge ..	Minyip	10.8.11	E.A.K.
116/2	Don McDonald ..	F. Mentha ..	Horsham ..	11.7.11	R.N.J.
117/2	Dunmore's Pride ..	A. and J. H. Young	Horsham ..	11.7.11	R.N.J.
157/2	Eaton Ensign ..	M. J. Caffrey ..	English Exam. ..	24.11.11	
115/2	Federal Scot ..	A. W. Andrews ..	Agricultural Offices (Special)	6.7.11	R.G.
134/2	Gold Link.. ..	C. Rhodes ..	Casterton ..	23.8.11	R.N.J.
118/2	Hampton Lad ..	A. and J. H. Young	Horsham ..	11.7.11	R.N.J.
133/2	Hero's Pride ..	W. Dowling ..	Kerang	23.8.11	E.A.K.
139/2	Keim's Champion ..	Wm. Luby ..	Ballan	26.8.11	E.A.K.
148/2	Legislator ..	C. W. Ludemann ..	Dookie	31 8.11	R.N.J.
150/2	Lord Ronald ..	E. J. Rickey ..	Royal Show ..	4.9.11	R.N.J.
158/2	Lymm Prime Minister	M. J. Caffrey ..	English Exam. ..	24.11.11	
144/2	Major Calbourne ..	Chas. Heal ..	Tungamah ..	29.8.11	R.G.
114/2	Masher	W. R. Smith ..	Agricultural Offices	27.5.11	G.S.B.
119/2	Merry Hampton ..	A. and J. H. Young	Horsham ..	11.7.11	R.N.J.
124/2	Morang Fashion ..	D. McKenzie ..	Newmarket ..	24.7.11	G.S.B.
126/2	Perfection ..	J. Poulton and Sons	City Horse Bazaar	26.7.11	R.N.J.
142/2	Pride	J. M. Phillips ..	Shepparton ..	25.8.11	R.G.
129/2	Prince Henry ..	A. Parish ..	City Horse Bazaar	26.7.11	G.S.B.
151/2	Prince of Albyn ..	P. O'Donnell ..	Kyneton ..	12.9.11	R.G.
152/2	Roseneath King ..	Jno. Jamieson ..	Yarram ..	18.9.11	R.N.J.
135/2	Royal Main ..	Stock Bros. ..	Casterton ..	23.8.11	R.N.J.
131/2	Scottie	H. Schmidt ..	Nhill	16.8.11	E.A.K.
121/2	Scottish Prince ..	Jesse Stokes ..	City Horse Bazaar	24.7.11	R.N.J.
138/2	Sir Donald ..	J. R. Jackson ..	Hamilton ..	24.8.11	R.N.J.
154/2	Sir Roger	J. Allison ..	Leongatha ..	20.9.11	R.N.J.
132/2	The Laird ..	F. C. Thomas ..	Nhill	16.8.11	E.A.K.
143/2	Upward	J. M Phillips ..	Shepparton ..	25.8.11	R.G.
153/2	Young St. Albans ..	P. Mason ..	Yarram ..	18.9.11	R.N.J.
120/2	Young Tatton ..	P. Byrne ..	City Horse Bazaar	22.7.11	R.N.J.

THOROUGHBREDS.

Cert. No.	Name of Horse.	Owner.	Parade.	Date of Examination.	Officer.
137/2	Scotch Mixture ..	W. C. Bayley ..	Hamilton ..	24.8.11	R.N.J.

LIGHT HORSES.

Cert. No.	Name of Horse.	Owner.	Parade.	Date of Examination.	Officer.
145/2	Dreadnought ..	A. Hunter ..	Seymour ..	1.9.11	E.A.K.

PONIES.

Cert. No.	Name of Horse.	Owner.	Parade.	Date of Examination.	Officer.
156/2	Commodore ..	W. L. Webb ..	Narre Warren (Special)	5.12.11	R.G.
149/2	Gentleman Charlie ..	F. Gunner ..	Royal Show ..	4.9.11	R.N.J.
155/2	Major Melrose ..	W. Woodmason ..	Agricultural Offices	2.12.11	G.S.B.
141/2	Scottie	W. W. Vincent ..	Wangaratta ..	28.8.11	R.G.

STALLION PARADES, 1912.

TIME TABLE.

District and Date.	Place.	Time.	Officer Arrives.	Officer Leaves.
SPECIAL.				
16th to 20th July ..	City Horse Bazaar	10 a.m.		
22nd to 27th July ..	Newmarket Horse Bazaar	10 a.m.		
Every Saturday, 29th June to 14th Dec.	Agricultural Offices	10 a.m. to 12 noon		
WIMMERA No. 1.				
2nd to 3rd July ..	Horsham* ..	10 a.m.		
MALLEE No. 1.				
Wednesday, 17th July	Sea Lake* ..	2 p.m. ..	9.55 p.m. (16th)	6.40 am. (18th)
Thursday, 18th July	Charlton* ..	2 p.m. ..	12.3 p.m. ..	12.23 p.m. (19th)
MALLEE No. 2.				
Tuesday, 30th July ..	Quambatook†	10 a.m. ..	6.35 p.m. (29th)	11.5 a.m.
Tuesday, 30th July ..	Boort* ..	3 p.m. ..	12.29 p.m. ..	6.10 a.m. (31st)
Wednesday, 31st July	Bendigo* ..	3 p.m. ..	11 a.m. ..	12.15 p.m. (1st Aug.)
Friday, 2nd Aug. ..	Wycheproof†	10.30 a.m.	6.5 p.m. (1st Aug.)	11.20 a.m.
WIMMERA No. 2.				
Tuesday, 30th July ..	Hopetoun ..	10.15 r.m.	10.15 a.m. ..	11.20 a.m.
Wednesday, 31st July	Murtoa† ..	2 p.m. ..	4.50 p.m. (30th)	6.20 p.m.
Thursday, 1st Aug.	Beulah ..	10.30 a.m.	9.10 p.m. (31st)	12.40 p.m.
Friday, 2nd Aug. ..	Warracknabeal†	1.30 p.m.	2.25 p.m. (1st Aug.)	2.55 p.m.
WESTERN No. 1.				
Tuesday, 30th July ..	Balmoral* ..	3 p.m. ..	11.30 a.m. ..	11 a.m. (31st)
Thursday, 1st Aug. ..	Portland* ..	3 p.m. ..	1.2 p.m. ..	8.10 a.m. (2nd)
WIMMERA No. 3.				
Wednesday, 31st July	Goroke* ..	3 p.m.	2.20 p.m. ..	6.30 a.m. (1st Aug.)
Thursday, 1st Aug. ..	Edenhope*	3 p.m. ..	12 noon ..	2.30 p.m. (2nd)

At places marked * a lecture can be arranged for the night of the Parade.
At places marked † a lecture can be arranged for the night before the Parade.

Stallion Parades, Time Table—*continued.*

District and Date.	Place.	Time.	Officer Arrives.	Officer Leaves.
WIMMERA No. 4.				
Monday, 5th Aug. ..	Stawell ..	3 p.m. ..	2.38 p.m. ..	10.13 p.m.
Tuesday, 6th Aug. ..	Rainbow ..	2 p.m. ..	1.15 p.m. ..	8 p.m.
Wednesday, 7th Aug.	Jeparit ..	2 p.m. ..	9.13 p.m. (6th)	5.17 p.m.
Thursday, 8th Aug. ..	Minyip ..	2 p.m. ..	6.53 a.m. ..	4.8 p.m.
Friday, 9th Aug. ..	Ararat ..	1.30 p.m.	9.25 p.m. (8th)	3.39 p.m.
MALLEE No. 3.				
Monday, 5th Aug. ..	Heathcote ..	2 p.m. ..	11.41 a.m. ..	8.17 p.m.
Tuesday, 6th Aug. ..	St. Arnaud ..	3.30 p.m.	3.22 p.m. ..	9.42 p.m.
Wednesday, 7th Aug.	Donald ..	2 p.m. ..	10.52 p.m. (6th)	6 p.m.
Thursday, 8th Aug. ..	Watchem† ..	2 p.m. ..	7.27 p.m. (7th)	7.20 p.m.
Friday, 9th Aug. ..	Birchip† ..	10 a.m. ..	8.5 p.m. (8th)	12.25 p.m.
MALLEE No. 4.				
Monday, 5th Aug. ..	Pyramid* ..	3 p.m. ..	2.36 p.m. ..	3.28 p.m. (6th)
Wednesday, 7th Aug.	Swan Hill*	2 p.m. ..	7.15 p.m. (6th)	11 a.m. (8th)
Thursday, 8th Aug. ..	Kerang* ..	2 p.m. ..	12.39 p.m. ..	6 a.m. (9th)
Friday, 9th Aug. ..	Elmore ..	2 p.m. ..	1.11 p.m. ..	4.55 p.m.
CENTRAL No. 1.				
Monday, 12th Aug. ..	Marybo-rough*	2 p.m. ..	12.32 p.m. ..	6.5 a.m. (13th)
Tuesday, 13th Aug. ..	Inglewood ..	11 a.m. ..	8.40 a.m. ..	2.10 p.m.
Tuesday, 13th Aug. ..	Dunolly* ..	4 p.m. ..	3.50 p.m. ..	9.17 a.m. (14th)
Wednesday, 14th Aug.	Clunes ..	2 p.m. ..	1.43 p.m. ..	6.45 p.m.
Thursday, 15th Aug.	Geelong ..	2 p.m. ..	12.10 p.m. ..	5.50 p.m.
NORTH-EASTERN No. 1.				
Monday, 12th Aug. ..	Benalla* ..	2 p.m. ..	11.15 a.m. ..	7.41 p.m.
Tuesday, 13th Aug. ..	Wangaratta*	2 p.m. ..	5.24 p.m. (12th)	12.34 a.m. (14th)
Wednesday, 14th Aug.	Myrtleford*	3 p.m. ..	2.54 p.m. ..	7.17 a.m. (15th)
Thursday, 15th Aug.	Euroa ..	3 p.m. ..	11.11 a.m. ..	6.32 p.m.
Saturday, 17th Aug. ..	Castlemaine	11 a.m. ..	10.20 a.m. ..	12.56 p.m.
WIMMERA No. 5.				
Wednesday, 14th Aug.	Nhill* ..	2 p.m	1.31 a.m. ..	8.10 a.m. (15th)
Thursday, 15th Aug.	Kaniva* ..	2 p.m. ..	1.30 a.m. ..	5.52 a.m. (16th)
Friday, 16th Aug. ..	Dimboola* ..	2 p.m. ..	1.14 a.m. ..	2.18 a.m. (17th)
WESTERN No. 3.				
Tuesday, 20th Aug. ..	Coleraine†	2 p.m. ..	6.35 p.m. (19th)	10 a.m. (21st) (Driving)
Wednesday, 21st Aug.	Casterton*	2 p.m. ..	12 noon (Driving)	8.15 a.m. (22nd)
Thursday, 22nd Aug.	Hamilton ..	2 p.m. ..	1.50 a.m. ..	4.35 p.m.
Friday, 23rd Aug. ..	Penshurst†	1.30 a.m.	7.33 p.m. (22nd)	10.17 a.m.
Saturday, 24th Aug.	Ballan ..	10 a.m. ..	8.18 a.m. ..	12.2 p.m.

STALLION PARADES, TIME TABLE—*continued.*

District and Date.	Place.	Time.	Officer Arrives.	Officer Leaves.
GOULBURN VALLEY No. 1.				
Tuesday, 20th Aug. ..	Daylesford ..	2 p.m. ..	11.50 a.m. ..	3.25 p.m.
Wednesday, 21st Aug.	Rochester ..	11 a.m. ..	10.58 p.m. (20th)	1.36 p.m.
Wednesday, 21st Aug.	Echuca* ..	3 p.m. ..	2.15 p.m. ..	5 a.m. (22nd)
Thursday, 22nd Aug.	Murchison ..	9.30 a.m...	8.30 a.m. ..	10.58 a.m.
Thursday, 22nd Aug.	Rushworth	2 p.m. ..	11.48 a.m. ..	5.20 p.m.
Friday, 23rd Aug. ..	Cobram ..	2 p.m. ..	1.57 p.m. ..	3.10 p.m.
GOULBURN VALLEY No. 2.				
Monday, 19th Aug. ..	Dookie ..	2 p.m. ..	12.52 p.m. ..	4.11 p.m.
Tuesday, 20th Aug. ..	Nathalia ..	2 p.m. ..	1.40 p.m. ..	3.25 p.m.
Wednesday, 21st Aug.	Numurkah†	2 p.m. ..	4.10 p.m. (20th)	4.43 p.m.
Thursday, 22nd Aug.	Tatura ..	10 a.m. ..	8.30 p.m. (21st)	11.42 a.m.
Thursday, 22nd Aug.	Kyabram ..	2 p.m. ..	12.50 p.m. ..	4.20 p.m.
Friday, 23rd Aug. ..	Shepparton†	2 p.m. ..	8.23 p.m. (22nd)	5.49 p.m.
NORTH-EASTERN No. 2.				
Monday, 26th Aug. ..	Rutherglen	2 p.m. ..	1.48 p.m. ..	3.22 p.m.
Tuesday, 27th Aug. ..	Yarrawonga	10 a.m. ..	10.22 p.m. (26th)	2.45 p.m.
Tuesday, 27th Aug. ..	Tungamah*	4 p.m. ..	3.28 p.m. ..	7.45 a.m. (28th)
Wednesday, 28th Aug.	Seymour ..	2 p.m. ..	12.5 p.m. ..	8.33 p.m.
Thursday, 29th Aug.	Yea‡ ..	9.30 a.m.	10.20 p.m. (28th)	10.40 a.m.
Thursday, 29th Aug.	Mansfield. ..	2 p.m. ..	1.53 p.m. ..	3.25 p.m.
Friday, 30th Aug. ..	Alexandra ..	2 p.m. ..	12.35 p.m. ..	4.40 p.m.
CENTRAL No. 2.				
Wednesday, 28th Aug.	Beaufort ..	2 p.m. ..	12.27 p.m. ..	5.28 p.m.
Saturday, 31st Aug.	Melton ..	11 a.m. ..	8.35 a.m. ..	1.21 p.m.
ROYAL SHOW.				
Tuesday, 3rd Sept. ..	Royal Show Grounds	8 a.m. to 10 a.m.		
WESTERN No. 2.				
Monday, 9th Sept. ..	Terang* ..	2 p.m. ..	12.44 p.m. ..	10.38 p.m.
Tuesday, 10th Sept.	Port Fairy ..	10 a.m. ..	1.4 a.m. ..	1.30 p.m.
Wednesday, 11th Sept.	Camperdown*	2 p.m. ..	5.5 p.m. (10th)	10.3 p.m.
Thursday, 12th Sept.	Warrnam-bool*	2 p.m. ..	11.55 p.m. (13th)	7.11 a.m. (15th)
Friday, 13th Sept. ..	Colac ..	2 p.m. ..	10.4 a.m. ..	6.52 p.m.
Saturday, 14th Sept.	Werribee ..	10 a.m. ..	7.17 a.m. ..	1.25 p.m.

‡ Lecture after.

STALLION PARADES, TIME TABLE—*continued.*

District and Date.	Place.	Time.	Officer Arrives.	Officer Leaves.
GIPPSLAND No. 1.				
Monday, 9th Sept. ..	Morwell* ..	2 p.m. ..	11.52 a.m. ..	12.20 p.m. (10th)
Tuesday, 10th Sept.	Mirboo ..	2 p.m. ..	2 p.m. ..	4.15 p.m.
Wednesday, 11th Sept.	Traralgon ..	11 a.m. ..	9.4 p.m. (10th)	12.20 p.m.
Wednesday, 11th Sept.	Bairnsdale* ..	3.30 p.m.	3.25 p.m. ..	9.30 a.m. (12th)
Thursday, 12th Sept.	Sale ..	2 p.m. ..	12.15 p.m. ..	4.33 p.m.
Friday, 13th Sept. ..	Lilydale ..	2 p.m. ..	1.34 p.m. ..	5.35 p.m.
Saturday, 14th Sept.	Bacchus Marsh	11 a.m. ..	8.55 a.m. ..	12.59 p.m.
CENTRAL No. 3.				
Tuesday, 10th Sept.	Whittlesea ..	2 p.m. ..	12.50 p.m. ..	8 p.m.
Wednesday, 11th Sept.	Berwick ..	11 a.m. ..	9.8 a.m. ..	12.16 p.m.
Wednesday, 11th Sept.	Dandenong ..	2 p.m. ..	12.35 p.m. ..	3.49 p.m.
Wednesday, 11th Sept.	Cranbourne ..	4.30 p.m.	4.7 p.m. ..	7.19 p.m.
Thursday, 12th Sept.	Smeaton ..	3 p.m. ..	3 p.m. ..	6.8 p.m.
Friday, 13th Sept. ..	Kyneton ..	11 a.m. ..	9.19 a.m. ..	2.9 p.m.
GIPPSLAND, No. 2.				
Monday, 16th Sept. ..	Foster ..	12.45 p.m.	12.38 p.m. ..	2.21 p.m.
Monday, 16th Sept. ..	Leongatha* ..	4 p.m. ..	3.56 p.m. ..	7.25 a.m. (17th)
Tuesday, 17th Sept.	Lang Lang ..	3 p.m. ..	9.25 a.m. ..	7.26 p.m.
Wednesday, 18th Sept.	Korumburra* ..	3 p.m. ..	8.30 p.m. (17th)	10.42 a.m. (19th)
Thursday, 19th Sept.	Yarram* ..	4 p.m. ..	3.45 p.m. ..	10.55 a.m. (20th)
Saturday, 21st Sept.	Frankston ..	11 a.m. ..	9.34 a.m. ..	1.1 p.m.
NORTH-EASTERN No. 3.				
Monday, 16th Sept. ..	Wodonga ..	2 p.m. ..	1. p.m. ..	3.5 p.m.
Tuesday, 17th Sept.	Tallangatta* ..	2 p.m. ..	4. p.m. (16th)	5 a.m. (18th)
Wednesday, 18th Sept.	Corryong* ..	3.30 p.m.	3.30 p.m. ..	7 a.m. (19th)
GIPPSLAND No. 3.				
Monday, 16th Sept. ..	Romsey ..	2 p.m. ..	10.10 a.m. ..	5.25 p.m.
Tuesday, 17th Sept.	Trafalgar ..	2 p.m. ..	11.16 a.m. ..	6.51 p.m.
Wednesday, 18th Sept.	Warragul* ..	3 p.m. ..	7.25 p.m. (17th)	6.15 a.m. (19th)
Thursday, 19th Sept.	Bunyip ..	10 a.m. ..	6.46 a.m. ..	11.25 a.m.
Saturday, 21st Sept.	Ballarat ..	11.15 a.m.	11.5 a.m. ..	3.5 p.m.
Thursday, 26th Sept.	Kilmore ..	2 p.m. ..	9.30 a.m. ..	8.40 p.m.
Tuesday, 3rd Oct. ..	Orbost* ..	3 p.m. ..	2 p.m. ..	8.2 a.m. (4th)

SMALL RURAL INDUSTRIES.

A.—LAVENDER CULTIVATION.

By Joseph Knight.

The establishment of the essential oil industry, like many others of a similar nature, has been attempted in this State, but, from various causes, has not been followed up—notwithstanding that liberal assistance was offered by the State Government, and satisfactory results as to yields, &c., obtained. Things are now, however, becoming more satisfactory for the grower in this regard, and, with proper care and attention, it may well

· LAVENDER (LAVENDERA VERA).

take its place amongst the profitable minor industries of the rural population. The producer should be content to produce the flowers and dispose of them to the distiller, or where this is inconvenient, distill them and dispose of the oil to the wholesale chemist, and not try to manipulate it further by attempting the making up of perfumes. Such attempts have often been made heretofore and failed.

Lavender (*Lavendera Vera* or *Levendula Augustifolia*) is one of the hardiest of herbaceous plants, and thrives under a wide range of conditions of both soil and climate—even poor, sandy, or loamy soils are agreeable to it, and these conditions are recognised as resulting in the production of the finer class of essential oil. One condition of soil is very necessary, and that is, it should be free from possibility of water-logging. Excessive moisture at the roots soon causes the plant to perish. Low, wet land should, therefore, be avoided, unless it is well drained.

RAISING PLANTS.

Plants may be obtained from either seed or cuttings, but the best method of propagating is by cuttings, and these should always be selected from the best plants available. Slips from 4 to 5 inches long—no matter how fine or small—may be planted out in a nursery bed, close in the rows, even touching. If the cutting be 4 or 5 inches long, 1 inch to 1½ inches above the ground is sufficient. The nursery rows should be sufficiently far apart to permit of the ground being kept loose and clean. The cuttings should be planted early in the autumn, when they will reach the stage in which they may be planted out in their permanent place in the following spring. A few blooms will show up sufficient to indicate what the plant is like.

PLANTING OUT.

In planting out permanently the distance apart must be regulated by the class of labour to be subsequently employed. If horse labour is to be used in the after cultivation the distance between the rows should be from 4 to 5 feet. If manual labour only is available then the plants may be grown closer, say, 3 to 4 feet, or, if it can only be ploughed or worked one way with the aid of horse labour, then the plants may stand 4 feet x 5 feet or 3 feet 6 inches x 5 feet. The plant, when developed, will spread out to cover ground from 1 foot 6 inches to 2 feet in diameter. There is no economy in close planting—the plant should have sufficient feeding ground, or it will become stunted, and the yield of flowers small and pinched.

The securing of proper cuttings is important, and care should be taken in this respect. There are a number of mother patches available, and a limited quantity may be obtained from the Labour Colony, Leongatha, by writing to the manager, who will supply them in bundles f.o.b. rail Leongatha at 3s. 9d. per 1,000 cuttings. In commencing this business it is important that plants should be secured early. Cuttings may be planted out at any time in the autumn or spring, but, if too late in autumn, the growth will be retarded by the cold, wet bed, and, if late in spring, with dry, hot weather. In planting, little can be done by way of regulating the length of stem above or below, but deep planting should be avoided. The plant should stand the same depth as when in the nursery bed ; mistakes are made in this respect frequently, and the plant too much buried. Spread the roots well and tramp the soil firm. Avoid planting when soil is wet or otherwise out of condition.

PREPARATION OF SOIL.

As the profitable lifetime of the plant runs for seven or eight years the soil should be properly prepared prior to planting, as it is impossible to do much after, beyond cleaning and ploughing shallow betwixt the plants. The plant will repay the labour for subsoiling, as the roots will be enabled to penetrate to a depth that will enable it to withstand the changes of excessive drought and wet. Subsoiling is preferable to deep, single plough-ing, as the surface soil should be kept to the surface ; and the cold, stub-born bottom soil should not be brought to the surface, as this soil is usually infertile and difficult to work. Whatever system is adopted, the soil should be well worked and pulverized to a fair depth, so that the young plant may be enabled to push its roots freely.

CUTTING OR HARVESTING.

The flower opens out on the stem somewhat irregularly, so care should be taken, when harvesting, to take them when the maximum amount of flower has opened out. The flowers are gathered in one hand and cut with a hook (see illustration here) or knife below the bloom and above the foliage, and laid out on sheets of hessian, but not exposed to the burning

sun any more than can be helped, as the essential oil is apt to escape. If intended for sale in the green state, the cut flowers may be spread out for a few hours in the shade, but the quicker it is taken to the still the better for all concerned. Avoid placing in bags, as it heats readily, and damages. If sending it away any distance it should be sent in crates and packed in thin layers—not more than 2 or 3 inches thick, so as to avoid pressure. The present price for this form of produce is 3d. per lb. in the green state, delivered in Melbourne. If it is inconvenient to market it in this form the flower may be spread out on trays, boards, or hessian in the shade, and dried, when it may be packed carefully, so as to save the blooms, which separate freely from the stem. As the bloom is the most valuable portion of the product, care must be taken in this respect. The dried flowers, with stems, are valued at about 5d. per lb., but buds alone are also sold for a price much beyond that.

The cutting of lavender commences about December, and arrangements should be made beforehand with the distilleries, as their intake must be regulated by their capacity for treating same. Failure in this respect may mean the loss of the crop.

TREATMENT OF THE FLOWER.

As stated above, the flowers are gathered and laid out on hessian and taken to the still. If they are sold to the distiller they must reach him in a sound condition, and it would be advisable, where they cannot be delivered within twenty-four hours or so, to spread them on some kind of trays, in a thin layer, so as to avoid heating, which destroys the blooms. It is better to market in boxes, fitted with trays inside, to prevent the weight of flowers pressing on each other. The depth of these on the boards, or netting, should not be over 3 inches, and they should carry their own weight of flowers separately. By this means there would be little danger of it damaging by heating. It is frequently the case that flowers are gathered and put up in sacks and sent on; on arrival at the destination they are found heated and black, and, of course, valueless.

It is desirable to market green if possible, but when this cannot be done then the flower may be spread out on any clean bottom and dried, and marketed dry, but the drying should be done in the shade, and not in the sun.

The other alternative is distilling—particulars of which are given below —and, as but little skill is necessary, women and youths can be intrusted with the work, and, with proper appliances, should be light and pleasant employment.

FIRST YEAR PLANTING.

SECOND YEAR PLANTING.

THIRD YEAR PLANTING.

After Treatment of Plant.

The annual cutting back of this low, bushy plant forces out a super-abundance of branches, and the plant becomes so close and dense that it is readily attacked by fungoid and other diseases; and, in order to avoid this, the plant should be thinned out during the dormant season, and the air let in. This will considerably improve its vigor and increase the yield of blooms, which is the object aimed at. The pruning should be done as low down as possible so as to avoid the production of superfluous buds, and much may be done by robbing these when going through the plants. Lavender, like most other plant-life, when employed for man's use, will repay for a little attention.

Yield.

It is somewhat difficult to give actual yields, as much depends on the varying conditions under which they are produced. For instance, the Governor of Pentridge, Mr. Cody, planted out a small area, about half-an-acre or so, and the returns given from this were highly satisfactory, but, as portions were taken from one, two, and three year old plantings, the actual returns would be of little service. Suffice it to say that, on his retirement from the Government service, he is entering into lavender cultivation on a much larger scale. The yield of flowers per acre varies, but may be put down to about 3 to 4 tons. The price at present is 3d. per lb., and gives over £50 per acre.

Mr. J. Blogg, of Messrs. Blogg Brothers, Melbourne, the well-known perfumers, estimates the yield of oil at 40 lbs. per acre. The late Mr. Slater, who was well-up in this business, gave the yield at 56 lbs., but when we come to the price of this we are lost. Some time back I had a parcel of a few lbs. to dispose of on behalf of the Department, and I invited quotations from three or four firms. One offer was made to me at 7s. per lb., and another at 14s. per lb. The third said he would give me the market value, but could not say what that was until testing it, so, on the second offerer rising to 15s. per lb., his offer was accepted. The third man then complained, and said he was prepared to go to 20s., or 21s., had I given him a chance. Herein lies the difficulty in dealing with all such special products, viz., the want of an established market value to regulate the price; but this will remedy itself when the trade becomes more established.

Distilling.

Where it is intended to extract the oil a still may be secured for about £20—sufficient for 4 or 5 acres. There is no licence or fee to be paid, but a permit must be obtained from the Customs Department, and a guarantee furnished to the extent of £100, that the Excise laws will not be violated. The skill necessary for this industry is not beyond ordinary capacity, and instructions can be obtained by calling at my office, 581 Flinders-street, Melbourne.

The following information is supplied by the Customs Department to those desiring to obtain a permit to hold a still :—

Commonwealth Instructions re *the use of Stills for purposes other than for Distilling Spirits.*

1. Any person making a still without the written permission of the collector is liable to a penalty of £100.
2. Any person having a still in his possession or custody, without lawful authority, is liable to a penalty of £500.

3. Any person who intends to use a still for any purpose, other than the distilling of spirits, must give notice in writing to the Collector of Customs, and furnish full details respecting the size or capacity of the still, the specific purpose for which it is to be used, and the place where it is to be used. Form of notice may be obtained on application to the collector.

4. Security in a sum not exceeding £100 that the still shall not be used for distilling spirits must be entered into.

5. When due notice has been given, and the security has been duly completed, the collector will furnish an acknowledgment of the receipt of the notice and security, and the acknowledgment must, at any time, on demand by an officer, be produced by the person using the still.

6. If any person intends to use more than one still a notice and security must be given for each still.

7. The still, or stills, must not be sold or removed to any place without the written permission of the Collector of Customs. The penalty for selling or removing a still, without written permission of the collector, is £100.

8. When written permission is given to remove a still a fresh notice and security must be furnished.

GENERAL REMARKS.

There are other species of lavender grown, but none other than the one under review can be recommended for commercial purposes, as the class of oil produced is low in value. *Lavendera Vera,* or *Lavendula Augustifolia,* is the only one worthy of consideration, and this, like many other plants or animals, may be improved by careful selection and other means. This should be the aim of all entering into its cultivation. With the aid of a small test still individual plants may be treated, and those of the best quality carefully selected for propagation. No doubt, if this were carried out systematically, the yield would be much improved.

If we look over a field of lavender in bloom we cannot help noticing the great variation of colour of flower and form and quantity of bloom on each, and, no doubt, the oil that each contains would vary equally so. Some plants are much more robust than others, but the plant is hardy, and gives but little trouble if properly handled. If neglected, it suffers from an attack of fungus, which appears to kill out portions of the plant, but if kept open, as advised, and air admitted freely, there will be little ground for complaint on this score.

BASIS WINES.

By F. de Castilla, Government Viticulturist.

Wines manufactured in England from such materials as dried grapes (currants, raisins, &c.), evaporated grape juice and sterilised must are known as basis wines, since they are mainly used as a basis in blends of various kinds.

It has long been evident that such wines could be manufactured in England under far more favorable conditions than those under which it is possible for Australian wine-makers to operate, the raw material paying little or no duty, whilst fermented wines must pay a duty of 1s. 3d. per gallon, on entering the United Kingdom. Basis wine manufacturers enjoy a further advantage in the way of lesser freight charges, owing to the concentrated form in which the raw material is carried.

Seeing the evident unfairness of such a state of affairs to our wine-growers, the attention of the Director of Agriculture was drawn to the matter by the Government Viticulturist in October last, with the result that the Agent-General was asked to obtain information on the following points :—

(1) Currants imported into England for manufacturing purposes.
(2) Evaporated grape juice imported.
(3) The quantity of wine manufactured in England.
(4) The amount of duty payable on evaporated grape juice.
(5) Any further information obtainable on the subject.

A despatch was received from the Agent-General dated the 8th December, accompanied by a return showing importations of grape juice or must as follows :—

Years.	Quantities.	Value.	Approximate value per gallon.
	Galls.	£	
1906–7	78,659	10,346	2/7½
1907–8	99,230	12,206	2/5½
1908–9	78,447	7,548	1/11
1909–10	88,203	9,419	2/1⅓
1910–11	183,494	16,047	1/9

A recent very marked increase is here shown, the figures for 1910-11 being more than double those for the previous twelve months, an increase for which the steady decline in value is, no doubt, largely responsible.

Further information was promised by the Agent-General, and a despatch has recently been received by the Honorable the Minister for Agriculture, dated 5th January, as follows :—

" Following up my despatch of the 8th ultimo, the Customs Department inform me that they have no information as to the disposal of currants after the payment of duty. The quantities and value of currants imported are shown in the *Annual Statement of Trade of the United Kingdom*, and are as follows, namely :—

	1906.	1907.	1908.	1909.	1910.
Quantity, cwts. ...	1,458,159	1,188,481	1,297,157	1,071,209	1,310,361
Value, £ ...	1,648,410	1,392,271	1,464,091	1,156,118	1,708,710

" *Evaporated Grape Juice.*—This, I am advised, is not separately recorded in the official statistics. Any such imports will be classified under the general heading ' Grape Juice or Must,' the imports and value of which are given in the *Annual Statement of Trade* as follows, namely :—

	1906.	1907.	1908.	1909.	1910.
Quantity, gallons ...	43,510	109,831	85,601	67,090	163,838
Value, £	5,422	15,047	8,527	7,967	16,513

" *Wine Manufactured in England.*—The Customs Department inform me that the quantity of wine made by licensed manufacturers of the United Kingdom was in the year ended 31st March, 1911, 1,234,512 gallons.

" There is no duty chargeable on grape juice or must as such.

" I am sending you a copy of the Finance Act passed in the last few days of the session. You will observe that section 10 of the Act imposes certain restrictions on the use of British wine for blending purposes. Regulations as to the registration of the sales of British wines by manufacturers have not yet been issued, but as soon as they are I will send you a copy. It is possible that under the new regulations we may be able to obtain further information to assist us in the matter.

"I regard the registration of the sales of British wines by manufacturers as being important. This will enable us to watch and report as to what is going on.

"(Signed)   J. W. TAVERNER,
"Agent-General."

Though it has long been known that "Basis wine" was manufactured on a large scale the fact, that 1,234,512 gallons of wine were made in England last year will probably come as a surprise to many. In this is included, no doubt, a certain quantity of British fruit wines, such as Gooseberry, Blackberry, &c. To the manufacture of such *bonâ fide* products no exception can be taken; they have been made since time immemorial, from British-grown fruit; but, that foreign-grown grape-juice should be able to compete with our wine, over which it enjoys the advantage of a Customs duty of 1s. 3d. per gallon, must appear somewhat of an anomaly to Australian wine-growers.

The quantity of *bonâ fide* British fruit wines made cannot be considerable, and it would appear that the production of "Basis wine" is at least equal to our annual shipments from the Commonwealth to the United Kingdom. Judging from the recent increase in the imports of "Grape Juice or Must" the industry appears to be expanding.

That the English wine trade is not in sympathy with such manipulations is evident. The London *Wine Trade Review*, of 15th February last, devotes a leading article to the question, referring to it as "The 'Basis wine' evil, which has so much disturbed legitimate business for the past ten or fifteen years." It reproduces the official circular which was recently sent to the trade, as follows :—

The Commissioners of Customs and Excise desire to make known to all traders concerned that, in pursuance of the powers vested in the Commissioners by section 10 of the *Finance Act* 1911, they are about to issue regulations, to come into force on 1st April next :—

> (1) restricting within certain specified limits the mixing of British with foreign wine, and
> (2) prohibiting the sale of wine so mixed, except such as may be mixed under the conditions prescribed in the regulations.

In order to avoid as far as possible inconvenience to traders, a period which the Commissioners, as at present advised, propose to fix at three months, will be allowed for the disposal of existing stocks of mixed wine remaining in hand on 1st April.

It expresses the hope "That the contemplated regulations will not lack in definiteness" so that traffic may no longer continue "In a fabrication. . . . which can, by exemption from the full duty applicable to imported wines, be used to cut into legitimate trade or to detrimentally affect the revenue." It uses such expressions as "Those counterfeits of foreign wine which find their way as cheapening factors into blends with the imported article," and, further, states that there is reason for the suspicion that "The 'basis' counterfeit" is used to mix with spirits. It concludes by noting with pleasure "That the opinion of the trade, as exemplified by the recent circulars of leading firms, is wholly in favour of the powers conferred on the Customs and Excise, and that the trade is already looking forward to a considerable revival in the demand for the cheaper classes of wine; more especially as regards clarets and Tarragona."

Further information as to the exact wording of the regulations should come to hand shortly.

FINAL RESULTS OF

VICTORIAN EGG-LAYING COMPETITION, 1911-12,

CONDUCTED AT BURNLEY HORTICULTURAL SCHOOL.

(Concluded from page 200.)

H. V. Hawkins, Poultry Expert.

No. of Pen.	Breed.	Name of Owner.	April to Feb.	March.	Total to date (12 mths)	Position in Competition.
31	White Leghorn	R. W. Pope	1,473	93	1,566	1
12	,,	W. G. Swift	1,456	90	1,546	2
40	,,	A. J. Cosh (S.A.)	1,419	120	1,539	3
20	,,	H. McKenzie	1,360	69	1,429	4
37	,,	E. Waldon	1,324	77	1,401	5
33	,,	Range Poultry Farm (Qld.)	1,275	56	1,331	6
39	,,	A. W. Hall	1,246	55	1,301	7
18	,,	T. Brundrett	1,188	78	1,266	8
24	,,	F. Hannaford	1,147	104	1,251	9
10	Black Orpington	H. A. Langdon	1,138	102	1,240	10
19	White Leghorn	A. Jaques	1,155	73	1,228	11
13	Black Orpington	D. Fisher	1,162	60	1,222	} 12
50	White Leghorn	C. H. Busst	1,137	85	1,222	
21	,,	R. L. Appleford	1,162	50	1,212	} 14
9	,,	J. O'Loughlin	1,137	75	1,212	
28	,,	John Campbell	1,118	93	1,211	16
2	,,	E. P. Nash	1,139	60	1,199	} 17
3	,,	K. Gleghorn	1,117	82	1,199	
11	Brown Leghorn	F. Soncum	1,097	98	1,195	19
55	White Leghorn	W. G. McLister	1,117	76	1,193	20
46	Minorca	G. W. Chalmers	1,127	65	1,192	21
25	White Leghorn	B. Mitchell	1,121	68	1,189	22
32	Silver Wyandotte	Mrs. M. A. Jones	1,075	96	1,171	23
38	White Leghorn	Mrs. C. R. Smee	1,111	51	1,162	24
62	,,	P. Hodson	1,091	63	1,154	25
45	,,	T. Kempster	1,098	55	1,153	26
67	,,	C. L. Sharman	1,085	112	1,147	27
49	,,	W. J. Thornton	1,089	57	1,146	28
22	Black Orpington	P. S. Wood	1,043	95	1,138	29
44	,,	T. S. Goodisson	1,070	66	1,136	30
1	White Leghorn	A. Brebner	1,099	34	1,133	31
65	,,	H. Hammill (N.S.W.)	1,048	81	1,129	32
36	,,	F. A. Sillitoe	1,097	25	1,122	33
57	,,	G. E. Edwards	1,031	85	1,116	34
35	,,	J. H. Brain	1,012	90	1,102	35
4	Golden Wyandotte	H. Bell	1,037	63	1,100	36
60	White Leghorn	J. J. Harrington	1,022	73	1,095	37
47	,,	C. W. Spencer (N.S.W.)	1,040	49	1,089	38
66	White Wyandotte	J. E. Bradley	1,021	64	1,085	39
43	White Leghorn	W. B. Creilin	1,015	59	1,074	40
5	,,	L. C. Payne	1,047	20	1,067	41
8	,,	T. W. Coto	1,022	35	1,057	42
41	,,	Morgan and Watson	994	56	1,050	43
6	Silver Wyandotte	Mrs. H. J. Richards	952	93	1,045	44
64	White Leghorn	J. D. Read	964	78	1,042	45
51	,,	J. B. McArthur	979	62	1,041	46
34	,,	E. Dettman	965	75	1,040	47
58	Faverolles	K. Courtenay	971	59	1,030	48
59	White Leghorn	W. H. Dunlop	972	56	1,028	49
30	Black Orpington	Rodgers Bros.	932	81	1,013	50
53	White Leghorn	A. Stringer	977	33	1,010	51
63	Black Orpington	A. J. Treacey	948	48	996	52
42	White Orpington	P. Mitchell	929	66	995	53
52	White Leghorn	W. J. McKeddie	955	36	991	54
27	,,	Hill and Luckman	952	21	973	55
16	Silver Wyandotte	Miss A. Cottam	862	74	936	56
56	White Leghorn	Mrs. C. Thompson	896	36	932	57
23	Golden Wyandotte	G. E. Brown	849	73	922	58
61	Silver Wyandotte	J. Reade	844	75	919	59
7	White Leghorn	H. Stevenson	900	18	918	60
26	,,	F. H. Seymour	885	31	916	61
54	,,	F. Hodges	856	58	914	62
17	,,	W. J. Eckershall	759	56	815	63
14	Black Orpington	W. J. Macauley	723	72	795	64
15	Minorca	H. R. McChesney	638	29	667	65
48	,,	C. James	578	39	617	66
			68,998	4,327	73,325	

STATISTICS.

Rainfall in Victoria.—First Quarter, 1912.

TABLE showing average amount of rainfall in each of the 26 Basins or Regions constituting the State of Victoria for each month and the quarter, with the corresponding monthly and quarterly averages for each Basin, deduced from all available records to date.

Basin or District.	January.		February.		March.		Quarter.	
	Amount.	Average.	Amount.	Average.	Amount.	Average.	Amount.	Average.
	points.	points.	points.	points.	points.	points	points.	points.
Glenelg and Wannon Rivers	16	121	98	87	155	167	269	375
Fitzroy, Eumeralla, and Merri Rivers	36	145	111	158	178	179	325	482
Hopkins River and Mount Emu Creek	25	145	68	100	167	178	260	423
Mount Elephant and Lake Corangamite	20	150	76	103	151	189	247	442
Cape Otway Forest ...	57	210	82	142	155	268	294	620
Moorabool and Barwon Rivers	23	145	92	112	135	184	250	441
Werribee and Saltwater Rivers	28	142	142	128	85	188	255	458
Yarra River and Dandenong Creek	87	228	133	166	138	278	358	672
Koo-wee-rup Swamp ...	69	240	120	154	73	270	262	664
South Gippsland	82	227	117	166	114	307	313	700
Latrobe and Thomson Rivers	118	233	113	162	118	280	349	675
Macallister and Avon Rivers	73	159	107	142	72	202	252	503
Mitchell River	84	248	110	210	70	214	264	672
Tambo and Nicholson Rivers	48	211	154	155	73	269	275	635
Snowy River	63	269	152	209	117	265	332	743
Murray River	46	114	100	97	54	161	200	372
Mitta Mitta and Kiewa Rivers	68	170	143	135	121	305	332	610
Ovens River	127	173	78	*124	108	286	313	583
Goulburn River	89	135	70	97	70	180	229	412
Campaspe River	21	116	86	91	60	160	167	367
Loddon River	14	96	113	80	62	126	189	302
Avon and Richardson Rivers	1	71	79	59	68	111	148	241
Avoca River	4	70	80	60	68	122	152	252
Eastern Wimmera	3	85	49	68	88	145	140	298
Western Wimmera	4	67	28	57	62	115	94	239
Mallee District	3	57	68	55	30	98	101	210
The whole State	48	133	91	107	86	179	225	419

100 points = 1 inch.

17th April, 1912.

H. A. HUNT,
Commonwealth Meteorologist.

ORCHARD AND GARDEN NOTES.

E. E. Pescott, Principal, School of Horticulture, Burnley.

The Orchard.

There are indications that the coming planting season will be one of considerably increased activity. The prospects for the fruit trade were never so good, and it is anticipated that this industry will advance in many ways in the near future. Such being the case, it will be wise not to unduly rush the planting of the trees, but to make every endeavour to have them planted in soil which has been well and truly prepared for their reception.

The months of June and July are the most favourable for planting in this State; the warmer the climate, the earlier the planting season.

There is thus ample time for preparing the land thoroughly before the planting is done. The land must be in a first class physical condition for the planting of the young trees. The first and foremost necessity is good soil drainage; and this may be accomplished by a deep system of subsoiling, or by the laying down of tile, timber, or cinder drains.

In the northern plain areas it is very often difficult to initiate a drainage system, owing to the level condition of the country. In such districts it is certainly advisable to carry out a scheme of deep subsoiling.

After clearing and ploughing, the subsoil should be well ploughed by following the furrows with the plough having the mould-board removed. This allows for the stirring of the clay without turning it over or bringing it to the surface.

This breaking up of the clay serves the dual purpose of placing it in the condition that a good water percolation or soil drainage is allowed, and that the tree roots are able to work and travel better in the loose subsoil. Where the subsoil is of a gravelly character or otherwise porous nature, the subsoiling work is not an urgent necessity. Should the drainage be satisfactory under natural conditions, it would be superfluous to carry out this work. What is required is that the soil shall be loose and friable enough to admit of the drainage of all superfluous water, and that the roots shall be able to travel with comparative ease.

For the purpose of fruit culture, soil fertility is dependent to a far greater extent on the suitable physical soil condition than on the richness of the soil.

The second factor in soil fertility is the richness or the quality of the soil.

It is only fair to assume that whatever is removed from the soil by the trees should be replaced, if the soil is to maintain its original fertility. The most useful material for this purpose is stable or farmyard manure. Where this is not obtainable, leguminous green manures are certainly the best substitute.

It is not advocated that solid masses of farmyard manure should be ploughed into the soil; quite the reverse. Light dressings annually or even biennially are the most suitable. To plough into the soil heavy and compact masses of manure is wasteful, and is liable to set up sour and unhealthy soil conditions.

It is the practice of many successful orchardists to manure their orchards every other year with either stable or green manure; and to use such artificial fertilizers as bonedust, sulphate of potash, and superphosphate in the alternate years.

Where it is not intended to manure this season, or even some time after manuring, a top dressing of lime will greatly improve soil conditions.

Pests.

It is now a favourable time to spray the trees where such pests as Bryobia mite, woolly aphis, scale species, and peach aphis have been or are prevalent.

Any of the recognised sprays are suitable, these being red oil, crude petroleum, kerosene emulsion, or lime-sulphur wash. The latter wash is again becoming popular, partly owing to its effectiveness, and also to its possessing certain properties as a fungicide.

Flower Garden.

The month of May is a suitable one for the preparation of new flower beds. In starting on this important work, the first essential is good drainage. The fertility of the soil depends so much on its ability to free itself of all surplus and unnecessary water, by being in a good mechanical condition.

This is of far greater importance than increasing the value of the soil by the addition of organic manures. The latter is by no means to be despised, but a correct condition, with good drainage is the first necessity.

The new beds should be well trenched into the clay, or the subsoil. It is not advocated that the trenching shall be excessively deep. Much labour has been lost in the past by deep trenching, and no very definite results have been produced.

The subsoil surface should be trenched so that the soil moisture may soak into it, and so that the plant roots may be able to penetrate into the subsoil. Then the surface soil and loam should be thoroughly cultivated and broken up. These remarks apply especially to the preparation of rose beds. If new ground is being broken up, the addition of from 4 to 5 cwt. of lime will be a distinct advantage. The lime should be well worked into the soil. The addition of stable manures to the soil may now be carried out. Too heavy dressings are not advised, as an accumulation of manure in the soil is likely to set up sour and unhealthy conditions. The manure should be thoroughly mixed with the soil.

It is not too late to sow sweet pea seeds, but the best results come from early planting. The planting of these seeds should not be delayed. Sweet pea results are generally poor if the plants are over-crowded. The individual plants should be given ample room, planting the seeds at least an inch apart. The training of the young plant is also an important matter. It should not be allowed to trail or to lie on the ground. As soon as the tendrils appear on the young plants, they should be given support so that they may be encouraged in the climbing habit at once. A good sap flow is necessary to good growth, and the stem of the plant should be trained as upright as possible to allow of this. Stable manure is one of the most useful of plant foods for sweet peas; but if a chemical manure is needed, sulphate of potash in very small quantities may be used. It must be understood that this manure is used to produce good and free growth in the plant itself. If this be obtained, good flowers will naturally follow.

Several inquiries have been received regarding the condition of the sweet pea seeds. Some of the varieties produce very inferior looking, spotted and wrinkled seeds. These are not to be discarded, as they will produce good and free flowering plants.

At the end of the month a start may be made with the autumn digging, pruning, and clearing up. Manure may be dug into the beds, well below the surface. All leaves and light litter should also be dug in. If necessary, a light top-dressing of lime may be given after the digging has been completed.

As much garden litter as can be saved should be rotted down for future use; the rough litter and strong stems should be burned and the ashes returned to the soil.

Flowering shrubs should be pruned only after the flowering season for each plant has passed.

Vegetable Garden.

The remarks in the Flower Garden notes referring to preparation of new beds also apply to the kitchen section; this being the time for good soil work. Only, where deep rooting vegetables are to be grown, such as carrots, and turnips, the soil and subsoil should be deeply worked so as to allow a ready root run for these vegetables.

A dressing of lime will be of great value in every section of the kitchen garden. This will especially help to minimize future attacks of insect and fungus pests.

All asparagus plots should be cleaned out, cut down, and kept in good order. A light dressing of stable manure may be given to the beds.

Plantings may be made of all seedlings, such as cabbage, cauliflower, lettuce, onions, &c. ; and seeds of carrot, leek, lettuce, onion, peas, radish, turnip, parsnip, broad beans, &c., may be sown.

REMINDERS - FOR JUNE.

LIVE STOCK.

HORSES.—Those stabled can be fed liberally. Those doing fast or heavy work should be clipped; if not wholly, then trace high. Those not rugged on coming into the stable at night should be wiped down and in half-an-hour's time rugged or covered with bags until the coat is dry. Old horses and weaned foals should be given crushed oats. Grass-fed working horses should be given hay or straw, if there is no old grass, to counteract the purging effects of the young growth. Old and badly-conditioned horses should be given some boiled barley.

CATTLE.—Cows, if not housed, should be rugged. Rugs should be removed in the daytime when the shade temperature reaches 60 degrees. Give a ration of hay or straw, whole or chaffed, to counteract the purging effects of young grass. Cows about to calve, if over fat, should be put into a paddock in which the feed is not too abundant. Calves should be kept in warm dry shed. Cows and heifers for early autumn calving may be put to the bull.

PIGS.—Supply plenty of bedding in warm, well-ventilated styes. Keep styes clean and dry. Store pigs should be placed in fattening styes. Sows in fine weather should be given a grass run. Young pigs over two months old should be removed from lucerne run.

SHEEP.—Wherever possible, castrate all ram lambs intended for export soon after they are a few days old. Leave tailing till later. Ewes should have succulent fresh feed. Class out all inferior-fleeced and ill-shaped ewes; ear-mark and dispose of these. Lamb-raising flocks should be classed similarly to merino flocks. Apply early to breeders for rams required for next season.

POULTRY.—Forward pullets should now be placed in winter scratching shed, fed liberally, and given fresh water daily. Supplies of shell, grit, and charcoal should always be available. Rest the breeding pens; dig them up and sprinkle lime throughout. Sow a mixture of English grass and clover; this not only removes taint in soil, but provides excellent green fodder for stock. Where possible, lucerne should now be sown for summer feed. Meat (cooked) and maize are aids to egg production during cold weather. Feed hot mash at daybreak. Clean drains.

CULTIVATION.

FARMS.—Plough potato land. Land to be sown later on with potatoes, mangolds, maize, and millet should be manured and well worked. Sow malting barley and finish sowing of cereals. Lift and store mangolds, turnips, &c. Clean out drains and water furrows. Clean up and stack manure in heaps protected from the weather.

ORCHARD.—Finish ploughing; plant young trees; spray with red oil or petroleum for scales, mites, aphis, &c.; carry out drainage system; clean out drains; continue pruning.

VEGETABLE GARDEN.—Prepare beds for crops; cultivate deeply; practise rotation in planting out; renovate asparagus beds; plant out all seedlings; sow radish, peas, broad beans, leeks, spinach, lettuce, carrot, &c.; plant rhubarb.

FLOWER GARDEN.—Continue digging and manuring; dig all weeds and leafy growths; plant out shrubs, roses, &c.; plant rose cuttings; prune deciduous trees and shrubs; sow sweet peas and plant out seedlings.

VINEYARD.—Thoroughly prepare for plantation land already subsoiled for the purpose. Remember that the freer it is kept from weeds from this forward, the less trouble will there be from cut-worms next spring. Pruning and ploughing should be actively proceeded with. In northern districts plough to a depth of seven or eight inches. Manures should be applied as early as possible.

Cellar.—Rack all wines which have not been previously dealt with. Fortify sweet wines to full strength.

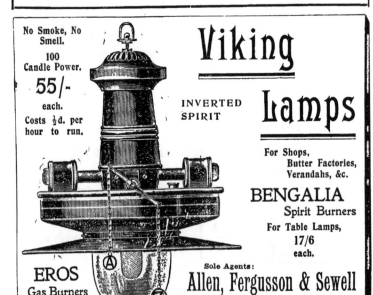

The Journal of

THE DEPARTMENT OF

AGRICULTURE

OF VICTORIA, AUSTRALIA.

June, 1912.

A PROLIFIC HAY CROP.

PRICE THREEPENCE. (Annual Subscription—Victoria, Inter-State, and N.Z., 3/-; British and Foreign, 5/-.)

THE JOURNAL

OF

THE DEPARTMENT OF AGRICULTURE,

VICTORIA, AUSTRALIA.

CONTENTS.—JUNE, 1912.

COPYRIGHT PROVISIONS AND SUBSCRIPTION RATES.

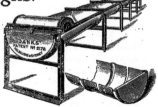

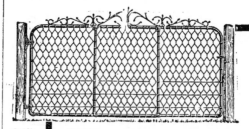

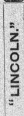

Alston's Patent Windmills

—AT THE ROYAL SHOW.—

At the recent Royal Show a fine collection of **Windmills** was exhibited by **James Alston,** of **Queen's Bridge, Melbourne.** Mills of all diameters, from 6 ft. to 25 ft. were shown at work, suitable to all requirements of farmers or stock raisers, the small Mills being suitable for lifting moderate supplies from shallow wells, while the larger sizes are capable of dealing with almost any depths. A splendid Mill, 25 feet diameter on a 50-ft. Steel Tower, working an 18″ pump, and throwing a stream of water of about 15,000 gallons per hour, attracted much attention. This, we believe, is the largest Mill ever shown on the Show Ground. **Alston's Patent Steel Windmills** have all the most up-to-date improvements in their construction. Pumps of many descriptions were shown, including the latest Draw Plunger Pumps for bore use, which admits of the plunger being drawn without disturbing the pipes in the bore.

THE JOURNAL

OF

The Department of Agriculture

OF

VICTORIA.

Vol. X.   Part 6.   **10th June, 1912.**

WHEAT AND ITS CULTIVATION.

(*Continued from page 274.*)

No. 5.—METHODS OF CULTIVATION.

By A. E. V. Richardson, M.A., B.Sc. (Agric.), Agricultural Superintendent.

The nature of the Australian climate is such as to render thorough tillage a prime factor in successful wheat cropping. A glance at the rainfall map of Australia will reveal the fact that the large wheat-growing areas of the Commonwealth are situated in districts with a limited annual precipitation. To make the fullest use of these areas, systems of cultivation must be practised which aim at conserving as much of the scanty rainfall as possible.

More, however, is required than this. No system of cultivation can be permanently effective and adequate unless it makes provision for the maintenance of the fertility of the soil. The fact that fallowing is so largely practised in the drier areas is proof that the former aspect is appreciated. The fact that there are wheat lands in this young State which practical farmers and the press frequently describe as " worn-out," shows that the latter aspect is frequently ignored.

No system of cropping can be complete and adequate under our conditions, unless it provides both for the conservation of soil moisture and for the conservation of soil fertility. Methods which lead to the conservation of moisture, but not to the conservation of soil fertility, may be temporarily effective and profitable, but ultimately they must be disastrous both to the farmer and to the community.

Two points, therefore, require consideration in discussing the merits or demerits of any system of cultivation for wheat growing under dry condifions, namely—

  (1) Conservation of moisture,
  (2) Conservation of fertility.

6004.   M

Attention will be directed to the former in considering the practice of fallowing, whilst the latter aspect will receive special consideration in considering the question of crop rotation and soil fertilization.

Wheat may be grown under three different systems of cropping—

    1. Continuous cropping with wheat.

    2. Wheat after bare fallow,

    3. Wheat in rotation with other crops.

We shall consider these seriatim.

I.—Continuous Cropping.

Continuous cropping with wheat is very general in countries where methods of cultivation are *extensive* rather than *intensive*. It is, therefore, very general in the Argentine, in parts of Canada, and the United States, and it is not uncommon in Australia.

In the early stages of a new country, lands are cheap, and even free; capital and human labour comparatively scarce and dear. To suit these circumstances, large areas are sown under pioneer conditions of culture. Large areas under crop and small average returns per acre are the rule. As population increases and land values in the settled districts rise, the margin of cultivation is gradually extended into new territory, the large holdings in process of time become subdivided, and an era of intensive culture in the more densely settled localities is gradually ushered in. In these localities the individual areas under crop are small, but the average yield is high, and the system of cultivation changes from continuous cropping to a highly developed rotation, in which far more labour and much better-directed labour is required.

Such is the history of agriculture in every civilized country of the world, and such will be the progress of agriculture in Victoria.

However expedient and profitable it may be in a new agricultural country where pioneer conditions prevail, the sowing of wheat year after year on the same land is condemned, by both theory and practice. While it may be said that continuous growing of wheat on the same land year after year is not good practice, the results obtained in the Broadbalk field at the Rothamsted Experiment Station show that it is possible. For example, wheat has been grown continuously in the Broadbalk field for over 60 years. The highest yield was obtained from Plot 8, viz., 37.1 bushels per acre; but in order to secure this result a liberal dressing of nitrogenous phosphatic and potassic manures was applied each year.

The next best result was on Plot 2, which gave 35.5 bushels per acre; but to get this result 15.7 tons of farmyard manure per acre had to be annually applied.

The unmanured plot gave an average for 55 years of 12.9 bushels, whilst the average of the last five years was but 10 bushels. While continuous cropping with wheat has been practised at Rothamsted for upwards of 60 years for purely experimental purposes, it must not be supposed that such practices could be followed with profit in the drier areas of this State.

In considering the results obtained at Rothamsted, it is necessary to bear in mind that the average annual rainfall is not only heavy, but is also well distributed throughout the year. Thus, for 51 years, the average is 28.21 inches, of which the fall from January to March is 5.94 inches, April-June, 6.47 inches; July-September, 7.76 inches; and October-December, 8.04 inches. Continuous cropping has been practised at Roseworthy College (South Australia) on seven different plots in the Permanent

Experimental Field. The results are highly interesting, and indicate what is likely to take place in districts with a similar rainfall (17 inches).

TABLE I.—Showing average returns from Seven Plots continuously under Wheat (1905-7) compared with averages of plots under Wheat after Bare fallow. (Roseworthy College, S.A.).

Plot.	Rainfall.	Grain per acre.		Total Produce per acre.		
	inches	bush.	lbs.	tons	cwts.	lbs.
1. 1904—						
(a) Average of seven plots (fallowed 1903)	16·71	29	19	2	17	54
(b) Wheat after bare fallow ..	..	28	30	2	11	68
2. 1905—						
(a) Continuously cropped plots ..	19·72	9	15	1	8	0
(b) Wheat after bare fallow ..	..	20	3	2	3	12
3. 1906—						
(a) Continuously cropped plots ..	15·05	3	53	0	7	21
(b) Wheat after bare fallow ..	..	16	8	1	2	35

* Professor Perkins, in commenting on these plots, says—" We see here clearly demonstrated the futility of attempting to grow wheat continuously under local conditions. The grain crop fell from over 29 bushels per acre to a little over 9 bushels in the second year, and to not quite 4 bushels in the third year. In the second year the yield of plots continuously under wheat was about 11 bushels below the average of the plots that had been treated as bare fallow the preceding season; and in the third year about 12 bushels below. We shall not be blamed for having thrown up the experiment."

II.—WHEAT AFTER BARE FALLOW.

Bare fallowing is the most popular method of preparation for wheat in all but the most humid portions of the State. According to the *Year Book of Victoria*, 1910-11, the ratio of bare fallow to the area under wheat in 1900 was 13.88 : 50, *i.e*, 1 acre of bare fallow to every 4¼ acres of wheat. Ten years later the ratio had risen to 24.32 : 43.38, *i.e.*, more than 1 acre of bare fallow for every 2 acres of wheat.

The fact that the area under bare fallow in this State annually exceeds 1,000,000 acres is a silent testimony to the effectiveness of this mode of cultivation under the conditions prevailing in the wheat areas. Still the fact that there is such a large area of wheat in the drier portions of Victoria still sown on stubble land seems to indicate that the importance of fallowing in a dry climate is not yet fully appreciated.

ADVANTAGES OF BARE FALLOWING.

1. *Bare Fallowing conserves the Soil Moisture.*—The great advantage of bare fallowing in a dry climate is that it enables the cultivator to make the utmost use of a limited rainfall. In the drier districts the rainfall during the growing period is not sufficient to ensure high yields but, by a good system of bare fallowing, a considerable proportion of the rainfall from the previous year is conserved and carried over to augment the supply which falls during the period of growth of the crop.

Just how much moisture may thus be conserved under a given rainfall depends on the nature of the soil and the efficiency of cultivation. The

---

* Fourth Report on the Permanent Exp. Field, Roseworthy College, Bulletin No. 65, Dept of Agric., South Australia.

amount conserved and carried over is considerable when the land has been early fallowed, and the surface mulch maintained through the summer.

Some idea of the amount conserved may be gained from some preliminary observations at Rutherglen and Longerenong this season. In both instances the land was not fallowed till late in the season September, so that the moisture contents are not nearly as high as what might have been expected had fallowing been commenced, say, in June.

TABLE II.—Percentage of Moisture (in terms of dry soil) on Fallowed and Non-fallowed land prior to seeding, 1st May, 1912 (Rutherglen Viticultural College), Victoria.

Depth of Sample.	Fallowed.	Non-fallowed.	Difference.
	%	%	%
0 to 12 inches	7·62	3·12	4·50
12 inches to 24 inches	16·37	10·52	5·85
24 inches to 36 inches	16·68	12·28	4·40
36 inches to 48 inches	21·26	19·68	1·58
Average content of first 4 feet ..	15·48	11·40	4·08

Thus the fallowed land had 4.08 per cent. more moisture in the first 4 feet than the non-fallowed land.

Assuming the weight of 1 acre foot of dry soil to be approximately 3,500,000 lbs., it follows that in the first 4 feet of the Rutherglen fallow there were 571,200 lbs. more water per acre in the fallowed than in the non-fallowed portion, *i.e.*, an amount equal to approximately 2½ inches of rain.

Table III. summarizes the moisture content of fallowed and non-fallowed land at Longerenong Agricultural College at various depths during the summer and autumn of 1912.

TABLE III.—Moisture content of Fallowed and Non-fallowed land at Longerenong, 1912.

Depth of Sampling.	5th January, 1912.		25th March, 1912.		1st May, 1912.	
	Fallowed.	Non-fal-lowed.	Fallowed.	Non-fal-lowed.	Fallowed.	Non-fal-lowed.
	%	%	%	%	%	%
1. 0 to 12 inches	31·49	16·66	25·84	17·94	26·39	16·92
2. 12 inches to 24 inches ..	33·46	23·31	34·41	24·12	28·75	20·26
3. 24 inches to 36 inches ..	31·46	26·79	33·69	27·25	27·81	25·16
4. 36 inches to 48 inches ..	31·34	29·47	33·18	33·61	28·65	32·07
5. 48 inches to 60 inches ..	33·14	30·31	35·67	36·74	33·78	34·27
Average first 5 feet ..	32·18	25·31	32·56	27·93	29·07	25·74

It will be noted from the tables that, while there are considerable variations at corresponding levels at different periods, the average moisture content of the fallowed portions was considerably in excess of that of the non-fallowed portions. The difference in favour of the fallowed portion immediately before seeding amounted to 3.33 per cent.; this means that in the first 5 feet the fallowed portion has moisture equal to 2.6 inches of rain more than the non-fallowed portion.

In connexion with these tables, the following figures dealing with the rainfall from 1st July, 1911, at Rutherglen and Longerenong will prove interesting :—

TABLE IV.—Monthly rainfall, Rutherglen and Longerenong, from July, 1911, till 1st May, 1912.

						Rutherglen.	Longerenong.
						inches	inches.
July, 1911	..	..	..	..	..	1·33	1·51
August ..	..	..	..	..	..	1·27	·84
September	..	..	..	..	..	1·32	3·69
October ..	..	..	..	..	..	·29	·48
November..	..	..	..	..	..	·40	·07
December	..	..	..	..	..	2·05	2·25
January, 1912	..	..	..	..	..	·44	·00
February ..	..	..	..	..	..	·19	·47
March ..	..	..	..	..	..	·49	·55
April ..	..	..	..	..	..	·14	·67
Total	..	..	..	..	..	7·92	10·53

Comparing the extra water saved by fallowing (Tables II. and III.) with rainfalls (Table IV.), it will be seen that at both stations the water saved formed a considerable percentage of the rainfall for the preceding ten months, and this, too, although the fallowing commenced too late in the season. As moisture conservation is one of the principal objects aimed at in bare fallowing, we shall now consider more closely the means whereby this object may be attained.

In considering how to store and make effective the maximum quantity of moisture possible in the soil under any given rainfall, three points must be kept in mind.

(*a*) Every facility must be given to allow the moisture that falls to penetrate the soil, and not run off the surface, collect in pools, or evaporate.

(*b*) Provision must be made to allow moisture to move freely within the body of the soil and sub-soil in all directions, *i.e.*, the soil must be got into good capillary condition.

(*c*) No moisture must be allowed to evaporate from the surface by injudicious or careless handling of the soil.

These points are, of course, simple enough, but the question is how to make them materialize in practice.

(*a*) So far as the penetration of moisture is concerned, it will be apparent that any hard, compact, unbroken surface of soil is not calculated to admit moisture readily. In fact if heavy rains fall a large proportion runs rapidly off the surface, collects in pools, and much becomes lost by evaporation. On the other hand a loose broken surface allows moisture to penetrate readily, and, by acting as a mulch, conserves whatever moisture happens to be in the soil. Many farmers, realizing this, are beginning fallowing operations early in autumn by discing the land to catch the early rains as a preliminary to subsequent ploughing in June or July. The important point, however, is that ploughing should begin, more especially in a dry district, as soon as possible after seeding, so that ready penetration is afforded to the heavy winter rains.

(*b*) The next essential is to get the soil in such condition as to enable the imprisoned moisture to move freely within the soil. It must be remembered that the soil particles are solid bodies, devoid of pores, and, consequently, they cannot hold moisture interstitially, as a sponge. Moisture is held by the soil in the form of films surrounding the soil particles. The water holding capacity of a soil is dependent on its physical constitution, *i.e.*, the amount of organic matter, clay, sand, &c., present, and also on the minuteness of subdivision of the soil particles, *i.e.*, the tilth of the soil. A soil in a good state of tilth is not only capable of conserving a maximum of moisture, but it is also in the best possible capillary condition, *i.e.*, the moisture from the subsoil is able to move up more freely than in a similar soil with a poor tilth, composed of large cloddy particles. Consolidation of the soil is an important factor, because the presence of large air spaces in the soil promotes evaporation and interferes with the movements of capillary water. The method of achieving this will be referred to later. A finely divided and firmly consolidated stratum of soil resting on the well-moistened subsoil is in the very best condition not only for the storage of moisture, but for the movement of that moisture upward by capillary action.

(*c*) The moisture must be prevented from evaporating at the surface. A shower of rain readily causes the surface to run together and set. The hard surface then enables unbroken capillary connexion between the moisture-laden subsoil below and the dry crust at the top. By breaking the continuity of these capillary tubes by means of a cultivator the soil is effectively mulched, and evaporation is reduced to a minimum. In this connexion it may be mentioned that it is not necessary, from the point of view of moisture conservation, to have the surface of the soil finely pulverized. We often observe farmers harrowing away at the surface of the soil until the tilth is like an onion bed. The important point is to have the finely divided and firmly consolidated soil below; and it is not of great moment if the surface be rather rough and cloddy, provided only that it is loose.

2. *Bare Fallowing Increases the Supply of Available Plant Food.*—One indirect result of the moisture conserved by the process of bare fallowing is that during the summer months many chemical and biological changes take place within the body of the soil, and result in the liberation of plant food.

Just exactly what these changes are has not been completely demonstrated. There is no doubt, however, that the process of nitrification goes on rapidly in well-tilled bare fallows under Victorian conditions. By this process, nitrogenous organic matter is slowly converted by three stages into nitrates, and the action is brought about by specific bacteria. It has been estimated that at Rothamsted 80 lbs. of nitrogen as nitric acid are formed in 1 acre of land during a year of bare fallow. Further, losses through drainage over a period of thirteen years was 37 lbs. per acre. The rate of nitrification under Victorian conditions has not yet been completely worked out, but, owing to the high-soil temperature during summer, it is fairly rapid in our well-tilled bare fallows. For example, in the fallowed land at Longerenong, on 7th December, 1911, there were 57.75 lbs. per acre of nitrogen present as nitrate in the first 5 feet. On 1st April, 1912, this amount had increased to 105 lbs. in the same volume of soil.

In addition to the increase in nitrates, there can be little doubt that other important plant foods, particularly potash and phosphoric acid, are converted from unavailable to available forms.

3. *Bare Fallowing Distributes the Farm Work evenly through the Year.*—One of the great advantages of bare fallowing is in the fact that it enables the wheat-grower to have ready in autumn large areas in the best

state of tilth to receive the seed, as soon as the weather conditions are favorable for seeding.   This is a matter of considerable importance in the drier portions of the State where the normal seeding season is so restricted.

When favorable conditions for seeding exist, it is necessary for the Victorian farmer to concentrate his energy, not on the ploughs, but upon the drills.

If ploughing has to be done at seed time, the subsequent seeding must be delayed, and danger arises from the ill effects of a non-consolidated seed bed.

Those who relied this season on the early autumn rains to get their ploughing done, have had an experience they will not readily forget.   Such an abnormally dry autumn as we have just experienced brings home very forcibly the benefits obtained by having land ready for seeding when the rains fall.

(4) *Subsidiary advantages* of bare fallowing are that it cleans the land of weeds, increases the amount of available plant food formed in the soil, and enables a consolidated seed bed to be formed.

The experienced wheat-grower knows the value of a firm, consolidated seed bed for the wheat crop.   The consolidation necessary for success is not effected in a week or a month.   Time is a necessary factor of the process.   The consolidation is effected by the packing action of the rain and frequent cultivation, and is one of the benefits accruing from early fallowing.   A firm seed bed is an essential for the effective utilization of the subsoil moisture by capillarity.

Limitations of Bare Fallow under Australian Conditions.

1. *Unnecessary and Unprofitable in Humid Districts.*

It must be obvious, from the recital of the advantages of fallowing that it can only be completely successful in the drier portions of this State, and in a relatively dry climate.   Obviously the most serious drawback to bare fallowing is that only one crop can be grown in two years, and the crop must be debited with two years' rental value of the land.   Wherever large areas of land are held, and land values are low, and the climate relatively dry, this is not really a very serious matter, for the difference between the crop grown on fallow and that grown on stubble land may be so great as to make the two years' rental which the fallow crop bears an item of little importance.

On the other hand, in districts where land values are high, the loss of a crop is a matter of great importance.   High land values, however, are restricted to the relatively humid areas of the State, where considerations of moisture conservation are of secondary importance.   In such cases, where the annual rainfall is sufficiently high to enable heavy crops to be taken off annually fallowing is unnecessary, and even unprofitable, and should be substituted by a skilled system of rotation and catch cropping, if the soil resources are to be fully utilized.   What must be remembered in such cases is that the nitrates formed during the process of bare fallowing are, on the one hand, extremely soluble in water, and, on the other, the soil has no power to hold them.   Unless bare fallow, therefore, is supplanted by a fallow crop, or by a catch crop, the practice must result in a loss of the soil nitrates.

Evidence both of the extent to which bare fallowing is practised and the effectiveness in various districts may be gathered from figures collected from the *Year-Book of Victoria.*

Table V.—Wheat grown on fallowed and unfallowed land in Victoria, 1908.

| | Manured Land. | | | |
| | Fallowed. | | Non-fallowed. | |
	Area.	Average Yield.	Area.	Average Yield.
	Acres.	Bushels.	Acres.	Bushels.
Wimmera	69,834	11·82	27,520	5·75
Mallee	31,963	5·75	20,908	2·62
Northern	41,110	9·50	28,946	4·06
Western	4,821	17·93	5,993	13·47
	147,728	10·07	83,367	4·93

It will be noted that the three relatively dry districts in the Wimmera, Mallee, and Northern the yield of fallowed land was in all cases more than double that of the non-fallowed land. On the other hand, in the Western District, which as a whole is considerably more humid, the benefits of fallowing, though considerable, were relatively less marked than those of the three former districts. Unfortunately, these statistics were only taken in four districts, and for the one year, 1908.

2. *Bare Fallowing Leads to Depletion of Organic Matter.*

A continual alternation of wheat and bare fallow must ultimately lead to the depletion of the organic content of the soil. As a permanent practice it is, therefore, inadequate. To the natural depletion of the humus brought about by oxidation in well-tilled fallows must be added the further depletion caused by the burning of the straw. Any serious lessening of the organic content must inevitably result in a lowering of the crop-producing power of the soil. This depletion of organic matter is, to a large extent, counteracted by the practice of interposing a period of pasture between the wheat crop and the bare fallow. The merits of such simple rotations, however, lie outside the scope of the present article.

When to Fallow.

Early v. Late Fallowing.

When it is considered that the success of a bare fallow depends mainly on the amount of moisture conserved, it will be readily seen that, generally speaking, fallowing should commence as soon as other important operations permit. Inasmuch as the whole team strength of the farm is usually concentrated on seeding operations, it is rarely possible to commence fallowing simultaneously with seeding.

The general advantage of early fallow is that it exposes the soil to the ameliorating influences of the atmosphere for a longer period than late fallow, and that heavy winter rains readily penetrate the subsoil and are conserved. Moreover it is easier to effect a satisfactory consolidation of the seed bed with early than with late fallowed land.

As was remarked above, time is a most important factor in the con-solidation of the seed bed, and the most effective consolidation results from early fallowing.

With late spring fallowing much of the winter rain may be lost by evaporation and surface drainage, and the main benefit accruing from fallowing thereby lost. Unfortunately, results of continued and exhaustive local experiments on this important subject are wanting. Those, however, who annually fallow large areas of land, know by experience how prominently early fallowed land shows up against late fallowed land, especially when the fallowing season happens to be at all dry. Though early fallowing is justified as a general principle in wheat-growing areas, it must be remembered that with some soils it is not always practicable. Heavy clays, which tend to break down rapidly under the influence of winter rains, and set like a macadamized road with equal rapidity with the advent of dry weather, should be better left till the lighter types of soil have received attention.

The practice of early autumn discing as a preparation for winter plough-ing is frequently adopted in the drier areas with very satisfactory results.

The disc is put over the land in February or March, and the ploughing done at leisure after seeding. This not only provides a satisfactory mulch early in the season, but it enables autumn rains to readily penetrate the subsoil. Ploughing operations are greatly facilitated, and the loose, finely divided mulch turned over by the plough to the bottom of the furrow slice greatly aids in establishing a satisfactory capillary connexion between the subsurface soil and the moisture-laden subsoil.

The practical difficulty in carrying out this process is that in many parts of the State the soil sets so hard in the dry summer weather that discing is precluded. Otherwise there is no reason why the operation should not be commenced as soon after harvest as possible.

Depth of Working.

In deciding the depth to which he should plough and work his land, the farmer must be guided mainly by the character and depth of the soil and subsoil.

No arbitrary rules can be laid down, but each must decide for himself. Obviously deep working would be quite undesirable wherever the soil was shallow, or where is rested on an inferior type of subsoil. It is also very undesirable to bring a crude, raw clay subsoil to the surface. On soils that are naturally deep, however it is well to give, wherever possible, a good stiff furrow. Provided that the soil is of sufficient depth, and the subsoil is satisfactory, deep working is better suited to the requirements of an arid climate than shallow working. Such working materially increases the storage capacity of the soil for moisture, and provides for an inter-play of moisture and air at a greater depth than shallow working, and thus leads directly to the formation of a greater supply of available plant food. Of course the beneficial effects of such deep working are not always immediately apparent, and in conducting investigations into the relative merits of deep and shallow working the test should be continued for at least a number of years. Wherever deep working is practised it is neces-sary, if wheat is to be sown, that the ploughing should be done many months before seeding. No plant suffers more from the effects of a loose, open, non-consolidated seed bed than wheat, and if it is intended to give deep tillage, care must be taken to see that fallowing is started early in the season. The full benefit of the packing action of the rain, and of the settling of the seed bed by cultivation is thus secured.

The question frequently arises as to whether the soil should be worked down immediately after ploughing, or left in the rough for some time.

As a general principle, land should be left rough during the winter in a wet district, whilst in the very dry areas the sooner the land is worked down the better.

Much, of course, depends on the area one has to fallow and the number and strength of the teams available. In most districts, and on most soils, it will generally be found best to plough a considerable area before working down, especially if an early start is made. With the approach of spring, however, the stores of moisture in the soil must be jealously guarded, and the soil should be worked down with a scarifier or cultivator to make a loose, but lumpy, surface mulch.

SUMMER CULTIVATION.

Under no circumstances should a hard crust be allowed to form on the surface. A crusty top will, by aiding capillary action, rapidly drain the subsoil of its reserves of moisture A loose crumbly layer of soil will, however, act as a mulch and reduce the losses by evaporation to a minimum. Such a soil mulch is maintained by cultivating as often as the summer rains bring about a consolidation of the surface. Frequently summer cultivation is over done. The soil may be reduced by continual cultivation to the condition of an onion bed. This is a source of trouble on fine clay soils, and may assist rather than retard capillary activity.

(To be continued.)

The fattening ox spends about 77 per cent. of the food digested for heat and work, the sheep 74, and the pig 57.   The pig is the most economical meat producer, but it requires a ruminant to deal effectively with hay and fibrous crops.

YIELD OF RECONSTITUTED VINEYARD AT THE RUTHERGLEN VITICULTURAL COLLEGE.

Vintage 1912.

By G. H. Adcock, F.L.S., Principal.

Following the practice adopted during recent years the vintage returns for the Viticultural College vineyard, for the current season, are here submitted for the information of readers of the *Journal:*—

In justice to all concerned it will be necessary to remember that the vineyard is on the comparatively poor soil, typical of so many acres in this and other auriferous areas. While not specially suited for general agriculture, yet it adapts itself to viticulture readily. The vines in the College vineyard are planted 10 feet x 3 feet, trellised, and pruned on the rod and spur system. The grafted rootlings were planted immediately on the spot where vines, dead and dying with phylloxera, were uprooted. All round them were phylloxerated vines. Hence, the test as to their resistance was as severe as could have been devised.

This season has been the opposite extreme from last, and this has naturally influenced the yield very considerably. The 1911 returns constitute a record, as far as this vineyard is concerned. Unlike the previous one, last winter brought frosts. Only those that come after the vine-shoots have started, are feared by vignerons. Unfortunately, last Spring, we had two of these late frosts that cut back the shoots of the vines in the vineyard, and of the grafts in the nursery, entailing, in each case, serious losses.

Some varieties suffered severely, much more than others, and, consequently, these returns are reduced very much.

Nor were late frosts our only perplexity. The season, generally, has been as unfavorable as the preceding one was favorable. This has been one of the driest summers experienced here for some time. For months no appreciable quantity of rain has fallen. Our domestic water-supply ran out, and we had to cart from Rutherglen. Many of our well-established ornamental trees, have succumbed. Indigenous trees, *e.g.*, Grevilleas. Hakeas, Acacias, &c., have died, owing to the dry weather and the long-continued heat. Under such circumstances vintage and other yields have been greatly reduced. The adverse conditions prevailing here have extended considerably beyond the limits of our own State, and the vintage is a short one almost everywhere.

Again, we have suffered from the depredations of birds. This year, for the first time, the Starlings caused us trouble. Previously we had only had odd birds to contend with. As they are rapidly increasing in the district it is likely, judging by the present season, that they will make their influence severely felt in the future. As usual, too, pilferers have caused us loss.

Grapes are now freely purchased at high rates by several local winemakers. Up to, and occasionally more than, £8 per ton can be obtained. This is an immense advantage to the small grower who may not have the experience necessary to turn out a marketable wine, nor the capital to provide the plant for the purpose. It is also a distinct gain to the industry, for a product of uniform character and exactly suited to the requirements of the trade is assured.

The thorough cultivation, which is a feature in the College vineyard, has been kept up. This has paid, as it always does. As far as possible

RESISTANT VINE NURSERY, WAHGUNYAH, VICTORIA,

we also replenish the material removed by the crop, and we are strongly impressed with the efficiency of green manuring. As in the previous year we have carried out experiments with fertilizers, supplied by the manager of the Potash Syndicate, Sydney. The test plots, which are the same as those treated in 1911, are each ¼-acre in extent. The results are as follow :—

Plot.	Manure per Acre.	Yields per Acre.
		lbs.
No. 1	Unmanured	4,680
No. 2	{ Superphosphate, 2 cwt. .. .. { Sulphate of Ammonia, ¾ cwt.	4,724
No. 3	{ Superphosphate, 2 cwt. .. .. .. { Sulphate of Ammonia, ¾ cwt. .. .. { Sulphate of Potash, 1 cwt.	6,360

This shows a gain of exactly three-quarters of a ton between the unmanured and plot No. 3. The value of this extra yield, at current rates, is £6. while the total value of the crop, from the fully-manured acre, is worth £22 14s. 3d.

In tabulated form are given the yields of the grapes from each stock. Once again a caution must be given against attributing the disparity in returns to the stocks. As previously pointed out the crop recorded on Rupestris du Lot is not fair to that stock, for, being next to the road, much of the produce does not reach our weighing machine. Growers will also note that some of the stocks, used when the College vineyard was replanted to test their value, are now discarded as not quite satisfactory. Of the new varieties we have, as far as possible, made the wine separately. We have 16 lots of these varying from 5 to 10 gallons each. Winemakers will realize the immense amount of trouble and labour the careful handling of so many small quantities has entailed, but will, we think, appreciate the results. Some of the newer table varieties of grapes are in cool storage to test their keeping qualities, and, consequently, their suitability for the export trade.

Of the newer varieties, from which wine was made, we have the following :—

Variety.	Sp. Gr. of Must.	Quantity Made.
Furmint	1·110	5 gallons
Pinot Chardonnay	1·120	2 ,,
Pinot Fin	1·120	5 ,,
Semillon	1·106	5 ,,
Melon	1·102	5 ,,
Colombard	1·110	10 ,,
Sauvignon	1·120	5 ,,
Aramon	1·090	18 ,,
Corbeau	1·095	10 ,,
Aspiran Bouschet	1·085	10 ,,
Chenia blanc	1·110	5 ,,
Folle blanche	1·092	10 ,,
Picpoul	1·095	10 ,,
Montils	1·090	10 ,,
Rousette	1·094	10 ,,
Terret Bourret	1·080	10 ,,

VINTAGE AT RUTHERGLEN VITICULTURAL COLLEGE, VICTORIA.

The following are the yields for vintage, 1912:—

Variety, Date of Planting, and Stock.	Sp. Gr. of Must.	Yield per Vine.	Yield per Acre.	Value per Acre at £8 a ton.
		lbs.	tons cwt. qrs. lbs.	£ s. d.
Shiraz (1903)—				
Hybrid, 3306	1·108	12·16	2 19 0 7	23 12 6
Rupestris Metallica (Cape) ..	1·108	9·64	2 6 3 8	18 14 7
Hybrid, 3309 ..	1·112	8·55	2 1 2 4	16 12 4
A.R.G.1	1·110	6·84	1 13 0 24	13 5 8
Rupestris du Lot ..	1·117	6·03	1 9 1 4	11 14 4
Burgundy (1904)—				
Riparia Grand Glabre ..	1·114	8·78	2 2 2 16	17 1 2
Hybrid, 3309 ..	1·113	6·47	1 11 1 21	12 11 6
Malbec (1904)—				
Riparia Grand Glabre ..	1·113	9·9	2 8 0 10	19 4 9
A.R.G.1	1·105	9·77	2 7 1 23	18 19 8
Hybrid, 3309 ..	1·110	7·56	1 16 2 27	14 13 10
Rupestris Metallica (Cape) ..	1·110	6·8	1 13 0 3	13 4 3
Hybrid, 101[14] ..	1·114	6·0	1 9 0 16	11 13 2
Rupestris du Lot ..	1·108	4·16	1 0 0 23	8 1 8

The following table gives the yields from the various stocks for the years 1909-1912, inclusive:—

Variety, Date of Planting, and Stock.	Yield per Acre 1909.	Yield per Acre 1910.	Yield per Acre 1911.	Yield per Acre 1912.
	t. cwt. q. lbs.	t. cwt. q. lbs.	t. cwt. q. lbs.	t. cwt. q. lbs.
Shiraz (1903)—				
Hybrid, 3306	2 5 2 0	2 8 3 23	3 2 1 0	2 19 0 7
Rupestris Metallica (Cape)	1 15 3 4	2 2 2 22	4 0 1 27	2 6 3 8
Hybrid, 3309	1 14 0 0	1 15 1 3	2 14 2 9	2 1 2 4
A.R.G.1	1 9 0 1	1 18 0 10	2 18 0 18	1 13 0 24
Rupestris du Lot ..	1 5 3 14	1 15 1 17	2 10 0 5	1 9 1 4
Burgundy (1904)—				
Riparia Grand Glabre ..	1 5 1 23	1 14 2 25	1 5 2 20	2 2 2 16
Hybrid, 3309	1 1 2 11	1 15 3 19	1 0 3 23	1 11 1 21
Malbec (1904)—				
A.R.G.1	2 3 0 8	3 1 2 3	4 17 0 6	2 7 1 23
Riparia Grand Glabre ..	1 18 3 12	2 16 1 5	4 11 1 17	2 8 0 10
Hybrid, 3309	1 16 1 26	2 4 1 20	3 19 1 19	1 16 2 27
Rupestris Metallica (Cape)	1 16 1 20	2 4 3 9	3 8 1 16	1 13 0 3
Hybrid, 101[14]	0 14 3 14	1 9 2 0	2 19 3 12	1 9 0 16
Rupestris du Lot ..	..	1 6 1 0	2 0 0 18	1 0 0 23

PROPAGATION OF FRUIT TREES.

(Continued from page 211.)

C. F. Cole, Orchard Supervisor.

DISEASES.

In compiling the diseases, both insect and fungi, to be found at times attacking the stocks and young trees during and after their development in the nursery, the writer wishes to strongly impress upon propagators the importance of keeping a sharp look-out for the first signs of attack, and of taking immediate steps to check the spread or eradicate the disease. To do this, and be successful, it is essential to have a sufficient knowledge of the different diseases with regard both to their life history and their methods of attack. As there are several illustrated and instructive works published dealing with destructive insects and fungus pests, and a special staff of experts attached to the Department of Agriculture, growers or those interested have no excuse for remaining ignorant of such subjects. To be fully conversant with the habits, the manner in which diseases obtain their food, and the season of attack, is to be forewarned, and if the propagator is intelligent, he will be prepared for an attack by being forearmed with the necessary appliances and chemicals needed, which, if used correctly, and at the right time, will give him the victory. The insect pests dealt with will be arranged according to the manner in which they attack the plants to obtain food, those that eat the foliage, twigs, or bark being called chewing, whilst those that puncture to obtain the sap being called suctorial. Upon classifying them as such will depend how they are to be attacked and destroyed.

With chewing insects it will be necessary to control them by applying with a fine spray poison to their food, so that when taken internally it will cause death. With suctorial insects it is necessary to bring them in direct contact with a suitable insecticide which causes death by smothering, combined with its caustic action. By the enumeration of the following insect and fungus pests, the novice or those about to start propagation should not be frightened, as in a nursery conducted upon sound lines, and where care is exercised in securing the buds, scions, or rooted stocks from clean trees or localities there is very little likelihood of diseases giving serious trouble. Many of the diseases adapt themselves to certain localities where the weather and other conditions are more suitable for their development. But it should be borne in mind that if such diseases are transferred from one locality to another, and the conditions are favorable, there will be trouble, *e.g.*, take the root-rot fungus (*Armillaria mellea*). Although it is commonly found in cool mountainous and timbered localities having a fair rainfall, yet, if transferred upon rooted stocks from such localities to a warm dry one, and the spring or summer following planting is suitable for its development, it will cause trouble if immediate steps are not taken when first noticed to check its spread. As most of our insect pests multiply with astonishing rapidity, delay in attacking them is dangerous; by destroying the first brood whole days of toil will be saved. It is generally through neglecting this brood that future trouble is brought about, and instead of a few insects to fight in a few days or weeks there are thousands. A nurseryman should have a suitable spray pump, an 8 or 10 gallon hand-pump will answer the purpose, and also keep many of the necessary chemicals, &c., to combat diseases on hand. Always keep the old adage well in mind—" A stitch in time saves nine." The few illustrations of diseases are from original photographs.

CHEWING INSECTS.

The Pear and Cherry Slug (Selandria Cerasi).—This small, dark-green or, at first sight, blackish-looking, slimy caterpillar usually makes its appearance about the latter end of October or early in November, and attacks the foliage of the cherry and pear, and, later on, the cherry plum family, the quince, occasionally the plum. The eggs are readily discernible, being deposited upon the upper side of the leaves, and are of a yellowish colour, about the size of a pin's head. The perfect insect is a glossy black small fly belonging to the saw fly order, *Hymenoptera*, readily seen upon the foliage. The William's Bon Chretien pear is generally the first to be attacked in the nursery row. If this pest is neglected, the larvæ will quickly destroy the foliage by eating off all of the epidermis or upper surface of the leaves, thereby checking the growth, and bringing about debilitated conditions. *Treatment.*—Spray as soon as detected with any of the leading brands of arsenate of lead—strength 1 lb. to 25 gallons of water—or Hellebore powder, 1 lb. to 30 gallons of water. Moisten the powder with a little water to make a paste before adding the full quantity of water; strain before using; keep well agitated whilst applying. Spray upon a fine dry day.

FIG. 69.

Pinara Apple Grub (Pinara Nana).—The larvæ of this pest are most voracious, stripping the young apple trees of their foliage in a very short while; also eating the tops of the growing shoots. The loss of the foliage gives the trees a serious check through interfering with the assimilation and elaboration of the sap and plant food. Upon noticing the first signs of attack the propagator should carefully examine along the stems of the young shoots and branches for the larvæ, which, owing to their protective colour, resembling that of the bark, combined with their habit of lying close to the bark, make them hard to detect. The larvæ when full grown are about 2 inches in length. From observations the writer finds that this pest feeds chiefly at night, lying close to the bark during the day-time. *Treatment.*—As a serious attack from this pest in the nursery is of rare occurrence, the destruction of the few larvæ when first detected generally suffices to check its spread. If indications point to a severe attack, spray with arsenate of lead. If the well-known native bird, black-faced cuckoo shrike, *Graucalus Melanops* (Lath.) is in the locality, it should be rigidly protected, as the writer has upon many occasions watched these birds doing great service in a nursery eradicating this pest.

Painted Apple Moth (Teia Anartoides) (Walk).—The small hairy caterpillar " larvæ " of this moth have an especial liking for the foliage of the apple, eating off the upper portion, or epidermis, very quickly, at times

leaving only the midrib of the leaves. Figure 69 shows the caterpillars
at work upon an apple stock. The loss of foliage seriously affects the
elaboration of the sap. This pest does not confine its attack solely to the
apple, but attacks the foliage of other kinds of fruit trees, and at times the
skin of the fruit. *Treatment.*—Very often killing the first few caterpillars
with the thumb and finger will prevent a further attack. Spraying the
foliage thoroughly with arsenate of lead will have the desired effect of
getting rid of this pest.

Cherry Green Beetle (Diphucephala Colospidoides) (Gyll).—A visitation from these small, handsome green beetles is to be taken seriously.
If coming in swarms, they very soon strip the young cherry trees of their
foliage, and cause great damage to the young growing trees and cherry
stocks. When first noticed immediate action should be taken. The trees
and stocks should be thoroughly sprayed with arsenate of lead, strength
1 lb. to 25 or 30 gallons of water.

Vine Moth (Agarista Glycine) (Lewis).—This common pest is very
easily recognised and kept in check, but, if neglected, the caterpillars will
very soon defoliate the vines. Spraying the young vines in early summer
with arsenate of lead generally suffices to keep this pest in check for the
whole vegetative period. Strength, 1 in 25 to 30 of water; or Hellebore
powder at the same strength recommended for pear or cherry slugs.

Silver Striped Vine Moth (*Chaerocampa Celerio*) (Stephen).—This
pretty but peculiar looking caterpillar rarely gives trouble, the writer once
only having had occasion to spray the vines. *Treatment.*—Spray with
arsenate of lead, or Hellebore powder.

Slugs.—During the spring, and when the buds begin to move in the
nursery row, slugs are one of the worst pests that the propagator has to
deal with, destroying hundreds of buds in a single night, if neglected.
Treatment.—If there are any signs of this pest during late autumn or
the winter months, no time should be lost in clearing away any weed
growths in the rows, particularly before the buds start to elaborate. One
of the chief factors in combating this pest is to keep the nursery free from
anything likely to harbor them. The soil should be kept well stirred
between the rows, applying freshly slackened lime immediately after. This
will be the means of destroying large numbers that harbor and breed beneath the clods of earth. Slugs being nocturnal in habit, just after dark is
the best time to attack them, particularly if rain has fallen during the day,
and the evening turns in mild.

Treatment of Lime.—Secure lump lime; slacken by sprinkling with
water. If using any quantity place the lump lime in a hole or pit made in
the earth for the purpose, half fill with lime, applying sufficient water to
slacken. Lime should be prepared in the morning, using it the same evening. Bag the slackened lime during the afternoon, placing the bags in
convenient positions in the nursery. Under no conditions allow the lime
to get damp or wet, before or after slackening, or any time previous to
being applied. Always use freshly slackened lime. Apply by placing
sufficient slack lime in a piece of hessian or a 70 lb. sugar-bag. Walk between the rows, jerking the bag up and down smartly, directing the dense
lime dust caused by these actions chiefly over the buds. If a dark night, it
will be necessary to carry a lantern whilst performing this operation. If
help is available to carry the light, this work can be accelerated by using
a dusting bag in each hand. Failing help, place the lantern in the centre,
i.e., between two rows of buds, and walk whilst dusting straight towards
the light. Stirring and dusting lime upon the soil during the day-time, and
following up the dusting process after dark, has been found by the writer

to be the most effective method, particularly if the area to be treated is of any extent. Besides destroying this pest, the lime is very beneficial to the soil, especially if it is deficient in this constituent. To be effective the lime must fall direct upon the slugs. Once it becomes moist, its power of killing is gone. When liming wear old boots and clothes. Apply lime when the weather is fine and calm, if possible, but remember that delay is dangerous to the buds.

SUCTORIAL INSECTS.

Some of the most difficult insects to eradicate coming under this heading are those known as scale, and belonging to the family Coccidae. Some species confine their attacks chiefly, if not solely, to deciduous trees and plants, whilst others only to evergreen ones. Some species attack many kinds of plant life both evergreen and deciduous. When treating evergreen trees, or any that are vegetative, the operator should be very careful to use a wash at a strength that will not defoliate or injure the growth of the young trees. No wash should be used that is not correctly made and tested, nor applied unless the operator has had previous experience or secures practical advice upon the particular wash to be used. One important factor that should not be overlooked before applying a caustic wash is the physiological condition of the tree or plant at the time it is to be sprayed, such condition varying according to the season, the weather, and the growth. Evergreen trees and plants when fully active and making growth cannot stand the same strength as when in a more dormant stage, or when the weather is cool and equable. With deciduous trees and plants, a far greater strength can be used in the late autumn, or when they have shed their foliage in the winter, than

FIG. 70.

any time during their vegetative period. Two or three somewhat weaker applications given at regular intervals are far more effective, and the risk of causing injury less, than if one application at the ordinary strength is given.

Olive Scale (Lecanium Oleæ).—This common scale insect, when fully developed, is hemispherical in shape (see Fig. 70), colour brownish black, is easily detected, and attacks the bark and foliage. Trees and plants badly attacked have a sooty appearance caused by the fungus known as sooty mould (*Capnodium Citricolum*). This fungus lives upon the sugary secretion from the scale insects. Another indication of attack is the appearance of ants and flies upon the trees or plants attacked, in quest of this sugary secretion. It is the commonest scale found attacking the citrus family, is very partial to the pear and quince, and is to be found attacking numerous species of plant life both evergreen and deciduous. *Treatment.*—If attacking deciduous trees, seed and stone fruits in the nursery row during their vegetative period, spray with kerosene emulsion, strength, 1 in 10 or 12. If attacking citrus trees or other hard-foliaged evergreens, spray with resin wash. The best time to spray the citrus is the winter months, and after the spring growth has hardened, and before the autumn growths start. Citrus and deciduous fruit trees standing in the nursery row during the winter months may be sprayed with red oil or crude petroleum oil emulsion, but great care should be taken to see that the emulsion is properly made, otherwise injury will be done to the trees. Strength, red oil, 1 in 40; crude petroleum oil, 1 in 30.

Greater Vine Scale (Lecanium Berberidis)—This large brown-coloured scale insect does not confine its attack to the vine, but is to be found severely attacking many kinds of our fruiting trees, chiefly the apricot, cherry. plum, Japanese plums, mulberry, and persimmon, also many of our ornamental trees, shrubs, and creepers. Owing to its size is easy to detect, and attacks the bark of the branches and twigs. Spreads rapidly, but is the easiest of all the scale insects to destroy. *Treatment.*—Spray the vines or fruit trees if attacked during the vegetative period with kerosene emulsion. Strength, 1 in 10 or 12, giving several applications, if necessary. When the trees or vines are dormant in the winter, spray with red oil or crude petroleum oil emulsion. Strength, red oil, 1 in 40; crude petroleum, 1 in 30.

Red Orange Scale (Aspidiotus Coccineus).—Scale insects belonging to the genus Aspidiotus are probably the hardest of all scale insects to eradicate by spraying. Fumigation by hydrocyanic acid gas is the most effective treatment where it is possible to carry it out. Although a small scale, it is easy to detect owing to its colour, and attacks the bark, fruit, and foliage. When badly attacked, the foliage becomes sickly and yellowish in colour, the twigs and young growth die. If this pest should make its appearance upon the citrus trees in the nursery row, immediate steps should be taken to thoroughly eradicate it. By exercising a little care when and where selecting the buds and grafts, a nursery should be kept free from this pest. *Treatment.*—Spray thoroughly and often with resin wash until eradicated. If the scale is very bad, give one or two sprayings with red oil or crude petroleum oil emulsion during the winter months, or in January and February, continuing later on, if necessary, with the resin wash. Strength, red oil, 1 in 45; crude petroleum, 1 in 35.

Black Flat Scale (Aspidiotus Rossi).—A very common scale. Attacks hard foliaged evergreen trees, &c. Once it is firmly established is hard to eradicate. From its shape and colour, it is readily detected upon the foliage, hence its name. In a nursery producing fruiting trees, this scale is not likely to give serious trouble; to the writer's knowledge, the only species of fruit attacked belonged to the citrus family, viz., pomelo or grape fruit, the bitter-sweet and Seville variety. *Treatment.*—The same as Red Orange Scale.

Wax Scale (Ceroplastes Ceriferus).—This scale is easy to detect by its resemblance to small pieces of white wax, and sticks close to the bark upon the boughs and twigs. The wax substance is secreted by the insects to protect and cover the body. Because of the waxy covering, the pest is difficult to destroy. This scale readily attacks the citrus family. *Treatment.*—Spray with 1½ lbs. of washing soda dissolved in 2 gallons of water, or resin wash when the scale insects are young. Apply using high pressure.

San Jose Scale (Aspidiotus Perniciosus).—This scale is one of the most difficult species to detect, owing to its small size and the closeness with which it sticks to the bark. To the propagator of deciduous fruiting trees this scale insect is to be feared most. Once it becomes established, it is hard to dislodge. The writer's observations are that when full grown this scale varies somewhat in colour. Where found attacking the plum and walnut, it is lighter, resembling more the colour of the bark than when found upon the apple, pear, &c. Small rusty red-coloured spots upon the bark, the scale insect occupying the central position, are usually one of the first indications of attack upon the apple, pear, peach, and cherry plum. Description.—General colour, sooty black, with a yellowish-brown spot in the centrè; shape, round. If the bark directly beneath these red spots is cut, it is generally a carmine shade down to the cambium. With badly infested trees the bark has a scurfy appearance, occasionally being pitted. This pest does not confine its attack to fruiting trees, but has a liking also for the hawthorn, &c. *Treatment.*—As there have been several outbreaks of this pest in different parts of the State, all buds or scions secured from an orchard should be thoroughly examined, particularly about and behind the buds, with a pocket magnifier. If there are any suspicious signs of attack or scale insects to be seen, destroy by burning. Trees or stocks badly infested should at once be destroyed by burning. If the trees are vegetative, spray thoroughly with kerosene emulsion, strength 1 in 10. Follow up with further applications at not more than ten days intervals. Further, treat in late autumn and the winter months with red oil or crude petroleum oil emulsion. Strength, red oil, 1 in 30; crude petroleum, 1 in 25. No trees should be sent out of the nursery until examined by some person who has an expert knowledge of this disease.

To be continued.

WATER REQUIREMENTS OF CROPS.

By John W. Paterson, B.Sc., Ph.D., Experimentalist.

Of the various requirements for the growth of a crop the most obvious is a sufficient supply of water. Ordinary experience points to the conclusion that the quantity required must be large. Green-house plants require frequent watering or they shrivel and dry up. A crop of lucerne cut in the morning is soon withered, because it ceases to receive water from the roots. Year after year the yields from dry farming depend more upon rainfall than, practically speaking, upon anything else. In the drier wheat areas of Victoria the soil may not receive enough rainfall to grow a crop every year, but, by fallowing in alternate years the water may sufficiently accumulate to grow a crop every second.

To determine exactly how much water is required by growing crops, attempts have been made by different investigators in different countries of the world. In all such investigations, apart from those of botanical interest only, the method is the same. The amount of water evaporated or "transpired" by a crop during its entire growth is found by weighing. At harvest, the crop is cut off close to the ground and dried. When the weight of water transpired is now divided by the weight of crop, there is found what is called the "transpiration ratio." This gives the number of pounds (parts) of water transpired by the crop during growth for each pound (part) of dry matter produced.

In such investigations the water transpired is found by growing the plants in pots. A pot is filled with a certain standard weight of soil (usually from 20 to 120 lbs.) of a certain wetness, and the crop is planted or sown. The pot is watered, usually daily, or four times a week; and this is done on the scales.   At watering, the loss of weight since the previous watering is noted down, and the pot is then brought up to its standard weight again by adding more water.   The water lost from a cropped pot will include water transpired by the plant, also water evaporated directly from the soil.   The latter is most simply discounted by setting up similar pots without a crop, and deducting the losses there from the losses on the cropped pots throughout the season.   In transpiration experiments the pots must be protected from rain in order to reserve control of the water supply.   This is usually done by placing the pots on low trolleys standing on rails, so that they can be run under cover at night and on wet days.

Proceeding on the general lines of investigation indicated, the following results have been obtained by different workers :—

TABLE I.

——	Lawes (1) (England).	Hellriegel (2) (Germany).	King (3) (United States).	Leather (4) (India).
Wheat	247	338	..	850
Barley	257	..	393	680
Oats ..	..	376	522	870
Rye ..	..	353	..	..
Maize ..	..	..	310	..
Beans ..	209	282	..	..
Peas ..	259	273	477	830
Clover	269	310	453	..
Buckwheat	..	363	..	..
Rape ..	..	329	..	..

(1) Jour. Horticultural Soc., V. (1850).
(2) Grundlagen des Ackerbaues, p. 622, *et seq.*
(3) Rep. Wisconsin, Expt. Stn., 1894, p. 248.
(4) Mem. Dept. Agric., India. Chemical series.   Vol. I., No. 8, p. 179.

The figures state the transpiration ratios found by different observers. Before going on to discuss them, it is necessary to glance briefly at the uses of water to the plant.

Water enters the plant body by the roots, passes upwards through the stem, and is evaporated by the leaves during transpiration.   In its passage through the plant, the water performs certain useful work.   It carries dissolved phosphates, nitrates, &c., from the soil into the plant; it is necessary for the life and growth of the protoplasm or living part of the plant, and for the action of ferments ; a small part of the water absorbed enters chemically into organic material in the process of carbon assimilation.

Carbon assimilation is the process whereby green plants feed from the carbon dioxide gas of the air and from water.   About 95 per cent. of the dry matter of crops is formed from air and water in this way.

It is difficult to say in which of its uses to the plant it becomes necessary that so much water should pass through it during the period of growth.   The inward passage of soil constituents probably does not altogether require it, as the water current and the soil nutrient movement are within inside limits independent.   It is more likely that the partial parching of a crop restricts growth, in the first instance, by increasing the difficulty of carbon assimilation. This up-hill chemical change requires the presence of very much water in the plant leaf, in addition to the relatively small amount which is decomposed there.

Transpiration of water takes place chiefly through little pores or openings called stomata,* which are most abundant on the under side of the leaf. These pores or stomata open and close automatically, according as the water supply is greater or less; but sun and wind modify their control by tending to open them. With the pores open, transpiration proceeds apace, but is naturally more rapid with a dry than a humid atmosphere. It is also very much greater in light than darkness, and plants wilted at night may appear fresh in the morning.

Looking to the effect of sun, wind, and a dry atmosphere upon evaporation from the leaves of plants, one would expect that the amount of water lost would in large measure be dependent upon the climate. It has been mentioned that much water is essential to carbon assimilation. This takes place in the green leaves, and only by day. As water is continually passing through the leaves on its way out by day, it follows that the water is only available as an aid to assimilation in the course of its passage. Now, as transpiration from the leaves is more active in a dry sunny climate, it would seem that more water must pass through the plant to maintain a suitable supply for carbon-assimilation in such a climate than in a dull humid one where it lingers longer in the leaf. In other words, a definite amount of water may be necessary for carbon-assimilation at its best, in a certain plant, under a certain intensity of light, and at a given instant, but as transpiration is more rapid in a dry climate, a larger amount of water must be absorbed there than in a humid one in order to maintain equally good water conditions in the leaf.

Returning now to the figures of Table I., it will be seen that an attempt has been made in each case to fix the transpiration ratio as a specific character of the crop. If however as we have endeavoured to show, the usefulness of water is dependent, in the first degree, upon the length of time the leaf is able to retain it, it becomes obvious that the transpiration ratio is less a factor depending upon the kind of crop than upon the climatic conditions of the country in which the experiments are carried out. Comparison of the results of the different workers bears in a rough way this theory out. The transpiration ration for production seems to be lowest in the country with the most humid climate, and differences due to crop are generally small as compared to differences due to country.

While the rate of transpiration from plants is largely dependent upon the physical conditions of climate which determine rate of drying, it cannot be supposed to be altogether so. The cells of the stomata respond to sun and wind, but this response bears no relation to their drying effect. Consideration of the vigour or tone of the plant also comes in. Nevertheless it is certain that the climatic conditions which cause drying have a very great influence upon the transpiration ratio of growing crops, and that by knowing the relative rates of evaporation from a free water surface at two places the transpiration requirements at one place could be approximately calculated for the other.

---

* *See* Wheat and its Cultivation, by A. E. V. Richardson. Jour. Dept. Agric., Vic., 1912, p. 187, *et seq.*

As transpiration experiments of other countries seemed unlikely, for the reasons stated, to be of direct application to Australian conditions, some test pots were set out at Burnley Horticultural Gardens during the past season. Wheat and oats were selected, and the general method adopted was that already described. The pots, which were adapted to the Wagner pattern, contained 37 lbs. 1 oz. of dry soil, made up to contain 18.5 per cent. of water (equal to 50 per cent. of the total water-holding capacity reckoned on the soil volume). The pots were watered on the scales with a fine spray. The amount of water transpired by the plants was got by deducting the loss of weight in similar fallow pots. To avoid rain, the pots were placed under cover in the best position available; but, soon after starting, it was evident there was too little light, and the wheat pots were discarded. The growing oats suffered less. The experiments lasted 159 days, starting from 6th September. Fig. 1 shows some of the pots at the time of harvesting, on 13th February.

Fig. 1.

At harvest, the crops were cut off close to the ground, dried, and the transpiration ratios calculated out. The results were as follows:—

TABLE II.

		Total Water Lost (159 days).	Excess over Average of Fallow Pots.	Weight of Dry Crop.	Transpiration Ratio.
		Grams.	Grams.	Grams.	
Pot 4 (Fallow) ..	..	12,785	..	..	..
Pot 4' (Fallow) ..	..	12,729	..	..	..
Pot 29 (Oats) ..	..	17,832	5,075	10·32	492
Pot 29' (Oats) ..	..	18,342	5,585	11·76	475

On comparing the results with those given for other countries on Table I., it will be seen that the ratio is higher than those obtained for cereals in Europe, but lower than American and Indian results. It cannot be said, however, that the comparison with the Burnley pots is quite satisfactory. In the earlier stages of growth the crops suffered from undue shading, and in the latter stage from the same influence at certain hours of the day. It has already been mentioned that transpiration is most active in bright light, and practically ceases at night. In connexion with this, it would be expected that the transpiration ratio would be higher for plants grown in the open air than in plants partially shaded most of the time. It has recently been shown by Dr. H. Brown that it would be about one-half greater. Accepting this figure instead of the average figure 483, we should then have a transpiration ratio of 725 for oat plants grown in the open. The Indian figure for oats is 870, and it appears likely that 725 more nearly expresses the ratio for the Australian climate than the results given in the table.

In discussing the question of assimilation it has been pointed out that the transpiration ratio is chiefly dependent upon the climate, but that it is not altogether so. In this connexion an important practical point was recently established by Dr. J. W. Leather of the Agricultural Research Institute, Pusa. In the dry climate of India the transpiration ratio tends to be high. It was found, however, that crops grown with manures made a better use of the water than crops with no manure, as is seen by the decreased ratios in every case.

TABLE III.

——	Unmanured.	Manured.
Wheat	850	550
Barley	680	480
Oats	870	550
Peas	830	530
Maize	450	330

The first four are cold weather crops, in which evaporation is rapid, the last a monsoon crop, during which season the atmosphere is humid and moist giving generally low ratios. In discussing the results the author points out that not only does superphosphate have effect in narrowing the ratio, but that nitrates also, if required for plant food, and as might not be anticipated, have a like effect. After an elaborate series of experiments lasting some years, it is stated that " the effect of a suitable manure in aiding the plant to economize water is the most important factor which has yet been noticed in relation to transpiration."

In concluding consideration of this subject it should be pointed out that the provision of a pot-culture house, on lines similar to those erected in other countries, is essential if the influence of local conditions upon the water relations of plants in Victoria is to be successfully studied. At Burnley a large number of pot cultures failed owing to the want of suitable equipment, and the results from those few which have completed have had to be discussed with reserve.

The following conclusions have been arrived at :—

1. In cold humid climates, from 200 to 300 tons of water is lost by transpiration for each ton of dry crop yield.

2. Experiments in different countries indicate that this ratio is increased in drier climates.

3. In Victoria the ratio for crops of moderate development possibly lies somewhere about 700.

4. Suitable manures, by rendering the plants more vigorous, reduce the transpiration ratio, and enable them to make a better use of available moisture.

5. Local conditions indicate that about 600 tons of water ($= 6''$ rain) must pass through a 13-bushel crop of wheat during its period of growth.

BUNYIP AGRICULTURAL SOCIETY.

By B. A. Barr, Dairy Supervisor.

This society merits the keen appreciation of all progressive dairymen in having introduced and conducted a dairy cow test in the district. From such test much benefit must result. It has a very wide-spreading educational influence. It amply demonstrates that the key to payable dairying is sufficient fodder of the proper kind, and careful attention, so that the activities of milk secretion may be maintained to the highest capacity dependent upon individual development; also it shows a record of each cow's yield, and the earnings of the lactation period are known. The only way to determine the cash return of each cow is by the continued use of the scales and the Babcock tester.

Such a contest as this acts as an incentive to others to emulate the achievements of the winner, and, consequently, is of great influence in improving the productivity of district herds. It also brushes aside the so-called records of incredible yields. The results of the competition are such as one would find in any ordinary herd. The tests for morning's milk —which is usually somewhat lower than evening's milk—are good. The deductions to be drawn from the results are consistent with known local dairying conditions. More feed and weigh the milk, so that the exact amount can be scheduled, are the lines to follow.

The Bunyip Agricultural Society is to be congratulated for undertaking this dairy cow test, and it is hoped will continue to hold one yearly, when it is suggested that the milk of two consecutive milkings be taken. The number of entries for a first occasion is encouraging.

RESULTS.

Name.			Milk in Morning.	Test.	Butter Fat.	Order.
Fleming, J.	..	..	21·5	5·1	1·09	1
Downes, J.	..	..	22·0	4·2	0·92	2
McIvor, P.	..	..	25·0	3·6	0·90	3
Jenkin, W. H.	..	..	23·5	3·6	0·84	..
Smethurst, J. H.		..	18·5	4·5	0·83	..
Strafford, T.	..	..	21·0	3·9	0·81	..
Greaves, F.	..	..	19·75	4·0	0·79	..
Cook, T. M.	..	..	16·25	4·0	0·73	..
Greaves, F.	..	..	16·25	3·8	0·61	..
Field, M.	..	..	18·0	2·9	0·52	..

The winner is a cow 15 years old.

BEE-KEEPING IN VICTORIA.

(*Continued from page 228.*)

By F. R. Beuhne, Bee Expert.

V.—HIVE FLOORS AND COVERS.

FLOORS.

The hive stand generally sold by manufacturers and dealers consists of a single board 22 inches long, 13⅞ inches wide, and ⅞-inch thick, nailed on to a piece of 3in. x 2in. at each end, as shown in Fig. 5 of the previous article. On the top of this board, along two sides are nailed strips of wood 19⅛ inches long, ⅞-inch wide, and 5-16-inch in thickness. A piece of like dimensions, but only 13⅞ inches long, is nailed across one end. These three cleats raise the hive body 5-16-inch, and form a bee-space between the bottom bars of the frames and the hive-stand, and, at the same time, constitute the entrance to the hive. This entrance is 12½in. x 5-16-in., and may be contracted in winter by blocking it for one-half or two-thirds with pieces of ⅞in. x 5-16in. wood. It is not advisable to have entrances larger than 5-16-inch, as mice may enter and destroy any combs not occupied by bees. This hive stand is fairly satisfactory, but rather expensive. The projection, which serves as an alighting board at the entrance, is also a somewhat objectionable feature, as it prevents close packing of hives in shifting colonies by road or rail.'

A hive stand can be made of half the weight, and at only two-thirds the cost, by substituting ½-in. x 6-in. white Baltic lining boards for the ⅞-in. shelving, and a frame of ⅞-in. x 6-in. white Baltic flooring for the pieces of 3in. x 2in. This frame should be made the length and width of the hive, and 2 inches high, the lining boards being nailed on top, and the three cleats on top again. A detachable alighting board, sloping down to the level of the ground, takes the place of the projection. This stand rests on the ground all round, and the exclusion of draught underneath compensates for less thickness of the floor. If pressed down tight on to levelled ground, it affords no harbor for spiders and other vermin, nor a hiding place for queens (where queens are clipped) at swarming time.

In some districts, particularly in forest country, trouble occurs with hive stands, and even hives, through white ants entering the wood of the stand where it touches the ground, and destroying it, and unless checked, eventually the hive. At a trifling expense in the first instance, this risk may be entirely avoided, by saturating those pieces of the stands which come into contact with the ground with a solution of sulphate of Copper, generally known as Bluestone. In a box ½-inch longer, inside, than the longest pieces to be treated, and made water-tight by running boiling wax over all the joints, dissolve sufficient Bluestone in water to make a saturated solution, so that in about a day, with occasional stirring, some of the crystals remain undissolved. The wood to be saturated should be thoroughly dry, and be packed into the box of solution, with bits of stick between the pieces to keep them apart, and a weight on the top to keep them under. Immersion for 24 hours will be sufficient, when the wood may be exposed to air and sun to dry. After the stands are made up the pieces impregnated should be painted or tarred to prevent the bluestone being soaked out by rain water.

COVERS.

In the matter of hive covers there is perhaps more neglect on the part
of beekeepers than in anything else; and yet upon the cover depends in
a great measure, not only the prosperity and health of the colony, but
the durability of the hive itself. When hives, however well made, are
covered with bags, palings, bark, or pieces of tin and iron, which materials
either absorb the rain or conduct it into the hive by soakage around the
edges, one need not wonder to find hives gaping open at the joints with
boards warped or cracked, and mouldy combs inside. A hive cover should
be watertight above all things, but it should also be constructed so that it
will throw the water clear of the hive walls, and prevent the fierce heat
of summer and the frost of the winter penetrating from the top. A flat,
single board cover cannot fulfil these requirements. Even when kept well
painted on the outside and strongly cleated at the ends it will warp, twist,
or crack in the heat of summer, and will then not fit down close on to the
hive all round. This will give rain water entrance to the interior of the
hive and robber bees an opening to hover round during a dearth of nectar.

A gable cover with base board resting flat on the hive surmounted by
a pitched roof with eaves projecting down a little below the top of the
hive, is most effective, and keeps the hive dry and cool in summer, and
warm in winter. This cover, is however, somewhat troublesome to construct, and not suitable for migratory beekeeping, being bulky and of an
awkward shape for transporting. After using extensively for a number of
years about six different patterns of hive covers, I find that a flat one
covered with plain galvanized iron is the best all round. This is made
of two layers of boards such as may be got from kerosene and jam cases.
The boards of one layer run crosswise to the other, and are nailed together
to form an oblong of 20½in. x 14¾in., that is ½ inch longer and wider
than the hive. Strips of board wide enough to project ½ inch all round
on the lower side of the cover are nailed to the edge of it. The whole is
then covered with a piece of galvanized (plain) iron, No. 26 gauge,
measuring 28in. x 18in., and cut in at the corners to allow of it being
turned down at right angles and secured at the eaves. A sheet of 26-gauge
plain galvanized iron 72in. x 36in., which is a trade size, will thus cover
six hive roofs. A hive cover of this description, will outlast any other kind.
It requires no paint, as the wood is not exposed. There is no warping,
as one layer of boards checks the other; it is water and fire-proof; and if
layers of non-conducting material, such as paper, are inserted between iron
and wood, it is also heat and frost-proof.

(To be continued.)

Fat occurs in milk as little globules measuring from .0006 inches in
diameter downwards. Fleischmann reckons their number at about 50,000
millions in a pint of milk.

GENERAL NOTES.

PIG FEEDING—

In the last *Annual Report* of the Secretary of Agriculture, U.S.A., reference is made to feeding tests recently concluded at the North Dakota Station. It was found that barley produced a better quality of pork than maize corn, but it required 18 per cent. more of barley than of corn to produce a given gain in weight. Another test showed that ground rejected wheat produced good gains when fed to swine with shorts. In comparison with maize corn it required 8.9 per cent. more rejected wheat than corn to produce the same gains, but the quality of pork produced was better than that produced on corn.

IRISH BLIGHT—

There is pretty general agreement among potato growers that the injury to be expected from Irish blight, once it has established itself in a country, will depend in large measure upon the wetness of the season. For the last 20 years experiments on spraying for the control of potato diseases have been carried out at the Vermont Experiment Station, U.S.A.; and in *Bulletin 159* of that institution the relation of rainfall to blight is discussed. There is said to be a close connexion between the two, and in general a rainy season is likely to be accompanied by an epidemic of blight and rot. However in 1901 the rainfall was small, and it was one of the worst seasons on record both as to the damage done to the foliage and to the tubers. Looking to this report one could wish that other weather observations besides rainfall had been included in the discussion. Absence of bright sunshine and a humid atmosphere would probably come next to excessive rainfall in encouraging a spread of the disease, but the data for these in 1901 are lacking. Altogether from the records, one seems warranted in believing that conditions of moderate rainfall and plenty of sun, are likely to act as powerful checks to the blight, while dull muggy, and wet weather will encourage it.

THE FERTILITY OF HEN EGGS—

How long after the removal from the pen of the male bird will the eggs laid by the hens prove fertile? The subject was essentially one for experiment, and the results of some tests at the Roseworthy Poultry Station are reported in the *Journal of Agriculture of South Australia.* The male bird was removed on 12th December, and each day's eggs were dated as gathered. It was intended to test 10 eggs each day, but the moulting season caused irregular laying. The eggs laid on 24 successive days were used in the tests. For the first week after the removal of the male bird the results were good, nearly all the eggs proving fertile. Thereafter there was a gradual falling off, the eggs of the tenth day hatching just 50 per cent. From the 14th day there were no fertile eggs, but the 15th yielded two and the 16th one. Thereafter none of the eggs proved fertile. The general rule is to allow seven days as the extreme limit up to which eggs may be set. In this test the fertility was high.

CARE OF CALVES—

Take a little better care of those humped-up discouraged-looking young calves that stand shivering in the yard all day. The first winter is the cheapest and easiest time to make substantial gains. Calf fat once lost is rarely made up, even though extra care be given later in life. A stunted calf means a dwarfed cow. A mossy-coated, thick-fleshed calf is a pleasure and a money maker, while the hat-rack type is a reproach to the farm and farmer.—*The Practical Farmer, Philadelphia.*

BREEDING CROP PLANTS—

The time has gone by when any kind of seed will do in farming, and if the industry is to hold its own it must procure the best for each purpose. The difference in yield from good and from indifferent seed often amounts to more than the annual value of the land. Much can be done by grading and selection from existing types, but in many cases the selective process must be preceded by artificial crossing in order to obtain the characters desired. The cross-breeding of plants follows the same laws as the cross-breeding of animals, but it is a more tedious affair, and it has another drawback in the eyes of the farmer. A good breeder of live-stock can obtain high prices for his annual drafts for stud purposes, and hope to do as well again next year, but the plant breeder when he begins to sell, ruins his market. The difference lies in the nature of the case. It seems to be for this reason that improvement in live-stock has progressed under private enterprise, while a corresponding improvement in crop plants must be sought for under public control. In the *Arb. Deut. Landw. Gesell.* 1910, appears a history of German plant breeding, including a description of the work carried on at the present time in both public and private institutions. As pointed out in this work, Germany has to-day 43 breeders of winter rye, 3 of spring rye, 61 of winter wheat, 23 of spring wheat, 5 of winter barley, 60 of spring barley, 53 of oats, 23 of fodder beets, 21 of sugar beets, 17 of potatoes, 4 of kale, carrots, and similar crops, 8 of clovers and grasses, and 28 of leguminous plants. As the best variety of any crop for one country is rarely the best for the conditions of another, there is an immense field for the breeder of Australian types.

COLD STORAGE—

The United States Department of Agriculture (*Annual Report, 1911*) has just concluded a special investigation into the economic results of cold storage. The business has assumed large proportions. Of the total production during the last year 13½ per cent. of the eggs were placed in cold storage; fresh beef over 3 per cent.; mutton over 4 per cent.; fresh pork 11½ per cent.; creamery butter 25 per cent. The cost of storage includes charge for space (either by month or season), interest on the value of the stored produce, and lastly insurance. When these three costs are combined they amount per month to 0.437 of 1 cent for fresh beef; for mutton 0.352; for pork 0.398; poultry 0.446; and for butter 0.571, all per lb. For eggs the costs are 0.593 of 1 cent per dozen per month. Cold storage has with certain commodities shown a strong tendency to equalize the monthly prices throughout the year particularly in regard to butter, eggs, poultry, and fresh mutton. This fact was established by converting the mean price of each commodity for each month into a percentage of the mean price for the whole year, and then comparing the monthly variations in 1902-11 with the variations before 1893 when cold storage first became able to affect prices. For butter and eggs, besides equalizing prices from month to month, cold storage has raised the average prices for the whole year; the calculations involved here were complicated and were not applied to the other commodities. An aspect of cold storage referred to is the facility which it affords for speculation in perishable goods by wholesale dealers holding for a rise, and it is concluded that "this business of storing goods has grown to such proportions that consumers have a rightful concern with its management for economic as well as sanitary reasons."

THE WEEDS, NATURALIZED ALIENS AND POISON PLANTS OF VICTORIA.

By Alfred J. Ewart, D.Sc., Ph.D., F.L.S., Government Botanist and Professor of Botany and Plant Physiology in the Melbourne University.

Watsonia Meriana, Mill. Var. Iridifolia (Irideæ).

This plant, often known as Merian's Bugle Lily, is a native of South Africa, which was first recorded as a permanent naturalized alien in 1907 (*Victorian Naturalist*, vol. 24, page 16). The plant is a rather handsome one, and was cultivated in gardens long before this, thence spreading and running wild, until in some parts it is quite a troublesome weed, particularly in neglected pastures which are moist or somewhat swampy during a portion of the year. It also shows a special predilection for growing along the banks of small water-courses, even where these are dry for the greater part of the year. Although it likes moisture, it is able to remain green over prolonged periods of dry weather, and at such times the green colour appears sometimes to attract stock and lead to their eating the plant, although it is surprising how little of it is usually eaten, in spite of its externally attractive and succulent appearance.

The plant is often reported as having exercised an injurious or poisonous action upon stock, and since it belongs to an order which includes such poison plants as the Cape Tulip (*Homeria collina*), as well as many which are injurious without being strictly poisonous, all such cases are worthy of critical experimental investigation. The Iris itself, for instance, contains, particularly in the rhizome, a peculiar acrid oleo-resin, sometimes known as Irisin, which, apparently, consists of a mixture of a bitter acrid fixed oil or soft resin, a volatile crystallizable oil, and other extractives. This oleo-resin of Iris appears to exercise an irritant action on the mucous membrane of the alimentary canal, and, hence, acts as a purgative, as well as a powerful stimulant to the liver. It also has emetic and diuretic properties, such as are possessed by the extracts from many other plants belonging to the same order. In the case of the Cape Tulip, it is probable that the plant contains a similar oleo-resin to that present in Iris, but that it is either more intense in its action or more abundant.

It is evident, therefore, that the reports as to Watsonia being poisonous could not be dismissed without full investigation. Accordingly, Dr. Rothera undertook to investigate the supposed poisonous character of this plant, and his results are published in brief in the Journal for November, 1910. He found that sheep, goats, and rabbits eat it readily, and that no harmful after-effects were noticeable. He could detect no alkaloid either in the bulbs or in the green parts, while injections of extracts designed to contain active principles if present, produced no apparent poisonous action. One possibility still, however, remained open. In some cases, as, for instance, in the case of the Darling Pea (*Swainsona galegifolia*), a poisonous action may be exercised in the course of time by plants from which it is exceedingly difficult or impossible to extract any poisonous principle, and if such plants are only eaten for a short period of time, no evil effects may result. In the case of the Swainsona, four to six weeks are required to produce serious symptoms, when the plant is eaten in moderate amount mixed with other food, and the effects are

similar to those produced by slow poisoning with alcohol and certain
toxic proteids, namely, peripheral neuritis and degeneration of the nerve
endings, accompanied by a loss of muscular control.   In addition, Professor Gilruth showed that after one to two months' continuous grazing on
Ragwort, cattle and horses, and, to a less extent, sheep may develop
cirrhosis of the liver, and ultimately die as the result of it.   Experiments
on another Senecio in South Africa showed that four to eight ounces a
day caused death in oxen in a few days to a month, the action being
usually a little slower on horses, and one result being the production of
cirrhosis of the liver.

Accordingly, an experiment was tried to determine whether with prolonged feeding, any general poisonous action was exercised by Watsonia.
Owing to the quantity of material required, small animals, namely guinea
pigs, were used for the test, which was begun on June 30th, and extended
to the 7th of September; that is, nearly eleven weeks.   During the first
half of this period, each guinea pig received mixed bran and pollard, and
as green food an average of 18 grams a day of the green leaves of
Watsonia.   These were taken fresh as required from a large bed
of the plants grown for this purpose in the Herbarium garden.   The
controls received ordinary green feed, together with bran and pollard.
At first, the guinea pigs did not eat the Watsonia very readily, and hence
were not given more than 10 to 12 grams a day apiece.   By the end of
the first week, however, they eat it readily, and received from 15 to 18
grams per day during the first five weeks.   During the latter half of
the experiment they were fed with as much as they would eat, which
varied from 20 to 40 grams a day apiece.   The average amount consumed
by each animal during the whole period was 1326 grams; that is, more
than the total body weight.   The animals remained healthy and normal
during the whole period of the experiment, showed no signs of any
poisonous action whatever, and one pair produced a batch of young
towards the latter part of the experiment, which were apparently normal,
but were destroyed and partially devoured by the parents, probably as the
result of confinement or of fright, and not as the result of any nutritive
hunger.   In any case, the experiment is sufficient to show that Watsonia
does not contain any poisonous principle capable of exercising any general,
slow, accumulative poisonous action.

In order that those unfamiliar with the plant may be able to recognise
it, the following brief description is appended :— .

It is a tall erect plant, usually 2 to 3 feet high, but sometimes
reaching a height of 5 feet on rich moist soils.   The underground base
of the stem is swollen into a hard bulb (corm), 1 to 2 inches in diameter,
covered with brown fibrous coats.   The leaves are somewhat like those
of an Iris, and arise at the base of the stem.   There is a single erect
flowering stem, sometimes slightly branched at the upper end, bearing
numerous rather large pink, red, or very occasionally white flowers, which
are sometimes partly or entirely replaced by clusters of small, fleshy,
pointed bulbils.   The bulbils when they fall off are able to strike root
and produce new plants.   The plant has no special smell or taste by
which it can be recognised, but once seen, it is not likely to be mistaken
for any other plant.   The flowers are much like those of a Gladiolus,
with a curved tube and the stamens all just falling short of the tips of its
segments.

SMALL RURAL INDUSTRIES.
B.—MINT CULTIVATION.
(By Joseph Knight.)

Mint (*Mentha*) includes the Penny-royal (*Mentha Pulegium*), also Spearmint (*Mentha viridis*), which is cultivated for culinary purposes, besides other species. Our business here is with the plant commonly known as Black Mint (*Mentha piperita*). From this is produced the well-known Oil of Peppermint, which is largely used in medicine, confectionery. and in the manufacture of cordials.

Black Mint is cultivated largely in England and other countries for the extraction of oil, it is a hardy plant, loving a cool moist climate and a free soil. It thrives well on the hillsides in Gippsland and similar situations, is easily managed, and gives good return for labour bestowed on it.

The following is a brief description of its cultivation and treatment :—

PLANTING AND CULTIVATION.

The plant used to establish a crop consists of pieces of the stolons or runners taken from the parent plant; like most of the " Mint " tribe, it is very prolific in producing these runners.

BLACK MINT (MENTHA PIPERITA).

Slips with three or four joints are sufficient—they should be well rooted, and the stronger they are the more prolific the first year's crop will be. The runners are planted ·out in well prepared soil, and should stand about 15 to 18 inches apart from plant to plant each way. The land should be clean and free from weeds, as the distillation afterwards of the produce renders foreign matters undesirable. Care with the first crop will save much trouble in future working, as the plant, when once established, will, to a large extent, protect itself from any intrusion of weeds.

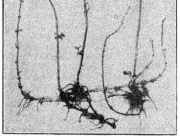

STOLONS OR RUNNERS.

Fairly deep cultivation is necessary. The plant is chiefly a surface feeder, but requires some depth of soil in order to obtain the best results. The land should be well worked to a fine tilth

6004.   N

and smooth surface, otherwise the cutting is difficult.   Little. in the way. of cultivation can be done after planting, but the soil round the crop may be kept stirred with a fork, so as to give the young plant freedom in pushing out its runners for the summer cutting.   In some cases, in fairly level land and dry situations, furrows are run between the rows and water run down ; but where there is danger of "scour," this must be avoided. Light forking will materially assist the plant in its development prior to cutting.

The sets may be dropped in a shallow furrow and the soil turned down with a plough at the distance decided upon, but the land must be left with a level surface for the reason stated above.   The time of planting must depend largely on the parent plant, as the runners have to be taken from the season's growth, and it is undesirable to rob it to the extent of impairing its yield for the coming harvest.   In Gippsland, and other timbered localities, early in November would be time enough, in ordinary seasons. . If the treatment of the soil has been suitable, there should be a fair cutting in March, and this may be treated for oil extraction straight away.   The yield should then be sufficient to meet the expenses of labour for the first year's working.

After cutting the first year, the plants are, in some cases, covered up with a little loose earth, which gives them a start in making runners for producing the second crop.   When the plants have been set out at a sufficient distance apart a cultivator should be worked between the rows. It will be found more economical to arrange this distance and employ horse labour, than to work by hand.   After the second cutting, the land may be ploughed and the plants covered, and being well established they will stand rough treatment as far as the cultivation is concerned ; this applies to all subsequent seasons.   It may be found advantageous to renew the plantation every five or six years, as new fields will be found to give better results.

HARVESTING.

The time of harvesting cannot be definitely stated but the crop should be taken in full bloom.   This is usually late in spring or early in autumn. The crop is usually cut with a hook, sometimes with a short-bladed scythe, frequently with a nipping machine ; it is gathered in rows, then placed on sheets of hessian, and carried direct to the still.   While many allow it to dry somewhat, asserting that there is no loss of oil, but only moisture, in the evaporation, others again claim that this is a mistake.   It may not always be convenient to distill the whole crop in the green state ; but there is no doubt that, where this can be done, it is advisable to do so.   Whatever is done, care must be taken to prevent self heating of the produce, which readily occurs if it is kept in heaps while green ; and it must not be permitted to get wet by rain and become mouldy, as the oil is affected thereby, both in quantity and quality.

AFTER TREATMENT.

The bulky nature of the mint crop necessitates the treatment of it on or near the place at which it is produced.   For this purpose, a fair-sized still is necessary—the size must be regulated by the amount of crop.

A 400-gallon still will be sufficient for 20 acres or so. The cost of the still depends on the nature of the material employed, and other such conditions.

The late Mr. Slater, of Mitcham, Victoria, who was a successful grower of plants for essential oils, and who had considerable experience of these in England, carried out his distillation work with the ordinary iron malt tanks—400 gallons each—which he found to answer the purpose well. A tank was set in on bricks (roughly) in such a way as to admit of a fire being placed underneath. The whole of the top of this tank was movable, and in it was fitted a cage lined with wire netting to hold the material. This cage was let down into the tank, which was filled with water. The lid had a goose-necked cone to convey the steam and oil to another tank holding the condenser, which

PERFUME STILL MADE BY DONDEY AND TESTRO.

was simply a spiral of tin-lined copper piping. The lid of the first tank was made to screw down tightly on a rubber ring, in order to prevent any escape of steam, except through the condenser. The second tank was open, and contained the condenser only ; and as a stream of water was not available to run into this, a third tank was employed to supply a current of cold water to keep the condenser cool. A steady stream of water was delivered to the bottom of the condensing tank, which, of course, as it heated, rose to the top and found its way to the overflow.

These simple and inexpensive appliances answered the purpose, but where a more elaborate outfit is desired, many of our coppersmiths can supply it. Messrs. Dondey and Testro, South Melbourne, have a very convenient still, made of the latest pattern, and no doubt will be reasonable in their charges. Their experience in still-making should be a warranty that a suitable article will be supplied. The illustration given here is for a small still about twenty-five (25) gallons. The design can be made to any size required.

The treatment of the various plants from which oil is extracted by distillation is carried out in the same manner as the product now under consideration. There is one thing very necessary when changing from one product to another—a thorough deodorizing and cleaning must take place, otherwise much of the product will be destroyed.

DISTILLING.

This operation is looked upon as being somewhat difficult, but it only requires a little practice to get good results. It may be mastered by the most inexperienced person with a few trials.

The oil contained in the leaves and stems is lighter than water, and it has also a lower boiling point. When heat is applied the oil rises and passes off with a little steam before the boiling point of the water is reached. The finer and better part of the oil escapes first, and here it is that care and skill is required to make the most of the product, and to secure a first and second quality of oil.

The steam, water, and oil which passes through the condenser referred to, passes out through the lower portion of the cooling tank into a receiver known as the "Florentine." This somewhat resembles a teapot without a handle. The oil and water dropping into the top of the receiver separate, the oil floating on the top whilst the water escapes slowly at the spout. As the outlet is at the bottom of this receiver and the top of the spout a little below the mouth or level of the receiving portion of the "Florentine," the water and oil are separated.

One mistake frequently made is in forcing the distillation. The boiling should be slow, so as to avoid forcing over objectionable matter. A tank of 400 gallons should be allowed four or five hours to boil; after the first two hours the receiver should be changed, as the oil to follow is of secondary quality, and should be marketed separately. It is said that whatever oil the stalks contain is inferior in quality, and, being the last to be driven off, the heat must be regulated and the boiling a simmer only.

In distilling, it is much preferable to heat the water in the boiling tank with superheated steam, as it is more under control. This is done by having a steam generator close by, and running steam through a perforated coil placed in the bottom of the still. The heat can then be regulated to a nicety. Some eucalyptus distillers run hot steam through their leaves without water, but this does not meet with general approval for the finer essential oil plants. When applying direct heat greater attention is required than in using steam.

YIELDS AND PRICES.

A good crop of well-established mint will yield from five to six tons per imperial acre. As to the yield of oil, some growers give 3 to 4 lbs. per ton, whilst others state 5 to 6 lbs.; nothing definite can be given in this respect. At the Dunolly and Leongatha Government Scent Farm mint was the last crop to receive attention, and it was not sufficiently established to give any reliable data to quote from.

EXTRACT FROM THE ROYAL COMMISSION'S REPORT ON VEGETABLE PRODUCTS.

(Evidence given by the late Joseph Bosisto, Esq., C.M.G., M.P.)

Now peppermint will grow on loamy and moist lands, and grow in abundance; but, like everything else, it wants proper gardening, taking care of, and keeping free from weeds. Its habitat is in loamy and moist lands. If this be neglected, it will soon lose its fragrance and flavour. The districts of Melbourne, Mount Macedon, and North Gippsland were tried, and that from North Gippsland was the best. Even in England the qualities vary in value; thus Mitcham oil realizes 40s. per lb., while Cambridge brings only 33s. per lb., American 16s. per lb., and French 10s. per lb. I sent home to London a large quantity that I myself distilled, but other persons grew. I offered to distil it free, provided they would supply me with the material, and many of them did so—four or five—and here are the reports which I received from home relative to the peppermint. I forwarded several samples, together with the following letter :—

"I herewith send you a sample of an essential oil of peppermint, distilled from the green and cultivated plant grown in the mountainous districts of Victoria, with a request that you will favour me with an opinion as to its quality and marketable value if forwarded in large quantities."

Here are the reports. One is from W. J. Bush and Company, one of the largest essential oil buyers in England :—

"We consider it very good quality—about equal to our Cambridge mint. We had submitted to us lozenges (Meggeson and Company), three kinds : one lot containing Mitcham oil, another lot containing Australian, and another containing Hatchkiss' (America). We picked out those made with the American at once as the worst, but were wrong with the other two, for we judged the Australian oil-made lozenges to be the Mitcham and *vice versâ*. We think 25s. to be an outside price to be expected at first, but will afterwards improve in price. There is a herby flavour about it that may be got over by cultivation."

Messrs. Price and Hickman report :—

"We have examined the Australian oil of peppermint, and consider it to be of excellent quality, and but little inferior to Mitcham oil. If it could be produced a trifle less yellow in colour, we have no doubt we could dispose of it in this market at about 27s. 6d. per lb. In its present state, we think it would be worth 25s."

Another firm report :—

"It certainly is the best foreign oil we have seen; but still it is foreign, and we doubt if at first it can compete with the English. We think it will soon take a high place."

Now Cambridge mint is the second quality, only second to the best Mitcham

FUMIGATION FOR THE DESTRUCTION OF SCALE INSECTS.

By A. A. Hammond, Orchard Supervisor.

For many years the Red Scale (*Aspidiotus Coccineus*) was known to be present in the Doncaster district. When first noted, only a few trees. in one large plantation were infected. For a long time, the scale made no headway, and consequently growers took but little notice of its presence. About five years ago, however, the pest began to multiply and spread to an alarming extent, notwithstanding that every effort was made to destroy it by spraying. Emulsions of kerosene, crude petroleum and red oil were used, as well as several patent spraying mixtures ; but it was found that, although spraying checked the pest for a time, it soon became as bad or worse than ever, and continued to spread. No matter how carefully spraying is done, only about 80 to 90 per cent. of the scale is destroyed on evergreen trees, because it is practically impossible to spray the under-side of every leaf and fruit.

It may be well to state here that red oil emulsion, 1 in 30, properly prepared, gave the best results. Scalecide also gave fair results, but is more expensive than fumigation, to be equally effective.

In 1909, soon after I had taken charge of the Doncaster district, the Red Scale was found in most of the citrus plantations. The Olive Scale was also causing a good deal of trouble.

When it was demonstrated to the Doncaster growers that fumigation was a thoroughly effective means of destroying scale insects, and the cost, in the long run, less than spraying, the leading citrus-growers adopted it.

To Mr. Ferdinand Finger is due the credit of being the first in the Doncaster district to demonstrate the efficiency and practicability of fumigation. Mr. Finger had five sheets made from strong unbleached calico selected by me. I supervised and assisted in the fumigation of several orange and lemon trees, on 26th March, 1909. These trees were infected with Red Scale, and, on examining the trees a few days later, all the scale were found to be dead. The charge used was 1 ounce each of cyanide and sulphuric acid to every 180 cubic feet of inclosed space. Mr. Finger and his son continued the fumigation at intervals during April and May. The Red Scale, on all trees treated, was destroyed ; but the charge was insufficient to kill Olive Scale fumigated early in May. In all subsequent demonstrations, 1 ounce each of cyanide and sulphuric acid to 160 cubic feet was used, and was found to be effective against both the Red and the Olive Scales, as well as the eggs of the latter. It is inadvisable, however, to use the stronger charge when treating orange-trees, unless they are treated on cloudy days, or at night, as they are much more susceptible to injury than lemons or mandarins.

The value of fumigation was further demonstrated in July, 1909. In the latter end of June of that year, I discovered the San Jose Scale in a Doncaster orchard.

As this dreaded pest had not previously been found in the district, and was confined to one orchard, it was decided to have the infected trees fumigated.

VIEW OF MR. JOHN FINGER'S CITRUS PLANTATION, DONCASTER, VICTORIA.

The work was carried out in July. One ounce each of cyanide and acid to 120 cubic feet was used, *i.e.*, about a quarter stronger than that used on evergreen trees. The scale was completely stamped out. It is now nearly three years since the trees were treated, and, although a careful inspection of the orchard where the outbreak occurred has been frequently made, no trace of the scale could be found.

Fumigation for Woolly Aphis was also tried in Mr. Finger's orchard in May, 1909. A charge of the same strength as that used for citrus trees was given. On examining the trees a month later, live aphis were found in the knots and excrescences, though examination immediately after treatment revealed no living aphis. These were, no doubt, protected in the interstices of the bark from the action of the gas.

FUMIGATION OUTFIT.

Sheets, either octagonal or square, made of strong closely woven unbleached calico, are recommended. The octagonal sheets require less material to cover a tree of a given size than a square sheet, but there is more trouble in making them up, and, consequently, the square sheets are more favored. A tree 13 feet high can be covered by a sheet 36 feet square, and one 11 feet high by a 30-ft. square sheet. It requires 72 yards of calico, double width, to make the former, and 50 yards the latter. The cost of the calico is about 1s. 3d. per yard. Before making up the sheets, growers should measure the height of their trees, and the height multiplied by 2¾ gives, roughly, the size of the sheets required.

Loops of rope or rings should be attached to two sides of the sheet, about 15 feet apart, and equal distances from the corners. These are required in which to insert the poles when placing the sheet over the tree.

CHEMICALS REQUIRED.

Cyanide of potassium (the best quality) and sulphuric acid, are the chemicals used for generating the gas. Both are sold by avoirdupois weight, but the quantities given in the fumigation table are ounces avoirdupois and fluid ounces respectively.

This has to be taken into account when ordering the chemicals. There are but 9 fluid ounces of sulphuric acid in 1 lb. avoirdupois, so, in ordering, it is required to get 16 lbs. of acid for every 9 lbs. of cyanide. The cost of the cyanide is 9d. to 10d. per lb., and sulphuric acid 1½d. per lb. The cost of a charge for a tree 11 feet high by 11 feet in diameter is about 4d.

A pair of scales is required to weigh the cyanide, and a measuring glass for the sulphuric acid and water. The scales should be accurate and in good order.

PLACING SHEETS OVER TREES, CHARGING, ETC.

Two light strong poles 12 to 15 feet long, according to the height of the trees, are required. These should be pointed at one end, and have a fork at the other.

The forked end is wanted to insert in the loop or ring attached to the sheet, and the pointed end prevents the poles from slipping on the ground.

Two men can with these easily raise the sheet and draw it over the tree. The operators should, if there is a breeze, work towards it, when the sheet will float over the tree without danger of being damaged.   The sheet should be sufficiently large to allow of a foot or so to lie on the ground all round the tree.   Soil is then thrown over this to prevent the escape of gas, except a few feet, which is left for the purpose of placing in the charge.

When branches of the tree lie on the ground, care must be taken not to cover them up when tucking the sheet around the tree, otherwise, scale occurring on these parts will not be destroyed, owing to the protection afforded by the tent and soil.

To ascertain the charge required, measure the height and diameter of the tree after the sheet is on.   A rod marked plainly off in feet is used for this purpose.

PLACING SHEET OVER TREE.

Should the tree be very irregular in shape, it is advisable to take the diameter two ways, and then take the mean diameter.   This also applies in measuring the height.   It is usually sufficient to take the extreme height and diameter, but when the margin of safety is small, as is the case when treating orange trees in the day time, particularly large ones, a good deal must always be left to the judgment of the operator.

After the height and diameter have been taken, a reference to the fumigation table will show the charge required.

In preparing the charge, the water is first placed in an enamel or earthenware vessel large enough to hold the liquid without danger of boiling over.   The sulphuric acid is then slowly added to the water, and the vessel placed well under the tree.   When all is ready, and the tent closed down, with the exception of the place where the charge is put in, the cyanide is dropped gently into the vessel.

The operator should not put his head inside the tent when placing the cyanide in the acid, as the fumes are very deadly. As soon as the cyanide is dropped in, the sheet should be quickly closed down and covered. The sheet should be left on for 45 minutes.

As a certain amount of gas escapes through the sheets, it is advisable when fumigating for the operators to work towards the wind, so that the gas fumes are blown away from them.

It is inadvisable to fumigate when it is very windy, or when the sun is hot. There is also a danger of burning if the foliage is wet.

TIME FOR FUMIGATION.

The best time to fumigate is in March. I have found that both the Red and Olive Scales are much more easily destroyed at this time of the year than when the cold weather sets in. This applies particularly to the

CHARGING.

Olive Scale, as in March and early April the majority of the scales are young, and easily destroyed. The foliage, too, at this season is tougher, and not so liable to injury. On the other hand, in Spring and early Summer, the foliage is tender, the insects more difficult to destroy, and if a few escape destruction, they multiply during the late Summer and Autumn. The Red Scale can be effectively treated in Winter, but the ground is then sloppy, and the weather usually unfavorable.

Another objection to winter treatment is that, although the scale on the fruit is killed, it will not fall off, whereas, if done in early Autumn, the expanding fruit throws it off before picking time.

The tables which have been prepared will probably be sufficient for all requirements, but the required charge for larger trees will be found by squaring the diameter, multiplying by $1\frac{1}{4}$, then by $\frac{9}{10}$ of the height, and dividing by 160 for the stronger charge as given in No. 1 table, or by

180 as given in No. 2 table. For example, if a tree is 20 feet high by 18 feet in diameter, the formula is $18 \times 18 \times \frac{1}{11} \times 20 \times \frac{9}{10} \times \frac{1}{100} = 28\frac{2}{3}$ nearly. The charge therefore is $28\frac{2}{3}$ ounces of cyanide, 29 ounces of sulphuric acid, and 87 ounces of water. It will be noticed that $\frac{1}{2}$-oz. weights are often required in weighing the cyanide. As these are not always obtainable, a penny can be used, which weighs exactly $\frac{1}{3}$ ounce.

Observation of the result of fumigating trees varying considerably in size, show that small trees are rarely overcharged, whilst with large trees this often happens when the margin of safety is small. Great care, therefore, must be taken with the measurements in treating large trees, especially oranges, during the day.

It has been noted that, when the sheet has been taken off a small tree after being on for 45 minutes, the odour of the gas has been scarcely

FUMIGATING FOR RED SCALE MR. RIESCHIECK'S PLANTATION,
DONCASTER, VICTORIA.

perceptible; whereas, in the case of large trees, the odour of the gas was strong.

The reason of this is that the area of the sheet enveloping a large tree is, in relation to the space enclosed, less than the area of the sheet enclosing a small tree. As there is an escape of gas through the undressed calico, the wastage of gas is relatively greater in small than in large trees.

In fumigating deciduous trees during winter for San Jose Scale, a charge one quarter stronger is necessary. This is found by multiplying the quantity of cyanide given in No. 1 table by 4, and dividing by 3. Sulphuric acid and water are increased proportionately. The cyanide should always be carefully weighed, and the exact charge given. A little more than the prescribed quantity of sulphuric acid can be given without harm, and this is done when small fractions are involved.

Cyanide is a deadly poison, and should be handled with great care. It should be kept in a secure place, and air-tight, when not in use. Sulphuric acid is dangerous also, and care should be taken not to allow it to come in contact with the clothing or the sheets. After handling the acid bottle, the operator should wipe or rinse his hands before touching the sheets.

When breaking the cyanide, which is in lumps, be careful that none gets into the eyes.

Always place the water in the vessel first, then slowly add the acid. When the vessel is in position under the sheet, gently drop the cyanide in. Hold the breath till the tent is closed down. Should the cyanide be very fine, it should be wrapped in paper, and paper and all put in. This prevents the too rapid generation of the gas. When large charges are given, it is advisable to place a board a few inches above the generator for the purpose of spreading the gas. The foliage immediately above the generator is sometimes damaged when this is not done.

Avoid treating orange trees on a warm sunny day, and never fumigate when the foliage is wet. Always dry the sheets well before storing them away. Fumigation can be done at any time of the year, but is safer and more effective in autumn.

There is no doubt that fumigation is superseding spraying as a means of destroying the scale in citrus trees. It is, in the long run, cheaper than spraying, and is thoroughly effective if properly done. Trees are invigorated by fumigation, but continual spraying injures them, more or less.

As has been stated, the San Jose Scale was stamped out in the Doncaster district by fumigation. There is no reason why the Red Scale could not also be stamped out if the fumigation is as carefully and as thoroughly carried out.

Reinfection is often caused through leaving a few trees in the plantation untreated which were thought to be clean. It should be remembered, also, that pear trees will harbor both the Red and the Olive Scales, and these should, when growing near citrus trees, be either fumigated or well sprayed with red oil, 1 in 25, in the winter.

Citrus trees have been reinfected through neglecting to treat infected pear trees which were growing among them.

Herewith, the opinions and experiences of the leading citrus-growers of the Doncaster district, who have adopted fumigation for the destruction of scale insects in citrus trees, are given :—

C. Gill writes :—"Besides getting rid of the scale, it improved the trees, also the fruit was far superior, commanding a better price on the market, and a readier sale. I may state that I am not quite free from it yet ; but it was not the fault of the fumigation. I discovered that some of the branches that were on the ground got covered up with the dirt when packing round the tent ; therefore, the fumes did not get at them. I may state that one tree in the badly affected part got missed, and it was marvellous the difference in that tree and the ones around it."

Mr. Wm. Rieschieck, Doncaster, writes :—" I found the fumigation tables, which you supplied me with, quite satisfactory. The ' No. 1 ' table was quite right for lemons, destroying both the Olive and the Red Scale. I tried the ' No. 1 ' table for oranges in the day time, but found it too strong. The ' No. 2 ' table, however, did no harm, and was, as far as I can see, effective. A lad and myself did 60 trees per day comfortably, using five sheets. The largest sheet used was 30 feet by

30 feet, which will cover a tree 12 feet high by 14 feet in diameter. And now accept my best thanks for helping me with the fumigation, as I knew nothing about it at the start."

Other orchardists have written in appreciation of fumigation, as carried out under instruction from the Department.

FUMIGATION TABLE NO. 1.

Height.	Diameter.	Capacity.	Cyanide.	Sulphuric Acid.	Water.
ft.	ft.	cub. ft.	ozs. av.	fl. ozs.	fl. ozs.
4	5	71	¾	1	2
4	6	102	¾	1	2
5	4	57	¾	1	2
6	4	68	¾	1	2
7	4	79	¾	1	2
5	5	88	¾	1	2
6	5	106	¾	1	2
7	5	124	¾	1	2
8	5	141	1	1	3
5	6	127	1	1	3
6	6	153	1	1	3
7	6	178	1¼	1½	4
8	6	204	1⅓	1½	4
9	6	229	1⅓	1½	4
6	7	208	1⅓	1½	4
7	7	242	1½	1½	5
8	7	277	1⅔	2	5
9	7	312	2	2	6
10	7	346	2¼	2½	6
6	8	271	1⅔	2	5
7	8	317	2	2	6
8	8	362	2⅓	2½	7
9	8	407	2½	2½	7
10	8	452	3	3	9
11	8	498	3¼	3½	10
12	8	543	3½	3½	10
6	9	344	2¼	2½	7
7	9	401	2½	2½	8
8	9	458	3	3	9
9	9	515	3¼	3½	10
10	9	573	3½	3½	11
11	9	630	4	4	12
12	9	687	4¼	4½	13
7	10	495	3¼	3½	10
8	10	565	3½	3½	11
9	10	636	4	4	12
10	10	707	4⅓	4½	13
11	10	778	4¾	5	14
12	10	848	5⅓	5½	16
13	10	919	5⅔	6	17
14	10	990	6¼	6½	19
8	11	684	4⅓	5	13
9	11	770	4¾	5	14
10	11	855	5⅓	6	16
11	11	941	5¾	6	17
12	11	1,026	6½	7	20
13	11	1,112	7	7	21
14	11	1,197	7½	8	22

Height.	Diameter.	Capacity.	Cyanide.	Sulphuric Acid.	Water.
ft.	ft.	cub. ft.	ozs. av.	fl. ozs.	fl. ozs.
9	12	916	5⅔	6	17
10	12	1,018	6⅓	7	19
11	12	1,120	7	7	21
12	12	1,221	7½	8	22
13	12	1,323	8¼	9	25
14	12	1,425	8¾	9	26
15	12	1,527	9⅓	9½	28
16	12	1,629	10¼	10½	31
9	13	1,075	6¾	7	20
10	13	1,195	7½	7½	23
11	13	1,314	8¼	8½	25
12	13	1,433	9	9	27
13	13	1,553	9¾	10	29
14	13	1,672	10½	10½	31
15	13	1,792	11¼	11¼	34
16	13	1,911	12	12	36
17	13	2,031	12⅔	13	38
10	14	1,385	8⅔	9	26
11	14	1,524	9½	9½	28
12	14	1,663	10⅓	10½	31
13	14	1,801	11¼	11½	34
14	14	1,940	12¼	12½	37
15	14	2,078	13	13	39
16	14	2,217	13¾	14	41
17	14	2,355	14⅔	15	44
18	14	2,494	15⅓	15½	46
10	15	1,590	10	10	30
11	15	1,749	11	11	33
12	15	1,909	12	12	36
13	15	2,068	13	13	39
14	15	2,227	14	14	42
15	15	2,386	15	15	45
16	15	2,545	16	16	48
17	15	2,704	17	17	51
18	15	2,863	18	18	54
11	16	1,991	12¼	12½	37
12	16	2,171	13½	13½	40
13	16	2,352	14⅔	15	45
14	16	2,533	15⅔	16	47
15	16	2,714	16¾	17	50
16	16	2,895	18	18	54
17	16	3,076	19	19	57
18	16	3,257	20	20	60
13	17	2,656	15¾	16	47
14	17	2,860	17¾	18	53
15	17	3,064	19	19	57
16	17	3,269	19¾	20	59
17	17	3,473	21½	21½	64

FUMIGATION TABLE No. 2.

Height.	Diameter.	Capacity.	Cyanide.	Sulphuric Acid.	Water.
ft.	ft.	cub. ft.	ozs. av.	fl. ozs.	fl. ozs.
4	5	71	⅔	1	2
4	6	102	¾	1	2
5	4	57	½	½	2
6	4	68	⅔	1	2
7	4	79	¾	1	2
5	5	88	⅔	1	2
6	5	106	¾	1	2
7	5	124	¾	1	2
8	5	141	1	1	3
5	6	127	1	1	3
6	6	153	1	1	3
7	6	178	1	1	3
8	6	204	1	1	3
9	6	229	1¼	1½	4
6	7	208	1	1	3
7	7	242	1⅓	1½	4
8	7	277	1½	1½	5
9	7	312	1⅔	2	6
10	7	346	1¾	2	6
6	8	271	1½	1½	5
7	8	317	1⅔	2	6
8	8	362	2	2	6
9	8	407	2¼	2½	7
10	8	542	2½	2½	7
11	8	498	2¾	3	9
12	8	543	3	3	9
6	9	344	1¾	2	6
7	9	401	2¼	2½	7
8	9	458	2½	2½	7
9	9	515	2¾	3	9
10	9	573	3¼	3½	10
11	9	630	3½	3½	10
12	9	687	3¾	4	12
7	10	495	2¾	3	9
8	10	565	3¼	3½	9
9	10	636	3½	3½	10
10	10	707	4	4	12
11	10	778	4⅓	4½	13
12	10	848	4¾	5	15
13	10	919	5	5	15
14	10	990	5½	6	18
8	11	684	3¾	4	12
9	11	770	4⅓	4½	13
10	11	855	4¾	5	15
11	11	941	5¼	5½	16
12	11	1,026	5¾	6	18
13	11	1,112	6¼	6½	19
14	11	1,197	6⅔	7	21
9	12	916	5	5	15
10	12	1,018	5⅔	6	18
11	12	1,120	6¼	6½	19
12	12	1,221	6¾	7	21
13	12	1,323	7⅓	7½	22
14	12	1,425	8	8	24
15	12	1,527	8½	8½	25
16	12	1,629	9	9	27
9	13	1,075	6	6	18
10	13	1,195	6⅔	7	21
11	13	1,314	7⅓	7½	22
12	13	1,433	8	8	24
13	13	1,553	8⅔	9	27
14	13	1,672	9⅓	9½	28
15	13	1,792	10	10	30
16	13	1,911	10⅔	11	33
17	13	2,031	11¼	11½	34
10	14	1,385	7⅔	8	24
11	14	1,524	8½	9	27
12	14	1,663	9¼	9½	28
13	14	1,801	10	10	30
14	14	1,940	11¼	11½	34
15	14	2,078	11½	12	36
16	14	2,217	12⅓	12½	37
17	14	2,355	13	13	39
18	14	2,494	13¾	14	42
10	15	1,590	8¾	9	27
11	15	1,749	9¾	10	30
12	15	1,909	10½	10½	32
13	15	2,068	11½	11½	34
14	15	2,227	12⅓	12½	37
15	15	2,386	13¼	13½	40
16	15	2,545	14¼	14½	43
17	15	2,704	15	15	45
18	15	2,863	16	16	48
11	16	1,991	11	11	33
12	16	2,171	12	12	36
13	16	2,352	13	13	39
14	16	2,533	14	14	42
15	16	2,714	15	15	45
16	16	2,895	16	16	48
17	16	3,076	17	17	51
18	16	3,257	18	18	54
13	17	2,656	14¾	15	45
14	17	2,860	16	16	48
15	17	3,064	17	17	51
16	17	3,269	18	18	54
17	17	3,473	19⅓	19½	57

REVIEW OF THE VICTORIAN DAIRYING SEASON AND BUTTER EXPORT TRADE, 1911-12.

By R. Crowe, Exports Superintendent.

Another record has been broken.   The prices realized for export butter during the season 1911-1912 have far exceeded any enjoyed during the history of the trade.   The highest average comes out in the neighbourhood of 125s. per cwt., against 110s. for the previous season, and the mean average may be placed at 120s., against 105s. for the year before.   It is to be regretted that the same cannot be asserted in regard to production. This year's exports from Victoria to all destinations total 20,082 tons, worth £2,409,840.   Included in this, however, are 805 tons of butter from Tasmania, so that Victoria can be credited with 19,277 tons, valued at £2,313,240, against 25,793 tons for the year before, worth £2,666,265. The butter exported from Victoria this season represents more than half the total shipped from Australia.

In the previous season two springs were encountered, and it was more than could be reasonably expected that the present season's output would reach the previous phenomenal record.   At the moment, however, grave results are being experienced in the northern districts of the State which tend to discount next year's prospects.   There are two causes responsible for this—a scarcity of food due to want of rain, and overstocking.'   There were more stock in Victoria this year than in the previous one, which was so bountiful, by 1,125,218 head, made up of 975,139 sheep, 99,558 cattle, 35,733 horses, and 14,788 pigs.   Most stock-owners have yet to learn that it is essential to provide fodder to carry them over the dry months.   Horses are never expected to work the year round without hand-feeding, and it is strange indeed that the great majority of dairymen expect cows to continue giving milk and keep alive without any assistance whatever.   In an average season, the grass dries up in January, and no new natural growth can be relied upon until the month of May or later.   It should therefore be regarded as essential to provide and conserve fodder during that period at least; stock should also be cared for during the winter months.   Fortunately, two-thirds of the State is not so badly off, and everything is fairly prosperous in the Western and Gippsland districts.   .

GRADING.

The amended Commerce Regulations came into operation at the commencement of last season, and these provided for an altered standard—a reduction in the maximum for moisture from 16 per cent. to 15 per cent., and the packing of 56½ lbs. of butter in boxes marked 56 lbs., together with compulsory grade-stamping.   In previous years, " Superfine " and " First Grade " butters were stamped as such, when exporters made special request to have it done.   During the present year all butters submitted for export were graded, and the " Superfine " and " First Grades " were stamped accordingly.   Grave and serious results were anticipated by a number who objected to the innovation, but after the season's experience it is found that grade-stamping did not produce the dreadful results apprehended by the opponents to its introduction.   The system is running well and smoothly.

Shortly after it came into force some exporters, whose output was wanting in uniformity, with some justification pointed out that when different grades were found in one consignment it was unfair to place the whole parcel in accordance with the lowest one. It was agreed that in such cases shippers should be notified and given an opportunity of separating the churn marks of different grades. It was held that one of the objects of grading and grade-stamping was to secure uniformity of quality and encourage the grading of cream in line with the standards recognised under the Commerce Act. It was certainly unreasonable to expect the Department to perform work which should have been done in the factory when the produce was in the cream stage. Already a great step in advance has been achieved under this heading. Factories which previously put all qualities under one brand are now grading their cream and covering each grade with a different brand corresponding in quality with the Government grades. Naturally the outcome will be the adoption of a differential rate of payment for cream, so that the suppliers of best-conditioned cream will not have to carry on their shoulders the product from careless producers. Payment for cream according to its suitability for making a good or bad butter will have a strong tendency to make all dairymen improve the care and treatment of the milk and cream.

CHURN MARKS.

Unfortunately, makers were left to employ their own system of churn-marking, and at the height of the season the method became most complex and difficult to follow. It was found necessary to issue a circular recommending the adoption of a uniform method, and quite a long time elapsed before much headway in that direction was achieved. Towards the end of the season, however, uniformity was reached with the great majority, to the relief of all concerned. It is to be hoped that managers will see the necessity for carefully applying the churn marks in the prescribed place on both ends of the boxes. It will be to the advantage of every one connected with this work if the requirements be fully complied with. In a few instances it was discovered that the same churn mark covered different grades. This result indicated that the application of the mark was either loose or intended to mislead. No points are gained by such a practice, as it is patent that the manufacturer has everything to gain by the application of identification marks. The graders' reports on each mark enable him to discover weaknesses and promptly apply remedies to eradicate same.

BRANDS AND MARKS.

It is becoming more apparent that something will have to be done to distinguish unsalted butters from salted. The consignments reach the Stores bearing the same brand, portion of which is marked " U.S.", indicating unsalted. The Department cannot be expected to separate the " U.S." portion from the rest, and it is taken for granted that the numbers indicated on the advice note under each heading are correct. When shipped, the shipping companies specifically exonerate themselves in the bill of lading from all responsibility regarding sub-marks, and accept the goods here, and deliver them in London under the leading brand alone. Everything comes out all right when the factory engages one agent only, but if the unsalted portion be consigned to one agent and the salted to another, trouble is encountered at every stage. Complaints from London are referred to me for investigation in consequence of firms getting salted butter when they bargained for unsalted, and *vice versâ.*   It will therefore be seen that some better method of distinguishing salted butter from unsalted will have to be adopted.   The word unsalted indelibly impressed on each end of the boxes is the least effective method that might be employed.   A better plan would be to have a separate brand covering the unsalted butter; 57.52 per cent. of the butter exported from the State to oversea destinations was salted, whilst 42.48 per cent. of the butter was unsalted.

Mould in Butter.

Mould was discovered on some butters upon opening for examination. Certain consignments were so bad that every box had to be re-papered and packed after scraping about $\frac{1}{4}$ inch off the surface through which the mould had penetrated, and making good the consequent shortage in weight. In no case did the managers fail to overcome the trouble upon their attention being drawn to it, and instructions given as to the proper care of butter paper.   The proprietor of a certain factory was greatly concerned about the mould reported on consignments from his factory.   One day an officer of the Department, when speaking to him, saw the paper over the office stool fronting a desk for the buttermaker's use.   Presently the butter-maker, whose garments were not too clean, came and sat on the paper to make an entry at the desk.   A few minutes afterwards the same paper was utilized for lining the butter boxes, and although this action may not have been directly responsible for the contamination of the butter paper, yet it clearly showed that the user did not appreciate the necessity for keeping it away from dust pending its being brought into requisition.

Butter Fat.

Only one consignment, representing nine boxes, was re-worked under supervision to comply with the standard before shipment.   In the previous season there were 45 contraventions, representing 1,697 boxes.

Short Weight.

Fifty-six consignments, representing 1,915 boxes, were intercepted from shipment on account of short weight.   By checking these packages, 1,479 were passed as correct and released, the remaining 436 having had their contents amended under supervision before export.   In the previous year, 62 consignments, representing 3,276 boxes, were intercepted from shipment, out of which 947 were found short weight.   It will be seen, therefore, that less than half the contraventions under this heading were encountered during the present season.   Under the new regulations it is necessary to brand any butter weighing less than $56\frac{1}{4}$ lbs. at time of checking with the words "Bare Weight."   Thirty-nine consignments, representing 1,649 boxes, were intercepted from shipment under this heading, 1,072 of which were passed on checking and released.   Of the remainder, 372 boxes had their contents amended under supervision, and one consignment only of 205 boxes had the words "Bare Weight" indelibly impressed on the outside covering.   The amended regulations under the Commerce Act have undoubtedly brought about a better condition of affairs in regard to weights. A margin is essential to insure the butter turning out satisfactorily at the port of destination.   This matter is further dealt with later on.

MOISTURE CONTENTS.

The average moisture contents of all samples analyzed is 13.91 per cent., against 13.82 per cent. for 1910-11.

District.	Average.	Co-operative.	Proprietary.
	%	%	%
Western District	14·12	14·09	14·15
Gippsland	14·06	14·12	13·89
North and North-east	14·01	13·96	14·16
City	13·74		

One hundred and thirty-one consignments, representing 5,008 boxes, contained over 15 per cent. The following is a summary of the 3,394 samples analyzed:—

> Over 16 per cent., 45 samples, 1.33 per cent.
> Over 15 per cent., 154 samples, 4.53 per cent.
> Over 14 per cent., 1,458 samples, 42.96 per cent.
> Over 13 per cent., 1,231 samples, 36.27 per cent.
> Under 13 per cent., 506 samples, 14.91 per cent.

It was forecasted by many that with the reduction in the maximum provided under the amended Commerce Regulations which came into force at the commencement of the season, the dairymen of the State would be greatly handicapped in consequence. Increased buildings, refrigerating machinery and plant were recommended in some quarters. It was pointed out by me at the time that a little more care and attention would enable manufacturers to comply with the new order of things without any sacrifice. Their average percentage was sufficiently below the proposed reduced maximum to leave them a safe working margin, and this proved to be the case. The butter submitted for export was found to contain more moisture than that for the previous season, when the maximum allowed was 1 per cent. higher.

BORIC ACID.

Only 35 results of analyses were received regarding boric acid, the average of which comes out at 0.46 per cent. These, of course, do not include butters analyzed for freedom from boric acid. Eleven consignments, representing 247 boxes, were found to contain more than the maximum 0.5 per cent., and withheld from shipment until the percentage was reduced.

INVESTIGATION REGARDING THE EFFICIENCY OF BORIC ACID AS A PRESERVATIVE.

During the season it was intimated that the State Pure Foods Committee intended recommending the abolition of boric acid in butter, and the authorities were induced by the trade to defer action in regard to the matter. Every butter-factory manager in Victoria at some time or other carried out tests to ascertain the effect of different preservatives in varying proportions. Without exception, the butter to which boric acid preservative was added in the process of manufacture to an extent not exceeding 0.5 per cent., was found to be more palatable at the end of six or eight weeks than the control samples in which none was used. Some years back the belief was entertained by the most advanced managers that a set of conditions could be created which would obviate the necessity for the use of preservatives—sanitary conditions on the farms, cleanliness, low temperatures, and prompt delivery of the milk at the skimming stations, would enable the product to come within expert control under the most favorable conditions.

Extreme care in manufacturing and low temperatures immediately afterwards were expected to complete the precautions.   The butter so made was exported as well as being placed on the local market, but it never at any time gave the same satisfaction to retailers, and lower prices had to be accepted.   The result of these experiments was so scattered and difficult to collect to put in convincing form, that it was arranged to carry out a new series on the widest lines.   A circular was issued to all butter factories asking them to make up from one churning two boxes of butter containing boric acid within the limit allowed under the Commerce Regulations and by the authorities in Great Britain, and two boxes without any.   One of each set was shipped per R.M.S. *Orama* on the 10th January last, and examined in London on the 26th February.   A cable was received reporting the market value up to 8s. per cwt. in favour of butter with preservative. Table A shows the difference in results between the butter containing boric acid and butter without any, together with the composition of each.   The average points scored by all the butters containing boric acid was 90, and the average of the control samples 87.4, giving a difference of 2.6 points in favour of the use of boric acid.   The average boric acid contents was 0.183 per cent., and 0.003 per cent., in the control samples, due to a number having been found to contain a small percentage.   The average fat content of the boric acid samples was 84.92 per cent., and of the control samples 85.65 per cent.; moisture contents, 12.88 per cent. in the boric acid samples, and 12.19 per cent. in the control samples; salt, 1.16 per cent. in the boric acid samples, and 1.27 per cent. in the control samples; curd, 0.92 per cent. in the boric acid samples, and 0.85 per cent. in the control samples.   A study of these results, which relate to 100 boxes of butter, besides proving interesting, will provide food for reflection to those so inclined for months, if not years, to come.   All my spare time for the last month has been devoted to it, and tables were taken out bearing on different aspects of the subject, to see if any definite result or principle could be deduced other than the primary one for which the test was made.   For instance, the fourteen brands showing the least average difference between the grading of B and C, and the fourteen showing the greatest average difference.   This table involved the taking out and re-arranging of the full details of 56 of the 100 returns, and it was found that the butter to which the greatest percentage of boric acid was added showed least deterioration; in other words, the greatest difference between the scoring of the boric acid samples and control samples.   The butters showing the least difference contained relatively a small percentage of boric acid, that is to say, butters which had comparatively a small percentage of boric acid added to them deteriorated to nearly the same extent as the control samples.   Ten butters containing the highest fat content were compared with ten showing the least fat content. This involved taking out all details of 40 of the samples.   Likewise, ten with the highest moisture content and ten with the lowest moisture content were compared.   The same was done from a salt point of view, without, however, eliciting data of much value.   The curd, on the other hand, gave positive results.   The butters containing the highest percentage of curd showed the largest variation in the score; in other words, the control sample deteriorated more in the case of butters found to contain a high percentage of curd than they did with those having lower percentages.   Finally, the ten brands showing the highest boric acid content and ten showing the least boric acid content were tabulated, and gave results confirming the first extract relating to scores, viz., that there was less difference in the score between the boric acid and control samples with those containing a low percentage of boric acid than was the case with those containing the higher percentage.

(*Concluded on page* 384.)

BUTTER ANALYSIS.

TABLE A.—SHOWING DIFFERENCE IN RESULTS BETWEEN BUTTER CONTAINING BORIC ACID AND BUTTER WITHOUT ANY, TOGETHER WITH THE COMPOSITION OF EACH.

No. and Mark.		Fat.	Moisture.	Salt.	Curd.	Boric Acid.%			Points Awarded.		
						B.	C.	Difference.	B.	C.	Difference.
		%	%	%	%						
1	B	83·74	13·88	1·43	·90	·047	..	...	86	..	..
	C	85·77	11·65	1·71	·87	..	..	·047	..	85	1
2	B	89·02	9·62	·47	·75	·142	..	...	91	..	..
	C	84·30	14·46	·37	·87	..	..	·142	..	90	1
3	B	85·13	12·10	1·55	1·07	·153	..	...	89	..	..
	C	84·12	13·18	2·03	·67	..	..	·153	..	86	3
4	B	84·73	13·18	1·25	·80	·035	..	...	91	..	..
	C	84·25	13·39	1·75	·61	..	..	·035	..	89	2
5	B	84·47	14·05	·60	·72	·167	...	·159	88	..	..
	C	85·81	13·00	·43	·75	..	·008		..	87	1
6	B	85·45	11·34	1·38	1·62	·210	..	...	90	..	..
	C	83·18	13·25	2·07	1·50	..	..	·210	..	85	5
7	B	82·29	14·19	1·82	1·62	·078	...	...	88	..	..
	C	83·90	13·47	1·79	·83	..	·011	·067	..	87	1
8	B	84·97	12·93	1·37	·63	·103	...	...	90	..	..
	C	87·00	11·20	1·30	·50	..	·004	·099	..	86	4
9	B	82·82	13·53	2·33	1·00	·319	..	...	88	..	..
	C	83·03	13·95	2·10	·92	..	..	·319	..	84	4
10	B	84·35	12·65	1·66	1·12	·220	...	...	90	..	..
	C	85·37	11·47	2·15	1·00	..	·007	·213	..	88	2
11	B	85·89	11·22	1·55	1·23	·107	..	...	88	..	..
	C	84·40	12·72	1·90	·98	..	..	·107	..	86	2
12	B	84·94	13·62	·49	·66	·293	...	...	94	..	..
	C	87·54	11·42	·40	·63	..	·007	·286	..	92	2
13	B	85·21	13·08	·33	1·02	·361	..	...	95	..	..
	C	86·95	11·93	·32	·80	..	..	·361	..	92	3
14	B	84·78	14·05	·45	·60	·118	..	...	86	..	..
	C	85·85	13·35	·25	·55	..	..	·118	..	86	0
15	B	85·94	11·85	1·21	·87	·132	..	...	88	..	..
	C	86·86	11·06	1·49	·59	..	..	·132	..	87	1
16	B	84·41	14·10	·49	·68	·319	..	...	95	..	..
	C	84·94	14·18	·28	·60	..	..	·319	..	93	2
17	B	84·00	12·15	1·70	1·80	·347	..	...	92	..	..
	C	86·98	10·40	2·07	·55	..	..	·347	..	90	2
18	B	86·49	11·93	·36	1·08	·142	..	...	88	..	..
	C	87·48	10·32	1·47	·73	..	..	·142	..	86	2
19	B	83·92	14·50	·43	1·06	·092	..	...	90	..	..
	C	86·62	11·95	·90	·53	..	..	·092	..	90	0
20	B	84·27	14·07	·74	·63	·293	...	...	91	..	..
	C	87·06	11·93	·30	·70	..	·007	·286	..	89	2
21	B	86·27	11·02	1·64	·86	·213	..	...	93	..	..
	C	87·92	9·48	1·42	1·18	..	..	·213	..	88	5
22	B	83·93	14·28	·52	1·02	·252	..	...	87	..	..
	C	84·90	13·97	·35	·78	..	..	·252	..	85	2
23	B	85·02	12·53	1·59	·73	·128	..	...	89	..	..
	C	86·25	10·44	2·37	·94	..	..	·128	..	86	3
24	B	84·82	13·70	·53	·73	·224	..	...	92	..	..
	C	86·71	12·57	·20	·52	..	..	·224	..	88	4

TABLE A.—SHOWING DIFFERENCE IN RESULTS OF BUTTER, ETC.—*continued.*

No. and Mark.	Fat.	Moisture.	Salt.	Curd.	Boric Acid.% B.	C.	Difference.	Points Awarded. B	C	Difference.
	%	%	%	%						
25 B	82·29	13·97	2·36	1·26	·125	..	..	90	..	
C	83·37	12·82	2·48	1·33	·..	..	·125	..	86	4
26 B	85·59	11·83	1·71	·66	·206	..	..	91	..	
C	82·48	14·48	2·06	·98	..	..	·206	..	87	4
27 B	84·02	12·48	2·02	1·21	·276	..	..	89	..	
C	85·68	11·49	1·94	·87	·..	·021	·255	..	88	1
28 B	85·77	13·13	·33	·65	·107	..	..	92	..	
C	88·11	10·70	·73	·45	..	·007	·100	..	91	1
29 B	84·32	14·55	·40	·66	·128	..	..	91	..	
C	85·74	13·33	·33	·60	..	..	·128	..	90	1
30 B	84·21	14·35	·55	·60	·296	..	..	95	..	
C	86·21	12·83	·46	·50	..	..	·296	..	92	3
31 B	83·44	15·23	·50	·67	·160	..	..	95	..	
C	87·47	11·61	·32	·60	·..	..	·160	..	94	1
32 B	83·24	13·43	2·17	·88	·286	..	..	88	..	
C	84·58	12·41	1·62	1·37	·..	·018	·268	..	84	4
33 B	86·94	11·57	·47	·80	·220	..	..	90	..	
C	86·12	12·80	·35	·72	..	..	·220	..	89	1
34 B	81·65	14·50	2·55	1·05	·251	..	..	92	..	
C	85·01	11·92	2·20	·87	..	..	·251	..	90	2
35 B	81·62	14·55	2·65	1·05	·135	..	..	88	..	
C	84·68	12·52	1·97	·83	..	..	·135	..	84	4
36 B	83·68	13·33	2·05	·85	·092	..	..	92	..	
C	85·30	11·35	1·66	1·68	..	·007	·085	..	85	7
37 B	88·10	9·87	1·15	·87	·007	..	..	87	..	
C	88·68	9·00	1·55	·77	..	..	·007	..	87	0
38 B	87·86	11·33	·15	·51	·146	..	..	87	..	
C	86·4	12·93	·17	·50	..	..	·146	..	85	2
39 B	84·94	13·63	·23	·92	·286	..	..	89	..	
C	86·55	12·63	·24	·58	..	..	·286	..	85	4
40 B	87·74	9·53	1·82	·70	·213	..	..	86	..	
C	87·22	9·85	2·15	·78	..	·010	·203	..	82	4
41 B	85·45	13·37	·33	·70	·149	..	..	90	..	
C	85·40	13·78	·20	·62	..	..	·149	..	89	1
42 B	88·54	10·67	·22	·50	·074	..	..	89	..	
C	86·50	12·83	·30	·37	..	..	·074	..	86	3
43 B	82·07	12·70	2·26	2·73	·238	..	..	87	..	
C	83·16	13·45	1·88	1·51	..	..	·238	..	80	7
44 B	85·92	12·90	·38	·55	·255	..	..	91	..	
C	85·25	13·75	·44	·55	..	·011	·244	..	89	2
45 B	83·80	13·07	2·22	·65	·262	..	..	89	..	
C	84·63	12·58	2·08	·70	..	·007	·255	..	86	3
46 B	82·07	13·90	2·30	1·60	·132	..	..	89	..	
C	84·83	10·87	2·62	1·68	..	..	·132	..	86	3
47 B	83·95	14·47	·47	·68	·231	..	..	93	..	
C	86·54	10·00	2·38	·85	·..	·046	·185	..	92	1
48 B	85·74	13·37	·24	·65	·231	..	..	90	..	
C	83·51	13·63	1·63	1·18	·..	..	·231	..	86	4
49 B	88·58	10·13	·44	·85	..	..	..	90	..	
C	86·23	9·97	2·27	1·53	..	..	..	..	89	1
50 B	85·61	12·83	·41	·93	·217	..	..	91	..	
C	86·06	12·90	·21	·83	..	..	·217	..	83	8
Average B	84·92	12·88	1·16	·92	·183	..	..	90	..	
C	85·65	12·19	1·27	·85	..	·003	·18	..	87·4	2·6

TABLE B.—SHOWING MELBOURNE AND LONDON WEIGHTS OF 98 BOXES OF BUTTER FROM 49 DIFFERENT FACTORIES LOCATED IN VARIOUS PARTS OF THE STATE, TOGETHER WITH THE DISCREPANCY, AND MOISTURE AND SALT CONTENTS IN EACH.

No. and Mark.	Melbourne Weights.		London Weights.		Loss in Transit.	Moisture Contents.	Salt Contents.
	Lbs.	ozs.	Lbs.	ozs.	Ozs.	%	%
1 B	56	10	56	4	6	13·88	1·43
C	56	11	56	5	6	11·65	1·71
2 B	56	15	56	10	5	9·62	0·47
C	56	14	56	11	3	14·46	0·37
3 B	56	14	56	9	5	12·1	1·55
C	56	11	56	5	6	13·18	2·03
4 B	56	13	56	7	6	13·18	1·25
C	56	15	56	7	8	13·39	1·75
5 B	56	9	56	5	4	14·05	0·6
C	56	5	56	1	4	13·0	0·43
6 B	56	15	56	6	9	11·34	1·38
C	56	13	56	11	2	13·25	2·07
7 B	57	9	57	5	4	14·19	1·82
C	57	9	57	6	3	13·47	1·79
8 B	56	13	56	9	4	12·93	1·37
C	56	15	56	10	5	11·20	1·30
9 B	56	12	56	8	4	13·53	2·33
C	56	10	56	5	5	13·95	2·10
10 B	56	8	56	5	3	12·65	1·66
C	56	2	56	0	2	11·47	2·15
11 B	56	11	56	5	6	11·22	1·55
C	57	0	56	9	7	12·72	1·90
12 B	56	12	56	4	8	13·62	0·49
C	56	14	56	4	10	11·42	0·40
13 B	56	10	56	4	6	13·08	0·33
C	56	14	56	9	5	11·92	0·32
14 B	56	13	56	4	9	14·05	0·45
C	56	13	56	6	7	13·35	0·25
15]B	57	6	56	13	9	11·85	1·21
C	57	0	56	7	9	11·06	1·49
16 B	56	12	56	5	7	14·10	0·49
C	56	10	56	5	5	14·18	0·28
17 B	57	0	56	10	6	12·15	1·70
C	57	2	56	13	5	10·40	2·07
18 B	57	5	56	15	6	11·93	0·36
C	56	15	56	8	7	10·32	1·47
19 B	58	9	58	2	7	14·50	0·43
C	57	10	57	4	6	11·95	0·90
20 B	56	9	56	3	6	14·07	0·74
C	56	10	56	4	6	11·93	0·30
21 B	56	15	56	6	9	11·02	1·64
C	56	15	56	7	8	9·48	1·42
22 B	57	3	56	13	6	14·28	0·52
C	57	6	57	2	4	13·97	0·95
23 B	56	7	56	3	4	12·52	1·59
C	56	8	56	4	4	10·44	2·37
24 B	56	12	56	5	7	13·70	0·53
C	57	1	56	11	6	12·57	0·20

TABLE B.—SHOWING MELBOURNE AND LONDON WEIGHTS OF BUTTER, ETC.—*continued.*

No. and Mark.		Melbourne Weights.		London Weights.		Loss in Transit.	Moisture Contents.	Salt Contents.
		Lbs.	ozs.	Lbs.	ozs.	Ozs.	%	%
25	B	56	12	56	6	6	13·95	2·86
	C	56	12	56	7	5	12·82	2·48
26	B	56	10	56	2	8	11·83	1·71
	C	56	5	55	13	8	14·48	2·06
27	B	56	8	56	3	5	12·48	2·02
	C	56	8	56	3	5	11·49	1·94
28	B	57	9	57	1	8	13·13	0·33
	C	57	8	57	1	7	10·70	0·73
29	B	56	11	56	6	5	14·55	0·40
	C	56	14	56	8	6	11·33	0·33
30	B	56	12	56	6	6	14·35	0·55
	C	56	6	56	2	4	12·83	0·45
31	B	56	6	56	3	3	15·28	0·50
	C	56	5	56	3	2	11·61	0·32
32	B	56	11	56	3	8	13·43	2·17
	C	57	0	56	9	7	12·41	1·62
33	B	56	7	56	2	5	11·57	0·47
	C	56	10	56	3	7	12·80	0·35
34	B	57	1	56	5	12	14·50	2·55
	C	57	2	56	8	10	11·2	2·20
35	B	57	0	56	12	4	14·55	2·65
	C	57	0	56	13	3	12·52	1·97
36	B	57	0	56	11	5	13·33	2·05
	C	57	1	56	11	6	11·35	1·66
38	B	56	8	56	5	3	11·33	0·15
	C	56	8	56	5	3	12·93	0·17
39	B	56	3	55	14	5	13·63	0·23
	C	56	7	56	1	6	12·63	0·24
40	B	57	4	56	14	6	9·53	1·82
	C	57	4	56	12	8	9·85	2·15
41	B	56	10	56	6	4	13·37	0·33
	C	56	9	56	5	4	13·78	0·20
42	B	57	2	56	12	6	10·67	0·22
	C	57	5	56	12	9	12·33	0·30
43	B	56	12	56	7	5	12·90	2·26
	C	57	7	57	3	4	13·45	1·88
44	B	56	15	56	11	4	12·90	0·38
	C	56	11	56	7	4	13·75	0·44
45	B	56	10	56	6	4	13·07	2·22
	C	56	10	56	6	4	12·58	2·08
46	B	56	11	56	6	5	13·90	2·30
	C	56	1	56	11	6	10·87	2·62
47	B	56	14	56	6	8	14·47	0·47
	C	56	10	56	6	4	10·00	2·38
48	B	56	12	56	8	4	13·37	0·24
	C	56	14	56	9	5	13·63	1·13
49	B	56	10	56	3	7	10·13	0·44
	C	56	12	56	3	9 ·	9·97	2·27
50	B	56	11	56	3	8	12·83	0·41
	C	56	11	56	3	8	12·90	0·21
				Average	..	5·765	12 59	1·20

LOSS OF WEIGHT IN TRANSIT.

Advantage was taken to have the matter of weights investigated. The question of loss in transit had never been satisfactorily determined. The weight of each box was carefully recorded before shipment, and a request made that the Agent-General should have the same done in London before they were examined. Table B gives all the particulars of 98 boxes. The average loss in weight encountered during transit was 5.765 ozs. In this table are included the moisture and salt contents of each, as it might reasonably be expected that these would have some influence on the loss. The average loss in weight during transit comes to 5.765 ozs. per box, the maximum being 12 ozs. and the minimum 2. The average moisture contents was 12.59 per cent., and salt 1.2 per cent.

By taking out the ten showing the greatest loss in weight during transit, Nos. 67, 24, 68, 11, 27, 29, 30, 41, 82, and 96, the average loss amounts to 9.5 ozs., the average moisture contents of which are 11.87 per cent., and salt contents 1.38 per cent. The ten showing the smallest loss in weight, Nos. 62, 12, 20, 4, 14, 61, 70, 73, 74, and 19, give an average discrepancy of 2.7 ozs. per box, whilst the average moisture contents are 12.89, and salt 1.11 per cent. From these results it appears that no inference can be drawn as to the cause of the marked difference in losses in weight. Those encountering the least loss contained 1 per cent. more moisture than the ones which gave the greatest loss, whilst the salt contents were only 0.27 per cent. more in the case of butters which showed the most pronounced discrepancy.

The ten boxes showing the highest percentage of moisture, Nos. 61, 69, 57, 37, 67, 52, 91, 4, 59, and 43, show the average loss of 6.2 ozs., whilst the average moisture contents were 14.54 per cent., and salt 1.5 per cent. The ten containing the lowest percentage of moisture, Nos. 42, 77, 3, 78, 96, 92, 95, 36, 34, and 46, indicate an average loss of 6.3 ozs. per box, whilst the average moisture contents are 9.97 per cent., and salt 1.68 per cent. It appears from this comparison that butter containing a high percentage of moisture is not more subject to loss in weight during transit than butter containing a low percentage.

The ten boxes containing the highest percentage of salt, Nos. 69, 90, 97, 50, 92, 46, 49, 17, 89, and 96 contained an average of 2.43 per cent. salt, the loss in weight during transit averaging 5.9 ozs. per box, whilst the moisture contents averaged 12.45 per cent. The ten boxes with the lowest percentages of salt, Nos. 9, 73, 74, 80, 48, 98, 81, 75, 76, and 93 show an average salt content of 0.19 per cent.; the average loss in weight per box was 4.9 ozs., whilst the moisture contents are 12.78 per cent. The ten butters containing the highest percentages of salt held 0.33 per cent. less moisture and lost 1 oz. per box more during transit than the boxes showing the lowest percentages of salt.

CONCLUSION.

From this review, it will be seen that the dairy produce export trade is now well organized, and the elimination of the various faults found is quite an easy matter if managers concerned direct their attention to them. They can rest assured that departmental officers, all of whom are enthusiastic, and have their heart in their work, will report faithfully on every churn-mark, and all details. It therefore only requires the mutual co-operation of producers, manufacturers, and others concerned, to lift the reputation of Victorian butter on to the highest possible plane. A greater need than this, however, is that the producers should profit by repeated sad experiences, and provide fodder in the season of plenty to carry them safely through the time of scarcity.

SECOND VICTORIAN EGG-LAYING COMPETITION, 1912-13,

Commencing 15th April, 1912.

CONDUCTED AT BURNLEY HORTICULTURAL SCHOOL.

H. V. Hawkins, Poultry Expert.

No. Pen.	Breed.	Name of Owner.	Eggs laid April 15 to May 14.	Position in Competition.
40	White Leghorns	Brown, S.	111	1
47	„	Bradley, J. E.	109	2
8	Black Orpingtons	Fisher, D.	107	3
44	White Leghorns	Hall, A. W.	103	4
70	„	Beatty, C. J.	101	5
23	„	McLister, Wm.	99	6
30	„	Stevenson, Mrs. H.	93	7
31	„	Edwards, G.	91	8
1	„	Campbell, J.	88	9
7	„	Padman, A. H.	87	10
48	„	Cant, Griffin	86	11
46	Black Orpingtons	Langdon, H. A.	85	12
20	White Leghorns	Waldon, E.	84	13
9	„	Spotswood, J. S.	83	14
62	„	Pope, R. W.	80	15
28	„	Eagleton, F. G.	77	16
42	„	Kempster, Mrs. T. E.	76	17
3	Black Orpingtons	King and Watson	75	18
29	White Leghorns	Brigden, J. B.	71	} 19
45	„	Wooldridge Bros.	71	
39	„	Swift, W. G.	69	21
38	„	Moy, Richard	67	} 22
58	„	Stock, W. J.	67	
64	„	Merrick, H.	65	24
24	„	Sargentri Poultry Yards	63	25
6	„	Macarthur, J. B.	58	} 26
33	„	McKenzie, H.	58	
50	„	Ahpee, A.	53	28
35	„	Buust, C. H.	52	29
53	„	Hodges, H.	49	30
15	„	Steer, Mrs. W. H.	47	} 31
14	„	Wright, J. H.	47	
56	„	Monk, M. A.	46	33
2	„	Rowlinson, B.	44	} 34
12	„	Stafford, T. H. C.	44	
37	„	Bertelsmeier, C. B.	41	} 36
63	„	Walker, Percy	41	
41	„	Stringer, A.	39	38
21	„	O'Loughlin, J.	38	39
25	„	Appletord, R. L.	35	} 40
4	„	Blackburn, J.	35	
13	„	Crellin, W. B.	32	42
61	Black Orpingtons	Ogden, Jas.	29	43
49	White Leghorns	Purvis, W.	27	44
59	„	Seabridge, W.	25	45
52	Black Minorcas	Chalmer Bros.	23	} 46
19	White Leghorns	Cowan Bros.	23	
43	„	Purton, G.	21	48
54	„	DeGaris, F. R.	20	} 49
16	Silver Wyandottes	Jobling, R.	20	
68	White Leghorns	McKeddie, W. J.	20	
69	„	Morgan and Watson	19	52
36	Old E. Game	Barrett, K. J.	18	} 53
27	White Leghorns	Nash, E.	18	
65	„	Thompson, A. H.	17	55
66	„	Moloney, J.	14	56
5	„	Brain, J. H.	13	} 57
18	„	Mitchell, B.	13	
22	„	Ling, W. N.	11	} 59
60	„	Ryan, Miss B. E.	11	
57	„	Walker, B.	7	61
32	„	Brundrett, S.	6	62
10	R.C. Brown Leghorns	Giles, S. P.	4	63
17	White Leghorns	Childs, S.	1	64
11	Black Orpingtons	Goodisson, T. S.	..	
51	White Leghorns	Hammill, H.	..	} 65
67	Anconas	Manning, A. E.	..	
55	Brown Leghorns	Matheson, J.	..	
34	White Leghorns	Moore, Reg. F. B.	..	
26	..	(Reserved)	..	
		Total ..	3 227	

STATISTICS.

Fruit, Plants, Bulbs, Grain, &c.

Imports and Exports Inspected for Quarter ending 31st March, 1912.

Description of Produce.	Imports.		Exports.	Description of Produce.	Imports.		Exports.
	Inter-State.	Oversea.	Oversea		Inter-State.	Oversea.	Oversea.
Apples and Pears ...	1,171	1	269,979	Mace	—	91	—
Bananas, bunches ..	98,014	30,773	—	Maize	—	53	—
Bananas, cases ...	2,222	11,111	—	Mangoes ...	9	—	—
Barley	60,626	6,066	—	Melons	9	—	—
Beans	—	260	—	Nutmegs ...	—	253	—
Blackberries ...	763	—	—	Nuts	56	4,107	—
Black Currants ...	293	—	—	Oats	49,382	18,739	—
Bulbs	28	200	—	Oranges	516	2,771	—
Cherries	1	—	—	Passion	1,035	—	—
Chillies	—	468	—	Peaches	6	—	—
Cocoa beans ...	—	1,058	—	Pepper	—	34	—
Cocoanuts ...	—	6	—	Peas, dried ...	6,496	66	—
Coffee beans ...	—	432	—	Persimmons ...	136	—	—
Copra	—	317	—	Pineapples ...	15,786	29	166
Cucumbers ...	5	—	—	Plants, Trees, &c.	64	296	45
Dates	—	4,953	—	Plums	7,598	—	515
Egg Fruit ...	1	—	1	Pomelos	—	18	—
Figs	—	601	—	Potatoes	137	1	750
Fruit—				Prunes	—	939	—
Canned ...	—	—	7,524	Quinces	—	—	50
Dried ...	—	115	4,728	Rice	3,559	75,473	—
Mixed ...	2	152	—	Seeds	1,149	9,536	55
Grapes	32	—	437	Spice	—	128	—
Green ginger ...	—	695	—	Strawberries ...	2	—	—
Hops	—	237	—	Tomatoes ...	332	—	4
Jams, Sauces, &c. ...	—	—	631	Vegetables ...	774	347	—
Lemons ...	402	2,900	—	Wheat, Grain, &c.	3,215	—	—
Lentils	—	23	—				
Linseed ...	—	462	—				
Logs	327	—	—	Totals ...	254,198	173,711	284,885

Total number of packages inspected for quarter ending 31st March, 1912 = 712,794.

E. MEEKING, *Senior Fruit Inspector.*

Perishable and Frozen Produce.

Description of Produce.	Exports from State (Oversea).		Deliveries from Government Cool Stores.	
	Quarter ended 31.3.12.	Quarter ended 31.3.11.	Quarter ended 31.3.12.	Quarter ended 31.3.11.
Butter ... ... lbs.	12,066,660	15,304,656	13,309,016	13,499,416
Milk and Cream ... cases	2,899	1,325	10	21
Milk and Cream (dried) "	1,203	...	...	...
Cheese ... ... lbs.	34,440	127,080	17,850	135,529
Ham and Bacon ... "	102,720	78,240	...	...
Poultry ... ... head	4,170	2,890	2,923	2,511
Eggs... ... ... dozen	...	...	8,182	12,276
Mutton and Lamb carcases	436,564	247,045	13,078	18,963
Beef ... ... quarters	8,041	4,039	232	...
Veal ... ... carcases	1,075	1,304	13	35
Pork... ... ... "	2,319	1,942	1,134	1,373
Rabbits and Hares ... pairs	155,676	34,464	86,984	21,936
Sundries ... ... lbs.	...	...	24,393	77,225

R. CROWE, *Superintendent of Exports.*

THE VICTORIAN WHEAT HARVEST.

Tne following return, showing the actual area and yield of wheat for the seasons 1911-12 and 1910-11, has been issued by the Government Statist (Mr. A. M. Laughton):—

Counties Geographically Arranged.	Area in Acres.		Produce in Bushels.		Average per Acre in Bushels.	
	1911–12.	1910–11.	1911–12.	1910–11.	1911–12.	1910–11.
Grant	17,565	38,747	183,982	695,526	10·47	17·95
Talbot	14,751	29,500	162,168	471,586	10·99	15·99
Grenville	43,657	41,036	516,402	774,856	11·83	18·88
Hampden	20,333	18,993	195,258	322,585	9·60	16·98
Ripon	68,162	98,446	554,715	1,571,914	8·14	15·97
Lowan	160,384	180,275	1,592,602	1,766,688	9·93	9·80
Borung	315,468	336,633	3,760,294	5,314,410	11·92	15·79
Kara Kara	127,289	127,104	1,541,418	1,880,603	12·11	14·80
Weeah	66,332	46,515	328,113	582,394	4·95	12·52
Karkarooc	332,984	351,509	1,943,436	4,011,903	5·84	11·41
Tatchera	217,603	261,972	1,410,192	3,259,777	6·48	12·44
Gunbower	38,351	40,716	380,245	656,148	9·91	16·12
Gladstone	122,830	124,462	1,428,613	1,760,662	11·63	14·15
Bendigo	128,601	135,897	1,571,500	2,571,624	12·22	18·92
Rodney	124,905	152,827	1,436,022	2,3£6,845	11·50	15·23
Moira	279,761	290,409	3,028,612	4,718,602	10·83	16·25
Delatite	12,316	18,101	123,713	296,963	10·04	16·41
Bogong	41,714	46,209	400,242	826,578	9·59	17·89
Remaining Counties	31,060	58,738	334,350	1,003,355	10·76	17·08
Cut for Grain	2,164,066	2,398,089	..	..	..	..
Cut for Hay	304,388	240,026	..	..	..	..
Total	2,468,454	2,638,115	20,891,877	34,813,019	9·65	14·52

NOTE.—The requirements for seed and consumption in 1912 are estimated at 9,000,000 bushels.

ORCHARD AND GARDEN NOTES.

E. E. Pescott, Principal, School of Horticulture, Burnley.

The Orchard.

PLANTING.

The time has now arrived when the general planting of deciduous fruit trees will take place. The soil should have previously been well ploughed and subsoiled, and, as far as possible, drained. Certainly, to insure satisfactory results, the orchard must be subsoiled. Where expense is a consideration, drainage may be left for subsequent years; but once the orchard has been planted, it will be impossible to subsoil.

When planting out, the distance between the trees will be determined by the kinds to be planted. For ordinary deciduous fruiting trees it is the custom in this State to plant them 20 feet apart in the rows, the rows also being 20 feet apart. Results have proved this to be a satisfactory practice. Almond trees may be planted 15 or 16 feet apart each way; while walnuts, owing to their spreading habit, require a distance of 30 feet each way.

Deep planting is not advocated, the general practice being that the depth of planting in the nursery should be followed. If holes are dug, they should be shallow, the bottom being merely loosened to allow a comfortable friable bed for the tree roots. A good practice is to dig the whole strip along which the trees are to be planted, merely removing sufficient soil when afterwards planting. Another satisfactory custom is to plough furrows 20 feet apart, and to plant the trees in the furrows, filling in the soil over the roots and trampling well down.

Before planting, the roots of the young tree should be well trimmed, shaped to an even form, and cleanly cut. As a result of their removal from the nursery beds, the roots are generally more or less damaged; and numbers of the fibrous roots, becoming dry, shrivel and die. These all require a clean trimming. Then it is often desirable to remove some of the roots so as to balance the root system. The trimming of the roots gives the young tree a clean root system, and it is enabled to establish itself with young vigorous roots

After planting the top should be well cut back, so as to leave three or four arms, with there or four buds on each. Where it is not possible to have this number of arms or limbs it is frequently advisable to cut back to one stem, allowing the buds to break out strongly and frame the tree after planting. In some localities, the custom of not cutting back the trees the first year is favoured. Local experience has not resulted in favour of this practice, as it is found to be inadvisable to unduly strain the young tree by leaving a heavy top to be supported by the weak-growing root system.

A selection of varieties will be determined by the district, some fruits thriving better in one locality than in others. For a good general list, reference may be made to the *Journal* for June, 1911. It is unwise to plant a large number of varieties in a commercial orchard, but due consideration should be given to planting varieties that have a favorable influence on each other for cross-fertilization purposes.

A number of good commercial fruits have been found to be either wholly or partially self-sterile, requiring other varieties near them to enable them to set their fruit. For this purpose it is necessary that the bloom periods should be somewhat coincident.

SPRAYING.

The dry summer and autumn have been favorable to the increase of certain scale insects, woolly aphis, and the bryobia mite in some localities. The use of red oil has been advocated for these pests; and, as well, crude petroleum, kerosene, and other oil emulsions have proved satisfactory. Some years ago the use of the lime, sulphur, and salt spray was much in vogue as a winter spray. Owing, however, to the difficulty of preparing the spray, and to its caustic effects on the skin, it was practically abandoned as an insecticide. Even then it was claimed, and rightly so, that this spray was, to a certain extent, a very good fungicide. The use of this mixture as a winter wash, with the omission of the salt, which has been found to be an unnecessary ingredient, is now being revived; and as the lime-sulphur wash is now on the market in the form of proprietary mixtures, it is likely that this spray will again become popular. It is searching in its action, very adhesive, and certainly very effective. Its claims too, as a fungicide, are not without foundation, as some years ago, when used in orchards on peach trees for scale insect troubles, it was subsequently found that the trees were very much more free from leaf curl and shot hole than during previous seasons.

It possesses objectionable features in its corrosive effects upon any iron or steel on pumps and harness ; and in its caustic effects on exposed parts of the body. These may be somewhat obviated by greasing the metal, and by rubbing the hands and face with olive oil or vaseline prior to spraying. The hindquarters of the horse, too, should be covered with a sack.

Experiments carried out in Pennsylvania in 1909 proved conclusively that in addition to being an excellent insecticide, it was considerably helpful in reducing the effects of fungus diseases on apples, pears, cherries, peaches, and plums.

GENERAL WORK.

All ploughing should now be completed ; if not, it should be finished before spraying and pruning operations are proceeded with.

Any autumn manuring or liming should also be now carried out. This, too, should be finished before spraying and pruning. Before spraying with oils or with lime-sulphur wash, all rough bark on apple and pear trees should be scraped off ; this will mean the certain destruction of any codlin moth larvæ hiding underneath.

Flower Garden.

General cleaning up and digging will be the work for this month in the flower section and shrubbery. Where the soil is heavy or sour, or where sorrel is plentiful, the garden should be given a heavy dressing of fresh lime, giving a fair dusting all over the surface. Lime should not be used in conjunction with leaves, garden debris, leafmould, stable manure, or any other organic matter used for humus. These should be first disposed of by digging well into the soil ; then shortly afterwards a top-dressing of lime may be given. Should no humic material be used, the lime may be dug in with the autumn digging.

In cleaning up the gardens, all light litter and dead foliage should either be dug in, or, better still, it should be placed in an out of the way corner to form a compost heap. Leafmould is especially useful in any garden, and where such plants as Azaleas, Rhododendrons, Liliums, &c., are grown, or for pot plant work, it is exceedingly valuable. In forming the compost heap, no medium whatever should be added to help the rotting down of the leaves, unless it be a little sand. Any chemical added will render the mould unsuitable for its special objects.

Any hardy annuals may be planted out, such as stocks, pansies, wall-flowers, &c., and cuttings of roses and hard-wooded shrubs may also be planted. In planting out cuttings, it is very important that all the eyes should be removed from the part of the cutting which is to be below the ground. If this be not done, there will always be the subsequent danger of the plant suckering.

Roses and any summer and autumn flowering shrubs that have finished flowering may be pruned. If the spring flowering shrubs have not previously been pruned, they should be allowed to remain until after the next flowering season. This especially applies to such plants as Spireas, Philadelphus (Mock Orange), Deutzia, Prumus Mumé, and other early flowering shrubs. To prune these now would mean the certain loss of a great proportion of their flowers.

In pruning, the shrubs may be well thinned out, especially removing any weak upright, or old flowering growths ; keep the shrub always at an outward growth, inclining to a broad bushy type, instead of to an upright habit. By this means, the lower regions will always be furnished with good growth. Shrubs and trees of all descriptions should never be allowed to become too crowded ; they require to be opened, so as to allow sunlight and air into the interior, where it is most needed. This is one means by which this class of plants may be kept healthy and free from disease. Very few shrubs resent pruning, and the majority of them, including Australian shrubs, such as Acacias, are very amenable to the pruning knife.

In rose pruning, the rule is that strong growing plants require less severe cutting than weak-growing ones. As roses always flower on new wood; it is essential that to have good blooms the bushes must be pruned regularly. All weak growths, exhausted and worn-out wood, must be removed, retaining only the vigorous growths. It is generally advisable to always prune to four or five eyes or buds, so as to have subsequent strong growths, always pruning into the previous season's wood. Spindly growths, especially in the centres of the bushes, should be removed, the plants being trained with an open and angular habit.

To prevent loss by decay, it will be advisable to lift and store such herbaceous plants as delphiniums, perennial phlox, rudbeckias, &c., also dahlia tubers, chrysanthemums, cannas, and perennial sunflowers and asters. Failing the possibility of doing this, they should be lifted gently with a fork, so as to allow of a slight air space under the crown.

Vegetable Garden.

If not previously done, asparagus beds should be well cleaned out, and a top-dressing of manure given. To insure good drainage, the soil from the paths, or between the beds, may be thrown up on to the beds, so as to deepen the surface drainage, and to consequently warm the beds. This will mean earlier growths. A heavy dressing of manure should be given, and the beds well and roughly dug over.

Plant out seeds of tomatoes, and the pumpkin family in the frames; and sow in the open, seeds of peas, lettuce, spinach, broad beans, raddish, onion, carrot, and leek. Asparagus crowns, rhubarb roots, tubers of Jerusalem artichokes, shallots, and onions may now be planted out. Celery should still be earthed up, taking care not to have the beds too wet.

ANSWERS TO CORRESPONDENTS.

The Staff of the Department has been organized to a large extent for the purpose of giving information to farmers. Questions in every branch of agriculture are gladly answered. Write a short letter, giving as full particulars as possible, of your local conditions, and state precisely what it is that you want to know. *All inquiries forwarded to the Editor must be accompanied by the name and address of the writer.* This is very necessary, as sometimes insufficient information is furnished by the inquirer.

SUNFLOWER SEED FOR POULTRY FEEDING.—G.G.B. asks :—What are the food elements in sunflower seed, and generally as to its utility as food for poultry?

Answer.—Food elements consist chiefly of Albuminoids, 13.0; Carbo hydrates, 17.7; Fats, 21.0; Water, 8.0; and Ash, 3.0. In excess it is injurious to poultry, being too rich in heating and fattening properties. Useful if fed sparingly during moulting period.

CRAMPS IN TERRIER.—T.F.C. asks how to treat his fox terrier for cramp, which attacks it after a journey or much swimming. Seems in great pain and froths at the mouth?

Answer.—Try the effect of a dose of areca nut, 20 grains in the form of a pill, for three consecutive mornings.

POTATOES.—"New Chum" wishes to know if it is advisable to soak seed potatoes in a solution of formalin, and, if so, what is the right strength?

Answer.—Formalin, 1 lb. to 30 gallons of water steeped for two hours.

For spraying plants :—

    Bordeaux—6 lbs. sulphate of copper (bluestone); 4 lbs. lime; 50 gallons water.

    Burgundy—8 lbs. sulphate of copper; 10 lbs. washing soda; 40 gallons water.

    Time of application—When plants are about 8 inches high; after that according to weather conditions as often as necessary.

FUNGUS IN RASPBERRY CANES.—W.J.S. asks if any cure has been discovered for fungus in raspberry canes?

Answer.—No absolute cure known. The Government Pathologist discovered that the chief factors in prevention were drainage, and liming of the soil, and burning and removing all diseased plants. A mixture of two parts of lime and one of salt is highly recommended.

RHUBARB.—E.J.W. writes that he procured four years ago root of giant rhubarb. This plant has gradually deteriorated until leaves are no longer than ordinary rhubarb.

Answer.—As rhubarb is a gross feeder annual dressings of stable manure in considerable quantities should be given each autumn. Also a light dressing of bone dust and blood manure in early spring. The beds must be well drained.

SUPERPHOSPHATE AS A CATTLE LICK.—A.C. writes to know if it would be harmful to give cows No. 1 Superphosphate as a lick instead of bone meal?

Answer.—Superphosphate may be used as a cattle lick prepared as follows :— Superphosphate, 6 lbs.; slaked lime, 6 lbs.; sheep salt, ½ cwt.; placed in accessible boxes protected from the weather.

CEMENT BRICKS, MACHINE-MADE.—E.S.D. asks as to stability and suitability of machine-made cement bricks made of 1 cement and 6 sand?

Answer.—One to six is too wide for foundations. One to four is advised, and bricks should set well before using..

LEGHORNS FOR CENTRAL GIPPSLAND.—G.G.B. asks if it is advisable to rear leghorns in Central Gippsland?

. *Answer.*—Black orpingtons, silver and white wyandottes, and Plymouth rocks will thrive better in Gippsland than any of the Mediterranean breeds. The latter should be kept during winter months well housed on dry straw or any litter. Protection from wet grass and cold wind is, in all cases, important.

EYE BLIGHT IN COWS.—B.H.L. writes that his cows are affected with eye blight, which seems to be carried from one to another by flies. Symptoms are, water running from eyes, swelling, and finally a white film forms on pupil.

Answer.—Bathe eyes with warm water and boracic acid, and drop into the eyes a few drops of the following twice daily :—Zinc sulphate, 4 grains, tincture of belladonna, 15 drops; distilled water, 1 ounce.

DRAIN PIPES UNDERGROUND.—C.N.W. asks whether drain pipes underground must have an outlet to the surface at some point to carry off such drainage?

Answer.—The pipes ultimately pass to an open drain, which takes the water from the lowest portion of the field to a neighbouring creek, dam, lagoon, &c., into which the field is drained.

ATRIPLEX LEPTOCARPA, SLENDER-FRUITED SALTBUSH.—A.L.M.G. forwards specimen.

Answer.—The above is a native perennial plant which is drought-resisting, and yields a fair amount of forage. Stock of all kinds fond of it. When not too closely fed down, produce seed in abundance, germinating readily under ordinary conditions.

ARTIFICIAL MANURES TO WHEAT-GROWING LAND.—L.G. asks whether long-continued application injuriously affects the soil even when the land is cropped only every third year?

Answer.—The continued application of phosphates to wheat-growing land will not injuriously affect the soil. What will happen is, that if the amount of phosphate acid applied be continually in excess of the requirements of the crop, the phosphoric acid will accumulate, until a point is reached, when further applications will cease to be profitable. The soil will then be comparatively rich in phosphoric acid, but may be deficient in nitrates or in potash, in which case the money invested in phosphates will be more profitably employed in adding these other deficient elements. In any case the intelligent farmer should occasionally test his land by means of small experimental plots to find just what the soil requirements are.

ERAGROSTES BROWNII, " COMMON LOVE GRASS."—" Grass Seed " forwards specimen.

Answer.—A variable native perennial grass, valuable as a pasture grass, producing for many months of the year abundance of palatable and nutritious fodder. Stands drought well even in poor soil, and bears hard feeding. In cultivated ground (orchards, &c.), it is easily kept down by ploughing and clean cultivation.

SOYA BEAN.—J.S.McN. asks where to get Soya Bean, what quantity of seed per acre to sow, nature of soil, and if it is good for pigs and fowls?

Answer.—Can be purchased from the leading Melbourne seedsmen, half a bushel of seed per acre is the quantity sown, the soil best suited for it is a sandy loam with plenty of lime. It is good feed for pigs mixed with other food, such as maize. Fowls do not take readily to the matured beans, but eat them green with advantage.

REMINDERS FOR JULY.

LIVE STOCK.

HORSES.—Those stabled can be fed liberally. Those doing fast or heavy work should be clipped; if not wholly, then trace high. Those not rugged on coming into the stable at night should be wiped down and in half-an-hour's time rugged or covered with bags until the coat is dry. Old horses and weaned foals should be given crushed oats. Grass-fed working horses should be given hay or straw, if there is no old grass, to counteract the purging effects of the young growth. Old and badly-conditioned horses should be given some boiled barley.

CATTLE.—Cows, if not housed, should be rugged. Rugs should be removed in the daytime when the shade temperature reaches 60 degrees. Give a ration of hay or straw, whole or chaffed, to counteract the purging effects of young grass. Cows about to calve, if over fat, should be put into a paddock in which the feed is not too abundant. Calves should be kept in warm, dry shed. The bull may now run with the cows.

PIGS.—Supply plenty of bedding in warm, well-ventilated styes. Keep styes clean and dry. Store pigs should be placed in fattening styes. Sows in fine weather should be given a grass run. Young pigs over two months old should be removed from lucerne run.

SHEEP.—The general classing of merino and lamb-raising ewe flocks should be commenced; none but roomy thick ewes, carrying a bulky fleece, should be kept. Class rams; keep only the best in shape and fleece, castrate all others; do not allow them to go entire to be used by those who think any ram good enough. Deep and narrow forequartered rams are responsible for many carcases dressing and freezing plainly, although often good sheep from a wool point. Sell aged or barren fat ewes from breeding flocks. Clean filth from breech of ewes of British breeds now commencing to lamb. Wherever possible, send lambs weighing 60 lbs. live weight to market. Early prices are always best; avoid waiting until the rush of the season.

POULTRY.—Mating of birds intended for breeding purposes should receive immediate attention. Ten second-season Leghorns or Minorcas, or six of the heavier birds, such as Orpingtons, Plymouth Rocks, and Wyandottes (preferably in their second year), with a vigorous unrelated cockerel will be found satisfactory. Table birds bred in July and early August will pay handsomely prior to the Cup Carnival. A tonic in drinking water as a preventive against chicken pox and other ailments is advantageous.

CULTIVATION.

FARM.—Finish sowing barley, peas and beans, and late white oats in backward districts. Trim hedges. Fallow for potatoes, maize, and other summer crops; in early districts, plant potatoes. Graze off early crops where possible.

ORCHARD.—Continue to plant deciduous fruit trees, bush fruits, and strawberries. Continue cultivating and pruning. Spray for mites, aphides, and scales.

FLOWER GARDEN.—Plant shrubs, climbers, and permanent plants, including roses; also annuals and herbaceous perennials, Gladioli, Liliums, Iris, and similar plants. Continue digging, manuring, trenching, and liming.

VEGETABLE GARDEN.—Plant out seedlings. Sow seeds of carrots, parsnips, cauliflowers, onions, peas, broad beans, and tomatoes. Dig all vacant plots.

VINEYARD.—Proceed with pruning, burning off, and ploughing. Complete, as early as possible, the application of manures other than nitrates and sulphate of ammonia if not already done. Mark out land for new plantations. If ground is in good order and not too wet, proceed with plantation of young vines (unpruned). Remove cuttings or scions from vines previously marked, and keep fresh by burying horizontally in almost dry sand in cool, sheltered place. Permanently stake or trellis last year's plantations.

Cellars.—Rack all young wines, whether previously racked or not. Rack older wines also. For this work choose, as much as possible, fine weather and high barometer. Fill up regularly all unfortified wines. This is a good time for bottling wine.

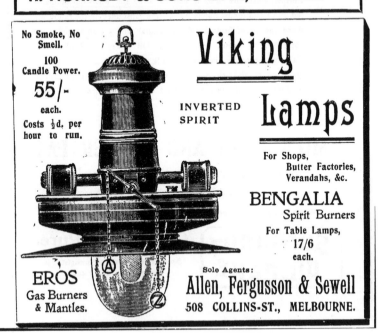

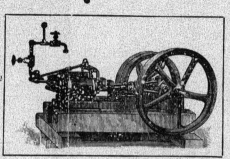

LITERATURE FOR AGRICULTURISTS.

PLAN AND SPECIFICATION OF SHEEP-SHEARING SHED. 2s. 6d. *Postage*, 1d.

MILK CHARTS (Monthly and Weekly), 6d. per dozen, post free. When ordering, dairy farmers should mention " Monthly " or "Weekly."

By Professor A. J. Ewart, Government Botanist.

WEEDS, POISON PLANTS, AND NATURALIZED ALIENS OF VICTORIA. 2s. 6d. *Postage* : Commonwealth, 1½d. ; N.Z., 5d. : British and Foreign, 10d.

PLANTS INDIGENOUS TO VICTORIA. Vol. II., 10s. *Postage :* Com., 2d. ; N.Z., 8d. ; Brit. & For., 1s. 4d.

By C. French, F.E.S., Government Entomologist.

DESTRUCTIVE INSECTS OF VICTORIA. Parts I., II., III., IV., V. 2s. 6d. each. *Postage :* Parts I. and III., C., 1d. ; N.Z., 3d.; B. & F., 6d. each. Parts II. and IV., C., 1½d. ; N.Z., 4d. ; B. & F., 8d. each. Part V., C., 1d. ; N.Z., 4d. ; B. & F., 7d.

By D. McAlpine, Government Vegetable Pathologist.

RUSTS OF AUSTRALIA. 5s. *Postage :* C., 2d. ; N.Z., 8d. ; B. & F., 1s. 4d.

SMUTS OF AUSTRALIA. 4s. *Postage :* C., 2½d. ; N.Z., 9d. ; B. & F., 1s. 6d.

FUNGUS DISEASES OF CITRUS TREES IN AUSTRALIA. 2s. *Postage :* C., 1d. ; N.Z., 3d. ; B. & F., 6d.

FUNGUS DISEASES OF STONE FRUIT TREES IN AUSTRALIA. 2s. 6d. *Postage :* C., 1½d. ; N.Z., 5d. ; B. & F., 10d.

SYSTEMATIC ARRANGEMENT OF AUSTRALIAN FUNGI. 3s. *Postage :* C., 2d. ; N.Z., 8d. ; B. & F., 1s. 4d.

THE DEPARTMENT OF AGRICULTURE,
MELBOURNE, VICTORIA.

Remittances from places outside the Commonwealth to be by Money Order only.

Pamphlets obtainable from the Director of Agriculture, Melbourne, Free on Application.

NEW SERIES.

1. SILO CONSTRUCTION. *A. S. Kenyon, C.E.*
2. HINTS FOR NEW SETTLERS. *T. A. J. Smith.*
* 3. APPLE GROWING FOR EXPORT. *P. J. Carmody.*
* 4. BOOKKEEPING FOR FARMERS. *W. McIver, A.I.A.V.; A.S.A.A., Eng.*
* 5. CIDER MAKING. *J. Knight.*
* 6. FARM PLUMBING. *C. H. Wright.*
7. CITRUS FRUIT CULTURE. *E. E. Pescott.*
* 8. BUILDING HINTS FOR SETTLERS. *A. S. Kenyon, C.E., and others.*
9. TOBACCO CULTURE. *T. A. J. Smith.*
*10. SILOS AND SILAGE. *G. H. F. Baker.*
11. THE BEET SUGAR INDUSTRY AND CLOSER SETTLEMENT. *H. T. Easterby.*

* Not yet available.

REPORT ON EGG-LAYING COMPETITION, 1911-12.

Vol. X.

Part 7.

The Journal of THE DEPARTMENT OF AGRICULTURE OF VICTORIA, AUSTRALIA.

July, 1912.

PENS

EGG LAYING COMPETITION, BURNLEY.

PRICE THREEPENCE. (Annual Subscription—Victoria, Inter-State, and N.Z., 3/-; British and Foreign, 5/-.)

THE JOURNAL

OF

THE DEPARTMENT OF AGRICULTURE,

VICTORIA, AUSTRALIA.

CONTENTS.—JULY, 1912.

COPYRIGHT PROVISIONS AND SUBSCRIPTION RATES.

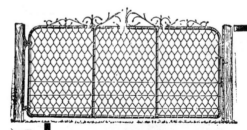

THE JOURNAL

OF

The Department of Agriculture

OF

VICTORIA.

Vol. X.   **Part 7.**   **10th July, 1912.**

INFLUENCE OF CERTAIN SOIL CONSTITUENTS UPON NITRIFICATION.

By John W. Paterson, B.Sc., Ph.D., Experimentalist, and P. R. Scott, Chemist for Agriculture.

Nitrification is the process whereby nitrates are formed in soils. Some other forms of nitrogen can be used by crops, but the nitrate form is required in order to get a paying crop. The nature and conditions of nitrification were described in the May issue of this *Journal*. Experiments were quoted showing how the moisture conditions of the soil affected the change.

In one of the soils used in the moisture experiments there appeared to be a deficiency of lime as revealed by chemical analysis, and on this soil nitrification was somewhat slow even under the best moisture conditions. It seemed desirable, therefore, to set up a new set of experiments with the soil in question in order to find whether an addition of lime would accelerate matters. The results form the principal subject of this report.

Lime is usually applied to land in one of two forms. It is applied as burnt, hot, or caustic lime—lime proper—and this is the most active form in which to apply lime. Again, it may be applied as chalk or ground limestone—carbonate of lime—and this form of lime is milder in its action. Slaked lime is a third chemical form of lime, but it acts just like hot lime, and is one-third heavier than hot lime, without containing more lime.

In these experiments, hot lime has been tried on the soil in two different quantities. Mild lime has also been tried in two quantities, equivalent in each case to an application of hot lime. With pure materials 56 parts of hot lime contain the same lime as 100 of mild lime.

7431.   o

Besides hot and mild lime, a number of other substances have also been tried to find their effect upon nitrification. These include gypsum (sulphate of lime) and superphosphate (phosphate of lime), both of which are generally available for application to land. Then magnesium carbonate, which often occurs as impurity in limestone, has been tested. Ferric hydrate or iron rust is present more or less in practically all soils, and it has been tried as to its effect upon nitrification. It can neutralize some acids as lime does, but is altogether less active. Common salt, excess of which is injurious to crops, has been included. Citric acid was used in order to imitate the acidity of sour land, which lime can be applied to sweeten. Finally, sugar and starch were used to find the effect of too much fresh humus in soil, and also when the soil is badly aerated.

The scheme of experiments is set forth in Table I.

TABLE I.

Test Number	Constituent added to Soil.	Percentage Present in Soil.	Chemical Equivalents.	Character of Materials.
1	Nothing			
2	Carb. of Lime ..	2·00	..	Commercial whitening, 99 per cent.
3	,, ,, ..	0·59	..	,, ,, ,,
4	Carb. of magnesia ..	1·08	= Test 2	Carbonate and Hydrate, MgO = 40·62 per cent.
5	,, ,, ..	0·42	= ,, 3	,, ,, ,,
6	Gypsum	3·44	= ,, 2	Chemically pure
7	,, ...	0·86	= ,, 3	,,
8	Lime	1·12	= ,, 2	Freshly ignited, 99 per cent.
9	,, ...	0·28	= ,, 3	,, ,,
10	Ferric hydrate ..	1·43	= ,, 2	Precipitated, washed, and dried
11	Common salt ..	0·125		Chemically pure
12	,, ..	0·25	= 2 x Test 11	
13	Citric acid ..	0·104	= Carbte. in soil	Commercial crystals
14	,, ..	0·213	= Carbte. in soil plus $\frac{1}{10}$ per cent.	,, ,,
15	Starch	1·14	..	Specially prepared—water, 12·1 per cent.
16	Sugar	1·00	= Org. matter in 15	Castor sugar, 99·5 per cent.
17	,, ..	1·00	(Sealed)	,, ,, ,,
18	Superphosphate ..	0·0025	= 100 lb. plus acid per acre foot	Phos. acid, 20 per cent. (17.1.2)

The first ten tests supply equivalent amounts of lime, magnesia, or iron in large or moderate doses. Regarding the use of magnesia, which in amount here is about one-sixth too little, reference is made later on. The amount of citric acid in 13 was estimated from the combined carbonic acid found on an analysis of the soil, and to 14 was applied 0.1 per cent. over and above the amount required for neutralizing. Each of the materials was used in a finely powdered condition.

The soil used was that described as "sandy" in the previous article, and was taken from the same bulk. The chemical and mechanical analysis of this soil has already been published.

The method of experiment was essentially the same as that adopted in the earlier investigations. Air-dry soil, equal to 300 grams of dry soil, including the added substance, if any, was wetted up to 60 per cent. of its water-holding capacity, and 5 c.c. ammonium sulphate solution containing 0.1 gram nitrogen was mixed with the wetted soil. This nitrogen equalled 333.33 parts per million of dry soil. After adding the ammonia the soil was transferred to a bottle, and compacted by tapping to a uniform volume in each case. With any substance, there were always two bottles, one getting ammonia, and one getting no ammonia (control). Where ammonia was given, the water of solution was part of the water required to

ASPIRATING THE BOTTLES.

give the desired moisture. The bottles were corked during the incubation period, and were placed in a dark cupboard where the temperature was read daily at 9 a.m. and 5 p.m. Twice weekly the bottles were uncorked, and aspirated for five seconds with a suction pump in order to maintain fresh air. Number 17, however, was sealed, and kept closed throughout the whole course of the experiments.

The eighteen tests, with their controls, required thirty-six bottles. Another set was filled similar to these, making seventy-two bottles. In addition, four extra bottles of Nos. 1 and 2 were placed aside in order to get some idea when the time had arrived to begin the full analyses.

The methods of analysis adopted have already been described. The work was performed by Mr. W. C. Robertson, chief deputy chemist, who also attended to the filling of bottles and keeping of records.

The four extra bottles of Nos. 1 and 2 were filled on 22nd February, and tested on 8th March. Period of incubation, fifteen days; average temperature, 72.9 degrees F. The results are stated in Table II.

TABLE II.

Test Number	Constituent Added.	Nitrate Nitrogen per 1,000,000 parts Dry Soil.			Percentage of added Ammonia Nitrified.
		Control Blanks.	Ammonia Bottles.	Excess with Ammonia.	
1	Nothing	29·40	75·72	46·32	13·89
2	Carb. of lime	42·62	352·67	310·05	93·01

·It was seen from these observation bottles that the addition of mild lime had very greatly increased the rate of nitrification, and it was decided therefore to commence one of the main series as soon as possible.

Table III. gives the results. The period of incubation here was twenty-one days ; average temperature, 72.1 degrees F.

TABLE III.

Test Number	Constituent Added.	Nitrate Nitrogen per 1,000,000 parts Dry Soil.			Percentage of added Ammonia Nitrified.
		Control Blanks.	Ammonia Bottles.	Excess with Ammonia.	
1	Nothing ·, ..	22·01	94·33	72·32	21·69
2	Carb. of lime	38·02	347·37	309·35	92·86
3	,, ...	33·26	299·38	266·12	79·83
4	Carb. of magnesia	22·01	55·12	33·11	9·93
5	,, ,·	26·40	52·75	26·35	7·90
6	Gypsum	16·51	94·33	77·82	23·34
7	,, ...	13·20	82·45	69·25	20·77
8	Lime	3·27	4·04	..	..
9	,, ...	14·61	4·39	..	..
10	Ferric hydrate	14·61	94·33	79·72	23·91
11	Common salt	16·50	26·37	9·87	2·96
12	,, ...	13·20	4·40	..	..
13	Citric acid	6·53	73·20	66·67	20·00
14	,, .. ·.	3·92	33·02	29·10	8·73
15	Starch	Nil	Nil	..	...
16	Sugar	Nil	Nil	..	..
17	,, ...	Nil	Nil	..	..
18	Superphosphate ..· ..	19·01	94·33	75·32	22·59

Referring to the figures, it was apparent that the acceleration of nitrification found in twenty-one days scarcely extended beyond the carbonate of lime, consequently it was decided to leave the duplicate set for another month. The figures of Table III. stand in an interesting relation to the final results, and will be referred to later.

At the end of fifty-one days, the remainder of the bottles were analyzed. Mean temperature of periods, 69.98 degrees F. The results were as shown on the following page.

TABLE IV.

Test Number	Constituent Added.	Nitrate Nitrogen per 1,000,000 parts Dry Soil.			Percentage of added Ammonia Nitrified.
		Control Blanks.	Ammonia Bottles.	Excess with Ammonia.	
1	Nothing	33·03	108·99	75·96	22·79
2	Carb. of lime	54·00*	412·83*	358·83	100·00
3	,, ,,	39·92*	329·97*	290·05	87·01
4	Carb. of magnesia	38·02	329·97	291·95	87·60
5	,, ,,	66·53	299·97	233·44	70·03
6	Gypsum	33·02	139·59	106·57	31·97
7	,,	29·35	131·97	102·62	30·78
8	Lime	3·92	4·37	..	..
9	,,	38·02	13·09	..	..
10	Ferric hydrate	26·37	188·89	162·52	48·75
11	Common salt	26·37	68·90	42·53	12·75
12	,,	26·37	29·94	3·57	1·07
13	Citric acid	10·93	70·09	59·16	17·74
14	,,	Nil	59·99	59·99	17·99
15	Starch	10·93	55·84	44·91	13·47
16	Sugar	2·85	92·66	89·81	26·94
17	,,	Nil	Nil	Nil	..
18	Superphosphate	29·35	136·62	107·27	32·18

* The soil of these 4 bottles was inadvertently missed, and refilled after 21 days.

WEIGHING THE MATERIALS.

We may now proceed to consider the practical lessons of these experiments.

Carbonate of Lime.—This material had the best effect on nitrification of all the substances tried. Not only did it give the best result ultimately, but its action was also the soonest felt. It gave a better result in fifteen days (Table II.) than any other application in fifty-one days. The quantity applied—2 per cent.—is larger than would be applied in practice, yet there is no danger of giving too much of the substance at one time. Indeed, the heavier application (No. 2) was better than the lighter (No. 3), which, however, was also good. The beneficial action of mild lime on nitrification is not new, but it is very clearly demonstrated in these results.

Tables II. and III. show that about 93 per cent. of the ammonia nitrogen given was nitrified after using carbonate of lime within three weeks. This is probably as large an amount as will ever be recovered in practice.* The final analysis shows a higher figure, but the bottles of Nos. 2 and 3 were emptied by mistake, and refilled at the time of the second analysis, and these particular results are therefore nitrated.

Increased production of nitrates following upon the use of carbonate of lime is one of the chief, if not the chief, reason for its beneficial effect on crops. The results obtained in this experiment may be confidently expected in the field where the land is deficient in lime, and sufficiently dry. When two soils in Trinidad were limed, and subsequently examined, a striking increase in the percentage of nitrates was shown over similar unlimed land.†

Caustic Lime (Nos. 8 and 9) had a bad effect in the fresh state, and practically stopped all nitrification. The larger application did most harm. There was some unavoidable loss of ammonia in filling and aerating these bottles, but as care was taken to wet the soil before adding the ammonia, the loss was only partial, and cannot be held to explain the result. Table III. shows clearly the folly of applying hot lime with, or shortly before, the seed of any crop, as thereby the nitrate factory is effectively closed down. Table IV. indicates that the smaller application was beginning to recover at the end of fifty-one days, but the large one was not. The lesson is that hot lime should be applied some months before seeding, and the heavier the dressing the longer the time should be. When hot lime lies a few months in the soil, it unites with carbonic acid, and is then present as carbonate of lime. The beneficial effects of carbonate of lime have already been noted. Any injurious effect of applying hot lime at the wrong time may be expected to disappear by the second year.

Hot lime eventually will stimulate nitrification just like mild lime, because it will be converted into mild lime. Using small quantities, it may indeed give a better result the second year, because it will be better distributed over the soil particles. For the same reason, its effect would be sooner expended.

Gypsum had a moderate effect in encouraging nitrification, but was not at all equal to carbonate of lime. The heavier application (No. 6) was a trifle better than the smaller (No. 7), but nothing to abide by. It is sufficient to group the results, and note that gypsum has certainly been of benefit, but that it was slow (Table III.) in beginning to act. Gypsum contains lime, but in union with sulphuric acid, and on this account gypsum will not generally repair the deficiencies of a soil requiring lime as quickly as the other forms, hot or mild.

Carbonate of Magnesia (Nos. 4 and 5) seems to behave in a curious manner. It was intended to apply the neutral carbonate, but by mistake the " magnesii carbonas levis " of the pharmacopœia was used. This contains hydrate as well as carbonate of magnesia, and is weakly alkaline. At the first period, therefore (Table III.), this material delayed nitrification

* *Die Stick-stoffdüngung der landw., Kulturpflanzen*, by Dr. Paul Wagner, Berlin, 1892.
† *Bul. Dept. Agric. Trinidad* 9 (1910), No. 66, pp. 239, 240.

somewhat after the manner of hot lime, which is strongly alkaline. After a longer period (Table IV.) apparently it had all become converted into the neutral carbonate; and it then exercised a fine effect somewhat resembling mild lime. Excess of magnesium carbonate may be harmful to crop plants, but apparently this effect will not be exercised through its influence on nitrification.

Superphosphate has appreciably increased the nitrification of added ammonia as compared to the soil receiving no application (No. 1), and on referring to the chemical analysis of the soil, it is seen to be very poor in phosphoric acid (.032 per cent.). The result is interesting as showing that phosphates may help to nourish the nitrifying organisms as well as the crop. Still the nitrate production is very far behind that of several other materials which have been considered. Where it is not required to nourish the organisms, superphosphate being acid will probably do harm. This particular subject has been investigated by Dr. Fraps in America.* Working with ten different soils, he found that phosphatic acid decreased the nitrate supply from 100 to 70 on the average of five soils, and increased it from 100 to 196 on the average of the five others.

Ferric Hydrate (No. 10) has been distinctly favorable to nitrification, although it was slow, and the effect was chiefly noticeable at the later date. Some recent investigations at Rothamsted, by Ashby, indicate a similar beneficial effect of iron rust (ferric hydrate) on nitrification.† These experiments were conducted in water cultures, and it is interesting to confirm the result here under soil conditions. Red and chocolate soils contain most ferric hydrate, and this may contribute to their fertility.

Common Salt had a bad effect all round, and the larger application (¼ per cent.) was worse than the smaller (⅛ per cent.). Crops fail on salt or alkali soils, and no doubt the effect is produced in part by the influence of this constituent in checking nitrification.

Citric Acid (Nos. 13 and 14) hindered nitrification very seriously, and the heavier application had a bad effect on the nitrate production throughout. It is noticeable with these sour soils that the nitrate production in the controls was reduced in an exceptional degree. These controls received no ammoniacal manure. Looking to the bad effect of acidity, and comparing it with the effect of mild lime, the advantage of liming sour land and neutralizing its acid becomes manifest.

Starch and Sugar in the aerated bottles (Nos. 15 and 16) did not help nitrification at the first (Table III.), but they destroyed the nitrates already present—denitrification. This may happen at times after ploughing in green or fresh stable manure, especially on stiff wet soils. At the close of the experiments, the soils showed no trace of either starch or sugar by chemical tests. These had apparently rotted away, and the sugar would rot fastest. If that were so, then the sugar bottle would soonest be able to re-start nitrification, and at the close indeed it contained considerably more than the other.

The sugar bottle kept sealed (No. 17) never showed nitrates anywhere, and one may conclude that working and tillage to admit air will stimulate nitrification. This will be particularly useful when green or stable manure has been applied some time before.

While conducting these experiments, an interesting point arose as to the probable effect of dry storage of soil upon the vigour of the nitrifying organisms contained in it. Four bottles were set up with a special soil,

* *Bul. Texas Agric. Exp. St.* 159 (1908), *pp.* 15, 16.
† *Jour. Agric. Sci.*, Vol. II. (1907-8), pp. 52 *et. seq.*

which had been air-dried, and stored at the laboratory for three months. Two of those bottles marked A were put away dry on 23rd February, while other two marked B were wetted to 60 per cent. of the saturation capacity, and put away on the same day. After fifty days (13th April), the contents of both A bottles were also wetted, and at the same time one of A and one of B received 0.1 gram ammonia nitrogen as sulphate. The bottles were again set aside, and after twenty-three days (6th May), the progress of nitrification was determined with the following results:—

TABLE V.

Test Mark.	Constituent Added.	Nitrate Nitrogen per 1,000,000 parts Dry Soil.			Percentage of added Ammonia Nitrified.
		Control Blanks.	Ammonia Bottles.	Excess with Ammonia.	
A	Wetted 13th April ..	33·50	90·75	57·25	17·17
B	,, 23rd Februray ..	41·50	307·50	266·00	79·80

The soil was a poor one, and there was little difference in the unmanured blanks. Where ammonia was given, nitrification, however, went on much more quickly on the soil previously kept wet, showing that continued existence in a dry soil impairs the vigour of the germs, but that under moister conditions, they recover. This question does not affect the influence of added substances, where the same soil is used throughout. What it shows is that after a long dry spell, nitrifying activity will not immediately revive with the rain because the organisms require some time to recover their normal vigour.

SUMMARY.

1. Mild lime is an effective means of promoting nitrification, and its action begins at once.
2. It is a safe dessing both as regards quantity and time of application.
3. Caustic lime requires greater caution in its use.
4. It should not be applied too near the time of seeding.
5. It should not be applied during the growth of any crop.
6. It should be used in smaller quantities than mild lime.
7. It will probably have a similar action to mild lime eventually.
8. Magnesium carbonate in a limestone may or may not damage crops, but it appears to favour nitrification.
9. Red and brown soils, other things being equal, favour nitrification, as they contain a slow-acting base in the form of iron rust.
10. Gypsum is a slow form in which to apply lime.
11. Superphosphate may prove a useful aid to nitrification on some soils.
12. Salt delays nitrification.
13. Sour soils are very unfavorable to nitrification.
14. Ploughing in of green or fresh stable manure may cause a temporary shortage of nitrates, particularly on damp soil.
15. The nitrifying organisms are weakened by continued drought, and where the surface soil becomes unduly parched in a dry spell, nitrification will begin slowly after rain comes.

ERUPTIVE DISEASE, OR "EXANTHEMA" OF ORANGE TREES IN AUSTRALIA.

By C. C. Brittlebank, Vegetable Pathologist's Office.

From time to time specimens of diseased oranges, together with their leaves and branches, have been forwarded to the office of the Vegetable Pathologist, with a request that a determination of the disease be made, and, if possible, a remedy suggested.   When on a recent visit to the capital of a sister State, a request was made by several fruit-growers that I should visit a number of orange groves in which an unknown disease had appeared.   As this was causing serious trouble to the growers, so much so that they intended to grub out their trees if relief could not be obtained. During this interview I was informed that they could not obtain any information as to the cause or control of the disease.   A visit was paid to the district and an examination of the diseased trees made.   This, together with the knowledge gained from specimens forwarded to Melbourne, soon convinced me that the trouble was physiological, and not due to any special fungi.

DESCRIPTION OF THE DISEASE.

A most striking feature of this disease is the general healthy appearance of the trees, the leaves of which are of a beautiful dark-green, and frequently nearly twice the normal size.   This apparent symptom of health is followed by a yellowing of the young tender shoots, from which the leaves fall.   Soon after, or concurrent with the fall of the leaves, the shoots turn reddish-brown, owing to the middle layers of the bark becoming engorged with a resin-like substance.   Twigs affected as described die back for a length of from 6 to 12 inches.   Numerous bushy twigs arise from the smaller branches, these however soon die away, giving the characteristic appearance to diseased trees.   When a number of affected shoots are borne on a larger branch the bark of the latter is often blistered, split, and ruptured to such an extent that the injured portions become almost confluent. (Plate I., Fig. 1.)   From these injuries a hard rusty-coloured resin-like gum exudes; this granulates on the edges of the injuries and does not run or collect in tears, as in some other citrus diseases. (Plate I., Fig. 11.)

An examination of the bark shows that the actual ruptures do not extend into the cambium or sapwood, but generally only affect the middle layer of the bark outwards.   However, beneath the ruptures numerous minute gum pockets are formed in the sapwood directly beneath the ruptures These appear as clear glass-like specks, if a shaving be removed and held against the light. (Plate II., Fig. IV.)   Sometimes even before the tree shows any sign of disease in leaf or shoot, it can be detected by the pale unhealthy colour of the fruit, which often falls before becoming mature. Oranges borne on affected branches are frequently stained by the reddish-brown exudation which hardens the skin, causing them to split or crack. (Plate II., Fig. IIIA.)   In some instances the diseased fruit becomes quite hard, and in others it falls early.   Even those which remain ripen prematurely, and are of a pale-greenish-lemon yellow, and quite insipid to taste, as are also the green immature oranges.

NATURE OF SOIL IN AFFECTED AREAS.

As nearly all soils are determined by the nature of the underlying geological formation, and as the main mass is composed almost entirely of

1. Orange branch showing ruptured bark.
11. Confluent blisters on small twig.

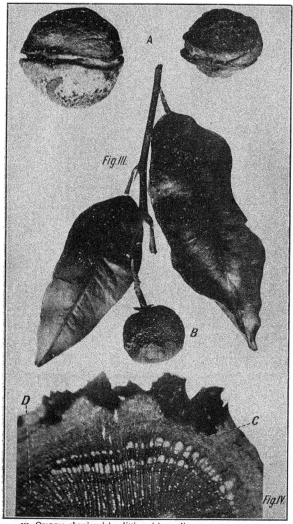

III. Oranges showing (A) splitting, (B) woodiness.
IV. Transverse section of twig gum pockets at (C), normal tissue at (D).

siliceous sandstone, this is broken down and is then washed from the higher levels and deposited on the lower slopes at the foot of the hills. From the nature of its source and deposition it is, as would be expected, of a light porous nature. As this soil was being formed, more or less vegetable matter was brought down and mixed through it, but this would be, comparatively speaking, quickly removed, more especially if the surface soil be kept free from plant growth.

Several of the orange groves are on this type of soil, some of these were planted many years ago, and as a consequence they have withdrawn a large quantity of the available plant food within their reach.

Even in the area of a single plantation the deficiencies of plant food in the soil vary to a considerable extent, affecting both the growth and yield of the trees. Generally speaking this is perhaps one of the most fertile sources of trouble as the weakened vitality and starved condition of the trees lay them open to attack from various citrus diseases. So far as I could ascertain no manure, with the exception of bone-dust, had been used in the affected area. That this disease is more prevalent in those areas which are of a dry porous nature and in which there is a lack of organic matter is easily seen. Trees growing in a more retentive soil are in this case not affected with " Exanthema," although they may be, and often are, attacked by collar-rot and other diseases. All the evidence collected in the field points to the lack of organic matter and an open porous sandy soil being the chief factors in causing this trouble.

Methods Suggested for the Control of the Disease.

Such being the case methods must be adopted which will render the soil more retentive of moisture and at the same time supply food for the trees. Ploughing in green crops of oats, barley, rye, or wheat, which have been previously manured with superphosphates would be the easiest and best method to adopt. Nitrogenous manures should be used sparingly, if at all, on the diseased areas, as they appear to have a deleterious effect upon the trees. Discretion must be left to the growers as to the best method of cultivation and crop suited to the district.

Care should also be taken that no bud wood be taken from trees which have been affected, as they might possibly be more susceptible if placed under favorable conditions for the development of the trouble.

The conditions favouring the development of the disease are—1. Porous light deep, coarse or sandy soil, lacking organic matter, and which quickly dries out after rain. 2. Continued drought followed by heavy rain. 3. Large amounts of nitrogenous manures.

THE OLIVE.

L. Macdonald, Horticulturist, Dookie Agricultural College.

(Continued from page 217.)

Pests.

The Olive in the older European countries is subject to the attack of a number of enemies; fortunately, however, it is endowed with a constitution specially fitted for the resistance of such attacks, otherwise it would not to-day be in its proud position in the forefront of economic trees.

Probably the worst pest in the countries referred to is the Olive Fly (*Dacus oleæ*). This insect attacks the matured and partially matured fruit. In some years it works enormous damage. The Olives in Australia appear, so far, to be free from its attack; yet it is possible, nay probable, that in the warmer districts one or the other of the fruit flies will take its place. Plantation owners and prospective growers must look with serious concern at the possibility of the introduction of this fly. For when once established under genial conditions, it is one of the most difficult to suppress.

A closely related species, "The Queensland Fruit Fly" (*Dacus (Tephritis) Tryoni Frogg*), is one of the most formidable pests with which the fruitgrower in the Northern States has to contend. Any insect such as this little fly, that directs its attack towards the matured or nearly matured fruit, is usually most difficult to suppress. Its presence is usually not suspected until it is so well established that it is difficult to cope with. Although the presence of the "The Queensland Fruit Fly" (*Dacus (Tephritis) Tryoni Frogg.*), "The Mediterranean Fruit Fly" (*Halterophora (Ceratitis) capitata,* Wied.), and "The Guava Fruit Fly" (*Tephritis psidii*) may cause serious forebodings in the Northern States, they are not be feared so much in Victoria. Our climatic conditions do not appear to be entirely suited to their development. Doubtless many of the larve were imported into Victoria in oranges and bananas before the present system of inspection was instituted, but they do not appear to have survived and multiplied. Although the Mediterranean Fruit Fly has been found in several places in the Goulburn Valley during the last five or six years, it seems to have had a somewhat precarious existence and to have done comparatively little damage. It would seem that it is only in those years when the summer and autumn are especially dry that its attack is to be feared. As a rule, the zone of its activity does not reach so far south. The vigilance of growers should not, however, be relaxed on that account, as it is possible that it may in time become acclimatised.

The three worst pests attacking the Olive in Australia at the present time are, "The Curculio Beetle," "The Olive Scale," and "The Red Scale." This being so, the prospective planter has not very serious cause for alarm. Providing he takes care in obtaining trees or cuttings that are free from any of these pests, he is not likely to have any trouble for years, unless he is adjoining an infected area. It may be mentioned here, that it is the writer's intention to deal chiefly with those diseases that are at present infesting the Olive groves in Australia, on'y slight reference being made to those pests that have not, so far, gained a foothold here. These will be dealt with separately, as they represent different classes of pests and call for different methods of treatment.

The Curculio Beetle (*Otiorhynchus cribricollis*):—This pest is undoubtedly becoming one of the most serious of those attacking the Olive in this country. Of late years it has been doing a considerable amount of damage in the olive plantations, nurseries, and gardens of South Australia. The writer has not so far met with it in the olive groves of this State, although it is possible that it may be present in some places. It is to be hoped that every precaution will be used against its introduction, and if it gains admittance, towards its suppression, because it appears to be almost omnivorous, and when once established is most difficult to suppress. When one food is not present it appears to turn its attention with equal zest to another, attacking practically all kinds of fruit trees

to a greater or lesser degree as well as a number of garden plants.   It
is, however, probable that on the whole the trees that suffer most from
its attack at the present time are Olives, Almonds, and Figs.

Owing to its shyness and nocturnal habits this insect is particularly
hard to cope with.   In many places its ravages were observed long before
the real cause of the trouble was discovered.   Growers, being at a loss
to understand the cause of the damage done to their trees, attributed the
mischief, in some cases, to innocent, inoffensive insects that happened to
be present at the time.   The gnawed and ragged edges of the leaves,
noticeable where it has attacked, are unfailing indications of the presence
of a chewing or mandibulate pest.   Nevertheless, its extreme shyness
in hastily dropping to the ground, its precipitate efforts at concealment,
and its cunning instinct in feigning death in the presence of danger, have
often robbed the grower of any suspicion that he may have had regarding

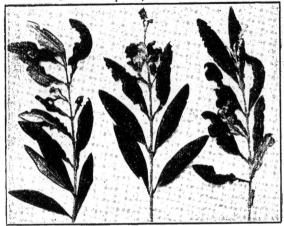

FIG. 19. TERMINALS OF OLIVE SHOOTS ATTACKED BY "CURCULIO" BEETLE.

its destructive work, and he has allowed it to go unharmed.   This power
of simulating death, the natural colour of the adult insect, and its tendency to seek a hiding place in the darkened interstices of the soil or among
decaying vegetable matter similar in colour to itself, have often aided it
in escaping detection.

"The Curculio Beetle" belongs to the great family (*curculionidæ*) or
weevils, which comprises some of the worst pests with which the horticulturist has to contend, such as the apple root borer (*Leptops hopei*); the
plum curculio (*conotrachelus nenuphar*), etc.   With seed of various
kinds, and trees and plants, both indigenous and exotic, the members of
this family have done incalculable damage, and are likely to continue
their destructive work for some time to come owing to the many difficulties
in the way of their suppression.

The adult insect usually measures about 5-16th of an inch in length.
That is from the tip of the snout to the posterior end of the wing cases,

and about an inch across the back or dorsal surface of the wing cases. The beetles are of a reddish-black or brownish-black colour, varying to almost solid black in some of the older insects.   They usually appear about November and continue their ravages through the summer months, disappearing again about March.

As far as the writer can ascertain, it appears that little information is available regarding the life history of this particular pest under our conditions.   In all probability its life history is similar in many respects to that of some other members of the same family with which we are more familiar.   That is, the eggs are laid close to the surface in sheltered parts of the soil, chiefly around the base of those trees or plants that provide the food of the mature insect.   The larvæ hatch out and live on adjacent roots, pupating in early spring, after which the beetles soon make their appearance.   In some cases the adult insects have been found hibernating in crevices around trees or other hiding places during winter.

Owing to the meagreness of the information regarding the habits of this insect, there is not sufficient evidence to show whether the larvæ live on the roots of the plants attacked by the beetle, or on decaying vegetable matter, or on the roots of weeds and grasses.   This lack of definite knowledge regarding the habits of this pest is a disadvantage in undertaking any means of combating its destructive work.   It appears to be fairly certain though, from the habits of the adult insects, that a portion of its life has been a subterranean one. The nocturnal habits, the strong aversion to bright daylight, and the instinct in seeking a hiding place in the soil, seem to point that way.

FIG 20. THE CURCULIO BEETLE (*magnified*).

This insect cannot fly.   In consequence its distribution has been somewhat restricted.   In some of the Olive groves where it is present its attack is confined to limited patches, but there is always a tendency to spread, even if slowly.

In Fig. 19 is depicted a few terminals of twigs picked by the writer at random, in one of the largest South Australian plantations.   They give a fair idea of the usual nature of this insect's attack on olive trees. The beetles crawl up the trees when darkness arrives and, reaching the terminals of the branches, usually cling from the underside or edge of the leaves and eat into them from the margin, giving them a jagged, irregular appearance somewhat similar to that due to the attack of the leaf cutting bee.   The attack depicted on the above plate is not a very bad one.   In extreme cases all the green fleshy cellular tissue of the leaves is consumed and nothing but the stalk and ribs are left.   The remnant of the leaves left in such cases on such trees as figs presents an appearance somewhat like those of melons that have been badly attacked by the black banded pumpkin beetle.

Treatment:—This should be based on what we know of the habits of the insect and should be carried out in the most economical and effective way possible.   It should be borne in mind that the beetles do their work at night, that they are chewing insects, that they cannot fly, and that they take shelter during the day under any cover adjacent to their host. The fact that they are nocturnal feeders present some difficulties in the way of treatment.   It seems like hitting in the dark trying to combat a pest that makes its attack at night.   This disadvantage is, however, counterbalanced by the inability of the insects to make their escape in flight and by their natural inclination to find a refuge during the day somewhere close to the trees.

Since they are unable to fly they must find their way on foot to the trunk of the trees and climb up to get at their food supplies. The return journey is made before the next day. Hence the use of a bandage around the trunk of each tree is a means of diminishing the pest. Crinoline bands of plate tin in conjunction with bagging will be found useful in this respect. The tin bands are cut about 3 to 4 inches in width and sufficiently long to go around the trees and provide for a little lap. In putting on such bands the uppermost edge is fitted as close as possible to the bark all around the trunk, thus preventing any beetle from squeezing between it and the bark in going up. The lower edge is spread out at some distance from the main stem. If the bandages are put on correctly and are of the right class of material, the beetles will fail to negotiate them during the night, and numbers will be found in the early morning underneath the bands. These should be collected and destroyed. Bandages of bagging may also be used lower down than the tin bands as a trap. Tanglefoot papers, strips of cloth or paper smeared with a strong adhesive will often serve well, although it should be remembered that all forms of adhesive bandages should be carefully tended and frequently renewed as they are somewhat troublesome to keep in a proper state of efficiency.

Frequent cultivation close to the trees will also kill out numbers of the pest, especially when in the larvæ or pupa stages. Many of the adult insects will also be injured and dislodged in this way.

In conjunction with bandaging of the trunks and frequent cultivation, spraying with arsenical compounds should be carried out. This latter operation is probably the most effective and economic way of dealing with this class of pest, and I would recommend the use of arsenate of lead for the purpose. This may be obtained in prepared form, there being quite a number of good brands on the market. In every case, however, the spray should be applied at high pressure and through a fine nozzle; care being taken to strike every part of the foliage. It is also advantageous to use strong solutions.

If the grower is making up his own materials they should be prepared in the following quantities :—

> 12 ozs. acetate of lead, 5 ozs. arsenate of soda, 50 gallons of water.
> Prepare in the following way :—Dissolve the 12 ozs. of acetate of lead in 2 quarts of water and the 5 ozs. of arsenate of soda in 3 pints of water in separate vessels, wooden or earthenware, for preference. Then pour the separate solutions into 50 gallons of water.

This formula may be increased in strength up to double quantities, *i.e.*, 24 by 10 by 50 and used without fear of scorching the foliage. In cases where the pest is very bad it is advisable to use a strong solution.

(To be continued.)

One inch of rain over 1 acre equals 101 tons of water. Therefore, the weight of 1 point of rain to the acre is approximately 1 ton.

At Rothamsted a soil growing barley lost 9 inches more water from the top 54 inches than a corresponding bare fallow.

GENERAL NOTES.

EXPORT OF GRAPES FROM SPAIN—

The official bulletin of the Algerian Government, in its issue of 1st February last, gives the following information concerning the exportation of fresh grapes from Almeria (Spain) during 1911 :—2,450,593 barrels in all were shipped, or 422,625 more than in 1910.

The quality of the fruit was superior, but growers appear to have been unable to regulate supply and demand, so that excessive quantities were shipped to certain markets with the usual disastrous results. Prices were as follows :—

In England	.. .. 8s. to 10s. per barrel (40 lbs. nett).
	(Special lots up to 22s. per barrel.)
In America	.. .. $3 to $4 (12s. to 16s.)
In Germany	.. .. 9·50M to 10·50M. (9s. 6d. to 10s. 6d.)

The shipments were as follows :—

					barrels.	b arrels
United Kingdom—						
Liverpool	..	..	..	..	537,716	
London	..	..	..	..	358,158	
Glasgow	..	..	..	..	125,379	
Hull, Newcastle Bristol, Cardiff, and Manchester				..	159,504	
						1,180,757
United States—						
New York	..	..	..	..	808,717	
Philadelphia and Boston	..	..	..	..	11,837	
						820,554
Germany—						
Hamburg	..	..	..	..	364,665	
Bremen	..	..	..	..	23,288	
Other Ports	..	..	..	..	61,329	449,282
Total	..	..	..	..	..	2,450,593

In addition to the above, 17,948 half-barrels were exported to different ports.

Rice husks were experimented with as a substitute for granulated cork by some shippers, but the results were disastrous.

CATTLE BREEDING AND DAIRY RECORDS—

It is absolutely impossible for a cow, which is yielding large quantities of solid matter in her milk up to within five or six weeks of calving, to do full justice to the reproduction of her own species, and thus it is that so many bulls obtained from high-yielding cows are a failure at the stud. The practice on the Government Stud Farm has been to subordinate milk yields to the production of the species in a high order. In other words, once a cow has shown herself to be first-class there is no effort to continue to obtain from her a large quantity of milk and butter per year. *Agricultural Gazette*, New South Wales.

Ripe seeds contain about 12, felled timber 40, grass 75, potatoes 75, and turnips 90 per cent. of water. There is 3 per cent. more water in turnips than in milk.

Animals give out carbonic acid when they breathe, and plants form the greater part of their substance from this gas. It has been estimated that an acre of forest producing 2 tons of dry matter annually will consume the carbonic acid produced by 12 men.

A LAND OF SMALL HOLDINGS—

Japan is a country of which the agricultural system consists chiefly of small holdings. As many as 55 per cent. of those who make a living out of the soil cultivate less than 2 acres each, 30 per cent. less than 3 acres, and 15 per cent. 4 acres or more. Few of the small farmers own horses or other traction animals, and their implements are of a very primitive description, but as large quantities of manure are used, and the soil is cultivated to a good depth and frequently, the yield obtained is very abundant. Usually two or three crops are taken off in the course of twelve months. Rice is the principal crop, and occupies about two-fifths of the arable land of the country, although the mulberry and tea are also largely grown. Most of the farmers have some subsidiary occupation, such as breeding silkworms and weaving silk. They are a hardy, contented people, and do well except in times of severe drought, which in some seasons causes great suffering.—*Mark Lane Express.*

EFFECT OF DROUGHT ON THE QUALITY OF STRAW—

In Europe cereal straw, especially oat straw, forms a considerable and useful part of the winter rations for cattle. Last year owing to a remarkably dry summer the straw in many districts took on a peculiar violet tinge, and farmers were anxious to know whether it could be fed to animals without danger. The matter was investigated by Professor Menard, who has communicated his views to the *Journal d'Agriculture Pratique.* He says that the discoloration of the stalks is due to growth having been suddenly checked by drought, and that the organic matter formed in the foliage, instead of passing as usual into the heads to fill the grain, has remained in some measure in the stalks. From this it appears that not only is the straw safe, but that it is of better quality than the straw of normal seasons. Analyses showed that the albuminoids, which normally formed about 3 per cent. of the straw, were nearly doubled (5.8 per cent.) by the dry weather. This finding arouses speculation as to the possible value of Victorian straws compared to those of wetter countries where threshed straw forms a staple article of fodder. The matter is worthy of investigation, and has possibilities of application in a greater use of mixed rations and the sacrifice of a smaller part of the cereal area for hay purposes than is at present the fashion.

EARLY FALLOWING—

Speaking at the Annual Conference of the Northern Branches of the Agricultural Bureau of South Australia, the Director of Agriculture (Professor Lowrie) gave good advice, which is equally applicable to the drier districts of this State :—" A subject round which there had been considerable controversy was the time of the year at which to begin working the fallow. If year after year farmers would note the returns per acre from the land that they fallowed in June, and compared the results with those from land which they fallowed in late August or September, it would very nearly convince them that it would pay to procure an extra team in order to get the fallowing done in good time. It was also necessary, for the benefit of the next year's crop to get on to the fallow as early as possible, and so gather the moisture and get it down into the land."

BEE MOTHS.

By C. French, Junior, Acting Government Entomologist, and F. R. Beuhne, Bee Expert.

Bee or Wax Moths are undoubtedly one of the worst pests beekeepers have to contend with in Victoria. There are two species, the " Larger Bee Moth " (*Galleria mellonella*) and the " Lesser Bee Moth " (*Achræca grisella*) ; both species are frequently found in the same apiary ; and these pests are present in most parts of the world where bee-keeping is carried on. The larvæ of both moths are great enemies to bees, and may become very destructive. They perforate the comb with burrows, thereby destroying the cells, and often cover it with a network of silken threads. The destruction of the cells, and the impediments caused by the silken network, partly smother the larvæ, and, as the adult bees are greatly hampered by the threads in feeding them, the larvæ are liable to be starved.

The " Larger Bee Moth," which measures about 1 inch in length, is of a dark brown colour, and the under wings are a light grey on the margin, with a lighter colour towards the centre. When young, the caterpillars are yellowish in colour, and when fully grown, are a dull greyish colour.

The " Lesser Bee Moth " is a uniform coloured drab-grey moth, with a yellow head. The larvæ are whitish, with a brown head. They are usually found in Spring, on the floor of hives, amongst the waste wax, which consists chiefly of the caps of the honey cells, emptied by the bees during the Winter. The floor of the hive should, therefore, be scraped clean at the first examination of hives in Spring, and the *débris* removed and burnt. When quilts or mats are used over the frames the larvæ and cocoons of the lesser wax moths are often found between the top bars and the quilt.

In Victoria there are least four broods in a season ; the first, appearing in early Spring from caterpillars that have passed the Winter in a semi-dormant condition, is not so destructive as the others appearing later, because the larvæ, being smaller, eat less than those of the larger sort, and also because they do not spin quite so profusely. Italian or Ligurian bees are not attacked to any extent.

PREVENTION AND REMEDIES.

A good hive, filled with a strong colony of Italian bees, is the best preventative against these pests. Cleanliness is of the greatest importance, and to obtain this use frame hives. All moths, cocoons, and larvæ should be destroyed when found. All hives should be made of timber sufficiently thick to prevent splitting or warping, and the boxes should fit closely to the bottom board. If the timber is cracked it will enable the moths to enter, and deposit their eggs near the honeycomb.

Empty, or partly filled, combs, removed from the hives at the end of the season, should be at once put beyond the reach of the wax moth. If left standing about, even for a few hours, the odour of the combs attracts the female moths, who deposit their eggs on the combs. The eggs hatch in the following Spring to the surprise of the beekeeper, who carefully secured his combs against moths, and probably only left them about for a little time. The cocoons are attacked by a small species of parasitic wasp which helps to keep them in check.

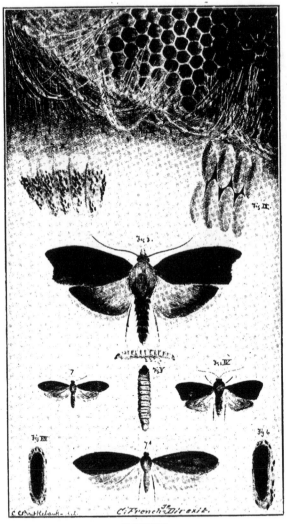

BEE MOTHS.

It is assumed by many bee-keepers that wax moths do some good by destroying the combs of bees in trees or neglected hives which had succumbed to foul brood. Experiments made by Dr. E. F. Phillips, of the United States of America Department of Agriculture have proved, however, that the spores of foul brood still remain capable of producing disease after the combs have been totally destroyed by wax moths, and the only point in favour of these moths from the bee-keeper's point of view is therefore disproved.

EXPLANATION OF PLATE.

BEE MOTHS.

" The Larger Bee Moth." (*Galleria mellonella,* Linn.)
" The Lesser Bee Moth." (*Achræa grisella,* Fab.)

Fig.   I.   Honeycomb showing appearance when attacked. Natural size. From Nature
Fig.   II.   Cocoons of *Galleria mellonella.* Natural size. From Nature
Fig. III.   Perfect Insect. Male. Magnified. From Nature.
Fig.   IV.   Perfect Insect. Female. Natural size. From Nature.
Fig.   V.   Larvæ of *Galleria mellonella.* Natural size. From Nature.
Fig.   VI.   Pupa of *Galleria mellonella.* Enlarged. From Nature.
Fig. VII.   Perfect Insect of *Achræa grisella.* Natural size. From Nature.
Fig. VII.A.   Perfect Insect of *Achræa grisella.* Magnified. From Nature.
Fig. VIII.   Pupa of *Galleria mellonella.* Natural size. From Nature.
Fig.   IX.   Cocoons of *Galleria mellonella.* Natural size. From Nature.

BEE-KEEPING IN VICTORIA.

F. R. Beuhne, Bee Expert.

(*Continued from page* 356.)

PART VI.—WATER FOR BEES.

Few beekeepers are aware what amount of water is required by a colony of bees during the summer months, and how important it is that a permanent supply should be available within a reasonably short distance of an apiary.   As a general rule, bees are left to themselves to get their supply of water wherever they can. There is usually a natural watercourse. dam, or waterhole somewhere in the neighbourhood, and if permanent and within a few hundred yards of the apiary, such sources answer well enough. When, however, water is not permanently available within a quarter of a mile, it is greatly to the advantage of the apiarist to provide an artificial supply as near the apiary as convenient. I do not think that the time occupied by the bees in carrying water over a longer distance need be seriously considered, but the greater liability of being caught by birds and insects, blown down during strong winds, or caught in rain-squalls during the longer journey is a serious matter.   At the margins of dams and water-holes hundreds of bees are often destroyed within a few minutes by cattle or horses stamping them into the mud or swamping them through the plunging of the animals into the water. Where many bees are kept, and the water supply is limited, they become a nuisance to stock, and sometimes a source of ill-feeling between neighbours in consequence.   Bees are also very annoying about the apiarist's own home, round water-taps, tanks, and the drinking dishes of poultry, when the weather is hot, and any other supply of water rather far from the apiary.   The writer was confronted with all the troubles enumerated when first establishing his apiary in its present location; an automatic artificial supply close to the apiary has overcome these difficulties, and has now been working continuously for fourteen years without a hitch.

The water is obtained from the roof of the honey house and stored in two tanks of 1,000 gallons each.   An iron water-pipe, laid underground (18 inches deep) so as to keep it cool in summer, conducts the water to the drinking troughs, which are at a distance of about 100 feet from the building, and the same distance from the nearest hives.   This distance is necessary, otherwise the bees, when flying to and from the water, interfere with work in the apiary, and also cause confusion at swarming time.   There are two drinking troughs; they are placed on a stand at a height of 3 feet from the ground, in order to prevent poultry going to them, and to keep drifting leaves and other material out as much as possible.   Each trough measures 36 inches x 24 inches inside, with a depth of 6 inches, and consists of a frame made of 6 x ⅞ white Baltic flooring boards, with a bottom of 6 x ½ lining boards.   It is lined with plain galvanized iron, No. 26 gauge, neatly fitted inside the wooden casing, to which it is secured at the top with fine tacks.   It is better to have two or even three of such troughs instead of a large one of the same surface area as the two or three combined.   If only one large trough is used the bees are too much concentrated, and a good deal of fighting and stinging takes place occasionally.   It is, therefore, better to have several troughs a little distance apart, and if they are placed on the same level and connected by means of a piece of garden hose attached to a stud at the bottom of each, one stand pipe, with automatic tap, will supply them all.   On the top of each trough floats a raft, upon which the bees alight to drink, and it is so constructed that they cannot drown, and even dead bees cannot drop into the water and thus pollute it.   The raft is made of slats of ½-in. lining boards, 35⅝ inches long, 15-16th inch wide, and ½ inch thick.   The edges on the upper side are planed away at an angle of 45 degrees, so that when the slats are placed side by side they form V-shaped gutters, with an opening 1-16th inch wide at the bottom. Twenty-four of these slats are nailed on to three cross-pieces of ⅞-inch flooring board 23½ inches long and 2 inches wide, in such a way that the thin bottom edges of the slats are 1-15 inch apart.   The raft is then fitted into the trough and dressed till a space of not more than ⅛ inch remains all around between the raft and the lining of the trough.   To keep the raft always at the proper level, that is, with the water not higher than about ⅛ inch between the slats, air-cushions are fastened underneath the raft, one at each end.   They are made of light zinc, such as the lining of piano or drapery cases.   Fold a piece of this material, cut to the correct dimensions, over a piece of wood 35 inches x 5 inches x 1 inch, solder the joints, and, after withdrawing the board, also the end.   It may be tested as to being air-tight by pressing it under water to see whether air-bubbles escape; if so, there is a leak which has to be re-soldered.   In soldering zinc, raw spirits of salt, diluted somewhat with water, should be used, not killed spirits (chloride of zinc); this rule also applies to galvanized iron.   The solder-iron should be clean, well faced with solder, and only just hot enough to melt the solder, but not the zinc; this is only possible if the solder is of good quality.   If the air-cushions raise the raft too high at first the latter should be weighted down to the proper level by means of small stones evenly distributed, and as the wood becomes saturated with water they may be removed as required.   The raft of the trough, which is under the stand-pipe, has an upright iron rod pivoted to it in the centre.   This rod connects by means of a hinge-joint with a lever fastened to the head of the water tap, which is screwed into the stand-pipe, so that the cone of the tap is in a horizontal position, and, therefore, lowering the lever will open the tap, and raising close it.   No dimensions for rod and lever can be given, as these depend upon the height of the tap above the raft, its distance from the centre of it, and the size and passageway of the tap itself.   The measurements and the angle of bend in the tap lever can, however, be easily ascertained.   The tap should be completely shut when the raft is within an inch of the top of the trough, but should begin to run as soon as the raft sinks and draws down the lever, when the water level is reduced by the bees drinking.

*The accompanying illustration will give a general idea of the arrangement.   The troughs shown are of the dimensions stated, and give drinking accommodation for 150 colonies.   When the season is very hot and dry, and the colonies strong, a third trough is added by means of a hose connexion, as stated before.   The roof of the honey house, with a ground measurement of 21 feet by 18, collects with a rainfall of 20 inches sufficient water for the bees and the ordinary requirement of extracting, &c.

There are many well-timbered areas in Northern Victoria where beekeeping could be carried on successfully, but which remain vacant owing to the absence of a water supply for the bees.   Every beekeeper requires a dwelling and a building for the requirements of his business ; if these are constructed in time to get a supply of water for the following season, and if the roof area is sufficient to give the required quantity with the rainfall of the locality selected, there is nothing to prevent some of the waterless, but for beekeeping, otherwise excellent country, being utilized.

To be continued.

REARING OF CALVES.

A. Kyle, Dairy Supervisor.

In building up a good dairy herd, there are other things to be considered besides the dam and sire.   Provided there are cows and bulls with all the breeding and quality necessary for the foundation of a good dairy herd, great attention must be paid to the offspring if the herd of the future is to be improved.   If a heifer when born was ready for milking, perhaps every attention would be shown ; but, as she is not profitable for about three years, she is oftentimes neglected, or even subjected to very bad treatment, it is always well to bear in mind that from poor, half-starved, pot-bellied creatures the dairy herds of the country cannot be raised successfully.

Few dairy farmers have enough land to enable them to rear all the calves dropped on a place, and the males are generally sold for veal, or killed and fed to pigs.   Many heifers born should share the same fate, as they will never make good dairy cows, and only take the milk from those which have all the milking qualities desirable.   Each heifer calf should be examined as soon as possible after its birth, and it is a sign of future inferiority if the teats are small and huddled together.   If, on the other

---

* Illustration will appear in August issue of *Journal.*

hand, the teats are a nice length, good colour and shape, and well separated, it is indicative of milking capacity, and she may be depended on
to come into the bail on calving with a nice-shaped udder and teats.

The newly-born calf is usually straightway introduced to the poddy
pen, and it is here, in most cases, that trouble arises. It should first be
allowed to suck the mother dry. This not only provides the calf with a
laxative to clear the digestive organs, but eases the cow, often preventing
after troubles.

Care and patience should be exercised in giving the calf its first drink
from the bucket ; if taken quietly, it can nearly always be induced to drink
without even giving it the finger. After allowing it to suck the mother
dry, leave it in the pen for twenty-four hours, then, with a little patience,
the calf can readily be made to drink, especially if the mouth is
wetted with milk, or a little milk dropped from the fingers into the
mouth. New milk should be fed to the calf for the first two weeks in
small quantities at frequent intervals ; for the next two weeks, half new and
half skim ; then skim, with the addition of some recognised food. The

HERKES CALF-FEEDER.

best calves the writer ever saw were fed according to this plan, and afterwards on skim-milk and boiled linseed. The linseed was boiled in a kerosene tin, and when cool it thickened to a jelly. A cupful of the jelly was
added to the skim-milk for each-calf. These calves were pictures of
health, and the cost of feeding was very small ; there were no signs of
scouring, and their coats were sleek and glossy.

One of the most important things in the rearing of calves is to keep
them going, and not allow them to get a check, for every time the calf is
thrown back, through scours or other causes, it is a drag on the system,
which is hard to make up ere they are introduced into the milking yard ;
therefore, every attention should be given to the avoidance of scours and
the like set-backs.

A calf, that is bred for the dairy herd, is by-and-by going to have a
big strain on the system, and that system should be well nourished from
the very first, so that all the organs of the body may grow and develop.

In serving the feed out, it should be seen that each calf gets its proper
allowance, for, if all are allowed to rush the feed together, the strongest
calves get the most ; then, again, some calves stand sucking another's

ear instead of drinking, and in the end are left without a drink at all. Each calf, then, should get its proper allowance, which should always be out of clean, sweet vessels. The best method of feeding is to construct a set of small bails, and arrange by means of rubber teat attached to stout piping, a system whereby the calf has to suck up its milk, this insures more certain digestion, and the accompanying illustration shows the "Herkes" calf-feeder in operation. Failing this, a tin should be provided for each calf (kerosene tins, cut in half, make good buckets for this purpose). The attendant can then see that each gets its proper allowance, and there will be no ear-sucking; if ear-sucking is resorted to after they are allowed out of the bails, the ears may be smeared with a solution of aloes.

Good, warm sheds, with clean straw bedding, should be provided at night. Even if straw has to be purchased clean, it will pay, as there is a return for the money in manure, in the value put on the calves, in the prevention of the onset of scour and other filth-induced ailments.

The straw should be thrown into the pens about three times a week, and the whole cleaned out once a week, and stacked for manure.

When a calf, properly reared, comes into the bail, it comes in robust fully grown, and ready to stand the years of milking that are before it; therefore, all the time that is devoted to calves is time well spent, and a herd of long-milking, strong, and healthy cows may be established. A half-nourished calf will grow into a weedy cow, and in turn bear a weedy calf, hence the great necessity of plenty of attention and proper feeding during the growing period.

THE INFLUENCE OF RADIO-ACTIVE MINERAL ON THE GERMINATION AND ON THE GROWTH OF WHEAT.

By Alfred J. Ewart, Ph.D., D.Sc., &c. (Professor of Botany and Plant Physiology in the Melbourne University).

A long series of experiments carried out by Victor Nightingall, Government Research Scholar in the Botanical Laboratory of the Melbourne University, have shown that, under suitable conditions, a distinct accelerating action is exercised upon the germination of wheat and other cereals when exposed to the rays emanating from a strongly radio-active mineral.* The details of these experiments are not yet ready for publication, but the accelerating action was, in some cases, so pronounced that it was considered worth while to proceed without delay to field trials. The results of plot experiments on a small scale are published in the *Journal* for 1911, page 155. Though somewhat indecisive, they indicated that there was a possibility that field trials might give a beneficial result. It must, however, be remembered that the results obtained in the laboratory were, for the most part, obtained by the use of quantities of radio-active mineral, which it would be impossible to apply on the same relative scale in a field trial. In addition, it does not always follow that a substance which accelerates germination will necessarily benefit the plant during its whole development, or even give it any permanent advantage. Furthermore, if the presence

---

* The mineral in question came from the Olary Hill mine, South Australia, and it contained 0·218 per cent. of phosphoric acid (P_2O_5), 0·740 of potash (K_2O), 0·400 of calcium (CaO), and 2·14 per cent. of magnesia (MgO).

of radio-active mineral in the soil injuriously affected the development of useful soil bacteria, it might, on the whole, injure the final harvest, although it favoured the early stages of germination.

In order that these questions might be answered by a trial in the field, the Council of Agricultural Education consented to the establishment of test plots at Longerenong, and the Director of Agriculture to a series of similar plots being used for the tests at Rutherglen. I have to thank Mr. Sinclair, the late Principal of the Longerenong Agricultural College, and Mr. Adcock, Principal of the Viticultural College, Rutherglen, for the interest they have taken in these experimental plots.

THE INFLUENCE OF RADIO-ACTIVE MINERAL ON THE DEVELOPMENT OF BACTERIA.

The first point to be determined was the amount of radio-active mineral required to influence the development of soil and other bacteria, or if any action at all was exercised. To determine this, a series of flasks each containing 100 c.c. of nutrient boullion were each infected with 1 c.c. of a watery extract from garden soil, and kept at a temperature of approximately 15 degrees centigrade. At the end of fourteen days $\frac{1}{10}$ of a c.c. was withdrawn from each, and added to 50 c.c. of sterilized water. The same quantity of this mixture was then transferred to a gelatine plate culture, and from the number of organisms developed upon the plate, the number per c.c. of the culture fluid was estimated. The results were as follow :—

—	Quantity of Radio-Active Mineral.	In Five Days.	In Fourteen Days.	Number of Organisms per c.c. of Culture Fluid.
A.	50 grams ..	Bacteria abundant ..	Liquid very nearly clear ..	115,000
B.	10 grams ..	,, ,, ..	Liquid nearly clear ..	375,000
C.	1 gram ..	Bacteria very abundant	Fairly clear	1,610,000
D.	0·1 gram ..	,, ,,	About equally turbid	11,200,000
E.	0·05 grams ..	,, ,,		17,250,000
F.	0·005 grams ..	,, ,,		18,500,000
G.	10 grams for one day and then the liquid poured off	,, ,,		12,600,000

These results show that bacteria are able to develop even in the presence of large quantities of radio-active mineral, but that, nevertheless, a distinct retarding action is exercised which becomes more pronounced with longer exposures.

Liquefying organisms were relatively more abundant in A, B, and C, in the order given than in the other cultures. Possibly organisms of the bacillus subtilis type may be more resistant to the rays of radio-active mineral than are other bacteria.

That the retarding influence was really due to the rays of the mineral and not to any poisonous substance dissolved from it is shown by experiment G.

The flasks were then sealed, and opened after two months. The liquid contents were distilled, and the distillate tested for formaldehyde. Faint traces were detected in A and B, there were doubtful traces of formaldehyde in the distillate from C and G, and none at all in those from D, E, and F. Apparently, however, in the presence of bacteria, carbon dioxide and water, the rays from a radio-active mineral present in sufficient quantity are able to cause a formation of small amounts of formaldehyde. The cultures were in darkness during the whole of the time, so that the action could not be due to the influence of ordinary light energy.

Whether the retarding action is a direct one, or is due to the formation of traces of formaldehyde is not quite certain, but the amount produced of the latter seems to be altogether too small to wholly explain the retarding action. In any case, however, a strong retarding action is exercised, but only if a relatively large amount of the mineral is used, and it remained to be determined whether any pronounced action was exercised in the field with dressings of radio-active mineral applied in the quantities customary for other mineral manures. Accordingly, samples of the soil were collected from the field plots, three months after sowing, and the numbers of the bacteria present determined. From each of the quarter-acre plots forty samples of soil were taken, and thoroughly mixed together. Five grams of the mixture were then shaken up with 40 c.c. of sterilized water, allowed to settle for five minutes, and then $\frac{1}{25}$ of a c.c. of the water inoculated on to gelatine plates. The number of organisms developing on the plates at 20 degrees centigrade was counted, and hence the number of the organisms present in a c.c. of the soil was calculated. These tests were carried out by Dr. Bull in the Bacteriological Laboratory at the Melbourne University. The following are the results :—

Plots.	Number of Organisms, one c.c. of Soil.	Remarks.
LONGERENONG PLOTS.		
Small plot, 9 square yards—		
A. ½ lb. radio-active mineral per square foot*	17,250,000	Many liquefying organisms
One-third acre plots—		
B. No manure	750,000	Fewer liquefying than non-liquefying organisms
C. 1 cwt. radio-active mineral per acre†	900,000	Numerous liquefying organisms
D. 56 lbs. superphosphate per acre†	1,800,000	Bacillus coli-communis present, very numerous liquefying organisms
RUTHERGLEN PLOTS.		
Small plot, 9 square yards—		
A. ¼ lb. of radio-active mineral per square yard*	450,000	Liquefying and non-liquefying organisms and ten moulds
Quarter-acre plots—		
B. 59 lbs. superphosphate and 56 lbs. radio-active mineral per acre†	1,125,000	Less liquefying organisms than on D.
C. 1 cwt. radio-active mineral per acre†	1,800,000	More liquefying organisms than on D.
D. 59 lbs. superphosphate per acre†	1,800,000	

* Applied as top dressing.　　† Drilled in with the seed.

In the case of the two plots A, owing to the smallness of them, only a few samples could be taken. A subsequent microscopic examination from the Longerenong plot A showed the presence of an unusual amount of decaying vegetable matter, which is probably the explanation of the unusually high number of organisms. The Longerenong samples were also tested on agar at body temperature. The sample A then appeared to contain fewer organisms than B, C, and D, and they consisted mainly of Bacillus subtilis, which is commonly associated with rotting hay or straw. Assuming this to be the correct explanation, the other figures would show that an enormously heavy dressing such as $\frac{1}{2}$ lb. per foot does reduce the number of soil organisms, but to nothing like the extent that might be expected, while ordinary dressings do not appear to produce any distinct action that can be separated from the normal range of fluctuation.

The Rutherglen samples contained more mould spores than those from Longerenong, possibly owing to their proximity to an orchard and vineyard with deciduous trees.

Field Test with Radio-Active Mineral as a Manure.
Longerenong Plots.

Four drill width strips were used for this experiment, each with a total area of approximately $\frac{1}{3}$ of an acre. The wheat used was "Yandilla King," and the manure and wheat were drilled in together. Plot 1 received $\frac{1}{2}$ cwt. of superphosphate per acre; plot 2 received $\frac{1}{2}$ cwt. of superphosphate and $\frac{1}{2}$ cwt. of finally divided radio-active mineral per acre; plot 3 received $\frac{1}{2}$ cwt. of radio-active mineral per acre, and plot 4 was unmanured.

No distinct sign was shown of any acceleration of germination by the radio-active mineral at any of the early stages of growth. A month after planting the plots 1 and 2 appeared to be about equal. They were much ahead of plots 3 and 4, were a darker green, and had generally a more healthy appearance. Two months after planting, the same differences were noticeable. Plots 1 and 2 were about equal, and far ahead of plots 3 and 4, which were about equally backward, and a lighter green than plots 1 and 2. Apparently, therefore, in quantities capable of practical application, the radio-active mineral does not appreciably affect the early stages of germination of wheat. Unfortunately, the season was a bad one for wild oats, and these developed to such an extent on the plots as to spoil them for harvesting. As far as could be judged, however, the plots 1 and 2 remained ahead right up to harvesting, and these two plots with equal amounts of superphosphate, and one with and one without radio-active mineral were about equal.

Rutherglen Plots.

A similar series of four plots was used in this case, each 4 yards 2 feet broad (two drill-widths), and approximately $\frac{1}{4}$ of an acre in area. Plot 1 received 59 lbs. of superphosphate per acre; plot 2 received 59 lbs. of superphosphate, and 59 lbs. of radio-active mineral per acre; plot 3 received 1 cwt. of radio-active mineral per acre; plot 4 was unmanured. In addition, one small square plot received $\frac{1}{2}$ lb. of radio-active mineral per square foot as a top dressing. On the large plots the mineral and manure were drilled in with the seed, using the single drill which deposits manure and seed together. In this case, "Federation Wheat" was used, and was planted on 5th May, 1911. Six weeks afterwards, plots 1 and 2 were much ahead of plots 3 and 4, were greener, stooled better, and were slightly taller. The small plot was best of all, but weeds were thriving better on it than on the other plots.   Just before harvesting, it could be seen that on the small, very heavily dressed plot, the wheat averaged 4 to 6 inches more in height than on the large plots, the straw was paler and stouter than is usual for " Federation Wheat," but on all the large plots the straw was normal in colour except in the case of a few odd plants.   The harvesting results from the large plots are given beneath :—

Plot.	Manure.	Wheat.	Straw.
1	59 lbs. superphosphate per acre	257 lbs.	495 lbs.
2	59 lbs. superphosphate and 59 lbs. radio-active mineral per acre	234 ,,	330 ,,
3	1 cwt. radio-active mineral per acre	76 ,.	165 ,,
4	Unmanured	121 ,,	330 ,,

There is no evidence here to indicate any beneficial action of the radio-active mineral upon the growth and germination of wheat, when quantities wh'ch could be used in agricultural practice are employed.   Any stimulating action which it might exercise when first applied, seems, if anything, to be converted into an injurious action when in prolonged contact.   There is nothing, therefore, in these results to show that radio-active mineral is of the least benefit to wheat when applied in the same manner as manure, and the hopes that had been raised by the stimulating action of large quantities upon the early stages of germination, that this substance might be of use in the field, have failed to be established by experiment as regards wheat, at least.   Whether results of value may be obtained with other plants is, of course, another question, but the radio-active mineral does not appear to have any direct value for the growth of wheat.

"METALLICA CAPE."

The following is an extract from the Preliminary Report of the Committee appointed by the Department of Agriculture of the South African Union to inquire into the suitability of the American stocks thus far used to reconstitute the vineyards in the Cape Province.   This report appeared in the South African *Agricultural Journal* of 12th April last.

Though " Metallica Cape " has not been very extensively used in Victoria, many growers are well satisfied with it—perhaps after too short a trial.

Such an authoritative expression of opinion from South Africa—the only viticultural country where this stock is well known—should serve as a warning to our growers.

" Metallica rupestris, also called Constantia metallica, is a stock that cannot stand much moisture in the soil, and that suffers easily from drought.   It, therefore, does well in fairly deep, loose, cool soils that have never too much and never too little moisture.   As such soils are rather rare to find, the result is that many thousands of vines grafted on this stock are suffering visibly and gradually dying.   Thus in the reddish Karroo soils in the Robertson and Worcester districts, in clay soils near Darling, Tulbagh, and at Bosjesmansvlei, near Botha's Halt in the Breede River Valley, grafted vines on Metallica are worthless.   In many instances the roots are infested with phylloxera, and the vines are dying off in patches.   In a fairly deep, coarse, sandy soil in Dal Josaphat (Paarl district) these vines have done so badly that they will be taken out this year.

In most of the Goudini and similar soils, Metallica can be safely used ; but in most soils it is a bad stock, and hence grafting on Metallica ought not to be continued in future."

SUPPLEMENTARY LIST OF FERTILIZERS REGISTERED AT THE OFFICE OF THE SECRETARY FOR AGRICULTURE UNDER THE ARTIFICIAL MANURES ACTS.

Description of Manure.	Brand.	Nitrogen.	Phosphoric Acid.				Price asked for the Manure per Ton.	Where Obtainable.
			Water Soluble.	Citrate Soluble.	In-soluble.	Total.		
Mly Phosphoric, but containing Nitrogen, also Phosphoric Acid difficultly Soluble.		% 4·50	% ..	% 10·00	% 5·00	% 15·00	£ s. d. 6 15 0	
Blood and Bone	Wischer's Blood and Bone							Wischer and Co., Melbourne
Phosphoric Acid difficultly Soluble.								
Bone Fertilizer ..	Elsworth's Bone Fertilizer	3·00	..	6·00	12·00	18·00	5 15 0	John R. Elsworth, Ballarat East
Bone Fertilizer ..	Compass .. Hoskin's Bone Fertilizer	5·46	..	7·00	3·40	10·40	5 5 0	Harbor Trust Commissioners, Geelong
		3·36	..	6·66	12·84	19·50	5 10 0	E. T. Hoskin, Eagle Point, Balmsdale
Animal Fertilizer	Wifco	7·50	..	5·50	4·00	9·50	5 15 0	Wimmera Inland Freezing Co. Ltd., Murtoa

Description of Manure.	Brand.	Nitrogen.	Phosphoric Acid.	Mechanical Condition.		Price asked for the Manure per ton.	Where Obtainable.
				Fine.	Coarse.		
Containing Phosphoric Acid and Nitrogen, Phosphoric Acid moderately Soluble.		%	%	%	%	£ s. d.	
Bonedust	A.D.B. ..	3·60	19·65	24·50	76·00	5 10 0	A. Day, Bendigo
,, ...	H.B. ..	3·14	20·46	65·50	34·50	5 15 0	Heinz Bros., Ballarat
,, ...	Brown Hill	2·90	18·00	27·00	73·00	6 0 0	Turner Bros., Ballarat East

Office of the Secretary for Agriculture,
Melbourne, 7th May, 1912.

S. S. CAMERON,
Acting Secretary for Agriculture.

LIST SHOWING RESULTS OF ANALYSES OF SAMPLES OF ARTIFICIAL MANURES COLLECTED IN VICTORIA UNDER THE PROVISIONS OF THE ARTIFICIAL MANURES ACTS.

Label No.	Description of Manure	Manufacturer or Importer	Moisture Found	Nitrogen		Phosphoric Acid								Potash		Price asked for the Manure per Ton.
						Water Soluble		Citrate Soluble		Insoluble		Total				
			Found %	Found %	Guaranteed %	Found %	Guaranteed %	Found %	Guaranteed %	Found %	Guaranteed %	Found %	Guaranteed %	Found %	Guaranteed %	£ s. d.
869	Blood Manure	Melbourne City Council	9·95	9·20	7·50							1·70	1·00			4 3 9
1008	Bone Fertilizer	J. Cockbill	5·58	3·73	3·50			5·43	3·00	12·89	14·75	18·32	18·25			5 15 0
1007	Superphosphate	Cuming, Smith, and Co.	5·65	5·20	5·00	18·57	17·00	0·93	1·00	1·00	13·00	20·80	16·00			6 15 0
1004	Superphosphate	P. Rohs	5·86			16·89	16·85	1·27	1·70	0·25	2·00	18·41	16·00			6 17 6
1002	Dissolved Bones and Super-phosphate	P. Rohs	9·62	0·93	1·00	12·26	10·01	1·92		5·92	0·45	20·10	20·00			4 12 6
872	Dissolved Bones and Super-phosphate	Cuming, Smith, and Co.	6·82					6·80	3·88	9·00	5·48	15·80	19·00			4 2 6
1009	Blood, Bone, and Super-phosphate	Cuming, Smith, and Co.	8·35	2·21	2·62	10·04	8·50	2·36	0·50	4·45	5·50	16·85	19·37			5 7 6
867	Bone and Superphosphate	A. H. Hasell	2·15	0·92	0·80	11·42	12·75	2·00	1·25	4·50	5·50	17·92	19·50			5 0 0
868	Bone and Superphosphate	Mt. Lyell M. and R. Co.	2·50	1·79	1·50	7·88	9·00	1·73	1·00	11·29	5·50	20·90	19·50			5 5 0
873	Bone and Superphosphate	P. Rohs	4·93	1·83	1·50	8·42	8·50	3·06	1·50	9·58	9·00	21·06	19·00			5 5 7
865	Bone and Superphosphate	Aust. Explosives and Chem. Co.	3·87	2·53	1·50	8·26	8·00	5·13	4·00	8·49	5·50	21·88	17·50			5 5 0
1011	Special Grain Manure	Mt. Lyell M. and R. Co.	4·84			17·23	16·50	1·04	1·00	3·06	2·00	21·33	19·50	0·68	0·75	4 15 0
010	Maize Manure	Mt. Lyell M. and R. Co.	8·46	3·20	3·00	14·37	11·00	0·82	1·25	1·30	1·75	16·49	14·00	1·35	1·00	6 0 0

LIST SHOWING RESULTS OF ANALYSES OF SAMPLES OF ARTIFICIAL MANURES, ETC.—*continued.*

Label No.	Description of Manure	Manufacturer or Importer.	Mois-ture Found.	Nitrogen.		Phosphoric Acid.		Mechanical Condition.				Price asked for the Manure per Ton.
								Fine.		Coarse.		
				Found.	Guaran-teed.	Found.	Guaran-teed.	Found.	Guaran-teed.	Found.	Guaran-teed.	
			%	%	%	%	%	%	%	%	%	£ s. d.
1000	Bonedust	A. Day	5·80	4·50	3·60	20·45	19·65	53·00	24·00	47·00	76·00	5 10 0

Agricultural Laboratory,
Melbourne, 16th May, 1912.

P. RANKIN SCOTT,
Chemist for Agriculture.

Albuminoids contain 16 per cent. of nitrogen. The cereal grains each contain about 12 per cent. of albuminoids, while leguminous seeds—beans, peas, lentils, and vetches—have just double this amount. The albuminoids in the latter are also more digestible.

It has been found that barley, maize, and pea meal are more nourishing for pigs when given dry than when cooked. The albuminoids in foods are rendered less digestible by cooking.

PROPAGATION OF FRUIT TREES.

(Continued from page 349.)

By C. F. Cole, Orchard Supervisor.

DISEASES *(continued).*

Black Peach Aphis, *Myzus Cerasi* (Fabr.)
Green Peach Aphis, *Myzus sp.*

The black and green peach aphis are two of the worst insect pests the propagator of the peach and other stone fruits has to contend with. Insects belonging to the family *Aphdidæ* multiply very rapidly by depositing living young ; under certain conditions they propagate by means of eggs. If immediate action is not taken to check their spread when first noticed, they will give trouble, causing serious damage to the seedlings, budded stocks, and growing buds. Like most aphides, these two species (black and green) usually attack the under parts of the twigs and shoots first, finally covering all parts as they multiply. The earliest to make its appearance is the black species, which arrives in the autumn or early winter, during mild weather. The period of attack, if unchecked. extends into the spring, or early summer. These insects disappear after the first few hot days. The writer made careful observations during November, 1908, on the habits of the black aphis. The females of the last spring brood become oviporous, depositing small oval glossy-black eggs behind the buds, in cracks and crevices upon the trees. and upon the roots. The eggs remaining unhatched during the hot summer months were hatched in the autumn or early winter. With the green species, the period of attack is much later than the black. The first appearance is usually in the early spring when the trees are vegetative, and the young tender shoots and foliage are preferred to the matured twigs.

EGGS OF BLACK PEACH APHIS. + 30.

There is very little doubt that the life history of the green species is similar to that of the black species. *i.e.*, the last brood of females deposit eggs. So far the writer has failed to find any trace of the green aphis eggs, and has not met any person who has. Several indications warn of a coming attack. With the black species, if the winged insects are to be seen in late autumn upon the underside of the foliage, and while the trees are shedding their leaves, it is a sure sign of coming trouble. In the winter. when trees are badly attacked, they have the appearance of being covered lightly with soot. Another sure sign is ants and flies upon the trees in quest of a sweet liquor which distils from the aphis. It is owing largely to this liquid, which covers the body of the aphis. that a wash has to be applied with force in order to destroy the pest.

Young and growing shoots curl when attacked by either species (black or green). If the leaves become crinkled and curled near the terminal end the presence of green aphis will be detected upon a close examination. Owing to the leaves curling and protecting the insects. the green species is hard to combat ; such foliage conditions make it hard to apply a wash that will come in direct contact with the insects. which is necessary if the operation is to be successful.

Treatment.—If the young trees are attacked in the autumn, early winter, or previous to being lifted. in the winter, spray them thoroughly with one of the following preparations :—1 lb. of soft soap boiled in 10 gallons of tobacco water, applied warm, if possible; or 1 lb. of Lowe's soaparine boiled in 15 gallons of tobacco water; or kerosene emulsion— using 1 part emulsion to 10 of water. Directions for the preparation of spray fluids are given below.

If the budded stocks are attacked during the autumn, spray as advised for young trees; but if attacked after the foliage is off. reduce back to the inserted bud, gather up the tops, and burn at once. The butts of the reduced stocks carrying the inserted buds should be treated; if necessary; examine well round the inserted buds to see that no aphides are concealed in or about the old incision mark that was made in budding. If the presence of aphis is detected, treat by spraying or hand soaping. When spraying, drive the fluid well into the insects, using high pressure, and follow up the first application with a second the same day, or not later than the day following. If the seedlings, growing buds, or shoots, are attacked in the spring, they may be treated by a method called hand soaping. To do this, dissolve soft soap at the rate of 1 lb. to 4 gallons of water by boiling, and place sufficient of the liquid in a kerosene tin or ordinary bucket. Make a swish by tying several fruit-tree cuttings together. Thrash the liquid up smartly until a good foam is obtained. Apply by taking enough of the foam in both hands, and work it well in amongst the foliage, and along the stems with the fingers to the affected parts. This method is very effective, thorough, and economic. If found practicable, almonds, nectarines, or peaches, should. not be grown twice upon the same soil in succession, seed fruits should follow stone, and *vice versâ.* Those kinds of fruits subject to root attack, if succeeding a similar crop, are more prone to attack than those planted and grown upon virgin soil, especially if the first crop were attacked. The only feasible explanation to this is that the insects exist upon those parts of the roots left behind in the soil when removing the young trees. The following will bear out this statement :—During the month of July, 1911, a prepared bed was planted with selected almond nuts. During early November, and when the seedlings had attained an average height of 6 inches, numbers of them started to die back from the tips, the foliage becoming yellow. in colour and drooping. There being no signs of insect or fungoid disease above ground, and indications pointing to root trouble, several of the seedlings were carefully removed; and, upon examination, the roots were found to be badly attacked by the black peach aphis. The crop previous to the seedling almonds were peaches. Soil that is going to be replanted with stone fruit should be allowed to remain in fallow through the summer, should receive a good dressing of lime, and be kept stirred in the autumn. Use a suitable chemical fertilizer when planting. Before planting peach or other stocks liable to attack from aphis, it is advisable to dip them wholly into a decoction of strong tobacco water, or tobacco and soft soap mixture.

Orange Aphis (Siphonophora? Sp.).—This pest usually makes its appearance in early autumn, but it is not unusual to find trees attacked during the summer months particularly if the weather be cool and unseasonable. Standard or established citrus trees in an orchard should not receive any great hurt from an attack by these aphides, as they are so easily controlled; one application, if thoroughly applied, generally is sufficient to arrest their spread. With growing buds or young and tender autumn growths upon citrus trees in the nursery, this aphis can do severe damage.

Their method of attack is similar to that of the green peach aphis. The insects concentrate at the ends of the young and tender growths which curl, wilt, and die back. This pest is easily recognised. The majority of the

FIG. 71.

insects are of a blackish colour, whilst some are brownish and others are green.

Treatment.—The methods recommended for peach aphis attacking seedlings, growing buds, &c., should be followed.

Woolly Aphis or American Blight—Schizoneura lanigera (Hausman).
—This aphis is one of the greatest pests the apple-grower has to contend
with. If detected in the nursery, no time should be lost in dealing with
it. The presence of woolly aphis is easily detected by the white woolly
matter produced by the insects, such matter forming a protective covering,
beneath which the aphides cluster and carry on their work. When commencing operations, they usually choose the under or sheltered side of the
branches or twigs close to or around the buds, gradually extending along
the whole branch or twig. By forcing a beak or sucker into the bark, they
are enabled to live upon the plant sap. The irritation produced by this
piercing operation causes swellings or excrescences to form, eventually
spoiling the tree. Fig. (71) shows the result of a neglected attack. Under
and upper view of growths.

   Treatment.—In a well-conducted nursery this pest should give little
or no trouble. If its presence should be detected during the vegetative
period of the young trees, first paint the parts attacked with a brush
dipped into kerosene emulsion, and then spray thoroughly, using the emulsion 1 part to 10 of water. Place the nozzle of the sprayer close up to
the disease, driving the emulsion on with force so as to break down the
woolly barrier, and get the emulsion well into the insects ; follow up the
first application by another the same day. If any trees should be badly
attacked, cut them out, and burn and spray those in the immediate vicinity.
If attacked in late autumn, or during the winter, use red oil or crude
petroleum oil emulsion instead—strength, red oil, 1 in 25 ; crude petroleum,
1 in 20. This pest should be practically unknown in a nursery during
the winter, and no trees should leave the nursery affected by it. Any
grower or propagator who fails to treat it during the summer, or when
the trees are vegetating, has very little chance of keeping it in check.
Upon rare occasions, the woolly aphis has been found attacking the pear.

   Bryobia Mite (Red Spider).—Usually, the propagator of fruit trees
gives this insect but litle thought, owing, no doubt, to the fact that it
causes little or no check to growth, and to all appearance does no harm.
Therefore, why worry? But the orchardist has a different tale to tell.
The life history of this spider is simple. Small round red eggs are deposited in thousands around the collars of the branches, buds,
and in cracks and crevices of the trees during the late
spring and summer months. These hatch in early spring, the
hatching beling largely influenced by the weather and the sap flow.
The eggs deposited upon trees that vegetate early hatch sooner than those
upon the later varieties. On emerging from the eggs, small reddish-
coloured mites swarm upon the young and tender foliage, and the expanding blooms. They suck up the natural juices, thus causing the foliage
to become sickly, yellowish in colour, and the edges of the leaves to dry
and curl. Instead of the trees producing strong, bold blooms, the organs
of the blossoms are weakened, and the setting of the fruit is interfered
with. When badly attacked in the spring or early summer, the foliage
has a scorched look. If trees in the nursery rows are attacked, and no
steps be taken to eradicate this pest, it simply means that the onus of fighting it will eventually fall on the grower.

   Treatment.—The best time to attack is when the insects are hatched and
moving about. Use soft soap and tobacco water, or tobacco water by
itself, or kerosene emulsion—the latter 1 in 15 of water. Drive the spray
well into the insects, following up the application at weekly intervals if
necessary. For a winter application use red oil or crude petroleum oil

emulsion ; strength, red oil, 1 in 30, crude petroleum, 1 in 25, applying the final application just before the buds start growth in early spring.

The following directions will enable growers to prepare the insect washes which have been recommended : —

Red Oil and Crude Petroleum Oil Emulsion.—Slice and boil 1 lb. of Lotus soap in 1 gallon of water until dissolved, remove from fire, add 1 gallon of oil, stir, and replace on the fire until it comes to the boil. Remove from fire again. and work up thoroughly with a hand syringe or force pump until thoroughly emulsified, and no signs of loose oil appear on the surface. To test whether the emulsion is properly made, take a small quantity of the emulsion and add to it five times the quantity of cold water ; if properly emulsified the effect will be similar to pouring milk into tea, if otherwise, the oil will separate and float on the surface. Soft or any other hard soap may be used in making an emulsion. Lotus soap is cheap, and contains a lot of soda, which assists emulsifying. A properly made and diluted emulsion may be kept some time before using, but it is always better to apply when freshly diluted. When diluting, take 1 part of the emulsion and add the required quantity of cold water, *e.g.*, 1 pint emulsion to 20 pints of water.

Kerosene Emulsion.—This is made in the same manner as red oil or crude petroleum oil emulsion, except that it is not replaced on the fire after the oil is added. If diluting with cold water, agitate well with a syringe or force pump while gradually adding the first of the water. If the standard or undiluted oil emulsion is allowed to get cold, boil and work it up again before diluting.

Resin Wash (No. 1).—Pulverised resin 2 lbs., washing soda 2 lbs., soft soap 1 lb. Boil 1 or 2 gallons of water and add the soda ; when dissolved add gradually the resin, stirring and boiling until dissolved. Add soft soap when dissolved ; make up to 10 gallons.

Resin Wash (No. 2).—Pulverised resin 16 lbs., caustic soda 8 lbs., fish oil 3 pints (raw linseed oil may be used as a substitute). Boil the caustic soda in 10 gallons of water, then add gradually the resin, stirring and boiling until dissolved. Add the oil, and keep boiling for another ten minutes ; then make up to 100 gallons. Warm water is only to be used. After using resin wash, all vessels used in mixing, including the spray pump and nozzle, should be thoroughly washed out with boiling water, otherwise the resin will clog the nozzle, &c., when dry.

Soft Soap and Tobacco.—Boil 1 lb. of soft soap in 1 gallon of tobacco water ; when dissolved make up to 10 gallons with tobacco water ; soak tobacco in cold water and let it infuse ; use at the strength of strong tea, and strain before adding to soap water.

Arsenate of Lead.—Dissolve 11 ozs. acetate of lead in half a gallon of water. In another vessel dissolve 4 ozs. arsenate of soda in half a gallon of water. Pour the soda solution into the lead solution, stir, and add from 40 to 50 gallons of water. Hot water dissolves these chemicals more rapidly and completely than cold water. Wooden pails should be used. This wash has a distinct advantage over all other arsenical preparations. It is practically harmless to foliage, remains longer in suspension, and is more adhesive. The process of manufacture is simple enough, but as there is often a difficulty in getting chemicals of proper purity, it is possible that the grower may prefer some of the leading brands of arsenate of lead now on the market in paste form.

To be continued.

REPORT ON FIRST EGG-LAYING COMPETITION AT BURNLEY, 1911-12.

By H. V. Hawkins, Poultry Expert.

On Sunday, the 31st March, the first Burnley Egg-laying Competition came to a close, and the result, both as to the high standard of egg-production attained, and the general health of the birds engaged in the test, was in every way satisfactory.

The Egg-laying Competition has proved beyond doubt that Victorian fowls are second to none in Australia for productiveness, and this is also tantamount to saying that in utility they are equal, if not superior, to anything in the poultry world. That this should be so is only a reasonable outcome of the efforts that have been made for years past by poultry-keepers to obtain breeds, and strains of such breeds, whose powers in relation to egg-production were above the common.

The recent competition was not the first instituted in this State. Some few years since two very successful egg-laying trials were held at the Dookie Agricultural College. The work done there was of an interesting and educative nature. The experience gained showed that poultry to pay must be carefully bred for the purpose, and attended to in an intelligent manner and by proper methods. There were 396 birds entered for the competition, all, or nearly all, the leading breeds being represented, as will be seen by the following table:—

Breed.						Pens.
White Legnorns	...	...	...	...	...	46
Brown Leghorns	...	...	...	...	...	1
Black Orpingtons	...	...	...	...	...	7
White Orpingtons	...	...	...	...	...	1
Silver Wyandottes	...	...	...	...	...	4
Golden Wyandottes		...	...	...	...	2
White Wyandottes	...	...	...	...	...	1
Minorcas	...	...	...	...	...	3
Faverolles	...	...	...	...	...	1
						66

WHITE LEGHORNS.

The great number of White Leghorns entered indicates the popularity of the breed. A note of warning should, however, be sounded in respect to them. It has been found that they are far more difficult to handle than many of the heavier types. This is largely due to a considerable amount of in-breeding which has been going on for some time; whilst the system of housing in small sheds the whole year round has, no doubt, a tendency to soften the birds—resulting in loss of stamina, and rendering them liable to catarrhal troubles and diarrhœa. Many pullets were brought into the competition that had never tasted green grass, nor had any of nature's favours, such as insect life, and the many varieties of seeds which usually abound during the breeding season. In nearly every case those birds raised by the shedding system were only moderately successful, and were the cause of much anxiety. Some of them broke down, and most of the deaths that occurred were amongst these. This grand breed runs a great risk of falling in public favour if the system referred to is carried

to further extreme. Many of these birds were delicate feeders. Some
of them refused maize, others oats; some would not look at soft food;
and so on; whilst some had never even been on a perch. The result of
this was that, in some cases, the hens did not settle down to work for
from four to six weeks. Breeders would be wise to develop stronger con-
stitutions in the young birds by giving them absolute liberty to pick up
insects, seeds, &c., in the natural way—thus building up frame work with
plenty of stamina to back them up when they are required for the laying
shed or pen.

ORPINGTONS.

Next to the White Leghorns in numbers come the Orpingtons, and with
these no trouble was experienced. They were docile, blocky, good feeders;
and in no case was it necessary to handle a bird, save putting the leg bands
on their shanks when they arrived. Not a single death or replacement took
place, and they showed a better margin of profit on the market price of
eggs from time to time than any other breed in the competition; the
average gross return per hen among the Black Orpingtons being shown
in the following table:—

Table showing Average Gross Return from Different Breeds.

Black Orpingtons	...	...	...	19s. 7d. per hen.
White Leghorns	...	..	...	18s. 0d. per hen.
Wyandottes and Faverolles	...		...	15s. 1d. per hen.
Minorcas	...	...	...	...	11s. 5d. per hen.

Another point to bear in mind is that, after their season of usefulness
for laying has passed, this breed commands good prices as boilers; and
the cockerels double the returns one may receive when marketing White
Leghorns. Orpingtons lay a large, rich, brown egg, and are, on an
average, the best winter layers. They make good mothers, and are not
so liable to disease.

WYANDOTTES.

Next in importance to the White Leghorns and Orpingtons come the
Wyandottes—at one time not long since the most favoured breed, not
only as an all-round fowl, but one much sought after on account of its
nice plump size and beautiful marking. Three varieties of this breed
were represented, *i.e.*, Silver, White, and Golden—the former holding
pride of place. They gave little trouble; and during the cold weather,
and again in the autumn, they produced good results. They are found a
useful utility fowl—cockerels at seven months weighing up to 7 lbs.—and
sickness amongst them is scarcely known. Wyandottes in pen No. 32
did the breed credit, going through the twelve months' test without an ailment, and with no replacement, producing the bulk of eggs at a time of
the greatest scarcity; and it is interesting to compare in the table herewith the market value of eggs laid by this pen. Some others, which,
though laying more eggs, were of less value by some shillings—as example
in pens Nos. 3, 11, 28, and 50.

MINORCAS.

There were only three pens of Minorcas in the competition—two of
them being positive failures, due probably to the desire to obtain high,
upstanding birds with large bodies, heavy combs, and coarse heads for
the show bench; characteristics which have a tendency to make the breed

GENERAL VIEW OF PENS SHOWING SHELTER FRAMES.

lazy, and, consequently, not so fertile. It is regrettable that the old type Minorca with lighter head gear, which used to produce an egg averaging 2¼ ozs. in weight, has almost ceased to exist.

Size of egg is a matter of heredity, and should be carefully considered when mating up the breeding pens; it is of quite equal importance as numbers. It is not uncommon to get a 1½d. dozen more for a guaranteed 2-oz. egg than for those mixed lots too often seen in the sale rooms. A few years back Denmark was threatened by the English buyer, that unless the eggs improved in size, the British public would look elsewhere for the hen product. The Danes set to work to remedy the complaint; and in a few seasons produced what is known at the present time as 19 lbs. weight for long hundreds (120), and her cash receipts for hen eggs from England is estimated at nearly £3,000,000 per annum. Australian poultry breeders would be wise to carry this fact in mind.

Method of Housing.

To accommodate the competing birds commodious pens were built. The ground on which they were placed was cleared and drained. They

RESERVE PEN SHOWING CONSTRUCTION SHELTER FRAME AND YOUNG TREE
BUDDLEIA FORMOSA.

were built under the supervision of the Public Works Department; the dimension of each pen was 30 feet by 12 feet. The pens are separated by plain sheet iron, 3 feet high, and this is again surmounted by wire netting (4 feet by 2½ mesh inches). No top rail finishes off these partitions, and consequently there is no inducement for the fowls to reach obstacles that afford no foothold. The plain sheet iron which surrounds the runs gives excellent shelter from winds, and induces quietude amongst the birds. In a corner of each pen is a galvanized iron house 8 feet by 4 feet—the frame work being outside. The only wood seen in the inside of the house are two pieces of jarrah 15 inches high and a 4-ft. length which drops into slots in the uprights and forms a perch. These can be easily removed

for cleansing and periodical soaking with kerosene to prevent vermin.
On the floor is 6 inches of sand, which goes to produce both cleanliness
and comfort to the birds. It is also a safeguard against dirty or broken
eggs.   Outside each shed a triangular sand bath was provided which,
during the hot weather, was kept damp. A tin is kept full of fresh
water, and vessels are also placed conveniently for charcoal, shell and
earthenware grit. It is amazing the quantities of these aids to digestion
which the birds consume. Oaten hay is placed in each pen, and feed is
scattered amongst this to induce exercise.   Young trees (Buddleia formosa)
were planted in the centre of each pen ; and as it could not be expected
they would provide any shade during the first year, collapsible frames of
light timber were made and covered by hessian. These frames, standing
like an inverted V (see plate) provided excellent shelter from the blazing
sun during summer, and allowed free circulation of air ; and it is pleasing
to note that no deaths occurred from heat apoplexy during the whole competition.   The general health of the birds has been good throughout, with
the exception of an outbreak of chicken pox during the early period.

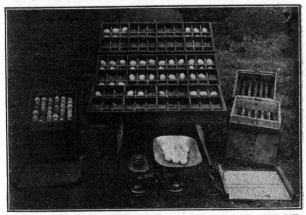

SHOWING TRAYS USED IN COLLECTING AND EGG BOXES FOR DESPATCH.

Twelve deaths occurred throughout the competition, principally on account
of troubles of the reproductive organs ; and a few replacements of birds
took place owing to other causes incapacitating them. Of the three leading pens, Mr. Pope's passed through without sickness or replacement ;
Mr. Cosh had to replace one—a wing of one of the hens having been
broken ; and Mr. Swift had also to replace one, owing to rupture of the
oviduct.

EGG PRODUCTION.

During the year the total number of eggs produced was 73,325, and
these were sold to the Victorian Railways at 1s. per dozen—the average
market price for the term being 1s. 2.38d. per dozen. This value is based
on the figures supplied by the Western District Co-operative Association,
and ranges from 8¾d. on 17th October, to 1s. 11d. on 11th May.

FEEDING.

The principal constituents of all food are proteids, fats, and carbo-hydrates—each of which plays an important part in the ration. They all assist in producing heat to the animal body, though fats have more than ·double the heat power of either the other two. Protein is mainly for the repair of tissue, and is considered the most essential part of a ration. Carbo-hydrates are mainly responsible for the maintenance of body heat. To obtain the best results, these substances must be present in a well-balanced proportion. An excess of any one of them, besides being a waste of food, becomes a danger to the birds consuming. The proportion in which they should exist in a food is found by dividing the proteids present into the sum of the fats multiplied by $2\frac{1}{4}$, plus carbo-hydrates. The result is known as the albumenoid ratio. Just as this ratio is narrow (1 to 3) or wide (1 to 12), so we have a rich or poor food. If too rich, the organs of digestion become weak and the system over-laden; whilst if too poor, the organs are over-taxed in an endeavour to obtain sufficient nourishment for the system. When the hen is required to yield a large number of eggs, the ratio should be narrow; whilst when eggs are not required, she may be fed on a wider ratio. A certain amount of moisture is required, which, if in excess, and the food sloppy, has a tendency to pass through the system too rapidly, and even to induce scouring—this should be avoided at all costs. The system of feeding mash in the evening and grain in the morning—followed by some poultry-keepers in order to save a little time—is one which does not induce the best results. The hot meal in the morning has a more stimulating effect, carrying the bird through the day in good fettle; and the grain fed at night, being somewhat slower of digestion, keeps up the body temperature for a longer period through the night.

ANALYSES OF FOOD USED.
Digestible Constituents in 100 lbs.

	Protein.	Carbohydrates.	Fat.
Pollard	12.2 ...	53.4 ...	3.8
Bran (Wheat)	12.2 ...	39.2 ...	2.7
Branning (Oats)	14.9 ...	51.8 ...	7.9
Rye	9.9 ...	67.6 ..	1.1
Oats	9.2 ...	47.3 ...	4.2
Maize	7.9 ...	66.7 ...	4.3
Wheat	10.2 ...	69.2 ...	1.7
Lucerne chaff	11.0 ...	39.6 ...	1.2
Bullock's liver	20.7 ...	1.5 ...	4.5

The feeding of the birds was conducted along common-sense lines, guided in all cases by scientific principles, and using only those foods which breeders in any part of the State could obtain. There has been no forced feeding of the birds by means of spices or expensive ingredients at any time. The *régime* of feeding throughout the competition has been as follows:—

At 7 a.m. a hot mash was fed, consisting of two parts pollard (20 lbs.), one part of oat-branning (6 lbs.), and one part of lucerne chaff (4 lbs.), which was scalded over night. To this was added 25 lbs. of boiled bullock's liver finely chopped—the whole then being mixed together to a crumbly consistency by adding sufficient of the liquid in which the livers were boiled. Care is necessary, in order to have the mash as friable as possible. The ratio of such a mixture is 1 : 2.36, which is a narrow one.

Each pen received, approximately, 15 ozs. of this mash. Two or three times a week 10 per cent. of raw onion was added, and this was found to be highly beneficial.

PEN NO. 31. R. W. POPE'S WHITE LEGHORNS.
1st in competition, greatest number of eggs, viz., 1,566   Value, £7 6s. 2d.   Net profit per hen, 17s. 10½d.   1st prize, greatest weight of eggs, 193¼ lbs.

At mid-day green feed in the form of lucerne, chick-weed, thistles, and clover mowings, &c., from the lawns in the Burnley Gardens were given;

PEN NO. 12. W. G. SWIFT'S WHITE LEGHORNS.
Winners of Winter Test.   2nd in competition, 1,546 eggs laid.   Value £7 3s. 9½d.
Cost of feed, £1 18s. 10½d.   Profit per hen, 17s. 6d.

whilst in the cold, wet weather a small quantity (approximately 5 ounces to each pen) of mash, made of equal parts of pollard and wheat bran was added.

The evening meal was composed of a grain mixture—4 parts wheat (approximately 19½ lbs.), 3 parts broken maize (approximately 11½ lbs.), and 2 parts of short oats (approximately 6½ lbs). The allowance to each pen was, approximately, 12½ ozs. A ratio is obtained from this food of 1 : 8.6, or an average for the day of 1 : 4.13.

VARIATIONS IN FEEDING.

It is impossible in dealing with a large number of birds to adhere to any strict rule-of-thumb methods throughout a twelve-months' competition. The above ration may, however, be taken as typical of that given during the cold weather. Under warmer conditions variations were made, as, for example, the meat ration was reduced, and only 12 lbs. of meat used in place of the 25 lbs., whilst the quantity of lucerne chaff was increased; also, the mid-day mash was omitted, and a handful of grain scattered in each pen to induce exercise. For the evening meal the maize ration was reduced, and in some cases wheat only would be given. Pens containing heavier breeds received a slightly increased quantity; whilst occasionally it would be found that a pen would become slightly sluggish in appetite, and under such circumstances it was necessary to reduce the ration until their avidity for food returned. Discretion is necessary in such matters to prevent the bringing about of digestive derangements; and a large measure of the success achieved is attributable to care in this matter, for in no cases throughout the competition was "sour crop" or other digestive troubles encountered. A constant supply of shell grit, charcoal, &c., was maintained in separate receptacles, placed within easy reach of the birds.

Amount of Food Purchased.

Bran, 117½ bushels ...	...	...	...	...	£5	5	7
Pollard, 440 bushels	...	...	...	...	25	13	8
Pea meal, 4 cwt. 1 qr. 12 lbs.	...	...	...	1	15	5
Maize, 60 bushels .	.	...	...	...	8	10	9
Wheat, 251¾ bushels	...	...	...	...	44	19	7
Rye, 30½ bushels ...	...	...	...	...	4	5	0
Branning, 220 bushels	...	...	..	...	8	3	0
Oats, 17 bushels ...	...	...	.	...	4	19	9
Onions, 5 cwt.	...	...	...	...	0	15	0
Lucerne chaff, twelve bags ...	...	...	...	3	0	0
Shell grit, charcoal, bone-meal, &c., 16 cwt. 2 qrs.	...	3	14	9
Meat ...	...	...	...	...	32	0	0

$$£143 \quad 2 \quad 6$$

At the close of the competition there was on hand 1 bag maize, 1 bag of lucerne, 1 charcoal, 2 of oats 5 of bran, 2 of pollard, 5 of wheat, and half a bag of bone-meal £9 2 4

The cost of feeding prior to the opening of the competition while the birds were in the pens was ... 5 3 2

The cost of feeding Pen No. 29 (disqualified) for fourteen weeks was 0 11 0

$$£14 \quad 16 \quad 4$$

Therefore, the cost of feeding 66 pens throughout the competition was £128 6 2

If allowance were made for the amount of food eaten by rats, which were, unfortunately, somewhat numerous at times, the cost of feeding would be appreciably less.

PRIZE LIST.

The prizes offered in the competition were :—.

(1) *The Greatest Number of Eggs Laid.*

Prize.		Winners.		Breed.	Number of Eggs.
1st—£10	..	R. W. Pope	..	White Leghorns..	1,566
2nd—£5	..	W. G. Swift	..	,, ,, ..	1,546
3rd—£3	..	A. J. Cosh	..	,, ,, ..	1,539

(2) *Winter Test—Greatest Number of Eggs Laid for Four Months.*

1st—£4	..	W. G. Swift	..	White Leghorns..	479
2nd—£2	..	A. J. Cosh	..	,, ,, ..	470

(3) *Greatest Weight of Eggs Laid.*

1st—£3	..	R. W. Pope	..	White Leghorns..	3,075¾ ozs.

It will be seen from the accompanying table that Mr. Cosh's pen put up the rather remarkable record of over 100 eggs each month throughout

PEN NO. 40. A. J. COSH'S WHITE LEGHORNS.
2nd Prize Winter Test, 470 eggs.   3rd Prize competition; eggs laid, 1,539.
Value £7 5s. 8¾d.   Net profit per hen, 17s. 9d.

the year. It would be interesting to know how often, if ever, this has been done in any Government competition. The record of three separate pens in the competition attaining a score of over 1,500 eggs each is also worthy of note. The table also shows the actual number of eggs laid by each pen, together with those which were rejected for being under weight or soft-shelled. It will be seen that a total of 42 was rejected for being under weight, and 64 for being soft-shelled. Though some of the pens do not show an average weight of 24 ozs. per dozen on the twelve months' work, no pen was disqualified at the end of the first four months, all pens having conformed to the rule relating to this aspect of the competition.

Concerning the weight of eggs, it should be pointed out that the figures are actual weights—not those based on averages at intermittent weighings. The eggs laid each day were weighed and recorded daily. The winner's score of 192¼ lbs. was a fine performance, averaging 34 lbs. of eggs from each hen (a hen may be estimated to weigh 5 lbs.), and thus showing a return of practically seven times their own weight in eggs.

As has already been stated, the eggs were sold at 1s. per dozen. This, however, was not the market price. The table given at a later stage is worked out on the actual market price obtainable for fresh eggs twice in every week during the competition. It will be seen from the table that the market value of the eggs was £319 11s. 7¼d., or an average of £4 16s. 10½d. per pen, and 16s. 1¾d. per bird. The cost of feeding was 6s. 6d. per hen, so that an average profit of 9s. 7¾d. is shown. The highest score—pen No. 31—shows a return of £7 6s. 2d.; consequently, the profit over feeding was £5 7s. 3½d., or 17s. 10½d. per bird; while the lowest pen, No. 48, with a return of £2 7s. 11½d. shows a profit of only 9s. 1d. for the pen, or 1s. 6d. per bird,

Broodiness.—The number of broodies amongst the Leghorns and Minorcas was 27; the heavier breeds occupied the coops frequently. In no case was there much difficulty in breaking them—the system, as shown in the photo, being to enclose them in a small coop, which was left in

SHOWING THE BROODY CAGE.

their own yard. By following this system it is claimed that they return more quickly to the lay, for the excitement of moving them from their companions and excessive handling is avoided, and they are found to return to egg-production within seven or eight days.

Weather Conditions.—Taken as a whole, the weather conditions were favorable. During the early months some unpleasant days and nights were experienced, considerable rain fell, and many days were muggy; later some wind and frost was experienced. During the summer months many changes occurred, frequently extremes following in quick order from high temperatures one day to cold the next. In the early summer, in order to keep the houses as cool as possible, they were painted with a cooling compo, which had the effect of reducing the temperature very considerably.

SUMMARY.

Number of pens, 66.
Number of birds, 396.
Total number of eggs laid, 73,325.
Average market value per dozen, 1s. 2·38d.
Market value, £319 11s. 7¼d.
Cost of feed, £128 6s. 2d.
Profit over feeding, £191 5s. 5¼d
Greatest number of eggs laid, 1,566.
Average number per hen, 261.
Second greatest number of eggs laid, 1,546.
Third greatest number of eggs laid, 1.539.
Highest score by pen, one week, 41.
Highest total score for week, 2,072.
Highest total score for day, 316.
Average number of eggs per pen, 1,110.9.
Average number of eggs laid per hen, 185.1.
Average cost of food per hen, 6s. 6d.
Average profit over cost of feeding, 9s. 7¾d.
Highest profit obtained per hen, 17s. 10½d.
Lowest profit obtained per hen, 1s. 6d.
Weight of eggs laid by winning pen—1 cwt. 2 qrs. 24 lbs. 3¾ ozs.
Weight of eggs laid by second pen—1 cwt. 2 qrs. 22 lbs. 4½ ozs.
Weight of eggs laid by third pen—1 cwt. 2 qrs. 23 lbs. 0¾ oz.

PEN NO. 58. FAVEROLLES.
Laid 1,030 eggs.   Value, £4 10s. 6d.   Profit, 8s. 7½d. per bird.

RECORD OF EGGS LAID.

Pen No.	Competitor.	Breed.	April.	May.	June.	July.	August.	September.	October.	November.	December.	January.	February.	March.	Total.	Not Recorded. Under Weight	Not Recorded. Soft.	Gross Weight each Pen.	Average Weight per Dozen.	Market Value of Eggs Produced.
																		ozs.	ozs.	£ s. d.
1	A. Brebner ..	White Leghorns	54	55	73	91	107	133	134	129	125	104	94	34	1,133	..	1	2,481¾	26·2	5 0 2¾
2	E. P. [redacted]h ..	,, ,, ..	96	65	61	35	61	141	152	150	138	130	110	60	1,199	1	1	2,475	24·7	5 7 5¾
3	K. Gleghorn ..	,, ,, ..	21	25	95	90	130	131	142	134	129	111	109	82	1,199	..	1	2,521¼	25·2	5 4 4½
4	H. Bell	[redacted]en Wyan-[redacted]tes	..	13	95	125	137	135	131	112	102	96	91	63	1,100	1	..	2,174	23·7	4 13 9½
5	L. C. Payne ..	[redacted]ite Leghorns	22	51	71	95	110	128	132	134	127	108	70	19	1,067	..	..	2,198½	24·7	4 11 3
6	[redacted] H. J. Richards	[redacted]er Wyandottes	..	2	78	55	132	135	150	110	97	101	89	96	1,045	..	..	2,089¼	23·9	4 8 7
7	H. Stevenson ..	White [redacted]ns	16	37	22	55	103	123	130	134	123	110	47	18	918	..	..	2,065½	27	3 13 6¼
8	T. W. [redacted].. ..	,, ,, ..	82	73	28	46	114	107	140	128	127	106	71	35	1,057	..	1	2,222¼	25·2	4 12 4
9	J. [redacted]in ..	,, ,, ..	45	73	59	89	126	130	141	130	121	122	103	75	1,212	..	..	2,565	25·4	5 7 2
10	H. A. Langdon ..	Black [redacted]s	28	37	88	110	139	121	136	137	118	121	103	102	1,240	..	..	2,513¾	24·3	5 9 10
11	F. Soneum ..	Brown Leghorns	20	22	39	83	122	136	134	141	139	136	125	98	1,195	2	..	2,458½	24·7	5 1 1¼
12	W. G. [redacted]ft ..	White Leghorns	137	127	102	113	136	162	164	153	152	132	85	87	1,546	6	4	3,044½	23·6	7 3 9½
13	D. Fisher	Black Orpingtons	63	54	109	122	137	124	127	117	121	104	84	60	1,222	1	..	2,526¾	24·8	5 11 3¾
14	W. J. [redacted]ey ..	,, ,, ..	..	..	32	50	120	114	119	96	74	65	63	72	795	..	..	1,700¾	25·6	3 5 2¼
15	H. R. [redacted]ey ..	Black [redacted]as ..	2	..	13	29	81	105	121	105	83	66	31	31	667	..	..	1,633¼	29·3	2 10 5½
16	Miss A. Cottam ..	Silver Wyandottes	29	38	38	42	120	135	113	104	87	79	77	74	936	..	..	1,920¼	24·6	4 0 2
17	W. J. Eckersall ..	White Leghorns	6	7	14	59	109	112	125	104	88	74	61	56	815	..	..	1,839	27	3 4 9¼
18	S. Brundrett ..	,, ,, ..	112	67	95	112	120	131	138	121	114	97	81	78	1,266	..	6	2,700	25	5 17 7¾
19	A. [redacted]es	,, ,, ..	49	75	62	62	123	133	128	120	132	141	120	83	1,228	..	..	2,557¾	25·5	5 11 1
20	H. [redacted]ie ..	,, ,, ..	110	75	83	95	142	151	163	141	148	138	114	69	1,429	..	..	2,954½	24·8	6 8 10¾
21	R. L. Appleford ..	,, ,, ..	80	125	69	43	108	139	154	126	128	113	77	50	1,212	5	4	2,544¼	25·2	5 10 9¾
22	P. S. [redacted]d ..	Black Orpingtons	52	25	61	110	123	117	142	116	118	87	92	95	1,138	..	4	2,415½	25·4	5 0 7¼
23	G. E. Brown ..	Golden Wyan-dottes	34	36	38	57	117	120	109	88	84	87	79	73	922	..	1	1,900½	24·7	4 0 3¾
24	F. Hannaford ..	White Leghorns	27	64	83	84	121	119	123	148	137	135	106	104	1,251	1	4	2,516	24·1	5 11 10½
25	B. [redacted]ll ..	,, ,, ..	2	81	97	121	120	143	138	127	102	107	83	68	1,189	..	..	2,479½	25	5 5 11½
26	F. Seymour ..	,, ,, ..	4	18	60	77	93	117	119	125	115	87	70	31	916	..	..	2,215¾	29·0	3 15 9¾
27	Hill [redacted]d Luckman ..	,, ,, ..	43	48	58	76	116	127	125	107	101	81	42	49	973	..	..	2,071¼	25·5	4 4 6¼
28	J. Campbell ..	,, ,, ..	58	21	32	87	141	141	148	135	136	114	107	91	1,211	1	1	2,651½	26·2	5 3 7
29	.. .. ..	.. ..	11	37	33	19	..	..	..	..	..	..	..	..	..	..	..	..	..	..
30	Rodgers Bros. ..	Black Orpingtons	53	25	60	18	126	144	128	112	96	105	65	81	1,013	..	..	2,270¾	26·9	4 6 7¼
31	R. W. Pope ..	White Leghorns	123	111	103	113	138	145	168	161	143	145	123	93	1,566	2	..	3,075¾	23·6	7 6 2
32	M. A. [redacted]es ..	Silver Wyandottes	30	76	98	114	126	128	124	101	113	88	79	94	1,171	2	..	2,387¾	24·5	5 7 8¾
33	[redacted]e Bros. ..	White Leghorns	104	114	99	86	128	143	152	130	134	114	71	56	1,331	..	..	2,797¼	25·2	6 4 0
34	E. Dettman ..	,, ,, ..	11	37	31	66	106	121	136	122	121	117	97	75	1,040	..	1	2,489¼	28·7	4 8 6¾
35	J. H. Brain ..	,, ,, ..	7	6	5	73	117	135	145	143	121	130	130	90	1,102	1	..	2,354¾	25·6	4 9 10

Journal of Agriculture, Victoria. [10 JULY, 1912.

RECORD OF EGGS LAID—*continued.*

Pen No.	Competitor	Breed	April	May	June	July	August	September	October	November	December	January	February	March	Total	Not Recorded Under Weight	Not Recorded Soft	Gross Weight each Pen.	Average Weight per Dozen.	Market Value of Eggs Produced.
																	ozs.	ozs.	£ s. d.
36	F. Sillitoe	White Leghorns	38	128	64	54	106	131	131	128	117	117	88	25	1,122		2	2,476½	26·4	5 1 3
37	E. Waldon	"	78	109	81	51	136	141	151	143	141	136	114	70	1,401			2,894	24·7	6 8 1¼
38	M. C. R. Smee	"	2	32	89	115	137	138	149	138	130	00	81	51	1,162		·6	2,445½	25·2	4 18 8¼
39	A. W. Hall	"	53	43	80	98	132	133	154	140	150	145	112	55	1,301			2,688½	23·8	5 13 5¼
40	Morgan and Watson	"	123	107	108	132	142	143	125	109	131	132	111	120	1,639			3,056½	24·5	7 5 8¾
41	A. J. Cbh	"	18	49	43	114	112	112	116	89	D8	114	84	76	1,060	2		2,142¾	24·7	4 10 7¼
42	P. B. Crellin	White Orpingtons		35	48	138	111	121	140	123	187	D9	82	56	995	1		2,394	25·7	4 10 6¾
43	W. B. Crellin	White Leghorns	33	91	26	67	130	127	146	138	93	118	68	59	1,074			2,416	26·3	4 5 3
44	T. S. Goodison	Black Orpingtons	68	73	74	13	128	127	146	131	136	95	68	66	1,136		·6	2,740½	25·5	4 5 7
45	T. Kempster	White Leghorns	50	54	51	128	128	140	146	114	95	124	84	55	1,153			2,416	28·5	5 3 2
46	G. W. Chalmers	Minorcas	80	44	90	89	139	151	133	104	135	98	64½	65	1,192	1		2,366	24·8	4 19 10
47	C. W. Spencer	White Leghorns	51		62	50	111	134	136	141	87	112	69	49	1,089		·2	2,254	27·6	5 7 6½
48	G. James	Minorcas		15	40	15	68	91	104	114	135	76	82	39	617			1,420	24·7	2 13 1
49	G. J. Thornton	White Leghorns	55	40	37	62	127	146	157	148	87	129	118	57	1,222	12		2,381½	24·1	5 7 11¼
50	G. H. Best	"	40	48	83	89	124	126	139	104	135	123	85	85	1,146			2,224	24·9	4 16 3
51	J. J. McKeddie	"	54	44	82	118	118	136	128	100	100	93	80	62	1,041			2,224	25·6	4 14 1
52	W. J. McKeddie	"		1	31	103	139	138	128	106	106	93	64	36	991			2,112½	25·5	4 19 0
53	A. Ser	"	4	8	D9	81	132	128	128	135	113	75	71	33	1,010			2,154	25·4	4 3 0
54	P. Hodges	"	51	41	50	81	115	99	87	124	89	114	84	58	914		1	1,844½	24·2	4 1 4
55	W. G. Mer	"	69	68	76	97	146	140	146	115	115	119	80	76	1,193			2,346½	26	5 4 0
56	Mrs. C. Thompson	"		63	8	39	112	119	129	130	D0	D0	85	36	932			3,019½	24·5	3 14 3¼
57	E. Edwards	"	71	12		24	134	134	155	114	124	119	85	36	1,116	2		2,282	24·5	4 10 6¼
58	K. E. Courtenay	Faverolles	50	50	44	78	131	133	145	146	145	118	49	55	1,030		1	2,176½	25·6	4 5 6¾
59	W. H. Dunlop	White Leghorns		45	70	69	131	133	138	126	122	94	97	73	1,028			2,176	26	4 13 10
60	J. J. Harrington	"	17	25	21	88	123	132	105	128	113	D9	90	75	1,095		·3	2,368½	24·9	4 15 9½
61	P. Reade	Silver Wyandottes			17	24	124	119	105	87	D8	103	105	63	919			1,908½	24·9	4 3 15 9¼
62	P. Hodson	White Leghorns	61	52	99	128	124	136	149	149	143	131	55	48	1,154	1		2,380	23·5	4 11 5
63	A. J. Treacey	Black Orpingtons	43	40		24	129	95	101	92	80	86	130	80	996		1	1,951½	24·7	4 11 10½
64	J. D. Read	White Leghorns	1	1	45	59	128	127	144	146	148	130	106	64	1,042		2	2,327	26·8	4 10 10¼
65	H. Hamill	"	50	50	40	102	127	115	109	128	85	85	92	64	1,029			2,172	24	4 5 0
66	J. E. Bradley	White Wyandottes	67	45	40	81	131	133	127	118	93	84	93	102	1,085	1		2,436½	25·4	5 3 4
67	C. L. Sharman	White Leghorns	62	83											1,147					
															78,325					**319 11 7½**

VERNACULAR NAMES OF VICTORIAN PLANTS.

Communicated by Alfred J. Ewart, D.Sc., Ph.D., F.L.S., Chairman, and C. S. Sutton, M.B., Ch.B., Secretary, of the Plant Names Committee of the Victorian Field Naturalists' Club.

In the *Journal of Agriculture* for 1911, a list of the vernacular names for approximately one-third of the Victorian flora was given. The present list comprises the second third of the flora extending from Dilleniaceae to the Myrtaceae. As in the previous list opportunity has been taken at the same time to add data in regard to the economic value or use of all the native plants mentioned. In some cases in particular it is surprising what little importance is attached to many native plants of pronounced decorative value for garden purposes, and in hardly any case have our native plants been used for selective garden cultivation, although there can be no doubt that it would be possible to raise from many of them garden plants equal in interest and beauty to any at present known. Such genera as Pultenaea and Acacia afford an almost unlimited opportunity for the activities of the plant breeder in search of garden novelties, and our native Violets, Boronias, Phebaliums, Eriostemons, and others, particularly among the Papilionaceae, are not only worthy of garden cultivation in their present form, but should improve under cultivation from a gardener's point of view.

Even in the case of plants for which a definite economic value has been recognised, it cannot be said that in all cases full recognition of their economic value has been made. For instance, although the value of salt-bushes as fodder plants for dry districts is recognised in theory, it is certainly not always recognised in practice, since in many districts the more useful saltbushes have been allowed to be eaten right out by stock, and it is only very rarely indeed that any attempt at replanting has been made. The fact that large quantities of saltbush seed have been exported abroad, particularly to America, is sufficient to show that other countries have recognised the value of these plants for fodder in dry districts, and have found it profitable to plant them and encourage their spread. Even in the case of the Acacias, which are among the best appreciated of our native plants, it is surely an anomaly that Australia should be importing wattle-bark from Australian Acacias, grown in other countries. Apart from the Acacias, the present list does not include many native timber trees, but the Sheokes, Bulokes, and Belar, the Myrtle Beech, and the Yellow Wood, are of more or less importance as supplying firewood or timber for special purposes.

In regard to the vernacular names, the present list, like the previous one, is provisional, and is open to suggestions or criticisms. Many criticisms or suggestions have already been received, discussed, and, in some cases, adopted by the Committee, but for the most part the names put forward have met with general approval, and seem likely to be generally accepted. The working Committee has undergone but little alteration since the last issue. Mr. McLennan, owing to his appointment to the Principalship of the Agricultural School at Warragul, has been unable to take an active part in the work of the Committee. The remaining active members of the Committee by whom the final decisions have been made are :—

Chairman : A. J. Ewart, D.Sc., Ph.D., F.L.S.
Honorary Secretary : C. S. Sutton, M.B'., Ch.B.
Committee : Messrs. F. G. A. Barnard, J. A. Leach, M.Sc., F. Pitcher, P. R. H. St. John, and J. R. Tovey.

In addition to those mentioned in the previous list, the following have forwarded valuable suggestions or criticisms :—Messrs. R. Kelly, G. Weindorfer, A. G. Campbell, J. P. Eckert, C. French, senior, and minor suggestions have been received from a large number of correspondents. One point which may be emphasized is that the Committee prefers criticism to indifference, and, in fact, some valuable suggestions have come from correspondents who disapprove entirely of the encouragement of the use of vernacular names for native plants.

DICOTYLEDONEÆ.

Botanical Name.	Popular Name.	Use or Character.
	CHORIPETALEÆ HYPOGYNÆ.	
DILLENIACEÆ.		
Hibbertia—		
densiflora, F.v.M.	Silky Guinea Flower	
stricta, R.Br.	Erect Guinea Flower	
humifusa, F.v.M.	Mountain Guinea Flower	
Billardieri, F.v.M.	Trailing Guinea Flower	
acicularis, F.v.M.	Prickly Guinea Flower	
serpyllifolia, R.Br.	Thyme-leaved Guinea Flower	Amost all very common bush plants, all bearing bright yellow flowers.
pedunculata, R.Br.	Stalked Guinea Flower	
procumbens, D.C.	Spreading Guinea Flower	
fasciculata, R.Br.	Bundled Guinea Flower	
virgata, R.Br.	Twiggy Guinea Flower	
linearis, R.Br.	Showy Guinea Flower	
diffusa, R.Br.	Rigid Guinea Flower	
dentata, R.Br.	Toothed Guinea Flower	
RANUNCULACEÆ.		
Clematis—		
aristata, R.Br.	Greater Clematis	Charming climbers. The first is one of the most beautiful features of the vegetation of our moist gullies and riversides, and the last of the coast and drier districts, like the Mallee.
glycinoides, D.C.	Erect Clematis	
microphylla, D.C.	Smaller Clematis	
Myosurus—		
minimus, L.	Mousetail	No known economic value.
Ranunculus—		
parviflorus, L.	Small-flowered Buttercup	
hirtus, Banks & Sol.	Hairy Buttercup	
rivularis, Banks & Sol.	River Buttercup	All are acrid and unpalatable to stock and *R. rivularis* has been suspected of being poisonous. When dried in hay, the acrid properties are largely lost.
Muelleri, Bentham	Felted Buttercup	
lappaceus, Smith	Common Buttercup	
Gunnianus, Hook.	Tufted Buttercup	
anemoneus, F.v.M.	Snowy Buttercup	
Millani, F.v.M.	Dwarf Alpine Buttercup	
aquatilis, L.	Water Buttercup	
Caltha—		
introloba, F.v.M.	Alpine Marsh Marigold	Of no known economic value.
CERATOPHYLLACEÆ.		
Ceratophyllum—		
demersum, L.	Common Hornwort	A troublesome water weed in ponds and small slowly flowing streams.

VERNACULAR NAMES OF VICTORIAN PLANTS—*continued.*

Botanical Name.		Popular Name.		Use or Character.

DICOTYLEDONEÆ –CHORIPETALEÆ HYPOGYNÆ—*continued.*

Botanical Name.		Popular Name.		Use or Character.
NYMPHACACEÆ.				
Brasenia— Schreberi. Gmelin	..	Water Shield	..	The leaves are astringent, have been employed in medicine.
MAGNOLIACEÆ.				
Drimys— aromatica, F.v.M.		Mountain Pepper	..	The fruit is sometimes used as a substitute for pepper or allspice. The leaves and bark also have a hot biting cinnamon-like taste.
ANONACEÆ				
Eupomatia— laurina, R.Br. ..		Bolwarra	..	A small tree. The wood is soft, close coarse grained.
MONIMIACEÆ.				
Atherosperma— moschatum, Labill.	..	Southern Sassafras	..	The wood is close grained, useful for cabinet making, &c.
Hedycarya— Cunninghami, Tulasne		Austral Mulberry	..	The wood is close grained and tough, suitable for cabinet making.
LAURACEÆ.				
Cassytha— glabella, R.Br. ..	..	Tangled Dodder-laurel		These unsightly parasitic plants often have a detrimental effect on the growth of the trees and shrubs which they infest.
pubescens, R.Br.	..	Downy Dodder-laurel	..	
phaeolasia, F.v.M.	..	Long-spiked Dodder-laurel		
paniculata, R.Br.	..	Ribbed Dodder-laurel	..	
melantha, R.Br.	..	Large Dodder-laurel	..	
MENISPERMACEÆ.				
Sarcopetalum— Harveyanum, F.v.M.	..	Bigleaved Vine ..	..	Hardy evergreen climbers, sometimes grown in gardens.
Stephania— hernandifolia. Walpers	..	Stephania	..	
PAPAVERACEÆ.				
Papaver— aculeatum, Thunb.	..	Austral Poppy ..	..	A weed, perhaps feebly poisonous.
CAPPARIDACEÆ.				
Capparis— Mitchellii, Lindley	..	Desert Caper ..	..	Fruit 1 to 2 inches in diameter. The pulp is eaten by the natives.
CRUCIFERÆ.				
Nasturtium— terrestre, R.Br.	..	Yellow Water-cress		When luxuriant, may be used as a pot-herb
Barbarea— vulgaris. R.Br.	..	Bitter Water-cress	..	Of no known economic value.
Arabis— glabra. Crantz. ..	..	Smooth Rock-cress	..	
Cardamine— stylosa, D.C. ..	..	Long-styled Bitter-cress ..		Of slight fodder value, but generally considered to be weeds.
dictyosperma, Hooker	..	Forest Bitter-cress	..	
laciniata. F.v.M.	..	Jagged Bitter-cress	..	
hirsuta, L. ..	..	Hairy Bitter-cress	..	
eustylis, F.v.M.	..	Dwarf Bitter-cress	..	

Vernacular Names of Victorian Plants—*continued*.

Botanical Name.	Popular Name.	Use or Character.

Dicotyledoneæ —Choripetaleæ Hypogynæ—*continued*.

Cruciferæ—*continued*.

Botanical Name.	Popular Name.	Use or Character.
Malcolmia—		
africana, R.Br. ..	Malcolmia ..	Allied to the Virginian stock.
Blennodia—		
trisecta, Benth.	Woody Blennodia ..	Has a certain fodder value for sheep, but gives an unpleasant flavour to the milk and butter of cows. *B. lasio-carpa* is perhaps the most readily eaten.
nasturtioides. Benth.	Yellow Blennodia ..	
Lucae, F.v.M. ..	Robust Blennodia ..	
cardaminoides, F.v.M.	Sand Blennodia ..	
eurvipes, F.v.M.	Curved Blennodia ..	
brevipes, F.v.M.	Short Blennodia ..	
lasiocarpa, F.v.M.	Hairy Blennodia ..	
alpestris, F.v.M.	Mountain Blennodia	
Alyssum—		
minimum, Pallas	Desert Alyssum ..	
Stenopetalum—		
velutinum, F.v.M.	Velvety Thread-petal ..	
lineare, R.Br. ..	Narrow Thread-petal ..	
sphaerocarpum, F.v.M	Pea Thread-petal ..	
Geococcus—		
Pusillous, D. & H.	Earth Cress	All have a slight pasture value, but are generally classed as useless weeds.
Menkea—		
australis, Lehmann	Fairy Spectacles ..	
Capsella—		
elliptica, C.A. Meyer	Oval Shepherd's Purse ..	
antipoda, F.v.M.	Southern Shepherd's Purse ..	
pilosula, F.v.M.	Hairy Shepherd's Purse ..	
Lepidium—		
leptopetalum, F.v.M.	Slender Pepper-cress ..	
phlebopetalum, F.v.M.	Veined Pepper-cress ..	
monoplocoides, F.v.M.	Winged Pepper-cress ..	
papillosum, F.v.M.	Warty Pepper-cress ..	Of very slight pasture value, but usually classed as weeds.
foliosum, Desvaux	Leafy Pepper-cress ..	
ruderale, L. ..	Rubble Pepper-cress ..	
Cakile—		
maritima, Scopoli	Sea-rocket	

Violaceæ.

Botanical Name.	Popular Name.	Use or Character.
Viola—		
betonicifolia, Smith	Purple Violet	All are pretty plants, and might be improved by cultivation in gardens.
hederacea, Labill.	Common Violet ..	
Caleyana, G. Don.	Forest Violet	
Hybanthus—		
floribundus, F.v.M.	Shrub Violet	
Vernonii, F.v.M.	Erect Violet	
filiformis, F.v.M.	Slender Violet	
Hymenanthera—		
Banksii, F.v.M.	Tree Violet	A shrub adapted for formation of close hedges. Stands clipping well. Flowers very fragrant.

Pittosporaceæ.

Botanical Name.	Popular Name.	Use or Character.
Pittosporum—		
*undulatum, Andrews	Sweet Pittosporum ..	Wood close grained. Easily wrought and well adapted for turners' purposes. Flowers give a fragrant volatile oil on distillation. A useful hedge plant.
revolutum, Aiton	Curled Pittosporum ..	No special economic value, but might be used for hedges.
phillyraeoides, D.C.	Weeping Pittosporum ..	A valuable stand-by for stock in drought time. Timber very hard, makes excellent tool handles, and can be recommended for wood engraving.
bicolor, Hook ..	Banyalla	Useful for hedges.
Bursaria—		
spinosa, Cavanilles	Sweet Bursaria ..	Varies from a shrub to a small tree. Would form a fragrant hedge. Foliage eaten by sheep. Often covered with a sooty fungus (*Capnodium*).

* Plants marked thus are listed either as growing plants or as seeds by one or more of our florists.

VERNACULAR NAMES OF VICTORIAN PLANTS—*continued.*

Botanical Name.	Popular Name.	Use or Character.

DICOTYLEDONEÆ—CHORIPETALEÆ HYPOGYNÆ—*continued.*

PITTOSPORACEÆ—*continued.*

Marianthus—

procumbens, Benth.	White Marianth	Might repay garden cultivation.
bignoniaceus, F.v.M.	Orange Bell-climber	One of our most beautiful climbers.

Billardiera—

longiflora, Labill.	Purple Apple-berry	
scandens, Smith	Solid Apple-berry	}All are worthy of cultivation in gardens.
cymosa, F.v.M.	Sweet Apple-berry	

Cheiranthera—

linearis, Cunningham	Finger Flower	

DROSERACEÆ.

Drosera—

indica, L.	Desert Sundew	
Arcturi, Hook	Alpine Sundew	
glanduligera, Lehmann	Scarlet Sundew	
pygmaea, D.C.	Tiny Sundew	The leaves of all the species capture
spathulata, Labill	Spoonleaved Sundew	and digest insects. Sometimes
binata, Labill.	Forked Sundew	stated to be dangerous to stock,
Whittakerii, Planchon	Scented Sundew	but on unsatisfactory evidence.
auriculata, Backhouse	Tall Sundew	
peltata, Smith	Erect Sundew	
Menziesii, R.Br.	Climbing Sundew	

ELATINACEÆ.

Elatine—

americana, Arnott	Water-pepper	

Bergia—

ammannioides, Roxb.	Water-fire Tree	}Of no known economic value.

GUTTIFERÆ.

Hypericum—

japonicum, Thunb.	Small St. John's Wort	A useless weed.

POLYGALACEÆ.

Polygala—

sibirica, L.	Dwarf Milkwort	Of no known economic value.

Comesperma—

scoparium, Steetz	Broom Milkwort	Possibly worthy of garden cultivation.
volubile, Labill.	Love Creeper	A hardy evergreen twiner.
retusum, Labill.	Mountain Milkwort	
ericinum, D.C.	Heath Milkwort	
calymega, Labill.	Blue Spiked Milkwort	}Some are possibly worth growing in
defoliatum, F.v.M.	Leafless Milkwort	gardens.
polygaloides, F.v.M.	Small Milkwort	

TREMANDRACEÆ.

Tetratheca—

ciliata, Lindley	Variable Pinkeyes	}Among the best known and most
ericifolia, Smith	Heath Pinkeyes	admired plants of our bush.
pilosa, Lab.	Hairy Pinkeyes	

RUTACEÆ.

Zieria—

laevigata, Smith	Angular Zieria	}Might be worth adding to the list of
aspalathoides, Cunningh.	Hairy Zieria	our garden plants.
cytisoides, Smith	Downy Zieria	
Smithii, Andrews	Sandfly Zieria	The yellow inner bark of this species is suitable for dyeing.
veronicea, F.v.M.	Pink Zieria	Well worth adding to the list of our garden plants.

VERNACULAR NAMES OF VICTORIAN PLANTS—*continued.*

Botanical Name.	Popular Name.	Use or Character.

DICOTYLEDONEÆ—CHORIPETALEÆ HYPOGYNÆ—*continued.*

RUTACEÆ—*continued.*

Boronia—

algida, F.v M. ..	Alpine Boronia ..	
*pinnata, Smith ..	Pinnate Boronia	The boronias are well known for their beauty or fragrance, and although the best come from West Australia, some of our species such as *B. pinnata*, *B. pilosa*, and *B. clavellifolia*, are very well worth cultivation.
pilosa, Labill. ..	Hairy Boronia ..	
coerulescens, F.v.M.	Blueish Boronia	
polygalifolia, Smith	Waxy Boronia ..	
anemonifolia, A.Cunn.	Anemone Boronia	
parviflora, Smith	Swamp Boronia..	
filifolia, F.v.M. ..	Thread Boronia	
clavellifolia, F.v.M.	Desert Boronia ..	

* Plants marked thus are listed either as growing plants o ras seeds by one or more of our florists.

SECOND VICTORIAN EGG-LAYING COMPETITION, 1912-13.

The Second Burnley Egg-laying Competition was commenced on 15th April, 1912. The decision to tar-pave the houses was responsible for this delay. The houses are now perfectly dry ; and as the floor has been raised by means of ashes, well above the level of the surrounding ground, it will remain dry and increase the comfort of the birds. Sixty-nine pens were allotted ; and in the majority of cases the birds arrived in excellent condition. One or two that showed symptoms of chicken pox and roup were immediately isolated, and not placed in pens until after the infection had passed. One Inter-State pen arrived in bad condition ; one of the birds died soon after arrival. It was considered this was caused by the kindly but mistaken action of some individual feeding them with large whole white maize while on the journey.

As regards type, the birds appear on the average to be superior to those of last year. Some of the birds have gone into a false moult, due, no doubt, to the removal from the sandy soil of their homes to the heavy clay at Burnley ; whilst the leading pen, bred in a cold climate with a heavy soil, has received no set-back.

All things taken into consideration, the number of eggs laid up to the present can be considered entirely satisfactory.

FEEDING.

The morning mash, given at daylight, is prepared by mixing two parts pollard, one of oatmeal branning, and one of lucerne chaff, scalded over night ; three or four mornings of a week 25 lbs. of bullock's liver finely chopped is added to this—2½ ozs. approximately being given to each bird. At mid-day equal parts of pollard and wheat bran mash is prepared, 5 ozs. being allowed each pen, followed by a handful of green food— grass, clover, &c. The evening meal consists of four parts wheat, three of broken maize, and two of white oats, 2 ozs. approximately being given to each bird. Occasionally, wheat only is given in the evening.

WEATHER.

The weather has been mild, isolated showers having fallen. A few of the birds of heavier breeds have shown broodiness

SECOND VICTORIAN EGG-LAYING COMPETITION, 1912-13.

Commencing 15th April, 1912.

CONDUCTED AT BURNLEY HORTICULTURAL SCHOOL.

H. V. Hawkins, Poultry Expert.

No. Pen.	Breed.	Name of Owner.	April 15 to May 14.	May 15 to June 14.	Total to Date (2 months).	Position in Competition.
40	White Leghorns	S. Brown	111	136	247	1
70	,,	C. J. Beatty	101	121	222	2
47	,,	J. E. Bradley	109	105	214	3
23	,,	W. McLister	99	113	212	4
31	,,	Geo. Edwards	91	114	205	5
9	,,	J. S. Spotswood	83	119	202	6
20	,,	E. Waldon	84	117	201	7
28	,,	F. G. Eagleton	77	123	200	8
3	Black Orpingtons	King and Watson	75	118	193	9
7	White Leghorns	A. H. Padman	87	105	192	} 10
30	,,	Mrs. Stevenson	93	99	192	}
48	,,	Griffin Cant	86	103	189	} 12
62	,,	R. W. Pope	80	109	189	}
1	,,	J. Campbell	88	100	188	14
44	,,	A. W. Hall	103	83	186	15
8	Black Orpingtons	D. Fisher	107	63	170	16
46	,,	H. A. Langdon	85	84	169	17
38	White Leghorns	R. Moy	67	100	167	18
24	,,	Sargenfri Poultry Yard	63	99	162	19
6	,,	J. B. Macarthur	58	103	161	20
39	,,	W. G. Swift	69	90	159	21
29	,,	J. B. Brigden	71	85	156	} 22
45	,,	Wooldridge Bros.	71	85	156	}
25	,,	R. L. Appleford	35	112	147	24
37	,,	C. B. Bertelsmeier	41	105	146	} 25
42	,,	Mrs. T. Kempster	76	70	146	}
50	,,	A. Ahpee	53	99	143	27
2	,,	B. Rowlinson	44	96	140	28
35	,,	C. H. Busst	52	78	130	} 29
33	,,	H. McKenzie	58	72	130	}
63	,,	Percy Walker	41	88	129	} 3
14	,,	J. H. Wright	47	82	129	}
64	,,	H. Merrick	65	55	120	33
49	,,	W. Purvis	27	88	115	33
58	,,	W. J. Stock	67	47	114	35
13	,,	W. B. Crellin	32	74	106	36
56	,,	M. A. Monk	46	59	105	37
15	,,	Mrs. W. H. Steer	47	56	103	38
53	,,	H. Hodges	49	51	100	39
27	,,	E. Nash	18	80	98	40
19	,,	Cowan Bros.	23	74	97	41
61	Black Orpingtons	Jas. Ogden	29	64	93	42
12	White Leghorns	T. H. Stafford	44	48	92	43
41	,,	A. Stringer	39	51	90	44
5	,,	J. H. Brain	13	69	82	} 45
43	,,	G. Purton	21	61	82	}
4	,,	J. Blackburne	35	43	78	47
54	,,	F. R. DeGaris	20	52	72	48
51	,,	H. Hammill	..	71	71	} 49
65	,,	A. H. Thomson	17	54	71	}
52	Black Minorcas	Chalmers Bros.	23	40	63	} 51
57	White Leghorns	B. Walker	7	56	63	}
22	,,	W. N. Ling	11	51	62	53
21	,,	J. O'Loughlin	38	19	57	54
32	,,	S. Brundrett	6	50	56	} 55
59	,,	W. J. Seabridge	25	31	56	}
10	R.C. Brown Leghorns	S. P. Giles	4	51	55	57
60	White Leghorns	Miss B. E. Ryan	11	44	55	} 57
69	,,	Morgan and Watson	19	33	52	59
68	,,	W. J. McKeddie	20	30	50	60
16	Silver Wyandottes	R. Jobling	20	29	49	} 61
18	White Leghorns	B. Mitchell	13	36	49	}
36	Old English Game	K. J. Barrett	18	22	40	} 63
66	White Leghorns	J. Moloney	14	26	40	}
11	Black Orpingtons	T. S. Goodisson	..	31	31	65
55	Brown Leghorns	J. Matheson	..	18	18	66
17	White Leghorns	S. Childs	1	10	11	67
34	,,	Reg. F. B. Moore	..	3	3	68
67	Anconas	A. E. Manning	..	..	..	69
26	,,	(Reserved)	..	..	..	..
		Totals	3 227	4.844	8.071	

A NEW PEST TO MAIZE.

HARLEQUIN FRUIT BUG.

(*Dindymus versicolor.*)

C. French, jun., Acting Government Entomologist.

During the last few weeks letters have been received by the Entomological Branch from Mr. J. A. Bayford, State School, Omeo, Gippsland, in reference to insects causing damage to maize cobs. On asking for specimens he kindly forwarded me a supply, together with a damaged maize cob. On examination I found the insects were the well-known Harlequin Bugs, which are natives of Australia. They are occasionally destructive to apples, &c., as they insert their rostrum or beak into the fruit, causing it to become spotted. The markings resemble the disease known as "Bitter Pit."

Mr. Bayford says :—"I am sending a specimen known here as the Soldier Beetle, which is doing much damage. To-day the local surveyor showed me how they were destroying his maize cobs wherever the outside covering had been loosened in any way that gave them a chance to get at the maize inside. The maize cobs were covered with these insects."

"I am forwarding with this a maize cob from the patch I mentioned to you. You will notice that the bugs have damaged the end of the cob, and if I have succeeded in imprisoning anything like the number that was on the cob when I picked it, you will be able to realize how they are swarming in the garden. Quite a large percentage of the cobs are damaged in the same manner as the one I am forwarding. They have done very much damage in this particular garden, attacking tomatoes, strawberries, raspberries, and other plants. Another garden-owner tells me that they

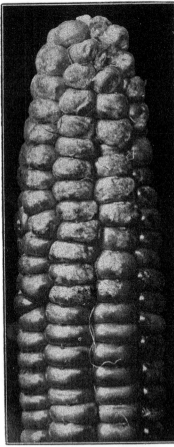

MAIZE COB SHOWING UPPER PORTION
DAMAGED BY HARLEQUIN BUG.

caused almost all his peaches to fall off before they were ripe by attacking the fruit near the stem."

The maize cob submitted to me was attacked towards the top, the damaged grain being of a dirty white colour, caused by the bugs sucking its juice.

PREVENTION AND REMEDIES.

Should the insects obtain a footing in the maize-growing districts of Victoria, they will cause losses to growers; therefore, when the bugs are first noticed, means should be at once taken to prevent their spread.

As the insects deposit their eggs amongst rubbish, and under logs, stones, old posts, &c., it is advisable that the maize field be kept as clean as possible. All weeds should be destroyed by burning. They should not be heaped round the maize field, as they form favourite breeding places for these pests.

HARLEQUIN FRUIT BUG.

Benzole emulsion spray, being particularly deadly to all bugs, is strongly recommended. As a deterrent coal tar water is useful. Boil 1 lb. of coal tar in 2 gallons of water, and while hot add from 50 to 100 gallons of water.

STATISTICS.

LIVE STOCK.

The following return of the live stock in Victoria at the end of March, 1912, has been issued by the Government Statist (Mr. A. M. Laughton) :—

Districts.	Horses.	Cattle.			Sheep.	Pigs.
		Dairy Cows (milking and dry).	Other Cattle.	Total.		
Central	100,156	133,973	128,922	262,895	1,191,787	60,881
North-Central ..	30,848	44,886	57,931	102,817	1,109,763	19,809
Western	75,057	170,054	181,370	351,424	4,399,158	75,044
Wimmera ..	70,050	24,253	32,237	56,490	2,264,108	11,962
Mallee	41,305	18,254	31,385	49,639	809,654	12,063
Northern.. ..	100,005	89,009	121,984	210,993	2,027,841	44,832
North-Eastern ..	40,138	65,054	157,929	222,983	880,024	27,624
Gippsland ..	50,254	154,072	235,814	389,886	1,175,469	95,854
Total March, 1912	507,813	699,555	947,572	1,647,127	13,857,804	348,069
Total March, 1911	472,080	668,777	878,792	1,547,569	12,882,665	333,281
Increase ..	35,733	30,778	68,780	99,558	975,139	14,788

AGRICULTURE IN VICTORIA.

ACREAGE AND CROP.

AREA AND PRODUCE, 1911–12 AND 1910–11.

The following agricultural statistics for the State of Victoria have been issued by the Government Statist (Mr. A. M. Laughton) :—

Name of Crop.	Area.		Produce.		Average per Acre.	
	1911–12.	1910–11.	1911–12.	1910–11.	1911–12.	1910–11.
	acres.	acres.	bushels.	bushels.	bushels.	bushels.
Wheat	2,164,066	2,398,089	20,891,877	34,813,019	9·65	14·52
Oats	302,238	392,681	4,585,326	9,699,127	15·17	24·70
Barley (malting)	36,748	30,609	725,803	804,893	19·75	26·30
Barley (other)	16,793	22,078	298,781	535,494	17·79	24·25
Maize	18,223	20,151	*	982,103	*	48·74
Rye	1,098	2,640	9,981	32,647	9·09	12·37
Peas and Beans	11,535	11,068	181,113	223,284	15·70	20·17
			tons.	tons.	tons.	tons.
Potatoes (early crop)	†5,142	5,606	17,498	21,140	3·40	3·77
Potatoes (general crop)	42,550	57,298	*	142,172	*	2·48
Mangel-wurzel	797	1,254	9,568	17,654	12·01	14·08
Beet, carrots, parsnips, turnips for fodder	658	872	4,953	7,481	7·53	8·58
Onions	3,652	6,161	20,911	37,484	5·73	6·08
Hay (wheaten)	304,388	240,026	357,379	333,711	1·17	1·39
Hay (oaten)	535,146	575,791	648,846	929,781	1·21	1·61
Hay (lucerne, &c.)	20,671	16,852	26,072	28,918	1·26	1·72
			cwt.	cwt.	cwt.	cwt.
Grass cut for seed	1,188	1,295	1,697	2,904	1·43	2·24
Green fodder	75,177	71,826	..	..	..	..
Vines	24,193	23,412	..	..	..	..
Orchards and gardens	59,985	57,375	..	..	..	..
Market-gardens	10,331	10,778	..	..	..	..
Other tillage	5,662	6,208	..	..	..	..
Total Area under Crop	3,640,241	3,952,070	..	..	..	..
Land in Fallow	1,469,608	1,434,177	..	..	..	..
Total Cultivation	5,109,849	5,386,247	..	..	..	..

* Not yet available.
† The early crop relates to potatoes dug before 1st March.

AREA UNDER POTATOES IN PRINCIPAL COUNTIES. 1911–12 AND 1910–11.

Principal Counties.	Area in Acres.	
	1911–12.	1910–11.
Bourke	5,228	7,230
Grant	8,205	9,451
Mornington	5,618	6,877
Dalhousie	2,687	3,891
Talbot	6,870	8,590
Villiers	3,758	7,256
Buln Buln	3,612	6,371
Remainder of State	11,714	13,238
Total	47,692	62,904

ORCHARD AND GARDEN NOTES.

E. E. Pescott, Principal, School of Horticulture, Burnley.

The Orchard.

PLANTING.

The planting of deciduous fruit trees will still be continued on the lines laid down in last month's notes. Care should be taken to have the soil thoroughly sweetened and aerated, the roots should be well trimmed, and the young tree firmly planted. Owing to the time that elapses between the removal of the tree from the nursery row and the planting of the tree in its permanent situation, practically the whole of the fibrous and feeding root system has been destroyed. It will be well to remove all of the finer roots, and to thoroughly trim back the stronger ones; this will allow the tree to make a new root system for itself.

Stringfellow's method of removing the whole of the roots, leaving only a stub, as referred to in the *Journal* for July, 1909, is not advocated, but a modification of this might be adopted, whereby the root system of the young tree will be vigorously pruned, in order that no detrimental effect will remain as a result of the transplanting of the tree. It should be borne in mind that a vigorous root trimming will require a corresponding severe pruning of the head. In trimming or cutting the roots, all cuts should have a downward face; this will allow, when the wound calluses, of a downward growth of roots from the callus. If the wound or cut be on the upper side of the root, in all probability suckering will result.

In planting a commercial orchard, it has been previously advised that the number of varieties should be limited, and that, as far as possible, these varieties should have a corresponding bloom period. The necessity for cross-fertilization is becoming more apparent each year, and it is now definitely known that cross-fertilization results in greatly increased crops, and also in fruit of an increased size. In the experiments of Waite on the " Pollination of Pear Flowers," and of Lewis and Vincent on " The Pollination of the Apple," their results were invariably that the largest fruits were crosses. Fruit-growers in this State have observed that where blocks of different varieties of the same kind of fruit have been planted alongside of each other, the adjoining rows of the two varieties have always carried the heaviest crops. Experience is thus against the planting of large blocks of any one variety; at the same time, the varieties must not be multiplied indefinitely.

The Jonathan apple is generally considered to be a consistent bearer and self-fertile; but even this prolific variety may be made to largely increase its yield by intermingling with another variety having a similar bloom period; and it has been found that the Sturmer Pippin is one of the best for the purpose. Dumelow's Seedling, Reinette du Canada, and Stone Pippin also flower at the same time. For fuller information on this subject reference may be made to the articles in the *Journal* for January, 1911.

PRUNING.

Pruning operations will now be in full swing. In pruning the young trees, heavy pruning will be required in order to produce strong growth and a good frame; but as the tree advances in age, the pruning will be reduced considerably. It should be remembered that strong, heavy pruning results in wood growth, and that weak pruning steadies the tree, and promotes an even growth. When framing and building a tree, the former consideration is observed, and when the tree is coming into fruit bearing or is mature, it will be pruned according to the latter. Any operation that will cause the tree to produce less wood growth will induce the tree to become more fruitful, provided the tree be in a healthy condition; so that when trees are mature, pruning operations, as a rule, should not be severe, but rather the reverse.

Old fruiting wood, and dead and dying wood should always be removed, and aged spurs should be considerably reduced, in order to make them produce new growths; crowded and overlapping laterals should be shortened back; fruit bearing in the higher portions of the tree should not be encouraged; and due consideration should be given to the admission of light and air to all parts of the tree.

Where varieties of fruit trees are prone to bearing crops every second year, their lateral system should be pruned so that they will not produce too heavy a crop in the fruiting year; and at the same time they will produce wood in their fruiting year to give a crop the subsequent season.

A model tree will always be light on its topmost leaders, bearing the major portion of the crop in the lower regions of the tree. The main point to be noted is that a heavy wood growth in the upper portion of the tree tends to reduce the bearing capabilities of the tree in its most useful parts.

SPRAYING.

Spraying should be carried out on the lines indicated in last month's notes, and it should be completed by the end of the month.

Flower Garden.

The cleaning up and digging will be continued this month. A good top dressing of stable manure may be given before digging, and all leaves and litter should be dug into the beds.

Herbaceous plants may be lifted and stored till springtime; they should not be allowed to become too dry. Shrubs and small perennial plants may now be removed if necessary, lifting evergreen ones with a good ball of earth.

The planting of roses will now be carried out. The soil should have been well sweetened and seasoned beforehand. The plants require to be firmly planted in the soil, and after planting, a vigorous pruning should be given to each.

Gladioli corms for early blooming may be planted; and, as well, plants of the Japanese Iris, *I. Kæmpferi*, and the German and English " Flag " Irises.

Hardy annuals may be transplanted, and where these have been sown in the open, the clumps should be considerably thinned out. The young plants should be given ample room; better flowers will result if fewer plants are grown, so as to give the individual plants more room, and to prevent overcrowding of roots. In cool districts, a few seeds of late sweet peas may still be sown, and seedlings of this class of plant may be transplanted.

Roses will now require pruning. In rose pruning, the rule is that strong-growing plants require less severe cutting than weak-growing ones.

As roses always flower on new wood, it is essential that to have good blooms the bushes must be pruned regularly. All weak growths, exhausted and worn-out wood, must be removed, retaining only the vigorous growths. It is generally advisable to prune to four or five eyes or buds, so as to have subsequent strong growths, always pruning into the previous season's wood. Spindly growths, especially in the centre of the bushes, should be removed, the plants being trained with an open and angular habit.

Vegetable Garden.

The addition of gypsum to the vegetable plots prior to digging will rid the soil of a large number of insects that infest the vegetables in spring; and thus numbers of vegetable pests, such as caterpillars, aphis, &c., will be killed. The gypsum may be dug into the soil, at the rate of about 2 ozs. per square yard. Another trouble in the vegetable garden at this season of the year is the snail and slug pest. The article on slugs and snails in the December, 1910, *Journal* may be consulted, but one means of reducing this pest is to keep the plots free of weeds. As hoeing is generally out of the question in winter, the weeds should be hand pulled. Where any foliage is in direct contact with the ground, it should be lifted occasionally, and a light dusting of lime sprinkled underneath.

All seedlings of sufficient size should now be planted out; this includes onions, asparagus, lettuce, cabbage, cauliflower, &c. A planting of broad beans may be made, and also all varieties of peas. Seeds of summer cabbage, lettuce, leek, onion, radish, parsnip, may now be sown. Tubers of Jerusalem artichokes should be planted out, and also a few early potatoes.

Seeds of tomatoes may be planted in the frames; and also, towards the end of the month, seeds of melons, cucumbers, marrows, pumpkins, may be sown under glass on the hot-bed.

REMINDERS FOR AUGUST.

LIVE STOCK.

HORSES.—Those stabled can be fed liberally. Those doing fast or heavy work should be clipped; if not wholly, then trace high. Those not rugged on coming into the stable at night should be wiped down and in half-an-hour's time rugged or covered with bags until the coat is dry. Old horses and weaned foals should be given crushed oats. Grass-fed working horses should be given hay or straw, if there is no old grass, to counteract the purging effects of the young growth. Old and badly-conditioned horses should be given some boiled barley.

CATTLE.—Cows, if not housed, should be rugged. Rugs should be removed in the daytime when the shade temperature reaches 60 degrees. Give a ration of hay or straw, whole or chaffed, to counteract the purging effects of young grass. Calves should be kept in warm, dry shed. Those on the bucket should be given their milk warm. The bull may now run with the cows.

PIGS.—Supply plenty of bedding in warm, well-ventilated styes. Keep styes clean and dry, and the feeding troughs clean and wholesome. Store pigs should be placed in fattening styes. Sows in fine weather should be given a grass run.

SHEEP.—Apply to breeders for rams needed. Ask for good backed sheep, both in flesh and fleece, whether British breeds or merinos. Fat lambs weighing 60 lbs. live weight will sell best now—avoid the rush of the season. Stud ewe flocks should be gone through carefully; put out second-rate ewes, and enter approved young ewes in stud books.

POULTRY.—When yards become damp and difficult to clean a little lime sprinkled on surface will sweeten soil, and also act as a germicide. Keep the breeders busy— oaten hay scattered about will make them exercise. As the hens eat twice as quickly as the male bird, feed the latter by himself; tack a piece of wire netting on a light frame, and place it across an angle to make a small enclosure for him whilst he is eating. Overhaul incubators; see that the capsule or thermostat acts properly; thoroughly clean lamps, egg drawers, and chimneys. Test machine for two days before putting valuable eggs in. It is also advisable to have thermometer tested. When additional incubators are required, it is more satisfactory to keep to the one make.

CULTIVATION.

FARM.—Second fallow where necessary for summer crops. If required, roll or harrow crops. Plant very early potatoes in forward districts. Sow mangolds. Apply slow-acting fertilizers, such as blood and bone manures, for maize.

ORCHARD.—Complete planting and pruning of deciduous trees. Watch for peach aphis, and spray with tobacco solution, if present. Prepare for planting citrus trees. Spray for woolly aphis with strong tobacco solution.

FLOWER GARDEN.—Finish digging and pruning of roses, &c. Leave pruning of shrubs till after flowering. Keep weeds in check; weed out seed beds. Divide and plant out all herbaceous plants, such as phlox, delphiniums, rudbeckia, &c. Plant out gladioli. Complete planting of shrubs. Mulch young plants.

VEGETABLE GARDEN.—Top-dress asparagus beds; plant new asparagus plots. Plant herb divisions, and potatoes. Sow cabbage, cauliflower, peas, carrots, beans, radish, and lettuce seeds. Sow tomato seeds in a hot frame. Finish digging.

VINEYARD.—August is the best month for planting vines (grafted or ungrafted). This should be actively proceeded with and completed before end of month. Scions for field grafting may still be preserved as detailed last month, or better still by placing them in cool storage. They should all be removed from vines before end of month, at latest. Conclude pruning and tie down rods. Where black spot has been very prevalent, apply 1st acid iron sulphate treatment (see *Journal* for July, 1911). Apply readily soluble nitrogenous manures (soda nitrate or ammonium sulphate) towards end of month.

Cellar.—Rack again, towards end of month, wines which have as yet only been once racked (spring racking). Fill up regularly all unfortified wines. Clean up generally in cellar and whitewash walls, woodwork, &c.

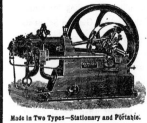

By Authority : ALBERT J. MULLETT, Acting Government Printer, Melbourne.

LITERATURE FOR AGRICULTURISTS.

PLAN AND SPECIFICATION OF SHEEP-SHEARING SHED. 2s. 6d. *Postage,* 1d.

MILK CHARTS (Monthly and Weekly), 6d. per dozen, post free. When ordering, dairy farmers should mention " Monthly " or " Weekly."

By Professor A. J. Ewart, Government Botanist.

WEEDS, POISON PLANTS, AND NATURALIZED ALIENS OF VICTORIA. 2s. 6d. *Postage :* Commonwealth, 1½d. ; N.Z., 5d. ; British and Foreign, 10d.

PLANTS INDIGENOUS TO VICTORIA. Vol. II., 10s. *Postage :* Com., 2d. ; N.Z., 8d. ; Brit. & For., 1s. 4d.

By C. French, F.E.S., Government Entomologist.

DESTRUCTIVE INSECTS OF VICTORIA. Parts I., II., III., IV., V. 2s. 6d. each. *Postage :* Parts I. and III., C., 1d. ; N.Z., 3d.; B. & F., 6d. each. Parts II. and IV., C., 1½d. ; N.Z., 4d. ; B. & F., 8d. each. Part V., C., 1d. ; N.Z., 4d. ; B. & F., 7d.

By D. McAlpine, Government Vegetable Pathologist.

RUSTS OF AUSTRALIA. 5s. *Postage :* C., 2d. ; N.Z., 8d. ; B. & F., 1s. 4d.

SMUTS OF AUSTRALIA. 4s. *Postage :* C., 2½d. ; N.Z., 9d. ; B. & F., 1s. 6d.

FUNGUS DISEASES OF CITRUS TREES IN AUSTRALIA. 2s. *Postage :* C., 1d. ; N.Z., 3d. ; B. & F., 6d.

FUNGUS DISEASES OF STONE FRUIT TREES IN AUSTRALIA. 2s. 6d. *Postage :* C., 1½d. ; N.Z., 5d. ; B. & F., 10d.

SYSTEMATIC ARRANGEMENT OF AUSTRALIAN FUNGI. 3s. *Postage :* C., 2d. ; N.Z., 8d. ; B. & F., 1s. 4d.

THE DEPARTMENT OF AGRICULTURE,
MELBOURNE, VICTORIA.

Remittances from places outside the Commonwealth to be by Money Order only.

Pamphlets obtainable from the Director of Agriculture, Melbourne, Free on Application.

NEW SERIES.

1. SILO CONSTRUCTION. *A. S. Kenyon, C.E.*
2. HINTS FOR NEW SETTLERS. *T. A. J. Smith.*
* 3. APPLE GROWING FOR EXPORT. *P. J. Carmody.*
* 4. BOOKKEEPING FOR FARMERS. *W. McIver, A.I.A.V., A.S.A.A., Eng.*
* 5. CIDER MAKING. *J. Knight.*
* 6. FARM PLUMBING. *C. H. Wright.*
7. CITRUS FRUIT CULTURE. *E. E. Pescott.*
* 8. BUILDING HINTS FOR SETTLERS. *A. S. Kenyon, C.E., and others.*
9. TOBACCO CULTURE. *T. A. J. Smith.*
*10. SILOS AND SILAGE. *G. H. F. Baker.*
11. THE BEET SUGAR INDUSTRY AND CLOSER SETTLEMENT. *H. T. Easterby.*
12. WORMS IN SHEEP. *S. S. Cameron, D.V. Sc., M.R.C.V.S.*

* Not yet available.

[Registered at the General Post Office, Melbourne, for transmission by Post as a Newspaper.]

The Journal of THE DEPARTMENT OF AGRICULTURE OF VICTORIA, AUSTRALIA.

August, 1912.

SCENT INDUSTRY.

THE JOURNAL

OF

THE DEPARTMENT OF AGRICULTURE,

VICTORIA, AUSTRALIA.

CONTENTS.—AUGUST, 1912.

COPYRIGHT PROVISIONS AND SUBSCRIPTION RATES.

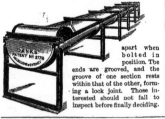
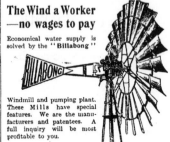

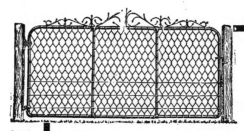

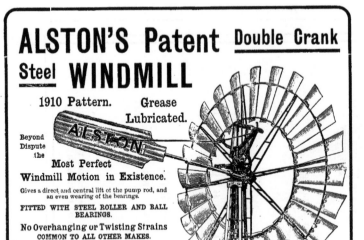

THE JOURNAL

OF

The Department of Agriculture

OF

VICTORIA.

Vol. X. Part 8.	10th August, 1912.

WHEAT AND ITS CULTIVATION.

 (Continued from page 338.)

No. 6.—METHODS OF CULTIVATION.

By A. E. V. Richardson, M.A., B.Sc. (Agric.),
Agricultural Superintendent.

In the preceding article, consideration was given to the practice of continuous cropping with wheat, and to the practice of barefallowing. Continuous cropping with wheat year after year stands condemned, both by theory and by practice. Under pioneering conditions it may be justifiable as a temporary expedient, but under normal conditions of cultivation it should be abandoned. Under pioneering conditions, land is usually cheap, whilst capital and labour are comparatively dear, and the pioneer, therefore, substitutes the cheaper factors of production for the more costly. Hence the initial system of farming is invariably *extensive*, for as much land and as little labour and capital as possible are used in production. The individual areas are relatively large, and the average yield relatively small. Continuous cropping is commonly resorted to, and the soil is of such virgin richness that it will produce large crops in spite of the comparatively crude methods of cultivation. When the soil begins to show signs of diminished fertility and production, the pioneer frequently wanders further afield, and leaves the problem of soil improvement to others than himself.

The Hill River Estate, in 1875, as shown in the accompanying illustrations, is a typical example of the extensive methods of cultivation practised in the pioneering days. In 1875, the estate was 60,000 acres in extent, and carried 50,000 sheep. The cultivated land was in large fields, one of which was 3 miles long, and contained, in 1873, no less than 4,250 acres of wheat in one block. According to Harcus' "History of South Australia (1876)," the ploughing was performed, in 1874, by "Thirty four-horse teams drawing a double plough, and five single ploughs striking out. The seed, which was of several kinds, to ascertain the best, was sown

8805.　　　　　　　r

EXTENSIVE WHEAT CULTURE ON HILL RIVER ESTATE, SOUTH AUSTRALIA, IN 1875.

NO. I.—PLOUGHING.

the first week in June with six of Adamson's 22-ft. broadcast machines, sowing 40 acres a day each. The pickling used is bluestone, and an ingenious dipping apparatus is used by which a bag at a time can be done with great rapidity. The lands are ploughed in 1-chain widths, and harrowed by fifteen sets of six-leaved harrows, doing a land in two turns. The harrowing is done at the 1ate of 500 acres a day. As harvest approaches, 2-chain wide strips are cut by mowing machines, at intervals, cutting the wheat into 200-acre blocks, and then the strips are ploughed, for the prevention of fire. Thirty-seven strippers are used to take off the crop (1874). Three crops were taken off in succession, and then the land was laid down to pasture.''

Four years later, there were 850 working horses fed under cover every day; the amount of land under crop was 11,000 acres per annum; and 65 strippers were used in taking it off. I am indebted to Mr. John Emery, of Adelaide, formely Resident Manager of the estate, for the photographs illustrating the teams at work.

From continuous cropping to bare-fallowing is a natural transition, especially in a relatively dry district. Continual cropping with the same crop encourages weeds to such an extent as to ultimately render a period of rest and cleaning absolutely necessary.

The marked advantages of this period of rest and cleaning must have appealed very strongly to the early pioneers. So far as barefallowing is concerned, we have already seen that it is an indispensable preparation for a maximum crop in all districts where the rainfall is relatively low, and that it enables the wheat crop to make the very utmost use of a limited rainfall. It was noted, too, that in the more humid districts problems relating to moisture conservation are of minor importance, and that barefallowing is unnecessary, and should be replaced by a skilled system of catch cropping and rotation. Finally, it was noted that in the dry districts no system of cultivation can be permanently effective

EXTENSIVE WHEAT CULTURE ON HILL RIVER ESTATE, SOUTH AUSTRALIA, IN 1875.

NO. 2.—HARROWING.

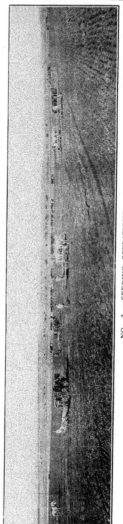

NO. 3.—SEEDING OPERATIONS.

Q 2

unless it provides, not only for the conservation of moisture, but also for the conservation of fertility. Attention was concentrated on the former principle in the preceding article. Let us now consider the latter principle. The weak point in the practice of barefallowing is that it tends to deplete the soil of organic matter. Organic matter—by which is meant vegetable or animal matter in the process of decay—is the soil's most valuable constituent. It has an important physical, chemical, and biological effect upon the soil. It acts physically, by increasing the capacity of the soil for holding moisture, and by improving its texture; chemically, by supplying nitrogen necessary for the growth of the crop and by unlocking the dormant stores of plant food and making them available; and, biologically, by affording the necessary material for the promotion of vigorous bacterial growth within the soil.

It may readily be understood, therefore, that the presence of this important ingredient in ample quantity will mean success, whilst its absence will mean disaster, and when the organic content of the soil becomes lessened, the crop-producing power will be seriously impaired.

Alternate barefallowing and wheat cropping, without a period of rest or pasturage, will ultimately deplete the soil of its organic matter, and this depletion will be hastened by the practice of burning the stubble. Local figures are wanting as to the rate at which organic matter is lost by slow oxidation in the process of fallowing; but there can be little doubt that the loss in dry, hot districts is considerable. The loss through burning of the stubble of a 15-bushel crop, however, may be set down at 1,145 lbs. of organic matter per acre (*vide* page 203). To counteract these losses should be the aim of every practical farmer. It is a matter of common observation that many of our old wheat lands are becoming more difficult to plough and reduce to a satisfactory tilth compared with virgin land of the same character in the same locality. This is one illustration of the effect of a reduction of the organic content of the soil. There are three general ways of supplying the soil with the organic matter necessary to maintain its fertility—

(1) By the application of farmyard manure.
(2) By pasturing and by rest.
(3) By green manuring.

Under the conditions that obtain in the wheat areas, the application of farmyard manure as a *practical* means of counteracting the depletion of organic matter is out of the question. The average wheat holding is far too large to be appreciably affected by the totality of farmyard manure produced on the farm. In districts where intense culture is practised, however, and where individual holdings are relatively small, the use of farmyard manure as a means of restoring organic matter becomes practicable. The average wheat-farmer, with his relatively large holding, must, therefore, depend either on pasturing, rest, or green manuring for the maintenance of the organic content of his soil.

III.—Rotation Systems for Wheat.

Thus arises the necessity for some sort of rotation in a system of cropping. Continuous cropping with the same crop, and the biennial system of cropping and barefallowing, have been shown to fall short of the requirements of a permanent system of agriculture. It is very rarely, however, that a wheat-farmer follows the strict practice of alternate cropping and fallowing. Sheep have now become an integral part of every wheat farm, and portion, at least, of the area is therefore periodically reserved for pasture, and a more or less regular rotation is practised.

Advantages of Rotation.—The most important advantages accruing from a rational system of crop rotation is that it leads to the best possible utilization of the resources of the soil, and makes for maximum crops. Different crops vary very widely in the manner in which, and the depth at which, they obtain their nutriment from the soil. Some obtain it from relatively shallow depths, whilst others are deep rooted, and, by alternating such crops, the store of fertility is more evenly used up. A well-planned system of rotation leads to a better and more economical distribution of labour throughout the farm year, and thus enables a farmer to offer permanent, instead of casual, employment to farm hands. Moreover, it aids in preventing the ravages of disease, for crops susceptible to the attack of specific fungoid pests are less liable to be attacked when grown in rotation with other crops. An illustration of this may be seen with regard to "take all" in wheat. It enables land to be cleaned without the employment of special labour, for where one kind of crop is grown repeatedly, the weeds favoured by that crop cannot be kept in check. Finally, it provides a means whereby the fertility of the soil may, by rational treatment, be maintained, and even increased.

A regular system of rotation—by which is meant that different kinds of crops are made to succeed one another on the same ground in regular order—is a feature of the advanced forms of agriculture practised in the older countries of the world. We must not fall into the error of assuming that because certain rotations are found profitable in the densely populated countries of Europe, that they would be equally applicable in a new country like Australia, with a relatively sparse population.

The most advanced and profitable rotation for us will be that which is best adapted to the exigencies of our peculiar climatic and economic conditions. What are the conditions obtaining in the wheat areas? The climate is such that the greater part of the rain falls during the winter months. The spring and summer rains are irregular, and rarely copious. Hence, in the wheat areas proper, the growing of summer crops is more or less risky and uncertain, and for securing suitable crops for rotating with wheat we are driven back to the use of winter-growing forages or cereals.

Among the economic considerations, the labour problem is of great importance. To break away from an extensive system of culture and adopt intensive methods is to change from a system in which a minimum of labour is required to one necessitating the employment of a maximum of labour. To rear and feed a large number of live stock, to rotate and diversify crops, and to follow the hundred-and-one practices of the intensive farmer, imply the expenditure of additional capital and labour. In densely crowded countries, the latter factor of production is usually abundant. In a sparsely populated country, in which immigration cannot keep pace with local requirements, trained farm labour is at a premium. The increasing cost of, and difficulty in securing, efficient local labour are already inducing many farmers to lessen the area devoted to cultivation, and increase the area devoted to grazing.

The size of the holding is obviously an important factor in determining the method of cultivation adopted, for the smaller the holdings, the more intense must be the methods of cultivation. According to the *Year-Book of Victoria* for 1910-11, more than one-half of the total area, *i.e.* 2,916,671 acres, devoted to cultivation in the whole State was confined to holdings in which the amount of privately owned land varied from 500 to 2,500 acres.

The values of farming land in the wheat areas have an important bearing on the methods of cultivation followed. Throughout the wheat areas, land values have considerably appreciated during the past decade, and this appreciation has been largely due to the increased productive power of the soil, brought about by improvements in cultivation, crop rotation, and in the adoption of artificial manures. It may be contended that the present prices represent high-water mark, and that values are not likely to ascend beyond the present limits. This belief, however, would imply that we have reached such a high stage of development in wheat growing that further improvements are impossible. It implies that the system of agriculture practised at the present time, which, by the way, is quite normal in a country occupied by a mere handful of people, must be a permanent characteristic of a country with an ever expanding population. High though the land values may be, it is certain that they must ultimately continue to rise with the pressure of population, and those who find themselves unable to make satisfactory interest on the enhanced capital values will gradually make way for those who can.

Let us now consider the rotations practised under existing economic conditions, and endeavour to see whether we may reasonably expect improved rotations in the future. A very widely practised rotation in the wheat areas is that of wheat, pasture, barefallow. This practice enables but one crop in three years to be taken off a given piece of land. One-third of the farm area is devoted to pasture for sheep and lambs, whilst the remainder, for a portion of the year, is under barefallow. Obviously, such a rotation could only be practised in a district where land values are relatively low, and where individual holdings are considerable. Since but one crop is taken off in three years, and the crop is fallowed by a year of pasture, the system is not exhausting, and with careful working one would expect a succession of heavy crops for many years. The preparatory year of careful barefallow guarantees the success of the wheat crop, but whether, under ordinary conditions, the year of pasture will accumulate sufficient organic matter to cover losses through fallowing has not been determined. Of course, only a portion of the organic and mineral constituents of the pasture is returned in the animal droppings, and under ordinary conditions the lambs and the wool are sold off the farm. The important point about this rotation is that it requires a minimum of labour, and is well adapted for a district in which holdings are large, and land is relatively cheap, and the rainfall scanty.

It must be noted, however, that with the increasing land values the time must come when, in the more favoured wheat districts, the returns will be insufficient under this system of rotation, to cover expenses, and leave a profitable margin of interest. While land is, say, £3 to £10 an acre, one 15-bushel crop in three years may yield a fair rate of interest over and above expenses, but the contrary might be the case if the monetary value of the land doubles.

A modification of this rotation is largely practised in the Wimmera, and consists of Wheat: Oats (for pasture): Pasture: Barefallow. The wheat is sown on well-prepared barefallow, and after the wheat is harvested, oats are disced in the autumn on the stubbles, and utilized for pasture. After oats, the paddock is depastured for sheep and lambs, and the rotation brought to a close by a season of barefallow. Under this scheme of rotation there can be little doubt that the organic content of the soil may be maintained, as two years of pasture are given for every year of crop. As will be shown later, however, the nitrogen content of the soil is not likely to increase unless legumes, such as trefoil and clover, regularly appear in the pasture. As with the three course rotation the labour difficulty is reduced to a minimum. The area of wheat actually in crop will be smaller than if the former rotation were practised, but the number of sheep that may be safely kept on the farm will be much greater than with the corresponding three-course rotation. These may be regarded as the prevailing rotations at present in vogue in the wheat areas, and it will be seen that they fit in well with the existing economic conditions in the wheat areas.

From time to time various forage crops, such as peas, rape, rye and vetches, barley, &c., have been grown in more or less regular rotation with wheat and barefallow in the drier areas, and the results have been such as to render it extremely probable that these crops will play an important part in the future of wheat growing, more especially as the lamb industry is now firmly established. Many individual cases are on record where farmers have been strikingly successful in combining the cultivation of these crops with that of wheat to the great benefit of the latter. As yet. however, no regular and definite rotation of forage crops with wheat and barefallow has been applied to any considerable area of the wheat belt proper. In this direction there is scope for much useful experimental work. A systematic test of different rotations of forage crops, with cereals and barefallow, extending over a sufficient period of years to eliminate the error effect of season and climate, would provide data of very material value for deciding the merits of different rotations. for the drier districts. and would indicate whether it is possible to get more than one crop in three years or one crop in four years.

The fundamental weakness of alternate cropping and barefallowing was seen to be the depletion of the organic content of the soil. It is only when the soil is rich in organic matter that the highest yields may be obtained from barefallowing, and the feeding off of forage crops, grown in systematic rotation with wheat, provides the grower with a means of preventing the depletion of the organic content of his soil. The growing and feeding down of forage crops should, therefore, be made to supplement barefallowing, and the problem to solve is " What are the best forage crops to grow in dry districts, and what should be their position in a rotation? "

This can only be determined by systematic experimentation, *i.e.*, by trying all possible combinations of forage crops, barefallowing and wheat. and determining accurately the monetary net return from each possible combination. A modest effort has been made this season at Rutherglen to test the merits of different systems of crop rotation for wheat. These will probably be extended next season. and provision made for tests under drier conditions than Rutherglen. For the present season the following rotations have been laid down :—

    (1) Wheat and barefallow, alternately.
    (2) Wheat, pasture, barefallow.
    (3) Wheat, oats, pasture, barefallow.
    (4) Wheat, rape, fallow.
    (5) Wheat, non-leguminous forages. leguminous forages.
    (6) Wheat, forage crops, alternately.
    (7) Wheat, forage crops, fallow.
    (8) Wheat, forage crops, barley or oats, legumes.
    (9) Wheat, rape or kale, barley or oats, rye and vetches mixed.
    (10) Wheat, non-leguminous forage crop, leguminous forage crop, barley, fallow.
    (11) Wheat, oats, green manure.

It is not, of course, expected that all these rotations will succeed. Indeed, some of them must obviously be of little value in the district. The systematic recording of the results of the tests over a period of years, however, should throw considerable light on the subject of crop rotations for wheat in dry districts. The best rotation, of course, will be the one which continues to yield the best financial returns over a period of years, under the economic and climatic conditions of the district.

The restoration of organic matter to the soil can be brought about by *green manuring*, as well as by the feeding down of forage crops. Green manuring, *i.e.*, the ploughing in of green crops such as peas, rye, and vetches, &c., is a much more *effective* method of restoring organic matter to depleted soils than the feeding down of forage crops. As, however, the feeding value of a green crop is usually greater than its manurial value, the general practice is to convert the crop into milk, mutton, or beef, instead of ploughing it under.

Crop rotation must be supplemented by Soil Fertilization.—Before leaving the subject of crop rotation there is one important point to bear in mind. No system of crop rotation—however well conceived and carried out—can make up for any shortcomings in either cultivation or manuring. There are many who think that crop rotation is a substitute for manuring, *i.e.*, rotation of crops in itself will maintain the fertility of the soil. *Crop rotation alone, without adequate manuring, will not increase, nor even maintain, the soil's fertility.* No system of crop rotation can add one single pound of any of those *inorganic* elements so essential for plant growth. Moreover, unless legumes are grown, or unless they appear naturally in the pastures, even the nitrogen content will not be maintained. A rational system of crop rotation *does* increase the *organic* content of the soil, simply because the plant can obtain its organic matter from the carbon dioxide of the atmosphere. We have already seen (P. 201) that 95 per cent. of the dry weight of the plant is obtained from the air, and, therefore, when a crop is ploughed in as a green manure, or fed down on the land with stock, the soil is enriched by the organic matter which the plant has secured from the atmosphere. But no scheme of crop rotation, in itself, can add one iota to the *inorganic* portion of the soil. Rotation of crops must, therefore, be supplemented by the application of inorganic manures, if the fertility of the soil is to be maintained or increased. Nothing could be clearer on this fundamental point than the results obtained during the last seventy years at the Rothamsted Experimental Station. The results obtained in the Agdell field represent the world's best information on this point. In the Agdell field the famous Norfolk four-course rotation—turnips, barley, clover, wheat—has been practised for over seventy years. In any one year there were three plots for each crop, viz. :—

(1) Unmanured.
(2) Manured regularly with phosphates.
(3) Manured regularly with phosphates and nitrogen.

The following table shows very clearly that (1) on Section I., where rotation was carried on without soil fermentation, the yields in turnips, barley, and wheat have regularly and continually declined. After the first year the turnip yield on this plot never exceeded 3 tons per acre, *i.e.*, they were always grown at a *loss*. The barley average dropped from 46.5 to 13.7 bushels, whilst the wheat dropped from 29.7 bushels to 18.9.

SUMMARY OF RESULTS OF CROP ROTATION IN ADGELL FIELD,
ROTHAMSTED, SINCE 1848.

	Section I. Unmanured.			Section II. Phosphates.			Section III. Phosphates and Nitrogen.		
—	Turnips.	Barley.	Wheat.	Turnips.	Barley.	Wheat.	Turnips.	Barley.	Wheat.
(1) First Crop, 1848	lbs. 19,584	bush. 46·5	bush. 29·7	lbs. 25,004	bush. 36·3	bush. 30	lbs. 25,032	bush. 35·9	bush. 30·3
(2) Average of first 20 years ..	5,264	38·0	29·6	18,561	36·8	32·5	31,198	46·3	35·3
(3) Average of second 20 years ..	1,723	22·5	21·1	17,669	28·1	30·1	31,790	41·1	32·0
(4) Average of third 20 years ..	967	13·7	18·9	25,275	22·2	38·9	41,739	29·2	36·4

(2) On Section II. the application of phosphates has maintained the yield of turnips, and has increased the wheat yield by 25 per cent., while on the unfertilized plot the yield of turnips dropped to less than ½ ton per acre. the plot manured with phosphates has averaged nearly 12 tons per acre during the last twenty years. The barley crop shows a falling off, but it remains twice the average of the unfertilized barley crop.

(3) The turnip crop, on Section III., manured with phosphates and nitrogen, has increased from 12 tons to 20 tons per acre. The barley crop, which follows the turnips, seems to have suffered from the increased demands made by the heavy crops of turnips. The average yield, however, is more than twice that of the unfertilized plot. Finally, the high initial wheat yield, 30.3 bushels, has not only been maintained throughout the whole sixty years, but has even increased during the last twenty years to 36.4 bushels. Soil fertilization is, therefore, bound up with crop rotation, and is indispensable for the maintenance of soil fertility.

(To be continued.)

THE OLIVE.

By L. Macdonald, F.R.H.S., Horticulturist, Dookie Agricultural College.

(Continued from page 408.)

PESTS—*continued.*

The Brown or Black Olive Scale (*Lecanium oleæ*) : This pest is said to be the most general among our olive trees. Owing to its adaptability to various conditions and its disposition to attack such a large number of plants, it is found to be one of the worst to cope with. Citrus trees, many of our garden shrubs, and even deciduous fruit trees, are liable to its attack. Usually it is accompanied by another serious trouble, the Sooty Mould Fungus. This pest appears to be the natural concomitant of the olive scale living as it does on the sugary secretion of the scale insects.

The eggs, pinkish in colour, are very minute, and hard to distinguish. The colour and appearance of the scales vary through the different stages of their life history. The young insects that have just hatched out have also a pinky, somewhat transparent appearance. As the scales begin to grow they assume a yellowish colour with darker markings; gradually, as they mature, they become grey, brown, and black, and vary considerably in size, some of the adult insects being quite large.

The adult female usually occupies the whole of the space under the shell-like covering, but when egg-laying begins—and it continues for some time—a gradual diminution takes place in her size, until there is practically nothing left but a filament of skin, the eggs occupying the whole of the space under the covering.

With regard to the number of eggs laid by an adult female, some difference of opinion appears to exist, between 200 and 300 are said by some authorities to be about the average. In observations on this point

FIG. 21.—BLACK OLIVE SCALE (MAGNIFIED).

carried out by the writer, the number of eggs found under each scale was much greater. In no case, in fact, was the number less than 700, and in the greater number of cases noted considerably over 1,000 were found. It must be stated, though, that all examined were well-developed specimens, living somewhat isolated from others. Probably the number of eggs found under the average scale shell, where they are crowded together, would be much less, and would more likely approximate the numbers first mentioned. However this may be, it is certain that this insect is fairly prolific, and will soon spread if left unmolested.

The usual methods of combating this pest, and those of a similar kind, are by spraying or fumigation. In spraying petroleum compounds are most favoured; they are cheap, easy to prepare, and, if properly applied, effective in reducing the pest.

Red oil, crude petroleum oil emulsion, and kerosene emulsion are all prepared in the following way:—Boil 1 gallon of water and 1 lb. of sliced-up hard soap, or 2 lbs. of soft soap, until the soap is dissolved. Remove from the fire and add 2 gallons of the oil, thoroughly agitate with a force syringe for about five minutes, or until emulsified, replace on the fire again after adding the oil. The greatest care should be taken that it does not boil over or drip into the fire, as, owing to its inflammable nature, it is exceedingly dangerous.

If the mixture has been properly prepared, it will set when cool, and no free oil will be noticeable on top. The presence of free oil indicates either an insufficiency of soap or of emulsification. Sufficient stock may be prepared at once in the above way to last all through the season. In making up for use the stock should be heated up or diluted in hot water.

In applying the red oil preparation use at the rate of 1 in 20 to 1 in 30, according to the time of application. In autumn or late summer, or on badly infested trees the stronger strengths may be used, while the

FIG. 22.—TERMINALS OF SHOOTS ATTACKED BY BLACK OLIVE SCALE.

weaker solutions should be used in spring, when the new growth is on the trees. The olive, being an evergreen tree, will not bear the winter strengths used on deciduous trees. Crude petroleum and kerosene emulsion should be used at strengths from 1 in 12 to 1 in 15.

Resin wash and the lime and sulphur wash may also be used. Although all these sprays are of value in reducing the pest, it is very rarely that they succeed in completely eradicating it on evergreen trees. The only effective method of doing this economically is by fumigation with hydrocyanic acid gas. Full particulars of this method appear in the *Journal of Agriculture*, June issue, 1912, pages 366 to 374.

The chemicals used and the gas generated are exceedingly dangerous poisons, and should be handled with the greatest care. The gas should never be inhaled. The chemicals should be securely locked away when not in use.

The Red Scale (*Aspidiotus rossi*): This pest must not be confused with the "Red Orange Scale" (*Aspidiotus aurantii*). It belongs to the great family coccididæ, the members of which are responsible for a great amount of damage every year to both fruit and ornamental trees. It is one of the most common of the scale here. It appears to flourish somewhat better in the coastal regions than in the inland areas; this is due, in part, perhaps, to the presence of more succulent vegetation, more equable conditions, and the greater shelter in the dense foliage of southern woodlands.

This scale differs considerably from *Lecanium olea*, inasmuch as it appears to secrete very little honeydew, consequently very little of the black fumagine that lives on this secretion, and is so conspicuous a feature of the latter's presence, is noticeable.

FIG. 23.—OLIVE LEAVES SHOWING ATTACK OF SOOTY MOULD.

The treatment adopted for the Black Olive Scale should be applied also for this one.

The White or Oleander Scale (*Aspidiotus nerii*): This scale sometimes attacks the olive as well as a number of other evergreen trees. It has a very wide distribution, and is very hard to dislodge when once well established. It is greyish white in colour, often changing to greyish brown. The scales are about 1-25th to 1-12th of an inch in diameter. The female-puparium is almost circular and somewhat larger than that of the male, which is small and elongated. Owing to the absence of the "Sooty Mould Fungus" with this and *Aspidiotus rossi*, it is more difficult to detect an early attack than in the case of, for instance, *Lecanium oleæ*. When once they are discovered, however, no time should be lost in applying the most effective remedies.

Treatment.—This should be carried out with contact sprays or fumigation, as is recommended for *Lecanium oleæ*.

A small parasitic fly is found to be attacking this scale, and lending a hand towards its suppression. However, the grower must as yet look to other means of effectively combating it.

The Sooty Mould Fungus.—This fungus is known in many places as (*Meliola camelliæ*, Sacc.). Some difference of opinion exists as to whether this is its right name. It does not appear to be definitely settled which of the species of this fungus—if they are various—feeds on the honeydew of the scale insects on different trees. It is very probable, as pointed out by Mr. McAlpine, that different species cause the trouble in different countries and on different trees. The Black Blight (*Capnodium citricolum*, McAlp.) which attacks citrus trees in this country, appears to live, like allied forms, on the sugary secretions of aphides and scale insects. However this may be, it will usually be found sufficient for the purpose of the horticulturist to know that the various forms of this fungus have a similar effect in injuring the functions of the leaves, and that if the trees are kept free from the presence of scales or aphides the fungus also ceases to exist.

FIG. 24.—OLIVE TWIG ATTACKED BY RED SCALE (ASPIDIOTUS ROSSI).

Trees attacked by the Black Olive Scale are usually easily distinguished by the dark appearance given them by the presence of the Sooty Mould Fungus; the leaves also become shiny and sticky in cases where the attack is severe. The chief injury caused by the fungus is the clogging up of the stomata of the leaves, and in cases where there is a bad attack the branches and leaves become almost completely covered with an incrustation of this fungus, and, consequently, cannot properly perform their functions.

Treatment.—Since this disease derives its food supplies from the secretions of aphides or scale insects, it is obvious that by destroying such insects you also do away with the food supplies of the fungus; and, as a result, it soon disappears. Hence the grower should direct his attention firstly to the destruction of the scales. However, to hasten the removal of the fungus a weak solution of some fungicide—such as Bordeaux mixture—may be used in conjunction with the spray that is used for the treatment of the scales.

The Olive Tree Bug (*Froggattia olivina*).—This bug does not appear to have claimed the attention of growers in this State. According to Mr. Froggatt, it has a wide distribution in New South Wales, where its native host plant is the mock olive (*Notelea longifolia*), and since this tree is also native to this State, it is possible that the olive bug may also be present. Though instances are recorded in New South Wales of this bug having transferred its attention from the native olive to the cultivated olive, it has so far done little damage ; nevertheless, where sufficiently numerous, a great deal of damage can be done. The bug itself is very small (being about 1-16th of an inch in length), and dark brown in colour, and although it can hardly be regarded as one of the olive pests here, it may possibly become one, and growers should be on the look out for its appearance, especially in those districts where the native olive grows. Where it is once detected precautionary measures should be immediately adopted against its extension.

Tuberculosis (*Bacillus oleæ*).—It is found that this disease causes the formation of various sized tubercules or nodules on the main branches. They, of course, interfere with the healthy development of the shoots, and if allowed to remain will gradually multiply. The trouble takes place in the wood-fibres under the bark, consequently it is difficult to apply any remedy effectively. The affected parts should be cut out and burned. This disease is prevalent in the Mediterranean countries, but does not appear to have been found in this country.

The Olive Fly (*Dacus oleæ* ossi).—This is probably the most dreaded of all the olive pests in the groves adjoining the Mediterranean. For years it has worked enormous damage. Owing to its habits and method of attack it is one of the most difficult to cope with. Its life history and mode of attack appear to be very similar to that of the closely allied species, the Mediterranean Fruit Fly (*Ceratitis capitata*, Weid). The fly itself is about one-fifth of an inch in length, yellowish red in colour, with dark stripes on the abdomen. The eggs are of a golden hue. The pest is most prevalent about the time of the fruits ripening, and if the affected fruits do not fall by the time the larvæ have developed sufficiently to enter the pupating stage they fall to the ground and seek some harbour in which to pupate. The larvæ, which are hatched out in a few days, burrow through the fruit, breaking down its tissues and quickly rendering it unfit for use.

As before stated, the method and period of this fly's attack render it very difficult to carry out any effective method of combating it. Since the insect is concealed in the pulp of the fruit during those stages of its life history where its damaging work is carried out, it cannot be attacked by means of a spray, methods of suppression must be directed chiefly against the moth itself. The traps used for other fruit flies would probably be found of value for this one. They are made of shallow tins with a little kerosene in them, and hung in the trees. Experiments made with various chemicals would reveal something which would attract the flies and prove of value in minimizing the pest; spraying with sweetened poisoned solutions has been carried out in Italy with some degree of success.

The Olive Moth (*Oruga minadora*).—The caterpillar of this moth is responsible for some degree of damage in the older countries, but so far as the writer can ascertain it is not doing any damage in the plantations here. It attacks chiefly the branches at the butt, sometimes also the fruit. Its attack is noticeable by the formation of galls on the shoots. The fully-grown insect is greenish white in colour and the larvæ yellowish.

The Olive Twig Borer (*Polycaon confertus*).—This beetle is reddish brown in colour and about ⅜ inch in length. It makes its attack by boring into the twigs, usually close to the axile of the leaves. So far as can be ascertained, it is not present in this country, and in America, where it is found, it has as yet done so little damage that it has received very little attention.

Thrips.—During the flowering season of the olive countless millions of these tiny insects swarm over the trees. It is hard to estimate the extent of the damage that may be attributed to their presence, or to what extent they affect the setting of the fruit. It is doubtful whether they interfere to any great extent in the latter case, as heavy crops have been observed in seasons when the insects were excessively numerous. Several species of the family (*Thripidæ*) are native to Australia, but the imported ones are most commonly met with. Judging by the varying appearance and size, there usually appears to be more than one species present on the olive.

Treatment.—Owing to the number and variety of our spring blooming plants, Thrips have every opportunity of multiplying during the flowering season of the olive, so that it seems well nigh impossible to suppress them. The Cape Weed proves a great harbour for them, and, consequently, it should be got rid of among the trees. Fumigating with hydrocyanic acid gas will, no doubt, prove an effective remedy, if it can be economically applied. Mr. French recommends the use of " Benzole Emulsion," or white oil soap (1 pound to each gallon of water used, and applied at 130 degrees Fahr.).

Dry-Rot.—The Californian (Station) Report for 1895-96, 1896-97 (p. 235), gives the description of a disease which is not definitely named, but which causes a gradual rotting of the fruits in spots. It appears in that State to attack chiefly the Nevadillo olives. Reference is also made to a similar disease in Bulletin 62 of the Arizona Experiment Station. In this case it appears more commonly on the Columbella olives. A similar, or identical, trouble is occurring here in a mild form on two varieties of olives. It appears first, just when the fruit is ripening, by a slight indentation or contraction of the skin of the fruit, gradually as the fruit becomes riper the spots become more marked, and they become darker in colour, extending in diameter and depth, and reaching right to the stone. The affected parts subside greatly, and tissues become dry and brown, similar in some respects to the effects of Bitter Pit. The trouble usually occurs towards the apex of the fruit, and is more marked in the wet years than in the dry   According to Mr. McAlpine, it is one of the Micro-diplodia. Since it has confined itself to two varieties, and then appears only in a very mild form, it has not called for any special investigation.

(*To be continued.*)

BEE-KEEPING IN VICTORIA.

(Continued from page 415.)

F. R. Beuhne, Bee Expert.

VI.—WATER FOR BEES.

DRINKING TROUGHS FOR BEES.
Illustration of article appearing in July issue of *Journal,* page 413.

VII.—HOW TO MAKE A START.

How to make a start in beekeeping will depend upon whether the beginner is taking up bee-culture as a business, or as a side issue of some other occupation.   If it is intended to adopt it as the only calling, then the best way is to go as a working pupil with an up-to-date apiarist for a season or two.   Even if a premium has to be paid for the first year, it will be less costly than the experience gained by failure.   After the first season, a pupil will have learned enough to entitle him to some pay for the second year, or he may be competent enough to run a small apiary on shares with the owner.   By the end of the second year, sufficient confidence and experience will have been acquired to make an independent start.

When means or circumstances do not permit of taking a position as pupil in an established apiary, or when beekeeping is to be only a side issue, then it is best to start in quite a small way.   Begin with two or three hives, and as experience is gained by practice, and knowledge by reading, gradually increase the number of colonies.   A book of reference, such as A. I. Root's *A. B. C. of Bee-culture*, will greatly assist in mastering the principles of beekeeping, and will supply solutions to nearly all the problems which usually present themselves to the novice.   Any opportunity to visit an apiary, or to personally consult an apiarist of some standing, should be made good use of whenever it occurs.

FIG. 1.

Everybody handling bees requires two things to start with, namely, a bee-veil, and a smoker. A veil will cost about 1s. 6d., a smoker 4s. to 7s., according to size, and whether tin or brass. There are two kinds—one straight, the other with a bent nozzle. I strongly recommend the latter (Fig. 1), because any kind of fuel may be used in it without risk of glowing embers dropping from it when directing smoke downwards. Dry decayed wood or bark is better smoker fuel than bagging, rags, or fresh wood, the former giving a cooler smoke and less tar in the smoker.

There are several ways of making a start in a small way:—(1) Full colonies; (2) Swarms; (3) Box-hives; (4) Nuclei. With which of these to start will depend upon the amount of money it is proposed to expend at once, and whether bees are obtainable in one form or another.

1.—*Full Colonies of Bees.*

Hives with finished combs and brood, and sufficient bees to cover all the combs, may be obtained from supply dealers advertising in the Melbourne weekly papers, at prices ranging from 30s. per stock for Black or Hybrid bees, to 45s. for Italians, with tested Queen. Bees in frame-hives can often be purchased direct from owners; but for a beginner this involves some risk of getting disease or hives with poor combs to start with. It is usually the neglected hives which are for sale.

2.—*Swarms.*

Where starting with natural swarms, and new hives, all danger of introducing disease is avoided. Swarms are obtainable from the end of September to the end of December, at 10s. to 15s. each, according to weight, 2s. 6d. per lb. being the price usually charged by dealers, or they may be advertised for and bought direct from beekeepers having a surplus. With swarms there is little danger of disease being conveyed, even though the bees come from a diseased hive. When obtained from a distance the boxes in which they are sent should be about the size of a kerosene case, with wire screen covering an opening of one-third of the surface on two opposite sides. The hives and frames should be bought beforehand, and be ready. When the swarms arrive they should be placed in a cool and well-aired spot till towards evening, when a cloth or bag is spread out in front of the hive entrance upon which the swarm is dumped out of the transit box. As a rule the bees will quickly run into the hive; if they cluster outside without entering some should be brushed off with a large feather, and a little smoke used on all of them to start them running in. If swarms are emptied out of transit boxes during the warm hours of the day or left hanging outside the hive overnight they will sometimes rise and cluster in some inconvenient place, or may even abscond. If several days of inclement weather follow the hiving of the swarms, the bees should be feed with sugar syrup made by dissolving sugar in an equal weight of

boiling water.   This is given inside the hive in a wooden feeder supplied
by dealers.

FIG. 2.

Single story hives, made up and painted, containing eight wired frames
supplied with strips of comb foundation cost 10s. each, or if bought in

the flat and nailed together and painted at home 8s. each.   The hives
when placed in position ready to receive the bees should stand perfectly
level crossways to the frames, otherwise the combs may have the wires
on the outside instead of in the centre, because comb is always built perfectly perpendicular by the bees.   The hives should, if possible, be sheltered from the south, with entrances facing east, north, or west.   When
the combs are nearly down to the bottom bars of the frames (Fig. 2) a
super or upper story must be put on.   It may be of the same size as the
lower one or of half depth with shallow frames.   Unless full sheets of
foundation are used instead of starters in the frames of an upper story
a queen-excluding honey board (Fig. 3) should be inserted between the
two boxes to prevent the queen depositing eggs in drone comb usually built
from starters in the super.   To start the bees building comb above, it
will be necessary to hang a comb or two from the lower into the upper
story taking care to leave the queen below and to fill the space below with
a frame or two from above.

3. *Box-hives.*

Good colonies in box-hives or unworkable frame hives may sometimes
be bought cheaply, and if free from disease the bees may be drummed up
into a frame hive, placed, with-
out its bottom board, on top of
the inverted box-hive.   If the
combs containing worker brood
are fairly straight they may be
cut out and fitted into frames
in which they are held in position by string tied over the outside of the frame.   When these
combs have been fastened to
the frames by the bees the
string may be removed, and
when the colony is strong
enough the combs may be hung

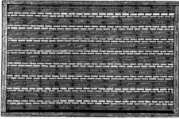

FIG. 3.

in the super over a queen excluder till all brood is hatched, when they
can be taken away and melted up for wax.

If a box-hive is strong and it is early in the season the most convenient
way of transferring the bees to a frame hive is to let them swarm, hive
the swarm in a frame-hive on the spot where the box-hive stood, and remove the latter some distance if it is desired to make two colonies; if not,
leave it near the new hive but facing in a different direction.   Just three
weeks later all the worker brood in the box-hive will have hatched out,
and a new queen will be laying.   The bees may now be drummed out
into another frame-hive or into the hive containing the swarm, as the case
may be.   The old box containing only combs without brood should be
taken indoors and secured against bees, and as soon as convenient the
combs boiled down for wax.   If there is any suspicion that a box-hive
colony is diseased, it is best to drum it off at once, and destroy the box
and old combs by burning.   The bees themselves will be clean in their new
hive provided they do not get access to any honey or comb from the old
box after being driven off.

4. *Nuclei.*

Beekeeping may also be commenced with nuclei colonies.   A nucleus
is a small colony of bees with a queen and two or three frames of comb

with brood, and some stores. When received it is transferred to a hive and frames with starters or full sheets of foundations added to fill the box. Three-frame nuclei may be obtained of Italian bees at 15s. to 25s., according to the kind of queen chosen with them, and black or hybrid bees at 10s. to 20s., or either may be bought in full-sized hives with the additional frames in position for 5s. each extra. Under favorable conditions, if obtained early enough in the season, nuclei will rapidly build up into full colonies and have the advantage that the beginner is not troubled with hiving, and possibly losing swarms during the first season.

The first cost of hives, frames, and comb-foundation appears high, and many beginners think that money can be saved by making their own hives and frames. It will be found, however, that when timber of the proper quality is purchased in small quantities the cost per hive is very little less than that of one bought already prepared. In any case, it is advisable to purchase at least one hive and frames so as to have a pattern to work by. Californian red wood is decidedly the best timber for hives, it is free from knots, shrinks very little, does not warp, and is never eaten by white ants, which in some localities are very destructive to hives.

If the first cost has to be cut down to a minimum, temporary hives may be made out of kerosene or petrol cases. The frames which should be of the self-spacing kind (Hoffman) had better be bought, as they require to be made very accurately, so that later on they can be transferred to permanent hives. To construct a frame hive out of a kerosene case, one of the broad sides is taken off, while the opposite one serves as a floor for the hive. The original lid of the case is nailed on as a side, the former bottom of the case forming the other. At the bottom at one end an opening 6 in. by ⅜ in. is cut out as an entrance for the bees, and a strip of wood ⅜ in. thick (such as the thin boards of the case), is nailed to the inside of the ends of the case ⅜ in. from the upper edge. This is to suspend the frames from. A roof for this hive may be made out of the broad side taken off the case. It should, however, be covered with some waterproof material and shaded to prevent excessive heat melting the combs in the hives. Hoffman, or other full-depth frames should always be wired, as without wires new combs often break out in handling the frames, or fall down in hot weather. When two sets of half-depth or shallow frames are used wiring may be dispensed with.

If in making two shallow bodies out of a kerosene case, ¾ in. is cut off the ends of the case crossways before sawing it in two lengthways the resulting half-depth bodies will exactly fit on an eight-frame hive, on which it may be used as a super when a proper hive is adopted. A difficulty usually experienced by beginners is that, not wishing to purchase a honey extractor right away, they attempt to raise comb-honey in 1 lb. sections. It is well known amongst apiarists that the profitable production of section honey requires considerable skill and a good honey locality. In the case of beginners both these factors are usually absent, with the result that the bees sooner than start work in the sections will repeatedly swarm, and the season will be over before the swarms have become strong enough to store any surplus of honey, whereas if frames had been used in the super instead of sections swarming would have been prevented to a great extent, and a fair amount of honey secured. With shallow unwired frames the honey may be obtained by cutting out the comb, leaving about ½ in. on the top bar to act as a guide for a new comb. The dimensions of shallow frames are:—Top bar, 19 in. long, 1 in. wide, ⅜ in. thick; bottom bar, 17⅝ in. long, 1 in. wide, ⅜ in. thick; side bars, 3¾ in. long, 1⅜ in. wide, ⅜ in. thick, nailed together as shown in Fig. 4.

Locality.

It must be understood that although bees may be kept almost anywhere, even near cities, and when properly managed some return may be secured, no one should take up beekeeping for profit or as a sole means of living unless prepared to go into the country as soon as the elementary knowledge and some experience in handling bees have been acquired.   As wheat-growing is profitable only where fair-sized areas of easily tilled land are available, so beekeeping requires a wide range of honey-producing flora

FIG. 4.

to make it a paying occupation.   To supplement the insufficient honey resources of a locality by growing flowers specially for bees is impracticable.   The land available for this purpose in the neighbourhood of cities and towns is too limited in area, and too valuable.   While in remoter localities where large areas of bee-pasture might be planted, the expense would be out of proportion to the return secured even if neighbours' bees and wild bees could be prevented from trespassing.   Australia has such a splendid honey-producing flora, if beekeepers will only go to it, there is no need whatever to raise plants specially for honey.   In Victoria only a fraction of the nectar produced annually by our native flora is at present being gathered by bees.

(To be continued.)

SMALL RURAL INDUSTRIES.

C.—ROSE CULTIVATION.

By Joseph Knight.

Possibly there is no plant grown which is more popular than the rose, nor any perfume produced which finds more favour than the Oil of Rose, or, as it is generally known, " Attar of Roses."

Its cultivation is simple. If grown under healthy conditions, the plant adapts itself to almost any soil or climate, and there is but little trouble with insect and fungoid pests.

ROSA CENTIFOLIA (PROVENCE ROSE).

The work of gathering the flowers lasts but a few weeks — generally from four to five — after which the plant may be left to itself. All that is necessary is to prune in the autumn, and cultivate the soil sufficiently to keep weeds in check. It takes about 4 tons of blooms to make 1 lb. of oil, and the present wholesale price of the oil in Melbourne is £3 per oz., or £48 per lb. It is well, therefore to look whether regular labour can be obtained to gather the blooms every second day, as this is necessary to ensure success. The work is light, and where the united efforts of a family may be utilized, rose cultivation has much to recommend it. This brief paper is written as a guide to those who wish to give rose-growing for essential oil production a trial.

Varieties Suitable.

In dealing with this question, only those which have been tested in this State, and found to be satisfactory, will be considered.

The late Mr. F. Mellon, who had experience of essential oil production in the South of France, was employed many years ago by the Department to establish a Scent Farm, and provide plants. He introduced the variety known as the " Provence Rose," which is much cultivated in the large rose-producing district of Grasse, in the South of France.

Mr. Mellon, in giving his evidence before the Royal Commission on Vegetable Products, in answer to the question of the suitability of Victorian soil and climate, stated that it was much better than that of the South of France. He stated that in the town of Grasse, which is said to be the centre of the world's floriculture, there were 52 distilleries, some of them employing 500 people at a time. With this experience before him, Mr. Mellon was careful to introduce the best rose for his purpose when stocking the first scent farm established in this State. He discarded all others but the one referred to, this he named " Rose de Grasse," which is identical with " Rosa centifolia," or " Provence Rose."

On Mr. Mellon's departure, the writer took charge of this Farm, and can say that this variety supplies all requirements, as it is hardy and easily cultivated. and, with proper attention in pruning, gives a large amount of blooms. .

Another variety of rose will be dealt with separately later on.

SOIL.

Many rose-growers assert that special soils with clay. or a "clay bottom," are necessary. Possibly this may be the case with some varieties, but with the " Provence Rose " it is not necessary. A warm, dry situation, whether sand, loam, or clay, answers the purpose quite well. The only situation which I have found unsuitable is one with a wet bottom.

CLIMATE.

Most parts of Victoria are suitable for rose cultivation, Those that do not experience excessive rain, but sufficient to allow the plant to mature its blooms, give the best results in "oil." Rain on the blooms has a detrimental effect.

At the Dunolly Flower Farm, North-western District, the crop could be harvested without danger of rain ; while at Leongatha, Southern District, the reverse was the case, considerable rain falling during the four or five weeks the plants were in bloom ; but under these conditions the plants were more vigorous, and gave a much greater yield of blooms.

As to the yield of oil, I had no opportunity of judging, as the farm was closed down before a proper experiment with distillation was made. It is recognised that the more sunshine the greater is the amount of oil, providing there is sufficient moisture for the proper development of the plant.

Plants were distributed to almost every part of Victoria, and so far as growth is concerned, I know of no place where there has been a failure. The " Provence Rose " can be recommended to any part of this State.

PLANTS.

Plants may be obtained from shoots, or what is known as " suckers." The latter may be obtained from any plantation which has been established for three or four years. when the plant is being thinned out. When growing from cuttings, pieces 6 or 7 inches long are planted out in a well-prepared nursery bed in autumn, and left until well rooted ; they may be put out in late spring, or carried over until the following autumn. When well rooted suckers can be obtained, they will be better, as they can be planted out in their permanent place at once. The plants should be well cut back when being planted out, and it is advisable to prune back straggling or wounded roots. The stem and side shoots should be trimmed first of all, both above or below the surface, with the exception of two or three on the top. These should not be more than 1 foot to 15 inches above the surface, as it is desirable to have a good strong stem to build the plant on, so that it can fill the space allotted to it. In selecting plants, it is well to take only from those that are of healthy growth.

CULTIVATION.

The soil for rose culture should be cultivated to some depth. If ploughed, it should be subsoiled, as in most cases it is better to keep the surface soil on the top, and loosen the subsoil to a depth of at least 10 or 12 inches. The soil should be well pulverized before planting, and, where convenient, it would be better to lie fallow for a few months before putting plants out. Where drainage is necessary, it should be attended to as early as possible, as a " wet bed " is most objectionable. All that is necessary in the after treatment is surface cultivation by light ploughing— 3 or 4 inches deep—and extermination of weeds.

The plants of the " Provence Rose " should be set out in rows about 4 to 5 feet apart, and the space in the rows should be about 3 to 4 feet. Where it is intended to employ horse labour, the wider distance between the rows should be selected, or even more, say 6 feet. The bush develops considerably under favorable conditions; if planted too close, it would be most difficult both to gather the flowers and cultivate the land.

Care should be taken not to plant too deep, for if it is planted too deep the crop becomes stunted and unhealthy. This is a mistake commonly made by those having no experience of rose culture. The roots should be near the surface, well spread out, and running down at an angle of about 45 degrees, and the fine surface soil pressed down on them tightly. This should give the plant a good start, and go a long way to the successful establishment of a plantation of this kind.

PRUNING.

Rose pruning generally is a much debated point, and methods differ; but with oil extraction as the object, the form of bloom or quality as a rose is of no consequence. What is required is "quantity." The bush should be cut back so as to produce an abundance of young growth on which the blooms can develop. Care must be taken to cut out the thinner growth, and admit light and air through the plant, and at the same time strengthen the leading shoots so as to keep it in proper form. The season in which this should be carried out is important, as late pruning does not give time for strong shoots to develop before the flowering season is due. The usual time for rose pruning about the city is July and August, but June, or early in July, is to be preferred when pruning for the purposes of oil distillation. The work should be done thoroughly, so as to give free scope to work the land.

GATHERING OF BLOOMS.

The blooms must be gathered every second day, and the best time for this operation is early in the morning before the sun gets at its height; the earlier the better. The blooms should be taken off before they are fully expanded, but not before they are opened sufficiently to show the petals. There is less risk of bruising or loosening them by shaking if it is done at this time. Care in this respect is necessary if the best results are to be obtained.

The blooms should be cut as near to the flower as possible, as any matter beyond the petals reduces the quality of the oil, and is useless. When gathered. blooms should be taken direct to the still-room and not exposed to the sun's rays, or rain, or moisture of any kind.

Distilling.

Rose distillation is similar to that of other essential oil-producing plants, but somewhat more delicate, and extreme care must be taken not to force the "boiling." This is, perhaps, difficult where direct heat is applied, but with superheated steam it is easily regulated, and where it can be done, this method is the best way of raising the temperature.

In Bulgaria, small stills are scattered all over the flower-growing districts, but it is said that nothing like as good results are obtained as in the South of France, where the work of distillation is carried out in large and well-equipped establishments, which sometimes handle 150 tons of roses a day. Nevertheless, with proper care in applying the heat, and attention to little details, good results can be obtained with the ordinary still and direct heat.

In distillation, two methods are adopted. The oil is contained on the surface of the petals. Either the petals are stripped from the calyx and distilled separately, or the whole flowers are employed. The former method gives a superior product, but it is doubtful whether the extra labour is repaid.

The time during which the boiling should continue depends on the size of the still. In a 20-gallon still, the bulk of the oil, and the best, would be passed over within one hour from the time of boiling, but it should be carried on for another hour at least. The still which has been illustrated and described on page 363 of this journal, is suitable for treating roses, and when the first lot of water has passed over into the "Florentine," the receptacle should be removed, and another placed in position to secure the balance. The two lots should be kept separate. The second lot is usually returned to the still with the next lot of flowers.

In rose distillation, delay must be avoided as much as possible; the flowers should be treated within 24 hours from the time of gathering, and care should be taken not to submit the roses to more rough treatment than is absolutely necessary. The place of treatment should be free from offensive or other odours. A good supply of cold water is necessary to supply the cooler. and where a running stream is not available it must be supplied from a well or tank by pumping; this water may be used over and over again.

Many small growers along the Mediterranean coast make rose water without the second distillation or extracting the oil in any way. As there is no licence-fee demanded for holding a still in the Commonwealth, but a permit only, with a guarantee against any imposition or infraction of the Excise laws, it may be worth while for some of our young ladies to try this as a pastime, as there is a ready sale for Rose Water if properly prepared. It is used largely for many purposes.

Enfleurage and Maceration.

Roses grown in France and elsewhere are also utilized for perfume extraction by the processes known as "Enfleurage and Maceration." In the latter case pure olive oil is generally used The oil is placed in a large vat, and the rose petals are submerged in it; they are stirred up occasionally, and after about 24 hours drawn out, and the oil pressed from the spent petals, and the same process is repeated with fresh petals until the oil is sufficiently impregnated with the scent of the flower, when it is stored, and the essence extracted by some highly rectified spirit solvent.

The "Enfleurage System" is very popular in France, and a very considerable amount of "Pomade" is made and used in this form.

"Red Rose."
Rosa Gallica.

This rose is cultivated in England and elsewhere for its flowers, which are gathered in the bud. The lower portion of the calyx is cut off, and it

is dried in this form. Mr. Slater states that it finds a ready sale at 3s. 6d. per lb. The wholesale chemist and druggist purchases freely, and there should be a good opening by way of export.

It is recommended in the *British Pharmacopœia*, but, like many other articles, to have its proper standing, plants must be cultivated in Great Britain. This rose has but little perfume in its fresh state, but develops a beautiful fragrant odour when dried.

The drying is extremely simple and inexpensive. The bud when gathered and trimmed should be spread out so that the air can pass through

ROSA GALLICA (RED ROSE).

the leaves. The most suitable method is to make a few trays, about 3 feet long by 2 feet wide, with strong hessian for a bottom. The buds are spread evenly over this, and a temporary stand is made after the style of a "three-sided clothes-horse"; then these trays can be laid across the two side bars, and the whole built up to whatever height is desired, and if just sufficient room is left between each tray for the air to pass through, the drying can be completed without further trouble. This may be carried on in the open air or within doors; if out of doors, there should be some sort of cover to protect from rain or dews. The quicker the drying is done the better will be the result; the blooms should not be exposed to the direct rays of the sun.

Mr. Slater speaks highly of this industry, having supplied the Melbourne trade with this product many years ago. I am not aware that further steps have been taken to continue the supply.

GENERAL NOTES.

SUGAR BEET—

The sugar beet production of the United States has become one of the great farm factors, and promises to utilize many thousands of acres of land, especially in the irrigated States. There are now 61 factories making sugar from beets. They have an annual output of about 510,000 tons of granulated sugar, and the area planted to beets aggregates almost 400,000 acres. —*Californian Cultivator.*

FEEDING FOR BUTTER FAT—

It used to be held that the feeding had a considerable influence upon the richness of milk, but more accurate investigations go to show that it has very little to do with it. The subject is discussed by Dr. Crowther, of Leeds University, in the *Journal of the Board of Agriculture* (London). He finds that, provided the ration is sufficient to maintain the milk yield and general " condition " of the animal, the composition of the milk can, in general, be but little affected by changes in the nature of the foods. Even in the case of underfeeding, the composition of the milk is, as a rule, but little affected until the condition of the animal has been very seriously reduced. The common view that turnips or brewer's grains give watery milk has received but litle support from experimental investigations, although the long-continued use of these foods will probably lead ultimately to a general weakening of the organs of the body, and result in poorer milk. Ability to yield rich milk is born into the cow, and if more butter fat is to be got from any cow, it can only be done by feeding to get a greater yield of milk of the same quality.

TOP DRESSING PASTURES—

For some years past, the manuring of second-class pastures has found much favour in Great Britain, the application usually consisting of Thomas phosphate, or of a mixture of ordinary superphosphate and lime. Reference has been made to the matter in these notes. In the *Massachusetts Station Report*, 1910, the result of top-dressing cow pastures in America is described. The manuring consisted of 500 lbs. Thomas phosphate and 300 lbs. low-grade sulphate of potash per acre. The author notes that the preference of the cows for the forage of the treated plots resulted in their being more closely grazed late into the Autumn than was favorable to their best development. Nevertheless, a thick mat of clover appeared the following spring in place of a dull, lifeless, moss-infested turf, thickly starred with " bluets " (*Houstonia cærulea*). In other pasture tests on mowing land at the Station, the yield of grass was rather more than doubled by the use of Thomas phosphate and potash. The proportion of clover was increased. Altogether, the experiments suggest that trial applications of Thomas phosphate, or of superphosphate and lime, would be desirable for many farmers in this State owning second-class land. Unless on soils of a very light sandy nature, the potash can probably be omitted. Winter is the best time to apply these manures, and stock should be kept off until the herbage has been washed by rain.

BENEFITS OF BARE FALLOW—

It is a deplorable fact that proportionately less land was fallowed last year in the Southern district than there was in 1909 and 1910. The reason for this is that the phenomenal seasons of 1909 and 1910 have made farmers careless in their methods. Fair crops were obtained in these two years on unfallowed land, but surely practical men must know that such seasons are abnormal and not likely to recur often. The season just concluded has been a bitter lesson to those who put their faith in non-fallowed land. Thousands of acres have yielded less than 6 bushels per acre, not sufficient to cover cost of putting in and taking off the crops. Side by side in every district in the south are to be met instances where the crop on non-fallowed land is hardly worth stripping, whereas the yield on adjoining fallowed land is 20 bushels or more per acre. . . . Let every wheat farmer make a firm resolution, no matter what happens, to fallow at least two-thirds of the area he is prepared to put under crop.— *Agric. Gazette,* New South Wales.

HIGH-GRADE BUTTER—

To produce high-grade butter the cream must be free from faults and taints, and an extension of the system whereby cream is graded and paid for according to quality at the butter factory appears to be most desirable. A system of uniform prices for butter fat removes the incentive to care and cleanliness on the farm, and helps towards a general lowering down rather than towards improvement in the condition of cream deliveries. This important matter is discussed by Mr. E. Graham in the *Queensland Agricultural Journal* for April, and the following extracts indicate the line of argument :—" Most factories receiving at least three distinct qualities of cream from their patrons pay a uniform price for the resultant butters. This method of making average payments to cream suppliers is not equitable, and positively destroys the chief incentive to produce high-quality cream. It is not surprising to find producers negligent in the production and handling of milk-products while the above custom of payments prevails. Milk or cream should be graded and paid for by the factories in strict accordance with its quality. The redemption of quality requires a united effort. At the height of the season, fully 80 per cent. of the butter manufactured in Queensland is sold on the over-sea markets. It is particularly under the stress of export conditions that the butters made from creams of inferior quality behave unsatisfactorily, and unduly deteriorate in quality. The local consumption of low-grade butter is very limited, and it naturally follows that almost all the butter of this character is forced into the export list. Although such butters have a market value, they are not of sufficient merit to build up any good reputation for the State."

Many Victorian soils contain about 1 ton each of nitrogen, phosphoric acid, and potash per acre in the top 9 inches of soil, but by far the greater bulk is in a form which the crop cannot utilize.

The nitrogen in humus must be changed into ammonia and nitrates before it is available to crops. Fresh vegetable residues undergo this change more readily than old humus matters. Lime hastens the change.

DESTRUCTIVE SCALE INSECTS.

Mealy Bugs (Dactylopius) Destroyed by Lacewings (Chrysopa).

By C. French, junior, Acting Government Entomologist.

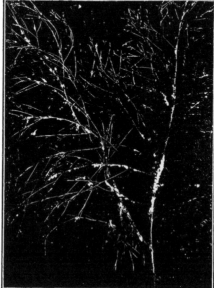

Some time, my attention was drawn to some fine native cherry trees (*Exocarpos eupressiformis*), which were infested with white mealy-looking insects. On examination I found the trunks, stems, and branches to be simply covered with mealy-bugs. The trunks were almost perfectly white, and in the distance looked as if a snowstorm had covered them. (See illustrations 1 and 3.) It was one of the worst infestations of mealy bug I have seen. The leaves of the trees were dying owing to the insects sucking out the sap.

Wishing to send a few perfect specimens of the scales to a specialist for naming,

1. MEALY BUGS ON BRANCHES AND LEAVES OF NATIVE CHERRY TREE.

I again visited the locality a few weeks later, and was surprised to find that the larvæ of the lacewings had been at work, and partly destroyed every scale; in fact, I was unable to obtain a single perfect insect.

Cocoons of the lacewings (illustration 2) were in dozens over the tree, showing that the larvæ had pupated after finishing their useful work. It is the larvæ, which have strong jaws, that destroy such large numbers of aphids and scale insects. The fully-grown lacewings have beautiful greenish veined, gauzy wings, and golden coloured eyes. At times, lacewings are exceedingly plentiful.

1.   **2.**

2. LACEWINGS (AFTER FROGGATT).
1. Full grown 2. Larva. (Magnified).

and do a great amount of good in keeping insect pests in check. They should therefore be protected.

As mealy bugs are very destructive to our valuable wattles, a sharp look-out should be kept for them, and, if seen, it would be advisable to spray with weak kerosene emulsion, benzole emulsion, or red oil.

3. MEALY BUGS ON TRUNK AND STEMS OF NATIVE CHERRY TREE.

Specimens of the insects mentioned in this short article can be seen at the Entomological and Ornithological Museum belonging to the Agricultural Department.

ARSENATE OF LEAD.

For the purpose of comparison and guidance to all interested in this spray, an examination has been made of the different brands obtainable on the market at the present time. This list, as can be seen, is of a fairly comprehensive character, as it contains not only the ordinary moist samples, but also some of the dry powder, which would appear to be making some headway—there being three different brands of that grade. The ordinary samples are evidently made, some by using Acetate of Lead and others by using Nitrate of Lead, as the lead base.

A pure dry sample of Arsenate of Lead made by the use of these ingredients, by calculation, would give the following percentages :—

	Arsenic Acid.	Oxide of Lead.
Arsenate of Soda + Acetate of Lead	30·07 per cent.	69·93 per cent.
Arsenate of Soda + Nitrate of Lead	34·94 ,,	65·60 ,,

ANALYSIS OF LEAD ARSENATE.

Original Sample.

Brand.	Agent.	Mois-ture.	Arsenic as Arsenic Acid.	Oxide of Lead.	Water-Soluble Portion.		
					Arsenic Acid.	Oxide of Lead.	Total Water Soluble.
Merks ..	Blackham & Co., King-street	·20	20·37	75·08	·07	Nil	4·49
Electro	Vic. Orchardists' Co-op. As-sociation	·44	31·34	63·49	·09	·04	2·39
Our Jack ..	J. W. Moss & Co., William-street	·30	28·95	68·19	·48	Nil	2·54
Paragon ..	J. G. Mumford, Flinders-lane	64·39	16·38	21·16	5·12	..	10·70
Our Jack ..	J. W. Moss & Co., William-street	41·44	18·35	39·62	·43	..	·88
Vocal ..	Vic. Orchardists Co-op Association	41·84	19·23	38·72	·17	..	·23
Blue Bell ..	F. W. Prell, Queen-street ..	45·34	17·60	35·34	·40	..	·98
Cobra ..	Chandler & Co., Brunswick-street, Fitzroy	47·04	15·00	37·10	·31	..	·48
Hemingways	F. H. Brunning, Elizabeth-street	51·66	16·26	31·44	·18	..	·27
Carlton ..	F. R. Mellor, Elizabeth-street	37·77	17·18	43·12	·54	·09	1·59
Magpie ..	F. R. Mellor, Elizabeth-street	39·68	19·08	38·48	·52	Nil	1·99
Elephant ..	A. Ferguson & Co., Collins-street	44·37	15·90	37·75	·42	..	1·53
Swift ..	Rocke, Tompsitt & Co., Flin-ders-street	43·29	15·49	39·74	·16	..	1·64
E. De Haens	Heyne, Keislin & Co., St. James-street	53·94	13·11	31·78	·18	..	·80

On Dry Basis.

Brand.	Agent.	Arsenic as Arsenic Acid.	Oxide of Lead.	Water-Soluble Portion.		
				Arsenic Acid.	Oxide of Lead.	Total Water Soluble.
Merks ..	Blackham & Co., King-street ..	20·41	75·23	·07	Nil	4·50
Electro ..	Vic. Orchardists' Co-op. Association ..	31·48	63·77	·09	·04	2·40
Our Jack ..	J. W. Moss & Co., William-street ..	29·04	68·40	·48	Nil	2·55
Paragon ..	J. G. Mumford, Flinders-lane ..	46·00	59·42	14·38	..	30·05
Our Jack ..	J. W. Moss & Co., William-street ..	31·34	67·66	·73	..	1·55
Vocal ..	Vic. Orchardists' Co-op. Association ..	33·06	66·57	·29	..	·55
Blue Bell ..	F. W. Prell, Queen-street ..	32·20	64·66	·73	..	1·80
Cobra ..	Chandler & Co., Brunswick-street, Fitz-roy	28·32	70·06	·58	..	·90
Hemingways	F. H. Brunning, Elizabeth-street ..	33·64	65·03	·38	..	·55
Carlton ..	F. R. Mellor, Elizabeth-street ..	29·60	69·29	·86	·14	2·55
Magpie ..	F. R. Mellor, Elizabeth-street ..	31·63	63·80	·86	Nil	3·30
Elephant ..	A. Ferguson & Co., Collins-street ..	28·58	67·86	·75	..	2·75
Swifts ..	Rocke, Tompsitt & Co., Flinders-street	27·31	70·08	·29	..	2·90
E. De Haens	Heyne, Keislin & Co., St. James-street	28·46	69·02	·39	..	1·25

From the chemical composition, as determined by analysis, all the brands appear to be of good quality, with one exception, the " Paragon." It contains an excessive amount of water-soluble arsenic, which would be, no doubt, harmful in its effect on the plant, while the others all contain a small percentage of water-soluble arsenic. Any brand may be considered safe to use so long as the percentage of soluble arsenic does not exceed 1 per cent. The matter of choice can be left to the individual fancy as far as the quality of the different brands is concerned. The difference in the arsenic acid content between the respective brands is only one of many points connected with the efficiency of the spray, and one should not judge any arsenate by its arsenic content, but rather by its proved effectiveness, which can only be ascertained by practical experience.

P. RANKIN SCOTT,
Chemist for Agriculture.

13th July, 1912.

BASIS WINES.

The Hon. the Minister for Agriculture has received from the Agent-General a copy of the new regulations which were foreshadowed in the letter we reproduced in our May issue (p. 322).

It will be noted with satisfaction that these provide protection against fraudulent practices, which were previously only too easy.

The full text of the regulations is as follows:—

BRITISH WINES.

The Commissioners of Customs and Excise, in pursuance of the powers vested in them by Section 10 of the *Finance Act* 1911, hereby prescribe the following Regulations which are to be observed on and after the first day of April, 1912 :—

1. A manufacturer for sale of British wines or sweets or made wines (hereinafter referred to as British wine) must not—
    (a) mix any British wine with any foreign wine except in the course of manufacture ; or
    (b) in course of manufacture mix with any British wine any foreign wine in any quantity exceeding the proportion of 15 gallons of foreign wine to 100 gallons of British wine ; or
    (c) mix any spirits with any British wine except for the sole purpose of fortifying the wine.

2. Every manufacturer for sale of British wine must, on sending out any British wine, enter in the entry book obtained by him from the Officer of Customs and Excise the following particulars, that is to say :—
    (a) The name and address of the person to whom wine is sent out ; and
    (b) the quantity and description of the wine sent out ; and
    (c) the date when the wine is sent out.

The entries must be made before the expiration of the day on which the wine is sent out, and are additional to the entries required to be made in the book. pursuant to the regulations made on the 8th day of August, 1906, under sub-section (2) of section 7 of the *Revenue Act* 1906.

3. A dealer in or retailer of foreign wine or British wine must not—
    (a) mix for sale any foreign wine with any British wine ; or
    (b) sell or expose for sale any British wine which contains foreign wine in any quantity exceeding the proportion of 15 gallons of foreign wine to 100 gallons of British wine ; or
    (c) sell or expose for sale any British wine to which spirits have been added except for the sole purpose of fortifying the wine.

4. A rectifier or compounder of spirits must not mix any British wine with any spirits, either for the manufacture of British compounds or for any other purpose.

5. A dealer in or retailer of spirits must not mix any British wine with any spirits except for the sole purpose of colouring or fining the spirits.

6. British wine manufactured in conformity with these Regulations must not, by reason of the admixture therewith of foreign wine, be sent out or sold or exposed for sale, otherwise than under the designation of a British wine.

Dated this 8th day of March, 1912.

Signed by order of the Commissioners of Customs and Excise.

J. P. BYRNE, Secretary.

Custom House, London.

Sec. $\frac{7278}{1911}$.

Stable manure when stored in heaps may soon lose about one-half of its nitrogen. This loss is greatly diminished by compacting and wetting the heap, and covering it with a thin layer of earth until it can be applied to the land.

THE ETIOLOGY OF CONTAGIOUS DISEASES.

W. A. N. Robertson, B.V.Sc.

(Paper read before the Farmers' Convention at Warrnambool, July, 1912, illustrated with lantern slides.)

There is, unfortunately, a feeling amongst a large number of the farmers of this State that, though there may be something in germs, those Government officers, whose duties are somewhat inspectorial, are germ-mad, and delight in imposing upon the farmers a lot of restrictions which, at first sight, appear unnecessary, and are a source of annoyance. This, in many cases, leads to a desire on the part of those who are unfortunate enough to be visited by an outbreak of some contagious disease to keep it as quiet as possible.

It is hardly necessary to point out the folly of such an attitude, either from the legal point—for it is a punishable offence—or from the moral aspect, and harm likely to follow in a district where certain restrictions are not imposed. The subject of contagious diseases dealt with in a general way would, therefore, not be out of place. Apart from the aspect of controlling diseases existent in Australia is another, and, in many ways, more important one, viz., the prevention of the introduction of disease

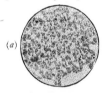

FIG. 1.   (*a*) STAPHYLOCOCCUS.   (*b*) STREPTOCOCCUS.

from other parts of the globe. What the result would be if the scourges of India and Africa were introduced to this land it is hard to picture; for the introduction of a disease into a new land is always found a much more severe affliction than in the land from which it came; as exampled by the terrible effect of *Pleuro-pneumonia-contagiosa* when it first appeared in Australia.

Later the causes of some of these diseases may, therefore, be lightly touched upon. That they can only lightly be dealt with will be understood when it is realized that each and every disease could by itself be made the subject for a lecture, and some of them, indeed, the subject for a series.

That some considerable degree of confusion exists in the minds of many as to a realization of the actual cause of disease must be admitted.

Organisms or germs are bodies capable of life and death, and of producing during their cycle poisons in the same way as our own bodies do, and it is the poisons which are produced which are mainly the cause of the symptoms we recognise in disease. They exist in many forms, all of which are classified, and receive names indicating their forms, &c. The most common forms are small round cellular bodies to which the name of "Coccus" is applied. They may be grouped in different manners, as, for example, in clusters or in chains (Fig. 1), singly, in pairs, fours, and so on, each form being suitably named with a name out of all proportion to the size of the germ ; for it must be clearly understood that these organisms are very minute.

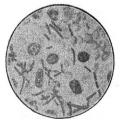

FIG. 2. BACILLUS ANTHRACIS
IN SPLEEN.

Those responsible for the formation of the pus or " matter " found in an abscess vary in size from 1/51,000th to 1/12,000th of an inch in length ; that is to say, 12,000 to 51,000 of them placed side by side would be required to measure 1 inch. They may also exist in the form of small rods, termed " Bacilli," which vary in size so that from 3,000 to 256,000 end to end would measure 1 inch. One of the largest—the " Anthrax Bacilli " (Fig. 2) is from 1/3,000th to 1/20,000th of an inch. This organism is one of a type which has two stages of life: First, the bacilli, the actual cause of the sudden deaths which occur ; the other stage, the spore which represents the resting stage, and, as such, is very difficult to eradicate from certain districts because of its long life and the resistance of the spore to the influence of destructive agencies.

It is recorded that these spores are capable of living in the soil for many years. Cold has no effect upon them, for they can live through freezing at minus 110 degrees Cent., and require boiling for some hours to destroy them all. Another of these spore-bearing organisms is seen in the bacillus of tetanus (Fig. 3), which varies in length from 1/8,550.h to 1/5,100th of an inch, and 1/12,600th of an inch broad. This bacillus is also an organism which it is extremely difficult to deal with, owing to the fact that the spores which occupy one end of the bacillus and give it the appearance of a minute drum-stick, are capable of prolonged life outside the animal body

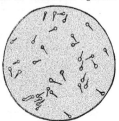

FIG. 3. BACILLUS OF
TETANUS WITH SPORES.

living in the soil, particularly in dirty, undrained stables. On entering the animal system once more, they are capable of producing the original

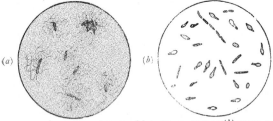

FIG. 4. BACILLUS OF BLACKLEG : (a) WITH FLAGELLA ; (b) WITH SPORES.

bacillus, the toxins of poison from which give rise to the chain of symptoms known as " lock-jaw." Another organism somewhat similar is the bacillus of Blackleg (Fig. 4). It differs in that the bacilli have originally a large number of fine filaments or flagellæ surrounding them, which, by rapidly moving, are capable of producing motion in the organism; whilst later in their life history they assume a type similar to that of tetanus, and go into sporulation, and in this form are difficult to eradicate from the soil.   There are various types and forms of bacilli in which flagellæ are present, such as typhoid, cholera, &c.   Organisms are widely distributed through nature in the earth, air, and water, and nearly all differ somewhat from others in their food requirements; also in the temperature in which they will both live and thrive.   Those which are disease producing, or pathogenic—for it must be understood that not all are harmful —grow most rapidly at about the temperature of the human body. That they are capable of living under a wide variety of circumstances, however, is shown by the fact already mentioned in respect of anthrax. Germs may gain access to the system in various ways through the alimentary canal, lungs, skin, mucus membrane, &c., but they are not capable of producing any harmful effect unless there is a predisposition on the part of the animal to suffer from the products of the organism introduced —as, for example, swine fever in

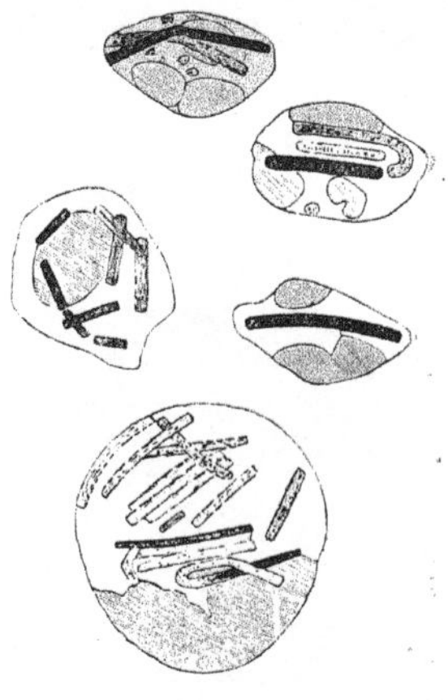

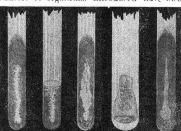

FIG. 5. PHAGOCYTOSIS SHOWING DESTRUCTION OF ANTHRAX BACILLI BY WHITE CELLS OF BLOOD.

pigs, blackleg in cattle.   As factors of their power to do harm, the channel by which they are introduced must be considered, as many of them grow only in certain tissues.   The physical condition of the part and the number of organisms introduced have also to be considered, whilst, for ever fighting against the introduction of organisms into the system, there are the white cells of the blood (Fig. 5).   These have the power of seizing and practically digesting within themselves nearly all classes of organisms.   The process is known as *phagocytosis.* Should the vitality of the animal be lowered, or the organisms introduced in excessive numbers, this power is not sufficient to check

FIG. 6. TEST TUBES WITH CULTURES.

them in their progress, and the result is that disease develops.   As has already been stated, organisms are extremely small bodies; so small, that special methods have to be adopted in order to recognise them.   In the first place, special staining is necessary in order to display their form.

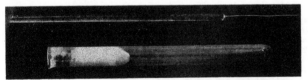

FIG. 7. A. TUBE WITH STERILE MEDIA.   B. INOCULATING NEEDLE.

FIG. 8. INCUBATOR.

Dyes are used, and counter stains, it being found that different tissues absorb or dye more readily with certain colours than others.   It is thus possible to obtain contrasts. They then have to be magnified very considerably under a microscope.   Consequently, it can be readily understood that very few of the organisms can be definitely recognised by merely examining them under the microscope, and further means are necessary for identification.   These include cultivation, for nearly all organisms are capable of growth outside the body on special soil (Fig. 6) *media*.   Just as it is necessary for the farmer, when sowing his wheat in a field, to have nourishment, moisture, and warmth for the growth of the wheat, so it is necessary for these three things to be present in order to produce a crop of organisms.   A great difference, however, exists in the time occupied in growth, and also in the number which can be produced from the original amount introduced into the medium.   The

method is—Glass test tubes are taken, and material, of which gelatine forms a basis, is introduced into them. Certain " food " is added in the shape of meat broth, egg albumen, &c., and all life is destroyed in this substance by means of heat.   That all life is destroyed may be shown by the fact that

FIG. 9. PLATE CULTURES WITH CHARACTERISTIC GROWTHS.

a tube will remain sterile for an indefinite period, providing unfiltered air does not gain access to the tube (Fig. 7). The method of cultivating is to take a small quantity of the material under

FIG. 10. HIPPOBOSEA
RUFIPES.

A transmitter of Trypano-
somes.

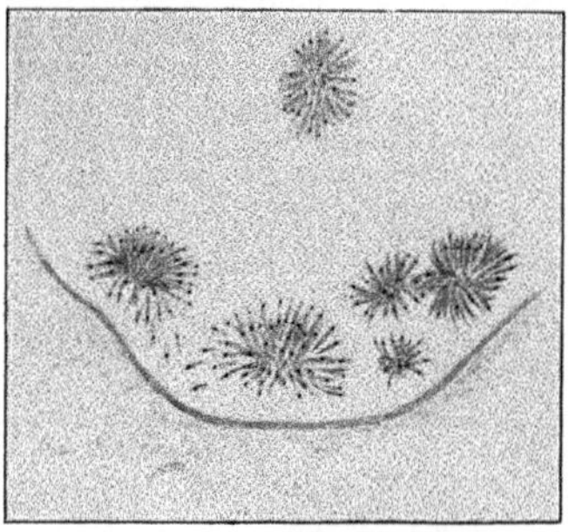

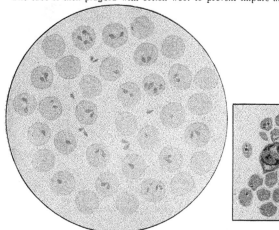

FIG. 11. PARASITES IN HIND GUT
OF FLEA.

consideration on the point of a fine needle (figure) previously heated to destroy life on it. This is introduced carefully into the test tube and the surface of the gelatine slightly touched (figure). The tube is then plugged with cotton wool to prevent impure air entering,

FIG. 12. PIROPLASM IN RED BLOOD CELLS.

and warmth is supplied by means of an incubator (Fig. 8), and within a few hours a crop will appear on and around the side that has been touched by the needle. The growths that result—or, as they are termed, "cultures"—have, in many cases, characteristic appearances, which assist considerably in arriving at a correct diagnosis. This culture method can go on through many generations, and though the first may be somewhat mixed—that is to say, contain more than one distinct organism—it is possible by sub-cultures to eventually obtain a perfectly pure culture of the organism concerned. Microscopical examination of these cultures from time to time will reveal the organism originally inoculated into the tube. They may be also grown on plates (Fig. 9). In order to prove that a micro-organism is the cause of a disease, it is necessary (1) that the organism in question, as recognised by its form, mode of growth, or products, be found constantly associated with the disease at least in the earlier stages and in sufficient numbers to account for the symptoms;

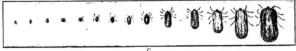

FIG. 13.

A. Mature female and eggs.
B. Hide showing cattle ticks.
C. Various stages of cattle ticks.

(2) that pure cultivation of this organism through sufficient generations be made, until it may reasonably be supposed that everything else which could possibly have been taken from the animal that yielded the organism has disappeared, (3) that other susceptible animals be inoculated with the cultivated organism, and that the disease be reproduced; (4) that the same organism be found in the tissues of the successfully inoculated animals in such numbers, and with such a distribution, as to account for the disease. In many cases it is necessary for the organism which produces disease to be transferred from one animal to another by means of intermittent hosts, such as biting flies, ticks, mosquitoes, fleas, &c. (Figs. 10, 11); as an example, the disease known, at any rate by name, to nearly all, as "Texas" or "Tick Fever" in cattle. This is caused by a small organism—from 12,000 to 80,000 being required to measure 1 inch (Fig. 12)—which gains access to the red blood corpuscles of the animal, and produces a train of symptoms, of which fever and red water are constant. The organism is carried from animal to animal by means of the tick (Fig. 13).

Another disease, which many in the northern districts will be familiar with, is tick fever in poultry (Fig. 14). The organism in these cases assumes

FIG. 14. BLACK LEGHORN HEN SUFFERING FROM ACUTE SPIROCHAETOSIS.

the form of a spirillum (Fig. 15). and is transferred from bird to bird by means of the tick; it is from 1/600th to 1/1,600th of an inch long. The difficulty in eradicating these diseases is apparent, for so long as the tick remains in a district, it is capable of continuing the spread; and as some of the ticks are capable of long life, even without food, the difficulties are increased.   The tick concerned in the spread of the disease in poultry is capable of living for a period of three years or more without food.

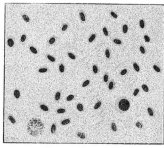

FIG. 15. FOWL SPIROCHAETOSIS. FREE SPIROCHAETES AND TANGLES DURING THE ACUTE STAGE.

A variety of parasite, which, fortunately, is not present in Australia producing any pathogenic effect, is the *Trypanosoma* (Fig. 16). These organisms live in the blood of various hosts and cause a variety of symptoms. Some of the diseases produced may be familiar by name, as example, "Surra"

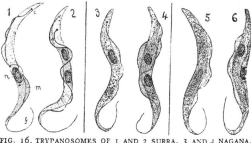

FIG. 16. TRYPANOSOMES OF 1 AND 2 SURRA, 3 AND 4 NAGANA. 5 AND 6 MAL DE CADERAS.

—a disease which produces a form of anæmia with intermittent fever, wasting, œdema of the limbs and belly, weakness, and paralysis. It lasts in the horse from one to two months, whilst camels have been known to be affected with it for as long as three years. Dogs are also susceptible. It is a disease which has caused great havoc, being present in India, China, Burmah, South Africa, Dutch Indies, Mauritius, Philippines, the Malay States, and Persia. In Mauritius the first outbreak

was recorded during 1902, and by June of the same year the mortality was appalling — the majority of the draught animals having succumbed. It was introduced by a cargo of cattle in September, 1901; and in June, 1902, Dr. Lesur wrote —" The epizootic at first appeared to be almost exclusively confined to oxen; then it attacked dogs, mules, donkeys, and horses. The destruction of draught

FIG. 17. TABANUS.

animals has gone to such an extent that farmers are anxiously asking themselves whether they will be able to gather in the harvest." By 29th January, 1903, the ruin was complete. " Horses and mules had practically disappeared, and at Port Louis it had become necessary to hand over the work of scavengering to prisoners, who, under the supervision of policemen, were used to pull the carts. The organism which produces this death is about 1/1,000th of an inch in length, and 1/51,000th of an inch in width. It is known to be carried from animal to animal by various biting flies." (Fig. 17.)

FIG. 18. DOURINE SHOWING CHARACTERISTIC PLAQUE.

Another disease which this parasite is responsible for is " Dourine." It is a disease of horses that is peculiar in that it is transmitted only by coitus. Its presence has been recorded in Spain, Germany, Switzerland, Austria, Russia and Turkey, Morocco, Algeria, Asia-Minor, Persia, India, United States, and Java. The first sign of the disease appears in from 11 to 20 days after coitus; it shows with swelling at the lower part of the sheath, extending along the abdomen. From 40 to 45 days after plaques are noticed on the skin (Fig. 18). The duration of these is very

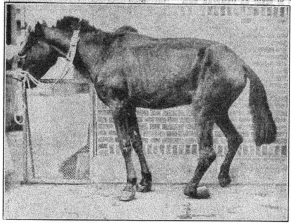

FIG. 19. HORSE SUFFERING FROM DOURINE AT THE END OF THE SECOND STAGE.

variable; wasting then sets in, the animal can rise only with difficulty, and the limbs are paralyzed (Fig. 19). The duration is usually from two to six months. In exceptional cases it lasts from one to four years. It has been recorded that certain breeds of horses can retain the power to spread the disease in their system for one or four years. It is estimated that 70 to 80 per cent. of affected mares die of the disease in India.

"Nagana," another of these diseases, occurs in horses, donkeys, oxen, dogs, and cats, and varies in duration from a few days or weeks to many months. It is invariably fatal in horses, donkeys, and dogs. It is present almost throughout the whole of Africa, except Cape Colony and the Transvaal.

Glanders, which all are familiar with by name, can, fortunately, be detected in

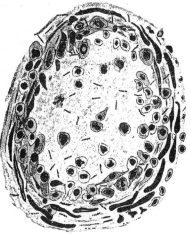

FIG. 20. BACILLUS OF GLANDERS PENETRATING WALL OF PULMONARY ARTERY.

the system by the Mallein test long before symptoms appear, so that it may be reasonably hoped we will keep our shores clear of this pest, which has been responsible for enormous losses in countries in which

FIG. 21. EPIZOOTIC LYMPHANGITIS SHOWING EYE LESIONS.

FIG. 23. EPIZOOTIC LYMPHANGITIS SHOWING LESIONS ON LEG.

it has appeared. Great Britain in 21 years—1887 to 1907—lost 40,936 head, which, valued at £20, equals £818,720. The organism is from 1/8,000th to 1/5,000th of an inch (Fig. 20).

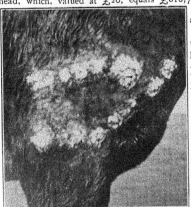

FIG. 22. EPIZOOTIC LYMPHANGITIS SHOWING LESIONS ON SHOULDERS.

"Epizootic lymphangitis" (Figs. 21, 22, 23) is present in India, Africa, Japan, China, France, Sweden, Russia, Germany, and parts of the United States, and is produced by an organism some 1/6000th to 1/8,000th of an inch in diameter. The incubation period varies from three weeks to fourteen months or more. Apparent recovery may occur, and later the disease re-appears. The mortality is low, only about 10 per cent. dying; but the after effects are serious, thickened tendons, &c., causing great depreciation.

Next there are a series of diseases which, whilst causing serious havoc, are produced by an organism so small that it cannot be seen except in

FIG. 24. COWS AFFECTED WITH FOOT AND MOUTH DISEASE.

culture masses. An example is seen in foot and mouth disease in cattle (Fig. 24). In 1883 500.000 animals were affected in Great Britain; in

FIG. 25. FOOT AND MOUTH DISEASE. BURIAL OF CARCASES OF CATTLE IN DEEP TRENCH.

Bavaria, 100,000. In Germany, in 1890, 800,000 were affected, and in 1892 over 4,000,000. Though the mortality is not high in the disease, the loss from wasting, fever, &c., is enormous; so much so, that a system of slaughter of all affected and in contact animals is carried on as the cheapest method of checking its ravages (Figs. 25, 26). Its seriousness may be gauged from the cablegrams appearing in the press of the last outbreak in Great Britain.

FIG. 26. FOOT AND MOUTH DISEASE. CARCASES OF CATTLE PILED WITH WOOD READY FOR BURNING.

No lecture on contagious diseases would be complete without some reference to tuberculosis, the disease upon which there is more literature than on almost any other subject. It is known as the "White Plague," and has been regarded by scientists as the only disease which is capable of exterminating the human race, and this mainly because of its insidious nature; for it is possible for one to contract the disease in youth or infancy and to be quite unaware of it until later in life—say upon gaining maturity, when, owing to some debilitating influence, the protection afforded up to that time by the white corpuscles of the blood is broken down, and the organism spreads through the system, bringing with it that train of symptoms

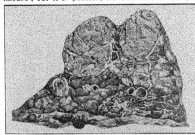

FIG 27. CHRONIC CHEESY TUBERCULOUS PNEUMONIA. SECTION OF LOBE OF COW'S LUNG.

which so many are familiar with either through the loss of relatives or friends from consumption (Figs. 27, 28).

The organism responsible for the disease is from 1/4,000th to 1/12,000th of an inch long, and from 1/24,000th to 1/72,000th of an inch broad (Fig. 29). The disease is communicable from animal to man, and *vice versa*, and, unfortunately, in the early stages, does not produce any visible symptoms (Figs. 30, 31). The symptoms are usually recog-

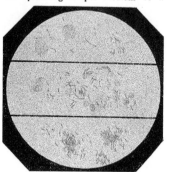

nised only when the disease is well advanced, and most are familiar with the wasting, cough, &c., produced (Fig. 32). A very common method of spreading is per medium of a

FIG. 28. LUNGS AND LIVER OF A COW AFFECTED BY TUBERCULOSIS.

FIG. 29. BACILLUS OF TUBERCULOSIS.

milk supply (Figs. 33, 34). A cow may be dangerously tubercular, yet continue to look and act like a healthy animal; she may show neither symptoms of disease nor discomfort; her appetite may be

FIG. 30. COW APPARENTLY HEALTHY, STRONG AND VIGOROUS, GIVING A LARGE QUANTITY OF MILK. KNOWN TO BE AFFECTED WITH TUBERCULOSIS FOUR YEARS.

good; she may conceive and milk like an ordinary cow, and may even be the sleekest and fattest in the herd. The illustrations shown are those of cows apparently in the best of health; some of them,

indeed, in fat condition. They were, however, known to be affected
with tuberculosis, distributing the bacilli through their fæces, and some
of them through their milk. The necessity for cleanliness in milking

FIG. 31. COW APPARENTLY HEALTHY, GOOD CONDITION FOR DAIRY COW.
KNOWN TO BE TUBERCULOUS FOUR YEARS. DUNG OF THIS COW CAUSED
TUBERCULOSIS IN PIGS THAT WERE PERMITTED TO EAT IT.

methods in the yard, and hind-quarters of the cow, is thus evident; for
it will readily be seen how milk can be contaminated where operations are
carried on under insanitary conditions, and where cows, whose flanks are
covered with manure, which may possibly contain large numbers of

FIG. 32. ADVANCED TUBERCULOSIS.

the organisms, are milked. The spread of the disease to the pig also
occurs when they are allowed to roam at will and root about in the manure
heap contaminated, possibly, by only one cow in a herd.

FIG. 33. LONG-STANDING CASE OF TUBERCULOSIS WITH TUBERCULAR
SWELLING IN UDDER.

Since the Milk and Dairy Supervision Act has been in operation some
500 cows out of dairy herds have been destroyed. It is, indeed, difficult

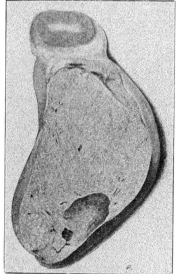

FIG. 34. TUBERCULOUS UDDER OF COW.

to say what saving of human life will result from this; but if only one
life is saved for every cow, it cannot be regarded as other than a great
work.

UNPROFITABLE ORCHARDS: REASONS AND REMEDIES.

E. Wallis, Orchard Supervisor.

Many orchards throughout the State are unprofitable, owing to one or more of the following causes :—

Area too large.
Unprofitable varieties.
Want of proper soil drainage.
Lack of systematic cultivation and manuring.
Improper pruning methods.
Unsuccessful eradication of insect and fungus pests.

AREA OF ORCHARD.

Large areas under orchard require much manual labour, horse and mechanical power, to bring them into and sustain them in a highly profitable condition. In many instances these necessary factors to profit-earning are not provided, and thus some essential part of the orchard's well-being is neglected. It may be cultivation, manuring, pruning, or spraying, but whatever it is, the orchard suffers. Thus it cannot possibly yield the same quantity or quality of fruit as if properly managed. Of course, large places worked thoroughly under proper organization, yield large profits. Unless, however, one has command of the necessary capital and labour, it would be better for him to be placed on a small holding, which could be thoroughly worked in every detail. Concentration is quite essential to success, and without it the orchard will fail to yield its maximum profits.

UNPROFITABLE VARIETIES.

There is no greater drawback to the profit-earning capacity of many established orchards than unprofitable varieties. It may be that when the trees were planted, their adaptability to the climatic and soil conditions of the locality was not understood. As a result of this want of knowledge, much labour is often expended without any appreciable result in the way of profitable crops. In most cases, none can be expected. Yet some growers persevere year after year with such trees, thinking that at some time their profitless career will end, and their profitable one commence. As a rule, their perseverance remains unrewarded. This is especially so with such varieties of apples as Cleopatra and Munro's Favourite when grown in the southern districts of Victoria. When, however, these splendid varieties are grown under congenial climatic conditions, such as obtain in the northern parts of the State, they produce fruit of high-grade quality without being subject to the characteristic scab and cracking which affect them in the south. Should these or any other varieties unsuitable to the locality be established, no time should be wasted with them. They should be cut back and worked over with some variety or varieties known to do well in the particular place concerned. This method is shown in Plate No. 1. The trees shown here are two-year-old grafts of Rome Beauty worked on eight-year-old stems of Munro's Favourite. In another two years, they should be capable of bearing a good crop. These Munro's Favourite trees were cut back on account of the fruit cracking badly, and thus rendered unfit for market. This is not a singular case, but one of many which has come under the writer's notice in the Diamond Creek and other districts south of the Dividing Range.

I. ROME BEAUTY GRAFTS ON MUNRO'S FAVOURITE STEMS.

There are other varieties of fruits which often prove unprofitable on account of their non- or partial fruiting. This sterility or partial sterility is to a great extent a varietal characteristic due to underlying causes which may sometimes be remedied by cross-fertilization, whilst in other cases the thinning out of the fruit spurs has often the desired result. In the Diamond Creek district, Keiffer pear is extensively grown, and in many cases is worthless as a cropper. This unprofitable condition generally occurs where the trees are planted in rich soil, producing very vigorous perpendicular growth, and isolated from other varieties blossoming simultaneously. When planted in poor country, the vigorous growth is checked, and trees often bear well. This variety is very susceptible to the influence of cross-fertilization. Such varieties as Harrington's Victoria, Howell, Le Coute, and others have proved suitable as a cross with Keiffer. Where this variety is established and has proved sterile or partly so, a sufficient number for cross-fertilizing purposes should be cut down and re-worked with one of the above varieties. Bailey's Bergamot is another variety often barren of fruit, though blossoming profusely each season, but the writer has brought it into a state of fruitfulness by crossing with Williams' Bon Chretien. Spur-pruning is advised as a remedy for want of bearing in Winter Nelis pear. Early Guigne cherry often proves a very light cropper when grown isolated from other helpful varieties. It, however, appears to be very favourably influenced by such varieties as Black Bigareau and Early Lyons.

Coe's Golden Drop plum also is prone to barrenness. No definite results have so far been obtained by crossing, but Pond's Seedling is recommended as a variety likely to prove beneficial as a cross. In the case of a young orchard being established containing any of these self-sterile or partially self-sterile varieties, suitable trees should be planted near them for cross-fertilization purposes.

DRAINING OF ORCHARDS.

It has been said that the better the drainage, the surer the water supply. This is sound advice, for land well drained and worked is enabled to draw up by capillary action, and hold, sufficient water for the use of the trees. Undrained land is cold, and being filled with water in winter time, the beneficial influences of soil aeration are absent.

In hot weather such soil is generally caked, hard, and dry, and under such conditions it is not difficult to understand the reason why so many trees " go off " in orchards, and become unprofitable during the existence of such conditions.

Orchards, to prove highly profitable, must be established under the best possible conditions of soil drainage, either natural or artificial. Few are naturally drained ; parts of them may be, but generally weak or rather wet patches exist, and the trees " go off " in those places. Plate No. 2 shows a Reinette du Canada apple tree growing vigorously. This tree was placed in a badly-drained situation, and did not make any satisfactory growth until a drain was laid and the tree cut back. The strong growth seen in the photo. is the direct result of the work.

In a perfectly-drained orchard, the trees develop uniformly. In fact, when looking along the rows of trees in such orchards, it is difficult to notice any difference in the general appearance of the trees of same variety and age. Plate No. 3 shows two rows of such trees. It will be seen that these trees are thrifty in growth and even in general development. This is the kind of orchard that proves profitable—every tree being able to produce maximum crops.

Of course, it is better to do the necessary work of draining when the orchard is being established, but old orchards, not too far gone, respond to the work of draining, even when done late in their existence.   Old and stunted trees have sometimes become quite thrifty in growth after the orchard has been drained.

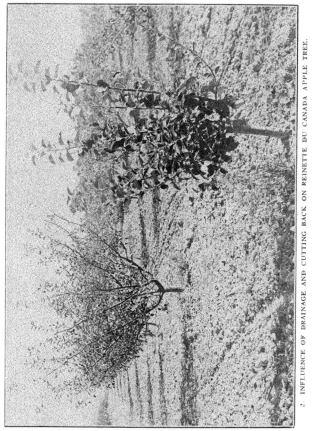

INFLUENCE OF DRAINAGE AND CUTTING BACK ON REINETTE DU CANADA APPLE TREE.

The system of drainage must vary according to local conditions. Speaking generally, however, if the soil is stiff and compact, the drains require to be placed at smaller distances apart than in ground of a more open texture.   Again, if the surface is fairly level, more drains are required than in land having a good slope.   Drains should be arranged so that soakage may be caught in the easiest and most complete way.

Pipe drains should be placed mid-way between the rows about 20 or 40 feet apart, and usually parallel to the fall. These pipe drains should lead into the main open drain that follows the natural water-course.

3. ROWS OF APPLE TREES GROWING UNDER IDEAL DRAINAGE CONDITIONS.

In laying pipe drains, they should be placed well into the subsoil to draw off water freely. It is a good plan to lay them on sand if readily available. Sand makes a good bed for pipes, and they are then not so apt to become displaced as when put on a hard bottom. In laying them, extreme care must be taken not to have any unevenness between successive pipes to allow of the collection of sediment in the interior of the pipe drain.

MANURING.

It is too commonly believed that fruit trees thrive well in the poorest of soil. This idea is not correct, for when the trees are called upon to bear heavy crops, they require a liberal supply of the necessary plant-food constituents. Soil of poor quality may certainly be beneficial in bringing trees into bearing quickly or in checking the over-vigorous growth of some varieties; but continued cropping will surely soon exhaust the required elements of plant-food in such soil, so that the trees will soon become incapable of producing a profitable crop of fruit. The evils of soil-exhaustion may be seen in many orchards, as evidenced by the stunted growth of trees, depleted buds, and fruit of very inferior quality. In fact, it may be said that the profits of the majority of orchards are considerably lessened by the lack of systematic manuring. The appearance of trees is the best guide to their manure requirements. Young trees should make regular and thrifty growth. Any defect in this respect should be remedied by the application of manure rich in nitrogen. Nitrogenous manures are very effective in producing growth, either in young trees or in old and stunted ones. No better manure can be used for general purposes than farm-yard manure, which, when properly prepared, is rich in all the essential elements of plant-food —nitrogen, potash, and phosphoric acid. In addition, the organic part of it has a very beneficial physical effect upon soil. It is, therefore, known as a *general* manure in contrast to *special* manures which contain one, two, or more constituents of plant nutriment, but which are not capable of maintaining the general fertility of the soil. The chief value, however, of special manures is to supply the soil with some plant food which it lacks. In order, then, to apply such manure profitably, the soil deficiency should be first ascertained, otherwise it may do no good. Sometimes a soil may fail through the absence of one or more of the essential elements. The reason of failure in such a case is because the minimum governs the whole in the same way as the strength of a chain is governed by its weakest link.

The mechanical effect of farm-yard manure upon soil texture is very marked, making it either more open or compact, as the case may be. Soil of heavy texture is opened up by the decomposition of the straw, which forms channels, and through them moisture, air, and the roots of trees penetrate.

As there is generally a difficulty in obtaining sufficient quantities of farm-yard manure, a system of green manuring is strongly recommended for soils deficient in humus. Such soils are light-coloured, dry, and harsh to the touch. Those containing it in proper proportions are dark-coloured, moist, and mellow. The properties of humus are that it renders heavy soils lighter, more open, and porous, while, on the other hand, soils of a loose sandy character are made denser and better enabled to absorb and retain moisture. Hill orchard land generally requires a liberal application of manure to bring about ideal humus conditions.

In addition to the production of humus, green manure of leguminous crops is rich in nitrogen. This is produced by the action of bacteria working in the root nodules of legumes, such as beans, peas, lucerne, &c. It will thus be seen that by the use of green manure, not only is the soil benefited physically, but also one of the most expensive manures—nitrogen— is added to the soil.

Green crops should be sown in the autumn, and ploughed into the soil when in flower. Special manures, such as nitrate of soda, sulphate of ammonia, sulphate of potash, and superphosphate, are soon rendered soluble, and thus should be applied to soil when trees are becoming active in early spring.

Bonedust is a valuable manure for fruit trees. It is not easily rendered soluble, therefore should be applied in autumn or winter.

PRUNING.

This all-important factor in making or marring the profits of an orchard cannot be dealt with at any length in such an article as this. However, no article bearing on unprofitable orchards would be complete without reference to the common mistakes made and which cause so much profit-leakage in many orchards.

Young Trees.—Instead of cutting leading growths of young trees hard back, some growers merely tip them; the result is a weakly framework which cannot bear the weight of fruit after the tree has come into bearing, the limbs often break off, and irreparable injury is done. Young trees should be hard cut back for a few years, in order to form a strong frame-work capable of bearing heavy crops.

Leaders.—Frequently the leading growths are improperly placed, and too many allowed to remain. The leaders should be spaced as equi-distant as possible and rise obliquely at an angle of about 45 deg; generally speaking, about 12-16 leaders are sufficient.

Laterals.—A thorough knowledge of the fruiting habits of different kinds and varieties is essential to successful pruning. A good general policy is to spare the knife on all well-placed light lateral growths. If allowed to remain for a season to ripen and develop fruit buds, they can then be shortened in as required. Especially does this apply to such varieties of apples as Jonathan and Rome Beauty. Many instances are met with where these splendid varieties have been made barren, or partly so, by the improper use of the secateur on laterals. A good plan is to observe carefully the result of last season's cuts. By this means a mistake should be made only once—not repeated.

Pruning the Peach.—Many peach orchards are silent witnesses to improper pruning methods. The light wood growth of the tree is often merely a tangled mass at ends of leading shoots, instead of being well regulated and placed in the most suitable positions.

As a result of such management, or lack of management, fruit of an uncertain quantity and quality is produced.

The peach bears its fruit on new growth, and only once on the same spur. Thus a regular supply of well-placed fruiting wood is essential. This can be obtained and maintained by the judicious use of the secateur—only possible when there is a thorough knowledge of the different kinds of buds and growth.

In pruning the peach, care must be taken to supply wood-growth for the succeeding year's crop as well as the regulation of spurs for the development of large fruit during the year the pruning is carried out. All dead wood should be removed as well as the over-weakened laterals. Cuts should be made clean to permit of free healing.

TREATMENT OF INSECT AND FUNGUS PESTS.

This subject has been dealt with in the *Journal* from time to time, and the Orchard Supervision Branch is always available to give instructions to growers in this important detail of orchard work.

HERD TESTING.

Government Certification of Standard Cows.

By W. A. N. Robertson, B.V.Sc.

The desire of the members of the Victorian branch of the Jersey Herd Society to introduce a scheme for the official registration of records of the Jersey cow, affording as it did an opportunity for putting into practice the principle advocated by the officers of the Department of Agriculture, was responsible during 1911 for the meeting of a committee of their mem-. bers, representatives of the Royal Agricultural Society, and officers of the Department, at which the more important features of such a scheme were discussed.   Later this led to a deputation waiting upon the Hon. G. Graham, Minister of Agriculture, and placing their request for assistance from Government officers before him.   Being in accord with the principle, the Minister, after due consideration, agreed to the issuing of certificates to all cows of any pure breed attaining a definite standard.   Eventually regulations were drawn up, which are reproduced herewith.   The testing is to apply to any pure breed, but only to those animals registered in a recognised herd book, whilst every such animal in a herd must be entered. A fee of £1 per herd and 5s. per cow tested will be made.   The test will occupy nine calendar months, commencing one week after calving, and cows attaining the standard as shown in Rule 11 will be granted certificates whereon all the information possible as showing her value will be recorded.   A list of all cows gaining the standard will be published annually.   As a cow must enter for testing within one week of calving, it is advisable that all owners desirous of participating in the scheme should enter their herds as early as possible, for it will be seen that some months must elapse before even the majority of animals in a herd are undergoing the test, and those which are calving at the present time will be handicapped by missing the lactation period of the present year.

REGULATIONS CONCERNING HERD TESTING FOR THE GOVERNMENT CERTIFICATION OF STANDARD COWS.

Entrance—

1. The owner of any herd of pure bred dairy cattle may submit his herd for certification.
2. Only those cows registered in a recognised herd book or pure stock register will be accepted, and all such cows in the herd must be tested, with such exceptions as are set out in Clauses 14, 15, and 16.
3. An annual fee of £1 per herd and 5s. per cow tested shall be paid to the Department of Agriculture on demand.
4. Any cow entered for certification may be branded in such manner as to insure identification, and all standard cows will be marked on the inside of an ear with the Government tattoo mark and an identification number.

Lactation Period—

5. Testing and recording shall occupy a period of nine calendar months, commencing one week from date of calving, excepting under such circumstances as set forth in Clause 18.   This period shall be recognised as the official lactation period.

Recording—

6. The milk from each cow entered shall be weighed separately immediately after each milking by means of tested and approved scales, and the weight recorded on a printed chart supplied for the purpose, which shall remain the property of the Department.   Such scales and chart shall be available for inspection by a Government Dairy Supervisor when required.

Supervision—

7. A Government Dairy Supervisor, under the direction of the Chief Veterinary Officer, will make periodical visits for the purpose of checking records and taking samples of milk for testing. There shall be not less than nine visits during the official lactation period, and not more than thirty days shall elapse between any two visits. Additional visits may be made at any time by the Supervisor for the purpose of taking supplementary records and samples for testing as often as may be deemed advisable.

8. Every facility shall be afforded Government officers in carrying out their duties under these Regulations, and accommodation must be provided over night when required.

9. Particulars as to date of calving, service, drying off, hours of milking, manner of feeding, must be supplied for record purposes on request of the Dairy Supervisor. If deemed necessary in any case, the owner may be called upon to furnish a statutory declaration as to the correctness of such or any particulars.

Testing—

10. In collecting samples for testing, the morning and evening milk will be taken; the tests will be made by the Chemist for Agriculture or his deputy from a composite sample containing quantities of the morning and evening milk proportionate to the respective yields; and the results, unless shown to be abnormal, shall be considered as the average for the period intervening since the next previous normal test. If apparently abnormal, the results may be discarded, and further samples taken and tests made.

Standard Cows—

11. Standard cows under these Regulations shall be those which, during the official lactation period, yield—

   (a) in the case of cows commencing their first lactation period and being then *under 3 years of age*—150 lbs. of butter fat;

   (b) in the case of cows commencing their first lactation period and being then *over* 3 years of age—200 lbs. of butter fat;

   (c) in the case of cows of *any age* commencing *any* lactation *period other than* the *first*—200 lbs. of butter fat.

Certification—

12. A Government certificate shall be issued in respect of all standard cows. Such certificate shall show the breed, the age at entry, brands, the official lactation period recorded, and date of completion; the weight of milk given, the amount of butter fat and commercial butter (estimated on a 14 per cent. over-run), and the weight of milk given on the last day of the official lactation period.

13. The certificate issued in respect of any standard cow shall, if she attain the standard during any subsequent official lactation period, be returned to the Department, when a fresh certificate will be issued, which shall show her record for each and every lactation period in which she was tested.

Exemptions—

14. Cows eight years old or over whose yields have been recorded for three official lactation periods may be exempt.

15. Aged or injured cows in the herd at time of entry and kept for breeding purposes may be exempt on the recommendation of the Government Supervisor. Any injury interfering with lactation received subsequent to entry may be recorded on certificate issued.

16. Any cow which on veterinary examination is found to be affected with tuberculosis shall be withdrawn from the test, and her milk shall not be allowed to be used for sale, or for the preparation of any dairy produce for sale.

17. Any cow which on veterinary examination is found to be affected with actinomycosis of the udder, or any other disease or condition which may temporarily render her milk injurious, may remain in the herd for testing, but her milk shall not be used for sale or for the preparation of any dairy produce for sale without permission of the Supervisor.

18. When any newly-calved cow is rendered temporarily unfit for testing by being affected with milk fever, mammitis, retention of placenta, or other ailment affecting newly-calved cows, the period elapsing between the calving and entrance to the official lactation period may be extended on the recommendation of a Veterinary Officer or Supervisor, but such period shall not exceed one month from date of calving.

19. Any interpretation or decision in respect of these Regulations, or in respect of any matter concerning the certification which receives the written approval of the Director of Agriculture shall be final.

20. Should the owner of any herd entered not conform to these Regulations, such herd shall be subject to disqualification for such period as the Minister shall determine. The Minister retains the right to withdraw any certificate when to his satisfaction good and sufficient cause is shown.

ORCHARD AND GARDEN NOTES.

E. E. Pescott, Principal, School of Horticulture, Burnley.

The Orchard.

If the winter spraying has been delayed, it should be completed as quickly as possible, and before the buds begin to swell and burst.

It is not advisable to spray stone fruits with the red oil emulsion at this time, as there will be the danger of burning and destroying any early buds that may be swelling, and consequently loosening their outside scales. It will be safe, if the work be done at once, to spray apple, pear, and quince trees with this spray, especially where the Bryobia mite. scale insects, or woolly aphis are prevalent.

If it is intended that the lime and sulphur wash will be the specific for these and other pests, it may still be used with safety, although the spraying should be completed as early as possible. This mixture has a certain value as a fungicide, and it is well worth trying on peach trees that have previously been affected with leaf curl; more especially in view of the fact that in some districts severe burning has occurred in peach orchards as a result of using Bordeaux mixture late in the season.

Where peach aphis has appeared, it will be advisable to spray at once with a strong nicotine solution. Tobacco stems should be soaked in cold water for some days, adding a teaspoonful of caustic soda to a cask of steeping stems. The liquid may be used strong, and every endeavour should be made to kill out the first insects that appear.

The pruning of deciduous trees should be at an end this month. Pruning of evergreens, such as oranges, lemons, and guavas, may be left until later.

Young deciduous trees should be planted not later than this month, according to the directions given in last month's notes. The soil should be trodden firm around the roots, and, when planting has been completed, the trees may be headed back to three or four buds on each arm.

Preparation may be made for planting citrus and other evergreen trees. The soil should be well ploughed and sweetened in anticipation of planting in September and October.

In root-borer affected districts, the beetles will begin to appear during the latter part of the month. A close observance should be kept, and the insects should be regularly collected and destroyed.

Vegetable Garden.

The plots should be well dug over at this time, adding gypsum or lime where any pests have been prevalent. In other beds, stable manure should be well worked into the soil.

The soil should be rich, well worked, and warm, so that a quick growth may result. Vegetables grown quickly are generally more tender than slowly grown ones; and frequent changes of crops in the plots will give better results. At this season, the weeds will require constant checking; frequent use of the hoe will therefore be necessary, and, in the rows, hand weeding should be resorted to.

All seedlings should be planted out, especially seedlings of cabbage, cauliflower, lettuce, and onion. Seeds of peas, carrots, parsnips, radish, lettuce, tomato, and broad beans may be sown.

Where they can be sheltered and protected from frosts, young tomato plants may be planted out for early fruiting. One method of managing these early plants is to place the young plant a few inches below the surface, and then place a box, 8 or 9 inches deep, with top and bottom removed, over the plant at ground level. This can then be covered loosely with a piece of glass whenever necessary.

Potatoes, artichokes, and asparagus crowns may still be planted. Asparagus beds should be kept free from weeds, they should have a loose surface, and a light top dressing with old manure would be beneficial.

In the frames, cucumber, vegetable marrow, melon, pumpkin, water and rock melon seeds may be planted. These are best planted in pots, placing three or four seeds in each pot. They then suffer no check when being transplanted into the beds.

Flower Garden.

Rose pruning should now be completed. At this time the buds are beginning to swell and show some prominence, and no check should be put in the way of their full development. A careful watch should be kept for the appearance of aphis, which should be washed off as soon as it is noticed. It is advisable to have a specific always at hand, ready made up, so as to kill the aphis when noticed. The aphis is a very rapid breeder, and delay of a few days means an enormous increase of this pest. Quite a number of specifics are useful in combating the aphis— Soaperine, tobacco emulsion, strong soapsuds, Robinson's pine spray, and pestend solution are among the useful remedies. Whatever is used, a good application should be given, and it should be repeated at frequent intervals, if the aphides remain.

All herbaceous and similar plants may now be planted out in the beds; these include delphinium, cannas, shasta daisy, rudbeckias, salvias, perennial phlox, &c. These plants should be well fed, so as to allow them to make a rapid and vigorous growth.

Weeds will need frequent attention, as they must be kept in check at this time of the year; they should be prevented from seeding in the beds.

The planting out of shrubs may now be continued and completed as early as possible, so as to allow the roots to get a good hold of the soil before the hot weather sets is. Gladioli may be planted for early flowering, and, as well, a few divisions or tubers of dahlias.

SECOND VICTORIAN EGG-LAYING COMPETITION, 1912-13.

H. V. Hawkins, Poultry Expert.

Monthly Report.

The past month has been characterized by cold bleak weather, with at times heavy rain and occasional frosts, the drinking vessels being frozen on several mornings. The lighter breeds have felt the cold very much; on the other hand, the 30 Orpingtons competing have scored remarkably well, and appear to relish the cold weather. A few cases of sickness have occurred, principally amongst the White Leghorns; up to the present one White Leghorn has died through accident, and one Silver Wyandotte succumbed to heart disease. There has been one replacement, due to paralysis, and one to wasting, in both cases White Leghorns. The scoring of the present team of birds compares favorably with the previous year's competition, as may be seen from the following figures:—

Comparative Table of Eggs Laid.

	1911–12 (396 Birds).		1912–13 (414 Birds).	
	No. of Eggs.	Average per Pen.	No. of Eggs.	Average per Pen.
1st Month	2,958	44·8	3,227	46·7
2nd ,, ...	3,139	47·5	4,844	70·2
3rd ,, ...	3,873	58·6	5,688	82·4

Feeding.

Owing to the cold weather experienced, there has been an increase in the amount of meat allowed, the bullock's liver being given four times a week; whilst on cold days or on approach of cold nights an extra ration of maize has been given, reversing the amount of maize and wheat that was given last month, *i.e.*, 4 parts maize, 3 parts wheat, and 2 parts oats, instead of 4 parts wheat, 3 parts maize, and 2 parts oats. In other respects, the feeding has been along the lines indicated in the July issue of the *Journal*.

Very few of the birds have shown signs of broodiness, and the general health has been good, and only few are in the moult, as is indicated by the increased egg yield. Keen interest is being shown in the contest this year, due to the equality of a number of the contestants; although the leading pen, No. 40, has maintained its position, there are many reasonably close.

Unfortunately, a few of the leading pens have laid a number of double-yolked eggs; this will handicap them as the warmer weather approaches, and possibly be a cause of loss.

SECOND VICTORIAN EGG-LAYING COMPETITION, 1912-13.

Commencing 15th April, 1912.

CONDUCTED AT BURNLEY HORTICULTURAL SCHOOL.

Pen.	Breed.	Name of Owner.	April 15 to June 14.	June 15 to July 14.	Total to Date (3 months).	Position in Competition.
40	White Leghorns ..	S. Brown ..	247	111	358	1
31	,,	Geo. Edwards ..	205	123	328	2
23	,,	W. McLister ..	212	115	327	3
70	,,	C. J. Beatty ..	222	100	322	} 4
28	,,	F. G. Eagleton ..	200	122	322	
47	,,	J. E. Bradley ..	214	100	314	6
3	Black Orpingtons ..	King and Watson ..	193	120	313	7
9	White Leghorns ..	J. S. Spotswood ..	202	102	304	8
20	,,	E. Waldon ..	201	102	303	9
48	,,	Griffin Cant ..	189	99	288	10
1	,,	J. Campbell ..	188	94	282	11
62	,,	R. W. Pope ..	189	91	280	12
8	Black Orpingtons ..	D. Fisher ..	170	110	280	13
46	,,	H. A. Langdon ..	169	109	278	14
30	White Leghorns ..	Mrs. Stevenson ..	192	72	264	15
24	,,	Sargenfri Poultry Yards	162	98	260	} 16
39	,,	W. G. Swift ..	159	101	260	
38	,,	R. Moy ..	167	92	259	18
7	,,	A. H. Padman ..	192	64	256	19
37	,,	C. B. Bertelsmeier ..	146	108	254	20
25	,,	R. L. Appleford ..	147	106	253	21
50	,,	A. Ahpee ..	143	105	248	} 22
29	,,	J. B. Brigdon ..	156	92	248	
45	,,	Wooldridge Bros. ..	156	92	248	
44	,,	A. W. Hall ..	186	56	242	25
2	,,	B. Rowlinson ..	140	100	240	26
6	,,	J. B. Macarthur ..	161	75	236	27
14	,,	J. H. Wright ..	129	104	233	28
49	,,	W. Purvis ..	115	110	225	29
63	,,	Percy Walker ..	129	89	218	30
13	,,	W. B. Crellin ..	106	110	216	31
15	,,	W. H. Steer ..	103	109	212	32
53	,,	H. Hodges ..	100	103	203	33
33	,,	H. McKenzie ..	130	71	201	34
35	,,	C. H. Busst ..	130	70	200	35
19	,,	Cowan Bros. ..	97	101	198	} 36
64	,,	H. Merrick ..	120	78	198	
56	,,	M. A. Monk ..	105	90	195	38
42	,,	Mrs. T. Kempster ..	146	47	193	39
61	Black Orpingtons ..	J. Ogden ..	93	88	181	40
5	White Leghorns ..	J. H. Brain ..	82	85	167	41
10	R.C. Brown Leghorns	S. P. Giles ..	55	110	165	} 42
51	White Leghorns ..	H. Hammill ..	71	94	165	
58	,,	W. J. Stock ..	114	46	160	44
12	,,	T. H. Stafford ..	92	66	158	45
54	,,	F. R. DeGaris ..	72	83	155	} 46
60	,,	Miss B. E. Ryan ..	55	100	155	
43	,,	G. Purton ..	82	71	153	48
4	,,	J. Blackburne ..	78	72	150	} 49
65	,,	A. H. Thomson ..	71	79	150	
27	,,	E. Nash ..	98	51	149	51
52	Black Minorcas ..	Chalmers Bros. ..	63	76	139	52
18	White Leghorns ..	B. Mitchell ..	49	89	138	53
59	,,	W. J. Seabridge ..	56	79	135	54
41	,,	A. Stringer ..	90	41	131	55
69	,,	Morgan and Watson ..	52	69	121	56
16	Silver Wyandottes ..	R. Jobling ..	49	71	120	57
32	White Leghorns ..	S. Brundrett ..	56	63	119	58
11	Black Orpingtons ..	T. S. Goodisson ..	31	75	106	59
22	White Leghorns ..	W. N. Ling ..	62	43	105	60
57	,,	B. Walker ..	63	39	102	61
21	,,	J. O'Loughlin ..	57	42	99	62
68	,,	W. J. McKeddie ..	50	47	97	63
55	Brown Leghorns ..	J. Matheson ..	18	72	90	64
36	Old English Game ..	K. J. Barrett ..	40	41	81	65
66	White Leghorns ..	J. Moloney ..	40	34	74	66
17	,,	S. Childs ..	11	37	48	67
67	Anconas ..	A. E. Manning ..	..	44	44	68
34	White Leghorns ..	Reg. F. B. Moore ..	3	40	43	69
26	..	(Reserved) ..	..	..	..	..
		Totals	8,071	5,688	13,759	

VICTORIAN PRODUCE.

The Government Statist (Mr. A. M. Laughton) has issued the following return of the area and produce for 1911-12 and 1910-11:—

POTATOES.

Principal Counties.	Area in Acres.		Produce in Tons.		Average per Acre in Tons.	
	1911–12.	1910–11.	1911–12.	1910–11.	1911–12.	1910–11.
Bourke	5,228	7,230	13,686	17,315	2·62	2·39
Grant	8,205	9,451	21,813	27,595	2·66	2·92
Mornington	5,618	6,877	14,695	17,166	2·62	2·50
Evelyn	860	1,333	1,952	2,806	2·27	2·10
Dalhousie	2,687	3,891	4,855	6,615	1·81	1·70
Talbot	6,870	8,590	16,599	21,648	2·42	2·52
Grenville	1,310	1.324	2,699	3,639	2·06	2·75
Polwarth	768	1,227	2,640	4,174	3·44	3·40
Ripon	1,219	1,208	2,976	4,281	2·44	3·54
Villiers	3,758	7,256	10,559	20,386	2·81	2·81
Normanby	1,253	1,368	3,246	5,709	2·59	4·17
Delatite	1,202	1,348	2,122	4,545	1·77	3·37
Buln Buln	3,612	6,371	10,218	11,929	2·83	1·87
Remainder of State	5,102	5,430	11,032	15,504	2·16	2·86
Total*	47,692	62,904	119,092	163,312	2·50	2·60

* These figures include 5,142 acres of early crop in 1911-12, which yielded 17,498 tons, being an average of 3·40 tons per acre, and 5,606 acres in 1910–11, which yielded 21,140 tons, an average of 3·77 tons per acre.

MAIZE.

Principal Counties.	Area in Acres.		Produce in Bushels.		Average per Acre in Bushels.	
	1911–12.	1910–11.	1911–12.	1910–11.	1911–12.	1910–11.
Delatite	241	619	3,369	25,670	13·98	41·47
Bogong	999	733	23,217	21,470	23·24	29·29
Croajingolong	2,634	3,160	156,960	113,476	59·59	35·91
Tambo	3,197	3,827	159,562	174,473	49·91	45·59
Dargo	4,228	4,498	174,024	219,547	41·16	48·81
Tanjil	5,063	5,320	225,860	331,383	44·61	62·29
Buln Buln	617	785	17,745	50,381	28·76	64·18
Remainder of State	1,244	1,209	31,923	45,703	25·66	37·80
Total	18,223	20,151	792,660	982,103	43·50	48·74

MILLET, CHICORY, AND HOPS.

Crop.	Area.		Produce.		Crop.	Area.		Produce.	
	1911–12.	1910–11.	1911–12.	1910–11.		1911–12.	1910–11.	1911–12.	1910–11.
Chicory	Acres. 399	Acres. 467	Tons.* 333	Tons.* 432	Millet (broom)	Acres. 286	Acres. 680	Cwt.† Cwt.‡ 1,652 1,147	Cwt.† Cwt.‡ 3,663 4,000
Hops	122	121	Cwt. 777	Cwt. 936					

* Dry.   † Fibre.   ‡ Seed.

NOTE.—Millet is principally grown in the county of Delatite; chicory in counties Mornington, Dargo, and Tanjil; and hops in counties Delatite, Bogong, Dargo, and Tanjil.

Perishable and Frozen Produce.

Description of Produce.			Exports from State (Oversea).		Deliveries from Government Cool Stores.	
			Quarter ended 30.6.12	Quarter ended 30.6.11.	Quarter ended 30.6.12.	Quarter ended 30 6.11.
Butter	...	lbs.	625,184	7,507,892	874,664	7,780,584
Milk and Cream	...	cases	148	2,056	1,205	30
Milk and Cream (dried)		"	2	...	...	...
Cheese	...	lbs.	26,040	194,160	4,800	219,730
Ham and Bacon	...	"	38,520	98,010	...	...
Poultry	...	head	3,705	2,910	2,224	1,898
Eggs...	...	dozen	...	...	25,149	24,574
Mutton and Lamb		carcases	171,469	35,155	11,520	1,328
Beef ...	...	quarters	3,397	1,427	230	...
Veal ...	...	carcases	777	772	65	163
Pork...	...	"	287	1,530	820	648
Rabbits and Hares	...	pairs	183,444	70,272	130,361	14,044
Sundries	...	lbs.	...	...	24,316	78,014

R. CROWE, *Superintendent of Exports.*

Fruit, Bulbs, Plants, Grain, &c.

Imports and Exports Inspected for Quarter ending 30th June, 1912.

Goods.	Imports.		Exports.	Goods.	Imports.		Exports.
	Inter-State.	Oversea.	Oversea		Inter-State.	Oversea.	Oversea.
Apples (Custard) ...	18	—	—	Mace	—	44	—
Apples and Pears ...	1,384	1	37,749	Melons	—	—	6
Apricots ...	—	—	257	Nutmegs ...	—	195	—
Bananas, bunches ..	71,720	16,891	—	Nuts	254	3,211	—
Bananas, cases ...	2,867	14,325	—	Oats	26,824	175,340	—
Barley ...	10,907	31,533	—	Olives ...	5	—	—
Beans ...	42	478	—	Onions ...	—	125	2
Blackberries ...	48	—	—	Oranges ...	54,251	224	61
Bulbs ...	—	28	32	Passion ...	1,310	—	25
Chillies ...	—	387	—	Paw Paws ...	9	—	—
Cocoa beans ...	—	1,385	—	Peaches ...	—	—	6
Cocoanuts ...	—	489	—	Pepper ...	—	160	—
Coffee beans ...	—	4,144	—	Peas, dried ...	17,917	319	—
Copra ...	—	212	—	Persimmons ...	68	—	—
Cucumbers ...	111	—	—	Pineapples ..	14,958	—	79
Dates ...	—	2,667	—	Plants ...	261	133	510
Figs ..	—	50	—	Plums ...	—	—	14
Fruit—				Potatoes ...	233	—	718
Canned ...	—	—	3,395	Prunes ..	—	200	—
Dried ...	—	175	4,698	Quinces ..	1,113	—	23
Mixed ...	34	7	25	Rice ...	3,863	92,425	—
Grapes ...	15	—	6	Seeds ...	1,222	15,850	211
Ginger ...	58	1,005	—	Spice ...	—	132	—
Hops ...	—	473	—	Tomatoes ...	50	—	—
Jams and Sauces, &c.	—	—	2,024	Vegetables ...	5,286	277	11
Lemons ...	1,003	60	1,398	Wheat, Grain, &c.	4,673	155	—
Lentils ...	—	122	—	Yams ...	44	—	—
Linseed ...	—	449	—				
Logs ...	763	117	—	Totals ...	221,316	363,788	51,250

Total number of packages inspected for quarter ending 30th June, 1912 = 636,354.

E. MEEKING, *Senior Fruit Inspector.*

STATISTICS.

Rainfall in Victoria.—Second Quarter, 1912.

TABLE showing average amount of rainfall in each of the 26 Basins or Regions constituting the State of Victoria for each month and the quarter, with the corresponding monthly and quarterly averages for each Basin, deduced from all available records to date.

Basin or District.	April.		May.		June		Quarter.	
	Amount.	Average.	Amount.	Average.	Amount.	Average.	Amount.	Average.
	points.	points.	points.	points.	points.	points	points.	points.
Glenelg and Wannon Rivers	226	217	124	290	211	357	561	864
Fitzroy, Eumeralla, and Merri Rivers	302	248	202	325	211	373	715	916
Hopkins River and Mount Emu Creek	246	204	135	260	194	305	575	769
Mount Elephant and Lake Corangamite	231	200	120	246	167	274	518	720
Cape Otway Forest ...	437	319	238	407	313	460	988	1,186
Moorabool and Barwon Rivers	226	209	113	240	227	266	566	715
Werribee and Saltwater Rivers	167	194	77	216	215	243	459	653
Yarra River and Dandenong Creek	330	307	189	317	224	382	743	1,006
Koo-wee-rup Swamp	297	306	184	315	277	384	758	1,005
South Gippsland	350	386	243	313	270	427	863	1,126
Latrobe and Thomson Rivers	267	295	217	285	267	384	751	965
Macallister and Avon Rivers	112	166	118	155	132	257	362	578
Mitchell River	208	212	184	229	99	290	491	731
Tambo and Nicholson Rivers	170	165	271	186	123	262	569	613
Snowy River	209	223	291	269	187	414	777	906
Murray River	28	143	10	188	250	268	288	599
Mitta Mitta and Kiewa Rivers	92	211	35	309	408	510	535	1,030
Ovens River	85	229	16	349	435	529	536	1,107
Goulburn River	78	183	53	261	271	357	402	801
Campaspe River	61	164	65	260	247	317	373	741
Loddon River	38	141	38	200	237	250	313	591
Avon and Richardson Rivers	28	122	32	184	246	222	306	528
Avoca River	23	132	24	187	270	223	317	542
Eastern Wimmera	89	142	43	240	274	302	406	684
Western Wimmera	41	163	50	218	263	265	354	646
Mallee District	18	107	12	160	281	181	311	448
The whole State	132	185	94	238	253	306	479	729

100 points = 1 inch.

H. A. HUNT,

10th July, 1912.   *Commonwealth Meteorologist.*

REMINDERS FOR SEPTEMBER.

LIVE STOCK.

HORSES.—Still continue to feed stabled horses well; feed green-stuff if available. Continue rugging to encourage the shedding of the coat; good grooming will also be beneficial. Continue giving hay or straw to grass-fed working horses. Feed old and badly-conditioned horses liberally

CATTLE.—Cows should still be rugged, but coverings should be removed frequently, in order to enable the animal to get rid of the old coat; or, better still, a good curry-combing may be given. Continue hay or straw. Give calves a good warm dry shed. Give the milk to young calves at blood heat.

PIGS.—Supply plenty of bedding in warm well-ventilated styes. Keep styes clean and dry, and feeding troughs clean and wholesome. Sows may now be turned into grass run.

SHEEP.—Prepare for shearing. Clean yards to minimize dust; also remove all straw, chaff, &c., from sheds and wool bins. For superior wools, procure special packs; for ordinary wools, the usual kind will do. Clean all excessively "daggy" sheep before bringing them on to the shearing board.

POULTRY.—September is one of the best for hatching. Incubators should be kept going, and broody hens set. Care must be taken to keep down vermin, as they now breed quickly; use sprays in houses and Insectibane or Pestend in nests—nothing stunts chickens quicker than vermin. The food for young chicks should be fine oatmeal, stale bread crumbs, a little calcined (dry) bone, and a pinch of powdered charcoal. Slightly moisten with skim milk, and add very finely pulped raw onion. Make the whole friable, and feed frequently ("little and often") just as much as they will readily eat, as an excess of food only sours and disturbs their digestive organs. Do not feed animal food yet. Skim milk is safer, and answers same purpose. Keep chicken's feet dry—wet grass causes a chill; and once the birds are chilled, trouble may be expected.

CULTIVATION.

FARM.—Plant early potatoes, and work up fallow for the main crop. Keep fallow for summer forage crops well worked up with the disc and harrows. Make early sowings of mangolds, beet, field carrots, and turnips. Push on with the fallowing in the Northern Districts. Prepare land for tobacco seed beds by burning rubbish on the site; afterwards work up to depth of three or four inches.

ORCHARD.—Commence spring ploughing; plough in leguminous crops for green manure as soon as the plants are in full flower. Finish grafting early in the month. Spray peach and apricot trees with Bordeaux mixture as the blossom buds are opening, as a preventive against "leaf curl" and "shot hole" fungi; watch for peach aphis, and spray when present with tobacco solution.

FLOWER GARDEN.—Cultivate and work up the surface to a fine tilth—clear out all weeds. Water newly planted shrubs, &c., if the weather is dry. Plant out cannas, early dahlias, chrysanthemums, gladioli, and other herbaceous plants.

VEGETABLE GARDEN.—Plant out seedlings. Sow seeds for summer use, such as tomatoes, cucumbers, marrows, pumpkins, melons, &c. Plant out tomatoes, and shelter till frosts are over. Hoe and work up the soil surface.

VINEYARD.—Plantation of young vines (grafted or ungrafted) should be concluded before the commencement of September; pruning of old vines likewise. Prune vines recently planted just before buds commence to swell (if not pruned when planted), cutting strongest cane back to two buds. Do not delay this work until buds have shot, as this seriously weakens the young vine. Towards end of month, field grafting may be commenced, if weather be fine and warm. If cold and wet, postpone until October. Swab with acid iron sulphate vines which showed signs of Black Spot last season. To avoid burning, this must be completed before the buds commence to swell.

Cellar.—Conclude spring racking early in month, if not already done. Fill up, regularly, all unfortified wines.

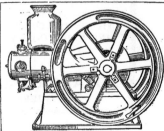

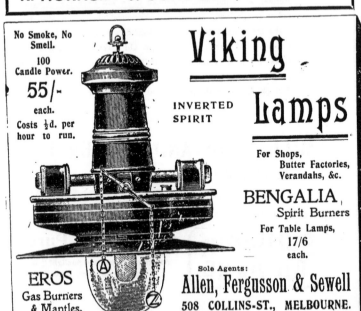

LITERATURE FOR AGRICULTURISTS.

PLAN AND SPECIFICATION OF SHEEP-SHEARING SHED. 2s. 6d. *Postage*, 1d.

MILK CHARTS (Monthly and Weekly), 6d, per dozen, post free. When ordering, dairy farmers should mention " Monthly " or " Weekly."

By Professor A. J. Ewart, Government Botanist.

WEEDS, POISON PLANTS, AND NATURALIZED ALIENS OF VICTORIA. 2s. 6d. *Postage :* Commonwealth, 1½d. ; N.Z., 5d. ; British and Foreign, 10d.

PLANTS INDIGENOUS TO VICTORIA. Vol. II., 10s. *Postage :* Com., 2d. ; N.Z., 8d. ; Brit. & For., 1s. 4d.

By C. French, F.E.S., Government Entomologist.

DESTRUCTIVE INSECTS OF VICTORIA. Parts I., II., III., IV., V. 2s. 6d. each. *Postage :* Parts I. and III., C., 1d. ; N.Z., 3d.; B. & F., 6d. each. Parts II. and IV., C., 1½d. ; N.Z., 4d. ; B. & F., 8d. each. Part V., C., 1d. ; N.Z., 4d. ; B. & F., 7d.

By D. McAlpine, Government Vegetable Pathologist.

RUSTS OF AUSTRALIA. 5s. *Postage :* C., 2d. ; N.Z., 8d. ; B. & F., 1s. 4d.

SMUTS OF AUSTRALIA. 4s. *Postage :* C., 2½d. ; N.Z., 9d. ; B. & F., 1s. 6d.

FUNGUS DISEASES OF CITRUS TREES IN AUSTRALIA. 2s. *Postage :* C., 1d. ; N.Z., 3d. ; B. & F., 6d.

FUNGUS DISEASES OF STONE FRUIT TREES IN AUSTRALIA. 2s. 6d. *Postage :* C., 1½d. ; N.Z., 5d. ; B. & F., 10d.

SYSTEMATIC ARRANGEMENT OF AUSTRALIAN FUNGI. 3s. *Postage :* C., 2d. ; N.Z., 8d. ; B. & F., 1s. 4d.

THE DEPARTMENT OF AGRICULTURE,
MELBOURNE, VICTORIA.

Remittances from places outside the Commonwealth to be by Money Order only.

Pamphlets obtainable from the Director of Agriculture, Melbourne, Free on Application.

NEW SERIES.

1. SILO CONSTRUCTION. *A. S. Kenyon, C.E.*
2. HINTS FOR NEW SETTLERS. *T. A. J. Smith.*
* 3. APPLE GROWING FOR EXPORT. *P. J. Carmody.*
* 4. BOOKKEEPING FOR FARMERS. *W. McIver, A.I.A.V., A.S.A.A., Eng.*
5. CIDER MAKING. *J. Knight.*
* 6. FARM PLUMBING. *C. H. Wright.*
7. CITRUS FRUIT CULTURE. *E. E. Pescott.*
8. BUILDING HINTS FOR SETTLERS. *A. S. Kenyon, C.E., and others.*
9. TOBACCO CULTURE. *T. A. J. Smith.*
10. SILOS AND SILAGE. *G. H. F. Baker.*
11. THE BEET SUGAR INDUSTRY AND CLOSER SETTLEMENT. *H. T. Easterby.*
12. WORMS IN SHEEP. *S. S. Cameron, D.V. Sc., M.R.C.V.S.*

* Not yet available.

GOVERNMENT STUD BULLS.

AVAILABLE FOR SERVICE OF COWS BELONGING TO BONA-FIDE SETTLERS UNDER THE CLOSER SETTLEMENT ACTS.

Fee, 5s. per cow.

Jersey Bull **"DREADNOUGHT"**; CALVED, 22nd October, 1908.
  Sire:—Sir Jack (188).   *Dam :*—Lady Kitchener, by Lord Melbourne.
    (In charge of Mr. H. Crumpler, Block 148, Bamawm.)

Jersey Bull **"ROSE FOX"**; CALVED, 19th August, 1909.
  Sire:—Starbright Fox (190).   *Dam:*—Tuberose, by Magnet's Progress (54 A.J.H.B.).
    (In charge of Mr. W. W. Vickers, Bamawm).

Jersey Bull **"VERBENA'S BOY"**; CALVED, 10th January, 1908.
  Sire:—Acrobat.   *Dam:*—Verbena 2nd, by Snowdrop's Progress 2nd.
    (In charge of Messrs. Laing and Mundie, Block 70, Bamawm.)

Jersey Bull **"NOBILITY"**; CALVED, 2nd April, 1910.
  Sire:—Lucy's Noble of Oaklands.   *Dam:*—Winnie of Melrose 3rd, by Royal Blue.
    (In charge of Mr. E. T. Partington, Block 136, Bamawm.)

Jersey Bull **"MILKY WAY"**; CALVED, 20th June, 1909.
  Sire:—Starbright Fox (190).   *Dam:*—Milkmaid 34th (590), by Plinlimmon (imp. 62 A.H.B.).
    (In charge of H. Macauley, Nanneella.)

Jersey Bull **"GOLD MEDAL"**; CALVED, 3rd April, 1910.
  Sire :—Golden Fox (142 A.J.H.B.).   *Dam:*—Melba, by Greystanes **2nd.**
    (In charge of Mr. W. F. Hill, Blocks 43 and 44, Nanneella.)

Jersey Bull **"MAGNET'S FOX"**; CALVED, 6th November, 1909.
  Sire:—Fox's Laddie.   *Dam :*—Magnet 28th, by Defender (imp.) (2288 H.C.J.H.B.).
    (In charge of Mr. C. C. Woods, Block 29, Koyuga.)

Jersey Bull **"ZODIAC"**; CALVED, 10th November, 1908.
  Sire:—Starbright Fox (190).   *Dam:*—Zoe 4th (805), by Handsome Hero.
    (In charge of Mr. R. J. Chappell, Block 12F, Swan Hill.)

Jersey Bull **"GAY FOX"**; CALVED, 12th May, 1909.
  Sire:—Starbright Fox (190).   *Dam :*—Floss, by Plinlimmon (imp. 62).
    (In charge of Mr. Dyer, Swan Hill.)

DEPARTMENT OF AGRICULTURE,
VICTORIA.

GOVERNMENT STUD BULLS.

AVAILABLE FOR SERVICE OF COWS BELONGING TO BONA-FIDE SETTLERS UNDER THE CLOSER SETTLEMENT ACTS—*continued.*

Fee, 5s. per cow.

Jersey Bull "WILLIAM OF AYRE"; CALVED, February, 1910.

Sire:—Favourite's Fox 2nd. *Dam:*—Bessie McCarthy, by Snowflake's Progress.

(In charge of Mr. J. S. Dickinson, Block 13, Nyah.)

Jersey Bull "FOX'S LAD"; CALVED, 5th October, 1908.

Sire:—Fox, by Snowdrop's Progress 2nd. *Dam:*—Pansy 2nd, by Duke.

(In charge of Mr. Ernest E. Borley, Block 6, Nyah.)

Ayrshire Bull "PETER OF WILLOWVALE"; CALVED, 30th Sept., 1909.

Sire:—Annetta's Pride (243). *Dam:*—Madge 2nd (Appendix A.H.B.), by Red Chief (359).

(In charge of Mr. F. McIvor, Block 12F, Swan Hill.)

Particulars of extended pedigrees, milking records, &c., can be obtained from each bull holder, from the resident Dairy Supervisors **(Mr. O'KEEFE, Rochester, or Mr. S. J. KEYS, Swan Hill),** or from **The Department of Agriculture, Melbourne.**

AVAILABLE FOR SERVICE OF COWS THE PROPERTY OF SETTLERS ON WYUNA ESTATE.

Red Danish Bull "CLAUDIUS"; CALVED, 10th November, 1909.

Sire:—Ernst Bellinge (imp.) *Dam:*—Kirsten IX. (imp.).

Fee, 5s.

Red Danish Bull "HAMLET"; CALVED, 1st August, 1910.

Sire:—Ernst Bellinge (imp.). *Dam:*—Marianne IV. *G. Dam:*—Marianne III. (imp.).

Fee, 5s.

Particulars of extended pedigrees, milking records and prizes may be obtained from. and arrangement for service made with, **Mr. E. R. EMERY,** Manager, Government Farm, Wyuna, where the bulls are kept.

AVAILABLE FOR SERVICE OF COWS THE PROPERTY OF BEET GROWERS AT BOISDALE.

Red Polled Bull "TABACUM"; CALVED, 12th November, 1908.

Sire:—Acton Ajax (imp.). *Dam:*—Janet, by Primate by Laureate (imp.).

Fee, 7s. 6d. (available to 20 cows).

Application to Mr. E. STEER, Herdsman, at the Homestead, Block 21.

DEPARTMENT OF AGRICULTURE,
VICTORIA.

Burnley Horticultural School.

E. E. PESCOTT,   Principal.

ANNOUNCEMENT.

The curriculum and management of the Burnley Horticultural School have now been arranged so that greater advantages and facilities will be given to students of both sexes in Horticulture and allied subjects.

The present course of Horticulture for male students includes a two years' course, students being charged a fee of £5 per annum.

Classes have been formed at Burnley, whereby students of both sexes may receive instruction on two afternoons of each week—Tuesdays and Fridays.

Instruction includes theoretical and practical work, and will commence at 2 p.m. This will be a two years' course, and the fee charged will be £2 per annum.

It has also been arranged that several short lecture courses shall be given on subjects which are suitable adjuncts to Horticulture, such as Poultry Farming, Bee-keeping, and Fruit Preserving, and these courses will be open and free to the general public. The subjects and dates of the Short Course Lectures will be announced monthly in this Journal.

STUDENTS SHOULD ENROLL WITHOUT DELAY.

APPLICATION FOR ADMISSION SHOULD BE MADE TO

The Director of Agriculture, Public Offices, Melbourne,

OR TO THE PRINCIPAL.

By Authority: Albert J. Mullett, Acting Government Printer, Melbourne.

VICTORIAN RAILWAYS.

SPECIAL NOTICE.

Show Visitors and Others

ARE INVITED TO CALL AT THE

Government Tourist Bureau, Corner Collins and Swanston Sts., Opposite Town Hall, Melbourne.

THE GOVERNMENT TOURIST BUREAU.

:: :: Full :: ::
Information

freely given
respecting
Rail,
Coach, and
Steamer
Travel,
and Tourist
Accommo-
dation.

:: Cheap ::
Excursions

List of
Trains, &c.,
Tourist Hand-
books, Maps,
and Country and
Melbourne and
Suburban Hotel
and Boarding
House Guides
free on
application.

Ask for Particulars of Trips to the Buffalo Plateau (all the year round); and to the Gippsland Lakes, Buchan Caves, Victorian Alpine District, Daylesford and Midland District, Healesville, Warburton, Dandenong Ranges; and to Queenscliff, Lorne, and other Seaside Resorts (from 15th Nov. till 30th April).

WHEN IN TOWN RING UP THE GOVERNMENT TOURIST OFFICER.

TELEPHONE 174 CENTRAL.   E. B. JONES, Acting Secretary for Railways.

[Registered at the General Post Office, Melbourne, for transmission by Post as a Newspaper.]

The Journal of THE DEPARTMENT OF AGRICULTURE OF VICTORIA, AUSTRALIA.

September, 1912.

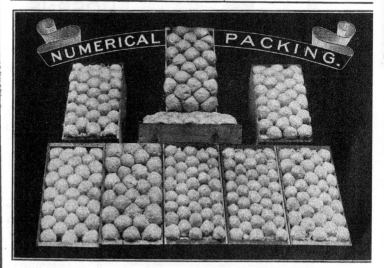

NUMERICAL PACKING.

PRICE THREEPENCE. (Annual Subscription—Victoria, Inter-State, and N.Z., 3 -; British and Foreign, 5/-.)

THE JOURNAL

OF

THE DEPARTMENT OF AGRICULTURE,

VICTORIA, AUSTRALIA.

CONTENTS.—SEPTEMBER, 1912.

COPYRIGHT PROVISIONS AND SUBSCRIPTION RATES.

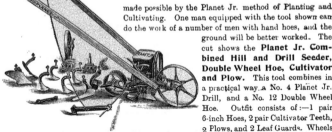

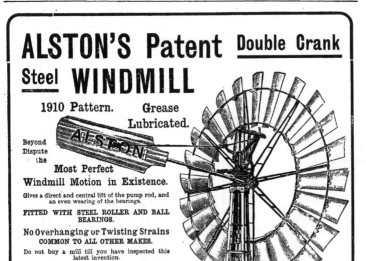

THE JOURNAL

OF

The Department of Agriculture

OF

VICTORIA.

Vol. X.   Part 9.   10th September, 1912.

SOME RESULTS IN FALLOWING LAND.

*By John W. Paterson, B.Sc., Ph.D., Experimentalist, and P. R. Scott,
Chemist for Agriculture.*

The most pressing demands of an ordinary crop are for water, phosphates, and nitrates. The importance of these arises from their comparative scarcity in the soil. The deficiency of phosphates is most easily made good by applying some phosphatic manure along with the seed, The deficiency of water and nitrates can usually best be remedied by some system of fallowing the land.

SCHEME OF EXPERIMENTS.

In order to find how two systems of fallowing affected the water and nitrate content of a soil, three plots were staked off on the farm of Sparrovale, Geelong, last September. The plots each measured 10 by 5 yards, and lay side by side with 2 yards space between them. The land had been sown down to Algerian oats at the end of June, and the crop was well brairded in September, when the plots were laid off. The scheme of the experiments was as follows :—

Plot A.—Dug over on 12th September, and the surface kept stirred from 16th October onwards.

Plot B.—Dug over on 12th September, and no further cultivation given.
Plot C.—Oat crop left growing.
The experiments continued until the 28th February of the present year.

WORKING PLAN.

The effect of fallowing and cropping upon the supply of water and nitrates was determined by sampling the soil of each plot at intervals of about six weeks. The samples were taken with a spade from a freshly exposed surface in holes dug on the central line of each plot. One of us was always present. They were forwarded for analysis in suitable bottles the same day. The holes were filled in as soon as the samples had been taken, and on any plot the next periodical sampling took place 2 yards further along the central line of the plot.

At the outset, each plot was sampled at six successive depths of 9 inches, $1\frac{1}{2}$ to $4\frac{1}{2}$ feet. Later on, it became apparent that the lower subsoils varied so considerably in character that it was useless to continue sampling to that depth. Attention was then confined to the upper 18 inches, where the d fferences of soil were naturally less pronounced.

In conducting the analyses, water was determined by drying to constant weight in a steam oven. Nitrates were determined according to the method described in a previous article by Mr. W. C. Robertson, Chief Deputy Chemist.

FALLOWING AND SOIL MOISTURE.

Table I. gives the percentage of water in the top 18 inches of soil at each date of sampling. The results are calculated on the dry soil.

TABLE I.

—				Worked Fallow.	Neglected Fallow.	Oat Crop.
				per cent.	Per cent.	Per cent.
October 16	..	..	..	25·22	24·27	24·95
November 28	..	..	..	19·62	15·95	15·22
January 17	..	..	..	20·66	11·61	10·01
February 28	..	..	..	21·67	12·38	10·06

In viewing the results the conditions regulating the loss of water on good fallow, bad fallow, and on crop may be briefly recapitulated. Water rises in a moist soil somewhat rapidly by capillarity. In a good fallow, the upper layer of soil is kept loose and dry by cultivation, so that its capillary power is lost. This loose, dry layer protects the water within the capillary zone underneath from sun and wind. In a bad fallow, the surface is compact, and also damper, so that capillary action is continued right through to the top, which is unprotected from drying influences. A crop requires much water for its growth, which must come from the soil. Experiments bearing upon the water losses through plants were previously reported.*

INFLUENCE OF WEATHER.

Table II. gives the weekly rainfall at Sparrovale from 19th August until the close of the experiments.

TABLE II.

Week ending.		Points.	Week ending.		Points.	Week ending.		Points.
August 26	..	5	October 14	..	10	December 16	..	150
September	2 ..	124	,, 21	..	9	,, 23	..	61
,,	9 ..	158	,, 28	..	13	,, 30	..	32
,,	16 ..	15	November 4	..	85	January 13	..	8
,,	23 ..	70	,, 25	..	27	February 10	..	42
,,	30 ..	165	December 2	..	14	,, 24	..	20
October	7 ..	12	,, 9	..	63	,, 28	..	0

In the weeks omitted no rain fell. September was a wet month, and the plots showed a fair degree of uniformity at the first sampling on 16th October. With more moderate but fairly distributed falls in the next period, the water contents of the soils varied considerably at 28th November. The first fallow was hoed over thrice during the period, and the oat crop was growing rapidly. These circumstances explain the tendency of the results at the second sampling. On 27th December, the crop was cut, and yielded at the rate of 2 tons 4½ cwt. hay per acre. From this date until the last samples were taken (two months), a total of 80 points of

---

* June, 1912.

rain fell on four dates. It was a dry spell, and gave no chance to equalize matters. At the final sampling, the cropped plot contained less than half the water present in the worked fallow; the neglected fallow was also bad. It had become caked on the surface, and carried a fair cover of weeds, both of which reduced its water content.

When taking samples at the later dates, it was evident to the eye that the worked fallow had much more water than the others. The assistants also noticed it when digging the holes. The worked fallow could be

TAKING SAMPLES OF SOIL.

dug easily with a spade, while the other plots required a pick to get down to them.

THE RESULTS BY WEIGHT.

By weighing the earth from a measured hole, it was estimated that 1 acre of the so l to a depth of 18 inches equalled 2,270 tons in the dry condition. Employ ng this figure, the water percentages at the different dates may be converted into tons.

TABLE III.

——				Worked Fallow.	Neglected Fallow.	Oat Crop.
				Tons.	Tons.	Tons.
October 16	..	..	..	572	551	566
November 28	..	..	..	445	362	345
January 17	..	..	..	469	263	227
February 28	..	..	..	492	281	228

At the close of the experiments, the cropped soil contained 264 tons, and the neglected fallow 211 tons less of water per acre in the first 18 inches than the corresponding worked fallow. One ton of water to the acre equals almost exactly one point of rain.

RESULTS OBTAINED ABROAD.

While it did not appear useful to carry the moisture investigations at Sparrovale deeper than 18 inches, there are indications in the above figures that the effect of cropping and fallowing upon water content would be felt at much greater depths. Experiments conducted elsewhere support this inference. Moisture determinations of the soil under barley and bare-fallow respectively were made at Rothamsted in the dry summer of 1870. Table IV. gives the results, which are stated as percentages of the wet soil. [†]

TABLE IV.

—	Bare Fallow.	Barley Crop.
	Per cent.	Per cent.
First 9 inches	20·36	11·91
Second ,,	29·53	19·32
Third ,,	34·84	22·83
Fourth ,,	34·32	25·09
Fifth ,,	31·31	26·98
Sixth ,,	33·55	26·38

Similar results have since been obtained by King and others in America. As the result of three years' trials at Nebraska, Burr reported "that land under summer tillage or thorough cultivation had accumulated from 5.5 to 7 inches (557 to 709 tons) more water in the first 6 feet of soil than similar land growing a crop."[‡]

EFFECT OF AUSTRALIAN CLIMATE.

While the Rothamsted figures and those quoted from America bear out the general conclusion that water-saving is effected to considerable depths by a good fallow, it is probable that they understate the relative advantage to be expected in Australia. Further investigations on the subject are now proceeding. Fallowing operations and the formation of mulches are most required where the drying conditions are most powerful, and the result is the same, whether the evaporation is from the soil direct or by influencing the transpiration of plants.[§] From a table published by Hilgard,[||] it would seem that the climate of Australia is somewhat unique in causing evaporation, and it is primarily to prevent such losses that fallowing is carried out. The figures are given in Table V. The first column states the number of years during which observations were made; the second column gives the inches of water evaporated from a free surface of water during twelve months.

TABLE V.

—	Years.	Inches.
Rothamsted (England)	9	17·80
London (England)	14	20·66
Munich (Germany)	(?)	24·00
Emdrup (Denmark)	10	27·09
Syracuse (New York)	1	50·20
Fort Collins (Colorado)	11	41·00
San Diego (California)	1	57·60
Pekin (China)	(?)	38·80
Bombay (India)	5	82·28
Demerara (South America)	3	35·12
Kimberley (South Africa)	(?)	98·80
Alice Springs (South Australia)	(?)	103·50

[†] *The Soil.* By A. D. Hall. London. John Murray. 1903.
[‡] Univ. of Nebraska, Bul 114, by W. W. Burr.
[§] Water Requirements of Plants. Jour Agric., Vic., June, 1912.
[||] *Soils.* By Prof. Hilgard. New York. The Macmillan Co. 1906.

While the figures for Alice Springs cannot be regarded as typical, being, according to figures published by the Meteorological Office,[*] about one-half greater than those for the drier wheat areas, still the rate of evaporation in Australia is undoubtedly very great, and there is almost no country where an equal need for fallowing occurs, nor where greater saving in soil moisture may be expected from good cultivation.

RELATION OF FALLOWING TO NITRATES.

Leaving the effect of fallowing upon moisture, the nitrate contents of the plots next call for notice. Table VI. states the results obtained in lbs. per acre of nitrate nitrogen for each plot at the different dates of sampling. Depth, 18 inches.

TABLE VI.

——			Worked Fallow.	Neglected Fallow.	Oat Crop.
			lbs.	lbs.	lbs.
October 16	..	.. ..	14·04	17·58	trace
November 28	..	.. ..	43·20	44·35	3·31
January 17	..	.. ..	123·09	60·29	28·06
February 28	..	.. ..	148·61	58·63	32·49

Up to 16th October, the worked and the neglected fallow had received the same treatment, and the results show that the worked fallow had no original advantage. Nevertheless, at the end of February, the neglected fallow contained just 39 per cent. of the nitrate present in the worked plot.[†] The latter was seen to be much moister during the latter half of the experiments, and the extra nitrates are probably due in large measure to this extra moisture encouraging nitrification. This is in accord with the results of experiments recently reported in this *Journal*.[‡] Sufficient moisture will be of greatest benefit in aiding nitrification during the hot months of the year. In addition to the extra water present, the better aeration of the worked fallow would also encourage the production of nitrates.

NITRATES USED BY CROP.

On the cropped plot the nitrate content was only a trace at the date of the first sampling. Comparing it with the fallow plots, this could not be due to lack of moisture, as at that date the moisture content of each plot was approximately identical. It appears that the nitrates of this plot had been absorbed to supply the wants of the growing crop. Apparently the crop in the early part of its growth was taking all the nitrates it could find. This fact indicates the importance of nitrates in the soil, and the probability that the supply often fails to meet the demand.

RESULTS OBTAINED ABROAD.

Similar results showing the demand for nitrates by cereals were obtained in America by King.[§] On 20th June (summer) a strip of land 8 by 120 feet in a growing oat crop was cleared by shaving everything off just beneath the surface. At this date nitrates were determined on the cleared strip and also on the adjacent land growing oats, and similar determinations were made again after nineteen days. Table VII. gives the results in lbs. of nitrate nitrogen for each date at successive depths of 1 foot.

[*] *Commonwealth Year-Book*, 1911.
[†] This is exclusive of 25 lb nitrate nitrogen in the worked fallow and 4½ lb. in the neglected fallow found below the 18 inch level at the last sampling.
[‡] May, 1912, p. 275.
[§] Univ. of Wisconsin. Agric. Exp. St. Bul. 93.

TABLE VII.

		Commencement of Fallowing.		After 19 Days.	
		Ground Fallow.	Oat Crop.	Ground Fallow.	Oat Crop.
		lb.	lb.		
First foot ..	..	3·81	3·78	57·87	3·32
Second foot ..	..	2·78	2·70	2·74	0·00
Third „ ..	..	19·23	21·37	13·12	3·08
Fourth „ ..	..	41·64	43·07	42·52	25·13
Totals	..	67·46	70·92	116·25	31·53

While the cleared or fallow strip made a gain of 49 lbs. nitrate nitrogen, the cropped land lost 39 lbs.

NITRATES FORMED NEAR SURFACE.

Looking to Table VII., it will be seen that the increase of nitrates in the fallowed strip during the nineteen days was confined to the top foot of soil. The reason is that nitrate production requires plenty of fresh air, and the less porous the soil the more superficial will the action be. Where any considerable supply of nitrates is found below the second foot of soil, they will have passed down by diffusion and drainage. As the upper portion of a soil in particular may become very dry under a crop or neglected fallow (Table IV.), it is the more necessary in a dry climate that the land be well supplied with nitrates before the vegetative period commences.

At Sparrovale the oat crop was the third in succession on the ground. On the cropped plot during the experiments no nitrates were ever found below 18 inches at any date of sampling. The same was true for all the plots at the first sampling, and the oat crop undoubtedly started growth under bad nitrate conditions. Had September not been exceptionally wet (532 points) it would have been still worse. The interposition of a fallow between two crops allows the soil to lay up a store of nitrates. With moderate winter rains, these will pass more or less downwards in the soil, and can be drawn upon by next season's crop for the purposes of growth.

NITRATES AVAILABLE FOR NEXT CROP.

That the nitrates produced in fallow must exercise a beneficial effect upon the next crop is clearly indicated in a table by King and reproduced by Hall. Analyses were made in spring of two similar soils, one of which had been fallowed and the other cropped during the previous year. The figures represent lbs. of nitrate nitrogen per acre.

TABLE VIII.

		1st Foot.	2nd Foot.	3rd Foot.	4th Foot.
		lb.	lb.	lb.	lb.
Land previously fallow ..	..	212	56	22	13
Land previously cropped ..	..	25	15	10	7

Warington* estimated that " the production of nitrates for the next crop is probably the mo.t important result of a bare fallow." While this is no doubt true for England, it hardly holds for Australia, where moisture conservation takes the first place. At the same time we have the authority of Warington added to King for stating that fallowing greatly increases the nitrate supply available for the next season's crop, and the analyses of the Sparrovale soils (Table VI.) indicate that the third oat crop grown on the land started its life with too small a supply of nitrates.

A Manurial Test.

On 2nd November two small plots of $\frac{1}{80}$ acre were staked off in the oat crop adjacent to the plots laid down for sampling the soils. One cwt. of

WEIGHING SAMPLES FOR MOISTURE CONTENTS.

nitrate of soda per acre was broadcasted on one plot, while the other received no manure. The object was to determine whether the addition of nitrate to a soil, which had proved so poor in nitrate at the previous sampling, would benefit the crop. The oats were then 6 inches high. The crops were harvested and weighed on 27th December, when the yield from the nitrated plot was increasd by 228 lbs. dry hay per acre, or 2 cwt. (nearly). There had been a fair rainfall after the application of the manure, but the crop was probably too far advanced to make a good use of it.

In concluding this report, we desire to thank Mr. Baird, manager at Sparrovale, for granting facilities for these experiments, and for furnishing us with the rainfall records.

[*Summary next page.*]

* *Chemistry of the Farm.* By R. Warington. London. Vinton & Co.

Summary.

1. A well-worked fallow prevents much loss of soil-moisture during dry weather.

2. A fallow may do little good if neglected.

3. A crop leaves the soil extremely dry in the autumn.

4. This lack of moisture must affect the succeeding crop unless the winter be exceptionally wet.

5. The Australian climate indicates in a special degree the need for fallowing.

6. Land growing a crop may contain only a trace of nitrates.

7. This deficiency may starve a crop.

8. Nitrate formation stops when the surface soil becomes too dry.

9. A growing crop dries up the surface soil.

10. It is desirable, therefore, that a crop should start with a ready-formed nitrate supply in the soil and subsoil.

11. Such a nitrate supply will also favour a downward development of the roots.

12. A well-worked fallow meets the nitrate requirement of the succeeding crop.

13. Fallowing serves the double purpose of storing soil-moisture and supplying nitrates.

LUCERNE PLANTS.

Samples of lucerne plants obtained from a paddock sown nine months previously in the Rochester irrigation district. They show most effectively the prolific growth possible on suitable land under proper methods of irrigation.

BEE-KEEPING IN VICTORIA.

(Continued from page 477.)

F. R. Beuhne, Bee Expert.

Part VIII.—The Use of Comb-foundation.

Comb-foundation is the base or midrib of the combs in the frames of the modern bee-hive. It consists of a thin sheet of beeswax impressed on both sides with the shape of the basis of the cells of honey-comb, and is supplied to the bees with the object of obtaining a larger yield of honey than would be possible were they allowed to build their combs in their own way. The better results obtained by the use of full sheets of comb-foundation, instead of a comb-guide or narrow strip of embossed wax, are due to three factors :—1. A stronger force of worker bees and very few drones. 2. The faster building of the combs for brood and the storage of honey. 3. Stronger and straighter combs.

1. *Stronger Colonies.*

By the use of full sheets of comb-foundation, the number of worker bees is greatly increased, and the number of drones reduced to a minimum,

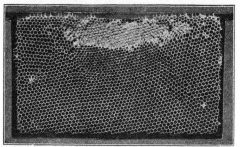

FIG. I.—COMB BUILT FROM STARTER, NEARLY ALL DRONE CELLS.

and as the former are producers and the latter consumers only, the profits of bee-keeping depend to a very large extent upon the ratio of worker bees to drones, and this is best regulated by the prevention of the building of drone-comb. The combs built by bees consist of two kinds of cells, one 1·5 inch in diameter, and known as worker cells, the other $\frac{1}{4}$ inch, called drone cells, the former being the cradle of the worker bee, the latter that of the drone.

In a state of nature a large percentage of the comb consists of drone cells, and immense numbers of drones are raised, a provision of nature to insure the fertilization of the queen from one hive by a drone from another colony, which, when bees are in their wild state, is often a considerable distance away. In the meeting of the sexes, which always takes place in the air often a considerable distance from the hives, a further safeguard against inbreeding is the aversion of the young queen to drones which come from her own hive, and have the same family odour. When a number of colonies occur close together, as in an apiary, the necessity of large numbers of drones ceases, as a limited number are always raised in each hive. Notwithstanding all efforts to suppress their production, the aggregate number is quite sufficient under the conditions of closer proximity of colonies.

A sheet of foundation is embossed with the pattern of worker comb, 25 cells to the square inch, and as the inside dimensions of a standard' frame are 17 inches by 8 inches, there are 3,400 cells on each sire, a total of 6,800. Making a liberal allowance of cells for the storage of honey and pollen around the brood, a comb of all worker cells produces fully 4,500 worker bees (1 lb. live weight) in one generation, while the same comb, but composed of drone cells, would, with the same allowance for storage cells, produce 2,900 drones. The amount of food and labour necessary for the raising of 4,500 workers is probably the same as for 2,900 drones, but while the workers, from a few days after hatching onwards, engage in productive work, the drones remain consumers to the end.

Further, the presence of large numbers of drones in the hive stimulates the swarming impulse of bees by causing crowding of the brood combs and that condition of the colony which precedes swarming. It will be seen from the above that the use of all worker combs not only increases the amount of surplus honey, but also counteracts in a large measure the

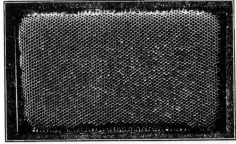

FIG. 2.—COMB FROM FULL SHEET OF FOUNDATION, ALL WORKER CELLS.

swarming propensity of bees. Under certain conditions, which will be dealth with later on, the use of starters instead of full sheets is not only permissible but even advisable.

2. Faster Comb-building.

Apart from the advantages of using full sheets of foundation enumerated above, the saving of the time of the bees by the quicker building of the combs and the consequent greater and earlier storing of surplus honey will amply repay the extra cost of foundation. Up to a few years ago it was assumed that when given full sheets of foundation the bees used no wax of their own secretion and wasted that which they secrete involuntarily when swarming, while quite recently the prevention of the exercise of one of their natural functions, the secretion of wax, has been held responsible for impaired vitality and consequent predisposition to disease. Experiments have shown, however, that no wax is wasted, and wax secretion not interfered with. A sheet of foundation of the grade generally used weighs 2 ozs., while the finished comb built from it weighs 3½ to 4 ozs., showing that an equal or nearly equal quantity of wax of their own secretion was added by the bees. In another experiment, when foundation of a different colour to that of the wax secreted by the bees was used, a cross-section of the resulting comb showed that nearly one-half of the total was newly-secreted wax.

As half the wax composing the combs is given to the bees and the other half secreted by them, it follows that without any interference with their natural functions, double the amount of comb is produced in a given time, thus bringing the colony much sooner into the condition for storing surplus honey. The speed of comb-building is also accelerated by the larger surface to work upon presented by full sheets as compared to combs from starters.

3. *Stronger and Straighter Combs.*

The importance of good combs for the raising of brood as well as for extracting cannot be overestimated. Even under the most favorable conditions, the combs built from starters are rarely equal to those from full sheets for either purpose. To get the full benefit of the frame-hive system, all combs should be interchangeable without in any way interfering with their utility. This result can only be obtained when the combs are perfectly straight. The correct spacing of the brood combs is $1\frac{3}{8}$ inch from centre to centre; this distance is necessary to allow of all the cells being used for brood, even when the combs are quite straight. When crooked combs are

FIG. 3.—COMB SHOWING CELLS SEALED BY THE BEES.

interchanged, the projecting portions prevent that part of the adjoining comb immediately opposite being occupied by brood. This also occurs in combs adjoining drone-brood. To get the maximum number of worker bees reared in the combs of the brood chamber, they should not only be of all worker cells, but also perfectly straight. When the surplus honey is taken by means of the extractor, and the empty combs returned to the hive to be refilled by the bees over and over again, straight combs are not only much easier to uncap, but suffer less damage in the process than crooked combs, particularly those built from starters, while much time is saved to the operator in uncapping and to the bees in repairing damaged combs. Combs built from full sheets of foundation are also less liable to melt and break down in hot weather, owing to the stronger midrid in the comb and the fastening to the bottom bar of the frame, and no bee-keeper should use starters except under conditions as set forth below.

Worker Comb from Starters.

To get worker comb built from starters, it is necessary to understand the factors governing comb-building. Worker comb is built so long as cells are required by the queen to deposit worker eggs in; under all other conditions more or less drone comb is produced. The production of worker

cells, therefore, depends upon the rate of egg-production by the queen and
the absence of worker comb already built. The ideal condition is that of
a· newly-hived swarm with a prolific queen. If the queen is defective in
laying owing to age or lack of vigour, and cannot keep pace with the comb-
builders,· drone comb will be built. The same result will occur when the
bees from the first-laid eggs hatch out before the combs completely fill the
frames. As soon as bees hatch out, the queen again deposits eggs in the
cells, neglecing the new comb which is in course of construction, and thus.
causing the building of drone cells. After having hived a swarm on a set·
of frames with starters, and allowed them to work for four or five days,
some of the frames in which little or no work has been done should ·be·
removed, and the number thus reduced to what they are likely to fill with
comb in the first three weeks after hiving. This rule also applies to colonies·
which have been shaken down, that is, deprived of their combs, on account
of foulbrood. Once bees begin to hatch from the new combs, it is extremely
difficult to get further worker combs built from starters, except by removing
all the combs but one or two, a procedure better left alone, as it would tend
to run the colony down to a very small one. Additional worker combs are·

FIG. 4.—TWO SHALLOW FRAMES OF SEALED COMB.

best secured by frames with full sheets of foundation given either above or
alongside the existing combs.

In a good district with a fair honey flow on, large swarms with vigorous
queens may fill a section super with honey while building their brood combs
from starters, but a queen-excluder should be used between sections and
frames. Such favorable conditions do not often obtain, however, and
most bee-keepers prefer to hive their swarms on drawn combs of the previous season, and when these combs are occupied, put a set of frames with
full sheets on top to get combs for the next season and for extracting purposes. Once two or three sets of combs for each colony are in existence,
there is no necessity for further comb-building, as colonies can be kept fully·
occupied by extracting the combs whenever they are ready for it and return.
ing them to be refilled, while all the wax secreted is required for the
capping of the full combs.

It should be understood that the less drone comb there is in a hive, the·
more likely will drone comb be built when starters are given to an estab.
lished hive between finished combs. Such a comb is shown in Fig. 1 of
the illustrations. Fig. 2 is an unsealed comb built on a full sheet of
foundation. Fig. 3 a comb completely sealed over, and Fig. 4 capped·
combs in half-depth or shallow frames.

(To be continued.)

GENERAL NOTES.

DRILLING *VERSUS* BROADCASTING OF MANURES.

Phosphatic manures have a special effect in encouraging the growth of a crop in its early stages and thus establishing a good plant. In order to exercise this effect the manure must be somewhere in the vicinity of the seed as the young plant has no wide-spreading roots. Drilling the manure with the seed gives the desired conditions with the smallest expenditure of manure. Experiments were conducted in Hungary to find whether drilling or broadcasting superphosphate gave the better return on cereal crops, and the results are described in the *Deut. Landw. Presse, 38* (1911). Barley, oats, wheat, and rye were the crops grown, and it was found that 102 lbs. of superphosphate applied with the drill gave better results than 307 lbs. applied broadcast on the average of all the tests.

MEAT EXPORTS.

Four of the Australian States sent meat to the United Kingdom in 1911, the non-exporters being Tasmania and Western Australia. The exports totalled 1,962,008 carcases of mutton, 1,649,043 of lamb, and 521,654 quarters of beef. Compared with the figures for 1910, the exports show a decrease of 28 per cent. in mutton, an increase of 12 per cent. in lamb, with beef nearly steady. In the case of each class of produce, more than one-half of the total export came from one particular State. Thus New South Wales sent 59 per cent. of the mutton, Victoria 65 per cent. of the lamb, and Queensland 95 per cent. of the beef shipped from the Commonwealth. The Agent-General in London reports the prospects for trade with the United Kingdom in 1912 to be "very satisfactory" from the Australian point of view. From time to time during the last six years, efforts have been made to induce the Continental Governments to allow the import of frozen meat into their dominions, but regarding this he states:—"Speaking generally of European countries, I fear that they are all impervious to external pressure in the matter of the removal of trade restrictions. There are many thousands of workmen in all the great industrial countries who rarely taste fresh meat; it cannot be supposed that this condition will last for ever, and when the barriers against the importation of frozen meat are broken down, it will be by pressure from within." The position is encouraging to those who take long views.

DRAINING WITH DYNAMITE.

A good deal has been heard recently of the use of dynamite and other high explosives in the removal of tree stumps and for breaking up hard subsoils in the orchard, but the latest application of the explosives is in the drainage of swamps. Such swamps are often caused by the surface waters which collect on low ground failing to percolate through a comparatively thin layer of impervious clay. The water is held as in a saucer. A Kansas farmer owned a 40-acre swamp of this kind on his land, and he proceeded to tap it. Across the lowest part, where the water was about 3 feet deep, he blasted a row of holes. In a few days the water had disappeared, and in the following season he is said to have reaped 1,600 bushels of oats from the 40 acres. Since then he has produced four cuttings of lucerne annually on this land.

SPRAYING AGAINST POTATO DISEASES.

Experiments have been conducted for twenty years on potato spraying at the Vermont Experiment Station, U.S.A., and *Bulletin 159* gives a summary account of the results. It is stated that by the application of Bordeaux mixture there was an average increase for the twenty years of 105 bushels per acre, equal to 64 per cent. gain. The gain from the use of the spray ranged from 18 per cent. in 1910 when there was no disease, up to 215 per cent. in 1901 when diseases were very prevalent. While the figures quoted show most satisfactory results, it has to be recollected that much depends on the time and manner of applying the spray, and also upon the climatic conditions. In the absence of disease, Bordeaux mixture is believed to increase the yield by toning up the plant.

SEED TESTING

A knowledge of the quality of seed sown is necessary in the case of any crop, but it is particularly necessary in the case of the smaller seeds such as grasses and clovers. There are two respects in which samples may fall short. First, the sample may have a low percentage of purity due to the presence of foreign and weed seeds. Second, the true seeds in the sample may show a low percentage of germination. Dealing with this question, a number of examples of the need for seed-testing are given in the *Journal of the New Zealand Department of Agriculture.* One of these may be quoted. The price for a certain line of white clover was 1s. 1d. per lb., and good white clover could be purchased for 1s. 6d. The cheaper sample gave a purity of 64 per cent., and a germination of 33 per cent. From these figures it is apparent that 100 lbs. of the "seed" contained just over 21 lbs. of pure white clover capable of growing. The germinating capacity of the weed seeds is not stated, but it is asserted that the greatest factor in the spread of weeds in New Zealand is the use of impure seeds. Cheap seed is *always* bad, and there are no "bargains" in the seed trade. The sowing of cheap, weed-infested seed is the most expensive policy that a farmer can adopt, and the germination of grass and clover seeds should be ascertained before buying.

MANURING FOR MILK.

Experiments on the manuring of cow pastures were started in 1909 by the Midland Agricultural and Dairy College, England. In the spring of that year, 8 acres were dressed with 10 cwt. ground lime per acre. A few days later one-half of this area received 4 cwt. superphosphate and 1½ cwt. sulphate of potash per acre. The two 4-acre plots were then separately fenced off, and no further applications of manure have been made to them. The method of the experiments was to graze cows on the plots each summer and note the respective milk yields. At first two cows were allotted to each plot, but it was found later that three could be carried. The two lots of three cows exchanged plots every fortnight in order to eliminate differences in the milking capacity of the cows. The experiments have completed their third year, and each year the manured section has yielded most milk. The original cost of the manures was £1 9s. per acre, and over the three years the gross revenue from the manured section has been increased by £6 5s. 6d. per acre, leaving a net profit of £4 16s. 6d. per acre from the use of the manures. It is estimated that the manures are not yet exhausted.

THE MISCHIEVOUS DODDER.

Perhaps no more striking instance of the necessity for seed cleaning could be advanced than that of clover seed. When it is delivered from the threshing machine, it is no more fit to send out to farmers for sowing than so much sand or sawdust. To begin with, the seed is mixed up with quantities of foreign matter—earth, small stones, vegetable fibres, fragments of wood, and the like. Of course, this miscellaneous collection is not, in itself, injurious to the prospective crop; but it serves to "make weight" in a manner entirely derogatory to the interests of the buyer. So all these odds and ends must be carefully sifted from the seed. Nor is this all. For among the newly-threshed seed, presumably clover, there is certain to be a considerable quantity of seed which will germinate and spring up as weeds of different varieties—all, of course, harmful to the clover crop. Among these injurious seeds is an exceedingly minute one, to detect which the seed merchant must be constantly alert. The plant which springs from it is a veritable blood-sucker, and is known as the dodder. Now, the dodder is not, as some suppose, a fungus, but a true flowering plant, which has acquired the parasite habit. Out of its germinating seed comes a little club-shaped root, which seeks the soil, while its young leafless stem grows upward like a thin thread, slowly moving round in sweeping circles. Should this stem fail to come into contact with a clover plant, it eventually falls prone upon the earth, and the embryo dodder soon dies. But let it once touch its prey—the clover— and it grips it with all the tenacity of the well-known bind-weed, to which it is nearly related. Moreover, it not only holds to the clover for support, but actually drives its "sucking roots" right into the substance of the clover's stem, and absorbs the vital sap of its helpless host.

As soon as the dodder has thus taken hold, its root dies away. Thereafter it has no connexion with the soil, as in the case of an ordinary plant; nor does it produce a single leaf. It becomes a rapidly-growing mass of red, hair-like fibres, twisting about its victim the clover, and sending out sucker roots at every possible point of contact. Thousands of tiny white flowers are produced, each destined to mature many seeds; but the increase of the dodder is an unmixed evil, for it is a hopeless hanger-on in the economy of nature. Fortunately, the seed of dodder does not ripen very freely in England; but this saving clause fails to apply to seed brought from abroad. Thus it is of the utmost importance that the agriculturist shall be acquainted with the history of his clover seed when he makes a purchase, or else make it a rule only to buy such seeds from firms of recognised standing.

The seed of dodder, as already mentioned, is exceedingly small, and the aid of an expert microscopical botanist must be invoked before a given quantity of clover seed can be pronounced "free." All big seed merchants are scrupulously particular on this point. After the clover seed has been passed through delicately adjusted machinery, which extracts the seeds of weeds, parasites, and every particle of rubbish in a manner as unerring as instinct, numerous samples are taken from the bulk, and subjected to the closest scrutiny through the microscope. If this final test fails to reveal impurity of any kind, then the clover seed is pronounced "clean," and guaranteed as such.—(From the *Southland Times*.)

CLEANLINESS comes next after godliness. Some say that in the dairy it should come before it.

PROPAGATION OF FRUIT TREES.

(*Continued from page 429.*)

C. F. Cole, Orchard Supervisor.

FUNGUS DISEASES.

Fungi, like mosses, are a low form of plant life. They belong to the great cryptogamic group, which includes plants that are flowerless and hence do not produce seed. In fungi, propagation is by spores of various kinds.

Fungi live on the substance of other plants. Some draw their nourishment from living plants (parasites). Some live on dead plant substance (saprophytes). When a parasite can live for a time on dead plant tissue it is called a facultative saprophyte. This property is of importance in securing the survival at times of parasitic infection.

An attack by plant fungus differs from an attack by insect life in the following particulars:—Generally with insects the attack is gradual and may be noticed from the earliest stages. The seriousness of an attack is generally controlled by the rapidity with which they perpetuate their

FIG. 72.—PEACH BUD ATTACKED BY LEAF CURL FUNGUS.

kind. But with most of the fungi, their presence is not observable until the harm is actually done. It is thus specially incumbent upon growers to apply a suitable fungicide at a time which will prevent the spores from germinating, and so destroy the fungus in its early stages of growth.

The germination of spores and the growth of fungi attacking fruit trees is largely controlled and influenced by the climatic conditions prevailing at the season suitable for their development. During a phenomenally wet spring, summer, or autumn, some species of fungi cause considerable damage that, in normal seasons, would do little or no harm. Dry weather conditions are adverse to their growth, whilst damp soil, bad drainage, excessive irrigation, and a moist, humid atmosphere are all favorable.

Peach Curl (Exoascus deformans, Fckl.).—This parasitic fungus disease is confounded with the crimping and curling of the foliage and twisting of the terminal ends of young shoots, caused by an attack from Peach Aphis (black and green species). However, a very slight practical knowledge of this fungus will serve to distinguish its workings from that of Aphides When the growing buds are attacked, the leaves, and very often the stems, become swollen, fleshy, distorted, and curled, changing in colour from green to a ruddy or dirty grey, whilst from aphis attack, the foliage and shoots become crimped and curled only. If neglected and the weather and other conditions are favorable, this fungus will spread rapidly, and do considerable damage to the growing peach and nectarine buds. Some varieties are more susceptible to attack than others. If neglected the inroad of the disease on the well-known variety of peach, Elberta, is so severe that the growing buds either die out or become weakened and useless as a sound type for planting out.

Treatment.—When selecting buds in the autumn for propagation purposes, secure them, if possible, from trees that were free from attack, or trees that were well sprayed in the spring, strictly avoiding any growths having a distorted or swollen appearance. The buds should receive a spraying with Bordeaux mixture or Lime-sulphur wash as soon as they start to move in the spring. Place the nozzle of the spray close to, and direct the wash well into the buds, using high pressure. This is an all-important factor when attacking this fungus and, indeed, most other disease of a like nature.

The buds should be closely watched, and if there is the slightest sign of attack a further spraying should be given. This will be when the growth of the buds, which is rapid, is from 1 inch to 6 inches in length. If no steps have been taken to spray as a deterrent, and the buds are attacked, all swollen or distorted leaves should be cut away and burnt, and spraying proceeded with at once to prevent spreading. If the stem is attacked, reduce the growth back into healthy wood and at a basal bud. (See Fig. 73.)

FIG. 73.—METHOD OF TREATMENT.

If the stem is attacked along its whole length, the growing bud is ruined and worthless. Having to cut away diseased leaves or reduce back the growth at all, like Fig. 73, is a very poor secondary operation to fall back upon. This check to the growing bud is generally so severe that at best only a poor type of tree is produced. The disease is more prevalent in wet, cold districts, and where trees are growing in wet, cold, and undrained soils. Well-drained and aerated soil is an all-important factor in the propagation and cultivation of the peach and nectarine. Yearling pruned trees in the nursery row should be sprayed when the buds are bursting and again when the leaves are developing.

Prune Rust (Puccinia pruni, Pers.).—To the kinds of stone fruit trees subject to attack, this disease seldom causes serious harm in the nursery row. As a fact, the fungus usually appears after the trees have made their full growth. If weather conditions are at all favorable after a good rainfall in late summer or early autumn, the rust may spread rapidly, attacking first the lower leaves upon the branches, and working upwards to the terminal ones, the result being that the trees are divested of their foliage. If the attack is confined solely to the leaves, the loss of foliage, being somewhat gradual, may be looked upon as of no great detriment to the young trees growing in the nursery at this time of the year.   To a very large extent this is true so far as the propagator is concerned, but if such trees were to be left standing in the nursery row, and untreated for a limited period, the continuous premature shedding of the foliage would have such an injurious effect upon the health of the trees that they would become very much weakened.   By neglecting this disease in the nursery it is disseminated to the planter, as the winter spores shelter behind or around the buds. One of the causes that may induce the buds of stone fruits to drop away from the sheath after unity has taken place with the stock, is found in this disease.   Buds selected from trees attacked are weak and prematurely hardened through the loss of healthy leaf actions and exposure.

The disease is easily recognised.   The upper surface of the foliage becomes covered, or partly so, with yellowish-coloured blotches, and if the under-surface of the leaves be examined directly beneath these yellow patches, numerous small dark-brown spots, known as pustules will be found.   *Treatment.*—Spray with Bordeaux mixture or Lime sulphur wash just before the buds burst and again when the foliage is fully expanded, directing the fungicide well beneath the leaves. The time and number of sprayings will be controlled by the climatic conditions prevailing at the time.   Upon the first signs of attack, spraying should be proceeded with at once.   Growers, when planting stone fruits such as almonds, apricots, nectarines, peaches, plums, should spray the young trees before or after planting with one of the already-mentioned fungicides, either as a deterrent or to destroy or prevent germination of any fungus spores that may be concealed upon any parts of the young trees.

Leaf Scald or Fruit Spot (Entomosporium maculatum Lev.).—This fungus disease, which has been shown to exist in Australia by Mr. D. McAlpine no further back than the year 1911, is in respect of appearance and method of attack identical with an old leaf trouble which attacked seedling pears and at times worked varieties in the nursery row, and was well known to many old propagators who termed it pear leaf rust.   The virulence of this leaf trouble is controlled by the weather conditions prevailing during midsummer and early autumn.   If the seasons happen to be wet, this leaf rust soon defoliates the stocks or trees attacked, but in normal weather little harm is done.   After the discovery and actual proof was made known, the writer submitted pear leaves to Mr. McAlpine, secured from seedling stocks, where this old leaf rust trouble was known to exist for many years, and it was diagnosed as *Entomosporium maculatum.*   Like the prune rust, its attack is usually too late in the nursery row to cause serious trouble, but if untreated there is the danger of transmitting it to the grower, consequently serious harm may be done to the pear crop.   The disease is readily recognised, and the following description by Mr. McAlpine will enable its presence to be detected in the nursery row :— " The foliage becomes pale in colour, spotted all over, chiefly upon the upper surface, and falling away early.   The spots are very definite and distinct, generally circular in outline at first, of a ruddy colour, then they run into one another, and become brownish, and ultimately the black, slightly-projecting fructification of the fungus appears upon them." *Treatment.*—Spray with Bordeaux mixture or Lime sulphur wash as a deterrent when the buds are bursting or as soon as the presence of this disease is detected. When selecting buds from mature trees for propagation purposes, only select growths that carry healthy foliage. In some localities, if no steps are taken to prevent its spread, this pest may make its appearance upon the seedling pear stocks early enough to prevent successful budding operations being carried out.

Powdery Mildew of Apple (Podosphaera leucotricha Salm.).—This fungus disease is troublesome at times in moist localities, or where favorable conditions prevail, causing damage to the growths of apple stocks and growing buds in the nursery row. It is recognised by attacking the terminal ends of the growing shoots. The surface of the leaves and twigs appear as if covered with white felt, caused by the great quantity of spores present, hence the name of powdery mildew. The result of an attack is that the foliage becomes dried up, and the terminal end of the growths and branchlets die back. If this disease is not recognised early, the trouble may be attributed to root or other causes. *Treatment.*— If discovered and recognised in its early stage, spray at once with Bordeaux mixture or Lime sulphur wash. If in an advanced stage, cut away diseased parts and burn, following up by spraying with either of the already-mentioned fungicides. Flowers of sulphur or freshly slaked lime will destroy this pest if dusted on as soon as detected in its early stages of development.

Root Rot (Armillaria mellea, Vahl.).—This deadly fungus is not to be treated lightly. It confines its attack to the roots and that portion of the stem below the surface of the soil, and very soon brings about a state of debility and ultimately death. It is an indigenous fungus preying upon many forms of native trees and shrubs, and is prevalent in cool, moist, timbered localities, particularly mountainous ones. *Symptoms of Attack.*—The foliage of stocks or young trees attacked in the nursery row becomes sickly in colour, finally falling if the attack is severe, and the terminal ends of the shoots die back. Upon removal from the soil the bark upon the stem or roots will be found to be dead, dying, or decayed, according to the progress of attack, the black cord-like mycelial strands of the fungus covering the roots like a dense felt or network. If the dead or decaying bark is removed from the roots or stem then white sheets of mycelium are to be found between the inner bark and wood. *Treatment.*—When clearing and breaking up virgin soil for planting, all roots, bark, &c., should be carefully gathered up and burnt. If any signs of white mould or felt-like substance is seen upon the bark or roots when clearing, the soil should be given a good dressing of fresh lime when ploughing, if planting is to follow close upon clearing and breaking up. Soil should be broken up before or in the spring, and allowed to remain in a rough state through the hot weather to sweeten and aerate until the autumn, when it should be well disced and finally worked into a suitable state of tilth for planting. The roots of stocks, &c., secured from a locality favorable to root rot should be dipped into a fungicide such as 1 lb. of sulphate of iron dissolved in 4 gallons of water or Bordeaux mixture 6—4—·50 formula. Any stocks or young trees showing symptoms of attack should be carefully dug up and burnt. Then the soil from where they were removed should be stirred up and watered with either of the above-mentioned fungicides, or a good dressing of fresh lime given to prevent its spread to other stocks, &c., close by. As there are several fungi causing root rot, all stocks and trees showing any signs of a whitish mould about the roots should be dipped before planting. Although an attack by this fungus may not have been noticed until the trees have become vegetative and are well on into the growing season, the actual damage to the roots or stem may have been caused in late autumn or during the winter months, and then, owing to the root action being interfered with in supplying moisture to the active top at a season when moisture is all-essential, symptoms as already described are brought about. Good drainage plays an all-important part in controlling and checking the spread of this pest. Very often the damage done is attributed to root-borers, bad drainage, or similar conditions, when the true cause is *Armillaria mellea.* Excessive moisture in the soil through irrigation or natural causes during hot weather may be the means of developing this fungus rapidly. The writer's experience is that, if introduced upon stocks or trees to a clean locality, this fungus will remain in a dormant state, or nearly so, for at least two years without the stocks, &c., showing signs of attack. As soon as conditions favorable to it are brought about, through irrigation or other causes, its spread is rapid, and death to the trees certain.

Collar Rot (Fusarium limoms, Brois.)—Lemon Bark Blotch (Ascochyta Corticola, McAlp.).—*Root Rot of Lemon (Phoma omnivora,* McAlp.).— The worst fungus diseases that the propagator and grower of citrus trees have to contend with are those known as Collar Rot, Lemon Bark Blotch, and Root Rot of Lemon. Although the same conditions favour the development and spread of them all, in appearance they are different. Collar Rot, which is probably the best known, is no doubt often confounded with Bark Blotch.

Collar Rot.—The first symptom is the exudation of small particles of gum from the bark at the seat of trouble. The bark eventually becomes usually deep brown in colour. It is generally when the bark is changing colour that the physiological conditions of the tree is noticed to be undergoing a change. The foliage appears to be sickly and pale-yellowish in colour. Matured trees generally show signs of heavy fruit production. *Bark Blotch.*—The symptom of attack with this disease is very similar to that of Collar Rot, the difference being that the diseased bark is usually sooty black in colour, instead of brown, and that gumming is absent. The bark eventually cracks, and peels off. *Root Rot.*—Generally the first symptom of attack is observed through the foliage becoming unhealthy and pale in colour. Upon the soil being removed around and close to the butts, the bark, if attacked, will have an unhealthy appearance, and upon scraping the bark lightly it will be found to be dead or decaying. Such conditions generally start at the extremity of the roots, working upwards to the ground level. At times this disease works rapidly in the nursery row if over-irrigation is practised. The leaves then suddenly droop, have the appearance of requiring moisture, and if a tree attacked in the nursery row is pulled it will leave the soil, and sometimes the freshly-decayed bark upon the roots will be left behind.

Trees once attacked with Root Rot rarely recover if the attack of the fungus is general upon all the roots. In some instances the attack is confined to the roots upon one side of the tree only. If conditions favorable for the development and spread of this fungus remain for any length of time, its action is rapid and deadly. Should anything occur to change these conditions, then the trees attacked may linger for years before dying out, and indeed, in rare instances, may even regain their vigour, particularly those branches upon the side of the tree opposite to that part of the trunk or roots attacked. With Root Rot, if the upward spread of the disease should become checked before too serious harm is done, very often fresh roots strike out from the healthy basal parts.

Amongst growers there is a diversity of opinion as to the prevention of Collar Rot. The following are some of the theories :—(No. 1) Worked trees are more susceptible than those propagated by layers or cuttings. (No. 2) Trees worked low down upon the stocks, particularly those grafted, are more subject to the disease than budded trees. (No. 3) Only certain stocks should be used for propagation purposes. (No. 4) No trees should be propagated from one that had, or one that has got, Collar Rot. If so, all such trees will die sooner or later from the disease, arguing that the disease is hereditary.   After close observation it is found that with trees growing in a certain soil, locality, position, and receiving certain treatment, these theories to some extent are sound; but if the same class of trees is grown under different conditions with regard to soil, locality, &c., opposite results are obtained.   Take the stock theory. Trees worked upon a certain stock, grown in a certain soil, with a free natural drainage, receiving no artificial irrigation, thrive well and remain very free from the fungus diseases mentioned. But when grown under artificial irrigation, upon another class of soil, the trees become diseased or die out. No hard-and-fast rules can be laid down from any of these theories.

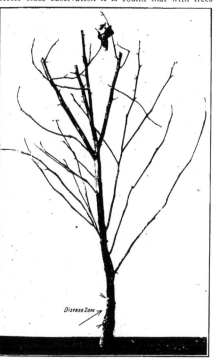

FIG. 74.—LEMON TREE ATTACKED BY COLLAR ROT.

The chief factor in growing and propagating citrus trees is to have a thorough knowledge of the class of soil to be planted, the locality, and conditions under which trees are to be grown, and the class of propagated tree whether suited or not to such conditions. When propagating citrus trees in the nursery row, great care should be taken that the soil is a friable one, naturally or easily drained, and that over-irrigation is not practised, as the chief causes of developing the fungus diseases mentioned are bad drainage, unsuitable soils, and excessive irrigation. With the citrus tree we have so far no universal stock for propagation purposes suitable for all conditions.

Treatment.—Seedling stocks or young trees attacked in the nursery row by any of these three fungus diseases should be dug up and immediately burnt. If standard trees are attacked by Collar Rot or Bark Blotch, the diseased part should be cut away as soon as detected, care being taken to see that all diseased and discoloured bark and wood is removed. Then paint the wound with equal parts of liquid carbolic and Stockholm tar. Give a good dressing of lime before replanting stocks in soil in which trees have died from fungus diseases. Rank weed growths should be kept down, and no mulch allowed to lie about the trunks, particularly during late autumn, winter, or early spring as damp and decaying matter close to the butts favours the development of fungus disease. If using stable manure or other matter as a mulch during the dry season, keep it away from the butt about 6 inches, and remove the mulch not later than the following April by raking it away from beneath the trees to the centre of the rows, either to decay or be ploughed in. When the trees have attained a fair size, plough only the one way each time; cross-ploughing should be avoided. Ploughing close to the trees should not be practised. Dusting lime upon the butts and beneath the trees is very beneficial to the health of citrus trees. Spraying the butts with a fungicide once or twice a year is also good. Gross growth in the nursery row or citrus grove should not be encouraged. The trees should be kept in the best of heart, and if a fertilizer is required the following mixture will be beneficial :— Sulphate of potash, 4 cwt.; blood and bone manure, 16 cwt. It is far better to apply a fertilizer twice in the year than all at one time; early spring and autumn are the suitable seasons. The quantity per tree is controlled by its condition and size—roughly, a tree ten years old, of average size, should receive 5 to 6 lbs. at each dressing.

The following will enable growers to prepare the fungus washes which have been recommended :—*Bordeaux Mixture.*—Bluestone (sulphate of copper), 6 lbs.; fresh unslaked lime, 4 lbs.; water, 50 gallons. Slake the lime with a small quantity of water, and then make up to 25 gallons. Pulverize the bluestone and dissolve in a small quantity of hot water, then make up to 25 gallons. Stir lime and bluestone water, and run evenly through a strainer into a third vessel. Stir well, and apply with a fine spray. *Lime-Sulphur Wash* (Stock Mixture).—Best lime, 10 lbs.; sulphur, 20 lbs. The lime is added to 2 gallons of water placed on a fire; when slaking is well started the sulphur is added, and water to make all to a thin paste is then poured in. When slaking and mixing are complete, 10 gallons of water are added and the mixture boiled for an hour stirring all the time. At the end of the hour there must be 10 gallons of mixture. Covering the stock mixture with paraffin oil will prevent air-crusting. When diluting for spraying take 1 gallon of stock mixture and dilute to 8 gallons with water.

Lime-Sulphur Wash is used on trees when dormant or just when buds are beginning to open at a density of 1.03 and at a density of 1.01 when buds have burst. The strengths given in the foregoing 1 in 8 and 1 in 25 give approximately these respective densities, if the mixture is made as directed. It must be pointed out, however, that Lime-Sulphur Wash is still in an experimental stage and should not be given preference over Bordeaux Mixture. *Caution.*—Lime-Sulphur Wash when buds &c. are vegetative should only be used at a strength of 1 in 25.

(Concluded.)

WHEAT AND ITS CULTIVATION.

(Continued from page 465.)

No. 7.—MANURIAL PROBLEMS.

A. E. V. Richardson, M.A., B.Sc., Agricultural Superintendent.

It has already been demonstrated that the most important requirement of a permanent system of agriculture is the maintenance of the productive power of the soil, and that the permanent efficiency of any given method of cultivation must be determined by its effect on soil fertility.

Under a good system of farming the soil will gradually increase in productive power. Poor soils may be improved and rich soils made richer.

Bad methods of cultivation, however, will gradually deplete the soil of its fertility, and render rich soils incapable of producing other than mediocre crops.

Factors Involved in Soil Fertility.

Soil fertility, in practical language, is the cropping capacity—the productive power—of the soil. It is a complex of many factors—some external—some internal.

Obviously, the climate is the most important external factor, and the amount of rainfall, its seasonable distribution, the range of temperature, &c., are controlling influences in successful farming. Excluding these climatic considerations, however, as entirely beyond human control, we may say that the fertility of a soil is dependent on the *chemical, physical,* and *biological* nature of the soil. Let us consider these points seriatim.

Chemical Composition.—One of the most common characteristics of a fertile soil is that it contains, in a soluble or available form, a sufficiency of those elements necessary for the nutrition of plants. These are ten in number (p. 200), namely, carbon, hydrogen, oxygen, nitrogen, sulphur, phosphorus, potassium, iron, magnesium, calcium (lime). The first three are obtained from the air and water, the remaining seven are obtained from the soil.

All these elements are essential plant foods. Fortunately, seven of these ten essential constituents are present in most soils in overflowing quantities. The other three—nitrogen, phosphorus, and potash—are frequently wanting or deficient. As the yield of the crop is governed by the amount of the most deficient element present, it is obvious that a study of the three substances referred to is of immediate practical importance. Lime sometimes becomes of considerable practical importance in assisting production, but the necessity for lime invariably arises from a faulty physical and biological condition of the soil, and not because it is actually required for plant food.

In the case of the wheat crop (straw and grain), of the total amount of food taken in by the crop—

(1) No less than $93\frac{1}{2}$ per cent. is obtained from the air and from the rain.

(2) $3\frac{1}{2}$ per cent. consists of mineral substances with which the soil is abundantly supplied.

(3) About 3 per cent. consists of nitrogen, phosphoric acid, and potash, which the soil contains in strictly limited quantities.

Hence, that portion of the plant's needs which man may require to supply is only a small fraction of that which is yielded by crops. But it is an indispensible fraction, and, as will be seen later, on this simple fact rests the whole practice of manuring.

So far as chemical considerations are concerned, it would appear that a fertile soil is one which contains a sufficiency of plant foods—and particularly nitrogen, phosphoric acid, and potash—in an *available* or soluble form. Emphasis must be laid on the presence of available plant food, because the greater portion of the plant food is locked up in inert forms, *i.e.*, in forms incapable of being used by the plant. It may, therefore, he readily understood that, while a soil may contain large reserves of nitrogen, phosphoric acid, and potash, it may yet be unable to support the growth of a decent crop. Such a soil would possess potential fertility, but could only become really fertile by methods of soil treatment which would bring about a conversion of the dormant plant food into available forms.

It must be clear, also, that under certain circumstances the amount of available plant food in the soil may be reduced to such a low level that there is insufficient for the requirements of a normal crop. Under these circumstances, the soil is said to be " worn out," or " exhausted."

It was formerly supposed that the fertility of a soil could be determined by chemical analysis. Soils were analysed, and the analyses referred to arbitrary standards, and judgment was given on the agricultural possibilities of the soil under review. If, for example, a given soil was analysed and found to contain 0.1 per cent. of nitrogen, 0.1 per cent. of phosphoric acid, and 0.2 per cent. of potash, it was judged to be a good soil. But no agriculturist who knew his business would attempt to judge a soil merely by the results of its chemical analysis, and to say what crops should be grown and what manures should be applied.

Soil analysis can tell us the total reserves of food stored up in the soil, or it may inform us as to the amount of food soluble in dilute solution of citric acid, but it can throw very little light on the forms in which the elements of plant food actually exist in the soil, and as to the amount actually available for a wheat crop.

Physical Condition of the Soil.—A soil exceedingly rich in total nitrogen, phosphoric acid and potash, and also in its available plant food, may yet be incapable of growing a blade of grass, much less a satisfactory crop. This may be the case with naturally rich but badly drained soils, and sour land, such as, *e.g.*, one would expect in a swamp.

Hence, to be fertile, a soil must not only be rich in plant food, but it must possess a satisfactory physical condition. However rich a soil may be in plant food—total or available—its fertility will be low, if it is sour, or in need of draining, unretentive of moisture, or of poor texture, and low capillary power. The physical condition of the soil, if unsatisfactory and inimical to successful cropping, may be improved by tillage, drainage, and the use of soil amendments. These, however, lie outside the scope of the present article.

Closely correlated and intimately bound up with the physical condition and chemical composition, is what may be termed the biological condition of the soil.

Biological Condition of Soil.—The soil used to be regarded as a mere inert mass of matter void of all vitality. We now know that it is really a vast laboratory swarming with millions of microscopic bacteria, and that these bacteria play a most important part in the nutrition of plants. The importance of these lowly organisms may be appreciated by briefly referring to the functions of the more important bacteria found in every soil.

Perhaps the most important group of organisms are the nitrifying bacteria. The nitrogen required by the wheat plant can only be taken in by the root in the form of nitrates. These nitrates are formed from the organic matter of soil by three distinct processes, each process involving a distinct set of bacteria. The process by which this organic nitrogen is converted into nitrates is called nitrification. Detailed experiments relating to this process have already appeared in this *Journal*.* It is interesting to note, in this connexion, that these nitrifying organisms require for their full development—(*a*) air ; (*b*) warmth—they thrive best at 99 degrees F., and are ten times more active at that temperature than at 57 degrees F.† ; (*c*) moisture ; (*d*) presence of lime ; (*e*) organic matter.

Opposed to these nitrifying organisms are the denitrifying bacteria, which undo the valuable work of the nitrifying organisms, and are most active when the soil is deficient in air, as a result of bad drainage or want of tillage. When these bacteria are active, the soluble nitrates quickly disappear, and even dissipate to free nitrogen, and crop yields are reduced. Every effort should be made, therefore, to reduce the activity of these organisms to a minimum.

Again, in well-tilled well-drained soils, the organic matter of the soil becomes slowly oxidized by a group of putrefactive bacteria to carbon dioxide and other products. It is through the direct action of several form of bacteria and through the indirect effects of the products of these organisms, that a large portion of the insoluble mineral plant foods of the soil are rendered available for the use of crops.

In badly drained soils, where the organic matter decomposes in the absence of air, marsh gas and organic acids are formed, and sourness and acidity in the soil thereby result.

On the roots of well-grown specimens of the *Leguminosæ*—the pea family of plants—colonies of bacteria of great economic importance exist. The curious nodules or wart-like growths on the roots of clover, peas, beans, and lucerne, are the dwelling-places of teeming millions of organisms. They live in a sort of partnership with the legume, and have the power of fixing free nitrogen from the air and making it available for the plant in return for a supply of carbonaceous food given by the plant. Thus, they enable a farmer to supply his soil with its most expensive plant food free of cost. This interaction is called symbiosis, and may be described as a kind of partnership in which two organisms, differing widely in character, live together for the advantage of both.

Organisms have been isolated by Winogradsky and Beyerinck which are able to fix the nitrogen of the air without associating themselves with any leguminous plant. These organisms secure the food necessary for their energy from the decaying organic matter of the soil.

Finally, recent research has revealed the presence of numerous organisms called *protozoa*, which prey on the various bacteria in the soil. It would appear that these organisms—the natural enemies of the bacteria—are destroyed by exposure to moderately high temperatures, leaving a free field for the development of the bacteria.

The tendency of this teeming bacterial population of the soil is to arrive at a state of equilibrium appropriate to the nature of the soil, and its physical condition. In well-tilled soils, in good " heart " and condition, containing adequate supplies of carbonate of lime, the useful types of bacteria predominate. In badly-tilled soils, sour through want of drainage,

* *Journal of Agriculture.* Victoria. pp. 275 and 393.
† Schloesing and Muntz.

7

6 *Journal of Agriculture, Victoria.* [10 Sept., 1912.

or from an absence of lime, moulds, fungi, and harmful types of bacteria flourish to the exclusion of the useful forms.

Summing up, we may say that a soil, to be fertile, must be satisfactory from three points of view :—

(a) It must contain a sufficiency of plant food in a properly assimilable form.

(b) It must possess a satisfactory physical constitution, *i.e.*, be of good texture, mellow, well drained, retentive of moisture, and good capillary power.

(c) It must be in good biological condition, so that free play may be given to the development of those bacteria which work for the advantage of the crop.

Formerly, the importance of the chemical aspect of the question was greatly exaggerated. To-day it is recognised that many important problems connected with the treatment of soils and manuring of crops, which hitherto have been incapable of explanation by the chemist, may, in the near future, be satisfactorily explained by the biologist.

Manuring.

The object of manuring is to supplement the supplies of plant food in the soil to such an extent as to enable a full crop to be grown.

The substances requiring special attention are those in which the soil is likely to be deficient, namely, nitrogen, phosphoric acid, and potash.

Occasionally, however, manures are applied with a view of improving the physical and biological condition of the soil rather than augmenting the supplies of plant food. This is the case when soil amendments, such as lime, gypsum, and green manures, are used.

If the soil is deficient in any one of the necessary ingredients, no amount of tillage can put it into good "heart;" and, as the yield of the crop is governed by the amount present of the most deficient soil ingredient, it is imperative that the deficiency be made good by the direct application of fertilisers if satisfactory crops are to be obtained.

How to Determine Soil Deficiencies.

In view of the fact that soils vary very considerably in their chemical composition, it is most important that every farmer should be able to determine for himself in what elements his soil is deficient. It has already been observed that chemical analysis is of little value for this purpose.

The most practical method of determining the soil requirements is establishment of a simple set of experimental plots. By this means, the farmer puts questions to the soil, and the answers to the questions are indicated by the amount of growth and the yield of the crop for each separate treatment.

A simple and effective scheme is to arrange for the sowing of a series of plots at seed time with the following treatment :—(a) No manure; (b) phosphates alone; (c) nitrates alone; (d) potash alone; (e) phosphates and nitrogen; (f) phosphates and potash; (g) phosphates, nitrogen, and potash. If the growth and development of these be carefully observed, and the yields from each separately determined, the experiments will be able to determine what class of manures is likely to prove profitable under his particular conditions. On badly drained, sour soils, lime supplemented by phosphates, should be included. Having determined which ingredient is deficient in his soil, the farmer may now proceed to determine, in a similar manner, the most profitable and economical form in which this ingredient may be applied, under his conditions, as well as the most profitable rate at which it may be applied.

CLASSIFICATION OF MANURES.

Manures may be divided into two general classes. Those which supply the soil with elements in which the soil is deficient are called Direct manures; whilst those which act by improving the physical and biological condition of the soil rather than by augmenting the supply of plant food are called Indirect manures. Again, Direct manures may supply all the elements of plant food, in which case they may be called General manures; or they may contain one dominating plant food ingredient such as phosphorus, potash, or nitrogen, in which case they may be called Special manures. Finally, the Indirect manures may be either vegetable in character, such as green manures, or mineral, such as lime, gypsum, salt.

The following tabulated statement may assist in making the matter clear :—

$$
\text{Manures} \begin{cases} \text{Direct} \begin{cases} \text{Special} \begin{cases} \text{1. Nitrogenous} \\ \text{2. Phosphatic} \\ \text{3. Potassic} \end{cases} \\ \text{General—Farmyard manure} \end{cases} \\ \text{Indirect} \begin{cases} \text{Mineral—Lime, gypsum} \\ \text{Vegetable—Green manures} \end{cases} \end{cases}
$$

We will consider these seriatim :—

NITROGENOUS MANURES.

The most striking and fundamental difference between the manurial practice of Europe and that of Australia is that, in the Old World, nitrogenous manures are all important, whilst in Australia they are generally unnecessary and unprofitable. In European agriculture, the controlling factor for successful cropping is the amount of available nitrogen present in the soil. In Australia, assuming the rainfall be sufficient, the limiting factor in crop production is the amount of available phosphoric acid.

The importance of this distinction is obvious. The cereal farmer of the Old World must supply the all-important nitrogen, either through the medium of costly nitrogenous manures, or by providing a regular scheme of rotation in which leguminous crops play an important part.

The cereal farmer of Australia finds expensive and costly nitrogenous manures, like nitrate of soda and sulphate of ammonia, quite unnecessary, and he is thereby saved the great expense incidental to their application.

His manure bill amounts to 2s. 6d. to 4s. 6d. per acre, and this amount is expended on the purchase of soluble phosphates.

Why Nitrogenous Manures are Unnecessary.

Why is it that nitrogenous manures are unnecessary, and even unprofitable. in the wheat areas of the State? At first sight, one might be inclined to the belief that our soils were richer in supplies of nitrogen than those of Europe. Examination of typical soils in the wheat areas, however, prove that such is not the case.

Many instances might be quoted of Australian soils which have proved unresponsive to the application of nitrates, even though they would be regarded as lamentably deficient in total nitrogen if judged by European standards of fertility.

The soils in our wheat areas have not been under cultivation for such a length of time as to reduce the supply of available nitrogen below the yearly requirements of crops. Moreover, it is extremely probable that, owing to our peculiar climatic and soil conditions, the percentage of nitrogen in an available form is considerably higher than under the wet conditions of Europe, where nitrates are so very necessary. Under European conditions, the heavy rainfall causes considerable losses of nitrates by leaching, and large quantities of nitrates are found in the drainage waters. In contrast to this, underground drainage is quite unnecessary over the greater portion of our wheat areas, and the losses of nitrates by leaching are reduced to a minimum.

Again, our system of cropping is not as intensive as that which obtains in Europe. Owing to the fact that but one crop is grown in two, or even three, years in the wheat areas, the demands made by the crop on the soil are not nearly so heavy as in European countries, where heavy crops are annually removed.

Finally, the conditions of soil and climate, and mode of cropping in our wheat areas, are conducive to rapid nitrification of the organic matter, resulting in the formation of a sufficiency of available nitrates for all demands of the cereal crop.

Most of the wheat sown in this State is on fallowed land, and during the progress of fallowing nitrification proceeds at a very rapid rate. (Page 335.)

Some idea of the amount of nitrates produced in well-tilled fallows may be gained from the results of investigations at Longerenong during the past eight months. Incidentally, the figures conclusively show why, in districts similarly situated to Longerenong, nitrates prove unresponsive when sown on fallow land.

TABLE I.—FORMATION OF NITRATES IN FALLOWED AND NON-FALLOWED LAND AT LONGERENONG AGRICULTURAL COLLEGE (VICTORIA), 1911-12.

(Nitrate nitrogen in parts per million).

Depth of Soil Sample.	(1) 7th December, 1911.		(2) 4th January, 1912.		(3) 6th February, 1912.		(4) 28th March, 1912.		(5) 20th May, 1912 (at seeding).		(6) 7th August, 1912.	
	Fallowed.	Non-fallowed.	Fallowed.	Non-fallowed.	Fallowed.	Non-fallowed.	Fallowed.	Non-fallowed.	Fallowed.	Non-fallowed.	Fallowed (now under crop).	Non-fallowed.
(1) 0" to 12"	10·3	Not tested.	13·28	3·20	25·2	1·60	20·5	2·10	20·60	1·07	18·07	2·34
(2) 12" to 24"	Trace		3·12	2·27	2·4	Trace	3·7	1·10	Trace	1·00	5·40	1·35
(3) 24" to 36"	1·4		3·16	1·65	1·63	Trace	2·40	2·8	Trace	Trace	0·72	0·46
(4) 36" to 48"	3·1		1·71	1·67	1·77	1·41	1·40	2·02	3·46	1·67	0·72	1·44
(5) 48" to 60"	1·9		1·73	2·10	2·78	2·47	2·02	1·70	2·17	2·31	0·72	0·82
Average nitrogen content of first 5 feet	3·4		4·6	2·18	6·76	1·10	6·00	1·94	5·25	1·20	5·12	1·28

Table I. shows the amount of nitrates found in each of the first 5 feet of soil when fallowed, and when allowed to lie in pasture   The soil samples were taken in two parallel lines, the distance between the fallowed and non-fallowed portions being 10 yards, whilst the distance between each successive sampling was 5 yards.

The nitrogen determinations were made by Mr. P. R. Scott, Chemist for Agriculture.

In the above tables, it will be noted that the amount of nitrate present in each layer is continually changing.   These changes follow closely on the changes in the moisture content of the soil.   With heavy showers, the nitrates get washed down to lower depths.   Under hot dry spells, they tend to concentrate near the surface.

The table clearly shows that, throughout the whole period during which the investigations were made, the fallowed land contained far more nitrate than the adjacent non-fallowed portion.   If these tables are condensed, and the figures reduced to pounds per acre, this point may be more clearly seen.

TABLE II.—TOTAL NITRATE NITROGEN IN THE FIRST FIVE FEET OF FALLOWED AND NON-FALLOWED LAND UNDER ORDINARY FIELD CONDITIONS AT LONGERENONG (VICTORIA), 1912.

Date of Sampling.	Amount of Nitrate Nitrogen. (In Parts per Million.)		Amount of Nitrogen. (Reduced to lbs. per Acre.)	
	Fallowed.	Non-fallowed.	Fallowed.	Non-fallowed.
			lbs. per acre.	lbs. per acre.
(1) 7th December, 1911 ..	3·4	Not taken	59·5	Not taken
(2) 4th January, 1912 ..	4·6	2·18	80·5	38·15
(3) 6th February, 1912 ..	6·76	1·10	118·3	19·25
(4) 28th March, 1912 ..	6·00	1·94	105·0	33·9
(5) 20th May, 1912 ..	5·25	1·20	91·87	21·0
(6) 7th August, 1912 ..	5·12*	1·28	89·6	22·4

* Now under crop.

From this table it will be seen that the amount of nitrate in the fallowed land gradually rose from 59½ lbs. in December, to 118.3 lbs. in the first week in February, after which it gradually fell to 91.87 lbs. per acre, as contrasted with 21 lbs. in the non-fallowed portion.   As a 15-bushel wheat crop removes in its grain and straw about 21 lbs. of nitrogen (p. 203) per acre, it will be observed that there was four and a half times more available nitrogen in the fallowed portion at seed time than was required for a 15-bushel crop.

On the other hand, in the non-fallowed portion there was barely enough nitrogen to supply the requirements of one such crop even assuming that every particle of nitrate nitrogen in the first 5 feet could have been used by the crop.

Moreover, at seed time, the nitrate nitrogen in the fallowed land amounted to 71 lbs. per acre above that of the non-fallowed portion.

If nitrate of soda containing 15 per cent. of nitrogen be worth 14s. per cwt., then the cash value of this extra nitrate content of the fallowed land over that of the unfallowed portion amounted to no less than £2 19s. 2d. per acre.

We see at a glance from these figures the reason why, in the northern areas, under the existing methods of cultivation, the application of nitrogenous manures are unnecessary and unprofitable.

In the Southern and Western Districts of Victoria, however, the same climatic and soil advantages as regards nitrate production do not hold, for in these districts fallowing is far less common (p. 336), and the rainfall is heavier, and in these districts it might be inferred that nitrogenous manures would prove of some value.

The needs of the North and South in this respect have already been made the subjects of separate inquiry by this Department.

Experiments conducted in 1902, and following years, brought out their differences as resulting from climate. Thus, in the Northern Wheat Areas. the addition of soluble nitrogenous manures (sulphate of ammonia) to phosphate gave an increase of only 3 lbs. of wheat per acre, on the average of 94 farms, and in no single case of the twelve local groups into which the 94 farms were divided did the nitrogenous manure repay the cost of its purchase. In many cases, it did actual harm—probably as a result of increased leafage causing too rapid a drain on the soil moisture.

In the moister Southern Districts, the need for some nitrogenous manure was apparent in the experiments, for an increase was obtained in 47 of the 50 farms by its use.

On the average of the 50 farms, 1 cwt. of nitrate of soda increased the yield of hay by nearly 6 cwt., and 1 cwt. of sulphate of ammonia by exactly 8 cwt. per acre.

To summarize, then, it may be said that the need for nitrogenous manures in this State is, to some extent, dependent on the length of time the land has been under cultivation, but is, in a very large measure, also dependent upon the climate. In the drier portions of the State, the use of nitrogenous manures does not seem to be called for, and it may even prove harmful. In the wetter districts, a limited call for nitrogenous manures exists at the present time, and this may be expected to develop as cultivation becomes of older date.

Manures Containing Nitrogen.

The principal nitrogenous manures are nitrate of soda, sulphate of ammonia, blood manure, calcium cyanamide, and nitrate of lime.

Nitrate of Soda is obtained principally from the nitre beds of Chili and Peru, and Bolivia. The commercial article contains about 15½ per cent. of nitrogen.

It is extremely soluble in water, and is very readily leached out of the soil by excessive rains. For these reasons, it is generally applied as a top dressing, more especially in districts with a heavy rainfall. In order to insure its uniform distribution, it should be mixed with two or three times its weight of dry loam, and broadcasted over the crop. According to Lawes and Gilbert, nitrate of soda applied in early winter is never as effective as when applied in spring.

Nitrate of soda can only give the best results when the soil is well supplied with phosphates and potash, and is deficient in available nitrogen. If it is to be used in conjunction with superphosphate, it is inadvisable to mix the manures together long before sowing, as a loss of nitric acid may result.

The most profitable rate of application for any particular soil and crop can only be determined by experiment. Generally speaking, however, from ½ to 1 cwt. per acre is used for hay crops where nitrates have been proved to be necessary.

It is generally held that nitrate of soda stimulates the vegetative rather than the grain-bearing power of cereals, and that it appears to exercise a retarding influence on vegetation which, in our climate, must always prove more or less detrimental. Experience at the Roseworthy Agricultural College during the past six years (*vide Journal of Agriculture of South Australia*, Aug., 1911) shows that, under Australian conditions, the nitrate of soda has not stimulated straw and flag growth at the expense of grain yield, nor has it had a retarding influence on the general character of the vegetation and the ripening of the crop.

Sulphate of Ammonia is a by-product in the destructive distillation of coal, and is obtained from the " gas liquor " of gasworks by neutralizing it with sulphuric acid. The commercial article is a greyish-white crystalline salt, extremely soluble in water.

It contains about 20 to 21 per cent. of nitrogen, and is the most concentrated and expensive of nitrogenous manures. If pure, it should entirely volatilize when placed on a red hot spoon. Lawes and Gilbert have used it with great success in the cultivation of wheat at Rothamsted, and have demonstrated that, for every 5 lbs. of ammonia added to the soil, an extra bushel of wheat was produced. It is similar in its action to nitrate of soda, but before being used, it must first undergo nitrification.

It is more readily held by the soil than nitrate of soda, and is therefore preferable to nitrate of soda in wet seasons and on soils of a light loamy character. On clay soils, it is best replaced by nitrate of soda. The continued application of sulphate of ammonia to soils deficient in lime leads to the removal of some of the lime in the form of gypsum, and the soil becomes acid and unsuitable for the growth of crops.

It may be safely mixed with superphosphates, but not with Thomas' phosphate, or manures containing free lime, as portion of the ammonia may be lost. It may be applied, like nitrate of soda, as a top dressing, but should be used rather earlier in the season than nitrate.

Dried Blood is a highly nitrogenous organic manure, containing about 10 to 12 per cent. of nitrogen. It is not so rapid in its action as nitrate of soda, as it must first undergo a preliminary nitrification before it becomes available. It is of considerable value in light loamy soils, and is an excellent manure for market-gardening purposes.

Calcium Cyanamide and Nitrate of Lime.—In 1898, Sir William Crookes suggested that, by the utilization of water-power, electrical energy might be generated at such a cheap rate as to make the fixation of the nitrogen of the air by electrical means a financial success.

His suggestion has been adopted, and at Nottoden, the Norwegian Nitrogen Company are now manufacturing nitrate of lime electrically from the nitrogen of the air.

The fertilizing powers of nitrate of lime and nitrate of soda for equal amounts of nitrogen are approximately the same. Experiments have recently shown that, on sandy soils deficient in lime, nitrate of lime has a more beneficial effect than nitrate of soda.

Calcium Cyanamide or Nitro-lime is prepared from the nitrogen of the air by causing it to combine with calcium carbide at the high temperature of the electric furnace.

This substance has already found its way to Victoria, and experimental plots have been laid out at Rutherglen to test the efficacy of these various forms of nitrogen. It is stated that the after effects of nitro-lime are far greater than other nitrogenous manures. Experience this season at Rutherglen demonstrates unmistakably that it must not be sown with the seed, as the germination is seriously affected. The future of these two manures will depend on whether they may be produced at such a rate as to compete with sulphate of ammonia and nitrate of soda.

(To be continued.)

A PROFITABLE DAIRY COW.

The illustration herewith is a typical dairy cow of pure Ayrshire breeding, the property of Mr. T. Cook, "Carpentaria," Glenroy. For the season just ending, covering a period of seven months, she has produced 5,530 lbs. of milk.

This cow, Edith 2nd, was purchased from the breeder, Mr. J. Thompson, "Hazelmount," Krowera, near Loch, Gippsland, by Mr. Cook's father at the Royal Show sales, September, 1905, for the purpose of supplying milk and butter to the household.

Mr. Cook has weighed and recorded this cow's milk night and morning, with the following result:—

Calved.	Dried off.	Period of Milking.	Age at Calving.		Milk.
		months.	yrs.	mths.	lbs.
Oct. 16, 1905	Oct. 29, 1906	12½	2	0	7,786
Jan. 28, 1907	Mar. 15, 1908	13½	3	4	8,512
June 22, 1908	May 4, 1910	22½	4	8	13,065½
Sept. 26, 1910	Sept. 28, 1911	12	7	0	9,023
Nov. 15, 1911	June 14, 1912	7	8	1	5,530½
					43,917

Average per milking period   ...   ...   8,783 lbs.
Average per annum   ...   .   6,273 „

The Editor will be glad to receive, and, when authenticated, to publish records of cows or herds of exceptional merit. — EDITOR.

THE VINE MOTH CATERPILLAR PARASITE.

By C. French, jun., Acting Government Entomologist.

During the months of January, February, March, and April last, many shrivelled-up Vine Moth caterpillars were noticed on the vine leaves. They were of a dark colour. On investigating the matter, I noticed that a parasite had been at work, so I made further search, and found that all the live caterpillars had clusters of larvæ on their backs. The colour of these larvæ is at first orange yellow, but when more fully grown, it is brownish yellow.

When the eggs of the parasite are first deposited on the caterpillars, they are exceedingly small, but soon develop. The larvæ grow fairly rapidly, and spread all over the backs of the caterpillars. The time occupied from the eggs being deposited until the larvæ are fully grown, is about a week. About the second day after the larvæ are hatched, the caterpillars cease eating, and remain in the one place, and at the end of the week they are simply sucked dry by the parasite.

When the caterpillars are dried up, the parasites cover them with a silken covering, and form their cocoons, emerging from same as perfect insects in a couple of weeks' time.

When the perfect Hymenopterous insects were hatched out in the observation box, live caterpillars of the Emperor Gum Moth, and several species of Cutworm Moth larvæ were placed in the box, but the parasite did not deposit eggs on them.

These parasites are reported to be doing good work this season in many parts of Victoria, and it is hoped that they will keep the Vine Moth in check.

Chalcid.

Fig.   I. Perfect vine-moth. Natural size. From nature.

Fig.   II. Pupa of vine-moth. Natural size. From nature.

Fig.   III. Vine leaf with vine-moth larvæ. Natural size. From nature.

    (a) Full grown larva in healthy state. Natural size. From nature.

    (b) Sickly larva owing to development of parasite fly, larvæ from deposited eggs. Natural size. From nature.

    (c) Sickly larva owing to development of parasite fly. larvæ from deposited eggs. More developed state. Natural size. From nature.

    (d) Further. Natural size. From nature.

    (e) Larva killed by the parasite. Natural size. From nature.

    (f) Larva with parasite larvæ changing to pupae. From nature.

    (g) With pupae of parasitic fly. Natural size. From nature.

Fig. IV. Parasitic fly. (Dorsal view.) Natural size. From nature.

Fig.   V. Parasitic fly. (Side view.) Natural size. From nature.

Fig.   VI. Parasitic fly. (Enlarged.) From nature.

10543.   T

VINE MOTH CATERPILLAR PARASITE.

HOW TO MAKE A BLOOD SMEAR.

By W. A. N. Robertson, B.V.Sc.

Numerous inquiries are made annually to the Stock Department for information as to the probable cause of deaths amongst stock which occur throughout the State. Occasionally, in addition to describing the symptoms of sickness, specimens of parts of organs, blood, &c., are forwarded, in the hope that some information can be obtained. Such specimens, however, are almost useless, as changes, due to putrefaction, commence during transit, and the organism responsible for this change either masks or destroys any organism which may have been present as the cause of mortality. Useful information, however, can be obtained from an examination of blood and tissues if correctly taken; consequently the accompanying description of "How to make a Blood Smear" will prove useful if kept for reference. The description is given of how to make a smear on microscopic slides; these are, of course, not always obtainable by the farmer, but any slip of flat glass will answer the purpose equally well, and the smear may be made with the end of a clean, unburnt wooden match. The essentials to be borne in mind in following the method described are cleanliness and attention to detail, especially in regard to the drying of the smear in the air. Glass upon which is a wet smear should never be put against another slip; each slip must be dried separately and wrapped in a piece of paper by itself before forwarding. In addition, a very careful description of the symptoms of sickness should be recorded, and on *post-mortem* examination a minute description of the appearance of all the organs given. No detail is too small to record if an accurate diagnosis is to be made.

To Make a Blood Smear.

(a) *From the Living Animal.*

Blood may be taken from one of the veins which run along the upper surface of the ear. The animal's head should be firmly secured, and the ear washed in solution of washing soda. A prominent vein should then be pricked with a needle (an ordinary clean sewing needle will do) or with the point of a clean, sharp knife, or a fine incision can be made on the margin of the ear. As soon as the blood flows the smears should be made; if delay occurs in spreading the film the blood will coagulate and the smear be a failure. Do not squeeze the vein in order to make the blood flow; it should occur quite naturally.

(b) *From the Dead Animal.*

Having opened the carcass, blood should be taken from the spleen or lymphatic glands, and in the forwarding letter it should be stated from which organ the smear was made. Cut the organ with a clean knife, and scrape a small piece of the cut surface off with the edge of the glass slide.

The first thing to be done is to prepare the glass slides on which the blood is to be spread. The glass should be thoroughly cleaned, kept free from dust, and should be polished with a cloth or handkerchief immediately before use.

To make the film, a very small drop of blood, about the size of a millet seed, should be put on one end of the slide by means of either the end of a wooden match or by the point of a knife, or by the needle used for pricking the ear, or by one of the corners of another glass slide.

Then place a second slide over it, arranging that the two slides together form an acute angle wherein the blood drop lies; the inclined glass slide should touch the drop, and the blood will then run along the edge of the slide, and the inclined slide should then be immediately drawn along the horizontal slide, as shown in illustration when the required film will result.

Scrapings from the organ made with the short edge of the slide can be drawn over the horizontal slide in the same manner. It is very easy to spoil a smear by making it too thick, and the film should always be made *as thin as possible.* A rough way of ascertaining whether the blood film is too thick or not is to hold the slide with the blood smear on it up to the light, and if the colours of the rainbow can be seen on the glass the film can be considered as being thin enough. When the smear has been made, allow the blood on the glass to dry in the air; when dry, wrap each glass in a small piece of thin paper, pack carefully and forward to

THE CHIEF VETERINARY OFFICER,
Department of Agriculture,
Melbourne.

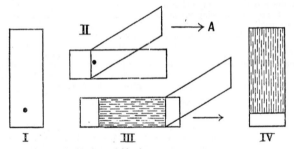

Fig. I.—Glass slide with drop of blood.
Fig II.—First position showing position of slides.
    A. Direction in which top slide is drawn.
Fig. III.—Second position of slides after blood smear is drawn out as indicated.
Fig. IV.—Slide showing blood smear.

RED POLLS AS BUTTER PRODUCERS.

(Season's Milk and Butter Record of the Government Herd.)

In continuation of the returns published in the November, 1911, issue of the *Journal*, the tables following, compiled by Mr. C. K. Harrison, Dairy Supervisor, show the milking record for the 1911-12 season of the Government herd of Red Polled Cattle stationed at Boisdale, Gippsland. These returns furnish some very interesting data, both as regards butter fat, and quantity of milk. During the period under review the herd has been fed on the natural pastures without hand feed of any kind except for less than 10 tons of lucerne hay and 5 tons of sugar beet offal, given during the dry autumn and towards the end of the milking period.

On referring to table A, it will be noticed that the majority of the cows show an increase in milk yield this season over that of 1910-11. The only cows producing less milk this season being "Connecticut," "Bullion," "Virginia," and "Havana." The three last-named were also below their butter-fat returns of last season, whereas "Connecticut's" butter-fat yield for this season shows an increase of 95 lbs. This cow's test in 1910-11 was 4.2 per cent. to 4.6 per cent., and in 1911-12 from 4.6 per cent. to 6.2 per cent.; such a case as this, and indeed some of the others also emphasizes the necessity of systematic weighing and testing from year to year, and not resting content with one year's records. The money values of the returns this year show a considerable increase over those of last year, partly due to the higher market price of butter-fat during the past season. The average monthly increase in the price since September, 1911, over the corresponding period this year was 3.1d. per lb. of butter-fat.

The weights of the daily milk yields were recorded, and weekly fat tests made by Mr. E. Steer, Dairy Herdsman, who has taken a keen interest in the herd and managed it with success. The butter-fat tests have been checked by the Senior Dairy Inspector (Mr. R. T. Archer) and the Chemist for Agriculture (Mr. Rankin Scott).

The stud bull "Tabacum" has been made available to settlers' cows on the Boisdale Beet Farms. The plan has been adopted of selling the bull calves under one year old at prices based on the preceding season's butter-fat return of the dam. For instance, the cow "Muria" returned 240 lbs. of butter-fat, which, reckoned at 1s. per lb., equals £12—the price realized for her calf. This is considered a fair basis for fixing the value of a bull intended for dairy purposes. After all is said and done, the value of a bull is in his potentiality for getting good milking heifers, and the hereditary influence in this direction possessed by the bull can probably be best estimated to the extent of one-half at any rate by the yielding capacity of the dam. This basis of sale seems likely to become popular, as last year's crop of bull calves have met a ready sale under it.

The yearling bull "Vuelta's Son" (sire "Tabacum," dam "Vuelta") has, however, been reserved from sale, notwithstanding a very tempting offer for him received from a breeder of Red Polls in New Zealand after reading the record of the dam. Prior to this it was decided to reserve the bull for stud purposes and breeding experiments on the Central Research Farm about to be established at Werribee. On referring to the tables, it will be seen that the dam "Vuelta" is a phenomenal producer. In the season 1910-11 she gave 556½ gallons of milk, returning 405 lbs. of butter-fat, value £17 10s. 10d.; and in the past season she yielded 485 lbs. of butter-fat from 775 gallons of milk, with a money value of £26 5s. 9d. During the month of November (twenty weeks after calving) "Vuelta" averaged 19 lbs. 4 ozs. of butter-fat per week.

The herd has recently been augmented by the purchase from Captain Philip Charley, of Belmont, Richmond, New South Wales, of twelve females and a young bull, "Nicotine," sired by the imported bull "Acton Dewstone," dam "Chessie," by "Magician" (imported). These cattle are descended from deep milking strains in the Old Country, and appear to have the milking qualities well developed; but as weighing and testing the milk is the only reliable proof of individual milking qualities, it will remain for their records to show to what extent the augmentation of the herd in this way is advantageous.

Table A.

COMPARATIVE SUMMARY OF YIELDS AND RETURNS OF THE GOVERNMENT HERD OF RED POLL DAIRY CATTLE.

(Seasons 1910–11 and 1911–12.)

Cow.	Season 1910–11.						Season 1911–12.					
	Weeks in Milk.	Milk in Gallons.	Butter Fat.	Values.			Weeks in Milk.	Milk in Gallons.	Butter Fat.	Values.		
			lbs.	£	s.	d.			lbs.	£	s.	d.
Vuelta ..	38½	556·5	405·1	17	10	10	41¼	775·2	485·1	26	5	9
Connecticut ..	40½	818·2	269·0	11	17	4	40½	678·2	364·0	19	11	10
Bullion ..	40½	773·3	356·7	15	17	10	43½	694·8	344·0	18	10	7
Beulah ..	39¾	646·5	342·6	15	3	6		(Not c	omplet	ed.)		
Cuba ..	40½	526·9	231·8	10	5	11	43½	701·4	337·8	18	10	4
Cigarette ..	34	504·4	211·6	8	18	9	41½	648·1	285·9	15	14	6
Sumatra ..	4¼*	43·6	19·6	0	19	2	42	666·2	284·2	15	6	2
Kentucky ..	36½	531·1	225·9	9	12	7	39½	669·5	277·7	15	1	1
Muria ..	40½	548·9	240·7	9	14	9	41	580·2	275·7	14	14	10
Pennsylvania	38½	461·9	189·7	8	4	3	45½	634·8	271·9	14	13	10
Carolina ..	40½	570·5	253·1	11	3	4	32¼	580·6	254·3	13	11	4
Virginia ..	40½	636·2	254·7	11	5	1	39½	551·2	221·7	12	0	7
Havana ..	40½	575·5	229·9	10	5	0	37½	535·6	215·3	11	15	4

* Short lactation period due to accident.

Table B.

YIELDS AND RETURNS OF THE GOVERNMENT HERD OF RED POLL DAIRY CATTLE.

(Season 1911–12.)

Cow.	Days in Milk.	Weeks in Milk.	Milk in Gallons.	Tests.	Butter Fat.	Prices.	Values.		
					lbs.		£	s.	d.
Vuelta	289	41¼	775·2	5·2–8·2	485·1	12¼–14½	26	5	9
Connecticut	283	40½	678·2	4·6–6·4	364·0	12¼–14½	19	11	10
Bullion	305	43½	694·8	4·8–6·2	344·0	12¼–14½	18	10	7
Beulah	278	39¾	646·5	4·9–6·4	342·6	9½–12½	15	3	6
Cuba	304	43½	701·4	4·4–8·4	337·8	12¼–15	18	10	4
Cigarette	291	41½	648·1	4·0–5·6	285·9	12¼–15	15	14	6
Sumatra	293	42	666·2	4·0–5·0	284·2	12¼–15	15	6	2
Kentucky	277	39½	669·5	4·0–4·8	277·7	12¼–15	15	1	1
Muria	286	41	580·2	4·5–7·0	275·7	12¼–14½	14	14	10
Pennsylvania ..	318	45½	634·8	4·0–5·2	271·9	12¼–15	14	13	10
Carolina	226	32¼	580·6	4·0–5·0	254·3	12¼–14½	13	11	4
Virginia	277	39½	551·2	3·9–4·6	221·7	12¼–15	12	0	7
Havana	262	37½	535·6	3·8–4·5	215·3	12¼–15	11	15	4

YIELDS AND RETURNS OF INDIVIDUAL COWS.

(SEASON 1911-12.)

Month.	YIELD FOR EACH MONTH. Milk in Gallons.	Test.	Butter Fat.	Price.	Value.	TOTALS FROM CALVING TO DATE. Days in Milk.	Milk in Gallons.	Butter Fat.	Value.
			lbs.	d.	£ s. d.			lbs.	£ s. d.
Vuelta (due to calve 7th July, 1912).									
August ..	53·9	5·2	28·0	12¼	1 8 7	15	53·9	28·0	1 8 7
Sept. ..	109·8	5·2	57·0	12¼	2 18 2	45	163·7	85·0	4 6 9
Oct. ..	125·7	4·7	59·0	12½	3 1 5	76	289·4	144·0	7 8 2
Nov. ..	118·7	7·0	83·0	12½	4 6 5	106	408·1	227·0	11 14 7
Dec. ..	94·9	7·0	66·4	13	3 11 11	137	503·0	293·4	15 6 6
Jan. ..	95·6	6·8	65·0	13½	3 13 1	168	598·6	358·4	18 19 7
Feb. ..	68·1	7·0	47·6	13¾	2 14 6	197	666·7	406·0	21 14 1
March ..	61·8	7·0	43·2	13½	2 8 7	228	728·5	449·2	24 2 8
April ..	28·6	7·4	21·1	14½	1 5 6	258	757·1	470·3	25 8 2
May ..	18·1	8·2	14·8	14¼	0 17 7	289	775·2	485·1	26 5 9
Connecticut (due to calve 9th July, 1912).									
August ..	23·1	4·6	10·5	12¼	0 10 8	9	23·1	10·5	0 10 8
Sept. ..	113·7	4·6	52·3	12¼	2 13 4	39	136·8	62·8	3 4 1
Oct. ..	129·5	4·6	59·5	12½	3 1 11	70	266·3	122·3	6 5 11
Nov. ..	112·1	6·4	71·7	12½	3 14 8	100	378·4	194·0	10 0 7
Dec. ..	88·3	6·0	52·9	13	2 17 3	131	466·7	246·9	12 17 10
Jan. ..	66·6	5·8	38·6	13½	2 3 5	162	533·3	285·5	15 1 3
Feb. ..	50·9	5·4	27·4	13¾	1 11 4	191	584·2	312·9	16 12 7
March ..	51·2	5·2	26·6	13½	1 9 11	222	636·1	339·5	18 2 6
April ..	26·1	5·6	14·6	14½	0 17 7	252	662·2	354·1	19 0 1
May ..	16·0	6·2	9·9	14¼	0 11 9	283	678·2	364·0	19 11 10
Bullion (due to calve 17th July, 1912).									
August ..	81·1	5·2	42·1	12¼	2 2 11	30	81·1	42·1	2 2 11
Sept. ..	87·4	4·8	41·9	12¼	2 2 9	61	168·5	83·0	4 5 8
Oct. ..	104·3	4·8	50·0	12½	2 12 1	92	272·8	134·0	6 17 9
Nov. ..	97·6	5·0	48·8	12½	2 10 10	122	370·4	182·8	9 8 7
Dec. ..	86·0	5·0	43·0	13	2 6 7	153	456·4	225·8	11 15 2
Jan. ..	72·1	4·8	34·6	13½	1 18 11	184	528·5	260·4	13 14 1
Feb. ..	57·4	4·8	27·5	13¾	1 11 6	213	585·9	287·9	15 5 7
Mar. ..	58·8	5·0	29·4	13½	1 13 0	244	644·7	317·3	16 18 7
April ..	30·7	4·8	14·7	14½	0 17 9	274	675·4	332·0	17 16 4
May ..	19·4	6·2	12·0	14¼	0 14 3	305	694·8	344·0	18 10 7

Month.	YIELD FOR EACH MONTH. Milk in Gallons.	Test.	Butter Fat.	Price.	Value.	TOTALS FROM CALVING TO DATE. Days in Milk.	Milk in Gallons.	Butter Fat.	Value.
Beulah (due to calve 8th February, 1913).									
Feb. ..	96·6	5·0	48·3	9¾	1 19 3	33	96·6	48·3	1 19 3
March ..	105·9	5·0	52·5	9½	2 1 11	64	202·5	101·2	4 1 2
April ..	99·0	5·2	51·4	9¾	2 1 10	94	301·5	152·7	6 3 0
May ..	72·3	5·0	36·1	10	1 10 1	125	373·8	188·8	7 13 1
June ..	70·8	4·9	34·6	10¼	1 11 9	155	444·6	223·5	9 4 10
July ..	69·6	5·3	38·8	11½	1 14 6	186	514·2	260·3	10 19 4
August ..	65·9	6·2	40·8	12¼	2 1 7	217	580·1	301·1	13 0 11
Sept. ..	44·7	6·2	27·7	12¼	1 8 3	247	624·8	328·8	14 9 2
Oct. ..	21·7	6·4	13·8	12½	0 14 4	278	646·5	342·6	15 3 6

YIELDS AND RETURNS OF INDIVIDUAL COWS—*continued.*

(Season 1911–12.)

	Yield for each Month.					Totals from Calving to Date.			
Month.	Milk in Gallons.	Test.	Butter Fat.	Price.	Value.	Days in Milk.	Milk in Gallons.	Butter Fat.	Value.
			lbs.	*d.*	£ *s.* *d.*			lbs.	£ s. *d.*
				Cuba (due to calve 25th September, 1912).					
Sept. ..	89·5	4·7	42·0	12¼	2 2 10	30	89·5	42·0	2 2 10
Oct. ..	113·2	4·6	52·0	12½	2 14 2	61	202·7	94·0	4 17 0
Nov. ..	112·2	4·6	51·6	12½	2 13 9	91	314·9	145·6	7 10 9
Dec. ..	94·5	4·4	41·5	13	2 4 11	122	409·4	187·1	9 15 8
Jan. ..	74·2	4·6	34·1	13½	1 18 4	153	483·6	221·2	11 14 0
Feb. ..	60·1	4·6	27·6	13¾	1 11 7	182	543·7	248·8	13 5 7
March ..	66·4	4·6	30·5	13½	1 14 3	213	610·1	279·3	14 19 10
April ..	49·4	5·0	24·7	14½	1 9 10	243	659·5	304·0	16 9 8
May ..	30·6	8·0	24·4	14¼	1 8 11	274	690·1	328·4	17 18 7
June ..	11·3	8·4	9·4	15	0 11 9	304	701·4	337·8	18 10 4
				Cigarette (due to calve 14th September, 1912).					
Sept. ..	17·7	4·2	7·4	12¼	0 7 6	17	17·7	7·4	0 7 6
Oct. ..	115·8	4·2	48·6	12½	2 10 7	48	133·5	56·0	2 18 1
Nov. ..	114·8	4·6	52·8	12½	2 15 0	78	248·3	108·8	5 13 1
Dec. ..	96·2	4·6	44·2	13	2 7 10	109	344·5	153·0	8 0 11
Jan. ..	81·6	4·0	32·6	13½	1 16 8	140	426·1	185·6	9 17 7
Feb. ..	57·5	4·2	24·1	13¾	1 7 7	169	483·6	209·7	11 5 2
March ..	71·9	4·2	30·1	13½	1 13 10	200	555·5	239·8	12 19 0
April ..	49·8	4·5	22·4	14½	1 7 0	230	605·3	262·2	14 6 0
May ..	30·2	5·6	16·9	14¼	1 0 0	261	635·5	279·1	15 6 0
June ..	12·6	5·4	6·8	15	0 8 6	291	648·1	285·9	15 14 6
				Sumatra (due to calve 7th August, 1912).					
August ..	25·1	4·4	11·0	12¼	0 11 2	9	25·1	11·0	0 11 2
Sept. ..	98·2	4·4	43·2	12¼	2 4 1	39	123·3	54·2	2 15 3
Oct. ..	99·6	4·2	41·8	12½	2 3 6	70	222·9	96·0	4 18 9
Nov. ..	96·3	4·4	42·3	12½	2 4 0	100	319·2	138·3	7 2 9
Dec. ..	84·3	4·4	37·0	13	2 0 1	131	403·5	175·3	9 2 10
Jan. ..	70·9	4·0	28·3	13½	1 11 10	162	474·4	203·6	10 14 8
Feb. ..	58·0	4·0	23·2	12¾	1 4 7	191	532·4	226·8	11 19 3
March ..	64·6	4·0	25·8	13½	1 9 0	222	597·9	252·6	13 8 3
April ..	39·6	4·4	17·4	14½	1 1 0	252	636·5	270·0	14 9 3
May ..	26·5	4·8	12·7	14¼	0 15 1	283	663·0	282·7	15 4 4
June ..	3·1	5·0	1·5	15	0 1 10	293	666·2	284·2	15 6 2
				Kentucky (due to calve 11th October, 1912).					
Sept. ..	88·0	4·0	35·2	12¼	1 15 11	29	88·0	35·2	1 15 11
Oct. ..	117·8	4·2	49·4	12½	2 11 5	60	205·8	84·6	4 7 4
Nov. ..	115·6	4·2	48·5	12½	2 10 6	90	321·4	133·1	6 17 10
Dec. ..	95·1	4·0	38·0	13	2 1 2	121	416·5	171·1	8 19 0
Jan. ..	79·1	4·0	31·6	13½	1 15 6	152	495·6	202·7	10 14 6
Feb. ..	60·9	4·2	25·5	13¾	1 9 2	181	556·5	228·2	12 3 8
March ..	57·0	4·2	23·9	13½	1 6 10	212	613·5	252·1	13 10 6
April ..	29·7	4·4	13·0	14½	0 15 8	242	643·2	265·1	14 6 2
May ..	24·4	4·8	11·7	14¼	0 13 10	273	667·6	276·8	15 0 0
June ..	1·9	4·8	0·9	15	0 1 1	277	669·5	277·7	15 1 1

YIELDS AND RETURNS OF INDIVIDUAL COWS—*continued.*

(SEASON 1911–12.)

Month.	Yield for each Month. Milk in Gallons.	Test.	Butter Fat. lbs.	Price. d.	Value. £ s. d.	Totals from Calving to Date. Days in Milk.	Milk in Gallons.	Butter Fat. lbs.	Value. £ s. d.
Muria (due to calve 19th August, 1912).									
August ..	24·2	4·5	10·8	12¼	0 11 0	12	24·2	10·8	0 11 0
Sept. ..	111·1	4·5	49·9	12¼	2 10 11	42	135·3	60·7	3 1 11
Oct. ..	107·7	4·6	49·5	12½	2 11 6	73	243·0	110·2	5 13 5
Nov. ..	86·7	4·8	41·6	12½	2 3 4	103	329·7	151·8	7 16 9
Dec. ..	67·3	4·8	32·3	13	1 15 0	134	397·0	184·1	9 11 9
Jan. ..	57·8	4·6	26·5	13½	1 9 9	165	454·8	210·6	11 1 6
Feb. ..	46·0	4·8	22·0	12¾	1 3 4	194	500·8	232·6	12 4 10
March ..	43·9	5·0	21·9	13½	1 4 7	225	544·7	254·5	13 9 5
April ..	23·6	5·4	12·9	14½	0 15 7	255	568·3	267·4	14 5 0
May ..	11·9	7·0	8·3	14¼	0 9 10	286	580·2	275·7	14 14 10
Pennsylvania (due to calve 16th September, 1912).									
August ..	37·4	4·5	16·8	12¼	0 17 1	14	37·4	16·8	0 17 1
Sept. ..	99·3	4·5	44·6	12¼	2 5 6	44	136·7	61·4	3 2 7
Oct. ..	103·1	4·4	45·3	12½	2 7 2	75	239·8	106·7	5 9 9
Nov. ..	97·1	4·0	38·8	12½	2 0 5	105	336·9	145·5	7 10 2
Dec. ..	67·9	4·2	28·5	13	1 10 10	136	404·8	174·0	9 1 0
Jan. ..	63·8	4·0	25·5	13½	1 8 8	167	468·6	199·5	10 9 8
Feb. ..	52·3	4·0	20·9	12¾	1 3 11	196	520·9	220·4	11 13 7
March ..	52·5	4·2	22·0	13½	1 4 9	227	573·4	242·4	12 18 4
April ..	27·6	4·5	12·4	14½	0 14 11	257	601·0	254·8	13 13 3
May ..	23·2	5·0	11·6	14¼	0 13 9	288	624·2	266·4	14 7 0
June ..	10·6	5·2	5·5	15	0 6 10	318	634·8	271·9	14 13 10
Carolina (due to calve 13th August, 1912).									
August ..	8·6	4·0	3·4	12¼	0 3 5	7	8·6	3·4	0 3 5
Sept. ..	115·7	4·0	46·2	12¼	2 7 2	37	124·3	49·6	2 10 7
Oct. ..	114·6	4·0	45·8	12½	2 7 8	68	238·9	95·4	4 18 3
Nov. ..	100·5	5·0	50·2	12½	2 12 3	98	339·4	145·6	7 10 6
Dec. ..	83·2	5·0	41·6	13	2 5 0	129	422·6	187·2	9 15 6
Jan. ..	66·1	4·2	27·7	13½	1 11 2	160	488·7	214·9	11 6 8
Feb. ..	45·5	4·2	19·1	13¾	1 1 10	189	534·2	234·0	12 8 6
March ..	45·1	4·4	19·8	13½	1 2 3	220	579·3	253·8	13 10 9
April ..	1·3	4·5	0·5	14½	0 0 7	226	580·6	254·3	13 11 4
Virginia (due to calve 11th July, 1912).									
Sept. ..	64·4	3·9	25·1	12¼	1 5 7	29	64·4	25·1	1 5 7
Oct. ..	104·6	3·9	40·7	12½	2 2 4	60	169·0	65·8	3 7 11
Nov. ..	93·9	4·0	37·4	12½	1 19 0	90	262·9	103·2	5 6 11
Dec. ..	77·5	3·9	30·2	13	1 12 8	121	339·4	133·4	6 19 7
Jan. ..	63·9	4·0	25·5	13½	1 8 8	152	403·3	158·9	8 8 3
Feb. ..	52·1	4·2	21·8	13¾	1 4 11	181	455·4	180·7	9 13 2
March ..	52·1	4·4	22·9	13½	1 5 9	212	507·5	203·6	10 18 11
April ..	27·0	4·2	11·3	14½	0 13 7	242	534·5	214·9	11 12 6
May ..	15·1	4·4	6·6	14¼	0 7 10	273	549·6	221·5	12 0 4
June ..	0·6	4·6	0·2	15	0 0 3	277	551·2	221·7	12 0 7

YIELDS AND RETURNS OF INDIVIDUAL COWS—*continued.*

(SEASON 1911–12.)

Month.	Milk in Gallons.	Test.	Butter Fat. lbs.	Price. d.	Value. £ s. d.	Days in Milk.	Milk in Gallons.	Butter Fat. lbs.	Value. £ s. d.

Havana (due to calve 18th August, 1912).

Month.	Milk in Gallons.	Test.	Butter Fat. lbs.	Price. d.	Value. £ s. d.	Days in Milk.	Milk in Gallons.	Butter Fat. lbs.	Value. £ s. d.
Sept.	15·6	3·8	5·9	12¼	0 6 0	15	15·6	5·9	0 6 0
Oct.	98·8	3·9	38·5	12¼	2 0 1	46	114·4	44·4	2 6 1
Nov.	96·4	4·2	40·4	12½	2 2 1	76	210·8	84·8	4 8 2
Dec.	86·4	4·0	34·5	13	1 17 4	107	297·2	119·3	6 5 6
Jan.	68·3	4·0	27·3	13¼	1 10 8	138	365·5	146·6	7 16 2
Feb.	59·6	4·0	23·8	13¾	1 7 3	167	425·1	170·4	9 3 5
March	64·1	4·0	25·6	13½	1 8 9	198	489·2	196·0	10 12 2
April	29·2	4·0	11.6	14½	0 14 0	228	518·4	207·6	11 6 2
May	16·3	4·5	7·3	14¼	0 8 8	259	534·7	214·9	11 14 10
June	0·9	4·0	0·4	15	0 0 6	262	535·6	215·3	11 15 4

RED POLL DAIRY HERD, BOISDALE.

PASPALUM FOR HILL PASTURES.

By R. G. Threlfall, Dairy Supervisor, Yea District.

During a season of drought such as the greater portion of this State has lately experienced, the question of improving the natural pasture by the introduction of drought-resistant grasses cannot fail to command the serious attention of every one interested in the breeding and keeping of stock.

While the cultivation and conservation of fodder crops in the form of hay and silage is absolutely necessary to enable stock-owners to carry their herds and flocks safely through a prolonged period of drought, yet it is plain that much may be done in the way of increasing the stock-carrying capacity of the pasture lands. There are thousands of acres of grass land in this and other districts which could be made to support at least twice or three times the quantity of stock carried on the natural grasses. That this can be done was clearly demonstrated to the writer while recently inspecting several paddocks of *Paspalum dilatatum* grass on "Glenmore" sheep station, owned by Colonel McLeish and his brother, Mr. Thomas McLeish. The station is situated about 12 miles from Yea, and that portion of the land referred to is fairly typical of thousands of acres in the Upper Goulburn district, being composed of high flats of second quality soil, overlying a dense and clayey subsoil, with very little natural drainage.

About four years ago, the Messrs. McLeish Bros. had a small paddock ploughed and sown down with *Paspalum dilatatum*, and so successful did the experiment prove that they have since added one paddock after another, until up to the present time 120 acres have been planted, and it is intended to considerably add to this area in the near future.

The method of planting was to plough and harrow to a fine tilth, then sow on the surface from 6 to 8 lbs. of the seed, and lightly cover with brush harrows. It is recommended that a few pounds of some of the winter-growing grasses, such as the Subterranean and Alsyke clovers, rye grass, and *Phalaris commutata*, be sown with the Paspalum to provide feed during the months from May to September, when the last-named grass is making comparatively little growth.

Spring or early summer is found to be the best time for sowing the *Paspalum*, as the hotter the weather the quicker the seed germinates, providing, of course, that the necessary amount of moisture is present in the soil. If, after sowing, the land remains in a dry state for the greater part of the summer, the seed will not be lost, as it will be found to sprout safely the following season. Even in swampy and rough places that could not be ploughed, but where the seed was lightly scattered among the tussocks and grass, the *Paspalum* has taken complete possession. Where the grass has been growing for three or four years, it has formed a complete mat of herbage which, during the spring, summer, and autumn months, has carried stock equivalent to a bullock to the acre. Owing to the matted nature of the crown and stems, it is found that no amount of heavy stocking will eat it out; in fact, it appears to spread much better and be more succulent when kept eaten close to the ground than if allowed to grow in the form of tussocks. Though little growth takes place in the winter, the severest frost or flooding will not kill it. The writer was shown a swamp where the *Paspalum* is fast killing out the tussocks and reeds. The grass has been known to be under water for weeks at a time in the winter, and then strike into luxuriant growth when the water-level was lowered in the summer. It is also growing well on the more hilly land, where the seed was scattered among the bracken fern. In many places the ferns are found to be thinning out and giving way before the ever-spreading *Paspalum*. All stock are very fond of the grass, horses, sheep, and cattle alike preferring it to the natural grasses. It is found to respond freely to irrigation.

It is not recommended that *Paspalum* should be sown as a rotation crop in cultivation land, as, owing to its tenacity of life, considerable trouble would be experienced in breaking up land once overgrown with it. Nor is it advisable to sow *Paspalum* in well-drained soil suitable for lucerne or rye-grass, and other finer grasses; but, as it thrives under dry conditions, it is possible it would greatly improve the grazing capacity of the poorer hill pastures.

THE FRUIT TRADE OF VICTORIA.

ITS PRESENT STATUS FROM A COMMERCIAL STAND-POINT.

By E. Meeking, Senior Inspector of Fruit.

PART 1.

Introductory.

" It has at last been realized that too much attention has been given in the past to the business of inducing people to plant fruit trees, and not enough consideration has been given to the selling of the crop, and the finding of a profitable market for the fruit that is already on hand. The one great object in growing fruit is to sell at a profit. Fruit-growing is a business, and as such is dependent upon business methods and principles quite as much as the manufacture and sale of boots and shoes, of steel implements, or of other articles."

The above were the terms in which the officer in charge of fruit transportation in the United States of America reported to the Secretary for Agriculture on the unsatisfactory condition of the fruit-growing industry in that country, which had resulted from the Government Immigration Agencies encouraging new settlers to undertake the business of fruit-growing without paying sufficient attention to the matters of handling, transporting, and marketing of the fruits when raised. This state of affairs eventually promised to create such financial embarrassment of fruit-growers in some of the States that the Government undertook to investigate the matter. As a result, the application of combined businesslike and scientific methods is now widely adopted in connexion with the marketing of fruits, and the position of the fruit trade in the United States has, from a commercial point of view, been much improved.

It is to be feared that, unless more attention is given to the proper handling, distribution, and marketing of our fruits, the fruit trade in Victoria will drift into the same unsatisfactory condition as was the case with the trade in the United States some years ago. Fruit-growing is now becoming such a popular branch of agronomy in this State, and has developed so rapidly during recent years, that, unless the demand can be made to keep pace with the supply, the position of the local fruit-grower may, in the future, be very unenviable. The predilection amongst our agriculturists to take up fruit-growing as a livelihood is accounted for by the following :—

1. The suitability of our soils and climate.
2. The profits which have been obtained from fruit-growing in the past.
3. The attractive nature of the occupation.

Suitability of Victoria for Fruit-Growing.

Any one acquainted, from a horticultural point of view, with Victoria will readily agree as to the suitability of our soils and climate, for here may be grown in profusion a wide variety of fruits of superior quality and fascinating flavour. The physiographic diversity which obtains in different portions of the State furnishes a range of climate which renders possible the successful cultivation of many kinds of stone, pip, and " berry " fruits. So much is this so, that many districts have become noted for producing some particular variety of paramount quality. Thus, the vernacular terms " Bendigo Tomatoes," " Merrigum Peaches," " Mildura Navels," " Goulburn Valley Gordos," " Wandin Raspberries," " Trentham Black Currants," may often be heard voiced by the retailers in our markets, and the barrowmen in the streets. In short, there is scarcely any portion of Victoria where, by planting varieties suitable to the locality, and under proper management, a prolific and healthy orchard may not be established. In spite of this, it must be confessed that our fruit industry, as a whole, is at present in anything but a satisfactory condition. This is by no means due to want of knowledge on the part of our growers, in so far as their part of the business is concerned. In pruning, spraying, cultivation, and all matters incidental to the production of prime quality fruit, it is questionable whether fruit-growers in any country are more advanced than those in this State. Our orchardists, as a whole, are intelligent, observant, and painstaking, with the result, as before stated, that our fruits, both from the stand-point of quality and quantity produced per acre, compare more than favorably with those grown elsewhere.

When we view the subject from a commercial stand-point, however, the position is not nearly so satisfactory. This is primarily due to want of organization amongst those concerned. The consequence is an absence of necessary collective attention to the matters of exploiting new markets, disposal of fruits to the best advantage in the markets already secured, the best methods of harvesting, handling, and transporting fruits, and many other minor details, each apparently unimportant, but each requiring attention in order to obtain the best results.

Special Methods Required for Handling and Transporting Fruits.

The perishable nature of fruit obviously renders necessary the application of special methods to its harvesting, transportation, and marketing. If those desiderata of the grower—absence of gluts and regular prices—are to be brought about, every factor which tends to shorten the life of fruits from the time of their severance from the tree until they reach the consumer, must be eliminated as far as possible. The longer fruits can be held in good condition, and the further they can be transported, the greater their relative value to the producer. These facts have long been realized ; but the possibility of holding even the better keeping varieties of fruits over extended periods until suitable markets may be obtained, has not, until recent years, been considered practicable. The growers of this State now appear to be awakening to a realization of what may be accomplished in this direction. This is evidenced by the movement towards the erection of cold storage accommodation in many of our fruit-growing centres. In this regard, Victoria is well ahead of the other States. These cool stores are, at present, to a limited degree, serving an excellent purpose in providing the means whereby fruit, intended for local sale, or Inter-State export, may be held until such time as the surplus crop has been disposed of locally, exported to other States, or oversea countries. The present accommodation, however, still falls far short of requirements, and last year many thousands of cases of fruits were sold at extravagantly low prices through the necessity which existed amongst growers to rush these on the market within a limited period. This would have been avoided in a large measure had sufficient cold 'storage been available in which to hold the fruits

The Relative Importance of Cold Storage.

Cold storage accommodation in the various fruit-growing centres, however, is only a link in a series of arrangements which must be entered upon, and the carrying out of which must be carefully observed, both wholly and in detail, if we wish to extend the industry on profitable and businesslike lines. Although our local markets could, if our fruits were brought into more direct touch with the consumer, at present almost absorb our total supply, yet these markets cannot be expected to keep pace with our increasing production. Even were there sufficient cold storage available to hold all our early apples and pears each season, it may be doubted whether prices, all round, would be much enhanced without the aid of a regular oversea export trade. In any case, these prices would certainly be much below the average which would be obtained were the whole of our available surplus crop exported each season. This argument applied with particular force in the case of our fruit crop last year, and was proved by the results of the "Somerset" shipment of pears. The prices realized for this shipment ranged from 13s. to 19s. per bushel. At the time these prices were being obtained on the London markets, pears of equal quality, and belonging to the same varieties, and, in many instances, picked, no doubt, from the same trees, were being disposed of locally for prices ranging from 6d. to 1s. 6d., per bushel. The removal of some 6,000 cases from this market contributed very little towards easing the local over-supply; but had this shipment been followed by further consignments during the weeks when the local markets were glutted, and pears here were practically valueless, the markets would have been eased, and the losses occasioned by the glut would have been avoided. The cabled reports of the prices realized for the *Somerset* shipment, arriving as they did at a time when similar pears were locally being sold as low as 6d. per bushel, furnished a forcible commentary upon the necessity on the part of our growers and exporters to open up a profitable trade in the regular oversea export of pears. The results of the *Somerset* shipment show what may be achieved, and help to confirm the belief expressed during the past four years through the *Journal of Agriculture* that not only pears, but soft fruits, such as peaches and nectarines, may, if proper conditions in picking, packing, and transportation are observed, be safely and profitably exported to oversea markets.

The Example of Other Countries.

For years past, certain oversea countries have been showing our growers that thousands of cases of oranges, lemons. apples, and even soft fruits, such as peaches, plums, and the softer varieties of pears, may be successfully shipped over long distances, and that uniformly good prices may be realized by carrying out specialized methods of picking, packing, handling, transportation, and marketing; the application of low temperatures to fruits as soon as possible after their severance from the tree; the uniform maintenance of these low temperatures until the arrival of fruits at their final destination; and, lastly, organized methods of disposal to the consumer. It is the intention of this article to show that this is possible, and that. at the same time, the status of the industry generally may be raised, and that the huge percentage of waste and deterioration which annually occurs may, in large measure, be avoided.

Before dealing with these matters, it will be as well to briefly outline the present conditions which obtain in connexion with the local, inter-State, and oversea disposal of our fruits in order to ascertain, if possible, our shortcomings. By this means, any suggestions for improvement should be more readily apprehended, and the criticisms of such suggestions be rendered more easy of accomplishment.

(To be continued.)

VERNACULAR NAMES OF VICTORIAN PLANTS.

(Continued from page 448.)

Communicated by Alfred J. Ewart, D.Sc., Ph.D., F.L.S., Chairman, and C. S. Sutton, M.B., Ch. B., Secretary, of the Plant Names Committee of the Victorian Field Naturalists' Club.

DICOTYLEDONEÆ—*continued.*

Botanical Name.	Popular Name.	Use or Character.

DICOTYLEDONEÆ—CHORIPETALEÆ HYPOGYNÆ—*continued.*

RUTACEÆ—*continued.*

Phebalium—

pungens, Benth.	Prickly Phebalium	
phylicifolium, F.v.M.	Mountain Phebalium	
dentatum, Sm. ..	Umbellate Phebalium	
Ralstoni, Benth.	Shy Phebalium ..	
bilobum, Lindl.	Truncate Phebalium	
lamprophyllum, Benth. ..	Shining Phebalium	
amplifolium, F.v.M.	Broadleaved Phebalium	
diosmeum, A. Juss.	Slender Phebalium	
ozothamnoides, F.v.M.	Everlasting Phebalium	
glandulosum, Hook	Desert Phebalium	
squamulosum, Vent.	Scaly Phebalium	
stenophyllum, F.v.M.	Narrowleaved Phebalium	There is hardly an unattractive member in this group, and *Eriostemon obovalis, Asterolasia Muelleri, Phebalium bilobum, P. Billardieri, P. glandulosum, Eriostemon difformis,* and *E. myoporoides (Eriostemon nervifolius* of the florists' catalogues) are specially recommended for cultivation.
podocarpoides, F.v.M.	Alpine Phebalium	
Billardieri, A. Juss.	Satinwood Phebalium	
ovatifolium, F.v.M.	Ovate Phebalium	

Microcybe—

pauciflora, Turcz	Microcybe Phebalium	

Asterolasia—

Muelleri Benth ..	Lemon Star-bush	

Pleurandropsis—

phebalioides, Baill.	Downy Star-bush	
trymalioides, F.v.M.	Leathery Star-bush	

Crowea—

exalata, F.v.M. ..	Crowea	

Eriostemon—

lanceolatus, Gaertner	Lance-leaved Waxflower	
trachyphyllus, F.v.M.	Blunt-leaved Waxflower	
*myoporoides, D.C.	Long-leaved Waxflower	
obovalis, Cunningham	Fairy Waxflower	
scaber, Paxton ..	Rough Waxflower	
difformis, Cunningham	Small-leaved Waxflower	

Correa—

aemula, F.v.M. ..	Hairy Correa	
alba, Andrews ..	White Correa	
speciosa, Andrews	Red Correa	All the species of correa are worthy of cultivation in gardens, particularly some forms of *Correa speciosa.*
speciosa, var. normalis	Green Correa	
speciosa, var. glabra	Smooth Correa ..	
Lawrenciana, Hook	Mountain Correa	

Geijera—

parviflora, Lindley	Wilga ..	Yields valuable feed for stock in time of drought, sheep being particularly fond of it. Timber light coloured, hard, close grained, and used for naves of wheels, blocks, &c.

Acronychia—

laevis, R. & G. Forster ..	Yellow Wood ..	Timber light coloured, close grained, but is not much used.

* Plants marked thus are listed either as growing plants or seeds by one or more of our florists.

Vernacular Names of Victorian Plants—*continued.*

Botanical Name.	Popular Name.	Use or Character.
Dicotyledoneæ—Choripetaleæ Hypogynæ—*continued.*		
ZYGOPHYLLACEÆ.		
Nitraria— Schoberi, L.	Nitre Bush	It produces fruit of the size of an olive, of a red colour, and agreeable flavour.
Zygophyllum— apiculatum, F.v.M. glaucescens, F.v.M crenatum, F.v.M. iodocarpum, F.v.M.	Pointed Twinleaf Pale Twinleaf Notched Twinleaf Violet Twinleaf	} No known economic value. A suspected poison plant, but stock usually avoid it.
ammophilum, F.v.M. Billardieri, D.C. fruticulosum, D.C.	Sand Twinleaf Coast Twinleaf Shrubby Twinleaf	} No known economic value.
Tribulus— terrestris, L'Obel	Caltrops	Has been said to kill stock if eaten when starving, possibly owing to the prickly fruits.
LINACEÆ.		
Linum— marginale, Cunningham	Wild Flax	Though only a small plant, it yields a fibre of good quality, and is used by the blacks for making fishing nets and cordage.
GERANIACEÆ.		
Geranium— dissectum, L.	Cut-leaved Geranium	Stock very fond of the succulent herbage of this plant
sessiliflorum, Cav.	Mountain Geranium	Of slight pasture value.
Erodium— cygnorum, Nees	Blue Erodium	Affords good herbage in the young state. Can be made into capital hay and might be turned into ensilage with good results.
Pelargonium— australe, Willd. Rodneyanum, Mitchell	Austral Pelargonium Rosy Pelargonium	} Might be improved by garden culture.
OXALIDACEÆ.		
Oxalis— magellanica, G. Forster corniculata, L.	White Wood-sorrel Yellow Wood-sorrel	} Usually avoided by stock. The leaves resemble clover but are acid.
MALVACEÆ.		
Lavatera— plebeja, Sims	Austral Hollyhock	Stock very fond of this in its young state. Root edible. Fibre can be prepared from the inner bark.
Plagianthus— pulchellus, A. Gray	Hemp Bush	The fibre is soft and glossy and should form a good warp yarn
spicatus, Bentham	Salt Plagianth	When in seed, if eaten in quantity, may injure stock by inflaming the stomach.
glomeratus, Bentham microphyllus, F.v.M.	Thorny Plagianth Small-leaved Plagianth	} Of no known economic value.
Sida— corrugata, Lindley intricata, F.v.M.	Dwarf Sida Bushy Sida	
Abutilon— otocarpum, F.v.M. Avicennae, Gerard	Desert Chinese Lantern Swamp Chinese Lantern	Several of these are worth the notice of our florists.
Howittia— trilocularis, F.v.M.	Shrub Mallow	
Hibiscus— Krichauffi, F.v.M. †Trionum, L.	Desert Hibiscus Bladder Hibiscus	Sometimes grown in gardens.

† Naturalized in Victoria from the other States, where it is native.

VERNACULAR NAMES OF VICTORIAN PLANTS—*continued.*

Botanical Name.	Popular Name.	Use or Character.
DICOTYLEDONEÆ —CHORIPETALEÆ HYPOGYNÆ—*continued.*		
STERCULICEÆ.		
Brachychiton—		
*populneus, R.Br.	Kurrajong	The tap-roots of young trees are used as food by the aborigines. In drought periods the leaves and branches are used as fodder. A strong fibre is obtained from the bark. Timber is soft, fibrous, and useless.
Ruelingia—		
pannosa, R.Br	Kerrawan	The timber is comparatively close grained and fairly hard, but is difficult to season.
Commersonia—		
Fraseri, J. Gay	Blackfellow's Hemp	Sometimes grown in gardens.
Thomasia—		
petalocalyx, F.v.M.	Paper Flower	No known economic value.
Lasiopetalum—		
dasyphyllum, Siebar	Shrubby Velvet Bush	
Behrii, F.v.M.	Pink Velvet Bush	
parviflorum, Rudge	Small-flowered Velvet Bush	Some species may prove worthy of garden cultivation.
Baueri, Steetz	White Velvet Bush	
ferrugineum, Smith	Rusty Velvet Bush	
Schulzenii, F.v.M.	Drooping Velvet Bush	
ELAEOCARPACEÆ.		
Elaeocarpus—		
holopetalus, F.v.M.	Black Olive-berry	The wood is white, close grained, and good for joiners' work.
*cyaneus, Ait.	Blue Olive-berry	Wood dark coloured ; very tough ; makes good handles and poles.
EUPHORBIACEÆ.		
Euphorbia—		
erythrantha, F.v.M.	Red Spurge	Frequently stated to poison sheep, but in the case of *E. Drummondii,* this has been shown to be incorrect. *E. eremophila* may be actually poisonous.
Drummondii, Boissier	Flat Spurge	
eremophila, Cunn.	Desert Spurge	
Poranthera—		
ericoides, Klotzsch.	Heath Poranthera	
corymbosa, Brongn.	Clustered Poranthera	
microphylla, Brongn.	Small-leaved Poranthera	
Micrantheum—		
hexandrum, Hook. f.	Box Micrantheum	No known economic value.
Pseudanthus—		
ovalifolius, F.v.M.	Oval-leaved Pseudanthus	
divaricatissimus, Benth.	Round-leaved Pseudanthus	
Beyeria—		
viscosa, Miquel	Sticky Wallaby-bush	Is considered a poison plant in N.S. Wales. The wood is very hard, and is used for turnery.
lasiocarpa, F.v.M.	Large Wallaby-bush	No known economic value.
opaca, F.v.M.	Small Wallaby-bush	
Ricinocarpus—		
pinifolius, Desfont.	Wedding-bush	A handsome shrub, well worth cultivating in gardens.
Bertya—		
Cunninghamii, Planchon	Sticky Bertya	Yields a clear gum-resin, but its economic value is unknown.
oleæfolia, Planch.	Olive Bertya	
‡(Mitchelli, J. Mueller)		
Findlayi, F.v.M.	Mountain Bertya	
Amperea—		
spartioides, Brongn.	Broom Spurge	
Phyllanthus—		
Fuernrohrii, F.v.M.	Sand Spurge	No known economic value.
lacunarius, F.v.M.	Lagoon Spurge	
trachyspermus, F.v.M.	Dwarf Spurge	
thymoides, Sieber	Thyme Spurge	
Gunnii, Hook. f.	Shrubby Spurge	

* Plants marked thus are listed either as growing plants or as seeds by one or more of our florists.
‡ Now included in B. oleæfolia.

VERNACULAR NAMES OF VICTORIAN PLANTS—*continued.*

Botanical Name.	Popular Name.	Use or Character.
DICOTYLEDONEÆ—CHORIPETALEÆ HYPOGYNÆ—*continued.*		
EUPHORBIACEÆ—*continued.*		
Claoxylon— australe, Baillon ..	Brittlewood	Wood, light yellow colour, hard, close grained, useful for cabinet-work.
Adriana— tomentosa, Gaudich. ..	Woolly Bitterbush ..	} No known economic value.
quadripartita, Gaudich. ..	Common Bitterbush ..	
Omalanthus— Leschenaultianus, A. de Jussieu	Poplar Spurge	A suspected poison plant, but no poisonous substance has been extracted.
URTICACEÆ.		
Trema— aspera, Blume	Rough Hemp Nettle ..	Is generally considered poisonous to stock in dry seasons, but probably is only mechanically injurious.
Ficus— scabra, G. Forster ..	Sand Paper Fig ..	Of no known economic value, but might be used for polishing or scouring.
Parietaria— debilis, G. Forster ..	Forest Pellitory ..	} Useless weeds, of which the last has severe stinging properties.
Australina— Muelleri, Wedd... ..	Smooth Nettle	
Urtica— incisa, Poiret.	Scrub nettle	
FAGACEÆ.		
Fagus— Cuninnghamii, Hooker ..	Myrtle Beech	Useful for sash and door-work and all kinds of light joinery, also for furniture.
CASUARINACEÆ.		
Casuarina— *quadrivalvis, Labill. ..	Drooping Sheoke ..	All the casuarinas can be pollarded for cattle fodder. Foliage eagerly eaten by cattle. and useful to stock of all sorts in drought time.
lepidophloia, F.v.M. ..	Belar	A first-class fuel wood.
Luehmanni, R. T. Baker..	Buloke	A hard close grained wood, useful for cabinet and ornamental work.
*glauca, Sieber	Grey Buloke	Of rapid growth. Wood valuable for staves, shingles, &c. Useful as forage for stock in time of drought.
*suberosa, Otto & Dietrich	Black Sheoke	Timber tough, coarse-grained and useful for many purposes. Stock fond of the young growth.
paludosa, Sieber ..	Marsh Sheoke	} Of some fodder value in times of scarcity.
distyla, Ventenat ..	Stunted Sheoke ..	
nana, Sieber	Dwarf Sheoke	
CELASTRACEÆ.		
Celastrus— australis, Harvey & F.v.M.	Staff-climber	A hardy evergreen climber.
SAPINDACEÆ.		
Nephelium— *leiocarpum, F.v.M. ..	Smooth Ramboutan ..	Greedily eaten by stock when other herbage is scarce. Wood hard and useful for tool handles.
Heterodendron— oleaefolium, Desfont. ..	Berrigan	Wood a yellowish colour with a black or dark brown heart; used for rollers and rolling pins.

*Plants marked thus are listed either as growing plants or as seeds by one or more of our florists.

VERNACULAR NAMES OF VICTORIAN PLANTS—*continued.*

Botanical Name.	Popular Name.	Use or Character.
DICOTYLEDONEÆ—CHORIPETALEÆ HYPOGYNÆ—*continued.*		
SAPINDACEÆ—*continued.*		
Dodonaea—		
triquetra, Wendl.	Large-leaved Hopbush	Wood light coloured, close grained.
*viscosa, L.	Giant Hopbush	Wood of a brown colour, close grained and hard. Used in India for tool handles, &c.
procumbens, F.v.M.	Trailing Hopbush	No known economic value.
lobulata, F.v.M.	Tall Hopbush	Timber hard, tough, close grained. One of the best forage shrubs. Sheep are particularly fond of it.
calycina, Cunningham	Angular Hopbush	⎫
bursarifolia, Behr. & F.v M.	Lesser Hopbush	⎪
Baueri, Endlicher.	Crinkled Hopbush	⎬ No special economic value, but some formerly provided a substitute for hops.
humilis, Endlicher.	Dwarf Hopbush	
boronifolia, G. Don.	Hairy Hopbush	
tenuifolia, Lindley	Thin-leaved Hopbush	⎪
stenozyga, F.v.M.	Desert Hopbush	⎭
STACKHOUSIACEÆ.		
Stackhousia—		
pulvinaris, F.v.M.	Alpine Stackhousia	⎫
linarifolia, Cunning.	Creamy Stackhousia	⎪
flava, Hook.	Yellow Stackhousia	⎬ Herbs of some decorative value.
viminea, Smith	Slender Stackhousia	⎪
spathulata, Sieber	Coast Stackhousia	⎭
FRANKENIACEÆ.		
Frankenia—		
pauciflora, D C.	Seaheath	Of no known economic value.
PLUMBAGINACEÆ.		
Statice—		
australis, Spreng.	Yellow Sea-lavender	Might be worthy of addition to the list of garden plants.
PORTULACACEÆ.		
Portulaca—		
oleracea, L.	Common Purslane	⎫
Calandrinia—		⎪
volubilis, Benth.	Twining Purslane	⎪
calyptrata, Hook. f.	Pink Purslane	⎬ Of slight pasture value when better fodder is scarce, but generally classed as useless weeds.
corrigioloides F.v.M.	Strap Purslane	
brevipedata, F.v.M.	Short-stalked Purslane	
pygmaea, F.v.M.	Dwarf Purslane	⎪
Claytonia—		⎪
australasica, Hook. f.	White Purslane	⎭
Montia—		
fontana, L.	Waterblinks	No known economic value.
CARYOPHYLLACEÆ.		
Stellaria—		
pungens, Brongn.	Prickly Starwort	⎫
palustris, Retzius	Marsh Starwort	⎪
flaccida, Hook.	Limp Starwort	⎬ See over page.
multiflora, Hook.	Many Flowered Starwort	⎪
Sagina—		⎪
procumbens, L.	Spreading Pearlwort	⎪
apetala, L.	Small Pearlwort	⎭

* Plants marked thus are listed either as growing plants or as seeds by one or more of our florists.

VERNACULAR NAMES OF VICTORIAN PLANTS—*continued.*

Botanical Name.	Popular Name.	Use or Character.

DICOTYLEDONEÆ—CHORIPETALEÆ HYPOGYNÆ - *continued.*

CARYOPHYLLACEÆ—*continued.*

Colobanthus—		
subulatus, Hook. f.	Alpine Colebanth	
Billardieri, Fenzl.	Coast Colebanth	
Scleranthus—		The native members of this order have no special commercial, pastoral, or horticultural value, except perhaps a variety of *Stellaria palustris*, which would make a pretty edging to flower-beds. The species of *Stellaria* and *Sagina* though sometimes troublesome as weeds of cultivation have a slight fodder value in pastures.
pungens, R. Br.	Prickly Knawel .	
diander, R.Br. ..	Tufted Knawel .	
minusculus, F.v.M.	Cushion Knawel	
biflorus, Hook. f.	Twin-flowered Knawel	
mniaroides, F.v.M.	Mossy Knawell ..	
Gypsophila—		
tubulosa, Boissier	Chalkwort	
Spergularia—		
rubra, J. & C. Presl.	Sand Spurrey ..	
Drymaria—		
filiformis, Benth.	Thread Spurrey	
Polycarpon—		
tetraphyllum, L.	Four-leaved Allseed	

AMARANTACEÆ.

Alternanthera—		
nodiflora, R.Br.	Joyweed	No known economic value.
Trichinium—		
obovatum, Gaud.	Silvertails	All the species of *Trichinium* have a certain decorative value, and some are eaten by stock, particularly in dry seasons (especially *T. obovatum,. T. nobile,* and *T. erubescens*).
alopecuroideun, Lindl.	Long Tails	
nobile, Lindl. ..	Yellow Tails	
macrocephalum, R.Br.	Feather Heads ..	
exaltatum, Benth.	Lamb Tails	
erubescens, Mog.	Hairy Tails	
spathulatum, R.Br.	Pussy Tails	
Amaranthus—		
macrocarpus, Benth.	Desert Amaranth	No special economic value.

(To be continued.)

A GOOD SALT HOUSE, LICK, AND DEVICE FOR FOOT ROT.

During the past season there have been many deaths from starvation,. impaction, &c., and in the latter case many animals have been in good condition. Numerous licks have been recommended in these columns from time to time, and it is of interest to know that favorable reports on their use are being made. Mr. Temple Smith, Chief Field Officer, in a recent visit to the North-Eastern District found one farmer who, having lost a considerable number of cattle and sheep, resorted to a lick made of 100 lbs. coarse salt, 10 lbs. slaked lime, 10 lbs. bone meal, 3 lbs. sulphur, ½ lb. sulphate of iron, and molasses sufficient to allow of the whole being made into a stiff lolly. After this he only lost two head of cattle, although the weather and general conditions had gone from bad to worse. A great saving of life was attributed to the use of the lick by farmers. who had adopted it early in the season. Salt and sulphur encourage-

salivation, and thus assist as an aid to digestion. The latter is also a laxative; the lime and bone meal supply certain elements of food, and the sulphate of iron is a good tonic for the blood; while the molasses makes the mixture more palatable and is a food that helps to supply warmth to the animal body.

One farmer who has had great success has arranged an ingenious method of supplying the lick and at the same time a method of treatment for foot rot. A shed made of bush timber and roofed with iron, shingles, or bark, has been made in each paddock to protect the lick from the weather. The dimensions are 9 feet by 3 feet by 3 feet in height to the eaves, with an overlap of the roof of at least 1 foot at the eaves. Rails and saplings are nailed to the sides and ends, through which the sheep gain access to the salt, without being able to stand in the troughs in which the mixture is placed. For cattle a higher shed, with rails so fixed that they can be reached over, is constructed. A still further addition for the treatment of foot rot is the placing of trays on each side of the shed

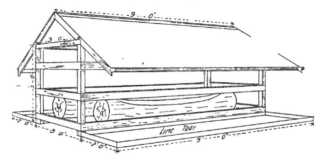

2 inches deep and 2 feet wide, in which burnt lime is spread from time to time, and in which the sheep must stand while engaged at the lick. This has been found of excellent assistance in keeping in check the disease, though not a cure in bad cases, where more stringent treatment is necessary. The lime carried away by the sheep and spread in the paddocks is also beneficial to the land, and in time, when sufficient quantity has been used, will materially improve the quality of the grasses, encouraging the growth of trefoils and clovers, and generally sweetening the soil. The sketch appended will give some idea as to the construction of the sheds.

The troughs can be hewn out of a log, the depth of the cut being not more than 5 inches for sheep and 10 inches for cattle. They should be raised off the ground a few inches to preserve them from rotting. The trays for holding lime can be made of strong galvanized sheet iron. Spouting should be provided to prevent water from the roof dripping into the trays.

SECOND VICTORIAN EGG-LAYING COMPETITION, 1912-13.

H. V. Hawkins, Poultry Expert.

The Winter Test, in connexion with the Second Burnley Egg-laying Competition, came to a conclusion on the 14th August.

As will be seen, White Leghorns again won the prize for the greatest number of eggs laid during the period (first four months). The Black Orpingtons, however, have scored well, and for many weeks past have put up the highest weekly scores.

During the last month many frosts have been experienced, together with cold, sleety showers. The necessity for providing good accommodation for profitable results—a feature, too, often overlooked in the selection of a poultry farm site—has been well emphasized, for, in spite of the elements, the yield of eggs has been very satisfactory ; 21,182 having been laid, or an average number of 307 per pen, as against 15,021 laid last year, or an average of 224 per pen, when Mr. W. G. Swift's pen won the contest with a total of 479 eggs.

The prizes offered in connexion with the Winter Test are for the greatest total number of eggs laid by a pen during the first four months of the competition, terminating on the evening of 14th August—the first prize being £4 4s., and the second £2 2s. : —

	No. eggs
First Prize—Mr. Samuel Brown, Gembrook South ; White Leghorns	480
Second Prize—Mr. George Edwards, Mentone, White Leghorns ...	456
Mr. W. McLister, Melbourne-road, Spotswood, White Leghorns	454
Mr. F. G. Eagleton, Ballarat Hospital, Ballarat, White Leghorns	451

The winning pen opened the competition in perfect condition, and established a lead which has been well maintained.

One pen, under Rule 12, has been disqualified on account of not having attained the standard weight of 24 oz. to the last dozen eggs laid. This was pen No. 36 (Old English Game).

The remainder of birds competing are producing eggs ranging from 24 to 27 ozs. per dozen.

Within the last month very few birds have become broody, due, no doubt, to the cold weather experienced. Two replacements have occurred—one of the birds became paralyzed, and one, due to wasting, had to be returned to the owners.

Feeding has been carried out on practically the same lines as published in the August issue of the *Journal*—the only alteration being an increase of one part of maize to the evening meal to compensate for the extremely cold weather being experienced.

SECOND VICTORIAN EGG-LAYING COMPETITION, 1912-13.

Commencing 15th April, 1912.

CONDUCTED AT BURNLEY HORTICULTURAL SCHOOL.

Pen.	Breed.	Name of Owner.	Eggs laid during competition.			Position in Competition.
			April 15 to July 14.	July 15 to Aug. 14.	Total to Date (4 months).	
40	White Leghorns	S. Brown	358	122	480	1
31	,,	Geo. Edwards	328	128	456	2
23	,,	W. McLister	327	127	454	3
28	,,	F. G. Eagleton	322	129	451	4
47	,,	J. E. Bradley	314	127	441	5
70	,,	C. J. Beatty	322	113	435	6
20	,,	E. Waldon	303	127	430	7
9	,,	J. S. Spotswood	304	122	426	8
3	Black Orpington	King and Watson	313	100	413	9
1	White Leghorns	J. Campbell	282	126	408	10
46	Black Orpingtons	H. A. Langdon	278	124	402	11
8	,,	D. Fisher	280	118	398	12
48	White Leghorns	Griffin Cant	288	105	393	13
62	,,	R. W. Pope	280	105	385	14
37	,,	C. B. Bertelsmeier	254	126	380	15
24	,,	Sargenfri Poultry Yards	260	119	379	16
45	,,	Wooldridge Bros.	248	127	375	17
25	,,	R. L. Appleford	253	117	370	} 18
29	,,	J. B. Brigden	248	122	370	
38	,,	R. Moy	259	109	368	20
2	,,	B. Rowlinson	240	124	364	21
30	,,	Mrs. Stevenson	264	99	363	22
14	,,	J. H. Wright	233	129	362	23
39	,,	W. G. Swift	260	100	360	24
50	,,	A. Ahpee	248	106	354	25
6	,,	J. B. McArthur	236	116	352	26
49	,,	W. Purvis	225	125	350	27
13	,,	W. B. Crellin	216	132	348	28
44	,,	A. W. Hall	242	105	347	29
15	,,	W. H. Steer	212	127	339	30
63	,,	Percy Walker	218	120	338	31
61	Black Orpingtons	J. Ogden	181	152	333	32
7	White Leghorns	A. H. Padman	256	69	325	33
33	,,	H. McKenzie	201	118	319	34
19	,,	Cowan Bros.	198	116	314	35
56	,,	M. A. Monk	195	118	313	36
35	,,	C. H. Busst	200	112	312	37
42	,,	Mrs. Kempster	193	112	305	38
53	,,	H. Hodges	203	101	304	39
5	,,	J. H. Brain	167	127	294	40
10	R.C. Brown Leghorns	S. P. Giles	165	121	286	41
64	White Leghorns	H. Merrick	198	86	284	42
51	,,	H. Hammill	165	118	283	43
60	,,	Miss B. E. Ryan	155	114	269	44
54	,,	F. R. DeGaris	155	106	261	45
43	,,	G. Purton	153	106	259	46
58	,,	W. J. Stock	160	93	253	47
65	,,	A. H. Thomson	150	97	247	48
16	Silver Wyandottes	R. Jobling	120	123	243	49
52	Black Minorcas	Chalmers Bros.	139	103	242	} 50
57	White Leghorns	B. Walker	135	107	242	
27	,,	E. Nash	149	86	235	} 52
12	,,	T. H. Stafford	158	77	235	
4	,,	J. Blackburne	150	84	234	54
69	,,	Morgan and Watson	121	112	233	55
32	,,	S. Brundrett	119	112	231	} 56
11	Black Orpingtons	T. S. Goodisson	106	125	231	
41	White Leghorns	A. Stringer	131	79	210	58
18	,,	B. Mitchell	138	70	208	59
68	,,	W. J. McKeddie	97	109	206	60
55	Brown Leghorns	J. Matheson	90	115	205	61
21	White Leghorns	J. O'Loughlin	99	77	176	62
66	,,	J. Moloney	74	95	169	63
22	,,	W. N. Ling	105	59	164	64
59	,,	W. J. Seabridge	102	51	153	65
36	Old English Game	K. J. Barrett	81	69	150	66
67	Anconas	A. E. Manning	44	103	147	67
17	White Leghorns	S. Childs	48	60	108	} 68
34	,,	R. F. B. Moore	43	65	108	
26	..	(Reserved)	..	..	..	..
		Totals ..	13,759	7,423	21,182	

HINTS TO SETTLERS.

By J. Wilson, Silo Builder.

A.—Six-bail Milking and Feed Shed.

The accompanying illustrations are for a 6-bail milking and feed shed.
The following is a list of material required :—

Hardwood.

4 inches x 1½ inches, thirty-nine 9-ft. Wall Studs.
4 inches x 3 inches, two 11-ft. Front Studs.
4 inches x 4 inches, five 7-ft. and five 6-ft. 6-in. Bail Posts.
4 inches x 2 inches, five 11-ft. Bail Rails.
3 inches x 2 inches, seven 5-ft. and six 6-ft. Studs and Tongues.
3 inches x 1½ inches, four 9-ft. and four 17-ft. Runners for Bails.
4 inches x 2 inches, two 17-ft. Collar Ties.
4 inches x 2 inches, eighteen 12-ft. Rafters.
3 inches x 2 inches, two 17-ft. and two 9-ft. Capping for troughs.
3 inches x 1½ inches, ten 17-ft. and ten 9-ft. Purlins.
6 inches x 1 inch, two 14-ft. Ridge.
4 inches x 2 inches, four 17-ft. and four 14-ft. Plates.
4 inches x 3 inches, one 17-ft. and one 10-ft. Plates.
3 inches x 1 inch, four 17-ft. and four 20-ft. Braces.
4 inches x 2 inches, 50-ft. Gable Studs.
3 inches x 1½ inches, thirteen 1-ft. 9-in. Trough Bearers.
3 inches x 2 inches, thirteen 4-ft. 6-in. Trough Studs.
3 inches x 1½ inches, thirteen 1-ft. 3-in. Trough Studs.

Red Deal.

Weatherboards, 1,400 feet.
Barge and Cover Boards, 6 inches x ⅞ inch, T. & G., eight 13-ft.
Flooring, 6 inches x ⅞ inch, T. & G., for Feed Troughs and Door, 260 feet.
Angle stops, 3 inches x 1½ inches, four 9-ft.

Ironmonger, &c.

Iron for Roof, 56 sheets, 6 feet, 26-gauge, galvanized, corrugated.
Ridging, galvanized, 16 inches, 26-gauge, five lengths.
Spring-head Nails, ten packets.
Wire Nails, 6 lbs. 4 inch ; 8 lbs. 3 inches ; 42 lbs. 2 inch.
T Hinges, one pair, 18 inches.
Bolts, 6 inches x ½ inch., six.
Spouting, galvanized, 5 inches, O.G., ten lengths.
Down Piping, galvanized, 2 inches, seven lengths.
Brackets for 5-in. Spouting, two dozen.

At present price of material in Melbourne it would cost £24 landed
on trucks at Spencer-street station. If the walls are covered with iron
instead of weatherboards, 10 more packets of spring-head nails will be
required, also 32 sheets of 9-ft. galvanized corrugated iron and battens
for iron 3 inches x 1½ inch hardwood—four 13-ft., four 17-ft. (Weatherboards and nineteen 9 ft. 4 in. x 1½-in. wall studs would not be required
or any 2-in. wire nails.) The difference in cost of weatherboard and iron
walls is £1 for material, but there is a big saving in labour if iron is
used and fixed to the inside of the walls. The need for limewashing is
done away with, and the smooth surface can be more quickly and effectively
cleaned by swabbing it at required intervals with a swab or broom.

Specifications for Shed.

The studs of back and two end walls are 4-in. x 1½-in. hardwood,
spaced 18 inches centre to centre, checked in ⅜ of an inch into 4-in. x 2-in.

Section

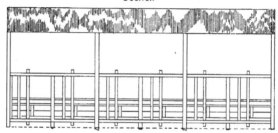

Front Elevation

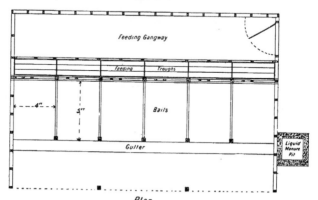

Plan

SIX BAIL MILKING AND FEED SHED.

plates set on blocks sunk in ground 2 feet and spaced not more than 4 ft. centres. The front top plate is of 4-in. x 3-in. hardwood carried by two 4-in. x 3-in. studs sunk 2 feet in the ground as shown, fix a collar-tie on each of these studs. All studs to be well nailed and braced with 3-in. x 1-in. battens, and cover the studs externally with weatherboards showing a 5½-in. weather to each board, and fix an angle-stop 3 inches x 1½ inch at each corner. If iron is used for walls the studs are then 3 feet centre to centre. The top and bottom plates will do to fix the ends of iron and divide the space between with two horizontal 3-in x 1½-in. battens, sinking them in flush with studs. The rafters of 4-in. x 2-in. hardwood, spaced about 3 ft. centres, well nailed to top plate and ridge (ridge 6-in. x 1-in. hardwood). Fix purlins, 3-in. x 1½-in. hardwood to carry iron spaced not more than 3 feet, and well nailed to rafters. Cover the roof with 26-gauge galvanized corrugated iron, allowing a 6-in. lap at joint cover Ridge with 16-in galvanized ridging, use 2½-in galvanized spring-head nails for fixing on iron.

Bails are formed with 4-in. x 4-in. posts sunk 2 feet in ground and mortised to receive the partition rails, 4-in. x 2-in. hardwood. Fix runners of 3-in. x 1½-in. hardwood. The first one from floor to top edge of runner is 9 inches, and the second comes level with top edge of bail post 5 feet from the floor. The posts will require to be checked out to receive runners, leaving 2¼ inches on posts to allow the bail tongues to work freely. Fix studs as shown; the first stud is 12 inches from post, then allow 7 inches between this stud and bail tongue, when the bail is closed a 6-in. bolt is provided for tongue. The feeding troughs are made as shown on plan; studs of 3 inches x 2 inches sunk 1 foot in floor, and spaced about 2 feet apart; fix bearers (3 inches x 1½ inches), keeping the top edge of bearer 18 inches from ground. Cover framing with 6-in. x ⅞-in. T. and G. flooring. Make a movable partition for each bail, which when removed will allow the troughs to be cleansed from end to end. Caps of 3 inches x 2 inches rounded on one side are well fastened to top edges of trough. The quantity of concrete required to cover the floor as shown, 5 inches deep, is 4 cubic yards, and the approximate cost of labour and material £1 15s. per cubic yard. The whole woodwork on outside of building should have at least two coats of paint, but paint or wash should not be applied until the timber is thoroughly seasoned, otherwise it will hasten the decay.

B.—A Durable White-wash.

The following is a durable white-wash (American Congress recipe), used on White House, Washington :—Slack ½ bushel of unslacked lime with boiling water, covered to keep in steam. Strain through fine sieve. Add a peck of salt previously dissolved in warm water. 3 lbs. ground rice, boiled to a thin consistency ; lb. powdered whiting ; 1 lb. clean glue previously dissolved. Boil the mixture one hour in a small kettle, then add 5 gallons of hot water, stir it well and let it stand for a few days, and put on hot with a brush. It remains brilliant for many years. Colouring matter may be added if desired. One pint covers one yard.

C.—Concrete for Cow-sheds, &c.

In mixing concrete it is just as important to select good stone, sand, and clean water as to choose the brand of cement. Experience proves that the most reliable stone is basalt.

The cement, sand, gravel, or broken stone, should first be thoroughly mixed in a dry state, and then again when moistened with water. A watering can with a rose can be used for the purpose. The proportions for concrete for general purposes is one part cement, three parts sand, and six parts broken stone, gravel, or ashes. All concrete should be lightly rammed and a surplus of water should be avoided, as otherwise the strength and density of the concrete is affected. The proportion of water is correct if after only light ramming the liquid appears on the surface. Care should be taken to prevent the quick drying of concrete by protecting it from the direct rays of the sun and sprinkling from time to time with water. When placing a second layer of concrete, it is best to do so before the first is dry, otherwise the first layer will require to be scratched, cleaned, and wetted, so as to insure a firm hold. Three inches of concrete, with $\frac{1}{2}$ inch of facing, is sufficient for silo floors; while for cow-sheds and other floors, where there is a lot of traffic, 4 to 6 inches of concrete, with 2 inches of facing, is required. The facing for cow-shed floors should be made with a greater proportion of cement than ordinary concrete, and the metal should be finer and the surface have a slightly rough finish; this will prevent the cows from slipping.

To prepare the floor it should be levelled off, well rammed, then covered with 2 inches of sand; this should be well wetted. The concrete is laid in sections, dividing each section with a batten, which is removed when the concrete is set, and the spaces where battens are taken from are grouted in with cement mortar; this prevents cracking caused by the shrinkage of concrete. The facing should be put on before the concrete is set. Gutters, corners, and edges should be rounded off. For cement mortar the cement and clean sharp sand (not too fine) should be thoroughly mixed in a dry state. Cement mortar of one part cement and two parts sand is used when a high degree of strength and density is required, such as machinery foundations, damp cellars, &c., but for masonry, plastering, and general purposes, one part cement and three parts sand is a suitable mixture. A smooth surface or platform is required for mixing. A board for this purpose can readily be made from any surplus timber available. Gauge boxes are necessary for measuring the quantities; and in making boxes it is advisable to allow the side boards to project past the ends of the box, so as to form handles for shifting the boxes. Do not make more concrete than can be used in half-an-hour; set or hardened cement mortar or concrete is quite useless. Its initial set should not be disturbed. Cement work should never be applied on dry or absorbent surfaces, unless those surfaces have been previously wetted.

ORCHARD AND GARDEN NOTES.

E. E. Pescott, Principal, School of Horticulture, Burnley.

The Orchard.

The winter seasonable works, such as pruning and planting, with the exception of Citrus fruits in the latter case, will now be completed; and the time has arrived for the new season's work to be commenced.

The spring ploughing should now be proceeded with as early as possible, so as to conserve all soil moisture. If the ploughing be delayed, it frequently happens that, owing to dry weather setting in, the soil surface becomes hardened and compacted, and in that condition it is very difficult to turn over. Cultivation should quickly follow ploughing, so that there shall be no lumps or clods on the surface. Where it is intended to use stable manure, or to spread fresh soil in the orchard, this should be done before ploughing, so that it may be well ploughed under.

As soon as cover crops are in full flower, they should also be ploughed in.

If the soil be warm, Citrus trees of all descriptions may be planted, the ground having been previously prepared for their reception. The planting of these trees may be spread over September and October; and in cooler districts they may even be left until November.

Spraying.

Peach aphis will be making its appearance on peach, nectarine, and Japanese plum trees, if it has not already done so. As soon as it appears, frequent sprayings with a nicotine solution will be required to keep it in check. It is advisable to spray early, and to spray a second time a few hours after the first spraying has been completed. After the first spraying, the aphides that remain alive generally endeavour to find a more congenial position. These moving ones, as well as the weakened ones, are then readily dealt with by the second application. Red oil emulsion should not be used, as this is only a winter spray.

As soon as the flower buds of the apple and pear are opening, these trees should be sprayed with Bordeaux mixture for black spot. Peach and nectarine trees will need a Bordeaux spraying for leaf curl; and plum trees also, for plum or prune rust.

In spraying peach trees for peach aphis and leaf curl, or for aphis and prune rust, the tobacco solution and Bordeaux mixture may be safely used as a mixture without any fear of damage to the trees.

In some cases the copper-soda spray is preferred by orchardists, in lieu of Bordeaux mixture. It is certainly good in many instances; and, where fresh lime is not procurable, or where the climate is dry, the copper-soda mixture is useful as a fungicide. It is, however, not so adhesive as Bordeaux, and is readily washed off by rain or heavy dews. The copper-soda mixture should not be used on stone fruits, particularly peaches, as the foliage of these trees is too delicate for the use of this spray. The recognised formulæ are :—

> Bordeaux : 6 lbs. bluestone, 4 lbs. fresh lime, and 50 gallons of water.
> Copper-soda : 6 lbs. bluestone, 8lbs. washing soda, and 50 gallons of water.

If the winter spraying for the Bryobia mite has been neglected, the trees should be given a good spraying with a nicotine solution, or with Robinson's Pine Spray, Soaperine, or some other similar preparation.

The work of grafting should be completed early in the month. The most useful method of re-working old trees is to cut the head right away, leaving only the stump. Then grafts can be put in according to the fancy of the grower. The old method of cleft grafting has been superseded by the bark or crown graft. The latter method does not cause any damage to the wood, and thus, with care, no rotting can take place. The best method of bark grafting is the saddle graft; that is, the graft is inserted in the bark, and a strip of bark is carried right across the trunk and inserted in the bark on the opposite side. This method is much slower than the ordinary bark graft, but it insures a much quicker healing over of the old stump.

Vegetable Garden.

The vegetable plots should be cleaned from all weeds, having the light weeds dug in and the stronger ones pulled out and rotted in the compost heap.   The surface should be worked up to a very fine tilth after digging : it must be kept constantly loose with the hoe to keep the soil cool ; and prior to digging it will be advantageous to give a top dressing of lime.

If the weather be dry or windy. all newly-planted plants should be frequently watered.   In transplanting seedlings, it is a help to dip the whole plant in water before planting.

Any seedlings that are ready may be planted out ; tomato plants may be planted out under shelter until the frosts are over.   At the end of the month a sowing of French bean seeds may be made.   Seeds of peas, broad beans, beet, cabbage, Kohl rabi, radish, turnip, cauliflower, lettuce, carrot, parsnip, &c., may be sown in the open.   Seeds of melons, cucumbers, pumpkins, marrows, and similar plants may be planted in frames for transplanting after the frosts have gone.

Flower Garden.

After digging, the surface must be kept constantly stirred with the hoe, so as to have it loose and friable for cooling and for moisture conserving purposes.   All weeds must be kept down, as they are robbers of plant food and moisture at this season of the year.

Shrubs of all kinds may still be planted out, and these should be well watered after planting.

Rose and other aphides must be watched for, and treated according to instructions given in last months' notes.   Rose scale should be sprayed with lime-sulphur wash, or with kerosene emulsion.   This pest will soon disappear if the bushes are kept open to admit the air and the sunlight freely. Rose mildew will now be appearing, and the plants as well as the soil should be sprinkled with liberal dustings of sulphur.   Sulphide of potassium is also a good specific for this fungus trouble, using it at the rate of 1 ounce to 3 gallons of water.

Cannas, early chrysanthemums, and early dahlia tubers may be planted out, as well as all kinds of herbaceous plants, such as delphiniums, perennial phlox, and asters, &c.   The clumps of these should be well divided, and in planting they should be fed with a liberal quantity of stable manure.   Beds should be prepared and well dug over for exhibition chrysanthemums and dahlias.

Wattles of all kinds may be planted out, and many of these are suitable for garden work.   For trees, *Acacia Baileyana* (Cootamundra), *A. saligna* (West Australian willow wattle), *A. spectabilis* (weeping), *A. verniciflua*, *A. lunata*, *A. prominens*, *A. leprosa*, *A. longifolia*, *A. cultriformis*, and *A. elata* are all useful.   While as shrubs, the following may be grown :— *A. rubida*, *A. Farnesiana*, *A. myrtifolia*, *A. acinacea*, *A. Mitchelli*, and *A. podylarifolia*.

Acacias may be readily pruned, the work being done after flowering : and if this work be commenced when the plants are fairly young, they may be trained into beautiful and shapely bushes and trees.

It is also a good time to sow the seed.   The outer covering of acacia seed is very hard, and the growing root is not able of its own accord to penetrate it.   The seed must, therefore. be immersed for a few moments in boiling water, and allowed to soak for at least twelve hours.   After this, they may be planted direct into the garden or into pots for subsequent transplanting

SUGAR BEET.

The phenomenal sugar beet root represented upon the opposite page was produced by a local syndicate of Maffra growers upon their land in the Sale-road. The beet measured from the crown to the tip 48 inches, and is properly shaped, that is, it is of the type desired in factory operations. This shape of beet can only be secured by deep subsoiling, which is one of the prime essentials in beet root cultivation.

ANSWERS TO CORRESPONDENTS.

The Staff of the Department has been organized to a large extent for the purpose of giving information to farmers. Questions in every branch of agriculture are gladly answered. Write a short letter, giving as full particulars as possible, of your local conditions, and state precisely what it is that you want to know. All inquiries forwarded to the Editor must be accompanied by the name and address of the writer. This is very necessary, as sometimes insufficient information is furnished by the inquirer.

HAND-REARING A FOAL.—N.L.S. wishes to know what food to give to hand-rear a foal?

Answer.—Give at blood heat 9 pints new milk (whole) six feeds daily. Sugar may be added at the rate of a teaspoonful to a pint. When a month old give 3 quarts of milk in three feeds, gradually increase milk and decrease number of feeds as foal gets older. At two months old work skim milk into ration, until at four months old it is all skim milk, to which 1 lb. of linseed jelly, or boiled oatmeal has been added. After this give 1 lb. oats for each month of age.

CHESTNUT AS A SHELTER TREE.—F.C.B. asks if chestnut is a good shelter tree suitable for Gippsland Lakes district?

Answer.—A good shelter tree from the sun, being deciduous, is no shelter in winter from weather. Would grow in district.

LUCERNE, PROPER TIME FOR SOWING.—B. Bros. ask the best time to sow lucerne?

Answer.—Best time of year to sow lucerne is either in autumn with a light cover crop, such as half a bushel of oats, or in early spring, without any covering. If district subject to heavy frosts, it can do without cover crop in autumn, but young plants are very susceptible at early stages of growth to frosts. As to manures, if soil deficient in lime a dressing of 3 to 5 cwt. per acre of lime a month before seeding will be found advantageous. If no lime required, 70 lbs. sulphate of potash and 100 lbs. mixed super and bone dust per acre applied a month before seeding will be sufficient to give the crop a good start.

WORMS IN YEARLINGS.—Farmer wishes to know how many doses of liquor arsenicalis prescribed for complaint must be given?

Answer.—The length of time treatment with liquor arsenicalis should be continued is guided largely by the improvement shown by the animal. Generally speaking, treatment may be discontinued when progressive improvement in appetite and general condition are shown.

DESTROYING ANTS' NESTS.—J.G.V. asks how to destroy ants?

Answer.—The best remedy is to make a hole in the centre of the nest with a stick and pour into it a cup of bisulphide of carbon. Soil should be immediately thrown into the hole and stamped firmly down. This will destroy all ants and their larvae.

WOOD LICE OR SLATERS.—E.J.S. would like to know how to destroy same?

Answer.—Poisoned parsnips, carrots, or beetroot. Cook in a solution of arsenic and place in haunts of the wood lice, they will eat the poisoned material greedily and be destroyed. Traps may be made by filling 10-inch flower pots with half-dry horse droppings, and placed where insects are most numerous. Once a week turn droppings into the fire and put fresh into pots. If this is persisted in, a riddance will soon be made. Spraying cabbage, lettuce, or any other vegetable leaves, with arsenate of lead in places frequented by wood lice will soon get rid of the pest. The poisoned leaves must be kept out of the reach of cattle.

DOUGLAS MIXTURE.—E.W.H. would like the formula of Douglas mixture.

Answer.—100 drops sulphuric acid (poison); 2½ ozs. sulphate of iron; 2 gallons of water. Thoroughly stir and after an hour's time stir again; then give birds to drink without further diluting. Earthenware vessels should be used. Give to birds one day each week.

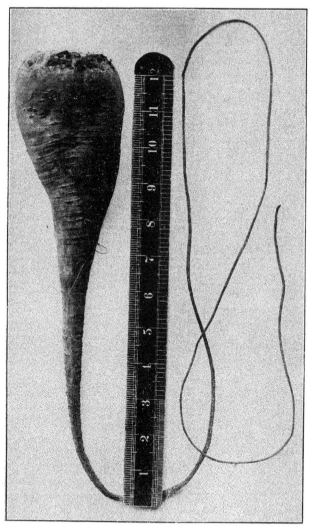

SUGAR BEET.

REMINDERS FOR OCTOBER.

LIVE STOCK.

Horses.—Continue to feed stabled horses well; add a ration of greenstuff. Rug at night. Continue hay or straw, chaffed or whole, to grass-fed horses. Feed old and badly-conditioned horses liberally. If too fat, mares in foal should be put on poorer pasture.

Cattle.—Except on rare occasions, rugs may now be used on cows at night only. Continue giving hay or straw Give calves a warm dry shed and a good grass run. Continue giving milk at blood heat to calves.

Pigs.—Supply plenty of bedding in warm well-ventilated styes. Keep styes clean and dry, and feeding troughs clean and wholesome. Sows may now be turned into grass run.

Sheep.—When shearing is in progress, well-bred fleeces should be skirted carefully—the better the class of wool the greater the need. Where the wool is burry, take the heaviest off, keeping bellies and pieces, &c., separate. In country free from burr, only the heavy fribs from arm and flank need be removed. It is better management to have ample table room, and extra men skirting carefully, than to hurriedly tear off unnecessary wool and then employ men at the piece table to sort what is known as "broken fleece" or "first pieces." All stains must come off fleeces, and weather stains from bellies. With crossbreds, separate all coarse fleeces from the finer sorts; and, with merinoes, the yellow and mushy ones from the shafty and bright. Skirt off any rough thighs from crossbred fleeces. Press in neat bales; avoid "sewdowns." Brand neatly. If any likelihood of lambs not going for export before dry feed comes, shear at once.

Poultry.—Incubation should cease this month—late chickens are not profitable. Devote attention to the chickens already hatched; do not overcrowd. Feed a little lightly-boiled liver, chopped finely and mixed with mash. Also add plenty of green food to ration, ordinary feeding to be 2 parts pollard, 1 part bran, a little dry bonemeal, and plenty of finely-cut raw onion. Mix with the gravy from liver. Give a little three or four times a day, according to the weather. Feed crushed wheat or hulled oats at night for a few days; whole wheat may then be given. Avoid whole oats. Grit (broken crockery) should be available at all times. Variety of food is important to growing chicks; insect life aids growth. Remove brooders to new ground as often as possible; tainted ground will retard development.

CULTIVATION.

Farm.—Plant main crop of potatoes in early districts and prepare land for main crop in late districts. Fallow and work early fallow. Sow maize and millets where frosts are not late, also mangolds, beet, carrots, and turnips. Sow tobacco beds and keep covered with straw or hessian.

Orchard.—Ploughing and cultivating to be continued, bringing surface to a good tilth, and suppressing all weeds. Spray with nicotine solution for peach aphis, with Bordeaux mixture for black spot of apple and pear, and with arsenate of lead for codlin moth in early districts.

Vegetable Garden.—Sow seeds of carrot, turnip, parsnip, cabbage, peas, French beans, tomato, celery, radish, marrow, and pumpkins. Plant out seedlings from former sowings. Keep the surface well pulverized.

Flower Garden.—Keep the weeds down and the soil open by continued hoeing. Plant out delphiniums, chrysanthemums, salvia, early dahlias, &c. Prepare ground by digging and manuring for autumn dahlias. Plant gladioli tubers and seeds of tender annuals. Spray roses for aphis and mildew.

Vineyard.—This is the best month for field grafting. If stocks bleed too copiously, cut off 24 hours before grafting. Field grafts *must* be staked, to avoid subsequent straining by wind and to insure straight stem for future vine. Stakes are also necessary for grafted rootlings for same reasons. Temporary stakes 3 feet long will suffice. Keep a sharp look-out for cut worms. (See *Journal* for July, 1911.) Disbud and tie up all vines, giving special care to young plantations. Beware of spring frosts. (See *Journal* for September, 1910.)

Conclude spring cultivation (second ploughing or scarifying and digging or hoeing round vines). Weeds must be mastered and whole surface got into good tilth. Sulphur vines when shoots 4 to 6 inches long.

Cellar.—Taste all young wines; beware of dangerous symptoms in unfortified fruity wines, which may need treatment. Fill up regularly all unfortified wines.

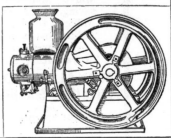

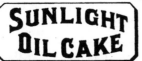

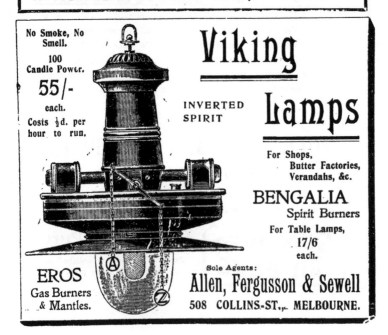

LITERATURE FOR AGRICULTURISTS.

PLAN AND SPECIFICATION OF SHEEP-SHEARING SHED. 2s. 6d. *Postage*, 1d.

MILK CHARTS (Monthly and Weekly), 6d. per dozen, post free. When ordering, dairy farmers should mention " Monthly " or " Weekly."

By Professor A. J. Ewart, Government Botanist.

WEEDS, POISON PLANTS, AND NATURALIZED ALIENS OF VICTORIA. 2s. 6d. *Postage :* Commonwealth, 1½d. ; N.Z., 5d. ; British and Foreign, 10d.

PLANTS INDIGENOUS TO VICTORIA. Vol. II., 10s.   *Postage :* Com., 2d. ; N.Z., 8d. ; Brit. & For., 1s. 4d.

By C. French, F.E.S., Government Entomologist.

DESTRUCTIVE INSECTS OF VICTORIA. Parts I., II., III., IV., V.   2s. 6d. each.   *Postage :* Parts I. and III., C., 1d. ; N.Z., 3d.; B. & F., 6d. each.   Parts II. and IV., C., 1½d. ; N.Z., 4d.; B. & F., 8d. each.   Part V., C., 1d. ; N.Z., 4d. ; B. & F., 7d.

By D. McAlpine, Government Vegetable Pathologist.

RUSTS OF AUSTRALIA. 5s. *Postage :* C., 2d. ; N.Z., 8d. ; B. & F., 1s. 4d.

SMUTS OF AUSTRALIA. 4s. *Postage :* C., 2½d. ; N.Z., 9d. ; B. & F., 1s. 6d.

FUNGUS DISEASES OF CITRUS TREES IN AUSTRALIA. 2s. *Postage :* C., 1d. ; N.Z., 3d. ; B. & F., 6d.

FUNGUS DISEASES OF STONE FRUIT TREES IN AUSTRALIA. 2s. 6d. *Postage :* C., 1½d. ; N.Z., 5d. ; B. & F., 10d.

SYSTEMATIC ARRANGEMENT OF AUSTRALIAN FUNGI. 3s. *Postage :* C., 2d. ; N.Z., 8d. ; B. & F., 1s. 4d.

THE DEPARTMENT OF AGRICULTURE,
MELBOURNE, VICTORIA.

Remittances from places outside the Commonwealth to be by Money Order only.

Pamphlets obtainable from the Director of Agriculture, Melbourne, Free on Application.

NEW SERIES.

1. SILO CONSTRUCTION. *A. S. Kenyon, C.E.*
2. HINTS FOR NEW SETTLERS. *T. A. J. Smith.*
* 3. APPLE GROWING FOR EXPORT. *P. J. Carmody.*
* 4. BOOKKEEPING FOR FARMERS. *W. McIver, A.I.A.V., A.S.A.A., Eng.*
5. CIDER MAKING. *J. Knight.*
* 6. FARM PLUMBING. *C. H. Wright.*
7. CITRUS FRUIT CULTURE. *E. E. Pescott.*
8. BUILDING HINTS FOR SETTLERS. *A. S. Kenyon, C.E., and others.*
9. TOBACCO CULTURE. *T. A. J. Smith.*
10. SILOS AND SILAGE. *G. H. F. Baker.*
11. THE BEET SUGAR INDUSTRY AND CLOSER SETTLEMENT. *H. T. Easterby.*
12. WORMS IN SHEEP. *S. S. Cameron, D.V. Sc., M.R.C.V.S.*

* Not yet available.

DEPARTMENT OF AGRICULTURE,
VICTORIA.

GOVERNMENT STUD BULLS.

AVAILABLE FOR SERVICE OF COWS BELONGING TO BONA-FIDE SETTLERS UNDER THE CLOSER SETTLEMENT ACTS.

Fee, 5s. per cow.

Jersey Bull **"DREADNOUGHT"**; Calved, 22nd October, 1908.
Sire:—Sir Jack (188).   *Dam:*—Lady Kitchener, by Lord Melbourne.
(In charge of Mr. H. Crumpler, Block 148, Bamawm.)

Jersey Bull **"ROSE FOX"**; Calved, 19th August, 1909.
Sire:—Starbright Fox (190).   *Dam:*—Tuberose, by Magnet's Progress (54 A.J.H.B.).
(In charge of Mr. W. W. Vickers, Bamawm).

Jersey Bull **"VERBENA'S BOY"**; Calved, 10th January, 1908.
Sire:—Acrobat.   *Dam.*—Verbena 2nd, by Snowdrop's Progress 2nd.
(In charge of Messrs. Laing and Mundie, Block 70, Bamawm.)

Jersey Bull **"NOBILITY"**; Calved, 2nd April, 1910.
Sire:—Lucy's Noble of Oaklands.   *Dam:*—Winnie of Melrose 3rd, by Royal Blue.
(In charge of Mr. E. T. Partington, Block 136, Bamawm.)

Jersey Bull **"MILKY WAY"**; Calved, 20th June, 1909.
Sire:—Starbright Fox (190).   *Dam:*—Milkmaid 34th (590), by Plinlimmon (imp. 62 A.H.B.).
(In charge of H. Macauley, Nanneella.)

Jersey Bull **"GOLD MEDAL"**; Calved, 3rd April, 1910.
Sire:—Golden Fox (142 A.J.H.B.).   *Dam:*—Melba, by Greystanes 2nd.
(In charge of Mr. W. F. Hill, Blocks 43 and 44, Nanneella.)

Jersey Bull **"MAGNET'S FOX"**; Calved, 6th November, 1909.
Sire:—Fox's Laddie.   *Dam:*—Magnet 28th, by Defender (imp.) (2288 H.C.J.H.B.).
(In charge of Mr. C. C. Woods, Block 29, Koyuga.)

Jersey Bull **"ZODIAC"**; Calved, 10th November, 1908.
Sire:—Starbright Fox (190).   *Dam:*—Zoe 4th (805), by Handsome Hero.
(In charge of Mr. R. J. Chappell, Block 12F, Swan Hill.)

Jersey Bull **"GAY FOX"**; Calved, 12th May, 1909.
Sire:—Starbright Fox (190).   *Dam:*—Floss, by Plinlimmon (imp. 62).
(In charge of Mr. Dyer, Swan Hill.)

DEPARTMENT OF AGRICULTURE,
VICTORIA.

GOVERNMENT STUD BULLS.

AVAILABLE FOR SERVICE OF COWS BELONGING TO BONA-FIDE SETTLERS UNDER THE CLOSER SETTLEMENT ACTS—*continued.*

Fee, 5s. per cow.

Jersey Bull "WILLIAM OF AYRE"; CALVED, February, 1910.

Sire:—Favourite's Fox 2nd.   *Dam:*—Bessie McCarthy, by Snowflake's Progress.

(*In charge of Mr. J. S. Dickinson, Block* 13, *Nyah.*)

Jersey Bull "FOX'S LAD"; CALVED, 5th October, 1908.

Sire:—Fox, by Snowdrop's Progress 2nd.   *Dam:*—Pansy 2nd, by Duke.

(*In charge of Mr. Ernest E. Borley, Block* 6, *Nyah.*)

Ayrshire Bull "PETER OF WILLOWVALE"; CALVED, 30th Sept., 1909.

Sire:—Annetta's Pride (243).   *Dam:*—Madge 2nd (Appendix A.H.B.), by Red Chief (359).

(*In charge of Mr. F. McIvor, Block* 12F, *Swan Hill.*)

Particulars of extended pedigrees, milking records, &c., can be obtained from each bull holder, from the resident Dairy Supervisors (**Mr. O'KEEFE, Rochester,** or **Mr. S. J. KEYS, Swan Hill**), or from **The Department of Agriculture, Melbourne.**

AVAILABLE FOR SERVICE OF COWS THE PROPERTY OF SETTLERS ON WYUNA ESTATE.

Red Danish Bull "CLAUDIUS"; CALVED, 10th November, 1909.

Sire:—Ernst Bellinge (imp.)   *Dam:*—Kirsten IX. (imp.).

Fee, 5s.

Red Danish Bull "HAMLET"; CALVED, 1st August, 1910.

Sire:—Ernst Bellinge (imp.).   *Dam:*—Marianne IV.   *G. Dam:*—Marianne III. (imp.).

Fee, 5s.

Particulars of extended pedigrees, milking records and prizes may be obtained from, and arrangement for service made with, **Mr. E. R. EMERY,** Manager. Government Farm, Wyuna, where the bulls are kept.

AVAILABLE FOR SERVICE OF COWS THE PROPERTY OF BEET GROWERS AT BOISDALE.

Red Polled Bull "TABACUM"; CALVED, 12th November, 1908.

Sire:—Acton Ajax (imp.).   *Dam:*—Janet, by Primate by Laureate (imp.).

Fee, 7s. 6d. (available to 20 cows).

Application to Mr. E. STEER, Herdsman, at the Homestead, Block 21.

DEPARTMENT OF AGRICULTURE,

VICTORIA.

Burnley Horticultural School.

E. E. PESCOTT, Principal.

ANNOUNCEMENT.

The curriculum and management of the Burnley Horticultural School have now been arranged so that greater advantages and facilities will be given to students of both sexes in Horticulture and allied subjects.

The present course of Horticulture for male students includes a two years' course, students being charged a fee of £5 per annum.

Classes have been formed at Burnley, whereby students of both sexes may receive instruction on two afternoons of each week—Tuesdays and Fridays.

Instruction includes theoretical and practical work, and will commence at 2 p.m. This will be a two years' course, and the fee charged will be £2 per annum.

It has also been arranged that several short lecture courses shall be given on subjects which are suitable adjuncts to Horticulture, such as Poultry Farming, Bee-keeping, and Fruit Preserving, and these courses will be open and free to the general public. The subjects and dates of the Short Course Lectures will be announced monthly in this Journal.

STUDENTS SHOULD ENROLL WITHOUT DELAY.

APPLICATION FOR ADMISSION SHOULD BE MADE TO

The Director of Agriculture, Public Offices, Melbourne,

OR TO THE PRINCIPAL.

By Authority: Albert J. Mullett, Acting Government Printer, Melbourne.

[Registered at the General Post Office, Melbourne, for transmission by Post as a Newspaper.]

The Journal of THE DEPARTMENT OF AGRICULTURE OF VICTORIA, AUSTRALIA.

October, 1912.

LIMING LAND.

PRICE THREEPENCE.   (Annual Subscription—Victoria, Inter-State, and N.Z., 3,-; British and Foreign, 5/-.)

THE JOURNAL

OF

THE DEPARTMENT OF AGRICULTURE,

VICTORIA, AUSTRALIA.

CONTENTS.—OCTOBER, 1912.

COPYRIGHT PROVISIONS AND SUBSCRIPTION RATES.

The Journal is issued monthly. The subscription, which is payable in advance and includes postage, is 3s. per annum for the Commonwealth and New Zealand, **and** 5s. for the United Kingdom and Foreign Countries. Single copy, Threepence.

Subscriptions should be forwarded to the Director of Agriculture, Melbourne. A complete list of the various publications issued by the Department of Agriculture will be supplied by the latter.

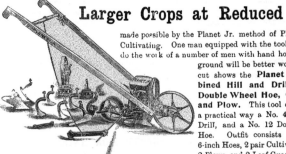

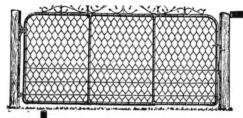

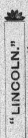

THE JOURNAL

OF

The Department of Agriculture

OF

VICTORIA.

Vol. X. Part 10.	10th October, 1912.

LIME IN AGRICULTURE.

I.

INTRODUCTION.

By the Director of Agriculture (Dr. S. S. Cameron).

It has become almost a commonplace to say, in respect of a large proportion of land in this State, that it would be the better for a dose of lime. In many ways, both direct and indirect, the liming of land has a proven beneficial influence in both the maintenance and enhancement of soil fertility.

It is the function of the agricultural specialists to explain and make clear the varied actions, physical, chemical and biological, as the case may be, by which lime produces its beneficial effects; but in a foreword to a series of articles on the subject by officers of the Department, it may not be out of place to indicate the character of the effort that is being made by the Department to demonstrate the exact value of lime in agricultural practice, and for the guidance of agriculturists in the profitable and economical use of it.

Hitherto the use of lime in this State has oftentimes been regarded by many practical agriculturists as an expensive luxury, and much the same incredulity has been expressed concerning its benefits as a regular means of maintaining or increasing soil fertility, as was voiced regarding the use of superphosphate at the time of its first introduction by Professor Cunstance of the Roseworthy Agricultural College (S.A.), and, indeed, until the experiments conducted by Mr. A. N. Pearson, formerly Chemist for Agriculture of this State, placed its value beyond doubt, and demonstrated the profitable quantities in which it could be economically and regularly used.

The fact is, that in the evolution of agriculture in this State, and from the stand-point of soil fertility, we have not yet quite reached unto the third stage. Our first was the cultivation of virgin land, unassisted by manure of any kind. The second stage was reached when it was realized that the surface soils of this continent were below the average in phosphatic content, and by frequent cropping became quickly depleted to a point below

12315. U

essential fertility of such as they contained naturally ; then the use of super-phosphate was advised and became general.   Now, the increase in market value of land demands that its productive value must be increased also ; and the continuous cropping and the use of superphosphate has tended to a " stiffening " and " souring " of the soil, which demands that further assist-tance shall be given in the maintenance of fertility.   One of the directions —and there are doubtless many, but in each case the cost or value ratio will be the prime consideration—in which this assistance may be given is in the judicious use of lime, at all events for the soils of certain districts.

As with the use superphosphate in the past, and as is inevitable for the amelioration of at present inferior soils by under-drainage in the future, so the liming of land is one of those refinements of agricultural practice which is always brought about whenever production has to be pushed in order to square increase of cost or compensate for competition.

It has been said repeatedly that the main thing standing in the way of the general use of lime was its cost.   Not so much its initial or actual cost as the cost of carriage on the railways.   Doubtless there is much in this con-tention, and the example of some American railway companies, and of the Government of New Zealand, in carrying lime at a loss, might well be followed by the Railways Commissioners of this State.   The increased freightage resulting from the more abundant production following on the use of lime would doubtless amply compensate the loss.   That there are other factors, however, operating against the more general use of lime in agriculture is obvious when last year's experience of the Maffra Sugar Fac-tory is related.   The factory had some hundreds of tons of high class lime on hand, as a by-product of the manufacturing operations.   Failing to secure local buyers, attention was drawn to it by paragraphs in the daily papers, and it was advertised in the weekly agricultural press for two months at 10s. per ton in bags f.o.r. Maffra.   Not a single application or offer was received, and such as was not required for departmental use was ultimately disposed of in one line to a Lyndhurst farmer at 4s. per ton.

One of the means of lessening the carriage cost of lime would be the opening up of lime quarries that could be practically worked in as many different localities as possible, so that each district requiring lime could be served from the nearest deposit.   There are, of course, scores of lime de-posits throughout the State, but many of them are composed of an inferior or unsuitable quality of lime.   Others are of high quality, but so small in extent as to be worthless to work, and others again, suitable as regards quality and extent, are so awkwardly situated as to be impossible of ex-ploitation.

In October last year, and as a step concurrent with the initiation of district liming experiments, this Department sought the aid of the Geological Branch of the Mines Department as to the location of lime deposits through-out the State of a character that could be profitably worked for agricultural purposes.   In response the Mines Department furnished the report published herewith, which may be regarded as both valuable and accurate, compiled as it is from the researches of such men as those whose names are attached to it.

Equally important as the matter of initial and carriage cost, and pos-sibly in a greater degree accounting for the small extent to which lime is at present used, is the uncertainty of knowledge as to the exact nature and re-lative value of the different limes available, and the uncertainty of know-ledge of the effect of lime in different districts, for different soils, in small or large quantities, for different crops, at long or short intervals, and so on. The application of lime has been advocated in a light and airy way by many advisers, but all sorts of confusing advice as to quantities, periodicity of application, and the like have been given. Farmers, however. with that conservative wisdom which is sometimes charged to their detriment, but which is really their abiding safeguard against irresponsible advisers and wasteful expenditure, have been loth to act on the exhortation of other than dependable investigators who can advance sound research and scientific proof for their guidance. So it was with superphosphate—so it will be as regards lime.

The demand of the moment, therefore, is that exact research should be undertaken to demonstrate :—

(*a*) the districts in which lime is likely to be generally required ;
(*b*) the soils in such districts that are already in a state of lime hunger, or are approaching thereto ;
(*c*) the varying or constant quantities, as the case may be, in which lime can be profitably applied ;
(*d*) the profitable or economical periodicity of application ;
(*e*) the proportion in which the yields of different crops are influenced by applications varying or constant in amount ;
(*f*) the form of lime best suited to different crops and different soils ;
(*g*) the season and method of application ;
(*h*) the cost of varying quantities relative to resultant crop yields.

Such work has not been previously undertaken in this State, or, indeed, in Australia. There have, doubtless, been fugitive experiments carried out in these directions, but the results, even when recorded, have been largely estimations or opinions or guesswork. Actual weighing of yields from treated and control areas, or comparative feeding off tests of results have not been carried out. and without these conclusions cannot be accurate, or other than speculative.

That such work has not been so undertaken may be charged as a sin against this and other State Departments of Agriculture. If so, it is not desired to extenuate the neglect further than to repeat what has been already said, viz. : — that the conditions of agriculture in this State have but recently become such as to require aid in this direction. and State Governments are not notoriously prone to authorize expenditure ahead of requirements.

Agricultural research is slow of process. There can be but one set of observations in each year, and these subject to so great a margin of experimental error as to be useless on which to base conclusions until they have been several times repeated under naturally varying seasonal conditions. particularly. rainfall; so that some years must elapse before definite data can be authoritatively pronounced concerning the problems for solution and the questions for answer set out above. Nevertheless, belated though it be (culpably so, some critics will smugly aver), a start has been made.

During last autumn the Agricultural Superintendent (Mr. A. E. V. Richardson, M.A.. B.Sc.) initiated a series of district experiments in different parts of the State, and also commenced in the North-Eastern district, at the Rutherglen Viticultural Station, and in the Goulburn Valley at the Wyuna Irrigation Farm, permanent lime plots designed to elucidate the problems that have been indicated. These will be elaborated in required directions from year to year, and at the Central Research Farm, at Werribee, they will be triplicated and extended. The objectives of these experiments are indicated by Mr. Richardson in his contribution to this brochure. in the article on " The Practice of Liming."

As year succeeds year the accumulating results will be published until, it is hoped, reliable data can be put forth as having stood the test of time and repetition under such a sufficiency of varying conditions as to be axiomatic for practice.

In the meantime, and in order that as much reliable information on the subject as possible may be made available for the benefit of farmers at the present time, it has been deemed desirable to put forward a concise compendium dealing with such of the aspects of the lime in agriculture question as is likely to prove informative and helpful in a practical sense to all who wish to undertake this method of soil renovation.

Accordingly, in addition to Mr. Richardson's article just mentioned, Mr. Rankin Scott, Chemist for Agriculture, deals with the chemistry of lime, and at the same time indicates a simplified nomenclature of the

CURDIE'S RIVER LIME COMPANY.   FIRST KILN.

various forms of lime which will be used throughout, and which it is hoped will tend to do away with the confusion that at present exists in the minds of farmers concerning the many forms in which lime may be purchased.

Dr. J. W. Paterson, B.Sc., Ph.D., Experimentalist, and Mr. Scott, deal with the "Relation of Lime to Soil Fertility," and indicate results of experiments already obtained in the laboratory.

The Viticulturalist (Mr. F. De Castella) supplies information with respect to the use of lime in viticulture; and Mr. Temple Smith, Chief Field Officer, as regards lime for tobacco land.

The Chief Orchard Superviser, Mr. P. J. Carmody, advises on the use of lime for orchard soils; and Mr. G. Seymour, the potato expert, relates practical experiences of the use of lime on certain classes of soil for potatoes.

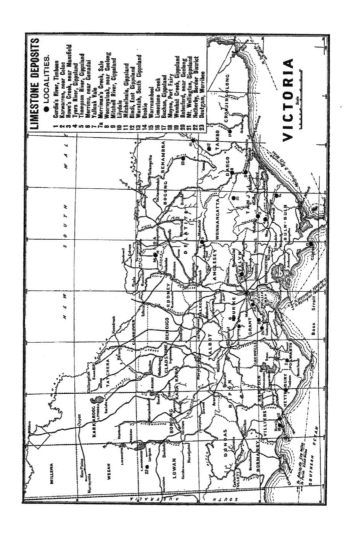

II.

VICTORIAN LIMESTONE DEPOSITS.

The information contained in this report was compiled from departmental records and Victorian scientific journals, the authorities being—E. J. Dunn, F.G.S., Director of Geology; R. A. F. Murray, F.G.S.; J. Stirling, F.G.S.; F. Chapman, A.L.S.; A. W. Howitt, F.G.S.; D. Mahony, F.G.S.; and Messrs. S. B. Hunter, W. Baragwanath, and W. H. Ferguson. The analyses were made by—J. Cosmo Newbery, B.Sc., and the Geological Survey laboratory officers.

A. W. Howitt,

30.7.1912.

Locality map attached.—A.W.H., 30.7.12.

(1) Curdie's River, Timboon.

Locality.—On Curdie's River, where the railway crosses it, parish of Timboon, in the county of Heytesbury.

Occurrence.—Tertiary calcareous strata carrying bands of limestone of varying quality.

Economic.—Large deposits occur in this locality, and have been specially examined at Tallent's Hill, on the railway line. Fuel is abundant, and the forest should be conserved, so as to provide a constant and cheap fuel.

Analyses.—Nos. 172 and 173, from Tallent's Hill—

	No. 173 (North face)	No. 173 (East face).
Ca CO_3	92.61%	88.39
Insol. Silica	3.54%	4.30
Magnesia	Trace.	Trace.

The analyses show that the limestone ranges from good to fairly good quality, and for agricultural purposes the deposit is most valuable.

(2) Kawarren, near Colac.

Locality.—These deposits are 29 chains west of Kawarren railway station, and 13 miles south of Colac.

Occurrence.—Tertiary deposits of sands and clays, &c., amongst which the limestone occurrence seems to be abnormal and different from the surrounding rocks. The deposit is composed of organic remains, corals, shells, &c.

Economic.—The limestone presents an abrupt face of eighty feet (80 feet) thick, and the quarry is eighty feet (80 feet) wide.

Fuel is abundant, and the occurrence of this deposit so close to the railway renders it a very valuable one.

Analysis.—No. 174—

Ca. CO_3	...	...	88.02
Insol. Silica	...	...	3.48
Magnesia	...	...	Trace

The analysis shows the limestone to be of fairly good quality, and quite good enough for agricultural purposes.

(3) Howes' Creek, near Mansfield.

Locality.—In allotments 94, 131, 132, and 133, parish of Loyola, and 6 miles from the Mansfield railway station. The quarry is known as Griffith's.

Occurrence.—There are 3 acres of blue dense limestone with small calcite veins. These limestone areas occur in Silurian formations, and they are fairly extensive, one being said to be 300 feet in length and 50 feet wide.

Economic.—This limestone has been worked in a small way from time to time, and yields an excellent lime. It is very similar to the Lilydale limestone, and is of value both for agricultural and building purposes.

Analysis (J. Cosmo Newbery)—

			Percentage.
Ca. CO_3	..	...	95.55
Mg. CO_3	...	...	Trace
Fe and Al	..	...	2.92
Clay and sand	..	...	1.53
			100.00

(4) Tyers River, Gippsland.

Locality.—Tyers River, 8 miles from the Traralgon railway station, in a deep gully emptying into the Tyers River.

Occurrence.—Grey, dense limestone, seamed with small calcite veins, and occurring in Silurian strata. There is a large formation of the limestone, which shows for 100 yards in length along the gully, and for a considerable height up either bank.

Economic.—It appears to be a first class limestone, and the analyses made by the late J. Cosmo Newbery, F.G.S., show that it is of high quality.

Analyses.—

		No. 1.		No. 2.
Ca. CO_3	...	96.20	...	93.50
Fe CO_3	...	1.25	...	1.47
Si O_2	...	1.70	...	4.00
Mg CO_3 ..	...	Trace	...	————
Moisture	...	0.50	...	0.70

(5) Thompson River.

Locality.—Thompson River, between Walhalla and Toongabbie, and about 10 miles in a westerly direction from Toongabbie.

Occurrence.—Several small areas occur on the Thompson River, east of the Deep Creek junction, and one on Deep Creek is several chains long and 200 feet high. Another small outcrop occurs nearer Walhalla, and close to the copper mine area. All are of Silurian age, and occur as a dense, compact limestone.

Limestone.—These deposits of limestone would be suitable for building or agricultural purposes.

Analyses.—Thompson River—

		No. 445.		No. 448.
Insoluble	...	0.75	...	0.72
Fe and Al	...	0.75	...	0.42
Ca CO_3	...	97.12	...	97.64
Mg CO_3 ..	...	1.63	...	1.11
H_2 O	...	c.08	...	0.05
		100.33	...	99.94

(6) Merrimu, near Coimadai.

Locality.—One mile east of the Lerderberg P. R., parish of Merrimu, county of Bourke.

Occurrence.—Limestone bands of Tertiary age. These bands have their partings of sand, clay, and gravel, and they rest on glacial formations.

Economic.—A considerable body of limestone occurs, and extensive works have been carried on here. About half-a-mile to the north-east of the main deposits, another deposit of workable size occurs.

The main deposit is over 24 acres in area and thirty feet (30 ft.) thick in one place. Mainly of use for building purposes.

Analysis—

Ca CO_3	..	...	...	55.00
Mg CO_3	..	..	...	41.00
Fe and Al	..	...	...	1.90
Si O_2 ...	...	...	...	2.05
H_2 O and	...	..	...	.05
				100.00

(7) Yaloak Vale.

Locality.—Southward from bores, Yaloak Vale, parish of Yaloak, Bacchus Marsh district.

Occurrence.—White, earthy limestone of Tertiary age. An extensive deposit occurs with harder bands of excellent quality.

(8) Merriman's Creek, Sale.

Locality.—Between Merton and Stradbroke, on Hodinots Creek, above the Sale-road.

Occurrence.—Dense grey Tertiary limestone, with soft layers.

Economic.—Yields excellent lime, similar to the Boggy Creek deposits.

(9) Woornyaloak.

Locality.—Near Duck Ponds railway station, Woornyaloak, and north from Geelong.

Occurrence.—Yellow, sandy limestone occurring over a large area, and twenty feet (20 ft.) thick in places.

Economic.—The limestone varies in character and quality, as can be seen from the following analyses:—

Analyses.—

	No. I.	No. II.	No. III.
Carbonate of lime	... 47.80	... 77.60	... 88.38
Carbonate of magnesia	... 26.70	... Trace	... 0.76
Carbonate of iron	... 2.90	... 4.05	... 0.51
Silica ...	... 18.10	... 11.15	... 7.02
Water ...	... 1.05	6.80	——
Alkaline salts ...	... 2.90	——	——

(10) Mitchell River.

Locality.—Over a wide area from west of the Mitchell River to the east side of Lake Tyers. At Lake Tyers showing as the banks of an estuary; and on the Mitchell River as banks bounding alluvial flats.

Occurrence.—Tertiary limestone. Being a yellow, friable calcareous rock to a hard, yellow limestone. It may be regarded as being about two hundred and fifty feet (250 ft.) thick in places, and has a slight dip towards the south-east.

Economic.—It affords a rich soil, and has been burnt for lime. For agricultural purposes it has been used at Hospital Creek in the natural state with benefit, the limestone being soft and friable.

Analysis.—No. 144 (Hospital Creek, 1910)—

Insoluble	...	...	... 4.28
Fe$_2$ O$_3$	...	...	... 2.65
Ca CO$_3$	...	..	... 84.10
Mg	...	...	... Trace

(11) Lilydale.

Locality.—Cave Hill, Lilydale district.   Allotment 20, parish of Mooroolbark, county of Evelyn.

Occurrence.—Blue-grey to pink-brown limestone of Silurian age. In texture it is a hard and semi-crystalline limestone, lenticular shaped and occurring between quartzite and shales.

Economic.—A large area occurs close to the railway line, but its exact extent is not known. In 1892 its greatest width was over three hundred feet (300 ft.). In good times it is reported that as much as seventy tons (70 tons) per day has been sent away.

Analysis (J. Cosmo Newbery).—

			Percentage.
Ca CO$_3$	...	...	... 92.60
Mg CO$_3$	...	...	... 0.36
Fe CO$_3$	...	..	... 2.12
Clay and sand	.	...	... 3.24
Other constituents		. .	... 1.68
			100.00

(12) Mitchellvale.

Locality.—At Ostler's, south of the junction of the Wentworth and Mitchell Rivers.

Occurrence.—Limestones shading into calcareous sandstone, and highly fossiliferous. Seams of calcite occur in places. Of Middle Devonian age.

Economic.—About 30 miles from the Lindenow railway station. The country is rough mountain ranges. No analyses have been made.

(13) Bindi.

Locality.—Old Hut Creek and Tambo River, parish of Bindi, in the county of Tambo, East Gippsland.

Occurrence.—Dense blue to grey crystalline limestone, with some chalky and impure lower calcareous beds. The formation is of Middle Devonian age, and covers about 18 square miles of country.

Economic.—It is nearly 80 miles by road from the Bairnsdale railway station ; but on the completion of the Orbost-Bairnsdale line, the distance from that line will be only about 55 miles.

Analysis.—There is no record of any analysis of the Bindi limestone. but the percentage of Ca CO$_3$ should be nearly as high as that found in the Buchan limestone.

(14) Waratah.

Locality.—On the west shore of Waratah Bay, and near Bird Rock, parish of Waratah, in the county of Buln Buln.

Occurrence.—Crystalline granular fine to coarse limestone. The deposit shows up to five chains (5 chs.) wide at the base and one hundred and ten feet (110 ft.) high. Of Silurian age.

Economic.—From an area of 2 acres over 1,000,000 bags of lime were obtained. There is every facility for direct shipment. It is easily worked, and upon burning yields a perfectly white lime. There are also large deposits of limestone at Bell Point and Point Grinder.

Analysis.—

Ca CO_3	...	...	... 94.90
Mg	...	...	... Trace
Fe	...	...	... 2.85
Si O_2	...	...	... 2.85
H_2O	...	...	... 0.50

(15) Dookie.

Locality.—Allotment 169, in the north-east of parish of Dookie, county of Moira.

Occurrence.—As a large calcite vein traversing diabase rocks. It appears to occupy a fissure, and is sometimes seen as a calcareous breccia.

Economic.—In one of the quarries the vein has been worked for a length of 3 chains, and to a depth of 10 feet, and 12 feet wide in places. Other quarries occur along the course of the vein for a total length of eight chains (8 chs.). This limestone was burnt and sent long distances in former years, and the old kiln is still standing.

Analysis.—

Ca CO_3 ... ... 94.10%

(16) Warrnambool.

Locality.—Between Warrnambool and Port Fairy, a distance of about fifteen (15) miles, county of Villiers.

Occurrence.—Extensive sand dunes up to 50 feet high in places. These sand dunes in many places consist almost entirely of small broken pieces of sea shells, and this shell sand has the composition of a fairly pure limestone.

Economic.—The deposits contain many millions of tons of finely-crushed limestone, apparently in a form most suitable for agricultural purposes. It is close to the railway line, and could be very cheaply handled; but before any operations are undertaken, the dunes should be thoroughly examined and sampled to determine the relative values of the various parts.

Analysis.—

Ca CO_3	...	...	... 84.46
Insol. (SiO_2)	...	...	... 5.10
Al_2O_3	...	...	... 0.57
Fe_2O_3	...	...	... 0.87
$Mg CO_3$ H_2O &c. (by difference)	...	9.00
Na Cl.	...	...	... Trace
P_2O_5 ...	...	...	... Trace

100.00

A bore at Albert Park, Warrnambool, was put down for a depth of 398 feet through 81 ft. 9 in. of limestone; at times this limestone contains flints. At a depth of 115 feet there was 9 ft. 5 in. of calcite.

(17) Limestone Creek.

Locality.—On Limestone Creek, 25 miles from Omeo Plains Station, parish of Enamo, in the county of Benambra.

Occurrence.—An extensive area of dense subcrystalline to white crystalline limestone and marble of the Middle Devonian series.

Economic.—One of the outcrops covers thirty-five (35) acres. The locality is over one hundred (100) miles from the Bairnsdale railway station.

Analysis (J. Cosmo Newbery).—

Ca CO_3	...	...	...	96.80
Mg CO_3	...	...	...	2.80
Soluble silica	...	...	...	0.20
Insol. silica	...	...	...	0.10
H_2O ...	...	...	...	0.10
				100.00

(18) Buchan.

Locality.—Buchan, in the county of Tambo, Eastern Gippsland, including Gelantipy, Buchan, South Buchan, Canni Creek, and New Guinea Point, Snowy River.

Occurrence.—Blue-grey limestone of Middle Devonian age, some extremely pure. It is by far the most extensive outcrop of limestone in Victoria, being in extreme length 15 miles, by 5 miles wide, and of great thickness.

Economic.—The southern area would be about 6 miles south of Buchan, and on the completion of the Bairnsdale-Orbost railway line this area will be more accessible.

Analyses.—

No. 395/1905 (Dr. Mackieson's, South Buchan).

Ca CO_3	..	...	...	93.20
Insol. ...	...	..	...	2.07
Fe and Al	...	...	...	0.60
Indeterminate	...	...	...	4.20
				100.07

No. 396/1905 (Spring Creek, Buchan).

Ca CO_3	...	...	...	92.97
Insol. ...	...	...	..	2.80
Fe and Al	..	...	...	1.80
Indeterminate	...	...	...	2.70
				100.27

(19) Moyne, Port Fairy.

Locality.—Hanging Rock Quarry, Moyne, Port Fairy. It is situated a little to the south of the Moyne siding, between Koroit and Port Fairy.

Occurrence.—Tertiary limestone exposed in a small quarry, and from the general appearance of the country there appears to be a very considerable amount of similar material to that submitted for analysis.

Economic.—Its position is convenient for transport, being about 1 mile from the railway, and the quality of limestone as collected for analysis is excellent.

Analysis.—No. 38/1907—

Ca CO_3 ...	...	...	...	90.6
Insol. ...	...	...	...	3.8
Al_2 O_3 Fe_2 O_3 ...	...	...	...	1.7
Mg CO_3 ...	...	...	...	0.7
H_2 O ...	...	...	...	0.3
Undetermined	..	...	...	2.9
				100.00

(20) Wombat Creek.

Locality.—On Wombat Creek, about 2 miles west of the Wombat-Mitta River junction, parish of Tongaro, in the county of Bogong.

Occurrence.—Blue to grey crystalline limestone bands of Silurian age. The area is extensive.

Economic.—The values of Ca CO_3 should be high, and somewhat similar to the other crystalline Silurian limestones as at Mansfield, &c. The locality is in rough mountain country, and too far from railway communication at present to be of commercial value.

(21) Batesford.

Locality.—Just east of the Dog Rocks, on the Moorarbool River, and about 1 mile south-east of the Batesford bridge, parish of Gheringhap, in the county of Grant.

Occurrence.—Yellow to reddish limestone of Tertiary age. A hill section shows—

	Feet.
Basalt	75
Incoherent sandy material with calcareous concretions	50
Yellow clay, with calcareous concretions	5
Polyzoal limestone	25
Orbitoidal limestone	20
	175

Economic.—The Upper Quarry shows a fairly hard limestone passing upward into a friable limestone, making about 45 feet in all.

The Dryden, or Filter Quarry, is about three-quarters of a mile lower down the Moorarbool, and here the deposits are very extensive, and are being worked by P. McCann and Sons, of Fyansford, for cement purposes, &c. The beds vary, being at one place 22 feet vertical of pure white, friable limestone, but generally less.

Analyses made by Mr. P. G. Bayly gave—

No. 735 (Upper Quarry) (Ca CO_3)	...	...	99.12
No. 736 (Filter Quarry)	...	...	96.66

(22) Mt. Wellington.

Locality.—Roan Horse Gully, near Dolodorook Creek, parish of Nap Nap Marra, county of Tanjil.

Occurrence.—Sub-crystalline grey limestone of Upper Cambrian age, forming a lenticular patch.

Economic.—There are three outcrops of limestone, one of which is said to be traceable at intervals for 1 mile in a south-west direction. Eventually this limestone should prove of great value for building purposes, and also for fertilizing the land. The locality is about forty (40) miles northward from the Heyfield railway station.

Analysis.—No. 412/1907—

Ca CO$_3$ ...	...	...	...	65.0
Insol. ...	..	...	...	23.0
Fe$_2$ O$_3$ Al$_2$ O$_3$		...	...	6.0
Mg CO$_3$	...	...	...	6.0

(23) Netherby.

Locality.—At Netherby, in the parish of Warraquil, county of Lowan, in the Horsham district.

Occurrence.—Tertiary friable limestone was proved in a bore, and was found to occur from a depth of 245 feet to 657 feet. In some other adjacent bores, the limestone beds were cut at a much shallower depth.

Economic.—An analysis of a sample of limestone from Netherby was as follows:—

Si O$_2$	...	...	...	2.883
Fe and Al	...	...	...	1.283
Ca CO$_3$	...	...	...	92.270
Mg CO$_3$	...	...	...	3.205
Unestimated and loss	...		...	.359
				100 000

(24) Deutgam (Werribee District).

Locality.—At a point 160 feet east of the north-west corner of allotment B, section III., parish of Deutgram, county of Grant, in Bore No. 4, which was put down under Government supervision in the year 1902.

Occurrence.—At a depth of forty-eight (48) feet from the surface large deposits of limestone were met with, and were as follows:—48 feet to 70 feet limestone and calcareous clay, 90 feet to 270 feet fossiliferous limestone, &c., and other beds at various depths, down to 606 ft. 5 in., where the bore was discontinued.

Economic.—These deposits are near the Werribee railway line, and the bore only 4 miles south-east of that station. There are no departmental analyses of these deposits.

III.

NOTE ON LIMESTONE DEPOSITS IN VICTORIA.

Will C. Robertson, Chief Deputy Chemist.

An extensive deposit of limestone of a fair degree of purity, say, 90 per cent. calcium carbonate, may be a valuable asset in any country, but from the stand-point of agriculture, especially in a State where closer settlement is in its infancy, this asset becomes dead stock if the environments preclude facilities for economical working.

The lime required by the builder is a different thing to the lime needed by the agriculturist, inasmuch as the former looks for a product with as high a percentage of lime as possible, and is prepared to pay a price for it. On the other hand, whilst the agriculturist would not say no to very pure lime, still, for the purposes for which he requires it, the high price that builders pay might not be justifiable. At present, therefore, the agriculturist is content with a product of a lower degree of purity supplied at a much cheaper rate. Consequently a limestone deposit, to be of any practical value to the agricultural community, must possess the following advantages—

(*a*) It must be of great extent.
(*b*) It must occur near the surface, and be easily quarried, thereby removing the difficulty of overburden, and minimizing the cost of labour.
(*c*) Means of railway or seaboard transport must be handy.
(*d*) An abundance of fuel adjacent.
(*e*) The percentage of calcium carbonate in the raw material should be at least 80 per cent. This would give on burning a product containing approx. 69 per cent. caustic lime.

These conditions are necessary if the limestone is to be burnt with the object of using " free caustic lime," but if " mild lime," in the form of ground limestone, is to be the object, then the same conditions apply with the single exception of fuel abundancy for which condition there needs to be substituted the provision of the raw material being of a soft tendency to permit easy grinding.

The chemist's branch of the Department of Agriculture has paid especial attention for years past to the all important subject of limestone deposits for agricultural purposes, and whenever possible, investigations have been conducted and analyses made, with the object of solving a very difficult problem.

A glance at the Mines Department list, showing the occurrences of limestone deposits in Victoria, elicits the information that 40 per cent. of these deposits are unavailable through the depth of occurrence and transport difficulty; amongst such are those situated at Mitchellvale, Bindi, Limestone Creek, Buchan, Wombat Creek, and Mount Wellington, whilst those at Netherby and Deutgam (Werribee) occur far too deep for economical working.

The deposits at Curdie's River, Coimadai, Dutson, Lilydale, Waratah and Batesford are being mined extensively, whilst those at Kawarren, Mansfield and Mitchell River are being worked in a smaller way.

The remaining deposits at the present moment are not being utilized. It will, therefore, be seen that, of the twenty limestone occurrences listed, 45 per cent. are being worked, 40 per cent. are unavailable, whilst the remaining 15 per cent. are in abeyance.

The analyses of the deposits show them to be of great purity with one exception, viz., Duck Ponds, Woornyaloak.

It should be noted that the Coimadai deposit is dolomitic, containing over 40 per cent. magnesia, which, according to authorities, somewhat detracts from its usefulness for agricultural purposes.

In addition to the limestone deposits mentioned above, there are marl beds, consisting mainly of calcium carbonate in an amorphous form, scattered through the limestone eras of the State, several of which are being quarried for agricultural purposes.

Some of these are situated in the Geelong district. whilst others are at Cobden. The following analyses of marl, from Mount Duneed and Cobden, may be of interest—

MARL FROM FORD'S PIT, MT. DUNEED.

	No. 1. Yellow Marl.	No. 2. Sample from 15ft. face.	No. 3. Underlying Clay.	No. 4. White Marl.
	%	%	%	%
Insoluble	86·01	60·61	78·62	12·17
$Fe_2O_3 \cdot Al_2O_3$	3·90	2·86	4·44	1·22
Lime	0·60	14·08	0·32	45·78
(= Ca. Carb.)	1·07	25·12	0·57	81·75
Magnesia	1·08	1·97	0·98	1·51
(= Mg. Carb.)	2·26	4·13	2·05	3·17

COBDEN MARLS.

	No. 1.	No. 2.	No 3.	No. 4.
Moisture	6·60	15·68	25·63	2·30
Insoluble	2·40	16·02	29·47	11·51
$Fe_2O_3 \cdot Al_2O_3$	0·82	2·80	3·65	2·55
Lime	50·05	35·30	21·40	46·25
(= Ca. Carb.)	89·37	63·03	38·21	82·59
Magnesia	0·22	0·52	0·40	0·50
(= Mg. Carb.)	0·46	1·09	0·84	1·05
SO_3	0·09	0·10	0·06	0·14
Phos. acid	Trace	Trace	Trace	Trace

Soft marl deposits have also been discovered in the Gippsland district. The following is an analysis of a sample from the Gippsland Lakes—

MARL FROM NICOLSON RIVER.

	%
Insoluble	2·47
$Fe_2O_3 \cdot Al_2O_3$	1·04
Lime	51·88
(= Ca. Carb.)	92·64
Magnesia	0·91
(= Mg. Carb.)	1·91

As will be noticed from the tables marls vary in lime content, and as a general rule white marls are the purer. The impression that the blue pug underlying these deposits contains the most lime is erroneous. and should be dismissed.

Marl deposits come as a boon and blessing locally, owing to the shallow depth at which they occur, and the easy manner in which the marl can be dug out, carted, and distributed. Unfortunately these deposits are never of very great extent, and they only serve a useful purpose in their own immediate locality, where the cost of handling is the only expense attached to their use.

A FARMER'S MARL PIT, GEELONG DISTRICT.   (See also page 610).

On the other hand, there is the deposit of limestone sand occurring as "Dunes" or "Hummocks," and running from the mouth of the Hopkins River, at Warrnambool, to Port Fairy—a distance of from 15 to 20 miles.

The following is a list of analyses of samples taken from various points around Warrnambool—

LIMESTONE SAND DUNES, WARRNAMBOOL.

	No. 1. Sand Dune near Pampas Plantation.	No. 2. Sand at Breakwater.	No. 3. Sand Dune near Rifle Butts.	No. 4. Sand Dune at Levy's Point.	No. 5. Waste from Steere's Quarry.
	%	%	%	%	%
Insoluble	16·06	9·39	5·26	11·28	2·79
$Fe_2O_3 \cdot Al_2O_3$ ..	1·02	1·04	1·26	1·40	0·96
Lime	42·12	46·28	47·21	44·48	52·88
(= Ca. Carb.) ..	75·21	82·64	84·31	79·43	94·43
Magnesia	3·54	3·17	3·88	3·72	1·29
(= Mg. Carb.) ..	7·43	6·65	8·15	7·81	2·71
Salt	Trace	Trace	Trace	Trace	Nil
Phos. acid	Trace	Trace	Trace	Trace	Trace

Regarding the quantity of this material available, suffice it to say that the Dunes are, in some places, a quarter of a mile wide and 80 feet high.

The deposit could be readily and cheaply worked by running a side line in from the main Port Fairy railroad, preferably on the Koroit side of Warrnambool, towards Levy's Point, or half-a-mile on the Melbourne side of the Warrnambool station, close to the Breakwater-road. The extremity of this side line could be made portable, and by means of a steam scoop the sand lifted and deposited in trucks at a very small cost, probably not more than a shilling per ton.

The Dunes on the seaward side only should be worked, for those extending inland are of much lower grade, being contaminated with *débris* and the adjacent soil.

The fine state of division makes burning for caustic lime out of the question. The degree of division, however, is hardly fine enough for agricultural purposes, and this is the main disadvantage of the deposit, and it is questionable whether grinding to a finer state of division would be a profitable undertaking. A test, conducted in the laboratory, showed the lime in Geelong marl to be more readily available than that in the sand dunes.

At Steer's limestone quarry, in the heart of Warrnambool, a certain amount of limestone sand and dust accumulates. This is available at 7s. per ton, and, although rather coarse in texture, it is a very pure material and well worthy of note.

Unfortunately, here again one is beset with the "quantity available" difficulty. From the stand-point of disintegration the soft yellow limestones, such as those occurring at Bellevue and Picnic Point, Bairnsdale, are more readily ground than the hard, dense, and compact blue and grey limestones occurring at Lilydale, Mansfield, and other parts. Some of the yellow limestones contain up to 1 per cent. phosphoric acid—an important advantage.

LIMESTONE SAND DUNES, WARRNAMBOOL, LOOKING TOWARDS PORT FAIRY FROM RIFLE BUTTS. (See also page 634).

Like unto the marl deposits, but more rare, are the beds of small sea or freshwater shells. The only deposit of this description at present being worked is that occurring on the Harbor Trust's Sparrovale property. The price charged for this shell deposit is 3d. per load.

STEER'S LIMESTONE QUARRY, WARRNAMBOOL, SHOWING ACCUMULATION OF LIMESTONE SAND IN THE FOREGROUND.

This shell grit is much more insoluble and unavailable than either marl or ground limestone, in that the glaze of the shell acts as a waterproof coating; and, together with the density, prevents the action of solvents. The deposits are small in extent.

IV.

THE CHEMISTRY OF LIME.

By P. Rankin Scott, Chemist for Agriculture.

Lime is a term somewhat loosely applied in a general way to various forms of compound substances which have for their base the oxide of calcium, represented by the chemical formula CaO, and commonly termed " lime."

Lime is therefore a compound of two elements, calcium (Ca) and. oxygen (O).   This compound possesses such a strong affinity for acids that it is never found free in nature.   Combined with carbonic acid gas (CO_2), however, large deposits of calcium carbonate ($CaCO_3$) are found in various forms, chief amongst which may be noted the limestones, marbles, chalks, and shells.   Any one of these deposits can be utilized for the production of calcium oxide (CaO) or quicklime by depriving it of carbonic acid gas by heat, thus $CaCO_3 + heat = CaO + CO_2$.   In actual practice there are three distinct forms of lime compounds applied to the soil, namely :—

> Calcium oxide (CaO) lime.
> Calcium hydrate (CaH_2O_2) slaked lime.
> Calcium carbonate ($CaCO_3$) chalk, limestone, shell, &c.

What these forms are and the relation they bear one to the other can be seen by means of the lime cycle :—

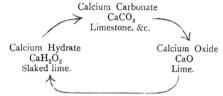

Calcium Carbonate
$CaCO_3$
Limestone, &c.

Calcium Hydrate
CaH_2O_2
Slaked lime.

Calcium Oxide
CaO
Lime.

The above cycle illustrates the changes of one form into the other. From calcium carbonate we obtain directly the oxide by driving off the carbonic acid gas, then the hydrate is formed by the combination of one part of water (H_2O) with the oxide, thus $CaO + H_2O = CaH_2O_2$, and finally the carbonate is formed by the substitution of one part of carbonic acid gas for one part of water, thus $CaH_2O_2 + CO_2 = CaCO_3 + H_2O$ The changes occurring are brought about by means of the following treatment : Lime is obtained when calcium carbonate is submitted to a red heat, the carbonic acid content is driven off as a gas, or is "burnt out," and lime remains.   Hence the term "burnt lime" as applied to the oxide of calcium (CaO). On the addition of water to the lime a chemical combination takes place, resulting in the formation of slaked lime.   This slaked lime when left exposed to the atmosphere combines gradually with carbonic acid gas, and continues to do so until all the lime is converted back again into calcium carbonate, identical in composition with the original material.   These changes can be explained more in detail by the use of chemical equations—

1st—

Calcium Carbonate		Calcium Oxide		Carbonic Acid
$CaCO_3$	=	CaO	+	CO_2

This change is brought about by heat ; the molecular weight of each substance being—

$CaCO_3$	=	CaO	+	CO_2
100	=	56	+	44

therefore, 100 lbs. of calcium carbonate yields 56 lbs. of calcium oxide, which remains as a solid, and 44 lbs. of carbonic acid, which is driven off as a gas.

2nd—

Calcium Oxide		Water		Calcium Hydrate
CaO	$+$	H_2O	$=$	CaH_2O_2

This change is brought about by wetting the (calcium oxide CaO) lime; the molecular weight of each substance being—

CaO	$+$	Water	$=$	CaH_2O_2
56	$+$	18	$=$	74

56 lbs. of calcium oxide and 18 lbs. of water yield 74 lbs. of calcium hydrate.

3rd—

Calcium Hydrate	$+$	Carbonic Acid	$=$	Calcium Carbonate	$+$	Water
CaH_2O_2	$+$	CO_2	$=$	$CaCO_3$	$+$	H_2O

This change is brought about by the carbonic acid of the air and soil; the molecular weight of each substance being—

CaH_2O_2	$+$	CO_2	$=$	$CaCO_3$	$+$	H_2O
74	$+$	44	$=$	100	$+$	18

therefore, 74 lbs. of calcium hydrate and 44 lbs. of carbonic acid yield 100 lbs. of calcium carbonate, and 18 lbs. of water. This was the quantity of water combined with the calcium oxide to form calcium hydrate, so the cycle is completed.

From the above results it is evident that heat applied to calcium carbonate alters its composition with reduction of weight; that the residue of lime left combines first with water to form calcium hydrate, and this calcium hydrate, if left exposed to the atmosphere, reverts back again to calcium carbonate, with no actual loss.

There is another important compound of lime which lies outside of the cycle given above, viz., the bi-carbonate of calcium $CaH_2(CO_3)_2$, formed by the addition of one part of water, and one part of carbonic acid gas to the ordinary carbonate, thus $CaCO_3 + H_2O + CO_2 = CaH_2(CO_3)_2$. It is through this form of lime compound that the chief losses of lime from the soil occur. Unlike the single carbonate of lime (chalk. limestone, &c.) this double carbonate is soluble in water, and when it is formed by the carbonic acid dissolved in the soil water coming in contact with particles of calcium carbonate, the latter is dissolved and passes away, or leaches out of the soil by means of drainage or in gravitational water.

Lime Proper or " Burnt Lime."

Lime (calcium oxide CaO) is always made commercially by taking advantage of the action of heat on limestone or other form of calcium carbonate. The general procedure adopted consists in burning the natural deposit in a specially constructed kiln, into which carbonate of lime and fuel are added in alternate layers from the top until the kiln is filled. The fuel is then ignited, and the process of burning can be kept on continuously by removing the burnt lime at the base of the kiln, replacing with a fresh supply of carbonate and fuel at the top. Natural deposits of limestone, &c., are never pure, but usually contaminated with varying proportions of carbonate of magnesia, iron and alumina and silica. The higher the percentage of these in the deposit, the less pure will be the lime produced on burning.

THE QUALITY OF LIME.

This depends upon several circumstances; impurities, as just mentioned, in the limestone, affect the quality. But quality may also be affected in other ways. If the lime is not thoroughly burned, pieces of imperfectly burned stone, which will not slake, will be contained in it. With limestone containing much silicious matter (sand), over-burning may take place, and calcium silicate be formed. Again, if some time has elapsed since burning, the lime will deteriorate owing to partial slaking, and subsequent formation of calcium carbonate as explained above. The essential points in connexion with lime burning is that limestone of good quality should be used, combined with careful burning. Well burned lime should contain practically all its lime as calcium oxide (CaO).

SLAKED LIME (Calcium Hydrate, CaH_2O_2).

Slaked lime is produced when freshly burned limestone is treated with water. The material will swell up considerably, and give off steam, owing to the heat generated by the chemical combination of the lime and water, thus, $CaO + H_2O = CaH_2O_2$. Eventually the mass will crumble into a fine powder.

AIR SLAKED LIME.

This material differs from the water-slaked lime, in that it is a mixture of slaked lime and calcium carbonate formed by reason of the fact that air contains both moisture and carbonic acid gas, both of which have a combining affinity with the burnt lime. The relative proportion of each constituent of air-slaked lime varies according to the time of exposure to the atmosphere after burning, for, as already mentioned, lime, if left long enough exposed, will eventually all become calcium carbonate again. This is the form of lime usually supplied as agricultural lime.

CARBONATE OF LIME.

This is present in agricultural lime, having been formed from slaked lime on exposure. Carbonate of lime is also obtained in chalk and all forms of limestone direct. If applied as a land dressing this form of lime, to be of the best service, must be in as fine state of division as possible, and, therefore, when purchasing limestone for such use it should be stipulated for, that it be finely ground. When finely ground, it can be more evenly distributed. Its effectiveness is also increased, owing in a great measure to the greater surface exposed by the fineness of the particles to the action of the soil acids. Some deposits of carbonate of lime are better adapted on that account for dressing soil than others. Chalk will easily crumble into a fine powder when dug out and allowed to become dry with exposure. Other forms which bear a striking resemblance to ordinary sandstone are also easily ground. Shells, both of fresh and salt water origin, are much denser in structure, and offer-considerable resistance to the grinding process. They are generally less bulky weight for weight, as compared with the more friable deposits, and proportionately less likely to disintegrate as readily in the soil.

GYPSUM (SULPHATE OF LIME).

Besides the natural deposits obtainable as carbonate of lime, considerable deposits exist of gypsum. Gypsum is lime (CaO) in combination with one part of sulphuric acid (H_2SO_4) and two of water (H_2O). It possesses the following formula:—

$$CaSO_4 \cdot 2H_2O$$

The molecular weight being :—

Sulphate of Calcium.	Water.		Oxide of Calcium (lime).		Sulphuric Anhydride.		Water
$CaSO_4$	. $2H_2O$	=	CaO	+	SO_3	+	$2H_2O$
172			56		80		36

therefore as 172 : 100 : : 56 : the percentage of lime (CaO)

$$\frac{56 \times 100}{172} = 32.54 \text{ CaO}$$

Thus, 100 lbs. of gypsum will yield 32.54 lbs. of lime. Gypsum being already in combination with an acid (H_2SO_4) does not possess the power of combining with and neutralizing the acids in the soil, so that it is useless as a dressing for sour land. Furthermore, as its lime content is only about one-third that of lime as shown above, its claims to recognition as a substitute for burnt lime can only be reasonably entertained when the price and convenience of the deposit are such as to counter-balance the extra cost of handling, rail, carriage, &c.

THE RELATIVE VALUE OF THE DIFFERENT FORMS OF LIME.

56 lbs. of fresh burnt lime contains the same amount of lime as—

   56 lbs. of fresh ground lime.
   74 lbs. of water-slaked lime.
   100 lbs. of carbonate of lime (as a powder—ground limestone, chalk, &c.).
   100 lbs. of old air-slaked lime.
   172 lbs. of sulphate of lime (as gypsum).

The equivalent value is, therefore, as follows:—

   100 lbs. of fresh burnt lime is equivalent to—

   135 lbs. of water-slaked lime
   178.6 lbs. of carbonate of lime (as a powder).
   307.3 lbs. of sulphate of lime (as gypsum).

STANDARDS.

Lime.—A good quality lime should contain at least 85 per cent. combined oxide and carbonate, of which not more than 10 per cent. shall be present as carbonate.

Slaked Lime.—A good quality slaked lime should contain at least 85 per cent. of combined oxide, hydrate, and carbonate. of which not more than 10 per cent. shall be present as carbonate.

Carbonate of Lime.—A good quality carbonate of lime should contain at least 85 per cent. of carbonate of lime, and pass through a sieve of 50 meshes to the linear inch.

Gypsum.—A good quality gypsum should contain at least 30 per cent. of calcium oxide.

All other grades should be sold on a guarantee, stating their calcium oxide content.

Money Value of Lime to the Farmer.

On some land the beneficial effect of lime may be worth £3 per ton. On other land it may be worth only £1 per ton, according to the greater or less ill-effect on the crop returns of the defect which it remedies. What, therefore, is the money value of lime delivered on the farm can only be ascertained as a result of experiment and careful record of the cost compared with the increase of crop returns over a period of years.

Assuming standard lime as above (75 per cent. CaO, and 10 per cent. $CaCO_3$) to be worth £1 10s. per ton on the farm, then—

Standard slaked lime (75 per cent. CaO and CaH_2O_2, and 10 per cent. $CaCO_3$) is worth £1 2s. 3d. per ton on the farm.

Standard carbonate of lime (85 per cent., finely ground $CaCO_3$ (ground limestone, &c.) is worth 16s. 10d. per ton on the farm.

Standard gypsum (30 per cent. CaO) is worth 9s. 9d. per ton on the farm.

It does not follow that if a farmer can get gypsum landed at the nearest railway station to him for 9s. 9d. per ton that it would pay him as well as to buy freshly burnt lime landed at the station at 30s. per ton, for the cartage to the farm and the cost of distribution would be three times as much in the former case as it would in the latter. Still less would it pay to buy the bulkier form of lime, paying the above rates at the sending end, for the freight of 3 tons would have to be paid for in the case of gypsum additional on the cost. as against the freight charges for 1 ton in the case of burnt lime.

Table showing the Names, Chemical Formula, and Synonyms of the Different Forms of Lime.

Name.	Chemical Formula.	Synonyms.
No. 1.—Lime	Calcium Oxide CaO	Quicklime, stone lime, lump lime, caustic lime, builders' lime, burnt lime, ground lime
No. 2.—Slaked Lime ...	Calcium Hydrate CaH_2O_2	Hydrate of lime, water-slaked, air-slaked, slacked lime
No. 3.—Carbonate of Lime	Calcium Carbonate $CaCO_3$	Limestone, chalk, marble, shell, shell-sand, marl, ground limestone
No. 4.—Gypsum ..	Calcium Sulphate $CaSO_4$ & $2H_2O$	Copi, sulphate of lime, land plaster

Note.—Nos. 1 and 2 are known as hot lime. Nos. 3 and 4 are known as mild lime. Hot lime is much stronger in its action in decomposing organic matter than the mild limes,

V.

THE PRACTICE OF LIMING.

By A. E. V. Richardson, M.A., B.Sc., Agricultural Superintendent.

The value of lime as a means of ameliorating, certain classes of soil has been known from the very earliest times, and was the subject of comment by many of the ancient writers. During comparatively recent times there are many instances on record where liberal dressings of marl and chalk have had a most marked and favorable effect on the fertility of the soil for generations. According to Hall, there are certain fields on the Rothamstead Experimental Station known to have received heavy applications of marl more than a century ago, which to-day exceed in productive value adjoining fields which were not so treated.

That the presence in the soil of a sufficiency of lime in the form of carbonate is a fair guarantee of its fertility and productive power is indeed generally recognised, and this view finds its expression in the well-known maxim, " A limestone country is a rich country."

In this article will be considered briefly the forms in which lime may be applied, its action on the soil, the rate, time, frequency, cost, and mode of application, and the method of determining the soil requirements with regard to lime.

1. Forms in which Lime may be Applied.

These will be dealt with in greater detail in Mr. Scott's article. It is only here necessary to mention that lime may be applied in four distinct forms :—

(1) As *Carbonate*, $CaCO_3$, in the form of ground limestone, marl, chalk, "unburnt lime," "dilute lime," shells, &c.

(2) As *Oxide*, CaO, in the form of quicklime, "hot lime," "caustic lime," or "burnt lime," "unslaked lime," "lump lime."

(3) As *Hydrate*, $Ca(OH)_2$, in the form of slaked lime.

(4) As *Sulphate*, $CaSO_4 . 2H_2O$, in gypsum, or "land plaster."

It is of importance to the farmer to realize that the relative value of these substances depends mainly on the percentage of lime present in the respective compounds. Now, if 178.6 lbs. of pure ground limestone (carbonate of calcium) are burnt in a kiln, 78.6 lbs. will disappear into the air as carbonic acid gas, and 100 lbs. of quicklime (oxide of calcium) will be left behind. That is to say, 100 lbs. of quicklime are equivalent to 178.6 lbs. of ground limestone or any other form of pure " carbonate of lime."

Again, if the 100 lbs. of quicklime be thoroughly slaked with water, 132 lbs. of slaked lime (hydrate of calcium) will be obtained. Finally, if this amount of slaked lime be properly neutralized with sulphuric acid 307 lbs. of "land plaster" or gypsum (sulphate of calcium) will be produced.

These figures are of practical importance It will be seen that there is precisely the same amount of "lime" in 178.6 lbs. of carbonate or ground limestone, 100 lbs. quicklime, 132 lbs. of slaked lime, and 307 lbs. of gypsum.

That is, if a farmer wished to purchase the equivalent of 1 ton of pure lime, he would require approximately the following quantities : — 1 ton of quicklime, 1.3 tons of slaked lime, 1.8 tons ground limestone, or 3.1 tons of gypsum.

2. Action of Lime on the Soil.

The object of applying lime to the soil is not the same as that involved in the application of ordinary fertilizers. Fertilizers, such as super-phosphate, Thomas' phosphate, guano, &c., supply the soil with elements of plant food in which the soil is actually deficient, and they are applied in relatively small amounts, *i.e.*, from $\frac{1}{2}$ cwt. to 1 cwt. per acre under ordinary farming conditions. Lime, however, is applied because of its indirect effect upon the soil, *i.e.*, because of the effect it produces upon the chemical composition and physical and biological condition of the soil, and not because it is actually wanted to supply the plants' immediate requirements. It is not in itself a plant food, as phosphoric acid is, except to a very limited extent, but nevertheless, the application of lime in suitable quantities has a most marked effect on soils wanting in lime.

Lime corrects soil acidity.—Perhaps the most important effect is that lime being alkaline neutralizes the acidity of the soil, and thus promotes vegetation. Most of our agricultural crops cannot thrive in a soil that is sour or acid, but must have a soil that is neutral or basic in character. Soils tend to become sour from various causes. In regions of heavy rainfall, lime is being constantly washed out of the surface layers. At Rothamstead this loss amounts to 800 lbs. of lime per acre per annum. Carbonic acid gas, which is present in all soil water, has the power of dissolving lime and carrying it off in the drainage waters. It is the presence of lime in solution that causes the "hardness" of certain waters, and it is owing to the power of the soil waters to dissolve lime that the formation of limestone caves is brought about.

Again, the organic matter or the humus of the soil is constantly under-going decomposition, and, as a result, various organic acids are formed in much the same way, as ensilage becomes acid and sour on exposure. Now, lime is the natural base by means of which these acid substances in the soil are neutralized. Hence, if for any reason the soil has become acid, then a dressing of lime is an indispensable preliminary for satis-factory crops. This is more particularly true of such leguminous crops as clover and lucerne, for these will not thrive on soils that are sour and acid in character.

Lime liberates plant food.—Lime is a very powerful soil stimulant, and is very effective in liberating plant food. Most of the phosphoric acid and potash present in the soil is present in insoluble combinations that cannot be used by the plant.

The application of liberal dressings of lime renders such insoluble compounds as iron and aluminium phosphates more susceptible to the solvent action of the soil water by converting them into phosphate of lime,[*] and thus making them immediately available to the crop.

Lime also replaces potash in its insoluble combinations in the soil, and this probably accounts for the beneficial action of lime, particularly when applied in the form of gypsum, on those crops which require relatively large amounts of potash, *e.g.*, lucerne. clover, and other legumes. The action of lime on the organic portion of the soil is extremely important. It hastens the decay and decomposition of the organic matter, and greatly promotes the process of nitrification.

Lime improves the mechanical condition of the soil.—The effect of lime on the physical constitution of the soil is very marked. Stiff clay soils are rendered more friable, far less adhesive. more open and porous

---

[*] Thénard.

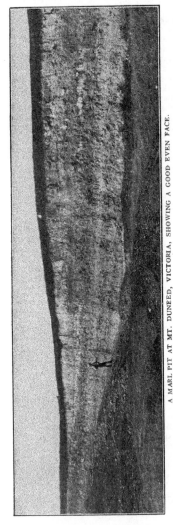

A MARL PIT AT MT. DUNEED, VICTORIA, SHOWING A GOOD EVEN FACE.

in character by the application of a liberal dressing of lime. Lime causes the very fine particles of silicate of alumina, which are responsible for the tendency of clay soils to set hard, to coagulate or curdle and aggregate into relatively large particles. Thus the soil becomes more open, its porosity and permeability are increased, and the soil tends to become drier, more friable, and more easily cultivated, and thus more congenial conditions for the development of the plants' roots are provided.

With light sandy soils quicklime should be used with discretion. When, however, lime is applied to such soils in the form of carbonate, it has the opposite effect to that exerted on clay soils, and tends to hold the soil particles together, and to increase the capacity of the soil for retaining moisture.

Lime improves the biological condition of the soil.—On rich peaty soils, lime may be used with considerable freedom. These soils are very liable to become sour owing to the decomposition of the large amount of organic matter they contain, and the consequent formation of various organic acids. This decomposition is brought about through the agency of countless millions of microscopic bacteria, and one may say that the fertility of any given soil is very largely dependent on the nature and activity of the teeming bacterial population it holds. The functions of some of these soil germs have been discussed elsewhere.* It need only be added that the presence of adequate supplies of lime in the form of carbonate will insure in the soil a vigorous and beneficial bacterial flora, and will consequently enhance the fertility and productive power of the soil.

* *Journal of Agriculture* (Victoria), September, 1912.

QUANTITY PER ACRE AND FREQUENCY OF APPLICATION.

The quantity of these various lime compounds to be used will depend on the nature of the soil, the object of the application, the form in which the lime is applied, and the cost of the material. The maximum dressing will be required on stiff clay soils, in which it is desired to effect an improvement in the physical condition, or on peaty soils rich in decaying organic matter. The minimum dressing is required for light open soils deficient in organic matter. On these latter soils, indeed, the use of quicklime, especially in large quantities, should be avoided. Ground limestone or "unburnt lime" will give far more satisfactory results.

For stiff clay soils or sour peaty soils which have *never* yet received any lime, very little material effect will be observable with a lighter dressing than 10 cwt. of quicklime, or its equivalent in slaked lime, while considerably heavier dressings may be applied with profit. To bring about a material improvement in the mechanical condition of very stiff clays from 1 to 2 tons of lime may be necessary for an initial dressing, and this will be sufficient for a number of years. Such a heavy dressing may seem at first sight a very unprofitable venture to farmers accustomed to an annual expenditure of 2s. 6d. to 5s. per acre for artificial manures. It must be remembered, however, that with a dressing of lime the effects last for a long period, and the initial cost must be spread over a period of years.

On lands rich in decaying organic matter, and in reclaimed swamps, a very liberal application of lime will also be necessary to insure the best results. On light soils, loose and open in character, application of lime must be smaller. If these soils are wanting in organic matter, carbonate of lime should be used in preference to quicklime or slaked lime. Carbonate of lime is mild in its action, and it may be applied to any soil without danger.

Marl, which is an impure form of carbonate of lime, is usually applied in very heavy dressings, amounting to tons per acre, but on account of freight its use must necessarily be confined to the neighbourhood of marl pits.

Many years ago it was the custom in Europe to apply lime in very large dressings at long intervals of time. Frequently 5 tons per acre were applied. Recent investigations in America have conclusively demonstrated the futility of this practice. It is now generally recognised that the secret of success in liming land is to apply the lime in comparatively small doses at *frequent* intervals and to *supplement* the dressing of lime with organic matter and phosphates.

Professor Wright, of Glasgow, carried out a series of experiments with lime over a period of eight years. He applied 4 tons of lime per acre in one, two, four, and eight applications to four different experimental plots. As a result of the first eight years' work, he says, "The largest increases of crops were obtained in this experiment from annual applications of 10 cwts. of burnt lime per acre. Applications of 5 to 10 cwts. per acre per annum gave profitable results, but larger dressings of 1, 2, and 4 tons proved very unprofitable."—(Tenth report, West of Scotland Agricultural College, 1911.) It must be added that the soil on which Professor Wright was working was a loam in high condition.

MODE OF APPLICATION.

Lime may be applied by hand, with ordinary fertilizer drills, or by means of specially constructed limespreaders. The advantages of the limespreaders are that comparatively small amounts may be spread with great regularity, and with the minimum of labour and of physical discomfort.

(*a*) If spread by hand, the lime may be placed on the ploughed land in small heaps at regular intervals, and covered with fine soil. If quicklime be used, it may be allowed to "air slack" by atmospheric moisture or by showers of rain, in which case a mixture of carbonate and hydrate is obtained; or it may be slaked quickly by the addition of sufficient water to break down the mass into fine powder. If this latter operation be judiciously performed, and excessive amounts of water be avoided, the whole mass will break down into very fine powder which will act most beneficially on the soil. After slaking, the lime may be mixed with earth (to facilitate evenness in distribution and render it less objectionable to handle), and then spread with a shovel and harrowed in.

Since lime naturally tends to "sink" in the soil and to be removed by solution from the surface layers, it is unadvisable to plough it in and thus place it at the bottom of the furrow. The better practice is to spread it on the surface and harrow it in.

FIG. I.—LIMESPREADER.

(*b*) Lime and ground limestone may be sown with an ordinary seed drill, but only in relatively small quantities, *i.e.*, a few cwt. per acre. If larger dressings are to be applied with the drill, it becomes necessary to go over the land twice, which obviously increases the cost of the application.

(*c*) There are, however, a number of specially constructed limespreaders now on the market, which will satisfactorily sow from 2 or 3 cwt. up to 2 tons per acre with great uniformity. The general principle of these spreaders is that the lime is fed into a V-shaped hopper containing a series of slots either at the bottom or side of the box, through which the lime is forced by means of a revolving chain, a set of teeth, or by a set of beaters. The amount of lime sown is regulated by an alteration in the size of the exit slots. Figures I., II., III. represent three limespreaders procurable on the Melbourne market. These limespreaders do very satisfactory work, and will spread from 3 cwt. to 2 tons of lime per acre with regularity and accuracy. It would be a distinct advantage to have larger hoppers, more especially when fairly liberal dressings are used, so as to avoid the necessity for filling up so often. The price of the spreaders also seems rather high, especially for the small settler. It is interesting to note that the farm dray is being adopted for limespreading. Figure IV. represents a limespreader, made by Mr. H. W. Kerle, of New South Wales, attached to the back of an ordinary dray; and Figure V. shows a field in the act of being limed with this machine. The advantage of this arrangement is that a good load of lime may be started with in the dray, and the hopper replenished as the spreading proceeds. I am indebted to Mr. Geo. Valder, Superintendent of Agriculture of New South Wales, for the photograph of this machine in action.

If a simple and cheap limespreading device could be made and attached to the back of an ordinary farm dray, and worked by a sprocket from the box of the wheel, it would be a great convenience to a farmer desirous of applying lime in liberal dressings.

Time of Application.

The most suitable time to apply lime is in the autumn—a month or two before seeding. Quicklime or slaked lime may interfere with the germina-

FIG. 2.—FORCE FEED LIMESPREADER.

tion of the seed if sown too close to seeding, but its power to injure seeds gradually disappears as it changes into the form of carbonate by contact with the soil, and in this form it is quite innocuous to germination or plant life. Quicklime and slaked lime may be applied at other seasons of the year, provided the lime is very thoroughly and uniformly worked into the soil by means of the harrows before the crop is sown. Carbonate of lime, *i.e.*, chalk, ground limestone, " unburnt lime " or ground limestone, may be applied at any time without risk, and the farmer may, therefore, consult his own convenience in applying these.

Cost of Material.

An important practical consideration to the farmer is the cost of the lime. At present, good agricultural lime containing over 90 per cent. of calcium oxide may be purchased for 25s. per ton. This agricultural lime is a by-product in the manufacture of builders' lime, which costs over £2 per ton. Now, as a source of lime, this burnt lime is relatively much cheaper than ground limestone, more especially when freights are taken into consideration. As previously stated, 1 ton of burnt lime is equivalent in lime content to 1.3 tons of slaked lime, and 1.8 tons of ground limestone or carbonate. Hence, if burnt lime is quoted at 25s. per ton, ground limestone, leaving freights out of consideration, is. worth, as a source of lime, only 14s. per ton. The present price is £1 per ton. The freight on a ton of burnt lime is 5s. 4d. per 150 miles. The freight on an *equivalent* amount of lime in the form of ground limestone would therefore be 5s. 4d. x 1.8 = 9s. 7d. In other words, if a farmer, situated 150 miles from a lime quarry, were to purchase the equivalent of a ton of pure lime in the form of burnt lime and ground limestone, his purchase would pan out as follows :—

> 1 ton of burnt lime at 25s., plus freight, 5s. 4d = 30s. 4d.
>
> Equivalent in ground limestone=1.8 tons at £1 per ton, freight, 9s. 7d.=£2 5s. 7d.

So that the lime in ground limestone would really cost him 50 per cent. more than in burnt lime. This should not be. With the vast deposits cf

FIG. 3.—LIMING LAND FOR LUCERNE.

high quality limestone in this State, and the improved rockgrinding machinery now available, it should be possible to bring the price of ground limestone to nearly half its present level. With an increasing demand for, and an increasing output of ground limestone, the price will doubtless drop considerably. The price must drop if it is to be used extensively. In other countries the ultimate cost to the farmer has been reduced by free haulage on the railways. Whether Victoria should follow in this regard is a matter of railway policy. It is to the farmers' interest, however, that lime and ground limestone or carbonate of lime should be railed at bedrock rates. It is also to the farmers' interest that the various lime compounds on the market should be sold on a guarantee basis just as is now done with phosphatic nitrogenous and potassic fertilizers.

What Form of Lime to Use.

We have already seen that lime may be applied in the mild form of carbonate, in the active form of burnt lime, slaked lime, or quicklime, and in the form of "land plaster" or gypsum. With regard to gypsum, it must be understood that on some soils it has little or no value. It improves the mechanical condition of stiff clay soils, and liberates large amounts of potash, but it does not correct the soil acidity. It is not alkaline, and therefore it *cannot* take the place of lime in acid soils. It has a value for stiff clay soils, and under certain circumstances for potash loving plants like clover and lucerne, but it will not relieve a soil of its sourness. Moreover, as a *source* of calcium, it is very expensive, containing but 34 per cent. of lime, and therefore worth about 8s. per ton compared with present market values of the other forms.

With regard to the remaining forms of lime, viz. :—lime (carbonate), and quicklime (oxide), much depends on the cost and the nature of the soil to which the compounds are applied. The relative cost of ground limestone and burnt lime has already been discussed.

It may be said that to the farmer in outlying districts, remote from limestone quarries, where freights must enter into consideration, the most concentrated form, *i.e.* burnt lime, will be cheapest. In the neighbourhood of marl pits and quarries, ground limestone or marl will probably be the most economical form to use.

FIG. 4.—LIMESPREADER ATTACHED TO A FARM DRAY.

On stiff clay soils, peaty lands, and reclaimed swamps, burnt lime is most efficacious. On other soils, carbonate of lime will give more beneficial and more lasting results.

The most extensive investigation ever made into the relative merits of burnt lime and ground limestone, in comparative tests, is that conducted by the Pennsylvania Experimental Station. Equivalent quantities of lime in the form of ground limestone and burnt lime were used every four years, and, as a result of 25 years' work, Dr. Frear says—"The yields from carbonate of lime (ground limestone) showed superiority under the conditions of this experiment over those following the application of an equivalent application of caustic lime."

Precautions to be Observed in using Lime.

Several matters need to be guarded against in applying lime—(1) Lime has a *constructive* and a *destructive* effect on the soil. Its constructive effect is observed in the correction of soil acidity, the stimulation of leguminous growth in the pastures, the promotion of nitrification and other bacterial activity, and the improvement of the mechanical condition of the soil. Its destructive effect is due to its caustic character. It rapidly destroys humus, and thus tends to rob the soil of its most valuable constituent. According to the Pennsylvania experiments quoted above, this loss was equivalent to the loss of 375 lbs. of nitrogen per acre in the first 9 inches of soil in sixteen years, *i.e.* equal to $37\frac{1}{2}$ tons of stable manure per acre. Hence, in liming, provision *must* be made for the restoration of this organic matter by green manuring or the use of organic manures, like farmyard manure, and also by the avoidance of stubble burning.

Furthermore, on soils deficient in organic matter, ground limestone or dilute lime should be used in preference to caustic lime.

(2) There is an old couplet which runs—

> " Lime and lime without manure
> Make both farm and farmer poor."

Liming must not be regarded as a *substitute* for manuring. Phosphates *must* be used in conjunction with lime to secure the best results, and the supply of organic matter or humus must also be maintained. Unless these points are borne in mind, liming will deplete the soil of its fertility.

When does a Soil need Lime.

1. The nature of the vegetation often indicates whether lime is wanting or abundant in a given soil. The habitual presence in the crops of such weeds as sorrel and plantain, which are fairly tolerant of acid soil conditions, is an indication of the lack of lime, just as the continual appearance of vigorous clovers and trefoils in the pastures is a fair indication of the presence of a sufficiency of lime. The nature of the vegetation is a reliable, but not an infallible indication of the requirements of a soil as regards to lime.

2. There are several simple tests which roughly indicate whether or not a soil is in need of lime. If a soil is acid or sour in character, it is deficient in lime. A rough practical method of determining whether a given soil is acid is to take a strip of blue litmus paper (which may be purchased from any druggist), and place it between the broken halves of a ball of moist soil. If, after standing for some little time, the litmus turns red in colour, the soil is clearly acid in character and in need of lime.

3. If a soil contains a sufficiency of lime in the form of carbonate, it cannot be acid in character. A rough test of the amount of carbonate of lime in a soil may be made by taking a hollowed out ball of soil and pouring in a few drops of strong spirits of salts or hydrochloric acid. If much lime in the form of carbonate exists, a brisk effervescence will take place, while, if small quantities only are present, only a few bubbles will appear.

4. Some idea of the requirements of a soil for lime may be gained by studying its chemical analysis. The total amount of lime present in the the soil may be determined with accuracy by chemical analysis, but such analysis can throw little light on the *form* in which the lime is present. If the greater portion of the lime is present in the form of phosphate, or silicate, or sulphate, it will be of practically little value in keeping the soil " sweet." Paradoxical as it may appear, some soils known to contain large quantities of lime have given increased returns when dressed with this ingredient; whilst, conversely, some soils with a relatively low percentage of lime have proved unresponsive to further applications. Hence the form in which the lime is present, rather than its total amount, is the important factor in deciding whether lime is required. The four

indicators described above all have their limitations, but to the experienced worker they are of service as rough guides in feeling the pulse of the land with respect to the need of lime.

5.—EXPERIMENTS WITH LIME.

By far the most satisfactory and practical method of testing the land is by the establishment of experimental plots with varying dressings of lime. By this means every farmer can test the requirements of the soils on his farm. In order that the information gained should be of value, it is absolutely necessary to conduct the experiments over a lengthy period. Indeed, the most satisfactory results can only be obtained when the plots are permanent in character, so that the effects of each particular dressing can be noted. The full effects of lime are never immediately discernible. Time must be allowed for the beneficial changes to be wrought.

Experiments were laid down last autumn at Rutherglen, Wyuna, and on private farms in the Western district, Central district, and in Gipps-

FIG. 5.—LIMING LAND.

land, to test the value of lime under varying conditions. The experiments were designed to seek definite information on the following points :—

    (*a*) The value of dressings of lime varying from 5 cwt. up to 2 tons per acre when applied to lucerne, barley, wheat, and rape crops, in order to determine the effect of lime, and the most suitable amounts to apply for legumes, cereals, and non-leguminous forages.

    (*b*) The periodicity of application that will lead to the most profitable results.

    (*c*) The value of lime when used in varying quantities with and without phosphates, nitrates, and potash, singly and in combination.

    (*d*) The effect of lime when used with and without green manures.

    (*e*) The effect of lime when used in various two, three, four, and five course rotations.

    (*f*) The relative merits of equivalent forms of lime when applied in the form of quicklime, carbonate of lime, and gypsum, to different crops and different soils, with and without supplementary dressings of phosphates and organic matter.

Some time must elapse before any definite conclusions can be drawn from these field experiments, but each year indications of value should be obtained. The experiments will be extended and laid down in permanent plots at the Central Experimental Farm, probably next autumn

Unfortunately, very little experimental work has been done on the lime question in Australia. It is admitted that there are wide divergences in Australian and European agricultural practice. This was referred to in dealing with the nitrogen question in the September issue.* It may so happen that in some details of liming, Australian soils may require special treatment. If so, the prosecution of definite experimental work in each of the climatically different districts of the State under varying conditions of soil treatment will indicate the direction in which improvements in existing and traditional practice may be brought about.

SUMMARY.

1. Lime may be applied in one of four forms : quicklime, slaked lime, ground limestone, and gypsum.

2. One ton of quicklime is equivalent to 1.3 tons slaked lime, 1.8 tons of carbonate of lime, and 3.1 tons gypsum.

3. Lime has an important chemical, mechanical, and biological effect on the soil.

4. It liberates phosphates and potash, decomposes organic matter, promotes nitrification, and corrects the soil acidity.

5. It makes clay soils more friable, and tends to bind sandy soils.

6. It stimulates bacterial activity, and promotes soil fertility.

7. It may be applied in dressings from 5 cwt. to 2 tons per acre, according to the kind of soil, kind of crop, and according to the frequency of application.

8. Small dressings frequently applied are more profitable than heavy dressings applied at long intervals.

9. Lime is best applied by special limespreaders. A good, handy man can make one to work from the back of a farm dray.

10. Quicklime and slaked lime are best applied in autumn, at least some weeks before the seed is sown. Carbonate of lime may be applied when convenient.

11. If quicklime can be purchased for 25s. per ton, then carbonate of lime is worth about 14s. per ton.

12. Quicklime and slaked lime give quickest results. Carbonate of lime is slower, but is ultimately the most profitable.

13. Lime destroys humus, therefore, keep up the supply of organic matter to the soil by green manuring.

14. Lime must be supplemented with phosphates to keep the soil productive.

15. There is urgent need for systematic and permanent experimental work in connexion with liming problems.

---

* *Journal of Agriculture* (Victoria), September, 1912. p. 543.

VI.

THE RELATION OF LIME TO SOIL FERTILITY.

By John W. Paterson, B.Sc., Ph.D., Experimentalist, and P. R. Scott, Chemist for Agriculture.

A manure is a substance used to supply a necessary plant food to the soil. Phosphoric acid is a necessary plant food which is often deficient in soil, and superphosphate may be employed to supply this. Superphosphate is thus a manure.

Lime is also a necessary plant food. But in practice a soil never contains too little lime to serve as plant food for the next crop. In the strict sense of the term, therefore, lime is not a manure.

The beneficial action exerted by lime in a soil is indirect. Lime is a strong base. An acid is a sour substance. When a strong base is added to an acid, it combines with it, and the sourness disappears. Most of the improvements effected in soils by lime are due to its basic character. Its action is to keep the land from getting sour.

Lime in Soils.

Lime exists in a soil in various forms, but always combined with an acid. It is combined with sulphuric acid in sulphate of lime (gypsum), with phosphoric acid in phosphate of lime (bones, super, &c.), and with silicic acid in silicates of lime of various degrees of complexity. In all these compounds the acids are strong, and they hold the lime firmly. In sulphate, phosphates, and silicates of lime, the lime is held so firmly that it is not available as a base. Gypsum or bones cannot remove soil acidity.

Carbonate of lime is another form of lime existing in soils. It is a compound of lime with carbonic acid. Carbonic acid is a weak acid, and is also volatile, so that it is easily driven out from carbonate of lime. When this happens the lime is available as a base.

So far as the lime content of a soil is concerned, carbonate of lime is, for most purposes, the only form that counts. It is valuable because it is easily decomposed, thus yielding free lime on demand. If a soil has not got a suitable supply of carbonate of lime, then liming is necessary.

Forms in which Lime may be Applied.

Lime may be applied to soils in various forms, viz., as free or hot lime, as slaked lime, or as carbonate of lime (see Mr. Scott's article herein). The value of lime in these forms lies in the fact that if not already carbonate of lime, they are soon changed to carbonate by the carbonic acid of the soil. The soil has then a supply of lime tied up as carbonate, but available when required.

Effect Depending on Fineness of Division.

When carbonate of lime in the soil is decomposed to furnish available lime, the action takes place on the outside of the particles of carbonate of lime. The larger these particles the smaller is the surface exposed for the same weight of carbonate, and the slower, consequently, will it act. The benefit derived from the presence of carbonate of lime in a soil depends, therefore, not only upon the quantity present, but also upon its fineness of division.

Burnt and slaked lime give very finely divided carbonate of lime in a soil because of the chemical action of slaking. Lime added as carbonate (ground limestone) is always more active the more finely it is ground. With this material it is recommended that at least 35 per cent. should pass a sieve with 10,000 meshes to the square inch. Fineness of grinding becomes more important when the quantity applied is small.

THE SOIL LOSES LIME.

Under natural conditions there is a marked tendency for the supply of carbonate of lime to diminish in the surface soil. Carbonate of lime is practically insoluble in pure water, but in water containing carbonic acid it goes into solution as bi-carbonate, which forms the chief ingredient in the drainage waters from many soils. Again, a certain quantity is removed in farm crops, while earth worms in certain cases contribute by gradually burying the coarser fragments. The use of certain manures such as superphosphate and the potash salts, and notably sulphate of ammonia, gradually deplete the soil in carbonate of lime. The combined result of these withdrawals may be very considerable, and it is estimated that certain of the experimental fields at Rothamsted have lost from the surface soil during the past 32 years carbonate of lime at the rate of 800 to 1,050 lb. per acre per annum.

It is an old saying that "lime sinks in the soil." So much is this the case that even soils on the limestone formation may be found to require a fresh application of lime at the surface.

QUANTITY OF LIME REQUIRED IN SOILS.

Discussing the percentage of carbonate of lime required in soil. Hall* places the danger limit between $\frac{1}{4}$ and $\frac{1}{2}$ per cent. Judging from numerous analyses of Victorian soils made by the Department, it is apparent that the great majority of them fall into the category of soils which require lime. Notable exceptions are found in the Mallee and in the dark soils of the Wimmera.

WHEN IS LIMING NECESSARY?

Chemical analysis can tell when a soil requires lime, because the percentage of carbonate of lime falls too low. It is a less sure guide as to when a soil does not require lime, because the carbonate of lime present may exist in relatively large lumps.

Clay and peaty soils require more lime to be present than do sandy soils low in organic matter to maintain them in good working order.

Litmus paper is stained blue with a vegetable colouring matter. Acids change the blue colour to red. If a little soil is placed on litmus paper, moistened, and left standing for a few minutes, the soil may be washed off and the paper examined. If the paper is clearly reddened, this indicates that the soil is acid and requires lime. But a soil may require liming when it fails to give the acid test.

There are limits to the usefulness, therefore, both of chemical analysis and of the litmus test, when we inquire whether or not a soil requires lime. The surest way to know is to make trial applications of lime, and watch the results. This matter will be referred to later on. Meanwhile it may assist to an understanding of the effect of such applications if we proceed to consider some of the more important actions exercised by lime upon the soil and crop.

* *Jour. Bd. Agric.,* Lond., 1906.

MECHANICAL EFFECT OF LIME.

When a clay deficient in lime is wetted it becomes sticky and swells up somewhat after the manner of starch paste or glue. On drying it becomes very hard. If lime, however, is added, the clay will not puddle well, and on drying it crumbles. Fig. 1 shows an ordinary clay from the Western Plains rubbed up with water. The photograph was taken 20 hours after the cylinders were set up. No. 1 had nothing added to the clay; the clay remains swollen up in the water, which is still muddy. In No. 2 the addition of lime has caused coagulation (sometimes referred to as flocculation) of the clay, which has then settled down as a fine powder. No. 3 got neutral carbonate of lime, which is practically insoluble, and hence had no immediate action. No. 4 got gypsum, which, like lime, is sufficiently soluble to act. Soluble lime compounds produce this coagulating effect on clay soils which then become more friable and porous, suffer

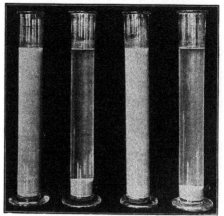

1. Control blank.   2. With lime.   3. Carbonate of lime.   4. With sulphate of lime.
FIG. 1.—COAGULATING EFFECT OF VARIOUS FORMS OF LIME.

less from working wet, and shrink and cake less on drying. Gypsum has not the other effects of lime in soils, but it has that of coagulating heavy clay. Hot lime will generally be preferred on stiff clay to all others— to gypsum because it has basic character and can correct sourness, and to ground limestone (carbonate) because the latter is slow to effect coagulation. In time, however, carbonate will also coagulate clay, as it gradually passes into solution as bicarbonate in the soil water.

Where gypsum can be obtained cheaply, it will form a useful application to heavy clay soils.

When the drainage waters from a district, and the water puddles in the fields remain long muddy, we have an indication of want of lime. Clear puddles in a clay district show sufficient soluble lime compounds to be present. The waters of the Lower Goulburn, for example, have obviously drained from an area deficient in lime.

Lime and Nitrification.

Lime is important in the production of nitrates. Where land shows signs of being "run down" or exhausted in fertility, this is more frequently due to its failure to produce sufficient nitrates than to anything else. Additional superphosphate manure will not help this, because if nitrates are deficient, extra phosphates given will not remove the defect. Lime does not contain nitrates, but it causes a more rapid production of nitrates from the supply of organic nitrogen within the soil.

The organic nitrogen in soils is not in a form which the crop can utilize. It is converted into the nitrate form by different kinds of bacteria. The changes may be viewed in two stages. The first stage results in the formation of ammonia from the organic matter ; the second stage results in the conversion of the ammonia into nitrates.

First Stage of Nitrification.

The first stage may be considered first. When fresh vegetable residues are incorporated in the soil, this kind of organic matter yields ammonia

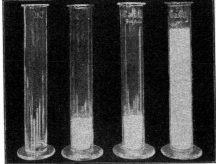

1. With lime. 2. Control blank. 3. With gypsum. 4. With carbonate of lime.

FIG. 2.—SHOWING HOW LIME HELPS NITRIFICATION.

with comparative ease. Where land has been long under cultivation without any return of fresh organic matter, the production of ammonia becomes each year a matter of greater difficulty. As it gets older, the soil organic matter gets "tougher," and the first stage in nitrate production, viz., the production of ammonia, becomes, in consequence, more difficult.

Lime helps the change. Ammonia is a product of the decomposition of soil organic matter, but it is only the last link in a chain of complex intermediate products. Except under specially favorable circumstances a certain amount of acidity is developed in these intermediate bodies, and where there is no lime as carbonate to neutralize the acid produced, the activity of the bacteria producing ammonia is greatly hindered. Bacteria cannot flourish when the reaction passes from neutral to acid, and when the acidity becomes marked, the decay processes are left to noxious fungi and moulds, which prefer an acid medium. Carbonate of lime by neutralizing the acid incidentally formed in the decay of soil organic matter, thus stimulates the production of ammonia from the relatively large supply of inactive organic nitrogen which all soils possess.

In the absence of lime, the production of ammonia is hampered by acidity. The evil will be most marked on stiff soils which are badly aerated, and on peaty soils rich in organic matter. These classes of soils, therefore, require heavier applications of lime than sandy soils poor in organic matter or humus.

SECOND STAGE OF NITRIFICATION.

The second stage in the production of soil nitrates, viz., the change from ammonia to nitrate, is also helped by lime. Fig. 2 shows the relative amounts of nitrate produced from ammonia in a soil during 21 days. The experiments from which these results are abstracted were conducted in the laboratory of the Department, and are fully described in the July issue of the *Journal of Agriculture*. No. 1 shows the nitrate formed where hot lime was added to the soil, No. 2 with no addition made to the soil. No. 3 with gypsum added, and No. 4 with carbonate of lime. In the tests free or combined lime was used in equivalent amounts.

On contrasting the cylinders, the different compounds of lime are seen to act in different ways. Gypsum was of but little help to nitrification, carbonate of lime increased it fourfold, while hot lime stopped nitrification altogether. Corroborative results were obtained in a second series of tests lasting 51 days.

The first and second stages of nitrification are alike due to bacteria both of them tend to produce acid, and in both the production of acid inhibits the organisms. The effects of lime upon the second stage may therefore be discussed with reference to the whole process of nitrate production from the organic matter of the soil.

THE BEST FORM OF LIME FOR NITRIFICATION.

The most effective form of lime is the carbonate. The soil organisms cannot endure acid, but neither can they endure free alkali or soluble base as this is present in hot lime. It is those facts which explain the results. Carbonate of lime removes any acid which may be produced, but it is not alkaline in reaction. Gypsum is not alkaline in reaction, but it is unable to neutralize acid substances produced by the germs. Hot lime can neutralize the acids all right, but it is too strongly alkaline to allow the bacteria to work.

In Great Britain the old usage in applying lime was to spread 4 or 5 tons of hot lime to the acre. It was a matter of common knowledge that such applications tended to diminish the yield for the first one or two years. The chief reason was that the land was rendered too alkaline for nitrification to proceed. During the first years the heavy dressing was gradually converted into carbonate of lime by the carbonic acid of the air and soil, and the lime then began to be of benefit.

Such heavy dressings of hot lime are now seldom employed in agriculture, about $\frac{1}{2}$ ton being a usual amount. Comparatively light dressings are quickly converted to carbonate, and in such cases a benefit is expected during the first year. Even light dressings, however, should not be applied with the seed of any crop, but are better put on several months before, in order that the hot lime may be converted into carbonate.

Direct applications of carbonate, as in ground limestone or marl, may be given at any time without danger to nitrification, and, practically speaking, to any amount.

Gypsum has no important action in stimulating the production of nitrates.

Journal of Agriculture, Victoria. [10 Oct., 1912.

OTHER RESULTS OF LIME.

While the effect of lime in liberating plant food from the soil is chiefly seen in an increased production of nitrates, it has also some effect in, rendering available the mineral constituents. This action is most important in connexion with potash and phosphoric acid, for both of which farm crops make considerable demands.

THE LIBERATION OF POTASH.

The effect of lime in liberating potash from insoluble compounds will be chiefly felt in the heavier class of soils. Like lime, potash is a base, and in the less stable hydrated double silicates of potash and alumina (zeolites) present in clay soils, lime and potash tend to change places. The liberation of potash by lime is less important for cereals than for roots and legumes, the latter of which require large amounts of potash. The largely increased yield of lucerne and clover which commonly follows an application of lime may often be traced to the liberation of potash within the soil.

THE LIBERATION OF PHOSPHORIC ACID.

The addition of lime also increases the availability of the soil phosphoric acid, particularly where this exists in union with iron and alumina.

FIG. 3.—SHOWING HOW LIME HELPS INSOLUBLE PHOSPHATES TO ACT.

Fig. 3 represents the stage, at the time of writing (15th September), of some experiments conducted by the Department during the present season. The primary object of these experiments is to test the relative efficiency of phosphates from different sources, but in certain cases lime has been introduced in order to obtain greater variety in the conditions. Pot 5 receives a native lime phosphate, Pot 6 the mineral Wavellite—an aluminium phosphate, and Pot 7 the mineral Vivianite—a phosphate of iron. The phosphates were ground up, but not dissolved. No lime was given in these pots. Pots 25, 26, and 27 received the same phosphates respectively as Pots 5, 6, and 7, but got carbonate of lime in addition. A uniform and sufficient quantity of easily available nitrogen and potash was applied to all the pots, and the phosphoric acid in each case was used in equivalent amounts. Federation wheat is the crop grown.

From the results at the present stage it appears that lime has increased the action of all the insoluble phosphates, but the improvement is more marked with the phosphates of alumina and iron than with the lime phosphate. Much of the phosphoric acid occurring in Victorian soils is combined with iron and alumina, and as there is a general deficiency of available phosphoric acid partly on this account, the liberation of phosphoric acid by lime may have considerable practical moment.

Effect of Lime on Plant Growth.

From the nature of the action which lime exercises in soils it would naturally be expected that the result would be seen in the character of the vegetation.   This is so both in regard to the quantity and quality of the produce.

Heavier Yields.

Fig. 3 represents a stronger growth of wheat following upon the use of lime.   Reference has already been made to the stimulating effect of lime upon lucerne and clover.   Several years ago a few experiments with lime were conducted by the Department in the northern wheat areas. On most of the farms an increase was recorded—this increase ranging from 0.67 to 3.25 bushels per acre.   Unfortunately, these tests lasted for one season only, and it is impossible to test the full effect of lime within one year.

Improved Quality in Roots.

In root and forage crops the effect of lime will often be seen in the better quality of the produce as much as in the quantity.   A few years ago some experiments were conducted in the south of Scotland to determine this point with turnips.*   At each of three farms 2 acres of turnips were grown, 1 acre with acid phosphate (super) and 1 acre with lime and phosphate.   After lifting, the roots were separately fed to equal lots of sheep, which were weighed at the beginning and again at the end of the feeding tests.   The same weight of turnips was given to each lot, and the feeding lasted twelve weeks.   The results were as follows :—

Name of Farm.			Number of Sheep fed.	Relative Feeding Values.	
				Acid-phosphate.	Lime and Phosphate.
Auchneel	..	..	80	100	114½
Awhirk	..	..	80	100	122
Torr ..	..	..	40	100	121

The roots from lime and phosphate were better feeding than the roots from superphosphate alone on every farm.

Profitable Returns from Pasture

In England a number of experiments have been carried out to find how the top-dressing of pastures affected its mutton-producing capacity.† The experiments with lime lasted nine years, and were conducted at three farms.   At each farm two separate blocks were fenced off, and each received 100 lb. phosphoric acid per acre the first year, and again in the fourth year.   In addition one block at each farm got ½ ton ground lime per acre in the first, third, and seventh years.   Each year the blocks carried what sheep they could feed, and the sheep were weighed when put on, and again when taken off.   The following table shows

* Bul. 23, W. of Scot. Agric. Col.   † Supp. Jour. Bd. Agric., Lond. Jan., 1911.

the aggregate gains in live-weight per acre fiom the limed and unlimed blocks at each farm at the end of nine years :—

	Cockle Park.		Sevington.		Ciansley.	
	No Lime.	Lime.	No Lime.	Lime.	No Lime.	Lime.
Mutton produced (9 years)	513 lbs.	713 lbs.	402 lbs.	435 lbs.	169 lbs.	402 lbs..
Increase due to lime ..	..	200 lbs.	..	33 lbs.	..	233 lbs-
Value of increase at 3d. per lb.	..	50s.	..	8s. 3d.	..	58s. 3d..
Cost of lime at 20s. per ton	..	30s.	..	30s.	..	30s.
Profit	..	20s.	..	*21s. 9d.	..	28s. 3d..

* = Loss.

At Cockle Park the lime returned a net profit of 66 per cent. after paying outlay for lime, and from the last yearly returns it appears to

FIG. 4.—LIMED PASTURES WILL OFTEN CARRY MORE SHEEP.

be not nearly exhausted. Sevington is on the chalk, and lime here gave a loss, because it was not required. Cransley shows 94 per cent. profit on expenditure ; here, however, the no-lime block was to some extent prejudicially affected by flooding in 1903.

CLOVER ENCOURAGED

In the Rothamsted pasture experiments the effect of lime has been to increase the percentage of clover in the mixed herbage. Here the relative value of the herbage is improved through a change in its botanical composition. Clovers have a higher nutritive value than grass.

LIME AND SORREL.

Some plants grow well on an acid soil. Such plants are always more or less worthless for stock. Sorrel and docks are acid-loving plants. A good application of lime is the surest method of eradicating them, and encouraging the kind of plants the farmer wants.

PRECAUTIONS IN USING LIME.

This article deals with the application of lime to land. We shall now conclude by drawing attention to certain precautions which should be observed in the use of lime.

Sufficient Phosphates Essential.

Lime will not give a good result on land which is too poor in available phosphoric acid.   This may occur very frequently.   Where lime is used, phosphates should be used just as usual.   On pasture land the need for lime cannot be determined until it has been tried with, as well as without, phosphates.   In Victoria lime will seldom fail to act because of a deficiency of potash.

Wet Land must first be Drained

It is no use applying lime to land that is swampy and requires draining.   On wet land, owing to the exclusion of air, the production of soil acids is too great for the land to be sweetened by ordinary applications of lime.   Drainage by admitting air removes the cause of extreme acidity, and lime can only remove the effect.   To continue liming wet soil in order to keep it sweet is like trying to keep a leaking bucket full of water.

Lime Diminishes Soil Humus.

An important constituent in a soil is the organic matter or humus which it contains.   Soil humus is important in that it increases the water-holding capacity of a soil, opens up stiff clays, and provided lime is present has a binding action on sands.   In its decay it also furnishes nitrates directly from itself, and mineral constituents of plant food, both directly and also indirectly from the fine rock masses of the soil.   Good soils are always well supplied with organic matters, and market gardeners rightly place great confidence in farm-yard manure because it forms humus.

Lime hastens the decay of the soil organic matter.   While fresh vegetable residues as in stubbles, green manures and, where practicable, farm-yard manure should be returned to cultivated land in any case, lime increases the necessity of doing so.   The farmer who neglects this matter is living upon his capital in so far as his land will steadily deteriorate under continued cropping.   If he still neglects it after using lime he will be living upon his capital more quickly than ever.

Lime may help to add Humus.

But while lime increases the need for returning fresh vegetable matters to the soil, it also makes the operation more easy.   It may do so in several ways   During the year of pasture. which is commonly allowed in the wheat areas between successive crops, the growth of clover and trefoil, where these are indigenous to the soil, will be stimulated.   Lime will also assist in giving a good stand of rape and rye, but particularly of vetches where these can be sown in autumn for feeding or ploughing-in in spring before the land dries out.   Phosphate should be used with those catch crops.   Then, again, if the use of lime brings the determination to plough in stubbles, instead of burning while preparing land for fallow, the lime will be a profitable investment.   Such ploughing should be overtaken early, so that in the damp soil the lime will help the stubble to rot.   Lime increases alike the practical feasibility, and the need, of returning fresh organic matter to the land.

When is Lime Required.

It is by the combined use of lime and organic or green manures that the regeneration of worn-out land will most frequently be accomplished. As to the question of whether any particular piece of land requires lime use may be made of the chemical analysis of the soil, or of the litmus

test, both of which have been described.   As a guide each has its uses
and its limitations, but in most cases the question can best be decided on
the spot.   To the practised eye the colour of the vegetation may often
indicate acid soil conditions, and here lime is required.   Such a result,
however, may simply be due to an excessively wet season, and in this case
and in all others where the need for lime is suspected the surest test is
to try.   For this purpose trial strips should be treated with lime at
different parts of the farm, and the situation of these plots should be
indicated by suitable marks.

Where the trial applications are made on grass land too much attention should not be paid to the bulk of herbage produced, as stock usually
prefer limed pasture, and eat it more closely down.

Summary and Conclusions.

1. Lime tends to leave the surface soil through various channels, and
fresh applications become necessary to maintain fertility.

2. Carbonate of lime is the best form of lime for the soil.

3. Burnt and slaked lime are rapidly changed to carbonate when
they are applied to land.

4. The rate at which lime acts depends on its fineness of division.

5. Lime, but especially hot lime, has a good effect upon the mechanical
condition of stiff clays.

6. Gypsum also coagulates clay, but it has not the beneficial action
of lime in other directions.

7. Lime greatly hastens the production of nitrates.

8. It has a good effect in liberating potash and phosphoric acid,
especially when the latter is combined with iron or alumina.

9. Where required by soil, lime produces larger crops.

10. It produces root crops, which are of greater feeding value per ton.

11. It may often be a profitable application to grass land

12. Lime kills sorrel, docks, and other acid-loving weeds.

13. It is specially stimulating to lucerne, clovers, and leguminous
plants.

14. Lime will not act if phosphates are deficient.

15. It increases the need, everywhere present, of ploughing in green
manures or stubbles.

16. It facilitates this operation.

17. The surest method of determining the need for lime is to dress
trial strips and await results.

VII.

THE USE OF LIME IN VICTORIAN VINEYARDS.

By François de Castella, Government Viticulturist.

The object of the present article is to briefly set out the reasons which
make it logical to anticipate that our vine-growing industry will benefit
quite as much as any other branch of our agriculture, from the judicious
application of lime to the soil.   As will be shown presently, the soils of
most of our vine-growing districts have a low lime contents.   Though
those of our vignerons who have planted their vines properly and cultivated them carefully have usually obtained profitable results, the progressive grower must ever strive to do better than he has done in the past,
and there appears every reason to anticipate that in the supplementing

of the lime content of soils lies an easy way of bringing about a very considerable improvement.

The application of lime to the soil of a vineyard may be considered from two distinct points of view, viz., as supplying a plant food and as affecting soil improvement.

LIME AS A PLANT FOOD.

The vine, like all other plants, demands a certain quantity of lime for its normal and healthy growth. Lime is, in other words, an essential plant food in the same way that nitrogen, phosphoric acid, and potash are. Notwithstanding its vital importance, however, it is a noteworthy fact that this phase of the question is scarcely ever considered by continental writers on vineyard manuring. Its utility as a soil improver is frequently mentioned; but its manurial value, or value as a plant food, the yearly removals of which must be returned to the soil, if production is to be maintained, receives no consideration whatever.

Perhaps the explanation is that, as compared with the other three plant foods, lime is usually present in such enormous quantities in European soils that there is no possibility of its ever being exhausted; under such conditions it cannot present any interest from a strictly manurial stand-point.

So generally rich in lime are the vine soils of France that excess of this constituent was, in the early days of reconstitution, a very frequent cause of non-success, until the introduction of stocks less sensitive to lime in excess than those first tried.

Nevertheless, the quantity of lime annually removed from each acre of vineyard is considerable. Though it naturally varies a good deal from one locality to another, according to yield, variety, climate, &c., the figures arrived at by Rousseau and Chappaz, as the result of their investigations in the Chablis district of France, will give some idea of the annual lime requirements of the vine as compared with the other plant food materials usually taken into account. The yield being at the rate of 320 gallons per acre, requirements would be similar to those of Victorian vineyards—

Fertilizing Substances Absorbed per Acre.

—					Nitrogen.	Phosphoric Acid.	Potash.	Lime.
					lbs.	lbs.	lbs.	lbs.
Dry leaves	..	..	lbs.	933·01	16·626	2·351	8·220	55·981
Dry prunings	..	..	,,	904·72	5·121	1·240	6·360	12·666
Marc	..	..	,,	·345·14	5·716	1·653	6·668	5·004
Wine	..	..	gals.	310·47	·833	·200	2·174	·345
Lees	..	..	,,	9·25	·584	·139	·699	1·114
					28·880	5·583	24·121	75·110

* Extract from " Etude sur le Vignoble de Chablis." By E. Rousseaux and G. Chappaz. *Revue de Vitioulture*, 23rd February, 1905.

From this table it will be seen that the vine extracts more of lime than of all the other plant food elements put together, and nearly three times as much lime as potash. It is true that the bulk of the lime is contained in the leaves; these, however, are largely blown away by the wind, only a small proportion returning to the soil.

The most striking difference between the soils of the greater part of Victoria and those of France, Spain, &c., is the low lime content of the former, and the very considerable quantity of it present in the latter. In European vineyards, except in a few isolated districts, it is rare to find a soil containing less than 5 per cent. of lime.   In Victoria, if we except the Wimmera, the Mallee, Geelong, and a few parts where vines are not extensively grown, it is unusual to find a soil containing 1 per cent. of lime, whilst the great majority contain less than .1 per cent.

Many of our vineyards are in auriferous country, and belong, geologically, to the silurian backbone of the State.   Such hilly formations, as well as the sedimentary valley soils resulting from their decomposition, are alike poor in lime.   So poor are they in this element that it is reasonable to question whether, in many Victorian vineyards, lime may not possess a real manurial value which it is not recognised as having under European conditions.

Lime Contents of Victorian Vineyard Soils.

Thanks to the co-operation of the Chemist for Agriculture, a good many analyses of typical vineyard soils have been made during the past three years.   On examining these it is possible to divide that portion of the State comprised between the main Dividing Range and the Murray River, which contains fully 95 per cent, of the vineyards of Victoria, into two distinct regions; in one of these the soil is remarkably poor in lime, whilst in the other this element is very plentiful.

The low lime region is of very considerable extent, and, if Mildura (in the high lime region) be excluded, it contains 92 per cent. of the remaining vineyards of the State.   It is separated from the high lime region by a somewhat irregular line from the junction of the Murray and Goulburn Rivers, near Echuca, to the Grampian Mountains.   As might be expected, the line of demarcation is not well defined, and in its vicinity soils of high, medium, and low lime contents are somewhat mixed up.

The following table contains analyses of typical vineyard soils throughout this extensive area; the North-East, Goulburn Valley, and Great Western being represented, as well as Whitfield, which is typical of the lower levels of the main Dividing Range:—

TABLE A.—Low Lime Region.

—	Nitrogen.	Phosphoric Acid.	Potash.	Lime.	Magnesia.
	Per cent.	Per cent.	Per cent.	Per cent.	Per cent.
Rutherglen. Hillside—					
1A Surface to 6 inches	·075	·057	·220	·132	·197
1B Subsoil, 6 to 15 inches	·064	·051	·255	·084	·223
1C „ 15 to 24 „	·061	·065	·281	·096	·267
Flat near Brown's Plains—					
2A Surface to 11 inches	·092	·083	·193	·136	·166
2B Subsoil, 11 to 24 inches	·050	·039	·239	·082	·196
Viticultural College Flat—					
3A Surface to 8 inches	·039	·022	·135	·080	·152
3B Subsoil, 8 to 14 inches	·040	·022	·154	·086	·185
3C „ 14 to 20 „	·040	·024	·335	·124	·263
3D „ 20 to 26 „	·030	·024	·350	·125	·367
Wahgunyah (sandhill soil)—					
4A Surface to 12 inches	·043	·043	·120	·099	·212
4B Subsoil, 12 to 24 inches	·028	·038	·134	·076	·213
4C „ 24 to 36 „	·019	·037	·140	·070	·260

TABLE A.—LOW LIME REGION—continued.

		Nitrogen	Phosphoric Acid	Potash.	Lime.	Magnesia.
	Whitfield.	Per cent.	Per cent.	Per cent.	Per cent.	Per cent.
5A	Surface to 12 inches ..	·137	·066	·289	**·080**	·180
5B	Subsoil, 12 to 24 inches ..	·050	·047	·238	·024	·125
	Goulburn Valley.					
	Shepparton Irrigation Settlement (loamy clay soil)—					
6A	Surface to 8 inches ..	·048	·023	·120	**·096**	·174
6B	Subsoil, 8 to 20 inches ..	·033	·026	·299	·276	·273
6C	,, 20 to 26 ,, ..	·028	·027	·334	·316	·697
	Tatura (stiff clay soil)—					
7A	Surface to 5 inches ..	·095	·068	·442	·308	—
7B	Subsoil, 5 to 12 inches ..	·055	·052	·626	·208	—
7C	,, 12 to 20 ,, ..	·042	·041	·656	·204	—
	Cobram (sand hill soil)—					
8A	Surface to 7 inches ..	·034	·023	·147	·132	·155
8B	Subsoil, 7 to 18 inches ..	·014	·013	·140	·096	·134
8C	,, 18 to 30 ,, ..	·011	·018	·134	·078	·138
	Tabilk (fairly sandy soil)—					
9A	Surface to 12 inches ..	·084	·067	·308	·182	·210
9B	Subsoil, 12 to 24 inches ..	·067	·060	·201	·118	·161
9C	,, 24 to 36 ,, ..	·050	·054	·161	·156	·277
9D	,, 36 to 48 ,, ..	·047	·056	·161	·096	·241
	Dookie (red soil)—					
10A	Surface	·095	·043	·319	**·156**	—
10B	Subsoil	·056	·043	·477	·248	—
	Cosgrove (exceptional lime soil)—					
11A	Surface	·238	·045	·386	**1·960**	—
11B	Subsoil	·210	·153	·379	13·240	—
	Great Western.					
12A	Surface to 7½ inches ..	·022	·012	·056	**·056**	·036
12B	Subsoil, 7½ to 14½ inches ..	·017	·013	·065	·048	·070
12C	,, 14½ to 20 ,, ..	·041	·022	·214	·108	·220
	Rhymney—					
13A	Surface to 8 inches	·106	·046	·108	**·250**	·290
13B	Subsoil, 8 to 18 inches ..	·078	·049	·088	·190	·349
13C	,, 18 to 25 ,, ..	·058	·055	·133	·202	·402
13D	,, 25 to 30 ,, ..	·045	·054	·258	·322	·544

An examination of Table A shows clearly the remarkable deficiency of lime which characterizes the soils of this large portion of the State. The great majority of the samples analyzed contain twice as much potash as lime. Isolated exceptions are, of course, to be met with occasionally, such as No. 11 A and B, at Cosgrove, near Dookie, which show up to 13 per cent. of lime in the subsoil. This is a local lime deposit of very limited area. Such cases are rare, and do not affect the main contention, that our silurian soils and the soils of valleys resulting from the decomposition of silurian formations are invariably poor in lime.

It is worthy of note that No. 13 A, B, C, and D, one of the few in which lime exceeds potash, is the heaviest bearing vineyard in the Great Western and Rhymney districts. It was, in fact, its excellent yields which led to the samples being taken for analysis.

Between the low and high lime regions there exists an intermediate zone shown in Table B in which, as yet, there are few vineyards. The following analyses show a marked increase in lime, the percentage of which slightly exceeds that of potash :—

TABLE B.—INTERMEDIATE LIME REGION.

—	Nitrogen.	Phosphoric Acid.	Potash.	Lime.	Magnesia.
	Per cent.	Per cent.	Per cent.	Per cent.	Per cent.
Bamawm.					
Pine ridge country—					
14A Surface to 12 inches ..	·042	·024	·089	·174	·189
14B Subsoil, 12 to 24 inches ..	·028	·027	·292	·214	·318
Medium soil—					
15A Surface to 9 inches	·045	·026	·199	·260	·245
15B Subsoil, 9 to 15 inches ..	·025	·026	·297	·280	·464
15C ,, 15 to 24 ,, ..	·022	·026	·509	·520	·490
Swan Hill.					
Red soil—					
16A Surface	·017	·056	·260	·466	·814
16B Subsoil	·014	·060	·307	·418	1·189
Black soil—					
17A Surface to 7 inches ..	·165	·048	·349	·390	·445
17B Subsoil, 7 to 18 inches ..	·070	·035	·335	·414	·576

In striking contrast with the soils of tables A and B are those of the Mallee and Wimmera districts shown in Table C—

TABLE C.—HIGH LIME REGION.

—	Nitrogen.	Phosphoric Acid.	Potash.	Lime.	Magnesia.
	Per cent.	Per cent.	Per cent.	Per cent.	Per cent.
Nyah.					
Mallee, pine, and honey-suckle—					
18A Surface to 10 inches ..	·059	·026	·403	·348	·487
18B Subsoil, 10 to 20 inches ..	·037	·025	·535	1·836	·769
18C ,, 20 to 30 ,, ..	·028	·027	·756	6·450	1·095
Wimmera.					
Longerenong (red soil)—					
19A Surface	·154	·026	·617	·213	·461
19B Subsoil	·118	·026	·960	·253	·620
Longerenong (black soil)—					
20A Surface	·151	·033	1·042	3·580	·137
20B Subsoil	·134	·045	1·070	4·300	·076
Mildura.					
Large Mallee—					
21A Soil	·069	·065	·529	3·500	—
21B Subsoil	·046	·051	·488	8·610	—
Blue Bush—					
22A Soil	·071	·069	·826	·820	—
22B Subsoil	·046	·050	·676	9·960	—
Murray pine—					
23A Soil	·022	·020	·261	·808	—
23B Subsoil	·024	·019	·293	5·480	—
Blue bush country—					
24A Surface to 8 inches ..	·089	·065	·571	9·160	·990
24B Subsoil, 8 to 22 inches ..	·058	·048	·497	19·360	1·150
24C ,, 22 to 36 ,, ..	.053	.045	.575	17·280	1.620

In this part of the State lime is almost everywhere present in abundance. Occasional exceptions, such as No. 19 A and B, where the potash exceeds the lime, are rare, and in a general way the soils of the Mallee and Wimmera contain enormous quantities of lime. They are in this respect similar to the bulk of European vine soils. Table C is given for the purpose of showing, by comparison, how very deficient in lime are the soils of table A, and that it is essentially logical to expect that the correction of this defect by liberal lime dressings cannot fail to have very beneficial results.*

South of the Dividing Range but few samples of soils have been submitted for analysis by the writer. Some of these reveal lime deficiency similar to that shown in table A. At Geelong, in many parts of the south-western district, and of Gippsland calcareous formations occur. It is scarcely necessary to point out the value of soil analysis in this connexion.

LIME AND MAGNESIA.

The arguments so far adduced in favour of the application of lime are based on the natural deficiency of this element in the soil. The analyses quoted above reveal another reason why such application should prove beneficial, viz., on account of the large quantity of magnesia many of our soils contain. Authorities on soils are agreed that it is desirable for lime to be present in greater quantity than magnesia. *Hilgard* is emphatic on the point—

"Soils containing large proportions of magnesia generally are found to be unthrifty, the lands so constituted being frequently designated as 'barrens.' Lowe finds that certain proportions of lime to magnesia must be preserved if production is to be satisfactory, the proportion varying with different plants, some of which (*e.g.*, oats) will do well when the proportion of lime to magnesia is as 1 to 1, while others require that that ratio should be as 2 or 3 is to 1, to secure best results. In general it is best that lime should exceed magnesia in amount." And again—

"In the case of soils containing much magnesia the proper proportion between it and lime may easily be disturbed by the greater ease with which lime carbonate is carried away by carbonated water into the subsoil, thus leaving the magnesia in undesirable excess in the surface soil. Hence the great advantage of having in a soil, from the outset, an ample proportion of lime. From this point of view alone, then, the analytical determination of lime and magnesia in soils is of high practical value."

On reference to table A it will be seen that the soils of the low lime region contain, very generally, from two to three times as much magnesia as lime. The correction of this defect by applications of lime appears to be most desirable.

LIME AS A POTASH LIBERATOR.

The whole of the analyses quoted above show that our vine soils usually contain a satisfactory proportion of potash. Some are exceedingly rich in this element, which, in view of the considerable quantities removed annually, in the shape of cream of tartar, is of great importance in viticulture.

---

* In the viticultural districts of France where lime is deficient excellent results follow its application to the soil. According to Guillon, for instance, "Granitic soils are nearly always rich in potash, but the majority, excepting those with calcic feldspar, are almost completely devoid of lime, and only become fertile if this element is brought to them in the course of soil improvement (*amendments*)." J. M. Guillon, Etude Générale de la Vigne, p. 349.

The question arises: Is this potash readily available? In the case of the soils of table A this appears doubtful. In view of the low lime contents a large proportion of the potash is probably held in zeolitic and other combinations, largely in the shape of double silicates. From such somewhat loose combination lime is able to displace potash. An application of lime is consequently equivalent to an application of potash, and when the very considerable difference in price in favour of the lime is taken into account, this means of unlocking the latent potash supplies, is thus, not only desirable, but financially easy. Such theoretical considerations receive practical confirmation in a striking manner in parts of the Goulburn Valley, where several growers are satisfied that they have obtained greater benefit from the application of lime than potash.

The Correction of Acidity.

Acidity or sourness is well known to be an undesirable condition in a soil; and yet very many Victorian soils present an acid reaction. The

Looking towards Hopkins River. The fringing sand dunes contain 80 per cent. calcium carbonate. Cross on the left shows position of railway line.

whole of the soils of which analyses are given in table A are more or less acid, with the exception of No. 11; on the other hand those of table B are neutral or alkaline, whilst those of table C are distinctly alkaline. Lime poverty and acidity are thus directly connected. Lime, being strongly alkaline, is a direct corrective of soil acidity as well as being the cheapest obtainable. Its use for this reason alone is most desirable in all soils, presenting the defect of an acid reaction.

Lime as a Soil Improver.

In addition to the chemical actions mentioned above, lime is capable of bringing about considerable physical improvement, especially in soils containing much clay. It flocculates or curdles this substance, thereby rendering soils containing it in considerable proportion more friable and more easy to work.

With the exception of sandy formations, such as the pine ridges occurring at intervals throughout Northern Victoria, the soils, and more especially the subsoils of the State, are of a clayey nature, and are capable of being much improved by the application of lime. A striking instance of this case may be given.   Mr. H. E. Ireland, of St. Leonard's vineyard, near Wahgunyah, planted with vines a block of land on which were a couple of small patches of unusually stiff land on which reeds grew.   Instead of leaving these patches unplanted, Mr. Ireland decided to attempt their correction by the use of lime.   Gypsum (sulphate of lime) was the form used; this was applied at the rate of about 5 tons per acre, about three years ago.   The result was entirely satisfactory, and at the present time these patches are completely transformed.   From on almost hopelessly stiff clay, which seemed unfit to grow vines, they have been converted into good friable soil, quite equal to the rest of the block.   The dressing was no doubt a very heavy one, but the cost of such could easily be borne in the case of a permanent and profitable culture, such as that of the vine.   The case was a rather exceptional one, and in view of the apparently intractable nature of the clay patches, an heroic dose was judged necessary.   Very much lighter applications would probably be ample in most clay soils.

The application of lime as a soil improver is often found advantageous in French vine soils, notwithstanding their being already well supplied. In those of our Victorian soils which are deficient in lime it is surely reasonable to look for far greater benefit.

Different Forms of Lime.

Lime may be applied to the soil in several distinct forms, each of which has its advantages and defects, and may be well suited or otherwise to any given case.   The three principal forms are—

1. Lime properly so called, or burnt lime. whether " quick " or " slaked."
2. Ground limestone or lime carbonate.
3. Gypsum or lime sulphate.

It must be remembered that the phosphatic manures in general use contain much lime; superphosphate contains nearly half its weight of lime sulphate, whilst Thomas' phosphate (basic slag) contains even more lime, but combined in a different form.

The first is the most concentrated, a given weight of burnt lime containing more lime (pure calcium oxide) than any other form; hence, at anything like equal price it is also the most economical, both as regards cost of the lime unit and carriage.   Being strongly alkaline it immediately neutralizes soil acidity, but being also caustic it is rather severe on the organic matter (humus) of the soil; for the latter reason the rate of application should not exceed half a ton per acre.   Used in conjunction with green manuring, to supply organic matter, we have in lime a most powerful means of increasing the fertility of our vineyards.

Ground limestone, containing considerably less calcium oxide than burnt lime. is a less economical form.   It parts readily with its carbonic acid in acid soils, and is therefore well suited for their neutralization.   Since it is not in any way caustic it may be supplied in almost any quantity without affecting humus.   Insolubility is its chief defect. but this is also shared by burnt lime, which rapidly becomes carbonated on exposure to the air.

Gypsum possesses undoubted good qualities as well as serious drawbacks.   A great part of its weight being made up of sulphuric acid and water, the unit cost of lime in this form is very high.   It is a neutral salt. and as such it is valueless for the correction of acid soils.   On the other hand its solubility is much greater than that of the carbonate (166 times); its dissemination throughout the soil is therefore more rapid. every shower carrying a certain quantity further into the subsoil. As a source of lime, where this element is deficient, as a potash liberator and as a soil improver, its efficiency is unquestionable. Its successful use in the latter connexion, at St. Leonard's vineyard. has already been mentioned. Gypsum is very highly thought of in France, where it enters into all the most popular vine manure formulas. Were it not for its high cost. perhaps even in spite of it, it would seem to merit further trial in our vineyards. Possibly a mixture of lime and gypsum, the former on account of alkalinity and cheapness. and the latter owing to its greater solubility, may prove the most suitable form for vinevard use

PRACTICAL RESULTS.

It is to be regretted that experiments to practically test the influence of lime as a means of increasing yield have not yet been carried out ; at least. not on a sufficient scale to give definite information. It is true that in some experiments conducted by the writer both lime and gypsum have been applied in conjunction with otherwise complete manures. In a general way the plots receiving either of these substances have yielded better crops than those to which complete manures without lime in any quantity were applied. Owing to the unevenness of the plots and their small number, the information, so far, is less definite than one could wish. Nor have the experiments been in force for a sufficient time. In vineyard manuring results are not so immediate as in the case of an annual crop.

Reference must be here made to the numerous practical growers who, as the result of their past experience of lime application, are quite convinced on the subject, and have become strong advocates of the practice.

Further experiments, in order to practically test the application of lime in its different forms, are to be shortly undertaken. It is confidently expected that the results will confirm the theoretical considerations outlined above, and that they will be in complete accordance with the experience of those progressive growers who already applied lime extensively to their vineyards.

VIII.

LIME FOR TOBACCO LAND.

By Temple A. J. Smith.

The value of lime for soils in which tobacco is produced has not yet been sufficiently recognised by growers in Victoria. Most of the land used for this purpose has been shown by analysis to be deficient in lime, and even where the land is known to have a fair percentage, applications, especially in some new form, have advantageous results.

The ash of the tobacco plant contains large proportionate amounts of lime and potash, with a low percentage of phosphoric acid, as the following figures show, viz. :—

Nitrogen	...	...	... 4.12
Potash	...	...	... 6.20
Phosphoric acid		...	... .62
Lime	...	...	... 5.50
Magnesia	...	...	... 1.67

Tobacco is evidently largely dependent on lime as a food, and for that reason alone a supply should be provided where it is known a deficiency exists. It is also necessary that considerably more than is actually required by the crop be present, as the period of growth is short, " being from twelve to twenty weeks," to enable the tobacco to obtain a full supply.

A crop of Connecticut seed leaf from 1 acre, including stalks and leaves, weighing 4,075 lbs. in all, takes from the soil :—

138 lbs. of potash.
94 lbs. of lime.
97 lbs. of nitrogen.
16 lbs. of phosphoric acid.
30 lbs. of magnesia.

The application of lime, apart from its value as a food in itself, is of even greater importance in regard to its effect in releasing and indirectly supplying potash and nitrogen for the crop's benefit. As the analysis shows that potash is the element of food taken in the greatest quantity from the soil, and, as is well known, lime has the effect of liberating and making available potash for the quickly growing crop, it is evident that for this purpose dressings of lime should be applied.

Potash in sufficient quantity is not only necessary to tobacco to insure a heavy yield, but its influence on the quality of the leaf is highly beneficial, counteracting the bad effect on the combustion or burn of tobacco caused by an excess of magnesia or chlorine in the soil. Lime also assists in supplying nitrogen indirectly, and at a greater rate, owing to its influence on nitrification, and the temperature of the soil is slightly increased, an important matter in regard to tobacco.

The mechanical effect of lime on the soil in relation to tobacco-growing is especially valuable. All tobaccoes thrive best, and are of better quality, when produced from free and well aerated soils, consequently the flocculating power of lime on those soils, liable to set closely, renders them more open and friable, bringing about the desired result.

Its effect on sour soils is highly beneficial in counteracting acidity, and in this way, not only inducing a better growth of the crop, but materially influencing the curing processes and fermentation later on in the sheds. this being due to the effect of the alkali supplied to the plant, which, if deficient in quantity, interferes with the development and action of the enzyme, or ferment, through whose agency the cure and fermentation of the leaf is perfected.

An application of lime will often save labour and loss from insect pests, killing the larvæ of cutworms, caterpillars, grasshoppers, &c. It is likewise to some extent a fungicide, and though not a cure for the disease known as blue mould, acts more or less as a preventive. Weeds of the most troublesome kind, such as sorrel, will not grow where lime is plentiful in the soil, another important consideration in tobacco-growing, where weeds must be kept out of the plot. Clovers and trefoils always grow more pro-fusely after liming practices are adopted, and very beneficial results follow. Tobacco is, as a rule, harvested in the early autumn, and if the trefoils grow well during the winter, they act as a catch rotation crop, sup-plying humus to the soil, and releasing potash and phosphoric acid, in addition to storing up nitrogen in the soluble form. Experience proves that tobacco in Victoria, and elsewhere, when grown in soils containing large amounts of lime, matures from four to eight weeks earlier than when grown in sour land. Quickly-grown tobacco leaf is generally of better quality, and naturally labour is saved in keeping down weeds and insect pests, and the risk of loss by frost, hail, &c., diminished.

The different forms of lime procurable have somewhat different effects on tobacco soils. Where heavy swamp land or peaty soils are cultivated, the use of builders' lime, "burnt lime," will be found most advantageous. Too much rough, organic matter in the shape of undecomposed roots, weeds, &c., has the effect of causing the tobacco to grow rank, and with too great a nicotine content. The builders' lime applied at the rate of from 5 cwt. to 10 cwt. per acre in the autumn will assist in decomposing this excess of vegetable matter, and render the soil sweeter and better fitted to produce good quality leaf. On clay or silty soils, the burnt lime also is desirable, as it improves the temperature in cold soils, and makes them more friable and open. On sandy loams, gypsum, "sulphate of lime," gives good results, as also on chocolate soils; larger amounts, however, should be used, from 10 cwt. to 2 tons, as its effects are not so pronounced as those of the burnt lime. In all soils short of humus, gypsum is safer to use than burnt lime, not having the caustic properties, and consequently not destroying the vegetable matter to the same extent.

Ground limestone is a valuable form of lime for tobacco land, and is more easily handled and applied than burnt lime. At the price, it will be found no more expensive than burnt lime, although it is necessary to use about twice the amount to obtain equal results; it is also slower in its effects.

On the whole, I am of opinion that lime for tobacco land is of more importance in Victoria, especially in the mountainous districts, than any other treatment, and that it would pay to use it. I have no doubt what-ever a larger crop of better quality would pay the cost of purchase and application of, say, 10 cwt. per acre, twice over in one year, and the effect of the lime would be felt over three years at least. For the seed-beds in which tobacco plants are raised, the use of lime as an insect and weed destroyer would be found useful, but the application should be made at least a month or six weeks before the seed is sown. Some of the best tobacco leaf produced in America is grown on limestone country, contain-ing as high as 17 per cent. lime, while it is used on all soils in which lime is deficient.

IX.

THE USE OF LIME IN POTATO CULTURE.

By Geo. Seymour, Potato Expert.

The use of lime in potato culture has not hitherto received much attention from the growers of this State. The reason generally assigned for this is that the cost of freight, added to that of the lime, makes it very expensive.

Though the potato crop removes a comparatively small quantity of lime from the soil, the haulm, like other plants, requires a considerable quantity. It is generally recognised that to have a satisfactory crop of tubers, we must have a vigorous and well developed plant, and there can be little doubt that the use of lime, in some soils, would contribute largely to that vigorous growth of the plant which results in an increased yield.

The following figures will show the difference in the quantities of lime per acre removed by a six-ton crop of potatoes and the haulm of the crop—

Potatoes.	Lime Removed per Acre.		
	Tubers.	Haulm.	Total.
6 tons per acre ..	2·9 lbs.	22·7 lbs.	25·6 lbs.

Taking the average of the Victorian crop of potatoes at 3 tons per acre the total loss would be nearly 13 lbs. per acre. This, it must be remembered, is often from a soil already deficient in lime, so that growers would do well to test the value of the use of lime on their potato fields.

The benefits of lime may be stated as follows:—

1. It acts as plant food.
2. It corrects the acidity of the soil. causing coarse vegetation to give place to more nutritious plants and discourages the growth of sorrel.
3. It acts rapidly on the organic matter in the soil, and prepares it for plant food by liberating the nitrogen which it contains.
4. It decomposes the dormant mineral matter of the soil, especially clay soil.
5. It improves the physical condition of heavy clay lands.

This Department carried out some experiments on the 5-acre forage fields in the seasons 1905/6 and 1906/7, the results of which are given in the table below. The soils embraced the following—Heavy clay soil, at Carrum ; clay loam. of a gravelly nature. at Digger's Rest ; peat, drained swamp. at South Bunyip ; heavy clay soil, at Turkeith (Colac).

The above soils were all, more or less, benefited by a dressing of 5 cwt. per acre. whilst the rich volcanic soil, at Illowa, and the light volcanic soil, at Kilmore, showed a decreased return, but looking at the returns from the peaty and heavy clay soils it will be seen that even so moderate a dressing as 5 cwt. proved beneficial. The action of lime on the peaty soil of the drained swamp at Bunyip South, in 1905/6, was repeated in a more emphatic manner in the 1906/7 operations with an increase to 12 cwt. per acre over the unlimed section. Its action was equally satisfactory in the clay loam at Digger's Rest, also in the stiff, heavy clays at the widely separated centres of Carrum and Turkeith, near Colac. The soils at the two latter places being almost identical.

The results of these experiments go to show that lime may be used with advantage to the potato crop on the soils which contain abundance of organic matter, such as the peaty soils of drained swamps and the heavy clay land, whilst it may do harm on the lighter soils.

District.	Class of Soil.	5 cwt. Lime.			No Lime.			+ −	Increase. Decrease.			Season.
		t.	c.	q.	t.	c.	q.		t.	c.	q.	
Digger's Rest ..	Gravelly clay loam	1	0	0	0	16	0	+	0	4	0	1905–6
Digger's Rest ..	Gravelly clay loam	0	16	0	0	12	0	+	0	4	0	1906–7
Whittlesea ..	Light loam ..	1	2	0	1	2	0	..				1905–6
Yarram ..	Light loam ..	0	10	0	0	12	0	−	0	2	0	1905–6
Bunyip South ..	Peat	2	2	0	1	18	0	+	0	4	0	1905–6
Bunyip South ..	Peat ..	3	4	0	2	12	0	+	0	12	0	1906–7
Condah ..	Gravelly loam volcanic soil	4	2	0	4	4	0	−	0	2	0	1905–6
Carrum ..	Heavy clay ..	4	18	0	4	8	0	+	0	10	0	1905–6
Turkeith ..	Heavy clay ..	2	4	0	1	18	0	+	0	6	0	1906–7
Illowa ..	Rich volcanic ..	3	16	0	4	0	0	−	0	4	0	1905–6
Kilmore ..	Light volcanic ..	4	4	0	4	16	0	−	0	12	0	1906–7

X.

LIME FOR ORCHARDS.

By P. J. Carmody, Chief Orchard Supervisor.

When it is considered that the average crop of fruit requires more plant food for its development than an average crop of wheat, and, moreover, that the fruit demands the same soil constituents year after year, the necessity for a sweet and favorable medium for root pasturage is apparent; and as no other application is at all comparable to the influence of lime for this purpose, its frequent use is urgently required. It is a matter of common observation that the fruit-buds of trees grown on sour soils are of a weak or indefinite character, while the bark is harsh and dry in appearance. and the growth more or less stunted. Under such conditions it is practically impossible to develop trees on the most profitable lines without first correcting soil acidity by the free use of lime in the same manner as requires to be adopted for other farm crops.

In many parts of the State insufficient attention has been given to this feature of soil management in the orchards. Particularly is this the case where fruit is grown on heavy clay soils. In these soils fruit trees grow through a lengthy period, so that a considerable quantity of immature wood is produced to the detriment of subsequent crops of fruit. Measures have not hitherto been adopted to definitely determine the actual effect of lime on the different parts of the tree; but investigations in other countries show that on soils rich in lime the wood is matured earlier and the fruit-buds are more stocky and robust than is the case with trees grown on soils deficient in lime. This is very apparent to any one acquainted with the fruit areas of many parts of Gippsland and other places in Southern Victoria, and one is struck with the unusual prominence or length of the fruit-buds, the relative distance between the nodes, and the softness of the wood in these districts when compared with the same varieties grown in fruit centres known to possess lime in abundance.

It may not, however, be correct to assign these differences solely to the effect of lime, as other soil constituents bear an important part on the character of the tree and its fruit-buds, particularly potash. It is generally recognised that the trees are not so manageable nor so prolific in bearing in soils where lime is deficient, and growers who have rectified this have had excellent results, though as artificial fertilizers were subsequently applied the same year, the relative value of the lime could not be ascertained. Though lime plays an important part in the apple and pear tree, it is in the stone fruits that its value is most apparent. It is a familiar fact that in soils rich in lime the stone fruits set their crops well, and are not so prone to cast off their fruit at the period of "stoning" as is otherwise the case. Where trees are making extensive wood growth with abundant foliage there is but little doubt that the application of lime at the rate of 7 to 8 cwt. to the acre would be of pronounced benefit.

No class of fruit is more eloquent in its request for specific soil constituents than the citrus. A light yellowish appearance of the leaves demands an application of nitrogenous manures, whilst the want of phosphoric acid is evidenced by many of the light laterals dying off. In a soil where lime is abundant the thinness of the rind, the deep colour and delicate aroma of the fruit are special features of the orange, so that beneficial effects are obtained by the use of lime in almost all classes of fruit.

ARTIFICIAL MANURES ACT, No. 2274.

Section 14.

NOTICE TO MANUFACTURERS AND IMPORTERS OF ARTIFICIAL MANURES.

Applications for registration of brands of all manures which are intended for sale during the ensuing season must, with declarations and regulation fees, be lodged with the Secretary for Agriculture on or before the 1st November.

SPRING CHEDDAR CHEESE-MAKING.

By G. C. Sawers, Cheese Expert.

As the season approaches for the making of cheese, it is important to overhaul the buildings, and have the interior, plant, &c., thoroughly renovated and brought up to date with modern utensils. Provision should be made for the supply of clean, sweet milk, perfect samples of which in such quantities as are accumulated at factories are far too rare, and those engaged in the manufacture of cheese commence their efforts under conditions which make perfection impossible.

Sometimes it is found that the milk when received appears in fairly good condition, but after the heat is applied to the curd in the whey, develops a very bad flavour. This is owing to some of the milk containing germs—probably entering in the milking shed by reason of insanitary and careless methods—which had not developed their characteristic odour at the time the milk was being received.

A good, clean-flavoured starter is one of the first essentials in the manufacture of prime cheese. Every utensil which comes in contact with the starter should be previously sterilized. Spring cheese is generally made too firm due mainly to it receiving the same treatment as that made from richer milk.

Curd from spring milk containing a comparatively small percentage of fat expels moisture more rapidly than curd from richer milk; therefore, it must be treated so as to retain more moisture, or the resulting cheese will be too firm and cure slowly.

A test of the milk should be made, and the treatment varied according to the quality. In spring, when the milk is testing low, it is found that setting at a lower temperature and using a correspondingly larger quantity of rennet, tends to make a quicker-curing cheese.

If it is intended that the cheese shall go into market in fourteen to twenty days, which is usually the case in the early part of the season, sufficient should be used to insure the process of coagulation commencing in from eight to ten minutes.

Spring milk testing 3 to 3.5 may be set at 82 to 84 degrees Fahr., and enough rennet used to have it ready for the knives in twenty to twenty-five minutes; this usually requires 4 oz. to 4¼ oz. rennet extract per 1,000 lbs. milk.

This treatment should only be for a few weeks, and should be gradually changed as the fat increases and the weather gets warmer. The setting temperature must then be raised and the quantity of rennet decreased, in order to get a firmer and slower-curing cheese.

The milk should be set in the vat early enough to allow the curd sufficient time to get fairly firm in the whey before the acidity develops. A great deal of curd is injured at this stage of the process. Cheese made from milk working fast will always tend to break down soft and weak in body.

Experience has shown that when the curd is not properly cooked, and the whey hurried off, the resulting cheese will go off-flavour much more readily than that from curd which has remained in the whey the proper length of time, and has been firmed and cooked. With spring milk good results will be obtained by heating or cooking to 96 or 98 degrees Fahr.

It is very important to know when the curd may be separated from the main body of whey. It is advisable, if the acidity is developing fast, or in hot weather, to draw off most of the whey before dipping, or racking, in order that the remainder may be drawn quickly when ready.

The proper test of acidity before racking is .19 to .195. The time taken between renneting and having the curd stirred dry on the racks is from two hours to two hours and a half; the richer the milk, the longer the time.

If too much acid develops in the curd before the whey is removed, it causes an extra loss of fat in the whey, consequently less cheese is made. which becomes dry and crumbly. When the curd is sufficiently matted together it should be cut in strips 6 to 8 inches wide, and turned every ten minutes, or often enough to avoid having whey pools forming between the pieces of curd.

If the curd is on the firm side it may be piled not higher than two deep, and kept at a temperature of about 94 degrees, until it becomes meaty, and the whey which comes away shows .7 to .75 per cent. of acid.

As a rule milling should come about half way between racking and salting. After the curd is milled it should be turned only often enough to keep it from matting and to have it well matured before salting.

The curd is in a fit condition to salt when it feels silky and mellow, and when the whey leaving the curd contains 1.0 to 1.5 per cent. acid.

The acidimeter test should be used to determine the time of salting and thus secure uniform results from day to day. The effects of salt on curd are to expel moisture, improve flavour, body, and texture of the cheese, to retard ripening or curing, and to add keeping quality.

Nothing but pure, clean-flavoured, dry salt should be used, coarser in the grain than used for butter, as curd contains more moisture to dissolve the salt, and less of the coarse salt will leave the curd and be lost. The amount of salt to be added depends upon the moisture in the curd, and upon the length of time for ripening; moist or tainted curd requires more salt, and quick-ripening cheese should have less. With spring milk and proper moisture and fair flavour, $2\frac{1}{4}$ to $2\frac{1}{2}$ lbs. per 1,000 lbs. of milk, according to butter fat test, is found to give good results.

The curd should be spread evenly over the bottom of the vat, and half the salt applied. After stirring this thoroughly and evenly through the mass of curd, the remainder should be put on and also be well mixed

In about twenty minutes after the salt has been thoroughly incorporated with the curd, and the harsh feeling caused by the salt removing the moisture has disappeared, it is ready for the hoops.

The temperature at this stage should not be lower than 84 degrees, as the curd cools rapidly when going to press.

In order to get uniformity in size of the cheese, the curd should be weighed in a bucket by means of a spring-balance suspended over the vat.

Pressure should be applied very gradually to the curd, following it up closely as the cheese slackens, until the maximum pressure is reached before leaving them for the night.

SECOND VICTORIAN EGG-LAYING COMPETITION, 1912-13.

Commencing 15th April, 1912.

CONDUCTED AT BURNLEY HORTICULTURAL SCHOOL.

No. of Pen.	Breed.	Name of Owner.	April 15 to Aug. 14.	Aug. 15 to Sept. 14.	Total to Date (5 months).	Position in Competition.
40	White Leghorns	S. Brown	480	142	622	1
23	,,	W. McLister	454	140	594	2
31	,,	Geo. Edwards	456	134	590	3
47	,,	J. E. Bradley	441	142	583	4
28	,,	F. G. Eagleton	451	130	581	5
9	,,	J. S. Spotswood	426	151	577	6
20	,,	E. Waldon	430	132	562	7
70	,,	C. J. Beatty	435	124	559	8
46	Black Orpingtons	H. A. Langdon	402	147	549	9
3	,,	King and Watson	413	134	547	10
1	White Leghorns	J. Campbell	408	133	541	11
62	,,	R. W. Pope	385	144	529	12
37	,,	C. B. Bertelsmeier	380	139	519	} 13
48	,,	Griffin Cant	393	126	519	
8	Black Orpingtons	D. Fisher	398	116	514	} 15
24	White Leghorns	Sargentri Poultry Yards	379	135	514	
45	,,	Wooldridge Bros.	375	137	512	17
25	,,	R. L. Appleford	370	134	504	18
29	,,	J. B. Brigden	370	132	502	19
38	,,	R. Moy	368	133	501	} 20
14	,,	J. H. Wright	362	139	501	
2	,,	B. Rowlinson	364	132	496	22
61	Black Orpingtons	J. Ogden	333	161	494	23
13	White Leghorns	W. B. Crellin	348	141	489	} 24
39	,,	W. G. Swift	360	129	489	
6	,,	J. B. McArthur	352	134	486	26
44	,,	A. W. Hall	347	137	484	27
30	,,	Mrs. Stevenson	363	120	483	28
49	,,	W. Purvis	350	132	482	29
50	,,	A. Ahpee	354	123	477	30
15	,,	Mrs. Steer	339	130	469	31
63	,,	Percy Walker	338	124	462	32
19	,,	Cowan Bros.	314	136	450	33
33	,,	H. McKenzie	319	130	449	34
7	,,	A. H. Padman	325	122	447	35
53	,,	H. Hodges	304	138	442	36
35	,,	C. H. Busst	312	127	439	37
56	,,	M. A. Monk	313	124	437	38
42	,,	Mrs. Kempster	305	126	431	39
5	,,	J. H. Brain	294	136	430	40
10	R.C. Brown Leghorns	S. P. Giles	286	127	413	41
64	White Leghorns	H. Merrick	284	128	412	42
51	,,	H. Hammill	283	128	411	43
60	,,	Miss B. E. Ryan	269	129	398	44
54	,,	F. R. DeGaris	261	126	387	45
43	,,	G. Purton	259	127	386	46
16	Silver Wyandottes	R. Jobling	243	139	382	} 47
65	White Leghorns	A. H. Thomson	247	135	382	
69	,,	Morgan and Watson	233	135	368	49
57	,,	B. Walker	242	124	366	50
32	,,	S. Brundrett	231	134	365	} 51
11	Black Orpingtons	T. S. Goodisson	231	134	365	
27	White Leghorns	E. Nash	235	125	360	53
4	,,	J. Blackburn	234	124	358	54
52	Black Minorcas	Chalmers Bros.	242	114	356	} 55
58	White Leghorns	W. J. Stock	253	103	356	
41	,,	A. Stringer	210	130	340	57
12	,,	T. H. C. Stafford	235	102	337	58
55	Brown Leghorns	J. Matheson	205	124	329	59
68	White Leghorns	W. J. McKeddie	206	101	307	} 60
18	,,	B. Mitchell	208	99	307	
66	,,	J. Moloney	169	130	299	62
21	,,	J. O'Loughlin	176	119	295	63
22	,,	W. N. Ling	164	113	277	64
67	Anconas	A. E. Manning	147	121	268	65
59	White Leghorns	W. J. Seabridge	153	106	259	66
36	Old English Game	K. J. Barrett	150	106	256	67
34	White Leghorns	R. F. B. Moore	108	118	226	68
17	,,	S. Childs	108	89	197	69
26	..	(Reserved)	..	..	..	..
		Totals	21,182	8,836	30,018	

SECOND VICTORIAN EGG-LAYING COMPETITION, 1912-13.

H. V. Hawkins, Poultry Expert.

REPORT FOR MONTH ENDING 14TH SEPTEMBER, 1912.

The month ending 14th September has been decidedly cold and gusty, with a fair rainfall. However, as the birds are well protected from wind and draughts, and provided with ample litter scattered in the pens, they have been kept busy, and the production of eggs has been well maintained. There has been no case of sickness.

Mr. S. Brown's White Leghorns still maintain pride of place, with a score of 622 for the five months; followed by W. McLister's White Leghorns, with 594.

A feature of the Competition during the past few weeks is that of a pen of Black Orpingtons, owned by Mr. Jas. Ogden. Their weekly record since 26th July is as follows :—33, 36, 35, 36, 33. 37, 37, and 39 respectively—making a total of 286 eggs in eight weeks. The total number of eggs laid is 30.018—an average of 435 per pen.

The feeding during the period under review has been on similar lines to that mentioned in my former report ; and there is no reason for any diminution of the meat or maize (heating foods) whilst the present cold conditions continue. Possibly next month we shall dispense with a part of the present grain ration, and reduce slightly the amount now used of animal food.

ORCHARD AND GARDEN NOTES.

E. E. Pescott, Principal, School of Horticulture, Burnley.

The Orchard.

Cultivation.

Orchard ploughing should now be finished, and the main work for the next few months will be an endeavour to keep the soil surface loose, friable, and well opened. The consolidation of the surfaces must be avoided ; as a hard, compact surface means the loss of much soil moisture by means of capillary attraction. So that after rains. heavy dews. spray pump and other traffic, it will be advisable to run the harrows through the orchard, to keep the surface well broken. so as to maintain a good earth mulch. If after ploughing it be found that the surface is cloddy, and that the harrows will not break the clods down. the soil must be well rolled with a spike or an ordinary round roller, and then afterwards harrowed.

Green manure crops should now be ploughed under ; if these crops are at all abundant in growth, they should be well rolled or dragged down with a chain, or they should be run over with a disc. Any of these means will assist in getting the whole of the crop underground. which is a desideratum.

In addition to the retention of soil moisture, cultivation of the orchards will suppress all weeds, which rob the trees of both water and food. The suppression of weeds is an important work in the spring and early summer, and they should be rigorously hoed or cultivated out.

Spraying.

Peach aphis will be claiming attention, as it will now be present in full force, if no winter spraying has been carried out. The spray for the present time is a strong nicotine solution, to be sprayed frequently, so long as the insects are present.

Until its action upon young foliage and fruit is well known, it will not be wise at the present time to spray with the lime-sulphur wash for either peach aphis, peach leaf-curl, or black spot of apple and pear. In all recent American experiments, this mixture has been used upon either dormant trees, or upon trees with mature foliage. Neither will it be wise to spray peach trees at this stage for leaf-curl with Bordeaux mixture. If this be done now, the trees will probably lose their foliage. For this disease and for shothole and scab of apricots, the trees should have been sprayed earlier in the season with Bordeaux mixture.

As apple and pear blossoms are bursting, the trees should be sprayed with Bordeaux mixture for black spot. If this has been delayed, the sulphate of copper may be added to the first arsenate of lead spraying for codlin moth, using one pound of copper sulphate to fifty gallons of the spray.

As soon as the apple and pear blossoms drop, it is time to prepare for the arsenate of lead spraying against the larvae of the codlin moth. Early applications are necessary; and one of two applications at the beginning of the season, while the apples are growing quickly, will be very efficacious.

General.

Grafts on young and old trees will need constant observation; they must not be allowed to become too dry; the sap and growth must not be restricted by the ties; and, if the growths become unduly long, they should be pinched back to make the growths sturdy, The foliage will always be benefited by a water spraying when the weather is hot, dry, or windy.

Citrus trees may be planted out; watering at planting and giving the foliage an occasional water sprinkling will be beneficial to the young trees.

Vegetable Garden.

The surface soil requires to be well pulverized at this time of the year; it should be kept well hoed, especially after the necessary frequent waterings, and all weeds must be suppressed. Apart from their harmfulness in robbing plants of food and moisture, the weeds, if allowed to remain and seed, become a menace to future economical work.

The top dressing and weeding of Asparagus beds will now be necessary; the beds should be well cut over as often as necessary, removing all growths, small and large. It is a mistake to allow the small stems to grow on, because they may be too small for cutting.

Plantings of tomatoes may now be carried out; all early planted plants should be fed, staked, and the laterals pinched back. A little bonedust or superphosphate may be given, but these are not equal to animal manures, if the latter are available. Chemical manures should only be given in a limited quantity. Six or seven cwt. per acre would be a heavy dressing, and this works out at nearly 3 ounces per square yard. Vegetable growers may easily try this for themselves, and it will soon be seen that 3 ounces scattered over a square yard of surface will appear to be a very light dressing.

French beans, carrot, parsnip, celery, radish, peas, and turnip seeds may now be sown. Seeds of cucumber, melon, and pumpkin family may now be sown in the open ground. All seedlings may be transplanted on favorable days, and it will be well to sprinkle the tops when planting out, as well as to water the roots.

Flower Garden.

As in other sections, there should be no clods on the surface, the soil should be friable, and no surface cracking should be allowed. As often as a watering is given, so a hoeing should succeed this work. Flowering plants suffer exceedingly through loss of soil moisture, and hard and compact surfaces are detrimental to their successful growth. It is always helpful to plants, and especially so on hot, sunny and windy days, to have the surface well hoed. In addition to conserving the soil water, it creates cool soil conditions, which is so helpful to good root action at this season of the year. Hoeing also keeps down the weeds, which need keeping down, and which should not be allowed to seed in the beds.

Roses will need attention, as both rose aphis and mildew will be making their appearance. For the former, strong tobacco and soap sprays, Robinson's pine spray, Benzole emulsion, and Soaperine are all very helpful in its eradication. For mildew the plants should be dusted with sulphur when the foliage is moist; a dusting of sulphur on the ground under the bushes will be useful as the fumes will be helpful in checking the fungus. All leaf eating insects on any plants may now be suppressed with arsenate of lead or with Paris Green.

Beds should be well dug over in preparation for chrysanthemum or dahlia planting; if these plants are not to be grown in separate beds, a few may be planted out for early flowering.

Bulbs that have finished flowering, and that have lost their foliage should be lifted and stored. The foliage must not be cut off while it is still green, as this means loss of sap and energy.

Tender and half-hardy and other annuals may be planted out for summer and autumn flowers. These include asters, zinnia, salvias, balsams, amaranthus, celosias, &c., lobelia, bedding begonias, iresines, and alternantheras may also be planted in the beds and borders.

Among the new garden plants now in cultivation one that is worthy of notice, and one that will be of great value for early spring and summer flowers is the new red perennial pea or Lathyrus Waratah. This is a fitting companion to the blue perennial pea, Lathyrus pubescens, now so popular. The colour is a rich Waratah red, and the plant is extremely floriferous. The flowers are larger than those of the blue pea; the plant is very hardy, and a good vigorous grower. It flowers at the same time as the Lathyrus pubescens, and is in every way worthy to be planted with it.

REMINDERS FOR NOVEMBER.

LIVE STOCK.

HORSES.—Continue to feed stable horses well; add a ration of greenstuff. Rug, at night. Continue hay or straw, chaffed or whole, to grass-fed horses. Feed old and badly-conditioned horses liberally. If too fat, mares in foal should be put on poorer pasture.

CATTLE.—Except on rare occasions, rugs may now be used on cows on cold and wet nights only. Continue giving hay or straw. Give calves a warm dry shed and a good grass run. Continue giving milk at blood heat to calves.

PIGS.—Supply plenty of bedding in warm well-ventilated styes. Keep styes clean and dry, and feeding troughs clean and wholesome. Sows may now be turned into grass run.

SHEEP.—Prepare for dipping. Powder and paste dips are most effective, particularly where lice are prevalent. Ascertain exact contents of bath before adding dip. Keep sheep in bath not less than half a minute. Submerge heads. Dip big sheep first, lambs last. Commence early in the day; sheep can then dry before nightfall. Do not dip sheep when heated or full. Clean out baths occasionally. Avoid having to travel sheep too far. Yard over night. Dip early in the day. Avoid filthy baths in dry areas particularly. Merino and fine comeback ewes are in season from middle of November. Join Lincoln and Leicester rams. English Leicester especially for small ewes, thick nuggety type for fat lambs preferable.

POULTRY.—Provide plenty of green food and shade. Watch for vermin; spray perches with kerosene and houses with a solution of 3 per cent. crude carbolic acid mixed with a little lime and soft soap. Keep water clean and cool. Discontinue feeding maize and reduce meat ration. Some Epsom salts should be placed in water weekly. Fresh skim milk, if available, should be given. Remove all male birds from the flock. Infertile eggs only should be used when pickling or when placed in cool storage.

CULTIVATION.

FARM.—Plant main crop of potatoes. Cut hay and silage. Weed early potatoes. Sow maize and millets. Weed tobacco beds, and water, if dry.

ORCHARD.—Ploughing, harrowing, and cultivating to be continued. Weeds to be kept down. Secure, pinch, and spray grafts with water. Spray frequently for codlin moth, pear and cherry slug, and peach aphis. Plant out citrus trees.

VEGETABLE GARDEN.—Hoe and mulch surface. Suppress weeds. Water where dry and hoe afterwards. Disbud and pinch back tomato plants. Sow celery, French beans, peas, lettuce, cucumber, melon, &c., seeds.

FLOWER GARDEN.—Water and mulch. Cultivate and keep down weeds. Thin out weak wood from roses. Prune early all flowering shrubs that have finished flowering. Lift and store bulbs. Plant out dahlias and chrysanthemums. Liquid-manure herbaceous perennials.

VINEYARD.—Cultural work, such as scarifying and hoeing, should be actively pushed forward, so as to provide as good a "mulch" as possible during summer. Proceed with tying up, stopping, and topping. Avoid excessive topping, summer pruning being usually more injurious than useful in warm, dry climates. Cincture Zante currant vines as soon as flower caps have fallen. Apply second sulphuring just before blossoming, wherever Oidium was prevalent last year.

Cellar.—Same as last month.

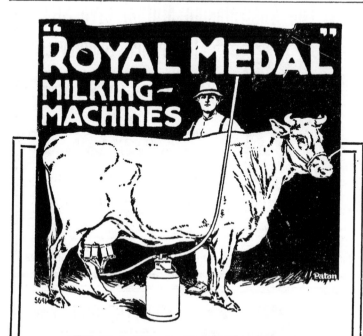

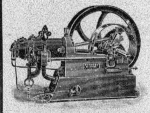

DEPARTMENT OF AGRICULTURE,

VICTORIA.

Burnley Horticultural School.

E. E. PESCOTT - Principal.

ANNOUNCEMENT.

The curriculum and management of the Burnley Horticultural School have now been arranged so that greater advantages and facilities will be given to students of both sexes in Horticulture and allied subjects.

The present course of Horticulture for male students includes a two years' course, students being charged a fee of £5 per annum.

Classes have been formed at Burnley, whereby students of both sexes may receive instruction on two afternoons of each week—Tuesdays and Fridays.

Instruction includes theoretical and practical work, and will commence at 2 p.m. This will be a two years' course, and the fee charged will be £2 per annum.

It has also been arranged that several short lecture courses shall be given on subjects which are suitable adjuncts to Horticulture, such as Poultry Farming, Bee-keeping, and Fruit Preserving, and these courses will be open and free to the general public. The subjects and dates of the Short Course Lectures will be announced monthly in this Journal.

BEE-KEEPING.

A series of Lectures on Bee-keeping will be given by Mr. F. R. Beuhne, the Bee Expert, on the following dates :—October 4th, 11th, 18th, 25th, at 2.30 p.m.

STUDENTS SHOULD ENROLL WITHOUT DELAY.

Application for Admission should be made to . .	THE DIRECTOR OF AGRICULTURE, PUBLIC OFFICES, MELBOURNE,	OR TO THE PRINCIPAL.

[Registered at the General Post Office, Melbourne, for transmission by Post as a Newspaper.]

The Journal of THE DEPARTMENT OF AGRICULTURE OF VICTORIA, AUSTRALIA.

November, 1912.

A WATTLE PLANTATION.

PRICE THREEPENCE.   (Annual Subscription—Victoria, Inter-State, and N.Z., 3/-; British and Foreign, 5/-.)

THE JOURNAL

OF

THE DEPARTMENT OF AGRICULTURE,

VICTORIA, AUSTRALIA.

CONTENTS.—NOVEMBER, 1912.

COPYRIGHT PROVISIONS AND SUBSCRIPTION RATES.

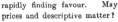

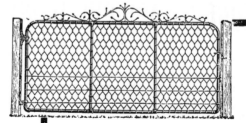

LITERATURE FOR AGRICULTURISTS.

PLAN AND SPECIFICATION OF SHEEP-SHEARING SHED. 2s. 6d. *Postage*, 1d.

MILK CHARTS (Monthly and Weekly), 6d. per dozen, post free. When ordering, dairy farmers should mention "Monthly" or "Weekly."

By Professor A. J. Ewart, Government Botanist.

WEEDS, POISON PLANTS, AND NATURALIZED ALIENS OF VICTORIA. 2s. 6d. *Postage :* Commonwealth, 1½d. ; N.Z., 5d. ; British and Foreign, 10d.

PLANTS INDIGENOUS TO VICTORIA. Vol. II., 10s. *Postage :* Com., 2d. ; N.Z., 8d. ; Brit. & For., 1s. 4d.

By C. French, F.E.S., Government Entomologist.

DESTRUCTIVE INSECTS OF VICTORIA. Parts I., II., III., IV., V. 2s. 6d. each. *Postage :* Parts I. and III., C., 1d. ; N.Z., 3d.; B. & F., 6d. each. Parts II. and IV., C., 1½d. ; N.Z., 4d. ; B. & F., 8d. each. Part V., C., 1d. ; N.Z., 4d. ; B. & F., 7d.

By D. McAlpine, Government Vegetable Pathologist.

RUSTS OF AUSTRALIA. 5s. *Postage :* C., 2d. ; N.Z., 8d. ; B. & F., 1s. 4d.

SMUTS OF AUSTRALIA. 4s. *Postage :* C., 2½d. ; N.Z., 9d. ; B. & F., 1s. 6d.

FUNGUS DISEASES OF CITRUS TREES IN AUSTRALIA. 2s. *Postage :* C., 1d.; N.Z., 3d.; B. & F., 6d.

FUNGUS DISEASES OF STONE FRUIT TREES IN AUSTRALIA. 2s. 6d. *Postage :* C., 1¼d. ; N.Z., 5d. ; B. & F., 10d.

SYSTEMATIC ARRANGEMENT OF AUSTRALIAN FUNGI. 3s. *Postage :* C., 2d.; N.Z., 8d. ; B. & F., 1s. 4d.

THE DEPARTMENT OF AGRICULTURE,
MELBOURNE, VICTORIA.

Remittances from places outside the Commonwealth to be by Money Order only.

Pamphlets obtainable from the Director of Agriculture, Melbourne, Free on Application.

NEW SERIES.

1. SILO CONSTRUCTION. *A. S. Kenyon, C.E.*
2. HINTS FOR NEW SETTLERS. *T. A. J. Smith.*
3. APPLE GROWING FOR EXPORT. *P. J. Carmody.*
* 4. BOOKKEEPING FOR FARMERS. *W. McIver, A.I.A.V., A.S.A.A., Eng.*
5. CIDER MAKING. *J. Knight.*
* 6. FARM PLUMBING. *C. H. Wright.*
7. CITRUS FRUIT CULTURE. *E. E. Pescott.*
8. BUILDING HINTS FOR SETTLERS. *A. S. Kenyon, C.E., and others.*
9. TOBACCO CULTURE. *T. A. J. Smith.*
10. SILOS AND SILAGE. *G. H. F. Baker.*
11. THE BEET SUGAR INDUSTRY AND CLOSER SETTLEMENT. *H. T. Easterby.*
12. WORMS IN SHEEP. *S. S. Cameron, D.V. Sc., M.R.C.V.S.*
*13. CHEESE MAKING (Cheddar). *C. S. Sawers.*
14. FARM BLACKSMITHING. *G. Baxter.*
15. BROOM FIBRE INDUSTRY. *T. A. J. Smith.*
*16. PIG INDUSTRY. *R. T. Archer.*
17. GOVERNMENT CERTIFICATION OF STALLIONS, 1911-12.
   W. A. N. Robertson, B.V. Sc.
18. REPORT ON FIRST EGG-LAYING COMPETITION AT BURNLEY, 1911-12.
   * Not yet available.   *H. V. Hawkins.*

THE JOURNAL

OF

The Department of Agriculture

OF

VICTORIA.

Vol. X.   Part 11.   11th November, 1912.

BEE-KEEPING IN VICTORIA.

(Continued from Page 532.)

F. R. Beuhne, Bee Expert.

IX. SWARMING.

Swarming is a natural impulse with bees, and the means of multiplying the species. In Victoria it occurs from September till December, October being the principal swarming month in most localities.

In abnormal seasons, when copious rains succeed a period of drought, swarming may take place a second time in January or February.

To the beginner the issue of swarms is a source of delight, and the most convenient way of increasing the number of his colonies. When, however, stocks have increased to the number intended to be kept, or to what the locality will carry with profit to the owner, then swarming becomes a trouble, involving a considerable amount of unprofitable work, and unless it is counteracted by re-uniting of swarmed stocks may result in the loss of all surplus honey. This is particularly so in districts having a plentiful supply of pollen in spring and a honey flow in early summer only. Taking as an illustration two colonies of equal strength, and assuming that one swarms several times, and that the other does not swarm at all, the worker force of the former is broken up into two, three, or more communities, none of which is in a condition to store surplus honey for a month or longer, because the parent colony is depleted of field bees by the issue of one or more swarms. The young queen, hatched after the swarm left, does not commence to lay for fourteen to twenty-one days, and this interruption in the succession of bee generations seriously affects the storing of honey later on, while every swarm put down in a separate hive has first to build sufficient comb to fill the frames of the lower story, establish a brood-nest, and accumulate stores before it is in a condition to store surplus honey. This point, at which productiveness commences, is in some localities, such as the country surrounding Melbourne, not reached till the main

13941.   Y

honey flow is practically over, and for the remainder of the season the bees are only able to gather sufficient to maintain themselves, and sometimes not enough to last them through the winter.   In the following season the colonies which survived will again undergo division by swarming, little or no honey will be obtained, and the owner will come to the conclusion that bees are not profitable in his locality.   It should be understood that increase of colonies always takes place at the expense of honey production, except in exceptionally good bee-country, with a late honey flow; but in passing it may be mentioned that in Spring bees are as much a saleable commodity as honey, that apiarists in the best honey districts of the State purchase swarms in large numbers, and that in localities better suited to the breeding of bees than the production of honey better profits may be obtained by the sale of bees than of honey.

Taking now the case of a colony which does not swarm at all, although of the same strength as another one which does, it will be seen that as the laying queen remains in the hive there is no interruption in the rearing of bees, and as all the work which is done by swarms during the first three or fours weeks is done by bees which come from the parent colony, it follows that when the total worker-force remains in the parent hive whatever would be needed in the establishment of the new colonies is available as surplus; in other words, the nectar available in the flora of the locality is, in one instance, turned into surplus honey for the benefit of the owner of the bees, and in the other into more bees which cannot do more than exist for the remainder of the season.

What has been said so far does not apply to the best honey districts of this State where the honey flow is heavy, and more or less continuous for the greater part of Spring, Summer, and Autumn; but even when the limit to increase is one of labour and material rather than of sources of nectar it is found more profitable to have the same total force of bees in a lesser number of colonies.   More surplus can be obtained from one colony containing 30,000 bees than from two containing 15,000 each, because the number necessary to attend to domestic work such as the rearing of brood, carrying water, &c., is practically the same in the smaller as in the larger colony, the latter has therefore a much larger number of bees available for the gathering of nectar and is less influenced by changes of temperature.

The prevention or control of swarming is one of the most difficult problems of bee culture.   Systematic efforts to eliminate the swarming impulse by breeding all queens from the mothers of non-swarming stocks have so far only resulted in reducing the percentage of swarming, owing to the inability of queen breeders to control the mating of the sexes as is done in the case of animals and birds.   Beekeepers are therefore compelled to confine their efforts to cope with the swarming problem to the removal of contributing causes and to counteracting the effects which swarming has on honey production.   Apart from the natural impulse, which is much stronger in some races, some strains, and even some individual colonies of bees than in others, climate, season, and flora have great influence upon the swarming propensity.   These are factors beyond the control of the beekeeper; there are, however, others which may be controlled, more or less, and excessive swarming prevented thereby.   The principal inducements for bees to swarm are—

    1. A crowded condition of the bees.
    2. The presence of large numbers of drones.
    3. An old or failing queen.

1. Hives may become crowded with bees early in September if wintered in single stories; as soon as the bees occupy all the combs, an upper story, with drawn empty combs, should be put on to allow the bees to spread out as their numbers increase and the weather becomes warmer. The beginner is at a great disadvantage in not having another set of combs, and the only thing he can do is to remove one or two combs from the brood chamber to the super (upper story) and put two frames with full sheets of foundation alongside the outside brood combs in the lower hive body. The bees will soon draw the foundation into comb, and the combs removed to the super will induce them to commence work there. Frames with starters only should not be used before swarming time, as drone comb is invariably built in them at this period. It must be pointed out that the addition of a set of frames with starters, or a section super, does not spread the bees out, because there is no connexion between the brood combs and the starters in the super. In a wild bees' nest, or when a set of drawn combs are given, the comb is continuous, and therefore, in the

FIG. I.—SPRING EXAMINATION OF HIVES.

latter case, accepted by the bees as part of their home as soon as required and the crowded condition relieved.

2. The presence of large numbers of drones is best avoided by the use in the brood chamber of combs built from full sheets of foundation, or combs which have been built by swarms during the first three weeks. The cutting out of drone comb or the shaving off of the heads of drone brood is of very little use, because drone comb is again built by the bees in the same space, and the queen again lays drone eggs into the cells from which the bees have removed the decapitated drones.

3. Old or failing queens may be discovered during the first or second examination of hives in Spring (Fig. 1) by noting the irregular way eggs are laid, as they are found scattered about instead of in compact circles. Colonies having three-year-old queens will be found most inclined to swarm; those with two-year-old queens less so, and the previous season's queens still less, while later on, when young queens of the same season's

rearing are laying, their colonies will not swarm the same season. Defective and old queens should be replaced as soon as ripe queen cells are available. In weak colonies the queen may be destroyed and a queen cell given at the same time, the interruption of brood rearing can be made good by giving a comb of brood a few days after the young queen hatched. If the colony contains sufficient bees it may be divided into two on the same stand, the old queen being kept laying in one till the young queen is laying in the other, when the former may be removed and the two stocks united by alternating the brood combs after smoking both. Uniting is best done at or after sunset.

Even when everything possible has been done to discourage swarming, there will be a number of swarms, but they will be larger (Fig. 2) than they would have been had the colonies swarmed earlier. Examining the hives once a week and destroying any queen cells that are found will, to some extent, prevent swarming or, at any rate, delay it. However, unless the bees are shaken off the brood combs every time, a small queen cell on the face of the comb, or one well covered with newly-built comb, is very likely to be over-looked and, if conditions continue favorable, colonies which have been thwarted will often swarm without having built cells. Taking into account the trouble involved by a careful weekly examination and the risk of failing to prevent swarming, it will be found best to allow

FIG. 2.—A LARGE SWARM, 10 LBS., OR ABOUT 45,000 BEES.

the swarm to come off and, if no increase but a yield of honey is desired, to re-unite the swarm and the parent colony. This is done in the following manner :—When the swarm has issued and clustered somewhere, hive it in a new box on a set of wired frames with starters on the spot occupied by the hive from which it came ; remove the latter a little to one side, with the entrance facing at right angles to its former position. All flying bees remaining in the parent stock, on returning from the fields, will join the swarm, because they will return to the spot they are used to. The swarmed colony will thus be so depleted of flying bees that usually the first virgin queen which hatches from one of the cells will be allowed by the bees to destroy the remaining queen cells. To make sure, however, that no after-swarms come off, it is best to examine the stocks within a day or two and destroy all the queen cells except one, selecting for the purpose one of the largest and most forward in development. In from fourteen to twenty-one days the young queen will be laying and, under normal conditions, the combs in the hive containing the swarm will have been built down to the bottom bar of the frames.   In the meantime the parent hive has been gradually turned round till it stands close alongside to the swarm, with the entrance facing the same way, and the two stocks may be united into one hive, the old queen (that with the swarm) being removed, the young queen taking her place on the new combs, with the old combs over a queen-excluder in the super to be extracted when full, or replaced by frames with full sheets of foundation, if unsuitable for further use.

As previously stated, uniting should be done towards evening, first blowing smoke between the combs of both colonies, and then alternating the frames of the two colonies, thus thoroughly mixing the bees.   They will have settled down by next morning, and will work peaceably together; the combs intended for the brood nest and the queen are then put in the lower chamber, the other combs in the super above a queen-excluder.

The old queen may be removed the day before uniting, which should not be attempted till the young queen has been laying for some days, as much stinging and balling of the queen may take place if uniting is done before ·or too soon after the young queen commenced laying.

The united stock is in the best condition for storing surplus honey, the brood combs have been renewed, and the queen being of the same season's raising, there will be no further swarming.

(To be continued.)

LUCERNE AND ENSILAGE.

By John W. Paterson, B.Sc., Ph.D., Experimentalist; and P. R. Scott, Chemist for Agriculture.

In order to determine the changes or losses which may occur in locally grown forage during the process of ensilage, a preliminary series of experiments was carried out at Geelong during the past summer.   The silo was of the reinforced concrete type, and in filling it the material was chaffed and elevated in the ordinary way.,   Second-cut lucerne was the crop employed.

.The method of working was simple.   About 50 lbs. of the material as it came from the cutter was well mixed on a clean floor.   From this 30 lbs. was sewed up in a clean Hessian bag and dropped in the centre of the silo where it was soon buried in the ordinary course of work.   At the same time 10 lbs. was weighed from the same heap and set out to dry as a thin layer in a lock-up room.   When dry this 10 lbs. was carefully collected and preserved for analysis.

The bag was placed in the silo on 27th December.   Chaffing went on from that time until the silage was from 10 to 12 feet deep over the bag at the end of three days.   The material was then fed to cows straight away, a quantity being taken from the silo daily.   On 27th February the bag was reached and it was then taken out and weighed.   It had been buried in the silo 62 days.

The silage when taken out weighed 25 lbs. 9 oz.   It was forwarded the same day in a sealed milk can for analysis.   At the same time the air-dried chaff from 10 lbs. of the original material was sent on as a separate parcel. One of us was present at all weighings on the farm to check the results.

The silage was of a brownish-green colour and had a somewhat pungent smell suggesting the presence of butyric acid. The dairy herd at the farm ate it readily. There was no mould of any sort on it and the farmer was well pleased with the general appearance of the material and the way it was turned out.

Table I. gives the percentage composition of the silage and dried chaff, and also of the original green lucerne as calculated from the dried chaff it produced. The items in the upper portion of the table are those ordinarily determined in stock food analysis, and they were determined in the ordinary way. In the lower division of the table the true protein was estimated by Stutzer's method, and the amides, &c., were then found by difference from the crude protein. Each of these represents nitrogen × 6.25. Sugar was determined by the gravimetric copper method. Furfurol was obtained by distillation with hydrochloric acid and subsequently precipitated by phloroglucin. Furfurol represents the pentosans and less resistant celluloses (oxy-celluloses) of the fodders, the latter being of most importance. The analyses were made by Mr. V. Deschamp, who has long experience of this class of work.

TABLE I.

	Green Lucerne.	Lucerne Hay.	Lucerne Silage.
	Per cent.	Per cent.	Per cent.
Water	74·63	9·80	75·00
Ether Extract	·83	2·94	1·29
Crude Protein	4·60	16·37	3·66
Sol. Carbohydrates	11·18	39·75	10·43
Woody Fibre	6·35	22·58	6·90
Ash	2·41	8·56	2·72
	100·00	100·00	100·00
Protein	3·31	11·75	2·19
Amides, &c.	1·29	4·62	1·47
Sugar	·27	·97	·02
Furfurol obtained	3·75	13·32	3·28

The percentage composition of the fodders indicates that chemically any one of them may be a useful feed for ruminants, but weight for weight they vary in the nutrients supplied. Comparing the green lucerne with the silage the latter contained less crude protein and considerably less true protein, while it contained a larger amount of amide or non-protein nitrogen. The silage had also somewhat less carbohydrates, and of the sugar which belongs to this group it had practically none while the furfurol shows that the more digestible cellulose was diminished. The silage had somewhat more fibre. It had more ether extract. Not much importance, however, should be credited to the ether extract in rough fodders of the kinds under review. While the ether extract of concentrated foods such as corn or linseed consists almost entirely of true fats which are wholly digestible and have a high value in feeding, the ether extract of rough fodders generally contains about 50 per cent. of chlorophyll and waxes which are indigestible. In silage it contains in addition a number of organic acids, such as lactic and butyric acid which have a low heat value and are in no way comparable to fats. The water in the silage happens to be about the same as in the original lucerne. Weight for weight the dried chaff is a much more concentrated food than the others, for the reason that it contained less water.

The important practical points in a comparison of silage, green fodder and hay lie not so much however in percentages as in the actual amounts of feeding material obtained from the different methods of curing. Thus it is conceivable that a gain in quality during ensilage might be purchased at too great an expense as regards the quantity of feed. Table II. shows for 100 lbs. of the original material how many lbs. of each food constituent were put in and how many taken out of the silo.

WEIGHING AT THE FARM.

TABLE II.

	Dry Matter.	Ether Extract.	Crude Protein.	Sol. Carbo.	Woody Fibre.	Ash.	Protein.	Amides, &c.	Sugar.	Furfurol Obtained.
Put in (lbs.) ..	25·37	·83	4·60	11·18	6·35	2·41	3·31	1·29	·27	3·75
Taken out (lbs.)	21·87	1·09	3·11	9·50	5·86	2·31	1·86	1·25	·02	3·28
Loss (lbs.) ..	3·50	·26*	1·49	1·68	·49	·10	1·45	·04	·25	·47
Loss (per cent.)	13·8	31·3*	32·4	15·0	7.7	4·1	43·8	3·1	92·6	12·5

* = Increase.

Of the total dry matter put in 13.8 per cent. was lost in 62 days. Of the soluble carbohydrates 15 per cent. was lost including all the sugar, and also, as the furfurol shows, the more decomposable cellulose. Analysis and theory alike indicate that during ensilage it is the most digestible part of the carbohydrates which are lost. The fibre showed less actual loss and the ash practically none. The bag was several feet from the floor of the silo. The most apparent loss, however, has been in the crude protein, and still more in the true protein of the silage. In the last case the loss approached 50 per cent. of the protein in the original material.

"Albuminoid ratio" is the ratio of the digestible albuminoids (proteins) to the digestible non-albuminoids in a food, the fat being multipled by 2.4 in making the calculation. Adopting Wolff's digestion coefficients for the fodders concerned the ratios work out at 1:3.3 for the fresh lucerne and 1:4.38 for the silage on the basis of crude protein; calculating from true protein the figures are 1:4.1 and 1:6.1 respectively. The American standard is 1:6—8, so that all the figures show the silage to be sufficiently rich in protein.

This result is obtained because fresh lucerne is particularly rich in protein as compared to ordinary forage. This however offers no reason why the protein should be wasted. Protein is the expensive constituent in a fodder. In the case of maize or the ordinary cereals there is less protein to start with—there is 66 to 50 per cent. less. These therefore are crops which seem more suitable for ensiling. They will lose less protein because they have less to lose.

WEIGHING AT THE LABORATORY.

Ensilage has its advantages and its disadvantages. When succulent food fails or at certain seasons in the dairy its advantages outweigh everything else. For ruminants succulent fodder is necessary to keep them in bloom, and continued dry feed is incompatible with heavy milking. The disadvantages of ensilage are connected with an inevitable loss of food materials. This indicates that it is wasteful to make silage to be used at a time when satisfactory green feed will be available. But the loss during ensilage falls more heavily upon certain of the constitutents of foods than upon others. From these experiments it seems to fall heavily upon the proteins. And as lucerne is particularly rich in protein it seems better that lucerne should be cured as hay rather than ensiled. Such hay would form an admirable addition to silage made from less nitrogenous fodders such as wheat, oats or maize.

There are few farms which do not produce a variety of forage crops. It is proposed to continue these investigations from the chemical side in order to find which crops can be converted into silage with greatest economy.

REPLENISHING THE DAIRY HERD.

By M. Thomas, Dairy Supervisor.

The dairy farmers of this State will, before many years have passed, have to face a serious situation unless a change in present methods is adopted. This will be how to replenish their dairy herds, which are continually being depleted by various causes.

The cutting up of large estates, under the Closer Settlement Act, into dairy farms, and the extension of the dairying industry generally throughout the State, has created a large demand for dairy heifers of good quality which seems very hard to satisfy.

This is a subject that requires very careful consideration on the part of our dairy farmers. The ruthless destruction of large numbers of heifer calves is, to my mind, a great waste of raw material, which should be utilized to better advantage especially in securing a certain supply of well-bred and well-reared heifers to replace any gaps that may occur in the herd.

When one thinks of the number of heifer calves, from cows of a 5, 6, and, in many cases, 7 gallons a day capacity, that are annually slaughtered for pigs' food, one can only conclude that eventually there must be a dearth of dairy heifers, and our herds, instead of improving, as they should do, will become of an inferior class. It, no doubt, seems to be the easiest way for the farmer to go to a cattle saleyard and purchase a few heifers, every now and then as wanted; but this is altogether wrong, for he is generally buying the calves that have been carelessly reared for three months, and then turned out to take their chance. The farmer who has fed his calves for five months, and reared them well, does not part with them unless forced to do so. For a good milking cow to stand the wear and tear on her system for years, a heifer must be reared from birth properly, so as to have stamina in her as a cow when she comes to the bail.

A lot of the heifers that are purchased in the saleyards are not so well reared as they require to be, and hence we often hear a farmer say, "I bought a couple of heifers in the yards a few weeks ago, but they are no good." This means that he will sell them for whatever sum the dealer likes to offer, and purchase others, from the same source, that possibly may turn out as bad, if not worse, than the first ones. Therefore the farmer who depends on this haphazard method of replenishing his herd will be far behind the careful farmer who rears the heifer calves from his own best cows, and rears them properly.

The correct method of rearing a calf has been described in previous issues of the *Journal*; it will, therefore, suffice to say that we have at our disposal many valuable, scientifically-tested, substitutes for the butter fat extracted from milk; whilst the farmer who will grow his own linseed will have all there is need of to rear good calves. Another important reason why the farmer should rear his own stock is to minimize the danger of introducing disease into his herd through purchasing a beast from an unknown and possibly infected source, and which may cause the loss of a whole year's profit to him.

In order to attain a high milking standard in a dairy herd, it is not essential that only pure-bred stock should be kept, for many of the most prolific milkers are of mixed breeds, and many of the pure-breds are

absolute failures at the bucket. It is, however, absolutely necessary that
prolific cows should be bred from along the lines of pure breeding, and
that instead of their offspring losing the milking character by being bred
from mongrel bulls, the function that is so well developed in the dam
should be made more and more of a fixed character by the use of a
pure-bred bull of milking strains. In no class of breeding is the influence
of the sire so well marked as in the breeding of dairy cattle. Therefore
serious attention should be given to the rearing of heifers, but they should
be only from the good cows of a herd, and got by none other than a
pure-bred bull.

IRRIGATION IN THE EARLY DAYS.

By A. S. Kenyon, C.E.

Recently a paragraph appeared in the daily press that the first attempt
at irrigation in Victoria was made at Kerang by the late Mr. W. J. W.
Patchell. No detraction from the credit due that enterprising settler is
intended in disputing that claim. That his was the first system which
was continuously successful is probable; but it was not the first attempt.

From the very outset of settlement on this continent, it was recognised
that its peculiar climatic conditions; its rivers—then known only as
" chains of ponds "—with their intermittent flows, rendered irrigation an
essential accompaniment to the full and profitable occupation of the
interior. The discovery of gold and the consequent dislocation for the
time of the ordinary conditions of life delayed the advent of irrigation,
for the efforts of the station gardener, generally a Chinaman, or of an
occasional pastoralist, in flooding some paddocks by damming the creeks,
are hardly worthy of the name, though in Tasmania a considerable amount
of work took place in the forties. It was not until the gold fever had
nearly run its course that the attention of the people was directed to
winning wealth from the soil by the less attractive but much more
profitable method of agriculture.

In the Victorian Government Prize Essays, 1860, Mr. William Storey,
in his essay upon the Agriculture of Victoria, says "Irrigation is pre-
destined to be a prominent feature in Australian husbandry, and though
it may seem paradoxical, it is, nevertheless, my impression that irrigation
will be more general, and will be earlier and better developed in Australia
than it would have been had its rivers been without drawback and fluvial
at all seasons of the year." Notwithstanding this and many similar
opinions, so little impression was made by the various efforts at irrigation
that Henniker Heaton, in his *Australian Dictionary of Dates,* 1879,
makes no reference to them whatever. Yet, in 1859, an extensive and costly
pumping scheme was being put into operation at Heidelberg, and in the
succeeding year an elaborate system was established at Adelaide Vale, on
the Campaspe River, for Messrs. Elms and Bladier. The following
extracts from the *Farmers' Journal and Gardeners' Chronicle,* a remarkably well-edited paper, will be of interest:—

" Irrigation is, perhaps, the most important subject that can engage
the study of the Australian farmer. In this dry climate, with its lengthened droughts and scorching hot winds, crops are often blighted and

destroyed before the grain has had time to ripen; and, again, the whole of the summer is lost, so far as production or vegetation is concerned. During the very months when the glowing heat of the sun would, with abundance of moisture, force and stimulate the most luxuriant vegetation, the whole face of the land is scorched and burnt up. The peculiarities of our climate, no doubt, arise, in great measure, from the vast extent of land we have on the one hand, and a wide ocean on the other. Any summer rains we have are not of much value, for the periods between one rainfall and another are so long that we have not only no summer vegetation, but the withered grass and dry herbage of the previous spring months are, in our opinion, often much damaged.

"If at any future time in the history of Victoria a general system of irrigation should be adopted and carried out, the greatest advantages would be gained by the agriculturists; and it is probable that the climate will become completely changed from a dry region to a land of showers and clouds and thunderstorms.

"Two days ago we paid a hurried visit to the farm of S. Ricardo, Esq., on the Yarra, near Heidelberg, for the purpose of inspecting his works for irrigating his land. That gentleman deserves very great credit for his enterprise in being the first in this Colony to employ irrigation on an extensive scale; but it is highly probable the undoubted gain the scheme will yield to him will come first, the credit afterwards.

"Mr. Ricardo's farm is 185 acres in extent, situated on the south bank of the Yarra, opposite to Heidelberg, and consists of two descriptions of soil—one of rich alluvial river flats, the other of sandy, undulating ground, with a clay substratum, bedded on rock of silurian formation. The highest ground is 120 feet above the river, and on it is formed the reservoir, which will, when full, contain 523,000 gallons. This reservoir is simply a square excavation, of about 30 yards by 60, and 5 or 6 feet deep. The soil and clay stripped from the rock form an embankment on all sides. From the engine-house, which stands by the river bank, a main pipe, sunk beneath the surface, leads the water up to the reservoir. To perform this work, a 12-horse-power engine, with double action pump, is provided. It was intended that this engine should force up 200 gallons per minute, but it has not been able to do this. Of course, the resistance to be overcome at each stroke is great—equal to about 60 lb. per square inch in 120 feet of elevation. Over a considerable extent of the rich river flats piping has been laid 2 feet under the surface, with plugs at intervals of 78 yards, so that two men with a hose can throw the water over the whole extent of intervening ground, and for this portion of the farm the water need not be taken from the reservoir, but may be supplied direct from the engine. In applying the water in this way, it, as a matter of course, falls upon the growing crop, and, under a burning sun, might be supposed likely to injure it; but such is not the case. Mr. Ricardo states that the water falling on the plants, even under the hottest sun, does them no harm whatever. Probably it is the radiation and reflection of heat from perfectly dry ground in the neighbourhood of plants that usually injures them if watered during sunshine.

"This mode of irrigation has been greatly recommended by Mr. Mechi, of Tiptree Farm. Mr. Ricardo, however, finds that it is a very imperfect method; that, in short, the supply is never equal to the demand; that the ground is no sooner watered than it requires to be watered again. Besides, he finds that the surface becomes caked by applying water from a jet or hose. He is, therefore, determined to irrigate the rest of the farm upon the Italian principle, or a modification of it. This consists in conveying the water along small open channels from the main pipe on various levels, allowing the liquid to flow gently and continually over the surface.

" Last summer the works were not completed early enough to test the full value of irrigation. Mr. Ricardo states, however, that he had a crop of turnips ready two months after sowing the seed.

" In reference to expense, he puts down the cost of pumping—that is, for fuel and attendance of one man—at 15s. per day. Two men, with hose, can water 5 acres per day. The whole cost of the works amounts to about £3,000; but a great deal of this sum might have been saved had all parties concerned possessed more practical knowledge of the subject, and had Mr. Mechi's stand-pipe system not been followed. The chief outlay should consist in raising the water to the required height, where such is necessary, and in making arrangements for its distribution by gravitation.

" At the present time the works in question are incomplete, and until next summer it will be impossible to say what will be the gain. Meanwhile, Mr. Ricardo has secured the services of a " duly qualified " Italian —one who thoroughly understands the practice followed in Italy, and he hopes, and, may we add, is certain, to obtain great results."— (7th July, 1860.)

Further particulars are given in the issue of 20th October, of the same year—

" The necessity for irrigation in this country is now a recognised fact. One of the first to discern this want and to take measures for supplying it is Mr. Ricardo, on whose farm at Heidelberg a system of irrigation by underground pipes, hose, and jet, similar to that practised in our streets, has been for some time in operation. This plan was projected by Mr. Mechi, the well-known agriculturist, of Tiptree Hall, Essex, but whatever the amount of success that may have attended its use under his auspices, it is now being discarded by Mr. Ricardo, on the ground, we believe, of its expensive working and general inefficiency. In its stead he has adopted the Italian system, which can be carried out at considerably less expense than the plan adopted by Mr. Mechi. The most difficult part of the ground, which, on account of its irregularity, requires a great amount of work in the way of levelling, has been under. taken for £15 per acre, while the more level portions of the farm will be completed for about £6 per acre. Mr. Mechi's system, on the other hand, costs something like £100 per acre.

" A portion of the works being sufficiently advanced to allow of a trial, the water was laid on last Tuesday, and the trial was in every respect a success. A steam-engine erected on the bank of the Yarra pumps the water into a tank capable of containing about 20,000 gallons. This tank is merely an excavation in the ground, and is, therefore, very inexpensive in its construction. It is 45 feet in length, 22 feet in width, and 4 feet in depth. From either end proceeds the main channel, 3 ft. 6 in. wide at top, 1 ft. 3 in. wide at the bottom, and 15 inches deep. Twenty-five chains only of this channel are yet finished, and they are intended for the irrigation of about 10 acres of land. The whole length of main channel required for the supply of the flat portion of the farm (about 100 acres) will be 110 chains. The experiment consisted in testing the efficiency of the part already completed. Several portions of land of about half-an-acre each having been ploughed, a flood-gate at the tank was raised and the channel was speedily filled to overflowing, irrigating the land regularly and most completely."

While claiming for Mr. Ricardo the honour of being the first irrigationist on a large scale, the names of Messrs. Robinson (Dutson), Eason (Buninyong), Vince (Bridgewater), Miller (Lerderderg), Pearce (Bacchus Marsh), Troy (Gannawarra), and Patchell (Kerang), should be placed on the roll of honour. The two first-named, though only irrigating on a small scale from springs, commenced in the fifties, the others not until the next decade. Any reference to the beginnings of irrigation in Victoria would hardly be complete without mention of Mr. Garden, of Cohuna, who, though not starting until 1882, was probably the most successful of all.

Footnote by the Hon. Geo. Graham, M.L.A., Minister of Agriculture and Water Supply.

I do not think the name of Messrs. Learmonth Bros., of Ercildoune, should be omitted from any list of early irrigators in Victoria. As far back as 1860, Mr. Thomas Learmonth prepared a piece of land about 1½ acres in extent, and, after carefully grading the same, had it planted with lucerne. He watered it by gravitation from a large reservoir situated on a hill at the back of the station, and irrigated with a system of mitre drains about 9 feet apart. To my personal knowledge he supplied a daily ration of lucerne to over 200 pigs for five months in the year from this small plot.

I saw the crop growing in February, 1861, when they were just preparing to take off the fourth cutting, and the lucerne was from 18 inches to 2 feet high.

What Mr. Kenyon has stated with regard to Mr. Ricardo is perfectly correct as I had the information from Mr. Ricardo himself many years ago. Mr. Ricardo was a very advanced and enthusiastic agriculturist, and was one of the very first men who purchased land in the Ballarat district for farming purposes.

MILK contains 4¾ per cent. of sugar. This milk sugar is not so sweet as cane sugar. On standing, bacteria form lactic acid from the milk sugar, and when the quantity becomes sufficient this acid causes the casein to coagulate. Casein can also be curdled by rennet, but the product is different to the curd produced by acid.

AN INSECT PEST OF THE "CURRAJONG" (BRACHYCHITON).

By C. French, Junr., Acting Government Entomologist.

From time to time, leaves of the native Currajong tree (Brachychiton populneum, R. Brown) are forwarded to the Entomological Branch by correspondents, who state, that the leaves are being discoloured by " insects which have white tails."   On examining the specimens I find them to be covered with the remarkable Psyllid (Tyora sterculiæ, Froggatt) which resembles an aphid and is often mistaken for one.

This insect was first discovered at Forbes, New South Wales, by Mr. W. W. Froggatt, Government Entomologist of New South Wales, and the following is a quotation from his description of the insect :—

" This is one of the most anomalous species I have found ; and the living psyllid with its bright green tints, delicate transparent wings, and long slender legs and antennæ, might easily be passed over at first sight as an aphis.   The deeply cleft head, absence of face lobes, and the peculiar venation of the wings render it a very distinctive insect.   The eggs are horn-colour, elongate-oval in form, and deposited in patches containing 30-40 in number on the upper surface of the leaves.   The larvæ and pupæ cluster together where they emerge from the eggs, the long filaments trailing out all round giving them a star-like appearance and each family makes a large white blotch on the foliage."

Many Currajong trees are now cultivated in Victoria, in large private gardens, public parks, avenues, &c.   They are fine, evergreen, shady trees, easily grown and very shapely.   The flowers are fairly large, downy on the outside, and on the inside red and yellow, variegated.   It is unfortunate that they are being attacked by an insect pest, which causes discoloration of the leaves and the trees themselves to become unsightly.

In times of drought, in some parts of the interior of Australia, starving stock have been saved by eating the leaves of these trees, and also the roots if they happen to be exposed.

REMEDIES.

The most effective means of dealing with this pest is to spray the trees with kerosene or benzole emulsion, pine oil spray, or any other mixture that kills insects by contact.   Formulas for any of these mixtures can be obtained on application to the Entomological Branch, Crown Law Offices, Melbourne.

EXPLANATION OF PLATE.

(Tyora sterculiæ, Froggatt.)

Fig.   I. Eggs. Magnified. From Nature.
Fig. II. Leaves with insects and cast skins. Natural size. From Nature.
Fig. III. Young leaves with cottony filaments. Magnified. From Nature.
Fig. IV. Pupa. Magnified. From Nature.
Fig. IVA. Pupa. Natural size. From Nature.
Fig. V. Perfect Insect. Magnified. From Nature.
Fig. VI. Antennæ. Magnified. From Nature.
Fig. VII. Leg, anterior. Magnified. From Nature.

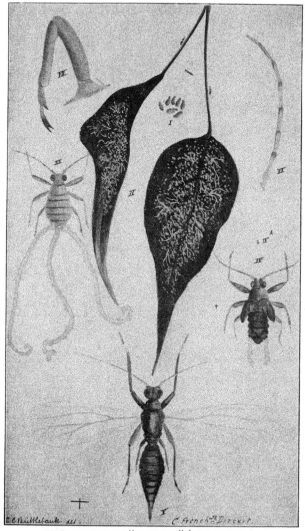

INSECT PEST OF THE "CURRAJONG" (BRACHYCHITON).

GENERAL NOTES.

THE FLY PEST—

A simple method of destroying house flies, which is well spoken of, is described in the *Agricultural Journal, Queensland.* Formalin is the agent employed. One ounce of commercial (40 per cent.) formalin is added to one pint of equal parts milk and water. A trace of sugar added makes it more attractive. The mixture is exposed in shallow plates, and a piece of bread or blotting paper in each plate offers more space for the flies to alight on. The preparation has been tried in cow houses, stables, dairies, and dwelling houses, and in most cases seems to have been very destructive. Mixed with syrup it was eaten by ants with impunity.

COMPARATIVE VALUES OF FOODS—

The unit-value system of ascertaining the prices of manures is described by the Chemist for Agriculture in the January issue of this Journal. It is useful as showing whether the purchaser of manures is getting value for his money according to current rates. From time to time proposals have been made for the application of the unit system to a comparison of food values, and *Leaflet 74* of the Board of Agriculture suggests the following method:—In a cattle food the ingredients commercially important are the albuminoids (proteids), fats, and carbohydrates. In working, multiply the percentage of albuminoids and fats by $2\frac{1}{2}$, and to the product add the percentage of carbohydrates. The result gives the number of food units in the material. Take an example. If a food contains 32 per cent. albuminoids, 11 per cent. fats or oils, and 34 per cent. carbohydrates, then $2\frac{1}{2}$ (32 + 11) + 34 = $141\frac{1}{2}$ food units. If the price is £9 per ton then each unit costs 1s. $3\frac{1}{4}$d. The same calculation may then be conducted for another food at another price in order to see which is purchasable at the cheaper rate per unit. In making this comparison between different foods it must be confined to foods of essentially the same character, and where each is dietetically suited to the purpose for which it is required. To compare, say, barley meal with oaten chaff under this method would give misleading results.

GOOD AND BAD PASTURE—

In any stretch of country one, pasture establishes a reputation as good fattening land, while another is known as only fit to carry store stock or lambing ewes. The reason for those differences is often hard to trace. In the Romney district of England there occur fields of permanent pasture capable of fattening six or eight sheep to the acre, while immediately adjoining may be found others of apparently the same character, which will only keep sheep in growing condition. In the *Jour. Agric. Sci.*, June, 1912, Mr. A. D. Hall and Dr. Russell, of Rothamsted, describe some investigations of this subject. They compared a good with an adjoining bad-feeding pasture at three stations. At each place both pastures were situated in flat silt land, and appeared to have been formed in the same way. There was no regular difference in the water content of the good and bad soils, and temperature differences were small. The ordinary chemical and mechanical analyses of the soils revealed nothing to account for their great differences in fertility; the good soils generally contained rather more total phosphoric acid, but not of citric acid soluble. Their investigations point to only one feature in which the good soils excelled in marked degree—they contained much more nitrates and ammonia early in the season. No reason could be given for this. Botanically, there was very little difference in the types of herbage. The feeding value of the pasture was thus largely independent of its botanical composition. Habit of growth appeared the important thing. On the good land, with plenty of nitrates and ammonia, the grasses were leafy, with little tendency to form heads; on the bad fields the herbage was stemmy, and flower heads came early and abundantly. Altogether the investigations indicate that the bacterial activity of pasture lands is of first-rate importance. They suggest that the application of lime (a germ tonic) would often bring marked improvement. Lime increases the natural supply of nitrates. Incidentally it helps clovers in another way. On some soils phosphates are required in addition to lime. It is by experimenting along these lines that the right means of improving poor pasture can be determined.

HERD TESTING—

Six years ago Mr. Burgess, a New Zealand farmer, started testing his dairy herd, and a lucid account of his experience appears in the *Journal of Agriculture* of the Dominion. In the first season of testing the cows averaged 198 lbs. of butter fat. As a result of always weeding out the worst cows, the average for the second season was 222 lbs.; for the third season 234 lbs; for the fourth, 241 lbs.; in the fifth season the yield was affected by the dry summer, and consequent scarcity of feed; in the sixth season the average was 261 lbs. Six year's testing thus increased the yield by 63 lbs. butter fat per cow. The cost of testing is calculated at 8s. 11d. per cow, including cost of apparatus and the farmer's own time at 1s. per hour. He estimates that improvement will continue, because in the period under review an exceptional number of heifers was introduced to replace culls. The herd was of mixed breeding, but at two dates a pure-bred Ayrshire bull of good milking strain was obtained. The writer would prefer pure breeds to work on as these perpetuate their qualities with greater certainty, but points out the difficulty of obtaining this class of stock with good records well authenticated. The scheme for officially testing pure herds recently introduced by this Department will furnish a guarantee to those purchasing pure-bred animals with the object of grading up their herds.

DRAINAGE LOSSES—

Phosphoric acid, potash, lime, and nitrogen are the soil constituents which the farmer wishes to conserve, and each of them stands in a different relation to drainage losses. A discussion of the subject and the analysis of drainage waters from the fields of five farms which appeared recently in the *Illustrated Landw. Zeit*, which serve to draw attention to the subject. The results were typical. There was no phosphoric acid lost by drainage. The loss of potash was not serious, but there was considerable loss of nitrogen (11.8 parts per million) almost wholly as nitrates. There was no loss of nitrogen as ammonia. The most serious loss was in lime, amounting to 215 parts per million. In nearly all cases lime will be the chief constituent in drainage waters. The loss is greater on cultivated land than on pasture, and most of the manures in use tend to increase it. The waste is inevitable, and in the long run must be made up by fresh applications of lime at the surface.

FRUIT TRADE OF VICTORIA.

ITS PRESENT STATUS, FROM A COMMERCIAL STANDPOINT.

(Continued from Page 567.)

LOCAL TRADE.

By E. Meeking, Senior Inspector of Fruit.

PART 2.

It is intended, in this number, to show the present position of the local fruit trade, and to point out some of the disabilities connected therewith. Suggestions will be furnished later as to the manner in which these may be, in large measure, surmounted.   Before doing so, it may be as well to indicate the channels whereby our fruits reach the consumer, in order that the suggestions for improving the present methods of disposal may be rendered more clear.

Approximately 50 per cent. of the total fruits raised in Victoria never leave the State, being consumed or otherwise dealt with locally.   Indeed, so far as the small fruits (berry fruits, currants, olives, &c.) are concerned, it may be confidently asserted that 99 per cent. of these are consumed within the State.   This is also true concerning a great proportion of the softer kinds of our large fruits, as the following figures will show :—

Low Consumption of Fruit in Victoria.

In the year 1910-11 (the latest year for which figures are available), a total of 3,641,977 bushels of fruits, exclusive of grapes, was raised in Victoria.   This total consisted of 3,583,059 bushels of large fruits, and 58,918 bushels of small fruits.   Of this total, a quantity of 484,413 bushels, or 13.5 per cent., was exported to the other States of the Commonwealth ; 318,297 bushels, or 8.8 per cent., were exported oversea ; 997,454 bushels, or 27.3 per cent., were manufactured into jams, jellies, &c., and 59,600 bushels, or 1.09 per cent., were converted into dried fruits.   This gave a total of 1,859,764 bushels exported, manufactured, or otherwise disposed of, and left a total of 1,782,213 bushels, or slightly under 50 per cent. of the total raised, to be consumed locally.   If we add to the quantity raised locally a quantity of 785,106 bushels imported from the other States, and 81,560 bushels imported oversea, we get a total of 2,648,879 bushels consumed in Victoria in the year 1910-11.

Taking the population of the State for the year under notice at 1,305,000 souls, it will be seen that approximately 80 lb. of fruit per head of population was consumed during the 12 months.   This gives a daily consumption of 3½ oz. of fruit per day per individual.   Comparing this consumption with the consumption of such staple articles of food as meat and bread, it would appear that the proportion of fruit consumed is relatively very small, as in 1910-11 there were consumed per head of population in Victoria 223 lb. of meat per annum, or 9.6 oz. per day, and 272 lb. of bread per annum, or 12 oz. per day.

Large Amount of Waste.

As no figures are available to indicate the amount of waste which annually takes place, the figures quoted do not allow for the fruits which are raised but never reach the consumer, and are either fed to stock or

carted to municipal rubbish tips.   There is every reason to believe, however, that this amount of waste is much larger than most people imagine,
and would be quite sufficient to bring the total consumption per head to
below 3 oz. per day.

Present Methods of Distribution.

The two points most forcibly emphasised by these figures are—firstly,
that we import a great deal of fruit which might be raised locally ; and,

A CORNER IN THE QUEEN VICTORIA MARKET.

secondly, that in a climate such as ours the use of fruit as a staple article
of diet is much less than it should be.   If we seek for reasons as to why
this state of affairs exists, the following facts would seem to indicate that
the causes are mainly due to the want of appreciation of the dietetic value
of fruit on the part of the public, and to improper methods of placing our
fruits before the consumer.   The latter cause may be chiefly attributed to

our incomplete methods of distribution.   Within the City of Melbourne·
and suburban radius, the total population of which in 1911 was estimated·
at 600,160, there are only three principal retail markets, viz., the Queen)
Victoria (situated within the city), South Melbourne, and Prahran Markets.
In addition to these three retail markets, one wholesale market, the Western·
Market, is situated between Market and William streets, Melbourne.   None·

RETAILING FRUIT, QUEEN VICTORIA MARKET.

of the markets, retail or wholesale, are connected with the railway.   The·
following are the number of fruit retailers in these different markets:—
Victoria Market, 450; South Melbourne Market, 35; Prahran Market, 20·
—a total of 505.   In addition to these, there are, on an average, 60·
barrowmen in the city, 20 in South Melbourne, and 90 in Prahran.   The
total number of fruiterers and greengrocers in the city and suburbs is 769.

The wholesale distributors, who are situated in, or adjacent to, the Western Market and Queen Victoria Market, number about 20. This gives a total of slightly over 1,400 distributors, or, approximately, one distributor to every 360 inhabitants in the metropolitan area.

IMPROVEMENT IN DISTRIBUTION NEEDED.

It would appear, from the above figures, that the number of distributors is quite sufficient to place the fruit before the public; but the

RETAILING VEGETABLES, QUEEN VICTORIA MARKET.

expensive and cumbersome methods by which these retail fruiterers and barrowmen are supplied add so much to the cost of the fruit as to render it a luxury, instead of being, as it should rightly be, a necessary article of diet. This contention will be rendered more clear when it is explained that the only means by which the suburban fruiterers and barrowmen can obtain their supplies is by attending the early morning markets, or by purchasing the fruit required at the Western Market, in the city. To compensate for the wear and tear incurred through the journey into the city and back, the long hours worked, and the great length of time occupied in obtaining his supplies, the retailer has necessarily to charge high prices for his fruit. This has the effect of lowering the average consumption, and also curtails the profits which would accrue if more direct methods were in force whereby the fruiterer could secure his goods. The necessity for working half the night during, at least, three nights of the week precludes the possibility of the fruiterer conveying his fruit to the houses of the consumers in his locality, and he has therefore to depend, in large measure, upon the residents calling at his shop to make their purchases. Many of the growers adjacent to the metropolis bring their fruit to the Queen Victoria and South Melbourne Markets and sell direct to the retailers and consumers. The growers other than those adjacent to the metropolis are dependent for the distribution of their fruit upon the Western Market alone. The retailers in the Prahran Market consist mostly of Chinese and Greek vendors of an itinerant type. The grower whose residence is so contiguous to the metropolitan markets as to enable him to convey his fruits to the city and sell these direct to the consumer would, at first sight, appear to possess an advantage over his fellow-grower who resides in a more distant portion of the State, as, by such direct sales, he is enabled to eliminate the profits of the middleman. When, however, the time occupied in travelling between the orchard and the market, in the disposal of his fruits, and in the return journey, and also the cost of wear and tear to his plant, is considered, the advantage is more apparent than real. The expense of placing his fruits on the markets is almost as great to the grower adjacent to the city as it is to the grower of the outlying district.

The foregoing facts tend to show that, consequent upon our cumbersome methods, the contingent expenses incurred in distributing our fruits for local sale are such as to lower the profits to the grower and raise the prices to the consumer. Whether the grower elects to convey his own fruits to the market and personally dispose of same, or whether he depends upon the wholesale merchant in the only wholesale market in the metropolitan area to dispose of these, the time and labour involved under our present methods of distribution are such as to render in some seasons both the production and consumption of fruits an unprofitable proposition. That fruit is a special product and needs special methods in connexion with its harvesting, handling, transportation and marketing has not yet been fully realized, and consideration also has not been given to the fact that our conditions are constantly changing, and that our methods of distribution should be altered accordingly.

The following outline of the marketing facilities and methods which have recently been adopted in Sydney since the erection of new municipal fruit markets there may serve to show, by comparison, how very urgent reform in our own methods is necessary. These markets cover a total area of 12½ acres of ground, and the section reserved for the disposal of fruit occupies 2½ acres. The market contains 34 stalls, of two stories, and 34 offices. The ground, or floor space, will accommodate 500 vendors, with ample room for the display and disposal of fruit. A branch fumigating chamber and cold-storage accommodation containing 30,000 feet of air space is also provided on the ground floor. The space on this floor is equally allotted to the grower and the agent, or fruit merchant. The two classes are divided by a central roadway running through the market. The growers are placed into five districts. The fruit is distributed to the public and shopkeepers and about 2,500 dealers, who have districts and sell both fruit and vegetables to the public.

In addition to the above-mentioned facilities, the municipality has erected, within 100 yards of the market, twenty large stores, of three stories, for the use of the large fruit merchant.

The market is connected with the rail, and fruit may be forwarded direct to it from country districts.

The method in which the fruit is distributed from the market throughout the city and suburbs is by cars and motor waggons.

It will thus be seen that at present the city of Sydney is much in advance of this city with regard to the disposal and marketing of fruit.

If the projected scheme in connexion with the new markets, which it is intended to shortly erect on the south side of the Yarra, is carried out as completely as proposed, Melbourne should then be well abreast of any other city in the Commonwealth with regard to the marketing and distribution of fruit.

(*To be continued.*)

SHEEP DIPPING.

By A. W. Curlewis, Inspector under Sheep Dipping Act.

As shearing time in this State is again approaching, a few words on sheep dipping may not be out of place.

A large majority of the sheep-owners of Victoria, including all who have had a lengthened experience on the subject, are fully aware of the benefits which accrue from careful and systematic dipping and strongly approve of the general provisions of the Sheep Dipping Act. The small minority consists, firstly—of those who are averse to taking any progressive steps which entail trouble and expense, and to measures taken to protect others from the effect of their carelessness and lack of management; and secondly, of those whose first experience of dipping has for some reason been unfortunate. And to the latter a few hints may be acceptable.

Various reasons may be given for the failure, or partial failure, of the operation, such as the use of inferior dipping medicaments, errors in mixing, over dilution with the false idea of economy, failure to keep the dip at the proper strength, and faulty methods of actual dipping.

Owners who have not had experience in dipping sheep are advised to procure a dip strongly recommended by one who has used it, to mix and use according to instructions received with it; if a powder, roll to break all lumps and mix in a paste over night, and in the morning complete mixing with the prescribed quantity of water, take care to keep dip at a uniform strength, use a plunger frequently whilst the sheep are going through to prevent any powder settling at the bottom of the dip. The sheep should be yarded over night and put through as early as possible; dipping should not be carried on in a fierce heat, and failing shelter trees being available rough shelter sheds should be provided near draining yard. When a small dip is used care should be taken to see that every sheep is thoroughly soaked, the head should be immersed a couple of times, and each sheep should be in about a minute. If it is necessary to drive the sheep away from the dip do so quietly, after allowing them to stand under shelter for a time, and avoid dusty roads until they are dry.

Numerous cases have come under notice the last few months of sheep which were dipped after last shearing and are nevertheless carrying ticks or lice. Imperfect dipping, together with the bad time most of them have gone through consequent on the drought, has had a good deal to do with it, the frequently expressed opinion is that " poverty breeds ticks and lice " ; and whilst this is not correct it is true that vermin thrive and increase best when their hosts are in low condition.

On the other hand, the freedom from lice and ticks observed in numbers of dipped sheep suffering from the effects of the bad season—recent yardings at Yarck and Nagambie for example—is very encouraging to all advocates of dipping, and goes to prove that poverty is not the only factor to be considered. One of the reasons why dipping does not absolutely eradicate vermin is the practice, followed by some who are not aware that they are infringing the Sheep Dipping Act, of leaving the lambs unshorn and undipped when the ewes are so dealt with ; the majority of the former may be marketed before they can infest dipped sheep, but others fatten late and some are not fattened at all. These are generally shorn and dipped later, but not before they have to some extent reinfested the flock. Granted that it is undesirable to dip lambs nearly fat and intended for early marketing, those which are to be kept any time after the dipping of the flock might well be shorn and dipped with the sheep and thereby secured from grass seeds and freed from vermin ; it should not be detrimental to their improvement or sale but the reverse, and as all sheep dipped should be immune from contagion from the early lambs up to the time the latter were sold, a great benefit should result to the flock.

Opinions vary very much as to the length of time which should intervene between shearing and dipping. Some dip "off the shears," but many prefer to put it off from three to six weeks, and others go so far as to object to the period allowed by the Act, *i.e.*, sixty days, as not long enough.

Whilst it is no doubt advisable when practicable to allow three or four weeks to elapse, especially in cases of machine shorn sheep, it is, I think, a mistake to leave them undipped longer than six weeks ; and in any case, farmers' sheep should be dipped before harvesting operations are commenced.

Dipping "off the shears" frequently gives excellent results ; as an example, I may instance cases of sheep which are depastured in the mountains near Alexandra. There being no facilities for holding the sheep near where they were shorn, they were mustered, shorn and dipped straight away and turned out in the hills again, and when mustered and offered for sale recently were found on being handled to be absolutely free from vermin, the wool being clean and bright.

When practicable, owners of, say, upwards of 200 sheep should have their own dipping baths ; it is a mistake to drive sheep far and have to return them over dusty roads, after being dipped. The cost of a dip suitable for small flocks is very moderate, portable iron baths are quoted at about £7, and with a small additional cost may be put down and small draining yards provided. Small brick and cement or concrete and cement dips and draining yards may also be constructed at from £10 to £15, which are permanent and answer the purpose admirably : it is only a question of a little more time in putting the sheep through.

The clubbing together of farmers and using a large dip between them is not altogether satisfactory, for the last to use the bath has a fouled wash and frequently has to wait his turn until late in the day ; the result is the sheep do not dry before night : this is very undesirable. In putting a flock through it is advisable for the largest sheep to go in first, the lambs and smaller ones last when the bath is shallower ; broken legs are avoided in this way.

Particulars of various styles of dips have already been given through these columns and directly to owners by the Department, and further details may be obtained on application. Finally, I strongly advise sheepowners, who have already been referred to as having had somewhat unfortunate experiences in the matter, to continue to dip, but to do so with care and judgment, and they need have no fear but that their trouble will be well repaid.

SHEARERS' HUT ACCOMMODATION ACT.

The Shearers' Hut Accommodation Act, No. 2341, came into operation on 1st July, when the Hon. the Minister for Agriculture decided that it should be administered by the Live Stock Division of the Department of Agriculture, and that the inspections necessary should be undertaken by the present staff, without additional appointments being made.

The first requirement was to define the districts, as ordered in Section 5 (1), and appoint inspectors thereto. This was done, and the Order in Council passed on 19th August, 1912.

The following table shows the districts defined, together with the names and addresses of the inspectors :—

Name of Inspector.	Address.	Shires under his Control.
Mathieson, John	Warrnambool..	Warrnambool, Portland, Belfast, Minhamite, Heytesbury, Colac, Mortlake, Hampden
Gresson, George Leslie	Casterton	Glenelg
Keys, Stanley Jeffrey ..	Coleraine	Wannon
Fisher, Albert William..	Hamilton	Mount Rouse, Dundas
Temple, John McVicar	Ararat	Ararat, Ripon, Lexton, Avoca, Stawell, Wimmera, Dunmunkle, Borung, Arapiles, Kowree
Wilson, Thomas	Melbourne	Lawloit, Lowan, Dimboola, Mildura, Karkarooc, Swan Hill, Walpeup
Edwards, Charles Basil	Bendigo	Wycheproof, Birchip, Charlton. Gordon, East Loddon, Korong, Kara Kara, Bet Bet, Kerang
O'Keefe, Peter Bernard	Rochester	Rochester
McKenzie, John William	Kyabram	Deakin
Henderson, George	Bendigo	Huntly, Strathfieldsaye
Close, John	Bendigo	Marong, Donald
Ash, Ethelbert Ebenezer	Castlemaine	Maldon, Metcalfe
Marshall, John Carlyle..	Melbourne	Tullaroop, Talbot, Creswick, Newstead, Mount Alexander, Mount Franklin, Glenlyon. Kyneton, McIvor, Newham and Woodend, Romsey, Springfield, Gisborne, Lancefield

DISTRICTS, ETC.—*continued.*

Name of Inspector.	Address.	Shires under his Control.
Ross, Alexander John	Ballarat ..	Ballarat, Bungaree
Kyle, Albert	Ballarat ..	Buninyong. Grenville
Kyle, John	Geelong ..	Meredith, Leigh, Corio, Bannock-burn
Thomas, Moses ..	Winchelsea ..	Winchelsea, Barrarbool
Madden, Thomas ..	Geelong ..	South Barwon, Bellarine
O'Bryan, Patrick Francis	Melbourne ..	Werribee, Braybrook
Morris, Edgar Gordon ..	Bacchus Marsh	Bacchus Marsh, Ballan, Melton
Budd, Hubert Walton	Melbourne ..	Broadmeadows, Bulla. Keilor
Comans. Michael ..	Melbourne ..	Preston, Merriang, Whittlesea. Epping
Gemmell, Thomas ..	Seymour ..	Seymour, Broadford. Kilmore, Pyalong
Parfitt, Henry Francis ..	Melbourne ..	Goulburn, Waranga, Euroa, Mansfield, Rodney, Shepparton, Numurkah, Tungamah, Violet Town, Yarrawonga
Porter, William Thomas ..	Wangaratta ..	Benalla, Oxley, North Ovens, Rutherglen, Chiltern. Wodonga, Yackandandah. Beechworth, Bright, Omeo, Towong
Threlfall, Robert George ..	Yea	Yea, Alexandra, Howqua
Younger, William ..	Melbourne ..	Heidelberg, Eltham, Doncaster, Healesville, Templestowe
McDougall, Edgar Wallace ..	Melbourne ..	Nunawading, Lilydale, Upper Yarra
Turner, Ernest James	Melbourne ..	Mulgrave, Fern Tree Gully, Dandenong
Sherlock, Samuel ..	Frankston ..	Moorabbin, Mornington, Frankston and Hastings, Flinders and Kangerong
McKenzie, George ..	Cranbourne ..	Cranbourne
McKenzie, Robert Taylor ..	Korumburra ..	Poowong and Jeetho, Phillip Island, and Woolamai
Grant, James ..	Leongatha ..	Woorayl
Morton, Charles James ..	Foster ..	South Gippsland
Fleming, James ..	Alberton ..	Alberton
O'Keefe, Dennis Francis ..	Berwick ..	Berwick
Corney, Charles Edwin Macdougall	Bairnsdale ..	Buln Buln, Warragul, Narracan, Morwell, Traralgon, Walhalla, Maffra, Rosedale, Avon, Orbost, Tambo, Bairnsdale, Mirboo
Curlewis, Alfred William ..	Melbourne ..	Whole of State

In order that all pastoralists may be made familiar with the operations of the Act, an epitome showing the principal provisions has been drawn up for circulation throughout the State. This epitome is in the following form:—

SHEARERS' HUT ACCOMMODATION ACT, No. 2341.

NOTICE TO EMPLOYERS OF SHEARERS.

Notice is hereby given that, in accordance with the provisions of the Shearers' Hut Accommodation Act, No. 2341, if six or more shearers* are to be employed in or about a shearing shed, the employer† must give to an Inspector at least three clear days' notice of intention to commence shearing—Section 12 (1). Penalty for failure to notify, £2—Section 12 (2). Shearing sheds where five or less shearers are employed and those situate in cities, towns, and boroughs, are exempt—Section 3.

An employer must provide sufficient accommodation for the comfort and health of shearers in buildings at least fifty yards from the shearing shed—Section 6 (1)—unless such accommodation has been provided prior to the passing of the Act, and conforms to the other requirements of the Act, which are—Section 6 (2) :—

(a) Separate buildings for sleeping accommodation of Asiatics;

(b) Sleeping bunks not placed one above another, and 240 cubic feet air space to each person;

(c) Sleeping-room apart from kitchen and dining-room; if cooking and serving is done in same room, then it must be at different ends thereof;

(d) Separate dining accommodation for Asiatics;

(e) Latrine not less than 25 yards from building, and 50 yards from water supply;

(f) Sufficient good drinking water;

(g) Meat house or safe constructed to keep out flies;

(h) Separate compartment for stores and rations;

(i) Sufficient clean straw or chaff for filling mattresses;

(j) Proper vessels for kitchen slops and refuse, and provision for disposal of same;

(k) Light and ventilation in sleeping and dining rooms;

(l) Floors of approved material;

(m) Proper cooking and washing vessels;

Tent accommodation to the satisfaction of an Inspector shall be deemed sufficient—Section 14.

Buildings must be kept clean by, and must not be damaged by the shearers. Where an employer is put to the expense of cleaning or repairing damage by shearers, the cost thereof, when certified to by an Inspector, may be deducted from the wages due to such shearer—Section 7 (1-5).‡

Where any expense is incurred by a tenant in providing any of the requirements of the Act, such expense shall be borne by the tenant and landlord, in the absence of any agreement to the contrary, in the following proportion—Section 15 (1) :—

If the tenant's interest is—

(a) for less than three years, the whole shall be payable by the landlord;

(b) for three years or less than five years, three-fourths by the landlord and one-fourth by the tenant;

(c) for five years or upwards, the whole by the tenant; provided that if the interest of a tenant be for less than five years, and he commences sheep-farming without the written consent of the landlord, the tenant shall bear the whole cost—Section 15 (2).

The Governor in Council may appoint Inspectors, who shall have free entry into any shearing shed or building provided for accommodation of shearers—Section 5 (1-2)—Penalty for obstruction, £20—Section 5 (3). Every Inspector shall carry a certificate of his appointment, which shall be shown to an employer on demand.

An Inspector may order the requirements of the Act to be complied with; failure to carry out same renders the employer liable to prosecution; and the penalty for not fulfilling the order of the Court entails a fine of £10, and £1 for each day in default—Section 11 (1-4).

By direction of the Hon. the Minister for Agriculture,

W. A. N. ROBERTSON, B.V. Sc.,

Live Stock Division, Department of Agriculture.

---

* " Shearer " means any person employed in work connected with shearing, but does not include regular employés or members of employers family.

† " Employer " means any person owning, having control of, or superintending at any shearing shed.

‡ The 1911 award of the Commonwealth Court of Conciliation and Arbitration provides that the employer may deduct such cost after notifying the shed representative in writing.

THE RELATIVE SOLUBILITY OF THE PHOSPHORIC ACID IN ROCK PHOSPHATE AND BONE-DUST.

W. C. Robertson, Chief Deputy Chemist.

The following table gives the results from an experiment recently conducted at the Agricultural Laboratory.

The object of the test was to ascertain the availability of the phosphoric acid in rock phosphate and bone-dust respectively.

A preliminary experiment was carried out by placing two perforated tin vessels containing pulverised rock phosphate and bone-dust respectively, in a garden soil and covering them to a depth of 12 inches.

The soil was watered every morning and, by a launder arrangement, the drainings were separately collected in two glass vessels.

After the expiration of one month, the drainage water in each vessel was tested for phosphoric acid, with the result that the drainings from the bone-dust gave a distinct affirmative reaction, whereas the test on the liquid from the rock phosphate gave an entirely negative result.

In the experiment under review, the mode of procedure was as follows :—

Two lots of virgin soil, each weighing 7 lbs., were placed in two earthenware jars having an outlet at the bottom.

From the latter, a tube with stop cock attached, led to a glass jar containing in one case 100 grammes of finely ground rock phosphate, and in the other the same amount of bone-dust.

The following diagram will serve to show the arrangement of the apparatus :—

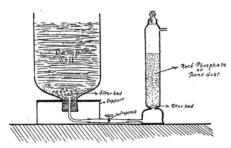

The soil in the earthenware receptacles was kept saturated with water and the drainage conducted through the outlet tube to the glass jars and thus allowed to act upon the material contained therein. The experiment was conducted over a period of four months, but progress analyses were conducted at the end of (a) one week, (b) one month, (c) four months.

The soil in the first instance was analysed for humus and available phosphoric acid and was found to contain 2.3 per cent. humus, whilst the available phosphoric acid content was infinitesimal. The soil water was of an acidity equal to .012 per cent. citric acid.

The subjoined table gives the results :—

Material Treated.	Per cent. of Total Phosphoric Acid dissolved in—			Ratio of Solubility.
	One Week.	One Month.	Four Months.	
Bone dust	per cent. ·41	per cent. ·75	per cent. 1·02	243
Rock Phosphate	Nil	·0019	·0042	1

The bone-dust originally contained 23.5 per cent. phosphoric acid, whereas the rock phosphate contained 37.91 per cent.

The result of the experiment shows the phosphate in bone-dust to be more soluble in soil water than the phosphate in rock phosphate.

SMALL RURAL INDUSTRIES.

D.—GERANIUM CULTIVATION FOR ESSENTIAL OIL.

By Joseph Knight.

The plant from which oil of geranium is obtained is known botanically as the pelargonium. It is a native of South Africa, where many different species are found. It is the intention of the present article to enter into a description of only two of these, namely, "The African," whose botanical name cannot readily be fixed, and "Pelargonium roseum." Both these varieties were grown at the Dunolly Scent Farm, and their value as essential oil producers has been established by actual experience. "The African" yields a large quantity of oil of a quality suitable for the use of soap-makers and other purposes, and should find a ready sale in this State.

"Pelargonium roseum," on the other hand, yields an oil of superior quality, but the quantity is so scanty that for practical purposes its cultivation at present need hardly be considered.

The illustrations show No 1 as "The African," and No. 2 "Pelargonium roseum."

SOIL.

Geranium will grow in any soil—either clay, loam, or sand. The richer the soil the greater will be the yield.

The natural situation of the plant is sandy loam, and in many parts it is cultivated on dry sandy hill-sides. The quality of the oil produced under these conditions is of a superior quality, but lately it is considered that when rich bottom land is employed the yield is considerably increased ; but the oil is said to be inferior, rank, and somewhat coarse. Irrigation, also, has been employed in many cases, and enormous cuttings obtained. Dry or well-drained soil will answer the purpose ; but the plant will not withstand excessive moisture at the roots.

CULTIVATION.

The soil, prior to planting, should be deeply stirred—subsoiling is preferable to trenching, as the bottom soil is usually stubborn and stiff to work. If rich low-lying land is chosen, then the drainage should be attended to.

Like some others of the essential oil-producing plants, rich soil is not absolutely necessary; but where there is poor or medium soil, its cultivation can be undertaken with the expectation of success. The only after-cultivation is the usual ploughing to keep the surface in good tilth and free from weeds.

The planting may be done either in autumn or spring. If a good bed of cuttings is put out in August or September these will be suitable to plant out early in March, or as soon as there is sufficient moisture to continue a growth.

Good results are also obtained by planting good strong cuttings in early spring, and this may be adopted where a bed of cuttings has not been provided. A bed should be well prepared and the set pressed firmly in at the base. A good solid tramping at the bottom is important, so as to exclude the air from the soil, but it should not be tramped on the surface.

NO. 1. THE AFRICAN.   NO. 2. PELARGONIUM ROSEUM.

The distance at which the plants should be placed in their permanent position should be regulated by the class of labour employed in the cultivation. The rows should stand about 4 feet apart, and the plants 3 feet in the rows; but if hand labour is to do the work, then 3 feet each way may be sufficient for carrying out operations. The plant is a strong grower and requires liberal feeding room, and nothing is lost by giving plenty of space.

PLANTS.

No plants are more easily raised—a geranium cutting of any size stuck into the ground grows rapidly into a strong plant—and if planted out in the autumn a fair clipping may be obtained the following summer.

Cuttings may be struck almost at any time. If planted out in a well-prepared bed in spring, they will give strong, well-rooted plants for the following autumn. When planting out, all that is necessary is to trim the top so as to give a well-balanced head, and all long trailing branches should be cut back—this should be accomplished without regard to the depleting of the top, as the plant will soon adjust any loss in this respect. All long trailing roots should also be trimmed off.

A well-balanced plant should be the aim, so that the growth will be even all over.

Season for Cutting.

The cutting season extends over two or three months, and the best time for this purpose is when the plant is in, or coming into, bloom; but it must be understood that no oil is obtained from the flower—but from the leaf and green portion of the plant. The plants should be matured, and this is indicated by the tinge of yellow that shows itself in the foliage.

The young, unmatured foliage does not give off that amount of oil which is obtained from the more matured portion of the plant. In many cases the plant will be found to throw out a second and third course of blooms when the cutting may be prolonged.

CUTTINGS FOR THE STILL.

The plant should be cut back every season, or it becomes coarse and woody.

The above illustration shows the parts which are cut for the still; the lower or strong portion of the plant should be shortened back, to give that bushy growth which alone is useful.

Distilling.

The treatment of this plant in the extraction of the oil is similar to that of others, which have been fully described in previous papers.

The boiling should be carried on slowly; and where a good class of oil is desired, the receiver should be changed when half is taken off, and the last received returned to the still, and the first put aside to cool, when the oil may be easily lifted off from the surface of the water. Unlike roses, no second distilling is necessary, as the oil separates freely.

In many cases the whole is run off in the one receptacle, and the operation completed at one time ; but as water has to be added to each charge, it is as well to utilize that which has a modicum of oil remaining in it, and the second portion of the distilling may be employed for that purpose.

The illustrations below represent vessels for receiving the discharge from the still, and are usually known as " Florentines."—Illustration No. 1. It will be seen that the discharge of water is taken from the bottom of this receptacle, whilst the oil is allowed to float on top.

Illustration No. 2 is a simliar vessel, but it is fitted with a special funnel when distilling oils that have a greater specific gravity than those already described. The object of this will be clearly seen. It is to check the downward tendency in the drop of the oil from the still, and to assist in the separation of the oil from the water by giving it an upward tendency.

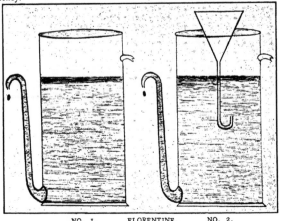

NO. 1.   FLORENTINE.   NO. 2.

There are various forms of these receptacles employed, and which are similar to those illustrated.

YIELD.

It is somewhat difficult to give the yield of oil per acre, as the character of the soil must be taken into consideration. At Dunolly the soil—as before stated—was so unsuitable for this, and other similar plants, that nothing of a reliable nature can be given ; but it is generally estimated that from 5 to 6 tons of green leaf stems may be cut to an average acre, and about 3 lbs. of oil may be obtained per ton. And, again, a second and third cutting can be obtained under ordinary con- ditions of growth. This may not be quite so heavy, yet help to swell the returns per acre.

In many parts where " geranium cultivation " is carried on, three crops in one season are obtained, and the operation of distilling extends over a considerable time. With the aid of irrigation in various parts of this State, there should be no difficulty in getting equally good, if not better, results.

LIST SHOWING RESULTS OF ANALYSES OF SAMPLES OF ARTIFICIAL MANURES COLLECTED IN VICTORIA UNDER THE PROVISIONS OF THE ARTIFICIAL MANURES ACTS.

Label No.	Description of Manure.	Manufacturer or Importer.	Moisture. Found. %	Nitrogen Found. %	Nitrogen Guaranteed. %	Water Soluble Found. %	Water Soluble Guaranteed. %	Citrate Soluble Found. %	Citrate Soluble Guaranteed. %	Insoluble Found. %	Insoluble Guaranteed. %	Total Found. %	Total Guaranteed. %	Potash Found. %	Potash Guaranteed. %	Price asked for the Manure per Ton. £ s. d.
1021	Superphosphate, Federal	Aust. Exp. and Chem. Co.	8·08	…	…	16·68	17·00	1·51	1·00	3·18	2·00	21·37	20·00	…	…	4 7 6
1035	Superphosphate, Florida	Cuming, r…h, and G.	11·45	…	…	17·10	17·00	1·12	1·00	2·44	2·00	20·20	20·00	…	…	4 7 6
1026	Superphosphate, Japan	A. H. Hasell	10·20	…	…	18·38	17·50	…	0·50	1·33	2·00	20·80	29·00	…	…	4 4 6
1023	Superphosphate	P. Rohs	9·76	2·60	…	16·94	16·85	0·56	1·70	0·56	0·45	18·06	19·00	…	…	4 12 6
1031	Blood and Bone Superphosphate	Cuming, Smith, and Co.	10·08	2·62	…	8·96	8·50	3·26	0·50	4·50	5·50	16·72	14·50	…	…	5 7 6
1033	Bone and Superphosphate	…t. Exp. and Chem. Co.	7·10	0·49	0·75	15·21	12·75	3·12	0·75	2·90	6·00	20·90	19·50	…	…	5 0 0
1032	Bone and Superphosphate, No. 1	„ „	4·94	1·52	1·50	10·95	8·50	3·19	0·50	4·19	10·00	18·33	19·00	…	…	5 0 6
1044	Bone and Superphosphate	J. …bill	9·04	1·35	1·50	13·15	12·75	2·42	1·50	3·78	4·75	19·35	19·00	…	…	5 5 0
1014	Dissolved Bones and Superphosphate	Cuming, Smith, and Co.	8·16	1·49	1·00	12·29	10·01	2·41	3·88	4·43	5·48	19·13	19·37	…	…	5 2 6
1024	Bone and Superphosphate, half and half	A. H. Hasell	9·30	1·42	1·50	9·59	9·00	0·65	1·00	9·94	9·50	20·18	19·50	…	…	5 6 6
1034	Bone and Superphosphate, No. 1	Mt. Lyell M. and R. Co.	6·63	1·80	1·50	7·98	8·50	4·27	1·50	8·23	9·00	20·48	19·00	…	…	5 7 6
1018	„ „	…er and G.	7·18	1·64	1·50	11·38	8·50	1·46	0·50	6·10	10·00	18·94	19·00	…	…	5 7 6
1042	„ „	S. and F. Bugg	7·23	1·54	1·50	8·72	8·50	5·00	0·50	4·78	15·78	18·50	21·45	…	…	5 5 6
1046	Bone Fertilizer	Cuming, Smith, and Co.	9·54	3·74	3·58	…	…	9·11	3·50	11·44	18·00	20·55	18·00	…	…	6 0 6
1019	„		6·45	3·10	3·00	…	…	5·04	2·35	12·35	15·42	17·59	18·00	…	…	5 17 6
1045	„		7·82	3·29	3·00	…	…	7·03	3·50	14·50	14·50	15·42	18·00	…	…	5 17 0
1029	„	J. R. „ Smith „	9·54	4·02	3·00	…	…	9·01	3·00	10·27	12·90	16·95	18·00	…	…	5 15 0
1016	„	A. Murphy	9·40	3·69	3·72	…	…	6·68	3·98	12·90	12·50	16·58	16·88	…	…	5 17 0
1041	„	Wischer and Co.	7·94	2·76	3·00	…	…	4·80	3·50	13·47	18·27	18·27	18·00	…	…	5 17 0
1022	Grass Manure	M. Lyell M. and R. Co.	12·45	…	…	11·85	7·00	6·30	11·00	2·9*	1·00	21·12	19·00	2·15	2·00	5 0 0

13941.   z

LIST SHOWING RESULTS OF ANALYSES OF SAMPLES OF ARTIFICIAL MANURES COLLECTED IN VICTORIA UNDER THE PROVISIONS OF THE ARTIFICAL MANURES ACTS—*continued.*

Label No.	Description of Manure.	Manufacturer or Importer.	Moisture. Found.	Nitrogen. Found.	Nitrogen. Guaranteed.	Phosphoric Acid. Found.	Phosphoric Acid. Guaranteed.	Mechanical Condition. Fine. Found.	Mechanical Condition. Fine. Guaranteed.	Mechanical Condition. Coarse. Found.	Mechanical Condition. Coarse. Guaranteed.	Price asked for the Manure per Ton.
			%	%	%	%	%	%	%	%	%	£ s. d.
883	Bonedust	Heinz Bros.	8·31	3·64	2·25	20·83	19·00	59·00	50·00	41·00	50·00	Incorrectly labelled
1036	„	Turner Bros.	6·96	2·92	2·90	22·90	19·00	50·00	30·00	50·00	70·00	Incorrectly labelled

Agricultural Laboratory,
Melbourne, 11th October, 1912.

P. RANKIN SCOTT,
Chemist for Agriculture.

A fat calf contains 65 per cent. of water, a half-fat ox 56 per cent., and a fat ox 48 per cent. In all animals the percentage of water diminishes with age, and especially during fattening.

One gallon of water weighs 10 lbs., and 1 gallon of milk weighs about 5 ozs. more.

Foods contain (1) albuminoids, (2) fats, (3) carbohydrates, (4) salts. Only the albuminoids (protein) can form lean tissue, and the fats and carbohydrates are oxidized to furnish animal heat and work. If not all required for heat and work, fats and carbohydrates can be laid on as fat. Albuminoids can go to form fat too.

SUPPLEMENTARY LIST OF FERTILIZERS REGISTERED AT THE OFFICE OF THE SECRETARY FOR AGRICULTURE UNDER THE ARTIFICIAL MANURES ACTS.

Description of Manure	Brand	Nitrogen	Phosphoric Acid				Potash	Price asked for the Manure per Ton	Where Obtainable
			Water Soluble.	Citrate. Soluble.	In-soluble.	Total.			
		%	%	%	%	%	%	£ s. d.	
Blood and Bone Fertilizer	Robs	7·50		1·75	7·75	1·25	0·50	6 10 0	P. Robs, Bendigo
Blood and Bone Manure	Siekle	5·25		2·10	4·20	9·50		6 5 0	Cuming, Smith, and Co., Melbourne
Blood and Bone Manure	M.L.	6·50		3·75	1·23	6·20		6 7 6	Mt. Lyell M. and R. Co., Melbourne
Bone Fertilizer	Kehuca	2·50		11·40	13·90	15·00		5 10 0	W. G. Boyle, Kehuca
	White Horse	2·50			13·90	23·30		6 0 0	F. W. Richards, Warrenheip
Mildura Citrus, No. 1	Siekle	1·39	3·79	0·92	8·80	12·81	16·20	8 0 0	Cuming, Smith, and Co., Melbourne
Mildura Citrus, No. 2	,,	2·02	5·52	0·32	12·80	18·64		8 12 0	,,
Mildura A. and P., No. 1	,,	3·46	9·41	0·55	1·10	11·06		5 12 6	,,
Mildura A. and P., No. 2	,,	4·45	12·11	0·71	1·42	14·24		9 7 5	,,
Mildura Vine, No. 1	,,	5·53	7·14	0·42	0·84	8·40	11·57	9 7 8	,,
Mildura Vine, No. 2	,,	7·13	7·14	0·54	1·08	10·80		10 5 0	,,
Mildura Vine, No. 3	,,	7·14	9·18	0·54	1·08	8·40	11·57	9 10 0	,,
Mildura Vine, No. 4	,,	9·20	10·60	0·62	1·37	8·80	11·57	10 15 0	,,
Vine Manure, "B."	,,	1·25	3·58	0·24	9·37	13·59	7·48	9 10 0	,,
Mildura Citrus, No. 1	M.L.	1·62	5·21	0·35	13·63	13·19	16·88	9 0 0	Mt. Lyell M. and R. Co., Melbourne
Mildura Citrus, No. 2	,,	2·36	6·73	0·45	1·03	19·19		8 0 0	,,
Mildura Vine, No. 1	,,	5·50	8·67	0·58	1·33	10·58	12·05	10 7 6	,,
Mildura Vine, No. 2	,,	5·80	8·67	0·58	1·03	8·21		7 17 6	,,
Mildura Vine, No. 3	,,	7·14	5·66	1·50	3·50	10·58	12·05	10 15 0	,,
Mildura Vine, No. 4	,,	6·70		1·68	6·18	8·21		7 15 0	,,
Mildura Vine, No. 5	,,	1·00	6·37	0·60	1·36	12·66	17·33	8 10 0	,,
Mildura Vine, No. 6	,,	1·12				14·23	13·00	8 12 6	,,
Mildura A. and P., No. 1	,,	3·46	8·88	0·60	1·36	10·84	12·05	8 12 6	,,
Mildura A. and P., No. 2	,,	3·70	11·43	0·77	1·75	13·05		6 5	,,

Description of Manure	Brand	Nitrogen	Phosphoric Acid	Mechanical Condition.		Price asked for the Manure per ton.	Where Obtainable.
				Fine.	Coarse.		
		%	%	%	%	£ s. d.	
Bonedust	Ox	3·15	22·00	33·00	67·00	5 15 0	Exrs. T. Brown, Hamilton.

Agricultural Laboratory,
Melbourne, 11th October, 1912.

P. RANKIN SCOTT,
Chemist for Agriculture.

ON WATTLES AND WATTLE-BARK.

Alfred J. Ewart, D.Sc., Ph.D., Professor of Botany and Plant Physiology in the Melbourne University.

The efforts of the Field Naturalists' Club and of the Wattle League have recently drawn considerable attention to our native wattles as plants of sufficient beauty to be regarded as the national flower of Victoria or of Australia, and also as being possessed of sufficient economic value to be worthy of cultivation and to be protected from destruction when growing wild. In regard to the question of the wattle as the national flower for Australia, several points of interest may be noted. In the first place, the name " wattle " is an instance of one of those misnomers, or at least words with altered meanings, which are so common in Australia. The word "wattle" is usually applied to the fleshy appendages hanging from the heads of such birds as fowls, and hence the Australian wattle bird receives its name, not from any association with the plants, but from the fleshy appendages which hang from its ears. The name wattle applied to acacias is derived from the Anglo-Saxon word " watel," meaning a hurdle, and hence came to be applied to the osier, *Salix viminalis,* one of the common European willows from whose flexible twigs hurdles were usually woven. The early colonists in New South Wales, using the branches of acacia for similar purposes and for stiffening the mud walls of their huts, applied to these acacias the name of wattle, which has since persisted and passed into general popular use. Strictly speaking, the name wattle should not be used as a general term for all acacias, but only to a certain limited number of species, and it would not be correct to apply it to acacias which grow outside Australia.

With regard to the wattle as the Australian national flower, this is of course entirely a matter for public opinion, and in time the latter is bound to crystallize around some particular plant. The wattle has much in its favour as regards beauty and fragrance as a national floral emblem. From a botanical stand-point, however, the acacias are not nearly as typically Australian as certain other genera, notably eucalyptus. Out of a total of 296 species of eucalyptus, only 25 occur elsewhere, and of these few species all are natives of districts not widely separated from Australia. On the other hand, out of a total of 767 species of acacia known to science, some 417 species are Australian, 112 species are native to Africa, and 234 species grow in other countries.

Hence there would be no valid cause of objection if any other country—South Africa, for instance—were also to adopt the wattle as its national flower; and although the eucalyptus is peculiarly Australian, it now grows in such abundance in many parts of the world as to form a characteristic feature of the forest flora, and to give rise to the possibility of its being adopted as a national flower for certain of the States in North America, or for some of the smaller Principalities in Europe, not as yet provided with a national floral emblem. As a matter of fact, botanical considerations usually play little part in the adoption of national flowers. There is, for instance, no special botanical reason why the rose should be the national flower for England, or the lily the national flower of France; while in the case of Scotland, the national flower a botanist would have selected would probably have been the heather.

In our own case, the special merit of the wattle probably lies in the fact that so many species flower at the same time, early in spring, forming a conspicuous feature in the landscape and giving the first relief from winter's floral monotony. Regarding the fears that have been expressed that the popularization of the wattle—if it needs any popularizing—and its adoption as the national flower may lead to its destruction, this is not a very serious danger. The adoption of the thistle as the national flower of Scotland has, for instance, not caused this plant to become extinct, nor have roses or lilies suffered in any way through being national flowers. Wattles in particular are easily planted and quickly grown, and are able to re-establish themselves year after year on ground where they have once grown, provided the conditions are suitable. It is probably no exaggeration to say that there are sufficient dormant wattle seeds lying in the surface soil of Victoria to cover the whole of Australia with a dense crop of wattles, if planted out and given the conditions necessary for development. The only damage done to wattles by people removing blossoms is when large branches are broken off, spoiling the symmetry of the tree and leaving a ragged injury aiding the penetration of borers or starting decay. Small, slender flowering branches may be cut or broken off without injuring the tree in the least; and, in fact, pruning off all the flowering branches each season would increase the life of the tree and give it a more compact growth. Most wattles can, in fact, be pruned much more severely than is generally imagined without suffering or being permanently injured, and in gardens a little judicious pruning will often considerably improve the appearance of various acacias, particularly when individual branches show signs of disease.

WATTLES FOR GARDENS AND PARKS.

Although wattles or acacias in general are well suited for garden cultivation, they are not suitable plants for street planting, particularly in large towns. For the most part they are very apt to become begrimed and dingy in appearance in an atmosphere which is at all smoky. In addition, the duration of life is short and also irregular. The best selected and tended avenue of acacias could rarely be relied upon for more than ten years, and after that time would need continual replanting as single trees died, so that the symmetry would always be broken by a series of gaps. Apart from the attacks of the borer beetle, the acacias in general are liable to the attacks of various plant and animal parasites, which may injure the trees or may completely distort its natural appearance. The natural habitat of most of our common acacias is on the fringes of forests, in open forest glades, and generally among other trees wherever a sufficient opening occurs. They do best, in fact, when given a certain amount of protection by other vegetation. This applies particularly to the species with tender leaflets and to a somewhat lesser extent to those with large flat phyllodes. The species with prickly or needle-like leaves, on the other hand, stand exposure much better, but have no special decorative or economic value for the most part.

Many of our Australian acacias are very suitable plants for cultivation in gardens and parks. A list of these was compiled by Mr. F. Pitcher, of the Botanic Gardens, and issued as a leaflet by the Wattle League. With a few slight alterations the list in question is given beneath, and though it does not entirely exhaust all the acacias which may be worthy of cultivation. it is sufficiently comprehensive for ordinary purposes.

Acacia acinacea, "Gold Dust Acacia." Approximate height, 5-8 feet. Victoria, New South Wales, and South Australia.

,, *armata,* "Hedge Acacia." 10-15 feet. Western Australia, South Australia, Victoria, New South Wales, and Queensland.

,, *Baileyana,* "Cootamundra Wattle." 10-15 feet. New South Wales.

,, *brachybotrya,* "Silvery Acacia." 4-8 feet. Victoria, New South Wales, and South Australia.

,, *buxifolia,* "Box Acacia." 3-5 feet. New South Wales and Queensland.

,, *cardiophylla,* "Wyalong Wattle." 8-10 feet. New South Wales.

,, *cultriformis,* "Knife-leaved Wattle." 8-15 feet. New South Wales and Queensland.

,, *cyanophylla,* "Blue-leaved Wattle." 12-20 feet. Western Australia.

,, *dealbata,* "Silver Wattle." 80-100 feet. Victoria, New South Wales. Queensland, South Australia, and Tasmania.

,, *decurrens,* "Early Black Wattle," or "Green Wattle." 10-20 feet. New South Wales, Victoria. and Queensland.

,, *diffusa,* "Spreading Acacia." 3-5 feet. Victoria, New South Wales, and Tasmania.

,, *discolor,* "Sunshine Wattle." 10-20 feet. Victoria, New South Wales, and Tasmania.

,, *elata,* "Cedar Acacia," or "New Year Wattle." 60-80 feet. New South Wales.

,, *homalophylla,* "Yarram Acacia." 15-40 feet. Victoria, New South Wales, Queensland, and South Australia.

,, *implexa,* "Lightwood Acacia." 30 feet. Victoria, New South Wales, and Queensland.

,, *iteaphylla,* "South Australian Wattle." 8-12 feet. South Australia.

,, *Jonesii,* "Jones Acacia." 5 feet. New South Wales.

,, *juniperina,* "Juniper Acacia." 8-10 feet. Victoria, New South Wales, Queensland, and Tasmania.

,, *leprosa,* "Leper Acacia." 15-30 feet. Victoria and New South Wales.

Acacia leprosa var. elongata, "Seville Wattle."   10-20 feet. Victoria.

  ,,   *linearis,* " Narrow-leaved Acacia."   5-8 feet.   Victoria, New South Wales, Queensland, and Tasmania.

  ,,   *lincifolia,* "Flax Acacia."   8-12 feet.   Victoria, New South Wales, and Queensland.

  ,,   *longifolia,* "Sallow Acacia."   15-30 feet.   Victoria, New South Wales, Queensland, South Australia, and Tasmania.

  ,,   *longifolia, var. floribunda,* " Marrai-us," or " Many-flowered Acacia."   8-12 feet.   Victoria and New. South Wales.

  ,,   *longifolia var. Sophorae,* " Coast Acacia." 3-8 feet.   Victoria, New South Wales, Queensland, South Australia, and Tasmania.

  ,,   *lunata,* "Crescent Acacia."   3-5 feet.   Victoria, New South Wales, and Queensland.

  ,,   *Macradenia,* " Mackay (Myall) Wattle."   10-12 feet. Queensland.

  ,,   *Maidenii,* "Maiden Acacia."   50 feet.   New South Wales and Queensland.

  ,,   *melanoxylon,* "Blackwood Acacia."   40-100 feet.   Victoria, New South Wales, South Australia, and Tasmania.

  ,,   *Mitchelli,* " Fringe Wattle."   2-6 feet.   Victoria and South Australia.

  ,,   *mollissima,* "Late Black Wattle."   30-100 feet.   Victoria, New South Wales, South Australia, and Tasmania.

  ,,   *montana,* "Mountain Acacia."   4-6 feet.   Victoria, New South Wales, and South Australia.

  ,,   *myrtifolia,* "Myrtle Acacia."   5-8 feet.   Victoria, New South Wales, Queensland, South Australia, Western Australia, and Tasmania.

  ,,   *oxycedrus,* "Spike Acacia."   3-10 feet.   Victoria, New South Wales, South Australia, and Tasmania.

  ,,   *pendula,* "Weeping Myall," or "Boree."   30-40 feet. New South Wales and Queensland.

  ,,   *penninervis,* "Hickory Wattle."   30-40 feet.   Victoria, New South Wales, Queensland, and Tasmania.

  ,,   *podalyrifolia,* "Queensland Silver Wattle."   10-15 feet. New South Wales and Queensland.

  ,,   *pravissima,* "Ovens Acacia."   10-20 feet.   Victoria and New South Wales.

  ,,   *prominens,* " Golden-rain Acacia."   10-15 feet.   New South Wales.

  ,,   *pruinosa,* "Frosty Acacia."   10-15 feet.   New South Wales.

  ,,   *pycnantha,* "Golden Wattle."   20-40 feet.   Victoria, New South Wales, and South Australia.

  ,,   *retinodes,* "Wirilda Acacia."   10-20 feet.   Victoria and South Australia.

Acacia Riceana, "Rice Wattle." 8-10 feet. Tasmania.

" *salicina,* "Willow Acacia." 15-25 feet. Western Australia, South Australia, Victoria, New South Wales, Queensland, and North Australia.

" *saligna,* "Western Wattle." 12-20 feet. Western Australia.

" *spectabilis,* "Showy Acacia." 8-12 feet. New South Wales and Queensland.

" *stricta,* "Straight-leaved Acacia. 2-10 feet. Victoria, New South Wales, and Tasmania.

" *strigosa,* "Hairy Acacia." 2-4 feet. Western Australia.

" *suaveolens,* "Sweet Acacia.' '6 feet. Victoria, New South Wales, Queensland, South Australia, and Tasmania.

" *verniciflua,* "Varnish Acacia." 5-10 feet. Victoria, New South Wales, South Australia, and Tasmania.

" *verticillata,* "Prickly Acacia." 8-15 feet. Victoria, New South Wales, South Australia, and Tasmania.

ECONOMIC VALUE OF ACACIAS.

Acacias have both a direct and an indirect economic value. Owing to the fact that they are plants which bear nitrogen-assimilating root tubercles, they are important agents in maintaining the nitrogenous constituents of a fertile soil, and hence making good the loss occasioned by forest fires. The hard seeds of various species of acacia are able to remain living in the soil for long periods of time. The following are a few of the longest records obtained by me for different species of acacia, whose seeds had been kept dry for the periods of time mentioned :—

		Age.		Germination.	
Acacia acinacea		51	years	4	per cent.
"	*alata*	30	"	4	"
"	*aneura*	20	"	56	"
"	*armata*	51	"	11	"
"	*bossiaeoides*	57	"	3	"
"	*brachybotrya*	57	"	4	"
"	*calamifolia*	18	"	80	"
"	*dealbata*	15	"	65	"
"	*decurrens*	17	"	63	"
"	*diffusa*	59	"	10	"
"	*doratoxylon*	20	"	6	"
"	*elata*	30	"	16	"
"	*Farnesiana*	15	"	5	"
"	*glaucescens*	20	"	46	"
"	*lanigera*	20	"	20	"
"	*leprosa*	51	"	28	"
"	*longifolia*	52	"	21	"
"	*longifolia*	68	"	5	"
"	*lunata*	48	"	8	"
"	*melanoxylon*	51	"	12	"

			Age.		Germination.
Acacia	*Merralli*	..	10 years	..	6 per cent.
„	*montana*	..	58 „	..	2 „
„	*myrtifolia*	..	55 „	..	5 „
„	*neriifolia*	..	17 „	..	4 „
„	*nervosa*	..	30 „	..	4 „
„	*Oswaldi*	..	10 „	..	50 „
„	*penninervis*	..	67 „	..	3 „
„	*pentadenia*	..	30 „	..	7 „
„	*Senegal*	..	51 „	..	5 „
„	*Simsii* .	..	31 „	..	15 „
„	*suaveolens*	..	51 „	..	4 „
„	*verniciflua*	..	41 „	..	4 „

In each sample of air-dried seeds it is the hard seeds which last longest, and in the soil it is only these hard, non-swelling seeds which can last for any length of time. In my paper on the "Longevity of Seeds," I have used the term "macrobiotic" to denote seeds of this character which are specially adapted for dispersal in time rather than in space.[*]

To some extent these macrobiotic seeds are adaptations to bush fires, which were probably of common occurrence long before the advent of civilized or even uncivilized man, and must have been far more frequent than at present when the lava was flowing from the volcanoes of Victoria.

Such bush fires, after burning off the humus more or less, not only partly expose the seeds, but leave behind an alkaline ash, which the next rain falling on the warm ground aids in softening the coats of the hard seeds, and bringing about their germination. When the ash is abundant and very alkaline the seedlings may be killed, but some will always survive. In addition, slight charring of the surface of the seed makes it permeable to water without necessarily destroying the vitality of the contents. The acacias or other leguminous plants, by the aid of their root-nodules, can grow in soil from which all, or nearly all, the humus has been burnt away, and the source of nitrates hence removed. They steadily enrich the soil again, and produce the conditions for the growth of large forest trees. These, if destroyed by a devastating bush fire, may once more be replaced by the humus-forming acacias, &c., whose seeds have lain dormant in the soil during part, at least, of the growth of the forest.

I have, in fact, found acacia seeds deeply buried in the soil of gum forests, where no other signs of their presence could be seen, and where no other acacias were present within at least a mile. In addition, the following data on page 690 may be given of the number of germinable acacia seeds per 2-in. cube of soil found at various depths under old acacias growing in undisturbed primeval bush.

A square pole of such soil would in the top 18 inches, in some cases, contain sufficient germinable seed to stock several square miles of territory, so that the amount of margin allowed for accident is very great, and even a very low percentage germination would suffice to re-cover the soil with the original vegetation after the severest bush

---

[*] See " Longevity of Seeds " in Proc. Roy. Soc. Vict., 21 (N.S.) Pt. 1 1908.

fire. The percentage germinations are high, because as soon as the seed becomes permeable in the course of time and swells, it either germinates or dies, so that in the deeper layers the only seeds found are likely to be hard macrobiotic ones. In fact, all the seeds found in the soil below the surface needed treatment with sulphuric acid to produce swelling and germination. Once they are swollen, the seeds are incapable of remaining long living in a latent condition without germinating, and this applies generally to the seeds of Leguminosæ, whether cuticularized or not.

	Depth.	Seeds Present in Eight Cubic Inches.	Number Germinable.	Per Cent.
	in.			
Acacia dealbata	3	28	26	93
,, ,, ...	6	17	13	77
,, ,, ...	9	16	10	63
,, ,, ...	12	11	9	82
,, ,, ...	18	3	3	100
,, *stricta*	4	1	1	100
,, ,, ...	8	2	2	100
,, ,, ...	12	0	0	0
,, *leprosa*	6	28	24	86
,, ,, ...	12	15	14	93
,, *melanoxylon*	4	11	10	91
,, ,, ...	8	5	4	80
,, ,, ...	12	2	2	100
,, *longifolia*	6	2	2	100
,, Var. *mucronata* ..	16	0	0	0
,, *verticillata*	4	32	26	81
,, ,, ...	8	5	4	80
.. ..	12	4	4	100

Hence it is not surprising to find that it has been found possible to establish a breakwind of acacias on land where they had previously grown by merely fencing off a broad strip of land, letting a fire run over the surface and then ploughing. Sufficient seed was present in the surface soil to germinate under this treatment and establish a good wind-break of acacias without any planting or seeding being necessary. It will, of course, only succeed on ground where acacias were formerly abundant, and the interval of time since acacias were originally present must not be too great, probably not much more than fifty years or so.

On new ground, acacias can only be established either by planting or sowing seed. Every sample of acacia seed will contain a variable percentage of hard seed according to the conditions under which the seed ripens, and occasionally all, or nearly all, the seed in a particular sample may be hard. This hardness is due to the impregnation of the outer skin, either the cuticle or also part of the epidermal layers, with a waxy substance, making the seed impermeable to water. If a little nick is made in the skin with a file, water enters the seed at this point, making it begin to swell and separating the particles in the wax layer, so that the whole seed is able to absorb water and swell..

The same effect may be produced by soaking the seeds in concentrated sulphuric acid for one to six hours until the waxy layer is eaten away, and then washing them well with water and lime water to remove or neutralize any traces of acid adhering to the skin. This method needs some care in its application, since the seeds must not remain either too long or too short a time in the acid, and this is best determined by a previous trial of a small sample. It is in all cases, however, best to test the seed by soaking in water a few of the seeds for a couple of days or so, and noting how many swell and how many become hard. If only 10 per cent. or so of the seeds remain hard, it is not worth while treating the bulk at all, but if only a minority of the seeds swell after two to three days in water, then unless the hard seeds are softened there will be great waste, since it is usually the hard seeds which give the best percentage germination when softened.

The simplest method of softening the seed is to drop them into water which has just boiled, and then allow them to remain in the water until it is cold. Seeds treated in this way should be planted at once, whereas those treated with sulphuric acid or filed can be kept dry for a considerable length of time. Filing the seeds, however, is, of course, only possible where small quantities are used.

Sowing seeds broadcast on ploughed or burnt land involves a considerable waste of seed, and is not always satisfactory in its results. Planting seedlings or individual seeds appears at first a more expensive and troublesome way of establishing a plantation, but is in the long run more satisfactory in its results, and enables the plants to be spaced out the proper distance apart without any subsequent thinning being necessary. If, however, the seedlings are grown in masses in trays, they are apt to suffer when planted owing to the disturbance of their roots. On the other hand, growing singly in pots in the ordinary way means considerable expense. For raising seedling trees on a large scale, the Forests Department uses a very cheap, ingenious, and indestructible pot. This consists of a strip of thin metal (tin, zinc, or galvanized iron may be used) something like an ordinary collar, but shorter and broader, and with the free ends bent over, one inwards and one outwards, so as to form an interlocking flange. When bent round and the flange interlocked, it forms a flower pot with sloping sides but no bottom. As it stands on a slab no bottom is necessary, and by the time the seedlings are large enough to plant out the roots have bound the soil in the pot together. When planting, a little lateral pressure unlocks the flanges, the strip of metal unrolls, and the roots, with the soil around them, can be planted with a minimum of disturbance. Another method is to raise seedlings in short lengths of bamboos filled with soil, simply splitting the bamboo and planting the whole in the soil when the seedling is old enough. The tubes should be 4 to 6 inches long, and hollow throughout. If the tube is already soft it need not be split before planting. Where preferred, however, plantations may be established by broadcasting the seed. In the case of the "Golden Wattle, *Acacia pycnantha,* Mr. Gill recommends ploughing to a depth of 6 inches or so, and broadcasting about half a pound of seed to a quarter of a bushel of sand, subsequently covering the seed to a depth of about an inch by using a light harrow if the land is rough, or a brush harrow if sandy. The sowing of the seed may take place during autumn or winter in light, well-drained soils; but in heavy, wet, cold land it is best to delay sowing until spring-time. Frequently, in thin or patchy forest land, the patches may be filled up with acacias by burning away the undergrowth and putting in seeds at distances of 8 or 10 feet. Mr. Gill states that, according to some, the best wattle-bark is usually obtained from wattles grown under the shelter of larger trees; but it is, of course, more difficult to protect such plantations from fire, cattle, and bark-strippers.

(To be continued.)

SECOND VICTORIAN EGG-LAYING COMPETITION, 1912-13.

H. V. Hawkins, Poultry Expert, report for month ending 14th October.

Good average results were obtained from the 69 pens engaged in the present competition for the month ending on the 14th inst. The weather has not been too favorable for high averages, due to the variations of temperature and at times rain squalls, accompanied by much wind, which has severely tried the light breeds. The general health of the birds has been good. Three deaths occurred during the month, all three being White Leghorns, due in each case to oviduct troubles; replacements were made according to the rules.

Mr. Samuel Brown's White Leghorns are well in front, having laid consistently for the half-year, and their condition is very satisfactory. As there are indications of broodiness amongst others which are well up in the list, Mr. Brown's pen may retain its position throughout.

The total number of eggs laid during the half-year is 38,621, an average of 559.7 per pen. The feeding has been somewhat changed, the meat ration being reduced one-half, due to the necessity of narrowing the ratio as the warmer weather approaches; very little maize has been fed during the past few weeks, wheat and short oats being used together with ample green lucerne, chopped finely.

The present test has so far again demonstrated the superiority of the small combed birds. The lowest pen in the competition is one of large-bodied, big-combed White Leghorns, coarse in the head, whilst the leading 20 pens have small combs, are more active, and will be found less subject to heat apoplexy as the hot weather approaches.

SECOND VICTORIAN EGG-LAYING COMPETITION, 1912-13.

Commencing 15th April, 1912.

CONDUCTED AT BURNLEY HORTICULTURAL SCHOOL.

No. of Pen.	Breed.	Name of Owner.	Eggs laid during competition.			Position in Competition.
			April 15 to Sept. 14.	Sept. 15 to Oct. 14.	Total to Date (6 months).	
40	White Leghorns	S. Brown	622	134	756	1
28	"	F. G. Eagleton	581	142	723	2
23	"	W. McLister	594	127	721	3
9	"	J. Spotswood	577	141	718	4
31	"	Geo. Edwards	590	126	716	5
47	"	J. E. Bradley	583	124	707	6
20	"	E. Waldon	562	134	696	7
70	"	C. J. Beatty	559	115	674	} 8
46	Black Orpingtons	H. A. Langdon	549	125	674	} 8
62	White Leghorns	R. W. Pope	529	142	671	10
1	"	J. Campbell	541	128	669	11
3	Black Orpingtons	King and Watson	547	121	668	12
37	White Leghorns	C. B. Bertelsmeier	519	138	657	13
45	"	Wooldridge Bros.	512	135	647	14
24	"	Sargenti Poultry Yards	514	131	645	15
48	"	Griffin Cant	519	123	642	16
25	"	R. L. Appleford	504	133	637	} 17
14	"	J. H. Wright	501	136	637	} 17
29	"	J. B. Brigden	502	127	629	19
13	"	W. B. Crellin	489	132	621	} 20
38	"	R. Moy	501	120	621	} 20
39	"	W. G. Swift	489	132	621	} 20
61	Black Orpingtons	Jas. Ogden	494	126	620	23
2	White Leghorns	B. Rowlinson	496	121	617	24
6	"	J. B. McArthur	486	127	613	25
44	"	A. W. Hall	484	126	610	26
50	"	A. Ahpee	477	129	606	} 27
49	"	W. Purvis	482	124	606	} 27
8	Black Orpingtons	D. Fisher	514	84	598	} 29
15	White Leghorns	Mrs. Steer	469	129	598	} 29
30	"	Mrs. Stevenson	483	111	594	31
33	"	H. McKenzie	449	137	586	32
7	"	A. H. Padman	447	138	585	33
63	"	Percy Walker	462	114	576	34
53	"	H. Hodges	442	130	572	35
19	"	Cowan Bros.	450	119	569	36
35	"	C. H. Busst	439	129	568	37
5	"	J. H. Brain	430	131	561	38
42	"	Mrs. Kempster	431	125	556	39
56	"	M. A. Monk	437	112	549	40
10	R.C. Brown Leghorns	S. P. Giles	413	126	539	41
51	White Leghorns	H. Hammill	411	125	536	42
64	"	H. Merrick	412	117	529	43
54	"	F. R. DeGaris	387	132	519	44
60	"	Miss B. E. Ryan	398	119	517	45
65	"	A. H. Thomson	382	128	510	46
16	Silver Wyandottes	R. Jobling	382	124	506	} 47
69	White Leghorns	Morgan and Watson	368	138	506	} 47
43	"	G. Purton	386	117	503	49
32	"	S. Brundrett	365	134	499	50
11	Black Orpingtons	T. S. Goodisson	365	133	498	51
27	White Leghorns	E. Nash	360	123	483	52
4	"	J. Blackburne	358	116	474	} 53
57	"	B. Walker	366	108	474	} 53
58	"	W. J. Stock	356	117	473	55
41	"	A. Stringer	340	131	471	56
12	"	T. H. Stafford	337	132	469	57
52	Black Minorcas	Chalmers Bros.	356	97	453	58
55	Brown Leghorns	J. Mathieson	329	120	449	59
68	White Leghorns	W. J. McKeddie	307	118	425	60
66	"	J. Molouey	299	125	424	61
21	"	J. O'Loughlin	295	117	412	62
18	"	B. Mitchell	307	103	410	63
22	"	W. N. Ling	277	125	402	64
67	Anconas	A. E. Manning	268	121	389	65
36	Old English Game	K. J. Barrett	256	116	372	66
59	White Leghorns	W. J. Seabridge	259	102	361	67
34	"	R. F. B. Moore	226	118	344	68
17	"	S. Childs	197	143	340	69
26	"	(Reserved)	..	..	..	..
		Totals ..	30,018	8,603	38,621	

WHEAT AND ITS CULTIVATION.

(*Continued from page* 552.)

No. 8.—MANURIAL PROBLEMS—*continued.*

A. E. V. Richardson, M.A., B.Sc., Agricultural Superintendent.

In the September issue consideration was given to the factors involved in Soil Fertility, and to the position of Nitrogen in Victorian agriculture.   It was shown that soils of the wheat areas of Victoria differed very widely from those of Europe, in regard to available nitrogen supplies, owing principally to the exceptional rate at which nitrification proceeds under the conditions which obtain in our wheat areas.   It is now necessary to consider the requirements of the wheat areas with respect to phosphoric acid and potash.

Phosphatic Manures.

Importance.—Phosphatic manures are of the greatest practical importance to the cereal farmer.   One striking peculiarity in Australian soils, as compared with those of Europe, is the uniformly low phosphatic content.

We need not here enter into a speculative discussion as to the probable causes of this deficiency.   It is sufficient to note that practical experience and experimental work throughout the wheat belt of Australia has conclusively demonstrated the value and necessity. of phosphates in cereal culture.   In many of the wheat areas the use of soluble phosphates is absolutely essential to secure a crop.   The importance of soluble phosphates in Australian cereal culture is strikingly demonstrated by the Commonwealth Statistics for 1911-12.   The following table, taken from the *Year-Book* for 1911-12, indicates the amount of artificial manure (nearly wholly phosphates) used in the four wheat-growing States of the Commonwealth, and the percentage of the manured area to the total area:—

State.	Artificial Manures used.	Total Area under Crop.	Area manured.	Percentage of Crop manured.
	Tons.	Acres.	Acres.	Per cent.
New South Wales ..	25,017	3,386,017	1,030,554	30·43
Victoria ..	86,316	3,952,070	2,714,854	68·69
South Australia ..	81,899	2,746,334	2,235,578	81·40
Western Australia ..	33,194	855,024	773,561	90·47

Sources of Phosphatic Fertilizers.—The most important sources of phosphorus are the minerals apatite and phosphorite, the various deposits of phosphatic guanos, and the widely distributed natural rock phosphates.   The inorganic portion of bones contains a large percentage of phosphates of lime, which is the principal fertilizing constituent of bone manures.

Another source of phosphates is the phosphatic slag obtained in the Bessemer process for making steel from iron ores rich in phosphorus.

From the mineral phosphates and bones, such manufactured phosphatic fertilizers as superphosphate, dissolved bones, concentrated superphosphate, are obtained.

Phosphates of Lime. —The calcium compounds are by far the most important of the compounds of phosphoric acid, and a knowledge of these is of practical importance to the farmer.

Phosphoric acid $(P_2O_5. 3H_2O)$ forms with lime three distinct compounds, namely, tricalcic, dicalcic, and monocalcic phosphate.

In these three compounds, one part of phosphoric acid combines with three, two, and one part of lime respectively. The degree of solubility of these compounds varies considerably. Thus, the tricalcic form $(3Ca, OP_2O_5)$ containing one part of phosphoric acid combined with three parts of lime, is insoluble in water, in weak organic acids, and is only soluble in mineral acids, such as sulphuric acid. It is the form found in bones and in rock phosphate and guano. It corresponds to the insoluble phosphate on the manure guarantee tags.

1.—GENERAL VIEW OF THE PERMANENT MANURIAL PLOTS, RUTHERGLEN EXPERIMENTAL FARM.

Dicalcic phosphate ($2CaO, H_2O, P_2O_5$) is insoluble in water, but soluble in weak organic acids and in citrate of ammonia. It is the form in which the phosphate is found in "reverted" superphosphate.

Monocalcic phosphate ($CaO, 2H_2O, P_2O_5$), so named because one unit of phosphoric acid is combined with one unit of lime, is freely soluble in water, and is of immediate value as plant food. It is the form found in superphosphate, dissolved bones, &c., and corresponds to the "water soluble phosphate" of the manure guarantees.

The following table summarizes these facts:—

Name.	Composition.		Formula.	Solubility.	Found in—
1. Tricalcic phosphate (insoluble phosphate)	Lime Lime Lime	Phosphoric acid	$3CaO\ P_2O_5$ or $Ca_3\,(PO_4)_2$	Insoluble in water and citrate of ammonia	Bones, guano, mineral phosphate
2. Dicalcic phosphate ("Reverted phosphate," "slowly soluble phosphate")	Lime Lime Water	Phosphoric acid	$2CaO\ H_2O\ P_2O_5$ or $Ca_2H_2P_2O_4$	Insoluble in water; soluble in citrate of ammonia	Reverted super.
3. Monocalcic phosphate (water soluble phosphate)	Lime Water Water	Phosphoric acid	$CaO\ 2H_2O\ P_2O_5$ or $CaH_4P_2O_4$	Soluble in water ..	Superphosphate, dissolved bones

NOTE.—In addition, there is a fourth form of phosphate called tetracalcic phosphate, which has the composition—$4CaO\ P_2O_5$—which is found in basic slag or Thomas' phosphate. The precise composition of Thomas' phosphate is not known, but it is possible that the phosphoric acid is present in the form of a double silicate and phosphate of lime, while smaller amounts are present as tetracalcic phosphate.

SUPERPHOSPHATE.

This is deservedly the most popular and profitable artificial manure used in the wheat areas of Australia at the present time. There are very few soils in the wheat areas proper which will not favorably and profitably respond to applications of super., and in dry seasons many soils fail altogether to produce a crop without soluble phosphates.

In 1840, Liebig, the great German chemist, suggested that insoluble tricalcic phosphate—the form in which phosphoric acid exists in bones and rock phosphates—could be changed into the soluble monocalcic phosphate by treatment with sulphuric acid. The product obtained as a result of this action is superphosphate.

The change which takes place may be simply represented thus. When the sulphuric acid acts on the tricalcic phosphate, two parts of lime are abstracted from the latter compound and two parts of water substituted. A mixture of monocalcic phosphate and gypsum is, therefore, formed, which constitutes the superphosphate of commerce. The action may be represented thus—

$$3CaO.P_2O_5 + 2\,(H_2O\ SO_3) = CaO\ 2H_2O\ P_2O_5 + 2CaSO_4$$

(Tricalcic phosphate)   (Sulphuric acid)   (Monocalcic phosphate)   (Gypsum)

Superphosphate.

"REVERSION" OF SUPERPHOSPHATE.

The rapidity of the action of superphosphate is due to its great solubility. But under certain circumstances the soluble phosphate in super. undergoes change and becomes converted into less soluble forms. This change in the solubility is known as " reversion." Such reversion, whatever may be its cause, obviously depreciates the value of the manure.

This reversion may be considerable in manures made from raw phosphate containing large percentages of iron and alumina compounds. For this reason, manufacturers generally refrain from using natural phosphates containing much iron and alumina. A slight amount of reversion may take place when super. is kept for any length of time. This is due to the fact that manufacturers usually use less sulphuric acid than is actually required to change the whole of the tricalcic phosphate to soluble phosphate, in order to avoid the presence of free acid in the manure. Hence, the undissolved tricalcic phosphate reacts with the soluble and forms reverted phosphate. When applied to the soil, however, the process of reversion goes on at a wholesale rate, due to

2.—A CORNER OF THE PERMANENT ROTATION PLOTS, RUTHERGLEN EXPERIMENTAL FARM.

Plot 31, Rape; 32, Barley; 33, Peas; 34, Wheat; 35, Rye and Vetches.

the action of. lime, alumina, and iron compounds. in the soil. If this is so, one might naturally ask why superphosphate is so superior to other forms of phosphate, if it begins to revert to more insoluble forms immediately it is applied to the soil; and, why should the manufacturer go to the trouble of converting it into water soluble phosphate?

The reason for the efficacy of the super. may probably be accounted for by the fact that when it is applied to the soil, the soluble phosphate is dissolved by the soil water or by the rains, and it immediately becomes thoroughly and intimately diffused through the soil before the process of reversion actually takes place. Moreover, in the form of a solution, the particles of monocalcic phosphate are in the finest state of sub-division possible—in a far more finely divided state than could ever be obtained by any process of grinding. It is owing to the infinitely minute state of subdivision of the soluble phosphate and its intimate mixture with the soil particles that its action is more rapid than the other phosphates.

Rate of Application of Superphosphate.—Opinions differ very widely as to the most suitable quantity of manure to use per acre for a wheat crop. Many farmers apply as little as 30 to 40 lbs. per acre, and consider the dressing quite sufficient; whilst there are many who use relatively heavy dressings, namely, 1 to 2 cwt. per acre. The rate of application will naturally vary with the soil and rainfall. In regions of light rainfall the dressings are generally reduced to a minimum, whilst in moister districts much larger quantities can be used with profit. In the drier districts heavy dressings may not infrequently lead to rank and vigorous growth, and in seasons of short rainfall transpiration from leaf and stem goes on so rapidly that the available moisture supplies give out with disastrous results to the crop. Obviously, such a contingency is less likely to happen with crops sown on well-prepared fallows. In considering the most profitable amount to apply, it must be remembered that conditions are such in the wheat areas that the farmer derives a considerable portion of his income from sheep. Consequently, in determining the most profitable dressing to apply, it becomes necessary to consider the indirect effect of the manure on the pasture as well as its mere direct effect upon the crop.

Now, it is a well established fact that relatively heavy dressings of superphosphate produce in Australian wheat soils a remarkable effect on the pastures. A marked stimulation of the leguminous growth on the stubble and pasture succeeding the wheat crop invariably results from heavy dressings of soluble phosphates, and the stock carrying capacity of the pasture is greatly increased.

Increased stock carrying capacity is quite as important to the cereal farmer as the direct effect of the manure on his crop, for, on the average wheat farm, the returns from sheep, wool, and lambs do not fall far short of those from wheat. This being the case, it would appear that, if the indirect effect on the pastures is taken into consideration, it is probable that, in moister districts at least, relatively heavy dressings will be far more profitable than light dressings.

Just what quantities may be most profitably applied in any given district can, of course, only be determined by actual trial. In such trials, however, we should look further ahead than the mere results on the season's crop.

The residual value of various applications should be carefully measured by their effect on the resultant stubble and pasture. Unfortunately, the residual value of various heavy and light dressings of super. on the sheep carrying capacity of the pasture has not been the subject of systematic and continued experiment in this State, and there is no local data as a guide.

In any case it is well to remember that, even if the value of the extra yield obtained from heavy dressings merely covers the increased cost of the manure, it will pay to use the heavy dressing, because the soil is being enriched in phosphoric acid without extra cost.

It may be thought that, if more soluble phosphates are applied than are really necessary for a wheat crop, the excess is lost for succeeding crops. Such, however, is not the case. Phosphates, unlike nitrates, are not generally found in the drainage waters. They become fixed in the soil shortly after their application. As explained above, soluble phosphates, when applied to the soil, become dissolved and intimately mixed with the soil particles, and then rapidly undergo conversion into less soluble forms. In this manner

3.—GENERAL VIEW OF THE FEEDING OFF EXPERIMENTS, RUTHERGLEN EXPERIMENTAL FARM.

they are fixed in the soil and prevented from becoming lost. This is borne out by the investigations of Dyer in the permanent plots of the Rothamsted experimental station. Dyer's results show that practically no loss of phosphoric acid has taken place on the plot heavily manured with super. for over fifty years.

It is often asked whether the continual use of superphosphate will impoverish or exhaust the soil. Real soil exhaustion, of course, can never take place. Bad farming practices, however, may reduce the fertility of the soil to such a low level as to render cropping operations unprofitable. For practical purposes we say that such a soil is "worn out" or "exhausted."

Now, the repeated use of superphosphate will not bring about any such soil exhaustion, if the farm operations are intelligently conducted. The continued use of phosphates will merely bring about a state of things in which further applications of phosphate will no longer prove profitable. The soil will not, however, be exhausted. It will merely contain an excess of phosphates, and it may then be necessary to apply other manures such as nitrates in order to maintain production at a high level.

In soils deficient in lime, the continual application of heavy dressings of superphosphate may cause the soil to become acid or sour in character, thus impairing vegetation. In such cases, however, this acidity may be corrected by suitable applications of lime (*vide Journal of Agriculture, Victoria,* October, 1912).

Time and Mode of Application.—In the majority of seasons the best results are obtained with superphosphate when the seed and manure are drilled in together in the normal seeding season.

Many farmers frequently sow the manure some weeks before seeding, either by means of a cultivator with a drill attachment or with the ordinary fertilizer drill. The cost of cultivation is slightly increased by sowing the seed and manure in two operations, but a compensating advantage is perhaps gained at seed time by the expediting of seeding operations. This is sometimes a matter of importance, especially where the seeding is likely to be delayed by want of strength, or by not having the land properly prepared.

The advantage of sowing seed and manure together is that the young plants very readily find the manure and make vigorous growth early in the season. They thus become well established and develop a good root system before the winter sets in—a point of great importance in relatively dry districts. If the autumn has been unfavorable to the destruction of weeds, the sowing of seed and manure gives the young crop a decided start, and materially assists it in overcoming the weeds.

BASIC SLAG.

This is obtained as a by-product in the manufacture of steel from iron ores rich in phosphorus. It is sold as a fine, heavy black powder. It is a very popular manure in Europe, both for wheat crops and for the improvement of pastures. It contains from 15 to 18 per cent. of phosphoric acid, and about 40 per cent. of lime.

In the wheat areas it is used at present only in relatively small quantities, and experience proves that, though a valuable manure, it is less effective than an equivalent amount of phosphoric acid in the form of superphosphate. The probable explanation of the superiority of superphosphate has already been indicated. It is not likely to displace superphosphate in the wheat areas, especially in districts where the soil has a high lime content. On sour peaty land, however, it will be found a most useful and valuable manure. The application of superphosphate alone to these latter soils would only aggravate their acidity. Basic slag, however, by reason of the lime it contains, tends to correct the acid conditions, and thus acts as a soil amendment as well as a phosphatic manure. Basic slag is extremely valuable in the top-dressing of impoverished pastures. The results of a large number of pasture experiments in Europe indicate that Thomas' phosphate does not always give a greater weight of herbage than super. The grazing value of the herbage, however. manured with Thomas' phosphate proved superior to that of super. A greater increase in live weight of sheep has been secured from the pastures manured with Thomas' phosphate

4.—CLOSER VIEW OF NO. 3, SHOWING PEAS FOR FEEDING OFF.

than those treated with super. The rate of application to wheat lands is similar to that of superphosphate.

BONEDUST.

Bone consists of an organic and an inorganic portion. The organic portion comprises about 40 per cent. of the raw bone, and consists of (*a*) ossein or bone cartilage, which is very rich in nitrogen; and (*b*) fat. The inorganic portion, comprising about 60 per cent. of the raw bone, consists principally of tricalcic phosphate (phosphate of lime).

Hence, the fertilizing principal constituents of raw bones are organic nitrogen and phosphate of lime.

The presence of fat is, however, highly objectionable, for, in addition to being useless as plant food, it prevents the bones from being finely ground, and also protects the fertilizing ingredients from being made available.   Hence, in the preparation of bonedust, the fat is first removed from the bones by steaming or by treatment with benzine, and the treated bone ground to fine meal.

The value of a bonedust will depend on its composition and its fineness of subdivision.   The purchaser should always insist on a guaranteed analysis for bonedust, for there is no fertilizer on the market so liable to vary in composition like the so-called bone fertilizers.

The phosphoric acid in bonedust is in a most insoluble condition. It is only very slowly made available in the soil, and therefore it has a very limited use in most of the wheat areas.   It gives best results on soils rich in organic matter, for with these there is a possibility of the insoluble phosphate being slowly made available.   On limestone soils in the drier districts, however, it has been proved of little value, because it takes so long for the tricalcic phosphate to be rendered available.

Other sources of phosphoric acid are the phosphatic guanos and raw ground phosphate rock.   In both these substances the phosphoric acid is insoluble, and they are of very little value in the majority of our wheat areas.

POTASH MANURES.

Potassic manures do not figure very largely in Australian manurial practice.   Most of the strong soils characteristic of the wheat areas are well supplied with potash, and further supplies in the form of artificial manures are generally unnecessary.   There are some soils, however, on which potash may possibly be of considerable benefit. These are the light, sandy loams, and possibly heavy, peaty soils. Dressings of potash are frequently necessary to secure a full crop from these soils, more especially with root crops such as potatoes, onions, beets, &c.   On the clay loams and stiff clay soils of the wheat areas, the application of potassic manures is generally unnecessary and unprofitable.   This may be gathered from the results of many field experiments conducted by the Department some ten years ago.   The addition of potassic manures to phosphates did not materially increase the yield. In fact, in many cases the effect of the application was to depress the yield, and resulted in actual loss.

The principal potassic manures are Sulphate and Muriate of potash and kainite.   These are obtained from the Stassfurt potash mines which form the principal source of the world's potash.

Sulphate of potash contains from 50 to 52 per cent. of potash, and costs from £13 to £14 per ton.

Muriate of potash contains an equivalent of 60-62 per cent. of potash, and is quoted from £14 to £14 10s. per ton.

Kainite is one of the crude potash minerals of the Stassfurt mines. Its composition varies considerably, but it generally contains from 12-13 per cent. of potash, most of which is in the form of sulphate, whilst a lesser quantity is present as chloride.   It is quoted at £5 per ton.

Potash is required in fairly large quantities by leguminous plants, such as clover and lucerne, but the drain on the soil reserves of potash by wheat crops is very small indeed. It is not likely to be of value in the wheat areas, except in the case of certain sandy soils deficient in this ingredient. With leguminous crops the most economical method of supplying potash will probably be the application of compounds, such as lime and gypsum, which will liberate the insoluble potash compounds and render them available. This matter, however, was discussed in the September issue of the *Journal*.

General Manures.

These supply all the elements required by plants for their perfect development.

The most important manures of this section are Stable and Green manures.

Stable Manure is one of the most valuable manures that can be applied to any soil to increase its fertility. In the older agricultural countries of the world the greatest care is taken in the preservation of

5.—FEEDING OFF OF BARLEY PLOT WITH SHEEP.

all the manurial resources of the farm. Under the conditions which obtain in the wheat areas of Australia at the present time, farmyard manure is practically neglected, and regarded as of minor importance. The average wheat holding at the present time is so large, and the amount of stable manure produced in a year so small, that the effect of the stable manure on the fertility of the farm will, for all practical purposes, be inappreciable. This state of affairs will not, however, continue indefinitely. With the rapidly increasing population, and the inevitable increase in land values ahead of us, individual holdings must gradually become much smaller in size, and the system of farming more diversified. Live stock will become more and more prominent; and ultimately the amount of farmyard manure produced on the farm will be sufficient to have a distinct effect on the fertility of the farm. On the dairy farm, however, as contrasted with the wheat farm, farmyard manure is of great importance. The majority of such farms are situated in the moister districts, where systematic rotation is possible.

Moreover, the average dairy holding is considerably smaller than the average wheat farm, and the number of live stock per unit of area considerably larger. Farmyard manure, therefore, becomes an item of considerable economic importance. It is of even greater importance to the small irrigation farm or orchard.

The composition of stable manure varies very considerably, as might be expected. The nature of the food eaten, kind of bedding used, the amount and nature of the fermentation, all have important bearing on the composition. Generally speaking, a good sample will contain about .6 per cent. of nitrogen, .35 per cent. of phosphoric acid, and .6 per cent. of potash, *i.e.*, about 13 lbs. of nitrogen, 7 lbs of phosphoric acid, and 13 lbs. of potash.

The most important principle to be observed in the care of stable manure is to prevent any loss of plant food constituents. No difficulty arises with regard to phosphoric acid and potash compounds, but it is almost impossible to prevent losses in nitrogen and organic matter.

The loss of nitrogenous organic matter may be avoided by the use of good absorbents for bedding purposes, and of substances, such as gypsum, which assist in fixing ammonia compounds and preventing loss by volatilization. Losses may also be reduced to a minimum by

(a) Controlling the fermentation of the manure, and

(b) By prevention of leaching.

If a plentiful supply of air is admitted to the manure heap, fermentation and nitrification proceed very rapidly, and the temperature quickly rises. Under these circumstances, a great deal of the organic nitrogen escapes as ammonia in its compounds, or even as free nitrogen.

The fermentation may be controlled by keeping the manure heap well compacted, and keeping it moist.

Losses by leaching may be avoided by building the manure heap on a raised cemented floor, with sloping sides. The liquid manure drains towards the side of the floor and collects in a pit, and is periodically pumped over the manure heap. This system of conserving manure is already practised on several large wheat farms.

Green Manuring.—The object of green manuring is to increase the organic content of the soil, which we have already seen is a dominating factor in soil fertility. There can be doubt that many of the soils in the wheat-growing areas, which have been under cultivation for a comparatively long period, have lost a considerable amount of the organic matter they formerly contained. This loss has been accentuated by the practice of bare-fallowing, and by stubble-burning. The restoration of this organic matter is a problem of fundamental importance to the wheat areas. Modes of restoration of this organic matter that are practicable in the wheat-growing areas have already been discussed. (*Jour. Agric.*, Victoria, 1912, p. 460.) The turning in of green crops is one of the most rapid methods of increasing the organic reserves in the soil. Whether this practice may be profitably worked in with the ordinary rotations in the wheat areas has not hitherto been the subject of experimental investigation. The crops to be used for this purpose may be nitrogen gatherers, such as peas, vetches. and other leguminous crops, or nitrogen consumers, such as rye, rape, mustard, &c.

The former crops restore to the soil all the organic matter secured from the carbon dioxide of the air during the course of their growth, but they also secure, for the use of the succeeding crop, a large quantity of combined nitrogen from the atmosphere. Thus they enrich the soil in organic matter and in nitrogen.

On the other hand, crops like rye, rape, mustard, &c., produce large quantities of organic matter, but they cannot make use of the free nitrogen in the air in the same manner as leguminous crops. In the wheat areas, however, at the present time, the most important requirement is organic matter. The increase of the nitrogen reserves is at present a secondary consideration. The important point to bear in mind is that crops which produce a maximum weight of green stuff that can be turned under in early spring, before the soil becomes too hard and dry to plough, should be grown rather than crops which give a relatively small yield of green stuff of high quality. Such crops require for our conditions to be sown early in autumn, so that they may be ready by August or September.

The immediate effect of these green manures is to greatly increase the water-holding capacity of the soil—a point of fundamental importance in arid agriculture—and to improve its mechanical condition.

FEEDING DOWN OF FORAGE CROPS.

The system of feeding down of crops, specially grown for livestock, provides a means for increasing the organic content of the soil. As the feeding value of a green crop is usually greater than its manurial value, the practice of raising green crops and converting them into mutton, beef, or milk, instead of ploughing them under, will be preferred to the practice of green manuring. For this purpose rape, mustard, peas, rye, vetches, &c., will be found extremely useful. Summer crops such as sorghum, millet, and maize, cannot be recommended in the drier wheat districts under ordinary farming conditions, as the yield of the succeeding wheat crop is invariably lowered, especially if the rainfall is short. Winter growing forages are most suitable for the wheat areas, and if these are sown early in autumn so as to germinate with the first rains they make a large amount of growth while the soil is still warm, and make invaluable winter forage for stock.

NOTES ON THE USE OF ARTIFICIAL MANURES.

Always Buy on Guarantee Analyses.—In purchasing artificial manures farmers should always study closely the guaranteed analyses of each manure. In the January number of the *Journal of Agriculture* each year the Chemist for Agriculture publishes a statement of all manures, registered under the Artificial Manures Act, together with their guaranteed percentages of the fertilizing ingredients present, and the unit values of nitrogen, phosphoric acid, and potash. These tables should be closely scrutinized by each farmer. The unit values will enable him to calculate the commercial value of any artificial manure selling on the market.

Mixing of Manures.

Care needs to be exercised in the mixing of manures. Fertilizers cannot be mixed indiscriminately without risk of loss, or of lowering the value of some of the plant food constituents.

With regard to nitrogenous manures, sulphate of ammonia, nitrogenous guanos, animal and blood manures, should not be mixed with substances of a strongly alkaline character.

Quicklime, slacked lime, wood ashes, Thomas' phosphate, or basic slag should, under no circumstances, be mixed with these manures, since considerable loss of ammonia will result.

With regard to nitrate nitrogen. loss is liable to occur with nitrate of soda if much free sulphuric acid is present in superphosphates; especially if the manures are mixed some time before application, and are kept in a warm place. Provided, however, the super is well made and dry, and the mixing is performed at the time of sowing, very little loss will occur.

6.—FEEDING OFF OF RAPE PLOT WITH SHEEP.

With regard to phosphatic manures, reversion will take place with soluble phosphates when placed in contact with lime, iron, or alumina compounds. This has already been referred to in dealing with the reversion of superphosphate.

In purchasing mixed manures attention should be paid to the guaranteed analyses.

The farmer should study particularly the guarantee for nitrogen and see whether it is in the form of nitrate, ammonia, blood, &c., also the percentage of water soluble, citrate soluble, and insoluble phosphate should receive close attention. Frequently the prices asked for certain mixed manures is out of all proportion to their real commercial value, and in such cases the mixing can be most profitably done by purchasing fertilizers separately, and mixing them on the farm. A study of the unit values published each year in the *Journal* will enable each purchaser to determine for himself whether the prices asked for a given mixed manure is reasonable.

Manuring not a Substitute for Tillage.

It must not be assumed that the application of artificial manures will relieve the farmer of the responsibility of thorough cultivation.

There are some who appear to think that heavily manured crops do not require the same amount of tillage as unfertilized crops. As a matter of fact, heavy dressings of manure cannot be used at a full profit without thorough preparatory tillage. Thorough tillage always was, and always will be, a prime factor for the production of heavy crops. Jethro Tull doubtless placed an exaggerated value on tillage operations when he stated, more than a century ago, that manures were absolutely unnecessary if tillage operations were thoroughly performed, and that thorough tillage was the best substitute for manure. We, in the twentieth century, should remember that while fertilizers are essential on many soils for the production of profitable crops, they do not give

7.—GREEN MANURIAL TESTS, RUTHERGLEN EXPERIMENTAL FARM.

their full measure of benefit unless the soil receives a thorough preparatory cultivation.

HOW TO DETERMINE SOIL DEFICIENCIES.

The most satisfactory and practical method of finding out the requirements of the soil is by systematic experimental work. The most important points requiring investigation with respect to manurial practice is to determine in each of the more important divisions of the State the value of the various phosphatic, nitrogenous, and potassic manures singly and in various combinations, the value of lime when applied in different forms, the cumulative as well as the immediate effect of each application, and the most economical method of restoring the organic matter. Permanent experimental plots have been laid down at the Rutherglen Experimental Farm with the object of securing exact information on these points. The results will be made available from time to time.

(To be continued.)

Perishable and Frozen Produce.

Description of Produce.		Exports from State (Oversea).		Deliveries from Government Cool Stores.	
		Quarter ended 30.9.12.	Quarter ended 30.9.11.	Quarter ended 30.9.12.	Quarter ended 30.9.11.
Butter	lbs.	1,397,160	4,823,228	1,564,976	5,148,752
Milk and Cream ...	cases	559	360	90	20
Milk and Cream (dried)	"	650	60	...	...
Cheese	lbs.	12,480	11,520	...	14,210
Ham and Bacon ...	"	13,200	28,560	...	...
Poultry	head	10,875	10,065	2,987	2,658
Eggs...	dozen	...	...	2,232	4,375
Mutton and Lamb	carcases	11,077	162,844	...	19,789
Beef	quarters	2,699	2,600	53	...
Veal	carcases	80	743	83	53
Pork...	"	...	1,009	289	1,476
Rabbits and Hares ...	pairs	676,176	909,390	320,184	198,545
Sundries	lbs.	..	...	72,803	14,010

R. CROWE, *Superintendent of Exports.*

Fruit, Plants, Bulbs, Grain, &c.

Imports and Exports Inspected for Quarter ending 30th September, 1912.

Goods	Imports.		Exports.	Goods	Imports.		Exports.
	Inter-State.	Oversea.	Oversea.		Inter-State.	Oversea.	Oversea.
Apples	18,514	—	259	Maize	1,715	2	—
Apples (Custard) ...	1	—	—	Millet	76	—	101
Bananas, bunches...	41,749	20,556	—	Nutmegs ...	—	205	—
Bananas, cases ...	4,371	17,622	—	Nuts	156	2,152	—
Barley	6,952	19,971	—	Oats	1,437	73,566	—
Beans	1	419	26	Oat Hulls ...	887	—	—
Bulbs	2	17	6	Onions	—	1,200	—
Chillies	—	446	—	Oranges	138,483	—	1,207
Cocoa beans ...	—	1,264	—	Passion	5,449	—	8
Cocoanuts ...	37	755	—	Paw Paws ...	37	—	—
Coffee beans ...	—	2,448	-	Pears	20	—	1
Copra	—	260	—	Peas, dried ...	3,434	94	1
Cucumbers ...	441	—	—	Pepper	—	318	—
Figs	—	8	—	Pineapples ..	17,455	—	301
Fruit—				Plants, Trees, &c.	547	221	406
Canned ...	—	—	2,903	Potatoes ..	774	196	329
Dried ...	—	89	7,425	Rice	7,983	9,003	—
Mixed ...	—	10	—	Seeds	1,636	6,174	159
Granadillas ...	7	—	—	Spice	—	89	—
Green Ginger ...	—	70	—	Strawberries ..	21	—	—
Hops	—	464	—	Tomatoes ..	2,579	—	—
Jams, Sauces, &c. ...	—	—	1,178	Turnips	5,350	21	—
Lemons ...	3,500	—	2,880	Vegetables ...	346	476	20
Lentils	—	82	—	Wheat, Grain, &c.	2	210	—
Linseed ...	—	1,255	—	Yams	19	—	—
Loquats	406	—	—				
Logs	173	—	—				
Mace	—	34	- —	Totals ...	264,560	159,097	17,209

Total number of packages inspected for quarter ending 30th September, 1912 = 441,466.

C. T. COLE, *pro. Senior Fruit Inspector.*

ORCHARD AND GARDEN NOTES.

E. E. Pescott, Principal, School of Horticulture, Burnley.

The Orchard.

SPRAYING.

The spray pump should now be in thorough working order, so that the various spring sprayings may be carried out with as little interruption as possible. It is always wise to clean out the pump after each spraying, so that it will be ready for the next mixture. Putting a different spray into a pump barrel that has not been washed out very often causes the formation of a sediment which blocks the nozzle and interrupts the work.

During November, it will be necessary to spray for codlin moth, peach aphis, pear slug, and various leaf-eating insects. In addition, black spot of the apple and pear, shothole, and other fungus diseases must be kept in check. Various sprays are required for all of these troubles, and the necessity of always having a clean pump will thus be admitted.

At the present time, the wisest spray to use for peach aphis will be a strong tobacco solution, and the same spray may also be used for the pear slug. Arsenate of lead is the better spray for this insect, but it should not be used when the fruit is approaching the ripening stage; hellebore may also be used for the slug with good effect.

As a preventive against codlin moth, the trees should be kept well sprayed with arsenate of lead. It has been definitely ascertained that this is the best remedy, and all other mixtures should be discarded in its favour. Its permanent qualities, combined with an effective killing strength, render this mixture invaluable; at the same time, it is easily mixed, and so very few brands leave any sediment, that the work of spraying is now reduced to a minimum.

If the spraying is careful and thorough, no bandaging need be carried out. The time spent in bandaging will be far better employed in an extra spraying. The first spraying should have been given at the time of the falling of the petals; the second spraying, owing to the rapid expansion of the fruit, should be given a fortnight later. After that, the grower must use his own judgment as to the necessity for subsequent sprayings. If the moths be at all prevalent, other sprayings will be quickly necessary.

Now that arsenate of lead is produced with such an excellent degree of killing strength, it is not necessary to spray nearly so frequently as it was in former years; and it may be found that four sprayings, and perhaps only three, will be sufficient to keep this pest in check. Last season, a number of Gravenstein apple trees at the Burnley Horticultural Gardens were sprayed once only, and out of 2,804 apples, including windfalls, only nineteen fruits were moth infected, which gives a percentage of only .67 of loss. Three Rokewood trees were sprayed twice, and 870 fruits, including windfalls, were gathered. Only three apples were moth infected, or a percentage equal to .35. One Mellon's Seedling tree was sprayed twice, and out of 202 apples gathered, also including windfalls, one fruit was moth infected, equal to .54 per cent. These figures must not be taken as conclusive, as it will be remembered that the attack of the codlin moth last season was very light.

As the woolly aphis is increasing at this season of the year, it will mean a saving of a good number of buds if this insect is sprayed. Nicotine solution or Pine Spray may be used with good effect.

Cultivation.

The work of ploughing and harrowing should be completed immediately. The frequent rains have rendered cultivation easy, and there should be no difficulty in carrying out this work at once. It is always advisable to have the land well tilled before the dry weather sets in.

All crops for green manure should be now under cover; and, if the orchard soil is at all heavy or sticky, the grower should make up his mind to grow a cover crop next season in order that this condition may be reduced.

The orchard should be kept free from weeds, not only for the conservation of moisture, but in order to do away with all hiding places of the Rutherglen fly, cut worm moths, &c.

General Work.

Grafted and newly planted trees should be frequently examined, and given an occasional watering and overhead spraying, in order to encourage their growth and to prevent loss of moisture from the foliage. It is also advisable to mulch young trees with light grass or straw mulching, not too rich in animal manure.

The disbudding of unnecessary shoots, and the pinching back or stopping of growths, to prevent them being unduly prolonged, may now be carried out. This work is particularly important on young trees.

Graft ties should be examined, and the ties cut wherever any growth is being made. Where the grafts are likely to make any long growth, they should be well staked and tied.

Citrus trees may be planted out, watering and mulching them after planting.

Vegetable Garden.

Tomato plants should now receive attention every day; laterals will require pinching back, crowded bunches and shoots should be thinned, the plants should be well tied to the stakes, and liberal supplies of water and manure should be given. One or two more plantings of tomato plants may still be made, so that there may be strong sturdy plants for the production of late fruits. By planting three or four successions of plants, it is possible to have a good supply of fruits from December to June.

Celery may now be sown for winter crops. French beans should be largely sown. Cucumber, melon, pumpkin, and all seeds of this family may now be sown in the open.

Where these plants are already growing the longest and strongest runners may be pinched back, to throw the strength into the flowering and lateral growths. Watch the plants for mildew, and use the sulphur freely wherever present, especially on the young plants.

Peas, lettuce, radish, turnip, cabbage, and sweet corn seeds may be sown this month. Seedlings from former sowings may be planted out, and it may be well to dip the whole plant in water before planting. This greatly assists the young plant while taking hold of the soil in its new location.

Frequent waterings and frequent cultivation will now be necessary; and all weeds must be hoed or hand-weeded out; mulching with stable manure will greatly assist the plants.

A few beds should now be deeply worked adding a liberal dressing of stable manure. These plots will be then ready for the celery, cabbage, and other seeds planted during this month.

Flower Garden.

Continue to plant out various bedding and foliage plants, corms of gladioli, tubers of dahlias, and seeds of such tender annuals as Phlox Drummondi. Balsam. Zinnia, Nasturtium. Celosia. Aster. Cosmos, and Portulaca.

While seeds germinate and grow fairly well planted out in the open, it is more advisable during the summer months to plant these in sheltered seed beds, or in a canvas or calico frame. The protection need only be on the one side, preferably the west or north-west; the seedlings are then protected during the hottest portion of the day. At the same time the shading is not sufficient to unduly " draw " them.

The seeds should not be deeply sown. and all waterings should be light. A little water and often should be the rule for seedlings. Annuals should be given plenty of room when planted out in the garden. Being quick growers, they are generally gross feeders, and they must have room to develop a good root system.

Feeding, too, with liquid manure is helpful when they are reaching the flowering stage.

Dahlias should now be planted out, either from tubers or from young rooted cuttings. These will give good summer blooms. For autumn and show blooms. the planting should be deferred until the middle of December.

Herbaceous and succulent plants should be staked for their protection; included in this section are Delphinia, Gladioli. perennial Phlox, Rudbeckia, &c. These plants will all benefit from liberal mulchings and watering with liquid manure when approaching the blooming period. Spring flowering bulbs, corms, and tubers should now be all lifted and stored.

The soil surfaces will now benefit from frequent hoeings and stirrings. Constant waterings will be required if the weather be hot or windy; the cultivation should quickly follow the waterings in order that the moisture may be thoroughly conserved. Mulching with stable manure is also beneficial at this season.

REMINDERS FOR DECEMBER.

LIVE STOCK.

HORSES.—*Stabled Horses.*—Over-stimulating and fattening foods should be avoided. Give water at frequent intervals. Rub down on coming into the stables overheated. Supply a ration of greenstuff to all horses. *Brood Mares.*—Those with foals at foot should be well fed. *Early Foals* may, with advantage, be given oats to the extent of 1 lb. for each month of age daily.

CATTLE.—Rugs may now be dispensed with. Supply succulent fodder. Milk should be given at blood heat to *calves.*

PIGS.—*Sows.*—Supply those farrowing with plenty of short bedding in well-ventilated sties. Those with litters old enough may be turned into grass run. *All* pigs should be given a plentiful supply of clean water.

SHEEP.—To insure even lambing, see that a sufficient number of rams run with the ewes for six weeks. In cases of non-pregnancy, this period admits of the ewes coming in season a second time whilst with the rams. Merino and fine come-back ewes have been in season for some weeks, whilst cross-bred ewes (*i.e.,* first cross) will now begin to come on. Coarse three-quarter bred ewes, and those approaching any of the British breeds, will not be in season until February. Ewes carry their lambs for five months.

POULTRY.—Add a little peameal to morning mash, and give less bran. Feed equal parts wheat and short white oats at night. Supply plenty of green food—at this time, lettuce is invaluable. Discontinue salts and condiments. Avoid salt meat of any description. Put Douglas mixture in drinking water. Keep ample supplies of sand, ashes, &c., in pens, and moisten same. This will enable the birds to keep themselves cool and clean. Top off geese, ducks, and cockerels for the Christmas markets. Hens will do better this month by having free range. Remove all male birds from flock.

CULTIVATION.

FARM.—Cut hay in late districts. Cut oats and barley in early places. Finish planting potatoes. Put in late maize for fodder, also millet and imphee. Plough fire-breaks where required. Get stackyard and stages ready for hay.

ORCHARD.—Keep the surface loose and free. Suppress weeds. Spray as often as necessary for codlin moth and pear slug. Mulch and spray young trees and grafts with water in the early morning during hot weather.

VEGETABLE GARDEN.—Keep the surface hoed, and allow the plants plenty of moisture. Stake, pinch out, manure, and water tomatoes. Pinch back long runners of pumpkin and melon family. Sow autumn and winter varieties of cabbage and cauliflower. Plant out seedlings in cool weather. Sow French beans. Cease cutting asparagus beds, and top-dress with manure.

FLOWER GARDEN.—Plant out dahlias for autumn blooming. Lift and store spring flowering bulbs. Stake, tie, and train growing plants. Sow zinnias and asters. Layer carnations, camelias, daphnes, &c. Water well and keep the surface loose.

VINEYARD.—Inspect young grafted vines (field or bench) and carefully remove any scion roots. Tie up young vines. Beware of cut worms on young vines—See *Journal* for July, 1911. Tying up of bearing vines, if practised, should be completed early in month. Avoid excessive and indiscriminate topping, far too frequent in Victoria. Scarify, if soil is not sufficiently loose, and after heavy rain. Look out for oidium and repeat sulphurings on first appearance of disease.

Cellar.—Fill up regularly and keep cellars as cool as possible.

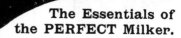

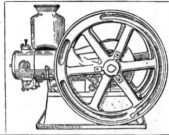

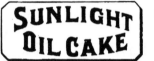

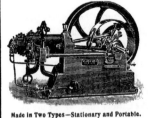

DEPARTMENT OF AGRICULTURE,
VICTORIA.

Burnley Horticultural School.

E. E. PESCOTT - Principal.

ANNOUNCEMENT.

The curriculum and management of the Burnley Horticultural School have now been arranged so that greater advantages and facilities will be given to students of both sexes in Horticulture and allied subjects.

The present course of Horticulture for male students includes a two years' course, students being charged a fee of £5 per annum.

Classes have been formed at Burnley, whereby students of both sexes may receive instruction on two afternoons of each week—Tuesdays and Fridays.

Instruction includes theoretical and practical work, and will commence at 2 p.m. This will be a two years' course, and the fee charged will be £2 per annum.

It has also been arranged that several short lecture courses shall be given on subjects which are suitable adjuncts to Horticulture, such as Poultry Farming, Bee-keeping, and Fruit Preserving, and these courses will be open and free to the general public. The subjects and dates of the Short Course Lectures will be announced in this Journal.

STUDENTS SHOULD ENROLL WITHOUT DELAY.

Application for . Admission should be made to . .	THE DIRECTOR OF AGRICULTURE, PUBLIC OFFICES, MELBOURNE,	OR TO THE PRINCIPAL.

By Authority: ALBERT J. MULLETT, Acting Government Printer, Melbourne.

The Journal of

THE DEPARTMENT OF AGRICULTURE OF VICTORIA, AUSTRALIA.

December, 1912.

PROVISION FOR THE FUTURE.

PRICE THREEPENCE. (Annual Subscription—Victoria, Inter-State, and N.Z., 3/-; British and Foreign, 5/-.)

THE JOURNAL

OF

THE DEPARTMENT OF AGRICULTURE,

VICTORIA, AUSTRALIA.

C.

CONTENTS.—DECEMBER, 1912.

COPYRIGHT PROVISIONS AND SUBSCRIPTION RATES.

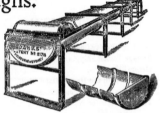

LITERATURE FOR AGRICULTURISTS.

PLAN AND SPECIFICATION OF SHEEP-SHEARING SHED. 2s. 6d. *Postage*, 1d.

MILK CHARTS (Monthly and Weekly), 6d. per dozen, post free. When ordering, dairy farmers should mention " Monthly " or " Weekly."

By Professor A. J. Ewart, Government Botanist.

WEEDS, POISON PLANTS, AND NATURALIZED ALIENS OF VICTORIA. 2s. 6d. *Postage :* Commonwealth, 1½d. ; N.Z., 5d. ; British and Foreign, 10d.

PLANTS INDIGENOUS TO VICTORIA. Vol. II., 10s. *Postage :* Com., 2d.; N.Z., 8d. ; Brit. & For., 1s. 4d.

By C. French, F.E.S., Government Entomologist.

DESTRUCTIVE INSECTS OF VICTORIA. Parts I., II., III., IV., V. 2s. 6d. each. *Postage :* Parts I. and III., C., 1d. ; N.Z., 3d.; B. & F., 6d. each. Parts II. and IV., C., 1½d. ; N.Z., 4d. ; B. & F., 8d. each. Part V., C., 1d. ; N.Z., 4d. ; B. & F., 7d.

By D. McAlpine, Government Vegetable Pathologist.

RUSTS OF AUSTRALIA. 5s. *Postage :* C., 2d. ; N.Z., 8d. ; B. & F., 1s. 4d.

SMUTS OF AUSTRALIA. 4s. *Postage :* C., 2½d. ; N.Z., 9d. ; B. & F., 1s. 6d.

FUNGUS DISEASES OF CITRUS TREES IN AUSTRALIA. 2s. *Postage :* C., 1d. ; N.Z., 3d. ; B. & F.. 6d.

FUNGUS DISEASES OF STONE FRUIT TREES IN AUSTRALIA. 2s. 6d. *Postage :* C., 1½d. ; N.Z., 5d. ; B. & F., 10d.

SYSTEMATIC ARRANGEMENT OF AUSTRALIAN FUNGI. 3s. *Postage :* C., 2d.; N.Z., 8d. ; B. & F., 1s. 4d.

THE DEPARTMENT OF AGRICULTURE,
MELBOURNE, VICTORIA.

Remittances from places outside the Commonwealth to be by Money Order only.

Pamphlets obtainable from the Director of Agriculture, Melbourne, Free on Application.

NEW SERIES.

1. SILO CONSTRUCTION. *A. S. Kenyon, C.E.*
2. HINTS FOR NEW SETTLERS. *T. A. J. Smith.*
3. APPLE GROWING FOR EXPORT. *P. J. Carmody.*
* 4. BOOKKEEPING FOR FARMERS. *W. McIver, A.I.A.V., A.S.A.A., Eng.*
5. CIDER MAKING. *J. Knight.*
* 6. FARM PLUMBING. *C. H. Wright.*
7. CITRUS FRUIT CULTURE. *E. E. Pescott.*
8. BUILDING HINTS FOR SETTLERS. *A. S. Kenyon, C.E., and others.*
9. TOBACCO CULTURE. *T. A. J. Smith.*
10. SILOS AND SILAGE. *G. H. F. Baker.*
11. THE BEET SUGAR INDUSTRY AND CLOSER SETTLEMENT. *H. T. Easterby.*
12. WORMS IN SHEEP. *S. S. Cameron, D.V. Sc., M.R.C.V.S.*
*13. CHEESE MAKING (Cheddar). *C. S. Sawers.*
14. FARM BLACKSMITHING. *G. Baxter.*
15. BROOM FIBRE INDUSTRY. *T. A. J. Smith.*
*16. PIG INDUSTRY. *R. T. Archer.*
17. GOVERNMENT CERTIFICATION OF STALLIONS, 1911–12.
W. A. N. Robertson, B.V. Sc.
18. REPORT ON FIRST EGG-LAYING COMPETITION AT BURNLEY, 1911–12.
H. V. Hawkins.

* Not yet available.

THE JOURNAL

OF

The Department of Agriculture

OF

VICTORIA.

Vol. X. Part 12.	10th December, 1912.

GOOD AND FAULTY CHEESES EXHIBITED AT THE ROYAL SHOW, 1912.

Report by G. C. Sawers (Cheese Expert).

Fig. 1.—This lot of cheese is regular in make and size, and most suitable for exporting to the London market. The English grocers prefer it to the smaller size, as they claim there is less waste in cutting up on the counter.

FIG. 1.—CHEESE FOR EXPORT.

Remarks.—The flavour is clean. body and texture solid, firm and smooth. Finish—neat with close rinds.

The flavour of a prime Cheddar cheese should have both the aroma and flavour of a nut. It should melt in the mouth, producing not only an agreeable flavour, but leaving a most pleasant after-taste. If either

17734   2 A

in smell or in taste, or in after-taste, there is anything the least unpleasant, such taste or smell is termed a taint.

The body and texture should be absolutely uniform, solid and smooth. Cheese open in body dries up more quickly when cut.

The finish should show close rinds with the bandage well pressed into the sides and ends of cheese, allowing not 'more than ½ inch lap each end.

FIG. 2.—CHEESE FOR LOCAL AND INTER-STATE TRADE.

Fig. 2.—This lot is the most suitable size for local and Inter-State trade.

Remarks.—The flavour is not so clean as lot Fig. 1; body and texture fairly close. Finish—fair.

The fault in flavour is due to a taint in the milk, or to the lactic acid starter being over-ripe. Body and texture being slightly open, and furry, is due to insufficient acid being developed in the curd before salting and hooping, and containing too much moisture. Too much

FIG. 3.—CHEESE IRREGULAR IN SIZE AND POORLY FINISHED.

cloth lapped over ends of cheese, which is liable to work loose, and give a rough and ragged appearance.

Fig. 3.—This lot is very irregular in size, a matter which cheese merchants dislike. For shipping they require special crates made to fit the cheese at extra cost.

The flavour is not clean, being very pronounced; body and texture too firm and dry. The finish is rough and very poor, showing cracks on sides of cheese and mold.

The fault in flavour is due evidently to lack of cleanliness, resulting in fermentations caused by bacteria, which develop only at a high temperature. Body and texture being too firm, dry, and rough, is due to over-cooking the curd in the whey, causing the curd to become greasy, and producing excessive loss of butter fat in pressing the cheese.

A cracky condition in the rind is due to over-cooking, or sour curd; the fat adhering to the outside preventing particles of curd from joining into one mass.

Fig. 4.—This lot is of very inferior make; only saleable at a very low price.

FIG. 4.—CHEESE OF VERY INFERIOR QUALITY DUE TO UNCLEANLINESS
PRIOR TO PRESSING.

Remarks.—The flavour is putrid, sour; body and texture weak, soft, and mealy. Finish—very poor.

The fault in flavour is due to lack of cleanliness, and holding the milk several days at a low temperature before being manufactured into cheese.

Body and texture weak, soft, and mealy, is due to the milk being sour—insufficient cooking allowing too much acid in the curd before drawing the whey off, causing excessive moisture; and at times leak on the shelf.

Cheese of this description dries up readily on the rind, and shrinks in size. It is shown as a striking example of what to avoid.

STORAGE TEST OF SHIPPING GRAPES.

F. de Castella, Government Viticulturist.

Experiments similar to those conducted last year, to test the keeping power of several varieties of grapes,* were again undertaken this year with a similar object, namely, to test the suitability, for exporting in a fresh state, of several recently introduced table grapes.

The grapes, which were all grown in the Rutherglen district, and without irrigation, were packed in granulated cork in ordinary export grape cases, West Australian pattern, holding 28 lbs. of fruit net. They were conveyed to Melbourne in ordinary fruit trucks (not cooled), actual transit occupying eight hours, but the total time spent in the truck was about 24 hours.

---

* See *Journal* for July, 1911.

Teneron du Cadenet (white), 8½ points.

Condition nearly as good as Ohanez.   Flavour superior.   In fact, this is one of the best flavoured grapes tried.

Trifère du Japan (black), 8 points.

This grape, which is identical with the one long known in Victoria under the name of Wortley Hall, has opened up in better order than previous trials would lead one to expect.   Though not in such good order as Ohanez, it flavour is superior.   The berries are of very fine size, and adhere fairly well in spite of their rather thin skin.

On arrival in Melbourne, they were placed in the Government Cool Stores, where they were kept at a temperature of 33 and 35 degrees F.

Four cases were experimented with ; three of these, from the Viticultural College, Rutherglen, went into the Cool Stores on 14th March, 1912 ; the fourth, grown by Mr. J. M. Grimmond, of Wahgunyah, went into the same chamber about a week later.   The time the grapes remained in cool storage was thus only a few days short of four months.

The cases were opened and contents examined on 9th July last, in the presence of several officers of the Agricultural Department, and some gentlemen interested in the shipment of grapes.

The cases from the College were somewhat at a disadvantage owing to the granulated cork being rather coarse ; occasional berries were injured by pressure by the angular fragments.

The case from Mr. Grimmond was packed in fine-grained cork.   On the other hand, it met with a slight mishap at the time of the Fruit and Floral Carnival, held from 26th to 30th March, having been sent thither in error with some other fruit.   The mistake was noticed on its arrival at the Exhibition Buildings, and it was placed in the working model cool store, where it remained until the close of the Exhibition, when it was returned to the Government Cool Stores.   It was not opened at the Exhibition.   Extra handling in transit and removal from cool storage do not appear to have injuriously affected the fruit.

The points awarded refer to marketable condition, according to a scale from 1 to 10.

College Grapes.

Case No. 1.—*Ohanez* (white), 9¾ points.

The fruit was in first class order   Practically no waste ; but a few berries were slightly wrinkled.

Case No. 2.—*Valensy* (white), 5 points.

Very poor order, about 50 per cent. waste.   The state of this case bears out last year's experience with the same grape.   It is not suited for lengthy storage.

Case No. 3.—Mixed case, containing the following varieties :—

Ohanez (white), 9½ points.

Almost in as good order as Case No. 1.   Probably the proximity of some grapes which had not kept so well, accounts for the slight difference in condition.

Raisin de Nöel (black), 8 points.

This grape has kept very well for a juicy variety.   It is quite black, round, and of medium size.   Seeing the demand for black grapes, it deserves further trial.

Mavron (pink), 7½ points.

Very fair order.   A remarkably crisp grape of peculiar texture.   Firm, and of good flavour.   Worthy of further trial.

Malvoisie des Chatreux (white), 7 points.

This has not kept so well as last year's trial lot.   A good many berries have decayed near the stalk.   Excellent flavour, almost as good as Teneron du Cadenet.

Malaga Rose, 7 points.

A medium sized very pale pink grape.   These dropped from the bunch somewhat, but were in fair order, and good flavour.

Olivette Rose, about 6 points.

Scarcely equal to last year's trial lot.

Kobou, 6½ points.

A juicy white grape of good flavour, but not very large.   It kept fairly well.

Valensy, 5 points.

About the same as the single case of this variety.

Sabalkanskoi, 3 points.

This large, elongated, pink grape, though remarkably handsome when freshly gathered, has proved itself to be a poor keeper.   Very few berries are altogether sound.   Even the sound berries are deficient in flavour.

Mr. Grimmond's Case.

This case contained the following four varieties :—

Red May, 9½ points.

Excellent order, practically as good as Ohanez.   This grape certainly appears to be a shipper.   It is a handsome bright red, somewhat oval grape, which does not detach easily, and is more juicy and of better flavour than Ohanez.

Red Portugal, 9 points.

This appears to be identical with Red Malaga.   Almost as good as Ohanez.

Grimmond's Black, 8½ points.

This black grape, the correct name of which is unknown, has stood the trial remarkably well.   The slight muscat flavour which characterizes it when fresh had almost disappeared after cool storage.   It is fairly juicy, and in good order.   Seeing the demand for black grapes on the English market, it is worthy of further trial.

Gros Colman (black), 7 points.

In fair condition.   Scarcely in as good condition as Wortley Hall referred to above.   It does not promise well as a shipping grape.

*   *   *   *

Seeing the accident referred to above, it is remarkable that Mr. Grimmond's grapes opened up in such good order.   Each of his bunches were broken up into several smaller ones when packing—a very desirable practice.   This, as well as the finer-grained cork, no doubt, contributed to the good condition in which this case opened up.   It must be noted, also, that Mr. Grimmond's grapes are grown on almost pure sand, whilst the College grapes are from very stiff soil.   Grapes grown on sand usually carry well.

GENERAL NOTES.

PIG FEEDING—

The Central Experiment Farm, Ottawa, has carried out a series of pig-feeding experiments, and the conclusions arrived at include the following points:—It will not pay to cook feed (grain and meals) for swine if economy of production is alone considered. More food is required to produce 1 lb. of gain after the live-weight exceeds 100 lbs., and the most economical time to slaughter swine is when they weigh 175 to 200 lbs. The average dressed weight of swine is about 76 per cent. of the fasted weight. Skim milk is a valuable addition to a grain ration where hard flesh is desired, and 700 lbs. skim milk equals 100 lbs. mixed grain, unless the milk is used in undue proportion. The greatest gains from a given amount of grain are made when the grain is ground and soaked for 24 hours. Mixed grains are more economical than grains fed pure.

PHOSPHATES ON PASTURE—

The soils of Victoria generally show a marked deficiency in available phosphates, and as a result the use of phosphatic manure upon cereal crops has become almost universal. As wheat and oats belong to the order of Grasses, one might infer that common pasture grasses would likewise benefit from an application of phosphatic manure. In this connexion the results obtained by the Federal Institution of Agriculture, at Lausanne, make suggestive reading. Two adjoining sections of pasture were selected, and one of them received 4 cwt. superphosphate each year, while the other got no manure. The experiments lasted three years. In the first year the yield on the unmanured plot was 9 cwt. and on the manured plot 14 cwt.; in the second year the yields were 6 cwt. and 18 cwt.; and in the third year 7 cwt. and 29 cwt. respectively. The size of the plots is not stated. Besides increasing the yield, the phosphate also improved the quality of the herbage, and at the close of the experiments clovers formed 45 per cent. of the herbage on the phosphate plot, as compared to 9 per cent. without manure. The profit from the superphosphate was calculated at £1 8s. 6d. per acre each year. It is pointed out that the soils here were rich in humus, and showed no deficiency of phosphates by chemical tests; consequently the only sure means of testing the need for phosphates was a trial in the field. The quantity of manure used at Lausanne is considerably in excess of that indicated for application to pastures in this State for reasons that are partly climatic and partly commercial. It is a well known law of manuring, however, that if a heavy dressing of manure yields a profit a small dressing will give a better return relatively to outlay, although the total profit may be less. For pasture trials in Victoria, from 1 cwt. to 2 cwt. superphosphate per acre would be a suitable dressing for the land.

CROPPING IN VICTORIA—

According to the latest volume of the *Commonwealth Year-Book*, Victoria, in 1910-11, had 3,952,070 acres under crop. This was equal to one-third of the total cropped area of the Commonwealth, and to 7 per cent. of the total superficial area of the State. Of the cropped area nearly 61 per cent. was devoted to wheat, 21 to hay, 10 to oats, while no other crop formed as much as 2 per cent. Among the various States, Victoria in wheat sowed the largest area, and reaped the largest crop—also in oats and barley. In maize (grain) Queensland planted nine times as much as Victoria, and New South Wales about eleven times as much, but in Victoria the yield per acre was double that of any other State. In beans and peas Victoria came second to Tasmania in point of area with 11,068 acres, and in rye with 2,640, second to New South Wales. In hay it cut 194,000 acres more than any other State. In orchards and fruit Victoria showed 57,375 acres, or about 10,000 in excess of New South Wales, which came second. In vines it tied with South Australia for first place at 23,412 acres. Victoria had most market garden, 10,778 acres, and the largest area under potatoes, 62,904 acres. In onions it had almost a monopoly—6,161 acres. Tobacco, 329 acres, was about one-sixth of the Australian total, and in hops Victoria was a poor second with 121 acres. Hops are chiefly grown in Tasmania. A poor place taken by Victoria was in the matter of green forage. In this it took third place with 71,826 acres, or nearly 110,000 acres below the figures for New South Wales.

BRITISH IMPORTS OF BUTTER—

In the year ending 30th June last there were imported into the United Kingdom 200,195 tons of butter, of which 52,857 tons, or 26 per cent came from British Dominions. Of the latter Australia contributed 33,677, Canada 2,997, and New Zealand 16,183 tons. In their eighteenth *Annual Review*, Messrs. W. Weddel and Company, Limited, mention some interesting facts in connexion with the dairy produce trade. So far as butter is concerned, Canada is dropping out from the export business. Of the European countries most have declined somewhat in butter exports to England in the last few years, Sweden alone showing a considerable increase. Holland has been sending increasingly to Germany. Imports from the Argentine shows a decrease in recent years, and United States exports are now small. Comparing the prices during the quinquennial period, 1893-98, with the prices for 1908-12, there has been a rise in butter from all countries, but it has not been uniformly distributed. In fifteen years Dutch butter has improved by 18s. 10d. per cwt., Russian by 18s. 3d., Irish by 15s. 6d., New Zealand 13s. 11d., Danish and Swedish 9s. 9d., Australian 8s. 10d., and French 5s. 2d. During the final period the prices were—Danish, 121s. 11d.; French, 120s. 6d.; Dutch, 118s. 7d.; New Zealand, 115s. 9d.; Irish, 115s. 7d.; Australian, 111s. 11d.; and Russian, 109s. 7d.—all per cwt. The process of cream pasteurization and careful handing in New Zealand is noted, and it is remarked that Australian butter has not given to buyers of finest quality the same complete satisfaction as New Zealand butter. As regards the markets in the coming season it is anticipated that prices will rule considerably lower than those for 1911-12, but will exceed the average of the preceding four years.

INSECT PESTS OF THE NEW ZEALAND FLAX
(*Phormium*).

The White Mussel Scale (*Phenacaspis eugeniae, Maskell*).

C. French, Jun., Acting Government Entomologist.

This scale, of which there are several varieties, is spreading in many parts of the State. Recently numbers of fine New Zealand flax plants (*Phormium tenax*) have been attacked; and, in some instances, especially after the predaceous insects have pulled the scales to pieces, the plants look as if a snowstorm had passed over them. (See plate 1.)

When the leaves are badly attacked, they develop a fungus which causes them to become rusty-red in colour, and in some instances they turn brown and curl up. Mr. C. C. Brittlebank, the Acting Government Pathologist, informs me that the fungus is one of the stages of Capnodium.

Numbers of the scales are attacked by parasitic wasps, other Hymenoptera, and Coccinellids (ladybirds), which help materially to keep them in check.

This scale insect is recorded from most parts of Australia, Ceylon, Japan, Hawaiian Islands, and has been found on various plants and trees, amongst which are the following:—Castor Oil Tree (*Ricinus communis*), Eugenias (a very ornamental and highly useful genus of plants), Palms, Tea Tree (*Leptospermum* and *Melaleuca*), Native Sassafras Tree (*Atherosperma moschatum*), &c.

Remedies.

A spraying with Pine Spray, Prepared Red Oil, Kerosene or Benzole emulsion will soon rid the plants of this pest. Formulas for any of the above sprays can be obtained by applying to the Entomological Branch, Department of Agriculture.

The Ivy or Oleander Scale (*Aspiditous hederae,* Vall').

This is another common scale, which attacks flax plants in Victoria. It causes similar damage to that done by the White Mussel Scale, and congregates on the leaves in larger numbers. In some instances leaves 5 feet in length are simply covered with them, the scales often overlapping each other.

When the young scales are hatched—generally in September and the following warm months—they are of a dark-yellow colour, and soon form a white round covering over themselves, which after a few weeks alters to a dirty white, greyish, or light-brown colour. This covering has a small cream-coloured dot in the centre.

This is a variable species, and has received considerably more than 40 names from writers on Coccids (scale insects). It has been found on oranges and lemons coming into Melbourne from foreign parts, bananas from Fiji, olives, palms, oleander, ivy, apples, cherry, plum, currant, grass, clover, and many other garden and native plants. It is found in most parts of the world.

Remedies.

The remedies recommended for the White Mussel Scale will suffice.

THE WHITE MUSSEL SCALE (PHENACASPIS EUGENIAE, MASKELL).

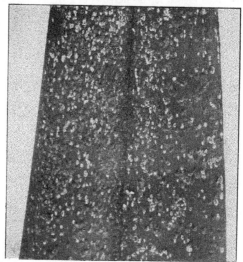

THE IVY OR OLEANDER SCALE (ASPIDIOTUS HEDERAE, VALL').

LEONGATHA LABOUR COLONY.

In presenting the Annual Report of the Leongatha Labour Colony, the Trustees desire to place on record a complete and comprehensive statement of the transactions and conduct of the farm for the year ending 30th June, 1912.

We wish to draw attention to the fact that this institution is now in the twentieth year of its existence, and during this term some 1,200 men have received assistance. In the case of those that have been physically fit a good sound training in agricultural work generally has been obtained. Many of the colonists have become competent farm labourers, and in a few instances successful farmers in the district.

In 1893 the farm comprised 822 acres of virgin land; since then some 400 acres have been disposed of at prices ranging from £12 to £25 per acre, and this land is to-day studded with prosperous farm houses. The portion retained for Colony purposes forms one of the best improved farms in South Gippsland. An additional 40 acres have recently been excised for the purposes of a High School, and the balance, consisting of 382 acres, is valued on the Colony books at £26 per acre. After taking full credit for the improvements effected, and the value of land sold and excised, the debit balance stands at £1,700. When the number of men relieved and the benefit received by them is taken into consideration, the position should be considered satisfactory.

For the year under review, 117 acres of land were put under cultivation, the whole of the produce being used on the farm as food for dairy stock and pigs. For the coming season, the following areas have been either put under crop or brought into a good state of cultivation preparatory to cropping:—

61 acres	Oats.	Estimate yield, 122 tons.
21 ,,	Oats and Tares, silage.	Estimate yield, 168 tons.
30 ,,	fallowed for Millet, Maize, and Sorghum.	Estimate yield, 300 tons.
23 ,,	Peas (10 acres in now).	Estimate yield, 445 bushels.
8 ,,	Pumpkins.	Estimate yield, 120 tons.
7 ,,	Mangels.	Estimate yield, 105 tons.
8 ,,	Potatoes.	Estimated yield, 40 tons.
15 ,,	Millet, for grazing purposes.	
13 ,,	New pasture sown down, Rye and Clover (mixed).	

The advantage in this respect will be readily understood when it is pointed out that the area the previous year was only 117 acres. The yield for the season just closing must, however, in view of the dryness experienced, the considered fairly satisfactory, the average returns being as follows :—

Oats for silage—yield, 5 tons per acre.
Peas—yield, 20 bushels per acre.
Hay (oats and wheat)—yield, 2 tons per acre.
Sorghum—yield, 10 tons per acre.
Maize and millet—fed off..
Potatoes—yield, 3 tons per acre.
Apples, exported—600 cases.
    „   local sales—667 cases.
Plums—28 cases.
Peaches—9 cases.
Quinces—8 cases.
Pears—4½ cases.
Strawberries—1,596 lbs.
Red currants—29 lbs.
Black currants—304 lbs.
Raspberries—397½ lbs.
Almonds—25 lbs.
Walnuts (green)—44 lbs.
Tomato plants—4,102.
Cabbage plants—920.
Rhubarb bunches—472.
Tomatoes—46 cases.
Lavender cuttings—32,600.

BUILDINGS.

The buildings consist of manager's house, stores and offices, staff and men's quarters, six men's huts, and dining-rooms, fruit-house, stables, barn, and implement sheds, engine and pumping plant building, dairyman's house, milking and shelter sheds, piggery and accommodation yards, milkers' and pigmen's huts, and several cattle shelter sheds. Most of these have been erected by colonists; they are complete and modern without being extravagant, and will bear comparison for economy and utility with similar farm buildings in any part of the State. These improvements are kept in thorough repair by the colonists. During the past year commodious piggeries have been erected on the farm capable of holding 150 pigs in the

GENERAL VIEW OF FARM.

fattening pens, in addition to convenient sheds and runs for the
brood sows and store pigs. The floors of the main building are of
machine-made bricks, cement grouted; the walls are on pivots to

INTERIOR OF NEW PIGGERY.

admit air and sunshine, with a lantern roof with glass lights for light
and ventilation. In every respect this building presents a model
of perfect hygiene in farm buildings, and accounts in a very great

measure for the freedom from disease that has been the happy experience of the farm. The two silos, which are capable of holding 250 tons of fodder, are kept constantly in use, and are usually filled twice a year. Persistent effort is put forth to conserve a full and complete ration for the dairy stock, a purpose for which the silos have been found indispensable. The cow shed is constructed on sanitary lines, and will accommodate 32 cows at a time; while shade and shelter sheds and water are provided in the yards for the cows waiting to be milked; those milked are turned direct into the paddocks. Stables, hay shed, fruit storage rooms, and men's quarters are substantial and convenient, the latter, in addition, being thoroughly sanitary.

Stock.

There are altogether 383 head of stock, including 120 dairy herd, 8 commercial cattle, 13 draught horses, 3 light horses, and 239 pigs; the total value being £1,879 14s.

INTERIOR OF MILKING SHED.

As evidence of the improved financial aspect of this institution since being handed over to the present management, it may be pointed out that in 1904, the year immediately prior to present control. the Government grant to carry on was between £4.000 and £5,000. while to-day it stands at £400 only. This means that the farm has. in the meantime, been made almost self-supporting, a fact considered most gratifying in view of the purpose it serves, and the fact that in many cases the unfortunates admitted have not for some time after admission been in a fit state to give labour adequate to the cost of

LITTER OF YORKSHIRE PIGS.

their keep. Every effort has, of course, been made to bring about this result by increasing the productiveness of the farm, and, at the same time, reducing expenditure by economical working.

The following is a statement of the revenue for each year from—

		£	s.	d.
1904-5	..	1,266	2	1
1905-6	..	1,172	4	8
1906-7	..	1,382	18	3
1907-8	..	1,408	3	10
1908-9	..	1,847	0	4
1909-10	..	2,111	7	8
1910-11	..	2,044	18	4
1911-12	..	2,212	5	2

Particulars of the transactions for the past year will be shown on a later page. Taking the particular items of revenue, *i.e.*, pigs, dairy, and garden, it is evident that the Colony's produce is earning a reputation for soundness and quality.

Pigs.

Although the receipts are less this year than the previous one, it must be borne in mind that the prices were fully 30 per cent. lower ; but, notwithstanding this fact, the undertaking shows a substantial profit. Pig raising and fattening is a fluctuating business, but it is felt that by keeping the stock up to the maximum at all times we will be enabled to reap the advantage when prices go up. It is anticipated that with the prospect of high prices a very large increase in receipts will be shown in the present year's transactions.

The class of pigs at present on the Colony are made up as follows :—

24 pedigreed Yorkshire sows.
2 pedigreed Yorkshire sows (young).
10 pedigreed Berkshire sows.
2 pedigreed Berkshire sows (young).
25 cross-bred sows.
3 pedigreed Yorkshire boars.
1 pedigreed Berkshire boar.
5 pedigreed Yorkshire boars (young)
40 porkers.
60 stores (large).
49 stores (small).
18 suckers.
——
239
——

The Berkshire - Yorkshire cross is used extensively, and the progeny of these breeds seem to meet the requirements of the trade, no difficulty being experienced in obtaining top market prices either on the Melbourne or local markets. A pleasing feature in connexion with our pig business is that not a single case of disease has occurred. This is attributed in a large measure to the fact that all the pigs are bred on the establishment, and that the conditions under which the animals are housed are of a thoroughly sanitary nature.

DAIRY.

The receipts for the year were £624 ; but we hope to increase this sum very materially in the future without adding to the number of cows, some 20 or 30 of which have been rejected with the object of filling their places with young heifers which are coming into profit,

YEARLING HERD.

and which are mostly from selected pure bred Jerseys, Ayrshires, and Jersey-Holstein cows by a Jersey bull. By this means it is anticipated that the future must show a satisfactory yearly increase in receipts.

Dairy cattle on the establishment number 120, made up as follows :—

Dairy cows ..	.. 82	
2-year-old Jerseys ..	.. 10	
2-year-old cross-bred Jerseys ..	.. 10	due to calve next autumn.
1-year-old Jerseys ..	.. 4	
1-year-old cross-bred Jerseys ..	.. 11	
4-year-old Jersey bull, pure ..	.. 1	
1-year-old Jersey bull, pure ..	.. 1	
2-year-old Ayrshire ..	.. 1	
	120	
also 8 commercial cattle	.. 8	
	128	

GARDEN AND ORCHARD.

This branch of the work has greatly improved under the present management, as some three years ago we were only able to make

JERSEY CALVES.

available for export 300 cases of apples, while during the past season 600 cases were despatched to London, which, considering the labour troubles that existed there, realized very fair prices, ranging from 8s. 9d. to 13s. 9d. per case. In addition, something like 800 cases were sold on the Melbourne and local markets, averaging about 6s. 6d. per case. Fruit and vegetables were provided for the consumption of the men on the Colony to the value of about £60 for the year.

It may be pointed out here that all our meat for food for the men and staff is purchased on the hoof and killed on the establishment, the average cost coming out at 11s. 8d. per 100 lbs.; and the sum of £93 8s. 1d. was received for the sale of hides and skins from same.

During the year under review 266 men have passed through the Colony, and 37 of these were still in residence on the 30th June, 1912. The table herewith shows the various occupations represented by the colonists. The task of adapting these men to work foreign to their training is one of the most difficult problems that the management has to solve, and, to a very great extent, minimizes the value of the labour which they perform :—

Labourers	87
Milkers	32
Cooks	18
Gardeners	10
Farm labourer, clerks	14
Drapers	5
Accountants, usefuls, engine-drivers, bakers	12
Ironmoulders, confectioners, miners	16
Kitchenmen, solicitors, farm hands, waiters, firemen, tinsmiths	27
Butchers, bullock-drivers, seamen, bootmakers, wheelwrights, tentmakers, frenchpolishers, bricklayers	16
Cabinetmaker, engineer, bushman, baker, engine-fitter, school teacher, bookkeeper, blacksmith, grocer, machinist, shearer, brass-fitter, boilermaker, sailor, printer, plumber, sailmaker, tailor, painter, plasterer, canvasser, &c.	29
	266

Their ages were as follow :—

Under 30 years of age	46
Between 30 and 40	78
Between 40 and 50	101
Over 50	41
	266

Work has been secured in the district at remunerative wages for about 40 per cent. of these men, others have left with sufficient money

COLONISTS HOEING BEANS.

earned on the establishment to carry them along while looking for employment; a few left without giving any notice of their intention to leave, and five were sent to Melbourne for medical treatment. Thirty-five were sent to work in and round Melbourne by the Secretary direct from the head office; this number is not, however, included in the

above list, as the men did not pass through the Colony. During the
onion season all colonists who were physically capable were sent out,
weeding and bagging, and were allowed on payment of a reasonable sum to board on the Colony. The men availed themselves of
this convenience readily, and the practice is much appreciated by
employers. The question of rationing the men is under the super-
'vision of the manager, and the following constitutes the bill of fare
for each day:—Meat, 1¼ lb.; bread, 1¼ lb.; potatoes, 1 lb.; sugar,
¼ lb.; tea, 2 oz.; oatmeal and rice, 2 oz.; treacle, 1 oz.; vegetables,
ad lib.; fruit, when in season; salt, pepper, mustard, and curry, as
required.

The existence of the Labour Colony is a great boon to the class
of people who avail themselves of its shelter. It is, indeed, pitiable
that there are so many men representing professions, trades, and

COLONISTS CUTTING FIREWOOD.

occupations who are unable to follow their usual avocations. Whilst
such a condition of affairs exists, so long will an institution similar
to the Labour Colony be required. Owing to the alienation from the
original area of land vested in the Trustees, and the highly improved
condition of the remaining portion, it is a matter of some difficulty
to find reproductive work for so many men. If it be proposed to
continue this form of relief, it will be necessary for fresh areas of
virgin land to be placed at the disposal of the Trustees so that the
work of reclamation, which is the more profitable as well as the more
suitable kind of employment for this kind of labour, may be undertaken. With the present farm as a base, much valuable work could
be carried out, and many of the initial difficulties likely to be
encountered when operating in an entirely new field would be obviated.
When such lands were sufficiently improved to warrant the plant and

management being transferred thereto, the present farm would no doubt be found immensely suitable for other purposes. and should prove a valuable asset to the State.   The reclaiming of land. which would not otherwise warrant the expenditure involved in clearing. would soon answer a double purpose by providing employment for the class of man the Colony caters for, while at the same time bringing into a state of productiveness land which would otherwise be of little use.   Such land would not produce any return for some time, and the expenditure would at first have to be met from a grant, which. as the land becomes profitable. could be gradually reduced, as has been done in the case of the Leongatha Labour Colony.

The Trustees naturally feel proud of the achievement of the farm as a revenue producer, and the financial improvement generally which has been manifested since it was handed over to them; while its benefit as an educational factor in the district has been evidenced by the large number of farmers and others interested in such pursuits in this and other parts of the world who have from time to time visited it and sought advice from the management regarding various phases of the work.   Requests have been made and granted for demonstrations in fruit culture, while the Farm Manager was chosen as a representative of the farmers on the Board of Control of the Agricultural High School at Leongatha.

The staff of the Labour Colony at present consists of Messrs. J. J. Willoughby (farm manager), A. P. Prout (gardener), J. Dick (dairyman), W. Wilson (general farm hand); and all of these have carried out their duties with zeal and intelligence.   The Trustees are also indebted to their Secretary (Mr. W. H. Crate) for the valuable assistance he has at all times given in the performance of his duties.

FARM MANAGER'S REPORT.

It will be observed that the rainfall for this season has been low as compared with the previous year, being 24.72 inches as against 43.16 inches for 1911; a difference of 19.56 inches.

Owing to the dry season and early autumn. the growth of crops and grass has been below the average.   These conditions proved advantageous in one respect, as they facilitated the work of ploughing and preparing land for sowing.

Nineteen acres, comprising different kinds of summer fodder crops, were sown last year, including sorghum, millet, mangolds. and pumpkins.   Of these, only the firstnamed (8 acres) gave any returns. the others being destroyed by the absence of rain and the prevalence of late frosts.   The sorghum was converted into silage, and produced 80 tons of that valuable fodder.   It is evident from the above that under adverse conditions sorghum is a more valuable summer crop in South Gippsland than either maize or millet.   It is necessary, however, to state that great care must be exercised in feeding to the stock, as it has been known to cause mortality as a result of the development of prussic acid at a certain stage of its growth.

The potato crop was attacked with eel worm and moth, and partly destroyed.

STATEMENT OF RECEIPTS AND EXPENDITURE FOR TWELVE MONTHS
ENDED 30th JUNE, 1912.

RECEIPTS.

1911.			£	s.	d.	£	s.	d.
July 1. Bank balance, Trust account	..	..	114	0	2			
Wages account			5	1	6			
						119	1	8
Grant from Treasury	..	..				400	0	0
Pigs	..	..	441	13	9			
Horses	..	..	86	8	6			
Dairy herd	..	..	27	4	3			
Dairy	..	..	624	12	5			
Nursery and garden	..	..	509	19	1			
Food (sale of hides, &c.)	..	..	93	8	1			
Colonists	..	..	164	18	7			
Boots and Clothing	..	..	62	3	9			
Tobacco	..	..	50	17	2			
Farm produce	..	..	16	9	9			
Stamps	..	..	0	5	9			
Rail fare (refunded)	..	..	5	1	10			
Stores	..	..	14	7	10			
Freights	..	..	1	4	0			
Board and lodging	..	..	113	4	5			
Grazing	..	..	0	6	0			
						2,212	5	2
						£2,731	6	10

PAYMENTS.

			£	s.	d.	£	s.	d.
Railway fares	..	..	88	15	7			
Railway freights	..	..	61	7	2			
Dairy	..	..	1	11	8			
Maintenance and plant	..	..	35	17	10			
Printing and stationery	..	..	4	18	0			
Building materials	..	..	5	13	11			
Stamps	..	..	8	9	2			
General expenses	..	..	46	18	11			
Furniture	..	..	2	10	9			
Insurance	..	..	36	10	3			
Implements..	..	..	59	0	0			
Fencing	..	..	1	1	0			
Tobacco	..	..	34	1	9			
Stores	..	..	185	9	5			
Food	..	..	204	17	0			
Boots and clothing	..	..	94	19	4			
Plant and tools	..	..	5	9	3			
Fodder, seeds, &c.	..	..	332	4	1			
Nursery garden	..	..	215	15	2			
Salaries and wages	..	..	1,034	16	4			
Dairy herd ..	..	..	6	6	0			
Horses	..	..	50	13	0			
Pigs	..	..	5	1	8			
						2,522	7	3
Less discounts allowed	..	..				13	7	0
						2,509	0	3
Bank balances, Trust account	..	..	188	17	6			
Wages account	..	..	33	9	1			
						222	6	7
						£2,731	6	10

VALUE OF STOCK, 30TH JUNE, 1912.

	£	s.	d.	£	s.	d.
Nursery, garden, &c.	132	14	3			
Boots and clothing	11	12	7			
Growing crops	145	10	0			
Water service	100	0	0			
Tanks	58	5	0			
Fencing	1	10	0			
Bedding	60	3	0			
Manure	47	16	6			
Printing and stationery	2	15	7			
Dairy	6	10	10			
Harness	60	17	0			
Furniture	121	18	9			
Implements	491	14	0			
Fodder, seeds, &c.	259	14	4			
Tobacco	11	4	4			
Stores	158	19	9			
Food	36	19	10			
Plant and Tools	447	6	0			
Building Materials	1	2	0			
Stamps	1	14	9			
Horses	454	10	0			
Cattle	860	15	0			
Pigs	532	9	0			
				4,006	2	6

PROFIT AND LOSS FOR TWELVE MONTHS ENDED 30TH JUNE, 1912.

Dr.

	£	s.	d.	£	s.	d
Boots and clothing	12	3	9			
Building materials	13	1	2			
Food	160	16	9			
Fodder, seeds, &c.	488	17	2			
Freight	48	8	9			
General expenses	46	4	7			
Harness	3	14	0			
Maintenance and plant	55	5	11			
Insurance	36	10	3			
Manure	17	6	0			
Printing and stationery	3	8	5			
Railway fares	58	14	5			
Salaries	575	8	0			
Stores	145	14	7			
Wages	285	15	0			
Water service	0	5	0			
				1,951	13	9

Cr.

	£	s.	d.	£	s.	d.
Board and lodgings	113	4	5			
Bedding	12	0	3			
Discounts allowed	13	7	0			
Dairy herd	49	19	3			
Dairying	625	7	9			
Fencing	0	1	9			
Furniture	9	19	6			
Growing crops	47	15	0			
Grazing	0	6	0			
Horses	18	3	0			
Implements	43	8	0			
Nursery, garden	171	19	2			
Plant and tools	30	15	4			
Pigs	492	17	7			
Tobacco	6	6	5			
				1,635	10	5

DISCING ON FORMER NEW ZEALAND FLAX LAND.

The present conditions are favorable to a plentiful season, and I anticipate much larger returns, which should result in an increase of revenue from the dairy and piggery. The pasture lands on the farm are very deficient, and require re-sowing. Having again got possession of the 50 acres of land which had been utilized by the Department of Agriculture for the purpose of carrying out flax-growing experiments, this has been placed under fodder crops and pasture grasses, which are growing splendidly. Strawberry clover is establishing itself in all the swampy lands, and improving the carrying capacity of the farm immensely.

IMPROVEMENT WORK.

Subdivision fences have been erected, and all old fences repaired, while six old gates have been replaced by new ones. All the land which was under New Zealand flax has been cleaned up and brought into a good state of cultivation. It is proposed to subdivide the flax ground and eventually get the whole of it under grass, the opinion being that this is the best pasture land on the farm. An additional 7 acres have been cleared of tussocks and stumps. The trees in the old orchard have been taken out, and the land prepared for cropping. Noxious weeds, such as ragwort and thistles, have been kept in check, and ferns cut twice. Portions of the low lands have been cleared up and sown with grass.

LABOUR.

Although the number of colonists has been up to the average, the value of their work is only a fractional part of what one would expect from the number, considerable difficulty being experienced in some cases in getting any returns at all. The absence of competent

OATS, PEAS, AND BEANS FOR SILAGE.

men to carry out the different branches of farming operations has been a severe handicap in the past. This difficulty has now to a great extent been overcome by the decision of the Trustees to permit of the

MIDDLE YORKSHIRE SOW.

engagement of a permanent farm hand. Ample evidence of the value of this departure is apparent on the farm to-day in the shape of advanced growing crops and thorough cultivation of the soil, in addition to which I am relieved of duties that hitherto have prevented me from exercising the close supervision necessary to get the best results.

STOCK.

The dairy herd consists of 117 head and 3 bulls, and 8 commercial cattle for killing purposes.   Twenty of the oldest and least profitable cows have been rejected from the milking herd, and will be used for beef or disposed of as opportunity offers.   The places of these will be filled by young heifers out of selected cows by the Jersey bull "Canary Lad IX."   The herd is being steadily improved both in character and yield, and many excellent young heifers by the above bull are on the farm at present.   A heifer, the progeny of this bull, on her first calf has given up to 3 gallons per day, with a test of 5.2 per cent. fat, and promises to be a much superior cow to her mother, whose test was 4.5 per cent.   This fact is of considerable importance, and very encouraging for the future, and I anticipate still better results in the direction of type as well as production.   The young Jersey bull

BERKSHIRE BOAR.

"Gold Brew," purchased by Mr. P. J. Carroll, Superintending Trustee, commands the admiration of every farmer who inspects him, and, having come from a noted butter producing family, should further enhance the value of the herd as butter-fat producers. Another valuable bull on the farm is the pure bred Ayrshire "Newport," out of that noted cow "Edith," whose photo and record appeared in the September number of the *Journal of Agriculture.* This bull is being mated with some Ayrshire and Ayrshire cross cows in addition to some of the Jerseys which it is thought would not mate to advantage with the Jersey bull.

Pigs.—The season just closed has not come up to expectations, chiefly on account of the slump in prices in pigs and the increased cost of food purchased. The number of pigs was, however, kept up to the full complement, and, with the advent of the high prices now prevailing, a good year in this branch of our farming operations is anticipated. The number of pigs on hand at present is 239.

Some splendid specimens of the breeds kept are at present on the farm, including boars and sows from imported strains purchased at the Royal Show of 1911. The progeny of these are much sought after by the dairymen along the line. Although very little thought or attention is given to the matter of exhibiting at the shows, we have been fairly successful where our pigs have competed, having secured second place with a Yorkshire boar at the Royal Show, 1911; champion, first, and second at Foster; and at Leongatha, five firsts and champion, three seconds, *and first for porkers and baconers.*

Horses.—There are 15 horses on the farm, 3 having been sold during the year; one, a ten-month old colt, realizing £25. The foals last year numbered 3, two draught and one light, all being good specimens and thriving well.

BROOD MARES.

A two-year old colt and a filly of the same age have been broken in and are working splendidly. Four draught mares have been served this year and have all proved in foal.

GENERAL REMARKS.

For the year, 266 men have been sent to the farm from the Melbourne office, excluding the 37 on the establishment at the commencement of the year. Of these, 37 remain on the farm at the present time. After putting in various terms, 266 have left, chiefly to accept employment in the neighbourhood. Every consideration is given to the farmers requiring labour, and they are permitted to select the best men on the farm for their own purpose at all times. I am pleased to say that some of those who have passed through the Colony are now farming on their own account. A large number of the men coming to the Colony are physically unfitted for hard work, and have to be given light employment which is not at all times of a reproductive character.

GARDENER'S REPORT.

Orchard.

On the whole, the health of the trees and plants is very good, though as a precaution the usual spraying had to be carried out. The worst diseases to be combated were woolly aphis and mussel scale, but by constant spraying these were kept in check and almost eradicated. Black spot proved a very difficult disease to cope with, more particularly on the pears, the trees having to be sprayed several times to keep it down; but, as the spraying was done at the right time, the result

PEAR TREE IN BLOOM.

was an almost clean crop. Codlin moth was also in evidence to a slight extent, but was no worse than in previous years. The old raspberry patch is gradually failing, but the young plants are looking very promising. The strawberries are looking very well, in spite of the hot dry summer just passed. Red and black currants are also thriving.

Yield.—As regards apples, last season was a record crop, a few of the old trees only being light. The pear crop was light, but had it not been for the destruction caused by the birds they would have

given a much better return.   The damage done to the pear and apple
crops by starlings was enormous, many of the trees, owing to this
pest, wearing a very sorry appearance; the only traces of fruit being
the skins left hanging on the trees.   Other fruit trees were only fair.
Bush fruits did fairly well on the whole, strawberries being very
prolific, yielding approximately 1,600 lbs. from 1-5th acre.   Red
currants fruited well, but the starlings made sad havoc with these,
and got most of the crop.   Black currants had a fair crop.   Raspberries were somewhat light, owing to the dry season.

Prices for all fruits were very good.   Strawberries sold from
4d. per lb. in the buckets to 9d. per lb. in baskets.   Raspberries
averaged 3½d. per lb., black currants 4d., and red currants 3d.
Apples sold locally and in Melbourne realized from 2s. to 6s. per case,
rejects for export bringing from 3s. to 5s.   The few pears which were
saved sold well.   We were fairly successful with our export of apples,
600 cases being shipped to London in three consignments, the fruit
being fair and of uniform size.   The best prices were realized by
Dumelow's Seedling, which brought from 9s. 6d. to 12s. 6d. per case,
Jonathans bringing 8s. 9d. only.   The fruit was all good, and
beautifully clean, especially the Dumelows, which evidently opened
up very attractively.   Jonathans were not so good, not having sufficient colour.   Next season it is proposed to keep Reinettes for local
sales, and ship mainly Jonathans, Five Crown, and Dumelows.   On
the whole, the shipment sold well, realizing as good prices as those of
other exporters.   The dock strike in London affected adversely the
sales of the last two shipments.

SHOWS.

A good exhibit of fruit and vegetables was staged at the local
Leongatha show, and secured first prize as a collection of garden pro-
duce; also eleven first prizes and two second prizes in the fruit section.
A very attractive exhibit was also shown at the Fruit and Floral
Carnival, in the Melbourne Exhibition, in March.   This secured a
certificate of merit, and was much admired by visitors.

NEW PLANTATIONS.

Since last year, a small plot of raspberry canes (1,500) was
planted.   These have made good progress, and should yield a fair
crop this season.   Three more rows of strawberries has also been
added.

OLD ORCHARD.

This has been abandoned, and the trees uprooted, the ground now,
being put under fodder crops.   The trees were very old, and for
many seasons have not been profitable.   In addition, they were a
menace to the clean trees in the main orchard; being old and very
weak they afforded excellent harbor for the various kinds of insect
and fungus pests.

VEGETABLE GARDEN.

In this section there was a slight decrease in the sales, the demand
for several lines falling off.   The spring crops were quite up to

expectations, but owing to the dry, hot summer the others were not so good. The onion crop was very satisfactory. Parsnips did not germinate as well as was expected, and were consequently short; but carrots did very well, and there is still a supply in hand. There was a successful crop of early cabbages, but those planted later were adversely affected by the very dry summer. Early peas yielded well, but late ones—like all late crops last season—were very light. Pumpkins, turks' caps, and marrows yielded fairly, and proved a good stand-by during the winter. There was not a very great demand for tomato plants. Fortunately, there were not many grown last season; and the balance, after sale of young plants, was planted out; the yield from these was good and prices were profitable.

Details of the yields of fruit and vegetables, together with prices obtained, will be found in the Manager's report. In addition to the sales of produce from the garden, a very large quantity is consumed on the Colony. When the value of this is taken into consideration, it will be found that the orchard and garden have proved profitable.

Finally, the year, on the whole has been very satisfactory. The area under fruit and vegetables is, approximately, 20 acres, the return from which, including sales and the value of produce used on the place, being estimated at £570.

The fruit trees, pears particularly, are looking exceedingly well, and show promise of a heavy crop during the coming season.

FODDER CROPS FOR NORTHERN AREAS UNDER IRRIGATION ON SMALL HOLDINGS.

By Temple A. J. Smith, Chief Field Officer.

There are various crops which can be grown in succession under irrigation which will not only supply constant green fodder for dairy cows or sheep, but will also prove a useful rotation so far as preserving the fertility of the soil is concerned, provided a system of manuring is adopted suited to the land, and such a system can be followed with slight expenditure. It is proposed to outline a rotation for the above purpose covering the whole of the year, giving the reasons from a restorative point of view as concerns the soil, and fodder values in relation to the crops produced. Cultivation must also be thorough in order to achieve the highest possible measure of success. Starting in the early autumn the land should be well fallowed to a depth of at least 6 inches unless the surface soil is shallower, under which circumstances the ploughing should not be so deep as to turn up the colder subsoil. The land should be worked down with cultivators or harrows after each day's ploughing, as it will be found that this practice conserves moisture better than where the ploughing is allowed to dry out, and a better tilth is obtained.

In April or May the land should be again worked with the one-way disc or cultivator to a depth of 3 or 4 inches if clean, or skim ploughed if dirty with weeds, and the following mixture sown for dairy cows or silage:—½ bushel rye; ½ bushel dun peas; 7 lbs. golden vetch; and ½ bushel of barley or white oats.

In many cases double the amount of rye and peas is sown on rich land. The peas are sown broadcast, and the rye, vetches, and oats, or barley drilled in to a depth of not more than 2 inches. A mixture of half-and-half bone dust and superphosphate, at the rate of 60 lbs. per acre, with 20 lbs. of blood manure or sulphate of ammonia is advisable, particularly on long-cultivated paddocks or poor land. If the soil is deficient in lime, and, in addition, of a heavy character, 10 cwt. of gypsum (sulphate of lime) or Thomas' phosphate in lieu of bone and super. will be found suitable. Quicker results are obtained if manures are applied three to four weeks before seed is sown. Care should be taken to sow the mixture while the land is still warm in order to give the crop a good start before the cold weather sets in. The advantages connected with the sowing of this combination of crops are many.

CHINESE MILLET GROWN AT NYAH.

In the first place a larger body of feed is produced as compared with separate seedings. The peas and vetches being legumes supply nitrogen in excess of their own requirements for the rye, oats, or barley, and the latter then naturally make greater growth.

A better balance ration is also secured, as the legumes supply a larger proportionate amount of protein, which element of food provides a larger milk supply or induces a better growth in lambs The rye and barley provide the carbohydrates which make for the fats and the warmth necessary to animal life.

The rye, peas, and vetches are useful rotation crops, the former owing to its greater rooting system, leaving more decaying organic matter in the soil than any of the other cereals, thus supplying humus. While all three have the effect of leaving the soil in better condition so far as available nitrogen is concerned for following crops.

Instances are on record of this mixture when cut yielding 28 tons of green fodder per acre, and better returns can always be had from cutting the crops than feeding off, though grazing is a practice often followed. Cutting can, if good autumn rains have fallen, or irrigation applied. be begun eight weeks after sowing, though full growth will not obtain until four weeks later.

If sheep only are to be fed, 3 lbs. of rape (Dwarf Essex variety) can be added, but where it is intended for cows and silage rape is not recommended. If, however, rape is sown, it should be broadcasted after the other seed is sown, and lighly harrowed. It is not unusual to find twelve to sixteen sheep fattened per acre on this fodder mixture, and either for cows or sheep feed will be available right up to the end of the spring. Meantime a second paddock should be under fallow for a spring crop with a view to a supply of green succulent fodder for the early and midsummer, so that no check in the milk supply or growth of lambs will ensue. The most suitable crops for this purpose are the Millets, Japanese, German, and Chinese, or White Millet. The first-mentioned is the hardiest, and gives from 6 to 10 tons of green fodder per acre. It should be sown after the danger of frosts is passed, in October and November, at the rate of 9 lbs. of seed per acre, in drills

LUCERNE, MILLET, AND MAIZE CROPS.

2 feet apart and 3 inches in the drill. Care must be taken not to put the seed down too deep, or it will perish, an inch to an inch and a half being the best depth to sow. The scuffler should be used between the drills until the crop is well established, commencing soon after the rows are well defined. This crop if cut before the seed is formed will come again two or three times if it gets rain or water after cutting and cultivation with the scuffler is followed, as soon as the land is sufficiently dry for the purpose. It can also be grazed if required, but the yield will not be so great if this course is followed. Any surplus can be made into fair hay or silage for cow feed. German Millet grows a finer straw, and gives a lighter yield, but makes a nice hay, and makes excellent grazing for sheep, seeding at the rate of 7 lbs. per acre is sufficient, broadcast. Chinese or White Millet should be sown in the same way as Japanese, and treated in the same manner, giving a heavy yield. The seed from all the millets is readily bought by seed merchants. The crop should be ready for the first-cut, about the middle

of December, and can be relied upon to keep things going until the end of February. Millets make good milk producers, and are easily handled; they are also suitable for silage. Farm manures suit the millets best. A third paddock should be in preparation for maize, which can be sown in September, October, November, and, where irrigation is possible, December. The best fodder varieties are Hickory King, Yellow Moruya, and Eclipse. These kinds give heavier yields, and keep green longer than most others, have a large leaf system with the least proportionate amount of woody fibre. The land should be fallowed and well worked, and seed sown at the rate of 20 to 30 lbs. per acre in drills 3 feet apart, and the seed 9 to 12 inches in the rows. two to three seeds in each place or hill as it is termed.

The rows should be worked between with the scuffler at intervals to conserve moisture, admit air, and keep down weeds until 6 feet high,

MAIZE CROP SOWN IN DRILLS.

the later working being shallow, when the crop itself should protect the soil from the sun's rays. Relays of seeding each month to keep a continuous supply should be sown, and the first cutting under favorable conditions should be ready about the end of January, and the last right into June. Broadcasting maize is a bad system, as if grown too thickly the lower leaves will dry off and become useless as fodder, and the stalk will be hard and woody, and less digestible; scarifying cannot be done, and the result is smaller and less succulent fodder. Yields of from 10 to 30 tons are possible per acre, and the best time to cut is when the crop comes into flower, and before the grain hardens in the cob. Maize is not only a fine fodder for cows and silage, but contrary to general opinion makes a fine fattening crop for sheep, especially crossbreds, if good fodder varieties are used, as they soon learn to straddle the stalks after cleaning up the bottom leaves, &c., and will eat it back to within a couple of feet

. of the ground. If the crop is not allowed to become too dry before they are turned in there is also very little waste after sheep. Broken-mouthed sheep should not be turned on to maize. Amber cane, Imphee, Farmer's Friend, are all treated for growth similarly to maize, except that less seed is required, 8 to 10 lbs. being sufficient per acre. They have a slight advantage over maize for winter fodder in that they are late, and of use after frost has attacked them in the early winter. They can also be cut, and stored dry, and fed through the winter to stock, or made into silage. In regard to the last three crops care must be taken to have good fences enclosing them, as they are liable to cause hoven or bloat if stock gain access to them before the ripening stage; if cut before ripe for fodder they should be allowed to wilt for a few hours in the sun before feeding. For very early winter feed skinless barley sown at the rate of 2 bushels per acre in early autumn will be found of value. Bonanza or Clydesdale oats are also early growers. They should be sown in the autumn while there is still warmth in the ground to get good results, and be well dressed with well-rotted manure ploughed in before sowing.

Adjuncts such as pumpkins, kale, mangels, turnips, can also be grown; the chief difficulty in regard to these root crops being the labour of handling. Pumpkins are easily grown on good river bottoms, and a cheap crop to produce; they are sown 10 to 12 feet apart, and. if a few shovelfuls of good farm manure are deposited at each hill will be found to give satisfactory returns. They are, however, not ideal food for cows, as their mushy condition prevents the act of rumination, and the seed is liable to pass into the second stomach and cause trouble.

Nothing has been said about lucerne, and there can be no doubt that as a fodder no better crop can be grown. The above system, if followed where lucerne cannot be successfully grown or as an adjunct, has proved a fine rotation. The addition of good oaten hay, chaff, and bran will improve the food value of all the green fodder crops dealt with, and a subdivision of at least four paddocks is necessary to properly carry out the system of rotation advocated. As each strip of the crop is finally cut the plough should be put in and the land well worked for the following crop; any delay means loss of moisture, and a prospect of weeds, and trouble. No mention is made as to the areas of each crop required as that will depend on the scale of operations of each individual, and the average yields of the crops will give a good idea as to the area to be planted; at the same time, a surplus would be always advisable. The average cow in milk will consume 70 to 100 lbs. of green fodder daily; a sheep 20 to 30. Where dairying is the main industry on the farm a silo is indispensable to make full use of surplus fodder crops to the best advantage.

HORSES and ruminants digest about the same percentage of albuminoids (protein) from a food, but the ruminants digest 10 per cent. more of the carbohydrates and 20 per cent. more of the fibre. They also make a better use of the fat.

RESULTS OF SPRAYING FOR IRISH BLIGHT.

By Geo. Seymour, Potato Expert.

Much difference of opinion exists among potato-growers as to whether it pays to spray their potato crops. It is well known that in Great Britain and Ireland, where the climate is more humid, and therefore more favorable to the development of late blight, spraying will check the disease, and increase the yield of sound tubers; but the majority of growers in this State argue that, with our dry climate, the disease is not likely to do much harm. This may be true; but spraying must be done regularly as it is impossible to foretell a visitation of the disease. Then again, if spraying is to do the greatest amount of good possible, it is necessary that growers should carry out the work simultaneously.

In order to gain reliable data, based on local conditions, it was decided by this Department to carry out experiments at different centres. For this purpose, plots were established at Crossley and Wollaston, near Warrnambool, for early crops. A plot on the same lines was established at Warragul, on the farm of Mr. S. McKay, for mid-season crop, and at Mr. P. H. Ibbott's farm, Pootilla, 2½ miles from Bungaree, for late crop. The scheme embraced five sections in each plot; three of these sections were sprayed from one to three times. In the case of the Warrnambool plot it was deemed advisable to divide the three-spray section, and spray half four times. This fourth spraying evidently had a beneficial effect, as this is the only section that was free of diseased tubers.

VARIETIES.

The varieties planted in the plots were as follow:—

New Zealand Pinkeye, at Crossley and Warrnambool.
Carman, at Warragul.
Snowflake, at Pootilla.

All the fields were carefully inspected before operations were commenced. Crossley and Warrnambool were inspected on October 3rd. Previous to this date the weather had been showery, and the soil was in a very moist condition, favorable to the development of the Late Blight, which was found evenly distributed in a mild form over the fields; but the tubers, which were just forming, had not been attacked. In the case of the mid-season plot at Warragul, a similar condition existed. In the late plot at Pootilla, the disease did not make its appearance at any stage.

The mixture used was copper-soda solution, or Burgundy mixture, of the following strength:—

12 lbs. sulphate of copper.
15 lbs. carbonate of soda.
100 gallons of water.

This mixture was applied at the rate of 80 to 100 gallons per acre. The latter quantity was found necessary when the plants were large and well grown. The cost of material worked out at about 3s. per acre for bluestone, and 1s. per acre for soda; total, 4s. per acre. The cost of

15584. 2 B

applying the mixture is regulated largely by the distance the water has to be carried and the supply of vessels for mixing, also the number of rows covered by the machine. The machine used in these experiments was a five-row "Fleming" sprayer. The total cost for spraying an acre works out at about 7s. 6d.

TABLE I.—PLOT 1.

SPRAYING EXPERIMENTS, 1911–12.

MR. P. CROWE'S PLOT, CROSSLEY, NEAR KOROIT.

Number of Times Sprayed.	Date of Spraying.	Yield per acre of Crop.			Weight of Diseased Tubers.	Proportion of Diseased Tubers.
		Tons	cwts.	lbs.	lbs.	Per cent.
Once	13th October	1	5	34	14	·6
Unsprayed		1	5	50	18	·6
Twice	13th October 21st October	1	3	56.	11	·4
Unsprayed		1	13	82	14	·3
Three Times	13th October 21st October 1st November	1	9	21	3	·09

In the case of the Crossley plot, it was found that about the time of the first spraying, on October 13th, the crop received a check. The set-back was very marked on the sprayed sections. The showery weather of the early part of October was followed by an exceptionally dry November, during which month rain only fell on seven days, giving 31 points at Crossley in six weeks. This dry spell, no doubt, checked the disease, and was responsible for the light yields. The Crossley plot was harvested during this month, and the Warrnambool

TABLE II.—PLOT 2.

SPRAYING EXPERIMENTS, 1911–12.

MESSRS. CALLAGHAN BROS. LTD., WOLLASTON, WARRNAMBOOL.

Number of Times Sprayed.	Dates of Spraying.	Yield per acre of Crop.			Weight of Diseased Tubers.	Proportion of Diseased Tubers.
		Tons	cwts.	lbs.	lbs.	Per cent.
Once	10th October	3	6	88	196	2·5
Twice	10th October 24th October	3	7	16	105	1·4
Unsprayed		2	10	4	213	4·3
Three Times	10th October 24th October 14th November	2	13	42	31	·5
Unsprayed		2	14	22	298	4·7
Four Times	10th October 24th October 14th November 22nd November	3	0	22	nil	..

plot a month later, the latter thus receiving the benefit of the December rain, which amounted to 393 points at Warrnambool.

The amount of disease in the Crossley plot was insignificant, the only indication of any benefit being a decrease in the percentage of Blight as the number of sprayings increased, but the average yield was in favour of the unsprayed sections by 13 cwt. 67 lbs.

The results of the Wollaston plot were more satisfactory, showing in a marked manner that spraying checks the disease even in a dry season. It will be noted that both the unsprayed sections have practically the same percentage of diseased tubers, viz., 4.3 and 4.7 per cent., whilst that sprayed only once has the largest amount of disease in the sprayed sections, viz., 2.5 per cent. Another spraying reduced the percentage to 1.4, the third to .5, and the fourth to *nil*.

In the case of the Wollaston plot, it will be noted that the yield showed an average increase of 12 cwt. 92 lbs. per acre in favour of the sprayed sections. This increase, no doubt, appears small; but, taking into consideration the very dry weather experienced during the growing period, it may be regarded as satisfactory, and *proves beyond doubt that spraying increases the quantity of sound tubers.*

TABLE III.

SPRAYING EXPERIMENTS, 1911–12.

PLOT 3.—MID-SEASON CROP.

Mr. S. Mackay, Warragul.

Variety—Carman.

Number of Times Sprayed.	Date of Spraying.	Yield per acre of Crop.			+ −	Increase Decrease.			Weight of Diseased Tubers.	Percentage of Diseased Tubers.	
		Tons	cwts.	lbs.	Tons	Tons	cwts.	lbs.			%
Once ..	2.12.11	4	1	28	−	0	9	84	Nil	Nil	10·8
Unsprayed ..	..	4	11	0	..		..		,,	,,	..
Twice {	2.12.11 16.12.11 }	3	13	22	−	0	17	90	,.	,,	14·6
Three Times {	2.12.11 16.12.11 12.1.12 }	2	12	20	+	0	3	48	..	..	·7
Unsprayed ..	..	2	8	84	+		..		..	..	*

PLOT 4.

Mr. Ibbott, Pootilla.

Variety—Snowflake.

Once ..	15.2.12	3	15	50	−	0	11	68	Nil	Nil	13·2
Unsprayed ..	..	4	7	6	..		..		..	,,	..
Twice {	15.2.12 7.3.12 }	3	12	80	−	0	14	38	..	,.	16·4

Reference to table 5 will show that at Warragul for the period embracing December, January, February, December had seventeen wet days, resulting in 704 points of rain, and January had eight wet days before the 11th, with 121 points, with only 5 points for the remainder of the month. Such conditions were favorable for the development of the disease, with the result that it made its appearance in the plants, but no disease was found in the tubers of the sprayed and unsprayed sections. It is very probable that the dry weather at the end of January and beginning of February checked the disease. That the dry weather had a marked influence on the crop is borne out by the yields obtained on sections 4 and 5 of plot 3, marked thus *, which were planted three weeks later than the sections 1, 2, and 3, consequently the results of sections 4 and 5 must be considered separately. In this case the sprayed section shows an increase of 7 per cent.

YIELDS.

The returns from plots 1, 3, and 4 show a marked decrease in the yield on the sprayed sections compared with the unsprayed, ranging from 7 per cent. to 16 per cent. The only increase is in plot No. 2, and the late planted portion of No. 3. This decrease is consistent throughout, and is greater in proportion to the number of sprayings.

TABLE IV.

AVERAGES OF SPRAYED AND UNSPRAYED SECTIONS.

Plot.	Sprayed.			Unsprayed.			Increase.			Decrease.
	Tons	cwt.	lbs.	Tons	cwt.	lbs.	Tons	cwt.	lbs.	cwt.
Mr. Crowe's ..	1	5	111	1	9	66		..		3·67
Mr. Callaghan's ..	3	1	98	2	9	6	0	12	92	..

From the above it will be seen that in one case spraying increased the yield ; in the other there is an apparent decrease.

SPRAYING EXPERIMENTS, 1911-12.

PLAN OF MR. CROWE'S PLOT AT CROSSLEY.

133 links.	50 links.	133 links.	50 links.	133 links.
Sprayed three (3) times	Unsprayed ..	Sprayed twice	Unsprayed ..	Sprayed once

Public road.

SPRAYING EXPERIMENTS, 1911-12.

PLAN OF PLOT AT MESSRS. CALLAGHAN BROS., WOLLASTON, WARRNAMBOOL.

285 links.	100 links.	285 links.	100 links.	285 links.	
Sprayed once ..	Unsprayed ..	Sprayed twice	Unsprayed ..	Sprayed three times	Sprayed four times.

It has been claimed for spraying that it is beneficial to the crop, apart from checking diseases, because it prolongs the life of the plant. It cannot be said to have had that result in any operations carried out by this Department. It has been noted that the sprayed sections kept green longer than the unsprayed, but it does not necessarily follow, because the leaves are green, that the crop of tubers will show an increased yield. The results of plot 4, at Pootilla, are interesting in this connexion, the section sprayed once showed a decrease of 11 cwt. 68 lbs. as compared with the unsprayed section, and the twice sprayed section a decrease of 14 cwt. 38 lbs.

In these experiments information has been sought on the following points:—

1. What effect has spraying on the disease?
2. How many times should the crop be sprayed?
3. Will spraying increase the yield of the crop?
4. Does it pay to spray?
5. What influence has the weather on the disease?
6. Data in regard to the rainfall during the growing period at different centres.

1. Spraying checks the disease and results in a larger percentage of sound tubers. The increase was in proportion to the number of times the crop was sprayed (see table, plots 1 and 2).

2. The number of times the crop requires to be sprayed must be determined by the weather conditions during the growing period. Results obtained on plots 1 and 2 in this experiment indicate very little difference between the section sprayed once and the unsprayed section, whilst the section sprayed four times was the only one free from disease.

3. In these experiments the balance of evidence is that spraying decreases the total yield of the crop, and that the decrease is in proportion to the number of times the crop is sprayed.

4. Judged by the results obtained in these experiments, the answer is No, but owing to the season being unfavorable for the development and spread of the disease, this reply must be considered in conjunction with question No. 1.

5. A prolonged dry period checks the disease in the plants, and is the controlling factor in its attack on the tubers. (See results of plot No. 3, sections 1 and 2). It has been stated that the disease was found in the plants of this plot before spraying commenced; but no disease was found in the tubers of the unsprayed sections.

6. Remarkable variations in the rainfall at different centres is revealed by table. Plot No. 1 had 44 wet days, with 658 points of rain; plot No. 2, 33 wet days, with 537 points; plot No. 3, 34 wet days, with 946 points; plot No. 4, 19 wet days, with 537 points, showing difference of 68 per cent. between the highest and lowest records.

THE WATER.

It was evident, in these experiments, that the quality of the water has a great deal to do with the effect of the copper-soda, and Bordeaux mixtures, on the plants. It is recognised that rain-water, or soft river-water, is best for preparing the solution; that used at Warrnambool

TABLE V.

The sites for the plots were selected with due regard to the rainfall and its effect on the crops maturing at different seasons ; Nos. 1 and 2, for the early Spring rains on the first early crop ; No. 3 for early Summer rain on the mid-season crop, and No. 4 for the late Summer and Autumn rains on the late crops. The following table will show the number of wet days and total rainfall during the growing period at each station :—

	1911.						1912.					
Station.	October.		November.		December.		January.		February.		March.	
	No. Wet Days.	Points.	No. Wet Days.	Points.	No. Wet Days.	Points.	No. Wet Days.	Points.	No. Wet Days.	Points.	No. Wet Days.	Points.
1. Crossley ..	17	166	7	31	20	411	..	..	..	..	..	..
2. Warrnambool	12	128	4	16	17	393	..	..	..	..	..	..
3. Warragul ..	..	..	..	..	17	704	9	126	8	116	..	..
4. Pootilla (Kirk's Dam)	..	..	..	..	..	..	5	47	4	119	7	155
Pootilla (Beale's Reservoir) ..	..	..	..	..	..	..	6	35	4	126	9	141

and Koroit was hard spring-water, highly mineralized, and required a much larger quantity of soda than the standard formula to precipitate the copper. On applying the litmus and cyanide test, the solution contained too much copper, and instead of the standard 6—7½—50, it required 6 lbs. soda-copper, 12 lbs. soda, to 50 gallons of water. At Warragul, with soft water, the proportions were 6 lbs. soda-copper, 8 lbs. soda, to 50 gallons of water. It is a question for the future whether it would not be better to use the lime-water preparation, which has proved quite as effective, and much cheaper. The latest formula is as follows :—

Copper-sulphate—10 ounces.
Lime-water—8½ gallons.
Add water to make up 50 gallons.

When considering the results of these experiments, it must be remembered that the season was an abnormally dry one, consequently the results are no indication of the benefit to be derived from early and systematic spraying, in such a season as 1910-11. The actual benefit to be derived from spraying every season is far from settled. In other countries, the results are not conclusive; in some seasons they are slightly in favour of the sprayed sections; and in others it is in favour of the unsprayed. But, allowing that the decreased yield in these experiments is due to the effect of the mixture on the plants, it amounts only to about 15 per cent., whilst the loss from the Blight in 1910-11 ranged from 25 per cent. to a total loss. As many fields were not harvested, it is safe to assume that if spraying had been undertaken early, and persistently followed up, many of these abandoned fields would have given a fair percentage of sound tubers. It is most desirable that those growers who have a spraying plant should be on the alert for any appearance of an outbreak in the coming season, and in carrying out the work are advised to have one or more unsprayed control sections.

I am indebted to the Commonwealth Meteorologist for the daily rainfall registered during the period of experiment at each centre. The thanks of this Department are also due to Mr. Crowe, Crossley; Messrs. Callaghan Bros., Warrnambool; Mr. S. McKay, Warragul; and Mr. Ibbott, of Pootilla, for setting apart portions of their crop for experimental purposes, and the assistance rendered in carrying out the work.

TABLE VI.

SPRAYING EXPERIMENTS, 1911–12.

RAINFALL AT KOROIT AND WARRNAMBOOL.

Early Fields.

Date.	Koroit.			Warrnambool.		
	October.	November.	December.	October.	November.	December.
	Points.	Points.	Points.	Points.	Points.	Points.
1	3	..	..	..	..	..
2	8	12	..	..	6	..
3	23	1	..	19	..	..
4	9	..	..	6	..	..
5	..	..	111	..	..	130
6	..	..	..	..	..	..
7	8	..	2	10	..	1
8	4	5	6	..	7	8
9	29	..	..	17	..	..
10	2	..	2	1	..	1
11	2	..	..	..	..	..
12	..	..	69	..	2	62
13	2	6	46	2	1	35
14	..	2	1	..	..	..
15	..	..	..	..	..	..
16	6	1	22	19	..	12
17	2	..	..	3	..	..
18	..	..	3	..	..	7
19	..	..	49	..	..	28
20	..	..	20	..	..	27
21	..	..	4	..	..	..
22	..	4	6	..	..	11
23	2	..	3	1	..	15
24	6	..	3	4	..	3
25	12	..	36	7	..	30
26	1	..	22	..	..	20
27	..	..	1	..	..	1
28	..	..	..	..	..	..
29	..	..	..	..	..	..
30	..	..	2	..	..	2
31	47	..	3	39	..	..
Total rain	166	31	411	128	16	393
	17 days	7 days	20 days	12 days	4 days	17 days

TABLE VII.

SPRAYING EXPERIMENTS, 1911–12.

	Mid-season Plot.				Late Plot.		
	Warragul.				Pootilla Plot. Records taken at Beale's Reservoir.		
Date.	1911.	1912.	1912.	Date.	1912.	1912.	1912.
	December.	January.	February.		January.	February.	March.
	Points.	Points.	Points.		Points.	Points.	Points.
1	..	9	..	1	10	..	..
2	..	14	..	2	1	..	..
3	..	..	..	3	..	..	..
4	71	47	..	4	3	..	1
5	12	4	..	5	8	..	2
6	8	..	4	6	..	..	..
7	..	6	75	7	..	62	..
8	..	..	5	8	..	24	..
9	..	16	..	9	..	..	62
10	..	17	..	10	10	..	25
11	94	8	..	11	3	..	..
12	149	..	..	12	..	..	3
13	12	..	..	13	..	..	..
14	..	..	..	14	..	..	..
15	29	..	..	15	..	..	..
16	22	5	15	16	..	..	..
17	2	..	..	17	..	..	..
18	50	..	..	18	..	..	..
19	40	..	..	19	..	..	..
20	4	..	..	20	..	..	..
21	67	..	..	21	..	..	..
22	21	..	..	22	..	..	..
23	..	..	6	23	..	..	..
24	..	..	5	24	..	36	..
25	88	..	2	25	..	..	..
26	34	..	..	26	..	..	..
27	1	..	4	27	..	4	8
28	..	..	..	28	..	..	25
29	..	..	..	29	..	..	13
30	..	..	..	30	..	..	2
31	..	..	..	31	..	..	..
Total Rain	704	126	116		35	126	141
Number of Days' Rainfall.	17	9	8		6	4	9

FRUIT PROSPECTS FOR THE COMING SEASON.

P. J. Carmody, Chief Orchard Supervisor.

The subjoined reports of the district supervisors indicate the fruit prospects of the coming year to be particularly good.

Owing to mild winter and to the fact that last season's crop was light, the trees are in excellent condition; and the bright and sunny weather prevailing at setting time has resulted in leading one to believe that a record yield will be harvested. In only a limited area have frosts been reported to be injurious.

Jonathan, the principal export apple of the southern part of the State, gives promise of a very heavy crop where the trees are under the influence of other varieties blooming at the same time. Where large areas of these apples are planted out on their own, crops are light and irregular. Rokewood, Yates, and Statesman are amongst those having the greatest influence in interpollination with the Jonathan, and it is remarkable to see young trees three and four years old with this advantage laden with fruit, while without it trees eight years old have but a few apples on them. It is advisable, not only with this variety, but with all other kinds of fruit, to adopt a method of planting whereby interpollinating influences can have the fullest scope.

Now that the work of spraying is facilitated by the general use of motor spray pumps, it is only reasonable to expect growers to take every precaution against diseases so that the fruit may be in a condition to bring remunerative prices on the market.

The reports from the different districts are as follow:—

Mr. H. W. Davey, Geelong and Western District, reports:—

Geelong, including Freshwater Creek and part of Moorabool Valley.—Apricots: from light to heavy, the average on the light side. Peaches: excellent. Plums: fair. Pears: very heavy. Apples: good.

Inverleigh, Native Creek, and Bannockburn.—Apricots from light to heavy, average a fair crop. Cherries and peaches: good. Plums: fair. Apples: good. Pears: heavy.

Mt. Cole.—Apricots: not much grown. Plums: good. Apples: good. Pears: heavy.

Ocean Grove, Fenwick, and Wallington.—Apricots: light to fair. Apples: good. Pears: heavy.

Portland, Gorae, and Bolwarrah.—Apricots: good, but little grown. Pears: very heavy.

Panmure.—Apricots: fair. Apples: good. Pears: heavy. Plums: fair.

Rokewood Junction.—Apricots: fair to good Apples: good. Pears: very heavy crops.

Warncoort and Yea.—Apricots: fair to good. Peaches: very little grown. Apples: good; some fine crops of Jonathans. Pears: heavy.

Mr. E. Meeking reports:—

Prospects of the coming season's fruit crop in the Mornington Peninsula are:—

Apples.—Jonathan: a good setting is the rule throughout the whole of the Mornington Peninsula and the greater part of South-eastern Gippsland.

Reinette du Canada: generally speaking, throughout the Mornington Peninsula and South-eastern Gippsland this useful and hardy variety has again set well.

Williams' Favorite: very fair all round.

Gravenstein: fair to medium in all the centres.

Rome Beauty: on the Mornington Peninsula there is promise of a fair crop; but with this particular variety it is rather early to speak definitely. In the Gippsland portion of the district the variety is not much cultivated.

London Pippin: this being a late variety, the remarks on Rome Beauty pertain to London Pippin also.

Delicious: where planted on the Peninsula, the setting has been very fair.

Sunnyside: a very fair setting in most of the centres.

Aesopus Spitzenberg: not a heavy setting in any of the centres.

Statesman: generally good everywhere.

Pears.—Williams' Bon Chrétien: the setting has been good; quite different from last season.

Beurré de Capiaumont: good generally.   Black Spot has made its appearance, and will tend to lessen the crop.

Beurré d'Anjou: usually a poor setter, this season there is promise of a fair crop.

Napoleon: a good setting.   Black Spot threatens to cause havoc.

Keiffer's Hybrid: promise of a very fair crop generally.

Beurré Bosc: a good setting wherever grown.

Apricots.—Oullin's Early Peach: a very fair promise.

Moor Park: a good promise.

Beuge: fair to good.

Plums.—All varieties have set well, and with favorable weather should yield a good harvest.

Strawberries.—Most varieties set well, but hailstorms caused a certain amount of loss.   The crop generally in Red Hill will be fair.

Mr. A. A. Hammond reports on the fruit crops in the Doncaster district:—

Apples.—Good.   All the leading varieties promise a good crop.

Apricots.—Good.   Very little grown, but the crop is the best for a number of years.

Pears.—Very good.

Peaches.—Very good. Late varieties are heavy. Brigg's and Hale's Early have only a medium crop, but on the whole the prospects of the peach crop are good.

Plums.—Light.   All the leading varieties are light.   The Washington, Greengage, and Late Black Orleans promise a medium to good crop, but these varieties are not so largely grown.

Lemons.—Good.

The prospects for the coming season's fruit crop are, on the whole, very satisfactory. With the exception of plums, all kinds of fruit trees are carrying a good crop.

The plum crop will probably be only about one-fifth to one-sixth of the 1910-11 season's crop.

Mr. J. Farrell reports:—

Bayswater.—Apples: all varieties medium to heavy. Pears: heavy. Plums: medium. Peaches: heavy. Apricots: light. Strawberries: heavy.

Blackburn.—Apples: medium to heavy. Pears: heavy. Peaches: heavy. Apricots: medium.   Plums: light.

Brighton.—Apples: heavy, particularly Fillbasket. Pears: Williams' Bon Chrétien, Keiffer's Hybrid, and Howell, heavy; others, medium. Peaches and apricots: medium.   Figs: light (first crop).

Burwood.—Apples: medium to heavy. Pears: heavy, particularly Williams' Bon Chrétien. Peaches and apricots: light. Plums: light to medium.

Croydon.—Apples: Jonathan, medium to heavy; Five Crown and Rome Beauty, heavy; other varieties, good.   Pears: Williams' Bon Chrétien, Howell, Keiffer, Beurré Bosc, and Beurré Capiaumont heavy; other varieties, medium to heavy.   Peaches, plums, and apricots: medium.

Emerald.—Apples: Five Crown and Rome Beauty, heavy; Jonathan, medium; others, light.   Pears: medium.   Plums: light to medium.   Strawberries: heavy.

Fern Tree Gully.—Apples: medium. Pears: heavy. Peaches: heavy. Plums: medium.   Strawberries: good.

Ringwood.—Apples: all varieties, medium to heavy.   Pears: heavy.   Plums: medium.   Peaches, heavy.   Apricots: light.   Strawberries: good.

Scoresby.—Apples: medium to heavy.   Pears: heavy.   Plums: medium. Lemons and oranges: medium.

Vermont.—Apples: medium to heavy.   Pears: heavy.   Plums: medium. Peaches and apricots: light.   Lemons and oranges: medium.   Strawberries: heavy.

Wandin.—Apples: medium.   Pears: heavy.   Plums, peaches, and apricots: light to medium.   Oranges and lemons: medium.   Quinces: heavy.   Loquats: medium.   Walnuts: light.   Almonds: medium.   Mulberries: heavy.   Figs: light.   Gooseberries: heavy, particularly Roaring Lion.   Passion fruit: very light.   Raspberries: show prospects of good crop.   Blackberries: all varieties look well for a crop.   Currants: medium.   Filberts: light.   Strawberries: Edith, Marguerite, Royal Sovereign, and Sunbeam, heavy; Up-to-date, medium; except where irrigated, heavy.

Waverley.—Apples: most kinds, medium to heavy.   Pears: heavy.   Plums: medium.   Peaches and apricots: light.   Lemons and oranges: medium.

Mr. E. Wallis reports:—

Diamond Creek, Doreen, Eltham, Greensborough, Research, South Morang, Tanck's Corner.—Apples: heavy.   Apricots: medium to heavy.   Peaches: heavy.   Pears: heavy.   Plums: heavy.   Quinces: medium to heavy.

Arthur's Creek, Kinglake, Running Creek, Strathewen, Wallan, Whittlesea.— Apples: heavy.   Apricots: medium.   Peaches: heavy.   Pears: heavy.   Plums: heavy.   Quinces: medium to heavy.

Allwood, Cottle's Bridge, Kangaroo Ground, Panton Hill, Queenstown, Summer Hill.—Apples: heavy.   Apricots: medium.   Peaches: heavy.   Pears: heavy. Plums: heavy.   Quinces: medium.

Digger's Rest, Keilor, Macedon, Riddell's Creek, Werribee.—Apples: heavy. Apricots: medium.   Peaches: medium.   Pears: heavy.   Plums: medium to heavy.

Mr. A. G. McCalman (Goulburn Valley) reports:—

Apricots both in the Goulburn Valley and North-east will be extremely light, especially Moor Park, the principal canning variety.   Total yield will probably not be one-fifth of last season's yield.

Peaches.—The early varieties Brigg's Red May and Hale's Early will be a light crop.   The later kinds, including all those suitable for canning and drying, will be a good crop, approaching that of last season, both in the Valley and North-east.   Of the late varieties of peaches, the Elberta has set well, but the Comet will be light; Foster is light.   Nicholl's Orange Cling, rather light; Pullar's Cling is light on the young trees, and light to medium crop on older trees; Lady Palmerston is light, and Late Orange Cling a very light crop.

Pears.—Williams' Bon Chrétien, the principal canning pear, will be extremely heavy, except at Toolamba and Ardmona, where the crops will be medium only.   The total will probably exceed that of any previous year, as many young trees are coming into full profit.   The yield of pears generally will be good.

Apples.—Heavy yields will be obtained with nearly all varieties in the Valley and North-east.

Plums.—Crops will be medium only in both districts.

Nectarines.—Crops will be good.

Oranges and lemons.—Promise of heavy yields, but it is too early to say.

Grapes.—Damaged by frost in many places. The total yield will be much lighter than last year.

Loquats have everywhere set heavy crops.

Almonds.—The crop will be very good, Hatch's Nonpariel having the biggest yield. The Jordan shows well in most places.

Mr. W. P. Chalmers reports on the various localities in his district:—

Bet Bet and Dunolly.—Apricots: very light. Peaches: early varieties, medium; late varieties, very heavy. Plums: medium. Apples: heavy. Pears: very heavy.

Amphitheatre, Elmhurst, Eversley.—Pears: heavy. Apples: medium.

Pomonal.—Apples: exceptionally light. Pears: heavy.

Horsham.—Apricots: exceptionally light. Peaches: early, light; late, heavy. Plums: medium. Apples: medium. Pears: heavy.

Guildford and Newstead.—Apples: heavy. Pears: very heavy.

Summary for District.—Apples: medium. Pears: very heavy. Plums: medium. Apricots: very light. Quinces: abundant.

Mr. S. A. Cock reports on the prospects of the fruit crop in the Bendigo district:—

Apricots.—The crop is a light one generally. Extremely light in the Bendigo district, and medium to light in the Murray district.

Apples.—Every variety is heavy, especially New York, Munroe, Newtown Pippin, and Jonathan. Harcourt should produce a record crop this season.

Citrus.—Oranges and lemons are showing abundant blossom, and the conditions favorable to setting a very heavy crop in all the northern irrigated areas.

Currants.—Black and red promise a good crop at Taradale, Woodend, and Kyneton.

Figs.—Bendigo and the Murray districts should produce a record first crop of figs. All varieties have set well.

Grapes.—Both table and drying grapes give excellent promise of a heavy crop at Bendigo and the Murray districts.

Gooseberries.—The crop is a medium to good one.

Loquats.—A good crop in the Bendigo district.

Pears.—The crop is light to medium; Williams' Bon Chrétien, Beurré de Capiaumont, and Eyewood are the heaviest, and Gansel's Bergamot and Winter Nelis extremely light.

Plums.—Early plums will be light, and late plums heavy. Generally, taking Bendigo and the Murray districts, the crop is medium to heavy.

Peaches.—Bendigo and the Murray districts should have a splendid crop in all varieties.

Quinces.—A heavy crop in all districts.

Strawberries.—At Campbell's Creek a good crop; and in the new irrigation settlements of the north, Tongala, Bamawm, Nanneella, and Swan Hill the promise is good.

Tomatoes.—A heavy crop at Echuca, Swan Hill, and all the Murray district. Bendigo a heavy crop, but late, owing to cold conditions of September and October. There is also a large planting in the irrigation settlements, and promise of heavy crops.

Mr. L. Pilloud reports on the fruit crop in the Gippsland district:—

Peaches are good at Bruthen, Bairnsdale, and Drouin; a heavy crop.

Pears.—Williams' Bon Chr tien, Keiffer's Hybrid, Josephine, Vicar of Wakefield are very heavy all through Gippsland.

Plums promise a good crop.

Quinces.—Not many grown; a good crop on the few trees here and there.

Apricots.—Not many grown; a good crop on those that have them.

Apples.—Jonathans and Yates will have a good crop.

Mr. J. T. Grossmann reports on the Mildura Settlement and adjacent orchards in the district:—

Apples promise a good yield in practically all the varieties grown. The early varieties, such as Red Astrachan, are yielding exceptionally heavy.

Pears.—Varieties grown are principally Bartletts. The older trees are promising a heavy yield. The younger trees in most cases are only showing light to fair.

Peaches.—Varieties cultivated are chiefly Elbertes, Lady Palmerston, and Crawfords. These three varieties in good peach land are promising a good crop, although not exceptionally heavy.

Apricots.—The varieties cultivated are Moor Park, Blenheim, Royal, and Oullin's Early Improved. The Moor Park are promising best, in some cases heavy; Blenheims are light; and Royals and Oullin's Early Improved only a sprinkling to fair generally.

Plums and *Prunes.*—Although not cultivated yet to any large extent, the season appears to be a favorable one for this fruit. The Sugar Prune is bearing heavy crops, also the Prune D'Agen, and most of the Japanese varieties are carrying a good crop.

Figs promise a good crop.

Almonds.—Principally Brandes Jordan and Nonpariel varieties are carrying a good crop.

Oranges.—Varieties, including the Washington Naval, Valencia Late, Mediterranean, sweet as well as the more common varieties, have all bloomed well, and, according to present appearances, promise a heavy crop for the coming year.

Lemons.—Chiefly Lisbon variety; good healthy trees, have also bloomed well, and, so far, the setting is equally good.

STRENGTH IN WHEAT—

A strong wheat is one which yields a strong dough in baking, and English wheats are lacking in this respect. Speaking at a conference recently, in Cambridge, Professor Biffen gave some interesting particulars as to the efforts of the Home Grown Wheat Committee to improve the strength of English wheats. Rating the best Canadian at 100 in strength, a good average wheat might be reckoned at 80, while ordinary English wheats could only be classed at 60. English wheat has, consequently, to be mixed with hard imported wheats in order to get the desired strength; and it is stated that strong imported wheat may be worth 10s. more per quarter to the inland miller than the home grown. In experiments conducted by the Committee it was found that neither soils nor manures can raise the quality of English wheats to the desired standard of strength, and that improvement must be sought in the introduction of new varieties. Of these many have been tested, seed being obtained from all parts of the world. In England the imported variety, however, has always deteriorated under cultivation with one exception—Red Fife—which was found to retain its strength.

BEE-KEEPING IN VICTORIA.

(Continued from page 653.)

F. R. Beuhne, Bee Expert.

X.—THE REARING OF QUEEN BEES.

The selection of a queen from which to breed for the purpose of super-seding old or inferior queens, or the queens of colonies showing a predisposition to disease, viciousness or some other undesirable trait, is not only of the greatest importance but also a most difficult problem.

It is upon the prolificness of the queen and the longevity and vigour of her worker progeny that the larger or smaller amount of surplus honey depends; but the most prolific queen is not necessarily the best to breed from. Experience has shown that the queen progeny of an exceedingly prolific queen rarely equal their mother; when they do, they produce workers which are constitutionally delicate, and these never yield the amount of surplus which one should expect from the great number of bees raised. A prolific queen producing vigorous long-lived workers is very soon restricted in egg production by the relatively large number of old field bees, the honey gatherers filling much of the comb with honey once the colony has attained normal strength. In the case of a colony having a queen producing short-lived workers the position is reversed. Many of the bees in such a colony die soon after reaching field bee age; therefore the young, the nurse bees, predominate. It is the work of the young bees to feed larvæ, prepare cells for egg-laying, and attend the queen. As the number of field bees bringing in honey is little more than sufficient to supply what is needed for immediate consumption, the colony will show a very large amount of brood in all stages right through the season but will store less honey for the apiarist than colonies which, with a smaller amount of brood, have far more old field bees.

As a breeder, I prefer the queen of a colony which has the maximum number of bees from a moderate amount of brood during a season. This results naturally in a good yield of honey, and indicates longevity of the bees. There are, however, other desirable characteristics, such as purity of race, gentleness, and absence of excessive swarming, which are needed. The number of queens which conform to all these requirements is, even in a large apiary, usually rather limited.

Important as the selection of the queen mother is, the raising of the young queens by the best possible method, and under the most favourable conditions, is not less so. Poor queens may result when queens are raised under unfavourable conditions, no matter how suitable the mother queen is. There are many different methods of raising queens and good queens may be obtained by any one of them if everything is just right. The difficulty is, that many bee-keepers fail to observe when conditions are suitable and when not. A prosperous condition of colonies, an income of pollen and honey, and a warm moist atmosphere, are essential. A heavy honey flow is not the best time for queen rearing, particularly when it occurs during hot dry weather. There may be both pollen and honey coming in, and yet the right conditions may not exist, even though atmospheric conditions appear favourable. This is probably owing to some deficiency in quality of the stores gathered. It may, however, be taken as an indication that conditions are favourable when the young larvæ are surrounded by a plentiful supply of pure white food. The colony selected for raising cells from the eggs or larvæ of the chosen breeding queen should be strong, particularly in nurse bees.

The " Doolittle " method of transferring young larvæ to artificial cell cups and getting the cells raised, either in a queenless colony or over the queen-excluding honeyboard in the super of a strong colony, has the advantage of enabling one to know exactly when the queen cells will hatch. The same advantage can be obtained by the " Alley " method without disturbing the young larvæ. Queenless bees are compelled to raise queen cells under the impulse of self-preservation, whether the conditions are suitable or not. Often they appear to raise them rather hurriedly. There is no doubt that good queen cells are produced by bees bent on swarming (in the proper season). They are raised deliberately, and only when conditions as to food supply and strength in bees are suitable. But the bees of queens from swarm-cells inherit the swarming impulse, which the best apiarists of all countries are trying to eliminate, and such queens are therefore not desirable in any numbers.

There is yet another impulse under which bees will raise good cells ; the superseding impulse. When a queen is in her third season, and long before the apiarist can notice any decline in her prolificness, the bees usually prepare to supersede her by raising one or more queen-cells. They do this at a time when the conditions are most favourable ; they are usually better

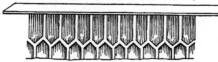

1. COMB CUT FOR QUEEN RAISING.

judges of this than their owner, excepting in the case of a queen suddenly failing from disease or accident. If the bees are inclined to swarm there may be a swarm issuing before or after the cell or first cell hatches. Where the bees are less inclined, the virgin queen on emerging from her cell will destroy all other cells but will take no notice of the remaining old queen, her mother.

The number of cells raised under the superseding impulse is not large —from one to three usually ; but they are invariably fine large cells producing splendid queens. For a number of years I have obtained some of my best queens in this way, but as the number is limited I could not get sufficient, till I made use of the superseding impulse for raising them from larvæ supplied repeatedly to the superseding colonies from selected breeding queens. For this purpose it is necessary to know the ages of all queens. Colonies having queens in their third year are examined periodically when conditions are favourable. If there are indications of superseding, the cells are removed and larvæ from the breeding queen, over which cell cups have previously been started by temporarily queenless bees, are given in place of those removed. The colony should naturally be populous and thriving enough to raise good cells. If the queens which are not up to standard are replaced every year irrespective of age, these three-year-olds are those which passed all the musters and there will be no lack of the necessary condition. Should none of the superseding colonies be of sufficient strength other strong ones may be made by exchanging queens between colonies with old queens and strong colonies with younger ones.

To have all the queen-cells mature at the same time, so as to be able to leave them where they are raised till the day before they hatch, it is necessary for the young larvæ from which the queens are to be raised to be all of the same age. This is not a difficult matter for any one knowing from experience the size of the grubs at different ages. At eighteen hours old, they are of about the size of the small c of ordinary type and will hatch on the twelfth day. For the purpose of obtaining larvæ of the right age in sufficient numbers, I do not find it necessary to insert an empty comb into the brood chamber of the colony with the selected queen, because, at a time suitable for queen rearing, sufficient larvæ for the purpose should be in every hive. To obtain the larvæ I cut a piece, four to six inches long and the width of three rows of cells, out of a comb in a

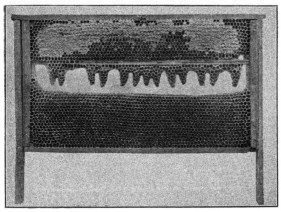

2. QUEEN CELLS GROUPED IN COMB.

suitable place. By cutting it again through the middle row of cells two single rows are obtained. These are fastened with liquid wax cell end on, to a thin strip of wood. The open row of cells is then cut down to half the depth (Fig. 1) by means of twirling a wooden match head first into the surplus larvæ. Those of the wrong age and any eggs which may be present are removed, leaving as far as possible one larva of the right age in every third cell. These strips of comb are then fixed in gaps cut into a comb and given to queenless bees for 6 to 12 hours to mould queen-cups round the larvæ. They are then fitted into an outside brood comb of the superseding colonies.

When the cells are sealed the strips may be removed and grouped into a comb, as shown in Fig. 2. This is placed into the super of a strong colony over a queen excluder where they may remain till distributed in cell protectors to nuclei about the tenth or eleventh day after they are started. Started queen-cells may again be given to the colonies which raised the cells as soon as the sealed cells are removed but the brood combs should be examined occasionally for a cell they may be raising on their own account.   Three to six cells are all I raise in a superseding colony at a time.   When greater numbers are raised they are not so perfect. The thirteen cells in Fig. 2 are on three strips, each from a different superseding colony.

The great advantage of this method of queen-rearing is that, having a laying queen in the hive, the bees will not raise the cells given, unless conditions are as they should be.   No inferior queens will therefore result.

(To be continued.)

PUTREFACTION AND DECAY.

Jno. W. Paterson, B. Sc., Ph. D.

It is a matter of everyday experience that when organic substances or mixtures such as milk, wines, flesh products, or wood are exposed to ordinary atmospheric influences they undergo chemical change and become unwholesome or useless.   At one time it was believed that those changes were due to instability in the complex chemical molecule, and that decay, therefore, was a spontaneous result.   More modern investigation has shown this view to be wrong, and that the whole series of changes variously known as souring, rotting, decay, fermentation and putrefaction are caused by various low forms of life. especially by bacteria and moulds.   As these latter are plants—bacteria are very small plants indeed—it will easily be understood why perishable commodities can be preserved in various ways.   As all plants—including bacteria—require water, it will be seen that dried milk or dried fish can be kept indefinitely.   Again, as all plants have a temperature at which they grow quickest—generally between 80 and 100 degrees F.— decay is quicker in warm weather.   Then, again, each plant—including bacteria—has a temperature below which it cannot grow—usually between 32 and 50 degrees F.—therefore, freezing prevents decay. Boiling kills all sorts of plants, and a tin of meat sealed up while hot is free from bacteria, and will keep indefinitely; but if a cold tin be opened decay soon starts because decay germs are floating about in the air.   Again, plants may be poisoned just like animals, and antiseptics are things which are poisonous to the bacteria causing decay. Borax, formalin, and carbolic acid are used in different cases to prevent decay—they are germ poisons.   Lastly, crops cannot grow in soils too salty because the soil water has too much dissolved matter— it is too strong a solution—to pass into the roots by osmosis.   It is for this reason that putrefactive germs cannot work in meat that has been made too salt for them; and also why jam and preserves keep all right when enough sugar has been used in the making.   Altogether, the many and different methods of preventing putrefaction and decay all have the same immediate object—it is to render the conditions of life unfavorable to the growth of the little plants which cause the damage.

STATISTICS.

Rainfall in ˙Victoria.—Third Quarter, 1912.

TABLE showing average amount of rainfall in each of the 26 Basins or Regions constituting the State of Victoria for each month and the quarter, with the corresponding monthly and quarterly averages for each Basin, deduced from all available records to date.

Basin or District.	July.		August.		September.		Quarter.	
	Amount.	Average.	Amount.	Average.	Amount.	Average.	Amount.	Average.
	points.	points.	points.	points.	points.	points.	points.	points.
Glenelg and Wannon Rivers	214	337	259	301	549	294	1,022	932
Fitzroy, Eumeralla, and Merri Rivers	162	374	275	322	538	310	975	1,006
Hopkins River and Mount Emu Creek	169	250	200	256	431	271	800	777
Mount Elephant and Lake Corangamite	126	239	165	244	455	268	746	751
Cape Otway Forest ...	275	407	362	400	696	388	1,333	1,195
Moorabool and Barwon Rivers	183	230	164	244	536	249	883	723
Werribee and Saltwater Rivers	207	194	131	210	324	248	662	652
Yarra River and Dandenong Creek	314	315	254	300	549	331	1,117	946
Koo-wee-rup Swamp	281	311	254	320	414	349	949	980
South Gippsland	247	371	258	381	554	407	1,059	1,159
Latrobe and Thomson Rivers	288	312	254	339	652	375	1,194	1,026
Macallister and Avon Rivers	337	146	89	218	272	204	698	568
Mitchell River	373	218	92	202	3.7	264	802	684
Tambo and Nicholson Rivers	427	194	93	180	188	237	708	611
Snowy River	522	286	139	241	201	317	862	844
Murray River	371	206	176	188	291	184	838	578
Mitta Mitta and Kiewa Rivers	586	435	256	322	701	310	1,543	1,067
Ovens River	610	456	272	340	446	327	1,328	1,123
Goulburn River	405	291	172	255	407	244	984	790
Campaspe River	369	267	141	245	516	258	1,026	770
Loddon River	256	188	135	194	378	183	769	565
Avon and Richardson Rivers	252	159	153	174	343	169	748	502
Avoca River	215	188	135	180	387	168	737	536
Eastern Wimmera	302	242	164	244	536	229	1,002	715
Western Wimmera	233	245	204	211	579	206	1,016	662
Mallee District	167	138	162	141	247	142	576	421
The whole State	291	250	185	235	407	241	883	726

100 points = 1 inch.

H. A. HUNT,

Commonwealth Meteorologist

HAYSTACK BUILDING.

T. A. J. Smith, Chief Field Officer.

As with all other arts, in haystack building proficiency is attained only by experience and practice. The builder requires a good eye for straight lines and the faculty of concentrating his mind on the work before him. The main purpose is so to build the stack that water will not penetrate it, and that it be able to resist the wind; but it is always desirable that it be symmetrical. A really well built stack is a fine sight.

FORMS OF STACKS.

There are various forms of stacks; they may be round, oblong, square, or oval, according to the fancy or purpose of the owner. As compared with small ones, large stacks have less waste in proportion. At the same time, small stacks have the advantage in being more easily built, and often obviate the necessity for opening a fresh stack; any size from 10 to 150 tons is the practice in this State.

The old practice of kneeing the sheaves is still followed by some builders, *i.e.*, kneeling on each sheaf, when placed in position. The majority of stacks, however, are now built with a short handled pitch fork, with which the sheaves are put in position by the builder. At least three hands are required for any fair-sized stack, viz., the pitcher from the load, the stack builder, and a sheaf turner. The business of the latter is, with a fork, to place the sheaf as received from the pitcher in a convenient position for the builder, so that the latter need not leave his place to reach for each sheaf in turn. A good sheaf turner can materially assist the builder and save valuable time and temper.

SITE.

The first consideration is the choice of a site for the stackyard, which should be a good solid piece of land, with drainage, either natural or artificial, on all sides. A substantial fence should be erected, leaving sufficient room for the stacks and a passage way around them for a dray after they have been completed. If the stacks are to be threshed, room for the straw stack should also be included. The size of the yard will depend on the amount of hay available. If more than four fair-sized stacks are necessary, it is best to have two yards, fifty or more yards apart, so that in the event of fire the whole of the crop will not be endangered.

Where the stacks are built on the ground, the grass and all rubbish should be scraped off to the extent of at least 4 ft. wider and longer than the stack itself.

BUILDING ON STAGE.

A better system is to build on a stage. This can be cheaply constructed, and will last for years. It should be erected on piles, 6 in. in diameter, of some durable hard wood; red gum, box, stringybark all stand well in the ground. They should be not less than 3 ft. in length; and, when erected, be 18 in. in the ground and not more than 4 ft. apart.

Before the floor or platform is built on the piles, a piece of galvanized iron, not less than 12 in. square, should be placed on the top of each pile to prevent mice climbing up and getting into the stack. A still better

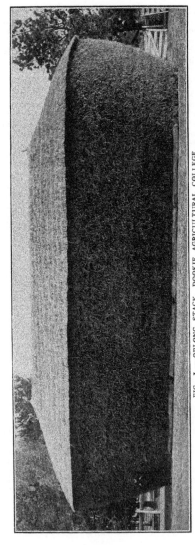

FIG. I.—OBLONG STACK, DOOKIE AGRICULTURAL COLLEGE.

practice is to cut the top out of a kerosene tin and place it upside down on the pile. When climbing up, mice will then get inside the tin, provided the piles are not larger than specified, and it will be impossible for them to jump to hanging straws or anything else that will carry them up to a stack. The floor of the stage is then built on top of the tins on joists laid across, and saplings, rails or slabs are put on the joists close enough together to form a good floor, which should be well nailed down. This stage will last for years, and will soon repay the cost in the saving of waste at the bottom, which is so common in stacks built on the ground, to say nothing of the damage done by mice.

A stage, 36 ft. long by 20 ft. wide, will be large enough for a stack of hay containing 50 to 60 tons, according to the height of the eaves, which should be 12 to 15 ft. when first erected. It is best to begin building from the outside, placing the sheaves with the butts to the outside. Keep a straight line along the edge of the staging, and the sheaves close together side by side, until the whole row right around is completed. At the corners, the best system is to draw the heads together so that only the butts are seen from outside as shown in Fig. 4. The next row of sheaves is placed with the heads outwards on top of the first row, lapping the outside sheaves to within a foot of the end of the butts, and so on with each row of sheaves until the centre of the stack is filled up. As the centre is approached, put the sheaves closer together, so as to make the middle of the stack tighter and higher than the outside ; always lap each succeeding row at least as far as the band on that preceding. From then on, as each fresh layer of sheaves is applied, keep the centre well trampled and slightly higher than the outside sheaves, and the butts of the sheaves in each row to the outside of the stack.

Many builders commence from the centre, especially on small stacks where no stage is used, and the practice is a good one, though the one

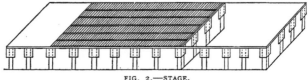

FIG. 2.—STAGE.

recommended will be found even better where a stage is built. Both styles of building are similar after the first two layers have been laid ; every fresh layer of sheaves should be commenced from the outside of the stack, always working to the centre and keeping the surface even with an elevation to the centre to give a pitch for any water that might penetrate the roof of the stack. If this is done and the middle well tramped, the stack should be safe from rain.

FIG. 3.—SYSTEM OF BEGINNING LAYERS AFTER FIRST TWO ARE PLACED.

The sheaf turner should always stand, as nearly as possible, in the centre of the stack, and should not trample on the outside row under any circumstances, as he will displace or push out the sheaves and spoil the shape of the stack. Each layer of sheaves should be put on in the same way as the first, except that, after the second layer is put down, the butts should be kept to the outside in the rows. The loose or ungainly sheaves should be used to keep up the middle. The very outside row of sheaves in each layer should not be as tightly packed as those towards the centre. This will admit of the outside settling as the stack progresses, and give a fall to the exterior which will allow the water to run

off.   The corners want carefully watching to see that they are even and
level.   As each load or so is put on, the builder should get down and
with a board, 12 in. by 10 in. nailed to a handle 7 ft. to 8 ft. long, pat
back any sheaves that work out from their position.   Keep the sides
perpendicular as the building is continued, and it will be found that the
stack will spread slightly of itself until, when the eaves are reached, the
width will be greater than when commenced.

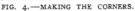

FIG. 4.—MAKING THE CORNERS.

It is better not to unload the waggon always from the same side or
position, as the constant tossing of the sheaves on to one portion of the
stack will harden that particular place; and, later on, it will not settle
uniformly and will become lopsided.   Where possible, it will be found
easier to toss the sheaves from the windward side.   A good ladder of not
less than 20 ft. in length will be necessary for the men to get on and
off the stack.

The building is continued until the eaves are, say, 14 ft. from the
floor of the stage.   When it is decided to put on the top, the last row

FIG. 5.—FIRST ROW.

of sheaves is projected 3 in. further than the previous outside row to
make an eave, after which each successive row is drawn in.

Roof.

The top or roof is made in the same way as the body of the stack,
except that each layer of sheaves is drawn in about 6 in.   Always remember to keep the centre of the stack closely packed and slightly higher
than the outside; this will give a gable end to the stack.   As
the roof is drawn in, the rows of sheaves become less until the

last sheaves are practically stooked along the top, being lightly packed together with the heads interlocked by opening them and dovetailing them into one another.   It will be found best to save a load of well-shaped sheaves of rather short length for finishing.   The biggest and roughest sheaves should go into the body of the stack.   After the top has been put on, it should be lightly raked down to remove all loose straws.   Provided due care has been taken to keep the middle high and solid, such a stack should resist any fall of rain, and the only waste should be the butts of the sheaves on the roof.

FIGS. 6 AND 7.—DIFFERENT STYLES OF RIDGING.

ROUND AND OBLONG STACKS.

Stacks of practically all shapes can be built on the lines indicated, with slight alterations such as square ends instead of gable.   The butts of the sheaves are kept out square with the end eave, instead of being drawn in with the sides.   Round stacks are perhaps the easies: to make, but are suitable only for small quantities, say, 15 to 25 tons of hay.

Round stacks and small oblong stacks are often started from the centre. Make a stook in the middle and gradually work out to a circle previously marked out on the ground on the stack site.   After the first layer of sheaves is laid each succeeding layer is started from the outside.   Work back to the centre and so continue until the stack is finished.

THATCHING.

All stacks that are to be kept for any length of time exceeding three months should be thatched to save waste, and insure immunity from the effects of rain.   This can be done with straw.   Rye straw is the best, and should be straightened out and tied in bundles.   The thatcher sits on a ladder thrown over the roof and anchored by a rope on the other side.   Operations are commenced by sewing on to the sheaves, with a

FIG. 8.—SEWING ON THATCH.

curved needle and twine, a layer of straw about 3 in. thick.   The straw is taken in the hand and each fresh handful laid close up against the preceding one.   The twine is taken over the top of the straw, about half way up the length, and through the one laid previously, the needle being brought a couple of inches further out, ready for the next handful.

The first layers of straw should project beyond the eaves and be afterwards trimmed with a pair of shears.   The second layer should lap over the first sufficiently to thoroughly cover the twine on the first, and so on until finished. The top or ridge can be finished by bending the straw over on both sides and sewing each, or by cutting the ends of the thatch square on the side from which the least rain comes, and bringing the thatch from the opposite side well up against the square end and projecting a few inches higher. The latter should then be trimmed.

Thatching machines can be bought for £7. With these, mats of thatch can be made, and these can be pegged on or sewn, simplifying the work very greatly.

If the winds are bad, or birds troublesome, it is a good plan to cover the whole roof with wire netting. This will keep the roof from being blown about, and also prevent birds from scratching or pulling it to pieces.

FENCING.

A fence of plain galvanized iron 2 ft. 8 in. high should be built all around the stack, at least 2 ft. away, to prevent access of mice. If built nearer than this it will be found as the stack spreads and settles it will be liable to injure the iron.

A good tarpaulin is of great use during building and afterwards. It should be 18 ft. by 24 ft., and made of good canvas, sufficiently close to prevent water penetrating. It often happens that a rainstorm will come up when a stack is in course of erection. A tarpaulin will be found most useful at such a juncture.

A good fence should be erected around the whole, at least 8 ft. from the stacks, with more room, if possible, and all should then be safe.

INSURANCE

Insurance is always advisable when stacks are kept for any length of time, and can be effected for periods ranging from one month to twelve months. The following system for measuring the contents of a stack is useful for insurance and other purposes :—

MEASUREMENT OF STACKS.

Scale showing the minimum number of cubic feet to be given to the ton, according to age and condition (coarse reedy stuff, besides being less valuable, is more bulky)—

Oblong Stacks—

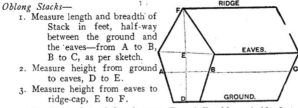

1. Measure length and breadth of Stack in feet, half-way between the ground and the eaves—from A to B, B to C, as per sketch.
2. Measure height from ground to eaves, D to E.
3. Measure height from eaves to ridge-cap, E to F.
4. To the number of feet between D and E add one-half of the number of feet between E and F.
5. Multiply length, breadth, and average height together, which will give the number of cubic feet in stack.
6. Divide this by the requisite number, as shown in scale below, to ascertain the number of tons.

Round Stacks—

Multiply half the circumference by half the diameter, and the sum of this by the height (ascertained in accordance with the rule already given).

Scale showing the minimum number of cubic feet to be given to the ton, according to age and condition (coarse reedy stuff, besides being less valuable, is more bulky)—

			Oaten Hay.		Wheaten Hay.	
			Sheaf.	Loose.	Sheaf.	Loose.
Immediately on completion of stack	...	...	350	400	400	500
One week after completion	...	...	325	375	375	450
One month after completion	...	...	300	350	350	400
Twelve months after completion	..	...	300	325	350	400

NOTES ON THE OCCURRENCE OF LIME IN VICTORIA.

Supplementary to the articles in the October issue of this *Journal,* Mr. A. S. Kenyon, Engineer to the State Rivers and Water Supply Commission, and formerly Engineer for Agriculture, furnishes the following:—

The list of limestone deposits given may be considerably increased. Mr. F. Chapman, A.L.S., in a paper on the "Victorian Limestones," *Journal of Proceedings,* Royal Victorian Institute of Architects. Melbourne, March, 1912, gives the following additional localities:—

Mornington.—Balcombe's Bay. Septarian nodules, and layers of an impure limestone. These have been worked for cement.

Waurn Ponds.—Rather impure limestone, of a snuff-brown colour. Analysis (Barnard and Dunn):—

			Percentage.
$CaCO_3$	..	..	79.60
$MgCO_3$	..	..	traces
$FeCO_3$	..	..	14.95
SiO_2	..	..	3.70
Water	..	..	0.25

Several quarries are worked both for building stone and builder's lime.

Torquay, Drysdale, &c.—Some of the yellow limestone of these
localities are very compact, and would form excellent
building stone.   Other beds in the series, which are more
friable, from their comparative purity would be suitable
for lime burning.   The marls used from the pits between
Geelong and Torquay run about 60 per cent. $CaCO_3$.   The
harder portions contain over 90 per cent., while the underlying clays, locally considered of value. only have about
2 per cent.

Flinders.—This deposit is of a very limited extent, and is, moreover, too soft to be of use for building purposes.   It occurs
in a low cliff on the ocean beach, near the point where the
extension of the main road from Bittern railway station
to Flinders strikes the coast.

Sorrento.—The greater part of the lime used in building Melbourne in the early days was burnt at Sorrento.   The
limestone occurs as dune rock.   It is also used for building
purposes.

Grange Burn.—This rock occurs along the valley of the Grange
Burn, near Hamilton, towards its junction with Muddy
Creek.   It is a polyzoal limestone of a conspicuous rose-
pink to yellow, and is composed of remains of polyzoa,
shellfish, and echinoids.   This limestone is of similar age
to the Batesford limestone.

Portland.—This is a whitish polyzoal limestone, which has a
reputation of hardening on exposure.   The yellow Portland stone is softer in texture, and, therefore, not so well
suited for a building stone.   Analyses (Barnard and
Dunn) :—

	White. Percentage.	Yellow. Percentage.
$CaCO_3$	94.50	91.10
$MgCO_3$	1.95	3.20
$FeCO_3$	1.05	2.20
SiO_2	3.20	1.50
Water	0.20	0.30
Alkaline salts		traces

Besides these quoted by Mr. Chapman there are many other occurrences.   At Marlo, near the mouth of the Snowy River, there are large
beds of tertiary limestone showing in the cliffs, probably connected
with the Bairnsdale beds.   No analysis is given in the October *Journal*
of the Merriman's Creek limestone.   The following is an analysis of
the marl or limestone found at Seldom Seen, in the same district:—

	Percentage.
$CaCO_3$	86.2
Fe_2O_3, Al_2O_3	2.9
Insoluble matter	6.4

Along the coast west of Torquay tertiary limestones exist at Airey's
Inlet, Cape Patten, Johanna River, Moonlight Head, and near Warrnambool.   In the Heytesbury and Otway forests there are many out-

crops of similar beds to those at Kawarren, Love's River, and Timboon. These vary in composition from 40 to over 90 per cent., and are largely availed of by the surrounding farmers. The following analyses are from various deposits on the Cobden to Princetown road:—

	Percentage.	Percentage.	Percentage.	Percentage.
$CaCO_3$	89.35	63.00	38.21	82.62
Fe_2O_3, Al_2O_3 ..	0.82	2.80	3.65	2.55
MgO	0.22	0.52	0.40	0.50
P_2O_5	trace	trace	trace	trace
SO_3	0.09	0.10	0.06	0.14
Insoluble ..	2.40	16.02	29.47	11.51
Organic matter..	0.52	1.87	2.57	0.38

On the north shore of Lake Corangamite there are deposits of both limestone and gypsum.

In addition to the polyzoal beds at Portland there are extensive dune rock deposits extending for some distance inland.

Along the Glenelg River from its mouth to above Dartmoor cliffs of tertiary limestone form the principal feature. Outcrops of similar formation as well as dune limestones are frequent throughout the districts between the Glenelg and the South Australian boundary.

Boring operations have proved the existence of beds of polyzoal limestone of many hundreds of feet in thickness from Portland to Wilcannia on the Darling River, New South Wales, underlying the whole of the Victorian mallee country and the county of Lowan, and that part of South Australia east of the Murray River, but they are of no industrial value owing to their inaccessibility.

The most extensive lime deposits in Victoria, however, are on the surface of the mallee country, and occur in three forms. Limestone rubble generally only a few feet in thickness and of concretionary origin, spread over the whole district. It is not very rich, but has been extensively used for building purposes. Analysis (limestone near Mildura) :—

	Percentage.
$CaCO_3$	57.45
Insoluble matter (sand)..	35.91
Undetermined ..	6.64

Fresh-water limestone deposits occur at Rainbow. Cow Plains, Ned's Corner, and at Sunset. These are very rich, but at Cow Plains, at any rate, are rather high in magnesia for agricultural use. They cover many square miles of country, and are 30 feet and over in thickness. Analysis (Cow Plains limestone) :—

	Percentage.
$CaCO_3$	67.89
$MgCO_3$	18.59
Insoluble (sand)	11.22

The third mode of occurrence is as gypsum, locally termed copi or cow, the aboriginal term for white. As a creamy-white floury powder, apparently amorphous, but really minute typical crystals, gypsum occurs as mounds of 20 or 30 feet in height, some few chains in width, and up to a mile or more in length at Ouyen, Cow Plains, Ned's Corner, The Raak, Yatpool (near Mildura), Lake Tyrrell, and Towan Plain (near Nyah). Smaller deposits are found throughout the mallee. The supply is enormous, and the quality exceptionally good. Although not quite within the confines of the mallee country, fairly large deposits of the floury form of gypsum are to be found near Natimuk and north of Mount Arapiles on some salt lakes. Large quantities have been excavated and used by the Mildura orchardists and the Melbourne manure manufacturers. Analyses:—

	Yatpool. Percentage.	Cow Plains. Percentage.
$CaSO_4 + 2H_2O$ ...	98.19 ...	94.01

It is also found in beds of large crystals at Boort, Boga, Lake Tyrrell, Cow Plains, &c. These deposits can be loaded on trucks for a nominal sum.

ORCHARD AND GARDEN NOTES.

E. E. Pescott, Principal, School of Horticulture, Burnley.

The Orchard.

As a preventive against codlin moth, apple and pear trees should be sprayed with arsenate of lead whenever there is danger from the prevalence of the moth.

By the use of arsenate of lead the codlin moth pest is very easily kept in check, and from being one of the most formidable of orchard troubles, it has come to be one of the least feared of all pests. By constantly spraying with arsenate of lead, the use of bandages as a trap for the codlin larvæ is now quite unnecessary. In fact, bandages, more often than not, become a harbor and a breeding ground. Further, the time spent in overlooking and attending to the bandages may be employed far more profitably by giving the trees an extra spraying.

There are a few growers who still make use of lamps at night time to destroy the codlin moth, irrespective of the fact, which has been pointed out again and again, that the codlin moth is not attracted by lamps or lights. These traps do incalculable harm to an orchardist, as they are responsible for the destruction of hundreds of lace-wing flies—insects that are most useful as destroyers of aphides and scales.

The question of trapping the codlin moth by means of attractive and sticky baits is again being advanced by growers and experimentalists. But it will be well to await definite results before this method is adopted to any large extent. Spraying has proved so effective that growers should hesitate before changing their methods for something new.

One of the secrets of success in codlin moth spraying is the destruction of as many as possible of the insects of the first brood.

Thus, if particular care is given to the early sprayings, keeping the fruit covered with spray for a month or six weeks after setting, this result is easily accomplished.   Some growers prefer to gather all fruit infected by the first brood, spraying only for the second and later broods.   Even if all the fruits attacked are gathered, which very rarely happens, the grower suffers from the loss of fruit, which he can ill afford, unless his crop be a heavy one.

Another feature for consideration is the fact that the presence of any arsenical spray on the foliage is responsible for the destruction of the pear and cherry slug, root-borer beetle, and all forms of leaf-eating insects.

Spraying the cherry trees for the slug will now be necessary. Arsenate of lead may be used, provided the fruit is not far advanced. Hellebore, and also tobacco water, are effective against this pest.

Cultivation.—All orchard soils should be kept well worked during the summer months.   It is very essential that the trees should have an abundant supply of moisture during the whole of the growing season.   The transpiration from fruit and foliage is considerable at any time; but during hot and windy weather the amount of moisture which is required by a tree, and which is ultimately transpired from the tree, is very exceptional.

Excessive transpiration is often the cause of loss of young trees and of new grafts.   They are found to part with a large amount of moisture, and are not able to retain or obtain sufficient for their nourishment; they then very soon wither and die.   The soil around these should always be kept well stirred; they may be also given a good straw or grass mulching, and an occasional overhead sprinkling will greatly benefit them.

The planting out of citrus trees may be continued, sheltering the tender plants from winds with hessian or breaks of scrub.

The general aims in summer cultivation should be to keep up a good loose earth mulch during the whole season, and to keep down all weeds and useless orchard growths.

Pruning.—Summer pruning may now be commenced, particularly on apple, pear, and plum trees.   The removal or reduction of surplus leader growths, the shortening of unduly long laterals, and the thinning out of crowded shoots, will all tend to strengthen other parts of the tree, and to increase the development of new fruit buds.

Vegetable Garden.

Tomatoes will require a good amount of attention at this time of the year.   If the plants have been well looked after, they should be making vigorous growth.   It will be to advantage to tie the plants to stakes, training them to two or three main growths, and pinching out all the laterals as they come.

The plants should be well watered, and occasionally a handful of bonedust and blood manure mixed should be forked in around the roots.   Where stable manure is used, it should be used as a mulch, forking it in every three or four weeks, and making a fresh mulch.

All plants of the cucumber and melon family should now be constantly supplied with ample water. Pinch out unnecessary lateral growths, and also the terminals.

The following seeds may now be sown:—French beans, cabbage and cauliflower for winter crops, parsnip, lettuce, and celery.

The side shoots of celery plants should be removed, afterwards earthing up the plants. Asparagus beds should be top-dressed, and allowed to grow without any more cutting. The vegetable beds will need frequent forking and hoeing to keep the soil sweet, and to keep down all weeds.

Flower Garden.

Plant out dahlias this month; tubers early, and plants grown from cuttings for exhibition blooms later in the month. Water well at planting, and keep well cultivated afterwards.

Rose bushes and beds may be given a good mulch with light stable manure, straw, grass, or lawn clippings. The beds should be kept rather dry, so as to allow the plants rest before the autumn period of growth.

Sow seeds of cosmos, asters, zinnia, balsams, cockscomb, and other late summer and autumn blooming annuals.

Cut down delphiniums that have yielded their first crop of flowers, so as to allow a succession of flowers to come.

Daffodil, hyacinth, tulip, ranunculus, anemone, and other bulbs and tubers may be taken up and stored; while gladioli corms may still be planted.

The garden must be kept well watered and well cultivated, so as to tide the plants over the hot and dry season.

SECOND VICTORIAN EGG-LAYING COMPETITION, 1912-13.

H. V. Hawkins, Poultry Expert.

Report for Month ending 14th November, 1912.

The past month has been for the most part dry, with some changes and showers of rain. The meat ration has been reduced and additional green feed, principally lucerne, has been given, save when the weather changed to cold and wet the maize was withheld, and then a small quantity was added to the wheat ration in order to maintain the body temperature. Unfortunately, three White Leghorns died during the month, pens 70, 44 and 15 each losing one, oviduct troubles being responsible. Broodies are more numerous now, and the heavy breeds are not laying as well as in October; this also applies in a lesser degree to the Leghorns. Mr. Samuel Brown's White Leghorns still continue in the lead with the good score of 897, although less than Mr. Swift's pen for the corresponding period in the first competition, yet they bid fair to reach good figures by the end of the test. The total number of eggs laid during the seven months was 47,172, an average of approximately 683.6 eggs per pen.

SECOND VICTORIAN EGG-LAYING COMPETITION, 1912-13.
Commencing 15th April, 1912.
CONDUCTED AT BURNLEY HORTICULTURAL SCHOOL.

No. of Pen.	Breed.	Name of Owner.	Eggs laid during competition.			Position in Competition.
			April 15 to Oct. 14.	Oct. 15 to Nov. 14.	Total to Date (7 months).	
40	White Leghorns	S. Brown	756	141	897	1
28	,,	F. G. Eagleton	723	132	855	2
23	,,	W. McLister	721	132	853	3
47	,,	J. E. Bradley	707	139	846	} 4
31	,,	Geo. Edwards	716	130	846	}
9	,,	J. Spotswood	718	127	845	6
20	,.	E. Waldon	696	136	832	7
62	,,	R. W. Pope	671	142	813	8
1	,,	J. Campbell	669	137	806	9
37	,,	C. B. Bertelsmeier	657	134	791	10
70	,,	C. J. Beatty	674	115	789	11
45	,,	Wooldridge Bros.	647	136	783	12
46	Black Orpingtons	H. A. Langdon	674	104	778	13
25	White Leghorns	R. L. Appleford	637	137	774	14
14	,,	J. H. Wright	637	131	768	15
3	Black Orpingtons	King and Watson	668	99	767	16
24	White Leghorns	Sargenfri Poultry Yards	645	120	765	17
48	,,	Griffin Cant	642	118	760	18
29	,,	J. B. Brigden	629	128	757	} 19
39	,,	W. G. Swift	621	136	757	}
61	Black Orpingtons	Jas. Ogden	620	136	756	21
13	White Leghorns	W. B. Crellin	621	132	753	} 22
49	,,	W. Purvis	606	147	753	}
38	,,	R. Moy	621	129	750	24
2	,,	B. Rowlinson	617	119	736	25
44	,,	A. W. Hall	610	122	732	26
50	,,	A. Ahpee	606	124	730	27
6	,,	J. B. Macarthur	613	116	729	28
33	,,	H. McKenzie	586	136	722	29
15	,,	Mrs. Steer	598	119	717	30
7	,,	A. H. Padman	585	130	715	31
53	,,	H. Hodges	572	140	712	32
63	,,	Percy Walker	576	133	709	33
30	,.	Mrs. Stevenson	594	109	703	34
5	,,	J. H. Brain	561	134	695	} 35
35	,.	C. H. Busst	568	127	695	}
19	,.	Cowan Bros.	569	115	684	37
42	,,	Mrs. Kempster	556	123	679	38
51	,,	H. Hammill	536	136	672	39
10	R.C. Brown Leghorns	S. P. Giles	539	128	667	40
8	Black Orpingtons	D. Fisher	598	66	664	41
64	White Leghorns	H. Merrick	529	129	658	42
56	,,	M. A. Monk	549	106	655	43
69	,,	Morgan and Watson	506	136	642	} 44
60	,,	Miss B. E. Ryan	517	125	642	}
32	,,	S. Brundrett	499	135	634	} 46
65	,,	A. H. Thomson	510	124	634	}
54	,,	F. R. DeGaris	519	111	630	48
16	Silver Wyandottes	R. Jobling	506	113	619	49
43	White Leghorns	G. Purton	503	115	618	50
11	Black Orpingtons	T. S. Goodisson	498	116	614	51
27	White Leghorns	E. Nash	483	127	610	52
12	,,	T. H. Stafford	469	133	602	53
41	,,	A. Stringer	471	130	601	54
4	,,	J. Blackburne	474	122	596	55
57	,,	B. Walker	474	115	589	56
58	,,	W. J. Stock	473	115	588	57
52	Black Minorcas	Chalmers Bros.	453	128	581	58
55	Brown Leghorns	J. Mathieson	449	116	565	59
66	White Leghorns	J. Moloney	424	127	551	60
68	,,	W. J. McKeddie	425	111	536	61
21	,,	J. O'Loughlin	412	114	526	62
22	,,	W. N. Ling	402	118	520	63
67	Anconas	A. E. Manning	389	122	511	64
18	White Leghorns	B. Mitchell	410	99	509	65
17	,.	S. Childs	340	137	477	66
59	,,	W. J. Seabridge	361	114	475	67
34	,,	R. F. B. Moore	344	124	468	68
36	Old English Game	K. J. Barrett	372	94	466	69
26	..	(Reserved)	—	—	—	..
		Totals	38,621	8,551	47,172	

REMINDERS FOR JANUARY.

LIVE STOCK.

HORSES.—*Stabled.*—Over-stimulating and fattening foods should be restricted. Water should be allowed at frequent intervals. Rub down on coming into stables in an overheated condition. Supply a ration of greenstuff to all horses. *Brood mares* should be well fed on succulent food if available; otherwise, oats and bran should be given. *Foals* may with advantage be given oats to the extent of 1 lb. for each month of age daily. Provision should be made for shade shelter for paddocked horses.

CATTLE.—Provide supply of succulent fodder, clean water, and shade shelter.

PIGS.—*Sows.*—Supply those farrowing with plenty of short bedding in well-ventilated sties. Those with litters old enough may be turned into grass run. *All* pigs should be given a plentiful supply of clean water.

SHEEP.—Disturb sheep as little as possible during hot spells. Remember, rams work mostly in the cool of the day, and crossbred ewes are only now coming in season. The older the feed becomes the greater the necessity for salt in northern areas; in wormy country it should be available at all times. If the least sign of worms exists, commence drenching weaners at once, and enable them to become strong before winter. Salt, 2 cwt.; Stockholm tar, 2 pints; and powdered resin, 1 pint (or 1 lb.); is a useful lick for young lambs in wormy areas.

POULTRY.—Separate the sexes; the cockerels should now be fattened and marketed. Grade the young stock according to age and size, otherwise the younger birds will not thrive. Avoid overcrowding. Do not force pullets too much with animal food; build them up with a good variety of food, but avoid maize, and give but little meat. Increase the green feed; thoroughly spray houses and perches. Keep water vessels in shady spot, and renew water twice daily. Moisten dust bath.

CULTIVATION.

FARM.—Get all crops harvested and stacked as soon as possible. Horse-hoe maize, potatoes and other summer crops. See to insurance of stacks of grain and hay.

ORCHARD.—Keep the soil well scarified and weed free. Cultivate after irrigation or rain. Do not allow the surface to become caked. Spray against codlin moth, pear slug, vine caterpillar, and woolly aphis. Summer prune strong growing shoots and laterals.

VEGETABLE GARDEN.—Plant out all seedlings when ready, from former sowings. Stir and mulch the surface. Dig each plot as it becomes vacant. Sow seeds of cauliflower, cabbage, peas, French beans, Kohl Rabi, &c.

FLOWER GARDEN.—Keep the soil moist and cool by watering, hoeing, and mulching. Stake tender and lengthy plants. Water and shade young plants. Sow pansy, Iceland poppy, cosmos, aster. &c.

VINEYARD.—This is the slackest month in un-irrigated vineyards—all ordinary work should be completed before Christmas. It is only exceptional operations, such as scarifying after rain or sulphuring in case of oidium, that must be carried out. In irrigated vineyards the application of water, and the cultivation it necessitates, must receive attention.

Cellar.—Fill up regularly and keep cellar as cool as possible. Towards end of month commence to make preparations for the coming vintage.

INDEX OF VOLUME X.

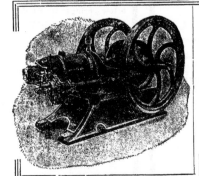
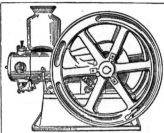

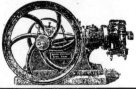
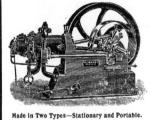

DEPARTMENT OF AGRICULTURE,

VICTORIA.

Burnley Horticultural School.

E. E. PESCOTT - Principal.

ANNOUNCEMENT.

The curriculum and management of the Burnley Horticultural School have now been arranged so that greater advantages and facilities will be given to students of both sexes in Horticulture and allied subjects.

The present course of Horticulture for male students includes a two years' course, students being charged a fee of £5 per annum.

Classes have been formed at Burnley, whereby students of both sexes may receive instruction on two afternoons of each week—Tuesdays and Fridays.

Instruction includes theoretical and practical work, and will commence at 2 p.m. This will be a two years' course, and the fee charged will be £2 per annum.

It has also been arranged that several short lecture courses shall be given on subjects which are suitable adjuncts to Horticulture, such as Poultry Farming, Bee-keeping, and Fruit Preserving, and these courses will be open and free to the general public. The subjects and dates of the Short Course Lectures will be announced in this Journal.

STUDENTS SHOULD ENROLL WITHOUT DELAY.

Application for . Admission should be made to . .	THE DIRECTOR OF AGRICULTURE, PUBLIC OFFICES, MELBOURNE,	OR TO THE PRINCIPAL.

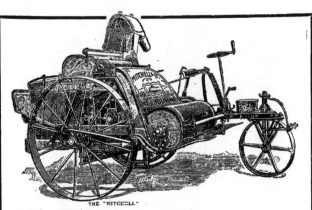
By Authority: ALBERT J. MULLETT, Acting Government Printer, Melbourne.